AMERICAN CONSTITUTIONAL DEVELOPMENT

Volume I

The Powers of Government

Richard S. Randall
New York University

New York   San Francisco   Boston
London   Toronto   Sydney   Tokyo   Singapore   Madrid
Mexico City   Munich   Paris   Cape Town   Hong Kong   Montreal

For Mal

Vice President/ Publisher: Priscilla McGeehon
Senior Acquisitions Editor : Eric Stano
Associate Editor: Anita Castro
Senior Marketing Manager: Megan Galvin-Fak
Production Manager: Charles Annis
Project Coordination, Text Design, and Electronic Page Makeup: WestWords, Inc.
Cover Designer/Manager: John Callahan
Cover Image: Courtesy Corbis
Manufacturing Buyer: Al Dorsey
Printer and Binder: Hamilton Printing Co.
Cover Printer: Lehigh Press, Inc.

Library of Congress Cataloging-in-Publication Data

Randall, Richard S.
    Americal constitutional development/Richard S. Randall.
        p. cm.
    Includes bibliographical references and index.
    ISBN 0-8013-2019-4
      1. Constitutional history—United States. 1. Title.

KF4541 .R36 2002
342.73'029—dc21   2001050440

Please visit our website at http://www.ablongman.com

ISBN 0-8013-2019-4

BRIEF CONTENTS

Detailed Contents
Preface
The Constitution of the United States
American Constitutionalism

Part I
The First Nation

Chapter 1   *The Groundwork for Revolution*
Chapter 2   *Independence and Confederation*

Part II
Union and Nation

Chapter 3   *The Framing*
Chapter 4   *The Formative Period*
Chapter 5   *Slavery and Civil War*

Part III
Constitutional Political Economy

Chapter 6   *The Republic of Bees*
Chapter 7   *Industrial Capitalism and the Middle Constitution*
Chapter 8   *The New Deal: Economic and Constitutional Crisis*

Part IV
The Modern Constitution

Chapter 9   *Presidential Power and Divided Government*
Chapter 10   *The New Federal System*
Chapter 11   *Property Rights in the Age of Regulation*

Appendices
Glossary
General and Supplementary Bibliography
Index of Cases
Index of Subjects

DETAILED CONTENTS

Preface   xi
The Constitution of the United States   xv

American Constitutionalism   1

Part I

The First Nation   5

Chapter 1 *The Groundwork for Revolution*   7
Colonial Society   7
The Economics of Empire   9
Religion and Religious Tolerance   10
Governing and Being Governed   11
Law and the Rule of Law   13
A Decade of Ferment   14
Sidebar: Grandfather of His Country   16
The Great Debate   18
One Revolution or Two?   19
FURTHER READING   20
SELECTION: THE DECLARATION OF INDEPENDENCE   21

Chapter 2 *Independence and Confederation*   25
The Revolutionary Government   25
British Defeat   26
The Articles of Confederation   27
Sidebar: The First Constitution   28
Republican State Constitutions   29
New Nation, Old Law   31
New Difficulties   32
The Road to Philadelphia   32
FURTHER READING   34

Part II

Union and Nation   35

Chapter 3 *The Framing*   37
Who Was There   37

Accord on Ends   38
In Convention   39
Scheme of the Constitution and Its
  Distribution of Powers   43
Done and Not Done   44
Sidebar: Original Intent   44
The Anti-Federalist Attack   47
The Constitution Defended   48
Sidebar: The Little Engine That Could   50
The Constitution Ratified   51
Ratification of the Constitution (map)   53
The Bill of Rights   54
The Second New Nation   55
FURTHER READING   56
SELECTION: THE FEDERALIST, NO. 10   57

Chapter 4 *The Formative Period*   63
The Federalist Regime   63
  Hamilton's Political Economy   64
  Constitutional Precedents
    in the Making   65
  Opposition of Jefferson and Madison   66
Sidebar: The Nation Builder   68
  An Unhappy Succession   69
The Early Supreme Court   71
  The Judiciary Act of 1789   71
  The Eleventh Amendment   72
  Constitutional Decisions   72
Republican Constitutionalism   73
  The Louisiana Purchase   74
Sidebar: Fixing a Mechanical Flaw   74
  Jefferson's Embargo   75
  Madison's War   76
  Internal Improvements   77
  End of an Era   78
Judicial Independence   79

Packing and Unpacking   79
The Marbury Case   79
Sidebar: Judicial Review   81
The Impeachment Attack   82
The Burr Treason Trial   82
Marshall's Nationalism   83
Sidebar: The Chief Justice   84
The Jurisdictional Challenge
  of States Rights   85
The Reach and Supremacy
  of National Power   86
Sidebar: Down the Interpretive Path   88
Jacksonian Democracy   91
The New Politics   91
The Strong Presidency   93
The Nullification Crisis   94
FURTHER READING   95
CASES
Chisholm v. Georgia   97
Marbury v. Madison   99
Eakin v. Raub   103
Martin v. Hunter's Lessee   104
Cohens v. Virginia   108
McCulloch v. Maryland   110
Barron v. Baltimore   116
Luther v. Borden   117

Chapter 5 *Slavery and Civil War*   121
Conflict and Compromise   121
Slavery and the Constitution   121
The New Political Economy of Slavery   122
The Missouri Crisis   123
The Issue Nationalized   123
The Abolitionist Movement   123
Sidebar: Ideas of the Iron Man   124
Fugitive Slaves   126
In the Supreme Court   127
Southwest Expansion   129
The Texas Question   130
War with Mexico   131
The Backlash   131
The Decade of Strife   132
A New Settlement   132
The Kansas Conflict   133

Three Compromises
  and a Decision (maps)   134
The Republican Party   136
The Nadir of the Presidency
  and the Court   137
Sidebar: Of Many Virtues and a Flaw   138
The Lincoln-Douglas Debates   139
From Politics to War   140
The Election of 1860   140
The Election of 1860 (map)   142
Secession Winter   142
Sidebar: Constitutionalism
  Confederate Style   144
War Government   145
Lincoln's Constitutional Dictatorship   146
Legal Status of the War   147
Internal Security and Civil Liberty   148
The Status of Slavery   150
Sidebar: The Constitution
  at Gettysburg   150
Growth of Federal Power   152
Reconstruction   153
The Presidential Plans   153
Congressional Reconstruction
  of Reconstruction   154
Johnson's Impeachment   156
The Problematic Court   158
The End of Reconstruction   160
FURTHER READING   162
CASES
Prigg v. Pennsylvania   164
Scott v. Sandford   166
Ableman v. Booth   170
The Prize Cases   172
Ex parte Milligan   174
Mississippi v. Johnson   178
Ex parte McCardle   179
Texas v. White   181

Part III
Constitutional Political Economy   183

Chapter 6 *The Republic of Bees*   185

Born Blessed 185
A Constitutional Door 187
The Transformation of American Law 188
The Obligation of Contracts 192
Sidebar: The Constitutional Lawyer 194
Toward a National Marketplace 196
The National Marketplace Modified 197
Sidebar: Scholar of the Law 198
New Property Versus Old 200
FURTHER READING 201
CASES
Fletcher v. Peck 202
Dartmouth College v. Woodward 203
Gibbons v. Ogden 206
Mayor of New York v. Miln 211
Charles River Bridge Co. v. Warren Bridge Co. 212
Cooley v. Board of Wardens 216

Chapter 7 *Industrial Capitalism and the Middle Constitution* **219**
The New Economic Order 220
Interconnecting a Continent 220
Organization of Big Capital 221
Response of Middling Government 223
Sidebar: A Creed for the Times 224
Laissez-Faire Constitutionalism 225
The Waite Court 227
Sidebar: Retreat from a Cause 228
The Fuller Court 229
Substantive Due Process and Liberty of Contract 230
Sidebar: The Brahman Skeptic 232
Regulation by Commission? Not Entirely 234
Trust-busting? Sometimes 235
Income Tax? Not at All 237
The Progressive Interlude 238
The New Reform 240
The White Court 241
Federal Police Power 241
Sidebar: Attorney for the People 242
State Regulation and the Brandeis Proof 245

Revitalization of the I. C. C. 246
Mobilization for World War 247
Return to "Normalcy" 249
Taft and His Court 250
No Again to Child Labor Reform 251
Liberty of Contract Renascent 251
Protecting Against Labor Insurgency 252
Property Versus Property: Regulation of Land Use 253
FURTHER READING 254
CASES
The Slaughterhouse Cases 255
Munn v. Illinois 260
United States v. E. C. Knight Co. 264
Pollock v. Farmers' Loan & Trust Co. 267
Champion v. Ames 270
McCray v. United States 274
Lochner v. New York 276
Muller v. Oregon 280
The Shreveport Rate Case 282
Hammer v. Dagenhart 284
Bailey v. Drexal Furniture Co. 288
Adkins v. Children's Hospital 289

Chapter 8 *The New Deal: Economic and Constitutional Crisis* **295**
The Great Decline 295
Failure of Policy and Imagination 297
Mandate for Change 299
The One Hundred Days 299
Sidebar: Repeal 300
The "Second" New Deal 302
Judicial Resistance 304
The Holdover Court 304
First Response 305
Sidebar: Public Servant Extraordinaire 306
"Black Monday" and Beyond 308
Battle Lost, War Won 310
Roosevelt's Plan 310
Sidebar: Longevity in the Robe 310
The Switch in Time 312
Aftermath 313
The Roosevelt Court 313
Sidebar: Justice of the Judicial Process 314
The New Constitutional Order 316

FURTHER READING   318
CASES
*Home Building & Loan Association
v. Blaisdell*   319
Schechter Poultry Corp. v. United States   323
Carter v. Carter Coal Co.   326
United States v. Butler   330
West Coast Hotel V. Parrish   334
*National Labor Relations Board v.
Jones & Laughlin Steel Corp.*   337
Steward Machine Co. v. Davis   341
United States v. Darby Lumber Co.   344
Wickard v. Filburn   347

Part IV

The Modern Constitution   **351**

**Chapter 9 *Presidential Power
and Divided Government***   **353**
War and National Security   355
Roosevelt's Wartime "Dictatorship"   355
Korea and the Cold War   357
Vietnam and Beyond   360
Diplomacy and Foreign Affairs   362
Treaties and Treaty-Making   362
Executive Agreements   363
Holding Office   365
Appointment   365
Removal   366
Term Limits   369

Sidebar: The President
and the Prosecutor   370

The Bounds of Office   372
Executive Privilege and Information   372
The Arrogation of Power   373
The Watergate Crisis   374
Immunities   376
Legislative Power Delegated
and Retained   378
Creation of the Administrative State 378
The Legislative Veto   379
Hybrid Offices and Mixed Functions   380
Congressional Investigation   381
Sidebar: The Man Who Followed Warren 382

McCarthyism   384
Later Issues   385
The Modern Court   386
Role in the Separation of Powers   386
Deciding to Decide   388
Sidebar: When the Supreme Court
Chose a President   390
Composition and Change   392
Sidebar: Reading (into) the Constitution 394
FURTHER READING   397
CASES
Missouri v. Holland   400
Humphrey's Executor v. United States 402
Curtiss-Wright Corp. v. United States 404
Korematsu v. United States   407
Youngstown Sheet & Tube Corp. v. Sawyer 411
Watkins v. United States   418
Baker v. Carr   424
Flast v. Cohen   429
Powell v. McCormick   432
United States v. Nixon   434
Dames & Moore v. Regan   439
*Immigration and Naturalization Service v.
Chadha*   441
Bowsher v. Synar   447
Morrison v. Olson   452
U.S. Term Limits v. Thornton   458
Clinton v. Jones   464
Clinton v. City of New York   468
Bush v. Gore   472

Chapter 10 *The New Federal System* **479**
The Reach of Federal Legislation   480
Police Regulation of Private Acts   481
Federal Regulation
of State Government   482
Sidebar: Chief Justice Conservative   484
Federal Supremacy: Preemption   484
Mutual Tax Immunities   487
Judicial Federalism   488
The Matter of Federal Common Law   489
Federal Supervisory Authority   490
State Regulation
of Interstate Commerce   493

Transport 493
Incoming Commerce 494
Outgoing Commerce
and State Resources 496
Interstate Relations 497
Full Faith and Credit 497
Privileges and Immunities 497
Rendition 498
Interstate Disputes 498
Interstate Compacts 499
FURTHER READING 499
CASES
Southern Pacific Co. v. Arizona 500
Pennsylvania v. Nelson 504
Heart of Atlanta Motel v. United States 506
Philadelphia v. New Jersey 509
Michigan v. Long 512
*Garcia v. San Antonio Metropolitan
Transit Authority* 515
Maine v. Taylor 520
South Dakota v. Dole 523
New York v. United States 525
United States v. Lopez 531
Printz v. United States 537
Alden v. Maine 542
Kimel v. Florida Board of Regents 548
Reno v. Condon 553
United States v. Morrison 556

**Chapter 11 *Property Rights in the Age
of Regulation*** **559**
Economic Due Process Interred 560
The Contracts Clause Revived 561
Eminent Domain
and the Takings Clause 562

Public Use 563
What Is a Taking? 563
Just Compensation 565
FURTHER READING 565
CASES
Williamson v. Lee Optical Co. 566
Ferguson v. Skrupa 567
United States Trust v. New Jersey 568
*Penn Central Transportation Co. v.
City of New York* 571
Hawaii Housing Authority v. Midkiff 575
Lucas v. South Carolina Coastal Council 577

Appendices
A Reading a Supreme Court Decision 581
B Law in the Library
and on the Internet 583
C Getting to the Court: The Supreme
Court and the American Judiciary 585
Figure C.1 The American Judicial
System, Lines of Appeal, Annual
Number of Cases 586
D Reaching a Decision: The Supreme
Court at Work 588
E Justices of the Supreme Court 590
F The Historic Supreme Courts 593
G American National Elections,
1788–2000 596

Glossary 599
General and Supplementary Bibliography 605
Index of Cases 613
Index of Subjects 617

PREFACE

Study of the Constitution is typically that of law and doctrine as developed in Supreme Court decisions. Though this "case method," borrowed originally from law schools, is appropriate for the material, difficulties with a purely legal model in undergraduate instruction abound. First, our clientele is different: Political science students are younger and less experienced academically, and often have had no other courses in law. Second, our mission is different, having integrity of its own to be honored. Law schools provide professional training in how to advise clients and win cases; political science instruction, as part of liberal arts education, offers an understanding of how the political system works and how it got to be the way it is. Our task is surely not a premolding of the "legal mind," once described by Thomas Reed Powell as a way of thinking "about a thing inextricably attached to something else without thinking of the thing to which it is attached." For those who go on to law school, that adroitness will come soon enough.

Most political scientists specializing in public law including many who, like the author, have had professional legal training, recognize these distinctions and have felt the constraints imposed by too narrow a focus on doctrine and by the formulaic topical organization that often characterizes law study. It is not surprising that many have called for greater attention to the historical aspects and the political dynamics of constitutional law.* Though many prefaces in new casebooks de-

---

* For example, Susan Gluck Mezey, "Introduction to the Law and Politics Book Review," *Law and Courts Newsletter,* The Law and Courts Section of the American Political Science Association, Fall 1992, 1–22, a collection of 13 reviews of recent editions of leading casebooks.

signed for undergraduate instruction echo this call, often more is promised than delivered.

This is especially true for the first or non-civil-liberties half of constitutional law, dealing, for the most part, with great issues settled some time ago. This half begs for a developmental presentation, especially since we can no longer assume that all or even most students know very much about American history. Yet, the organization of most books has remained steadfastly topical and thus politically and historically disjointed. Relatively minor matters or cases sometimes receive unusual attention or inordinate space at the expense of important shaping decisions or practices. The major teaching problem in the first half of constitutional law is to help students understand how we got from "there" to "here" in the real world of our national political life. Many casebooks do not do a very good job of that.

In both halves of constitutional law students are still confronted by an intimidating array of cases rigidly, often numbingly classified by legal topic or even by Constitutional section or clause. Too often topics have little connection with those preceding or following, and leaps forward and backward of 20, 50, even 100 years between consecutive cases within a topic are not uncommon. Links, if any, are usually those of doctrine. (It is symptomatic that many undergraduate casebooks contain no subject index.) Except for "background" in chapter introductions or headnotes, the political, social, economic, and cultural conflict out of which cases arise is lost and with it much about the conflict to which they return. Such isolation and fragmentation, in mimic of law school instruction, rob constitutional law of its full political vitality.

I have tried to deal with these problems by combining cases with an expansive text focusing on constitutional development. A low-level, non-intrusive analytic framework is used to ask the same kinds of questions of the Court's work that we ask about other institutional performance and policymaking in American government.

The text and cases in this volume are organized around two great problems in the American political experience in which the Constitution has played a central role: (1) the nature of the national union and (2) the protection and regulation of property and economic enterprise. These correspond to the scope of the traditional first half of a full-year course and are each organized developmentally rather than topically.

Certain topics receive somewhat greater attention than they do in most other books. The uncertain nature of the Union, the nation's salient political issue and ultimate constitutional question for nearly a century, is one (Chapters 3–5, Volume I). Chapters 6–8, Volume I emphasize constitutional political economy as a dominant feature of American political and social life from the antebellum period to the New Deal. Here the greatest geo-economic expansion in the history of nations transformed American law and the Constitution; its excesses led to hard questions of public control and to further legal transformations.

Immigration and the assimilation of diverse peoples have been vital in American economic and social life and will no doubt continue to be so. A separate chapter (18, Volume II) deals with this development and its constitutional reflection in questions of alienage and citizenship. The media, now in perpetual revolution, also receive separate treatment (Chapter 14, Volume II). As the politically critical "fourth estate" yet also one economic interest among many, they have come to dominate our culture and intrude upon functions of a range of institutions from political parties to the family. A separate chapter, "Privacy and Public Morality," (16, Volume II) deals with conflicts over moral preferences and "ways of life," aggravated as

they are by our natural social diversity and the media age in which we live. These struggles, often symbolic in their distributive effect, have unusual emotional valance for large numbers of persons and are certain to receive greater attention from the Supreme Court.

The text assumes that conflict and its adjustment or resolution lie at the heart of politics and government action and that all authoritative results—policies, programs, executive and administrative actions, statutes, judicial decisions, and constitutions themselves—have distributive effect, allocating gains, losses, benefits, and costs to those with interests at stake and, eventually, to others as well.

The Constitution, and interpretations of what it permits, requires, or forbids, is the most authoritative allocator of all, resolving or at least transforming major conflicts in the American political experience. Almost all the disputes in the Supreme Court's great cases began in non-judicial arenas and, receiving provisional resolution there, were cast or recast in legal terms by actors or parties defeated or dissatisfied. In the immediate, the Court distributes rights and obligations by granting or denying the former and by imposing or providing release from the latter. These fungible legal values are transformed into the gains and losses by which we measure the "scarce" resources of our world—wealth, power, status, security, expressive freedom, and the hegemony of moral preferences—at stake in the fundamental or underlying conflict. With the imprimatur of constitutional authority, the Court's settlements, often provisional themselves, have shaped American political development. In turn, the Court, judiciary, and the law have been affected by the same political, social, and economic forces that have borne upon other agencies of government, though not always in the same ways or at the same pace.

It is important for students to see and appreciate the interplay of decision and politics, for example, how the Constitution has shaped and been shaped by the political economy of an expansive Jacksonian marketplace and of later industrial capitalism, by the geopolitics of the slave question, the political ideology of the Cold War, the political sociology of segregation and racial discrimination, and the political culture of the late twentieth century's hyper-media age.

Institutionally, it is no less important for students to realize that the Supreme Court is not the sole or, at times, even chief agent of constitutional change. At all stages of constitutional development, never less than in our own time, important constitutional change has come about through actions initiated and carried out by the president and by Congress.

Cases are placed at the ends of chapters and include almost all those generally agreed to be "landmark" or chief secondary decisions in doctrinal development and political significance. They are edited to allow students to grasp the issues before the Court, the Court's analysis and reasoning and, where present and of note, disagreement among the justices. Their arrangement is chronological to permit either serial or selective assignment.

Along with occasional maps and figures, the text employs a number of sidebars to discuss relevant matters not easily incorporated in their detail in the narrative flow of the text. These include biographical or jurisprudential sketches of major figures; discussion of important concepts in constitutional law and interpretation; detail on constitutional events or mechanics, such as the Twelfth Amendment's repair of the electoral college and the operating flaws in the Confederate Constitution; and "internal" data about the Supreme Court. Each chapter is followed by a bibliography of leading works for reference or further reading.

Several appendices provide additional information and help. These include a scheme for case briefing with a developmental emphasis; a guide for doing legal research in the library and on the internet; a description of the American judiciary and how cases come to the Supreme Court; a description of the internal work of the Court; a line biography of the justices from Jay to Breyer; a list of the Justices by

"historic" Courts; and the results of American national elections, 1788–2000, including presidential vote and party division in Congress. The first four may be particularly useful to students at the beginning of a course, the last three throughout.

In most texts background on the Supreme Court and the American judicial system appears in the first few pages, but to maintain a narrative and developmental flow, I have included this information in appendix form (C and D), where it can be assigned at any time—the beginning of the course or when the Supreme Court is first discussed and cases read.

A general and supplementary bibliography goes beyond the sources at the end of each chapter. This includes works on American political and constitutional development, constitutional theory and interpretation, the Supreme Court as an institution, and judicial biography.

Cases have been edited with readability in mind. Most footnotes and citational references beyond case names have been omitted. In a few instances, I have summarized precedential lists or references that have been cut, in brackets. Verbal excesses or flourishes, such as "It is my opinion in the case before us today," have been eliminated, as have decorative Latin phrases or pure legalisms that add nothing to meaning. Nonetheless, only so much can be done with the scholarly exhibitionism of a Story opinion or the convoluted legalese often found in a Scalian. Where it made sense, the names of the parties to the case have been substituted for "respondent," "petitioner," "plaintiff in error," and the like. In a very few instances, I have taken the liberty of inserting a much needed comma. Any substituted words or punctuation are in editor's brackets.

For each case, questions dealing with political or doctrinal matters have been inserted before the Opinion of the Court, to serve as guide to reading or a basis for discussion. In most cases, essential facts are given in the opinion; where not, a brief statement of them appears before the opinion.

I have tried to remain sensitive to the problem that confronts every casebook author or editor, that of not saying too much or too little. Each of the cases excerpted is discussed, at least briefly, in the chapter text. A sharp student, reading only the text, would have a good sense of the importance of the case in constitutional development, but would probably not fully understand how the Court reached its decision nor many of the issues the justices debated. For that, there is no substitute for reading the opinion(s).

Though this book is the work of one person who bears all responsibility for errors and shortcomings, it has profited greatly from the suggestions and comments of many others. I would particularly like to thank Richard M. Pious, Barnard College; Kathleen M. Moore, University of Connecticut; John Fliter, Kansas State University; Paul Wice, Drew University; Robert C. Bradley, Illinois State University; Christopher P. Banks, University of Akron; Steven Puro, St. Lewis University; Michael Horan, University of Wyoming; Mark Landis, Hofstra University; Tim Luther, Catholic Baptist University; Danny M. Adkinson, Oklahoma State University; C. Scott Peters, University of Louisville; Paul Lermack, Bradley University; Richard A. Brisbin, Jr., West Virginia University; Mark C. Miller, Clark University; William A. Blomquist, Indiana University-Purdue University Indianapolis; and Tracey Gladstone-Sowell, University of Wisconsin–River Falls; who read all or part of the manuscript of Volume I.

I would like to thank, as well, various editors at Longman, including Pam Gordon, Peter Glovin, Eric Stano, and Anita Castro, and also Jennifer Maughan and Julie Hollist, production and copy editors at WestWords who have contributed importantly to this book at various stages and with whom it has been a pleasure to work.

Richard S. Randall

THE CONSTITUTION OF THE UNITED STATES

Preamble

We the People of the United States, in Order to form a more perfect Union, establish Justice, insure domestic Tranquility, provide for the common defence, promote the general Welfare, and secure the blessings of Liberty to ourselves and our Posterity, do ordain and establish this Constitution for the United States of America.

Article One

Section 1. All legislative powers herein granted shall be vested in a Congress of the United States, which shall consist of a Senate and House of Representatives.

Section 2. The House of Representatives shall be composed of members chosen every second year by the people of the several States, and the electors in each State shall have the qualifications requisite for electors of the most numerous branch of the State legislature.

No Person shall be a Representative who shall not have attained to the age of twenty five years, and been seven years a citizen of the United States, and who shall not, when elected, be an inhabitant of that State in which he shall be chosen.

Representatives and direct taxes shall be apportioned among the several States which may be included within this Union, according to their respective numbers, which shall be determined by adding to the whole number of free persons, including those bound to service for a term of years, and excluding Indians not taxed, three fifths of all other persons. The actual enumeration shall be made within three years after the first meeting of the Congress of the United States, and within every subsequent term of ten years, in such manner as they shall by law direct. The number of Representatives shall not exceed one for every thirty thousand, but each State shall have at least one Rep-

resentative; and until such enumeration shall be made, the State of New Hampshire shall be entitled to choose three, Massachusetts eight, Rhode Island and Providence Plantations one, Connecticut five, New York six, New Jersey four, Pennsylvania eight, Delaware one, Maryland six, Virginia ten, North Carolina five, South Carolina five and Georgia three.

When vacancies happen in the Representation from any State, the executive authority thereof shall issue writs of election to fill such vacancies.

The House of Representatives shall choose their Speaker and other officers; and shall have the sole power of Impeachment.

Section 3. The Senate of the United States shall be composed of two Senators from each State, chosen by the legislature thereof, for six years; and each Senator shall have one Vote.

Immediately after they shall be assembled in consequence of the first election, they shall be divided as equally as may be into three classes. The seats of the Senators of the first class shall be vacated at the expiration of the second year, of the second class at the expiration of the fourth year, and of the third class at the expiration of the sixth year, so that one third may be chosen every second year; and if vacancies happen by resignation, or otherwise, during the recess of the legislature of any State, the executive thereof may make temporary appointments until the next meeting of the legislature, which shall then fill such vacancies.

No person shall be a Senator who shall not have attained to the age of thirty years, and been nine years a citizen of the United States, and who shall not, when elected, be an inhabitant of that State for which he shall be chosen.

The Vice-President of the United States shall be President of the Senate, but shall have no vote, unless they be equally divided.

The Senate shall choose their other officers, and also a President pro tempore, in the absence of the

Vice-President, or when he shall exercise the office of President of the United States.

The Senate shall have the sole power to try all impeachments. When sitting for that purpose, they shall be on oath or affirmation. When the President of the United States is tried, the Chief Justice shall preside: And no Person shall be convicted without the concurrence of two thirds of the members present.

Judgment in cases of impeachment shall not extend further than to removal from office, and disqualification to hold and enjoy any office of honor, trust or profit under the United States: but the party convicted shall nevertheless be liable and subject to indictment, trial, judgment and punishment, according to law.

Section 4. The times, places and manner of holding elections for Senators and Representatives, shall be prescribed in each State by the legislature thereof; but the Congress may at any time by law make or alter such regulations, except as to the places of choosing Senators.

The Congress shall assemble at least once in every year, and such meeting shall be on the first Monday in December, unless they shall by law appoint a different day.

Section 5. Each house shall be the judge of the elections, returns and qualifications of its own members, and a majority of each shall constitute a quorum to do business; but a smaller number may adjourn from day to day, and may be authorized to compel the attendance of absent members, in such manner, and under such penalties as each house may provide.

Each house may determine the rules of its proceedings, punish its members for disorderly behavior, and, with the concurrence of two-thirds, expel a member.

Each house shall keep a journal of its proceedings, and from time to time publish the same, excepting such parts as may in their judgment require secrecy; and the yeas and nays of the members of either house on any question shall, at the desire of one fifth of those present, be entered on the journal.

Neither house, during the session of Congress, shall, without the consent of the other, adjourn for more than three days, nor to any other place than that in which the two Houses shall be sitting.

Section 6. The Senators and Representatives shall receive a compensation for their services, to be ascertained by law, and paid out of the Treasury of the United States. They shall in all cases, except treason, felony and breach of the peace, be privileged from ar-

rest during their attendance at the session of their respective houses, and in going to and returning from the same; and for any speech or debate in either house, they shall not be questioned in any other place.

No Senator or Representative shall, during the time for which he was elected, be appointed to any civil office under the authority of the United States which shall have been created, or the emoluments whereof shall have been increased during such time; and no person holding any office under the United States, shall be a member of either house during his continuance in office.

Section 7. All bills for raising revenue shall originate in the House of Representatives; but the Senate may propose or concur with amendments as on other bills.

Every bill which shall have passed the House of Representatives and the Senate, shall, before it become a law, be presented to the President of the United States; If he approve he shall sign it, but if not he shall return it, with his objections to that house in which it shall have originated, who shall enter the objections at large on their journal, and proceed to reconsider it. If after such reconsideration two thirds of that house shall agree to pass the bill, it shall be sent, together with the objections, to the other house, by which it shall likewise be reconsidered, and if approved by two thirds of that house, it shall become a law. But in all such cases the votes of both houses shall be determined by yeas and nays, and the names of the persons voting for and against the bill shall be entered on the journal of each house respectively. If any bill shall not be returned by the President within ten days (Sundays excepted) after it shall have been presented to him, the same shall be a law, in like manner as if he had signed it, unless the Congress by their adjournment prevent its return, in which case it shall not be a law.

Every order, resolution, or vote to which the concurrence of the Senate and House of Representatives may be necessary (except on a question of adjournment) shall be presented to the President of the United States; and before the same shall take effect, shall be approved by him, or being disapproved by him, shall be repassed by two thirds of the Senate and House of Representatives, according to the rules and limitations prescribed in the case of a bill.

Section 8. The Congress shall have power to lay and collect taxes, duties, imposts and excises, to pay the debts and provide for the common defence and general welfare of the United States; but all duties, imposts and excises shall be uniform throughout the United States;

To borrow money on the credit of the United States;

To regulate commerce with foreign nations, and among the several States, and with the Indian tribes;

To establish an uniform rule of naturalization, and uniform Laws on the subject of bankruptcies throughout the United States;

To coin money, regulate the value thereof, and of foreign coin, and fix the standard of weights and measures;

To provide for the punishment of counterfeiting the securities and current Coin of the United States;

To establish post-offices and post-roads;

To promote the progress of science and useful arts, by securing for limited times to authors and inventors the exclusive right to their respective writings and discoveries;

To constitute tribunals inferior to the Supreme Court;

To define and punish piracies and felonies committed on the high seas, and offenses against the law of nations;

To declare war, grant letters of marque and reprisal, and make rules concerning captures on land and water;

To raise and support armies, but no appropriation of money to that use shall be for a longer term than two years;

To provide and maintain a navy;

To make rules for the government and regulation of the land and naval forces;

To provide for calling forth the militia to execute the laws of the union, suppress insurrections and repel invasions;

To provide for organizing, arming, and disciplining, the militia, and for governing such part of them as may be employed in the service of the United States, reserving to the States respectively, the appointment of the officers, and the authority of training the militia according to the discipline prescribed by Congress;

To exercise exclusive legislation in all cases whatsoever, over such district (not exceeding ten miles square) as may, by cession of particular States, and the acceptance of Congress, become the seat of the Government of the United States, and to exercise like authority over all places purchased by the consent of the legislature of the State in which the same shall be, for the erection of forts, magazines, arsenals, dockyards, and other needful Buildings; and

To make all laws which shall be necessary and proper for carrying into execution the foregoing powers, and all other powers vested by this Constitution in the Government of the United States, or in any department or officer thereof.

Section 9. The migration or importation of such persons as any of the States now existing shall think proper to admit, shall not be prohibited by the Congress prior to the Year one thousand eight hundred and eight, but a tax or duty may be imposed on such importation, not exceeding ten dollars for each person.

The privilege of the writ of habeas corpus shall not be suspended, unless when in cases of rebellion or invasion the public safety may require it.

No bill of attainder or ex post facto law shall be passed.

No capitation, or other direct tax shall be laid, unless in proportion to the census or enumeration herein before directed to be taken.

No tax or duty shall be laid on articles exported from any State.

No preference shall be given by any regulation of commerce or revenue to the ports of one State over those of another: nor shall vessels bound to, or from, one State, be obliged to enter, clear, or pay duties in another.

No money shall be drawn from the Treasury, but in consequence of appropriations made by law; and a regular statement and account of the receipts and expenditures of all public money shall be published from time to time.

No title of nobility shall be granted by the United States; and no person holding any office of profit or trust under them, shall, without the consent of the Congress, accept of any present, emolument, office, or title, of any kind whatever, from any king, prince or foreign State.

Section 10. No State shall enter into any treaty, alliance, or confederation; grant letters of marque and reprisal; coin money; emit bills of credit; make anything but gold and silver coin a tender in payment of debts; pass any bill of attainder, ex post facto law, or law impairing the obligation of contracts, or grant any title of nobility.

No State shall, without the consent of the Congress, lay any imposts or duties on imports or exports, except what may be absolutely necessary for executing it's inspection laws: and the net produce of all duties and imposts, laid by any State on imports or exports, shall be for the use of the Treasury of the United States; and all such laws shall be subject to the revision and control of the Congress.

No State shall, without the consent of Congress, lay any duty of tonnage, keep troops, or ships of war in time of peace, enter into any agreement or compact with another State, or with a foreign power, or engage in war, unless actually invaded, or in such imminent danger as will not admit of delay.

Article Two

Section 1.   The executive power shall be vested in a President of the United States of America. He shall hold his office during the term of four years, and, together with the Vice-President chosen for the same term, be elected, as follows:

Each State shall appoint, in such manner as the legislature thereof may direct, a number of electors, equal to the whole number of Senators and Representatives to which the State may be entitled in the Congress: but no Senator or Representative, or person holding an office of trust or profit under the United States, shall be appointed an elector.

The electors shall meet in their respective States, and vote by ballot for two persons, of whom one at least shall not lie an inhabitant of the same State with themselves. And they shall make a list of all the persons voted for, and of the number of votes for each; which list they shall sign and certify, and transmit sealed to the seat of the government of the United States, directed to the President of the Senate. The President of the Senate shall, in the presence of the Senate and House of Representatives, open all the certificates, and the votes shall then be counted. The person having the greatest number of votes shall be the President, if such number be a majority of the whole number of electors appointed; and if there be more than one who have such majority, and have an equal number of votes, then the House of Representatives shall immediately choose by ballot one of them for President; and if no person have a majority, then from the five highest on the list the said House shall in like manner choose the President. But in choosing the President, the votes shall be taken by States, the representation from each State having one vote; a quorum for this purpose shall consist of a member or members from two thirds of the States, and a majority of all the States shall be necessary to a choice. In every case, after the choice of the President, the person having the greatest number of votes of the electors shall be the Vice-President. But if there should remain two or more who have equal votes, the Senate shall choose from them by ballot the Vice-President.

The Congress may determine the time of choosing the electors, and the day on which they shall give their votes; which day shall be the same throughout the United States.

No person except a natural born citizen, or a citizen of the United States, at the time of the adoption of this Constitution, shall be eligible to the office of President; neither shall any person be eligible to that office who shall not have attained to the age of thirty five years, and been fourteen years a resident within the United States.

In case of the removal of the President from office, or of his death, resignation, or inability to discharge the powers and duties of the said office, the same shall devolve on the Vice-President, and the Congress may by law provide for the case of removal, death, resignation or inability, both of the President and Vice-President, declaring what officer shall then act as President, and such officer shall act accordingly, until the disability be removed, or a President shall be elected.

The President shall, at stated times, receive for his services, a compensation, which shall neither be increased nor diminished during the period for which he shall have been elected, and he shall not receive within that period any other emolument from the United States, or any of them.

Before he enter on the execution of his office, he shall take the following oath or affirmation:

"I do solemnly swear (or affirm) that I will faithfully execute the office of President of the United States, and will to the best of my ability, preserve, protect and defend the Constitution of the United States."

Section 2.   The President shall be Commander-in-Chief of the Army and Navy of the United States, and of the militia of the several States, when called into the actual service of the United States; he may require the opinion, in writing, of the principal officer in each of the executive departments, upon any subject relating to the duties of their respective offices, and he shall have power to grant reprieves and pardons for offenses against the United States, except in cases of impeachment.

He shall have power, by and with the advice and consent of the Senate, to make treaties, provided two thirds of the Senators present concur; and he shall nominate, and by and with the advice and consent of the Senate, shall appoint ambassadors, other public ministers and consuls, judges of the Supreme Court, and all other officers of the United States, whose appointments are not herein otherwise provided for, and which shall be established by law: but the Congress may by law vest the appointment of such inferior officers, as they think proper, in the President alone, in the courts of law, or in the heads of departments.

The President shall have power to fill up all vacancies that may happen during the recess of the Senate, by granting commissions which shall expire at the end of their next session.

Section 3. He shall from time to time give to the Congress information of the State of the Union, and recommend to their consideration such measures as he shall judge necessary and expedient; he may, on extraordinary occasions, convene both houses, or either of them, and in case of disagreement between them, with respect to the time of adjournment, he may adjourn them to such time as he shall think proper; he shall receive ambassadors and other public ministers; he shall take care that the laws be faithfully executed, and shall commission all the officers of the United States.

Section 4. The President, Vice-President and all civil officers of the United States, shall be removed from office on impeachment for, and conviction of, treason, bribery, or other high crimes and misdemeanors.

Article Three

Section 1. The judicial power of the United States, shall be vested in one Supreme Court, and in such inferior courts as the Congress may from time to time ordain and establish. The judges, both of the supreme and inferior courts, shall hold their offices during good behavior, and shall, at stated times, receive for their services, a compensation, which shall not be diminished during their continuance in office.

Section 2. The judicial power shall extend to all cases, in law and equity, arising under this Constitution, the laws of the United States, and treaties made, or which shall be made, under their authority; to all cases affecting ambassadors, other public ministers and consuls; to all cases of admiralty and maritime jurisdiction; to controversies to which the United States shall be a

party; to controversies between two or more States; between a State and citizens of another State; between citizens of different States; between citizens of the same State claiming lands under grants of different States, and between a State, or the citizens thereof, and foreign States, citizens or subjects.

In all cases affecting ambassadors, other public ministers and consuls, and those in which a State shall be party, the Supreme Court shall have original jurisdiction. In all the other cases before mentioned, the Supreme Court shall have appellate jurisdiction, both as to law and fact, with such exceptions, and under such regulations as the Congress shall make.

Trial of all crimes, except in cases of impeachment, shall be by jury; and such trial shall be held in the State where the said crimes shall have been committed; but when not committed within any State, the trial shall be at such place or places as the Congress may by law have directed.

Section 3. Treason against the United States, shall consist only in levying war against them, or in adhering to their enemies, giving them aid and comfort. No person shall be convicted of treason unless on the testimony of two witnesses to the same overt act, or on confession in open court.

The Congress shall have power to declare the punishment of treason, but no attainder of treason shall work corruption of blood, or forfeiture except during the life of the person attainted.

Article Four

Section 1. Full faith and credit shall be given in each State to the public acts, records, and judicial proceedings of every other State. And the Congress may by general laws prescribe the manner in which such acts, records and proceedings shall be proved, and the effect thereof.

Section 2. The citizens of each State shall be entitled to all privileges and immunities of citizens in the several States.

A person charged in any State with treason, felony, or other crime, who shall flee from justice, and be found in another State, shall on demand of the executive authority of the State from which he fled, be delivered up, to be removed to the State having jurisdiction of the crime.

No person held to service or labor in one State, under the laws thereof, escaping into another, shall, in consequence of any law or regulation therein, be discharged from such service or labor, But shall be delivered up on claim of the party to whom such service or labor may be due.

Section 3.   New States may be admitted by the Congress into this Union; but no new States shall be formed or erected within the jurisdiction of any other State; nor any State be formed by the junction of two or more States, or parts of States, without the consent of the legislatures of the States concerned as well as of the Congress.

The Congress shall have power to dispose of and make all needful rules and regulations respecting the territory or other property belonging to the United States; and nothing in this Constitution shall be so construed as to prejudice any claims of the United States, or of any particular State.

Section 4.   The United States shall guarantee to every State in this Union a republican form of government, and shall protect each of them against invasion; and on application of the legislature, or of the executive (when the legislature cannot be convened) against domestic violence.

Article Five

The Congress, whenever two thirds of both houses shall deem it necessary, shall propose amendments to this Constitution, or, on the application of the Legislatures of two thirds of the several States, shall call a convention for proposing amendments, which, in either case, shall be valid to all intents and purposes, as part of this Constitution, when ratified by the Legislatures of three fourths of the several States, or by conventions in three fourths thereof, as the one or the other mode of ratification may be proposed by the Congress; provided that no amendment which may be made prior to the Year One thousand eight hundred and eight shall in any manner affect the first and fourth Clauses in the Ninth Section of the first Article; and that no State, without its consent, shall be deprived of it's equal suffrage in the Senate.

Article Six

All debts contracted and engagements entered into, before the adoption of this Constitution, shall be as valid against the United States under this Constitution, as under the Confederation.

This Constitution, and the laws of the United States which shall be made in pursuance thereof; and all treaties made, or which shall be made, under the authority of the United States, shall be the supreme law of the land; and the judges in every State shall be bound thereby, anything in the Constitution or laws of any State to the contrary notwithstanding.

The Senators and Representatives before mentioned, and the members of the several State Legislatures, and all executive and judicial officers, both of the United States and of the several States, shall be bound by oath or affirmation, to support this Constitution; but no religious test shall ever be required as a qualification to any office or public trust under the United States.

Article Seven

The ratification of the Conventions of nine States, shall be sufficient for the establishment of this Constitution between the States so ratifying the same.

Done in Convention by the unanimous consent of the States present the seventeenth day of September in the year of our Lord one thousand seven hundred and eighty-seven and of the Independence of the United States of America the twelfth, in witness whereof we have hereunto subscribed our Names,

George Washington,	*President and Deputy from Virginia*
New Hampshire:	*John Langdon* *Nicholas Gilman*
Massachustts:	*Nathaniel Gorham* *Rufus King*
Connecticut:	*William Samuel Johnson* *Roger Sherman*
New York:	*Alexander Hamilton*
New Jersey:	*William Livingston* *David Brearley* *William Paterson* *Jonathan Dayton*

Pennsylvana: *Benjamin Franklin*
       Thomas Mifflin
       Robert Morris
       George Clymer
       Thomas FitzSimons
       Jared Ingersoll
       James Wilson
       Gouverneur Morris

Delaware: *George Read*
       Gunning Bedford, Jr.
       John Dickinson
       Richard Bassett
       Jacob Broom

Maryland: *James McHenry*
       Daniel of St. Thomas Jenifer
       Daniel Carroll

Virginia: *John Blair*
       James Madison, Jr.

North Carolina: *William Blount*
       Richard. Dobbs Spaight
       Hugh Williamson

South Carolina: *John Rutledge*
       Charles Cotesworth Pinckney
       Charles Pinckney
       Pierce Butler

Georgia: *William Few*
       Abraham Baldwin

(Signed September 17, 1787)

Amendment I

(Amendments I–X were ratified December 15, 1791)

Congress shall make no law respecting an establishment of religion, or prohibiting the free exercise thereof; or abridging the freedom of speech, or of the press; or the right of the people peaceably to assemble, and to petition the government for a redress of grievances.

Amendment II

A well regulated militia, being necessary to the security of a free State, the right of the people to keep and bear arms, shall not be infringed.

Amendment III

No soldier shall, in time of peace be quartered in any house, without the consent of the owner, nor in time of war, but in a manner to be prescribed by law.

Amendment IV

The right of the people to be secure in their persons, houses, papers, and effects, against unreasonable searches and seizures, shall not be violated, and no warrants shall issue, but upon probable cause, supported by Oath or affirmation, and particularly describing the place to be searched, and the persons or things to be seized.

Amendment V

No person shall be held to answer for a capital, or otherwise infamous crime, unless on a presentment or indictment of a Grand Jury, except in cases arising in the land or naval forces, or in the militia, when in actual service in time of war or public danger; nor shall any person be subject for the same offence to be twice put in jeopardy of life or limb; nor shall be compelled in any criminal case to be a witness against himself, nor be deprived of life, liberty, or property, without due process of law; nor shall private property be taken for public use, without just compensation.

Amendment VI

In all criminal prosecutions, the accused shall enjoy the right to a speedy and public trial, by an impartial jury of the State and district wherein the crime shall have been committed, which district shall have been previously ascertained by law, and to be informed of the nature and cause of the accusation; to be confronted with the witnesses against him; to have compulsory process for obtaining witnesses in his favor, and to have the assistance of counsel for his defence.

Amendment VII

In suits at common law, where the value in controversy shall exceed twenty dollars, the right of trial by jury shall be preserved, and no fact tried by a jury, shall be otherwise re-examined in any court of the United States, than according to the rules of the common law.

Amendment VIII

Excessive bail shall not lie required, nor excessive fines imposed, nor cruel and unusual punishments inflicted.

Amendment IX

The enumeration in the Constitution, of certain rights, shall not be construed to deny or disparage others retained by the people.

Amendment X

The powers not delegated to the United States by the Constitution, nor prohibited by it to the States, are reserved to the States respectively, or to the people.

Amendment XI

(Ratified January 8, 1798)

The judicial power of the United States shall not be construed to extend to any suit in law or equity, commenced or prosecuted against one of the United States by Citizens of another State, or by citizens or subjects of any foreign State.

Amendment XII

(Ratified September 25, 1804)

The electors shall meet in their respective States, and vote by ballot for President and Vice-President, one of whom, at least, shall not be an inhabitant of the same State with themselves; they shall name in their ballots the person voted for as President, and in distinct ballots the person voted for as Vice-President, and they shall make distinct lists of all persons voted for as President, and of all persons voted for as Vice-President and of the number of votes for each, which lists they shall sign and certify, and transmit sealed to the seat of the Government of the United States, directed to the President of the Senate; The President of the Senate shall, in the presence of the Senate and House of Representatives, open all the certificates and the votes shall then be counted; the person having the greatest number of votes for President, shall be the President, if such number be a majority of the whole number of Electors appointed; and if no person have such majority, then from the persons having the highest numbers not exceeding three on the list of those voted for as President, the House of Representatives shall choose immediately, by ballot, the President. But in choosing the President, the votes shall be taken by States, the representation from each State having one vote; a quorum for this purpose shall consist of a member or members from two-thirds of the States, and a majority of all the States shall be necessary to a choice. And if the House of Representatives shall not choose a President whenever the right of choice shall devolve upon them, be-

fore the fourth day of March next following, then the Vice-President shall act as President, as in the case of the death or other constitutional disability of the President. The person having the greatest number of votes as Vice-President, shall be the Vice-President, if such number be a majority of the whole number of Electors appointed, and if no person have a majority, then from the two highest numbers on the list, the Senate shall choose the Vice-President; a quorum for the purpose shall consist of two-thirds of the whole number of Senators, and a majority of the whole number shall be necessary to a choice. But no person constitutionally ineligible to the office of President shall be eligible to that of Vice-President of the United States.

Amendment XIII

(Ratified December 18, 1865)

Section 1. Neither slavery nor involuntary servitude, except as a punishment for crime whereof the party shall have been duly convicted, shall exist within the United States, or any place subject to their jurisdiction.
Section 2. Congress shall have power to enforce this Amendment by appropriate legislation.

Amendment XIV

(Ratified July 28, 1868)

Section 1. All persons born or naturalized in the United States, and subject to the jurisdiction thereof, are citizens of the United States and of the State wherein they reside. No State shall make or enforce any law which shall abridge the privileges or immunities of citizens of the United States; nor shall any State deprive any person of life, liberty, or property, without due process of law; nor deny to any person within its jurisdiction the equal protection of the laws.
Section 2. Representatives shall be apportioned among the several States according to their respective numbers, counting the whole number of persons in each State, excluding Indians not taxed. But when the right to vote at any election for the choice of Electors for President and Vice-President of the United States, Representatives in Congress, the executive and judicial officers of a State, or the members of the Legislature thereof, is denied to any of the male inhabitants of such State, being twenty-one years of age, and citizens of the United States, or in any way abridged, except for participation in rebellion, or other crime, the basis of representation therein shall be reduced in the proportion which

the number of such male citizens shall bear to the whole number of male citizens twenty-one years of age in such State.

Section 3. No person shall be a Senator or Representative in Congress, or elector of President and Vice-President, or hold any office, civil or military, under the United States, or under any State, who, having previously taken an oath, as a member of Congress, or as an officer of the United States, or as a member of any State legislature, or as an executive or judicial officer of any State, to support the Constitution of the United States, shall have engaged in insurrection or rebellion against the same, or given aid or comfort to the enemies thereof. But Congress may by a vote of two-thirds of each House, remove such disability.

Section 4. The validity of the public debt of the United States, authorized by law, including debts incurred for payment of pensions and bounties for services in suppressing insurrection or rebellion, shall not be questioned. But neither the United States nor any State shall assume or pay any debt or obligation incurred in aid of insurrection or rebellion against the United States, or any claim for the loss or emancipation of any slave; but all such debts, obligations and claims shall be held illegal and void.

Section 5. The Congress shall have power to enforce, by appropriate legislation, the provisions of this Amendment.

Amendment XV

(Ratified March 30, 1870)

Section 1. The right of citizens of the United States to vote shall not be denied or abridged by the United States or by any State on account of race, color, or previous condition of servitude.

Section 2. The Congress shall have power to enforce this Amendment by appropriate legislation.

Amendment XVI

(Ratified February 25, 1913)

The Congress shall have power to lay and collect taxes on incomes, from whatever source derived, without apportionment among the several States and without regard to any census or enumeration.

Amendment XVII

(Ratified May 31, 1913)

The Senate of the United States shall be composed of two senators from each State, elected by the people thereof, for six years; and each Senator shall have one vote. The electors in each State shall have the qualifications requisite for electors of the most numerous branch of the State legislature.

When vacancies happen in the representation of any State in the Senate, the executive authority of such State shall issue writs of election to fill such vacancies: Provided, That the legislature of any State may empower the executive thereof to make temporary appointments until the people fill the vacancies by election as the legislature may direct.

This amendment shall not be so construed as to affect the election or term of any senator chosen before it becomes valid as part of the Constitution.

Amendment XVIII

(Ratified January 29, 1919)

Section 1. After one year from the ratification of this Amendment, the manufacture, sale, or transportation of intoxicating liquors within, the importation thereof into, or the exportation thereof from the United States and all territory subject to the jurisdiction thereof for beverage purposes is hereby prohibited.

Section 2. The Congress and the several States shall have concurrent power to enforce this Amendment by appropriate legislation.

Section 3. This Amendment shall be inoperative unless it shall have been ratified as an amendment to the Constitution by the legislatures of the several States, as provided in the Constitution, within seven years from the date of the submission hereof to the States by Congress.

Amendment XIX

(Ratified August 26, 1920)

The right of citizens of the United States to vote shall not be denied or abridged by the United States or by any States on account of sex.

The Congress shall have power by appropriate legislation to enforce the provisions of this Amendment.

Amendment XX

(Ratified February 6, 1933)

Section 1. The terms of the President and Vice-President shall end at noon on the twentieth day of January, and the terms of Senators and Representatives at noon on the third day of January, of the years in which such terms would have ended if this Amendment had not been ratified; and the terms of their successors shall then begin.

Section 2.   The Congress shall assemble at least once in every year, and such meeting shall begin at noon on the third day of January, unless they shall by law appoint a different day.

Section 3.   If, at the time fixed for the beginning of the term of the President, the President-elect shall have died, the Vice-President-elect shall become President. If a President shall not have been chosen before the time fixed for the beginning of his term, or if the President-elect shall have failed to qualify, then the Vice-President-elect shall act as President until a President shall have qualified; and the Congress may by law provide for the case wherein neither a President-elect nor a Vice-President-elect shall have qualified, declaring who shall then act as President, or the manner in which one who is to act shall be selected, and such person shall act accordingly until a President or Vice-President shall have qualified.

Section 4.   The Congress may by law provide for the case of the death of any of the persons from whom the House of Representatives may choose a President whenever the right of choice shall have devolved upon them, and for the case of the death of any of the persons from whom the Senate may choose a Vice-President whenever the right of choice shall have devolved upon them.

Section 5.   Sections 1 and 2 shall take effect on the 15th day of October following the ratification of this Amendment.

Section 6.   This Amendment shall be inoperative unless it shall have been ratified as an amendment to the Constitution by the legislatures of three-fourths of the several States within seven years from the date of its submission.

Amendment XXI

(Ratified December 5, 1933)

Section 1.   The eighteenth article of amendment to the Constitution of the United States is hereby repealed.

Section 2.   The transportation or importation into any State, Territory, or possession of the United States for delivery or use therein of intoxicating liquors, in violation of the laws thereof, is hereby prohibited.

Section 3.   The Amendment shall be inoperative unless it shall have been ratified as an amendment to the Constitution by conventions in the several States, as provided in the Constitution, within seven years from the date of the submission hereof to the States by the Congress.

Amendment XXII

(Ratified February 26, 1951)

Section 1.   No person shall be elected to the office of the President more than twice, and no person who has held the office of President, or acted as President for more than two years of a term to which some other person was elected President shall be elected to the office of the President more than once. But this Amendment shall not apply to any person holding the office of President when this Amendment was proposed by the Congress, and shall not prevent any person who May be holding the office of President, or acting as President, during the term within which this Amendment becomes operative from holding the office of President or acting as President during the remainder of such term.

Section 2.   This Amendment shall be inoperative unless it shall have been ratified as an amendment to the Constitution by the legislatures of three-fourths of the several States within seven years from the date of its submission to the States by the Congress.

Amendment XXIII

(Ratified June 16, 1960)

Section 1.   The District constituting the seat of government of the United States shall appoint in such manner as the Congress may direct:

A number of electors of President and Vice-President equal to the whole number of Senators and Representatives in Congress to which the District would be entitled if it were a State, but in no event more than the least populous State; they shall be in addition to those appointed by the States, but they shall be considered, for the purposes of the election of President and Vice-President, to be electors appointed by a State; and they shall meet in the district and perform such duties as provided by the twelfth Amendment of amendment.

Section 2.   The Congress shall have power to enforce this Amendment by appropriate legislation.

Amendment XXIV

(Ratified February 4, 1964)

Section 1.   The right of citizens of the United States to vote in any primary or other election for President or Vice-President, for electors for President or Vice-President, or for Senator or Representative in Congress, shall not be denied or abridged by the United States or any State by reason of failure to pay any poll tax or other tax.

Section 2. The Congress shall have power to enforce this Amendment by appropriate legislation.

Amendment XXV
(Ratified February 10, 1967)

Section 1. In case of the removal of the President from office or of his death or resignation, the Vice-President shall become President.

Section 2. Whenever there is a vacancy in the office of the Vice-President, the President shall nominate a Vice-President who shall take office upon confirmation by a majority vote of both Houses of Congress.

Section 3. Whenever the President transmits to the President pro tempore of the Senate and the Speaker of the House of Representatives his written declaration that he is unable to discharge the powers and duties of his office, and until he transmits to them a written declaration to the contrary, such powers and duties shall be discharged by the Vice-President as Acting President.

Section 4. Whenever the Vice-President and a majority of either the principal officers of the executive departments or of such other body as Congress may by law provide, transmit to the President pro tempore of the Senate and the Speaker of the House of Representatives their written declaration that the President is unable to discharge the powers and duties of his office, the Vice-President shall immediately assume the powers and duties of the office as Acting President.

Thereafter, when the President transmits to the President pro tempore of the Senate and the Speaker of the House of Representatives his written declaration that no inability exists, he shall resume the powers and duties of his office unless the Vice-President and a majority of either the principal officers of the executive department or of such other body as Congress may by law provide, transmit within four day to the President pro tempore of the Senate and the Speaker of the House of Representatives their written declaration that the President is unable to discharge the powers and duties of his office. Thereupon Congress shall decide the issue, assembling within forty-eight hours for that purpose if not in session. If the Congress, within twenty-one days after receipt of the latter written declaration, or, if Congress is not in session, within twenty-one days after Congress is required to assemble, determines by two-thirds vote of both Houses that the President is unable to discharge the powers and duties of his office, the Vice-President shall continue to discharge the same as Acting President; otherwise, the President shall resume the powers and duties of his office.

Amendment XXVI
(Ratified July 1, 1971)

Section 1. The right of citizens of the United States, who are eighteen years of age or older, to vote shall not be denied or abridged by the United States or by any State on account of age.

Section 2. The Congress shall have power to enforce this Amendment by appropriate legislation.

Amendment XXVII
(Ratified May 7, 1992)

No law, varying the compensation for the services of the Senators and Representatives, shall take effect, until an election of Representatives shall have intervened.

AMERICAN CONSTITUTIONALISM

Constitutionalism rests on ideas of limited government and rule by law. Constitutional principles date to the ancient world, but constitutionalism in practice is a fairly late and unique achievement. In the natural history of government, most authority has been established by force, justified, if at all, by notions of God's will, hereditary entitlement, the need to prevent anarchy, or other theories bending toward absolute or near absolute rule. Over the years, this has placed discretionary power in a wide range of hands, including those of benevolent despots, divinely ruling kings, military dictators, party elites, and totalitarian bureaucracies, to say nothing of an unfortunately rich variety of rogues, tyrants, and gangs.

These rulers and regimes may or may not have the best interests of their subjects—the governed—at heart, or even considered their subjects important, but they have had one thing in common. They have been under little or no operating restraint as a matter of their subjects' right; their power has not been prescriptively limited by laws duly made. Of all regimes ever established, relatively few have been under working constitutions and almost none until the last 200 years.

Constitutions limit political authority by creating and defining governing institutions, allocating powers to them, and setting out procedures for choosing those who will fill them. In such provisions, general boundaries are drawn against possible seizure or usurpation of power. Additionally, certain matters or acts may be specifically forbidden to government. These are often stated positively as rights, such as those protecting speech, worship, or private property. Constitu-

tions may also contain statements about the general ends or purposes of the government created.

Because constitutions define basically, they are usually said to be "higher law," commanding an obligation superior to that of ordinary enactments, decisions, or policies. Though not cast in concrete, constitutions are usually intended to be less easily changed than other law. Thus, along with their defining functions and superior legal status, constitutions are often seen to have at least a relative "permanence" not usually associated with governmental offices and the laws and policies of those who occupy them.

Most constitutions appear as codified statements, their systematic provisions arranged in a single document or text. But a few, such as Great Britain's, may be "unwritten" and refer to a collection of important political settlements that have been given primary statutory form and to certain basic rules and procedures growing out of long usage.

Modern constitutionalism is associated with democratic government and has often been advanced historically in successful struggles of the nongoverning "many" against the governing "few." But it does not necessarily require democracy, at least as that term is understood today. The British and American constitutions of the late eighteenth century, though affording wider political participation than almost any other regimes of their time, were not democratic by present-day standards. By requiring that political authority be limited, however, they facilitated later fuller development of government popularly chosen and held popularly accountable. Modern nondemocratic states, such as the People's Republic of China or the former Soviet Union, may have formal constitutions but not operating constitutionalism.

"A Machine That Would Go of Itself"*

The American federal constitution, the subject of this book, is the oldest and, by almost any measure, most successful operating written constitution in the world. At its framing in 1787, it was without precedent. No country had ever adopted a single document constitution based on consent freely and popularly given, that had the status of supreme law. In the two centuries or more since, that constitution has served as a model for scores of others.

As the world's leading constitutionalists, Americans may be forgiven a certain absorption with their creation. The British playwright, George Bernard Shaw once observed that "America is always talking about its constitution."[†] He meant it as a criticism, but it could as well serve to compliment. Preoccupation has had less to do with questions of whether the Constitution is good or bad or needs changing, than with whether some act of government does or does not conform to it. Many Americans might readily agree with the judgment of nineteenth-century British Prime Minister William Gladstone that the Constitution was, "The most wonderful work . . . ever struck off at a given time by the brain and purpose of man."[‡] So ingrained is the notion of the Constitution as a perpetual and benevolent higher law that American constitutionalism has often almost seemed to be a kind of secular religion, with the Constitution the scripture, constitutionality its orthodoxy, and justices of the Supreme Court, the interpreting

high priests. This veneration has given American politics a particularly distinctive turn.

Though it came into being as a political act and political considerations have shaped its development at every turn, the Constitution is usually seen as separate and at some remove from government and politics of the day. Legitimacy of government policy is apt to depend not merely on what that policy accomplishes politically, but also on whether seen as having held to constitutional particulars. Similarly, American political debate tends to be dominated by "the need to justify positions and proposals by reference to the Constitution."[*]

Because the Constitution's blessing is so critical, political considerations are often dressed in the mantle of legal and constitutional argument and inevitably weigh on the Constitution to affect what it means. The astute nineteenth-century French observer of American politics Alexis de Tocqueville concluded that "scarcely any question arises in the United States which does not become, sooner or later, a subject of judicial debate."[†] The greatest dispute in American history—that over the nature of the national union on the slavery question—was cast, even as it led to civil war, largely as an argument over which side, North or South, was in the constitutional wrong. The Constitution has been and is the judging ground on which American political ideas and values are revealed, renewed, and sometimes transformed.

Casting or recasting political and governmental disputes in constitutional terms puts a premium on declaring what the law, ultimately the Constitution, means. This "discovery" or interpretation has given the American judiciary, and the Supreme Court at its summit, an unusually important place in the American political scheme. Wisely or unwisely, we look to judges and justices to be particularly skilled at determining the meaning of the law while, at

---

* The phrase is probably first attributable to poet and diplomat James Russell Lowell, in a speech in 1888. Lowell used it to describe American overconfidence in the constitutional system, for him a disturbing national complacency. See, generally, Michael Kammen, *A Machine That Would Go of Itself*, (New York: Random House, 1986).

[†] Ibid., 256.

[‡] Ibid., 162.

---

* Michael Foley, *American Political Ideas*, (Manchester and New York: Manchester University Press, 1991), 203.

[†] Alexis de Tocqueville, *Democracy in America*, Henry Reeve translation, (New York: Oxford University Press, 1946), 207.

the same time, being distanced enough from partisan politics to be "objective." To what extent the Supreme Court has successfully played this role or can hope to play it, are questions to which we shall return often in this book.

The Constitution says much about separating power at the center, dividing it between the center and outlying parts we call states, and restraining both center and parts in the name of individual rights. But the same Constitution, born of political struggle, is also filled with compromises, ambiguities, and just plain blanks. Many of its uncertainties have been resolved, provisionally or otherwise, but others remain to be resolved, and many new ones may be revealed as the Constitution is applied to unique disputes in the future. Saying what the Constitution means is the log of constitutional development. To examine that log, we must consider not only the great disputes that called interpretations forth but also the political, economic, and social forces surrounding them. Constitutional decisions have shaped our political system and political life; many of the disputes they resolved, in turn, changed the meaning of the Constitution.

Often overlooked in our constitutional development, perhaps because it seems almost granted, is that the United States, except for the Civil War, has been a beacon of political stability. A telling example illustrates the point. There have been 54 presidential elections since the first in 1788. Each, including one during the Civil War, has been held on schedule and in each the winner took office. Though such apparently hum-drum consistency wins no prizes for political drama, it signifies a political environment populated by "good winners" and "good losers" accustomed to having political disputes peacefully brokered. In that environment, a reasonably predictable political morrow can be relied on. Because it can, valuable time and resources can be securely turned to other, nonpolitical matters of choice. Such stability has played no small part in the success of the Constitution; the Constitution

has had no small part in gaining and keeping that stability.

Three Constitutional Regimes

Stability is not constitutional stasis. In more than 200 years, the Constitution has been amended only 27 times (18, if the Bill of Rights, the first 10 amendments, is considered a single ratifying act), but it has been anything but an unchanging idea or fixed text. As one modern constitutional scholar has put it, it is "an evolving historical practice, constituted by generations of Americans as they mobilized, argued, and resolved their ongoing disputes over the nation's identity and destiny."*

The founding, in 1787 and 1788, created a republican government with functionally separated power at the center and a unique "federal" system dividing power between center and states. It settled the question of whether to have a central government stronger than that represented by the existing Articles of Confederation. It did not resolve the exact nature of that enhanced union, nor how much sovereignty and independence the states retained particularly on the subtext issue of slavery, which was to hold a more highly defined union constitutional hostage for nearly 75 years. On many other matters, however, this "first" Constitution was formative. Many of the basic institutional features of today's government and political economy got their first shaping in the nationalizing and "new property" decisions of the Marshall and early Taney Courts.

In ending slavery and establishing national supremacy over state sovereignty once and for all, the Civil War was constitutionally transforming. During the decade of Reconstruction that followed, the basic text was amended three times, placing important new restrictions on state power in the name of individual rights. The intended protection of former slaves went unrealized in fact, as a regional caste system based on segregation and racial discrimination succeeded slavery and was largely ignored constitutionally. At the same time, American constitutionality was

---

* Bruce Ackerman, *We the People: Foundations*, 1991, 34.

recruited into the service of what occupied the nation itself: the new political economy of industrial capitalism. On the important matter of the regulatory role of government, the Constitution was interpreted to embody essentially laissez-faire principles. Occasional victories in the Supreme Court for reform measures mitigating some of the excesses of entrepreneurial freedom, were but modest countercurrents to a constitutional mainstream uncommonly solicitous and supportive of property and property rights.

The middle Constitution ended with the economic crash of the 1930s and Franklin Roosevelt's New Deal response to it. The Great Depression, which saw millions of persons left unemployed and impoverished, undermined public confidence in leadership of the titans of industry and finance and called attention to the flaws of largely unregulated capitalism. The Constitution was once more transformed, this time not by war and amendment but by popularly supported legislative and administrative innovation that eventually, after capitulation of a recalcitrant Supreme Court, received constitutional imprimatur through new interpretation of text. The new constitutionality shifted power at the center to the president and, within the federal system, to the national government. In the economy, it gave blessing to much greater governmental intervention and regulation, including establishment of many large-scale welfare programs. The new era eventually brought new attention to civil liberties and civil rights, particularly during the Warren Court in the 1960s. This in-

cluded expansive interpretation of First Amendment freedoms and criminal justice rights and long overdue realization of equal protection rights against racial segregation and discrimination.

American constitutional development is not a story of linear progress but of many winding paths and changes of direction. We begin in Part I by reflecting briefly on political, social, and economic features of colonial life that contributed to republican constitutionalism, and then by considering the struggle for independence, which succeeded, and that for a first constitutional union, which did not. Part II deals with the great question of the nature of the Union as it was provisionally answered at the Constitutional convention in Philadelphia, then shaped and recast in the decades that followed yet remaining unresolved on the slavery issue, finding final solution only through military triumph in civil war. Part III focuses on constitutional political economy, first as it developed in support of new property rights in the antebellum period, then underwrote full blown laissez-faire industrial capitalism in the late nineteenth century before facing the economic and constitutional crisis of the Great Depression and the New Deal. In Part IV we deal at length with the modern Constitution, its new empowerment of the national government and the president within it, and how these transformations have affected both intergovernmental and intragovernmental balance of power, the relation of government to business and property, and the nation's conduct of foreign affairs.

I

THE FIRST NATION

1

THE GROUNDWORK FOR REVOLUTION

America—the American colonies and, later, the United States—is an offshoot of the civilization of Western Europe, but its course within that lineage has been unique. The cult of constitutionalism and the remarkable authority given to courts and judges are but two later and higher-level developments in a complex intersecting of social, economic, geographic, and religious forces and conditions, perhaps unrepeatable in history, that shaped the American political experience and set the country apart from almost every other nation.

Some elements were purely circumstantial. Americans "inherited" an enormously rich land with forest and mineral resources, fertile soil, swift streams, good harbors, and a temperate climate. The small, largely scattered indigenous population that was intruded upon and ousted, was not strong enough to defeat settlement and occupation. A vast ocean separated the colonies and, later, the nation from the wars and political strife of Europe. By the nineteenth century, only Britain among the international powers was strong enough to maintain an important presence in North America. The absence of powerful neighbors to the north, west, and south provided security from interference or attack that few other developing nations have had.

Other elements had more to do with the people themselves and the institutions they built. In this chapter, we consider some of the social, economic, religious, and legal circumstances that led to republican independence in a world of kings, emperors, and czars. With many years of self-governance behind them, rebelling Americans of 1776 could feel politically self-confident and entitled. The popular elements in the colonial polity were hardly democratic by today's standards, but they allowed Americans, who would soon become constitutional pioneers, to be leaders in representative government even earlier.

Colonial Society

Though many early settlers, including those who built along the Massachusetts coast, came to the New World to escape religious persecution and to form their own religious communities, most made the crossing with more worldly motives. A handful from the English upper classes were gentlemen adventurers or those simply down on their luck. A few were speculators having little or no interest in putting down roots. Most, however, were from the lower and middle ranks of European societies. "The rich," the Frenchman Crevecouer wrote, "stay in Europe; it is only the middling and the poor that emigrate." Many who could not afford passage arrived as indentured servants. Eventually more than 250,000 of them traded time at bonded labor—usually for four to seven years—for a ticket to a new life. Another group—perhaps as many as 30,000—were convicts, cost effectively shipped out from England. More than one established American family tracing its lineage has been chagrined to find a forbear or two who had stood in the dock at Old Bailey, London's legendary criminal court.

Most settlers were ambitious and they needed to be. With little more than high hopes and courage to sustain them, they found a life that was harsh and uncertain. Primitive and dangerous conditions tested will and survival itself. The early road to opportunity was seldom straight or smoothly paved.

For most, the vital units of social organization were family and small community. Patriarchically ruled, the family did not resemble the modern nuclear model; it was likely to include many dependent relatives and unrelated "boarders" or hands. Women were clearly subordinate, though being in short supply and needed for sharing the great labor of settlement gave them unusual influence. As in most agrarian societies, children were specially valued as helping hands; modern childhoods of play and education were rarities.

By the mid-eighteenth century, class structure differed markedly from that in most of Europe. A middle class of semiprosperous farmers, artisans, shopkeepers, and petty officials, though small by modern standards, was steadily expanding, with easy entry or exit in either direction. Celebrated by Benjamin Franklin for its virtues of industry, thrift, and self-reliance, this loosely bounded stratum furnished the social base for an increasingly self-confident self-governing polity. Sustained prosperity eventually produced an indigenous aristocracy. This small group of wealthy, sometimes pretentious men, having time and leisure to gain education and pursue science, philosophy, and the arts, provided much of the local political leadership. Though a few were loyalists when the Revolution came, most actively served the struggle for independence, often in its front ranks. The Adamses and Hancocks in Massachusetts, Schuylers in New York, Livingstons in New Jersey, Dickinsons and Morrises in Pennsylvania, Masons, Lees, and Randolphs in Virginia, and Pinckneys in the Carolinas were among those who risked their station by leading the rebellion.

Below the middle class were most of the new arrivals, many former indentured servants, and those who, for one reason or another, had not prospered or made economic headway. Lower standing was often temporary, ascent depending much more on material success than on ethnicity, family, or education. Most colonials found they had come a long way from the fixed stations that had bound their forbears in Europe.

For Africans the matter was altogether different. Almost all had arrived as slaves and all but a few thousand remained so. Their lot was immeasurably worse than lower strata whites and their opportunities almost nil. Though their labor was economically critical, they were scarcely thought to be members of society. The slave trade was prospering, and voices against it and the institution it fed were not yet audible.

Though many individual Indians were absorbed by colonial society, tribes were not. Many tribes had sold or given up their land or had it taken away. Some moved westward while others were enveloped and isolated by the spreading stream of settlers. Some tribes gained while others lost by being on one side or the other in several interior colonial wars against the French. Most remained foreign entities, usually by choice, rather than becoming assimilated parts of colonial life.

On the eve of the Revolution, white colonial society was probably the most open and fluid in the world. Mobility for the average person was unequaled anywhere, and foreign observers were apt to remark about the lack of condescension from above or deference from below. None of this implied a reign of perfect social harmony or solidarity. Class tensions and antagonisms were present and some had ugly local eruptions, usually over land ownership and easy money or the more purely political matters of representation and use of government. Such conflicts were more the overhead of a fast-growing society animated by extraordinary geo-economic conditions than they were deep fissures in the body politic. Some antagonisms were made worse by the Revolution; more often than not, they were submerged in its larger cause.

The Economics of Empire

Though the colonies were founded by religious dissenters and those seeking a better material life, they were also pawns in a complex international economy that was slowly moving from medieval feudalism to industrial capitalism. New World exploration fueled an already heated commercial rivalry among the European powers, making a race for productive colonies all but certain. If well located, colonies could be a perpetual source of foodstuffs, minerals, field and forest products, and other raw materials for the parent country while serving as a ready market for its finished goods and home to its excess population.

This form of economic nationalism, loosely called mercantilism, promised military protection, governance, and a kind of second-hand prosperity to the colonies in return for perpetual loyalty and subordination. The parent country had first, if not exclusive, rights to colonial products—its trade routes being funnels through which almost all exportable surplus flowed. To succeed, mercantilism also called for elaborate internal controls, including regulation of labor and production. Economic individualism and laissez-faire freedom from government intervention, so important in later American commercial practice, had little or no place in the mercantilist system.

New economic and political forces eventually undid mercantilism in the American colonies but not before it had run a century or more. The colonies prospered and England, developing the most powerful economy in the world, came to dominate European rivals in North America. These successes coupled with political unrest at home diverted parental attention from the internal life of the colonial offspring.

The colonies had not one economy but three. Only in the South, dependent on a few surplus agricultural staples—mainly tobacco, indigo, and rice—was there specialization suited to the mercantilist system. In the maturing economy of the middle colonies, agriculture was diversified, and settlers were more successful in setting up commercial enterprises and small manufacturing. In New England neither soil nor climate supported profitable surplus crops. Because of small compact farms, the region was better suited to commerce and manufacturing. Early industries to the middle and northern colonies were chiefly extractive, using the resources of sea and forest, but as their economies grew more balanced and diverse, many products began to compete with those made in England.

Two other conditions, common to all regions, also worked against the mercantilist system: cheap or free land and a chronic shortage of labor. It is almost impossible to overstate the importance of land in shaping American development. Its effect was economic and psychological. As humankind's basic form of wealth, fertile land was America's most compelling resource. The colonial position was nearly opposite the fixed, feudal-like order still having force in much of Europe. Cheap or free land favored a self-reliant individualism and, with it, local economic and political sufficiency, adverse to a mercantilist system.

Despite a steady stream of new settlers crossing the Atlantic, colonial prosperity and perpetual expansion created a demand for labor that was to mark American economic life until well into the twentieth century. The colonial working man's lot was hard and primitive by modern standards, but he was freer than his European counterpart from mercantilism's propensity for deflating wages and increasing hours. Constant need for "hands" led to wages and working conditions that were the world's best. "America," as William Penn put it, was "a good poor man's country." For whites, at least, this became more and more a settled fact.

The linchpin of imperial economic policy was control of colonial trade. Most colonial imports came from or passed through the parent country. Colonial consumers, not having the benefit of a fully free market, paid higher prices. Most colonial exports, including those eventually destined for non-English consumption, could be sent only to England or other English colonies. English merchants realized sizeable "middleman" profits in this scheme while colonial producers usually got less for their goods than they would have by direct competitive sale to French, Spanish, or other Continental buyers. Whenever colonial manufacture was seen to threaten similar home manufacture, Parliament was called on to regulate it. The Woolens Act of 1699, the Hat Act of 1732, and the Iron Act of 1750 were all aimed to eliminate or at least contain developing industries in the colonies. The Molasses Act of 1733 prevented New England rum distillers from buying sugar more cheaply from the French West Indies than they could from English Caribbean sources. This restriction, famously ignored, helped make smuggling a fixture in colonial economic life.

By the mid-eighteenth century it was clear nearly everywhere except London that a trade policy designed to keep the colonies in permanent dependency could not survive. Together, the 13 societies along the Atlantic seaboard were now too large, too prosperous, too aspiring and energetic, too competent and self-confident simply to serve the interests of another land 4,000 miles away. Equal partnership was in order but not in the offing.

Religion and Religious Tolerance

Religious divisiveness, which had plagued Europe for centuries and is still of consequence in many parts of the world today, was relatively subdued in America. A quest for religious freedom played an important part in the founding and development of several colonies. The Roman Catholic Lord Baltimore and the Quaker William Penn each got proprietary charters from the Crown to set up havens for their coreligionists, in Maryland and Pennsylvania. But it was Puritan settlement in New England that had the greatest influence on American political thinking and practice.

The Puritans were an extreme latter-day product of the turmoil created by the Protestant Reformation and its spiritual and ecclesiastical rebellion against rigidities of the Church of Rome. Though England had become the chief Protestant country in Europe by the late 1500s, the Puritans and other radical sects wanted to carry reform further, purifying the Church of England of all remnants of Catholic ritual and hierarchy. Some urged abolishing the state church entirely, in favor of separate local congregations; the Quakers, extending this, preached that every believer was his or her own church. These "dissenters," of whom the Puritans were among the most vocal and uncompromising, provoked both Church leadership and Crown, who then tried to impose greater orthodoxy.

The Puritans went into exile seeking religious freedom, but the colony they founded under John Winthrop and John Cotton at first offered little to anyone else. They set up a tight-knit theocracy in which individual life was wholly secondary to the good of the fellowship. The conformity served them well in the struggle against the wilderness, but was less suited to life in the more prosperous, socially diverse assemblage the colony later became.

The importance of the Puritans and other Separatists to American constitutional development—out of all proportion to their numbers—is not in their religion or misguided efforts at theocratic governing, but in their ideas about the legitimacy of authority. The contractual notion of covenant—of a church and later a community built on consent of the believers—and of a higher law, one superior to the mere enactments of men of the day, became cornerstones of later American thinking about government and politics.

Two other developments, unfolding after many stops and starts, were no less important: the growth of religious tolerance and a weakening of ties between church and state. Though tolerance had such outspoken champions as Roger Williams and William Penn, its progress was more the by-product of social and economic forces than the prize of inspired argument. Many early settlers had witnessed intolerance in England and were aware of its destructive possibilities. Later colonists, needing to adjust to many religious sects and beliefs, found that tension produced by disturbing beliefs and practices could be eased by distance—by the sheer amount of living space around them. Besides, religious strife was not compatible with economic growth. Intolerance got in the way of rational planning and was usually bad for business. It was not the first nor last time that conflict with high emotional valence would give ground to economic expediency.

Tolerance was also the product of a trend toward secularism. Spiritual life was important in the eighteenth century, but individuals were less apt to be consumed by religion and religious belief than in centuries past. Science, discovery, and rationalism challenged the certainty with which many beliefs were held. If the eighteenth century was not suddenly teeming with atheists and agnostics, at least its secular intellectual summons, new freedoms, and material opportunities turned many energies away from religious concerns.

Tolerance and diversity were antithetical to state support of one church over others, and would eventually call for separation of ecclesiastic and temporal authority. On the eve of the Revolution, nine colonies still had official churches, but the status had been eroding for some time. Independence quickly brought near complete disestablishment everywhere.

By mid-eighteenth century, religious freedom and disestablishment had advanced further in the colonies than in any society in history. For many colonists, religious tolerance helped to liberate an inner, spiritual life that matched new social and economic freedoms encountered in the external world.

Governing and Being Governed

Despite being founded under a variety of corporate and semifeudal proprietary charters, grants, and "compacts," the colonies soon developed similar patterns of government. Internal executive power was in the hands of a governor who, except in Connecticut and Rhode Island, came to be appointed by the Crown as the founding documents were gradually replaced by royal charters. More like viceroys than locally accountable administrators, they were agents of imperial authority and had various executive prerogatives. They appointed lower officers, headed the established church, commanded military forces, and had absolute vetoes over legislation.

Nearly every colony had a council, an advisory body to the governor appointed by the Crown. Designed as an analog of the House of Lords, it was supposed to represent the upper class and thus balance royal authority of the governor and the legislative power of ordinary citizens represented in the assembly. But without an hereditary aristocracy in the colonies, councils soon became anomalous. Where they survived, they gradually became a second elected legislative house.

Opposed to the governor was the assembly representing the people of the colony. These bodies grew from small, fairly exclusive, nonelected groups that were mainly consultative to agencies with a true popular base. They were the forerunners of American republican government and representative democracy. Eventually, they acquired general legislative power and, with it, control of the public purse.

Colonial government thus veered off from the English "mixed" model based on the post-feudal political sociology of English society in which monarchical, aristocratic, and democratic parts represented by King, Lords, and Commons, shared the tasks of governing. The more open social and economic conditions of colonial life produced a different kind of balance, one that separated power by executive, legislative, and judicial function, a division that became fixed in American constitutional organization.

Though suffrage was limited in early years—in Massachusetts, for example, it was tied to church membership—by 1700 it had grown to include most white males with modest property holdings. Since land was cheap, such asset qualifications were easily met. Depending on the colony, between 25 and 75 percent of white males were eligible to vote in elections of the assemblies, though perhaps only a quarter of them regularly did so. Today we would find such a franchise cramped and level of participation unimpressive, but in the oligarchic eighteenth century, it put the colonies in the democratic front ranks.

Colonial politics time and again was a running battle between governor and assembly. The constituencies of these vying institutions were almost as divergent as the interests they represented—imperial ends on the one hand, local needs and demands on the other. Some governors proved able and astute in manipulating the assemblies or at least in getting along with them. Others were stubborn, foolish, or simply well-connected incompetents sent out from London. The assemblies were often no bargains either. Their ranks produced some outstanding colonial leaders, but in too many cases they were filled simply with quarrelsome, small-minded men.

Because of his great official powers, the governor would have seemed to have had the better of it. In fact, however, the balance gradually shifted to the assemblies. Looking to London for instructions and support, the governors often got little of either. Years of imperial inattention to internal colonial governance had created empty political space that the assemblies readily filled. Control over appropriations and a growing moral authority gained from their popular base were important political assets. By the 1760s, the assembly was the dominant agency in almost every colonial government.

In representing the Crown, the colonial governor had important help from customs officials, postmasters, judges, and military and naval commanders, most of whom were Englishmen. The locus of highest imperial policymaking and administration, however, was London. Parliament placed authority for the colonies in the Privy Council, but most actual direction fell to the Council's committees and to the Board of Trade, formed in 1696 and having among its responsibilities the drafting of instructions to the governors. Imperial policy called for colonial laws to be submitted to the Council for approval or "royal disallowance." Of many thousand reviewed during the colonial period, only a few hundred—about five percent—were set aside. More often than not, those that were denied touched on England's commercial interests, rather than being of strictly internal concern. In later years, several colonies maintained agents in London to better represent their points of view. The best known and most effective of these lobbyists was Benjamin Franklin, who served Pennsylvania first, and later, other colonies.

The difficulties of governing a vast, populous territory 4,000 miles away without benefit of modern transport or communications, are obvious. But London's problems were also of its own making. Except for a brief period in the 1680s when James II tried to assert greater control over colonial affairs by centralizing their administration (a project that ended with his overthrow in the Glorious Revolution of 1688–1689), England had paid only enough attention to the colonies to insure their protection against France and Spain and the success of its mercantilist policies. Growing awareness of colonial growth and diversity gave rise to a more elaborate administration in the eighteenth century. But a cumbersome bureaucracy, diffused responsibility, and mediocre and sometimes corrupt personnel all weakened or simply confused administrative efforts. By the time Parliament acted decisively in the 1760s, the colonists (partly through their own efforts, partly through imperial default) had become masters of their local affairs.

Law and the Rule of Law

The original colonial charters and grants said almost nothing about everyday conflicts that might arise among the settlers over land, debt, promises, or anything else. Except in the Puritan theocracy, where it was believed the Bible, properly read, could offer guidelines for resolving most worldly quarrels, the early colonists were largely on their own. Because lawyers were few and courts rudimentary, settlement of disputes was apt to be informal, uncertain, and sometimes amateurish. This may have satisfied many early settlers, who wanted to keep things simple and had no great love for lawyers, but the growing complexity of economic and social life created a demand for law—for rules that were known and comprehensible and, when applied to disputes, yielded reasonably predictable results. Gradually, this need was met by development of a colonial bar, enactment of local statutes and codes and, not least, the borrowing of established judge-made English common law. By the end of the seventeenth century, most parts of the English legal system were firmly implanted, a matter of lasting consequence for American constitutionalism.

Despite this success, not all English substantive law proved suitable to colonial circumstances. That which did not was eventually recast by statute or modified by common law decision.

English land law, for instance, still reflecting the feudal notion that all real property was held under a tenured relationship to the King or his grantees, called for those working land to pay an annual quitrent—a form of taxation—to the King or overlord. Such a rule, useful perhaps in a society where land was limited and tightly held and expected to remain so, made less sense in the colonies where realty was cheap and abundant and had never been "owned" by the King. Quitrents were gradually abolished or came to have lax enforcement.

Decline of the rule of primogeniture was another tribute to the colonial world's unique social geography. English common law called for land to pass at death only to the eldest son, thus preventing the breakup of holdings into smaller and smaller parcels uneconomical to work. But where supply of land far exceeded occupancy, primogeniture lost much of its utility and became a symbol of an unwanted aristocratic land order. It was gradually abandoned, except in the more traditional Southern colonies, where it ended with the Revolution.

The idea and practice of limited government—the rule of law itself—proved the most important political part of the English legal heritage. It had shaped the complex of institutions, rules, practices, and customs that make up the English constitution. Its bounds included the Magna Carta, the source of modern substantive and procedural due process; such long-standing common law liberties as the writ of habeas corpus; hard-won Parliamentary supremacy; and the English Bill of Rights growing out of the Glorious Revolution of 1688. To this legacy of constitutionalism, the colonists added their unique codicil: the written statement of basic law, which was to come to full flower with the drafting of the Articles of Confederation in 1778 and the Federal Constitution in 1787.

Each colony was founded and later developed under a charter or other documentary basic law that distributed powers and set out privileges and responsibilities. In some sense, it was controlling law: Neither a colony's original sponsors or proprietors nor its later assembly could change its terms. The phrase "unconstitutional," destined to ring through American history, entered common political parlance to signify violated basic law. The charters were enough like constitutions that two—Connecticut's of 1662 and Rhode Island's of 1663—survived the Revolution to serve as state constitutions until well into the nineteenth century.

The idea that the people, in community or congregation, could themselves create a basic governing agreement—a social contract—was also part of the colonial experience, dating to the Mayflower Compact and covenants of the Separatist churches. Such agreements implied that the governed were politically competent and their willing consent was something that mattered, two notions that had not yet widely taken root in the European world.

Law and government by law were arguably the most important parts of the entire English colonial endowment. The parent country was the world's leader in legal and constitutionalist development. The colonists profited from that and, later, from their own experience in creating governments of laws.

A Decade of Ferment

After victory over arch-rival France in the Seven Years War (the French and Indian War in America) in 1763, Britain was unchallenged in North America, astride the greatest empire of modern times. But the triumph also set in motion forces that led to revolt of a large part of that empire. Drawn out and costly, the war left Britain with a debt of 137 million pounds to be paid off by unpopular and sharply higher taxes at home. Also, a vast new territory in North America was now to be policed, and the army, rather than being sent home, was kept in remote outposts at great expense. The cost of peace added to that of war was staggering.

It seemed reasonable to look to the colonies for financial help—after all, had not the war been fought partly for their protection and benefit? For the next 10 years British colonial policy was driven by this end. But what seemed natural and fair on one side of the Atlantic did not seem so on the other, and those policies, often heavy handed in application, were a calamity. They produced little revenue and pushed 13 colonies into revolt.

A year after war's end, Parliament passed the American Revenue Act—the Sugar Act, named after one of its specified commodities—which imposed or increased duties on an array of non-British imports. To put teeth into these measures, Parliament tightened what had been a notoriously lax customs enforcement in America. Prosecution of violators was taken out of the hands of local colonial courts, which often did not convict, and placed in a new vice-admiralty court in Nova Scotia. What Edmund Burke called the period of "salutary neglect" was over.

Colonial resentment mounted the following year when Parliament passed the Quartering and the Stamp Acts. The first, aimed at squaring the cost of the army, called for colonial authorities to provide barracks and supplies for the troops and to allow their billeting in inns and unoccupied buildings. The Stamp Act, the first direct levy imposed by Parliament in the colonies, placed taxes on newspapers, pamphlets, legal documents, insurance policies, and other records of commerce. Affecting many of the groups that carried the greatest weight in colonial affairs—lawyers, merchants, printers, and publishers—it could not have been better designed to provoke colonial opposition.

Reaction took three forms: boycotts of British-made imports, the formation of secret societies—the Sons of Liberty—for sabotage and other extra-legal acts, and calling the Stamp Act Congress, a protest meeting of colonial representatives in New York. Nonimportation, which began in Boston and eventually spread to most other port cities, was highly effective. When the volume of British exports to the colonies dropped markedly in 1766, Parliament repealed the Stamp Act but still asserted it had absolute power to make binding laws for its North American subjects.

In the Townshend Acts of 1767, Parliament, conforming to what had been the colonial position—that only external taxes might be imposed—placed new import duties on many products including glass, paint, lead, paper, and tea. Again, a colonial nonimportation boycott reduced trade and revenue. A new government in London in 1770 headed by Lord North repealed the Townshend duties on all items but tea. Though the remaining impost became critical, Parliament's retreat was a clear victory for the colonials.

New provocation came early in 1773 in passage of the Tea Act. Trying to bail out the imperially prized but near bankrupt East India Tea Company, Parliament subsidized sale of its tea in North America. Even with the tea tax, the company could now undersell other tea imported by law-abiding merchants or brought into the colonies by smugglers. Colonial response was swift and to the point. A group of Boston locals disguised as Mohawk Indians boarded *The Dartmouth* and two other tea ships holding consignments about to be landed and dumped the entire cargo into the Boston harbor. Other "tea disorders" followed in New York and Annapolis.

Parliament angrily responded to these offenses by passing the Coercive Acts, which closed the port of Boston until restitution should be made to the East India Tea Company and shielded Crown officials in Massachusetts from being tried in colonial courts on any charges arising from performance of their duties. More drastically, the acts all but annulled the Massachusetts Charter by requiring that members of the Governor's Council, until then elected by the assembly, be appointed by the King and giving the Governor power to appoint other officials formerly elected. Another provision, aimed directly at colonial op-

position, barred town meetings, which the wily agitator Samuel Adams and other radicals had used so effectively, without prior consent of the Governor.

However justified they may have seemed in London, these punitive and repressive measures proved to be miscalculations. Repeatedly Parliament had underestimated colonial unity and determination. It now misjudged how fast things were moving on the other side of the Atlantic. The colonials found they could communicate with each other up and down the continent and organize themselves locally for boycotts and forceful protest. When royal governors in several colonies dissolved the assemblies or refused to call them to session, oppositionists formed provincial congresses—rump sessions of the assemblies or newly elected groups—to serve as alternative legislatures. In defying British policy, the colonials also discovered they were far more affiliated across class lines than they or anyone else might have thought possible. Even before the Coercive Acts, a growing number of leaders of almost every station and colony believed things had gone beyond a point of no return.

Rising calls for an intercolonial conference led to a meeting of the first Continental Congress in Philadelphia in the early fall of 1774. Its 56 delegates representing every colony but Georgia went well beyond a show of moral support for Massachusetts. Voting by colony, they declared 13 Parliamentary acts since 1763 to have violated American rights and condemned extension of the vice-admiralty jurisdiction and the keeping of a standing army in the colonies. They then formed the Continental Association, pledging each colony to the boycott of British products and embargo of exports to Britain. It was an extraordinary meeting and an eye-opening glimpse of eventual national unity.

When it learned of the Congress's action, the North government introduced a conciliatory plan in Parliament that would recognize the Continental Congress and forbear further revenue measures, but it was defeated in the House of Lords. A watered down measure was passed

Grandfather of His Country

No American colonial was better known than Benjamin Franklin and probably none so embodied the qualities that set America apart from Europe. By any measure, Franklin was one of the most talented men alive, an authentic polymath. Having had only two years of formal education, he personified self-improvement in a land of self-made persons. He played a part in almost every important American political event for 30 years.

Born in 1706, the youngest of 17 children of a Boston candlemaker, he made his way to Philadelphia in his teens as a printer's apprentice. In a few years he was himself a successful publisher founding a newspaper and putting out the popular annual *Poor Richard's Almanack,* filled with witticisms and homespun "a penny saved is a penny earned" maxims. He was a main force in several civic projects including organization of the city's first police and fire departments, a circulating library, and an academy that later became the University of Pennsylvania. At 37, he was comfortable enough to "retire" to pursue science and invention. He read widely, taught himself three languages, made the first pair of bifocals, the lightning rod, and the Franklin stove. His work with electricity, popularly symbolized by his famous kite experiment, brought him international attention.

It was Franklin's public service as a statesman and diplomat in the last four decades of his long life that made him a vital figure in American independence and early nationhood. As a Pennsylvania delegate to the Albany Congress, which had been called by British authorities in 1754 to discuss ways to deal with the French and Indian threats, he drew up the visionary Albany Plan calling for union of the colonies under a president-general appointed by the Crown. A generation ahead of its time, the scheme was too radical in America and in London.

---

instead, including a declaration of Massachusetts to be in rebellion. By now both sides in that colony were preparing for hostilities. These occurred at Lexington and Concord in April 1775 when British forces, in a preemptive strike, tried to destroy the colonial militia's military stores. The troops were met in the two towns by local Minute Men, and the clashes left 100 or more dead and wounded on each side. When the British retreated to Boston, the militia laid siege to the city until the army evacuated it months later for New York.

In May, the Continental Congress reconvened in Philadelphia and began assuming basic functions of government. When delegates from Georgia arrived five months later, the Congress represented all 13 colonies for the first time. In one of its first acts, it adopted the colonial forces surrounding Boston as the new Continental Army and named George Washington of Virginia its commander-in-chief. Plans were made to raise additional companies of riflemen and to form a small navy of converted fishing boats. These efforts were paid for by issuance of bills of credit redeemable against the "Confederated Colonies." The Congress called on each colony to create new state governments. Repudiating imperial trade laws, it declared all American ports open to foreign trade.

At the same time, Congress put out a peace feeler that came to be known as the Olive Branch Petition. Addressed to King George III,

In the years following, Franklin served as postmaster-general for the colonies, a job in which he succeeded with typical thrift and ingenuity in improving delivery and ending the service's recurring deficits. Later, as colonial agent in London for Pennsylvania, Georgia, and Massachusetts, he helped persuade Parliament to repeal the Stamp Act. Back home, he was a member of the Second Continental Congress and helped draft the Declaration of Independence, of which he was a signer.

During the war, he was sent to France to negotiate loans and an alliance between France and the Revolutionary government. He returned to Paris in 1783 with John Adams and John Jay to negotiate the treaty with Britain that ended the war and completed American independence.

His last great public service was as a Pennsylvania delegate to the Constitutional Convention in Philadelphia in 1787. Now the country's elder statesman and in failing health, he was a conciliatory force among the delegates, most of whom were less than half his age. On the convention's final day, he made his famous harmony speech, praising the delegates for persevering through compromises, hoping that doubters among them—of whom there were many—might doubt their own infallibility, and urging all to maintain unity of their ranks for the task of ratification.

Like all public men, Franklin was not without critics. Where many persons were taken with his charm, affability, and wit, others saw a wily man of many masks. Indeed, Franklin was not above political indiscretion. As colonial agent in London, he had obtained, apparently in confidence, letters written by the Massachusetts governor Thomas Hutchinson (then the colony's Chief Justice) to the British ministry, seeming to give false advice on the troubles in the colony. Franklin sent these to the speaker of the Massachusetts House, saying they were not to be published or copied. They soon fell into the hands of the radical Samuel Adams—as Franklin perhaps knew they might—who made the most of them. For this "leak," he was reprimanded by the Privy Council; his influence in London was not the same again.

John Adams, not a constant admirer, once joked that after all the lies about the Revolution were told, "the essence of the whole will be that Doctor Franklin's electrical rod smote the earth and out sprang George Washington. That Franklin electrified him with his rod—and thence forward these two conducted all the policy, negotiations, legislatures, and war."* As Adams knew, he was also paying Franklin the highest tribute.

*Letter to Benjamin Rush, April 14, 1790, in Alexander Biddle, ed., *Old Family Letters, Copied from the Original for Alexander Biddle*, 2 vols (Philadelphia, 1892), vol I. 168–170, quoted in John Ferling, *John Adams, A Life* (New York: Henry Holt, 1992), 310.

it expressed the hope that harmony might be restored and asked him to discourage further action against the colonies until a plan of reconciliation might be agreed on. Refusing to receive the petition, the king declared the colonies to be in open rebellion. A motion in the House of Commons that the petition be the basis for rapprochement was soundly defeated.

Congress also set about exploring the possibility of help from abroad, particularly from Britain's long-standing imperial rivals, France and Spain. Leaders in the two nations were sympathetic and offered quantities of munitions and other military supplies. The French alliance proved vital throughout the war for independence.

Though about a third of the colonial population remained unsympathetic or, in the case of the Loyalists, openly hostile to the idea of rebellion, sentiment for a complete break had risen sharply by the spring of 1776. In June, the Virginian Richard Henry Lee offered Congress a resolution that the colonies "are and, of right ought to be, free and independent States." A committee made up of Benjamin Franklin of Pennsylvania, Thomas Jefferson of Virginia, John Adams of Massachusetts, Robert Livingston of New York, and Roger Sherman of Connecticut was directed to prepare a declaration of independence.

Jefferson wrote the draft with a few small changes added by Franklin and Adams. Without mentioning Parliament directly, it attacked the King as the sovereign, thus severing the basic cord of allegiance. On July 2, Congress voted on Lee's resolution: 12 colonies for, none against, New York abstaining. Two days later, on a date marked in history, the delegates approved Jefferson's Declaration by the same vote. Acceptance by New York's Provincial Congress the following week made unanimous the creation of the United States of America.

The Great Debate

The decade leading to the Revolution produced a widening colonial debate first about the constitutional powers of Parliament, then about organization of the British Empire, and finally about basic principles in the allegiance of men to government itself. It was also the first sustained exercise in political theorizing by Americans. Its terms were not formal and it brought forth no profound speculative treatises in the European grand style. Its medium was the pamphlet, newspaper article, sermon, oration, and state paper. Those who lent important voices to it at one time or other included James Otis, John Dickinson, James Wilson, Benjamin Franklin, John and Samuel Adams, Thomas Jefferson, Alexander Hamilton, Patrick Henry, Thomas Paine, and the Loyalists Daniel Leonard and Jonathan Boucher.

As they addressed their fellow citizens, the British government, and finally, as the Declaration put it, "the opinions of mankind," they reached for ideas and theories, opportunely, to justify or rationalize positions on the great division of the day. As arguments came more to invoke first principles or natural rights, these basic ideas became a political force of their own. It was not the first time nor last that philosophy and polemics marched shoulder to shoulder.

Parliament had testily stated the basic proposition in the Declaratory Act of 1766: It had "full power and authority to make laws and statutes of sufficient force and validity to bind the colonies

. . . in all cases whatsoever." Though almost no one claimed this meant total colonial subjection, it was not clear what, if anything, was to be conceded.

When it was argued that the Sugar and Stamp Acts were, in effect, "taxation without representation," Loyalists replied that the colonies had *virtual* representation in Parliament. Each member of that body could and did represent the interests of *all* Englishmen. Several English cities including Birmingham, Manchester, and Sheffield had no members in Parliament either, but the theory of virtual representation was no more persuasive with colonial protesters than it would be with modern democrats. Daniel Dulany, later himself a Loyalist, tellingly observed that not a single member of Parliament would be affected by taxation he might vote to impose on the colonies. Arthur Lee, colonial agent for Massachusetts in London, lamented that "Our privileges are all virtual; our sufferings are real."* And if some great cities of England were not in Parliament, James Otis said, then perhaps they should be!

Could the colonies actually be represented in Parliament? Otis and Franklin advanced such proposals, perhaps more as a logical extension of the no taxation without representation argument than from real conviction. They probably knew there was no chance Parliament would do anything so radically unsettling as admitting colonials, especially in proportion to their North American numbers. Others held that representation would be no guarantee against the passage of tax laws and, were such laws enacted, it would make them legally and morally binding.

More practically, the debate turned to differences between kinds of taxation: internal versus external; for revenue versus for regulation of trade. The first distinction condemned the offensive levies of the Stamp Act while acknowledging those placed on imports in the Sugar Act. For many colonials this conceded too

---

* Quoted in Clinton Rossiter, *Political Thought of the American Revolution* (New York: Harcourt, Brace and World, 1963), 20.

much, especially when Parliament exploited the difference by imposing an onerous array of new import duties in the Townshend Acts in 1767.

Those acts, plainly stating their aim of raising general revenue, led to a widening of the colonial argument to include purpose. Dickinson stated the position comprehensively in his widely read "Letters from a Pennsylvania Farmer": No internal taxes and no external taxes not directed to the regulation of imperial trade. But were these distinctions as sharp in reality as they appeared in theory and what if a regulation of trade in fact produced revenue? Dickinson's popular argument still left room for Parliamentary discretion.

Events were now moving faster than ideas. New tensions and hardened attitudes meant that the taxation arguments, which probably would have satisfied most colonials earlier, now seemed too accommodating. The debate moved to a new plane. Several writers, including Jefferson, Hamilton, John Adams and, most forcefully, Wilson, were now willing to deny Parliament *all* authority over the colonies, which, they argued, owed allegiance only to the King. This dominion theory of empire laid claim to home rule while letting the colonists remain English subjects. Prophetically, it was exactly the direction the Empire took a century later, but in 1774 the dominion theory was alien to London; neither King nor Parliament was ready to embrace so radical a constitutional change.

The only solution left was outside the British system. From the dominion theory to independence was a short step logically but a giant one psychologically and philosophically. The way was dramatically laid open early in 1776 with publication and wide readership of the pamphlet "Common Sense" by the English expatriate radical Thomas Paine. In it, Paine attacked the English constitution as a false repository of political wisdom and liberty and ridiculed the King and monarchical power.

Paine's iconoclasm openly expressed what a growing number of colonials had come to feel but were reluctant to fully admit. The conclu-

sion, Paine said, was obvious: "A government of our own is our natural right."*

Six months later in the Declaration of Independence (p 21), Jefferson argued the final step, drawing on the ideas of Locke who had philosophically transformed the liberal outcome of the Glorious Revolution of 1688 into universal moral criteria for all government. Gone now were contentions about representation and taxes, Parliament's constitutional authority, and imperial organization. In their place were ringing claims of the right of a people to revolt against oppressive government, of a right to be independent, and as individuals, of rights held inalienably from the Creator to pursue life, liberty, and happiness as they should choose. The great debate had moved from the constititutional rights of Englishmen to the natural rights of man. It ended with a fighting faith that would sustain the colonies through a long war, then spur a nation for more than 200 years.

One Revolution or Two?

We usually think of the American Revolution as having begun on July 4, 1776, or perhaps with the first shot on the Lexington Commons, and as ending with Cornwallis's Yorktown surrender or the Treaty of Paris. The six- or seven-year war for independence decisively marked the end of one era and the start of another. But it was made possible—inevitable perhaps—by another revolution that had already taken place.

By the 1770s, the colonies had the most open economy and fluid social system the world had seen. They had advanced further toward religious tolerance and humaneness than any society of their day. They were accomplished in the art and practice of constitutional self-government and had won a degree of liberty that other men and women could only hope for in a distant future, if at all. The great claim to a natural right to be free and independent in the Declaration of

---

* Philip S. Foner, ed., *The Compete Writings of Thomas Paine* (New York: Citadel Press, 1945) vol I, 29.

Independence made sense not simply as a final response to objectionable British policy, but as a cosmic entitlement already earned.

In looking back after 40 years, John Adams, one of the leading revolutionaries, had it exactly right:

> But what do we mean by the American Revolution? Do we mean the American war? The Revolution was effected before the war commenced. The Revolution was in the minds and hearts of the people . . . This radical change in the principles, opinions, sentiments, and affections of the people, was the real American Revolution.*

---

* Letter to Hezekiah Niles, February 13, 1818, reprinted in Daniel J. Boorstin, ed., *An American Primer* (1966), p. 248.

Those "principles, opinions, sentiments, and affections" did not spring into being suddenly or majestically in the 1770s as though from the brow of the Creator. They were the outcome of economic, social, political, and religious developments more than 150 years in the making.

As a result, the war for independence—the fighting revolution—was more a struggle to preserve than pull down or destroy. It differed strikingly from the French and Russian revolutions and perhaps from almost all other modern rebellions. The world was not to be made over—the year 1776 would be followed by 1777, not Year One of a new millennium. The colonial rebels were among the most conservative revolutionaries in history; they could be because they had already completed a radical revolution.

FURTHER READING

The Colonial Experience

Bailyn, Bernard, *The Peopling of British North America: An Introduction* (1986)

Barrows Thomas C., *Trade and Empire* (1967)

Botein, Stephen, *Early Law in American Society* (1983)

Draper, Theodore, *The Struggle for Power: The American Revolution* (1995)

Engerman, Stanley L. and Robert E. Gallman, eds., *The Cambridge Economic History of the United States*, vol. I, *The Colonial Era* (1996)

Fischer, David Hackett, *Albion's Seed: Four British Folkways in America* (1989)

Gipson, Lawrence Henry, *The British Empire Before the Revolution*, 15 vols. (1936–1970)

Jensen, Merrill, *The Founding of a Nation* (1968)

Jones, Alice Hanson, *Wealth of a Nation To Be: The American Colonies on the Eve of the Revolution* (1980)

Kammen, Michael, *Deputyes and Libertyes: The Origin of Republican Government in Colonial America* (1969)

Lutz, Donald S., ed., *Colonial Origins of the American Constitution: A Documentary History*

Maier, Pauline, *From Resistence to Revolution: Colonial Radicals and the Development of American Opposition to Great Britain, 1765–1776* (1972)

McCusker, John J. and Russell R. Menard, *The Economy of British America, 1607–1789* (1985)

Pole, J. R., *Political Representation in England and the Origins of the American Republic* (1966)

Rossiter, Clinton, *Seedtime of the Republic* (1953)

Wood, Betty, *The Origins of American Slavery: Freedom and Bondage in the English Colonies* (1996)

The Heritage of Ideas

Bailyn, Bernard, *The Ideological Origins of the American Revolution* (1967)

Fruchtman, Jack, *Thomas Paine and the Religion of Nature* (1993)

Pocock, J. G. A., *The Machiavellian Moment: Florentine Thought and the Atlantic Republican Tradition* (1975)

Rahe, Paul A., *Republics Ancient and Modern: Classical Republicanism and the American Revolution* (1992)

Stimson, Shannon C., *The American Revolution in the Law: Anglo-American Jurisprudence Before John Marshall* (1990)

White, Morton, *The Philosophy of the American Revolution* (1978)

Zuckert, Michael, *National Rights and the New Republicanism* (1994)

Independence Declared

Becker, Carl L., *The Declaration of Independence: A Study in the History of Political Ideas* (1942)

Jayne, Allen, *Jefferson's* Declaration of Independence: *Origins, Philosophy, and Theology* (1998)

Maier, Pauline, *American Scripture: The Making of the Declaration of Independence* (1997)

Wills, Garry, *Inventing America: Jefferson's Declaration of Independence* (1978)

Biographical

Brands, H.W., *The First American: The Life and Times of Benjamin Franklin* (2000)

Van Doren, Carl, *Benjamin Franklin* (1938)

THE DECLARATION OF INDEPENDENCE

In Congress, July 4, 1776
The Unanimous Declaration of the Thirteen
United States of America

When in the course of human events, it becomes necessary for one people to dissolve the political bands which have connected them with another, and to assume among the powers of the earth, the separate and equal station to which the laws of Nature and of Nature's God entitle them, a decent respect to the opinions of mankind requires that they should declare the causes which impel them to the separation.

We hold these truths to be self-evident, that all men are created equal, that they are endowed by their Creator with certain unalienable rights, that among these are life, liberty and the pursuit of happiness. That to secure these rights, governments are instituted among men, deriving their just powers from the consent of the governed. That whenever any form of government becomes destructive of these ends, it is the right of the people to alter or to abolish it, and to institute new government, laying its foundation on such principles and organizing its powers in such form, as to them shall seem most likely to effect their safety and happiness. Prudence, indeed, will dictate that governments long established should not be changed for light and transient causes; and accordingly all experience hath shown, that mankind are more disposed to suffer, while evils are sufferable, than to right themselves by abolishing the forms to which they are accustomed. But when a long train of abuses and usurpations, pursuing invariably the same object evinces a design to reduce them under absolute despotism, it is their right, it is their duty, to throw off such government, and to provide new guards for their future security. Such has been the patient sufferance of these Colonies; and such is now the necessity which constrains them to alter their former systems of government. The history of the present King of Great Britain is a history of repeated injuries and usurpations, all having in direct object the establishment of an absolute tyranny over these States. To prove this, let facts be submitted to a candid world.

He has refused his assent to laws, the most wholesome and necessary for the public good.

He has forbidden his Governors to pass laws of immediate and pressing importance, unless suspended in their operation till his Assent should be obtained; and when so suspended, he has utterly neglected to attend to them.

He has refused to pass other Laws for the accommodation of large districts of people, unless those people would relinquish the right of representation in the legislature, a right inestimable to them and formidable to tyrants only.

He has called together legislative bodies at places unusual, uncomfortable, and distant from the depository of their public records, for the sole purpose of fatiguing them into compliance with his measures.

He has dissolved Representative Houses repeatedly, for opposing with manly firmness his invasions on the rights of the people.

He has refused for a long time, after such dissolutions, to cause others to be elected; whereby the legislative powers, incapable of annihilation, have returned to the people at large for their exercise; the State remaining in the mean time exposed to all the dangers of invasion from without, and convulsions within.

He has endeavored to prevent the population of these States; for that purpose obstructing the laws for naturalization of foreigners; refusing to pass others to encourage their migration hither, and raising the conditions of new appropriations of lands.

He has obstructed the administration of justice, by refusing his assent to laws for establishing judiciary powers.

He has made judges dependent on his will alone, for the tenure of their offices, and the amount and payment of their salaries.

He has erected a multitude of new offices, and sent hither swarms of officers to harass our people, and eat out their substance.

He has kept among us, in times of peace, standing armies without the Consent of our legislature.

He has affected to render the military independent of and superior to the civil power.

He has combined with others to subject us to a jurisdiction foreign to our constitution, and unacknowledged by our laws; giving his assent to their acts of pretended legislation:

For quartering large bodies of armed troops among us:

For protecting them, by a mock trial, from punishment for any Murders which they should commit on the inhabitants of these States:

For cutting off our trade with all parts of the world:

For imposing taxes on us without our consent:

For depriving us in many cases, of the benefits of trial by jury:

For transporting us beyond seas to be tried for pretended offenses:

For abolishing the free system of English laws in a neighboring province, establishing therein an arbitrary government, and enlarging its boundaries so as to render it at once an example and fit instrument for introducing the same absolute rule into these colonies:

For taking away our charters, abolishing our most valuable laws, and altering fundamentally the forms of our governments:

For suspending our own legislature, and declaring themselves invested with power to legislate for us in all cases whatsoever.

He has abdicated government here, by declaring us out of his protection and waging war against us.

He has plundered our seas, ravaged our coasts, burnt our towns, and destroyed the lives of our people.

He is at this time transporting large armies of foreign mercenaries to complete the works of death, desolation and tyranny, already begun with circumstances of cruelty and perfidy scarcely paralleled in the most barbarous ages, and totally unworthy the head of a civilized nation.

He has constrained our fellow citizens taken captive on the high seas to bear arms against their country, to become the executioners of their friends and brethren, or to fall themselves by their hands.

He has excited domestic insurrections amongst us, and has endeavored to bring on the inhabitants of our frontiers, the merciless Indian Savages, whose known rule of warfare, is an undistinguished destruction of all ages, sexes and conditions.

In every stage of these oppressions we have petitioned for redress in the most humble terms: Our repeated petitions have been answered only by repeated injury. A prince, whose character is thus marked by every act which may define a tyrant, is unfit to be the ruler of a free people.

Nor have we been wanting in attention to our British brethren. We have warned them from time to time of attempts by their legislature to extend an unwarrantable jurisdiction over us. We have reminded them of the circumstances of our emigration and settlement here. We have appealed to their native justice and magnanimity, and we have conjured them by the ties of our common kindred to disavow these usurpations, which, would inevitably interrupt our connections and correspondence. They too have been deaf to the voice of justice and of consanguinity.

We must, therefore, acquiesce in the necessity, which denounces our separation, and hold them, as we hold the rest of mankind, enemies in war, in peace friends.

We, therefore, the Representatives of the United States of America, in General Congress, Assembled, appealing to the Supreme Judge of the world for the rectitude of our intentions, do, in the name, and by authority of the good people of these Colonies, solemnly publish and declare, That these United Colonies are, and of right ought to be Free and Independent States; that they are absolved from all allegiance to the British Crown, and that all political connection between them and the State of Great Britain, is and ought to be totally dissolved; and that as free and independent States, they have full power to levy war, conclude peace, contract alliances, establish commerce, and to do all other acts and things which independent States may of right do. And for the support of this Declaration, with a firm reliance on the protection of Divine Providence, we mutually pledge to each other our lives, our fortunes and our sacred honor.

New Hampshire: *John Hancock*
                      Josiah Bartlett
                      Matthew Thornton
                      William Whipple

Massachusetts Bay: *Samuel Adams*
                      Robert Treat Paine
                      John Adams
                      Elbridge Gerry

Rhode Island: *Stephen Hopkins*
William Ellery

Connecticut: *Roger Sherman*
William Williams
Samuel Huntington
Oliver Wolcott

New York: *William Floyd*
Francis Lewis
Phillip Livingston
Lewis Morris

New Jersey: *Richard Stockton*
John Hart
John Witherspoon
Abraham Clark
Francis Hopkinson

Pennsylvania: *Robert Morris*
James Smith
Benjamin Rush
George Taylor
Benjamin Franklin
James Wilson
John Morton
George Ross
George Clymer

Delaware: *Caesar Rodney*
Thomas M'Kean
George Read

Maryland: *Samuel Chase*
Charles Carroll
William Paca
Thomas Stone

Virginia: *George Wythe*
Thomas Nelson, Jr.
Richard Henry Lee
Francis Lightfoot Lee
Thomas Jefferson
Carter Braxton
Benjamin Harrison

North Carolina: *William Hooper*
John Penn
Joseph Hewes

South Carolina: *Edward Rutledge*
Thomas Lynch, Jr.
Thomas Heyward, Jr.
Arthur Middleton

Georgia: *Button Gwinnett*
George Walton
Lyman Hall

2

INDEPENDENCE AND CONFEDERATION

The Revolutionary Government

Between 1776 and 1781, the Second Continental Congress was the de facto central authority of the new independent states—the first American national government. It had no written constitution, no formally delegated powers, little or no money, and no direct popular base, because its delegates were chosen by the provincial governments, themselves often in disarray. Twice it was forced to flee its capital to evade British forces. Conditions of the war were such that it had to share effective governing power with the military under Washington and with the new state governments. Struggles with the states, which often acted on their own, rivaled efforts against the British.

Despite these problems, the inexperienced wartime government had some notable successes. In Washington it had chosen an able military leader lacking Caesar-like ambition. It set up committees and a rudimentary infrastructure to administer national affairs. It created a small diplomatic corps, sending its leading members—Benjamin Franklin, John Adams, and John Jay—to Europe to seek aid and alliances, a mission in

which they were largely successful. A postal service was organized, which did much to serve continental unity. Not least, it issued currency and borrowed money, eventually coordinating these efforts in a Department of Finance headed by the Pennsylvanian Robert Morris, a financial wizard who did much to strengthen public finances, sometimes using notes based on his personal credit.

Very early, Congress realized that gaining and keeping independence would call for a formal plan of union and central government—a constitution. In June 1776, three weeks before the signing of the Declaration of Independence, the delegates chose a committee, chaired by John Dickinson and having one member from each state, to draft a plan. Its proposal "The Articles of Confederation and Perpetual Union" was presented the following month, but quick approval proved elusive. The delegates debated its provisions for more than a year, disagreeing on questions of national fusion that would reappear at the federal convention a decade later: large versus small state interests, the basis for representation for voting and for allotment of taxes.

After several compromises, the plan was approved and sent to the states, the delegates hoping for a ratification that might be proclaimed on the second anniversary of the Declaration of Independence. Again, speedy assent proved impossible. The states moved cautiously, proposing many amendments all of which Congress turned down. By early 1779, 12 states had ratified, with only Maryland holding out because Virginia and other large states had not ceded their trans-Appalachian claims to the proposed confederacy. Since it called for ratification to be unanimous, Congress now had to decide whether to go ahead with a union of only 12 states. This matter was debated for nearly two years. When states opposing incomplete union proved adamant, the large states gave up their western claims.

Ratification of the nation's first constitution was finished on March 1, 1781, near the end of the war. The drawn out, contentious installation made it clear that the states still found it hard to value common interests except for the military one of defeating the British. Oddly enough, the very matter that had so delayed ratification now strengthened the sense of unity under the new government. An enemy in common had been succeeded by property held in common.

British Defeat

Each of the warring sides believed the rebellion would be short. In Congress, many delegates assumed that mere issuance of the Declaration of Independence would be enough to send the British home. In the Continental Army, many soldiers believed fighting could not last for more than a year. For their part, the British underestimated George Washington's tenacity and failed to see a widening of the war with entry of France, Spain, and Holland. Had either side clearly foreseen the extended costly struggle, it might have more readily embraced reconciliation or early compromise. The long conflict strained American unity. Probably at no time did more than 40 or 50 percent of the popula-

tion actively support the rebellion. Perhaps 15 to 30 percent were unsympathetic and about a third of that number were in active opposition as Loyalists. Thus the struggle had some features of civil war though not along the sectional lines of the conflict of 1861–1865. If the war was not universally popular in America, it was decidedly unpopular in England once early victory was denied and the growing cost in men and money became clear.

The strengths and weaknesses of one side complemented those of the other, in a strange way leaving the two combatants evenly matched. American forces were in the Continental Army, which never numbered many more than 18,000, and different state and local militia; they were supported later by French contingents. British forces were a mix of regular army, Hessian mercenaries, Loyalists, and Indian allies, in all probably not more than 35,000. As the world's leading superpower, Britain had an enormous naval advantage and used it to move troops around at will. Individual American privateers, combining patriotism with greed, took a toll of British merchant shipping, but it wasn't until France committed its strong West Indies fleet that the American cause had substantial concerted sea power at its disposal. The Continental Army had a gifted leader, but its ranks were often undisciplined, ill-clothed, ill-fed, unpaid, and on occasion mutinous. British regulars and mercenaries were better trained and equipped, but top leadership was often dilatory, rigid in engagement, and arrogant in underrating the opponent.

A British plan for an early knockout by splitting the colonies through capture of the Hudson Valley failed when a force under Gen. Burgoyne, advancing south from Canada to meet another British force moving northward from the coast, was defeated at Saratoga. The British made New York City, which they held throughout the war, their main base. From it they launched campaigns, at one time or other occupying every main port, including Philadelphia, the American capital. Washington's rag-tag army, not strong enough to oust the British from their coastal perimeters, proved much better at hit-and-run forays. Except in the South, the British had meager success when they moved inland, often finding themselves at war with the countryside, as militia groups materialized and disappeared in the best guerilla tradition.

The lingering stalemate ended in the spring of 1781 with a well coordinated land-sea attack on a large British force that, after a campaign through the Carolinas, had retreated to Yorktown in Virginia. Organized and led by Washington, combined American and French forces laid siege to the town at the mouth of the York River on Chesapeake Bay while escape by sea was blocked by a large French fleet that had sailed up from the Caribbean. Seeing the hopelessness of his situation, the British commander, Cornwallis, surrendered his entire army, about a third of all British forces committed to the war.

The coup led the government in London, painfully drawn by a war it could not win, to offer terms of peace. In the Treaty of Paris, which went into effect in early 1783, Britain recognized American independence and agreed to give up all claims south of Canada, north of Florida, and east of the Mississippi, stunningly generous terms since the territory was far more than Americans actually occupied. All debts due creditors of either side by citizens of the other were to be valid, and Congress was pledged to urge the states to fully restore the rights and properties of Loyalists.

Washington, who had served as commander in chief for nearly eight years without salary, rightfully emerged from the war as the hero of his new nation, held in deep respect and affection by almost all his countrymen. After overseeing the departure of the last British troops from New York and a moving farewell to his staff at Fraunce's Tavern, he went before a grateful Congress to resign his commission, and from there returned to his neglected estate at Mount Vernon. Scrupulous in his respect for civil authority, he was an American Cincinnatus, literally laying down sword for ploughshare. Not

only had Washington shown himself to be a great military strategist and tactician, he was an able "political" general. Holding his oft-grumbling army together, coordinating diverse allied forces, cajoling members of Congress, and ever pleading with state leaders for support called for skills of diplomat and statesman. More than a few seers saw that his greatest days of public service might lie ahead.

The Articles of Confederation

The nation's first constitution set out to build a formal "perpetual" union from an expedient de facto alliance. Yet the Articles of Confederation were a mirror of equivocations. A need for national government had been recognized by those wary of any power not within easy local reach. A collection of independent-minded, self-regarding states, bent on retaining their own sovereignty, had been willing to work on the accommodative, self-denying task of nation-building. The result was a loose, contradictory league of nearly autonomous political entities rather than a fusion of people. Though aimed at creating lasting union, the Articles proved to be no more than a transition. For all that, they remained a great advance in constitutionalism. In a single written statement they set out the bounds of national union and based it on the unanimous consent of 13 constituents.

In practical terms, the new government was not much different from the old. Power was in the hands of a Congress—still called the Continental Congress by many—in which each state, represented by two to seven delegates, had one vote. No provisions were made for an independent executive or for national courts. Reliably, Congress's chief powers dealt with national security and foreign affairs: making war and peace, sending and receiving ambassadors, entering into treaties and alliances.

By contrast, internal authority was attenuated, limited mainly to coining money, fixing standards of weights and measures, and establishing

The First Constitution

The Articles of Confederation declared a "perpetual Union" among 13 named states. The nation's first constitution, two-thirds as long as the later federal document, had 13 sections or articles. Unlike the later, Federal document, they were written in eighteenth century legalese. They are summarized here.

Article I. The new confederacy is named "The United States of America."

Article II. Primacy of the states is affirmed. Each state retains its "sovereignty, freedom, and independence," and all powers not expressly given to Congress.

Article III. The states are pledged to a "league of friendship with each other, for their common defense, the security of their liberties, and their mutual and general welfare."

Article IV. The states are pledged to comity and cooperation. Citizens of each are entitled to "all privileges and immunities of free citizens of the several states" and to "free ingress and regress to and from any other state." Fugitives from justice must be returned to states having jurisdiction over them. Each state must give "full faith and credit . . . to the records, acts, and judicial proceedings . . . of every other state."

Article V. Each state has one vote in Congress and must be represented by not fewer than two or more than seven delegates appointed and recallable by their state. Neither the travel of delegates to and from Congress nor their speech in Congress may be impeded.

Article VI. Without the consent of Congress, no state may send or receive ambassadors, enter into treaties, interfere with treaties made by Congress, maintain navy warships or armed forces (except for a militia), or make war unless actually invaded by enemies.

Article VII. In forces raised by a state in the common defense, all officers at the rank of colonel or below are to be appointed by the legislature of the state.

Article VIII. The cost of the central government is to be met from a "common treasury" supplied by the states in proportion to the value of property within each state. Taxes for meeting each state's allotment are to be levied by the legislature of that state.

Article IX. The powers of Congress include:
• The "sole and exclusive right" to make war and peace, send and receive ambassadors, and enter into treaties.
• The right to serve as "the last resort on appeal in all disputes and differences" between two or more states, according to a procedure described.
• The "sole and exclusive right and power of regulating the value of coin . . . fixing the standards of weights and measures . . . regulating and managing affairs with the Indians . . . establishing and regulating post offices" and appointing military and naval officers in forces serving the United States.
• The right to establish government administration by appointing a "Committee of the States" consisting of one delegate from each state that will sit in recess of Congress, and by appointing "other committees and civil offices as may be necessary for managing affairs of the United States."

But Congress shall not make war or treaties, coin or borrow money, or appoint a commander in chief of armed forces without agreement of at least nine states.

Article X. When Congress is in recess, the Committee of the States has authority to exercise whatever powers of Congress have been given to it with approval of at least nine states, but not those powers in Article IX for which approval of nine states is needed.

Article XI. Canada is invited to join the confederation, but no other colonies may be admitted unless agreed on by at least nine states.

Article XII. The debts of the Continental Congress are assumed by the new confederation.

Article XIII. The Articles may not be amended unless the proposed changes are agreed on in Congress and afterward approved by every state.

a post office. Congress was given the power to borrow money, but that, like its war, treaty, and coinage authority, needed approval of nine states. Conspicuously absent were powers to tax and to regulate commerce, matters at the heart of the struggle for independence. Without taxation authority, money for central operations was to be requisitioned from the states, with allotment determined by the value of property within each state. In place of an executive, Congress could appoint a "Committee of the States," made up of one delegate from each state, to do the work of government when Congress was not in session. Management became so burdensome that Congress later created five administrative "departments"—for foreign affairs, war, finance, admiralty, and the post office—each headed by a "secretary."

Despite the dogged emphasis on state sovereignty—the central government's enactments, for example, were not called laws of Congress but "determinations of the United States in Congress assembled"—the Articles did have integrating provisions dealing with comity and disputes among states. States were obliged to give "full ingress and egress: to citizens of other states and "full faith and credit" to the acts and records of other states. Congress was to be the "last resort on appeal: in disputes between two or more states, and an elaborate procedure was set out for such assignment.

Congress scored important successes in concluding peace with Britain and establishing relations with other European powers. Remarkably, its greatest legislative triumph—devising a policy for the western lands—went beyond its few prescribed powers. In the Northwest Ordinance of 1787, enacted at the very time the Philadelphia convention was at work to replace the Articles, Congress developed a plan for the vast area north of the Ohio and east of the Mississippi ceded by Britain. It set out provisions for territorial government that included a bill of rights and restrictions on slavery. By anticipating the creation of new states and prescribing ways statehood might be advanced, it avoided putting the

United States into a colonizing role. It also required new states be "on an equal footing with the original states in all respects," preventing invidious distinctions from arising. Out of the Northwest tract eventually came Ohio, Michigan, Indiana, Illinois, and Wisconsin; the ordinance served as a model for the progression of other territories to statehood.

During its short life, Congress had few other opportunities to be as creative, more from want of power than fault of its own. When remedies were proposed, the provision of Article Thirteen, that amendments had to be ratified by all 13 states, proved insurmountable.

Republican State Constitutions

While protractedly debating the kind of national union they could tolerate, Revolutionary Americans at the state level wasted no time in engaging in the greatest surge of constitution-writing in history. Except for Connecticut and Rhode Island, which retained their colonial charters with modest revisions, each of the other colonies quickly drafted a basic document setting out the powers and structure of government. In seven, new elections were held for legislative bodies that would also write the constitutions. In three others, revolutionary provincial congresses drafted the constitutions without seeking new authority. In none of the 10 was the constitution submitted to the people for approval. Only in Massachusetts was a special convention called and provision made for later popular ratification.

In replacing constitutional monarchy with republican government, the constitution-makers drew heavily on the colonial experience with democratic assemblies, though adding important innovations. Ten of the eleven new constitutions created a strong, popularly elected bicameral legislature while placing attenuated executive power in a governor. (Pennsylvania chose a unicameral legislature and plural executive.) Because of the difficulties with royal governors, it is not surprising that the executive office was kept deliberately weak. Terms were short—one year in seven states—election was by the legislature in eight, reeligibility limited in seven, the veto denied in nine, and the appointment power shared with the legislature in nine. The office was a bit stronger in New York and Massachusetts where the governor was popularly elected. Judges were appointed for terms of modest length or good behavior. All the constitutions imposed moderate property qualifications for ballot and office, and all provided for frequent elections (from semiannual for Rhode Island's lower house to four years for several upper houses). Most striking, perhaps, was the inclusion of bills of rights in all these documents. These were generally modeled on George Mason's "Declaration of Rights." which he had drafted for Virginia. This great statement of liberty, inspired by painful experience with imperial authority, included an array of criminal justice rights—among them trial by jury and freedom from self-incrimination, excessive bail, and cruel and unusual punishments—besides protections for freedom of worship and of the press.

The pairing of a strong legislature and weak executive was an important break with the English theory of mixed government in which power was supposedly balanced among Crown, Lords, and Commons. Having no established aristocracy to take into account and the monarchy now abolished, American constitution-makers could base the new state governments on the popular element in their legislatures. To keep the balance they believed necessary for limited government, they turned to the principle of separated powers. Functional authority—legislative, executive, judicial—was not to be mixed or shared as in England but kept institutionally apart, thus preventing one part of government from gaining control of the entire. Because it provided more points of access, the organizing principle was also well suited to the interests of rising but underrepresented groups competing with better-established interests.

But by empowering the legislature and reducing the executive, was it possible to go too far and so lose the very balance promised by separa-

tion of power? Many conservatives and persons of property thought so. They feared that rebellion against British power, taken further, might become a challenge to all authority and endanger property itself. Self-serving or not, they commonly believed that property and the hard effort often needed to get it were proof of virtue, that is, of economic and civic responsibility. Even with the best of intentions, revolutionary enthusiasm for popular government might end in a tyranny of its own.

The Revolution had released new forces and brought new men to political voice who found the open legislatures receptive. Aristocratic idealists such as Jefferson and Mason saw the accountable assemblies as representing the will of "the people" and being the agencies of government least dangerous to individual liberties. Others, more focused on social parity, did not believe the Revolution was fought simply to replace a royally sponsored oligarchy with a local ruling elite. Many with debtor concerns saw popular power as an opportunity for easy money policies. All could appeal to equality and natural rights that had been so powerfully proclaimed in the Declaration of Independence.

In republican constitution-making ideals mixed with interests. The fluid middle class nature of the American social structure moderated possible conflict, but social and economic tensions between its radical and conservative poles were evident. That conflict would help to shape the debate about government and the distribution of power under constitution for the next 200 years.

Even with hindsight it is hard to fully appreciate the extraordinary feat of Revolutionary constitution-making. In the late eighteenth century, Britain's constitutional scheme, with its interfusion of royal, aristocratic, and democratic power, was widely believed to be the model of limited, responsive government. The political world was filled with absolute monarchies, overbearing oligarchies, and other despotisms. To base power almost entirely on the democratic part in mixed government was radical within the model itself. In the eyes of many, including sympathizers, it was a noble or foolish experiment destined to end in mob rule or worse. Yet for Revolutionary Americans, it was but a small step in the art and science of government, less a departure than a progression.

New Nation, Old Law

In drafting new state constitutions Americans had moved quickly to fill the political space created by overthrow of imperial authority. But would Parliamentary acts and the common law decisions of English courts that had helped settle disputes over property, contracts, inheritance, and other private matters continue to be valid and binding? Patriotic antipathy to almost all things British produced a concerted attack on the common law. Once thought settled in colonial life, these rules of English origin now seemed a badge of dependence to be done without. Hostility was reinforced by those distrusting the common law generally—entrepreneurs who chafed under its rigidities or ordinary persons who saw it favoring the rich or being remote from their own lives. Many critics suggested that some other system of law, such as a Continental civil code, with its highly defined, systematic, legislative statement of the law, might now be adopted. Francophilic sentiment of the day made French law particularly attractive, even if few translations of its corpus were to be found.

Fortunately for the common law and perhaps for the legal system as well, expediency prevailed over fervor. Colonials had lived quite well under English rules, benefiting from the certainty and uniformity they brought to everyday life. To many persons, abolishing them because they originated in England made no more sense than abolishing the language simply because it too came from the same source. Important in this debate was the appearance in the colonies of a monumental work of legal scholarship, *Commentaries on the Laws of England* by William Blackstone, an Oxford don. Blackstone had collected and summarized the scattered, often confused mass of English legal precedent from hundreds

of courts over many centuries. Nothing like this had been done before; suddenly the common law was all there, organized, detailed, and indexed. Its four volumes—the rights of individuals, the wrongs to individuals (torts), the rights to things (property and contracts), and wrongs to the state (crimes)—were the first important systematic statement of the body of the common law. They sold astonishingly well in America, becoming a law library and a kind of law school for countless lawyers and judges.

Influence of the *Commentaries* went beyond their extraordinary reference value. There was something in them for radical and conservative alike. Blackstone's emphasis on absolute individual rights that were owed legal protection supported the patriot position in the Declaration of Independence and the state bills of rights. At the same time, the compendium of precedent gave new force to the stabilizing doctrine of *stare decisis,* in which rulings in earlier cases guide or determine those in later. Supposing a hierarchical arrangement of laws—those of God, nature, nation, and locality—Blackstone vested judges, then one of society's premier conservative groups, with power to decide whether lower law conformed to higher. This was, as well, an anticipation of the later American doctrine of judicial review.

The upshot of the debate over English law was that each new state government enacted a "reception" statute setting out what law would be taken as valid and what would not. With variations, these statutes typically embraced all English common law not in conflict with earlier colonial practices. They were less generous with acts of Parliament. For example, Virginia's statute did not recognize any enactment later than 1607. English common law decisions after 1776 were not to be binding.

By incorporating most pre-Revolutionary English common law, the reception statutes made possible an important continuity in rules governing everyday affairs. The line drawn by Independence also insured final Americanization. A generation or two later, the great common law commentaries of Chancellor James Kent and Justice Joseph Story, for example, were occupied with native precedent. Common law change is evolutionary, relying on continual small modifications by decision and statute. Yet the Revolutionary crisis had speeded legal experimentation and the adaptation of law to unique conditions. Its full effect was not felt until the early nineteenth century's explosive release of energy through the forces of economic individualism and acquisitive enterprise.

New Difficulties

Basic flaws in the constitutional system of the Articles became increasingly evident in the years following the war. In their new independence the states had ceded too little authority to the central government, and the need for amendments to be unanimous made it almost impossible to correct mistakes. As a result, Congress was left largely helpless in foreign affairs and in the domestic economy, two areas in which positive national government usually has its most important work.

Opportunities to make favorable trade treaties or to gain commercial concessions from European powers were lost when Congress could not guarantee that individual states would not impose their own import duties, a right reserved to them by Article IX. Britain refused to evacuate western forts in violation of the peace treaty, claiming that several states had hindered debt collection by British creditors or had refused to pay Loyalists for lands seized during the war. Congress had neither the military power to make the West secure nor the political means to force the states to abide by the treaty.

Without power to regulate commerce, Congress could not prevent states from imposing tariffs on goods from other states or head off commercial warfare among them. Without an independent taxing power, Congress lacked the stable resources to pay national debts including the back salaries of war veterans. The scheme for financing the central government by requisitions from the states broke down when many states were dilatory, put strings on their pay-

ments, or, in New Jersey's case, flatly refused to honor its allocation at all. To meet a mounting national debt, Congress resorted to borrowing money from abroad and issuing unbacked paper. The last soon became deflated, further weakening national credit.

Recognizing the growing difficulties, Congress made several proposals to amend the Articles. These included giving it power to impose a 5 percent duty on imports and to enact uniform navigation rules to reduce trade conflict among the states. Though these and other prescriptions had substantial support, in no instance could all 13 states be persuaded to act together. In the face of state jealousies, distrust of one another, and plain self-interest, the unanimity rule was fatal.

Congress' problems coincided with deepening financial unrest made worse by a depression in 1786. Falling farm income and tight money aggravated the normal conflict between debtor and creditor interests. Agrarian majorities captured control of several state legislatures and enacted debtor relief laws. Taxes needed to pay off public debt and restore financial stability were forgiven, lowered, or simply cut out. To make loan repayment easier, the radical legislatures authorized printing of money, with predictable inflationary results.

Massachusetts, where conservatives remained in office as the farmer's case worsened, was a tinderbox. In the summer of 1786, mobs of farmers in the western counties prevented courts from sitting in foreclosure or tax collection cases. As the insurgency widened, an armed force of 1,000 or more came under the reluctant leadership of Daniel Shays, a destitute farmer and former Revolutionary captain. His rag-tag group remained at large in the state until defeated by the militia the following February.

The Road to Philadelphia

For conservatives and a growing number of moderates, economic radicalism was not just a matter of democratic excess but a threat to order itself. Crushed though it was, Shays' Rebellion seemed to warn of the chaos to come unless stronger and more balanced government could be instated.

Many thoughtful leaders, including Dickinson, Washington, Hamilton, John Adams, and James Madison, had been troubled by the impotence of Congress and the growing domestic factionalism for some time. Though Shays' Rebellion served as a violent catalyst for serious consideration of constitutional change, the deliberative genesis of the Philadelphia constitutional convention lay in two earlier, more composed events.

Concerned with destructive commercial rivalry among the states, Madison and several of his fellow Virginia legislators arranged a meeting of Virginia and Maryland representatives in Washington's home at Mount Vernon to discuss long-standing disagreements about the use of the Potomac and Chesapeake Bay. The conferees made several recommendations to their legislatures, including one for an annual conference on commercial problems. Before the next meeting, scheduled in Annapolis in September, 1786, the two states agreed to broaden its base, first by asking neighboring states to take part, then, at Madison's urging, inviting all the states.

The Annapolis convention turned out to be something of a disappointment when representatives from only five states showed up. Deciding it would be useless to go ahead, the delegates instead issued a report drafted by Madison and Hamilton, who was a New York delegate. Boldly it called on each state to send delegates to a new convention the following May in Philadelphia to discuss *all* matters needed "to render the constitution of the federal government adequate to the exigencies of the union." Several months later, after Shays' Rebellion, Congress gave the invitation a cautious endorsement. Perhaps sensing that its own days might be numbered, it added the custodial instructions that the meeting be "for the sole and express purpose of revising the Articles of Confederation and reporting to Congress and the several legislatures such alterations and provisions therein."

In the spring of 1787, agreement was fast growing, at least among moderates and conservatives, that constitutional reform was needed. Hardly surprising, there was much less accord on exactly what that change should be.

In one revolution, 150 years in the making, Americans had become politically competent in the art of self-government. In a second revolution of less than a decade, they had overthrown imperial authority. They had established the first American nation, more constitutionally directed and nascently democratic than any other in the world. In that extraordinary achievement they invoked the federal principle—sovereignty balanced between a vital center and constituent parts—and that of the separation of powers—functional distribution of who has authority to do what—but failed to fully realize either. Still finding it easier to think of themselves as New Yorkers, Pennsylvanians, or Virginians than as Americans, the Revolutionaries had created a confederation of loosely allied states that retained most of their hard-earned sovereignty. Neither political authority nor political identifications were yet truly national; it was no surprise that many of the country's ablest leaders preferred to serve in their states rather than in Congress. Founded in a war against central authority, the new national government had much less power in dealing with the states than Britain had had in dealing with the colonies. It lacked the means to be militarily or diplomatically effective in the world of nations, or politically and economically effective in the world of states at home. It did not rest on a popular base as did the great republican authority of each of the states; it was a government of governments, not of people.

In creating republican government, the Revolutionaries had replaced socially balanced, mixed government with one of functionally separated powers. To be workable, the new arrangement needed reasonably strong executive and judicial agencies that could check and be checked by the legislature. This symmetry was exactly what the Revolutionaries were unwilling to concede. Instead, popular legislative power, which had been the core of colonial self-government, was carried to excess. In the new central government there was no executive or judiciary; in the early state constitutions, the governor and the courts were structurally and operationally weak, the legislatures often usurping their functions.

The question of union—where does sovereignty lie—divided Americans for the next 75 years and led the nation to civil war. The matter is now settled except for details, the reckoning eventually transforming the constitutional system. The question of distribution of power—who will govern and have their way—remains a matter of constitutional contention to our own day. It has included the familiar struggles of property against numbers, one kind of property against another, and conflict among a range of eco-nomic and social interests trying to realize material gain or the intangible ends of status, freedom, and social control.

The new nation had to go through a critical period to move from the plane of confederation and legislative supremacy to one where final sovereignty was national and power functionally balanced within government. It was almost providential that the crisis came as early as it did. Had the Articles been more easily amendable, they might have served well into the nineteenth century. By then, widening sectional differences over slavery would have made stronger political union next to impossible and a breakup into two nations all but certain.

FURTHER READING

The First Union

Bobrick, Benson, *Angel in the Whirlwind: The Triumph of the American Revolution* (1997)

Douglas, Elisha P., *Rebels and Democrats: The Struggle for Equal Political Rights* (1955)

Greene, Jack P., ed., *The Reinterpretation of the American Revolution, 1763–1789* (1968)

Jameson, J. Franklin, *The American Revolution Considered as a Social Movement* (1924)

Jensen, Merrill, *The Articles of Confederation: An Interpretation of the Societal-Constitutional History of the American Revolution, 1774–1781* (1940)

McDonald, Forrest E., *E Pluribus Unum: The Formation of the American Republic, 1776–1790* (1965)

McLaughlin, Andrew C., *The Confederation and the Constitution, 1781–1789* (1905)

Middlekaupf, Robert, *The Glorious Cause: The American Revolution, 1763–1789* (1982)

Morgan, Edmund S., *The Birth of the Republic, 1763–1789* (1958)

Morris, Richard B., *The Forging of the Union, 1781–1787* (1987)

Onuf, Peter S., *Statehood and Union: A History of the Northwest Ordinance* (1987)

Rakove, Jack N., *The Beginnings of National Politics: An Interpretive History of the Continental Congress* (1979)

Reid, John Phillip, *Constitutional History of the American Revolution: The Authority to Legislate* (1992)

_____, *The Constitutional History of the American Revolution: The Authority of Law* (1994)

Rakove, Jack M., *The Beginnings of National Politics: An Interpretive History of the Continental Congress* (1979)

Wood, Gordon, *Creation of the American Republic, 1776–1787* (1969)

The New States

Adams, Willi Paul, *The First American Constitutions: Republican Ideology and the Making of the State Constitutions in the Revolutionary Era* (1980)

Kruman, Marc W., *Between Authority and Liberty: State Constitution Making in Revolutionary America* (1997)

Lutz, Donald S., *Popular Consent and Popular Control: Whig Political Theory in the Early State Constitutions* (1980)

Nevins, Allan, *The American States During and After the Revolution, 1775–1789* (1924)

Biographical

Brookheiser, Richard, *Founding Father* (1995)

Flexner, James, *Washington: The Indispensible Man* (1974)

Ver Steeg, Clarence L., *Robert Morris: Revolutionary Financier* (1954)

(Additional sources in General Bibliography, p. 605)

II

UNION AND NATION

3

THE FRAMING

Who Was There

Twelve of the 13 states responded to the Annapolis invitation by appointing delegates to the Philadelphia meeting. Some acted readily, others with skepticism or suspicion. Only Rhode Island, where radical groups controlled the legislature, chose not to take part. Of 65 delegates selected, 10 never attended and 16 others dropped out along the way. The average present was about 30.

The delegates were not ordinary men. Twenty-eight had served or were then serving in Congress. Most of the others had been in their state legislatures at one time or other, many taking part in writing or revising the state constitutions. Three were governors. Eleven had been officers in the Continental Army. By occupation, thirty-three were lawyers, eight merchants, six planters, three physicians, and four college presidents or professors. Thirty were college graduates, a high proportion for the time. They were also young. Five were under 30, the youngest, merely 24; only six were over 60, the oldest, by 16 years, was Benjamin Franklin.

Among the leading public figures in their ranks were Rufus King and Elbridge Gerry of Massachusetts; William Samuel Johnson and Roger Sherman of Connecticut; Alexander Hamilton of New York; William Paterson of New Jersey; Franklin, Robert Morris, James Wilson, and Gouverneur Morris of Pennsylvania; John Dickinson of Delaware; George Washington, James Madison, George Mason, and Edmund Randolph of Virginia; John Rutledge, Charles Pinckney, and Pierce Butler of South Carolina. Two who surely would have been had they not been serving abroad were Thomas Jefferson, ambassador to France, and John Adams, ambassador to England.

The delegates did not represent the social, economic, or political diversity of the country. They were better educated and wealthier than most of their countrymen. In an agrarian economy, their financial interests were disproportionately in commerce. Few of those who gave the first state constitutions their popular character or who were most suspicious of political "consolidation" were among them. Advocates of

37

cheap money and other debtor interests were not represented at all.

Except for Washington, Franklin, Robert Morris, and two or three others, they were a different group from the Revolutionary leadership. Absent were the likes of Samuel Adams, John Hancock, Patrick Henry, and Richard Henry Lee. Only 7 of the 56 signers of the Declaration of Independence were among the 39 who eventually put their names to the Constitution. Most of the delegates had reached adulthood or built careers during the years of the Revolution and Confederation. Since their views were less apt to have been shaped by the local colonial struggles against imperial authority, their horizons tended to be more "continental." In all, they were younger, economically more conservative, politically less democratic and more nationalist than the Revolutionary leaders. But these differences were hardly the makings of counterrevolution. Background should not be confused with motive and design. The convention delegates had more in common with their elders and countrymen than not.

The convention began on May 25, 1787, 11 days later than scheduled but the first day on which delegates from seven states (a quorum) were present. It met in almost continuous session for 18 weeks, far longer than anyone had expected, through one of Philadelphia's hottest summers.

Washington, who had been publicly greeted as a returning hero when he arrived in Philadelphia, was unanimously chosen as the presiding officer. Though he did not speak in the substantive debates, his presence and leading role held the convention together during difficult days and ensured that anything it reported would be taken seriously by the nation. Getting Washington to take part was not easy. He was still struggling with his finances and now had illness in his family. Persuading him was a master stroke for which Madison and several of the general's close friends could take credit.

At the outset, the delegates voted unanimously to meet behind closed doors. There would be no public gallery, no statements to the press, and no interim reports. Individual delegates pledged themselves to be discreet outside the meeting hall and, for the most part, they were. Such secrecy would be unimaginable in the modern hyper-media age where the press is apt to regard itself as a participant on behalf of the public in the work of government. Yet the decision was defensible. Closed meetings were not unusual; the Revolutionary colonial assemblies had met in secret as had the First Continental Congress. Even the debates of the Confederation Congress were not reported. Knowing that public review of whatever they did would come later, they did not equate the public interest with the interest of the press or the immediate satisfaction of public curiosity. The closed meetings allowed opinions to be aired candidly and new and even unusual ideas to be considered free of the inflexible posturing that might come from having to defend positions in public. The shielding also made compromises easier to reach. Reflecting on the matter many years later, Madison remained convinced that "the Constitution would never have been adopted by the convention if the debates had been public."*

Accord on Ends

The delegates who framed the Constitution generally agreed about the fundamentals of government. If they doubted this when discussion grew heated, their mutual understanding was strong enough and the purposes important enough to allow them to reconcile most of their differences and finish the Constitution.

They agreed that central government needed to be strengthened. It was this end more than any other that had brought the convention into being. Only a handful of committed antinationalists had come to Philadelphia and all left well before the end. A stronger government would

* Clinton Rossiter, *1787, the Grand Convention* (New York: The New American Library, 1968) 142.

better secure the country's national interests, military and commercial, against the threats from abroad. It would ensure prosperity at home by controlling the destructive short-sighted trade restrictions states that were imposing on each other. Yet a stronger central government would require a stronger union than the loose confederation of semi-independent constituent states they now had. On this question, the possibilities ranged from complete consolidation in which the states would be totally subordinate, if not cut out, to a tighter confederation not unlike the present one. Only Hamilton and two or three others were willing to embrace total consolidation. Most delegates, doubting the political feasibility of recommending so radical a change, took positions between the two extremes. They would need to decide how sovereignty, which had always been assumed to be indivisible, could be assigned to two levels of government—that is, how it could be placed at the center yet retained in the parts.

With no feudal legacy, there was no monarchy or hereditary privilege to consider. The delegates agreed the government must be republican in which the executive and legislature were chosen directly or indirectly by the people. Here the spectrum of views ranged from rule by an accountable elite to total democracy. Except for a few delegates, most notably Mason and Wilson who favored direct choice by the people wherever possible, most of the others distrusted democracy and doubted that the "common people" had the needed wisdom and dispassion to govern. Almost all preferred an arrangement in which a "natural aristocracy" of educated, public-spirited leaders, who had gained their stations on merit, governed in the interests of the people.

They agreed power must be limited. But where should the balance be drawn between concentration and diffusion? Too much of the first might lead to oppression or tyranny; too much of the second to paralysis or impotence. Since the English mixed system would not do, the framers anticipated separating power by governmental functions—executive, legislative, and judicial—interlocking those them with checks and balances, the common arrangement in the state governments. Few favored legislative supremacy, which was associated with irresponsible and corrupt politics. Only one, Hamilton, argued for executive supremacy. Again, most were between the poles.

Lastly there was general agreement on the need to curb economic radicalism, which was believed to threaten not only property and enterprise but prosperity itself. Though this was not a "pure" constitutional matter as, say, the locus of sovereignty or distribution of power, most delegates believed it important enough to a well-ordered society for it to be dealt with in the basic governmental arrangement. Since most of the them were men of high or at least comfortable financial standing, the goal might seem self-serving. For some perhaps it was, but we must remember that almost all the delegates (and a large number of their countrymen) equated possession of property with civic virtue and saw in its protection the security of all liberties.

In Convention

Madison arrived in Philadelphia several days early. After meeting with Pennsylvania delegates and later with his fellow Virginians, he wasted no time in drafting a blueprint for government that could be put to the convention. His proposals were presented by Edmund Randolph, the Virginia governor, on May 29, the first day the delegates turned to substantive work. The Virginia Plan, as it came to be called, provided for a bicameral national legislature in which the states would be represented in proportion to population. The lower house would be elected by the people, the upper by the lower from nominees proposed by the state legislatures. A national executive would be chosen by the legislature. It also provided for a judiciary, including a supreme court, and a council of revision made up of the executive and several members of the judiciary that would have a veto over legislation. As the delegates recognized at once, the proposal went well beyond a mere amending of the Articles. From the first day, it took the convention into new constitutional territory and set the agenda for the rest of its work.

But it was soon apparent that any provision basing both houses of the legislature on population would be strongly opposed by delegates from the smaller states, who feared domination by Virginia, Pennsylvania, and Massachusetts, which together had almost half the country's population. After two weeks of debate, William Paterson of New Jersey introduced an alternative plan departing less radically from the Articles. Its main provision was for a unicameral legislature in which states would be represented equally, as they had been in the Continental Congress and in the present Congress. The plan did not satisfy the need felt by most delegates for more substantial change and it was easily defeated.

Yet the stubbornness of the smaller states on equal representation persisted, and it became clear the convention risked deadlock and possible failure over this issue. The matter was not resolved until mid-July when the delegates agreed on a two-house legislature, with the lower, the House of Representatives, based on population—representatives not exceeding one for every 30,000 inhabitants—and chosen by direct popular vote for two-year terms, and the upper, the Senate, based on the principle of state equality—two representatives for each state, chosen by the state legislature for six-year terms. This agreement—the Great Compromise, as it came to be called—was a partial defeat for the democratic principle, but it eased the chief anxiety of the small states about creating a stronger central government. It allowed the convention to continue and set an example for the resolution of other differences.

With the matter of state representation settled, the delegates were able to agree on a three-branch national government: the bicameral Congress, executive power vested in a President, and judicial power in a Supreme Court. The Virginia Plan's council of revision was dropped. None of the three branches was designated as superior or subordinate to the other two. The single executive would serve a four-year term and be eligible for reelection. The delegates rejected proposals for a plural executive, a seven-year term, and ineligibility for reelection.

In this heroic rendition of a meeting of the Constitutional convention in Philadelphia, George Washington is portrayed addressing the delegates, though as presiding officer he most often sat and said little. Elder statesman Benjamin Franklin is seated in front of the platform. James Madison, who said a great deal, is seated at the corner of the platform.

Members of the Supreme Court would be appointed by the President, rather than the Senate as the Virginia Plan had it, and would serve for life or good behavior.

After rejecting proposals that the President be chosen by popular vote or by the Senate, the delegates devised the curious two-step college of electors. The President would be chosen by electors in each state equal in number to the state's members of Congress and "in such manner as the legislature thereof may direct." If no presidential candidate got a majority of the electors' votes, the president would be chosen from among the five candidates with the most votes, by the House voting by state. Since the delegates thought that few nominees would get a majority of the electoral vote, they assumed most elections would be decided in the House of Representatives. Thus, the Electoral College was both a desirable indirect way of choosing the president and, at the same time, one more balanced between large and small states. The larger states having a greater number of electoral votes would supply most of the nominees while the smaller, voting in the House by state, would be decisive in choosing among the highest nominees.

The Congress was given the power to tax and to regulate commerce among the states, authority conspicuously missing in the central government under the Articles. These powers and several others, including that of borrowing money, raising an army and maintaining a navy, and declaring war, were enumerated. Congress was also authorized to enact whatever laws were "necessary and proper" to realize the enumerated powers. At the same time, it was expressly forbidden to enact bills of attainder, ex post facto laws, suspend the writ of habeas corpus except in cases of rebellion or invasion, tax exports, or levy "direct" taxes unless apportioned among the states.

Empowerment of the president was stated generally as taking care that "the laws be faithfully executed." Specifically he was designated commander in chief of the armed forces, given power to make treaties with advice and consent

of the Senate, appoint Justices of the Supreme Court, ambassadors, and other executive officers, veto acts of Congress, and grant pardons.

National judicial power was set out by describing the kinds of cases to which it would extend. The Supreme Court was given a limited original jurisdiction and an appellate jurisdiction "in all other cases." Lower national courts could be created by Congress.

The delegates did not set out property qualifications for holding national office, apparently sure that only financially responsible persons would be chosen. They were tempted at first to place such restrictions on voting for members of the House. In the end, they left the matter to the states, requiring only that voters have the same qualifications as those for the "most numerous" branch of the state legislature.

Discussion of the slave trade and how slaves were to be counted in apportioning seats for the House produced much rancor. Antipathy of many delegates to slavery was apparent, but they realized there was no chance of ending slavery and still form a union of the 13 states. Nor would a union without the slave states end slavery in those states. Focus turned to what seemed a more realizable goal—ending the slave trade. But when Georgia and South Carolina threatened to bolt, the matter was compromised: Congress was given the power to end importation of slaves from abroad but not allowed to exercise it for 20 years. (When that period ended in 1808, Congress promptly put a stop to the traffic though some illegal importation continued until the Civil War.)

Sectional conflict also arose over the question of counting the slaves, a matter of both moral and statistical importance, since the country's 650,000 slaves were nearly 20 percent of the population. Southern delegates argued for full counting and thus for more seats in the House. Most non-Southern delegates, observing that slaves had no political rights and not wanting to reward slave states for having slavery, argued for no counting. The result was the so-called three-fifths compromise in which slaves would be counted in 60 percent of their number. The formula, which was borrowed from the Articles of Confederation, had no internal logic being simply the ground upon which agreement could be reached. It was applied also in counting population for the apportionment of direct taxes.

Though the convention did not deal with the structure or internal workings of the state governments—to have done so would have been politically explosive—the delegates believed they needed to curb or end some state powers. To constrain economic radicalism, states were forbidden to coin money, issue bills of credit, make anything except gold or silver coin acceptable for the payment of debt, or impair the "obligation of contracts." To discourage the raising of interstate trade barriers to a national market, states were denied power to tax imports or exports except as needed for inspections. They were forbidden, as they were under the Articles, from entering into treaties or otherwise engaging in foreign affairs. Borrowed also from the Articles was the requirement that states give "full faith and credit" to the laws and judicial actions of other states and return fugitives from justice to the states having jurisdiction over them.

What if state and national law or action should be in conflict? And who should determine this? The Virginia Plan included a council of revision that would have a veto over state legislation. When this part of the plan was dropped, the delegates simply provided that the Constitution, national laws, and treaties "shall be the supreme law of the land and the judges in every state shall be bound thereby."

Determined that the new constitution would not suffer the immutability that burdened the Articles, the framers provided that amendments could be proposed by a two-thirds vote of Congress and later ratified by three-quarters of the state legislatures or state conventions or, alternatively, by an amending convention called by Congress upon the request of two-thirds of the states, with later ratification by the legislatures or by conventions of three-quarters of the states.

On September 10, the convention held its last day of debate and committed its "bundle of compromises" to a Committee of Style, consist-

ing of Madison, Hamilton, King, Johnson, and Gouverneur Morris, to draft all that had been agreed upon into a single document. The committee assigned the task to Morris, a natural-born writer. In two days, he produced the final draft of the Constitution, set out in seven Articles. In 87 sentences it was longer than the Articles of Confederation, but remarkably terse compared with later constitutions in the states and in countries abroad. Its language is elegant and almost free of legalese, a remarkable feat considering the precision of expression called for in instruments of law. Nowhere was this more evident than in the graceful, rhythmical Preamble:

> We the people of the United States, in order to form a more perfect union, establish justice, insure domestic tranquillity, provide for the common defense, promote the general welfare, and secure the blessings of liberty to ourselves and our posterity, do ordain and establish this constitution for the United States of America.

After a clause-by-clause examination and a few minor changes, the delegates, voting by state, unanimously approved the Constitution on September 17. It was signed individually by 39 of the 42 present. For various reasons, Mason, Randolph, and Gerry, each of whom had played an important part in the debates, did not sign. The document was then sent to the Congress in New York, to await consideration by ratifying conventions in each state as provided for in Article VII.

Probably no delegate was wholly satisfied with the Constitution—there had been too many compromises in which individual delegates or state delegations had to give up things they wanted. The unhappiest had left before the end, not to return. Benjamin Franklin probably spoke for most signers when he remarked on the final day that there was much in the Constitution he did not like and would never like, but he remained convinced that it was the best proposal of government they could put together. As they adjourned, the sense of accomplishment

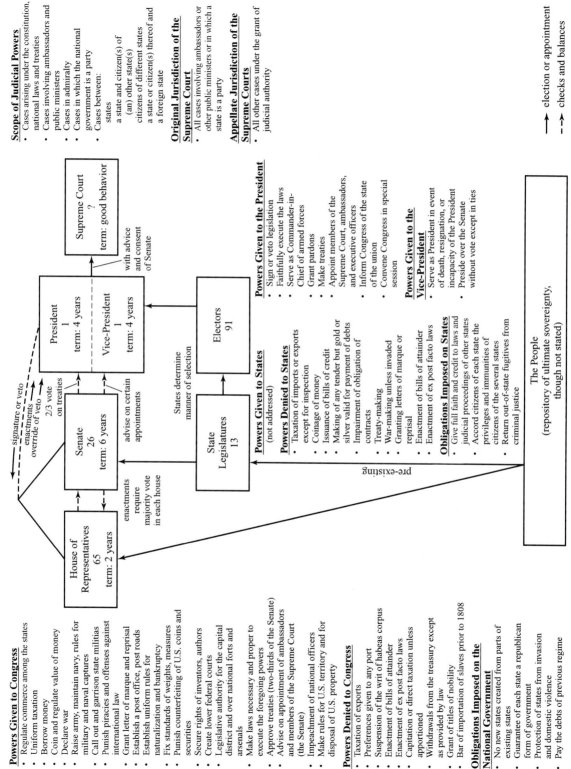

Powers Given to Congress

- Regulate commerce among the states
- Uniform taxation
- Borrow money
- Coin and regulate value of money
- Declare war
- Raise army, maintain navy, rules for military and naval captures
- Call out and garrison state militias
- Punish piracies and offenses against international law
- Grant letter of marque and reprisal
- Establish a post office, post roads
- Establish uniform rules for naturalization and bankruptcy
- Fix standards of weights, measures
- Punish counterfeiting of U.S. coins and securities
- Secure rights of inventors, authors
- Create lower federal courts
- Legislative authority for the capital district and over national forts and arsenals
- Make laws necessary and proper to execute the foregoing powers
- Approve treaties (two-thirds of the Senate)
- Advise on appointment of ambassadors and members of the Supreme Court (the Senate)
- Impeachment of national officers
- Make rules for U.S. territory and for disposal of U.S. property

Powers Denied to Congress

- Taxation of exports
- Preferences given to any port
- Suspension of the writ of habeas corpus
- Enactment of bills of attainder
- Enactment of ex post facto laws
- Capitation or direct taxation unless apportioned
- Withdrawals from the treasury except as provided by law
- Grant of titles of nobility
- Bar of importation of slaves prior to 1808

Obligations Imposed on the National Government

- No new states created from parts of existing states
- Guarantee of each state a republican form of government
- Protection of states from invasion and domestic violence
- Pay the debts of previous regime

Powers Given to States

- (not addressed)

Powers Denied to States

- Taxation of imports or exports except for inspection
- Coinage of money
- Issuance of bills of credit
- Making of any tender but gold or silver valid for payment of debts
- Impairment of obligation of contracts
- Treaty-making
- War-making unless invaded
- Granting letters of marque or reprisal
- Enactment of bills of attainder
- Enactment of ex post facto laws

Obligations Imposed on States

- Give full faith and credit to laws and judicial proceedings of other states
- Accord citizens of each state the privileges and immunities of citizens of the several states
- Return out-of-state fugitives from criminal justice

Powers Given to the President

- Sign or veto legislation
- Faithfully execute the laws
- Serve as Commander-in-Chief of armed forces
- Grant pardons
- Make treaties
- Appoint members of the Supreme Court, ambassadors, and executive officers
- Inform Congress of the state of the union
- Convene Congress in special session

Powers Given to the Vice-President

- Serve as President in event of death, resignation, or incapacity of the President
- Preside over the Senate without vote except in ties

Scope of Judicial Powers

- Cases arising under the constitution, national laws and treaties
- Cases involving ambassadors and public ministers
- Cases in admiralty
- Cases in which the national government is a party
- Cases between:
  - a state and citizen(s) of (an) other state(s)
  - citizens of different states
  - a state or citizen(s) thereof and a foreign state

Original Jurisdiction of the Supreme Court

- All cases involving ambassadors or other public ministers or in which a state is a party

Appellate Jurisdiction of the Supreme Courts

- All other cases under the grant of judicial authority

Figure 3.1 Scheme of the Constitution, September, 1787.

Original Intent

The claim that the Constitution should be interpreted, in its various phrases and provisions, according to the original intent of its framers, is familiar and full of controversy. In one sense, the claim has obvious and compelling merit. Since the Constitution formed a lasting union and is, by any measure, a remarkable political achievement, should we not honor the written and unwritten design and wisdom of the framers? And since the Constitution is supreme basic law, are we not all bound by its terms and intent, obliged neither to fall short of them nor go beyond? Proponents of the doctrine of original intent argue that it is part of the rule of law itself.

Attractive as the idea may be, original intent raises difficult questions of method and suitability. Many words and phrases of the Constitution, such as "direct tax," "appellate jurisdiction," "commerce among the states," are unclear, not because Gouverneur Morris was a careless draftsman, but because the framers either could not agree on more exact terms or wanted to leave them in general, open-ended language. Such lack of clarity was often a by-product of compromise. Many other great constitutional matters—for example, growth of national police power and a national common law, conflict between treaties and acts of Congress, the president's power to remove executive subordinates—were not dealt with at all because the framers did not fully anticipate them.

Only limited light can be shed on such questions by looking at the text or into the minds of the framers. No transcript of the Philadelphia convention exists. The best illumination is in the notes taken by James Madison himself, and not published until after his death. Madison edited these and, though he was probably faithful to the proceedings, he could record or chose to record only about 10 percent of what was said. Beyond this inventory we have only scattered remarks, reminiscences, and fragmentary records left by other delegates. Even if we had better information, weighing diverse individual understandings to arrive at a clarifying intent of the convention would be a bewildering task.

Things are more confounding when ratification is included. The delegates at Philadelphia merely proposed; those at the 13 state ratifying conventions—1,255 by count of final votes in favor—actually approved the Constitution. Since they can be said to have spoken as the "We, the People" of the Constitution's Preamble, their understanding of what they voted for would be critical to any search for original intent. But records of

was also tempered by the uncertainty of getting approval in the states. Few present on that cool late summer day in 1787 could have guessed that their work would serve as a model for scores of other constitutions around the world or that it would still be intact in a much different United States more than 200 years later.

Done and Not Done

Despite many differences over details, the framers realized their general aims. They created a stronger national government that could assert new powers at home and abroad, and it was this goal more than any other that had brought them together. It was impossible to say just how strong that government would be. For many committed nationalists like Hamilton, it was an important advance beyond the Articles but did not go nearly far enough in countering powers of the states. A few other delegates feared the convention had possibly created a political monster.

The framers applied the principles of representative government, already well-established in the states, to the union itself to form the largest republic in history. But lessons of the past were that republics, always difficult to create and sustain, had been small—city-states rather than the size of modern nations—and that most were short-lived. Here, too, success in realizing a general goal was attended by doubt.

the state convention debates are woefully incomplete and, in a few cases, even corrupted by later partisan revision. Also, many delegates spoke seldom, if at all, in the proceedings.

Critics of the doctrine of original intent raise another question even more challenging than that of method. Considering that we often face problems the framers could not foresee and that we have information they did not, should we be bound in all instances even where original meaning is clear or fairly so? Justice William Brennan, a leading liberal member of the modern Supreme Court, put the matter simply and candidly: "The genius of the Constitution rests . . . in the adaptability of its great principles to cope with current problems and current needs. What the constitutional fundamentals meant to the wisdom of other times cannot be the measure of the vision of our time."*

But what standards would reveal the "vision of our time" and who would apply them? Presumably the answer is a heavy dose of contemporary social values as understood by a majority of the Supreme Court. Here, proponents of original intent reply that standards outside the constitution, whether resting on a modern version of natural law, moral philosophy, or even some latter-day principles of Burkean conservatism, are no less ambiguous or more consensual than the original intent and text of the Constitution. Judges departing from the Constitution to "bring it up to date" are freed from the restraint of law and become themselves unelected philosopher-kings. Proponents point out that the Constitution has a carefully thought out amending procedure, resting on a popular base, to prevent it from becoming static.

Defending alternatives to original intent may be as hard as defending the doctrine itself. Each side has been better at attacking the other's theories. To show that intent matters is not the same as proving it can be fathomed in all cases or should control all cases. To show that original intent has flaws as a general theory of constitutional interpretation is not the same as proving a warrant to depart from text and intent where the latter are clear or giving them no weight where they are not.

Much of the debate over original intent is, at bottom, a dispute about how much discretion judges and justices of the day should have in interpreting the Constitution. And in that question—one of the oldest in American politics—often lie the "real" issues: differences over public policies. Perhaps there is no clearer example of the difficulties that lie in navigating the shoals of any "intent."

* William J. Brennan, "The Constitution of the United States, Contemporary Ratification," 27 *S. Tex. L. Rev.* 433, 438 (1986).

Legislative supremacy gave way to the principle of separation of powers. Instead of being vested in one branch, national authority was distributed among three—the House and Senate, the president, and the Supreme Court. The hybrid, containing several checks and balances, was more detailed than similar arrangements in most state constitutions. Nominally at least, each of the branches was a coequal of the other two.

The framers also gave effect to their political economy. By forbidding states to tax imports or exports and giving the central government power to regulate commerce among the states, the goal of a national marketplace was within reach. By denying states power to coin money, experiment with legal tender, or interfere with contracts, the framers had taken steps against inflationary monetary policy. They created a constitutional system far more congenial to business and commerce than the one they hoped to replace.

Many questions debated at Philadelphia were not acted upon. Three—voting qualifications for choosing members of the House and for choosing presidential electors, and the method by which the electors were to be chosen—were prudently left to the states. Others were not dealt with in the Constitution because their importance was not clearly recognized or because they were so devisive that pushing them through to decision would have risked wrecking the convention. Whether states might regulate interstate commerce, incidentally or otherwise, in the absence of national legislation would need to be settled by the courts in later years. Jurisdiction of inferior national courts, a contentious matter, was left to future Congresses. Failure to define citizenship or deal with the prospect of slavery in new territories or even with whether Congress had power on those matters probably avoided a sectional deadlock, but had grave consequences later as the slavery issue led to civil war.

Conspicuously missing was a bill of rights even though such inventories of protected liberties were fixtures in the state constitutions. The oversight was probably more a matter of not fully appreciating the need for such a provision than any antipathy to individual liberties. In fact many rights—the protection against bills of attainder, ex post facto laws, suspension of the writ of habeas corpus, and religious tests for public office—were included in the Constitution as were certain trial rights including that by jury in criminal cases. The crime of treason was carefully spelled out so that the charge of treason would not be abused. Many framers believed, perhaps too readily, that other individual liberties were safe because the central government was one of limited, enumerated powers. Why declare that things shall not be done which there is no power to do? Hamilton was to ask in *Federalist No. 84*. In any event, the matter was soon remedied without struggle through the addition of the first 10 amendments.

Leaving some matters in general, even ambiguous terms or not dealing with them at all also offered longer-term advantages. As the constitutional historian Forrest MacDonald put it, indefiniteness allowed power "to shift from one place to another, as time and circumstance should dictate,"* without the need of frequent formal revision. The Constitution has survived a civil war, two world wars, a "cold war," economic depressions, and profound social and technological change with only 27 amendments (18 if the first 10, the Bill of Rights, are taken as one),

remarkably few in a life of more than 200 years. Wisely or not, intentionally or not, the framers did not cover everything. They left many blanks that future generations might fill in to fit their circumstances.

They did create a new kind of government—a *federal* system. They devised a central government independent of the several states and gave it primacy in its empowered sphere without making the state governments totally dependent or subordinate. In effect, they divided the indivisible—sovereignty. Every citizen would live under two governments, each sovereign in its own right and each drawing its sovereignty from the same source—the people at large. The national government was supreme in its limited but now much enlarged authority. The states, as before, were free to do as they pleased so long as they did not confute national power or the Constitution. Familiar enough today, the arrangement was a radical departure from accepted notions of government at the time and, in the eyes of many, an invitation to trouble. For the framers it was not an experiment in political science but a device for cobbling together a union stronger than the existing league but not so "consolidated" that it would fail to gain and hold the young nation's approval. There would be much trouble. The nature of the union and the place of the states within it would be in dispute until resolved by the Civil War. And after that, the federal system—federalism—would continue to need balancing and fine-tuning.

Was the new government democratic or was it a retreat from the nascent popular forces of the 1780s? Clearly by today's standards the Constitution was not democratic, but neither was horse-and-carriage transport the equal of the modern airplane and automobile. Compared to the republican state governments, the Constitution was a partial retreat and intended to be so. The framers worried that unchecked popular power might lead to a "tyranny of the majority," which they felt had nearly seized several states. But they were not engaged in creating state governments; their task was constructing a national

* Forrest McDonald, *E Pluribus Unum* (Indianapolis: The Liberty Fund, 1979), 315.

one, and it is at that level that evaluating the democratic element makes the most sense. The framers had to design a constitution for a country of 4 million that stretched more than 1,000 miles along the Atlantic coast and almost as far inland—in area and population, 10 to 20 times larger than the largest states and 20 to 30 times the size of the revered city-state republics of the ancient world. In doing so, these skeptics of popular power created the most democratic large government in history.

Admittedly, they did put barriers between the citizenry and the government: indirect election of senators and of the president, life appointment of judges, and long terms of office. They also naively believed that a "natural aristocracy" based on education, merit, and property—one rather like themselves—should govern the country. Still, they placed ultimate sovereignty in the people rather than in the states as political entities. They provided direct popular election of one of the two houses of the legislature by an electorate in which nearly 95 percent of white males were eligible to vote. This alone carried popular participation further than in any other country. In letting the states decide how presidential electors were chosen, they also left open a door for greater popular voice in the selection of the president.

Nor did the framers try to force their notions of a natural elite on their countrymen. Except for certain requirements of age and one that the president be native born, they placed no restrictions on who might hold national office and none on who might vote. More important than any other provision in taking the democratic measure of the framers is the requirement in Article VII for popular ratification in conventions called in each state.

In its tone and terms the Constitution is conspicuously nondoctrinaire. It contains no longing for utopian solutions, no appeals to religious piety or exhortations to virtue. There is no reaching for cosmic first principles as in the Declaration of Independence. For better or worse, there were no true evangelicals among the framers, no Tom Paines, not even Thomas Jeffersons. Most thought of themselves as hard-headed realists who did not believe human beings were infinitely perfectible. They had gathered in disenchantment but worked with a cautious, pragmatic optimism. They were not demigods but inventive statesmen whose achievement was in practical more than theoretical politics.

After the Constitution was ratified and the new government instated, national leadership drew heavily from the ranks of the framers. Many were to fill the offices they had created. Two became presidents, one vice-president, five Supreme Court justices, four cabinet officers, four ambassadors, sixteen Senators, and eleven members of the House of Representatives.

The Anti-Federalist Attack

Debate about the Constitution began almost immediately and continued for the 10 months during which the state ratifying conventions were chosen and met. Proponents called themselves "Federalists," appropriating a term associated with confederation, thus avoiding such less popular labels as "nationalists" or the highly charged "consolidationists." Opponents were stuck with the negative "Anti-Federalist," and it was symptomatic of their position. Expecting only changes to the Articles of Confederation, they had readied no coherent alternative. They were left in the weak debating position of urging a rejection which, if obtained, would mean, at least for a while, continuing with things as they were.

Their dismay with the proposed scheme is easily understood. Out of a closed meeting in Philadelphia, called to revise the Articles, came a proposal for a new arrangement that shifted great powers from the states to the central government and needed approval of only nine states to become effective. Though they challenged almost every clause of the Constitution, their main objections were three: It was a plan for consolidated union, at best unworkable, at worst despotic; it would result in government by a privileged elite or, eventually, a monarch; it paid little or no attention to individual liberty.

The country was simply too big to be nationalized or consolidated in the way proposed. When an overland traveler might make only 30 to 40 miles a day in good weather on the best roads, the central government would be too remote from the people who were accustomed to authority closer at hand. There were too many persons—30,000—to be adequately represented by each member of the House of Representatives. Local desires would not be satisfied; corruption and influence would prevail. And had not Montesquieu, the authority on republics, warned that they could succeed only in small areas where people shared common interests? Having vast new powers and little accountability, the central government would become a tyranny.

Robert Yates, who had been a New York delegate to the convention but had left midway through not to return, argued that the powers given Congress were too far-reaching and ill defined. The taxation and borrowing authority would be unlimited. If taken with the provision that Congress had all powers "necessary and proper" to realize its enumerated powers, the national government would have a license to do almost anything it wanted. He and other Anti-Federalists maintained that Congress and the central government should have no power not _expressly_ granted to it.

The Marylander Luther Martin, another delegate who had quit the convention, challenged the very idea of a central government's sovereignty. The framers had declared the Constitution to be a compact among the people of the United States as _individuals._ But this was proper only if state governments did not exist, that is, only if all the people on the continent were forming government for themselves for the first time. The arguments of Yates and Martin failed in 1787–1788, but variations remained on the political table for years to come, to be dealt with in the Supreme Court and, on the matter of sovereignty, later on the battlefield.

Charges that the Constitution would lead to a monarchy or government by aristocracy often touched the emotions of a latent class antagonism. Patrick Henry feared the president, with command of the army and able to appoint executive officers, might easily become a king. Others believed the Senate was a blueprint for a privileged House of Lords and that powers of the appointed judiciary were dangerously vague. Terms of office of the President and members of Congress were too long. Having no annual elections, rotation in office, or limits on reeligibility, government would fall into the hands of a privileged few. Except for the concern about undefined judicial power, a worry destined for perpetuity, these fears would soon prove groundless.

The Anti-Federalists scored their most telling point in objecting to the absence of a bill of rights. The debates on this issue produced many thoughtful essays and speeches, including those by the Virginians Richard Henry Lee and George Mason, the Philadelphia delegate turned Anti-Federalist, on the importance of individual liberty in constitutional government. For other Anti-Federalists these arguments were vehicles for protecting local interests in the shift of power that might take place. Still, advocacy of a bill of rights was popular and put the Federalists on the defensive. Throughout the ratification debates, they had resolutely refused to yield to Anti-Federalist demands for amendments or for a second convention, But on a bill of rights they gave ground. Madison and other leading Federalists promised to seek amendments as a first order of business under the new government. The concession headed off conditional ratification in several states. If the Philadelphia Federalists framed the original Constitution, it is not too much to say the Anti-Federalists gave it its Bill of Rights.

The Constitution Defended

Proponents of the Constitution replied to the Anti-Federalists in public speeches and articles and in the state convention debates. Their most extensive defense come in *The Federalist Papers,* 85 serialized essays appearing once or twice a week for several months in New York newspapers. Written under the name "Publius," 51 were the work of Alexander Hamilton, who conceived the project, 29 of Madison, and 5 of John Jay.

Despite their genesis as campaign tracts and the haste in which many had to be written, the essays are probably the most powerful political thought America has produced. The authors first criticized the Articles of Confederation and argued the need for a national government strong enough to ensure security and prosperity. They then explained how the Constitution would work, almost clause by clause, and how it would achieve the ends set out. They went to lengths to reassure doubters and opponents that the Constitution reconciled power and liberty and remained faithful to republican principles.

In *Federalist No. 10,* which many political scientists view as the premier analysis of American politics, Madison answered the Anti-Federalist objection that the country was too large for workable republican government. In doing so, he also set out a theory of liberal democratic politics. No nation could rely solely on public virtue to achieve justice and avoid despotism. Factions—selfish interests formed by differences over property, commerce, religion, or almost anything else—were inevitable in a free, open society. Since they could be eliminated only by removing liberty itself, the "cure" instead lay in controlling their harmful effects. Where a faction was less than a majority, democratic government allowed the majority to defeat the faction by simple vote. But where a faction was large enough to include a majority, the democratic principle was helpless to prevent oppression of the minority outside the faction. This was the ultimate difficulty faced by republican government. It was not solved, Madison thought, by denying differences or selfish interests or by heroically trying to transcend them. The remedy lay in making it diffi-

cult for a majority faction to form at all, that is, for any interest to gain control of the entire government. Here Madison inverted conventional wisdom that republics could survive only if they were small. By having greater diversity and so more factions, a large republic made it harder for any single faction to gain all political power. The more factions or interests there were, the more they would act to check each other. Thus a large republic, which the Constitution created, was actually more viable than a small one.

Though the argument did not convince many hardened Anti-Federalists, it did free republican theory from the limits of scale, social homogeneity, and reliance on an idealized, publicly virtuous citizenry. Here, too, is the legitimacy for the pluralism and interest group liberalism that was then and now a norm of American politics. Heterogeneity in a large free society could actually be an asset rather than a hindrance. The growth of the United States from 4 million to nearly 300 million persons in two centuries shows how perceptive Madison was. But are things so simple? Might not a constitutional system in which power was widely distributed and thus difficult to fully marshal, also be one slow to respond to a profound public interest? Madison did not address this question—he probably would not have thought it much of a problem—yet it would be a recurrent and sometimes confounding one in American constitutional development.

To meet Anti-Federalist objections that the Constitution created a consolidated government while ignoring the states as older sovereignties, *The Federalist Papers* also provided a theory of federalism and sovereignty. In No. 39, Madison argued that the Constitution created a union that was neither wholly unitary nor wholly confederal, but had attributes of both. In giving the central government only limited, enumerated powers, the union was confederal; in allowing these powers to apply directly on individuals rather than operate through states, the union was unitary. This was the *federal* principle, and the division of

The Little Engine That Could

The only thing small about James Madison was his physical stature—he was 5 feet 2 inches tall and probably never weighed more than 100 pounds. His extraordinary public career of more than 40 years touched on so many important political events that his résumé reads like a biographic chronicle of the early history of the Republic.

He helped draft the Virginia Constitution in 1776 when he was only 25; was the youngest member of the Continental Congress in the 1780s; helped engineer the Philadelphia convention, wrote the Virginia Plan, and was the meeting's most effective member; was "campaign manager" for the Constitution during ratification debates and was its chief theorist in the *Federalist Papers;* served as a leading member of the new House of Representatives, where he introduced the Bill of Rights as the first amendments to the Constitution; organized the country's first opposition party with Jefferson in the 1790s; was framer of the Virginia Resolutions in reply to the Federalist Alien and Sedition Acts, 1798; served as Secretary of State in Jefferson's presidency, 1801–1809; was the nominal defendant in the Supreme Court's great Marbury case, 1803; served as the fourth president of the United States, 1809–1817 and in 1812, as its first war president.

Madison had to overcome frail health as a youth and later suffered periodic epileptic-like seizures

that may have been psychosomatic in origin. Called "Jemmy" by his friends, he was usually reserved and colorless. In an era in which public oratory was an art form and critical to success in public life, Madison often spoke so softly he could hardly be heard. Rejected by an early love, he was so wounded that he temporarily left public life and thought about living out his years as a scholar! He overcame his shyness with women and, in his forties, married the widow Dolley Todd, a remarkable extrovert, who later as First Lady became a legendary hostess at the center of the capital's social life and who, during the war, bravely rescued valuables from the White

sovereignty it required would be tested again and again in adjusting national and state authority to each other.

Madison argued ingeniously that the new government rested on popular sovereignty—its authority came from the people *outside of* government rather than from the states. In this view, the people were the ultimate source of power for both the states and central government. This relocation of sovereignty allowed the Federalists to sidestep the hard question of how sovereignty and power could be transferred from antecedent states to the center and what sovereignty, if any, was retained by the states. The idea that sovereignty rested in the people

and was granted by them through the Constitution to the central government and to the states was a powerful antidote to claims of an ultimate preexisting state sovereignty, in the years before the Civil War.

The Federalist Papers provided what the Philadelphia convention had not, a theoretical justification for the Constitution. They also offered valuable insight about the intentions of the framers. Their importance lies not in the number of minds they changed during the ratification debates, but in the shaping of American constitutional thought of the founding generation and those that followed. Through citation in many decisions, the Supreme Court has ele-

House minutes before British troops arrived to set it aflame.

Madison's subdued political style allowed him to collaborate successfully with strong men of such differing personalities as Washington, Hamilton, and Jefferson. He was unfailingly well-prepared on political issues, preferring to move cautiously, making sure interested parties were consulted and getting as much agreement as possible before taking final action. This often caused others to think him indecisive and, to their later regret, underestimate him. When he was able to tie his skill at organization to his great intellectual gifts, as he was at the Philadelphia convention, he was an extraordinarily effective leader. Similarly, he out-maneuvered and out-debated the formidable Anti-Federalist Patrick Henry at the Virginia ratifying convention.

At a time in which many public leaders were well-read in political philosophy and knowledgeable about comparative politics, Madison stood above the rest. As a scholar, he was probably the best political scientist and theoretician this country has produced. His *Federalist* essays provide not only a theory of government and political motivation, but keen insight into how American politics worked and would work.

When he became increasingly concerned about the aggressive nationalism of the Federalist government, he joined with his long-time friend Jefferson in forming the Republican (later the Democratic) Party to stand in opposition. Following Jefferson's presidential triumph in 1800, the party dominated American politics for 20 years. He succeeded Jefferson as president in 1809. His nomination of Joseph Story to the Supreme Court was one of the great judicial appointments in American history, though he failed to get the counterweight to Chief Justice Marshall he had hoped for. Madison was criticized by warhawks for his slowness to respond to British provocations in 1812, and when he did take the country into war, it was ill-prepared. The conflict came to be called "Mr. Madison's War" when things went badly at first. As the tide turned, Madison's popularity returned and he was hailed as the victorious leader.

After his second term, Madison retired to his Virginia home, the last of the generation of the framers to serve in public office. For the next 20 years, he was an active elder statesman, notably opposing the ideas of nullification and secession that were starting their upward climb on the American political agenda.

At his death in 1836, Daniel Webster said "He had as much to do as any man in framing the Constitution, and as much to do as any man in administering it."[*] The assessment was echoed by Henry Clay, "Mr. Madison rendered more important services to his country than any other man, Washington only excepted."[†]

[*] Quoted in Harold S. Schultz, *James Madison* (New York: Twayne Publishers, 1970), 5.
[†] Quoted in Irving Brant, *James Madison* (Indianapolis: Bobbs-Merrill, 1961), 521–522.

vated the *Papers* to near-official status in Constitutional law.

The Constitution Ratified

The seventh and last Article of the Constitution provided for ratification by state conventions rather than the state legislatures. The framers thought, no doubt correctly, that the Constitution had a much better chance of winning approval if it were given to new, ad hoc assemblies outside the legislatures. The chance of success was greatly improved by the proviso that if just nine states ratified the new government would go into effect for the ratifying states.

The first of these provisions violated Congress's instructions to the convention, which were that constitutional revisions be submitted to it. The second violated the spirit of the unanimity provision of the existing constitution. The new constitution was sent to Congress, but to inform not propose. Some members wanted to reject the document and censure the convention, but a majority, which included several of the framers, simply voted to send the Constitution on to the states without endorsement, so that state conventions might be called.

If a public opinion poll could have been taken in the winter of 1787–1788, the Anti-Federalists would probably have had the better of it. But electing delegates to the conventions was another matter, and in most of those bodies opponents of the Constitution were not as strong as in the population at large. The Federalists had some clear advantages. Besides holding the initiative, they were better organized and their support was more compact geographically, no small matter in getting voters to polling places. And though the Anti-Federalists had some able leaders, they could not match the names on the Federalist side, including the nation's two "living legends," Washington and Franklin, both closely associated with the Constitution. It was not simply that Washington had presided over the Philadelphia convention; it was universally assumed that should the new system be ratified, he would be its first president, a perception that quieted many fears. The Federalists not only had the proposal, they had the man.

Though some states—Delaware, New Jersey, and Georgia—ratified unanimously and quickly, the contests in several others, including the largest states—Pennsylvania, Massachusetts, Virginia, and New York—were close and acrimonious. Underlying class antagonism was visible in some of the popular feeling against the Constitution. Questionable tactics were used by both sides. Scurrilous attacks impugning motives were frequent. In Pennsylvania, several Anti-Federalist legislators were mistreated, and James Wilson, one of the leading framers, was beaten by an Anti-Federalist mob. In Massachusetts, Federalists won over the vainly ambitious John Hancock by falsely promising to support him to be the first vice-president. Anti-Federlists rioted in Albany and burned a copy of the Constitution in New York City, then the nation's capital.

The Constitution was ratified when New Hampshire became the ninth state to approve, in June 1788, but pragmatically it was not complete until Virginia and New York, important states because of their size and location, approved soon afterward. Six of the last seven states to ratify did so with accompanying "recommendations," mainly urging inclusion of a bill of rights. North Carolina rejected ratification and Rhode Island, the only state not to send delegates to Philadelphia, refused even to call a con-

vention. When the first Congress under the new regime met in March 1789, it quickly placed a tax on "imports" from the two states, in effect dealing with them as foreign countries. North Carolina soon reconsidered and ratified. In Rhode Island, the holdout populist radicals who controlled the state were not overcome until May 1790, nearly two years after the Constitution had gone into effect.

Economic concerns were often prominent in the motives and reasons for supporting or opposing the Constitution. Some were based on social station, others in calculation of interest. Federalists drew heavily from northern merchants, southern planters, those engaged in commerce and foreign trade, professionals, artisans, shopkeepers, and creditor interests. Anti-Federalists were stronger among self-sufficient "yeoman" farmers, common laborers, frontiersmen, and those with debtor interests, who were not necessarily the poor. Differences were also reflected in geography. Support for the Constitution was strongest along the coast and in the largest cities, which were also the areas that had been most directly involved in the War, and weakest inland, in western counties and less settled areas (Figure 3.2). In Virginia, for example, Federalists dominated the Tidewater, Anti-Federalists the Piedmont.

The emphatic ratification vote in Delaware, New Jersey, and Connecticut partly reflected fear that local economies were not strong enough to withstand annexation pressures from larger neighboring states. The need for national protection was strongly felt in Georgia where the Spanish in Florida occupied the state's southern flank and strong Creek Indians were in the west. The prospect that the new government might assume Revolutionary debts was a factor in South Carolina, which had been hit hard by the war and where the burden of debt was particularly heavy.

Many Anti-Federalists opposed the Constitution because of concern about republican principles and individual liberty, and many Federalists supported it because they were worried about national security and national well-being. At bottom, a great

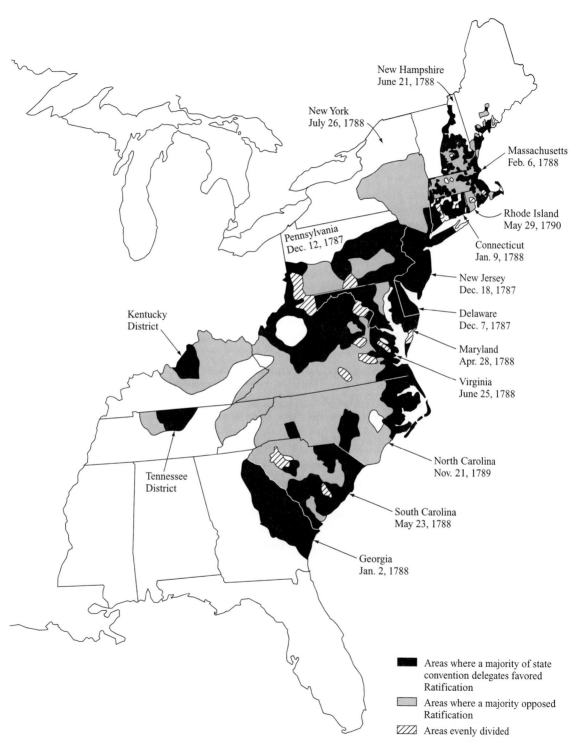

Figure 3.2 Ratifying the Constitution: Federalist and Anti-Federalist Majorities.

deal depended on one's own circumstances. Those with little knowledge of or interest in events beyond their local areas or states had less reason to be dissatisfied with conditions and less reason to take a chance on a new plan for a strong, distant government. Many leaders who had made their reputations locally saw the power shift the Constitution would bring as a threat to their political base. It is commonplace to see the Anti-Federalist cause, shaped by hostility, suspicion, and apathy, as standing in history's way. Yet it was also a commitment to a smaller, more personalized society pledged to the defense of traditional values—a stance that has never gone totally out of style. Supporters of the Constitution were apt to have more cosmopolitan views, the product of better education, wider travel, and a broader outlook generally; they tended to see politics in larger, continental terms. Many of their leaders were younger men who had less identification with their states and could easily imagine great national horizons.

Delegates to the state conventions were all popularly chosen. By best estimates, about 160,000 persons voted in these elections, about 100,000 for candidates favoring the Constitution. Though this turnout—roughly a sixth of eligible white males—is unimpressive by modern standards, ratification was one of history's great democratic events. No nation had ever before proposed a new government and then given that proposal to those who would be governed, for their approval or rejection. The popular base of the Constitution was thus more direct, more deliberative, and better established than that of either the Articles of Confederation or the Declaration of Independence. More than that, the process was carried through with little violence or coercion. No one was killed and few persons were physically hurt. The losers were not jailed, hanged, or politically disabled. They did not boycott, take up arms, or go into exile. They continued, as before, to be full and free citizens, but now living in a new republic. Several of their leaders actually served in the new government, one—

George Clinton, governor of New York—later twice as vice-president.

The Bill of Rights

Soon after the new government was instated with the election of the first Congress and of Washington as president, the Federalists set about fulfilling their ratification promise of adding a bill of rights to the Constitution. Madison, who had been elected to the House of Representatives, took the lead in preparing the first amendments. More than 200 recommendations had been made by the state ratifying conventions dealing with nearly 100 matters. Some had nothing to do with individual rights but were aimed at removing powers, such as taxation, from the central government. A few, such as one that objected to the elimination of religious tests for federal office because it might allow Jews or "infidels" to take over the government, were motivated by bigotry rather than liberty.

Many among both the Federalists and Anti-Federalists had genuine concern for individual rights, but the motives of others were complex and positions taken not always straightforward. Some Federalists who still believed a statement of rights was unnecessary supported the amendments simply from a sense of moral obligation. Some Anti-Federalists were in favor because they saw the amendments as one more way to tie down central power on behalf of the states. Many Federalists were in favor because they thought the amendments would head off pressures for another constitutional convention. A few Anti-Federalists were cynically opposed because they thought rejection would have the opposite effect.

The debate in Congress decided two matters of great long-term importance. Madison had proposed the amendments be limits on the state governments as well as the central. This was defeated by Anti-Federalists and others concerned about protecting states rights. As a result the Bill of Rights begins with the phrase "Congress shall make no law . . . ." Nearly 150 years would pass before parts of the Bill of Rights began to be interpreted as limits on state power. Despite this triumph, states-rights partisans were defeated in their attempt to limit central authority to powers *expressly* enumerated in the Constitution. "Expressly" was, in effect, expressly omitted from what became the Tenth Amendment, which now read: "Powers not delegated to the United States by the Constitution, nor prohibited by it to the states, are reserved to the states respectively, or to the people." Inclusion of "expressly" after "not" would have precluded the possibility of federal implied powers and perhaps radically changed the course of constitutional development.

In all, Congress sent 12 proposed amendments to the states for ratification. Two, dealing with adjustments in congressional representation and limits on the pay of members of Congress, failed to gain approval. Ratification of the others, now the first 10 Amendments, was completed in December 1791.

Though some members of Congress wanted to include lofty general statements of rights and liberty similar to those in the Declaration of Independence, the Bill of Rights is confined to concrete statements of traditional protections, many of which were in bills of rights in the state constitutions. The First Amendment contains protections for the freedoms of speech, press, assembly, and religious worship, and a bar to "establishment" of religion. The Second and Third Amendments deal with the right to bear arms and protection against quartering of troops. The Fourth sets out rights against arbitrary searches, seizures, and arrest. The Fifth guarantees certain rights to the criminally accused and against the public taking of property. The Sixth and Seventh set out various trial rights. The Eighth protects against excessive bail and cruel and unusual punishments. The Ninth, containing no substantive rights, declares that the liberties and protections listed do not preclude others "retained by the people." The Tenth Amendment, already noted, is less a statement of liberty than of distribution of power. Even

without the restricting term "expressly," the amendment became the great Constitutional source of states rights and ground for striking down federal legislation.

Many contemporaries played down the Bill of Rights as simply a restatement of the obvious, and in fact, the amendments had little immediate effect beyond declaration. But in the second half of the twentieth century, the Bill of Rights became in the eyes of many the most important part of the Constitution. Claims under its provisions and those of the later, Fourteenth Amendment account for nearly half the cases coming before the Supreme Court.

The Second New Nation

Debate over the Constitution was not about whether to have a union but about the kind of union to have. The Constitution represented a great shift of power, geopolitically from outer concentrations to the center, hierarchically from lower legal ranks to higher. Authority moved from republican state governments to a new republican central government where it was distributed among legislative, executive, and judicial agencies. This departure from the Articles of Confederation nationalized republicanism. These changes were not the product of violence, intimidation, or social displacement, but came out of a deliberative process later legitimated by consent widely and freely given. It was a great political triumph.

Yet even well-managed shifts of power bring changes in the fortunes and opportunities of interests, groups, and individuals. Gains and losses are not simply political but social, economic, and moral as well. Some of those were anticipated (not always accurately) by those on both sides of the Constitutional debate and gave that debate much of its intensity. Other consequences would become clearer later and some would profoundly affect the course of the nation socially and economically. Those bearing on the sectional conflict over slavery would raise the question of union itself as the ratification debate had not.

Failure of the union in 1861 should not obscure the presence of a great underlying consensus that allowed the formation of a new constitutional regime in 1787, as it had allowed the first nation to declare itself independent a dozen years before. Even as they combatively debated the Constitution, late eighteenth-century Americans shared a high degree of social, economic, and cultural unity, based on a common legal and political tradition and a common language. Economic and social cleavages were not as deep, fixed, or politically explosive as those in Europe. The social structure was fluid, and a great many persons were in the middle class. Religious differences had not been transformed into the kind of divisive conflict that had tormented England and other countries. The long experience with self-government had nurtured a remarkable political self-confidence that helped

community to flower. The historian Benjamin Wright observed, "It was not the consensus of ideology, or desperation, or crisis . . . that may temporarily unite a people, [but one] rooted in the common life, habits, institutions, and experience of generations . . . the consensus of contentment and success, not misery and oppression."*

Underlying unity permitted political continuity in the swing of the pendulum from Revolution to Constitution, from the radicals who rebelled conservatively in 1776 to the conservatives who innovated radically in 1787–1788. We can see now, as few did then, that the experiment with confederation, in between, was critical to making a stronger union. The first nation had to precede the second, just as the second would need to take hold to later withstand a brutal war within.

_____

* *Consensus and Continuity, 1776–1787* (New York: W. W. Norton, 1958) 57–58.

FURTHER READING

The Constitution Created

Anderson, Thornton, *Creating the Constitution: The Convention of 1787 and the First Congress* (1994)

Beard, Charles A., *An Economic Interpretation of the Constitution* (1913)

Brown, Robert E., *Charles Beard and the Constitution* (1956)

Farrand, Max, ed., *The Records of the Federal Convention of 1787,* 4 vols. (1911–1937).

Jillson, Calvin C., *Constitution Making: Conflict and Consensus in the Federal Convention of 1787* (1988)

Levy, Leonard, ed., *Essays on the Making of the Constitution,* 2nd ed. (1987)

Levy, Leonard W. and Dennis J. Mahoney, eds., *The Framing and Ratification of the Constitution* (1987)

McDonald, Forrest E., *We the People: The Economic Origins of the Constitution* (1958)

Rossiter, Clinton, *The Grand Convention* (1966)

Rossom, Ralph A. and Gary L. McDowell, eds. *The American Founding: Politics Statesmanship and the Constitution* (1981)

Warren, Charles, *The Making of the Constitution* (1929)

Ideas, Antecedent and Embodied

Banning, Lance, *The Sacred Fire of Liberty: James Madison and the Founding of the American Republic* (1995)

Casper, Gerhard, *Separating Power: Essays on the Founding Period* (1997)

Davis, S. Rufus, *The Federal Principle: A Journey Through Time in Quest of Meaning* (1978)

Gillespie, Michael A. and Michael Lienesch, *Ratifying the Constitution* (1989)

Hall, Mark David, *The Political and Legal Philosophy of James Wilson* (1997)

Huyler, Jerome, *Locke in America, The Moral Philosophy of the Founding Era* (1995)

Lerner, Ralph, *The Thinking Revolutionary: Principle and Practice in the New Republic* (1987)

Lutz, Donald S., *The Origins of American Constitutionalism* (1988)

Matthews, Richard K., *If Men Were Angels: James Madison and the Heartless Empire of Reason* (1995)

McDonald, Forrest E., *Novis Ordo Seclorum: The Intellectual Origins of the Constitution* (1985)

Pangle, Thomas L., *The Spirit of Modern Republicanism: The Moral Vision of the American Founders and the Philosophy of Locke* (1988)

Phelps, Glenn A., *George Washington and American Constitutionalism* (1993)

Rakove, Jack N., *Original Meanings: Politics and Ideas in the Making of the Constitution* (1995)

Rosen, Gary, *American Compact: James Madison and the Problem of Founding* (1999)

Sandoz, Ellis, *A Government of Laws: Political Theory, Religion, and the American Founding* (1990)

Sellers, M. N. S., *Roman Republicanism: Roman Ideology in the United States Constitution* (1994)

Sinopoli, Richard C., *The Foundations of American Citizenship: Liberalism, the Constitution, and Civic Virtue* (1992)

Sorenson, Leonard R., *Madison on the "General Welfare" of America: His Consistent Constitutional Vision* (1995)

West, Thomas G., *Vindicating the Founders: Race, Class, Sex, and Justice in the Origins of America* (1997)

Wright, Benjamin F., *Consensus and Continuity, 1776–1787* (1958)

The Constitution Attacked and Defended

Boyd, Stephen R., *The Politics of Opposition: Anti-Federalists and the Acceptance of the Constitution* (1979)

Conley, Patrick T. and John P. Kaminski, eds., *The Constitution and the States* (1989)

Epstein, David, F., *The Political Theory of 'The Federalist'* (1984)

Gillespie, Michael A. and Michael Lienesch, eds., *Ratifying the Constitution* (1992)

Hamilton, Alexander, Jay, John and Madison, James, *The Federalist* (1788)

Maine, Jackson Turner, *The Anti-Federalists: Critics of the Constitution, 1781–1788* (1961)

Riker, William, *The Strategy of Rhetoric: Campaigning for the American Constitution* (1996)

Rutland, Robert A., *The Ordeal of the Constitution: The Anti-Federalists and the Ratification Struggle of 1787–1788* (1966)

Storing, Herbert and Dry, Murray, eds., *The Complete Anti-Federalist*, 7 vols. (1981)

Wills, Garry, *Explaining America: "The Federalist"* (1981)

Biographical

Brant, Irving, *James Madison: Father of the Constitution* (1950)

Brookheiser, Richard, *Alexander Hamilton, American* (1999)

Flexner, James T., *George Washington and the New Nation, 1783–1793* (1969)

Rutland, Robert A., *James Madison, the Founding Father* (1987)

THE FEDERALIST, NO. 10
James Madison

To the People of the State of New York:

Among the numerous advantages promised by a well constructed Union, none deserves to be more accurately developed than its tendency to break and control the violence of faction.

The friend of popular governments never finds himself so much alarmed for their character and fate, as when he contemplates their propensity to this dangerous vice. He will not fail, therefore, to set a due value on any plan which, without violating the principles to which he is attached, provides a proper cure for it. The instability, injustice, and confusion introduced into the public councils, have, in truth, been the mortal diseases under which popular governments have everywhere perished; as they continue to be the favorite and fruitful topics from which the adversaries to liberty derive their most specious declamations.

The valuable improvements made by the American constitutions on the popular models, both ancient and modern, cannot certainly be too much admired; but it would be an unwarrantable partiality, to contend that they have as effectually obviated the danger on this side, as was wished and expected. Complaints are everywhere heard from our most considerate and virtuous citizens, equally the friends of public and private faith, and of public and personal liberty, that our governments are too unstable, that the public good is disregarded in the conflicts of rival parties, and that measures are too often decided, not according to the rules of justice and the rights of the minor party, but by the superior force of an interested and overbearing majority.

However anxiously we may wish that these complaints had no foundation, the evidence, of known facts will not permit us to deny that they are in some degree true. It will be found, indeed, on a candid review of our situation, that some of the distresses under which we labor have been erroneously charged on the operation of our governments; but it will be found, at the same time, that other causes will not alone account for many of our heaviest misfortunes; and, particularly, for that prevailing and increasing distrust of public engagements, and alarm for private rights, which are echoed from one end of the continent to the other. These must be chiefly, if not wholly, effects of the unsteadiness and injustice with which a factious spirit has tainted our public administrations.

By a faction, I understand a number of citizens, whether amounting to a majority or a minority of the whole, who are united and actuated by some common impulse of passion, or of interest, adversed to the rights of other citizens, or to the permanent and aggregate interests of the community. There are two methods of curing the mischiefs of faction: the one, by removing its causes; the other, by controlling its effects.

There are again two methods of removing the causes of faction: the one, by destroying the liberty which is essential to its existence; the other, by giving to every citizen the same opinions, the same passions, and the same interests.

It could never be more truly said than of the first remedy, that it was worse than the disease. Liberty is to faction what air is to fire, an aliment without which it instantly expires. But it could not be less folly to abolish liberty, which is essential to political life, because it nourishes faction, than it would be to wish the annihilation of air, which is essential to animal life, because it imparts to fire its destructive agency.

The second expedient is as impracticable as the first would be unwise. As long as the reason of man continues fallible, and he is at liberty to exercise it, different opinions will be formed. As long as the connection subsists between his reason and his self-love, his opinions and his passions will have a reciprocal influence on each other; and the former will be objects to which the latter will attach themselves. The diversity in the faculties of men, from which the rights of property originate, is not less an insuperable obstacle to a uniformity of interests. The protection of these faculties is the first object of government. From the protection of different and unequal faculties of acquiring property, the possession of different degrees and kinds of property immediately results; and from the influence of these on the sentiments and views of the respective proprietors, ensues a division of the society into different interests and parties.

The latent causes of faction are thus sown in the nature of man; and we see them everywhere brought into different degrees of activity, according to the different circumstances of civil society. A zeal for different opinions concerning religion, concerning government, and many other points, as well of speculation as of practice; an attachment to different leaders ambitiously contending for pre-eminence and power; or to persons of other descriptions whose fortunes have been interesting to the human passions, have, in turn, divided mankind into parties, inflamed them with mutual animosity, and rendered them much more disposed to vex and oppress each other than to cooperate for their common good. So strong is this propensity of mankind to fall into mutual animosities, that where no substantial occasion presents itself, the most frivolous and fanciful distinctions have been sufficient to kindle their unfriendly passions and excite their most violent conflicts. But the most common and durable source of factions has been the various and unequal distribution of property. Those who hold and those who are without property have ever formed distinct interests in society. Those who are creditors, and those who are debtors, fall under a like discrimination. A landed interest, a manufacturing interest, a mercantile interest, a moneyed interest, with many lesser interests, grow up of necessity in civilized nations, and divide them into different classes, actuated by different sentiments and views. The regulation of these various and interfering interests forms the principal task of modern legislation, and involves the spirit of party and faction in the necessary and ordinary operations of the government.

No man is allowed to be a judge in his own cause, because his interest would certainly bias his judgment, and, not improbably, corrupt his integrity. With equal, nay with greater reason, a body of men are unfit to be both judges and parties at the same time; yet what are many of the most important acts of legislation, but so many judicial determinations, not indeed concerning the rights of single persons, but concerning the rights of large bodies of citizens? And what are the different classes of legislators but advocates and parties to the causes which they determine? Is a law proposed concerning private debts? It is a question to which the creditors are parties on one side and the debtors on the other. Justice ought to hold the balance between them. Yet the parties are, and must be, themselves the judges; and the most numerous party, or, in other words, the most powerful faction must be expected to prevail. Shall domestic manufactures be encouraged, and in what degree, by restrictions on foreign manufactures? are questions which would be differently decided by the landed and the manufacturing classes, and probably by neither with a sole regard to justice and the public good. The apportionment of taxes on the various descriptions of property is an act which seems to require the most exact impartiality; yet there is, perhaps, no legislative act in which greater opportunity and temptation are given to a predominant party to trample on the rules of justice. Every shilling with which they overburden the inferior number, is a shilling saved to their own pockets.

It is in vain to say that enlightened statesmen will be able to adjust these clashing interests, and render them all subservient to the public good. Enlightened statesmen will not always be at the helm. Nor, in many cases, can such an adjustment be made at all without taking into view indirect and remote considerations, which will rarely prevail over the immediate interest which one party may find in disregarding the rights of another or the good of the whole.

The inference to which we are brought is, that the *causes* of faction cannot be removed, and that relief is only to be sought in the means of controlling its *effects*.

If a faction consists of less than a majority, relief is supplied by the republican principle, which enables the majority to defeat its sinister views by regular vote. It may clog the administration, it may convulse the society; but it will be unable to execute and mask its violence under the forms of the Constitution. When a majority is included in a faction, the form of popular government, on the other hand, enables it to sacrifice to its ruling passion or interest both the public good and the rights of other citizens. To secure the public good and private rights against the danger of such a faction, and at the same time to preserve the spirit and the form of popular government, is then the great object to which our inquiries are directed. Let me add that it is the great desideratum by which this form of government can be rescued from the opprobrium under which it has so long labored, and be recommended to the esteem and adoption of mankind.

By what means is this object attainable? Evidently by one of two only. Either the existence of the same passion or interest in a majority at the same time must be prevented, or the majority, having such coexistent passion or interest, must be rendered, by their number and local situation, unable to concert and carry into effect schemes of oppression. If the impulse and the opportunity be suffered to coincide, we well know that neither moral nor religious motives can be relied on as an adequate control. They are not found to be such on the injustice and violence of individuals, and lose their efficacy in proportion to the number combined together, that is, in proportion as their efficacy becomes needful.

From this view of the subject it may be concluded that a pure democracy, by which I mean a society consisting of a small number of citizens, who assemble and administer the government in person, can admit of no cure for the mischiefs of faction. A common passion or interest will, in almost every case, be felt by a majority of the whole; a communication and concert result from the form of government itself; and there is nothing to check the inducements to sacrifice the weaker party or an obnoxious individual. Hence it is that such democracies have ever been spectacles of turbulence and contention; have ever been found incompatible with personal security or the rights of property; and have in general been as short in their lives as they have been violent in their deaths. Theoretic politicians, who have patronized this species of government, have erroneously supposed that by reducing mankind to a perfect equality in their political rights, they would, at the same time, be perfectly equalized and assimilated in their possessions, their opinions, and their passions.

A republic, by which I mean a government in which the scheme of representation takes place, opens a different prospect, and promises the cure for which we are seeking. Let us examine the points in which it varies from pure democracy, and we shall comprehend both the nature of the cure and the efficacy which it must derive from the Union.

The two great points of difference between a democracy and a republic are: first, the delegation of the government, in the latter, to a small number of citizens elected by the rest; secondly, the greater number of citizens, and greater sphere of country, over which the latter may be extended.

The effect of the first difference is, on the one hand, to refine and enlarge the public views, by passing them through the medium of a chosen body of citizens, whose wisdom may best discern the true interest of their country, and whose patriotism and love of justice will be least likely to sacrifice it to temporary or partial considerations. Under such a regulation, it may well happen that the public voice, pronounced by the representatives of the people, will be more consonant to the public good than if pronounced by the people themselves, convened for the purpose. On the other hand, the effect may be inverted. Men of factious tempers, of local prejudices, or of sinister designs, may, by intrigue, by corruption, or by other means, first obtain the suffrages, and then betray the interests, of the people. The question resulting is, whether small or extensive republics are more favorable to the election of proper guardians of the public weal; and it is clearly decided in favor of the latter by two obvious considerations:

In the first place, it is to be remarked that, however small the republic may be, the representatives must be raised to a certain number, in order to guard against the cabals of a few; and that, however large it may be, they must be limited to a certain number, in order to guard against the confusion of a multitude. Hence, the number of representatives in the two cases not being in proportion to that of the two constituents, and being proportionally greater in the small republic, it follows that, if the proportion of fit characters be not less in the large than in the small republic, the former will present a greater option, and consequently a greater probability of a fit choice.

In the next place, as each representative will be chosen by a greater number of citizens in the large than in the small republic, it will be more difficult for unworthy candidates to practice with success the vicious arts by which elections are too often carried; and the suffrages of the people being more free, will be more likely to center in men who possess the most attractive merit and the most diffusive and established characters.

It must be confessed that in this, as in most other cases, there is a mean, on both sides of which inconveniences will be found to lie. By enlarging too much the number of electors, you render the representatives too little acquainted with all their local circumstances and lesser interests; as by reducing it too much, you render him unduly attached to these, and too little fit to comprehend and pursue great and national objects. The federal Constitution forms a happy combination in this respect; the great and aggregate interests being referred to the national, the local and particular to the State legislatures.

The other point of difference is, the greater number of citizens and extent of territory which may be brought within the compass of republican than of democratic government; and it is this circumstance principally which renders factious combinations less to be dreaded in the former than in the latter. The smaller the society, the fewer probably will be the distinct parties and interests composing it; the fewer the distinct parties and interests, the more frequently will a majority be found of the same party; and the smaller the number of individuals composing a majority, and the smaller the compass within which they are placed, the more easily will they concert and execute their plans of oppression. Extend the sphere, and you take in a greater variety of parties and interests; you make it less probable that a majority of the whole will have a common motive to invade the rights of other citizens; or if such a common motive exists, it will be more difficult for all who feel it to discover their own strength, and to act in unison with each other. Besides other impediments, it may be remarked that, where there is a consciousness of unjust or dishonorable purposes, communication is always checked by distrust in proportion to the number whose concurrence is necessary.

Hence, it clearly appears, that the same advantage which a republic has over a democracy, in controlling the effects of faction, is enjoyed by a large over a small republic,—is enjoyed by the Union over the States composing it. Does the advantage consist in the substitution of representatives whose enlightened views and virtuous sentiments render them superior to local prejudices and schemes of injustice? It will not be denied that the representation of the Union will be most likely to possess these requisite endowments. Does it consist in the greater security afforded by a greater variety of parties, against the event of any one party being able to outnumber and oppress the rest? In an equal degree does the increased variety of parties comprised within the Union, increase this security. Does it, in fine, consist in the greater obstacles opposed to the concert and accomplishment of the secret wishes of an unjust and interested majority?

Here, again, the extent of the Union gives it the most palpable advantage.

The influence of factious leaders may kindle a flame within their particular States, but will be unable to spread a general conflagration through the other States. A religious sect may degenerate into a political faction in a part of the Confederacy; but the variety of sects dispersed over the entire face of it must secure the national councils against any danger from that source. A rage for paper money, for an abolition of debts, for an equal division of property, or for any other improper or wicked project, will be less apt to pervade the whole body of the Union than a particular member of it; in the same proportion as such a malady is more likely to taint a particular county or district, than an entire State.

In the extent and proper structure of the Union, therefore, we behold a republican remedy for the diseases most incident to republican government. And according to the degree of pleasure and pride we feel in being republicans, ought to be our zeal in cherishing the spirit and supporting the character of Federalists.

Publius

4

THE FORMATIVE PERIOD

The Federalist Regime

In the first election under the Constitution, Washington was chosen president with the votes of all 69 presidential electors, who had been elected by popular vote in districts or at large in some states and chosen by the legislature in others. With each elector having two votes to cast, John Adams, with the next highest vote, 34, became the first vice-president. Washington's long trip from Mount Vernon to the capital in New York turned into an extraordinary procession. Tens of thousands of his countrymen, frustrated by what they saw as a lack of leadership and direction, turned out to cheer or pay honor to him. Arriving in New York, he was greeted by a singing of the familiar "God Save the King," the words being slightly edited for the occasion. Such adulation, which made Washington uncomfortable, might have been enough to turn the head of a lesser republican.

The new government began with a spirit of good will and cooperation. A handful of Anti-Federalists had been elected to Congress, but proponents of the Constitution had comfort-able majorities in both houses. Twenty-six of the 39 signers of the Constitution were in the new government; they made up more than half the Senate membership. But Washington and other Federalist leaders were not lulled. They knew that winning the right to instate new government was not the same as having that government's policies accepted by the people and by the states. For the moment, Anti-Federalist criticism was quieted, but suspicion remained and many saw the Constitution as merely provisional.

Much work needed to be done and seldom had a new government inherited fewer assets. Left over from the Confederation were a handful of clerks, an army of a few hundred officers and men and no navy, an empty treasury, and the burden of a staggering public debt. Congress quickly established three executive departments—Treasury, State, and War—and the offices of attorney-general and postmaster general. Washington appointed Jefferson, who had returned from France, as secretary of state; his old Continental Army colleague General Henry Knox as secretary of war; and Edmund Randolph as attorney general. For the Treasury Department, which nearly everyone assumed would be the most important in the new government, Washington preferred the experienced Robert Morris. But when he declined the offer, the president chose Alexander Hamilton, then only 34 years old. The appointment would be one of the most important in the nation's history.

The empty treasury and huge debt were the most pressing problems confronting the new government. Luckily, a favorable phase of the business cycle brought low interest rates to most of the country. But it was clear to most Federalists that the longer-term legitimacy of the new regime would depend on the success of its fiscal policies. Congress quickly used the central government's new taxing power to place duties on imports—tariffs—and on tonnage, that is, on vessels in trade. Though aimed mainly at raising revenue, the levies gave advantages to American manufacturing and shipping. It marked the start of the protective tariff and of a continuous conflict between manufacturing regions and those dependent on imports.

Hamilton's Political Economy

Soon after the revenue legislation, Congress asked the new Treasury secretary to prepare a report on the nation's credit. Hamilton seized the opportunity to draw up one of the great documents of public finance, "The First Report on Public Credit." In characteristically bold strokes he set out the principles of a nationalist political economy. Restoration of American credit, he argued, was essential not simply so that money might be borrowed in the future if needed but to develop new resources for agriculture and industry and to secure the nation against attack. The outstanding debt, the price nation had paid for liberty, should be fully honored to restore confidence in the government. To do this, he made two controversial proposals. First, the debts incurred by the Confederation should be paid off at par—full face value rather than at their much

depreciated market prices. Though some debt was held by the governments of France and Spain and by private bankers in the Netherlands, much that had been held by Americans was now in the hands of speculators. Objections arose to paying these last obligations at par, since they had been bought from their original, patriotic lenders for as little as 15 cents on the dollar. Hamilton replied that the Constitution, which required Confederation debts be assumed, made no distinction between assignees and original holders.

Hamilton's second proposal went further still: The central government should assume all outstanding state debts, also at face value. This provoked an extended debate in Congress. Such funding was not required by the Constitution, and a few states, like Virginia, had already paid off much of their debt. Now national taxes would be used to do what less conscientious states had failed to do. Hamilton, who believed restoration of public credit depended on liquidating all government debt, state and central, knew the states could not be compelled to tax themselves enough to pay off their debts. A deadlock on the issue was broken by a classic political "deal." opponents of the assumption of state debts, mainly Southerners, would drop their objections in return for an agreement to move the national capital southward, temporarily to Philadelphia, then to a permanent location in a special federal district on the Maryland bank of the Potomac.

Funding of state and Confederation obligations at face value swelled the national debt to more than $80,000,000, an astronomical sum at the time. Interest on it amounted to nearly 80 percent of the central government's spending. But the scheme was dramatically successful. Almost overnight American credit was restored abroad. New bonds of the United States sold *above* par in the Netherlands. When Europe plunged into turmoil following the French Revolution, American securities and, later, the American economy itself became safe havens for investment, roles they have continued to play ever since. At home, the funding helped to bind financial and creditor interests, whose support

Hamilton believed critical to survival of the Constitution, to the new central government. The funding was a fiscal triumph and a great nationalizing force.

Next, at Hamilton's urging, Congress created a 20-year charter for a national bank to help manage the public credit. As Washington debated whether to sign the legislation or not, his cabinet was deeply divided. Jefferson, nervous about broadening the central government's authority, argued the action was unconstitutional, since the government had no granted power to establish a bank. Hamilton answered that the bank was an allowable "necessary and proper" means in Article I-8 for realizing several granted powers including taxation and borrowing. But for Jefferson, the "necessary and proper" clause gave Congress only those implied powers that were *indispensable* rather than simply expedient to its granted powers. Hamilton took a position of broad construction: "Necessary and proper" gave Congress implied power to do all that was "needful, requisite, incidental, useful, or conducive" to execute its enumerated powers. After weighing the arguments carefully, Washington supported Hamilton, and in 1791 signed into law the First National Bank of the United States.

Later in the year, Hamilton submitted a third proposal, "The Report on the Subject of Manufactures," a bold program to make the United States economically independent of other nations. It called for encouragement of manufacturing through a protective tariff, bounties for agriculture, and internal improvements paid for by the central government. Amid growing concern in Congress about national power, the proposal was not enacted, though its chief points showed a remarkable grasp of the future political economy of the United States.

Constitutional Precedents in the Making

The Constitution created an outline of government that was flexible, open, and sometimes ambiguous. In the course of governing, Washington and Congress quickly discovered a great many blanks needed filling in. Many of their decisions and practices became traditions and so almost as much a part of the binding Constitution as the text the framers had drafted.

In setting up the executive departments, an early question arose of whether the president alone could dismiss executive officers. Except for impeachment, the Constitution was silent on removal. After much debate, Congress did not speak conclusively but inferred that the president had removal power free of consultation with Congress. The issue remained quiet until Congress tried to reclaim a role, in the Tenure of Office Act of 1867. It was not resolved definitively until the Supreme Court upheld presidential power in *Myers v. United States* in 1926.

Washington used the first presidential veto in 1791 to block a bill that would have allowed some states more than one representative in the House for every 30,000 persons, because he believed it to be unconstitutional. The veto was then used sparingly for many years, and not until Jackson's presidency was legislation rejected for reasons of policy rather than constitutionality.

Washington was a presiding leader *par excellence.* He preferred to seek advice widely and then act on choices put before him. Yet except for the Senate giving "advise and consent" on treaties and certain appointments, the Constitution did not provide for presidential consultation. And the Senate's role became attenuated after a painful attempt at interbranch cooperation. Early in his first term, Washington went to the Senate with a list of questions about a treaty being negotiated with the Creek Indians. He expected the Senate to supply him with expeditious "yes" or "no" answers while he sat. But the Senators, seeing themselves as a deliberative body, asked to study the matter and referred the questions to a committee, at which point Washington angrily left. Though the Senate did send answers in three days, Washington vowed to communicate with it in the future only through written messages. The misunderstanding ended any chance of the Senate becoming a fuller advisory body. Its role in treaty-making would usually be confined to a post hoc approval or rejection.

That the Supreme Court might act as a consultative body also came to nothing. In his second administration, Washington asked the Court for an advisory opinion on legal questions in a treaty. The Court courteously declined to give such an opinion, citing the separation of powers. The rebuff and the unfortunate experience with the Senate spurred Washington to consult the heads of departments—the cabinet—which raised no separation of powers question. The cabinet became a stable and moderately effective advisory body, though in practice presidents have also consulted other officials and even persons outside government.

The Constitution commits responsibility for foreign affairs to both the president and Congress without fully defining their roles. When war broke out between Britain and France in 1793, the country was divided about which side to favor without becoming a full belligerent. Washington wanted to establish official neutrality, but a constitutional debate arose over who should issue such a declaration, the president or Congress. In his cabinet, the pro-French Jefferson argued that because Congress had power to declare war, it must declare neutrality. Unsurprisingly, the pro-British Hamilton favored the executive: In foreign affairs, the president, as head of a nation dealing with other nations, had inherent executive powers—those beyond the grants of the Constitution. Without expressly accepting Hamilton's reading, Washington issued a proclamation of neutrality, in part because Congress had just adjourned and could not quickly be called back into session. The action raised a storm and opened the door to wide use of presidential power in foreign affairs. The balance of responsibilities between the president and Congress in foreign policy has never been settled definitively.

During the British-French conflict, Washington had sent John Jay to England to negotiate several outstanding Anglo-American issues. But when the war went in Britain's favor, Jay was un-

able to get terms as favorable as he had hoped. Though Jay's Treaty, as it became known, was unpopular, it was ratified by the Senate. But the following year, the last of Washington's administration, the House tried to foil the treaty by refusing to appropriate money needed for its enforcement. In doing this, it asked Washington to submit all executive documents on the treaty. Washington coolly refused, reminding the House that, unlike the Senate, it had no voice in treaty-making. His stand, asserted as executive prerogative, set a second important precedent in foreign affairs. Future presidents would often share treaty information with the House, not on demand but at their discretion.

Opposition of Jefferson and Madison

All important government actions distribute their benefits and costs unevenly and are often intended to do so. Hamilton's fiscal program, successful though it was, came at a price. Commercial and maritime interests were helped the most; small farmers, shopkeepers, frontiersmen, at least as they could see, hardly at all. That speculators had profited from the debt funding was widely resented. What made this opposition more dangerous for Hamilton was its coincident sectional bias. About 80 percent of the state and Confederation domestic debt had been held by residents of northern states. In the eyes of many, taxes were being imposed throughout the nation to benefit a section of it. That the perception was simplistic and ignored the longer-term national gains Hamilton's program offered, did not make it false. It aggravated the sectional division, the most serious faultline in pre-Civil War American politics.

Added to this was the first outright resistance to the new government. One of the excise taxes in Hamilton's program was a heavy duty on distilled whiskey. It fell hardest on western and rural areas where surplus corn was often converted into spirits, which made it easier to store or transport. The practice was so common that distilled whiskey often served as a medium of exchange. In 1794, Pennsylvania farmers in several western counties refused to pay the tax. They organized resistance that included intimidation of tax officials, disruption of local government, and threats to march on Pittsburgh and Philadelphia. Fearing spread of the insurgency, now known as the Whiskey Rebellion, Washington called out several state militia. A huge army of more than 13,000 responded, and the resistance was easily broken. Its leaders were captured and two were found guilty of treason, though they were later pardoned by the president. The government's swift and decisive action showed that it could meet internal crises. Despite this important triumph for civil order, the rebellion was one more sign of discontent with the distributive aspects of fiscal nationalism.

Jefferson worried about the effects of Hamilton's program and the aggressive nationalism that lay behind it. He believed Hamilton's broad reading of national and executive authority went beyond constitutional warrant. As a leader in Congress, Madison was also apprehensive and eventually broke with his old collaborator. After Jefferson resigned from the government, the two set about organizing an opposing voice. Supporters of the government's program were a loose coalition calling themselves Federalists. Jefferson and Madison organized opponents into the Republican Party, a constellation of Southern leaders and northerners like the New York governor George Clinton, who had been Anti-Federalists during ratification. When Washington's second term ended, the country had two opposing, easily identifiable national parties for the first time.

The Federalists' strength lay with manufacturing, commercial, and shipping interests who benefited from a capitalist economy, and were sympathetic to a broader reading of national powers. The Republicans, drawing support from the planting slaveholding interests in the South, frontiersmen in the West, and small farmers in all sections, were less national in outlook and favored a narrower construction of central power. Federalists were pro-British in foreign affairs, some seeing in the French Revolution in 1789 a chance for the United States to loosen ties to its former ally. Republicans were generally pro-French and remained so even after postrevolutionary events in France turned bloody and oppressive.

The ideas of Jefferson and Hamilton were the intellectual cores of the parties. Though a figure of many talents, broad interests, and great sophistication, Jefferson had little patience with high finance, of which he knew little, or with industrial possibilities. He saw a great agrarian democracy in the American future, built on the strong backs and civic virtue of the small farmer. It would be a republic of liberties and equal opportunities in which the focus of political life was local and the laws mild. Trust could be placed in the collective wisdom of the people, perfected by education. Hamilton, who respected Jefferson personally, regarded these ideas as sentimental nonsense. The nation's future lay in a strong union and diversified economy directed by an able, patriotic elite. The chief threat was not the tyranny that Jefferson feared but anarchy. In reality, of course, the country was close to neither. But the great programmatic changes the Federalists had brought were divisive. They dispensed gains and losses giving rise to opposing political camps with differing philosophies and contrasting visions of the future.

The Constitution does not mention political parties. To the extent the framers thought about them, they hoped the system they were creating would be discouraging. Parties were traditionally seen to be groups of like-minded persons who put their own interests above all—the factions that Madison had written about in *The Federalist, No. 10*. Yet, paradoxically, they were probably indispensable if the large new republic was to survive. Some organization was needed to mobilize and transmit public opinion to the government and, at the same time, identify candidates with programs so an electorate could choose among them. Within the government they served as a partial

The Nation Builder

Almost everything in Alexander Hamilton's life came early. In a young nation with many youthful leaders, he was the most precocious of them all. Born in the West Indies out of wedlock— "the bastard brat of a Scottish peddler," John Adams would later say—he was sent to the mainland in 1773 by a friendly minister to study at King's College (now Columbia University). Soon he was speaking on the patriot cause at public meetings and showing a surprisingly mature grasp of issues. His pamphlets became important entries in the great debate leading to the Revolution. When the war started, he organized an artillery company and so impressed Washington in the battle of New York that the general made Hamilton, at 22, his aide-de-camp and private secretary. He later asked for and was given a field command and led troops in the siege of Yorktown. He was a colonel at 26.

After the war, he began a law practice in New York City and married into the wealthy and landed Schuyler family. As a delegate to the Annapolis Convention, he joined Madison in calling for the Constitutional convention the following year. He represented New York at Philadelphia, though his effectiveness was limited by his own extreme views on both national and executive authority and by being outvoted by his fellow New York delegates, who were Anti-Federalists. During the ratification debates, he persuaded Madison and Jay to join in writing the *Federalist Papers,* of which he authored nearly two-thirds. He played a main role in New York's eventual ratification.

His working relationship with Washington resumed when the new president asked him to become, at 34, the first secretary of the treasury. In this post, which he held until 1795, Hamilton performed his greatest service. His bold plan for funding the national domestic and foreign debt at par and for national assumption of state war debt, swiftly reestablished American credit. In urging the creation of a national bank, he formulated the liberal theory of federal implied powers and broad

antidote to the rigidities of formally separated power by helping to coordinate actions among the parts and making coherent programs possible. Despite occasionally being vehicles for selfish interests, they became an important part of republican government, providing a generalized representation of opinion from the atoms of individual votes.

When Washington's second term ended in 1797, the country was probably more divided than when he took office. Yet, the governing system—the Constitution—was much less a source of conflict than eight years earlier. As the debate between Hamilton and Jefferson showed, there were sharp disagreements over what the Constitution meant and what it permitted, but now there were few attacks on it as a governing system and no calls for another convention. The regularity with which former Anti-Federalists— now likely to be Republicans—invoked its literal meaning to argue for limited national power, was dramatic testimony to how attitudes had changed. The Constitution had acquired a remarkable degree of legitimacy in just eight years. This was the great achievement of Washington's presidency.

construction of constitutional grants. His urging that tariff levies be not merely for revenue but also protection for developing domestic manufacturing laid a cornerstone for American industrial development. As Washington's chief minister, he built a fiscal system with a distinctly modern cast.

After returning to his New York law practice near the end of Washington's administration, he and John Adams vied for the leadership of the Federalist Party. When the presidential election of 1800 was thrown into the House of Representatives and the choice was between Jefferson, his old rival in Washington's cabinet, and Aaron Burr, a political rival in New York, Hamilton threw his support to Jefferson, whom he disliked but respected, against Burr, whom he disliked and distrusted. When Hamilton also helped deny Burr the New York governorship in 1804 and was severely critical of him in public comments, the furious Burr, still the nation's vice-president, challenged him to a duel with pistols. Hamilton foolishly accepted, though he did not believe in dueling and had no need to prove his courage. It is believed he deliberately shot over Burr's head. But Burr, less generous and ever the opportunist, mortally wounded Hamilton, who died the next day, only 49.

Hamilton's political time had already passed. He had expected Jefferson's regime to disintegrate as had the French Republic, and then, some critics said, he expected to step forward as an American Bonaparte to restore order and stability. Ironically, one of the reasons that nothing remotely approaching anarchy occurred was that Hamilton had built so well. The Hamiltonian System was a going concern and, to his lasting credit, Jefferson did little tampering with it.

The political economy Hamilton fashioned as secretary of the Treasury was a tribute to an extraordinary perception of what the American future could be in an fast evolving capitalist world. In this, Hamilton was both a visionary and an administrative genius, perhaps, as the historian Richard Morris has suggested, the greatest America has yet produced. He combined a quick and sharp perception of means with a confident sense of remote ends. Though he may have been the most modern of the nation's late eighteenth century leaders, Hamilton might not have made his way so easily in democratic politics. Arrogant and impatient, he did not suffer fools well and lacked the instinct for compromise and sensitivity to rights possessed by Jefferson. Appreciation of a kinder, gentler politics was not his forte. As one of his twentieth-century critics, the populist, agrarian scholar Vernon Parrington observed, he was a leader "to whom our industrialism owes a very great debt, but from whom our democratic liberalism has received nothing."* If it was impossible to have the leadership qualities of Hamilton and Jefferson in one man, the young nation was fortunate to have them in two.

* "Hamilton and the Leviathon State," in J. E. Cooke, ed., *Alexander Hamilton, A Profile* (New York: Hill and Wong, 1967), 149.

An Unhappy Succession

Washington retired after two terms, and the election of 1796 was between two parties and two candidates: Federalist John Adams and Republican Jefferson. Adams won the presidency with 71 electoral votes to Jefferson's 68, who became vice-president. Now in his sixties, Adams's public career was notable, going back to his pre-Revolutionary days as a patriot lawyer and writer. It had included service in the Continental Congress, as an ambassador to England, and eight years as vice president to Washington. Judged by his writings of 30 years, he was a student of politics second only to Madison. Yet his presidency was a troubled one.

Almost immediately he was confronted by a crisis with France. The aggressive postrevolutionary Directory government, reacting to Jay's Treaty with Britain, began systematically to interfere with American shipping and in a few months had captured more than 300 vessels. This undeclared naval war and a heavy-handed French diplomacy, which included the soliciting of a bribe, divided the country and Adams's party. Hamilton, his chief Federalist rival and no longer in the government, wanted an immediate declaration of war. Several holdover members of Adams's cabinet, including Timothy Pickering, the secretary of state, felt the same way. Without Adams's knowledge, they reported regularly to Hamilton, the apparent heir-in-waiting. This was not hard to do since Adams spent more than a quarter of his time at home in Massachusetts. When he discovered the treachery, he replaced all of Hamilton's allies. Like Washington, he wanted to keep the United States out of war with either European belligerent. He did this while building up American naval forces. It was the signal triumph of his administration.

But the neutral course did little to calm the waters. The Republicans, strongly anti-British and in sympathy with France, looked the other way on the French provocations and opposed any hostilities against the country's former ally. In the quasi-war atmosphere, the Federalist majority in Congress, with Adams's approval, pushed through the Alien and Sedition Acts of 1798, aimed at enemies at home. The first dealt with foreign agitators and with French immigrants who numbered about 25,000. It authorized the president to deport aliens thought to be dangerous and, in wartime, to round up and imprison any enemy alien. The Sedition Act, striking at Republican critics, made it a crime to conspire to oppose or interfere with any law or to write or speak against the president or Congress "with intent to defame or bring them . . . into disrepute or to excite against them . . . the hatred of the good people of the United States." The act allowed truth as a defense, but political criticism was, as always, often highly subjective and truth often impossible to discover.

Twenty-five persons were tried under the act; 10 were convicted including several Republican journalists and a member of Congress. Many trials were before arrantly biased Federalist judges. To objections that the free speech and press shields of the First Amendment prevented Congress from enacting such a law, Federalist lawyers argued that the amendment's protection included only the English common law bar to prior restraints—censorship before publication—not prosecution after the fact. However heavy-handed the Federalists were in attempting to silence criticism, they were close to the historical mark in this interpretation. A First Amendment reading that would make the Sedition Act unconstitutional today was nearly 150 years away.

The Republican response was a sweeping constitutional attack in the form of resolutions of two state legislatures, Virginia and Kentucky. Drafts of these statements were written anonymously by Madison in Virginia's case, and Jefferson in Kentucky's. They cast Republicans as defenders of freedom of speech, but it was the appeal to states rights that struck home. The Union was formed by a compact of states; under the Constitution, the federal government had limited power and was not the exclusive or final judge of its reach. If it went beyond its grants, a state could interpose itself between the national government and its citizens and so refuse to enforce such unconstitutional national laws.

Though the Virginia and Kentucky Resolutions were meant to be campaign salvos in the election of 1800, they came to have much greater importance. The ringing defense of states rights allowed them to be used later in the growing sectional conflict leading to the Civil War. Calhoun, for example, took them up in his doctrine of nullification in which secession was a last resort. Madison and Jefferson did not intend their argument to go that far, at least Madison later denounced state nullification. The resolutions were also another sign that the Constitution had gained acceptance—all sides could and did appeal to it even as the constitutional nature of the Union remained much in doubt.

The Sedition Act and the state resolutions were elements in the Federalist defeat in 1800. Though the party was never able to regroup, it had given the country 12 years of moderately strong government and a heavier dose of nationalism than almost anyone in 1788 would have thought possible. The thrust had reached a point of temporary exhaustion as a triumphant

Jeffersonian regime appeared ready to redress the balance of power between nation and state.

The Early Supreme Court

In setting out the judicial branch, the framers of the Constitution left most things to future legislation. They created a Supreme Court but did not specify its size or composition. They described in detail the Court's original jurisdiction—the right to hear trials—yet, except for the recital of "in all the other cases," left the Court's appellate jurisdiction to be determined by Congress. They created no lower national courts but authorized Congress to do so. They said nothing about the state courts or how they would fit with the new federal judiciary.

The Judiciary Act of 1789

It was not surprising that in 1789 the new Congress would make the judiciary its first order of business nor, in six months of proposals and debate, that lines would be drawn between nationalists and states rights advocates, including Anti-Federalists. Nationalists argued for a strong, pervading federal court system, opponents to keep as much judicial power in the states as possible. The definitive Judiciary Act of 1789, setting out a national court system, remains one of Congress's most important enactments, almost more an extension of the Constitution than ordinary legislation. Its chief architect, Oliver Ellsworth, one of the framers, struck a middle position between the nationalists and states rights members. The Supreme Court would have a chief justice and five associate justices. Two lower levels of courts were created: 13 one-judge district courts—one in each of the 11 states then in the Union and two territories—and 3 three-judge circuit courts made up of a district judge and two Supreme Court justices.

The fractious matter of jurisdiction was spelled out in detail. Exclusive federal jurisdiction was limited mainly to admiralty and mar-

itime cases in the district courts. Otherwise, the original jurisdiction of the district and circuit courts was concurrent with that of the state courts, a big concession to the states-rights advocates who feared federal exclusivity. But the jurisdiction of the circuit courts included litigation involving citizens of two or more states—the so-called diversity cases. This was a contentious matter because many Federalists believed that out-of-state plaintiffs, who were often trying to collect debts, would not get fair treatment in a state court. Lines of appeal from district court to circuit court to the Supreme Court and from the highest state courts to the Supreme Court were specified.

The Judiciary Act was an important compromise because it set up a network of federal courts without absorbing the state courts into a "consolidated" federal system. Most jurisdiction would be concurrent. Though the Act has been modified several times, the basic form of the system it created remains the same.

With the federal judicial structure in place, Washington appointed the first members of the Supreme Court. He chose John Jay, the veteran diplomat, as chief justice, and William Cushing of Massachusetts, James Wilson of Pennsylvania, John Blair of Virginia, James Iredell of North Carolina, and John Rutledge of South Carolina as associate justices. All were strong nationalists. Wilson, Blair, and Rutledge had been framers of the Constitution. The others played active roles in its ratification, Jay being one of the coauthors of the *Federalist Papers*. The Court met for the first time in February 1790 in New York. For most of its first three years it heard no cases and did little more than hire a clerk and swear in lawyers who would practice before it. Individually, the justices were active as members of the new circuit courts.

Two early matters helped to establish judicial independence by defining lines separating the courts from executive and legislature authority. A war veterans' pension act Congress passed in 1792 called for the circuit courts to rule on claims filed by disabled veterans. In

Hayburn's Case, Justices Wilson and Blair, sitting in the circuit court in Pennsylvania, held that Congress had imposed nonjudicial duties on the courts, violating the separation of powers. But to avoid a confrontation with Congress, they construed the law as naming the judges as commissioners; in that role they were willing to accept the task. The issue went no further because Congress, heeding the objections, repealed the statute the following year. The Court's refusal to give Washington an advisory opinion, already noted, helped define lines separating the judicial and executive branches and let the Court avoid committing itself to positions in advance of actual conflicts that might later be brought to the courts.

The Eleventh Amendment

The Court's first full decision, *Chisholm v. Georgia* in 1793, (p. 97) laid open the conflict between federal jurisdiction and ideas of state sovereignty. Exercising its original jurisdiction, the Court heard an action by two South Carolina citizens against the State of Georgia to recover property confiscated by the state during the Revolution. Though the Constitution committed jurisdiction in cases "in which a state shall be party" to the Court, it was generally assumed this referred to cases brought *by* states, not against them, and even Hamilton had admitted in the *Federalist Papers* that a state could not be sued without its consent. When Georgia refused to appear, the Court entered a default judgment for the plaintiff. This stirred up old state-rights fears of "consolidation" and of creditors with claims against states thronging the federal courts. A storm of protest gathered quickly and within days an amendment to undo the decision was introduced in Congress. Feelings ran so high in Georgia that its lower house passed a bill making any attempt to enforce the Court's decision a felony punishable by hanging "without benefit of clergy"!

The constitutional amendment, later ratified over Federalist opposition as the Eleventh, simply declared that "the judicial power of the United States shall not be construed to extend to any suit in law or equity commenced or prosecuted against one of the United States by citizens of another state or by citizens or subjects of any foreign state." For the first and only time, the Supreme Court's jurisdiction was limited by constitutional amendment. It was not a promising start for the Court and signaled how easily it could become embattled in the politics of federalism.

John Jay, who had earlier taken leave from the Court at Washington's request to negotiate a treaty with Great Britain, was elected governor of New York in 1795 and resigned as chief justice, having concluded that after the *Chisholm* reaction the Court was unlikely ever to be effective. Washington nominated Associate Justice Rutledge to succeed him, but after it was learned he had made a speech opposing Jay's Treaty, the Senate refused to confirm. Washington then turned to Oliver Ellsworth, who became the third chief justice in 1796.

Constitutional Decisions

Though the Court was under a heavy political cloud after *Chisholm,* its workload increased steadily and two of its next decisions dealt with interpretation of the Constitution. In *Ware v. Hylton,* 1796, the action of British creditors on a prewar debt against a Virginia citizen put state law squarely in conflict with a treaty. Virginia had sequestered British property during the war and given Virginia citizens who owed money to Brits the right to discharge such debt by paying it to the state treasury. Many state debtors, including Daniel Hylton, the defendant, did this in the vastly depreciated paper currency of the day. But the Treaty of Paris in 1783, which ended the war, made clear there should be no legal impediments to creditors on either side in collecting prewar debts. The Supreme Court, voting 4 to 0, conceded that states had a right to sequester property during war, but held the Virginia act contrary to the treaty, which under Article VI of the Constitution was part of the "supreme law of the land." The decision, reviving old debt owed to old enemies, was widely unpopular. But it did not produce the unnerving response *Chisholm* had, and it stands as an important early assertion of national supremacy.

In *Hylton v. United States,* the same year, the Court ruled on a tax Congress had placed on carriages rented or kept for personal use. Hylton (the same who challenged the treaty debt provisions) refused to pay the levy, contending that it was a "direct" tax under Article I-8 and so had to be apportioned among the states according to population rather than imposed uniformly on all owners of carriages. Congress, aiming to tax the wealthy, had assumed the levy was simply an excise, thus not needing apportionment. The Supreme Court agreed and held that direct taxes were limited to those on land and persons. The decision was a victory for the Hamiltonian financial system. Had the direct tax category been expanded, it would no doubt have undercut the national government's revenue power. Since apportioned taxes would fall on states unequally, they would be politically difficult to impose and would probably stoke animosities among the states. (If the carriage tax had been direct, for example, a state with 10 percent of the population but, say, only 5 five percent of the carriages, would need to tax each carriage at twice the average rate to meet its apportioned share.) The Court retreated from its theory of direct taxes only once, a century later, when it held a federal income tax to be direct, a decision later undone by the Sixteenth Amendment.

Hylton was important also because the Supreme Court had reviewed the constitutionality of an act of Congress for the first time. It upheld the statute but seemed to say that, should the occasion arise, it also had power to hold a national law to be in conflict with the Constitution. A few years later, it faced that question in *Marbury v. Madison.*

Despite its rulings in the two Hylton cases, the Court's first dozen years were not auspicious. Its first decision had produced a corrective constitutional amendment. When the Sedition Act was enforced in the federal courts, an increasingly strong Republican opposition came to see the Federalist-dominated national judiciary, including the Supreme Court, as an enemy agency. The Court already had three chief justices, one of whom quit to take another job. When failing health forced Ellsworth to resign near the end of Adams's term, John Jay refused the president's offer of reappointment, saying the Court lacked "energy, weight, and dignity." A fair description at the time, it was soon dead wrong as the Court, after a bit more buffeting, entered the most creative period of its history.

Republican Constitutionalism

The victory of Jefferson and the Republicans in 1800 marked one of the few times in the history of governments that power was transferred peacefully from those who had it to those who opposed them, by the will of those who were governed. Yet, many Federalists, familiar with Jefferson's rhetoric and political philosophy, worried that the constitutional system they had worked so hard to build would not survive in the hands of the man they had denounced as an "atheist" and "Jacobin" for his sympathies for the French Revolution. As things turned out, they had little to fear. Jefferson was a broadly educated Southern gentleman of many talents and wide-ranging curiosity, whose actions almost always spoke more pragmatically than his ideology. His notable inaugural address, welcoming defeated opponents back to the political family, set a tone of conciliation and disappointed some of his more zealous followers. In the backswing of the political pendulum, Jefferson rode a crest of personal popularity. He was generous in victory though he did not need to be and though Old World precedent would not have encouraged him to be. Anti-Federalists had set an example of being good losers a dozen years before; Jefferson now set one of a good winner. It was another triumph for political moderation.

The "Revolution of 1800" inherited a Hamiltonian political economy that was, in the main, working.

Fixing a Mechanical Flaw

Though the framers gave much time and thought to how the president should be chosen—8 of the original Constitution's 87 sentences, almost half of Article II, are taken up with it—the Electoral College never worked as they had intended. The idea was that electors in each state, who they assumed would be local political notables, would be chosen by popular vote or in other ways the state legislature might devise. Once chosen, they would meet in their state, more or less as a deliberative body, and each elector would use his own judgment to cast two votes. The votes from each of the states would then be forwarded to the president of the Senate for a later national tally. The candidate with the most electoral votes—provided it was a majority of the number of electors—would become the president, the candidate with the next highest, the vice president.

If no candidate got a majority, the election would be decided by the House of Representatives, voting by state and choosing from among the five candidates having the highest electoral vote. If two candidates got a majority but were tied, the election would also be given to the House to decide between them. In either case, the winner would be the candidate receiving the votes of a majority of states. The framers apparently believed that many, if not most, elections would be decided by the House, with the Electoral College acting like a nominating convention to winnow candidates.

But the framers did not anticipate the development of political parties. By the first competitive presidential election, 1796, two parties had formed: the Federalists, who nominated John Adams, and the Republicans, who nominated Jefferson. Electors were chosen because of their affiliation with one party and candidate or the other. They were not chosen to exercise their own judgment but to transmit the will of their constituents. This produced the discordant result of the victor's chief opponent—in this case, Jefferson—becoming vice president because he had the second highest electoral vote.

A proposal to amend the Constitution failed, and the electoral result of the next election, 1800, was even more erratic. The parties had nominated candidates for both offices: the Federalists, the incumbent Adams and Charles C. Pinckney for vice president; the Republicans, Jefferson and Aaron Burr. When the Republicans captured a majority of the electoral college, each of their 73 electors cast one vote for Jefferson and one vote for Burr, leading to a tie and sending the election to the House to choose between them. The matter should have been settled simply by a vote for Jefferson as president, leaving Burr to be vice president, as intended

A good revenue flow allowed the Republicans to remove the despised excise taxes at the same time that Jefferson was able to cut the national debt by nearly half. Only in his reaction to the Federalist judiciary (taken up in the next section), did he try to turn back the clock. Instead, it was the Republican's own constitutional tenets—the doctrine of states rights, the compact theory of the union, and the strict reading of national legislative and executive powers—that were tested and then modified by military and diplomatic realities.

The Louisiana Purchase

In 1802, France had reacquired the vast Louisiana territory that stretched from New Orleans north to Canada and from the Mississippi west to the Rockies. For Napoleon, it was to be a first step in the reassertion of French power on the North American continent. But after a military setback in the Caribbean and finding himself badly in need of cash to pursue European wars, he suddenly offered to sell the tract to the United States. Except for Indians, the area was largely uninhabited and would be a source of mineral and agricultural wealth. Possession would also open the mouth of the Mississippi for American trade and remove a European power from American borders. The prosperous young nation could easily afford Napoleon's price—$15,000,000.

But the obstacle, as Jefferson saw it, was the Constitution; it said nothing about a right of the central government to acquire lands. Article IV-3, giving Congress power to admit new

by the party and presumably by all who had voted for the 73 Republican electors. But the House, which got the matter in February 1801, was not the newly elected body but the outgoing one in which the Federalists were strong. Many in their ranks saw an opportunity for mischief and political gain by giving their support to Burr for president. This produced an acrimonious deadlock on the day and night of February 17 when 36 ballots were taken before some Federalists, at Hamilton's urging, switched their support to Jefferson allowing him finally to gain victory, 10 states to 8.

Since almost no one wanted to see this spectacle repeated, the Constitution was amended in time for the 1804 election. Though retaining most aspects of the Electoral College, the Twelfth Amendment made one vital change: One of the two votes of each elector must be cast for the choice of president, the other only for vice president. A small change was also included: If no candidate had a majority, the House would be asked to choose from among the highest three rather than five.

Only one other presidential election has gone to the House: the four-candidate race of 1824, which coincided with a lapse in the two-party system. The House chose John Quincy Adams even though he ran second to Andrew Jackson in both electoral and popular vote. Since parties offer slates of committed electors to the voters, it is improbable that another election will go to the House as long as presidential choice is dominated by competition between two major parties and state election laws (in 48 states) award all of a state's electoral votes to the winner of the popular vote.

Neither the Electoral College nor the Twelfth Amendment assures that a candidate or party winning the national popular vote will also have the greater electoral vote. Because of party slates of electors, a party winning the popular vote in a state usually captures all of that state's electoral votes, regardless of its percentage of the popular vote. Three times candidates who have finished second in the national popular vote have gotten a majority of the electoral vote: Rutherford B. Hayes defeating Samuel Tilden in 1876, Benjamin Harrison defeating the incumbent Grover Cleveland in 1888, and George W. Bush defeating Albert Gore in 2000. Hayes and Harrison had 48 percent of the popular vote, Bush slightly less than 50. Normally, however, the winner-take-all electoral vote mechanics gives the winner of the popular vote an even greater margin in the electoral vote. Proposals to end the Electoral College and elect the president directly by popular vote have consistently failed. They have met resistance from smaller states fearing being overwhelmed by more populous areas, and from the major parties fearing the encouragement of minor parties.

states and make rules for American territories, was assumed to refer only to territory already belonging to the nation at the time of ratification. Jefferson believed a constitutional amendment would be needed, but he was aware the mercurial Napoleon might change his mind before an amendment could be effected. Reluctantly he accepted the constitutional reasoning of Treasury Secretary Albert Gallatin that the United States had an inherent right to acquire territory as part of its national sovereignty; the means being implied in the delegated treaty-making power in Article II-2. Once acquired, Gallatin argued, new territory could be governed by power implied from Congress's grant in Article IV-3 to make all "rules and regulations" for such territory.

Republican constitutional scruples about strict construction were put aside to complete the greatest real estate deal in history. In the stroke of a treaty-making pen, the size of the United States was doubled and its future changed forever. The constitutionality of the purchase was never ruled on by the courts, but 20 years later, in *American Insurance Company v. Canter,* which brought to issue the purchase of Florida from Spain in 1819, the Supreme Court upheld the acquisition of territory through treaty.

Jefferson's Embargo

Resumption of the Napoleonic wars in Europe led to violations of American neutrality rights. These grew more numerous during Jefferson's second term when hundreds of American ships were seized or destroyed by the chief belligerents, Britain and France. Since Britain dominated the sea war, its provocations tended to be worse and included impressing many captured British-born American sailors who had become naturalized citizens into British service. Since Jefferson had cut back the navy earlier, the United States was unprepared to make a daunting military response. Long intrigued by the idea of commercial exclusion as a substitute for war, Jefferson chose economic sanctions. At his urging, the Republican Congress passed the Non-Importation Act in 1806, proscribing a long list of articles from Britain, most of which could be produced at home or imported from other countries. When the policy failed to change Britain's course, Jefferson asked for and got the more drastic Embargo Act, late the following year. It barred all exports by land or sea to all foreign nations; American ships were not allowed to leave for foreign ports.

Evasions were many, and Jefferson spent much of his last months in office focused on the problem. Smuggling across the Canadian border was furious. Opposition mounted, coming from the minority Federalists and a group of Republicans led by John Randolph, a Virginia senator. In New England, the region hardest hit by the shutdown, public demonstrations were commonplace and calls for secession heard.

The embargo raised two important constitutional questions, one involving Congress' power to regulate commerce, the other, the president's power to enforce the legislation. Though the Constitution gives Congress no direct power of embargo, Article I-8 vests it with the authority to regulate foreign commerce, and limited embargoes had been placed before. But did this regulatory power include the right to stop commerce completely or was it limited merely to regulations protecting commerce? The question would crop up repeatedly in the years to come. On the second, Congress had given Jefferson power to suspend the embargo at his discretion if it happened not to be in session. Critics argued this violated the separation of

powers because it gave the president power to alter legislation itself. Congressional delegation of legislative power was also destined to be a recurrent problem in constitutional law. Though the embargo was held constitutional by a lower federal court, the issue never reached the Supreme Court.

Congress repealed the act early in 1809, just before the end of Jefferson's presidency. It had been a great self-inflicted wound and hardly affected British or French policies. Politically, it divided Jefferson's party and put the Federalists in the unfamiliar position of opposing use of national and executive power.

Madison's War

James Madison, Jefferson's secretary of state, was elected to succeed him in 1808 and reelected in 1812, as Federalist strength continued to decline. As the Napoleonic wars continued in Europe, Madison faced the same diplomatic problems Jefferson had. British impressment of seamen and other provocations continued, and pressures on Madison to get into war increased. Though antiwar sentiment remained strong in New England, new young "warhawks" in Congress, like Henry Clay and John C. Calhoun, saw war as a chance to expand in the west at British expense and even to capture Canada. Failing to get diplomatic satisfaction from Britain, a divided and militarily unprepared United States declared war in June 1812.

Napoleon's abdication early in 1814 allowed Britain to reinforce its army in Canada and, later, to land on the American coast and attack Baltimore and Washington, leaving most government buildings in flames. The two sides eventually wearied of the indecisive struggle, the British public increasingly restless after years of European war. A treaty, the Peace of Ghent, was concluded in late 1814. The biggest American victory, the Battle of New Orleans, came two weeks after the war was over; news of the treaty had not reached the combatants. The late battle boosted American morale and made its hero, General Andrew Jackson, a future president.

The war produced an important constitutional issue and again stirred the pot of states rights. Republicans had allowed the prewar regular army to slip into a state of underfinanced neglect. When hostilities began, Madison, acting under earlier authority delegated by Congress, had called out the state militia. Though Article I-8 gives Congress power to summon the militia "to execute the laws of the Union, suppress insurrections and repel invasions," some states resisted Madison's order. Others added conditions refusing to allow their troops to be commanded by federal officers or to be used outside their borders.

The demurring states, mainly in New England, argued that the federal government had no power to nationalize state militia since there was no insurrection, invasion, or violation of federal laws. Determining whether such exigencies exist was not a task of the president or of Congress but was reserved to the states under the Tenth Amendment. Because of this resistance and before the regular army became restocked with volunteers, Congress debated the use of conscription, but strong opposition developed and no law was passed. Madison's militia action, though not settled during the war, was sustained by the Supreme Court many years later in *Martin v. Mott,* 1827. As commander in chief, the president alone had authority to decide whether the urgencies anticipated by the constitutional provision existed or not. The decision created an important precedent on which Lincoln relied in the early days of the Civil War. The constitutionality of conscription was upheld in the Selective Draft Cases, 1918, growing out of World War I.

Opposition to the war reached a crest with the Hartford Convention late in 1814. Led by Federalists, antiwar delegates from five New England states—Massachusetts, Rhode Island, New Hampshire, Vermont, and Connecticut—met behind closed doors. Though secession was debated, moderates prevailed and reported out proposals for seven constitutional amendments. Most of them would have put limits on federal power and executive authority and strengthened the rights of the states. A committee of three was appointed to "negotiate" with the federal government. But by the time the delegation reached Washington, the Peace of Ghent had ended the war and news of Jackson's New Orleans victory had arrived. Opposition collapsed and with it what remained of the Federalist Party.

Though the Hartford Convention was easily ridiculed or, worse, made a symbol of disloyalty, it retains a place alongside the Anti-Federalist objections of 1788 and the Virginia and Kentucky Resolutions of 1798 in the great vein of states rights, strict constructionist sentiment that has run so enduringly through American politics. In the pre-Civil War period, this persuasion almost always contained the implicit threat of secession. The Hartford Convention showed again how the ideology of states rights has served as a constitutional haven for those out of power nationally. The stunning reversal of Federalist and Republican constitutional philosophies during the administrations of Jefferson and Madison is another example of ideas serving power.

Internal Improvements

If Jefferson's presidency ended on the low note of the embargo disaster, Madison's ended on the high one of "victory" in an often humiliating war. After 15 years of responding to international events, the country's attention returned to domestic matters. Madison and many members of Congress recognized a need to improve transport, especially the roads, bridges, and canals that the ever-larger nation depended on for its commerce and economic well-being. A first step to these ends was reestablishment of financial order. The 20-year charter of the First National Bank, the symbol of Federalist government, had been allowed to lapse in 1811. But difficulties in financing the war convinced many Republicans that the bank was an important instrument of national security and prosperity. In 1816, the Second Bank was chartered for 20 years, with much less constitutional debate than that over establishing its predecessor.

Madison asked Congress to propose a constitutional amendment giving the federal government power to make internal improvements. But many members, including the powerful Clay and Calhoun, believed Congress already had such authority impliedly from its Article I-8 grants to establish post roads, regulate interstate commerce, and tax for the general welfare. They argued further that an amendment would be a dangerous admission that the government had no implied powers. Accordingly, Congress appropriated money for the construction of a number of roads and canals and for improvement of harbors. In his last act as president, Madison vetoed the measure on strict constructionist reasoning that it would give Congress a general power to legislate rather than one defined by its granted powers.

Madison's successor, his secretary of state and fellow Virginian, James Monroe, also supported a program of internal improvements and, like Madison, called for a constitutional amendment. Again, Congress refused to follow. When Monroe's objections shifted from a concern with Congress' constitutional power to that of federal internal improvements being an infringement on the rights of states, the way was open for compromise. Congress would appropriate money only with consent of the state affected and leave construction and operation of the improvements to the states. This federal-state cooperation would often lead to the incorporation of private groups under state law to do much of the work and assume responsibility for operation. Yet failure to enact a constitutional amendment left uncertainty about the legitimacy of the federal government acting alone in these matters. That question was eventually settled by the Supreme Court but not until well into the twentieth century.

End of an Era

Monroe was reelected in 1820, unopposed. With the demise of the Federalists, the country had a brief period of one-party politics; most important interests were contained within the Republican Party. But this "era of good feelings" as the 1815–1824 years are sometimes called, was de-

ceptive. A political transition and realignment was underway, though it would not be completed until later in the decade. John Quincy Adams became the sixth president in 1824, in the second and last election to be decided in the House of Representatives. He had run a poor second to the war hero Jackson in the popular vote and second also in the electoral vote, but Jackson did not have the majority of electors needed to win outright.

Adams, like his father, was an able statesman. As Monroe's secretary of state he could take chief credit for the Monroe Doctrine—the declaration (with Britain's complicity) that the Western Hemisphere should be free of further European colonization, thereby opening the door to Latin American independence and creating an American sphere of influence. But his own administration was not successful and coincided with the decline of Republicanism. Ignoring the constitutional qualms many persons still had, Adams urged on Congress a program of high-minded positive government in which an array of federal improvements would be undertaken through a liberal reading of national powers. As a minority president, he lacked the popular mandate for such bold proposals. The result was a strong opposing reaction in the name of states rights and strict construction.

The Republicans came into office as opponents of federal power and left as its champions. Faced with threats to national well-being and opportunities for national growth, they put aside their preferences for an agrarian society of small communities and states rights. Where they could not empower themselves as strict constructionists through constitutional amendment, they compromised and accepted powerful federal implied powers. Their triumph was the transition from opposition to responsible power. In that, they gave the constitutional system and the Hamiltonian political economy a legitimacy the Federalists alone could not have done. In governing for 28 years, they gathered national power without enthusiasm and, in doing so, allowed the nation to move slowly but importantly into an era of much wider democracy and economic opportunity.

Judicial Independence

Many Republicans including Jefferson himself harbored an abiding suspicion of judicial power. Under the Constitution, they saw the federal courts as instruments of national consolidation. Had not the Constitution needed amending to prevent subordination of states rights by these courts? As federal judgeships came to be filled with Federalists of nationalist persuasion, as they were by 1800 thanks to appointments by Washington and Adams, Republicans saw matters at their worst. Sedition Act prosecutions in the federal courts to silence opposition made the federal judiciary the enemy.

Packing and Unpacking

Long-standing antipathy became anger when a lame-duck Federalist Congress passed the Judiciary Act of 1801 five days before its term expired. Among other things, the Act created several new district and circuit courts and the judgeships, offices of marshals, clerks, and federal attorneys to go with them. At a lower level, 42 justices of the peace were created for the new capital district, the District of Columbia. Federal jurisdiction was expanded by making it easier to remove cases from state to federal courts. And the size of the Supreme Court was reduced from six to five to prevent Jefferson, the incoming president, from filling a vacancy. The oft-complained about circuit-riding duties of Supreme Court justices were lightened. Parts of the law were a sensible way of meeting the workload of the federal courts, which had risen markedly in 12 years. But as a last minute action of a politically rejected party, partisan motives were transparent. When John Adams spent his last presidential days and hours filling the new offices with loyal Federalists—the "midnight judges"—who would have life tenure, Jefferson

was incensed, accusing his defeated opponents of trying to retire to a judicial stronghold.

Another late Adams appointment, not affected by the Act, was his choice of a chief justice to succeed the ailing Oliver Ellsworth. Unable to persuade John Jay to accept reappointment, he turned to Secretary of State John Marshall. Though few would have thought so at the time, the act was the most important of Adams's presidency. Jefferson was not happy with the appointment of his fellow Virginian and distant cousin—it was one more that might have waited for the newly elected government—but the two figures had not yet become arch-opponents. Marshall was to serve 34 years as chief justice, one of the longest appointments in American history. He was to establish the Court as a true coequal branch and, through its decisions, do as much as anyone to shape the future of the nation.

The new Republican Congress repealed the 1801 Federalist act, but not without a constitutional debate. The Federalists, now a minority in Congress, argued that Article III-1 providing that "judges of both the Supreme Court and inferior courts shall hold office during good behavior," meant that the new judges could be removed only by impeachment. The Republicans cited the preceding provision in Article III-1, giving Congress power to create inferior courts. Since this grant could not have meant that such courts would be permanent, they argued, it impliedly gave Congress power to abolish whatever it may have earlier created. Repeal was a great blow to the Federalists. Later, the Republicans passed a judiciary act of their own, slightly expanding the circuit court system, restoring the size of the Supreme Court to six, and reinstating the justices to the burdensome tasks of circuit riding.

The Marbury Case

In the haste with which many of Adams's "midnight" appointments were made, several commissions of justices of the peace in the District of Columbia were not delivered to their recipients as required by law. When Jefferson discovered this on taking office, he ordered James Madison, who as the new secretary of state would have responsibility for delivering the commissions, to withhold them. The would-be recipients of three, including William Marbury, a Federalist flunky, sought a remedy in the courts. Marbury brought his case to the Supreme Court, itself under its original jurisdiction, asking for a writ of mandamus—an order requiring a government official to perform a nondiscretionary legal obligation—which the Court was empowered to issue under Section 13 of the Judiciary Act of 1789.

In the gathering storm over the courts, the case, trivial though its dispute was, loomed as a showdown between Jefferson and the Federalist judiciary. Jefferson thought Marshall would be politically trapped. If he admitted Marbury was not entitled to his commission, he gave the Republicans a victory. If he issued the writ in Marbury's favor, as was thought more probable, Jefferson would simply ignore it. In the face of such presidential disregard, the Court would be revealed as impotent, if not ridiculous, all of which might lead to Marshall's impeachment.

Marshall ingeniously averted both horns of the dilemma. Speaking for the entire Court, he declared that Marbury was entitled to his commission but the Court could not order Madison to deliver it! By authorizing the Court to issue writs of mandamus, Section 13 of the Judiciary Act of 1789, in effect, enlarged the Court's original jurisdiction. This Congress had no power to do because that jurisdiction was completely set out in Article III-2 of the Constitution and could be changed only by amendment. So, Section 13 was not constitutional.

Though Marshall shied away from the confrontation with Jefferson that would have followed issuance of the writ, he did use the first part of his opinion in the case to lecture the Republicans on the basic validity of Marbury's appointment. Jefferson was angered by the sermon, but he could do nothing because Marshall had ordered nothing. Marshall successfully

pulled back from the Court a small power and, doing so, indirectly claimed for it a far greater one—the right to declare an act of a coequal branch unconstitutional.

This was a master political stroke, but Marshall cannot be given such high marks for judicial professionalism. He ignored what are today several canons of good practice. First, he could easily have read Section 13 as referring only to the Court's appellate jurisdiction, which Congress may change, thereby saving the constitutionality of the provision. Modern courts usually avoid a ruling of unconstitutionality if they can. Second, when a court decides it has no power to grant the remedy requested, it will usually forego any discussion of the merits—the substantive aspect—of the case. In *Marbury,* the entire first half of Marshall's opinion is a discourse on why the commission was valid. Finally, a judge who has earlier played a role in a case now coming before him will usually recuse himself—refuse to take part in it. When Adams signed Marbury's commission, it was Marshall as secretary of state who had responsibility for seeing that it was delivered. One can hardly imagine a more intimate connection than that. Still, these canons of judicial practice were not so well established in Marshall's time as they are now, and it is hard to be too severe with the chief justice. *Marbury* was enmeshed in politics from its start, and Marshall responded in kind.

Since the Constitution is silent on judicial review—the power of courts to decide the constitutional validity of the laws or actions of government—many students of the Constitution have credited Marshall with staking out the power for the Supreme Court. This overstates matters. First, neither the idea nor practice of review were new; lower state courts had sometimes given constitutional review to state legislation. The Supreme Court itself had earlier reviewed an act of Congress in *Hylton v. United States* though it upheld the legislation. Striking down a law is more assertive than upholding one, but in *Marbury,* Marshall's action was de-

Judicial Review

Despite Marshall's triumph in *Marbury v. Madison*, the Supreme Court did not hold another act of Congress unconstitutional until the destructive Dred Scott decision 54 years later. The power of judicial review is far better established and more often exercised today than it was in the nation's first century. Of more than 100,000 cases heard by the Court since its first in 1793, nearly 150 have invalidated acts of Congress (all but 18 occurring since 1888) and more than 1,300 have struck down acts of state legislatures (all but 138 since 1888). The effect of the cases on public policy and on American society in general is far greater than their small percentages suggest. A judicial negative based on constitutional grounds is likely to be deterring on legislatures and other agencies of government. Thus, it is impossible to gauge the full impact of the Court's power to invalidate except to say that it is far greater than the relative infrequent use would indicate.

Controversy over judicial review today is no longer over whether the Court has or should have the power but over how active or restrained should be its exercise. Critics of activism argue that judicial review gives ultimate interpretive authority to a small group of unelected persons having life tenure. This gives the Court opportunity to thwart laws and policies made by elected officials representing a majority, perhaps a very large majority, of the nation. Defenders of activism contend that by the very fact of being removed from electoral politics the Court is able to protect the rights of individuals and the minority—defined by property, race, religion, or other status—from prejudices or excesses of a dominant majority.

Both the critics and the defenders of activism are correct. At times, the Court has stood in the way of majoritarian government, as it did in the Dred Scott case and in the early days of the New Deal in the 1930s. But the Court has also given effect to various rights and in the Bill of Rights and other parts of the Constitution where majoritarian government was unwilling or unable to do so. In this sense, neither judicial activism nor self-restraint is inherently liberal or conservative. As the legal scholar Philip B. Kurland observed, "An activist Court is essentially one that is out of step with the legislative or executive branches of government. It will be 'liberal' or 'conservative' depending on which role its prime antagonist has adopted."*

Despite the antimajoritarian implication of judicial activism, the Court, more often than not, has reflected majority opinion, at least on the leading issues of the day. The reason is that the justices themselves are selected and approved by elected officials: the president, who nominates, and the Senate, which must advise and consent. The times the Court is most apt to invalidate national policy—the early New Deal, for example—have been periods immediately following "critical" elections, in which massive electoral shifts and party realignment have occurred: 1800, 1828, 1860, 1896, and 1932. These elections brought new presidents and new Congressional majorities. But because the Court is not elected and vacancies on it occur only with the death or resignation of incumbents, there is an inevitable "lag" before a new electoral coalition is reflected in a new Supreme Court.

That the personnel on the Court will inevitably reflect major political shifts in the nation calls attention to the other side of the coin of judicial review. Even in its most activist periods, the Court has *upheld* acts of Congress and state legislatures much more often than not. In hearing a challenge to a law or policy some time after it has been passed or formulated and affirming it in a reasoned decision, the Court plays an important role in legitimating the decisions of majoritarian government. Judicial review is a deliberation on constitutionality in which the Court affirms or negates. Over the years, it has done much more yea-saying, as in *McCulloch v. Maryland,* than nay-saying, as in *Marbury v. Madison.*

* Philip B. Kurland, *Politics, the Constitution, and the Warren Court* (Chicago: University of Chicago Press, 1970), 17–18.

---

fensive; in a hostile political environment, the Court retreated. Also, the Marbury decision was consistent with the so-called department theory of constitutional interpretation that had wide currency at the time. In it, each of the three branches had power to decide constitutional questions that affected its own domain. In interpreting the Judiciary Act of 1789, the Court had done no more than that.

At the time, the constitutional aspects of *Marbury* were overshadowed by its immediate political importance. Yet Marshall's opinion, employing the grand deductive logic and a reasoning from constitutional first principles that were to characterize all his great decisions, gave definition to the interpretive role of the Court. His argument and rhetorical skill allowed later generations of judges, lawyers, and scholars to look to *Marbury* as the wellspring of the Court's great constitutional power.

The Impeachment Attack

For Jefferson and many Republicans the life-appointed Federalist judges in the national judiciary were the chief obstacle to completing the "Revolution of 1800." They feared the judges, many of whom were openly partisan on and off the bench, would undermine the Republican legislative program. But the Constitution offers no way for removing government officers except through impeachment. Article I-2 gives the House of Representatives sole power to bring impeachment charges. Article I-3 gives the Senate sole power to try such charges and requires a two-thirds vote for conviction. In such a case, the penalty is limited to removal from office, though it does not preclude a later criminal trial in the courts. Article II-4 specifies the grounds for impeachment: "treason, bribery, or other high crimes and misdemeanors."

Marshall's remonstrance in *Marbury* convinced Jefferson that the impeachment power should be used against the worst Federalist judges. One jurist had already been removed from the Pennsylvania state courts, and a week after the Marbury decision, the House voted impeachment charges against John Pickering, a federal district court judge who had a record of being drunk and intemperate on the bench and critical of Republicans. By the time of the Senate trial, it was clear that he was also insane. He was convicted by a party-line vote though he had not committed any of the offenses set out in Article II-4.

The House then brought impeachment charges against a much bigger quarry, Justice Samuel Chase of the Supreme Court. The Republican campaign against the judiciary was now in full swing and many thought charges against Marshall might not be far off. Chase, appointed to the Court by Washington, had been one of the signers of the Declaration of Independence. Though an able jurist, he had a weakness for using jury charges to attack political opponents. His Federalist partisanship had been blatant in the sedition cases, and in the election of 1800 he campaigned openly for Adams. But none of these "offenses" were the treason, bribery, or high crimes and misdemeanors the Constitution proscribed. Nor was Chase mentally deranged.

The Senate trial was a battle between the Republican regime and the Federalist judiciary, much as the Marbury case had been two years before. The chief constitutional question was whether impeachment, already used to remove an incompetent, should be broadened still further to remove a political partisan. Though Republicans now had a large majority in the Senate, thanks to a big victory in the 1804 election, the defection of several moderates kept the party from mustering the two-thirds majority needed for conviction. Failure ended Republican efforts to impeach federal judges, though it did not settle the scope of the impeachment power. That issue would arise dramatically again in the trial of President Andrew Johnson after the Civil War and again with the impeachment of Bill Clinton in 1999.

The Burr Treason Trial

As cunning a political scoundrel as America has produced, the New Yorker Aaron Burr served as vice president during Jefferson's first term. But he wrecked his political career by scheming to get the presidency when the election of 1800 was thrown into the House and later killing

Alexander Hamilton in a duel. When his term was over, he embarked on a murky venture in the West to recoup his personal and political fortunes. He organized a small expeditionary force whose purpose was never totally clear. Burr later claimed it was to wrest away part of Spanish-held Mexico for settlement. Others said it was the first step in a grandiose plan for detaching a large part of the United States to build a separate western empire with Burr as its head. Jefferson clearly believed the latter. He had the army capture Burr's party and bring Burr himself back to stand trial for treason. The government brought the case in the federal circuit court in Richmond, where Marshall himself presided in his circuit-riding duty.

The trial of the former vice president in the summer of 1807 riveted the country's attention and set the stage for yet another confrontation between Jefferson and Marshall, once more enmeshing the federal judiciary in political controversy. Going all out for a conviction, Jefferson virtually directed the prosecution himself. His fury with Burr soon extended to Marshall after the latter gave a narrow effect to the definition of treason in the Constitution. The Framers, fully aware that treason charges had been used broadly in Britain and other countries to decimate opposition, had taken pains to spell out the offense in Article III-3: "Treason against the United States shall consist only in levying war against them, or in adhering to their enemies, giving them aid and comfort."

Though the government had no evidence of Burr actually making war on the United States, it contended he was guilty of "constructive treason" because he had entered into a conspiracy, one of the purposes of which was to make war on the United States. Marshall rejected this theory and so refused to expand the framers' limited definition of the offense. Because of this statement of the law, the jury had little choice but to acquit Burr. Once again in the face of political pressure and an implicit threat of impeachment, Marshall stood his ground, this time in the name of fair criminal procedure. His ruling on treason remains valid to this day.

Though angry with Marshall, Jefferson soon found his attention taken up with problems of foreign policy. The threat posed to the federal judiciary by the "Revolution of 1800," which had worried many moderate Republicans, had passed, and a measure of judicial independence had been preserved. But the Jeffersonian attacks were chastening. Federal judges, and perhaps judges everywhere, were now mindful of the dangers posed by judicial partisanship. In the future, judicial independence would embrace a professionalism that disavowed the overt partiality of judges and justices.

Reconciliation of Republicans and federal judges was helped by three appointments Jefferson made to the Supreme Court: William Johnson in 1804, Henry Brockholst Livingston in 1806, and Thomas Todd in 1807. All were moderates and each found he could work well with Marshall. Jefferson had hoped Johnson would be a counterweight to Marshall. Though Johnson sometimes differed with the chief justice, becoming known as the "First Dissenter," the two agreed much more often than not in the 30 years they served together, especially on the need for a strong judiciary.

Marshall's Nationalism

Withstanding challenges from the Republican executive and Congress and asserting the co-equality of the judiciary branch were signal triumphs for Marshall's Court. But alone they did not secure the place of the federal courts in the federal system. That would depend on lines drawn between national and state power and, even more, on the nature of the union itself. Federalism was still in an experimental stage and many of its lines remained uncharted. As the new government entered its third decade, continuing political divisions gave the Marshall Court an unusual opportunity to shape the constitutional system. Its great influence on property and on economic development is discussed in Chapter Six.

The Chief Justice

Political antagonist Martin Van Buren once described John Marshall as the "ablest judge now sitting upon any bench in the world."* Whether this high tribute was deserved or not, Marshall had more to do with shaping the constitutional system and the nation itself than any other jurist and perhaps more than any other statesman. Had Jefferson been able to fill a vacant chief justiceship in 1801—only fair, since he had just won a momentous election—the early course of the nation would no doubt have been very different and the emergence of a strong nationalist union blocked, or at least much delayed.

Though Marshall entered a public career as a young man and rose rapidly in Virginia politics, few could have predicted his later greatness. Born in a log cabin on the Virginia frontier, he was a distant though poor relative of Jefferson, his later rival. Though well read, he had almost no formal schooling. When the Revolution began, Marshall and his father were among the first to enlist in Washington's Continental Army and took part in several early battles. Marshall later attended law lectures for six weeks at William and Mary College and began practice in Richmond, the path to the bar being shorter and simpler than it is today. He soon won a seat in the Virginia Assembly and, later, as a member of the state ratifying convention, was a leader in getting the Constitution approved. Though he declined Washington's later offer of the attorney generalship for financial reasons, he did perform diplomatic service for Adams. After being elected to Congress as a Federalist, he resigned to become Adams's secretary of state, the post from which he was appointed to the Supreme Court.

From his first constitutional opinion in *Marbury* to his last in *Barron v. Baltimore*, Marshall was the unquestioned leader of the Court, which came to speak

---

The Court's role was affected by its composition and working style. In 1811, Madison made his only appointments: Gabriel Duvall and Joseph Story. Like Jefferson's justices, Duvall was a moderate Republican with nationalist leanings. Story, at 32 the youngest person ever to sit on the Court, was nominally a Republican but his thinking was more in the Federalist vein. He was already an accomplished legal scholar, and his *Commentaries on the Constitution,* written while on the Court, is still an important treatise on the early constitutional system. His scholarship complemented Marshall's more pragmatic disposition, and he proved nearly as able a defender of national power and judicial independence as the chief justice.

Marshall ended the practice of seriatim opinions in which each justice stated his views separately. The Court was also more effective when it spoke, as it now did in most cases, with one voice—invariably Marshall's. The chief justice sought agreement and was highly persuasive in getting it. In the nearly 1,100 decisions during his tenure, only 70 had dissenting opinions, and only 22, concurrences. In any modern term of the Court, it is common for 60 percent of the cases to have dissents and 40 percent or more, concurring opinions. Though the Court is larger today and issues before it more diverse and complex, multiple opinions, so rare in Marshall's time, often cloud the law and dilute the Court's authority.

largely through his voice. Marshall wrote nearly half of the 1,100 opinions of the Court during his tenure and nearly two-thirds in cases with constitutional questions. This sway was all the more remarkable since he was eventually surrounded by colleagues appointed by presidents—Jefferson, Madison, Monroe, and Jackson—who held views on the meaning of the Constitution and the Union very different from his own. His personal attributes and reputation for absolute integrity were important assets. Though he was often in acrimonious battles with the Court's external antagonists, Marshall was personally convivial and, as his informal dress and spare but comfortable home gave witness, a man almost without pretense.

Marshall was neither a scholar of the law, like his friend and colleague Joseph Story, nor a careful follower of legal precedent, but he repeatedly reached for basic constitutional principles from which he made concise, compelling arguments with grace and eloquence. In this, he wrote almost as a latter-day framer, clarifying the Constitution's ambiguities and giving content to its omissions. He defended the Court against attack, expanded it jurisdiction, and established its integrity as a coordinate branch of government. He gave broad meaning to the constitutional grants to the central government and maintained the supremacy of those powers against the states. Insistent that authority for the Union rested in a compact of the people rather than the states, he did much to counter the emerging doctrine of state sovereignty. His constitutional jurisprudence also helped shape the nation's economic development. By reading the doctrine of vested rights into the contract clause, he helped defend property and risk capital against populist attacks. In limiting state regulation of interstate commerce, he took a giant step toward the creation of a Hamiltonian national market. Marshall did not have to confront the modern issue of *federal* regulation of property and the economy, by which he might have been confounded.

Another celebrated justice, Oliver Wendell Holmes, once wrote that Marshall's greatest achievement was simply "being there."[†] This is much too simple. Marshall was indeed in the right place and the right time, but the leadership and vision he brought to opportunity were extraordinary and they separate him from all other judges.

* U. S. House of Representatives, 19th Cong. 1st Session, April 17, 1826, quoted in Jean Edward Smith, *John Marshall, Definer of a Nation* (New York: Henry Holt and Co., 1996), 491.
[†] "John Marshall," *Occasional Speeches,* Feb. 2, 1901, 132, quoted in G. Edward White, *Justice Oliver Wendell Holmes: Law and the Inner Self* (New York: Oxford University Press, 1993), 355.

The Jurisdictional Challenge of States Rights

Two cases coming before the Court during Madison's first term were occasions for the assertion of federal judicial authority over the states. In *United States v. Peters,* 1809, a federal judge in Pennsylvania had allowed a ship owner to recover proceeds from the sale of a prize ship captured during the Revolution. But he did not enforce the decision after the state legislature authorized the governor to use force, if needed, to defy it. The plaintiff asked the Supreme Court for an order directing the judge to execute his decision. The Court complied, Marshall declaring that "If the legislatures of the several states may, at will, annul the judgments of the courts of the United States, and destroy the rights acquired under their judgment, the Constitution itself becomes a solemn mockery, and the nation is deprived of the means of enforcing its laws by the instrumentality of its own tribunals." [9 U.S. 115 at 136]

A year later in *Fletcher v. Peck,* the Court held a Georgia law rescinding several state land-grant contracts that had been procured through bribery, to be unconstitutional. Though the Court had already held against a state law in conflict with a treaty in *Ware v. Hylton,* the Fletcher case marked the first time it found a state law to violate a provision of the Constitution, here Article I-10, which forbade states from "impairing the obligation of contracts."

The economic regulatory consequences of this decision are discussed in Chapter Seven.

Direct confrontation between state and national judicial power arose from a land dispute dating to the Revolution. Virginia had confiscated vast amounts of property belonging to Loyalists, one of whom was Thomas Fairfax. Later, the state sold parts of Fairfax's holdings to David Hunter. However, when Fairfax died, his will passed the land to his nephew Denny Martin, a British subject. Martin claimed to be the rightful owner under terms of the Treaty of Paris, which had ended the war, and Jay's Treaty with Great Britain in 1794. Both protected Loyalist holdings and rights of British subjects in America.

The Virginia Court of Appeals ruled for Hunter, but on appeal in *Fairfax's Devisee v. Hunter's Lessee,* 1813, the Supreme Court overturned the decision and held for Martin citing the supremacy of a national treaty over state law. The Virginia court refused to give the decision effect, declaring that the appellate jurisdiction of the Supreme Court did not extend to cases in the highest state courts. Judge Spencer Roane, chief justice of the Virginia court and an ardent advocate of states rights, argued that Section 25 of the Judiciary Act of 1789, which gave the Supreme Court jurisdiction over the final decisions of the highest state courts on questions in federal laws or treaties, was unconstitutional. In taking this position, Roane, who had been Jefferson's choice for the chief justiceship of the Supreme Court had Adams not first appointed Marshall, raised once more the basic question of union. How could there be any state sovereignty, he asked, if final authority over state laws and decisions rested with the Supreme Court?

The Virginia challenge gave rise to a second appeal by Martin. This time, in *Martin v. Hunter's Lessee,* 1816, (p. 104) the Supreme Court, in an opinion written by Story, rejected Roane's theory of equal state sovereignty. The power to make final interpretation of the Constitution was the Supreme Court's. The decision was a definitive statement of federal judicial supremacy.

Five years later the Court was again entangled with the Virginia judiciary's claim of states rights. The brothers Phillip and Mendes Cohen were convicted of selling lottery tickets in violation of state law and fined $100. In *Cohens v. Virginia,* 1821, they appealed to the Supreme Court arguing that since the lottery had been authorized by Congress to pay for public improvements in the District of Columbia, their sales in Virginia were protected. Though the offense was trivial, Marshall took advantage of the issues to answer Roane's earlier states rights argument. He sustained Virginia's right to suppress lottery sales, but reiterated and extended the nationalism of the Martin case. Virginia had contended that since the state was a defending party, the Supreme Court was precluded from hearing the case by the Eleventh Amendment. Marshall disagreed, declaring that an appeal from a criminal conviction was not a case "commenced or prosecuted" against a state, thus narrowing the reach of the amendment. Though Virginia won the case—it could bar federal lottery tickets and the Cohens' convictions were sustained—it lost the constitutional issue, and states rights interests went unappeased.

The Reach and Supremacy of National Power

Important as they were, the jurisdictional battles between state and federal courts were overshadowed by clashes of state and national legislative power. The second issue became the focus of conflict growing out of Congress's recharter of the National Bank in 1815. The second bank was unpopular in many quarters much as its predecessor had been. Many states rights Republicans thought it a bastion of conservative monetary policy and a competitor of state banks. To them, it was the symbol of federal overreaching. Evidence of occasional corruption in its ranks won it no friends either. Intending to hinder the bank's operations in the state, the Maryland legislature levied a burdensome tax on the Baltimore branch. When James McCulloch, the cashier, refused to pay it, the stage was set for the most important case in American federalism, perhaps in the history of the Court.

After Maryland won a debt judgment against McCulloch in the state courts, he appealed in *McCulloch v. Maryland,* 1819, (p. 110) to the Supreme Court. The high stakes were evident from the start, and several of the nation's leading legal figures were on one side or the other: Luther Martin, who 32 years before had quit the Constitutional convention, and David Hopkinson for Maryland; William Wirt, U. S. attorney general, William Pinckney, and young Daniel Webster for the bank. Maryland's case was two-fold: First, the bank was unconstitutional because Congress had no granted power to establish banks; second, even if the bank were constitutional, Maryland as a sovereign state had a right to tax it. The first question raised the issue of implied powers and reached back to the debate between Hamilton and Jefferson over chartering the first bank. The second raised the issue of national supremacy in the federal system. Both called for definitive answers, and Marshall writing his greatest, certainly most eloquent opinion, supplied them.

The Court's decision upholding Congress's power and the reach of federal supremacy to protect that power from state interference went to the core of early nationalism. It provoked widespread criticism, particularly for the sweep of Marshall's opinion. Despite these misgivings, the decision showed how far the nation had traveled down the nationalist road and how much judicial independence had been won. Fifteen years earlier, the same decision would almost certainly have led to Marshall's impeachment. And though the bank did not survive—it's second rechartering was vetoed by President Jackson in 1832—*McCulloch v. Maryland* became the cornerstone for the Court's new nationalism after the Civil War. Later it was constitutional underpinning for extensive federal action in the economy and in social life, starting with the New Deal.

Some states disregarded *McCulloch.* Ohio persisted in trying to collect a crippling $50,000 annual tax on the bank's operations. When it

was not paid, the state auditor, Ralph Osborn, seized more than $100,000 from its branch in Chillicothe. The bank sued in federal court for return of the money. *Osborn v. United States,* 1824, was a reprise of *McCulloch* but with an added wrinkle. The Supreme Court ruled the state interference unconstitutional. But in answer to the state's argument that the bank, as plaintiff, was a citizen of another state and thus barred by the Eleventh Amendment from bringing suit against it in the federal courts, Marshall made a distinction only a lawyer could appreciate. The suit was not one against the state but against a state official who had committed a trespass and was thus *personally* responsible for his action. The decision violated the spirit of the Eleventh Amendment and, like the Cohens case, further narrowed its scope.

Though one of the Constitution's chief aims was to give the central government power to regulate interstate commerce, the matter did not come before the Supreme Court until *Gibbons v. Ogden,* 1824 (p. 206). New York had granted Robert Fulton, one of the inventors of the steamboat, a monopoly for steam navigation on the state's waters. Fulton in turn transferred part of the license to Ogden to operate steamboat service between New York and New Jersey. Conflict arose when Ogden's former partner, Gibbons, went into competition with him in violation of his lease from Fulton. For his part, Gibbons held a federal coasting license under a 1793 act of Congress regulating coastal navigation.

Like *McCulloch,* but without the attack of one government on another, the case raised the two great issues of American federalism: the valid reach of national power and the rights of states where state and national power were in conflict. Was "commerce" limited, for example, to buying and selling or did it include the means of commerce like transport and navigation? Did "among the states" in the commerce clause refer simply to commerce crossing state lines or did it include any business done in more than one state? Marshall interpreted the federal power expansively on both questions.

Down the Interpretive Path

In *Marbury v. Madison,* the Supreme Court claimed for itself the role of ultimate interpreter of a constitution written in very general terms and leaving many important things unsaid. In cases raising constitutional issues that role has allowed the Court to add meaning to the supreme document. It does this by applying straightforward textual provisions to new circumstances, by clarifying ambiguous provisions, and by filling in blanks left by the framers.

How much freedom the Court should have in interpreting the Constitution has been a matter of sharp debate. Those comfortable with judicial activism say it should have wide range including discretion to look beyond the "four corners" of the Constitution for help. Advocates of judicial self-restraint argue the opposite. To answer this question for ourselves, we must look closely at the Court's important interpretive cases and try to understand how its decisions were made. Unlike many other agencies of government, the Court usually goes to length to explain and justify its decisions, which are cast as rulings of law. Beyond its opinions, however, its work leaves few other footprints. In most instances, its explanations employ one or more traditional or established methods of interpreting legal materials, but other seldom acknowledged nonjuristic factors may also come into play.

All interpretation starts with the legal text itself, that is, with a reading of the "plain words" of the Constitution. The primacy if not sufficiency of this method is the basis for the doctrine of textualism or literalism. The Court has sometimes also looked to *The Federalist Papers,* treating their explication of particular constitutional provisions as approximate authority. It may also look to history for light on what words meant at the time they were written. Where some justices have found clarity, however, others see yet uncertainty. Not all words of the Constitution leave as little doubt as the provision of Article II-1-5 that a person must have "attained the age of thirty-five years," for presidential eligibility. By contrast, in *McCul-*

loch v. Maryland, the entire matter of implied powers and the future strength of the central government turned on the disputable meaning of "necessary" in Article I-8-18.

The search of history may go further than mere hunting for word clarity and seek to fathom the actual *intention* of those who drafted and ratified the Constitution. The importance of this inquiry is the basis of the doctrine of originalism. Proponents argue that constitutional interpretation should rest mainly, if not entirely, on text and founding intent. In Chapter 3, we noted the utility of original intent as well as the difficulties encountered in discovering and using it. (p. 44–45) It remains a method frequently cited by the Court. Chief Justice Marshall's conclusion in *Barron v. Baltimore* that the Bill of Rights did not limit state powers because its drafters, members of the first Congress, intended only to limit the national government, is an early example.

Another approach closely associated with those emphasizing text and intent, and one that Marshall used in many of his early nationalist decisions, is the drawing of rational inferences from the structure of the Constitution itself. In the second part of *McCulloch v. Maryland,* for example, he argued that the federal structure created by the Constitution would be subverted if a part of the whole—a state—could tax an agency of the whole and thus possibly control or destroy that agency. Yet nothing in the constitutional text or clearly evident in the framers' intent expressly disallowed such taxation.

Reference to precedent—binding rules established in previously decided cases—is the method the Court most often uses to explain its decisions. Here, the Court, using the doctrine of *stare decisis*—literally, let the decision stand—is controlled by its own doctrinal work. Following "well-settled" rules gives an aura of legitimacy to new decisions and lends an obvious and important stability and predictability to constitutional meaning. But the method may also lead to inflexibility. Though the Court has overruled itself nearly 300 times in its history, those decisions represent only about three-tenths of 1 percent of the cases it has heard.

But was Congress's commerce authority exclusive, as Daniel Webster argued for Gibbons, or did the states have a fully concurrent power to regulate interstate commerce, as Ogden claimed? Here, Marshall temporized. Rejecting Ogden's view but not fully embracing Web-

Precedent is seldom tidy, and the Court must often choose between cases cited as supporting one side and those claimed to underwrite the other. An earlier case that appears to be controlling may be *distinguished* as being different enough from a present case so not binding. Interpreting precedent is a skill—art is perhaps a better term—at which justices are adept, allowing them to reach a decision apparently determined by past cases or, distinguishing those cases, freedom to reach a different decision. How precedent is used and how closely it should be followed is a chief article in the debate over judicial activism.

In many of the Supreme Court's most important early opinions we find little reference to precedent, one reason being that the Court had decided relatively few cases. Another is that a strict following of precedent did not fit Chief Justice Marshall's judicial style and would have inhibited his chief constitutional projects, the establishment of judicial authority and independence and the advancement of nationalism. Most cases coming before the Court today, however, call up a rich collection of applicable past decisions.

So far, we have considered juristic explanations of constitutional meaning, those that follow accepted common law canons of legal interpretation. Most Supreme Court (and lower court) decisions appear to be based mainly, if not entirely, on these "objective" methods, yet to gain a full understanding of constitutional decisions we must sometimes go further and recognize that professional, objectively minded jurists are also political human beings.

Justices have values and preferences based on their professional and personal experience, some of which may be more or less integrated into a philosophy or ideology. For example, they are likely to have ideas on what the judicial role should be, on what is or is not prudent for the Court, on what is desirable or undesirable on particular issues of policy, and on broader political, social, and economic matters affecting the country as a whole. These views or attitudes may influence their legal or juristic analysis of a case. Several of Marshall's great opinions, for example, were driven by Hamiltonian ideas about the future of the American union and clearly shaped his use of interpretive canons.

The Supreme Court is also a small interactive group in which decisions are made collectively. No justice can resolve a constitutional issue alone and all are subject to the interplay of minds and personalities. Members of such collegial groups are unavoidably affected by personal relationships and by the need to negotiate with other members. Marshall's impressive personal qualities, for example, allowed him to work effectively with and even have unusual influence on such different colleagues as the formidable and prickly legal scholar Joseph Story and the strong-minded William Johnson, Jefferson's first appointee and hoped-for counterweight to the chief justice.

Like everyone else, justices also have personal biases. These may be about anything, including the parties to a case. Professionally, these biases are unacceptable in the decision-making equation and are expected to be controlled or overcome. But this demanding standard may not always be met; to the extent that biases are unconscious or barely conscious, it may fail altogether.

Except for views on judicial role or institutional prudence, nonjuristic elements are seldom visible in an opinion and almost never offered as a rationale. Explanations of constitutional decisions will almost always be cast in the language of law and employ, persuasively or not, accepted methods of judicial interpretation. For men and women trained in the law, as all justices have been, and who approach their work professionally and conscientiously, as most justices have, the proffered juristic explanation of a decision may often be close to a full explanation.

Reading the cases of this book requires awareness of the methods the justices use in interpreting the Constitution and explaining that work to us. We must keep in mind that the references to constitutional text, original intent, precedent, or the mandate of constitutional structure do not always command universal agreement among the justices, seldom self-evidently dictate a particular decision, and are sometimes inexact enough to allow their employ for other ends.

ster's, he held that New York's monopoly had to give way, not because states had no power over interstate commerce, but because the state grant conflicted with a national regulation under which Gibbons held his license. Whether states might regulate interstate commerce in the absence of corresponding Congressional action, was not definitively answered, though it was taken up and answered in the negative by Justice Johnson in a lone concurring opinion. Not until *Cooley v. Board of Wardens,* 1852, did the Court develop a formula for partitioning concurrent national and state power over interstate commerce.

The decision in *Gibbons,* like that in *McCulloch,* opened the door to wide federal regulation of economic activity, though the power was not much used until the twentieth century. The case's consequence for economic development is explored in Chapter Six.

Another line of federalism that needed to be drawn was that between state taxing power and the protection of commerce. A Maryland license tax on wholesale dealers of imported goods was argued to be in conflict with federal commerce power and to violate Article I-10, forbidding states from taxing imports. In sustaining the claim in *Brown v. Maryland,* 1827, Marshall formulated the "original package" doctrine: as long as goods remained in their original containers and were not yet mingled with the mass of property in the state, they were free of state taxation.

Jackson's election in 1828 brought a resurgence of state rights sentiment and, with the new president's appointments of John McLean in 1829 and Henry Baldwin in 1830, a change in the composition of the Court. In *Barron v. Baltimore,* 1833, (p. 116) the revamped Court filled another blank in the federal system by making an important ruling on the Bill of Rights. To improve its harbor, the City of Baltimore had made several street improvements, which lowered the water level around a wharf owned by Barron, leaving the structure all but useless. Barron made a novel claim that the City had, in effect, deprived him of property without the "just compensation" required by the Fifth Amendment in the Bill of Rights. But the argument was flawed—the Bill of Rights, inspired by the ratification debates, was clearly intended to limit the national government, not the states or their municipalities. This was the position Marshall and the Court took. In

doing so, they left states more or less unshackled in their use of the power of eminent domain to promote economic development, a matter discussed further in Chapter 11.

The decision's long-term effect on individual liberties was even more profound. Unless a right existed in the state constitution, its presence in the Bill of Rights was protection only from federal intrusion. This bifurcation of civil liberties began to change in 1925 after the Court declared freedom of speech in the First Amendment to be part of "due process of law" and protected against state interference through the due process clause of the Fourteenth Amendment. Today, nearly all the rights in the first 10 amendments are "incorporated" in due process and are applicable to both federal and state governments. This "nationalizing" of the Bill of Rights needed 17 cases and more than half a century to complete. Though made possible by an amendment—the Fourteenth—it is a premier example of constitutional change through judicial interpretation rather than formal altering of text.

The Georgia-Cherokee crisis gave Marshall his last opportunity for an important nationalist statement, but it was also one that led a president and a state to defy the Court. The large Cherokee tribe occupied much of the northwestern part of Georgia. Many Indians had taken up an agricultural way of life and were attending schools under the guidance of New England missionaries. The tribe had also adopted a written constitution and proclaimed itself an independent state. This troubled most Georgians, who had long resented the "permanency" of the Cherokees. After Jackson's first message to Congress in 1829 urging removal of all Southern Indians to lands west of the Mississippi, treaties notwithstanding, the state felt encouraged to assert jurisdiction over the tribe and speed up relocation.

The matter received constitutional focus in *Worcester v. Georgia,* 1832. Two missionaries had been convicted of not getting a license the state required of any white person living in Cherokee territory. Marshall's decision that the Cherokees were a distinct political community in which the laws of Georgia had no force, was in vain. Jackson, an old Indian-fighter who had little sympathy for Indian rights or presence, is supposed to have said in response, "John Marshall has made his decision, now let him enforce it!" Georgia openly ignored the Court's ruling and Jackson looked the other way. Eventually, under pressure from the state and the president, the Cherokees evacuated their land for Oklahoma in a humiliating trek known as the "Trail of Tears"—another sorry chapter in the often tragic Indian policies of the federal and state governments. Georgia's defiance of the Court's authority in the name of states rights was also an ominous hint of the nullification crisis to come over the protective tariffs of the late 1820s and early 1830s.

The legacy of Marshall's nationalism far outweighed the setback in *Worcester*. His Court had found 19 state or local laws or actions unconstitutional and had asserted its review over scores of others. It had given a definitively liberal effect to federal implied powers and asserted that a federal power, properly exercised, was superior to any state law or action. The result was a vast broadening of national rule. Marshall's constitutional jurisprudence pushed nationalism to the edge of the political envelope of his day. At his death in 1835, the United States was a stronger, more nationally directed federal union than almost anyone thought possible in 1801 when he joined the Court. This advance allowed the Union to withstand the increasingly virulent slavery-based states rights attack that ended in civil war.

Jacksonian Democracy

The framers of the Constitution did not create a modern political democracy, but in structure and operation the new constitutional system was radically democratic for its time. By the end of the first quarter of the nineteenth century,

powerful forces transforming American economic and social life would carry democracy much further still. Material opportunities appeared everywhere; the West was nearly wide open and commerce and manufacturing were thriving in older areas of the North and East. The cotton gin had transformed the regional economy of the South. The United States of the 1830s was a society that astonished the perceptive French observer Alexis de Tocqueville. In his classic work *Democracy in America* he celebrated the absence of class distinctions that were rife in the Old World: "In America men are nearer equality than in any other country." Democracy was the wave of the future, yet he worried that its tendency to reduce men and women to the lowest common denominator culturally might produce a "tyranny of the majority" politically. These seemingly contradictory forces of democracy were symbolized and partly molded by the presidency and political persona of Andrew Jackson.

The New Politics

In 1824, Jackson led four candidates in both electoral and popular vote but had a majority of neither. He was denied the presidency in the House of Representatives after Henry Clay, one of the also-rans, gave his support to John Quincy Adams, the runner-up. When Clay became secretary of state, Jackson and his supporters denounced the "corrupt bargain," a phrase that still rang four years later when Jackson won the presidency outright. By that time, the Republican Party had split into an Adams-Clay faction, known as National Republicans and later to reassemble as the Whig Party, and the dissident Jacksonians, calling themselves Democrat-Republicans, later simply Democrats, political forebears of the modern Democratic Party.

Though Jackson, the popular hero of the War of 1812, had once served in the Senate, he cast himself as an "outsider" against the effete incumbents. The latter, supposedly representing established and privileged interests, were said to be out of touch with the "common people." As the first president from truly humble origins, Jackson put together a new coalition, drawing its strength from western settlers and frontiersmen, Southern small farmers and strict constructionists, disaffected farmers and artisans in the North, and the swelling ranks of manual laborers everywhere. He won reelection easily in 1832, and his vice president and hand-picked successor, Martin Van Buren, won handily in 1836. By that time, the nation again had a competitive two-party system, Democrats and Whigs. The rivalry lasted until coming apart over the slavery and secession questions in the late 1850s.

The new spirit of democracy was reflected in political changes everywhere. Rising opposition to the "closed" Congressional caucus as the method of choosing presidential nominees led to candidates being nominated by state legislatures or state conventions. The movement to get rid of property or taxpaying qualifications for voting accelerated. Restrictions were dropped in New Jersey in 1807 and Maryland in 1810. Several new states—Illinois, Indiana, Alabama, and Maine, for example—had complete white manhood suffrage when admitted. Between 1815 and 1830, constitutional reform produced the same results in other states, including Connecticut, Massachusetts, and New York. The apportioning of seats in state legislatures was increasingly based on general population rather than the taxpaying part of it. More state and local offices, including many judgeships, became elective, and by 1828, all but two of the 24 states chose presidential electors by popular ballot rather than by vote of the state legislature.

The political party itself changed. The coalition that formed around Jackson's candidacies was the forerunner of the voter-mobilizing, nationally organized mass party of today. It aimed not merely to nominate candidates and coordinate efforts of like-minded persons in the government, but to recruit rank-and-file supporters, retain their loyalty, and, by winning elections, supposedly give voice to the will of the people. These goals called for a cadre, disciplined organization, and an identifying set of principles or policies. The new party was both a nationalizing and democratizing force. Winning a national election demanded cooperative effort that rose above state and local lines and parochial concerns. With its open ranks and emphasis on loyalty, the party offered a ready means for citizens to take part in politics. And the rewards of victory could be personal as well as collective, as the Jacksonians used the "spoils system" and its award of government jobs to bring patronage to a new plane in American politics. The principle of rotation in office, positing the average person's competency to handle most work of government, was another product of the new democratic ethos.

The Constitution presented no barrier to modern parties or to broadening suffrage, but a series of events in Rhode Island raised a question of the meaning of "a republican form of government," guaranteed to each state by Article IV-4. In contrast to its earlier reputation for radicalism, the state was the only one to resist liberalization of suffrage. By 1840, eligibility was still limited to freeholders and their eldest sons. Unchanged since pre-Revolutionary days, this franchise now excluded half the adult males. When the existing Charter government refused to consider reforms, leaders of the disenfranchised called an extra-legal constitutional convention and drafted a reform constitution. The Charter government refused to recognize the proceedings, and both sides held elections. The new constitutionalists chose Thomas Dorr governor, and for a brief time the state had two opposing governments before the older declared those of the newer to be in rebellion and imposed martial law. Both sides appealed to President John Tyler for military help under Article IV-4 requiring the federal government to protect states "against domestic violence." When Tyler refused but made clear his sympathies lay with the Charter government, the "rebellion" collapsed and Dorr and other leaders were arrested.

Several years later in *Luther v. Borden,* 1849, (p. 117) an appeal by one of the insurgents revived the legal challenge to the Charter government's actions. That government's refusal to reform itself and its repression of the constitutionalists, it was argued, violated Article IV-4's federal guarantee to each state of a "republican form of government." In effect, the Supreme Court was asked to decide which of the two governments was legitimate and so give substantive definition to "republican form of government." In refusing to do this the Court, now led by Roger Taney as Marshall's successor, formulated the "political questions" doctrine. The power to declare governments legal or illegal was not a judicial one, Taney wrote, but under Article IV-4 resided in the "political" branches— the president and Congress.

The doctrine has had long-term consequence and been used by the Court as an instrument of judicial self-restraint. Though narrowed in *Baker v. Carr,* 1962, in which the Court held long-standing malapportionment of state legislatures to be judicially reviewable, the doctrine retains much of its vitality. It has been used by the Court to defer to the other branches on many constitutional questions arising from foreign and military policy, including those of the Vietnam War.

The Strong Presidency

Though courtly and often charming in polite society, Andrew Jackson never lost his backwoods forthrightness and simplicity or rough-hewn identity with the "common man." Pugnacious, even violent as a personality, his approach to politics and most other matters was personal and instinctive. This makeup and frequent embattlement made him the most polarizing political figure of his day, and it is no surprise that he left a permanent mark on the office he held for two terms.

Jackson had more influence on legislation than any of his predecessors. He vetoed seven Congressional enactments—the presidential negative had been used only 10 times in the preceding 40 years. Two—that of the Maysville Road bill and the rechartering of the Second National Bank—were of constitutional significance. The Maysville enactment, the brainchild of the Kentuckian Henry Clay, chief spokesman in Con-

gress for the expanding West and Jackson's unsuccessful presidential rival in 1832, provided money for the construction of an important 60-mile highway in Kentucky. Though Jackson was not opposed to public underwriting of internal improvements, he based his veto on states rights grounds that echoed the earlier positions of Jefferson and Madison. Since the proposed road was entirely in one state, Jackson reasoned, the federal government had no power to support it unless granted the authority by constitutional amendment.

The bank veto, in 1832, had even greater consequence. Jackson, who knew even less about finance than Jefferson, was unable to appreciate the bank's importance in maintaining sound currency and a degree of financial stability in the perpetually expanding American economy. But he did recognize a symbol of monopoly and creditor privilege when he saw one. His veto message, drafted by Roger Taney, then his attorney general and chief theoretician, was an assertion of executive independence. Notwithstanding *McCulloch v. Maryland* 13 years before, the bank was unconstitutional; it was also inexpedient policy. The constitutional argument challenged the Supreme Court as the final interpreter of constitutional questions. Echoing the department theory of Jefferson's time, he claimed that each of the three branches must be "guided by its own opinion on the Constitution . . . the opinion of the judges has no more authority over Congress than the opinion of Congress has over the judges, and on that point the President is independent of both."* The policy argument also created misgivings in Congress. The Whig opposition pleaded unsuccessfully that basing a veto on anything other than constitutional reservations was law-making, in effect, and thus a breach of the separation of powers. Paradoxically, it has been the policy grounds

---

* Melvin I. Urofsky, *Documents of American Constitutional History,* vol I *From Settlement Through Reconstruction* (New York: Alfred A. Knopf, 1989),. 237.

for executive veto rather than the assertion of presidential coequality in constitutional interpretation that has had lasting effect on American political practice.

The bank issue gave Jackson a chance to assert executive control over the Treasury Department and authority to remove its officers at will. The Second Bank still had four years left in its 20-year charter, but Jackson, interpreting his easy reelection as an anti-Bank mandate, ordered its deposits removed and distributed to several state banks. Secretary of the Treasury William J. Duane refused, maintaining that he was authorized by Congress to use his own discretion. When Jackson replaced him with Roger Taney, who carried out the policy, the Senate was in an uproar. Jackson insisted the executive power was unitary and vested completely in the president, who was responsible for all subordinate executive officers and could remove them as he saw fit. Despite these battles with his coequal federal partners, Jackson's greatest display of presidential leadership came where one would have least expected it—against an aggressive states rights claim.

The Nullification Crisis

The tariff was a mainstay in the Hamiltonian fiscal system. Levies on imports not only all but paid off the national debt, they gave protection to various nascent and established American manufacturers. But as it became clear that manufacturing would evolve mainly in northern states, much of the agrarian, importing South came to see the higher prices for foreign and domestic manufactures as a huge and unfair tax on itself. This led to periodic battles in Congress over tariff rates, which in the revised levies of 1816, 1824, and 1828, grew progressively higher. The last, the Tariff of Abominations, as it came to be called, passed in the final year of John Quincy Adams's administration. Coinciding with low cotton prices, it was widely unpopular in the South. Hardest hit was South Carolina, the state most heavily dependent on cotton and one suffering substantial soil depletion. When the Jacksonian Congress finally got around

to revising it, rates were lowered only slightly. This disappointment touched off a wave of reaction. In South Carolina, a popularly elected convention, authorized by the legislature, met and adopted an ordinance declaring the Tariff Act of 1828 and its later revisions null and void. Another ordinance barred federal collection of duties in the state; any use of force by the federal government would be cause for secession.

Never shy of a fight, Jackson responded by ordering General Winfield Scott to take command of army forces in the state and issued a "Proclamation to the People of South Carolina" in which he defended the supremacy and indivisibility of the Union. No state could defy the laws of the land or leave the Union, and an attempt to do so by armed force would be treason. Jackson also asked Congress for power to collect the tariff duties by military force if needed. At this face-off, a compromise was engineered by Henry Clay, now representing Kentucky in the Senate. The so-called Force bill was passed giving Jackson the authority he sought, but the tariff was to be progressively reduced over nine years and its protective principle phased out. South Carolina accepted the lower tariffs but, in a face-saving action, "nullified" the now unneeded Force bill. Though the state was politically isolated during the crisis when other Southern states refused its call for a general convention, its obstreperousness did get the tariff lowered. For his part, Jackson had acted swiftly and firmly to proclaim the principles of federal supremacy and inviolability of the Union. The "lessons" of the crisis were mixed, but its portent was ominous.

The intellectual father of nullification was John C. Calhoun, who, in 1830 while serving as Jackson's vice president, had secretly written "The South Carolina Exposition," the fullest statement of the doctrine. Shortly afterward, Calhoun, breaking with Jackson, resigned the vice presidency and was elected to the Senate from South Carolina. The one-time nationalist then became the leading sectionalist of his day. In the Exposition, formally issued by the state legislature, he decried exploitation of the South through the tariff and proclaimed the right of individual states to nullify federal law. The mechanics for this were simple: If a federal law were found objectionable, the people of a state acting in a popularly elected convention could declare it null and void in that state. Congress could then either repeal the law or submit it to the states as a constitutional amendment. If three-quarters of the states approved, the objecting state could accept it or secede. Calhoun believed such arrangements were needed to protect the South against a permanent hostile majority at the federal level. As he saw it, the doctrine of nullification, though embracing secession as a last resort, was aimed at keeping dissidents in the Union by making the basic rules less unjust.

Though now discredited, the doctrine had a degree of plausibility and went to the heart of the debate over the Union. Calhoun ingeniously based his argument on the republican principle of sovereignty of the people. That sovereignty, he contended, had always been exercised in popular *state* conventions. Such meetings had ratified the Constitution, dissolved the ties with Britain, and formed the state constitutions. Nullification gave this popular source the constitutional means to make its voice effective. In this, Calhoun went be-

yond the Virginia and Kentucky Resolutions of Jefferson and Madison and their view of states rights as a limit on federal power. Calhoun had developed a theory not of state rights but of state *sovereignty*, based not on state power but on popular power within states. The constitutional union was a compact of popularly sovereign states.

By challenging the Union, the nullification crisis also affected nationalist thinking. Until then, defense of union was almost always utilitarian, with emphasis on the experimental, practical values of federalism. Now given voice by Daniel Webster and the Whigs and, later and even more dramatically, by Lincoln, the Union began to take on an organic, almost mystical character—a creation perpetual and indissoluble. Jackson's dual federalism had rejected both Calhoun's theory of state sovereignty and Whig ideas of centralization. The compromise on the tariff had avoided a constitutional showdown. But the matter of state sovereignty was anything but settled. "The next pretext," Jackson predicted, sensing the gathering storm, "will be the Negro, or slavery question."*

---

* Quoted in Samuel Elliot Morrison, *History of the American People* (New York: Oxford University Press, 1965), 437.

FURTHER READING

The Federalist Period

Banning, Lance, *The Sacred Fire of Liberty: James Madison and the Founding of the American Republic* (1995)

Casto, William R., *The Supreme Court in the Early Republic: The Chief Justiceships of John Jay and Oliver Ellsworth* (1995)

Cogan, Neil H., *The Complete Bill of Rights: The Drafts, Debates, Sources, and Origins* (1996)

Currie, David P., *The Constitution in Congress: The Federalist Period, 1789–1801* (1997)

Duncan, Christopher M., *The Anti-Federalists and Early American Political Thought* (1995)

Elkins, Stanley, and McKitrick, Eric, *The Age of Federalism* (1993)

Flaumenhaft, Harvey, *The Effective Republic: Administration and Constitution in the Thought of Alexander Hamilton* (1992)

Goebel, Jr., Julius, *The History of the Supreme Court of the United States,* vol 1, *Antecedents and Beginnings to 1801* (1971)

Levy, Leonard, *The Origins of the Bill of Rights* (1999)

Lloyd, Gordon and Margie Lloyd, eds., *The Essential Bill of Rights: Original Arguments and Fundamental Documents* (1998)

Marcus, Maeva, ed., *Origins of the Federal Judiciary: Essays on the Judiciary Act of 1789* (1992)

McNamara, Peter, *Political Economy and Statesmanship: Smith, Hamilton, and the Foundation of the Commercial Republic* (1997)

Miller, John C., *The Federalist Era, 1789–1800* (1960)

Rutland, Robert A., *The Birth of the Bill of Rights, 1776–1791* (1983)

Stourzh, Gerald, *Alexander Hamilton and the Idea of Republican Government* (1970)

Jeffersonian Republicanism

Abernethy, Thomas P., *The Burr Conspiracy* (1954)

Banning, Lance, *The Jeffersonian Persuasion: Evolution of a Party Ideology* (1978)

Currie, David P., *The Constitution in Congress: The Jeffersonians, 1801–1829* (2001)

Ellis, Richard E., *The Jeffersonian Crisis: Courts and Politics in the Young Republic* (1971)

Finkelman, *Slavery and the Founders: Race and Liberty in the Age of Jefferson* (1996)

Sloan, Herbert E., *Principle and Interest: Thomas Jefferson and the Problem of Debt* (1995)

Judicial Nationalism

Dewey, Donald O., *Madison v. Jefferson: The Political Background of* Marbury v. Madison (1970)

Faulkner, Robert K., *The Jurisprudence of John Marshall* (1968)

Gunther, Gerald, ed., *John Marshall's Defense of* McCulloch v. Maryland (1969)

Haskins, George L. and Herbert A. Johnson, *History of the Supreme Court of the United States*, vol 2, *Foundations of Power: John Marshall, 1801–1815* (1981)

Henderson, Dwight F., *Congress, Courts, and Criminals: The Development of the Federal Criminal Law, 1801–1829* (1985)

Hobson, Charles F., *The Great Chief Justice: John Marshall and the Rule of Law* (1996)

Johnson, Herbert A., *The Chief Justiceship of John Marshall, 1801–1835* (1997)

Newmyer, R. Kent, *The Supreme Court Under Marshall and Taney* (1968)

White, G. Edward, *History of the Supreme Court of the United States*, vols 3–4: *The Marshall Court and Cultural Change, 1815–1835* (1988)

Jacksonian Democracy

Ellis, Richard E., *The Union at Risk: Jacksonian Democracy, States' Rights, and the Nullification Crisis* (1987)

Freehling, William H., *Prelude to Civil War: The Nullification Controversy in South Carolina, 1816–1836* (1966)

Latner, Richard B., *The Presidency of Andrew Jackson: White House Politics, 1829–1837* (1979)

Mushkat, Jerome and Joseph G., Rayback, *Martin Van Buren: Law, Politics, and the Republican Ideology* (1997)

Peterson, Merrill D., *The Great Triumvirate: Webster, Clay, and Calhoun* (1987)

Schlesinger, Jr., Arthur, *The Age of Jackson*

White, Leonard D., *The Jacksonians: A Study in Administrative History, 1829–1860 (1954)*

Biographical

Beveridge, Albert J., *The Life of John Marshall*, 4 vols (1916–1919)

Brant, Irving, *James Madison: The President, 1809–1812* (1961)

———, *James Madison: Commander-in-Chief, 1812–1836* (1961)

Brookheiser, Richard, *Alexander Hamilton, American* (1999)

Burstein, Andrew, *The Inner Jefferson: Portrait of a Grieving Optimist* (1995)

Ellis, Joseph J., *American Sphinx: The Character of Thomas Jefferson* (1998)

———, *Founding Brothers: The Revolutionary Generation* (2000)

Hobson, Charles F., *The Great Chief Justice: John Marshall and the Rule of Law* (1996)

Kennedy, Roger G., *Burr, Hamilton, and Jefferson: A Study in Character* (1999)

Malone, Dumas, *Thomas Jefferson and His Time*, 6 vols. (1948–1977)

McCullough, David, *John Adams* (2001)

Morris, Richard B., *John Jay: The Nation and the Court* (1967)

Nagel, Paul C., *John Quincy Adams: A Public Life, a Private Life* (1997)

Randall, Willard Sterne, *Thomas Jefferson* (1992)

Remini, Robert, *Andrew Jackson*, 3 vols (1977–1984)

———, *Daniel Webster: The Man and His Time* (1997)

Shaw, Peter, *The Character of John Adams* (1976)

Smith, Jean Edward, *John Marshall: Definer of a Nation* (1996)

On Leading Cases

Baxter, Maurice J., *The Steamboat Monopoly:* Gibbons v. Ogden (1972)

Clinton, Robert L., *Marbury v. Madison and Judicial Review* (1989)

Magrath C. Peter, *Yazoo: Law and Politics in the New Republic* (1966)

Nelson, William E., *Marbury v. Madison: The Origins and Legacy of Judicial Review* (2000)

Norgren, Jill, *The Cherokee Cases: The Confrontation of Law and Politics* (1995)

Stites, Francis N., *Private Interest and Public Gain: The Dartmouth College Case* (1972)

CASES

Chisholm v. Georgia

2 U.S. 419 (1793), 4–1
Seriatim opinions: Jay, Wilson, Cushing, Blair
Dissenting: Iredell

Chisholm, executor of the estate of a South Carolina merchant who had sold war supplies on credit to the State of Georgia during the Revolution, sued the state to collect the unpaid debt in federal court. Georgia, denying it could be sued by a citizen of another state in the national courts, refused to appear.

Is the decision consistent with the intent of the framers of the Constitution? Given the state's refusal to appear and the storm of protest that followed the decision, should the Court have exercised self-restraint and refused to hear the case? Is any attempt made to calm states rights fears? Besides the parties to the case, who is likely to gain and who to lose as a result of this decision?

Justice Wilson:

This is a case of uncommon magnitude. One of the parties to it is a State; certainly respectable, claiming to be sovereign. The question to be determined is, whether this State, so respectable, and whose claim soars so high, is amenable to the jurisdiction of the Supreme Court of the United States? This question, important in itself, will depend on others, more important still; and, may, perhaps, be ultimately resolved into one, no less radical than this 'do the people of the United States form a Nation?'. . .

Whoever considers, in a combined and comprehensive view, the general texture of the Constitution, will be satisfied, that the people of the United States intended to form themselves into a nation for national purposes. They instituted, for such purposes, a national Government, complete in all its parts, with powers Legislative, Executive and Judiciary; and, in all those powers, extending over the whole nation. Is it congruous, that, with regard to such purposes, any man or body of men, any person natural or artificial,

should be permitted to claim successfully an entire exemption from the jurisdiction of the national Government? Would not such claims, crowned with success, be repugnant to our very existence as a nation? When so many trains of deduction, coming from different quarters, converge and unite, at last, in the same point; we may safely conclude, as the legitimate result of this Constitution, that the State of Georgia is amenable to the jurisdiction of this Court.

But, in my opinion, this doctrine rests not upon the legitimate result of fair and conclusive deduction from the Constitution: It is confirmed, beyond all doubt, by the direct and explicit declaration of the Constitution itself. 'The judicial power of the United States shall extend, to controversies between two States.' Two States are supposed to have a controversy between them: This controversy is supposed to be brought before those vested with the judicial power of the United States: Can the most consummate degree of professional ingenuity devise a mode by which this 'controversy between two States? can be brought before a Court of law; and yet neither of those States be a Defendant? 'The judicial power of the United States shall extend to controversies, between a state and citizens of another State.' Could the strictest legal language; could even that language, which is peculiarly appropriated to an art, deemed, by a great master, to be one of the most honorable, laudable, and profitable things in our law; could this strict and appropriated language, describe, with more precise accuracy, the cause now depending before the tribunal? Causes, and not parties to causes, are weighed by justice, in her equal scales: On the former solely, her attention is fixed: To the latter, she is, as she is painted, blind. . . .

Jay, C.J.:

The question we are now to decide has been accurately stated, viz. Is a State suable by individual citizens of another State? . . .

Any one State in the Union may sue another State, in this Court, that is, all the people of one State may sue all the people of another State. It is plain then, that a State may be sued, and hence it plainly follows, that suability and state sovereignty are not incompatible. As one State may sue another State in this Court, it is plain that no degradation to a State is thought to accompany her appearance in this Court. It is not therefore to an appearance in this Court that the objection points. To what does it point? It points to an appearance at the suit of one or more citizens. But why it should be more incompatible, that all the people of a State should be sued by one citizen, than by one hundred thousand, I cannot perceive, the process in both cases being alike; and the consequences of a judgment alike. Nor can I observe any greater inconveniencies in the one case than in the other, except what may arise from the feelings of those who may regard a lesser number in an inferior light. But if any reliance be made on this inferiority as an objection, at least one half of its force is done away by this fact, viz. that it is conceded that a State may appear in this Court as Plaintiff against a single citizen as Defendant; and the truth is, that the State of Georgia is at this moment prosecuting an action in this Court against two citizens of South Carolina.

The only remnant of objection therefore that remains is, that the State is not bound to appear and answer as a Defendant at the suit of an individual . . . This inquiry naturally leads our attention, 1st. To the design of the Constitution. 2nd. To the letter and express declaration in it.

Prior to the date of the Constitution, the people had not any national tribunal to which they could resort for justice; the distribution of justice was then confined to State judicatories, in whose institution and organization the people of the other States had no participation, and over whom they had not the least control. There was then no general Court of appellate jurisdiction, by whom the errors of State Courts, affecting either the nation at large or the citizens of any other State, could be revised and corrected. Each State was obliged to acquiesce in the measure of justice which another State might yield to her, or to her citizens; and that even in cases where State considerations were not always favorable to the most exact measure. There was danger that from this source animosities would in time result; and as the transition from animosities to hostilities was frequent in the history of independent States, a common tribunal for the termination of controversies became desirable, from motives both of justice and of policy.

Prior also to that period, the United States had, by taking a place among the nations of the earth, become amenable to the laws of nations; and it was their interest as well as their duty to provide, that those laws should be respected and obeyed; in their national character and capacity, the United States were responsible to foreign nations for the conduct of each State, relative to the laws of nations, and the performance of treaties; and there the inexpediency of referring all such questions to State Courts, and particularly to the Courts of delinquent States became apparent. While all the States were bound to protect each, and the citizens of each, it was highly proper and reasonable, that they should be in a capacity, not only to cause justice to be done to each, and the citizens of each; but also to cause justice to be done by each, and the citizens of each; and that, not by violence and force, but in a stable, sedate, and regular course of judicial procedure.

These were among the evils against which it was proper for the nation, that is, the people of all the United States, to provide by a national judiciary, to be instituted by the whole nation, and to be responsible to the whole nation.

Let us now turn to the Constitution. The people therein declare, that their design in establishing it, comprehended six objects. 1st. To form a more perfect union. 2nd. To establish justice. 3rd. To ensure domestic tranquillity. 4th. To provide for the common defense. 5th. To promote the general welfare. 6th. To secure the blessings of liberty to themselves and their posterity. . . .

The question now before us renders it necessary to pay particular attention to that part of the second section, which extends the judicial power 'to controversies between a state and citizens of another state.' It is contended, that this ought to be construed to reach none of these controversies, excepting those in which a State may be Plaintiff. The ordinary rules for construction will easily decide whether those words are to be understood in that limited sense.

This extension of power is remedial, because it is to settle controversies. It is therefore, to be construed liberally. It is politic, wise, and good that, not only the controversies, in which a State is Plaintiff, but also those in which a State is Defendant, should be settled; both cases, therefore, are within the reason of the remedy; and ought to be so adjudged, unless the obvious, plain, and literal sense of the words forbid it. If we attend to the words, we find them to be express, positive, free from ambiguity, and without room for such implied expressions: 'The judicial power of the United States shall extend to controversies between a state and citizens of another state.' If the Constitution really meant to extend these powers only to those controversies in which a State might be Plaintiff, to the exclusion of those in which citizens had demands against a State, it is inconceivable that it should have attempted to convey that meaning in words, not only so incompetent, but also repugnant to it; if it meant to exclude a certain class of these controversies, why were they not expressly excepted; on the contrary, not even an intimation of such intention appears in any part of the Constitution. It cannot be pretended that where citizens urge and insist upon demands against a State, which the State refuses to admit and comply with, that there is no controversy between them. If it is a controversy between them, then it clearly falls not only within the spirit, but the very words of the Constitution. What is it to the cause of justice, and how can it effect the definition of the word controversy, whether the demands which cause the dispute, are made by a State against citizens of another State, or by the latter against the former? When power is thus extended to a controversy, it necessarily, as to all judicial purposes, is also extended to those, between whom it subsists.

The exception contended for, would contradict and do violence to the great and leading principles of a free and equal national government, one of the great objects of which is, to ensure justice to all: To the few against the many, as well as to the many against the few. It would be strange, indeed, that the joint and equal sovereigns of this country, should, in the very Constitution by which they professed to establish justice, so far deviate from the plain path of equality and impartiality, as to give to the collective citizens of one State, a right of suing individual citizens of another State, and yet deny to those citizens a right of suing them. . . .

For the reasons before given, I am clearly of opinion, that a State is suable by citizens of another State; but left I should be understood in a latitude beyond my meaning, I think it necessary to subjoin this caution, viz, That such suability may nevertheless not extend to all the demands, and to every kind of action; there may be exceptions. For instance, I am far from being prepared to say that an individual may sue a State on bills of credit issued before the Constitution

was established, and which were issued and received on the faith of the State, and at a time when no ideas or expectations of judicial interposition were entertained or contemplated.

Marbury v. Madison

5 U.S. 137 (1803), 4–0
Opinion of the Court: Marshall (Chase, Paterson, Washington)
Not participating: Cushing, Moore

William Marbury was one of 42 justices of the peace appointed in the District of Columbia by President John Adams in his last days in office. To become effective, these commissions had to be delivered to their recipients by the secretary of state. In the last minute rush, the outgoing secretary, who happened to be John Marshall, failed to deliver several of the commissions including Marbury's. As Adams's successor, Thomas Jefferson ordered incoming Secretary of State James Madison to withhold the undelivered commissions. Marbury then brought an original action to the Supreme Court for a writ of mandamus asking that Madison be ordered to deliver his commission.

Since the Constitution does not expressly give the Court the power of judicial review, what constitutional justification does Marshall offer to support the power? Is the power limited to matters that affect the Court's own authority or does it extend to all constitutional questions? Is it logical for a coequal branch to have final say about the constitutionality of acts of other branches? Is it practical? Is it a threat to democratic government if unelected judges have, in effect, a constitutional veto over acts of elected officials? What checks might there be on the judges? Does Marshall's opinion address any of these last questions? Does the decision make the Constitution more flexible or more rigid?

Marshall, C.J., for the Court:
The peculiar delicacy of this case, the novelty of some of its circumstances, and the real difficulty attending the points which occur in it, require a complete exposition of the principles on which the opinion to be given by the Court is founded. . . .

In the order in which the Court has viewed this subject, the following questions have been considered and decided.

1. Has the applicant a right to the commission he demands?

2. If he has a right, and that right has been violated, do the laws of his country afford him a remedy?

3. If they do afford him a remedy, is it a mandamus issuing from this court?. . .

It is . . . decidedly the opinion of the Court, that when a commission has been signed by the President, the appointment is made; and that the commission is complete when the seal of the United States has been affixed to it by the secretary of state. . . .

Mr. Marbury, then, since his commission was signed by the President and sealed by the secretary of state, was appointed; and as the law creating the office gave the officer a right to hold for five years independent of the executive, the appointment was not revocable; but vested in the officer legal rights which are protected by the laws of his country.

To withhold the commission, therefore, is an act deemed by the Court not warranted by law, but violative of a vested legal right.

This brings us to the second inquiry; which is: If he has a right, and that right has been violated, do the laws of his country afford him a remedy?

The very essence of civil liberty certainly consists in the right of every individual to claim the protection of the laws, whenever he receives an injury. One of the first duties of government is to afford that protection. . . .

The government of the United States has been emphatically termed a government of laws, and not of men. It will certainly cease to deserve this high appellation, if the laws furnish no remedy for the violation of a vested legal right.

If this obloquy is to be cast on the jurisprudence of our country, it must arise from the peculiar character of the case. . . .

[Marshall allows that there are aspects of executive conduct (Madison's) that are not suitable for judicial examination, because they are committed to the executive's discretion.]

But where a specific duty is assigned by law, and individual rights depend upon the performance of that duty, it seems equally clear that the individual who considers himself injured has a right to resort to the laws of his country for a remedy. . . .

The question whether a right has vested or not, is, in its nature, judicial, and must be tried by the judicial authority . . . So, if [Marbury] conceives that by virtue of his appointment he has a legal right either to the commission which has been made out for him or to a copy of that commission, it is . . . a question examinable in a court. . . .

It is then the opinion of the court,

1. That by signing the commission of Mr. Marbury, the President of the United States appointed him a justice of peace for the county of Washington in the district of Columbia; and that the seal of the United States, affixed thereto by the secretary of state, is conclusive testimony of the verity of the signature, and of the completion of the appointment; and that the appointment conferred on him a legal right to the office for the space of five years.

2. That, having this legal title to the office, he has a consequent right to the commission; a refusal to deliver which is a plain violation of that right, for which the laws of his country afford him a remedy.

It remains to be inquired whether,

3. He is entitled to the remedy for which he applies. . . .

The act to establish the judicial courts of the United States authorizes the Supreme Court "to issue writs of mandamus, in cases warranted by the principles and usages of law, to any courts appointed, or persons holding office, under the authority of the United States."

The secretary of state, being a person holding an office under the authority of the United States, is precisely within the letter of the description; and if this court is not authorized to issue a writ of mandamus to such an officer, it must be because the law is unconstitutional, and therefore absolutely incapable of conferring the authority, and assigning the duties which its words purport to confer and assign.

The Constitution vests the whole judicial power of the United States in one supreme court and such inferior courts as Congress shall, from time to time, ordain and establish. This power is expressly extended to all cases arising under the laws of the United States; and consequently, in some form, may be exercised over the present case; because the right claimed is given by a law of the United States.

In the distribution of this power it is declared that 'the supreme court shall have original jurisdiction in all cases affecting ambassadors, other public ministers and consuls, and those in which a state shall be a party. In all other cases, the supreme court shall have appellate jurisdiction.'

It has been insisted at the bar, that as the original grant of jurisdiction to the supreme and inferior courts is general, and the clause, assigning original jurisdiction to the Supreme Court, contains no negative or restrictive words; the power remains to the legislature to assign original jurisdiction to that court in other cases than those specified in the article which has been recited; provided those cases belong to the judicial power of the United States.

If it had been intended to leave it in the discretion of the legislature to apportion the judicial power between the supreme and inferior courts according to the will of that body, it would certainly have been useless to have proceeded further than to have defined the judicial power, and the tribunals in which it should be vested. The subsequent part of the section is mere surplusage, is entirely without meaning, if such is to be the construction. If Congress remains at liberty to give this court appellate jurisdiction, where the Constitution has declared their jurisdiction shall be original; and original jurisdiction where the Constitution has declared it shall be appellate; the distribution of jurisdiction made in the constitution, is form without substance.

Affirmative words are often, in their operation, negative of other objects than those affirmed; and in this case, a negative or exclusive sense must be given to them or they have no operation at all.

It cannot be presumed that any clause in the Constitution is intended to be without effect; and therefore such construction is inadmissible, unless the words require it.

If the solicitude of the convention, respecting our peace with foreign powers, induced a provision that the Supreme Court should take original jurisdiction in cases which might be supposed to affect them; yet the clause would have proceeded no further than to provide for such cases, if no further restriction on the powers of Congress had been intended. That they should have appellate jurisdiction in all other cases, with such exceptions as Congress might make, is no restriction; unless the words be deemed exclusive of original jurisdiction.

When an instrument organizing fundamentally a judicial system, divides it into one supreme, and so many inferior courts as the legislature may ordain and establish; then enumerates its powers, and proceeds so far to distribute them, as to define the jurisdiction of the Supreme Court by declaring the cases in which it shall take original jurisdiction, and that in others it shall take appellate jurisdiction, the plain import of the words seems to be, that in one class of cases its jurisdiction is original, and not appellate; in the other it is appellate, and not original. If any other construction would render the clause inoperative, that is an additional reason for rejecting such other construction, and for adhering to the obvious meaning.

To enable this court then to issue a mandamus, it must be shown to be an exercise of appellate jurisdiction, or to be necessary to enable them to exercise appellate jurisdiction.

It has been stated at the bar that the appellate jurisdiction may be exercised in a variety of forms, and that if it be the will of the legislature that a mandamus should be used for that purpose, that will must be obeyed. This is true; yet the jurisdiction must be appellate, not original.

It is the essential criterion of appellate jurisdiction, that it revises and corrects the proceedings in a cause already instituted, and does not create that case. Although, therefore, a mandamus may be directed to courts, yet to issue such a writ to an officer for the delivery of a paper, is in effect the same as to sustain an original action for that paper, and therefore seems not to belong to appellate, but to original jurisdiction. Neither is it necessary in such a case as this, to enable the Court to exercise its appellate jurisdiction.

The authority, therefore, given to the Supreme Court by the act establishing the judicial courts of the United States, to issue writs of mandamus to public officers, appears not to be warranted by the constitution; and it becomes necessary to inquire whether a jurisdiction, so conferred, can be exercised.

The question, whether an act, repugnant to the constitution, can become the law of the land, is a question deeply interesting to the United States; but, happily, not of an intricacy proportioned to its interest. It seems only necessary to recognize certain principles, supposed to have been long and well established, to decide it.

That the people have an original right to establish, for their future government, such principles as, in their opinion, shall most conduce to their own happiness, is the basis on which the whole American fabric has been erected. The exercise of this original right is a very great exertion; nor can it nor ought it to be frequently repeated. The principles, therefore, so established are deemed fundamental. And as the authority, from which they proceed, is supreme, and can seldom act, they are designed to be permanent.

This original and supreme will organizes the government, and assigns to different departments their respective powers. It may either stop here; or establish certain limits not to be transcended by those departments.

The government of the United States is of the latter description. The powers of the legislature are defined and limited; and that those limits may not be mistaken or forgotten, the Constitution is written. To what purpose are powers limited, and to what purpose is that limitation committed to writing; if these limits may, at any time, be passed by those intended to be restrained? The distinction between a government with limited and unlimited powers is abolished, if those limits do not confine the persons on whom they are imposed, and if acts prohibited and acts allowed are of equal obligation. It is a proposition too plain to be contested, that the Constitution controls any legislative act repugnant to it; or, that the legislature may alter the Constitution by an ordinary act.

Between these alternatives there is no middle ground. The Constitution is either a superior, paramount law, unchangeable by ordinary means, or it is on a level with ordinary legislative acts, and like other acts, is alterable when the legislature shall please to alter it.

If the former part of the alternative be true, then a legislative act contrary to the Constitution is not law: if the latter part be true, then written constitutions are absurd attempts, on the part of the people, to limit a power in its own nature illimitable.

Certainly all those who have framed written constitutions contemplate them as forming the fundamental and paramount law of the nation, and consequently the theory of every such government must be, that an act of the legislature repugnant to the Constitution is void.

This theory is essentially attached to a written constitution, and is consequently to be considered by this court as one of the fundamental principles of our society. It is not therefore to be lost sight of in the further consideration of this subject.

If an act of the legislature, repugnant to the constitution, is void, does it, notwithstanding its invalidity, bind the courts and oblige them to give it effect? Or, in other words, though it be not law, does it constitute a rule as operative as if it was a law? This would be to overthrow in fact what was established in theory; and would seem, at first view, an absurdity too gross to be insisted on. It shall, however, receive a more attentive consideration.

It is emphatically the province and duty of the judicial department to say what the law is. Those who apply the rule to particular cases, must of necessity expound and interpret that rule. If two laws conflict with each other, the courts must decide on the operation of each.

So if a law be in opposition to the Constitution: if both the law and the Constitution apply to a particular case, so that the Court must either decide that case conformably to the law, disregarding the Constitution; or conformably to the Constitution, disregarding the law: the court must determine which of these conflicting rules governs the case. This is of the very essence of judicial duty.

If then the courts are to regard the Constitution; and the Constitution is superior to any ordinary act of the legislature; the Constitution, and not such ordinary act, must govern the case to which they both apply.

Those then who controvert the principle that the Constitution is to be considered, in court, as a paramount law, are reduced to the necessity of maintaining that courts must close their eyes on the constitution, and see only the law.

This doctrine would subvert the very foundation of all written constitutions. It would declare that an act, which, according to the principles and theory of our government, is entirely void, is yet, in practice, completely obligatory. It would declare, that if the legislature shall do what is expressly forbidden, such act, notwithstanding the express prohibition, is in reality effectual. It would be giving to the legislature a practical and real omnipotence with the same breath which professes to restrict their powers within narrow limits. It is prescribing limits, and declaring that those limits may be passed at pleasure.

That it thus reduces to nothing what we have deemed the greatest improvement on political institutions—a written constitution, would of itself be sufficient, in America where written constitutions have been viewed with so much reverence, for rejecting the construction. But the peculiar expressions of the Constitution of the United States furnish additional arguments in favor of its rejection.

The judicial power of the United States is extended to all cases arising under the Constitution.

Could it be the intention of those who gave this power, to say that, in using it, the Constitution should not be looked into? That a case arising under the Constitution should be decided without examining the instrument under which it arises?

This is too extravagant to be maintained.

In some cases then, the Constitution must be looked into by the judges. And if they can open it at all, what part of it are they forbidden to read, or to obey?

There are many other parts of the Constitution which serve to illustrate this subject.

It is declared that 'no tax or duty shall be laid on articles exported from any state.' Suppose a duty on the export of cotton, of tobacco, or of flour; and a suit instituted to recover it. Ought judgment to be rendered in such a case? ought the judges to close their eyes on the constitution, and only see the law.

The Constitution declares that 'no bill of attainder or ex post facto law shall be passed.'

If, however, such a bill should be passed and a person should be prosecuted under it, must the Court condemn to death those victims whom the Constitution endeavors to preserve?

'No person,' says the Constitution, 'shall be convicted of treason unless on the testimony of two witnesses to the same overt act, or on confession in open court.'

Here the language of the Constitution is addressed especially to the courts. It prescribes, directly for them, a rule of evidence not to be departed from. If the legislature should change that rule, and declare one witness, or a confession out of court, sufficient for conviction, must the constitutional principle yield to the legislative act?

From these and many other selections which might be made, it is apparent, that the framers of the Constitution contemplated that instrument as a rule for the government of courts, as well as of the legislature.

Why otherwise does it direct the judges to take an oath to support it? This oath certainly applies, in an especial manner, to their conduct in their official character. How immoral to impose it on them, if they were to be used as the instruments, and the knowing instruments, for violating what they swear to support!

The oath of office, too, imposed by the legislature, is completely demonstrative of the legislative opinion on this subject. It is in these words: 'I do solemnly swear that I will administer justice without respect to persons, and do equal right to the poor and to the rich; and that I will faithfully and impartially discharge all the duties incumbent on me as according to the best of my abilities and understanding, agreeably to the Constitution and laws of the United States.'

Why does a judge swear to discharge his duties agreeably to the Constitution of the United States, if that constitution forms no rule for his government? if it is closed upon him and cannot be inspected by him.

If such be the real state of things, this is worse than solemn mockery. To prescribe, or to take this oath, becomes equally a crime.

It is also not entirely unworthy of observation, that in declaring what shall be the supreme law of the land, the Constitution itself is first mentioned; and not the laws of the United States generally, but those only which shall be made in pursuance of the constitution, have that rank.

Thus, the particular phraseology of the Constitution of the United States confirms and strengthens the principle, supposed to be essential to all written constitutions, that a law repugnant to the Constitution is void, and that courts, as well as other departments, are bound by that instrument.

Eakin v. Raub

12 Sargent & Rawle 330 (Pa., 1825)

This Pennsylvania Supreme Court ejectment case dealt with the state court's power to invalidate a state law. Because its substantive issues are of no national constitutional importance, the facts and majority opinion have been omitted. However, Justice John Gibson's dissenting opinion is a formidable critique of Chief Justice Marshall's reasoning in Marbury v. Madison *and an early statement of judicial self-restraint. Gibson was a leading state court judge who was once considered for appointment to the U. S. Supreme Court. Ironically, in another case 20 years after this decision, he largely changed his mind, taking a more sanguine view of judicial review.*

Is Gibson persuasive in answering Marshall? What are the advantages and the drawbacks of the legislature having final say in judging the constitutionality of legislation? What role, if any, does Gibson concede to the courts in dealing with a statute of a coequal legislature? Suppose the president believed and asserted that an act of Congress was unconstitutional, who in Gibson's view would have authority to decide the matter? Suppose a majority of Congress believed a presidential act or policy was unconstitutional and passed a law declaring it to be so? Whose view would be constitutionally authoritative? What are the practical consequences to whatever your answer is?

Gibson, dissenting:

. . . [A] right to declare all unconstitutional act void, without distinction as to either state or federal constitutional, is generally held as a professional dogma . . . [A]lthough the right in question has all along been claimed by the judiciary, no judge has ventured to discuss it, except Chief Justice Marshall; and if the argument of a jurist so distinguished for the strength of his ratiocinative powers be found inconclusive, it may fairly be set down to the weakness of the position which he attempts to defend. . . .

The constitution is said to be a law of superior obligation; and consequently, that if it were to come into collision with an act of the legislature, the latter would have to give way; this is conceded. But it is a fallacy, to suppose, that they can come into collision *before the judiciary.*

The constitution and the right of the legislature to pass the act may be in collision, but is that a legitimate subject for judicial determination? If it be, the judiciary must be a peculiar organ to revise the proceedings of the legislature and to correct its mistakes; and in what part of the constitution are we to look for this proud preeminence? It is by no means clear that to declare a law void which has been enacted according to the forms prescribed in the constitution, is not a usurpation of legislative power. It is an act of sovereignty, and sovereignty and legislative power are said by Sir William Blackstone to be convertible terms. It is the business the judiciary to interpret the laws not scan the authority of the lawgiver, and without the latter, it cannot take cognizance of a collision between a law and the constitution. . . .

But it has been said to be emphatically the business of the judiciary to ascertain and pronounce what the law is and that this necessarily involves a consideration of the constitution. It does so but how far? If the judiciary will inquire into anything beside the form of enactment, where shall it stop? There must be some point of limitation to such an inquiry, for no one will pretend that a judge would be justifiable in calling for the election returns or scrutinizing the qualifications of those who composed the legislature.

It will not be pretended that the legislature has not, at least, an equal right with the judiciary to put a construction on the constitution; nor that either of them is infallible; nor that either ought to be required to surrender its judgment to the other. Suppose, then, they differ opinion as to the constitutionality of a particular law; if the organ whose business it first is to decide on the subject is not to have its judgment treated with respect, what shall prevent it from securing the preponderance of its opinion by the strong arm of power? . . .

But the judges are sworn to support the constitution, and are they not bound by it as the law of the land? The oath to support the constitution is not peculiar to the judges, but is taken indiscriminately by every officer of the government and is designed rather as a test of the political principles of the man than to bind the officer in the discharge of his duty; otherwise, it were difficult to determine what operation it is to have in the case of a recorder of deeds, for instance, who in the execution of his office has nothing to do with the constitution. But granting it to relate to the official conduct of the judge, as well as every other officer, and not to his political principles, still it must be understood in reference to support the constitution *only as far as that may be involved in his official duty;* and consequently, if his official duty does not comprehend an inquiry into the authority of the legislature, neither does his oath . . .

But do not the judges do a *positive* act in violation of the constitution when they give effect to an unconstitutional law? Not if the law has been passed according to the forms established in the constitution. . . . [T]he fault is imputable to the legislature, and on it the responsibility exclusively rests.

Martin v. Hunter's Lessee

14 U.S. 304 (1816), 6-0
Opinion of the Court: Story (Duvall, Johnson, Livingston, Todd)
Concurring: Johnson
Not participating: Marshall
The refusal of Virginia's highest court to enforce the Supreme Court's decision in Fairfax's Devisee v. Hunter's Lessee, resulted in this appeal by Martin.

Is the text of the Constitution or the intent of the framers of any help to the Court in deciding whether it has power to review the decisions of state courts on the constitutionality of state laws? On what basis does Story argue that Supreme Court review of state court decisions is necessary to national supremacy? Where does he find the power for such review? Does that power depend on the Court's earlier decision in Marbury v. Madison*? A century after* Martin*, a leading justice would say, "I do not believe that the United States would come to an end if we [the Supreme Court] lost our power to declare an act of Congress void. I do think the Union would be imperiled if we could not make that declaration as to the law of the several states."* Collected Legal Papers of Oliver Wendell Holmes *(1920), 295–296. Does* *this mean that Martin is a more important decision than Marbury? What would have been the consequences had the Court held the other way in the case?*

Story, for the Court:

This is a writ of error from the court of appeals of Virginia, founded upon the refusal of that court to obey the mandate of this court . . . The following is the judgment of the court of appeals rendered on the mandate: 'The court is unanimously of opinion, that the appellate power of the Supreme Court of the United States does not extend to this court, under a sound construction of the Constitution of the United States; that so much of the 25th section of the act of Congress to establish the judicial courts of the United States, as extends the appellate jurisdiction of the Supreme Court to this court, is not in pursuance of the Constitution of the United States.' . . .

Before proceeding to the principal questions, it may not be unfit to dispose of some preliminary considerations which have grown out of the arguments at the bar.

The Constitution of the United States was ordained and established, not by the states in their sovereign capacities, but emphatically, as the preamble of the Constitution declares, by 'the people of the United States.' There can be no doubt that it was competent to the people to invest the general government with all the powers which they might deem proper and necessary; to extend or restrain these powers according to their own good pleasure, and to give them a paramount and supreme authority. As little doubt can there be, that the people had a right to prohibit to the states the exercise of any powers which were, in their judgment, incompatible with the objects of the general compact; to make the powers of the state governments, in given cases, subordinate to those of the nation, or to reserve to themselves those sovereign authorities which they might not choose to delegate to either. The Constitution was not, therefore, necessarily carved out of existing state sovereignties, nor a surrender of powers already existing in state institutions, for the powers of the states depend upon their own constitutions; and the people of every state had the right to modify and restrain them, according to their own views of the policy or principle. On the other hand, it is perfectly clear that the sovereign powers vested in the state governments, by their respective constitutions, remained unaltered and unimpaired, except so far as they were granted to the government of the United States. . . .

The third article of the Constitution is that which must principally attract our attention. . . . It is the voice of the whole American people solemnly declared, in establishing one great department of that government which was, in many respects, national, and in all, supreme. It is a part of the very same instrument which was to act not merely upon individuals, but upon states; and to deprive them altogether of the exercise of some powers of sovereignty, and to restrain and regulate them in the exercise of others. . . .

This leads us to the consideration of the great question as to the nature and extent of the appellate jurisdiction of the United States. We have already seen that appellate jurisdiction is given by the Constitution to the Supreme Court in all cases where it has not original jurisdiction; subject, however, to such exceptions and regulations as Congress may prescribe. It is, therefore, capable of embracing every case enumerated in the constitution, which is not exclusively to be decided by way of original jurisdiction. But the exercise of appellate jurisdiction is far from being limited by the terms of the Constitution to the Supreme Court. There can be no doubt that Congress may create a succession of inferior tribunals, in each of which it may vest appellate as well as original jurisdiction. The judicial power is delegated by the Constitution in the most general terms, and may, therefore, be exercised by Congress under every variety of form, of appellate or original jurisdiction. And as there is nothing in the Constitution which restrains or limits this power, it must, therefore, in all other cases, subsist in the utmost latitude of which, in its own nature, it is susceptible.

As, then, by the terms of the Constitution, the appellate jurisdiction is not limited as to the Supreme Court, and as to this court it may be exercised in all other cases than those of which it has original cognizance, what is there to restrain its exercise over state tribunals in the enumerated cases? The appellate power is not limited by the terms of the third article to any particular courts. The words are, 'the judicial power (which includes appellate power) shall extend to all cases,' &c., and 'in all other cases before mentioned the supreme court shall have appellate jurisdiction.' It is the case, then, and not the court, that gives the jurisdiction. If the judicial power extends to the case, it will be in vain to search in the letter of the Constitution for any qualification as to the tribunal where it depends. It is incumbent, then, upon those who assert such a qualification to show its existence by necessary implication. If the text be clear and distinct, no restriction upon its plain and obvious import ought to be admitted, unless the inference be irresistible.

If the Constitution meant to limit the appellate jurisdiction to cases pending in the courts of the United States, it would necessarily follow that the jurisdiction of these courts would, in all the cases enumerated in the constitution, be exclusive of state tribunals. How otherwise could the jurisdiction extend to all cases arising under the constitution, laws, and treaties of the United States, or to all cases of admiralty and maritime jurisdiction? If some of these cases might be entertained by state tribunals, and no appellate jurisdiction as to them should exist, then the appellate power would not extend to all, but to some, cases. If state tribunals might exercise concurrent jurisdiction over all or some of the other classes of cases in the Constitution without control, then the appellate jurisdiction of the United States might, as to such cases, have no real existence, contrary to the manifest intent of the constitution. Under such circumstances, to give effect to the judicial power, it must be construed to be exclusive; and this not only when the *casus foederis* should arise directly, but when it should arise, incidentally, in cases pending in state courts. This construction would abridge the jurisdiction of such court far more than has been ever contemplated in any act of Congress.

On the other hand, if, as has been contended, a discretion be vested in Congress to establish, or not to establish, inferior courts at their own pleasure, and Congress should not establish such courts, the appellate jurisdiction of the Supreme Court would have nothing to act upon, unless it could act upon cases pending in the state courts. Under such circumstances it must be held that the appellate power would extend to state courts; for the Constitution is peremptory that it shall extend to certain enumerated cases, which cases could exist in no other courts. Any other construction, upon this supposition, would involve this strange contradiction, that a discretionary power vested in Congress, and which they might rightfully omit to exercise, would defeat the absolute injunctions of the Constitution in relation to the whole appellate power. . . .

But it is plain that the framers of the Constitution did contemplate that cases within the judicial cognizance of the United States not only might but would arise in the state courts, in the exercise of their ordinary jurisdiction. With this view the sixth article declares, that 'this constitution, and the laws of the United States which shall be made in pursuance thereof, and all treaties made, or which shall be made, under the authority of the United States, shall be the supreme law of the land, and the judges in every state shall be bound thereby, any thing in the constitution or laws of any state to the contrary notwithstanding.' It is obvious that this obligation is imperative upon the state judges in their official, and not merely in their private, capacities. From the very nature of their judicial duties they would be called upon to pronounce the law applicable to the case in judgment. They were not to decide merely according to the laws or constitution of the state, but according to the constitution, laws and treaties of the United States—'the supreme law of the land.' . . .

It must, therefore, be conceded that the constitution not only contemplated, but meant to provide for cases within the scope of the judicial power of the United States, which might yet depend before state tribunals. It was foreseen that in the exercise of their ordinary jurisdiction, state courts would incidentally take cognizance of cases arising under the Constitution, the laws, and treaties of the United States. Yet to all these cases the judicial power, by the very terms of the constitution, is to extend. It cannot extend by original jurisdiction if that was already rightfully and exclusively attached in the state courts, which (as has been already shown) may occur; it must, therefore, extend by appellate jurisdiction, or not at all. It would seem to follow that the appellate power of the United States must, in such cases, extend to state tribunals; and if in such cases, there is no reason why it should not equally attach upon all others within the purview of the constitution.

It has been argued that such an appellate jurisdiction over state courts is inconsistent with the genius of our governments, and the spirit of the constitution. That the latter was never designed to act upon state sovereignties, but only upon the people, and that if the power exists, it will materially impair the sovereignty of the states, and the independence of their courts. We cannot yield to the force of this reasoning; it assumes principles which we cannot admit, and draws conclusions to which we do not yield our assent. . . .

[The Constitution] is crowded with provisions which restrain or annul the sovereignty of the states in some of the highest branches of their prerogatives.

The tenth section of the first article contains a long list of disabilities and prohibitions imposed upon the states. Surely, when such essential portions of state sovereignty are taken away, or prohibited to be exercised, it cannot be correctly asserted that the Constitution does not act upon the states. The language of the constitution is also imperative upon the states as to the performance of many duties. It is imperative upon the state legislatures to make laws prescribing the time, places, and manner of holding elections for senators and representatives, and for electors of President and Vice-President. And in these, as well as some other cases, Congress have a right to revise, amend, or supersede the laws which may be passed by state legislatures. When, therefore, the states are stripped of some of the highest attributes of sovereignty, and the same are given to the United States; when the legislatures of the states are, in some respects, under the control of Congress, and in every case are, under the constitution, bound by the paramount authority of the United States; it is certainly difficult to support the argument that the appellate power over the decisions of state courts is contrary to the genius of our institutions. The courts of the United States can, without question, revise the proceedings of the executive and legislative authorities of the states, and if they are found to be contrary to the constitution, may declare them to be of no legal validity. Surely the exercise of the same right over judicial tribunals is not a higher or more dangerous act of sovereign power.

Nor can such a right be deemed to impair the independence of state judges. It is assuming the very ground in controversy to assert that they possess an absolute independence of the United States. In respect to the powers granted to the United States, they are not independent; they are expressly bound to obedience by the letter of the constitution; and if they should unintentionally transcend their authority, or misconstrue the constitution, there is no more reason for giving their judgments an absolute and irresistible force, than for giving it to the acts of the other coordinate departments of state sovereignty.

It is further argued, that no great public mischief can result from a construction which shall limit the appellate power of the United States to cases in their own courts: first, because state judges are bound by an oath to support the Constitution of the United States, and must be presumed to be men of learning and integrity; and, secondly, because Congress must have an unquestionable right to remove all cases within the scope of the judicial power from the state courts to the courts of the United States, at any time before final judgment, thought not after final judgment. As to the first reason— admitting that the judges of the state courts are, and always will be, of as much learning, integrity, and wisdom, as those of the courts of the United States, (which we very cheerfully admit,) it does not aid the argument. It is manifest that the Constitution has proceeded upon a theory of its own, and given or withheld powers according to the judgment of the American people, by whom it was adopted. We can only construe its powers, and cannot inquire into the policy or principles which induced the grant of them. The Constitution has presumed (whether rightly or wrongly we do not inquire) that state attachments, state prejudices, state jealousies, and state interests, might some times obstruct, or control, or be supposed to obstruct or control, the regular administration of justice. Hence, in controversies between states; between citizens of different states; between citizens claiming grants under different states; between a state and its citizens, or foreigners, and between citizens and foreigners, it enables the parties, under the authority of Congress, to have the controversies heard, tried, and determined before the national tribunals. . . .

This is not all. A motive of another kind, perfectly compatible with the most sincere respect for state tribunals, might induce the grant of appellate power over their decisions. That motive is the importance, and even necessity of uniformity of decisions throughout the whole United States, upon all subjects within the purview of the constitution. Judges of equal learning and integrity, in different states, might differently interpret a statute, or a treaty of the United States, or even the Constitution itself: If there were no revising authority to control these jarring and discordant judgments, and harmonize them into uniformity, the laws, the treaties, and the constitution of the United States would be different in different states, and might, perhaps, never have precisely the same construction, obligation, or efficacy, in any two states. The public mischiefs that would attend such a state of things would be truly deplorable; and it cannot be believed that they could have escaped the enlightened convention which formed the constitution. What, indeed, might then have been only prophecy, has now become fact; and the appellate jurisdiction must continue to be the only adequate remedy for such evils. . . .

[T]he appellate power of the United States does extend to cases pending in the state courts; and that the 25th section of the judiciary act, which authorizes the exercise of this jurisdiction in the specified cases, by a writ of error, is supported by the letter and spirit of the constitution. We find no clause in that instrument which limits this power; and we dare not interpose a limitation where the people have not been disposed to create one. . . .

It is the opinion of the whole court, that the judgment of the court of appeals of Virginia, rendered on the mandate in this cause, be reversed, and the judgment of the district court, held at Winchester, be, and the same is hereby affirmed.

Cohens v. Virginia

19 U.S. 264 (1821), 6-0
Opinion of the Court: Marshall (Duvall, Johnson, Livingston, Story, Todd)
Not participating: Washington
How does Marshall justify the Court's review of actions in state courts? Does his argument advancing judicial review differ at all from his reasoning in Marbury v. Madison *finding a federal law unconstitutional? How is his position similar to or different from Story's in* Martin v. Hunter's Lessee? *In what way does this decision extend the ruling in* Martin? *What theory of the Union does it embody?*

Marshall, C.J., for the Court:
The first question to be considered is, whether the jurisdiction of this Court is excluded by the character of the parties, one of them being a State, and the other a citizen of that State?

The second section of the third article of the Constitution defines the extent of the judicial power of the United States. Jurisdiction is given to the Courts of the Union in two classes of cases. In the first, their jurisdiction depends on the character of the cause, whoever may be the parties. This class comprehends 'all cases in law and equity arising under this constitution, the laws of the United States, and treaties made, or which shall be made, under their authority.' This clause extends the jurisdiction of the Court to all the cases described, without making in its terms any exception whatever, and without any regard to the condition of the party. If there by any exception, it is to be implied against the express words of the article.

In the second class, the jurisdiction depends entirely on the character of the parties. In this are comprehended 'controversies between two or more States, between a State and citizens of another State,' 'and between a State and foreign States, citizens or subjects.' If these be the parties, it is entirely unimportant what may be the subject of controversy. Be it what it may, these parties have a constitutional right to come into the Courts of the Union. . . .

The jurisdiction of the Court, then, being extended by the letter of the Constitution to all cases arising under it, or under the laws of the United States, it follows that those who would withdraw any case of this description from that jurisdiction, must sustain the exemption they claim on the spirit and true meaning of the constitution, which spirit and true meaning must be so apparent as to overrule the words which its framers have employed.

The American States, as well as the American people, have believed a close and firm Union to be essential to their liberty and to their happiness. They have been taught by experience, that this Union cannot exist without a government for the whole; and they have been taught by the same experience that this government would be a mere shadow, that must disappoint all their hopes, unless invested with large portions of that sovereignty which belongs to independent States. Under the influence of this opinion, and thus instructed by experience, the American people, in the conventions of their respective States, adopted the present constitution.

If it could be doubted, whether from its nature, it were not supreme in all cases where it is empowered to act, that doubt would be removed by the declaration, that 'this constitution, and the laws of the United States, which shall be made in pursuance thereof, and all treaties made, or which shall be made, under the authority of the United States, shall be the supreme law of the land; and the judges in every State shall be bound thereby; any thing in the constitution or laws of any State to the contrary notwithstanding.'

This is the authoritative language of the American people; and, if gentlemen please, of the American States. It marks, with lines too strong to be mistaken, the characteristic distinction between the government of the Union, and those of the States. The general government, though limited as to its objects, is supreme with respect to those objects. This principle is a part of the constitution; and if there be any who deny its necessity, none can deny its authority. . . .

The powers of the Union, on the great subjects of war, peace, and commerce, and on many others, are in themselves limitations of the sovereignty of the States; but in addition to these, the sovereignty of the States is surrendered in many instances where the surrender can only operate to the benefit of the people, and where, perhaps, no other power is conferred on Congress than a conservative power to maintain the principles established in the constitution. The maintenance of these principles in their purity, is certainly among the great duties of the government.

One of the instruments by which this duty may be peaceably performed, is the judicial department. It is authorized to decide all cases of every description, arising under the constitution or laws of the United States. From this general grant of jurisdiction, no exception is made of those cases in which a State may be a party. When we consider the situation of the government of the Union and of a State, in relation to each other; the nature of our constitution; the subordination of the State governments to that constitution; the great purpose for which jurisdiction over all cases arising under the constitution and laws of the United States, is confided to the judicial department; are we at liberty to insert in this general grant, an exception of those cases in which a State may be a party? Will the spirit of the Constitution justify this attempt to control its words? We think it will not. We think a case arising under the constitution or laws of the United States, is cognizable in the Courts of the Union, whoever may be the parties to that case. . . .

We think, then, that, as the Constitution originally stood, the appellate jurisdiction of this Court, in all cases arising under the constitution, laws, or treaties of the United States, was not arrested by the circumstance that a State was a party.

This leads to a consideration of the 11th amendment. . . .

The first impression made on the mind by this amendment is, that it was intended for those cases, and for those only, in which some demand against a State is made by an individual in the Courts of the Union. . . .

To commence a suit, is to demand something by the institution of process in a court of justice; and to prosecute the suit, is, according to the common acceptation of language, to continue that demand. . . . If a suit, brought in one Court, and carried by legal process to a supervising Court, be a continuation of the same suit, then this suit is not commenced nor prosecuted against a State. It is clearly in its commencement the suit of a State against an individual, which suit is transferred to this Court, not for the purpose of asserting any claim against the State, but for the purpose of asserting a constitutional defense against a claim made by a State. . . .

Where, then, a State obtains a judgment against an individual, and the Court, rendering such judgment, overrules a defense set up under the constitution or laws of the United States, the transfer of this record into the Supreme Court, for the sole purpose of inquiring whether the judgment violates the constitution or laws of the United States, can, with no propriety, we think, be denominated a suit commenced or prosecuted against the State whose judgment is so far re-examined. Nothing is demanded from the State. No claim against it of any description is asserted or prosecuted. The party is not to be restored to the possession of any thing. Essentially, it is an appeal on a single point; and the defendant who appeals from a judgment rendered against him, is never said to commence or prosecute a suit against the plaintiff who has obtained the judgment. . . .

It is, then, the opinion of the Court, that the defendant who removes a judgment rendered against him by a State Court into this Court, for the purpose of re-examining the question, whether that judgment be in violation of the constitution or laws of the United States, does not commence or prosecute a suit against the State, whatever may be its opinion where the effect of the writ may be to restore the party to the possession of a thing which he demands. . . .

If this writ of error be a suit in the sense of the 11th amendment, it is not a suit commenced or prosecuted 'by a citizen of another State, or by a citizen or subject of any foreign State.' It is not then within the amendment, but is governed entirely by the Constitution as originally framed, and we have already seen, that in its origin, the judicial power was extended to all cases arising under the constitution or laws of the United States, without respect to parties.

The second objection to the jurisdiction of the Court is, that its appellate power cannot be exercised, in any case, over the judgment of a State Court.

This objection is sustained chiefly by arguments drawn from the supposed total separation of the judiciary of a State from that of the Union, and their entire independence of each other. The argument considers the federal judiciary as completely foreign to that of a State; and as being no more connected with it in any respect whatever, than the Court of a foreign State. If this hypothesis be just, the argument founded on it is equally so; but if the hypothesis be not supported by the constitution, the argument fails with it. . . .

That the United States form, for many, and for most important purposes, a single nation, has not yet been denied. In war, we are one people. In making peace, we are one people. In all commercial regulations, we are one and the same people. In many other respects, the American people are one; and the government which is alone capable of controlling and managing their interests in all these respects, is the government of the Union. It is their government, and in that character they have no other. America has chosen to be, in many respects, and to many purposes, a nation; and for all these purposes, her government is complete; to all these objects, it is competent. The people have declared, that in the exercise of all powers given for these objects, it is supreme. It can, then, in effecting these objects, legitimately control all individuals or governments within the American territory. The constitution and laws of a State, so far as they are repugnant to the constitution and laws of the United States, are absolutely void. These States are constituent parts of the United States. They are members of one great empire—for some purposes sovereign, for some purposes subordinate.

In a government so constituted, is it unreasonable that the judicial power should be competent to give efficacy to the constitutional laws of the legislature? That department can decide on the validity of the constitution or law of a State, if it be repugnant to the constitution or to a law of the United States. Is it unreasonable that it should also be empowered to decide on the judgment of a State tribunal enforcing such unconstitutional law? Is it so very unreasonable as to furnish a justification for controlling the words of the constitution?

We think it is not. We think that in a government acknowledgedly supreme, with respect to objects of vital interest to the nation, there is nothing inconsistent with sound reason, nothing incompatible with the nature of government, in making all its departments supreme, so far as respects those objects, and so far as is necessary to their attainment. The exercise of the appellate power over those judgments of the State tribunals which may contravene the constitution or laws

of the United States, is, we believe, essential to the attainment of those objects. . . .

We are not restrained, then, by the political relations between the general and State governments, from construing the words of the constitution, defining the judicial power, in their true sense.

McCulloch v. Maryland

17 U.S. 316 (1819), 6-0
Opinion of the Court: Marshall (Duvall, Johnson, Livingston, Story, Washington)
Not participating: Todd

McCulloch, cashier of the Baltimore branch of the Second National Bank, was sued by Maryland when he refused to pay a tax levied by the state on certain operations of the bank.

What competing theories of (a) national power and (b) state power are argued in this case? Besides his textual interpretation of the meaning of "necessary and proper," on what does Marshall base his decision upholding national power? Does he suggest any limitations on the doctrine of implied powers? Who should determine what is "necessary and proper"? Is state taxation of a federal instrumentality necessarily destructive or challenging of national supremacy? Many years later, in Panhandle Oil v. Mississippi *(1920), Justice Oliver Wendell Holmes asserted that "power to tax is not the power to destroy as long as this Court sits." Is this an effective answer to Marshall's concern in this case? Why is this case viewed by many as the most important decision in the Court's history?*

Marshall, C.J., for the Court:
The first question made in the cause is—has Congress power to incorporate a bank?. . .

In discussing this question, the counsel for the state of Maryland have deemed it of some importance, in the construction of the constitution, to consider that instrument, not as emanating from the people, but as the act of sovereign and independent states. The powers of the general government, it has been said, are delegated by the states, who alone are truly sovereign; and must be exercised in subordination to the states, who alone possess supreme dominion. It would be difficult to sustain this proposition. The convention which framed the Constitution was indeed elected by the state legislatures. But the instrument, when it came from their hands, was a mere proposal, without obligation, or

pretensions to it. It was reported to the then existing Congress of the United States, with a request
that it might 'be submitted to a convention of delegates, chosen in each state by the people thereof,
under the recommendation of its legislature, for
their assent and ratification.' This mode of proceeding was adopted; and by the convention, by Congress, and by the state legislatures, the instrument
was submitted to the people. They acted upon it in
the only manner in which they can act safely, effectively and wisely, on such a subject, by assembling in
convention. It is true, they assembled in their several states—and where else should they have assembled? No political dreamer was ever wild enough to
think of breaking down the lines which separate the
states, and of compounding the American people
into one common mass. Of consequence, when they
act, they act in their states. But the measures they
adopt do not, on that account, cease to be the measures of the people themselves, or become the measures of the state governments.

From these conventions, the Constitution derives
its whole authority. The government proceeds directly
from the people; is 'ordained and established,' in the
name of the people; and is declared to be ordained,
'in order to form a more perfect union, establish justice, insure domestic tranquillity, and secure the blessings of liberty to themselves and to their posterity.'
The assent of the states, in their sovereign capacity, is
implied, in calling a convention, and thus submitting
that instrument to the people. But the people were at
perfect liberty to accept or reject it; and their act was
final. It required not the affirmance, and could not be
negated, by the state governments. The constitution,
when thus adopted, was of complete obligation, and
bound the state sovereignties . . .

The government of the Union, then (whatever
may be the influence of this fact on the case), is, emphatically and truly, a government of the people. In
form, and in substance, it emanates from them. Its
powers are granted by them, and are to be exercised
directly on them, and for their benefit.

This government is acknowledged by all, to be
one of enumerated powers. The principle, that it can
exercise only the powers granted to it, would seem
too apparent, to have required to be enforced by all
those arguments, which its enlightened friends, while
it was depending before the people, found it necessary to urge; that principle is now universally admitted. But the question respecting the extent of the

powers actually granted, is perpetually arising, and
will probably continue to arise, so long as our system
shall exist. In discussing these questions, the conflicting powers of the general and state governments
must be brought into view, and the supremacy of
their respective laws, when they are in opposition,
must be settled.

If any one proposition could command the universal assent of mankind, we might expect it would be
this—that the government of the Union, though limited in its powers, is supreme within its sphere of action. This would seem to result, necessarily, from its
nature. It is the government of all; its powers are delegated by all; it represents all, and acts for all. Though
any one state may be willing to control its operations,
no state is willing to allow others to control them. The
nation, on those subjects on which it can act, must
necessarily bind its component parts. But this question is not left to mere reason: the people have, in express terms, decided it, by saying, 'this constitution,
and the laws of the United States, which shall be
made in pursuance thereof,' 'shall be the supreme
law of the land,' and by requiring that the members
of the state legislatures, and the officers of the executive and judicial departments of the states, shall take
the oath of fidelity to it. The government of the
United States, then, though limited in its powers, is
supreme; and its laws, when made in pursuance of the
constitution, form the supreme law of the land, 'anything in the constitution or laws of any state to the
contrary notwithstanding.'

Among the enumerated powers, we do not find
that of establishing a bank or creating a corporation. But there is no phrase in the instrument
which, like the articles of confederation, excludes
incidental or implied powers; and which requires
that everything granted shall be expressly and
minutely described. Even the 10th amendment,
which was framed for the purpose of quieting the
excessive jealousies which had been excited, omits
the word 'expressly,' and declares only, that the
powers 'not delegated to the United States, nor prohibited to the states, are reserved to the states or to
the people;' thus leaving the question, whether the
particular power which may become the subject of
contest, has been delegated to the one government,
or prohibited to the other, to depend on a fair construction of the whole instrument. The men who
drew and adopted this amendment had experienced
the embarrassments resulting from the insertion of

this word in the articles of confederation, and probably omitted it, to avoid those embarrassments. A constitution, to contain an accurate detail of all the subdivisions of which its great powers will admit, and of all the means by which they may be carried into execution, would partake of the prolixity of a legal code, and could scarcely be embraced by the human mind. It would, probably, never be understood by the public. Its nature, therefore, requires, that only its great outlines should be marked, its important objects designated, and the minor ingredients which compose those objects, be deduced from the nature of the objects themselves. That this idea was entertained by the framers of the American constitution, is not only to be inferred from the nature of the instrument, but from the language. Why else were some of the limitations, found in the 9th section of the 1st article, introduced? It is also, in some degree, warranted, by their having omitted to use any restrictive term which might prevent its receiving a fair and just interpretation. In considering this question, then, we must never forget that it is a constitution we are expounding.

Although, among the enumerated powers of government, we do not find the word 'bank' or 'incorporation,' we find the great powers, to lay and collect taxes; to borrow money; to regulate commerce; to declare and conduct a war; and to raise and support armies and navies. The sword and the purse, all the external relations, and no inconsiderable portion of the industry of the nation, are entrusted to its government. It can never be pretended, that these vast powers draw after them others of inferior importance, merely because they are inferior. Such an idea can never be advanced. But it may with great reason be contended, that a government, entrusted with such ample powers, on the due execution of which the happiness and prosperity of the nation so vitally depends, must also be entrusted with ample means for their execution. The power being given, it is the interest of the nation to facilitate its execution. It can never be their interest, and cannot be presumed to have been their intention, to clog and embarrass its execution, by withholding the most appropriate means. Throughout this vast republic, from the St. Croix to the Gulf of Mexico, from the Atlantic to the Pacific, revenue is to be collected and expended, armies are to be marched and supported. The exigencies of the nation may require, that the treasure raised in the north should be transported to the south, that raised in the east, conveyed to the west, or that this order should be reversed. Is that construction of the Constitution to be preferred, which would render these operations difficult, hazardous and expensive? Can we adopt that construction (unless the words imperiously require it), which would impute to the framers of that instrument, when granting these powers for the public good, the intention of impeding their exercise, by withholding a choice of means? If, indeed, such be the mandate of the constitution, we have only to obey; but that instrument does not profess to enumerate the means by which the powers it confers may be executed; nor does it prohibit the creation of a corporation, if the existence of such a being be essential, to the beneficial exercise of those powers. It is, then, the subject of fair inquiry, how far such means may be employed.

It is not denied, that the powers given to the government imply the ordinary means of execution. That, for example, of raising revenue, and applying it to national purposes, is admitted to imply the power of conveying money from place to place, as the exigencies of the nation may require, and of employing the usual means of conveyance. But it is denied, that the government has its choice of means; or, that it may employ the most convenient means, if, to employ them, it be necessary to erect a corporation. . . .

The power of creating a corporation, though appertaining to sovereignty, is not, like the power of making war, or levying taxes, or of regulating commerce, a great substantive and independent power, which cannot be implied as incidental to other powers, or used as a means of executing them. It is never the end for which other powers are exercised, but a means by which other objects are accomplished. No contributions are made to charity, for the sake of an incorporation, but a corporation is created to administer the charity; no seminary of learning is instituted, in order to be incorporated, but the corporate character is conferred to subserve the purposes of education. No city was ever built, with the sole object of being incorporated, but is incorporated as affording the best means of being well governed. The power of creating a corporation is never used for its own sake, but for the purpose of effecting something else. No sufficient reason is, therefore, perceived, why it may not pass as incidental to those powers which are expressly given, if it be a direct mode of executing them.

But the Constitution of the United States has not left the right of Congress to employ the necessary means, for the execution of the powers conferred on the government, to general reasoning. To its enumeration of powers is added, that of making 'all laws which shall be necessary and proper, for carrying into execution the foregoing powers, and all other powers vested by this constitution, in the government of the United States, or in any department thereof.' . . .

But the argument on which most reliance is placed, is drawn from that peculiar language of this clause. Congress is not empowered by it to make all laws, which may have relation to the powers conferred on the government, but such only as may be 'necessary and proper' for carrying them into execution. The word 'necessary' is considered as controlling the whole sentence, and as limiting the right to pass laws for the execution of the granted powers, to such as are indispensable, and without which the power would be nugatory. That it excludes the choice of means, and leaves to Congress, in each case, that only which is most direct and simple.

Is it true, that this is the sense in which the word 'necessary' is always used? Does it always import an absolute physical necessity, so strong, that one thing to which another may be termed necessary, cannot exist without that other? We think it does not. If reference be had to its use, in the common affairs of the world, or in approved authors, we find that it frequently imports no more than that one thing is convenient, or useful, or essential to another. To employ the means necessary to an end, is generally understood as employing any means calculated to produce the end, and not as being confined to those single means, without which the end would be entirely unattainable. Such is the character of human language, that no word conveys to the mind, in all situations, one single definite idea; and nothing is more common than to use words in a figurative sense. Almost all compositions contain words, which, taken in a their rigorous sense, would convey a meaning different from that which is obviously intended. It is essential to just construction, that many words which import something excessive, should be understood in a more mitigated sense—in that sense which common usage justifies. The word 'necessary' is of this description. It has not a fixed character, peculiar to itself. It admits of all degrees of comparison; and is often connected with other words, which increase or diminish the impression the mind receives of the urgency it imports. A thing may be necessary, very necessary, absolutely or indispensably necessary. To no mind would the same

idea be conveyed by these several phrases. The comment on the word is well illustrated by the passage cited at the bar, from the 10th section of the 1st article of the constitution. It is, we think, impossible to compare the sentence which prohibits a state from laying 'imposts, or duties on imports or exports, except what may be absolutely necessary for executing its inspection laws,' with that which authorizes Congress 'to make all laws which shall be necessary and proper for carrying into execution' the powers of the general government, without feeling a conviction, that the convention understood itself to change materially the meaning of the word 'necessary,' by prefixing the word 'absolutely.' This word, then, like others, is used in various senses; and, in its construction, the subject, the context, the intention of the person using them, are all to be taken into view.

Let this be done in the case under consideration. The subject is the execution of those great powers on which the welfare of a nation essentially depends. It must have been the intention of those who gave these powers, to insure, so far as human prudence could insure, their beneficial execution. This could not be done, by confiding the choice of means to such narrow limits as not to leave it in the power of Congress to adopt any which might be appropriate, and which were conducive to the end. This provision is made in a constitution, intended to endure for ages to come, and consequently, to be adapted to the various crises of human affairs. To have prescribed the means by which government should, in all future time, execute its powers, would have been to change, entirely, the character of the instrument, and give it the properties of a legal code. It would have been an unwise attempt to provide, by immutable rules, for exigencies which, if foreseen at all, must have been seen dimly, and which can be best provided for as they occur. To have declared, that the best means shall not be used, but those alone, without which the power given would be nugatory, would have been to deprive the legislature of the capacity to avail itself of experience, to exercise its reason, and to accommodate its legislation to circumstances. . . .

That this could not be intended, is . . . too apparent for controversy . . . The clause is placed among the powers of Congress, not among the limitations on those powers. Its terms purport to enlarge, not to diminish the powers vested in the government. It purports to be an additional power, not a restriction on those already granted. . . .

The result of the most careful and attentive consideration bestowed upon this clause is, that if it does not enlarge, it cannot be construed to restrain the powers of Congress, or to impair the right of the legislature to exercise its best judgment in the selection of measures to carry into execution the constitutional powers of the government. If no other motive for its insertion can be suggested, a sufficient one is found in the desire to remove all doubts respecting the right to legislate on that vast mass of incidental powers which must be involved in the Constitution, if that instrument be not a splendid bauble.

We admit, as all must admit, that the powers of the government are limited, and that its limits are not to be transcended. But we think the sound construction of the Constitution must allow to the national legislature that discretion, with respect to the means by which the powers it confers are to be carried into execution, which will enable that body to perform the high duties assigned to it, in the manner most beneficial to the people. Let the end be legitimate, let it be within the scope of the constitution, and all means which are appropriate, which are plainly adapted to that end, which are not prohibited, but consist with the letter and spirit of the Constitution, are constitutional. . . .

If a corporation may be employed, indiscriminately with other means, to carry into execution the powers of the government, no particular reason can be assigned for excluding the use of a bank, if required for its fiscal operations. To use one, must be within the discretion of Congress, if it be an appropriate mode of executing the powers of government. That it is a convenient, a useful, and essential instrument in the prosecution of its fiscal operations, is not now a subject of controversy. . . .

But were its necessity less apparent, none can deny its being an appropriate measure; and if it is, the decree of its necessity, as has been very justly observed, is to be discussed in another place. Should Congress, in the execution of its powers, adopt measures which are prohibited by the constitution; or should Congress, under the pretext of executing its powers, pass laws for the accomplishment of objects not entrusted to the government; it would become the painful duty of this tribunal, should a case requiring such a decision come before it, to say, that such an act was not the law of the land. But where the law is not prohibited, and is really calculated to effect any of the objects entrusted to the government, to undertake here to in-

quire into the decree of its necessity, would be to pass the line which circumscribes the judicial department, and to tread on legislative ground. This court disclaims all pretensions to such a power. . . .

After the most deliberate consideration, it is the unanimous and decided opinion of this court, that the act to incorporate the Bank of the United States is a law made in pursuance of the Constitution, and is a part of the supreme law of the land. . . .

It being the opinion of the Court, that the act incorporating the bank is constitutional; and that the power of establishing a branch in the state of Maryland might be properly exercised by the bank itself, we proceed to inquire:

Whether the state of Maryland may, without violating the constitution, tax that branch? That the power of taxation is one of vital importance; that it is retained by the states; that it is not abridged by the grant of a similar power to the government of the Union; that it is to be concurrently exercised by the two governments—are truths which have never been denied. But such is the paramount character of the constitution, that its capacity to withdraw any subject from the action of even this power, is admitted. The states are expressly forbidden to lay any duties on imports or exports, except what may be absolutely necessary for executing their inspection laws. If the obligation of this prohibition must be conceded—if it may restrain a state from the exercise of its taxing power on imports and exports—the same paramount character would seem to restrain, as it certainly may restrain, a state from such other exercise of this power, as is in its nature incompatible with, and repugnant to, the constitutional laws of the Union. A law, absolutely repugnant to another, as entirely repeals that other as if express terms of repeal were used.

On this ground, the counsel for the bank place its claim to be exempted from the power of a state to tax its operations. There is no express provision for the case, but the claim has been sustained on a principle which so entirely pervades the constitution, is so intermixed with the materials which compose it, so interwoven with its web, so blended with its texture, as to be incapable of being separated from it, without rending it into shreds. This great principle is, that the Constitution and the laws made in pursuance thereof are supreme; that they control the constitution and laws of the respective states, and cannot be controlled by them. From this, which may be almost termed an axiom, other propositions are deduced as corollaries, on the truth or error of which, and on their application to this case, the cause has been supposed to depend. These are, 1st. That a power to create implies a power to preserve: 2d. That a power to destroy, if wielded by a different hand, is hostile to, and incompatible with these powers to create and to preserve: 3d. That where this repugnancy exists, that authority which is supreme must control, not yield to that over which it is supreme. . . .

The power of Congress to create, and of course, to continue, the bank, was the subject of the preceding part of this opinion; and is no longer to be considered as questionable. That the power of taxing it by the states may be exercised so as to destroy it, is too obvious to be denied. But taxation is said to be an absolute power, which acknowledges no other limits than those expressly prescribed in the constitution, and like sovereign power of every other description, is entrusted to the discretion of those who use it. . . .

The argument on the part of the state of Maryland, is, not that the states may directly resist a law of Congress, but that they may exercise their acknowledged powers upon it, and that the Constitution leaves them this right, in the confidence that they will not abuse it. . . .

That the power to tax involves the power to destroy; that the power to destroy may defeat and render useless the power to create; that there is a plain repugnance in conferring on one government a power to control the constitutional measures of another, which other, with respect to those very measures, is declared to be supreme over that which exerts the control, are propositions not to be denied. But all inconsistencies are to be reconciled by the magic of the word confidence. Taxation, it is said, does not necessarily and unavoidably destroy. To carry it to the excess of destruction, would be an abuse, to presume which, would banish that confidence which is essential to all government. But is this a case of confidence? Would the people of any one state trust those of another with a power to control the most insignificant operations of their state government? We know they would not. Why, then, should we suppose, that the people of any one state should be willing to trust those of another with a power to control the operations of a government to which they have confided their most important and most valuable interests? In the legislature of the Union alone, are all represented. The legislature of

the Union alone, therefore, can be trusted by the people with the power of controlling measures which concern all, in the confidence that it will not be abused. This, then, is not a case of confidence, and we must consider it is as it really is.

If we apply the principle for which the state of Maryland contends, to the constitution, generally, we shall find it capable of changing totally the character of that instrument. We shall find it capable of arresting all the measures of the government, and of prostrating it at the foot of the states. The American people have declared their constitution and the laws made in pursuance thereof, to be supreme; but this principle would transfer the supremacy, in fact, to the states. If the states may tax one instrument, employed by the government in the execution of its powers, they may tax any and every other instrument. They may tax the mail; they may tax the mint; they may tax patent-rights; they may tax the papers of the custom-house; they may tax judicial process; they may tax all the means employed by the government, to an excess which would defeat all the ends of government. This was not intended by the American people. They did not design to make their government dependent on the states. . . .

The question is, in truth, a question of supremacy; and if the right of the states to tax the means employed by the general government be conceded, the declaration that the constitution, and the laws made in pursuance thereof, shall be the supreme law of the land, is empty and unmeaning declamation. . . .

It has also been insisted, that, as the power of taxation in the general and state governments is acknowledged to be concurrent, every argument which would sustain the right of the general government to tax banks chartered by the states, will equally sustain the right of the states to tax banks chartered by the general government. But the two cases are not on the same reason. The people of all the states have created the general government, and have conferred upon it the general power of taxation. The people of all the states, and the states themselves, are represented in Congress, and, by their representatives, exercise this power. When they tax the chartered institutions of the states, they tax their constituents; and these taxes must be uniform. But when a state taxes the operations of the government of the United States, it acts upon institutions created, not by their own constituents, but by people over whom they claim no control. It acts upon the measures of a government created by others as well as themselves, for the benefit of others in common with themselves. The difference is that which always exists, and always must exist, between the action of the whole on a part, and the action of a part on the whole—between the laws of a government declared to be supreme, and those of a government which, when in opposition to those laws, is not supreme. . . .

The Court has bestowed on this subject its most deliberate consideration. The result is a conviction that the states have no power, by taxation or otherwise, to retard, impede, burden, or in any manner control, the operations of the constitutional laws enacted by Congress to carry into execution the powers vested in the general government. This is, we think, the unavoidable consequence of that supremacy which the Constitution has declared. We are unanimously of opinion, that the law passed by the legislature of Maryland, imposing a tax on the Bank of the United States, is unconstitutional and void.

This opinion does not deprive the states of any resources which they originally possessed. It does not extend to a tax paid by the real property of the bank, in common with the other real property within the state, nor to a tax imposed on the interest which the citizens of Maryland may hold in this institution, in common with other property of the same description throughout the state. But this is a tax on the operations of the bank, and is, consequently, a tax on the operation of an instrument employed by the government of the Union to carry its powers into execution. Such a tax must be unconstitutional.

Barron v. Baltimore

32 U.S. 243 (1833), 7-0
Opinion of the Court: Marshall (Baldwin, Duvall, Johnson, McLean, Story, Thompson)
Does the text of the Constitution give the Court all the information it needs to decide this case? Does Marshall look outside the Constitution? Is the decision consistent with the intent of Congress in recommending the Bill of Rights amendments to the Constitution? Is the decision consistent with the nationalism evident in so many of Marshall's other opinions? Though the case involved damage to realty, what bearing does the decision have on the issues surrounding slavery?

Marshall, C. J., for the Court:
The Constitution was ordained and established by the people of the United States for themselves, for their own government, and not for the government of the individual states. Each state established a constitution for itself, and in that constitution, provided such limitations and restrictions on the powers of its particular government, as its judgment dictated. The people of the United States framed such a government for the United States as they supposed best adapted to their situation and best calculated to promote their interests. The powers they conferred on this government were to be exercised by itself; and the limitations on power, if expressed in general terms, are naturally, and, we think, necessarily, applicable to the government created by the instrument. They are limitations of power granted in the instrument itself; not of distinct governments, framed by different persons and for different purposes.

If these propositions be correct, the fifth amendment must be understood as restraining the power of the general government, not as applicable to the states. . . .

The counsel for [Barron] insists, that the Constitution was intended to secure the people of the several states against the undue exercise of power by their respective state governments; as well as against that which might be attempted by their general government. It support of this argument he relies on the inhibitions contained in the tenth section of the first article. We think, that section affords a strong, if not a conclusive, argument in support of the opinion already indicated by the court. The preceding section contains restrictions which are obviously intended for the exclusive purpose of restraining the exercise of power by the departments of the general government. Some of them use language applicable only to Congress; others are expressed in general terms. The third clause, for example, declares, that 'no bill of attainder or ex post facto law shall be passed.' No language can be more general; yet the demonstration is complete, that it applies solely to the government of the United States. In addition to the general arguments furnished by the instrument itself, some of which have been already suggested, the succeeding section, the avowed purpose of which is to restrain state legislation, contains in terms the very prohibition. It declares, that 'no state shall pass any bill of attainder or ex post facto law.' This provision, then, of the ninth section, however comprehensive its language, contains no restriction on state legislation.

The ninth section having enumerated, in the nature of a bill of rights, the limitations intended to be imposed on the powers of the general government, the tenth proceeds to enumerate those which were to operate on the state legislatures. These restrictions are brought together in the same section, and are by express words applied to the states. 'No state shall enter into any treaty,' &c. Perceiving, that in a constitution framed by the people of the United States, for the government of all, no limitation of the action of government on the people would apply to the state government, unless expressed in terms, the restrictions contained in the tenth section are in direct words so applied to the states. . . .

If the original constitution, in the ninth and tenth sections of the first article, draws this plain and marked line of discrimination between the limitations it imposes on the powers of the general government, and on those of the state; if, in every inhibition intended to act on state power, words are employed, which directly express that intent; some strong reason must be assigned for departing from this safe and judicious course, in framing the amendments, before that departure can be assumed. We search in vain for that reason.

Had the people of the several states, or any of them, required changes in their constitutions; had they required additional safe-guards to liberty from the apprehended encroachments of their particular governments; the remedy was in their own hands, and could have been applied by themselves. A convention could have been assembled by the discontented state, and the required improvements could have been made by itself. The unwieldy and cumbrous machinery of procuring a recommendation from two-thirds of Congress, and the assent of three-fourths of their sister states, could never have occurred to any human being, as a mode of doing that which might be effected by the state itself. Had the framers of these amendments intended them to be limitations on the powers of the state governments, they would have imitated the framers of the original constitution, and have expressed that intention. Had Congress engaged in the extraordinary occupation of improving the constitutions of the several states, by affording the people additional protection from the exercise of power by their own governments, in matters which concerned themselves alone, they

would have declared this purpose in plain and intelligible language.

But it is universally understood, it is a part of the history of the day, that the great revolution which established the constitution of the United States, was not effected without immense opposition. Serious fears were extensively entertained, that those powers which the patriot statesmen, who then watched over the interests of our country, deemed essential to union, and to the attainment of those invaluable objects for which union was sought, might be exercised in a manner dangerous to liberty. In almost every convention by which the Constitution was adopted, amendments to guard against the abuse of power were recommended. These amendments demanded security against the apprehended encroachments of the general government—not against those of the local governments. In compliance with a sentiment thus generally expressed, to quiet fears thus extensively entertained, amendments were proposed by the required majority in Congress, and adopted by the states. These amendments contain no expression indicating an intention to apply them to the state governments. This court cannot so apply them.

We are of opinion, that the provision in the fifth amendment to the constitution, declaring that private property shall not be taken for public use, without just compensation, is intended solely as a limitation on the exercise of power by the government of the United States, and is not applicable to the legislation of the states. We are, therefore, of opinion, that there is no repugnancy between the several acts of the general assembly of Maryland, given in evidence by the defendants at the trial of this cause, in the court of that state, and the constitution of the United States. This court, therefore, has no jurisdiction of the cause, and it is dismissed.

Luther v. Borden

48 U.S. 1 (1849), 8-1
Opinion of the Court: Taney (Catron, Daniel, Grier, McKinley, McLean, Nelson, Wayne)
Dissenting: Woodbury

This case was a trespass action against Borden for breaking into Luther's house. Borden, a member of the state militia, argued that Luther had been in insurrection against the state government and the entry was therefore lawful for the purpose of searching and arresting of Luther. Luther argued that the government under which Borden acted had been displaced and annulled by the people of the state and, consequently, it was Borden who in arms against lawful authority.

Exactly what is a "political question"? Is the term apt or misleading? How else might the doctrinal principle of the case be described? What reasons does Taney give for declaring that it is Congress and not itself that should decide whether a state has a republican form of government? Is the Constitution clear on this question? Are courts not competent to decide such matters or are they simply not the best branch for doing so? Can Taney's decision be reconciled with Marshall's statement in Marbury v. Madison *that it is the responsibility of the judiciary to say what the law is?*

Taney, C.J., for the Court:

The evidence shows that the defendants, in breaking into the [Luther's] house and endeavoring to arrest him, as stated in the pleadings, acted under the authority of the government which was established in Rhode Island at the time of the Declaration of Independence, and which is usually called the charter government. For when the separation from England took place, Rhode Island did not, like the other States, adopt a new constitution, but continued the form of government established by the charter of Charles the Second in 1663; making only such alterations, by acts of the legislature, as were necessary to adapt it to their condition and rights as an independent State. . . .

In this form of government no mode of proceeding was pointed out by which amendments might be made. It authorized the legislature to prescribe the qualification of voters, and in the exercise of this power the right of suffrage was confined to freeholders, until the adoption of the constitution of 1843. . . .

[T]he question presented is certainly a very serious one: For, if this court is authorized to enter upon this inquiry as proposed by [Luther], and it should be decided that the charter government had no legal existence during the period of time above mentioned—if it had been annulled by the adoption of the opposing government—then the laws passed by its legislature during that time were nullities; its taxes wrongfully collected; its salaries and compensation to its officers illegally paid; its public accounts improperly settled; and the judgments and sentences of its courts in civil and criminal cases null and void, and the officers who carried their decisions into operation answerable as trespassers, if not in some cases as criminals.

When the decision of this court might lead to such results, it becomes its duty to examine very carefully its own powers before it undertakes to exercise jurisdiction.

Certainly, the question which [Luther] proposed to raise by the testimony he offered has not heretofore been recognized as a judicial one in any of the State courts. . . .

Moreover, the Constitution of the United States, as far as it has provided for an emergency of this kind, and authorized the general government to interfere in the domestic concerns of a State, has treated the subject as political in its nature, and placed the power in the hands of that department.

The fourth section of the fourth article of the Constitution of the United States provides that the United States shall guarantee to every State in the Union a republican form of government, and shall protect each of them against invasion; and on the application of the legislature or of the executive (when the legislature cannot be convened) against domestic violence.

Under this article of the Constitution it rests with Congress to decide what government is the established one in a State. For as the United States guarantee to each State a republican government, Congress must necessarily decide what government is established in the State before it can determine whether it is republican or not. And when the senators and representatives of a State are admitted into the councils of the Union, the authority of the government under which they are appointed, as well as its republican character, is recognized by the proper constitutional authority. And its decision is binding on every other department of the government, and could not be questioned in a judicial tribunal. It is true that the contest in this case did not last long enough to bring the matter to this issue; and as no senators or representatives were elected under the authority of the government of which Mr. Dorr was the head, Congress was not called upon to decide the controversy. Yet the right to decide is placed there, and not in the courts.

So, too, as relaters to the clause in the above-mentioned article of the Constitution, providing for cases of domestic violence. It rested with Congress, too, to determine upon the means proper to be adopted to fulfill this guarantee. They might, if they had deemed it most advisable to do so, have placed it in the power of a court to decide when the contingency had happened which required the federal government to interfere. But Congress thought otherwise, and no doubt wisely; and by the act of February 28, 1795, provided, that, 'in case of an insurrection in any State against the government thereof, it shall be lawful for the President of the United States, on application of the legislature of such State or of the executive (when the legislature cannot be convened), to call forth such number of the militia of any other State or States, as may be applied for, as he may judge sufficient to sufficient to suppress such insurrection.'

By this act, the power of deciding whether the exigency had arisen upon which the government of the United States is bound to interfere, is given to the President. He is to act upon the application of the legislature or of the executive, and consequently he must determine what body of men constitute the legislature, and who is the governor, before he can act. The fact that both parties claim the right to the government cannot alter the case, for both cannot be entitled to it. If there is an armed conflict, like the one of which we are speaking, it is a case of domestic violence, and one of the parties must be in insurrection against the lawful government. And the President must, of necessity, decide which is the government, and which party is unlawfully arrayed against it, before he can perform the duty imposed upon him by the act of Congress.

After the President has acted and called out the militia, is a Circuit Court of the United States authorized to inquire whether his decision was right? Could the court, while the parties were actually contending in arms for the possession of the government, call witnesses before it and inquire which party represented a majority of the people? If it could, then it would become the duty of the Court (provided it came to the conclusion that the President had decided incorrectly) to discharge those who were arrested or detained by the troops in the service of the United States or the government which the President was endeavoring to maintain. If the judicial power extends so far, the guarantee contained in the Constitution of the United States is a guarantee of anarchy, and not of order. Yet if this right does not reside in the courts when the conflict is raging, if the judicial power is at that time bound to follow the decision of the political, it must be equally bound when the contest is over. It cannot, when peace is restored, punish as offenses and crimes the acts which it before recognized, and was bound to recognize, as lawful.

It is true that in this case the militia were not called out by the President. But upon the application of the governor under the charter government, the President recognized him as the executive power of the State, and took measures to call out the militia to support his authority if it should be found necessary for the general government to interfere; and it is admitted in the argument, that it was the knowledge of this decision that put an end to the armed opposition to the charter government, and prevented any further efforts to establish by force the proposed constitution. The interference of the President, therefore, by announcing his determination, was as effectual as if the militia had been assembled under his orders. And it should be equally authoritative. For certainly no court of the United States, with a knowledge of this decision, would have been justified in recognizing the opposing party as the lawful government; or in treating as wrongdoers or insurgents the officers of the government which the President had recognized, and was prepared to support by an armed force. In the case of foreign nations, the government acknowledged by the President is always recognized in the courts of justice. And this principle has been applied by the act of Congress to the sovereign States of the Union.

It is said that this power in the President is dangerous to liberty, and may be abused. All power may be abused if placed in unworthy hands. But it would be difficult, we think, to point out any other hands in which this power would be more safe, and at the same time equally effectual. When citizens of the same State are in arms against each other, and the constituted authorities unable to execute the laws, the interposition of the United States must be prompt, or it is of little value. The ordinary course of proceedings in courts of justice would be utterly unfit for the crisis. And the elevated office of the President, chosen as he is by the people of the United States, and the high responsibility he could not fail to feel when acting in a case of so much moment, appear to furnish as strong safeguards against a willful abuse of power as human prudence and foresight could well provide. At all events, it is conferred upon him by the Constitution and laws of the United States, and must therefore be respected and enforced in its judicial tribunals. . . .

Undoubtedly, if the President in exercising this power shall fall into error, or invade the rights of the people of the State, it would be in the power of Congress to apply the proper remedy. But the courts must administer the law as they find it. . . .

Much of the argument on the part of [Luther] turned upon political rights and political questions, upon which the Court has been urged to express an opinion. We decline doing so. The high power has been conferred on this court of passing judgment upon the acts of the State sovereignties, and of the legislative and executive branches of the federal government, and of determining whether they are beyond the limits of power marked out for them respectively by the Constitution of the United States. This tribunal, therefore, should be the last to overstep the boundaries which limit its own jurisdiction. And while it should always be ready to meet any question confided to it by the Constitution, it is equally its duty not to pass beyond its appropriate sphere of action, and to take care not to involve itself in discussions which properly belong to other forums. No one, we believe, has ever doubted the proposition, that, according to the institutions of this country, the sovereignty in every State resides in the people of the State, and that they may alter and change their form of government at their own pleasure. But whether they have changed it or not by abolishing an old government, and establishing a new one in its place, is a question to be settled by the political power. And when that power has decided, the courts are bound to take notice of its decision, and to follow it.

5

SLAVERY AND CIVIL WAR

Conflict and Compromise

Forced labor of one sort or another was a central element of permanent settlement in the New World. Though African slaves had been sold to Virginia colonists as early as 1619, white indentured servants met intermittent labor shortages through most of the seventeenth century. Only after European indentures declined, were Africans imported in large numbers. By the Revolution, slavery was present in all 13 colonies, though only in the tobacco-growing upper South and the rice-growing lower region was it economically profitable. It was phased out in northern states in the two decades following the Revolution, partly for economic reasons and partly because of growing moral concerns. Many slaveholders in the upper South believed the system's days were numbered in that region as well. Manumissions—freeing of slaves by their owners—increased almost yearly.

Slavery and the Constitution

Though most delegates at Philadelphia opposed slavery, any attempt in the Constitution to abol-ish it would probably have ended all chance for a national union. The Constitution recognized slavery but did not mention it by name, which for some delegates was a way of opposing its permanence. Slaves were "all other persons" in Article I-2 and "persons held to service in labor" in Article IV-2. The slave trade was the "migration or importation" of persons in Article I-9. Most delegates, including many Southerners, believed that slavery would gradually be ended except possibly in Georgia and South Carolina, as it had been in northern states—by state law or economic dictate.

Twice impasses were resolved through compromises. In the first, slavery was allowed to remain a state or local matter simply by not granting the central government power over it. An exception was the African slave trade. Though Article I-9 forbade Congress from ending that trade before 1808, most delegates assumed, correctly, that its 20-year lease on life would not be extended. Congress ended it at first opportunity, though smuggling of slaves continued right to the Civil War.

The second—how slaves were to be counted in the apportioning of seats in the House of

Representatives and the levying of direct taxes among the states—was more difficult and had longer-run consequence. Many Southerners argued for a full counting in apportioning the House but no counting in apportioning direct taxes or capitations (head taxes). The bare-faced inconsistency of holding slaves to be property for one purpose and persons for another did not trouble Southern logic. Many Northerners took the opposite position. The result was the three-fifths clause, in which slaves were counted in 60 percent of their numbers for both apportionments. This formula was not new—it had been discussed in Congress four years before in connection with asking taxes of states in proportion to population. The coupling of capitations here with direct taxes to be apportioned by population was a victory for Southern delegates who feared a future Congress might place a prohibitive tax on slaves as property as a way of emancipating them.

One other aspect of slavery—what to do about fugitives or runaways—was dealt with in Article IV-2. Escaped slaves were to be returned to the "party to whom . . . service or labor may be due." But the powers or obligations this gave the central government were not spelled out and the matter later became one of great conflict. One question not addressed—whether the national government had power over slavery in acquired territories—became the country's leading constitutional issue in the antebellum period.

The New Political Economy of Slavery

Though a few slaves became house servants, nurses, drivers, millworkers, and skilled craftsmen, the vast majority toiled as field hands, planting and harvesting tobacco and rice. The economic utility of slavery was tied to those staples and so appeared limited. In fact, with soil depletion widespread, much of the southern economy was stagnant. This all changed quickly and radically with Eli Whitney's invention of the cotton engine or "gin" in 1793. The machine

simply but ingeniously separated cotton fibers from cottonseed by means of wire-toothed cylinders rotating in opposite directions. It was 50 times faster than tedious separating by hand, which had made large-scale cotton growing uneconomical. Cotton suddenly became immensely profitable and planting spread quickly throughout the South. Since that depended on intensive field labor, it also revitalized slavery.

In a few years, the South was the world's leading supplier of cotton, feeding northern mills and a huge British textile industry alike. By the 1850s cotton accounted for more than half the value of the nation's exports. The boom dashed any hope that slavery would soon die out. The slave population, estimated at 500,000 at the Revolution, was counted at 698,000 in the first national census in 1790. By 1820, it was 1,538,000, more than doubling in 30 years. In the South, slaves were a third of the population.

The profitability of cotton and exhaustion of soil in many older areas of the South spurred movement of planters westward to the Mississippi and beyond. This advance, part of the great westward expansion of the entire country in the second quarter of the nineteenth century, also meant the spread of slavery, earlier assumed to be contained. Opposition to slavery grew in northern and western states, based on moral objections and a new perception of it as a threat to free labor.

Ironically, the marching cotton economy hurt the South as a region in the longer run. The sustained boom committed Southerners to preserving and extending slavery and blocked development of a diversified economy. Planters continued to invest their profits in more land and more slaves, largely ignoring opportunities in manufacturing, shipping, banking, and other commerce. True, maximum profits were not the primary goal for many slaveowners, who saw northern industrial materialism as inferior to a slower paced, more genteel (for them at least) way of life. But the result was that by midcentury, the South economically lagged far behind the North. The disparity, perhaps as much as any other factor, contributed to its defeat in the Civil War.

The Missouri Crisis

Identity of the cotton economy with the southern regions gave the slave issue its hard geopolitical edge and helped make it unique in American politics. A powerful economic interest based on forced labor coincided with a sectional cleavage. Earlier balances at the national level grew unstable as new states were admitted to the Union. After Louisiana's entry as a slaveholding state in 1812, Missouri, which also permitted slavery, was the next territory from the vast tract acquired from France in 1803 to ask admission. Of 22 states in the Union in 1820, 11 were slave-holding and 11 not. Members of Congress from free northern and western states argued that Missouri should be admitted only if slavery were forbidden. Southerners contended that Congress had no constitutional power to place conditions on new states, which had the same freedom of action as the original 13 and, thus, could permit or disallow slavery as they chose.

The debate dragged on for four months in an atmosphere of growing mutual resentment. The deadlock might have continued even longer had not Maine, formerly a part of Massachusetts, also applied for statehood. Because the North had blocked Missouri, the South opposed Maine as a free state. Early in 1820, Henry Clay of Kentucky brokered an agreement that become known as the Missouri Compromise. The two territories would be admitted, Missouri with slavery, but the remaining Louisiana Territory north of the southern border of Missouri—the latitudinal line 36 degrees, 30 seconds—would forever be closed to slavery. Though the agreement brought slavery further north than in any new state before, Northerners won two main concessions: closure of more than 80 percent of the remaining Louisiana Purchase to slavery and, by that fact, acknowledgment that Congress had power to forbid slavery in the territories.

Yet, the Compromise was more truce than lasting settlement. It dealt with extension and containment rather than the underlying issue of slavery itself. For the next 30 years, the Compromise, though having no greater legal status than ordinary legislation, was treated more like a Constitutional amendment—a formula for balancing the national government between slave states and free. Before the arrangement unraveled in the 1850s, six new states had been admitted: Arkansas (1836), Texas (1845), and Florida (1845) with slavery; Michigan (1837), Iowa (1846), and Wisconsin (1848), without.

The Issue Nationalized

Because the issue of slavery in the territories and thus in future states seemed resolved, many believed the entire slavery question could be calmed and not again divide the nation. The Jacksonians, who relied on northern and southern support, had a keen interest in diffusing the issue and were more or less successful in keeping it out of national politics. The nullification crisis, which dangerously invoked the same economic questions and sectional energies that underlay slavery, had not been about slavery. It was successfully compromised, chiefly by a material redistribution—the lowering of tariff rates. But the idea that slavery could long be kept off the national agenda was a political chimera. Those hoping it might failed to see that the slave economy in the South and the capitalist-driven free labor economy in the North and West were not static systems. Their steeply rising trajectories were, in fact, on a collision course. Nor did the diffusers fully grasp the growing moral antipathy to slavery. In its aversion to legal or material compromises, that temper was to be a great destabilizing force in American politics.

The Abolitionist Movement

Sentiment for complete emancipation could be found throughout the eighteenth century and

Ideas of the Iron Man

Harriet Martineau, the astute nineteenth century English observer of American society, once described John C. Calhoun as "the cast-iron man, who looks as if he had never been born and never could be extinguished."* Tall, gaunt, with deep-set piercing eyes and a shock of iron-gray hair that in later years seemed to come out of his head in all directions like a lion's mane, Calhoun looked the other-worldly part. He had twice been vice president, once secretary of state, and for 17 years represented South Carolina in the Senate. Except for James Madison, he was probably the most original political thinker America has produced. He had been the chief theorist of nullification in the 1830s, but his more mature thought lies in two works published after his death in 1850, *A Disquisition on Government* and *A Discourse on the Constitution and Government of the United States.* Together, they are the philosophical undergirding of the Southern position on the Constitution and slavery.

Like Madison, he saw human beings as pursuing their personal ends, forming groups or factions, then coalitions, then, in a democracy, a majority that would hold power and govern. But where Madison saw safety in faction checking faction in a vast country and in the flexible, shifting majorities of republican government, Calhoun saw the possibility that a national majority formed around a great discovered common interest could become permanent and oppress the minority. Calhoun believed Madison's theory was flawed and that the system based on it had broken down. The North had found a common economic and social interest at the expense of the South, and because it was a majority, ordinary democracy would allow it to pursue that interest and leave the South helpless.

The solution, Calhoun believed, was a structural modification of the constitutional system, one that would "give to each division or interest, through its appropriate organ, either a concurrent voice in making and executing the laws or a veto on their execution."[†] He called this arrangement rule by the "concurrent majority" as opposed to that of the numerical majority. Since American society was divided into two sectional interests, the concurrent majority could be given simple effect by each electing a president having a veto over national legislation. In terms of political acceptability, the idea was an absurdity. But on another plane, it exposed long-felt misgivings about majority rule and touched something responsive in the American political sensibility. A correlative of the concurrent principle—the requirement of extraordinary majorities—already had a place in the constitutional system in the two-thirds needed for

gained strength during the Revolution. But it was not mobilized as a militant force until the founding of the American Antislavery Society in the 1830s by a group of whites and free blacks. Like so many other moral crusades in American history—temperance, women's rights (in the nineteenth and early twentieth centuries), pacifism, civil rights in the 1960s, and right to life—the abolitionist movement was nourished by religious revivalism and appeals to a fundamentalist Christian conscience. Its leaders were a varied and impressive group: the preacher Lyman Beecher; the agitator-editor William Lloyd Garrison, publisher of The Liberator; the intellectual critic and former slave Frederick Douglass; and the orator Wendell Phillips.

Congress to recommend a constitutional amendment, the three-quarters needed for its ratification by the states, and the two-thirds vote needed to override a presidential veto or convict for impeachment. The same logic was present in such in-house rules as the 60 percent requirement to close debate in the Senate.

Calhoun's analysis also anticipated the fuller development of interest group pluralism in the United States. At different times powerful interests or coalitions—labor, banks, farmers, segregationists, environmentalists, the "gun lobby," for example—have been able to exercise at least partial "vetoes" over national policies favored by numerical majorities.

Though designed to serve the immediate political ends of the South as a section, Calhoun's scheme was firmly attached to a view of society and its members that was congenial with the planter class he represented. He departed from Lockean individualism and natural rights so prominent in most American thinking about politics to argue that men and women everywhere live in societies and draw their rights only from societies, which are thus able to keep selfish individual pursuits in bounds. Within societies, individuals and classes were inherently unequal. The best organized societies recognized this and were stratified accordingly; the upper ranks, which produce great culture, lived off the backs of others. This was the natural order of things, and African slavery was but one example of it. Because the South's system of patriarchal slavery was based on a sense of community, it was more humane than the uncaring "wage slavery" of the North. Calhoun believed the economic and social system of the North, with its underlying atomistic individualism, would eventually be fractured by violent conflict between capital and labor. His emphasis on class tensions and their relation to economic organization led the political historian Richard Hofstadter to call him the "Marx of the mas-

ter class" and to suggest that Calhoun might have seen a common front of Northern conservatives and Southern reactionaries, in which the South would be a balance wheel against Northern labor agitation.[‡] But there is little evidence Calhoun sought such an alliance; he clearly would have felt uncomfortable in one.

Calhoun and Marx alike overestimated the revolutionary inclination of workers, the one fearfully, the other out of hope. Neither recognized the resilience of capitalism or that vast numbers of laborers would be brought into its affluent fold. Calhoun mistook the unrest and vulgarity of the Jacksonian period as a sign of coming upheaval. He failed to see that the democratizing of capitalism through new political and economic freedoms would make revolution improbable and draw a line between the vital North and the static South every bit as sharp as slavery itself. The North, stimulated by invention and industry and fortified by immigration, was prospering and filling up territory and marketplace alike. No concurrent majority veto would be allowed to stem that tide.

Though Calhoun was able to point to theoretical problems in Madisonian pluralism and majority rule, the minority for which he spoke was a unique geosocial one, a planter aristocracy that controlled and claimed to speak for a section in defense of its culture and its privileges.

[*] *Retrospect of Western Travel* (New York, 1838), vol I, 144–145, quoted in Merrill D. Peterson, *The Great Triumvirate: Webster, Clay and Calhoun* (New York: Oxford University Press, 1987), 236.
[†] Richard K. Cralle, ed., *John C. Calhoun, A Disquisition on Government* (New York: P. Smith, 1963), 23.
[‡] *The American Political Tradition* (New York: Vintage Books, 1959), 68–92.

Egged on by Garrison, abolitionists flooded the country, north and south, with antislavery propaganda. The barrage was polarizing, touching sympathetic chords and stirring moral indignation but also generating antagonism, which sometimes turned violent as when an abolitionist editor was murdered in Alton, Ill. In the South, where abolitionist literature was seen as

incendiary, reaction was uniformly harsh. Abolitionist agents were expelled, and one state, Georgia, made publication of material tending to incite slaves a capital offense. In 1835, the federal postmaster in Charleston, S.C., impounded a boatload of abolitionists tracts, which were later seized by a mob and burned. The U.S. Postmaster General Amos Kendall, though publicly declaring he had no power to keep abolitionist literature from the mails, privately urged local Southern postmasters to intercept it, saying, "We owe an obligation to the laws, but a higher one to the communities in which we live."*

Taking advantage of the First Amendment right to "petition the government for redress of grievances," abolitionists sent a stream of petitions to Congress calling for emancipation. They found an eloquent champion in former President John Quincy Adams, now serving in the House. When Adams disrupted business by insisting on reading the petitions on the floor, the House adopted a rule automatically tabling them. Many northerners supported the rule either because they believed Congress had no power to deal with slavery (even though some petitions called for an end to slave trade in the District of Columbia) or because they believed political harmony was more important. The "gag" rule remained in effect for eight years. Like many other attempts to silence political criticism or troubling opposition, before and since, the effort produced a backlash in public opinion and the rule was repealed in 1844. Though nothing came of the petitions legislatively, they heightened public awareness of the South's oppressive defense of slavery.

As the abolitionist movement grew, so did disagreements within it over the Constitution. A small, nationalist group held that slavery violated the guarantee of a republican form of government in Article IV-4 and the due process protection of "liberty" in the Fifth Amendment. A larger, moderate group, led by the Ohioan Salmon P. Chase, a future chief justice of the Supreme Court, accepted the Southern view that the Constitution gave the federal government no power to abolish slavery, but insisted on the corollary that it gave that government no power to establish or protect it either. Their strategy was one of containment—slavery should be kept out of the territories. This done, it would gradually

wither and die in the South. This position later merged with that of the Free Soilers and, later still, became a chief tenet of the Republican Party. For a third, radical group, led by Garrison and Phillips, any cooperation with institutions tolerating slavery was profane. Since the Constitution recognized slavery, they disavowed "the covenant with death." Garrison, who in a celebrated incident had publicly burnt a copy of the Constitution, called for northern states to secede from the Constitutional union.

Though abolitionists helped many slaves escape to freedom through the Underground Railroad and were important in gaining passage of state "personal liberty" laws, their chief influence was on attitudes and public opinion. By focusing on the moral wrongs of slavery, they raised the consciousness of much of the country. Their aggressive certitude kept the slavery issue before the country and on the political agenda at every level of government at a time when many leaders wanted it out of sight. Casting the issue as one of right and wrong, they also made compromise or other political resolution more difficult and eventual rupture of the Union more likely.

Fugitive Slaves

Runaway slaves escaping to free states raised one of the most vexing moral and political issues. For the slaveholding South, the matter was simply one of strayed property that, like other lost possessions, should be returned to rightful owners. But recapture of fugitives brought the South's errant institution dramatically into free northern communities.

The mandate in Article IV-2 for the return of escaped slaves left it unclear whether rendition was the responsibility of the federal government or the states. Because the clause appears in Article IV, which deals mainly with matters of interstate comity, and because Article I-8, setting out the granted powers of Congress, makes no reference to slavery, it could be argued that enforcement was a charge on the states. Congress

---

* Quoted in Forrest McDonals, *A Constitutional History of the United States* (New York: Franklin Watts, 1982), 112.

tried to clarify matters in the Fugitive Slave Act of 1793 by providing that runaways to other states might be seized by slaveowners or their agents and then brought before a state or federal court. Rendition would be ordered on proof of identity and ownership. By the inclusion of state courts, the act made state officials agents of enforcement.

For a while the law worked without difficulty, but as the number of fugitives increased, thanks in part to the Underground Railroad, slaveholders demanded more stringent rules. The repeated extension of slavery's arm into free states and the local sympathy for the escapees it produced put pressure on state officials not to cooperate in recaptures. Starting in the 1820s, many northern states passed personal liberty laws, requiring jury trials on the question of title and giving certain procedural rights to the seized fugitives. Where local antislavery sentiment was strong, these provisions often prevented slaveowners from making successful cases. Illegal acts were commonplace. Slave-catchers, unable to find the runaway, sometimes kidnapped free black citizens and took them South. In several spectacular incidents, fugitives who had been legally seized or were being legally returned, were "rescued" by mobs sometimes using violence.

Enforcement of the Constitution's mandate for rendition gave slavery extraterritorial effect. Here, officially at least, preservation of the slave system prevailed over state and local laws and public opinion supporting freedom. This produced a striking reversal of traditional constitutional positions. The South, believing the runaway problem could be solved only through strong federal action, took a stand for broad constitutional construction and against states rights. The North, trying to confine slavery, preferred to limit federal power and invigorate that of the states. The turnaround proved again the utilitarian relativism of the ideas of states rights and of broad versus strict constitutional construction. Each side was willing to forgo its traditional constitutional reading to defend important interests.

The stronger fugitive slave law enacted as part of the Compromise of 1850 met even more resistance and heightened sectional tensions right to the eve of the war. It also moved Harriet Beecher Stowe to depict sensationally the trials of slave life and ordeal of escape in *Uncle Tom's Cabin,* which in a few years sold an astonishing 1,200,000 copies. Though lacking great literary merit, it was probably the most politically effective novel ever written. On meeting Stowe during the Civil War, Lincoln is said to have remarked, "So you're the little woman who made this big war."*

In the Supreme Court

The legality of the African trade was the first aspect of slavery ruled on by the nation's highest court. A Spanish slave ship *The Antelope* had been captured by pirates near the North American coast. The pirates and the slave ship were later seized by an American revenue cutter and brought to Savannah. The incident raised questions of international law and of the fate of the enslaved Africans on board. Speaking for the Court in *The Antelope* in 1821, Chief Justice Marshall wrote that though the slave trade was "contrary to the laws of nature," it was not then inconsistent with the laws of nations. But since importation of slaves into the United States was now illegal, he ordered those Africans who appeared headed for American sale returned to their homeland; the others were remitted to their Spanish owners. Thus the Court permitted the prosecution of American traders but did not interfere with the slave trade of those countries in which it was legal.

The trade issue arose again several years later in a different form. Africans on the Spanish slaver *Amistad* had mutinied and killed most of the crew. The ship drifted into waters off Long Island and was seized by an American

---

* Herbert Mitgang, ed., *Abraham Lincoln: A Press Portrait* (Chicago, 1971), quoted in James M. McPherson, *Battle Cry of Freedom, The Civil War Era* (New York: Oxford University Press, 1988), 90.

naval vessel. In *United States v. The Amistad* in 1841, Justice Story held that since slavery was now illegal under Spanish law, the Africans could neither be tried for murder in American courts nor extradited to Spain. They were entitled to be freed and repatriated. Abolitionists, who had gotten John Quincy Adams to take the case before the Court, made it a *cause celebre*. They began educating the captives and converted several to Christianity. But ironically the leader of the mutiny, Joseph Cinqué, became himself a slavetrader after returning to Africa.

Two other cases in the early 1840s forced the Court to confront interstate trade of slaves and the fugitive slave question. Hoping to prevent an outflow of capital, Mississippi had amended its constitution to bar the purchase of slaves from other states. In *Groves v. Slaughter,* 1841, a default action on a contract for an out-of-state slave raised constitutional issues. The decision, resting on a technicality—the amendment could not be applied because the legislature had provided no way of enforcing it—was less important than the nervous concurring and dissenting opinions it produced.

Justice John McLean, a former politician with abiding presidential ambitions and the only member of the Court with abolitionist views, argued that a state could prevent the importing of slaves through its police power. What this point implied about containment of slavery was obvious and provoked other justices to state their opinions. Justice Henry Baldwin took nearly the opposite view: A state had no power to prevent the importing of slaves from other states because the federal government alone had authority over interstate commerce. But the mere suggestion of federal exclusivity was threatening to slaveholding interests, who feared an antislavery majority in Congress might exploit it (and the slaveholders' argument that slaves were property) to bar interstate slave trade. Partly for this reason, proslavery Chief Justice Roger Taney, was led to counter Baldwin: State power over

the ingress and egress of slaves was exclusive of federal involvement. The Court's inability to agree on constitutional issues or even silently avoid them reflected the lack of post-Marshall leadership and deep divisions among the justices themselves.

A year later in *Prigg v. Pennsylvania* (p. 164), the Court ruled on the constitutionality of the 1793 Fugitive Slave Act and of Pennsylvania's personal liberty law. Prigg, a professional slave-catcher, had followed and seized a Maryland fugitive and her children in Pennsylvania. He applied to a local magistrate for a certificate of removal, which was denied because of either higher evidentiary standards of the state law or simple antislavery bias. Prigg then returned the runaway to Maryland anyway. He was charged and found guilty of kidnapping in Pennsylvania.

Story's opinion of the Court, taken with six others filed in the case, showed again how the constitutional questions of slavery could remain muddied when the complexities of a federal system were before a divided Court. Story held the mandate of Article IV-2 gave the federal government exclusive power over fugitive slaves. Thus the 1793 Act was constitutional and Pennsylvania's law, by adding new conditions, was not. Had he stopped there, the decision would have been an important victory for slaveholding interests. But Story added that states could not be forced to take part in a federal fugitive slave program. In a concurrence, Taney argued that the fugitive slave law assumed the help of state officers, because too few federals were available for the police, magisterial, and detention work called for by recapture and rendition. He correctly predicted the free states would use the ruling to frustrate recaptures. The decision was hard to characterize as pro- or antislavery; Prigg was freed, but neither side was sure who had won. The case helped to nationalize and further polarize the fugitive slave issue.

Five years later, the 1793 Act was unsuccessfully challenged in *Jones v. Van Zandt*, 1847, a civil action against a "conductor" on the Underground Railroad for the value of fugitives he helped escape. The Court's decision is notable for its rejection of an appeal to conscience and its placement of positive law—rules made through duly constituted authority—above natural law or purely moral considerations. Justice Levi Woodbury, a New Englander and Story's successor, speaking for a unanimous Court, declared that the fugitive slave clause in Article IV-2 had been one of the "sacred compromises" in the Constitution, essential to the South's entry into the Union. The justices had no choice, Woodbury wrote, "but to stand by the Constitution and laws with fidelity to their duties and oaths." (46 U.S. 215 at 231) Whatever a judge's views of the morality of slavery, he could not refuse to uphold the law.

The sojourner aspect of slavery arose in the 1851 case of *Strader v. Graham,* a civil action against the operator of a ferry for helping three slaves escape from Kentucky to Ohio, where slavery had been banned in the Northwest Ordinance of 1787. In his defense, Strader argued that since their owner had several times allowed the slaves to go to Ohio to perform in minstrels, they were no longer slaves after they returned to Kentucky. The theory was rejected by Kentucky courts. On appeal, the Supreme Court, through Taney, refused jurisdiction, holding that the status of the blacks was a matter of state law to be decided by state courts alone. But then Taney added an ominous dictum. The laws of Kentucky could not be controlled by those of Ohio, nor could the Northwest Ordinance, enacted by the Confederation Congress and supposedly outlawing slavery forever in the territory from which Ohio and four other states had been formed, be controlling either. Its antislavery provision had no effect after the area was carved into states. The nationalizing proslavery implication of this dictum, deeply unsettling to many northerners, was a hint of worse to come from the Court.

That the Court was asked to address aspects of slavery was not unexpected. But its decisions were hardly satisfactory; they settled little and left much unclear. The Court cannot be faulted for being divided, since much of the country was itself. The difficulty lay, instead, in the nature of judicial power. The slavery question had become irrevocably politicized by the 1850s and had begun to cut deeper than the consensual underpinnings of the political system. Under such circumstances, resolution was almost certainly beyond the competence of courts, which, without army or treasury, must rely on the consensual appeal of legal and moral authority. The rent in the American union caused by slavery was so deep that even the stark bargaining resources of politics would not make it whole again. Yet the Court recognized little of this. Its increasingly proslavery stand—by which it tried to impose a strongly held minority's position on a strongly held majority's—was exactly the wrong one.

Southwest Expansion

The westward imperative was a main force in American life almost from the first day of settlement. Driven by quest for material profit, concern about national security, and a belief in an American providential mission, territorial expansion had become an all but irresistible force by the second quarter of the nineteenth century. Geopolitically, it was the nation's "manifest destiny" to push through to the Pacific and fill a continent. In 1819, Florida (72,000 square miles) had been acquired in a treaty with Spain. Between 1845 and 1853, four other acquisitions—the Texas annexation, the Oregon Territory through a treaty with Great Britain, the Mexican cession through conquest, and the Gadsden Purchase from Mexico—added 1,234,000 more square miles, increasing the size of the United States by two-thirds and bringing it to its present continental limits. Politico-economic consequences of this expansion for constitutional development are explored in Chapter 7; how expansion helped bring the question of slavery and Union to its final crisis is dealt with here.

The Texas Question

After independence from Spain in the 1820s, the new government of Mexico encouraged American immigration into the sparsely populated reaches of Texas, west of the Louisiana border. Within a decade, American settlers, who were mainly from Southern states, outnumbered resident Tejanos. Most brought slaves with them, though slavery had been made illegal under Mexican law. These facts, combined with incompetent Mexican local administration, created tension between the settlers and militarist central government under General Santa Ana in Mexico City. Chaotic fighting broke out in 1835 and, later, through the efforts of Stephen Austin, a provisional Texas government was set up. At first it called only for independent statehood within Mexico, but when that was rejected in Mexico City, full independence was declared in 1836. Santa Ana then led an army against the insurgents and won a costly victory at the Alamo in San Antonio, but was later defeated and captured by a main force of Texans under Sam Houston, in the Battle of San Jacinto.

Houston was elected president of the new republic of Texas, though voters made it clear they favored eventual annexation by the United States. Presidents Jackson and Van Buren opposed annexation, fearing it would bring on a war with Mexico and stir up strong antislavery opposition in the free states. For the next eight years, Texas remained an independent nation. Concern about British machinations in the Southwest and growing enthusiasm for expansion renewed the annexation issue and made it the center of the 1844 election. James K. Polk, a dark horse who favored annexation, edged out Van Buren for the Democratic nomination and defeated the Whig Henry Clay, who had equivocated on the issue. This "referendum" divided

both national parties, creating strains from which neither fully recovered. Many northern Democrats left the party and many Southern Whigs moved into it, leaving the party system dangerously congruent with sectional politics.

Texas obtained statehood in 1845, soon after Polk's inauguration, but not without an important constitutional debate. At first, antislavery opponents claimed the United States lacked constitutional authority to annex an independent nation. Previous annexations—the Louisiana Purchase territory and the Floridas—were areas that had been colonial dependencies of foreign powers. Weighed against this argument was the sweeping dictum Marshall had issued 17 years earlier in *American Insurance Co. v. Canter,* a case in which the constitutionality of the Floridas annexation had been an issue. In giving the government war and treatymaking powers, Marshall said, the Constitution recognized the power to acquire territory "either by conquest or by treaty." This authority was rooted in the existence of national government itself.

The constitutional debate is noteworthy also because Southerners like Calhoun, traditional advocates of strictly limiting national power; and Hamiltonian broad constructionists like Daniel Webster and John Quincy Adams; switched positions, reflecting again the imperatives of political interest. Views on the slavery question could overcome the most nicely held constitutional philosophy.

Regardless of the constitutional argument, annexation appeared to be doomed, since the president's treatymaking power in Article II-2 called for the concurrence of two-thirds of the Senate. An earlier annexation treaty negotiated by President John Tyler in 1844 had been voted down. But the following year, proponents got around the two-thirds requirement by proposing Texas not be annexed as a territory, as Louisiana and the Floridas had been, but be admitted directly as a state under Article IV-3, which gives Congress power to admit new states by ordinary legislation and so by simple majority vote. Opponents argued that a treaty was needed because Texas, as an independent nation, raised an issue of foreign affairs. Mexico, in fact, had warned that annexation would be interpreted as an act of war.

At the heart of all this, of course, was the slavery issue. Direct admission to statehood meant that Congress could not interfere with the legality of slavery in Texas. With admission of Louisiana in 1812, the principle of equality among the states was extended to new states. Whatever were the rights and privileges of existing states, including the right to have slavery (or to abolish it), so too were those of new states. Though the principle of new state equality is not addressed in the Constitution, the Supreme Court, starting with *Permoli v. New Orleans* and *Holland v. Hagan* in 1845, had treated it as though it were an inherent attribute of the federal union. Proponents of direct annexation to statehood prevailed, and Texas was admitted to the Union in 1845 as a slave state by joint resolution, that is, by a simple majority vote in both House and Senate. Though the new state lay well below the Missouri Compromise line, efforts to contain slavery had suffered a big setback.

War With Mexico

American relations with Mexico were problematic almost from the day of its independence. The government in Mexico City was weak and unstable and, though republican in form, dominated by militarists. It had never recognized Texas independence and after annexation it foolishly prepared to retake the territory. When clashes occurred in the disputed area between the Nueces and the Rio Grande early in 1846, Congress declared war. In nearly two years of fighting, American forces occupied the disputed Texas territory, cleared much of what is now New Mexico, captured California, and with General Winfield Scott's landing at Vera Cruz and march inland, occupied Mexico City. The expansionist Polk proved an aggressive war president, having deployed forces even before the declaration of war. Opponents of the war seized

on this action to raise unsuccessfully what later became an enduring constitutional issue: the power of the president to act on his own as commander in chief.

Support for the war had many footings. Besides fear for the safety of Texas, there was worry that Mexico might allow Great Britain to establish itself on the Pacific coast or possibly even transfer California to Britain in exchange for debt forgiveness. War was also an opportunity to expand in the southwest, perhaps all the way to the Pacific, and so give new meaning to "manifest destiny." Romantics like Walt Whitman and James Fenimore Cooper saw the war as a mission to carry American ideals to the world. Many proslavery southerners saw it, like Texas annexation, as an unusual chance to extend and thus better defend slavery. Abolitionists and many other northerners opposed to slavery were convinced the war was a slaveholders' conspiracy.

In the Treaty of Guadalupe Hidalgo, which ended the war early in 1848, Mexico recognized the loss of Texas south to the Rio Grande and ceded California and vast reaches of what is now the Southwest—in all more than 500,000 square miles. From this territory eventually came California, Arizona, New Mexico, Nevada, Utah, and parts of Wyoming, Colorado, Kansas, and Oklahoma. In return, the United States assumed all claims of its citizens against Mexico and paid Mexico $15,000,000 to help it achieve long-term financial stability. Whether slavery would be allowed in the new lands was debated even before the war was over, as the stakes of the slavery question were raised to new heights.

The Backlash

In August 1846, a few months after the war began when it was already clear the United States would gain much of northern Mexico, David Wilmot, an obscure Democratic Congressman from Pennsylvania, introduced an amendment to a war appropriations bill. It proposed to outlaw slavery in any territory gained in the war. Though similar to the antislavery provision in the Northwest Ordinance of 1787 and thus hardly innovative, it was nonetheless a political bombshell. Passed by the House, it met defeat in the Senate. Though there were later attempts to attach similar riders to other appropriations bills, the Wilmot Proviso, as these measures came to be called, never found its way into law. Still, it became a rallying cry for Free Soilers and abolitionists in the North and West.

The debate created a problem for the South. Since Congress had earlier admitted slavery to some territories and banned it from others, why could it not also legislate on the Mexican lands? Though the South had strongly argued for federal authority over fugitive slaves, it now took a different tack, fearing new introductions of the Wilmot Proviso. Led by their chief constitutional theoretician, Calhoun, Southerners now argued that Congress had no power to bar slavery in the territories but had a duty to protect it there. Lost in all of this was the old 36-30 line of the Missouri Compromise and the principle of balance between new free and new slave states. Both sides were now dissatisfied with that settlement, and each tried, defensively, to make its own position national. In the meantime, the Wilmot Proviso split the Democratic Party along sectional lines and cost it the election of 1848 when General Zachary Taylor, a hero of the war, was elected president as a Whig.

The Decade of Strife

The territorial question raised by the Mexican Cession was only one of several slavery issues demanding attention. California was so extensively settled that it was ready for statehood without going through the territorial stage. The South was concerned that since its settlers had rejected slavery, California's admission as a free state would upset the balance in the Senate. Agitation to end slave trade in the District of Columbia, over which Congress had undisputed authority, continued to grow. And the South persisted in its demand for a stronger fugitive slave law.

A New Settlement

In the face of mounting sectional antagonism, Henry Clay, the "Great Compromiser," now serving in the Senate, introduced a series of resolutions early in 1850. The chief parts were: California would be admitted as a free state; slave trade would be abolished in the District of Columbia; a much stronger fugitive slave law would include federal machinery for recapture and rendition; on the all-important territorial question, the new Utah and New Mexico regions would be organized as territories and once an area attained the needed population, it would achieve statehood "with or without slavery, as its constitution may prescribe," at the time of admission. These enacted provisions became known as the Compromise of 1850.

Congressional "silence" on the territorial question avoided inclusion of a Wilmot Proviso, which would have made the Compromise totally unacceptable to the South. By leaving the legality of slavery to "popular sovereignty," the Compromise tried to localize the issue and, in doing so, preserve national harmony. Tactically ingenious, it challenged neither the moderate Northern view that slavery was illegal in the territories unless made legal by positive enactment, nor the moderate Southern view that slavery followed the flag and was legal until made illegal by positive enactment. But did it really settle anything? Some farsighted members of Congress, such as Salmon Chase in the North and Alexander Stephens in the South, thought not and that the day of reckoning was yet to come. But first, the popular sovereignty formula would be tested.

The fugitive slave law was the most immediately explosive part of the new mix. By increasing federal responsibility, it aimed at more rigorous enforcement, at the same time avoiding flashpoints of local resistance that often occurred when reliance was on state authorities. But the tougher law also encouraged seizures, some occurring under pitiable circumstances, and loaded the legal dice against the runaway. All of this generated new Northern antagonism.

The South had not yet learned that the best way to quiet agitation was to let Northerners forget about slavery rather than throw it in their faces by hunting down fugitives in their streets and countrysides. Instead, the South was growing increasingly confident about using the threat of secession as a political instrument.

Except for determined abolitionists in the North and radical secessionists in the South, the Compromise of 1850 was widely accepted as the "final" or "permanent" solution to the slavery question. Each side got something important, and the public seemed relieved to have the country's most divisive issue out of the way. Both major parties, Whigs and Democrats, endorsed it in the election of 1852. The Free Soil Party, which did not, fared poorly, its presidential candidate receiving less that five percent of the vote.

Yet, partly obscured by optimism and hope of the moment, an important realignment of perceptions and ideas was taking place. As the historian David Potter observed, "Without embracing secession, the South had committed itself to the principle of secessionism; without embracing abolition, the North had committed itself to the principle of abolitionism." *

The Kansas Conflict

By 1853, with the Gadsden Purchase from Mexico, expansion of the United States to its present continental limits was complete. In 1846, northwest differences with Great Britain were settled by a treaty in which the United States took undisputed possession of the Oregon Territory from which the states of Washington, Oregon, and Idaho would later come. A transcontinental railroad was now an imperative, giving rise to a political battle over its route. The chief possibilities were a central course from Chicago to San Francisco and a southern one from New Orleans to Los Angeles. Ordinarily this sort of question, like that of locating a state capital, would be settled by the "normal" politics of material tradeoffs and adjustments. But this one was laid upon sectional differences, which meant it would be held captive to the slavery question.

To win support for the central route, which would have a commercially valuable terminus in his own state, Senator Stephen A. Douglas of Illinois introduced a bill early in 1854 to organize parts of the remaining Louisiana Purchase into two territories, Kansas and Nebraska. To win Southern support, he also proposed that in the lower of the two, the legality of slavery would be decided by "popular sovereignty," that is, by the settlers alone. Since both territories were north of the 36-30 latitudinal line represented by the southern border of Missouri and thus under the Missouri Compromise were to be free of slavery, the proposal was politically explosive.

Passed after three months of acrimonious debate, the Kansas-Nebraska Act expressly repealed the Missouri Compromise. To antislavery Northerners, the new law was a betrayal and a big step backward; slavery could now be brought to any of the new territories if approved locally. Popular sovereignty—government by the people—had almost been invented by Americans and served as a cornerstone of the Revolution and constitutional government. Here it was a code name for federal nonintervention. Ironically, if allowed to have one voice across the entire nation, popular sovereignty might well have outlawed slavery for the country. Now the hallowed principle was devolved to the territorial level where local vote could choose to make slavery legal.

Many historians have criticized Douglas as reckless and questioned his motives. He did speculate in western land and stood to profit personally by a central route for the railroad. More importantly, he had presidential ambitions and could easily believe the Kansas-Nebraska formula would capture the middle political ground. He was also convinced slavery would not be economical in most of the central and northern territories, and thus opponents of slavery really had

---

* David M. Potter, *The Impending Crisis 1848–1860* (New York: Harper and Row, 1976), 143–144.

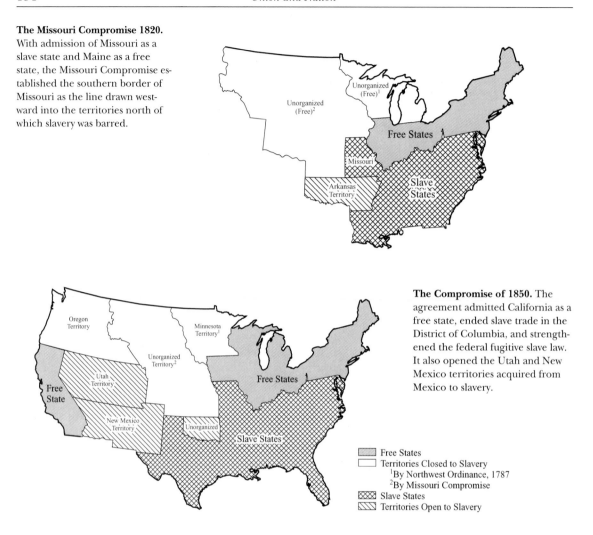

The Missouri Compromise 1820.
With admission of Missouri as a slave state and Maine as a free state, the Missouri Compromise established the southern border of Missouri as the line drawn westward into the territories north of which slavery was barred.

The Compromise of 1850. The agreement admitted California as a free state, ended slave trade in the District of Columbia, and strengthened the federal fugitive slave law. It also opened the Utah and New Mexico territories acquired from Mexico to slavery.

Figure 5.1 Three Compromises and a Decision: The Legality of Slavery in the Territories

little to worry about. But many others who knew that individual slaves had been trained for all sorts of skilled work believed that slavery could possibly be profitably adapted to growing grain on the prairie, mining ore in the Rockies, or ranching in the Southwest. Whether Douglas was right about the inexpedience of slavery, he deeply believed popular sovereignty was the only way to head off secession and war.

Whatever the assessment, the Kansas-Nebraska Act was a great miscalculation. Rather than removing the slavery question from the national agenda by devolving it, it stirred reaction to a new national intensity. The Act was another nail—nearly the final one—in the coffin of politics. Protests and demonstrations took place throughout the North, often focusing on what was closest at hand, enforcement of the new fugitive slave law.

Events in Kansas itself were appalling. Proslavery settlers and "visitors" flocked in from Missouri while antislavery or "free staters" came or were shipped in from different parts of the North, to win the race for "popular sovereignty." By late 1855, an antislavery government had

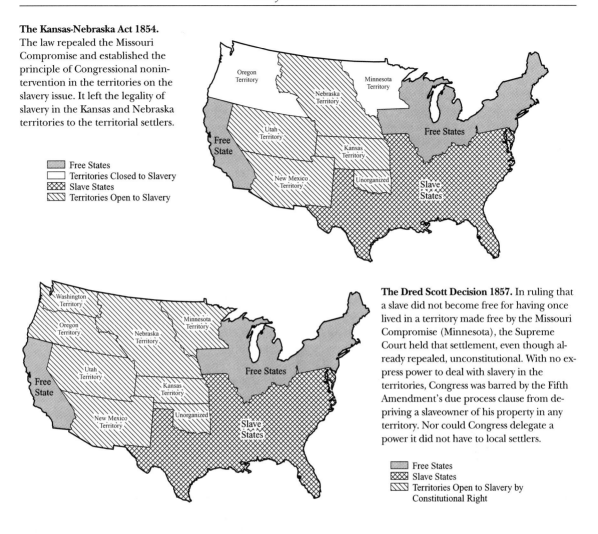

The Kansas-Nebraska Act 1854.
The law repealed the Missouri Compromise and established the principle of Congressional nonintervention in the territories on the slavery issue. It left the legality of slavery in the Kansas and Nebraska territories to the territorial settlers.

Free States
Territories Closed to Slavery
Slave States
Territories Open to Slavery

The Dred Scott Decision 1857. In ruling that a slave did not become free for having once lived in a territory made free by the Missouri Compromise (Minnesota), the Supreme Court held that settlement, even though already repealed, unconstitutional. With no express power to deal with slavery in the territories, Congress was barred by the Fifth Amendment's due process clause from depriving a slaveowner of his property in any territory. Nor could Congress delegate a power it did not have to local settlers.

Free States
Slave States
Territories Open to Slavery by Constitutional Right

Figure 5.1 Three Compromises and a Decision: The Legality of Slavery in the Territories (*Continued*)

been set up in Topeka and a proslavery one in Lecompton. Sporadic fighting broke out and, at one point, more than 1,000 Missouri "border ruffians" sacked Lawrence, an antislavery stronghold. A few days later the abolitionist religious fanatic John Brown murdered several proslavery settlers in retaliation. Fighting continued among roving bands right up to the Civil War, for which "bleeding Kansas," as the abolitionist press called it, was an all too apt rehearsal. In 1857, settlers voted down a proslavery constitution endorsed by President Buchanan, even

though it meant the territory might be denied statehood indefinitely.

The tear in the political fabric was symbolized by a disgraceful event in Washington. Senator Charles Sumner, a Whig and the first out-and-out abolitionist to sit in the upper house, was clubbed senseless by a Southern congressman, Preston Brooks, as Sumner sat helpless in his Senate seat. Sumner, a brilliantly articulate but often unpleasant personality whose role in the Senate was mainly agitational, had made a particularly intemperate speech. The beating left

Sumner permanently impaired, but he was instantly transformed into a northern martyr. Southerners rallied to Brooks's "defense of Southern honor," he resigned his seat in the House, but was later unanimously reelected by his district.

The Republican Party

The events in Kansas hastened the breakup and recombination of the party system. After the Kansas-Nebraska Act, most Southern Whigs either joined the Democratic Party or abstained from politics. In the North, a series of mass meetings in midwestern states, the most important in Ripon, Wis., brought together Whigs, Free Soilers, and disaffected Democrats. Out of these deliberations came proposals for the formation of a new party, later named the Republican. Among its leaders were Whigs like William Seward of New York, former Democrats like Salmon Chase of Ohio, and abolitionists like Sumner. Their political common ground rested on two constitutional principles. First, slavery could not exist where it was not allowed by positive law. This meant that it could be recognized in the South but nowhere else unless affirmatively enacted. Thus the territories were to be free from day one, which meant few slaveholders would risk bringing slaves into them at all. Second, the federal government was completely divorced from the slavery question. It had no power to establish, protect, or even abolish slavery; only states and local government could do that. This would mean the end of fugitive slave laws and give freedom for slaves escaping from the South. This constitutional ideology gave the party no chance of winning the slightest support in the South. It was a northern and western sectional party, and as such, further polarized the politics of the day.

The Democrats tilted further and further to an exclusively Southern point of view, despite the continued presence of northerners like Douglas. In 1856, the Democrat Buchanan, a Northerner with Southern sympathies, won a three-way race against the first Republican candidate, General John C. Fremont, who got a third of the popular vote and carried 11 of the 31 states, and the former president, Millard Fillmore, who finished a poor third on the American (Know Nothing) Party ticket. The South, in which there had been talk of secession if Fremont won, now saw that Calhoun's nightmare might be at hand: The North and West were populous enough that a determined antislavery majority could form and elect a Northern candidate to the presidency without Southern support.

The Nadir of the Presidency and the Court

In Buchanan, the nation got exactly what it elected—a Northerner who believed the chief problem dividing the country was not slavery but the agitation over slavery. His embarrassing support for the rejected proslavery Kansas constitution was consistent with his view that a territorial legislature could not prohibit slavery. Though he had been an experienced cabinet officer, diplomat, and Senator, he was a plodding and unimaginative president who opposed secession but was too politically flabby to deal with the deepening crisis. It was Buchanan who, as president elect, had learned in a private communication from his friend, Justice John Catron, that the Supreme Court was going to turn the relatively unimportant case of *Scott v. Sandford* into a great proslavery decision holding the Missouri Compromise unconstitutional. At Catron's request, Buchanan privately pressured his fellow Pennsylvanian, Justice Robert Grier, to go along with it. Knowing what the outcome would be, Buchanan made political use of the information in his inaugural address. Holding out hope that the Court would soon settle the slavery question, one way or the other, he declared "to their decision, in common with all good citizens, I shall cheerfully submit."*

---

* James D. Richardson, ed., *A Compilation of the Messages and Papers of the Presidents* (New York: 1897–1917), vol VII, 2,962, quoted in Harold M. Hyman and William M. Wiecek, *Equal Justice Under Law, 1835–1875* (New York: Harper and Row, 1982), 179.

In the 1830s the slave Dred Scott had accompanied his master, John Emerson, a Missouri army doctor, to successive postings in Illinois, a free state, and to Fort Snelling in what is now Minnesota in the northern part of the Louisiana Purchase, free territory under the Missouri Compromise. In 1840, he returned to Missouri with Emerson. Years later, after Emerson's death, Scott sued his widow for his freedom, alleging he had become free by having lived in a free state and a free territory. Though he won in a lower Missouri court, the state supreme court reversed on authority of *Strader v. Graham,* that regardless of previous sojourning, a slave continued to be a slave after he returned to a slave state. Those helping Scott then arranged his fictitious sale to a New Yorker John Sanford so that Scott's case could be brought into a federal court through the diversity of citizenship jurisdiction. This access called on them to allege the case was now between citizens of different states, Scott of Missouri and Sanford of New York. Losing in the lower courts, Scott eventually appealed to the Supreme Court, which handed down the infamous *Dred Scott v. Sandford* in 1857. (Sanford's name was misspelled in the Supreme Court's record of the decision.)

Apparently the Court at first intended to decide the case on the *Strader* precedent and assigned the opinion to Justice Samuel Nelson. But when Justices John McLean and Benjamin Curtis, who held strong antislavery views, said they would write dissenting opinions, the other justices, except for Nelson who filed his original opinion, decided the time was ripe to discuss outstanding slavery issues and to make the case definitive. Chief Justice Taney took over the opinion of the Court. Though six other justices agreed with his decision, they were not at one on the reasoning. The result was a scattered decision in which all nine justices filed opinions, six concurrences and two dissents. But all too clear were the overarching proslavery views of Taney and a majority of the justices.

In finding that Scott could not sue in the federal courts because he was a slave and thus not a citizen of Missouri, Taney reached the Missouri Compromise. Scott was still a slave not simply because he was back in a slave state, but because Congress could not abolish slavery in the territories. Such enactment not only violated the Fifth Amendment by taking property (of the slaveowner) without due process of law; it was beyond Congress's constitutional power since that body had no affirmative grant to deal with slavery in the territories. Congress's attempt to draw a line on slavery in the Missouri Compromise had been unconstitutional. Taney also struck at Douglas's popular sovereignty position by saying that Congress, not having power to interfere with slavery in the territories, could not empower a territorial government to do so.

Constitutionally, the decision opened all territories to slavery and killed the policy of containment that had been acceptable to most northerners. For them, slavery had existed only by force of state law; in effect, slavery was local and freedom national. Now matters were exactly reversed. Perhaps worse, Taney held that Congress, the nation's chief brokering institution, could not deal with the leading political issue of the day. In a great political conceit, the Court replaced Congress as the chief policymaker on slavery.

Though the decision allied the Supreme Court and the president in a new proslavery point of view that they misguidedly hoped would bring a new peace, it had the opposite effect. Its rejection of popular sovereignty split the Democratic Party. Douglas breaking with the administration, gave the rising Republicans new sectional ammunition. Praised in the South, the decision was denounced throughout the North where the Court lost nearly all credibility. It was, as Chief Justice Charles Evans Hughes was to say years later, a great "self-inflicted wound." As for Scott, he was manumitted after one of his supporters purchased him from Sanford. He died free, two-and-a-half years after the Court had held him a slave.

Of Many Virtues and a Flaw

Roger Brooke Taney, (he pronounced it TAWN-ey) born during the Revolution and dying during the Civil War, was the nation's fifth chief justice, serving 28 years, 1836–1864, longer than any other except John Marshall. Though his influence on American constitutional law and development is extensive and generally positive, in many minds he is linked irrevocably with the Dred Scott decision. The abolitionist Senator Charles Sumner was partly correct in predicting of Taney after *Dred Scott* that his name "would be hooted through the pages of history."* Yet in a respected modern survey of the careers of Supreme Court justices by the American Bar Association, Taney was among 12, including Marshall, Story, Holmes, and Brandeis, ranked as "Great." Taney, in fact, was a complex, contradictory man who had a mixed but generally distinguished record on the Court.

He came from a prominent slave-owning planter family in the Maryland tidewater. Since his elder brother stood to inherit the plantation, Taney studied law and embarked on a legal career, first in Annapolis, then Frederick. Though a Federalist in his youth, he became an early supporter of Andrew Jackson. As a Jacksonian, he was elected state attorney general in 1827 serving until summoned to Jackson's cabinet as U. S. attorney general. There he became the president's chief confidant and helped draft his famous message vetoing the recharter of the Second

National Bank, and later served briefly as secretary of the Treasury. Though Taney was now a controversial figure, Jackson appointed him to succeed Justice Gabriel Duvall in 1835, but the Senate refused to confirm. When Marshall died later the same year, Jackson stubbornly nominated him for the chief justiceship. Bitter Whig opposition in the Senate delayed confirmation eight months, during which time the Court was without a chief.

The new chief justice was the first Roman Catholic to serve on the Court. Paradoxically, given his later dogged defense of rights of slaveowners and slave states, Taney was personally opposed to slavery. He freed his own slaves and, at his own expense, con-

After *Dred Scott,* the Court handed down another constitutionally important antebellum decision. Sherman Booth, an abolitionist editor in Wisconsin, had been tried and found guilty of violating the 1850 Fugitive Act in leading a mob that helped a runaway escape from a federal marshal. However, he was freed by the Wisconsin Supreme Court, which held the Fugitive Slave Act unconstitutional—the first time a state court had declared a federal statute invalid. Ableman, a federal marshal, then got the U. S. Supreme Court to issue a writ to review the state court's action. In outright defiance, the state court refused to re-

ceive notice of the writ and ignored it entirely. In *Ableman v. Booth,* 1859, Taney spoke for a unanimous Court and upheld Booth's conviction and denied the state court's power to block the federal judiciary. In ringing nationalist phrases that would have made John Marshall proud, Taney asserted supremacy of the federal judiciary over the state, that without it there would be no Union at all. By this measure, the case stands today as an important nationalist decision, facing down nullificationist action. But, at the time, its defense of the Fugitive Slave Law stigmatized it everywhere but in the South. Whether or not Taney's decision

tinued to support those who were elderly or infirm for the rest of their lives. Though an urbane aristocrat, he was provincial in personal experience, seldom traveling far from the Maryland shore. He did not dominate the Court the way Marshall had—perhaps no one could—but on most issues he gave leadership to justices who were more divided than Marshall's colleagues had been. Taney ended Marshall's practice of the chief justice writing almost all the opinions and assigned many important ones to associate justices, a practice that has continued to the present.

Though Taney did not undo Marshall's nationalism or his doctrine of vested rights, as many feared he might, he did lead the Court to important modifications in the direction of states rights and democratic capitalism. The Charles River Bridge decision, unquestionably his greatest opinion, struck a Jacksonian blow against monopolies and exclusive grants, throwing open a door of economic opportunity. Legislative charters were to be strictly construed and not forever tie the hands of future lawmakers. "While the rights of property are socially guarded," Taney argued, "the object and end of all government is to promote the happiness and prosperity of the community." In *Cooley v. Board of Wardens* and other decisions, the Taney Court gave effect to another Jacksonian principle—dual federalism—in which the states and national government should share powers, most notably in the regulating of commerce. At the same time the Court reserved a role for itself in drawing the line between the two levels of government.

But Taney failed to navigate the treacherous currents of the slavery question. After the Court had cautiously refrained from passing on the basic issue for several years, his persuasion of a proslavery majority to try to settle the matter definitively in the Dred Scott case had unfortunate results for the country, the Court, and himself as its chief justice. The decision was defensible only if one believed the slavery question should be resolved on terms highly favorable to the South and that judges were the ones to do this. Taney badly underestimated opinion in the North and the moral depth it was gaining. He badly overestimated what judicial power could do, a curious blind spot given his earlier circumspect holding on it in *Luther v. Borden*.

Though two later opinions, the forceful *Ableman v. Booth* upholding supremacy of the national judiciary, and the eloquent *Ex parte Merryman* defending an important civil liberty, were noteworthy, each was motivated largely by Taney's unreconstructed sympathy for the Southern position. He remained loyal to the Union and, as chief justice, administered the presidential oath to Lincoln in 1861. But the last years were unhappy ones; he died four months before Lee's surrender, truculent and bitter.

* Quoted in Carl Brent Swisher, "Mr. Chief Justice Taney," in Allison Dunhan, ed., *Mr Justice* (Chicago: University of Chicago Press, 1964), 35.

---

could have been enforced given the growing evasion of the law became moot as the forum for the slavery issue shifted to the battlefield.

The Lincoln-Douglas Debates

Democrat Stephen Douglas ran for a third Senate term from Illinois in 1858. His Republican opponent was Abraham Lincoln, who had earlier served a term in the House but was almost totally unknown outside the state. Though Senators then were still chosen by state legislatures and not popularly elected until 1913, the two candidates took their campaign directly to the people, who would choose the members of the state legislature. They stumped every section of the state in a series of seven debates. Perhaps no other campaign oratory in American history has surpassed these debates in crisp, eloquent exposition of the chief issue of the day and in the search for deeper constitutional and moral questions. For the heavily favored Douglas, the dapper "Little Giant" and human dynamo an entire foot shorter than his gangling, plainly dressed, almost melancholic opponent, it was a chance to expound on the formula of popular sovereignty as the means of holding the Democratic Party together and avoiding the collision course of pro- and antislavery forces. This advocacy and Douglas's political stature gave the debates national attention.

Lincoln had grasped the lateness of the hour in his earlier "House Divided" speech in which he said prophetically that the Union could not continue to exist half-slave and half-free. In the long run it would became "*all* one thing or *all* the other." Douglas thought the choice could and should be avoided. Convinced that slavery was unsuitable for most territories, those settlements, if allowed to decide as Kansas had been, would choose to be free. But the important thing was local determination of domestic institutions—this was both a way out of the slavery impasse and an end in itself. In the debate in Freeport, Lincoln pointedly asked Douglas how popular sovereignty could be squared with the Dred Scott decision, which held the right of property in slaves must be protected everywhere. Douglas's reply, which became known as the Freeport Doctrine, was that slavery "cannot exist a day or an hour any where unless it is supported by local police regulations."* For Douglas, there was still visible room between not taking positive action to interfere with slavery and not taking positive action to support it.

Lincoln, in contrast, argued that slavery should be kept out of the territories—all territories—by Congressional action. This was radical enough, but he differed with Douglas on two other points, which elevated the debates to a new plane. He condemned slavery as "a moral, a social, and a political wrong," not merely in the territories but any place. He did not advocate disturbing it where it existed, but he looked forward to its "ultimate extinction." Douglas, who professed moral indifference to slavery, was willing, as Lincoln pointed out, to live with it forever. Lincoln grasped what Douglas would or could not: their debate was really for the mind and soul of antislavery America. Lincoln struck a

responsive chord by morally rejecting slavery. He lost the election, but it is fair to say he won the debates. He quickly became a national figure and a dark-horse candidate for the Republican presidential nomination.

Douglas believed he had staked out the middle ground with the unassailable principle of popular sovereignty. What he did not see was that there was precious little middle ground left. This was brought home with unmistakable clarity at the ballot box two years later. The center, whose seizure is usually the surest path to political success in America, had shrunk. Its normally bell-shaped distribution of political opinion and attitudes had become hopelessly inverted.

From Politics to War

The Election of 1860

The Republicans made important gains in the 1858 Congressional elections, edging the Democrats in the House. In their national nominating convention two years later, they chose Lincoln on the third ballot over the experienced New Yorker William H. Seward, not so much for Lincoln's unusal gifts of leadership, which were not yet fully apparent, but because he was more moderate on slavery and would run strongly in the West. The party platform called for an array of internal improvements, including a railroad to the Pacific, a homestead law, liberal immigration policy, and a protective tariff, but the real issue was slavery. On that, the line was drawn: no slavery in the territories, no interference within the states.

In their nominating convention in Charleston, Democrats split over the issue of popular sovereignty in the territories. Southerners, who believed the formula had cost them Kansas and felt betrayed by Douglas's Freeport Doctrine, walked out after Douglas forces refused to support active protection for slavery in the territories. With a two-thirds majority needed for nomination, the party was unable to arrive at a choice after 57 bal-

---

* Robert W. Johannsen, ed., *The Lincoln-Douglas Debates of 1858* (New York: Ford University Press, 1965), 88, quoted in Hyman and Wiecek, 197.

lots. It reassembled in Baltimore two months later and, after another Southern walkout, nominated Douglas. Delegates from eight Southern states, led by Jefferson Davis, held their own convention and nominated John C. Breckinridge of Kentucky. Border state remnants of the Whig and American parties, condemning sectional parties, formed a fourth—the Constitutional Union, and nominated John Bell of Tennessee for president and Edward Everett, president of Harvard, for vice president.

Not in American politics before or since has the country been more divided and never has the electorate been given such a menu of constitutional choices in the candidacies of the contenders. Except for ratification in 1788, the 1860 vote was the most consequential electoral event in American history.

Republicans argued that Congress had power over slavery in the territories, which meant the power to outlaw it if it chose to do so. Further, the due process clause of the Fifth Amendment—no person shall be "deprived of life, liberty, or property, without due process of law"—prevented Congress from establishing or abetting slavery in the territories. Lincoln did not embrace an abolitionist position nor did he advocate disobedience of the Dred Scott decision or urge impeachment of its majority justices. But he made it clear the decision should be overturned and, if elected, that he would appoint judges and justices committed to doing so.

In pressing for local sovereignty, Douglas and Northern Democrats appealed to a "higher law" that gave every community the right to decide what social institutions would be legally acceptable. In this, the people of each territory had as much power over slavery as did the people of each state. The appeal to local autonomy and self-determination drew upon an important element in the American political tradition but forced Douglas into a difficult constitutional circumlocution: Congress could invest the territories with power over domestic affairs but could not exercise such powers itself in the territories. To make this argument, Douglas had to ignore that the Confederation Congress, which, acting

for a much less empowered central government, had in fact barred slavery from the Northwest Territory.

The ad hoc Constitutional Unionists, fearing what might happen if either Lincoln or Breckinridge were elected, took the most traditional stand constitutionally. Arguing that Congress had power over slavery in the territories, they urged a return to the Missouri Compromise. Its 36-30 latitudinal line should be extended to the Pacific by a constitutional amendment. This would divide the territories and preserve the equilibrium in the Senate between slave states and free, as the old compromise had done for 30 years.

Southern Democrats, taking a fourth position, denied that either Congress or territorial settlers could prohibit slavery. That power rested only in the sovereign states. The laws of the states that had slavery must be given extrajurisdictional effect in the territories, if necessary being enforced by the federal government acting as agent for the sovereign states.

The election was a national referendum—the first—on slavery, at least on the territorial issue. Perhaps it might even be said to have been an expression of popular sovereignty at the level of the nation. The split among the Democrats made Lincoln's victory all but certain even though he was not on the ballot in 10 Southern states. The result was the following:

	Popular Vote	Per-cent	Electoral Vote	States Carried
Lincoln (Rep.)	1,865,908	39.8	180	17
Douglas (North. Dem.)	1,380,202	29.5	12	2
Bell (Const. Union)	590,901	12.6	39	3
Breckinridge (So. Dem.)	848,019	18.1	72	11

Though Lincoln's percentage of the popular vote was the lowest ever for a presidential winner, he won a clear majority in the North and West, failing only in New Jersey, Oregon, and

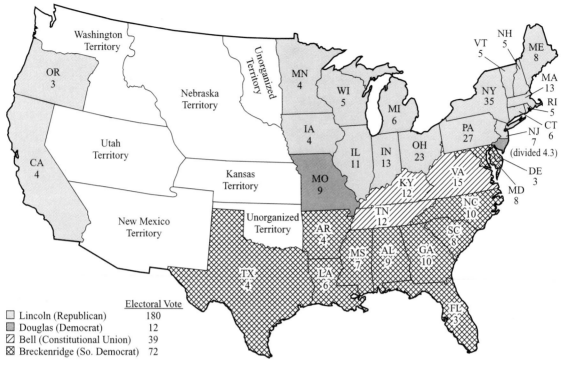

Electoral Vote
☐ Lincoln (Republican)   180
▓ Douglas (Democrat)   12
▨ Bell (Constitutional Union)   39
▨ Breckenridge (So. Democrat)   72

Figure 5.2 The Election of 1860

California. He carried the last two states with a plurality. Breckinridge won nine of the deep South states—Alabama, Arkansas, Florida, Georgia, Louisiana, Mississippi, North Carolina, South Carolina, and Texas—and two border states—Maryland and Delaware—where slavery was legal. Strongest in the border areas, Bell carried the slave states of Tennessee, Kentucky, and Virginia. Despite a good showing in the popular vote, Douglas won only New Jersey and Missouri.

As a minority president with less than 40 percent of the popular vote, Lincoln would have been a politically weaker winner had the Union remained intact. Without the South, his strength was unquestioned. Douglas, who campaigned tirelessly and heroically in every area—the only candidate to do so—was physically and politically spent. He died six months later, loyally discharging a war mission for Lincoln in the West, at age 48.

Secession Winter

For most Southerners, the handwriting was on the wall. They had come to believe, despite assurances otherwise, that the North's insistence on containment and its refusal to cooperate in returning runaways would eventually mean a political attack on slavery in Southern states. Moral condemnation of slavery, now no longer confined to the abolitionist fringe, signaled the long-run design. The North's faster-growing population, invigorated by immigration, would condemn the South to permanent minority status in the House of Representatives. Loss of the balance between free and slave states in the Senate, assured by the failure in Kansas, would allow a Northern antislavery majority to form. The loss of the presidency to a Northern sectional candidate was the final blow.

As soon as Lincoln's election became clear, the South Carolina legislature called a state convention. Meeting on December 20, 1860, it quickly and unanimously declared that "the union now subsisting between South Carolina and other states, under the name 'The United States of America' is hereby dissolved." It was natural for the state that had been home to Calhoun and the cradle of nullification 30 years earlier to take the lead. In the next six weeks, five others of the lower South—Alabama, Florida, Georgia, Louisiana, and Texas—took similar action. To be sure, there were those who expressed opposition or grave reservations, like Alexander Stephens in Georgia and Sam Houston in Texas, but they were a distinct minority. Where secession was put to direct popular vote, as it was in Tennessee, Texas, and Virginia, prosecessionist support ranged between 69 and 76 percent.

The seceding states called a convention that met in Montgomery, Ala., February 4. It drafted a constitution, set up a provisional government for the Confederate States of America, choosing Jefferson Davis, who had represented Mississippi in the Senate, as president, and Alexander Stephens as vice president.

The idea of secession was not new, and there was much to persuade the South that it was a valid constitutional instrument. It rested on the unsettled proposition that the Union was a compact of states, each of which retained its sovereignty. When Northern states violated the compact by refusing to protect slavery, which had been recognized in the Constitutional settlement, an aggrieved state could then assert its sovereignty by withdrawing from the Union. But the recognition of slavery was not so explicit or unambiguous as many Southerners claimed; the highest law had antislavery provisions as swell. On secession itself, it was silent. True, Madison had failed to persuade the framers to include a clause barring it. But presumptively weighing against secession were the grants of exclusive federal powers and the supremacy clause. Moreover, ratification had offered a choice between a government that was little more than a

league of sovereign states and a new regime in which many sovereign powers were ceded to the central government. In short, the constitutionality of secession, like many other claims arising in the lacunae of the basic law, was unclear, but it could not be wholly dismissed as illegal.

Four months separated Lincoln's election and inauguration.* Though President Buchanan declared secession unconstitutional because the Union was intended to be permanent, he said there was no constitutional power to stop it. Believing he could do nothing, he did nothing, hoping that Congress might effect an eleventh hour compromise. Moderates in the House and Senate worked toward that end. The most important result was the Crittenden Compromise, a series of resolutions introduced by the Kentucky Senator John J. Crittenden. They recommended constitutional amendments that would extend the Missouri Compromise line to the Pacific, deny federal power to interfere with domestic slave trade including that in the District of Columbia, and compensate slaveowners who were stopped from recovering runaways. The resolutions failed when Republicans would not accept any extension of slavery to the territories. For them to have done so would have subverted the outcome of the election and belied the party's reason for being.

Lincoln had been conspicuously silent during the interregnum. In his inaugural address on March 4—one of the greatest ones in presidential history—he was conciliatory but firm. There could be no compromise on the territorial question. As for slavery in the South, he repeated his campaign pledge not to interfere. The federal government had no power over Southern slavery, and he was willing to support a constitutional amendment to that end. Though not referring to the Dred Scott decision directly, he

---

* The "lame duck" period was not shortened until 1933 when the twentieth Amendment moved inauguration up to January 20.

Constitutionalism Confederate Style

Delegates of the six secessionist states meeting at the Montgomery convention in February 1861 drafted a Confederate Constitution, which was ratified in the states a month later. That it closely resembled the U. S. Constitution is not surprising. Southerners had lived under the older constitution for almost 75 years; their quarrel was not with it but with Northern interpretation of it. With a few exceptions, the new constitution reflected wishful Southern understanding of the old. Its Preamble made clear the sectional constitutional philosophy: "We the people of the Confederate States, each State acting in its sovereign and independent character." Article I set up a bicameral legislature and gave Congress nearly all the powers the U. S. Congress had with a few important exceptions. Protective tariffs, the granting of bounties, and the central financing of internal improvements—all long-time Southern grievances—were forbidden to Congress. Debating seats were given to members of the Cabinet. Article II limited the president to a single six-year term, but gave him an item veto and explicit power to remove executive officers. The judicial Article III, almost identical with that in the U. S. Constitution, incorporated the eleventh Amendment's provision against suits by citizens of one state suing another state in courts of the central government.

Unsurprisingly, slavery got specific attention. Slaveholders were given the right to enter and sojourn with their slaves in any state of the Confederacy. Bowing to European opinion, the constitution forbade African slave trade, but slavery was to be permitted and protected in any new territory acquired by the Confederacy.

States were given power to impeach officers and judges of the central government who held office solely within their boundaries—evidence that the spirit of nullification still lived. Three or more states could petition Congress for a constitutional convention, and amendments proposed by such a proceeding would require approval of two-thirds of the states. Congress was not given power to propose amendments. Most of the rights in the Bill of Rights were incorporated in Article I as limits on Congress.

Quickly adopting a constitution—one not very different from the U. S. Constitution—and having operating state governments already in place gave the Confederacy a great head start in trying to gain independence. In that endeavor it was in a much stronger position than that of the 13 colonies in 1776. Yet the constitutional philosophy behind the Confederate regime, reflecting as it did years of fealty to state sovereignty and states rights and suspicion of central power, was antithetic to the structural unity and political concentration needed to conduct a major war. Southern constitutional energies were centrifugal at a time they needed to be centripetal. The glorified compact of states needed to be the consolidated union that was politically and philosophically unacceptable.

Though Lincoln and Jefferson Davis, the Confederacy's president, had similar constitutional machinery to work with, Lincoln had the aid of a strong party system, which Davis did not. Lincoln's Republicans could bring factions and diverse views together and coordinate efforts not merely within the federal government but, all importantly, between it and the states. The party was a political antidote to localism and to the great diffusion of power in the American political system. It was, as well, the conveyer of opinion and information, aggregating it from people to government and dispersing it from government to the people, brokering differences along the way. It was kept cohesive by patronage and the threat of electoral loss to an active opposition party.

Though Davis learned to use many executive powers granted to him, they were no substitute for a party as a war tool. Without such informal infrastructure, he was often helpless in the face of state bickering and resistance to central initiatives. Nor did the Confederacy in its Southern suspicion of a central judiciary ever set up the Supreme Court provided for in its constitution. Thus it was also deprived of another instrument for settling internal disputes and gaining uniformity from differences resolved.

The South's constitutional system, nominally not very different from the North's, was much less suited to its end of gaining independence than the North's was to its end of preserving the Union.

said that each branch of government had power to decide constitutional issues itself. On secession he was emphatic, leaving no doubt that it would be resisted: "The Union of the States is perpetual . . . No State, upon its own mere motion, can lawfully get out of the Union . . . I shall take care, as the Constitution itself expressly enjoins upon me, that the laws of the Union shall be faithfully executed in all of the States."*

Lincoln's actions in the first weeks of his presidency were cautious. Eight slave states—Arkansas, Delaware, Kentucky, Maryland, Missouri, North Carolina, Tennessee, and Virginia—had not yet declared themselves. In the meantime, the sectional confrontation focused on the federally held Fort Sumter in Charleston harbor. South Carolina demanded its surrender. The garrison refused, at least until its supplies would run out in two days. Knowing that Lincoln was sending ships to reprovision the fort, Confederate shore batteries opened fire at 4:30 A.M., April 12, and the Civil War began. The garrison surrendered after running out of ammunition 36 hours later. Lincoln has been accused of deliberately maneuvering the South into being the aggressor. Whether he did or not, the attack on the fort galvanized the North and pushed Arkansas, North Carolina, and Virginia into secession. But Delaware, Kentucky, Maryland, and Missouri remained loyal. Keeping those states, in which Lincoln had gotten less than 6 percent of the vote in 1860, was a major political stroke and may have made a difference in the outcome of the war.

It is said that after Fort Sumter there was no turning back, but the point of no return may have been reached much earlier. Perhaps it was Lincoln's address, the Montgomery convention, Lincoln's election, the Dred Scott decision, the Kansas civil war, or events even more distant. By the spring of 1861, both sides expected hostili-

ties. Yet neither could have anticipated four years of the bloodiest war. If they had, each might have shrunk back and continued to search for political solutions.

War Government

With secession and the start of fighting, the political agenda and chief constitutional questions took a radical turn. The future of slavery, the salient issue for a quarter century, was now subsumed under the larger task of preserving the Union. The framers of the Constitution had made provisions for war, foreign invasion, and even "domestic violence." They gave Congress power to declare war, raise armies, and maintain navies, and they designated the president as commander in chief. But they had not planned on civil war and did not make provisions for emergency government. The North faced the task of regaining control of the seceded areas and restoring the Union. Whether the Constitution would impede that effort and whether it would survive it, were two questions for which answers were not immediately clear.

The scale of the conflict would be enormous, and each side had assets that offset the other's. In the North were 23 Northern and border states and a population of 23,000,000; in the South, 11 states with 9,000,000 of whom 3,500,000 were slaves. Allied with the South were several removed Indian tribes, some holding slaves, in the Oklahoma Territory. Fifty Unionist counties of the mountainous western section of Virginia, long at odds with Tidewater and Piedmont domination of the state, opposed secession and were later admitted to the Union as the separate state of West Virginia. Reinforcing the North's advantage in numbers was its far larger and more balanced economy, stronger banking institutions—more than 80 percent of all deposits were in Northern banks—a more extensive railway grid, and a dominant merchant marine. With an agrarian economy based on a

---

* Roy P. Basler, ed., *The Collected Words of Abraham Lincoln*, 9 volumes (New Brunswick N.J.: Rutgers University Press, 1952–1955). vol IV, 271.

few profitable staples, the South had an under-developed industrial base and poor transport. Worse, perhaps, its agricultural economy, dependent in the best of times on extensive foreign trade, was vulnerable to Northern naval interdiction.

The South had two important advantages. In the early period of the war, soldier-for-soldier it had a better fighting force with higher morale. Until the North found Grant and Sherman, it also had better generalship. Its second favor and the one by which it hoped to prevail, was strategic. To win, the North had to invade and subdue the South. Merely seeking independence, the South did not need to conquer the North to win the war.

In the end, perhaps, the North's highest card was political. In Lincoln, it had one of the great democratic crisis leaders of all time. Its developed constitutional system offered many ways for adjusting conflict, coordinating effort, and maintaining public support. It allowed the North to hold a free, open presidential election on schedule when the war was still much in doubt. That election, in which the war leader, opposed by his former commanding general sympathetic to making peace, had to stand judgment by the governed, was an extraordinary achievement in democratic politics and popular government. The South had no counterpart to the established politics of the North. That deficiency, though not apparent at first, took a heavy toll.

Lincoln's Constitutional Dictatorship

After Fort Sumter and the retention of four slave states Lincoln's actions were as bold as they had been cautious earlier. Congress, which was adjourned, was called into special session, but Lincoln set the date for July 4, almost three months away. This left him with total, daunting responsibility for dealing with the crisis. That it also gave him a free hand does not diminish his courage or the great introspective strength that set him apart from so many other leaders.

He called 75,000 state militia troops into immediate federal service, for which he had authority under Article II-2, and called for 42,000 regular army volunteers, for which he did not have authority, since that power is given to Congress. He refused to recognize the Confederacy as an independent nation, calling Southern hostilities an "insurrection" rather than a war. Yet he ordered a blockade of Southern ports, under international law an act of war between sovereign nations.

To deal with Confederate sympathy in the North, he ordered military commanders to arrest and hold without trial persons believed likely to engage in subversive acts. To prevent the suspects from challenging their detention and possibly being released by the courts, he ordered commanders to ignore writs of habeas corpus. Article I-9 says that the "writ of habeas corpus shall not be suspended, unless when in cases of rebellion or invasion the public safety may require it." The Constitution does not say who decides this, but placement of the matter in Article I rather than II suggests that it is Congress.

Lincoln's actions were constitutionally dubious, as he himself realized, but he was prepared to defend them. When Congress convened, he asked it to ratify his actions on two grounds: first, that he had undertaken them in an emergency to discharge his oath as president in Article II-1 to "preserve, protect, and defend the Constitution"; second, that none of the steps was "beyond the constitutional competency of Congress." After much debate, Congress declared Lincoln's actions to be "in all respects legalized and made valid, to the same intent and with the same effect as if they had been issued and done under the previous express authority and direction of Congress." This extraordinary act of Congressional deference, downplaying the separation of powers, masked some uneasiness. Later in 1861, in the face of military setbacks, Congress set up the Joint Committee on the Conduct of the War, partly as a restraint on the president and partly to affirm civilian control of the military. Though critical of Lincoln at times, the committee promoted cooperation with the executive branch throughout the war. Lincoln's theory of presidential emergency powers had no precedent, but it made one. It has been the basis for executive action by several twentieth-century presidents in the name of national security.

Legal Status of the War

Though hostilities between North and South quickly became a full-scale war, Lincoln continued to refer to the South's action as an insurrection. Naming the conflict was no idle matter. Its official status bore on a number of legal rights and responsibilities and had diplomatic consequence that could affect the outcome of the war. A "war" implied sovereignty of the belligerents. Such an international status for the Confederacy could mean diplomatic recognition by other nations and their aid or intervention, eventualities Lincoln wanted to avoid at all cost. If the conflict were simply a matter of suppressing an insurrection within the country, it would be of no concern to other nations. But hostilities quickly reached a scale that defied credulity to classify them as an uprising. Of necessity, Lincoln had to respond to them as being a full-scale war between two belligerents.

His blockade of Southern ports was part of the dilemma, since it was internationally an act of war, entitling the imposer to seize neutral ships trying to run or evade it. The matter took on a legal cast when the owners of several seized ships and cargoes sued for return of their property. They argued that since Lincoln had insisted the conflict was an insurrection and Congress had not been in session when the blockade was imposed and the ships seized, no state of war could have existed between North and South. Thus the Union had no right to hold the ships or their cargoes.

The Supreme Court received the claims, collectively known as the Prize Cases, in 1863 (p. 172), and handed down an important wartime decision, narrowly upholding the seizures. Justice Robert Grier, writing for the majority, gave the government all the advantages of a belligerent power without admitting that the Southern states were a sovereign nation. "A civil war," Grier wrote, "always begins by insurrection against the government." The president had a constitutional duty to suppress insurrections and, as commander in chief, could respond to them with whatever force was needed. Justice Nelson, dissenting, argued that a state of war that would legally justify a blockade could not exist without a declaration by Congress; the president alone could not make war.

In 1863, the Supreme Court was a different court from the one that decided *Dred Scott* six years before. It had four new justices: Nathaniel Clifford, a Maine Democrat appointed by Buchanan in 1858; and three Lincoln appointees—Noah Swayne, an Ohio Republican; Samuel Freeman Miller, an Iowa Republican; and David Davis, an Illinois Republican and close friend of Lincoln's. The Lincoln appointees joined Grier and holdover Justice James Wayne to form the majority. Clifford and the other holdovers—Chief Justice Taney and Justice Catron—joined Nelson in dissenting.

Constitutionally, the Prize Cases allowed the North to fight the Civil War as an international war, which it was in fact, without having to recognize the Confederate government as a sovereign belligerent. The president's power to make war or undertake war-like actions remains unsettled to the present. Three major American wars of the twentieth century—Korea, Vietnam, and the Persian Gulf—were never declared by Congress.

Whether the North-South conflict was war or insurrection also had important consequence for the status of captured combatants. If the conflict were an insurrection, a captured Confederate might be tried for treason, a crime punishable by death. But humanitarian considerations and the Southern threat to retaliate against Union captives forced the government, here at least, to concede belligerent status to the South. All captured Confederates were treated as prisoners of war rather than as traitors and so were entitled to certain protections under international law.

The insurrection theory remained intact in other respects. As the end of the war neared, the North persisted in demanding "unconditional surrender" without the terms or assurances that sovereign belligerents might expect. Surrender was in fact unconditional; no peace treaty was ever signed between North and South.

Internal Security and Civil Liberty

Neither the North nor the South was fully united during the war. Sympathies and loyalties did not completely follow state lines. Tens of thousands of Unionists were among the population of the South, particularly in its upper regions. Opposition was even greater in the North. Support for the Southern cause was strong in the border slave states that remained in the Union and in southern areas of states such as Ohio and Indiana, and among scattered individuals throughout the North. Dissident acts ranged from outspoken advocacy of making peace and recognizing the Confederacy to spying, sabotage, stealing military supplies, and recruiting for the South.

Such subversion raised both legal and practical problems for a government trying to win a war and preserve a union. If the conflict were an insurrection, disloyal acts of giving "aid and comfort" to the enemy were treason under Article III-3 and, under statutes in force since 1790, punishable by death. But the Constitution calls for the testimony of two witnesses in open court to convict; besides, many disloyal acts did not strike most persons as capital offenses. In any event, the number of persons disloyal or suspected of disloyalty was simply too large to use the courts to prosecute them for treason. (In the previous 72 years under the Constitution, no person had ever been executed for treason.

None were during the Civil War, a remarkable restraint in the history of governments.)

Lincoln's order to military commanders to arrest and detain persons suspected of disloyalty or who might commit disloyal acts resulted in thousands being held who had not done anything punishable. To make this roundup effective, he suspended the writ of habeas corpus. As a legal order from a court to an incarcerator to show why a person in custody is being held, the writ was designed to prevent arbitrary detention and to insure those detained speedy trials. The framers, aware of colonial experience with arbitrary British arrest and detention, believed the writ so important they provided in Article I-9 that it could be suspended only for reasons of public safety in cases of rebellion or invasion.

Suspension of the writ met bitter opposition from Democrats and gave rise to an early showdown between Lincoln and Chief Justice Taney. A Maryland secessionist, John Merryman, had been arrested by the army under suspicion of destroying a railway bridge and was held in Fort McHenry in Baltimore. He petitioned for a writ of habeas corpus to Taney sitting on circuit in Maryland. Taney issued the writ on the fort's commanding officer, General George Cadwalader, to have Merryman brought before him. On Lincoln's orders, Cadwalader ignored it. Taney then ordered the general to appear before him. When Cadwalader ignored this command as well, Taney issued his opinion in *Ex parte Merryman*, 1861.

He made three points. First, since the provision for suspension of the writ of habeas corpus was in the legislative Article I rather than the presidential Article II, only Congress could exercise the power. Second, even with the writ suspended, a civilian could not be militarily detained or brought to trial in a military proceeding because the Sixth Amendment guarantees a criminal defendant the right to "a speedy and public trial by an impartial jury." Finally, the president's constitutional obligation to faithfully execute the laws gave him a duty to come to the aid of judicial authority, assisting it in enforcing its judgments. From a civil liberties point of view, this was a ringing indictment of Lincoln's policy.

The president answered Taney indirectly in a message to Congress. He noted that the Constitution was silent on who had power to suspend the writ, but his main thrust was boldly and baldly pragmatic. The president had responsibility to see that "the whole of the laws" were faithfully executed and that because of subversive acts, these were not executed in a third of the states. "Are all the laws *but one,*" he asked, "to go unexecuted and the government itself to go to pieces lest one be violated?"*

The dialogue between Taney and Lincoln reveals the conflict between two constitutional obligations: protection of civil liberties, including those of many persons innocent of wrongdoing, and the civil emergency of winning a war. The same dilemma would confront the nation in the twentieth century in World Wars I and II, the Vietnam conflict, and in the long Cold War with the Soviet Union. For the most part, military arrest and detention during the Civil War was administered cautiously and with moderation. Many detainees were held only short periods of time and few were treated harshly. Lincoln believed the precautionary arrests kept many disloyal acts from occurring, thus possibly shortening the war and saving lives.

In 1863, Congress passed the Habeas Corpus Act, authorizing the president to suspend the writ, but also placing certain judicial restrictions on detention. In the meantime, Lincoln had ordered that disloyal persons be tried before military commissions, which were much like courts martial and not restrained by the traditions of civil justice. This produced a controversial test before the Supreme Court. A former Democratic Congressman and Southern sympathizer, Clement Vallandigham, was arrested and found guilty by a military tribunal for delivering a speech denouncing Union war policies and calling for a peace with the South. He appealed, arguing that he had

broken no law and, being a civilian, the military commission had no power to try him. But in *Ex parte Vallandigham,* 1864, the Court, now dominated by six Lincoln appointees, refused to hear the case on the circular reasoning that the Court's appellate authority did not reach military tribunals because they were not courts. Still tarnished by its Dred Scott decision, the Court chose throughout the war not to confront the president over military arrests and detention. Lincoln himself later ordered Vallandigham released and banished to the Confederacy.

The Court took a different position in an important case that came to it after the war. Lambdin Milligan, a prominent antiwar Democrat in Indiana, was convicted by a military tribunal of conspiracy to seize arms at a federal arsenal and liberate Confederate prisoners at several Northern prison camps. He was sentenced to be hanged. In *Ex parte Milligan,* 1866 (p. 174), the Court unanimously overturned the conviction, ruling that the military commission did not have jurisdiction over him. Justice Davis, speaking for a majority of five, held that the right to indictment by grand jury in the Fifth Amendment and to trial by an impartial jury in the Sixth, meant no civilian could be tried by the military as long as local civil courts were open and operating, as they had been in Indiana at the time of Milligan's arrest. Four concurring justices, joining in an opinion by Chief Justice Salmon Chase, refused to reach such a sweeping conclusion. They would have held for Milligan on statutory grounds: The Habeas Corpus Act called for detainees not indicted by a grand jury to be released. They argued that Congress had war power to authorize military trials of civilians if it concluded civil courts were incapable of punishing treason.

Though many modern commentators have hailed the case as a landmark because of Justice Davis's eloquent defense of civil trial rights, it remains that *Milligan* was decided after the war was over, Lincoln was dead, and the emergency he had to face, no more. The difficult questions raised in Chase's concurring opinion have never been fully answered. A later Court did not allow

---

* Ibid., 430.

The Constitution at Gettysburg

The battle of Gettysburg, fought during the first three days of July 1863, was the bloodiest of the Civil War—leaving more than 7,000 dead and 43,000 wounded between the two sides. Though the war was to continue nearly two more years, Gettysburg was a turning point. The battle was an unplanned part of General Robert E. Lee's strategy to capture and hold Northern territory, including the Pennsylvania capital, Harrisburg. The plan aimed to win foreign aid and recognition and, by bringing the war home to the North, convince it that subduing the South was too costly to continue. But Lee unwisely gave battle at Gettysburg and was defeated, his remaining force barely escaping back to Virginia. Any chance that Great Britain or France would give diplomatic recognition to the Confederacy or deliver war vessels to it was shattered.

Northern losses had been horrific, and on November 19 of the same year, a cemetery on the battlefield was dedicated. The principal commemorative address would be given by Edward Everett, the most renowned orator of his time. The president of the United States was also invited to speak. Everett delivered an eloquent two-hour memorial to the outdoor assembly of 15,000. Lincoln followed, speaking for less than three minutes not counting interruptions by applause. His brief remarks—272 words—constitute the most memorable of all American speeches. More than that, they changed the effective meaning of the Constitution, even before the guns had completed their work and the great postwar amendments were added to it.

In his perceptive study of the Gettysburg Address, *Lincoln at Gettysburg*, the American historian Garry Wills sees the speech as a calculated political and rhetorical act. (Lincoln did not casually write it on the back of an envelope on the train to Gettysburg, contrary to one of the many myths grown up around the address.) His aim was to give transcendental meaning to what the Union dead had fought for and thus to the war itself. In doing this he tried to reconcile the two great writs of American history—the Declaration of Independence and the Constitution. He used the first, which proclaimed equal liberty, to purify the second, which had recognized slavery.

Lincoln saw the Declaration and its statement that all men were created equal and had inalienable rights to life and liberty as the ideal on which the nation was founded. It was, in effect, a political North Star. He had earlier described it as "a standard maxim for free society . . . constantly looked to, constantly labored for, and even though never perfectly attained, constantly approximated, and thereby constantly spreading and deepening its influence, and augmenting the happiness and value of life to all people of all colors everywhere."*

This reading was more than Jefferson and the Revolutionaries of 1776 had intended. For them, the Declaration was an indictment of kingship and imperialism, not slavery. Yet Lincoln insisted on reading its ideals, so well phrased by Jefferson (who continued to own slaves), in the light of his own time and the crisis that enveloped it. As Wills observed, "the Declaration committed Americans to claims even more at odds with slavery than kingship."† The Constitution was the working law of the

the principles of the decision to stop President Franklin Roosevelt from ordering military internment of tens of thousands of West Coast Japanese-Americans during World War II.

The Status of Slavery

When the war began, abolition of slavery in the Confederate states was not a Union aim. The Republican Party platform had vowed no interference with slavery in the South, a pledge Lincoln restated in his inaugural address. The position made strategic sense at the time; transforming hostilities into a war to end slavery in the South would have severely weakened the Union's position in the loyal slave states and increased opposition among Northern Democrats. As late as August 1862, Lincoln wrote to the New York publisher Horace Greeley, "My paramount object in this struggle is to save the Union, and not

land, without which there would have been no Union. But its countenance of slavery had made it an imperfect and provisional embodiment of the ideal of equal liberty. At Gettysburg, without mentioning the Declaration or slavery by name, Lincoln spoke of the first birth of freedom "four score and seven years ago." The terrible war to preserve the Union would also redeem the Constitution and the nation. That was "the great task remaining before us . . . that these dead shall not have died in vain—that this nation, under God, shall have a new birth of freedom."

Lincoln gave the Declaration of Independence greater meaning than the Revolutionary genera-tion had imagined; he used it to give the war greater meaning than much of his own generation could imagine. The Union would be saved and the Constitution amended. Full equal liberty was not immediately realized and continues even now to be partly elusive. But Lincoln gave the nation a compass at Gettysburg that he used to find its way then and which later generations might use to find its way again.

* Speech in Springfield, Illinois, June 26, 1857, Basler, *Collected Works,* Vol II, 406.
† *Lincoln at Gettysburg: The Words that Remade America* (New York: Simon and Schuster, 1992), 100.

Union soldiers patrol rear of crowd awaiting Lincoln's remarks at the Gettysburg cemetery dedica-tion, November 19, 1863. The president, barely visible (center right of man wearing tall stove pipe hat) in this historic Matthew Brady photo, gave one of history's great addresses, and a post-slavery vision of a constitution informed by a new understnding of the Declaration of Independence.

either to save or destroy slavery. If I could save the Union without freeing any slave, I would do it; if I could save it by freeing all the slaves, I would do it; and if I could save it by freeing some and leaving others alone, I would also do that."*

But any possibility of leaving slavery undis-turbed was already diminishing out of military need. Slaves were being used in the Confederate effort to raise food, make munitions, and serve as teamsters and laborers for the army. Where Union forces penetrated Southern territory, many slaves escaped to Union lines. Returning them to their owners in rebellion was out of the question; some Union commanders, giving them food and protection, simply declared them to be free. As the war dragged on and the North suffered big reverses in 1862, forbearance

* Ibid., vol V, 388–389.

on abolition as a war aim in the hope of placating the South, was pointless. Pressures for emancipation rose and many Republicans now believed the slaveholders' rebellion against the Union had become a war of the Union against slavery itself. Congress had already taken a few steps. Early in 1862, it abolished slavery in the District of Columbia, compensating owners but below market value for their slaves, and it freed the few slaves in the territories without compensation to owners. It also declared freedom for slaves who had crossed to Union lines or had been liberated by Union advances if their owners were part of the rebellion.

On New Year's Day, 1863, Lincoln strategically played the emancipation card, issuing the historic order that slaves in states or parts of states still in rebellion "shall be then, thenceforward, and forever free." The Emancipation Proclamation was of questionable constitutional status. Issued without Congressional authorization, its only constitutional support was the war power of the president. Since it applied only to areas under Confederate control, it did not have much immediate liberating effect though, in the long run, it siphoned off part of the South's labor force by encouraging slaves to escape to Union lines. The Proclamation also authorized recruitment of freed slaves and free black persons as soldiers. In the last two years of the war, nearly 200,000 served in the Union army and navy, making an important contribution to final victory. Not least, the Proclamation had a vital propaganda effect abroad. Though Britain's textile industry had depended on cheap Southern cotton, British public opinion was strongly opposed to slavery. Emancipation reduced whatever chance there was for diplomatic recognition of the Confederacy by Great Britain. Above all, the Proclamation made the abolition of slavery an official war aim. The war to preserve the Union became one not merely to keep slavery out of the territories, but to end it once and for all.

Lingering constitutional doubts about the Proclamation and the fact that it did not cover all slaves caused Lincoln and Republicans in Congress to propose an amendment, the Thirteenth, which provided simply that "neither slavery nor involuntary servitude, except as a punishment for crime whereof the party shall have been duly convicted, shall exist within the United States or any place subject to their jurisdiction." The first formal change in the Constitution in 60 years was ratified December 6, 1865, by the needed three-quarters of the states, including provisional reconstruction governments of eight of the secessionist states.

Growth of Federal Power

The war lasted four years and was, to that time, the largest and deadliest in history. At one point or other, more than 1,500,000 men served in Union forces and more than 1,000,000 in Confederate. Fighting took place in 16 states and several territories. Union dead numbered 360,000, including 110,000 battle deaths; Confederate losses were 258,000, including 98,000 in battle. Between the two sides, an additional 400,000 were wounded. To prosecute and win such a conflict called for a government effort of unprecedented Herculean scope. Military needs disrupted civilian life and strained productive capacity well beyond anything required in the War of 1812 or the Mexican War. Mobilization more closely resembled that in World Wars I and II.

Centralization of power in the presidency, already noted, was accompanied by growth in the machinery of the national government and a new balance of power within the federal system between the states and the national government. Between 1800 and 1860, the country had grown from a mainly east coast nation to one of transcontinental size, and its population had risen sixfold to more than 31,000,000. But the federal government had grown hardly at all. Most persons and groups had looked to their states when public action or regulation was needed. In the early months of the war, the states supplied most of the soldiers and materials. But it was clear from the start that most functions, many of which were new and required a bureaucratic infrastructure, would need to be federal. Gradually, and sometimes reluctantly, Congress formulated centralized policies.

The most dramatic of these was the Conscription Act of 1863, the first comprehensive law for compulsory military service in the nation's history. Though necessary to meet the huge military manpower needs, it was extremely unpopular in many quarters and set off four days of bloody antidraft riots in New York City. Whether conscription was within Congress's power to raise an army was widely debated, but did not come before the Supreme Court. Not until World War I, when compulsory service was reinstated, was the power constitutionally upheld.

Financing the war also required centralized operations and machinery. Banking and currency had been mainly state matters after Jackson vetoed rechartering of the Second National Bank, but reserves in state banks were small and uncoordinated. One device Congress used was the issuance of unbacked paper money—"greenbacks"—making them legal tender for both public and private debt. By 1863, nearly $450,000,000 in such fiat money had been issued. The National Banking Act, passed early that year, set up a system of federally chartered banks to issue notes based on holdings of public bonds guaranteed by the federal government. To move toward a national uniform currency, Congress placed a 10 percent tax on state bank notes, putting them out of existence.

Compared with wartime standards in the twentieth century, private property went largely unregulated. The exceptions were railroads and telegraph. Congress authorized Lincoln to take nominal possession of roads and lines to assure military needs for transport and communication would be met. Military needs also brought a shift in attitudes toward federal sponsorship of internal improvements, as Congress set large sums aside for new railway construction.

Though the growth of federal power and activity slowed after the war, its wartime breadth set a precedent in government administration and in the public mind for wide use of central power in later years in war and peace. States rights survived the war and secession did not, but in the wheel of the federal system great power and responsibility had shifted from rim to hub.

Reconstruction

The Union had been preserved and secession defeated in a hard-won, unconditional victory on the battlefield. But restoration of that Union would prove nearly as difficult politically as winning the war had been militarily. Three great matters of constitutional status needed resolution: that of the seceded states, the Freedmen as the emancipated slaves were called, and the former Confederates who had made war against the Union. With these issues went two others: Who—the president or Congress—had chief power and responsibility for restoration and what should restoration achieve? Behind these questions was the stark reality of an economically devastated South and the prospect of a profound social revolution within it.

The Presidential Plans

Lincoln had a plan for reconstruction long before war's end. Based on his view that the Confederate states had never legally seceded, he assumed it was the president's task to decide when the rebellion was over so that legal government could be reinstated. With remarkable lack of vindictiveness, the program aimed to bind up the wounds of war. Its tone was captured in the familiar line from his second inaugural address, "with malice toward none, charity for all." Except for the highest ranking civil and military officers of the Confederacy, he would grant pardons to all Southerners willing to take an oath of loyalty to the Union. He would give executive recognition to state governments where 10 percent of the electorate took the oath and the state agreed to emancipation. Before the war was over, these conditions had been met in Union-occupied Arkansas, Louisiana, and Tennessee.

Congress's wartime views on restoration were less generous. In 1864, Lincoln refused to sign the Wade-Davis Bill, which called for a majority of the electorate in each state to take the oath and would have excluded anyone who had served in the Confederate army or government from immediate political participation. The bill looked to a much longer period of reconstruction.

Lincoln's assassination, April 11, 1865, a week after General Robert E. Lee had surrendered Southern main forces at Appomattox all but ending the war, brought Andrew Johnson to the presidency. A loyal Tennessee Unionist and Democrat, he had seemed the ideal "unity" running mate for Lincoln in 1864 when the war was far from over. Honest and generally well-intentioned, Johnson had a tendency to become embattled, a reputation for stubbornness, and few of Lincoln's political skills. As a Democrat, he lacked Lincoln's sway over the majority party in Congress and in the nation; as a "Southerner" his motives were not fully trusted. The Congress elected in 1864 was not scheduled to meet until December 1865, and Johnson, hoping to finish presidential reconstruction beforehand, did not call it into special session. What eventually followed was a careening of reconstruction from one extreme to another.

Johnson was particularly liberal in granting amnesty to individuals, who could then take part in political life. Under presidential supervision, provisional governments were set up in the remaining Southern states, and constitutional conventions called. Beyond being required to renounce secession, repudiate Confederate war debts, and ratify the thirteenth Amendment, these conventions were given pretty much a free hand. By the end of the year, Johnson was able to announce to the new Congress that postwar governments had been set up in every state but Texas, and that Reconstruction was virtually finished. All that remained was for newly elected Southern Senators and Representatives to be admitted to their seats in Congress.

Congressional Reconstruction of Reconstruction

Congress was in no mood to cooperate. For Radical Republicans, holding that the seceded states were out of the Union, the South was occupied territory until far-reaching social and political reforms could be made. Even moderate Republicans wondered whether things had gone too far too fast at the expense of goals for which the war had been fought. The two groups worried that the Freedmen were not well enough protected or given genuine opportunity to be economically free. In the meantime, an embarrassing number of former Confederate officers were elected in the South, and the new legislatures began to act in disturbingly old ways. Most of them quickly passed so-called Black Codes, whose aim was to freeze emancipated slaves in a status of permanent political, social, and economic subordination. These laws, which failed to give Freedmen the right to vote or sit on juries, restricted their entry into certain occupations and, in some areas, even limited public movement. In many of the former Confederate states, they were little more than warmed over versions of antebellum slave codes, minus only forced labor.

Such bad faith in the verdict of the war was more than enough to provoke Congressional reaction. The Republican majority refused to endorse Johnson's program or admit the new Southern representatives who, as though to add insult, included two former Confederate generals and Alexander Stephens, the former vice president of the Confederacy. As Republicans saw it, letting the Southern delegates take their seats would be tantamount to restoring the South, thus ending Reconstruction, before the new Congress had a chance to represent the will of the people. A committee of six Senators and nine Representatives— twelve Republicans and three Democrats—was set up to look at the issues of Reconstruction. The Joint Committee of Fifteen, as it was called, was dominated by Radical Republicans led by Charles Sumner and Thaddeus Stevens. The latter, an old-line abolitionist bitter in his hatred of the Confederate

South and sour on presidential reconstruction, became the most powerful figure in the government for the next two years as Congress replaced Johnson's program with its own. Retributive though it often was, the Joint Committee came closer to representing opinion in the North than did the president.

In its session year, 1866, Congress took three important steps. It enlarged the powers of the Freedman's Bureau, a federal office set up near the end of the war as a general relief agency. The Bureau was now given power to try before military commissions anyone accused of depriving Freedmen of civil rights. Johnson vetoed this enactment as being a war measure passed in peacetime, but was overridden. Congress then passed the Civil Rights Act, granting citizenship and other basic civil rights to black persons, including the right "to make and enforce contracts, to sue, and give evidence, to inherit, purchase, lease, sell, hold, and convey real and personal property." Johnson vetoed this bill arguing that the rights were a matter of state not federal responsibility, but again Congress overrode.

The constitutional doubts raised by Johnson and the recognition that the thirteenth Amendment, though abolishing slavery, could not alone guarantee rights of former slaves, convinced Congress to propose an additional amendment, ratified two years later as the Fourteenth. In it, national citizenship was defined for the first time and states were forbidden to "abridge the privileges and immunities of citizens of the United States" or "deprive any person of life, liberty or property without due process of law, nor deny to any person within its jurisdiction the equal protection of the laws." The amendment also annulled the three-fifths clause for representation in Congress. Ratification was made a condition for readmission of any former Confederate state.

Though it did not have great effect on Reconstruction, the Fourteenth Amendment became the most important of all the formal additions to the Constitution. Its due process provision—the most litigated clause in the Constitution in the

twentieth century—became the means for holding almost all protections in the Bill of Rights to be limits on state as well as federal power. Its equal protection clause became the constitutional basis for modern civil rights.

These Republican actions, the first steps in a tougher and more comprehensive Congressional reconstruction program, were inspired mainly by genuine humanitarian concerns about the freedom and security of black persons in a restored South. But Republicans had a self-interested motive as well. With the three-fifths clause cut out, a restored South would have greater representation in Congress than before, and Republicans feared a national revival of the Democratic Party. Having had no prewar strength in the South, they hoped to ally vast numbers of Freedmen with the party as voters and participating citizens.

Reconstruction was the chief issue in the Congressional campaign of 1866, perhaps the most important midterm election in American history. In most districts, a Radical Republican faced a Copperhead Democrat. President Johnson campaigned extensively and ineptly for Democrats, further estranging himself from Congressional Republicans. Republicans won 75 percent of the House seats and retained control of the Senate with an even greater margin. With majorities large enough to override presidential vetoes, the way was open for a still more aggressive Congressional program and a fateful showdown with the president.

The theory of Reconstruction had swung from Lincoln's (and Johnson's) idea that the rebellious states had never left the Union—a radical position during the war, but now conservative—to the Radical view that the seceded states had forfeited their rights and were now, in effect, "dead." In the latter view, those states, until restored, had only the rights granted to them by Congress. Tennessee, in which Unionist sentiment had always been strong, was now the only secessionist state to ratify the fourteenth Amendment, and doing so, was promptly readmitted by Congress. Other former secessionist states refused to ratify.

In the First Reconstruction Act, passed over Johnson's veto, Congress divided the South, Tennessee excluded, into five military districts subject to martial law and ruled by military governors with near-dictatorial powers. Though the program was nominally under direction of the president as commander in chief, actual control was exercised by Congressional leaders through Secretary of War Edwin M. Stanton, who refused to follow Johnson's orders. To be restored to the Union, a state needed to call a new constitutional convention, the delegates to which were elected by universal manhood suffrage, guaranteeing suffrage to the Freedmen, and denying it to former Confederate officials.

When Southern states refused to call such conventions, Congress authorized the military commanders to enroll voters. The South was reoccupied by 20,000 federal troops including units of black militia. The preceding governments set up by Johnson, which had been operating for a year or two, were dismantled. Eventually, 703,000 blacks and 627,000 whites, some of whom were Northerners—"carpetbaggers"—who had gone South to participate in Reconstruction and, in many cases, make their fortunes, were registered. New conventions were called in which Radical black-white alliances were dominant. The new constitutions drafted and later ratified were more democratic than those they replaced and, except for express guarantees of civil rights for Freedmen and disqualification of ex-Confederates, were similar to those in Northern states.

To make sure Congressional Reconstruction was not subverted by the president, Congress passed several laws to tie his hands. It required presidential military orders be executed only with approval of General of the Army Ulysses S. Grant. The Tenure of Office Act, passed over Johnson's veto, provided that executive branch officers appointed with Senate approval could not be dismissed without it. Having earlier reduced the size of the Supreme Court from ten to seven, Congress now refused to increase it, thereby denying Johnson appointment opportunities.

To protect black suffrage, Congress also proposed the Fifteenth Amendment, barring states from depriving citizens of the right to vote because of "race, color, or previous condition of servitude." This last of the three great post-Civil War Amendments was ratified early in 1870.

With new constitutions in place and operating governments now in the hands of Freedmen and Radical whites, Congress at last began readmitting the former secessionist states to full status. Seven—Arkansas, Alabama, Florida, Georgia, Louisiana, North Carolina, and South Carolina—were restored in 1868. Mississippi, Texas, and Virginia were readmitted in 1870.

Johnson's Impeachment

Congressional takeover of Reconstruction left the relationship between the president and Congress at its lowest ebb in history. A virtual state of war existed between the two branches. After sweeping the 1866 elections, Radical Republicans believed Johnson would cooperate fully with the Congressional program or resign. He did neither. With a dwindling political base, no more than modest leadership ability to go with an innate mulishness, he helped bring about the travesty that followed. Impeachment had been vaguely talked about for several months, but it was Johnson's decision to test the Tenure of Office Act that brought it to action. The president removed Secretary of War Stanton, a holdover from Lincoln's cabinet with close ties to the Radicals. Early in 1868 with a year left in Johnson's term, the House drew up formal articles of impeachment, and Johnson became the first president to stand trial in the Senate.

Of 11 Articles in the indictment, the first 8 dealt with Johnson's alleged violations of the Tenure of Office Act. The ninth charged him with giving military orders directly rather than going through commanding generals as Congress had required. In the thin-skinned tenth, he was accused of trying to bring Congress into "disgrace, ridicule, hatred, contempt, and reproach." The last Article, phrased in general terms, got to

A day in the Senate's impeachment of President Andrew Johnson, with Supreme Court Justice Salmon P. Chase presiding. The proceeding lasted seven weeks. March 30 to May 18, 1868, and ended in an acquittal. The vote against Johnson, 35-19, fell one short of the two-thirds necessary for conviction. Congress tried to carry on its regular business during trial recesses.

the basic reason for impeachment; it charged Johnson with obstructing enforcement of Congressional Reconstruction. Starting in March of 1868 and continuing for seven weeks, the country was treated to a full-dress political drama with a cast prescribed by the Constitution: the House as prosecutor; the Senate, the jury; and Chief Justice Salmon P. Chase, the presiding officer.

A central issue was the meaning of the Constitution's Article II-4, which makes executive officers impeachable for "treason, bribery, or other high crimes and misdemeanors." Johnson's attorneys, who included Benjamin Curtis, the former Supreme Court justice who had been one of the two dissenters in *Dred Scott,* forcefully argued that this provision limited impeachment to criminally indictable offenses and could not be used to remove a president merely because he was politically unacceptable to Congress. The House prosecutors, contending that a president could engage in obstructionist acts without technically committing a crime, urged a broader interpretation that would include actions "against the public interest." As precedent, they cited impeachment of the demented Judge Pickering in

1804, in which no crimes were charged at all. In truth, there was no constitutional model for impeaching a president or almost anyone else. The trial itself would decide the meaning of "high crimes and misdemeanors."

To the extent that the narrower, indictable offense view was persuasive, the alleged Tenure of Office Act violations were a weak foundation for impeachment. Johnson's attorneys argued that the Constitution is unclear on the president's power to remove executive officers, and what precedent there was favored the president—Andrew Jackson and other presidents had summarily removed officers who had been confirmed by the Senate. The president, they said, was simply defending what he believed were his constitutional powers and had as much right to do this as Congress did. (Years later, the Tenure of Office Act was repealed without ever going to the Supreme Court. However, in 1926, in *Myers v. United States,* the Court, ruling on another statute, held that Congress could not place conditions on the president's power to remove political officers from the executive branch.)

The Senate vote on impeachment—35 in favor, 19 opposed— fell one short of the two-thirds needed for conviction and removal. Acquittal turned on the votes of nine Republicans, who risked their political careers, to join the Senate's twelve Democrats. They have gotten high praise for their courage, but here again, political motivation is complex. Many were economic conservatives and feared the harebrained views on public finance of Senator Ben Wade who, under the presidential succession law in effect at the time, would have become president had Johnson been removed. Though acquitted, Johnson was ineffective in his last months in office.

Johnson's narrow escape did not establish once and for all that impeachment was limited to indictable offenses—the matter remains ambiguous as the trial of President Bill Clinton confirmed in 1999. But the acquittal did do two things. It saved the presidency from becoming, at least for a time if not permanently, an inferior branch whose occupant could be removed for political disagreement with a strong and determined Congressional majority. Congress did become ascendant—there were no truly strong presidents again until the twentieth century— but separation of powers and coequality remained basically intact. Though not apparent at the time, acquittal was the beginning of the end of Reconstruction. Military occupation continued in most parts of the South for several years more, but the resolute Congressional energies needed to sustain reformation began to wane after the Senate verdict.

The Problematic Court

The Supreme Court, totally discredited in the North after *Dred Scott*, was filled with Lincoln appointees by the end of the war. Besides Justices Swayne, Miller, and Davis, Lincoln named Stephen Field, a California Democrat, in 1863, and on Roger Taney's death in 1864, Salmon P. Chase, formerly his secretary of the Treasury, as chief justice. To add a tenth federal judicial

circuit on the West Coast and draw the new state of California closer to the rest of the Union during the war, Congress had increased the size of the Court to 10 in 1863. But, two years later, with Johnson as president and amid complaints that the Court's size was unwieldy, Congress reduced the Court to seven by not allowing the next three vacancies to be filled. As Congress proceeded with military reconstruction and conflict with the president deepened, constitutional questions about Reconstruction began to arise. The Court had been quiescent during the war, but many believed—Radical Republicans fearfully, Johnson and his Southern allies hopefully—that it would eventually strike down the Congressional program.

Certainly there were hints. Though not involving a Reconstruction law, the Court's ruling in *Ex parte Milligan* in 1866 cast doubt on the validity of many proceedings of the new military rule in the South, since civil courts there were open and operating and peacetime conditions prevailed.

In the Test Oath cases early in 1867, *Cummings v. Missouri* and *Ex parte Garland,* the Court's leaning seemed even clearer. The first dealt with a provision of the Missouri constitution requiring that to vote, hold public office, or practice any of several professions including that of the clergy, a person must take an oath to support the Constitution and swear they had always been loyal to the United States. Cummings, a Roman Catholic priest, was indicted for preaching without having taken the oath. In *Garland,* a federal law requiring lawyers to swear they had never borne arms against the United States, had been applied to a Confederate veteran, pardoned by Johnson, who wanted to practice before the Supreme Court.

These laws were intended to politically disable former rebels and their sympathizers. The Court overturned both, 5–4. Justice Field, a confirmed individualist who was later to have great influence on protection of property rights, broke with his fellow Lincoln appointees to join four pre-Lincoln justices. The Court held the laws to be bills of attainder (acts singling out individuals for punishment without trial) and ex post facto laws (acts creating retroactive crimes). As such, the federal statute violated Article I-9, and the Missouri provision, Article I-10.

In a few months, the Court was asked to rule directly on Congressional Reconstruction in *Mississippi v. Johnson* (p. 178) and *Georgia v. Stanton*. In each case it sidestepped the issue. In the first, representatives of the soon-to-be replaced Johnson provisional government in Mississippi sought an injunction, nominally against the president but really against the military commander who would be in charge of the state, to prevent the Congressional takeover. The Georgia suit, also brought by representatives of a provisional Johnson government, tried to enjoin the secretary of war and General of the Armies Grant for the same purpose.

Plaintiffs in both cases argued that Congress was annihilating a state and its government, thus depriving its citizens of their political and legal rights. But the Court refused to reach the substantive issues. In the Mississippi case, in which it was unanimous, it drew a distinction between "ministerial" duties, such as delivery of a commission to a duly appointed person, and "executive" ones. The first involved no discretion and, being all but mechanical, might be subject to a court order. But executive acts requiring discretion or political judgment were not. Enforcement of Congressional Reconstruction acts was clearly "executive" and thus beyond judicial reach. In the Georgia case, the Court, echoing its decision in *Luther v. Borden* 18 years earlier, held the issue a "political question"—one to be left to the other two branches for resolution.

Despite these decisions, Republican Radicals were still wary of the Court because it had agreed to hear the case of William H. McCardle, a Mississippi newspaper editor who, under Congressional Reconstruction acts, had been convicted in a military tribunal of disturbing the peace and inciting to insurrection. He asked the Court for a writ of habeas corpus under a Congressional act defining that right of appeal. Unlike the Mississippi and Georgia challenges, the case dealt with an individual's rights. Amid rumors the Court would use it to hold Congressional Reconstruction unconstitutional, Congress acted quickly to withdraw the kind of appeal McCardle had taken from the Court's jurisdiction. Thus, when the Court heard *Ex parte McCardle* (p. 179), it first had to decide whether Congress's action on jurisdiction affected a case already on the Court's docket that had progressed to formal argument. Speaking through Chief Justice Chase, it held unanimously that Congress's Article III-2 power to qualify the Court's appellate jurisdiction "with such exceptions and under such regulations as the Congress shall make" applied also to cases pending.

The same day it retreated in *McCardle*, the Court did reach an important Reconstruction issue, though not one involving Congress's power, in the unusual case of *Texas v. White* (p. 181). During the war, the Texas Confederate government sold a number of U.S. bonds that had been in the prewar state treasury and used the proceeds to pay for war supplies. After the war, the presidentially reconstructed state government sued the bondholders to recover the instruments. Because this was ostensibly a suit by a state against citizens of other states, it came directly to the Supreme Court under its original jurisdiction in Article III-2. White and the other defendants argued that the Court had no such jurisdiction in the case because Texas was not a state. Deciding the jurisdictional question meant ruling on the status of the provisional Johnson government and the old Confederate state government, thus giving the Court opportunity to analyze the theory of secession and of Reconstruction. In a larger sense, it was asked to rule on the nature of the Union itself.

For five members of the Court, Chief Justice Chase distinguished between a state and its government. Texas had standing to sue because when admitted in 1845 it had entered, in Chase's memorable phrase, "an indestructible Union of indestructible States." Despite secession and the state's altered postwar status, Texas had, in effect, never left the Union. Its secessionist government was illegal, as were acts taken by it to further the rebellion. The long debate about ultimate state sovereignty and the validity of secession, settled in fact on the battlefield, was now also settled as a point of law. Lincoln's theory of an organic, indissoluble Union, older even than the Constitution, became Constitutional doctrine.

The case did not call for the Court to rule on Congress's Reconstruction acts, but Chase made it clear that although the president might set up provisional governments, Congress had final authority under Article IV-4, which guarantees states a republican form of government, to restore states to their full status.

The Chase Court has drawn praise and criticism for its work during Reconstruction. Though in *Ex parte Garland* and a few other cases it ruled on enactments applied to individuals, it never held on the constitutionality of Congress's entire program including its draconian military measures. It left the matter political, to be thrashed out between the two other branches. Whether this was judicial statesmanship or faintheartedness is still a matter of debate. Had the Court tried to block Congressional Reconstruction, it seems clear it would have met with severe reprisal. A veto-proof Congressional majority with an electoral mandate, willing to impeach a president and alter the Court's appellate jurisdiction, might not have sat idly by while an unelected body with no final enforcement powers thwarted it on the leading issue of the day.

The End of Reconstruction

By 1870, all secessionist states were readmitted and all had state governments and constitutions acceptable to Congress, though it is doubtful much of this could have been achieved without military occupation and supervision. In 1868, General Grant, the Republican presidential nominee, defeated Horatio Seymour, the former Democratic governor of New York. He won easy

reelection in 1872 against Horace Greeley. The army remained in place, and for a brief period Southern state legislatures and governorships were controlled by an alliance of carpetbaggers, "scalawags" (Southern Republicans and former Unionists), and Freedmen. These governments, sometimes corrupt and almost always in inexperienced hands, did have some notable aims and accomplishments, including proposals for economic development, the checking of discrimination against the Freedmen, and the founding of the South's first public school system.

Yet their world was deceiving. Propped up by military force and dependent on a determined Congress for political help, they lacked support of most of the local white population, which chafed under high taxes and would not accept the political and social equality of former slaves. Local opposition mounted, and unreconciled whites, organized as "Redeemers," gradually regained control of the political machinery in several states. Secret societies, including the Ku Klux Klan and the Knights of the White Camellia, were organized to intimidate allegedly unruly blacks and their white allies. President Grant responded with military reoccupation of some areas evacuated earlier. Though more than 7,000 arrests were made, few convictions followed. In the meantime, Northern interest in Reconstruction began to ebb as attention turned—returned is probably more accurate—to the challenges of economic and territorial development. With the Southern states now fully represented in Congress, Democrats recaptured control of the House in 1874, setting the stage for a great shift in national policy.

The close presidential election of 1876 between the Republican Rutherford B. Hayes and the Democrat Samuel J. Tilden was rife with fraud and corruption on both sides. Tilden led in the popular vote with 51 percent, but because returns were disputed in four states—Oregon, Florida, Louisiana, and South Carolina—with 22 electors, neither candidate had a majority of the electoral vote. The three Southern states were the only ones of the South still "unredeemed," that is, still having Republican governments. After negotiations between Southern Democratic leaders and representatives of Hayes, a compromise was reached. Democrats would acquiesce in Hayes's election if Hayes, as president, would remove remaining federal troops from the South, in effect ceding control of the three Southern states to the Democrats. An election commission set up by Congress then accepted the Republican version of returns from the four disputed states, and Hayes was declared the winner, 185 electoral votes to 184. When he kept his part of the bargain the following year, Reconstruction was over.

The outcome left a long-lasting legacy, mostly negative. Politically, the machinery of government in the South passed into the hands of a reactionary ruling elite who played on white fears and animosity and stifled dissent. As Republicans all but disappeared from the region, the South became a one-party bastion until the 1960s, giving it great seniority power in Congress. Socially, slavery was replaced by a caste system based on racial segregation, discrimination in almost all parts of life, and sharecropping. Economically, the devastated region lagged for nearly a century. The political and social arrangements did not encourage capital or immigration. Occupied with race, Southerners were unable to best use the resources of white or black populations.

Against these developments were some notable achievements. Attempts of the Republican Congress to gain genuine freedom and equal rights for the Freedmen produced three constitutional amendments, extending national power to protect individual liberties. The fruits of these changes were not immediately reaped because of narrow interpretations first given them by the Supreme Court and because of federal indifference to their virtual nullification in the South. But starting in the late 1950s, they provided the legal and moral basis for a "Second Reconstruction" in the form of the civil rights movement.

Still, Reconstruction is a story of lost opportunity. How much was lost may depend on one's view of whether the social revolution called for by the battlefield triumph and constitutional settlement was possible all within one generation. Absent, perhaps understandably so, was a sense of moderation that might have tempered the unfortunate cycle of indifference, compensatory excess, reaction, and counter-reaction. It is all too true then that the murder of Lincoln may have taken from the country far more than just a great life. Perhaps Lincoln might have seen, as Johnson and Southerners did not, that abolition of slavery was not the end of changes wrought by the war but only the beginning. It is hard to believe he would not have found and championed ways of aiding the Freedmen that were less provoking and vindictive than those of the Radical Republicans and less likely to stir the depths of racial animosity.

If one war goal—freeing the slaves—was nominally achieved but only partly realized in four years of fighting and a decade of peace, the other—preserving the Union—was resoundingly won. No longer would there be nation-dividing arguments about ultimate state sovereignty, the right of secession or nullification, or whether the Union was a compact of states or of the people of the united states. It is no mere vicissitude of usage that after the Civil War "the United States," once a plural noun, became invariably singular.

Important questions of federalism would remain, including the perennial one of where the line between state and federal authority and responsibility was to be drawn. But the fundamental character of the Union was now beyond doubt. In Chief Justice Chase's Lincolnian thesis in *Texas v. White* (p. 181), the Union predated the Constitution. It was supreme and perpetual, organic, and almost mystical. "The Constitution was ordained 'to form a more perfect Union.' It is difficult to convey the idea of indissoluble unity more clearly than by these words. What can be indissoluble if a perpetual Union, made more perfect is not?" This rhetorical question needed no answer. Whether supported or not by historical fact, Lincoln's theory first written in blood, was now inscribed in the Constitution and in the hearts and minds of the people.

FURTHER READING

Slavery and Its Constitutional Issues

Ashworth, John, *Slavery, Capitalism, and Politics in the Antebellum Republic* (1996)

Berlin, Ira, *Free at Last: A Documentary History of Slavery, Freedom, and the Civil War* (1997)

Brandon, Mark E., *Free in the World: American Slavery and Constitutional Failure* (1998)

Campbell, Stanley W., *Slave Catchers: Enforcement of the Fugitive Slave Law, 1850–1860* (1968)

Ericson, David F., *The Debates Over Slavery: Antislavery and Proslavery Liberalism in Antabellum America* (2001)

Fehrenbacher, Don E., completed and edited by Ward M. McAfee, *The Slaveholding Republic: An Account of the United States Government's Relations to Slavery* (2001)

Finkelman, Paul, *An Imperfect Union: Slavery, Federalism, and Comity* (1981)

Genovese, Eugene D., *Roll, Jordan, Roll: The World the Slaves Made* (1974)

Harrold, Stanley, *The Abolitionists and the South, 1831–1861* (1995)

Jeffrey, Julie Ray, *The Great Silent Army of Abolitionism* (1998)

Lynd, Staughton, *Class Conflict, Slavery, and the U. S. Constitution* (1967)

Miller, William Lee, *Arguing About Slavery: The Great Debate in the United States Congress* (1995)

Morris, Thomas D., *Southern Slavery and the Law* (1996)

———, *Free Men All: The Personal Liberty Laws of the North, 1780–1861* (1974)

Newmyer, R. Kent, *The Supreme Court Under Marshall and Taney* (1968)

Noonan, Jr., John T., *The Antelope: The Ordeal of the Recaptured Africans in the Administration of James Monroe and John Quincy Adams* (1977)

Onuf, Peter S., *Statehood and Union: A History of the Northwest Ordinance* (1987)

Robinson, Donald L., *Slavery in the Structure of American Politics,* 1765–1820 (1979)

Sewell, Richard H., *Ballots for Freedom: Antislavery Politics in the United States, 1837–1860* (1976)

Stampp, Kenneth M., *The Peculiar Institution* (1956)

Thomas, Hugh, *The Slave Trade* (1997)

Tushnet, Mark, *The American Law of Slavery, 1810–1860: Considerations of Humanity and Interest* (1981)

Wiecek, William, *The Sources of Antislavery Constitutionalism in America, 1760–1848* (1977)

Wiethoff, William E., *The Peculiar Humanism: The Judicial Advocacy of Slavery in High Courts of the Old South, 1820–1850* (1996)

Sectional Conflict and Political Failure

Birkner, Michael J., *James Buchanan and the Political Crisis of the 1850s* (1996)

Gienapp, William E., *The Origins of the Republican Party, 1852–1856* (1987)

Hyman, Harold and Wiecek, William, *Equal Justice Under Law: Constitutional Development, 1835–1875* (1982)

Jaffa. Harry V. *Crisis in the House Divided: An Interpretation of the Lincoln-Douglas Debates* (1959)

Knupfer, Peter B., *The Union as It Is: Constitutional Unionism and Sectional Compromise, 1787–1861* (1991)

Potter, David M., *The Impending Crisis, 1848–1860* (1976)

Swisher, Carl B., *The Taney Period, 1836–1864* (1974)

Civil War

Ash, Stephen V., *When the Yankees Came: Conflict and Chaos in the Occupied South, 1861–1865* (1995)

Belz, Herman, *Emancipation and Equal Rights: Politics and Constitutionalism in the Civil War Era* (1978)

———, *Abraham Lincoln, Constitutionalism, and Equal Rights in the Civil War Era* (1998)

Bogue, Allan G., *The Earnest Men: Republicans of the Civil War Senate* (1981)

Cox, La Wanda, *Lincoln and Black Freedom: A Study of Presidential Leadership* (1981)

Davis, William C., *The Cause Lost: Myths and Realities of the Confederacy* (1996)

DeRosa, Marshall L., *The Confederate Constitution of 1861* (1991)

Fletcher, George P., *Our Secret Constitution: How Lincoln Redefined American Democracy,* (2001)

Harris, William H., *With Charity for All: Lincoln and the Restoration of the Union* (1997)

McPherson, James M., *Battle Cry of Freedom: The Civil War Era* (1988)

Randall, James G., *Constitutional Problems Under Lincoln,* rev. (1951)

Waugh, John C., *Reelecting Lincoln: The Battle for the 1864 Presidency* (1998)

Wills, Garry, *Lincoln at Gettysburg* (1992)

Wilson, Douglas L., *Honor's Voice: The Transformation of Abraham Lincoln* (1998)

Reconstruction

Belz, Herman, *A New Birth of Freedom: The Republican Party and Freedmen's Rights, 1861–1866* (1976)

Benedict, Michael Les, *The Impeachment Trial of Andrew Johnson* (1973)

———, *A Compromise of Principle: Congressional Republicans and Reconstruction, 1863–1869* (1974)

Bensel, Richard Franklin, *Yankee Leviathan: The Origins of Central State Authority in America, 1859–1877* (1990)

Brandwein, Pamela, *Reconstructing Reconstruction: The Supreme Court and the Production of Historical Truth* (1999)

Carter, Dan T., *When the War Was Over: The Failure of Self-Reconstruction in the South, 1865–1867* (1985)

Fairman, Charles, *History of the Supreme Court of the United States,* vols 6–7, *Reconstruction and Reunion* (1971, 1987)

Foner, Eric, *Reconstruction: America's Unfinished Revolution, 1863–1877* (1988)

Franklin, John Hope, *Reconstruction After the Civil War* (1961)

Goldman, Robert H., *Reconstruction and Black Suffrage: Losing the Vote in* Reese *and* Cruikshank (2001)

Hyman, Harold M., *The Impact of the Civil War and Reconstruction on the Constitution* (1975)

Kaczorowski, Robert J., *The Politics of Judicial Interpretation: The Federal Courts, Department of Justice, and Civil Rights, 1866-1876* (1985)

Kutler, Stanley I., *Judicial Review and Reconstruction Politics* (1968)

Maltz, Earl M., *Civil Rights, the Constitution, and Congress, 1863–1869*

McKitrick, Eric, *Andrew Johnson and Reconstruction* (1960)

Nieman, Donald G., *To Set the Law in Motion: The Freedmen's Bureau and the Legal Rights of Blacks, 1865–1868* (1979)

Perman, Michael, *The Road to Redemption: Southern Politics, 1868–1878* (1984)

Richards, David A. J., *Conscience and the Constitution: History, Theory, and Law of the Reconstruction Amendments* (1993)

Simpson, Brooks D., *The Reconstruction Presidents* (1998)

Woodward, C. Vann, *Reunion and Reaction: The Compromise of 1876 and the End of Reconstruction* (1951)

Biographical

Donald, David Herbert, *Lincoln* (1995)

Johannsen, Robert, *Stephan A. Douglas* (1972)

Niven, John, *John C. Calhoun and the Price of Union* (1988)

———, *Salmon P. Chase, A Biography* (1995)

Randall, James G., *Lincoln, the President,* 4 vols (vol 4 completed by Richard Current) (1945–1955)

Trefousse, Hans, *Thaddeus Stevens: Nineteenth Century Egalitarian* (1997)

On Leading Cases

Erhlich, Walter, *They Have No Rights: Dred Scott's Struggle for Freedom* (1979)

Fehrenbacher, Don E., *The Dred Scott Case: Its Significance in American Law and Politics* (1978)

———, ed., *Dred Scott v. Sandford: A Brief History with Documents* (1996)

Hyman, Harold M., *The Reconstruction Justice of Salmon P. Chase: In* Re Turner *and* Texas v. White (1997)

CASES

Prigg v. Pennsylvania

41 U.S. 539 (1842), 8-1
Opinion of the Court: Story (Catron, McKinley)
Concurring: Taney, C.J., Baldwin, Daniel, Thompson,
   Wayne
Dissenting: McLean

Edward Prigg, an agent for a Maryland slaveowner, pursued and captured an escaped slave. When denied a certificate for removal by a Pennsylvania court, Prigg forcibly returned the slave to Maryland. Here he appeals his conviction under a state law forbidding self-help in the return of fugitive slaves.

What is the disagreement between Story and Taney? What theories of the Union are represented in their opinions? Exactly what does the case hold with regard to federal power? State power? How does the decision settle the fugitive slave question? How does it not? Besides the parties to the case, who gains and who loses as a result of this decision?

Story, for the Court:

There are two clauses in the constitution upon the subject of fugitives, which stands in juxtaposition with each other, and have been thought mutually to illustrate each other. They are both contained in the second section of the fourth article, and are in the following words: 'A person charged in any state with treason, felony or other crime, who shall flee from justice, and be found in another state, shall, on demand of the executive authority of the state from which he fled, be delivered up, to be removed to the state having jurisdiction of the crime.' 'No person held to service or labor in one state, under the laws thereof, escaping into another, shall, in consequence of any law or regulation therein, be discharged from such service or labor; but shall be delivered up, on claim of the party to whom such service or labor may be due.'

The last clause is that, the true interpretation whereof is directly in judgment before us. Historically, it is well known, that the object of this clause was to secure to the citizens of the slave-holding states the complete right and title of ownership in their slaves, as property, in every state in the Union into which they might escape from the state where they were held in servitude. The full recognition of this right and title was indispensable to the security of this species of property in all the slave-holding states; and, indeed, was so vital to the preservation of their do-

mestic interests and institutions, that it cannot be doubted, that it constituted a fundamental article, without the adoption of which the Union could not have been formed. . . .

[U]nder and in virtue of the constitution, the owner of a slave is clothed with entire authority, in every state in the Union, to seize and recapture his slave, whenever he can do it, without any breach of the peace or any illegal violence. In this sense, and to this extent, this clause of the constitution may properly be said to execute itself, and to require no aid from legislation, state or national. . . .

If, indeed, the constitution guaranties the right, and if it requires the delivery upon the claim of the owner (as cannot well be doubted), the natural inference certainly is, that the national government is clothed with the appropriate authority and functions to enforce it. The fundamental principle, applicable to all cases of this sort, would seem to be, that where the end is required, the means are given; and where the duty is enjoined, the ability to perform it is contemplated to exist, on the part of the functionaries to whom it is intrusted. The clause is found in the national constitution, and not in that of any state. It does not point out any state functionaries, or any state action, to carry its provisions into effect. The states cannot, therefore, be compelled to enforce them; and it might well be deemed an unconstitutional exercise of the power of interpretation, to insist, that the states are bound to provide means to carry into effect the duties of the national government, nowhere delegated or intrusted to them by the constitution. On the contrary, the natural, if not the necessary, conclusion is, that the national government, in the absence of all positive provisions to the contrary, is bound, through its own proper departments, legislative, judicial or executive, as the case may require, to carry into effect all the rights and duties imposed upon it by the constitution. . . .

The remaining question is, whether the power of legislation upon this subject is exclusive in the national government, or concurrent in the states, until it is exercised by congress. In our opinion, it is exclusive; and we shall now proceed briefly to state our reasons for that opinion. The doctrine stated by this court in *Sturges v. Crowninshield* contains the true, although not the sole, rule or consideration, which is applicable to this particular subject. 'Wherever,' said Mr. Chief Justice Marshall, in delivering the opinion of the Court, 'the terms in which a power is granted to congress, or the nature of the power, require, that it should be exercised exclusively by congress, the subject is as completely taken from the state legislatures, as if they had been forbidden to act.' The nature of the power, and the true objects to be attained by it, are then as important to be weighed, in considering the question of its exclusiveness, as the words in which it is granted.

In the first place, it is material to state (what has been already incidentally hinted at), that the right to seize and retake fugitive slaves and the duty to deliver them up, in whatever state of the Union they may be found, and, of course, the corresponding power in congress to use the appropriate means to enforce the right and duty, derive their whole validity and obligation exclusively from the constitution of the United States, and are there, for the first time, recognized and established in that peculiar character. Before the adoption of the constitution, no state had any power whatsoever over the subject, except within its own territorial limits, and could not bind the sovereignty or the legislation of other states. Whenever the right was acknowledged, or the duty enforced, in any state, it was as a matter of comity, and not as a matter of strict moral, political or international obligation or duty. . . .

In the next place, the nature of the provision and the objects to be attained by it, require that it should be controlled by one and the same will, and act uniformly by the same system of regulations throughout the Union. If, then, the states have a right, in the absence of legislation by congress, to act upon the subject, each state is at liberty to prescribe just such regulations as suit its own policy, local convenience and local feelings. The legislation of one state may not only be different from, but utterly repugnant to and incompatible with, that of another. The time and mode, and limitation of the remedy, the proofs of the title, and all other incidents applicable thereto, may be prescribed in one state, which are rejected or disclaimed in another. One state may require the owner to sue in one mode, another, in a different mode. One state may make a statute of limitations as to the remedy, in its own tribunals, short and summary; another may prolong the period, and yet restrict the proofs. Nay, some states may utterly refuse to act upon the subject of all; and others may refuse to open its courts to any remedies in rem, because they would interfere with their own domestic policy, institutions or habits. The right, therefore, would never, in a practical sense, be the same in all the states. It would have no unity of purpose, or uniformity of operation. The duty might be enforced in some states; retarded or limited in others; and denied, as compulsory, in many, if not in all. Consequences like these must have been foreseen as very likely to occur in the non-slave-holding states, where legislation, if not silent on the subject, and purely voluntary, could scarcely be presumed to be favorable to the exercise of the rights of the owner. . . .

To guard, however, against any possible misconstruction of our views, it is proper to state, that we are by no means to be understood, in any manner whatsoever, to doubt or to interfere with the police power belonging to the states, in virtue of their general sovereignty. That police power extends over all subjects within territorial limits of the states, and has never been conceded to the United States. It is wholly distinguishable from the right and duty secured by the provision now under consideration; which is exclusively derived from and secured by the Constitution of the United States, and owes its whole efficacy thereto. We entertain no doubt whatsoever, that the states, in virtue of their general police power, possesses full jurisdiction to arrest and restrain runaway slaves, and remove them from their borders, and otherwise to secure themselves against their depredations and evil example, as they certainly may do in cases of idlers, vagabonds and paupers. The rights of the owners of fugitive slaves are in no just sense interfered with, or regulated, by such a course; and in many cases, the operations of this police power, although designed generally for other purposes, for protection, safety and peace of the state, may essentially promote and aid the interests of the owners. But such regulations can never be permitted to interfere with, or to obstruct, the just rights of the owner to reclaim his slave, derived from the constitution of the United States, or with the remedies prescribed by congress to aid and enforce the same.

Taney, C.J., concurring:

I concur . . . that the law of Pennsylvania, under which [Prigg] was indicted, is unconstitutional and void; and that the judgment against him must be reversed. But as the questions before us arise upon the construction of the Constitution of the United States, and as I do not assent to all the principles contained in the opinion just delivered, it is proper to state the points on which I differ. . . .

The . . . Court maintains that the power over this subject is so exclusively vested in congress, that no state, since the adoption of the Constitution, can pass any law in relation to it. In other words . . . the state authorities are prohibited from interfering, for the purpose of protecting the right of the master, and aiding him in the recovery of his property. I think, the states are not prohibited; and that, on the contrary, it is enjoined upon them as a duty, to protect and support the owner, when he is endeavoring to obtain possession of his property found within their respective territories. The language used in the Constitution does not, in my judgment, justify this construction given to it by the Court. It contains no words prohibiting the several states from passing laws to enforce this right. They are, in express terms, forbidden to make any regulation that shall impair it; but there the prohibition stops. And according to the settled rules of construction for all written instruments, the prohibition being confined to laws injurious to the right, the power to pass laws to support and enforce it, is necessarily implied. And the words of the article which direct that the fugitive 'shall be delivered up,' seem evidently designed to impose it as a duty upon the people of the several states, to pass laws to carry into execution, in good faith, the compact into which they thus solemnly entered with each other. The Constitution of the United States, and every article and clause in it, is a part of the law of every state in the Union; and is the paramount law. The right of the master, therefore, to seize his fugitive slave, is the law of each state; and no state has the power to abrogate or alter it. And why may not a state protect a right of property, acknowledged by its own paramount law? Besides, the laws of the different states, in all other cases, constantly protect the citizens of other states in their rights of property, when it is found within their respective territories; and no one doubts their power to do so. And in the absence of any express prohibition, I perceive no reason for establishing, by implication, a different rule in this instance; where, by the national compact, this right of property is recognized as an existing right in every state of the Union. . . .

I dissent, therefore . . . from that part of the opinion of the Court which denies the obligation and the right of the state authorities to protect the master, when he is endeavoring to seize a fugitive from his service, in pursuance of the right given to him by the constitution of the United States; provided the state law is not in conflict with the remedy provided by Congress.

Scott v. Sandford

60 U.S. 393 (1857), 7-2
Opinion of the Court: Taney
Concurring: Campbell, Catron, Daniel, Grier, Nelson, Wayne
Dissenting: Curtis, McLean

What is Taney's theory of the nature of the Union? Can it be reconciled with Marshall's in McCulloch v. Maryland? *This is the first case striking down a national law since* Marbury v. Madison. *How does Taney expand judicial review beyond that established by* Marbury? *Why did Taney find it necessary to declare the Missouri Compromise unconstitutional? Could the case have been decided on narrower grounds? What distinction does Taney make between federal and state citizenship? After this decision, what recourse is left open for black persons to become citizens? Is the decision a failure because it tried to impose a solution on the slavery question or because it tried to impose the wrong one?*

Taney, C.J., for the Court:

The question is simply this: Can a negro, whose ancestors were imported into this country, and sold as slaves, become a member of the political community formed and brought into existence by the Constitution of the United States, and as such become entitled to all the rights, and privileges, and immunities, guarantied by that instrument to the citizen? One of which rights is the privilege of suing in a court of the United States in the cases specified in the Constitution.

[T]he plea applies to that class of persons only whose ancestors were negroes of the African race, and imported into this country, and sold and held as slaves. The only matter in issue before the Court, therefore, is, whether the descendants of such slaves, when they shall be emancipated, or who are born of parents who had become free before their birth, are citizens of a State, in the sense in which the word citizen is used in the Constitution of the United States. And this being the only matter in dispute on the pleadings, the court must be understood as speaking in this opinion of that class only, that is, of those persons who are the descendants of Africans who were imported into this country, and sold as slaves. . . .

The words 'people of the United States' and 'citizens' are synonymous terms, and mean the same thing. They both describe the political body who, according to our republican institutions, form the sovereignty, and who hold the power and conduct the Government through their representatives. They are what we familiarly call the 'sovereign people,' and every citizen is one of this people, and a constituent member of this sovereignty. The question before us is, whether the class of persons described in the plea in abatement compose a portion of this people, and are constituent members of this sovereignty? We think they are not, and that they are not included, and were not intended to be included, under the word 'citizens' in the Constitution, and can therefore claim none of the rights and privileges which that instrument provides for and secures to citizens of the United States. On the contrary, they were at that time considered as a subordinate and inferior class of beings, who had been subjugated by the dominant race, and, whether emancipated or not, yet remained subject to their authority, and had no rights or privileges but such as those who held the power and the Government might choose to grant them. . . .

[W]e must not confound the rights of citizenship which a State may confer within its own limits, and the rights of citizenship as a member of the Union. It does not by any means follow, because he has all the rights and privileges of a citizen of a State, that he must be a citizen of the United States. He may have all of the rights and privileges of the citizen of a State, and yet not be entitled to the rights and privileges of a citizen in any other State. For, previous to the adoption of the Constitution of the United States, every State had the undoubted right to confer on whomsoever it pleased the character of citizen, and to endow him with all its rights. But this character of course was confined to the boundaries of the State, and gave him no rights or privileges in other States beyond those secured to him by the laws of nations and the comity of States. Nor have the several States surrendered the power of conferring these rights and privileges by adopting the Constitution of the United States. . . .

It is very clear, therefore, that no State can, by any act or law of its own, passed since the adoption of the Constitution, introduce a new member into the political community created by the Constitution of the United States. It cannot make him a member of this community by making him a member of its own. And for the same reason it cannot introduce any person, or description of persons, who were not intended to be embraced in this new political family, which the Constitution brought into existence, but were intended to be excluded from it. . . .

It is true, every person, and every class and description of persons, who were at the time of the adoption of the Constitution recognized as citizens in the several States, became also citizens of this new political body; but none other; it was formed by them, and for them and their posterity, but for no one else. And the personal rights and privileges guarantied to citizens of this new sovereignty were intended to embrace those only who were then members of the several State communities, or who should afterwards by birthright or otherwise become members, according to the provisions of the Constitution and the principles on which it was founded. . . .

It becomes necessary, therefore, to determine who were citizens of the several States when the Constitution was adopted. And in order to do this, we must recur to the Governments and institutions of the thirteen colonies, when they separated from Great Britain and formed new sovereignties, and took their places in the family of independent nations. We must inquire who, at that time, were recognized as the people or citizens of a State, whose rights and liberties had been outraged by the English Government; and who declared their independence, and assumed the powers of Government to defend their rights by force of arms. . . .

[T]he legislation and histories of the times, and the language used in the Declaration of Independence, show, that neither the class of persons who had been imported as slaves, nor their descendants, whether they had become free or not, were then acknowledged as a part of the people, nor intended to be included in the general words used in that memorable instrument. . . .

They had for more than a century before been regarded as beings of an inferior order, and altogether unfit to associate with the white race, either in social or political relations; and so far inferior, that they had no rights which the white man was bound to respect; and that the negro might justly and lawfully be reduced to slavery for his benefit. . . .

The opinion thus entertained and acted upon in England was naturally impressed upon the colonies they founded on this side of the Atlantic. And, accordingly, a negro of the African race was regarded by them as an article of property, and held, and bought and sold as such, in every one of the thirteen colonies which united in the Declaration of Independence, and afterwards formed the Constitution of the United States. The slaves were more or less numerous in the different colonies, as slave labor was found more or less profitable. But no one seems to have doubted the correctness of the prevailing opinion of the time.

The legislation of the different colonies furnishes positive and indisputable proof of this fact. . . .

We refer to these historical facts for the purpose of showing the fixed opinions concerning that race, upon which the statesmen of that day spoke and acted. It is necessary to do this, in order to determine whether the general terms used in the Constitution of the United States, as to the rights of man and the rights of the people, was intended to include them, or to give to them or their posterity the benefit of any of its provisions. . . .

And upon a full and careful consideration of the subject, the court is of opinion, that, upon the facts stated in the plea in abatement, Dred Scott was not a citizen of Missouri within the meaning of the Constitution of the United States, and not entitled as such to sue in its courts; and, consequently, that the Circuit Court had no jurisdiction of the case, and that the judgment on the plea in abatement is erroneous. . . .

We proceed, therefore, to inquire whether the facts relied on by [Scott] entitled him to his freedom. . . .

In considering this part of the controversy, two questions arise: 1. Was he, together with his family, free in Missouri by reason of the stay in the territory of the United States hereinbefore mentioned? And 2. If they were not, is Scott himself free by reason of his removal to Rock Island, in the State of Illinois, as stated in the above admissions?

We proceed to examine the first question.

The act of Congress, upon which [Scott] relies, declares that slavery and involuntary servitude, except as a punishment for crime, shall be forever prohibited in all that part of the territory ceded by France, under the name of Louisiana, which lies north of thirty-six degrees thirty minutes north latitude, and not included within the limits of Missouri. And the difficulty which meets us at the threshold of this part of the inquiry is, whether Congress was authorized to pass this law under any of the powers granted to it by the Constitution; for if the authority is not given by that instrument, it is the duty of this court to declare it void and inoperative, and incapable of conferring freedom upon any one who is held as a slave under the have of any one of the States.

The counsel for [Scott] has laid much stress upon that article in the Constitution which confers on Congress the power 'to dispose of and make all needful rules and regulations respecting the territory or other property belonging to the United States;' but, in the judgment of the court, that provision has no bearing on the present controversy, and the power there given, whatever it may be, is confined, and was intended to be confined, to the territory which at that time belonged to, or was claimed by, the United States, and was within their boundaries as settled by the treaty with Great Britain, and can have no influence upon a territory afterwards acquired from a foreign Government. It was a special provision for a known and particular territory, and to meet a present emergency, and nothing more.

A brief summary of the history of the times, as well as the careful and measured terms in which the article is framed, will show the correctness of this proposition. . . .

This brings us to examine by what provision of the Constitution the present Federal Government, under its delegated and restricted powers, is authorized to acquire territory outside of the original limits of the United States, and what powers it may exercise therein over the person or property of a citizen of the United States, while it remains a Territory, and until it shall be admitted as one of the States of the Union.

There is certainly no power given by the Constitution to the Federal Government to establish or maintain colonies bordering on the United States or at a distance, to be ruled and governed at its own pleasure; nor to enlarge its territorial limits in any way, except by the admission of new States. . . .

We do not mean . . . to question the power of Congress in this respect. The power to expand the territory of the United States by the admission of new States is plainly given; and in the construction of this power by all the departments of the Government, it has been held to authorize the acquisition of territory, not fit for admission at the time, but to be admitted as soon as its population and situation would entitle it to admission. It is acquired to become a State, and not to be held as a colony and governed by Congress with absolute authority. . . .

[A]nd as the people of the United States could act in this matter only through the Government which represented them, and the through which they spoke and acted when the Territory was obtained, it was not only within the scope of its powers, but it was its duty to pass such laws and establish such a Government as would enable those by whose authority they acted to reap the advantages anticipated from its acquisition, and to gather there a population which would enable it to assume the position to which it was destined among the States of the Union. The power to acquire necessarily carries with it the power to preserve and apply to the purposes for which it was acquired. The form of government to be established necessarily rested in the discretion of Congress. It was their duty to establish the one that would be best suited for the protection and security of the citizens of the United States, and other inhabitants who might be authorized to take up their abode there, and that must always depend upon the existing condition of the Territory, as to the number and character of its inhabitants, and their situation in the Territory. In some cases a Government, consisting of persons appointed by the Federal Government, would best subserve the interests of the Territory, when the inhabitants were few and scattered, and new to one another. In other instances, it would be more advisable to commit the powers of self-government to the people who had settled in the Territory, as being the most competent to determine what was best for their own interests. But some form of civil authority would be absolutely necessary to organize and preserve civilized society, and prepare it to become a State; and what is the best form must always depend on the condition of the Territory at the time, and the choice of the mode must depend upon the exercise of a discretionary power by Congress, acting within the scope of its constitutional authority, and not infringing upon the rights of person or rights of property of the citizen who might go there to reside, or for any other lawful purpose. It was acquired by the exercise of this discretion, and it must be held and governed in like manner, until it is fitted to be a State.

But the power of Congress over the person or property of a citizen can never be a mere discretionary power under our Constitution and form of Government. The powers of the Government and the rights and privileges of the citizen are regulated and plainly defined by the Constitution itself. And when the Territory becomes a part of the United States, the Federal Government enters into possession in the character impressed upon it by those who created it. It enters upon it with its powers over the citizen strictly defined, and limited by the Constitution, from which it derives its own existence, and by virtue of which alone it continues to exist and act as a Government and sovereignty. It has no power of any kind beyond it; and it cannot, when it enters a Territory of the United States, put off its character, and assume discretionary or despotic powers which the Constitution has denied to it. . . .

These powers, and others, in relation to rights of person, which it is not necessary here to enumerate,

are, in express and positive terms, denied to the General Government; and the rights of private property have been guarded with equal care. Thus the rights of property are united with the rights of person, and placed on the same ground by the fifth amendment to the Constitution, which provides that no person shall be deprived of life, liberty, and property, without due process of law. And an act of Congress which deprives a citizen of the United States of his liberty or property, merely because he came himself or brought his property into a particular Territory of the United States, and who had committed no offense against the laws, could hardly be dignified with the name of due process of law. . . .

Now, as we have already said in an earlier part of this opinion, upon a different point, the right of property in a slave is distinctly and expressly affirmed in the Constitution. The right to traffic in it, like an ordinary article of merchandise and property, was guarantied to the citizens of the United States, in every State that might desire it, for twenty years. And the Government in express terms is pledged to protect it in all future time, if the slave escapes from his owner. This is done in plain words—too plain to be misunderstood. And no word can be found in the Constitution which gives Congress a greater power over slave property, or which entitles property of that kind to less protection that property of any other description. The only power conferred is the power coupled with the duty of guarding and protecting the owner in his rights.

Upon these considerations, it is the opinion of the Court that the act of Congress which prohibited a citizen from holding and owning property of this kind in the territory of the United States north of the line therein mentioned, is not warranted by the Constitution, and is therefore void; and that neither Dred Scott himself, nor any of his family, were made free by being carried into this territory; even if they had been carried there by the owner, with the intention of becoming a permanent resident.

We have so far examined the case, as it stands under the Constitution of the United States, and the powers thereby delegated to the Federal Government.

But there is another point in the case which depends on State power and State law. And it is contended, on the part of [Scott], that he is made free by being taken to Rock Island, in the State of Illinois, independently of his residence in the territory of the United States; and being so made free, he was not again reduced to a state of slavery by being brought back to Missouri.

Our notice of this part of the case will be very brief; for the principle on which it depends was decided in this court, upon much consideration, in the case of *Strader v. Graham*. In that case, the slaves had been taken from Kentucky to Ohio, with the consent of the owner, and afterwards brought back to Kentucky. And this court held that their status or condition, as free or slave, depended upon the laws of Kentucky, when they were brought back into that State, and not of Ohio; and that this court had no jurisdiction to revise the judgment of a State court upon its own laws. This was the point directly before the court, and the decision that this court had not jurisdiction turned upon it, as will be seen by the report of the case.

So in this case. As Scott was a slave when taken into the State of Illinois by his owner, and was there held as such, and brought back in that character, his status, as free or slave, depended on the laws of Missouri, and not of Illinois. . . .

Upon the whole, therefore, it is the judgment of this court, that it appears by the record before us that [Scott] is not a citizen of Missouri, in the sense in which that word is used in the Constitution. . . .

Curtis, dissenting:

To determine whether any free persons, descended from Africans held in slavery, were citizens of the United States under the Confederation, and consequently at the time of the adoption of the Constitution of the United States, it is only necessary to know whether any such persons were citizens of either of the States under the Confederation, at the time of the adoption of the Constitution.

Of this there can be no doubt. At the time of the ratification of the Articles of Confederation, all free native-born inhabitants of the States of New Hampshire, Massachusetts, New York, New Jersey, and North Carolina, though descended from African slaves, were not only citizens of those States, but such of them as had the other necessary qualifications possessed the franchise of electors, on equal terms with other citizens. . . .

Did the Constitution of the United States deprive them or their descendants of citizenship?

That Constitution was ordained and established by the people of the United States, through the action, in each State, or those persons who were qualified by its laws to act thereon, in behalf of themselves and all

other citizens of that State. In some of the States, as we have seen, colored persons were among those qualified by law to act on this subject. These colored persons were not only included in the body of 'the people of the United States,' by whom the Constitution was ordained and established, but in at least five of the States they had the power to act, and doubtless did act, by their suffrages, upon the question of its adoption. It would be strange, if we were to find in that instrument anything which deprived of their citizenship any part of the people of the United States who were among those by whom it was established.

I can find nothing in the Constitution which . . . deprives of their citizenship any class of persons who were citizens of the United States at the time of its adoption, or who should be native-born citizens of any State after its adoption; nor any power enabling Congress to disfranchise persons born on the soil of any State, and entitled to citizenship of such State by its Constitution and laws. . . . [U]nder the Constitution of the United States, every free person born on the soil of a State, who is a citizen of that State by force of its Constitution or laws, is also a citizen of the United States. . . .

Ableman v. Booth

62 U.S. 506 (1859), 9-0
Opinion of the Court: Taney (Campbell, Catron, Clifford, Daniel, Grier, McLean, Nelson, Wayne)
Does Taney rely on text of the Constitution or on other factors as the grounds for this decision? Is the decision consistent with Prigg v. Pennsylvania? *Is it an extension of Dred Scott? If a decision can be both nationalist and proslavery in its effect, what does that say about the nature of the Union at the time?*

Taney, C.J., for the Court:

If the judicial power exercised in this instance has been reserved to the States, no offense against the laws of the United States can be punished by their own courts, without the permission and according to the judgment of the courts of the State in which the party happens to be imprisoned; for, if the Supreme Court of Wisconsin possessed the power it has exercised . . . it necessarily follows that they must have the same judicial authority in relation to any other law of the United States . . . And, moreover, if the power is possessed by the Supreme Court of the State of Wisconsin, it must belong equally to every other State in the Union, when the prisoner is within its territorial limits; and it is very certain that the State courts would not always agree in opinion; and it would often happen, that an act which was admitted to be an offense, and justly punished, in one State, would be regarded as innocent, and indeed as praiseworthy, in another.

It would seem to be hardly necessary to do more than state the result to which these decisions of the State courts must inevitably lead. It is, of itself, a sufficient and conclusive answer; for no one will suppose that a Government which has now lasted nearly seventy years, enforcing its laws by its own tribunals, and preserving the union of the States, could have lasted a single year, or fulfilled the high trusts committed to it, if offenses against its laws could not have been punished without the consent of the State in which the culprit was found.

The judges of the Supreme Court of Wisconsin do not distinctly state from what source they suppose they have derived this judicial power. There can be no such thing as judicial authority, unless it is conferred by a Government or sovereignty; and if the judges and courts of Wisconsin possess the jurisdiction they claim, they must derive it either from the United States or the State. It certainly has not been conferred on them by the United States; and it is equally clear it was not in the power of the State to confer it . . . for no State can authorize one of its judges or courts to exercise judicial power, by habeas corpus or otherwise, within the jurisdiction of another and independent Government. And although the State of Wisconsin is sovereign within its territorial limits to a certain extent, yet that sovereignty is limited and restricted by the Constitution of the United States. And the powers of the General Government, and of the State, although both exist and are exercised within the same territorial limits, are yet separate and distinct sovereignties, acting separately and independently of each other, within their respective spheres. And the sphere of action appropriated to the United States is as far beyond the reach of the judicial process issued by a State judge or a State court, as if the line of division was traced by landmarks and monuments visible to the eye. And the State of Wisconsin had no more power to authorize these proceedings of its judges and courts, than it would have had if the prisoner had been confined in Michigan, or in any other State of the Union, for an offense against the laws of the State in which he was imprisoned. . . .

The Constitution was not formed merely to guard the States against danger from foreign nations, but mainly to secure union and harmony at home . . . and to accomplish this purpose, it was felt by the statesmen who framed the Constitution, and by the people who adopted it, that it was necessary that many of the rights of sovereignty which the States then possessed should be ceded to the General Government; and that, in the sphere of action assigned to it, it should be supreme, and strong enough to execute its own laws by its own tribunals, without interruption from a State or from State authorities. . . .

But the supremacy thus conferred on this Government could not peacefully be maintained, unless it was clothed with judicial power, equally paramount in authority to carry it into execution; for if left to the courts of justice of the several States, conflicting decisions would unavoidably take place, and the local tribunals could hardly be expected to be always free from the local influences of which we have spoken. And the Constitution and laws and treaties of the United States, and the powers granted to the Federal Government, would soon receive different interpretations in different States, and the Government of the United States would soon become one thing in one State and another thing in another. It was essential, therefore, to its very existence as a Government, that it should have the power of establishing courts of justice, altogether independent of State power, to carry into effect its own laws; and that a tribunal should be established in which all cases which might arise under the Constitution and laws and treaties of the United States, whether in a State court or a court of the United States, should be finally and conclusively decided. Without such a tribunal, it is obvious that there would be no uniformity of judicial decision; and that the supremacy, (which is but another name for independence,) so carefully provided in the clause of the Constitution above referred to, could not possibly be maintained peacefully, unless it was associated with this paramount judicial authority. . . .

This judicial power was justly regarded as indispensable, not merely to maintain the supremacy of the laws of the United States, but also to guard the States from any encroachment upon their reserved rights by the General Government. And as the Constitution is the fundamental and supreme law, if it appears that an act of Congress is not pursuant to and within the limits of the power assigned to the Federal Government, it is the duty of the courts of the United States to declare it unconstitutional and void. . . .

And as the final appellate power in all such questions is given to this court, controversies as to the respective powers of the United States and the States, instead of being determined by military and physical force, are heard, investigated, and finally settled, with the calmness and deliberation of judicial inquiry. And no one can fail to see, that if such an arbiter had not been provided, in our complicated system of government, internal tranquillity could not have been preserved. . . .

No State judge or court, after they are judicially informed that the party is imprisoned under the authority of the United States, has any right to interfere with him, or to require him to be brought before them. And if the authority of a State, in the form of judicial process or otherwise, should attempt to control the marshal or other authorized officer or agent of the United States, in any respect, in the custody of his prisoner, it would be his duty to resist it. . . . No judicial process . . . can have any lawful authority outside of the limits of the jurisdiction of the court or judge by whom it is issued; and an attempt to enforce it beyond these boundaries is nothing less than lawless violence. . . .

[N]o power is more clearly conferred by the Constitution and laws of the United States, than the power of this court to decide, ultimately and finally, all cases arising under such Constitution and laws. . . .

[W]e are not willing to be misunderstood, it is proper to say that, in the judgment of this court, the act of Congress commonly called the fugitive slave law is, in all of its provisions, fully authorized by the Constitution of the United States. . . .

The judgment of the Supreme Court of Wisconsin must therefore be reversed.

The Prize Cases

67 U.S. 635 (1863), 5-4
Opinion of the Court: Grier (Davis, Miller, Swayne, Wayne)
Dissenting: Nelson, Catron, Clifford, Taney
Several owners of foreign ships and cargos seized by Union forces in the blockade of Southern ports in the first months of the Civil War sued to recover their property arguing that no state of war had been declared between the parties.

Was the military resistance of Southern forces to federal authority war? Exactly who has power to initiate war? To declare war? To continue war? What does Grier say was the source of Lincoln's power to take military action? Does the decision rest on Congress's express approval of Lincoln's action after the fact? On what constitutional grounds do the dissenters argue against the legality of the blockade? Is this case to be understood mainly as a decision addressed to unique circumstances or as the basis for an expansive and enduring theory of presidential power to deal with military threat?

Grier, for the Court:

There are certain propositions of law which must necessarily affect the ultimate decision of these cases, and many others, which it will be proper to discuss and decide before we notice the special facts peculiar to each. . . .

Had the President a right to institute a blockade of ports in possession of persons in armed rebellion against the Government, on the principles of international law, as known and acknowledged among civilized States? . . .

That a blockade de facto actually existed, and was formally declared and notified by the President on the 27th and 30th of April, 1861, is an admitted fact in these cases.

That the President, as the Executive Chief of the Government and Commander-in-chief of the Army and Navy, was the proper person to make such notification, has not been, and cannot be disputed.

The right of prize and capture has its origin in the *jus belli,* and is governed and adjudged under the law of nations. To legitimate the capture of a neutral vessel or property on the high seas, a war must exist de facto, and the neutral must have a knowledge or notice of the intention of one of the parties belligerent to use this mode of coercion against a port, city, or territory, in possession of the other.

Let us inquire whether, at the time this blockade was instituted, a state of war existed which would justify a resort to these means of subduing the hostile force.

War has been well defined to be, 'That state in which a nation prosecutes its right by force.'

The parties belligerent in a public war are independent nations. But it is not necessary to constitute war, that both parties should be acknowledged as independent nations or sovereign States. A war may exist where one of the belligerents, claims sovereign rights as against the other.

Insurrection against a government may or may not culminate in an organized rebellion, but a civil war always begins by insurrection against the lawful authority of the Government. A civil war is never solemnly declared; it becomes such by its accidents—the number, power, and organization of the persons who originate and carry it on. . . .

As a civil war is never publicly proclaimed . . . against insurgents, its actual existence is a fact in our domestic history which the Court is bound to notice and to know.

The true test of its existence, as found in the writings of the sages of the common law, may be thus summarily stated: 'When the regular course of justice is interrupted by revolt, rebellion, or insurrection, so that the Courts of Justice cannot be kept open, civil war exists and hostilities may be prosecuted on the same footing as if those opposing the Government were foreign enemies invading the land.'

By the Constitution, Congress alone has the power to declare a national or foreign war. It cannot declare war against a State, or any number of States, by virtue of any clause in the Constitution. The Constitution confers on the President the whole Executive power. He is bound to take care that the laws be faithfully executed. He is Commander in chief of the Army and Navy of the United States, and of the militia of the several States when called into the actual service of the United States. He has no power to initiate or declare a war either against a foreign nation or a domestic State. But by the Acts of Congress of February 28th, 1795, and 3d of March, 1807, he is authorized to call out the militia and use the military and naval forces of the United States in case of invasion by foreign nations, and to suppress insurrection against the government of a State or of the United States.

If a war be made by invasion of a foreign nation, the President is not only authorized but bound to resist force by force. He does not initiate the war, but is bound to accept the challenge without waiting for any special legislative authority. And whether the hostile party be a foreign invader, or States organized in rebellion, it is none the less a war, although the declaration of it be 'unilateral.' . . .

This greatest of civil wars was not gradually developed by popular commotion, tumultuous assemblies, or local unorganized insurrections . . . The President was bound to meet it in the shape it presented itself, without waiting for Congress to baptize it with a name; and no name given to it by him or them could change the fact.

It is not the less a civil war, with belligerent parties in hostile array, because it may be called an 'insurrec-

tion' by one side, and the insurgents be considered as rebels or traitors. It is not necessary that the independence of the revolted province or State be acknowledged in order to constitute it a party belligerent in a war according to the law of nations. . . .

Whether the President in fulfilling his duties, as Commander in chief, in suppressing an insurrection, has met with such armed hostile resistance, and a civil war of such alarming proportions as will compel him to accord to them the character of belligerents, is a question to be decided by him, and this Court must be governed by the decisions and acts of the political department of the Government to which this power was entrusted. 'He must determine what degree of force the crisis demands.' The proclamation of blockade is itself official and conclusive evidence to the Court that a state of war existed which demanded and authorized a recourse to such a measure, under the circumstances peculiar to the case. . . .

If it were necessary to the technical existence of a war, that it should have a legislative sanction, we find it in almost every act passed at the extraordinary session of the Legislature of 1861, which was wholly employed in enacting laws to enable the Government to prosecute the war with vigor and efficiency. And finally, in 1861, we find Congress *ex majore cautela* and in anticipation of such astute objections, passing an act 'approving, legalizing, and making valid all the acts, proclamations, and orders of the President, &c., as if they had been issued and done under the previous express authority and direction of the Congress of the United States.'

Without admitting that such an act was necessary under the circumstances, it is plain that if the President had in any manner assumed powers which it was necessary should have the authority or sanction of Congress, that on the well known principle of law, *omnis ratihabitio retrotrahitur et mandato equiparatur*, this ratification has operated to perfectly cure the defect. . . .

[T]herefore we are of the opinion that the President had a right, *jure belli*, to institute a blockade of ports in possession of the States in rebellion, which neutrals are bound to regard.

Nelson (Catron, Clifford, Taney), dissenting:

. . . [T]o constitute a civil war in the sense in which we are speaking, before it can exist, in contemplation of law, it must be recognized or declared by the sovereign power of the State, and which sovereign power by our Constitution is lodged in the Congress of the United States—civil war, therefore, under our system of government, can exist only by an act of Congress, which requires the assent of two of the great departments of the Government, the Executive and Legislative. . . .

So the war carried on by the President against the insurrectionary districts in the Southern States . . . was a personal war against those in rebellion . . . until Congress assembled and acted upon this state of things. . . .

[N]o civil war existed between this Government and the States in insurrection till recognized by the Act of Congress 13th of July, 1861; that the President does not possess the power under the Constitution to declare war or recognize its existence within the meaning of the law of nations, which carries with it belligerent rights, and thus change the country and all its citizens from a state of peace to a state of war; that this power belongs exclusively to the Congress of the United States, and, consequently, that the President had no power to set on foot a blockade under the law of nations, and that the capture of the vessel and cargo in this case, and in all cases before us in which the capture occurred before the 13th of July, 1861, for breach of blockade, or as enemies' property, are illegal and void, and that the decrees of condemnation should be reversed and the vessel and cargo restored.

Ex Parte Milligan

71 U.S. 2 (1866), 9-0
Opinion of the Court: Davis (Clifford, Field, Grier, Nelson)
Concurring: Chase, Miller, Swayne, Wayne
Lambdin P. Milligan, a Confederate sympathizer living in southern Indiana, had been tried and convicted by a military tribunal for a variety of treasonable acts including conspiracy to seize munitions at federal arsenals and free Confederate prisoners held in northern prison camps. He was sentenced to be hanged.

What is the disagreement between Davis and Chase in dissent? Would the decision of the Court have been different had Congress authorized civilian trials by the military? In the Prize Cases, the Court sustained great presidential war-making power; in this case it refused to sustain an important wartime power of the President. Are the two cases consistent? Would the result here have been

different had the war still been going on? Had Lincoln still been president?

Davis, for the Court:
The importance of the main question presented by this record cannot be overstated; for it involves the very framework of the government and the fundamental principles of American liberty . . .

The controlling question in the case is this: Upon the facts stated in Milligan's petition, and the exhibits filed, had the military commission mentioned in it jurisdiction, legally, to try and sentence him? Milligan, not a resident of one of the rebellious states, or a prisoner of war, but a citizen of Indiana for twenty years past, and never in the military or naval service, is, while at his home, arrested by the military power of the United States, imprisoned, and, on certain criminal charges preferred against him, tried, convicted, and sentenced to be hanged by a military commission, organized under the direction of the military commander of the military district of Indiana. Had this tribunal the legal power and authority to try and punish this man? . . .

Have any of the rights guaranteed by the Constitution been violated in the case of Milligan? and if so, what are they?

Every trial involves the exercise of judicial power; and from what source did not military commission that tried him derive their authority? Certainly no part of judicial power of the country was conferred on them; because the Constitution expressly vests it 'in one supreme court and such inferior courts as the Congress may from time to time ordain and establish,' and it is not pretended that the commission was a court ordained and established by Congress. They cannot justify on the mandate of the President; because he is controlled by law, and has his appropriate sphere of duty, which is to execute, not to make, the laws; and there is 'no unwritten criminal code to which resort can be had as a source of jurisdiction.'

But it is said that the jurisdiction is complete under the 'laws and usages of war.'

It can serve no useful purpose to inquire what those laws and usages are, whence they originated, where found, and on whom they operate; they can never be applied to citizens in states which have upheld the authority of the government, and where the courts are open and their process unobstructed. This court has judicial knowledge that in Indiana the Federal authority was always unopposed, and its courts always open to hear criminal accusations and redress grievances; and no usage of war could sanction a military trial there for any offense whatever of a citizen in civil life, in nowise connected with the military service. Congress could grant no such power; and to the honor of our national legislature be it said, it has never been provoked by the state of the country even to attempt its exercise. One of the plainest constitutional provisions was, therefore, infringed when Milligan was tried by a court not ordained and established by Congress, and not composed of judges appointed during good behavior.

Why was he not delivered to the Circuit Court of Indiana to be proceeded against according to law? No reason of necessity could be urged against it; because Congress had declared penalties against the offenses charged, provided for their punishment, and directed that court to hear and determine them. And soon after this military tribunal was ended, the Circuit Court met, peacefully transacted its business, and adjourned. It needed no bayonets to protect it, and required no military aid to execute its judgments. It was held in a state, eminently distinguished for patriotism, by judges commissioned during the Rebellion, who were provided with juries, upright, intelligent, and selected by a marshal appointed by the President. The government had no right to conclude that Milligan, if guilty, would not receive in that court merited punishment; for its records disclose that it was constantly engaged in the trial of similar offenses, and was never interrupted in its administration of criminal justice. If it was dangerous, in the distracted condition of affairs, to leave Milligan unrestrained of his liberty, because he 'conspired against the government, afforded aid and comfort to rebels, and incited the people to insurrection,' the law said arrest him, confine him closely, render him powerless to do further mischief; and then present his case to the grand jury of the district, with proofs of his guilt, and, if indicted, try him according to the course of the common law. If this had been done, the Constitution would have been vindicated, the law of 1863 enforced, and the securities for personal liberty preserved and defended.

Another guarantee of freedom was broken when Milligan was denied a trial by jury. The great minds of the country have differed on the correct interpretation to be given to various provisions of the Federal Constitution; and judicial decision has been often invoked to settle their true meaning; but until recently no one ever doubted that the right of trial by jury was fortified in the organic law against the power of attack. It is now assailed; but if ideas can be expressed in words, and language has any meaning, this right—one of the most valuable in a free country—is preserved to every one accused of crime who is not attached to the army, or navy, or militia in actual service. The sixth amendment affirms that 'in all criminal prosecutions the accused shall enjoy the right to a speedy and public trial by an impartial jury,' language broad enough to embrace all persons and cases; but the fifth, recognizing the necessity of an indictment, or presentment, before any one can be held to answer for high crimes, 'excepts cases arising in the land or naval forces, or in the militia, when in actual service, in time of war or public danger;' and the framers of the Constitution, doubtless, meant to limit the right of trial by jury, in the sixth amendment, to those persons who were subject to indictment or presentment in the fifth. . . .

It is claimed that martial law covers with its broad mantle the proceedings of this military commission. The proposition is this: that in a time of war the commander of an armed force (if in his opinion the exigencies of the country demand it, and of which he is to judge), has the power, within the lines of his military district, to suspend all civil rights and their remedies, and subject citizens as well as soldiers to the rule of his will; and in the exercise of his lawful authority cannot be restrained, except by his superior officer or the President of the United States.

If this position is sound to the extent claimed, then when war exists, foreign or domestic, and the country is subdivided into military departments for mere convenience, the commander of one of them can, if he chooses, within his limits, on the plea of necessity, with the approval of the Executive, substitute military force for and to the exclusion of the laws, and punish all persons, as he thinks right and proper, without fixed or certain rules.

The statement of this proposition shows its importance; for, if true, republican government is a failure, and there is an end of liberty regulated by law. Martial law, established on such a basis, destroys every guarantee of the Constitution, and effectually renders the 'military independent of and superior to the civil power'—the attempt to do which by the King of Great Britain was deemed by our fathers such an offense, that they assigned it to the world as one of the causes which impelled them to declare their independence.

Civil liberty and this kind of martial law cannot endure together; the antagonism is irreconcilable; and, in the conflict, one or the other must perish.

This nation, as experience has proved, cannot always remain at peace, and has no right to expect that it will always have wise and humane rulers, sincerely attached to the principles of the Constitution. Wicked men, ambitious of power, with hatred of liberty and contempt of law, may fill the place once occupied by Washington and Lincoln; and if this right is conceded, and the calamities of war again befall us, the dangers to human liberty are frightful to contemplate. If our fathers had failed to provide for just such a contingency, they would have been false to the trust reposed in them. They knew—the history of the world told them—the nation they were founding, be its existence short or long, would be involved in war; how often or how long continued, human foresight could not tell; and that unlimited power, wherever lodged at such a time, was especially hazardous to freemen. For this, and other equally weighty reasons, they secured the inheritance they had fought to maintain, by incorporating in a written constitution the safeguards which time had proved were essential to its preservation. Not one of these safeguards can the President, or Congress, or the Judiciary disturb, except the one concerning the writ of habeas corpus.

It is essential to the safety of every government that, in a great crisis, like the one we have just passed through, there should be a power somewhere of suspending the writ of habeas corpus. In every war, there are men of previously good character, wicked enough to counsel their fellow-citizens to resist the measures deemed necessary by a good government to sustain its just authority and overthrow its enemies; and their influence may lead to dangerous combinations. In the emergency of the times, an immediate public investigation according to law may not be possible; and yet, the period to the country may be too imminent to suffer such persons to go at large. Unquestionably, there is then an exigency which demands that the government, if it should see fit in the exercise of a proper discretion to make arrests, should not be required to produce the persons arrested in answer to a writ of habeas corpus. The Constitution goes no further. It does not say after a writ of habeas corpus is denied a citizen, that he shall be tried otherwise than by the course of the common law; if it had intended this result, it was easy by the use of direct words to have accomplished it. The illustrious men who framed that instrument were guarding the foundations of civil liberty against the abuses of unlim-

ited power; they were full of wisdom, and the lessons of history informed them that a trial by an established court, assisted by an impartial jury, was the only sure way of protecting the citizen against oppression and wrong. Knowing this, they limited the suspension to one great right, and left the rest to remain forever inviolable. But, it is insisted that the safety of the country in time of war demands that this broad claim for martial law shall be sustained. If this were true, it could be well said that a country, preserved at the sacrifice of all the cardinal principles of liberty, is not worth the cost of preservation. Happily, it is not so. . . .

[T]his is not a question of the power to proclaim martial law, when war exists in a community and the courts and civil authorities are overthrown. Nor is it a question what rule a military commander, at the head of his army, can impose on states in rebellion to cripple their resources and quell the insurrection. The jurisdiction claimed is much more extensive. The necessities of the service, during the late Rebellion, required that the loyal states should be placed within the limits of certain military districts and commanders appointed in them; and, it is urged, that this, in a military sense, constituted them the theater of military operations; and, as in this case, Indiana had been and was again threatened with invasion by the enemy, the occasion was furnished to establish martial law. The conclusion does not follow from the premises. If armies were collected in Indiana, they were to be employed in another locality, where the laws were obstructed and the national authority disputed. On her soil there was no hostile foot; if once invaded, that invasion was at an end, and with it all pretext for martial law. Martial law cannot arise from a threatened invasion. The necessity must be actual and present; the invasion real, such as effectually closes the courts and deposes the civil administration.

It is difficult to see how the safety for the country required martial law in Indiana. If any of her citizens were plotting treason, the power of arrest could secure them, until the government was prepared for their trial, when the courts were open and ready to try them. It was as easy to protect witnesses before a civil as a military tribunal; and as there could be no wish to convict, except on sufficient legal evidence, surely an ordained and establish court was better able to judge of this than a military tribunal composed of gentlemen not trained to the profession of the law. . . .

[T]here are occasions when martial rule can be properly applied. If, in foreign invasion or civil war, the courts are actually closed, and it is impossible to administer criminal justice according to law, then, on the theatre of active military operations, where war really prevails, there is a necessity to furnish a substitute for the civil authority, thus overthrown, to preserve the safety of the army and society; and as no power is left but the military, it is allowed to govern by martial rule until the laws can have their free course. As necessity creates the rule, so it limits its duration; for, if this government is continued after the courts are reinstated, it is a gross usurpation of power. Martial rule can never exist where the courts are open, and in the proper and unobstructed exercise of their jurisdiction. It is also confined to the locality of actual war. Because, during the late Rebellion it could have been enforced in Virginia, where the national authority was overturned and the courts driven out, it does not follow that it should obtain in Indiana, where that authority was never disputed, and justice was always administered. And so in the case of a foreign invasion, martial rule may become a necessity in one state, when, in another, it would be 'mere lawless violence.' . . .

The two remaining questions in this case must be answered in the affirmative. The suspension of the privilege of the writ of habeas corpus does not suspend the writ itself. The writ issues as a matter of course; and on the return made to it the court decides whether the party applying is denied the right of proceeding any further with it.

If the military trial of Milligan was contrary to law, then he was entitled, on the facts stated in his petition, to be discharged from custody by the terms of the act of Congress of March 3d, 1863. The provisions of this law having been considered in a previous part of this opinion, we will not restate the views there presented. Milligan avers he was a citizen of Indiana, not in the military or naval service, and was detained in close confinement, by order of the President, from the 5th day of October, 1864, until the 2d day of January, 1865, when the Circuit Court for the District of Indiana, with a grand jury, convened in session at Indianapolis; and afterwards, on the 27th day of the same month, adjourned without finding an indictment or presentment against him. If these averments were true (and their truth is conceded for the purposes of this case), the court was required to liberate him on taking certain oaths prescribed by the law, and entering into recognizance for his good behavior.

But it is insisted that Milligan was a prisoner of war, and, therefore, excluded from the privileges of the statute. It is not easy to see how he can be treated as a prisoner of war, when he lived in Indiana for the past twenty years, was arrested there, and had not been, during the late troubles, a resident of any of the states in rebellion. If in Indiana he conspired with bad men to assist the enemy, he is punishable for it in the courts of Indiana; but, when tried for the offense, he cannot plead the rights of war; for he was not engaged in legal acts of hostility against the government, and only such persons, when captured, are prisoners of war. If he cannot enjoy the immunities attaching to the character of a prisoner of war, how can he be subject to their pains and penalties?

Chase, C.J. (Miller, Swayne, Wayne), dissenting:
The Constitution itself provides for military government as well as for civil government. And we do not understand it to be claimed that the civil safeguards of the Constitution have application in cases within the proper sphere of the former.

What, then, is that proper sphere? Congress has power to raise and support armies; to provide and maintain a navy; to make rules for the government and regulation of the land and naval forces; and to provide for governing such part of the militia as may be in the service of the United States.

It is not denied that the power to make rules for the government of the army and navy is a power to provide for trial and punishment by military courts without a jury. It has been so understood and exercised from the adoption of the Constitution to the present time. . . .

[T]he power of Congress, in the government of the land and naval forces and of the militia, is not at all affected by the fifth or any other amendment. It is not necessary to attempt any precise definition of the boundaries of this power. But may it not be said that government includes protection and defense as well as the regulation of internal administration? And is it impossible to imagine cases in which citizens conspiring or attempting the destruction or great injury of the national forces may be subjected by Congress to military trial and punishment in the just exercise of this undoubted constitutional power? . . .

In Indiana, for example, at the time of the arrest of Milligan and his co-conspirators, it is established by the papers in the record, that the state was a military district, was the theatre of military operations, had been actually invaded, and was constantly threatened with invasion. It appears, also, that a powerful secret association, composed of citizens and others, existed within the state, under military organization, conspiring against the draft, and plotting insurrection, the liberation of the prisoners of war at various depots, the seizure of the state and national arsenals, armed cooperation with the enemy, and war against the national government.

We cannot doubt that, in such a time of public danger, Congress had power, under the Constitution, to provide for the organization of a military commission, and for trial by that commission of persons engaged in this conspiracy. The fact that the Federal courts were open was regarded by Congress as a sufficient reason for not exercising the power; but that fact could not deprive Congress of the right to exercise it. Those courts might be open and undisturbed in the execution of their functions, and yet wholly incompetent to avert threatened danger, or to punish, with adequate promptitude and certainty, the guilty conspirators.

In Indiana, the judges and officers of the courts were loyal to the government. But it might have been otherwise. In times of rebellion and civil war it may often happen, indeed, that judges and marshals will be in active sympathy with the rebels, and courts their most efficient allies.

We have confined ourselves to the question of power. It was for Congress to determine the question of expediency. And Congress did determine it. That body did not see fit to authorize trials by military commission in Indiana, but by the strongest implication prohibited them. . . .

We think that the power of Congress, in such times and in such localities, to authorize trials for crimes against the security and safety of the national forces, may be derived from its constitutional authority to raise and support armies and to declare war, if not from its constitutional authority to provide for governing the national forces.

Mississippi v. Johnson

71 U. S. 475 (1867), 9-0
Opinion of the Court: Chase (Clifford, Davis, Field, Grier, Miller, Nelson, Swayne Wayne)
What was the Court asked to do and why? What did it conclude with regard to presidential immunity? Why did it rule the President was immune from such suits? What would have been the likely immediate and long-run effects if it had ruled the other way? Suppose it had ruled the other way and the President refused to obey?

Chase, C.J., for the Court:

A motion was made, some days since, in behalf of the State of Mississippi, for leave to file a bill in the name of the State, praying this court perpetually to enjoin and restrain Andrew Johnson, President of the United States, and E. O. C. Ord, general commanding in the District of Mississippi and Arkansas, from executing, or in any manner carrying out, certain acts of Congress therein named.

The acts referred to are those of March 2d and March 23d, 1867, commonly known as the Reconstruction Acts.

The Attorney-General objected to the leave asked for, upon the ground that no bill which makes a President a defendant, and seeks an injunction against him to restrain the performance of his duties as President, should be allowed to be filed in this court.

This point has been fully argued, and we will now dispose of it.

We shall limit our inquiry to the question presented by the objection, without expressing any opinion on the broader issues discussed in argument, whether, in any case, the President of the United States may be required, by the process of this court, to perform a purely ministerial act under a positive law, or may be held amenable, in any case, otherwise than by impeachment for crime.

The single point which requires consideration is this: Can the President be restrained by injunction from carrying into effect an act of Congress alleged to be unconstitutional?

It is assumed by the counsel for the State of Mississippi, that the President, in the execution of the Reconstruction Acts, is required to perform a mere ministerial duty. In this assumption there is, we think, a confounding of the terms ministerial and executive, which are by no means equivalent in import.

A ministerial duty, the performance of which may, in proper cases, be required of the head of a department, by judicial process, is one in respect to which nothing is left to discretion. It is a simple, definite duty, arising under conditions admitted or proved to exist, and imposed by law.

The case of *Marbury v. Madison*, Secretary of State, furnishes an illustration. A citizen had been nominated, confirmed, and appointed a justice of the peace for the District of Columbia, and his commission had been made out, signed, and sealed. Nothing remained to be done except delivery, and the duty of delivery was imposed by law on the Secretary of State. It was held that the performance of this duty might be enforced by mandamus issuing from a court having jurisdiction . . . [N]othing was left to discretion. There was no room for the exercise of judgment. The law required the performance of a single specific act; and that performance, it was held, might be required by mandamus.

Very different is the duty of the President in the exercise of the power to see that the laws are faithfully executed, and among these laws the acts named in the bill. By the first of these acts he is required to assign generals to command in the several military districts, and to detail sufficient military force to enable such officers to discharge their duties under the law. By the supplementary act, other duties are imposed on the several commanding generals, and these duties must necessarily be performed under the supervision of the President as commander in chief. The duty thus imposed on the President is in no just sense ministerial. It is purely executive and political.

An attempt on the part of the judicial department of the government to enforce the performance of such duties by the President might be justly characterized, in the language of Chief Justice Marshal, as 'an absurd and excessive extravagance.'

It is true that in the instance before us the interposition of the court is not sought to enforce action by the Executive under constitutional legislation, but to restrain such action under legislation alleged to be unconstitutional. But we are unable to perceive that this circumstance takes the case out of the general principles which forbid judicial interference with the exercise of Executive discretion.

It was admitted in the argument that the application now made to us is without a precedent; and this is of much weight against it. . . .

The fact that no such application was ever before made in any case indicates the general judgment of the profession that no such application should be entertained.

It will hardly be contended that Congress can interpose, in any case, to restrain the enactment of an unconstitutional law; and yet how can the right to judicial interposition to prevent such an enactment, when the purpose is evident and the execution of that purpose certain, be distinguished, in principle, from the right to such interposition against the execution of such a law by the President?

The Congress is the legislative department of the government; the President is the executive department. Neither can be restrained in its action by the judicial department; though the acts of both, when performed, are, in proper cases, subject to its cognizance.

The impropriety of such interference will be clearly seen upon consideration of its possible consequences.

Suppose the bill filed and the injunction prayed for allowed. If the President refuse obedience, it is needless to observe that the court is without power to enforce its process. If, on the other hand, the President complies with the order of the court and refuses to execute the acts of Congress, is it not clear that a collision may occur between the executive and legislative departments of the government? May not the House of Representatives impeach the President for such refusal? And in that case could this court interfere, in behalf of the President, thus endangered by compliance with its mandate, and restrain by injunction the Senate of the United States from sitting as a court of impeachment? Would the strange spectacle be offered to the public world of an attempt by this court to arrest proceedings in that court?

These questions answer themselves.

It is true that a State may file an original bill in this court. And it may be true, in some cases, that such a bill may be filed against the United States. But we are fully satisfied that this court has no jurisdiction of a bill to enjoin the President in the performance of his official duties; and that no such bill ought to be received by us.

It has been suggested that the bill contains a prayer that, if the relief sought cannot be had against Andrew Johnson, as President, it may be granted against Andrew Johnson as a citizen of Tennessee. But it is plain that relief as against the execution of an act of Congress by Andrew Johnson, is relief against its execution by the President. A bill praying an injunction against the execution of an act of Congress by the incumbent of the presidential office cannot be received, whether it describes him as President or as a citizen of a State.

The motion for leave to file the bill is, therefore, denied.

Ex Parte McCardle

74 U.S. 506 (1869), 8-0

Opinion of the Court: Chase (Clifford, Davis, Field, Grier, Nelson, Swayne)

Is the judicial self-restraint evident in this decision based on an interpretation of the Constitution or on the Court's recognition of its political vulnerablity during Reconstruction? Is the decision consistent with Marbury v. Madison? *Does Chase suggest any limits to Congress's power to establish or change the Court's appellate jurisdiction? What does he say about the motives of Congress? Is the decision an admission by the Court that it is not truly a coequal branch? Sometimes? Always?*

Chase, C.J., for the Court:

The first question necessarily is that of jurisdiction; for, if the act of March, 1868, takes away the jurisdiction defined by the act of February, 1867, it is useless, if not improper, to enter into any discussion of other questions.

It is quite true, as was argued by the counsel for [McCardle], that the appellate jurisdiction of this court is not derived from acts of Congress. It is, strictly speaking, conferred by the Constitution. But it is conferred 'with such exceptions and under such regulations as Congress shall make.'

It is unnecessary to consider whether, if Congress had made no exceptions and no regulations, this court might not have exercised general appellate jurisdiction under rules prescribed by itself. For among the earliest acts of the first Congress, at its first session, was the act of September 24th, 1789, to establish the judicial courts of the United States. That act provided for the organization of this court, and prescribed regulations for the exercise of its jurisdiction.

The source of that jurisdiction, and the limitations of it by the Constitution and by statute, have been on several occasions subjects of consideration here. In the case of *Durousseau v. United States,* particularly, the whole matter was carefully examined, and the Court held, that while 'the appellate powers of this court are not given by the judicial act, but are given by the Constitution,' they are, nevertheless, 'limited and regulated by that act, and by such other acts as have been passed on the subject.' The Court said, further, that the judicial act was an exercise of the power given by the Constitution to Congress 'of making exceptions to the appellate jurisdiction of the Supreme Court.' 'They have described affirmatively,' said the Court, 'its jurisdiction, and this affirmative description has been understood to imply a negation of the exercise of such appellate power as is not comprehended within it.'

The principle that the affirmation of appellate jurisdiction implies the negation of all such jurisdiction not affirmed having been thus established, it was an almost necessary consequence that acts of Congress, providing for the exercise of jurisdiction, should come to be spoken of as acts granting jurisdiction, and not as acts making exceptions to the constitutional grant of it.

The exception to appellate jurisdiction in the case before us, however, is not an inference from the affirmation of other appellate jurisdiction. It is made in terms. The provision of the act of 1867, affirming the appellate jurisdiction of this court in cases of habeas corpus is expressly repealed. It is hardly possible to imagine a plainer instance of positive exception.

We are not at liberty to inquire into the motives of the legislature. We can only examine into its power under the Constitution; and the power to make exceptions to the appellate jurisdiction of this court is given by express words.

What, then, is the effect of the repealing act upon the case before us? We cannot doubt as to this. Without jurisdiction the Court cannot proceed at all in any cause. Jurisdiction is power to declare the law, and when it ceases to exist, the only function remaining to the Court is that of announcing the fact and dismissing the cause. And this is not less clear upon authority than upon principle.

Several cases were cited by the counsel for [McCardle] in support of the position that jurisdiction of this case is not affected by the repealing act. But none of them, in our judgment, afford any support to it. . . .

On the other hand, the general rule, supported by the best elementary writers, is, that 'when an act of the legislature is repealed, it must be considered, except as to transactions past and closed, as if it never existed.' And the effect of repealing acts upon suits under acts repealed, has been determined by the adjudications of this court. The subject was fully considered in *Norris v. Crecker,* and more recently in *Insurance Co. v. Ritchie.* In both of these cases it was held that no judgment could be rendered in a suit after the repeal of the act under which it was brought and prosecuted.

It is quite clear, therefore, that this court cannot proceed to pronounce judgment in this case, for it has no longer jurisdiction of the appeal; and judicial duty is not less fitly performed by declining ungranted jurisdiction than in exercising firmly that which the Constitution and the laws confer.

Counsel seem to have supposed, if effect be given to the repealing act in question, that the whole appellate power of the Court, in cases of habeas corpus, is denied. But this is an error. The act of 1868 does not except from that jurisdiction any cases but appeals from Circuit Courts under the act of 1867. It does not affect the jurisdiction which was previously exercised.

The appeal of [McCardle] in this case must be dismissed for want of jurisdiction.

Texas v. White

74 U.S. 700 (1869), 5-3
Opinion of the Court: Chase (Clifford, Davis, Field, Nelson)
Dissenting: Grier, Miller, Swayne
The question the Court addressed was whether the Reconstruction government of Texas could bring a suit as a state, under the Court's original jurisdiction.

What theory of the Union is developed in this case? Is it supported by the text of the Constitution? The intent of the framers? The outcome of war? Other factors outside the Constitution?

Chase, C.J., for the Court:

The first inquiries to which our attention was directed by counsel, arose upon the allegations . . . that the State, having severed her relations with a majority of the States of the Union, and having by her ordinance of secession attempted to throw off her allegiance to the Constitution and government of the United States, has so far changed her status as to be disabled from prosecuting suits in the National courts. . . .

If, therefore, it is true that the State of Texas was not at the time of filing this bill, or is not now, one of the United States, we have no jurisdiction of this suit, and it is our duty to dismiss it . . .

In the Constitution the term state most frequently expresses the combined idea just noticed, of people, territory, and government. A state, in the ordinary sense of the Constitution, is a political community of free citizens, occupying a territory of defined boundaries, and organized under a government sanctioned and limited by a written constitution, and established by the consent of the governed. It is the union of such states, under a common constitution, which forms the distinct and greater political unit, which that Constitution designates as the United States, and makes of the people and states which compose it one people and one country. . . .

The Republic of Texas was admitted into the Union, as a State, on the 27th of December, 1845. By this act the new State, and the people of the new State, were invested with all the rights, and became subject to all the responsibilities and duties of the original States under the Constitution.

From the date of admission, until 1861, the State was represented in the Congress of the United States by her senators and representatives, and her relations as a member of the Union remained unimpaired. In that year, acting upon the theory that the rights of a State under the Constitution might be renounced, and her obligations thrown off at pleasure, Texas undertook to sever the bond thus formed, and to break up her constitutional relations with the United States. . . .

The position thus assumed could only be maintained by arms, and Texas accordingly took part, with the other Confederate States, in the war of the rebellion, which these events made inevitable. During the whole of that war there was no governor, or judge, or any other State officer in Texas, who recognized the National authority. Nor was any officer of the United States permitted to exercise any authority whatever under the National government within the limits of the State, except under the immediate protection of the National military forces.

Did Texas, in consequence of these acts, cease to be a State? Or, if not, did the State cease to be a member of the Union? . . .

The Union of the States never was a purely artificial and arbitrary relation. It began among the Colonies, and grew out of common origin, mutual sympathies, kindred principles, similar interests, and geographical relations. It was confirmed and strengthened by the necessities of war, and received definite form, and character, and sanction from the Articles of Confederation. By these the Union was solemnly declared to 'be perpetual.' And when these Articles were found to be inadequate to the exigencies of the country, the Constitution was ordained 'to form a more perfect Union.' It is difficult to convey the idea of indissoluble unity more clearly than by these words. What can be indissoluble if a perpetual Union, made more perfect, is not?

But the perpetuity and indissolubility of the Union, by no means implies the loss of distinct and individual existence, or of the right of self-government by the States. Under the Articles of Confederation each State retained its sovereignty, freedom, and independence, and every power, jurisdiction, and right not expressly delegated to the United States. Under the Constitution, though the powers of the States were much restricted, still, all powers not delegated to the United States, nor prohibited to the States, are reserved to the States respectively, or to the people. And we have already had occasion to remark at this term, that the people of each State compose a State, having its own government, and endowed with all the functions essential to separate and independent existence,' and that 'without the States in union, there could be no such political body as the United States.' Not only, therefore, can there be no loss of separate and independent autonomy to the States, through their union under the Constitution, but it may be not unreasonably said that the preservation of the States, and the maintenance of their governments, are as much within the design and care of the Constitution as the preservation of the Union and the maintenance of the National government. The Constitution, in all its provisions, looks to an indestructible Union, composed of indestructible States.

When, therefore, Texas became one of the United States, she entered into an indissoluble relation. All the obligations of perpetual union, and all the guaranties of republican government in the Union, attached at once to the State. The act which consummated her admission into the Union was something more than a compact; it was the incorporation of a new member into the political body. And it was final. The union between Texas and the other States was as complete, as perpetual, and as indissoluble as the union between the original States. There was no place for reconsideration, or revocation, except through revolution, or through consent of the States.

Considered therefore as transactions under the Constitution, the ordinance of secession, adopted by the convention and ratified by a majority of the citizens of Texas, and all the acts of her legislature intended to give effect to that ordinance, were absolutely null. They were utterly without operation in law. The obligations of the State, as a member of the Union, and of every citizen of the State, as a citizen of the United States, remained perfect and unimpaired. It certainly follows that the State did not cease to be a State, nor her citizens to be citizens of the Union. If this were otherwise, the State must have become foreign, and her citizens foreigners. The war must have ceased to be a war for the suppression of rebellion, and must have become a war for conquest and subjugation.

Our conclusion therefore is, that Texas continued to be a State, and a State of the Union, notwithstanding the transactions to which we have referred. And this conclusion, in our judgment, is not in conflict with any act or declaration of any department of the National government, but entirely in accordance with the whole series of such acts and declarations since the first outbreak of the rebellion.

But in order to the exercise, by a State, of the right to sue in this court, there needs to be a State government, competent to represent the State in its relations with the National government, so far at least as the institution and prosecution of a suit is concerned. . . .

When the war closed there was no government in the State except that which had been organized for the purpose of waging war against the United States. That government immediately disappeared. The chief functionaries left the State. Many of the subordinate officials followed their example. Legal responsibilities were annulled or greatly impaired. It was inevitable that great confusion should prevail. If order was maintained, it was where the good sense and virtue of the citizens gave support to local acting magistrates, or supplied more directly the needful restraints. . . .

There being then no government in Texas in constitutional relations with the Union, it became the duty of the United States to provide for the restoration of such a government. . . .

A provisional governor of the State was appointed by the President in 1865; in 1866 a governor was elected by the people under the constitution of that year; at a subsequent date a governor was appointed by the commander of the district. Each of the three exercised executive functions and actually represented the State in the executive department.

In the case before us each has given his sanction to the prosecution of the suit, and we find no difficulty, without investigating the legal title of either to the executive office, in holding that the sanction thus given sufficiently warranted the action of the solicitor and counsel in behalf of the State. The necessary conclusion is that the suit was instituted and is prosecuted by competent authority.

The question of jurisdiction being thus disposed of, we proceed to the consideration of the merits . . . [The Court held that Texas was entitled to recover the bonds.]

III

CONSTITUTIONAL
POLITICAL ECONOMY

6

THE REPUBLIC OF BEES

Born Blessed

The constitutional system both succeeded and failed in the tasks of building a union and serving a polity. It failed in face of the deepening sectional conflict over slavery. Constitutional politics succeeded notably in accommodating political growth, including the widening of participatory opportunity represented first by Jeffersonian republicanism and later by Jacksonian democracy.

Antebellum constitutionalism was marked by yet a third great development: an economic and social expansion unique in the history of nations. The rapidity of this growth tested the early constitutional system no less than did the questions of union and democracy. Its legal and political accommodation made possible the modern economic and entrepreneurial colossus the American nation was to become.

The geopolitical circumstances of the nation were unique. In a half century from the Louisiana Purchase in 1803 to the Gadsden Purchase in 1853, its territory expanded threefold. The Revolution had left the United States the chief power in North America. Except for Britain, the states of Europe had a steadily declining colonial presence; all were occupied with upheavals on the Continent. Four thousand miles of ocean would also provide unparalleled national security. The West, stretching to the Pacific, was either unpopulated or thinly populated by native tribes most of whom did not want to be assimilated or were thought by whites not assimilatable. In either case, they were too few and too weak militarily to stand (or be allowed to stand) in the way. Nor would Mexico, the only national rival in the West, be able to stop a steady westward expansion to settle and exploit a rich continent.

The American population, less than 4,000,000 in the first national census in 1790, increased by a third or more in each of the next seven decades. A high birth rate and a steady stream of immigrants, averaging nearly 125,000 a year, brought the population to more than 30,000,000 by 1860. This sustained rate of growth in territory and people has had no parallel before or since.

The economy of the country was increasingly mixed though it remained regionally divided. Agriculture thrived. A 50-fold increase in the cotton crop from a mere 100,000 bales grown mainly within 100 miles of the seaboard in 1801, to more than 5,000,000 bales in 1859 in a belt stretching across the Southeast and into Texas, reinforced the slave economy. In the North and West, annual wheat production grew to 125,000,000 bushels and corn to more than 800,000,000 on the eve of the Civil War. Raising livestock, closely related to corn production, experienced similar growth. Productivity per farm worker rose dramatically with a host of inventions including the seeder, harrow, binder, reaper, harvester, thresher and cotton gin. The wooden plow was replaced with a cast-iron implement and, later, with one of tempered steel.

Impressive as these agricultural successes were, they were surpassed by those of industry. Compared to its gigantic growth later in the century, manufacturing was still mainly small scale, its units often being directed by a founder or single entrepreneur. But on the eve the Civil War, the value of manufactured products—nearly $2 billion—had surpassed that of the land for the first time. A protective tariff shielded many nascent industries from foreign competition as the economy became more diverse and self-sufficient.

Of particular importance were advances in the iron industry where mineral coal replaced charcoal and the closed furnace supplanted the open forge. These efficiencies and the higher quality of iron and steel were a boon to other manufacturing, especially machinery production. The steam boiler and the steam engine, undergoing their own development, were rapidly adapted to different kinds of manufacturing. Their effect on transportation was revolutionary.

In the late eighteenth century, the chief means of transport for both persons or goods was the horse-drawn carriage or wagon and the sailboat. Early efficiencies were realized through the building of better roads and turnpikes and use of canals, the digging of which boomed in the first quarter of the nineteenth century. The steam engine allowed development of the steamboat and the steam locomotive. The first gradually replaced sailing vessels and made upstream river transport a practical reality. The "iron horse" made possible a network of railroads that became the nation's chief means of long-distance transport by 1860 and were the most extensive in the world.

These gains in transportation spurred trade and promoted a more efficient division of labor within and among regions. In simplest terms, the South grew cotton, tobacco, and other staples; the Western plains produced food, and the Northeast turned out products.

But the growth road was not always smooth or straight. Expansion exaggerated the ebb and flow of the business cycle, its volatility producing higher peaks and deeper valleys. Eight major depressions occurred between Ratification and the Civil War. Two of them—1815–1821 and 1837–1843—lasted more than 70 months, nearly as long as the Great Depression of the 1930s.

Though a steadily increasing collective affluence was a salient economic fact, rapid growth had substantial and often unnerving distributive consequences. Great fortunes could be made, but competition was often keen, even ruthless. Rags-to-riches stories were commonplace, but it was also possible to go bust. For many of those who did there were opportunities to recoup or start over, if not at home, then by going West. If the United States was the land of first chance for most immigrants, it was one of the second chance for many Americans already in place.

Nor did everyone share in the collective gains equally. By modern standards, labor was exploited and working men and women were often prevented from organizing. Their best defense was the country's chronic labor shortage, which even steady immigration could not fully relieve. Many did not expect to be laborers for long. For the most resourceful, determined, or simply lucky, this faith was often justified.

In all, economic expansion of the antebellum period represented a tremendous release of creative energy. The new nation was likened by one early nineteenth century observer to a "republic of bees" whose citizens, resisting all foreign influence and nourished by "innumerable flowers," go about their uniquely productive ways.* As the twentieth century legal historian J. Willard Hurst put it, Americans were "a people going places in a hurry."

Favorable geography and demography found their complement in a favored social history. The United States was an offshoot of the societies of Western Europe, but it had neither the feudal nor the socialist traditions that complicated European political and economic growth. For liberal bourgeois capitalism to triumph in Europe, the political and economic hold of a conservative aristocracy and state church had to be broken. A new middle class then had to defend its gains against the claims of a peasantry gradually being transformed into a self-conscious working class or an alienated proletariat. In the United States, as in colonial America, the middle class was a much larger part of the polity and lines between classes were far more fluid. Though class conflict was hardly absent, middle class hegemony was never seriously contested.

With John Locke as its patron philosopher and Adam Smith its chief economist, a bourgeois liberal ideology took hold of the public mind in America to a degree it never had in Europe. Its tenets included the idea of a social contract among autonomous individuals, personal liberties and political participatory rights, the pursuit of rational self-interest, the protection of property and economic opportunity, and the maintenance of free markets. The wide consensus these principles commanded helped moderate economic conflict and made capture of the State and its levers of power seem much less important than in Europe.

---

* Jesse Root, quoted in Laurence M. Friedman, *A History of American Law,* (New York: Simon and Schuster, 1973), 97.

A Constitutional Door

History, geography, ideology, technology, and social conditions all conspired to make extraordinary economic development possible. Still, this growth would not have taken place in the degree and form it did were it not for an accommodating constitutional and legal system. The basic organizational premises of the Constitution—federally divided power between the states and national government, and centrally divided power among three coequal branches—was almost ideally suited for nascent capitalist development.

Though many of the framers were economic conservatives anxious to secure property and worried about radicalism in several of the states, it cannot be said that they created or intended to create a capitalist political economy, at least as that term is understood today.

Yet the Constitution they framed does contain several provisions supportive of such an economy, particularly when given favorable interpretation as they were by the Marshall and Taney Courts. Preventing state trade discrimination was the driving purpose behind Article I-10-2 provisions that forbade states to tax either imports or exports beyond levels needed to enforce inspection laws. As reinforcement, Article I-8 gave the power to regulate interstate commerce to the central government. Much later in the nineteenth century and following the New Deal crisis in the twentieth, the federal commerce power was used to modify or rein in operations of markets. But during the antebellum period, it was more often cited as reason why the marketplace should remain free of state restraints.

The Constitution did not prevent states from using what came later to be called police powers. Though unspecified, these were assumed to be among those reserved to the states under the Tenth Amendment. During the antebellum period, this state regulatory power was used as often to encourage capitalist endeavor as to restrict it.

A second constitutional curb on state intrusion on business affairs was the provision in

Article I-10-1 barring actions "impairing the obligations of contracts." The Contracts Clause, as the passage has become known, was added to the Constitution at the eleventh hour without much debate, apparently the brainchild of Gouverneur Morris and Alexander Hamilton, who were members of the drafting committee. Given little notice at first, it became the most invoked provision of the Constitution in cases before the Marshall and Taney Courts. Most often the courts used it to free commerce from restriction, though occasionally ways were found to accommodate state regulation.

Perhaps the most important Constitutional provision affecting economic development and the emergence of a capitalist economy was one that at first might seem to have little to do with such matters. In Article VI-1, all debts contracted before adoption of the Constitution "shall be valid against the United States under this Constitution, as under the Confederation." Making the new government responsible for money owed by the old was fiscally responsible and helped gain support for the Constitution in the debate over Ratification. Yet the provision said nothing about how this was to be done. That was left to the future, in this case, to Alexander Hamilton, the first secretary of the Treasury, and to the first Congress dominated by Federalists.

Hamilton's decision to monetize the public debt instead of conventionally retiring it out of accumulated revenue and taxes meant that the government replaced the old debt with new securities on which interest would be regularly and reliably paid (an obligation that governments of the world often failed to meet). These payments would establish creditor confidence that, in turn, would allow the securities to circulate as money.

Hamilton correctly anticipated that the new government securities would markedly appreciate. When he took office, the market worth of domestic public debt was about $15,000,000. A year later, it was about $45,000,000! Within two years, 40 new corporations—for banking, manufacturing, and canal digging—were chartered,

as many as had been founded during the entire colonial and Confederation periods. Almost all were financed from the sale of public securities. Monetizing the debt enormously increased investment capital, exactly the catalyst needed to underwrite the greatest economic expansion in history.

The Constitution alone did not create a capitalist political economy or insure rapid economic growth. These developments were far too complex economically, socially, and geopolitically to be the work of one political act or instrument however ingenious. But the Constitution did create a political and legal framework in which great, rapid economic development was made easier. In the immediate, it allowed plans like Hamilton's to be effected; later, it permitted special readings and interpretations by the Supreme Court that were no less favorable. And, affecting economic development, the Constitution would be affected by it.

The Transformation of American Law

The imperatives of economic expansion and efficiency challenged many settled rules of law. Growth often meant that one use of property opposed another. As economic development became a near universal goal, important changes took place in the judge-made common law of property, contracts, and torts and, through statute, in the law of incorporation and eminent domain.

At the end of the eighteenth century, two conceptions underlay the law of real property: natural use and prior use. The first and older assumed that owners of land were entitled to undisturbed enjoyment of it. Their protected rights were limited to uses that were "natural" or well settled. They were liable for damage done to other property through unusual or untraditional uses. The antidevelopmental bias of this static conception, was well suited to a stable, agrarian society. But by the early 1800s, "natural use" was being challenged in American law by "prior use," which held that a first or earlier development conferred the right to be free of (or to be compensated for) injury stemming from later, conflicting uses of other property. The rule rewarded those who were enterprising enough to undertake first development. Though it introduced the element of economic utility into the common law of real property, the long-term protection of the rights of the first developer came to have static consequences of its own.

In the early nineteenth century, American courts began to apply a third and more dynamic idea, that of "reasonable" use, to give protection, again in the name of economic utility, to innovative enterprise. The new doctrine, which all but ended that of natural use, had two important tenets. First, ownership of land carried with it a reasonable expectation of its use for business; second, liability for injuries inflicted on other property by such use was limited.

The legal historian Morton J. Horwitz has illustrated how this change affected all-important riparian rights as the boom in grain and textile mills increased the demand for energy released by falling water. Under traditional property law, a mill owner who built a dam to get greater water power was liable for all losses sustained by upstream owners whose lands were flooded. But under the new doctrine, such losses were balanced against developmental gains that mill construction offered. Protected "reasonable" use could often be established by showing the likelihood of economic advance or efficiency. Courts thus embraced the notion of *damnum absque injuria*—damage without legal injury—which distinguished actual economic or property loss from legal loss for which compensation could be gained.

These transformations were not the result of conflict between property and antiproperty interests but of one form of property with another. Their instrumentalism, which favored the side of development and "progress," had enormous distributive consequences, yet the changes took hold gradually in the case-by-case pace of the common law method. Skilled common law lawyers and judges often tried to retain the appearance of continuity in the law while allowing legal rules to undergo important change. This time-honored process was, as Oliver Wendell Holmes would later describe it in his definitive treatise *The Common Law,* "forever adapting new principles from life at one end, and it always retains old ones from history at the other."* In the matter of antebellum property rights, the front end clearly had the better of it.

The rules of contracts and torts were also adapted to the new economic realities and in turn helped to shape them. When most markets had been local and limited, commercial agreements or contracts, which were usually between parties who knew each other, were treated as an aspect of property law. In a bargain over a price for land, a horse, or bushels of wheat, ownership or title changed hands when the object actually passed from seller to buyer. If one party reneged or breached the agreement, the other could only go to court to try to compel the agreement be honored or recover the consideration—that which had been offered or given to make the bargain. Damages in the form of monetary compensation for lost opportunity were not available. Courts were also likely to consider whether the bargain had been fair or "sound" and intervene to protect one party from overreaching by the other. Such legal arrangements made sense where most transactions took place in a market that was intimate and not especially fluid.

As markets became larger and more complex and contracts were made between persons often at great distance from each other, traditional arrangements were often inconvenient. What if a buyer of a shipment of wheat refused to accept it because cheaper wheat was in the market? Normally, the seller (still having title to the shipment), would have to hold the perishable product at his own cost and risk until it could be decided whether the buyer had a legal obligation to accept it. But what if, instead, the seller

---

* Mark deWolfe Howe, ed., *The Common Law* (Cambridge, Mass.: Harvard University Press, 1963), 2.

sold the wheat to a third party at the lower market price and sued the original buyer for the difference? When courts began to recognize such actions, the law of contracts underwent a remodeling to fit a fast-developing burgeoning capitalist market economy. By allowing the seller to sue for damages, courts recognized that one or both sides to the bargain were speculating about the future worth of the wheat and that such contracts dealt in fungible rather than unique goods. In fluid, liquid markets, a breached contract need not be specifically enforced to get a just result. Instead, the loss suffered by the party against whom the breach was made could be calculated in money and the dispute settled in law on those terms.

The "will" theory of contract was an important corollary. Except where fraud or duress was present, courts gradually began to withdraw from examining the adequacy of consideration, that is, from looking at the fairness of the bargain. Validity came more to depend on whether a meeting of the minds had actually occurred, that is, on whether an agreement had been freely made. If it had, the fairness of the contract was left to the judgment of the parties and ceased to be a legal issue. The will theory created a "bargainer beware" environment, but it also eased the making of contracts and further privatized economic decisions. Not being an issue a judge might later raise, adequacy of consideration would be determined solely by the forces of supply and demand in the marketplace.

Changes in tort law, emphasizing individual self-reliance, also served the ends of development and efficiency. In traditional English common law, torts—noncriminal wrongs—implied strict or absolute liability. If someone accidentally or unintentionally injured another person or their property or was the owner of an object or animal causing injury, they were liable for the loss regardless of fault. With the growth of railways and the wide use of complex and often dangerous machines, torts emerged as a main class of legal disputes. To relieve owners and entrepreneurs of the heavy burden of absolute liability, the criterion of negligence or fault entered the law. An owner would incur no liability for workplace injuries unless a lack of care could be proven.

Further relief was given by development of three other rules. The doctrine of contributory negligence barred liability even where the employer was negligent if the injured employee had also been at fault. The fellow-servant rule had the same effect if the injury was shown to have been caused by the negligence of another worker. Finally, the doctrine of assumption of risk meant that a worker who knowingly undertook a dangerous job or assignment (for which he might have been paid higher wages) legally assumed the higher risk and could not hold his employer responsible should injuries follow.

These tort developments often produced harsh legal outcomes for injured workers and, later in the century, became the source of much pressure for reform through legislation. But by partly shifting the cost of workplace accidents away from the employer, the new tort doctrines eased one of the legal burdens associated with economic development and innovation.

Not all the great antebellum changes in the law were the work of the courts. Innovative statutes abetting enterprise were enacted by almost every state legislature. Those of incorporation and eminent domain were of particular importance. As a form of legal organization dating to medieval times, the corporation had been used to set up several of the early colonies. Typically it was a charter granted by the Crown or the legislature for a fixed number of years to achieve a particular charitable or public purpose. It permitted the pooling of resources and talents that were ordinarily beyond the means of individuals or simple partnerships.

In a new country rich in opportunities but perpetually short of capital to exploit them, the corporation was an ideal legal device. By providing a means for privately participating in a collective enterprise, it was also congenial with a political culture setting high value on democratic opportunity but remaining skeptical of governmental initiatives. Where only a handful of corporations operated before the Revolution, more than 300 had been charted by 1800, mainly for public works—building turnpikes, canals, and bridges. Soon charters began to be issued for manufacturing or such other purely commercial enterprise as banking and insurance, the main goal of which was private profit. Petitions for charters became so numerous that many states, starting with New York in 1811, enacted general incorporation laws, which removed much of the legislative discretion that was part of dealing with individual requests. The new laws also standardized corporate organization and its means of doing business, setting out rights of shareholders and creditors. Typically they also extended the corporation's life from a fixed number of years to perpetuity.

By making lobbying of the legislature unnecessary in most cases, general incorporation laws widened access to the legal advantages of incorporation and thus of entrepreneurship. Though legislatures might still grant special charters for public or quasi-public projects and confer additional benefits and privileges, increasingly most corporations were private in purpose. Still second to partnerships as the mode of commercial organization, they numbered in the thousands in the 1830s and the tens of thousands by the Civil War.

Traditionally in corporate law, each shareholder was responsible for all the debts and liabilities the organization might incur. A corporation's failure would expose all of a shareholder's private assets to the claims of creditors and others. By 1820, states had begun to limit this risk. Shareholders were held responsible only in proportion to the amount of stock they owned and usually for only as much capital as they had invested in the company. This benefit of limited liability, which offered individual shareholders a known discrete risk, made incorporation enormously attractive to investors and speculators alike and proved a boon in the raising of venture capital. The private profit-making corporation with limited liability was an American innovation, a legal and economic response to the demands of rapid development.

Corporate chartering also raised many concerns and occasional opposition. Some charters granting special privileges created monopolies that, even when not the product of political favoritism, were at odds with the ideal of democratic competitiveness. Despite the limits imposed by general incorporation laws, the private entities were not closely regulated, and the pursuit of private ends often clashed with public purposes. Limited liability could leave many creditors of failed corporations unpaid. And later, large corporations would often overwhelm their workers. These concerns were partly allayed by the laissez-faire belief in the existence of a self-regulating competitive marketplace. Whether ever justified by the facts, this notion would become increasingly dubious in the era of corporate consolidation and giant industrial capitalism following the Civil War.

The power of government to take private property for public purpose—eminent domain—had long been an attribute of sovereignty. It assumed that private property rights, though extensively protected, were not unlimited and might give way to the interest of the community or nation. The power had been used sparingly in colonial times, and owners of property seized were sometimes compensated at the discretion of the legislature. Though not mentioned by name in the Constitution, eminent domain is assumed in the Fifth Amendment's provision "nor shall private property be taken for public use, without just compensation." As already seen, the requirement had been held to apply only to the central government in *Barron v. Baltimore*, 1833.

Starting in the 1790s, many states exercised eminent domain on behalf of grain or textile mill owners who needed falling water to operate their machinery, by enacting laws permitting them to build dams. Upstream landowners who suffered permanent flooding were sometimes given the right to sue for damages but usually only up to an amount specified in the statute. They had no right to block construction of the dams or to prevent the flooding. These laws subsidized an economic development widely thought desirable at the expense of the right to a less productive use of land or an unproductive enjoyment of it.

With the spread of franchise corporations—railway, turnpike, and canal companies—states innovated further by devolving the power of eminent domain directly to these private entities. This allowed them to acquire the tracts they needed for building transport arteries while limiting their liability for damage to adjacent properties. Placing a sovereign power in private hands was one more example of the favoring of one kind of property—that with strong developmental possibilities—over others. By making private investment in railway, turnpike, and canal building more attractive, devolved eminent domain allowed public purposes to be realized through the pursuit of private profit and suited antebellum America's bias for private economic decisions over public.

Many questions growing out of the use of eminent domain—what was a use for "public purpose," a "taking" of property, and "just compensation" for other owners suffering a loss—were left to the courts. As a result, eminent domain cases became an important part of the American common law of real property.

The period between Ratification and the Civil War was one of the most creative in American law, legislatively and judicially. The strongly prodevelopment bias that entered the law cannot be understood simply as a protection of property or property rights. Transformation of the law, as the legal historian Willard Hurst aptly put it, "had less to do with protecting holdings than it had to do with protecting ventures."*

---

* J. Willard Hurst, *Law and the Conditions of Freedom*, (Madison: University of Wisconsin Press, 1956), 24.

The Obligation of Contracts

The changes in American commercial and property law were underwritten by important constitutional interpretations that enhanced economic opportunity. Salient in this development was the rise of the once obscure provision of Article I-10 barring states from "impairing the obligation of contracts." The specific intent of the clause was far from clear. Did it refer only to private contracts or did it include public grants and agreements to which a state itself was a party? Did "obligation" include only provisions in contracts already made or also those in all contracts that might ever be made? And did the curb on state power rest partly on extraconstitutional grounds of natural or vested rights?

Answers given by the Marshall Court reflect its nationalism and solicitation for property rights and mark one of its most creative thrusts. The clause was first applied in a dispute arising from the notorious 1794 land-grant scandal in which the Georgia legislature, nearly every member of which had been bribed, sold 3.5 million acres along the Yazoo River (now part of Alabama and Mississippi but then under Georgia's claim) to land speculators for 1.5 cents per acre. When the extent of the corruption became known the following year, indignant voters elected almost an entirely new body, which promptly rescinded the sale. But the land companies had already sold some tracts to third parties, some of whom were unaware of the original venality. One of those buyers, Robert Fletcher, sued to block the recission, arguing that it impaired his purchase contract.

After protracted litigation the case came before the Supreme Court as *Fletcher v. Peck* in 1810 (p. 202). Faced with upholding the new legislation at the expense of blameless third parties or upholding the corrupt grant and protecting later good faith contracts, Marshall chose the second path. The original sale was a contract that created vested property rights. That it was made by a state rather than a private party made no difference. Recission, then, was an impairment of contracts in violation of Article I-10. Further, Marshall argued, it violated principles of natural justice that protected private property from destruction by government.

The decision—the first in which the Court found a state law unconstitutional—led to the Contracts Clause becoming the chief constitutional curb on state regulatory power in the antebellum period and cast the Court as a nationalist interpreter. Despite a public uproar among defenders of states rights who believed there was nothing in the Constitution to prevent a legislature from undoing the mistake of a predecessor, Marshall's opinion was sensitive to the needs of investors in an age of economic expansion and scarcity of capital. Invoking the natural law doctrine of vested rights—"the general principles of which are common to free institutions"—the chief justice assumed that these rights, nowhere to be found in the Constitutional text, could and should guide constitutional interpretation.

The scope of the Contracts Clause was further enlarged in *New Jersey v. Wilson,* two years later. The New Jersey colonial legislature had granted certain lands to the Delaware Indians with a provision that they would be exempt from taxes. When the tracts were sold years later, the state tried to tax them. The Court held that the exemption was a contractual benefit annexed to the land and passed with it to later purchasers. Repeal impaired the obligation of contract.

But it was the world of corporate charters rather than land grants that allowed the Marshall Court to make its most far-reaching use of the Contracts Clause. Dartmouth College had been founded in 1769 in New Hampshire under a royal charter. In the early years of the republic, its board of trustees, a self-perpetuating body under the charter, became dominated by a Federalist elite. When Jeffersonian Republicans gained control of state government in 1816, they passed several laws affecting operations of the college, including enlargement of the board of trustees

and requiring that its members be politically appointed. The trustees challenged these acts as impairments of the obligation of contract. *Dartmouth College v. Woodward* (p. 203) reached the Supreme Court in 1819, with Daniel Webster, the leading constitutional lawyer of the antebellum period, arguing the case for his alma mater.

Marshall largely accepted Webster's brief. The College was a private corporation, its charter was a contract with the state as successor to the colonial government and was impaired by changes wrought by the new legislation. As he had in *Fletcher,* Marshall also summoned supra-Constitutional natural law principles. Even without the textual limit of the Contracts Clause, the new state laws compromised vested rights, violated political morality and were not "the exercise of a power properly legislative."

The decision had profound consequences for economic development. By declaring that charters of private corporations could not be impaired by state law, the Court gave capital and the corporate enterprise security against popular or partisan state interference. For the next 50 years, the Contracts Clause was the most frequently litigated provision of the Constitution.

Yet, a state's hands might not be completely tied. In a concurring opinion, Justice Joseph Story suggested the means by which the broad sweep of Marshall's theory might be circumvented. Legislatures could retain the right to later qualify corporate charters if that qualification were part of the charter when issued. They could include in the original contract, the right of one party—the state—to amend it later on. Eventually, such reservations became commonplace and were included in general incorporation statutes.

Two weeks after its Dartmouth decision, the Court applied the Contracts Clause to yet another area—debtor relief. In the financial and banking chaos that followed the War of 1812, many states, responding to debtor pressures, passed bankruptcy laws. Under New York's, once a bankrupt debtor had assigned his remaining

The Constitutional Lawyer

Daniel Webster twice served in the House of Representatives, first from New Hampshire, later from Massachusetts. From 1820 to 1840 and again from 1844 to 1850, he represented Massachusetts in the Senate where he was one-third of the Great Triumvirate that dominated Congress in the second quarter of the nineteenth century. He spoke for the Northeast as Henry Clay did for the West and John C. Calhoun for the South, in the sectional politics of the day. He was secretary of state under two presidents, 1841–1843 and 1850–1852, ranking as one of the ablest to serve in that office. With Henry Clay, he founded the Whig Party in the 1830s and for a time seemed headed to the presidency.

This impressive political record notwithstanding, Webster's greatest legacy lies in his constitutional lawyering. He was perhaps the most active and successful advocate ever to appear before the Court. He was counsel for one side or another in almost every important constitutional case of the later Marshall and early Taney Courts: *Dartmouth College, McCulloch v. Maryland, Cohens v. Virginia, Gibbons v. Ogden, Ogden v. Saunders, Luther v. Borden, Charles River Bridge Co. v. Warren Bridge Co., Swift v. Tyson,* and *West River Bridge v. Dix,* among them.

In his advocacy of nationalism and the protection of property rights, he probably had a greater shaping effect on the Constitution than all but a handful of the justices of the Court. His winning arguments

strengthened the federal government against the states, the judicial branch against the executive and legislative, and the interests of commerce and industry against agriculture. Marshall frequently adopted Webster's logic, and sometimes even his dramatic phrasing, as in the classic "a power to create implies a power to preserve . . . the power to tax involves the power to destroy," in *McCulloch v. Maryland.* In *Dartmouth College,* he successfully represented his alma mater in getting the Court to adopt a broad reading of the Contracts Clause. In *Gibbons,* he argued successfully for federal supremacy in the regulation of interstate commerce.

property to the state for benefit of creditors, he was discharged from liability that might remain unsatisfied after distribution of the surrendered assets. The law also abolished debtor imprisonment. These provisions came before the Court in *Sturges v. Crownenshield.*

Though the Constitution gave Congress power to enact bankruptcy laws, Marshall held this grant did not prevent states from legislating in the field, since Congress had not used its authority. But in eliminating *previously* acquired liability, the New York law was an impairment of the obligation of contracts; states could not retroac-

tively discharge debt. At the same time, Marshall upheld the abolition of debtor imprisonment, distinguishing between contractual obligations and legal remedies for their enforcement.

A main question left unsettled by the decision—whether a state insolvency law was valid as applied to contracts entered into after it was passed—was taken up in *Ogden v. Saunders,* 1827, involving a revision of the New York law. Speaking for a bare majority of four, Justice Bushrod Washington (a nephew of the first president), held that a contract made after enactment was subject to provisions of the law,

Webster's political and legal successes owed no small debt to his oratory. In an age that placed high value on public speaking, Webster had few peers. His intellectual power and natural eloquence moved judges, juries, Senators, and general audiences alike. A Jovian brow and dark, piercing eyes complemented the often spellbinding words to give him an Olympian presence as a speaker of dramatic force. In Stephen Vincent Benet's mythologizing short story "The Devil and Daniel Webster," Webster debates the ultimate adversary and wins. One observer called him "a living lie, because no man on earth could be so great as he looked."*

Webster's greatest oratorical and constitutional triumph was his Senate reply to Robert Y. Hayne of South Carolina in January 1830, in what still may be the most compelling debate in the Senate's history. Hayne had forcefully advanced the doctrine of state sovereignty and nullification. Deploring such disunionist views, Webster answered by expounding on the nature of the Union. States had sovereignty only so far as they were not limited by the Constitution; final sovereignty resided in the Constitution and the national government. A dispute between a state and the national government was to be settled through institutions provided by the Constitution: the federal courts, amendment, and elections. Speaking for two days, Webster ended with the now famous flourish, "Liberty and Union, now and forever, one and inseparable!" Lincoln could hardly have put the case better.

Like his two partners in the Triumvirate, Webster was to be denied the Presidency. Though he ran as one of three Whigs in 1836, the candidate of the Northeast wing of the party, he carried only Massachusetts. He failed to get the party's nomination in 1840 and 1844, perhaps having become too closely identified with a section and with large monied interests. In the slavery controversy he supported the Wilmot Proviso, which displeased Southerners, and the Compromise of 1850, which fatally alienated many of his Northeastern abolitionist supporters. Webster risked his popularity in choosing to see disunion as a greater evil than slavery.

Though he was the highest paid attorney of his time, the state of his personal finances was often precarious because of poor investments and high living. "Very expensive and always in debt," Ralph Waldo Emerson would say.[†] Webster's death at age 70 in 1852 was nearly a decade before the Union he defended so well broke in two. Though it would take a war to achieve what Webster hoped might be done by politics and persuasion, he is remembered best as the historian Richard Hofstadter wrote, "as the quasi-official rhapsodist of American nationalism.[‡]

* Quoted in John F. Kennedy, *Profiles in Courage* (New York: Harper and Row, 1956), 60.
† Quoted in C. M. Fuess, *Daniel Webster*, vol II, 1832–1852 (Boston: Little, Brown, 1930), 129.
‡ *The American Political Tradition* (New York: Vintage Books, 1959), 68.

which in effect became part of the contract. Marshall dissented with Justices Story and Gabriel Duvall. It was the only time in a long career that he found himself in a minority on a constitutional issue. He believed insolvency laws operating prospectively were as invalid as those with retroactive effect; they also violated a natural justice based on the morality of keeping agreements under all circumstances.

Ogden v. Saunders imposed the first important limitation on the Contracts Clause as a bastion of property rights against state power. No longer would it be an absolute bar to insolvency relief.

In times of economic crisis, states could now balance the plight of debtors and defaulters against the rights of lenders and investment capital. In the long run these state efforts proved to be uneven, and Congress enacted national bankruptcy legislation in 1898. As we will see in the next chapter, the Contracts Clause was eventually eclipsed as property's chief shield against state regulations by the Court's laissez-faire reading of the fourteenth Amendment's due process clause.

To term the Marshall Court's contracts clause jurisprudence conservative, as is often done, would be misleading. Though several of its decisions were unpopular, most critics were not opposed to property and vested rights so much as they were to encroachments on state power. Often those seeking economic benefits at the state level found themselves in conflict with interests pursuing them at the national. At the core of Marshall's opinions was not a defense of established or static wealth but the encouragement of new wealth through enterprise and economic growth. The state laws he struck down were not democratically inspired or passed to aid a working class. Their intended beneficiaries were persons of property and enterprising ideas who had had the bad luck or poor judgment to stumble financially and whose numbers in hard times often rose alarmingly.

Marshall's reference to natural vested rights, though unsuccessful in *Ogden v. Saunders,* laid groundwork for the Court later to apply a theory of substantive due process to read rights into the Constitution that were neither in its text nor part of the clear intent of the framers. In the late nineteenth and early twentieth centuries, the Court would discover a right to enter into commercial agreements free of government interference. Later, the Warren Court would hold many civil liberties and civil rights, also found nowhere in constitutional text or original intent, to be likewise beyond the reach of government.

Toward a National Marketplace

Unlike the Contracts Clause, which aimed at state power but had no clear specific intent, the constitutional grant to Congress of regulatory power over interstate commerce had very clear purpose—preventing the balkanization of trade—yet alone placed no restrictions on state authority. The absence of such central power under the Articles had been one of the chief weaknesses of the regime the framers replaced. Yet the early Congresses under the Jeffersonian spell of strict construction after 1800 had shown little bent for exercising this obviously important grant. States

were largely left alone in dealing with commerce that was interstate. Many enacted laws that discriminated, intentionally or not, against commercial interests in other states. Some, like the monopoly grant, were especially unpopular and often brought retaliation.

Such was the case with New York's exclusive grant to Robert Livingston and Robert Fulton, one of the inventors of the steamboat, to run steamers in New York waters. Aaron Ogden obtained a license from the Livingston-Fulton combine to operate a steamboat service between Manhattan and New Jersey. When his former partner, Thomas Gibbons, who held a federal coasting license, ran competing boats in the same waters, the stage was set for one of the Supreme Court's great shaping decisions.

As we saw in Chapter 4, *Gibbons v. Ogden* in 1824 was the Court's first ruling on the regulation of interstate commerce. Its holding that a state law could not abridge privileges granted under a federal law was one of Marshall's greatest and a classic statement of economic nationalism. Breaking the steamboat monopoly was widely popular and, in opening the door to competition, had great economic consequence. In 1824 American steamboat tonnage was about 22,000. It tripled in the next six years, tripled again by 1840, and reached nearly 900,000 at the start of the Civil War. In holding that Congress could keep interstate commerce free of state monopolies, the decision also cleared the way for development of a national railway system. It was, as the constitutional historian Charles Warren said, "the emancipation proclamation of American commerce."*

By curbing state authority, *Gibbons* also set out a broad base for the exercise of national regulatory power, though that power would not be used in an important way until after the Civil War. Marshall's constitutional doctrine, going far to free commerce from state-granted monop-

---

* Charles Warren, *The Supreme Court in United States History,* rev. ed., 2 vols, vol 1 (Boston: Little, Brown, and Company, 1935), 616.

olies, was not translated into positive federal programs or national policies during the antebellum period. Nor, presumably, would Marshall have wished it to be. The nation's political preferences, embodied in a Jacksonian dual federalism, decreed that there should be little or no federal regulatory activity.

The vexing unanswered question in *Gibbons*—whether a state might affect interstate commerce when there were no pertinent or opposing federal regulations—was taken up by the Court five years later in *Willson v. Blackbird Creek Marsh Co.* Delaware had permitted construction of a dam across a minor navigable stream so that a tidewater swamp might be drained. When Willson, who held a federal coasting license similar to Gibbons's, rammed and broke the dam with his sloop, the company sued for damages.

Willson's defense, that the state had unconstitutionally obstructed a navigable waterway, might have produced a decision simply on the authority of *Gibbons*. But Marshall sustained the Delaware action, finding no conflict with a directly related Congressional act and, by that, all but ignored the coasting statute. The waterway was commercially unimportant, but Marshall let the decision rest on a state's power to improve the health, well-being, and property of its citizens—authority that would later be called state "police power." The decision was a partial retreat from the breadth of *Gibbons*. Where Congress had not regulated, states might do so for their own ends. Because local situations in the developing nation were so diverse and states had valid public interests to satisfy, the decision was eminently reasonable; otherwise, the clamor of local needs might have taken up much of Congress's time and energy. Nonetheless, the decision left unresolved a host of subsidiary questions about the limits of concurrency.

The National Marketplace Modified

When Jackson appointed Roger Taney to the chief justiceship after Marshall's death in 1835, the Supreme Court had already begun to change. Jackson had earlier named three other justices: John McLean, Henry Baldwin, and James Wayne. Within a year of Taney's ascent, three more Jacksonians were appointed: Philip Barbour, John Catron, and John McKinley (the last by Jackson's presidential successor Martin Van Buren). By 1837, the new members had transformed the Court from the nationalist tribunal Marshall had built to one in which Jacksonian principles, including a higher regard for states rights, were ascendant.

Unsurprisingly, the more accommodating approach to state power evident in *Willson* commanded the new Court. In its first important case dealing with interstate or foreign commerce, *New York v. Miln*, 1837 (p. 211), it sustained a state law that called for ship captains who landed aliens to supply information on the immigrants and post bonds so that they would not become public paupers after entry. A majority of five justices chose to view the law not as a regulation of commerce but as exercise of police power—the first time the Court had actually used the term. This method side-stepped the lingering question of whether states had concurrent power to regulate interstate or foreign commerce. One concurring justice, Smith Thompson, finding no conflict with a federal statute, assumed there to be a concurrence of power. Justice Joseph Story, Marshall's old stalwart, took the opposite view in dissent: What Congress did not regulate, it intended to leave free. The majority's approach and differences among the justices again left the line between federal and state power uncertain.

Concerns about slavery clearly underlay some of the discord. That issue came to the surface five years later in *Groves v. Slaughter* over a state's power to forbid entry of slaves. There, too, a divided Court side-stepped ruling definitively on the concurrence issue.

In three cases from New England states, decided together as the License Cases, 1847, the Court upheld laws that taxed and otherwise regulated the sale of alcoholic beverages imported from other states. Though the enactments

Scholar of the Law

At 32, Joseph Story was the youngest person ever appointed to the Supreme Court. His service of 34 years (1811–1845) was one of the longest in the history of the Court. As a nationalist and advocate of an expansive federal judicial authority, Story was a natural ally of John Marshall and helped build the great record of the Marshall Court. His legal learning, unsurpassed by his colleagues on either the Marshall or Taney Courts, is probably rivaled among all justices only by Oliver Wendell Holmes and Felix Frankfurter. While on the Court, he managed to publish a dozen books on legal subjects and serve 16 years as a full-time professor of law at Harvard.

Story's appointment by Madison was problematic. Son of a doctor who had taken part in the Boston Tea Party, Story was a restlessly ambitious, often pugnacious youth. He entered Harvard at 16, graduating second in his class three years later. He had hoped to be a poet, but when his efforts were indifferently received, he turned to an apprenticeship in law, eventually setting up practice in Salem, Massachusetts. He was elected to the Massachusetts House and later to Congress as a Jeffersonian Republican. But his opposition to the disastrous 1807 presidential embargo earned him Jefferson's lifelong enmity. When Madison, as Jefferson's successor, failed in three attempts to fill a vacancy on the Court, he turned to the rising young Massachusetts lawyer. Jefferson cautioned him that Story's Republican loyalty was not to be trusted. The concern proved well founded as Story's broad constructionist nationalism, more congenial with Federalist-Whig principles, began to emerge.

On the Court, Story was an advocate of expanded federal jurisdiction. This was most dramatically evident in *Martin v. Hunter's Lessee* where Story, writing for the Court, upheld its power to review state court decisions. Though he failed to persuade his colleagues to establish a federal common law of crimes, he was able to enlarge federal admiralty and maritime jurisdictions. Later, in *Swift v. Tyson*, he led the Court in holding that the federal judiciary in diversity cases was not bound by state court commercial law but was free to establish an independent federal common law. The decision freed interstate commercial transactions that were brought into federal courts from idiosyncratic state holdings, thus helping to check a balkanizing of commercial law. Though the decision was reversed a century later in *Erie Railroad v. Tompkins*, it helped

favored local interests at the expense of out-of-state competitors, the Court sustained them as valid use of the police power to protect public health and morals. The Court was unanimous, but six justices filed opinions, again partly because of concerns about how the ruling might affect the slavery issue.

Multiple opinions also marked the Passenger Cases, two years later. At issue were New York and Massachusetts laws imposing taxes on incoming ship passengers including immigrants, the proceeds going to pay for support and medical care of immigrant paupers. The Court held the laws invalid, 5-4, as an interference with federal power over immigration, but failed to clarify the constitutional doctrine of the coexistence of national delegated power and state police power. That it had upheld a bond-posting requirement in *Miln*, but struck down a simple head tax in this case only added to the uncertainty.

to nationalize commercial rules and make them more uniform and predictable—goals close to Story's heart.

His attempts to balance the rights of vested property and the demands of economic expansion led him to formulate the doctrine of "reasonable use" in *Tyler v. Wilkinson*, 1827, a circuit court decision upholding dam construction rights of upstream mill owners against the damage claims by downstream landowners. Story's opinion showed the creative flexibility of the common law and the importance of law and thus of judges in accommodating economic change.

He and Marshall were close collaborators, but Story differed enough with his chief in the Dartmouth College case to write a concurring opinion showing how states might prospectively overcome the limits of the Contracts Clause by reserving in their original grants the right to make future changes. Though he feuded with some of his colleagues, particularly William Johnson and Henry Baldwin, the exuberant, energetic Story was second only to Marshall himself in impelling the great formative decisions that flowed from the Marshall Court.

When Marshall died in 1835, Story was a logical and popular choice to succeed him as chief justice, but President Andrew Jackson, having no desire for a Marshall II Court, nominated his trusted attorney general Roger Taney instead. Story soon found himself surrounded by Jacksonian associates and, despite his triumph in *Swift v. Tyson,* was often outvoted. In the Court's conferences, he argued in vain for federal exclusivity in interstate commerce matters. Though he believed dissenting opinions weakened the Court as an institution, he wrote a learned one in *Charles River Bridge,* favoring a strict

honoring of charter promises. His rearguard defense of Marshall's jurisprudence helped to moderate the new Court's impulses toward populist and states rights reforms.

Throughout his tenure on the Court, Story was politically active behind the scenes in Massachusetts and in national affairs, indefatigably giving advice on a range of political and legal issues. He collaborated often with his friend Daniel Webster and even helped draft Webster's reply to Jackson's veto message on rechartering the National Bank in 1832. Judicial conflicts of interest did not loom as large in nineteenth century America as they would today, and Story seems to have given little concern to the ethical questions such "dual" roles might raise. He heard cases involving the National Bank while he was president of its Massachusetts branch and participated in *Charles River Bridge* though he was a Harvard faculty member and a Fellow of the Harvard Corporation.

Even had Story not served on the Court, he would have left a lasting mark on American law through writing and teaching. His best known work, the three-volume *Commentaries on the Constitution,* published in 1833 and eventually translated into several languages, ranks with Chancellor James Kent's *Commentaries on American Law* as the most influential legal work of the antebellum period. So widely read were Story's books that by the early 1840s, the failed poet's royalty income was more than twice his judicial salary. At Harvard, Story was a strong advocate of university-based legal education and a curriculum of national law based on "rational" and uniform legal principles, particularly in commercial law. Several of his books became the standard fare of legal instruction.

By the 1850s the Taney Court had wrestled with the concurrence question for 15 years with little success. The enormous growth in the nation's economy had not been matched by Congressional regulatory attention to interstate commerce. The prevailing philosophy of laissez-faire, a strict constructionist understanding of the Constitution, and the anxiety of Southern slave interests wary of any federal expansion kept national legislation to a minimum. Congress had

plenary power over interstate commerce but had used it hardly at all.

On the other hand, state statute books were filled with all manner of provisions affecting commercial activity. In a growing, ever-more interdependent economy, that activity was often interstate in scope. That states could regulate commerce within their borders and could pass laws to protect the health, safety, and well-being of their citizens was well established. But the exercise of either authority often had a direct or indirect effect on interstate commerce and sometimes a discriminatory effect that favored local interests.

The doctrinal uncertainty over concurrence was at last substantially resolved in the Court's 1852 decision *Cooley v. Board of Wardens,* (p. 216) involving a Philadelphia pilotage rule that clearly burdened interstate commerce. All ships entering the city's harbor were required to take on a pilot or, alternatively, pay half the pilotage fee to an organization for pilot relief. For the first time, a majority of the Court (five of the eight justices participating) was able to agree on the doctrinal status of concurrence.

Justice Benjamin Curtis, a newcomer to the Court, announced what was to become known as the "Cooley rule." The power to regulate commerce embraced a "vast field, containing not only many, but exceedingly various subjects, quite unlike in their nature." Some called for a uniform rule operating equally everywhere. But others, such as harbor navigation, permitted diversity. Where uniformity was needed, regulatory power was exclusively that of Congress. Where it was not needed and Congress passed no preemptive or superseding legislation, a state was free to act.

The Cooley rule struck the seemingly pragmatic balance between nationalist and laissez-faire arguments for complete Congressional exclusivity (thus usually no regulation at all), and states rights and public interest arguments for complete concurrence. This important feat notwithstanding, the decision offered no guidelines for determining which subjects of commerce called for uniform rules and which did not. And it raised a new question: Who would make final decision on whether uniformity was called for, Congress or the Court?

These unanswered questions got an early test. In *Pennsylvania v. Wheeling and Belmont Bridge Co.* later the same year, the Court held that a railway suspension bridge across the Ohio River at Wheeling, authorized by Virginia (of which

Wheeling was then part), was an obstruction to interstate commerce because its low height interfered with steamboat passage. Congress responded by declaring the bridge to be of lawful height. A short time later the bridge was destroyed in a storm but then rebuilt at the same height. In a second suit of the same name in 1856, the Court, now faced with Congress's declaration, yielded to it.

Economically, these events represented a triumph for the railroads, which were now becoming the dominant means of transport, over steamboats. It was another victory for new development and technology over established ventures, and Congress later authorized the construction of many bridges over navigable waterways. But in many other areas of interstate commerce, Congress was to remain silent, often for many years, thus allowing the Court under its new Cooley rule to decide what interstate commerce needed and what it did not.

New Property Versus Old

No constitutional case better represents the course and spirit of American antebellum economic development than *Charles River Bridge Co. v. Warren Bridge Co.* (p. 212) Decided in 1837, it was Roger Taney's first opinion for the Court. No case better captures the Jacksonian hostility to special privilege and the conflict between economic competition and vested rights. Probably none better reveals the contrasting judicial methods of the Marshall and Taney Courts.

In 1785, Massachusetts had granted a corporate charter to a group of private investors organized as the Charles River Bridge Company to build and operate a toll bridge over the river between Boston and Charlestown. In 1828, with traffic having greatly increased, the state authorized another group of investors to build a second bridge, the Warren Bridge, a short distance away. They were to collect tolls but only until their investment had been paid off, at which time the bridge would revert to the state and become toll-free. Because the older bridge could not compete successfully with a free facility, the Charles River Bridge Company tried to enjoin the construction. It argued that by authorizing a new bridge, the state impaired its contractual obligation that impliedly gave the company an exclusive right to collect tolls in the line of travel.

Taney's majority opinion rejected the claim and with it the entire notion of implied privileges in corporate charters. Being state grants, such charters must be strictly construed. In the absence of an express agreement to the contrary, a state was free to make competing grants. If it were not, the economic development and thus the well-being of the community, in this case the easing of traffic, could not be served.

Despite this Jacksonian blow to privilege, there is no spirit of leveling in Taney's opinion or in his assumption that it was a task of government to act for the public good. There is no animus against property or rejection of its protection per se. Instead, Taney departs from the older, more exacting protection of vested rights, to accommodate and encourage new ventures.

The older view, which likely would have been Marshall's, found expression in Justice Story's dissent in which he stressed the "certainties of expectations." Property rights created by the original charter should not be destroyed by later grants. To do so, Story thought, would inject an unpredictability into capital enterprise that would discourage the undertaking of valuable public projects.

Though unpopular in established legal circles, the decision was not followed in the states by assaults on corporate property or by a slowing of economic growth. If anything, it had the opposite effect.

FURTHER READING

The Constitution and Economic Development

Ashworth, John, *Slavery, Capitalism, and Politics in the Antebellum Republic* (1996)

Corwin, Edward S., *The Commerce Power Versus States Rights* (1936)

Frankfurter, Felix, *The Commerce Clause Under Marshall, Taney, and Waite* (1937)

Howe, Daniel Walker, *The Political Culture of American Whigs* (1979)

Hyman, Harold and William M. Wiecek, *Equal Justice Under Law: Constitutional Development, 1835–1875* (1982)

Latner, Richard B., *The Presidency of Andrew Jackson: White House Politics, 1829–1837* (1979)

Mushkat, Jerome and Joseph G., Rayback, *Martin Van Buren: Law, Politics, and the Republican Ideology* (1997)

Schlesinger, Jr., Arthur, *The Age of Jackson*

Sellers, Charles, *The Market Revolution: Jacksonian America, 1815–1846* (1991)

Swisher, Carl B., *History of the Supreme Court of the United States*, vol 5: *The Taney Period, 1836–1864* (1974)

White, G. Edward, *History of the Supreme Court of the United States*, vols 3–4:*The Marshall Court and Cultural Change, 1815–1835* (1988)

White, Leonard D., *The Jacksonians: A Study in Administrative History, 1829–1860* (1954)

Wright, Benjamin F., *The Contract Clause and the Constitution* (1938)

Transformation of the Law

Balleisen, Edward J., *Navigating Failure: Bankruptcy and Commercial Society in Antebellum America* (2001)

Friedman, Lawrence M., *A History of American Law*, 2nd ed., (1985)

Hall, Kermit, *The Magic Mirror: Law in American History* (1989)

Horwitz, Morton J., *The Transformation of American Law*, 1780–1860, 2 vols (1977)

Hurst, J. Willard, *The Growth of American Law: The Law-makers* (1950)

Remini, Robert V., *Daniel Webster: The Man and His Time* (1997)
Swisher, Carl B., *Roger B. Taney* (1935)

Biographical

Baxter, Maurice, *Daniel Webster and the Supreme Court* (1966)
———, *Henry Clay and the American System* (1995)
Peterson, Merrill D., *The Great Triumvirate: Webster, Clay, and Calhoun* (1987)
McClellan, James, *Joseph Story and the American Constitution* (1971)
Newmyer, R. Kent, *Supreme Court Justice Joseph Story: Statesman of the Old Republic* (1985)

On Leading Cases

Baxter, Maurice, *The Steamboat Monopoly: Gibbons v. Ogden* 1864 (1971)
Kutler, Stanley L., *Privilege and Creative Destruction: The Charles River Bridge Case* (1971)
Magrath, Peter, *Yazoo: Law and Politics in the New Republic, the Case of Fletcher v. Peck* (1966)
Stites, Francis N., *Private Interest and Public Gain: The Dartmouth College Case* (1972)

CASES

Fletcher v. Peck

10 U.S. 87 (1810), 4-1
Opinion of the Court: Marshall (Washington, Livingston, Todd)
Dissenting in part: Johnson
Not participating: Chase, Cushing
In 1795, the Georgia legislature, bribed by land speculators, sold more than 35 million acres of public land near the Yazoo River to four companies for $500,000—less than 2 cents an acre. A year later after the corrupt details became known, Georgia voters elected a new legislature which then repealed the earlier sale. But the speculators had acted quickly and by the time of repeal, had sold most of their ill-gotten tracts to various persons throughout the country, most of whom presumably were unaware of the fraud. After many years, the controversy reached the Supreme Court. John Peck, a dealer in the Yazoo lands, had sold 15,000 acres to Robert Fletcher for $3,000. Fletcher sued Peck for recovery of his purchase money. Peck argued that the legislative repeal of the original sale was invalid.

Does Marshall base his decision on considerations beyond the Constitution? What are the various kinds of contracts to which the Contracts Clause might apply? Does the decision here mean that a state might never alter a grant once given or an agreement once made? Where does the public interest lie in this case?

Marshall, C.J., for the Court:

... The lands in controversy vested absolutely in James Gunn and others, the original grantees, by the conveyance of the governor, made in pursuance of an act of assembly to which the legislature was fully competent. Being thus in full possession of the legal estate, they, for a valuable consideration, conveyed portions of the land to those who were willing to purchase. If the original transaction was infected with fraud, these purchasers did not participate in it, and had no notice of it. They were innocent. Yet the legislature of Georgia has involved them in the fate of the first parties to the transaction, and, if the act be valid, has annihilated their rights also. ...

If a suit be brought to set aside a conveyance obtained by fraud, and the fraud be clearly proved, the conveyance will be set aside, as between the parties; but the rights of third persons, who are purchasers without notice, for a valuable consideration, cannot be disregarded. Titles, which, according to every legal test, are perfect, are acquired with that confidence which is inspired by the opinion that the purchaser is safe. If there be any concealed defect, arising from the conduct of those who had held the property long before he acquired it, of which he had no notice, that concealed defect cannot be set up against him. He has paid his money for a title good at law, he is innocent, whatever may be the guilt of others, and equity will not subject him to the penalties attached to that guilt. All titles would be insecure, and the intercourse between man and man would be very seriously obstructed, if this principle be overturned. ...

Is the power of the legislature competent to the annihilation of such title, and to a resumption of the property thus held?

The principle asserted is, that one legislature is competent to repeal any act which a former legislature was competent to pass; and that one legislature cannot abridge the powers of a succeeding legislature.

The correctness of this principle, so far as respects general legislation, can never be controverted. But, if an act be done under a law, a succeeding legislature cannot undo it. The past cannot be recalled by the most absolute power. Conveyances have been made, those conveyances have vested legal estate, and, if those estates may be seized by the sovereign authority, still, that they originally vested is a fact, and cannot cease to be a fact.

When, then, a law is in its nature a contract, when absolute rights have vested under that contract, a repeal of the law cannot divest those rights; and the act of annulling them, if legitimate, is rendered so by a power applicable to the case of every individual in the community. . . .

. . . The constitution of the United States declares that no state shall pass any bill of attainder, ex post facto law, or law impairing the obligation of contracts.

Does the case now under consideration come within this prohibitory section of the constitution?

In considering this very interesting question, we immediately ask ourselves what is a contract? Is a grant a contract?

A contract is a compact between two or more parties, and is either executory or executed. An executory contract is one in which a party binds himself to do, or not to do, a particular thing; such was the law under which the conveyance was made by the governor. A contract executed is one in which the object of contract is performed; and this, says Blackstone, differs in nothing from a grant. The contract between Georgia and the purchasers was executed by the grant. A contract executed, as well as one which is executory, contains obligations binding on the parties. A grant, in its own nature, amounts to an extinguishment of the right of the grantor, and implies a contract not to reassert that right. A party is, therefore, always estopped by his own grant.

Since, then, in fact, a grant is a contract executed, the obligation of which still continues, and since the constitution uses the general term contract, without distinguishing between those which are executory and those which are executed, it must be construed to comprehend the latter as well as the former. A law annulling conveyances between individuals, and declaring that the grantors should stand seised of their former estates, notwithstanding those grants, would be as repugnant to the constitution as a law discharging the vendors of property from the obligation of executing their contracts by conveyances. It would be strange if a contract to convey was secured by the constitution, while an absolute conveyance remained unprotected.

If, under a fair construction the constitution, grants are comprehended under the terms contracts, is a grant from the state excluded from the operation of the provision? Is the clause to be considered as inhibiting the state from impairing the obligation of contracts between two individuals, but as excluding from that inhibition contracts made with itself?

The words themselves contain no such distinction. They are general, and are applicable to contracts of every description. If contracts made with the state are to be exempted from their operation, the exception must arise from the character of the contracting party, not from the words which are employed.

Whatever respect might have been felt for the state sovereignties, it is not to be disguised that the framers of the constitution viewed, with some apprehension, the violent acts which might grow out of the feelings of the moment; and that the people of the United States, in adopting that instrument, have manifested a determination to shield themselves and their property from the effects of those sudden and strong passions to which men are exposed. The restrictions on the legislative power of the states are obviously founded in this sentiment; and the constitution of the United States contains what may be deemed a bill of rights for the people of each state. . . .

It is, then, the unanimous opinion of the court, that, in this case, the estate having passed into the hands of a purchaser for a valuable consideration, without notice, the state of Georgia was restrained, either by general principles which are common to our free institutions, or by the particular provisions of the constitution of the United States, from passing a law whereby the estate of the plaintiff in the premises so purchased could be constitutionally and legally impaired and rendered null and void.

Dartmouth College v. Woodward

17 U.S. 518 (1819), 5-1
Opinion of the Court: Marshall (Johnson, Livingston)
Concurring: Washington, Story
Dissenting: Duvall
How did Marshall characterize the college's charter as a contract? Why did he go to great lengths to try to demonstrate

that it was protected by the Constitution from state impairment? Does this decision mean that a state may contract away its police power and, once done, is forever bound by the agreement? How does Story answer that question? Given the general views of the framers on property rights and what is known of their intent, has Marshall broadened or narrowed the contracts clause or interpreted it largely as they understood it? Should this decision be considered a great victory for property rights or not? See Charles River Bridge Co. v. Warren Bridge Co. How would it be likely to affect economic development?

Marshall, C.J., for the Court:

This court can be insensible neither to the magnitude nor delicacy of this question. The validity of a legislative act is to be examined; and the opinion of the highest law tribunal of a state is to be revised . . . On more than one occasion, this court has expressed the cautious circumspection with which it approaches the consideration of such questions . . . But the American people have said, in the Constitution of the United States, that "no state shall pass any . . . law impairing the obligation of contracts." In the same instrument, they have also said, "that the judicial power shall extend to all cases in law and equity arising under the Constitution." On the judges of this court, then, is imposed the high and solemn duty of protecting, from even legislative violation, those contracts which the constitution of our country has placed beyond legislative control . . .

It can require no argument to prove, that the circumstances of this case constitute a contract . . . The points for consideration are (1) Is this contract protected by the Constitution of the United States? (2) Is it impaired by the acts under which [Woodward] holds?

On the first . . . That the framers of the Constitution did not intend to restrain the states in the regulation of their civil institutions, adopted for internal government, and that the instrument they have given us, is not to be so construed, may be admitted. The provision of the Constitution never has been understood to embrace other contracts, than those which respect property, or some object of value, and confer rights which may be asserted in a court of justice. It never has been understood to restrict the general right of the legislature to legislate on the subject of divorces. Those acts enable some tribunals, not to impair a marriage contract, but to liberate one of the parties, because it has been broken by the other. When any state legislature shall pass an act annulling all marriage con-

tracts, or allowing either party to annul it, without the consent of the other, it will be time enough to inquire, whether such an act be constitutional.

The parties in this case differ less on general principles . . . than on the application of those principles to this case, and on the true construction of the charter of 1769 . . . If the act of incorporation be a grant of political power, if it create a civil institution, to be employed in the administration of the government, or if the funds of the college be public property, or if the state of New Hampshire, as a government, be alone interested in its transactions, the subject is one in which the legislature of the state may act according to its own judgment, unrestrained by any limitation of its power imposed by the Constitution of the United States.

But if this be a private eleemosynary institution, endowed with a capacity to take property, for objects unconnected with government, whose funds are bestowed by individuals, on the faith of the charter; if the donors have stipulated for the future disposition and management of those funds, in the manner prescribed by themselves; there may be more difficulty in the case. . . .

Whence, then, can be derived the idea, that Dartmouth College has become a public institution, and its trustees public officers, exercising powers conferred by the public for public objects? Not from the source whence its funds were drawn; for its foundation is purely private and eleemosynary—not from the application of those funds; for money may be given for education, and the persons receiving it do not, by being employed in the education of youth, become members of the civil government. Is it from the act of incorporation? Let this subject be considered.

A corporation is an artificial being, invisible, intangible, and existing only in contemplation of law. Being the mere creature of law, it possesses only those properties which the charter of its creation confers upon it, either expressly, or as incidental to its very existence . . . [H]ow is it, that this artificial being, created by law . . . should become a part of the civil government of the country? Is it because its existence, its capacities, its powers, are given by law? Because the government has given it the power to take and to hold property, in a particular form, and for particular purposes, has the government a consequent right substantially to change that form, or to vary the purposes to which the property is to be applied? This principle has never been asserted or recognized, and is supported by no authority. Can it derive aid from reason? . . .

From the fact . . . that a charter of incorporation has been granted, nothing can be inferred, which changes the character of the institution, or transfers to the government any new power over it . . . The incorporating act neither gives nor prevents this control. Neither, in reason, can the incorporating act change the character of a private eleemosynary institution. . . .

From this review of the charter, it appears, that Dartmouth College is an eleemosynary institution, incorporated for the purpose of perpetuating the application of the bounty of the donors, to the specified objects of that bounty; that its trustees or governors were originally named by the founder, and invested with the power of perpetuating themselves; that they are not public officers, nor is it a civil institution, participating in the administration of government; but a charity-school, or a seminary of education, incorporated for the preservation of its property, and the perpetual application of that property to the objects of its creation.

Yet a question remains to be considered, of more real difficulty, on which more doubt has been entertained, than on all that have been discussed. . . . Can this be such a contract, as the Constitution intended to withdraw from the power of state legislation? Contracts, the parties to which have a vested beneficial interest, and those only, it has been said, are the objects about which the Constitution is solicitous, and to which its protection is extended . . .

This is plainly a contract to which the donors, the trustees and the crown (to whose rights and obligations New Hampshire succeeds) were the original parties. It is a contract made on a valuable consideration. It is a contract for the security and disposition of property. It is a contract, on the faith of which, real and personal estate has been conveyed to the corporation. It is, then, a contract within the letter of the Constitution, and within its spirit also . . .

On what safe and intelligible ground, can this exception stand? There is no expression in the Constitution, no sentiment delivered by its contemporaneous expounders, which would justify us in making it. In the absence of all authority of this kind, is there, in the nature and reason of the case itself, that which would sustain a construction of the Constitution, not warranted by its words? Are contracts of this description of a character to excite so little interest, that we must exclude them from the provisions of the Consti-

tution, as being unworthy of the attention of those who framed the instrument? Or does public policy so imperiously demand their remaining exposed to legislative alteration, as to compel us, or rather permit us, to say, that these words, which were introduced to give stability to contracts, and which in their plain import comprehend this contract, must yet be so construed as to exclude it?

Almost all eleemosynary corporations, those which are created for the promotion of religion, of charity or of education, are of the same character. The law of this case is the law of all. . . .

If the insignificance of the object does not require that we should exclude contracts respecting it from the protection of the Constitution; neither, as we conceive, is the policy of leaving them subject to legislative alteration so apparent, as to require a forced construction of that instrument, in order to effect it. These eleemosynary institutions do not fill the place, which would otherwise be occupied by government, but that which would otherwise remain vacant. They are complete acquisitions to literature. They are donations to education; donations, which any government must be disposed rather to encourage than to discountenance. . . . All such gifts are made in the pleasing, perhaps delusive hope, that the charity will flow for ever in the channel which the givers have marked out for it. If every man finds in his own bosom strong evidence of the universality of this sentiment, there can be but little reason to imagine, that the framers of our constitution were strangers to it, and that, feeling the necessity and policy of giving permanence and security to contracts, of withdrawing them from the influence of legislative bodies, whose fluctuating policy, and repeated interferences, produced the most perplexing and injurious embarrassments, they still deemed it necessary to leave these contracts subject to those interferences . . .

The opinion of the court, after mature deliberation, is, that this is a contract, the obligation of which cannot be impaired, without violating the Constitution of the United States. This opinion appears to us to be equally supported by reason, and by the former decisions of this court.

We next proceed to the inquiry, whether its obligation has been impaired by those acts of the legislature of New Hampshire, to which the special verdict refers?

From the review of this charter, which has been taken, it appears that the whole power of governing the college, of appointing and removing tutors, of fixing their salaries, of directing the course of study to be pursued by the students, and of filling up vacancies created in their own body, was vested in the trustees. On the part of the crown, it was expressly stipulated, that this corporation, thus constituted, should continue for ever; and that the number of trustees should for ever consist of twelve, and no more. By this contract, the crown was bound, and could have made no violent alteration in its essential terms, without impairing its obligation.

By the revolution, the duties, as well as the powers, of government devolved on the people of New Hampshire. It is admitted, that among the latter was comprehended the transcendent power of parliament, as well as that of the executive department. It is too clear . . . that all contracts and rights respecting property, remained unchanged by the revolution. The obligations, then, which were created by the charter to Dartmouth College, were the same in the new, that they had been in the old government. The power of the government was also the same. A repeal of this charter, at any time prior to the adoption of the present constitution of the United States, would have been an extraordinary and unprecedented act of power, but one which could have been contested only by the restrictions upon the legislature, to be found in the constitution of the state. But the Constitution of the United States has imposed this additional limitation, that the legislature of a state shall pass no act 'impairing the obligation of contracts.'

It has been already stated, that the act 'to amend the charter, and enlarge and improve the corporation of Dartmouth College,' increases the number of trustees to twenty-one, gives the appointment of the additional members to the executive of the state, and creates a board of overseers, to consist of twenty- five persons, of whom twenty-one are also appointed by the executive of New Hampshire, who have power to inspect and control the most important acts of the trustees. . . .

Between acting directly, and acting through the agency of trustees and overseers, no essential difference is perceived. The whole power of governing the college is transferred from trustees, appointed according to the will of the founder, expressed in the charter, to the executive of New Hampshire. The management and application of the funds of this eleemosynary institution, which are placed by the donors in the hands of trustees named in the charter, and empowered to perpetuate themselves, are placed

by this act under the control of the government of the state. The will of the state is substituted for the will of the donors, in every essential operation of the college . . . The founders of the college contracted, not merely for the perpetual application of the funds which they gave, to the objects for which those funds were given; they contracted also, to secure that application by the constitution of the corporation. They contracted for a system, which should, so far as human foresight can provide, retain for ever the government of the literary institution they had formed, in the hands of persons approved by themselves. This system is totally changed. The charter of 1769 exists no longer. It is re-organized . . . in such a manner, as to convert a literary institution, molded according to the will of its founders, and placed under the control of private literary men, into a machine entirely subservient to the will of government. This may be for the advantage of this college in particular, and may be for the advantage of literature in general; but it is not according to the will of the donors, and is subversive of that contract, on the faith of which their property was given . . .

[T]he acts of the legislature of New Hampshire . . . are repugnant to the Constitution of the United States . . . The judgment of the state court must, therefore, be reversed.

Story, concurring:

In my judgment, it is perfectly clear, that any act of a legislature which takes away any powers or franchises vested by its charter in a private corporation, or its corporate officers, or which restrains or controls the legitimate exercise of them, or transfers them to other persons, without its assent, is a violation of the obligations of that charter. If the legislature mean to claim such an authority, it must be reserved in the grant. The charter of Dartmouth College contains no such reservation; and I am, therefore, bound to declare, that the acts of the legislature of New Hampshire, now in question, do impair the obligations of that charter, and are, consequently, unconstitutional and void.

Gibbons v. Ogden

22 U.S. 1 (1824), 6-0
Opinion of the Court: Marshall, C.J. (Duvall, Johnson, Story, Todd, Washington)
Marshall's opinion contains one of the most tightly reasoned textual analyses in the Court's history. How did he

support his claim that commerce was not limited to traffic? That the commerce power did not stop at state lines? To what did he look for a definition of commerce? Does he place any limits on the commerce power? As a result of this decision, do states have any concurrent power over commerce when Congress is silent? In granting the steamboat franchise to Fulton et. al., the New York legislature believed it was rewarding enterprise and new invention. Does the Court's decision strike a blow against economic development? Is the case one of conflict between state and national power or between economic interests? How does the decision relate to McCulloch v. Maryland? *To* Dartmouth College v. Woodward? *Why might the decision be less popular in the South than elsewhere?*

Marshall, C.J., for the Court:

[The] clause in the Constitution which authorizes Congress to regulate commerce . . . contains an enumeration of powers expressly granted by the people to their government. It has been said, that these powers ought to be construed strictly. But why ought they to be so construed? . . . In the last of the enumerated powers, that which grants, expressly, the means for carrying all others into execution, Congress is authorized 'to make all laws which shall be necessary and proper' for the purpose. But this limitation on the means which may be used, is not extended to the powers which are conferred; nor is there one sentence in the Constitution . . . that prescribes this rule . . . What do [counsel for Ogden] mean, by a strict construction? . . . If they contend for that narrow construction which, in support or some theory not to be found in the Constitution, would deny to the government those powers which the words of the grant, as usually understood, import, and which are consistent with the general views and objects of the instrument; for that narrow construction, which would cripple the government, and render it unequal to the object for which it is declared to be instituted, and to which the powers given, as fairly understood, render it competent; then we cannot perceive the propriety of this strict construction, nor adopt it as the rule by which the Constitution is to be expounded. As men, whose intentions require no concealment, generally employ the words which most directly and aptly express the ideas they intend to convey, the enlightened patriots who framed our constitution, and the people who adopted it, must be understood to have employed words in their natural sense, and to have intended what they have said. If, from the imperfection of human language, there should be serious doubts

respecting the extent of any given power, it is a well settled rule, that the objects for which it was given, especially when those objects are expressed in the instrument itself, should have great influence in the construction . . . We know of no rule for construing the extent of such powers, other than is given by the language of the instrument which confers them, taken in connection with the purposes for which they were conferred.

The words are, 'Congress shall have power to regulate commerce with foreign nations, and among the several States, and with the Indian tribes.'

The subject to be regulated is commerce; and our constitution being, as was aptly said at the bar, one of enumeration, and not of definition, to ascertain the extent of the power, it becomes necessary to settle the meaning of the word . . . Commerce, undoubtedly, is traffic, but it is something more: it is intercourse. It describes the commercial intercourse between nations, and parts of nations, in all its branches, and is regulated by prescribing rules for carrying on that intercourse. The mind can scarcely conceive a system for regulating commerce between nations, which shall exclude all laws concerning navigation, which shall be silent on the admission of the vessels of the one nation into the ports of the other, and be confined to prescribing rules for the conduct of individuals, in the actual employment of buying and selling, or of barter. . . .

[T]his power [over navigation] has been exercised from the commencement of the government, has been exercised with the consent of all, and has been understood by all to be a commercial regulation. All America understands, and has uniformly understood, the word 'commerce,' to comprehend navigation. It was so understood . . . when the Constitution was framed. The power over commerce, including navigation, was one of the primary objects for which the people of America adopted their government, and must have been contemplated in forming it. The convention must have used the word in that sense, because all have understood it in that sense; and the attempt to restrict it comes too late.

[A]dditional confirmation is, we think, furnished by the words of the instrument itself.

It is a rule of construction, acknowledged by all, that the exceptions from a power mark its extent; for it would be absurd, as well as useless, to except from a granted power, that which was not granted—that which the words of the grant could not comprehend. If, then, there are in the Constitution plain exceptions

A drawing of Robert Fulton's early steamboat the *Clermont* in New York harbor. Fulton's invention revolutionized maritime commerce and led New York state to grant Aaron Ogden an exclusive franchise for steamboat passenger service between New Jersey and New York.

from the power over navigation, plain inhibitions to the exercise of that power in a particular way, it is a proof that those who made these exceptions, and prescribed these inhibitions, understood the power to which they applied as being granted.

The 9th section of the 1st article declares, that 'no preference shall be given, by any regulation of commerce or revenue, to the ports of one State over those of another.' This clause cannot be understood as applicable to those laws only which are passed for the purposes of revenue, because it is expressly applied to commercial regulations; and the most obvious preference which can be given to one port over another, in regulating commerce, relates to navigation. But the subsequent part of the sentence is still more explicit. It is, 'nor shall vessels bound to or from one State, be obliged to enter, clear, or pay duties, in another.' These words have a direct reference to navigation . . .

The word used in the Constitution, then, comprehends . . . navigation within its meaning; and a power to regulate navigation, is as expressly granted, as if that term had been added to the word 'commerce.'

To what commerce does this power extend? The Constitution informs us, to commerce 'with foreign nations, and among the several States, and with the Indian tribes.' . . .

The subject . . . is to commerce 'among the several States.' The word 'among' means intermingled with. A thing which is among others, is intermingled with them. Commerce among the States, cannot stop at the external boundary line of each State, but may be introduced into the interior.

It is not intended to say that these words comprehend that commerce, which is completely internal, which is carried on between man and man in a State, or between different parts of the same State, and which does not extend to or affect other States. . . .

Comprehensive as the word 'among' is, it may very properly be restricted to that commerce which concerns more States than one. The phrase is not one which would probably have been selected to indicate the completely interior traffic of a State, because it is not an apt phrase for that purpose; and the enumeration of the particular classes of commerce, to which the power was to be extended, would not have been made, had the intention been to extend the power to every description. The enumeration presupposes something not enumerated; and that something, if we regard the language or the subject of the sentence, must be the exclusively internal commerce of a State. The genius and character of the whole government seem to be, that its action is to be applied to all the external concerns of the nation, and to those internal concerns which affect the States generally; but not to those which are completely within a particular State, which do not affect other States, and with which it is not necessary to interfere, for the purpose of executing some of the general powers of the government. The completely internal commerce of a State, then, may be considered as reserved for the State itself.

But, in regulating commerce with foreign nations, the power of Congress does not stop at the jurisdictional lines of the several States. It would be a very useless power, if it could not pass those lines. The commerce of the United States with foreign nations, is that of the whole United States. Every district has a right to participate in it. The deep streams which penetrate our country in every direction, pass through the interior of almost every State in the Union, and furnish the means of exercising this right. If Congress has the power to regulate it, that power must be exercised whenever the subject exists. If it exists within the States, if a foreign voyage may commence or terminate at a port within a State, then the power of Congress may be exercised within a State.

This principle is, if possible, still more clear, when applied to commerce 'among the several States.' ... What is commerce 'among' them; and how is it to be conducted? Can a trading expedition between two adjoining States, commence and terminate outside of each? And if the trading intercourse be between two States remote from each other, must it not commence in one, terminate in the other, and probably pass through a third? Commerce among the States must, of necessity, be commerce with the States ...

We are now arrived at the inquiry—What is this power?

It is the power to regulate; that is, to prescribe the rule by which commerce is to be governed. This power, like all others vested in Congress, is complete in itself, may be exercised to its utmost extent, and acknowledges no limitations, other than are prescribed in the Constitution. These are expressed in plain terms ... If, as has always been understood, the sovereignty of Congress, though limited to specified objects, is plenary as to those objects, the power over commerce ... among the several States, is vested in Congress as absolutely as it would be in a single government, having in its constitution the same restrictions on the exercise of the power as are found in the Constitution of the United States ...

But it has been urged with great earnestness, that, although the power of Congress to regulate commerce with foreign nations, and among the several States, be co-extensive with the subject itself, and have no other limits than are prescribed in the Constitution, yet the States may severally exercise the same power, within their respective jurisdictions. In support of this argument, it is said, that they possessed it as an inseparable attribute of sovereignty, before the formation of the Constitution, and still retain it, except so far as they have surrendered it by that instrument; that this principle results from the nature of the government, and is secured by the Tenth Amendment; that an affirmative grant of power is not exclusive, unless in its own nature it be such that the continued exercise of it by the former possessor is inconsistent with the grant, and that this is not of that description ...

The grant of the power to lay and collect taxes is, like the power to regulate commerce, made in general terms, and has never been understood to interfere with the exercise of the same power by the State ... Although many of the powers formerly exercised by the States, are transferred to the government of the Union, yet the State governments remain, and constitute a most important part of our system. The power of taxation is indispensable to their existence, and is a power which ... is capable of residing in, and being exercised by, different authorities at the same time. We are accustomed to see it placed, for different purposes, in different hands ... Congress is authorized to lay and collect taxes to pay the debts, and provide for the common defense and general welfare of the United States. This does not interfere with the power of the States to tax for the support of their own governments; nor is the exercise of that power by the States, an exercise of any portion of the power that is granted to the United States. In imposing taxes for State purposes, they are not doing what Congress is empowered to do. Congress is not empowered to tax for those purposes which are within the exclusive province of the States. When, then, each government exercises the power of taxation, neither is exercising the power of the other. But, when a State proceeds to regulate commerce with foreign nations, or among the several States, it is exercising the very power that is granted to Congress, and is doing the very thing which Congress is authorized to do. There is no analogy, then, between the power of taxation and the power of regulating commerce.

In discussing the question, whether this power is still in the States, in the case under consideration, we may dismiss from it the inquiry, whether it is surrendered by the mere grant to Congress, or is retained until Congress shall exercise the power. We may dismiss that inquiry, because it has been exercised, and the regulations which Congress deemed it proper to make, are now in full operation. The sole question is, can a State regulate commerce with foreign nations and among the States, while Congress is regulating it? ...

Since ... in exercising the power of regulating their own purely internal affairs, whether of trading or police, the States may sometimes enact laws, the validity of which depends on their interfering with, and being contrary to, an act of Congress passed in pursuance of the Constitution, the Court will enter upon the inquiry, whether the laws of New York, as expounded by the highest tribunal of that State, have, in their application to this case, come into collision with an act of Congress, and deprived a citizen of a right to which that act entitles him. Should this collision exist, it will be immaterial whether those laws were passed in virtue of a concurrent power 'to regulate commerce with foreign nations and among the several States,' or, in virtue of a power to regulate their domestic trade and police. In one case and the other, the acts of New York must yield to the law of Congress; and the decision sustaining the privilege they confer, against a right given by a law of the Union, must be erroneous . . .

[T]he framers of our constitution foresaw this state of things, and provided for it, by declaring the supremacy not only of itself, but of the laws made in pursuance of it . . . and the law of the State, though enacted in the exercise of powers not controverted, must yield to it . . .

In the exercise of this power, Congress has passed 'an act for enrolling or licensing ships or vessels to be employed in the coasting trade and fisheries, and for regulating the same.' . . .

The act describes, with great minuteness, the various operations of a vessel engaged in it; and it cannot . . . be doubted, that a voyage from New Jersey to New York, is one of those operations . . .

The laws of New York, which grant the exclusive privilege set up by the respondent, take no notice of the employment of vessels, and relate only to the principle by which they are propelled. Those laws do not inquire whether vessels are engaged in transporting men or merchandise, but whether they are moved by steam or wind . . .

The real and sole question seems to be, whether a steam machine, in actual use, deprives a vessel of the privileges conferred by a license . . .

[T]he laws of Congress for the regulation of commerce, do not look to the principle by which vessels are moved. That subject is left entirely to individual discretion; and, in that vast and complex system of legislative enactment concerning it, which embraces every thing that the Legislature thought it necessary to notice, there is not . . . one word respecting the peculiar principle by which vessels are propelled through the water, except what may be found in a single act, granting a particular privilege to steam boats. With this exception, every act, either prescribing duties, or granting privileges, applies to every vessel, whether navigated by the instrumentality of wind or fire, of sails or machinery . . .

This act demonstrates the opinion of Congress, that steam boats may be enrolled and licensed, in common with vessels using sails. They are, of course, entitled to the same privileges, and can no more be restrained from navigating waters, and entering ports which are free to such vessels, than if they were wafted on their voyage by the winds, instead of being propelled by the agency of fire. The one element may be as legitimately used as the other, for every commercial purpose authorized by the laws of the Union; and the act of a State inhibiting the use of either to any vessel having a license under the act of Congress, comes . . . in direct collision with that act . . .

Johnson, dissenting:

The judgment entered by the Court in this cause, has my entire approbation; but having adopted my conclusions on views of the subject materially different from those of my brethren, I feel it incumbent on me to exhibit those views . . .

The 'power to regulate commerce,' here meant to be granted, was that power to regulate commerce which previously existed in the States . . . The States were, unquestionably, supreme; and each possessed that power over commerce, which is acknowledged to reside in every sovereign State. The definition and limits of that power are to be sought among the features of international law; and . . . that, 'unaffected by a state of war, by treaties, or by municipal regulations, all commerce among independent States was legitimate.' . . . The law of nations, regarding man as a social animal, pronounces all commerce legitimate in a state of peace, until prohibited by positive law. The power of a sovereign state over commerce, therefore, amounts to nothing more than a power to limit and restrain it at pleasure. And since the power to prescribe the limits to its freedom, necessarily implies the power to determine what shall remain unrestrained, it follows, that the power must be exclusive; it can reside but in one potentate; and hence, the grant of this power carries with it the whole subject, leaving nothing for the State to act upon . . .

It is impossible . . . to concur in the view which this Court takes of the effect of the coasting license in this cause . . . If there was any one object riding over every other in the adoption of the Constitution, it was to keep the commercial intercourse among the States free from all invidious and partial restraints. And I cannot overcome the conviction, that if the licensing act was repealed to-morrow, the rights of [Gibbons] to a reversal of the decision complained of, would be as strong as it is under this license . . . The inferences, to be correctly drawn, from this whole article, appear to me to be altogether in favor of the exclusive grants to Congress of power over commerce, and the reverse of that which the [Ogden] contends for.

New York v. Miln

36 U.S. 102 (1937), 6-1
Opinion of the Court: Barbour (Taney, C.J., McLean, Baldwin, Wayne, Barbour)
Concurring: Thompson
Dissenting: Story

In its 1824 Passenger Act, New York required captains of all incoming ships to provide certain information on all passengers landing and for those without means of support, to post a bond with New York City to indemnify it for three years should the passenger become a pauper and require public support. When William Thompson, captain of the Emily, and George Miln, the ship's receiver of goods, failed to provide the required information or post bond for about 100 passengers landed, the city sued to enforce the Act.

What is Barbour's theory of state power? How does he distinguish national from state power? Is his theory of state power consistent with Marshall's in Gibbons v. Ogden? *What is the basis of the disagreement between Barbour and Story? How might the thinking of the justices in this case been affected by the slavery question?*

Barbour, J., for the Court:

It is contended by Miln et. al that the act in question is a regulation of commerce; that the power to regulate commerce is, by the constitution of the United States, granted to congress; that this power is exclusive, and that consequently, the act is a violation of the constitution of the United States.

On the part of the [City], it is argued, that an affirmative grant of power previously existing in the states to congress, is not exclusive; except, 1st, where it is so expressly declared in terms, by the clause giving the power; or 2d, where a similar power is prohibited to the states; or 3d, where the power in the states would be repugnant to, and incompatible with, a similar power in congress; that this power falls within neither of these predicaments; that it is not, in terms, declared to be exclusive; that it is not prohibited to the states; and that it is not repugnant to, nor incompatible with, a similar power in congress; and that having

pre-existed in the states, they, therefore, have a concurred power in relation to the subject; and that the act in question would be valid, even if it were a regulation of commerce, it not contravening any regulation made by congress. But they deny that it is a regulation of commerce; on the contrary, they assert, that it is a mere regulation of internal police, a power over which is not granted to congress; and which, therefore, as well upon the true construction of the constitution, as by force of the tenth amendment to that instrument, is reserved to, and resides in, the several states.

We shall not enter into any examination of the question, whether the power to regulate commerce, be or be not exclusive of the states, because the opinion which we have formed renders it unnecessary: in other words, we are of opinion, that the act is not a regulation of commerce, but of police; and that being thus considered, it was passed in the exercise of a power which rightfully belonged to the states. . . .

If, as we think, it be a regulation, not of commerce, but police; then it is not taken from the states. To decide this, let us examine its purpose, the end to be attained, and the means of its attainment. It is apparent, from the whole scope of the law, that the object of the legislature was, to prevent New York from being burdened by an influx of persons brought thither in ships, either from foreign countries, or from any other of the states; and for that purpose, a report was required of the names, places of birth, &c., of all passengers, that the necessary steps might be taken by the city authorities, to prevent them from becoming chargeable as paupers. . . .

. . . In *Gibbons v. Ogden*, the law of the state assumed to exercise authority over the navigable waters of the state; to do so, by granting a privilege to certain individuals, and by excluding all others from navigating them by vessels propelled by steam; and in the particular case, this law was brought to bear in its operation directly upon a vessel sailing under a coasting license from the United States . . . [T]here is not, in this case, one of the circumstances which existed in that of Gibbons v. Ogden, which, in the opinion of the court, rendered it obnoxious to the charge of unconstitutionality . . .

But we do not place our opinion on this ground. We choose rather to plant ourselves on what we consider impregnable positions. They are these: That a state has the same undeniable and unlimited jurisdiction over all persons and things, within its territorial limits, as any foreign nation; where that jurisdiction is not surrendered or restrained by the constitution of the United States. That, by virtue of this, it is not only the right, but the bounden and solemn duty of a state, to advance the safety, happiness and prosperity of its people, and to provide for its general welfare, by any and every act of legislation, which it may deem to be conducive to these ends; where the power over the particular subject, or the manner of its exercise is not surrendered or restrained, in the manner just stated. That all those powers which relate to merely municipal legislation, or what may, perhaps, more properly be called internal police, are not thus surrendered or restrained; and that, consequently, in relation to these, the authority of a state is complete, unqualified and exclusive. . . .

Now, in relation to the section in the act immediately before us, that is obviously passed with a view to prevent her citizens from being oppressed by the support of multitudes of poor persons, who come from foreign countries, without possessing the means of supporting themselves. There can be no mode in which the power to regulate internal police could be more appropriately exercised. New York, from her particular situation, is, perhaps, more than any other city in the Union, exposed to the evil of thousands of foreign emigrants arriving there, and the consequent danger of her citizens being subjected to a heavy charge in the maintenance of those who are poor. It is the duty of the state to protect its citizens from this evil; they have endeavored to do so, by passing, amongst other things, the section of the law in question. We should, upon principle, say that it had a right to do so. . . .

We think it as competent and as necessary for a state to provide precautionary measures against the moral pestilence of paupers, vagabonds, and possibly convicts; as it is to guard against the physical pestilence, which may arise from unsound and infections articles imported, or from a ship, the crew of which may be laboring under an infectious disease. . . .

We are, therefore, of opinion . . . that so much of the section of the act of the legislature of New York, as applies to the breaches assigned in the declaration, does not assume to regulate commerce between the port of New York and foreign ports; and that so much of said section is constitutional.

Story, J., dissenting:
I admit, in the most unhesitating manner, that the states have a right to pass health laws and quarantine

laws, and other police laws, not contravening the laws of congress rightfully passed under their constitutional authority. I admit, that they have a right to pass poor-laws, and laws to prevent the introduction of paupers into the state, under the like qualifications. I go further, and admit, that in the exercise of their legitimate authority over any particular subject, the states may generally use the same means which are used by congress, if these means are suitable to the end. But I cannot admit, that the states have authority to enact laws, which act upon subjects beyond their territorial limits, or within those limits and which trench upon the authority of congress in its power to regulate commerce. . . .

. . . The nature and character of these laws were fully considered, and the true answer given to them, in the case of *Gibbons v. Ogden,* and though the reasoning there given might be expanded, it cannot, in its grounds and distinctions, be more pointedly illustrated, or better expounded. I have already said, that I admit the power of the states to pass such laws, and to use the proper means to effectuate the objects of them; but it is with this reserve, that these means are not exclusively vested in congress. A state cannot make a regulation of commerce, to enforce its health laws, because it is a means withdrawn from its authority. . . .

. . . The power given to congress to regulate commerce with foreign nations, and among the states, has been deemed exclusive, from the nature and objects of the power, and the necessary implications growing out of its exercise. Full power to regulate a particular subject, implies the whole power, and leaves no residuum; and a grant of the whole to one, is incompatible with a grant to another of a part. When a state proceeds to regulate commerce with foreign nations, or among the states, it is doing the very thing which congress is authorized to do.

Charles River Bridge Co. v. Warren Bridge Co.

36 U.S. 420 (1837), 5-2
Opinion of the Court: Taney, C.J. (Baldwin, Barbour, McLean, Wayne)
Dissenting: Story, Thompson
Is this decision pro- or antiproperty in its intent? In its effect? Which opinion, Taney's or Story's, is more faithful to the "principles of the Constitution"? Which is more attentive to practical considerations? What does each imply about the role of the courts? Under what circumstances, if any, would

Story have allowed the Warren Bridge to be built? Is the decision consistent with Dartmouth College v. Woodward? *Which is likely to have the greater effect on economic development? Besides the two bridge companies, what interests are likely to gain or lose as a result of this decision?*

Taney, C.J., for the Court:

The [proprietors of the Charles River Bridge] insist . . . that by virtue of the grant of 1650, Harvard College was entitled, in perpetuity, to the right of keeping a ferry between Charlestown and Boston; that this right was exclusive; and that the legislature had not the power to establish another ferry on the same line of travel, because it would infringe the rights of the college; and that these rights, upon the erection of the bridge in the place of the ferry, under the charter of 1785, were transferred to, and became vested in 'The Proprietors of the Charles River Bridge;' and that under, and by virtue of this transfer of the ferry-right, the rights of the bridge company were as exclusive in that line of travel, as the rights of the ferry. That independently of the ferry-right, the acts of the legislature of Massachusetts, of 1785 and 1792, by their true construction, necessarily implied, that the legislature would not authorize another bridge, and especially, a free one, by the side of this, and placed in the same line of travel, whereby the franchise granted to the 'Proprietors of the Charles River Bridge' should be rendered of no value; and [they] contend, that the grant of the ferry to the college, and of the charter to the proprietors of the bridge, are both contracts on the part of the state; and that the law authorizing the erection of the Warren bridge in 1828, impairs the obligation of one or both of these contracts. . .

But we are not now left to determine, for the first time, the rules by which public grants are to be construed in this country. The subject has already been considered in this court . . . that in grants by the public, nothing passes by implication. . . .

[T]he object and end of all government is to promote the happiness and prosperity of the community by which it is established; and it can never be assumed, that the government intended to diminish its power of accomplishing the end for which it was created. And in a country like ours, free, active and enterprising, continually advancing in numbers and wealth, new channels of communication are daily found necessary, both for travel and trade, and are essential to the comfort, convenience and prosperity of the people. A state ought never to be presumed to surrender this power, because, like the taxing power, the whole community have an interest in preserving it undiminished. And when a corporation alleges, that a state has surrendered, for seventy years, its power of improvement and public accommodation, in a great and important line of travel, along which a vast number of its citizens must daily pass, the community have a right to insist, in the language of this court, above quoted, 'that its abandonment ought not to be presumed, in a case, in which the deliberate purpose of the state to abandon it does not appear.' The continued existence of a government would be of no great value, if, by implications and presumptions, it was disarmed of the powers necessary to accomplish the ends of its creation, and the functions it was designed to perform, transferred to the hands of privileged corporations. . . . No one will question, that the interests of the great body of the people of the state, would, in this instance, be affected by the surrender of this great line of travel to a single corporation, with the right to exact toll, and exclude competition, for seventy years. While the rights of private property are sacredly guarded, we must not forget, that the community also have rights, and that the happiness and well-being of every citizen depends on their faithful preservation.

Adopting the rule of construction above stated as the settled one, we proceed to apply it to the charter of 1785, to the proprietors of the Charles River bridge. . . It confers on them the ordinary faculties of a corporation, for the purpose of building the bridge; and establishes certain rates of toll, which the company are authorized to take: this is the whole grant. There is no exclusive privilege given to them over the waters of Charles river, above or below their bridge; no right to erect another bridge themselves, nor to prevent other persons from erecting one, no engagement from the state, that another shall not be erected; and no undertaking not to sanction competition, nor to make improvements that may diminish the amount of its income. Upon all these subject, the charter is silent; and nothing is said in it about a line of travel . . . in which they are to have exclusive privileges. No words are used, from which an intention to grant any of these rights can be inferred; if the [proprietors are] entitled to them, it must be implied, simply, from the nature of the grant; and cannot be inferred, from the words by which the grant is made . . .

The relative position of the Warren bridge has already been described. It does not interrupt the passage over the Charles River bridge, nor make the way to it, or from it, less convenient. None of the faculties or franchises granted to that corporation, have been revoked by the legislature; and its right to take the tolls granted by the charter remains unaltered. In short, all the franchises and rights of property, enumerated in the charter, and there mentioned to have been granted to it, remain unimpaired. But its income is destroyed by the Warren bridge; which, being free, draws off the passengers and property which would have gone over it, and renders their franchise of no value . . . [I]t is not pretended, that the erection of the Warren bridge would have done them any injury, or in any degree affected their right of property, if it had not diminished the amount of their tolls. In order, then, to entitle themselves to relief, it is necessary to show, that the legislature contracted not to do the act of which they complain; and that they impaired, or in other words, violated, that contract, by the erection of the Warren bridge . . .

[D]oes the charter contain such a contract on the part of the state? Is there any such stipulation to be found in that instrument? . . . [T]here is none; no words that even relate to another bridge, or to the diminution of their tolls, or to the line of travel. If a contract on that subject can be gathered from the charter, it must be by implication; and cannot be found in the words used. Can such an agreement be implied? The rule of construction before stated is an answer to the question: in charters of this description, no rights are taken from the public, or given to the corporation, beyond those which the words of the charter, by their natural and proper construction, purport to convey. There are no words which import such a contract . . . and none can be implied . . .

Indeed, the practice and usage of almost every state in the Union, old enough to have commenced the work of internal improvement, is opposed to the doctrine contended for [by the proprietors]. Turnpike roads have been made in succession, on the same line of travel; the later ones interfering materially with the profits of the first. These corporations have, in some instances, been utterly ruined by the introduction of newer and better modes of transportation and travelling. In some cases, railroads have rendered the turnpike roads on the same line of travel so entirely useless, that the franchise of the turnpike corporation is not worth preserving. Yet in none of these cases have the corporation supposed that their privileges were invaded, or any contract violated on the part of the state. Amid the multitude of

cases which have occurred, and have been daily occurring, for the last forty or fifty years, this is the first instance in which such an implied contract has been contended for, and this court called upon to infer it, from an ordinary act of incorporation, containing nothing more than the usual stipulations and provisions to be found in every such law. The absence of any such controversy, when there must have been so many occasions to give rise to it, proves, that neither states, nor individuals, nor corporations, ever imagined that such a contract could be implied from such charters. It shows, that the men who voted for these laws, never imagined that they were forming such a contract; and if we maintain that they have made it, we must create it by a legal fiction, in opposition to the truth of the fact, and the obvious intention of the party. We cannot deal thus with the rights reserved to the states; and . . . take away from them any portion of that power over their own internal police and improvement, which is so necessary to their well-being and prosperity.

And what would be the fruits of this doctrine of implied contracts, on the part of the states, and of property in a line of travel, by a corporation, if it would now be sanctioned by this court? To what results would it lead us? If it is to be found in the charter to this bridge, the same process of reasoning must discover it, in the various acts which have been passed, within the last forty years, for turnpike companies. And what is to be the extent of the privileges of exclusion on the different sides of the road? . . . How far must the new improvement be distant from the old one? How near may you approach, without invading its rights in the privileged line? If this court should establish the principles now contended for, what is to become of the numerous railroads established on the same line of travel with turnpike companies; and which have rendered the franchises of the turnpike corporations of no value? Let it once be understood, that such charters carry with them these implied contracts, and give this unknown and undefined property in a line of travelling; and you will soon find the old turnpike corporations awakening from their sleep, and calling upon this court to put down the improvements which have taken their place. The millions of property which have been invested in railroads and canals, upon lines of travel which had been before occupied by turnpike corporations, will be put in jeopardy. We shall be thrown back to the improvements of the last century, and obliged to stand still, until the claims of the old turnpike corporations shall be satisfied; and they shall consent to permit these states to avail themselves of the lights of modern science, and to partake of the benefit of those improvements which are now adding to the wealth and prosperity, and the convenience and comfort, of every other part of the civilized world. Nor is this all. This court will find itself compelled to fix, by some arbitrary rule, the width of this new kind of property in a line of travel; for if such a right of property exists, we have no lights to guide us in marking out its extent, unless, indeed, we resort to the old feudal grants, and to the exclusive rights of ferries, by prescription, between towns; and are prepared to decide that when a turnpike road from one town to another, had been made, no railroad or canal, between these two points, could afterwards be established. This court are not prepared to sanction principles which must lead to such results . . .

The judgment of the Supreme Judicial Court of the Commonwealth of Massachusetts, dismissing the [proprietors'] bill, must, therefore, be affirmed, with costs.

Story, dissenting:
. . . I do not insist upon any extraordinary liberality in interpreting this charter. All I contend for is, that it shall receive a fair and reasonable interpretation; so as to carry into effect the legislative intention, and secure to the grantees a just security for their privileges. . . . The present grant is confessedly a contract . . .

Let us now enter upon the consideration of the terms of the charter . . . [N]othing can be more plain, than that it is a grant of a right to erect a bridge between Boston and Charlestown, in the place where the ferry between those towns was kept. It has been said, that the charter itself does not describe the bridge as between Charlestown and Boston, but grants an authority to erect 'a bridge over Charles river . . . where the old ferry was then kept;' and that these towns are not named, except for the purpose of describing the then ferry . . . [T]his seems . . . to be a distinction without a difference. The bridge is to be erected in the place where the old ferry then was. But where was it to begin? and where was it to terminate? Boston and Charlestown are the only possible termini, for the ferry-ways were there; and it was to be built between Boston and Charlestown, because the ferry was between them . . .

The argument of the defendants is, that the plaintiffs are to take nothing by implication. Either (say they) the exclusive grant extends only to the local limits of the bridge; or it extends the whole length of the

river, or, at least, up to old Cambridge bridge. The latter construction would be absurd and monstrous; and therefore, the former must be the true one. . . . The right to build a bridge over a river, and to take toll, may well include an exclusive franchise, beyond the local limits of the bridge; and yet not extend through the whole course of the river, or even to any considerable distance on the river. There is no difficulty, in common sense, or in law, in maintaining such a doctrine. But then, it is asked, what limits can be assigned to such a franchise? The answer is obvious; the grant carries with it an exclusive franchise, to a reasonable distance on the river; so that the ordinary travel to the bridge shall not be diverted by any new bridge, to the injury or ruin of the franchise. A new bridge, which would be a nuisance to the old bridge, would be within the reach of its exclusive right. . . .

I put it to the common sense of every man, whether if, at the moment of granting the charter, the legislature had said to the proprietors; you shall build the bridge; you shall bear the burdens; you shall be bound by the charges; and your sole reimbursement shall be from the tolls of forty years: and yet we will not even guaranty you any certainty of receiving any tolls; on the contrary; we reserve to ourselves the full power and authority to erect other bridges, toll or free bridges, according to our own free will and pleasure, contiguous to yours, and having the same termini with yours; and if you are successful, we may thus supplant you, divide, destroy your profits, and annihilate your tolls, without annihilating your burdens: if, I say, such had been the language of the legislature, is there a man living, of ordinary discretion or prudence, who would have accepted such a charter, upon such terms? I fearlessly answer, no. There would have been such a gross inadequacy of consideration, and such a total insecurity of all the rights of property, under such circumstances, that the project would have dropped still-born. And I put the question further, whether any legislature, meaning to promote a project of permanent, public utility . . . would ever have dreamed of such a qualification of its own grant, when it sought to enlist private capital and private patronage to insure the accomplishment of it? . . .

[T]he present grant carries with it a necessary implication, that the legislature shall do no act to destroy or essentially to impair the franchise; that . . . there is an implied agreement that the state will not grant another bridge between Boston and Charlestown, so near as to draw away the custom from the old one; and . . . that there is an implied agreement of the state to grant the undisturbed use of the bridge and its tolls, so far as respects any acts of its own, or of any persons acting under its authority. In other words, the state impliedly contracts not to resume its grant, or to do any act to the prejudice or destruction of its grant. . . .

[T]here exists no more right in the legislature of Massachusetts, to erect the Warren bridge, to the ruin of the franchise of the Charles River bridge, than exists to transfer the latter to the former, or to authorize the former to demolish the latter. If the legislature does not mean in its grant to give any exclusive rights, let it say so, expressly, directly, and in terms admitting of no misconstruction. The grantees will then take at their peril, and must abide the results of their overweening confidence, indiscretion and zeal. . . .

Upon the whole, my judgment is, that the act of the legislature of Massachusetts granting the charter of Warren Bridge, is an act impairing the obligation of the prior contract and grant to the proprietors of Charles River bridge; and, by the Constitution of the United States, it is, therefore, utterly void.

Cooley v. Board of Wardens

53 U.S. 299 (1851), 7-2
Opinion of the Court: Curtis (Catron, Grier, McKinley, Nelson, Taney)
Concurring: Daniel
Dissenting: McLean
Does the Court's decision deal effectively with questions left unanswered in Gibbons v. Ogden? Is Curtis clear about where a uniform rule would be required and where one would not? Will motivation for the local regulation be taken into account? Will the extent of its burden on interstate commerce? Since Congress had yet enacted few laws regulating interstate commerce, who will be the nation's chief policymaker where state or local regulations are challenged as burdening interstate commerce? Is the Court's decision a practical accommodation of commercial and geographical diversity in the country or an invitation to localism and protection? What effect, if any, could the decision be expected to have on economic development?

Curtis, for the Court:
It remains to consider the objection, that it is repugnant to the third clause of the eighth section of the first article. 'The Congress shall have power to regulate commerce with foreign nations and among the several states, and with the Indian tribes.'

That the power to regulate commerce includes the regulation of navigation, we consider settled. And when we look to the nature of the service performed by pilots, to the relations which that service and its compensations bear to navigation between the several states, and between the ports of the United States and foreign countries, we are brought to the conclusion, that the regulation of the qualifications of pilots, of the modes and times of offering and rendering their services, of the responsibilities which shall rest upon them, of the powers they shall possess, of the compensation they may demand, and of the penalties by which their rights and duties may be enforced, do constitute regulations of navigation, and consequently of commerce, within the just meaning of this clause of the Constitution . . .

[A] pilot . . . is the temporary master charged with the safety of the vessel and cargo, and of the lives of those on board, and entrusted with the command of the crew. He is not only one of the persons engaged in navigation, but he occupies a most important and responsible place among those thus engaged. And if Congress has power to regulate the seamen who assist the pilot in the management of the vessel . . . we can perceive no valid reason why the pilot should be beyond the reach of the same power. It is true that, according to the usages of modern commerce on the ocean, the pilot is on board only during a part of the voyage between ports of different states, or between ports of the United States and foreign countries; but if he is on board for such a purpose and during so much of the voyage as to be engaged in navigation, the power to regulate navigation extends to him while thus engaged, as clearly as it would if he were to remain on board throughout the whole passage, from port to port. For it is a power which extends to every part of the voyage, and may regulate those who conduct or assist in conducting navigation in one part of a voyage as much as in another part, or during the whole voyage . . .

[A] majority of the Court are of opinion, that a regulation of pilots is a regulation of commerce, within the grant to Congress of the commercial power . . .

It becomes necessary, therefore, to consider whether this law of Pennsylvania, being a regulation of commerce, is valid.

The act of Congress of the 7th of August, 1789, sect. 4, is as follows:

'That all pilots in the bays, inlets, rivers, harbors, and ports of the United States shall continue to be regulated in conformity with the existing laws of the states, respectively, wherein such pilots may be, or with such laws as the states may respectively hereafter enact for the purpose, until further legislative provision shall be made by Congress.'

If the law of Pennsylvania, now in question, had been in existence at the date of this act of Congress, we might hold it to have been adopted by Congress, and thus made a law of the United States, and so valid. Because this act does, in effect, give the force of an act of Congress, to the then existing state laws on this subject, so long as they should continue unrepealed by the state which enacted them.

But the law on which [this case is brought] was not enacted till 1803. What effect then can be attributed to so much of the act of 1789, as declares, that pilots shall continue to be regulated in conformity, 'with such laws as the states may respectively hereafter enact for the purpose, until further legislative provision shall be made by Congress'?

If the states were divested of the power to legislate on this subject by the grant of the commercial power to Congress, it is plain this act could not confer upon them power thus to legislate. If the Constitution excluded the states from making any law regulating commerce, certainly Congress cannot re-grant, or in any manner re-convey to the states that power. And yet this act of 1789 gives its sanction only to laws enacted by the states. This necessarily implies a constitutional power to legislate; for only a rule created by the sovereign power of a state acting in its legislative capacity, can be deemed a law, enacted by a state; and if the state has so limited its sovereign power that it no longer extends to a particular subject, manifestly it cannot, in any proper sense, be said to enact laws thereon ... [W]e are brought directly and unavoidably to the consideration of the question, whether the grant of the commercial power to Congress, did per se deprive the states of all power to regulate pilots. This question has never been decided by this court, nor ... has any case depending upon all the considerations which must govern this one, come before this court. The grant of commercial power to Congress does not contain any terms which expressly exclude the states from exercising an authority over its subject-matter. If they are excluded it must be because the nature of the power, thus granted to Congress, requires that a similar authority should not exist in the states. If it were conceded on the one side, that the nature of this power, like that to legislate for the District of Columbia, is absolutely and totally repugnant

to the existence of similar power in the states, probably no one would deny that the grant of the power to Congress, as effectually and perfectly excludes the states from all future legislation on the subject, as if express words had been used to exclude them. And on the other hand, if it were admitted that the existence of this power in Congress, like the power of taxation, is compatible with the existence of a similar power in the states, then it would be in conformity with the contemporary exposition of the Constitution (*Federalist, No. 32*), and with the judicial construction, given from time to time by this court ... to hold that the mere grant of such a power to Congress, did not imply a prohibition on the states to exercise the same power; that it is not the mere existence of such a power, but its exercise by Congress, which may be incompatible with the exercise of the same power by the states, and that the states may legislate in the absence of congressional regulations.

The diversities of opinion, therefore, which have existed on this subject, have arisen from the different views taken of the nature of this power. But when the nature of a power like this is spoken of, when it is said that the nature of the power requires that it should be exercised exclusively by Congress, it must be intended to refer to the subjects of that power, and to say they are of such a nature as to require exclusive legislation by Congress. Now the power to regulate commerce, embraces a vast field, containing not only many, but exceedingly various subjects, quite unlike in their nature; some imperatively demanding a single uniform rule, operating equally on the commerce of the United States in every port; and some, like the subject now in question, as imperatively demanding that diversity, which alone can meet the local necessities of navigation.

Either absolutely to affirm, or deny that the nature of this power requires exclusive legislation by Congress, is to lose sight of the nature of the subjects of this power, and to assert concerning all of them, what is really applicable but to a part. Whatever subjects of this power are in their nature national, or admit only of one uniform system, or plan of regulation, may justly be said to be of such a nature as to require exclusive legislation by Congress. That this cannot be affirmed of laws for the regulation of pilots and pilotage is plain. The act of 1789 contains a clear and authoritative declaration by the first Congress, that the nature of this subject is such, that until Congress should find it necessary to exert its power, it should be left to the legislation of the states; that it is local and not national; that it is likely to be the best provided for, not by one system, or plan of regulations, but by as many as the legislative discretion of the several states should deem applicable to the local peculiarities of the ports within their limits.

Viewed in this light, so much of this act of 1789 as declares that pilots shall continue to be regulated 'by such laws as the states may respectively hereafter enact for that purpose,' instead of being held to be inoperative, as an attempt to confer on the states a power to legislate, of which the Constitution had deprived them . . . It manifests the understanding of Congress, at the outset of the government, that the nature of this subject is not such as to require its exclusive legislation. The practice of the states, and of the national government, has been in conformity with this declaration, from the origin of the national government to this time; and the nature of the subject . . . is such as to leave no doubt of the superior fitness and propriety, not to say the absolute necessity, of different systems of regulation, drawn from local knowledge and experience, and conformed to local wants. How then can we say, that by the mere grant of power to regulate commerce, the states are deprived of all the power to legislate on this subject, because from the nature of the power the legislation of Congress must be exclusive. This would be to affirm that the nature of the power is in any case, something different from the nature of the subject to which . . . the power

extends, and that the nature of the power necessarily demands, in all cases, exclusive legislation by Congress, while the nature of one of the subjects of that power, not only does not require such exclusive legislation, but may be best provided for by many different systems enacted by the states, in conformity with the circumstances of the ports within their limits . . .

It is the opinion of a majority of the Court that the mere grant to Congress of the power to regulate commerce, did not deprive the states of power to regulate pilots, and that although Congress has legislated on this subject, its legislation manifests an intention, with a single exception, not to regulate this subject, but to leave its regulation to the several states . . . [T]his opinion must be understood to be confined. It does not extend to the question what other subjects, under the commercial power, are within the exclusive control of Congress, or may be regulated by the states in the absence of all congressional legislation; nor to the general question how far any regulation of a subject by Congress, may be deemed to operate as an exclusion of all legislation by the states upon the same subject . . .

We are of opinion that this state law was enacted by virtue of a power, residing in the state to legislate; that it is not in conflict with any law of Congress; that it does not interfere with any system which Congress has established by making regulations, or by intentionally leaving individuals to their own unrestricted action; that this law is therefore valid . . .

7

INDUSTRIAL CAPITALISM
AND THE MIDDLE CONSTITUTION

The Civil War settled the question of Union and ended slavery. In taking several hundred thousand lives, destroying hundreds of millions of dollars worth of property, and consuming vast amounts of stored wealth, it also halted the remarkable economic expansion of the nineteenth century's first half. When the fighting ended, the way seemed gloriously open for a return to growth and material advance. The nation, now spanning a continent, was no longer threatened by an issue that called its very existence into question. The South would remain an economically laggard region and the rights of black persons in it were compromised, but the national horizon most Americans saw seemed bright and beckoning.

In 64 years between Lee's surrender at Appomattox and the fateful stock market crash of 1929 and the Great Depression that followed, the United States achieved an economic development unparalleled in the history of nations. Capital-intensive industrialization was rapid and transforming, and the nation's political economy at the end of the period bore little resemblance to the one at the start. Though mitigated by an ever-rising standard of living, these changes placed formidable and often divisive strains on Americans struggling to adapt eighteenth-century institutions and ideas to the new order. Innate Jeffersonian preferences for localism and the least government were confounded by a world of Hamiltonian opportunity.

With ratification of the Thirteenth, Fourteenth, and Fifteenth Amendments after the war, the Constitution was formally changed for the first time in 60 years. In placing new restrictions on the states, the Fourteenth and Fifteenth created new rights and shifted power in the federal system toward the center. Yet, as the Supreme Court interpreted the Fourteenth, the most far-reaching of the three, it found not so much new powers for the national government or protection for former slaves as new rights for corporations and reasons for reading the entire Constitution through a laissez-faire lens.

This interpretation carried the old debate about what was secured against government and what was within its reach to a new plane. Where did the interests of the private capitalist and the public servant diverge? When did government move from being supporter and promoter to regulator? And within government's power, what was federal and what was state? As the Supreme Court came to grapple with these issues, it proved to be of several minds. This eventually produced important disparate decisions, but not before the Court went far to adapt the Constitution to large-scale industrial capitalism.

The New Economic Order

The Industrial Revolution began in England in the last decades of the eighteenth century with perfection of the steam engine and the coal-fired blast furnace for making iron. These developments led to manifold technological innovation, radically changing the production of material goods and eventually transforming Britain from a rural, agricultural society to an urban industrial nation.

The United States was not unaffected. It became a main market for British finished goods, especially hardware and cloth. A commercially symbiotic relationship developed between the huge British textile industry and the cotton-producing economy of the South. Eventually, the new industrial technologies themselves crossed the Atlantic, quickening antebellum growth and making possible large-scale American factories and mills.

Economists mark a second industrial revolution, taking place mainly in the United States and Germany, about a century after the first. It, too, was based on a wave of new technology and, in America, on important innovations in business organization and finance that greatly enlarged productive capacity.

Changes wrought by the new revolution were even greater than those of the first. New labor-saving machinery entered industry after industry. New, more efficient sources of energy were developed: Coal and petroleum replaced wood to fuel steam engines; electricity provided better illumination, cleaner urban transport, and the energy for precision machinery. With its assembly line, the forerunner of modern automation, the factory system made mass production and uniformity of product possible at lower unit cost. Thousands of engineers, chemists, and physicists were recruited to improve products and invent new ones in a seemingly unending wave of innovation. With improved machinery and techniques, farming became more productive particularly on the fertile soil of the West.

New products became the nuclei of great industries. Many pioneering companies became giant corporations with household names: Remington and National Cash Register in office machinery, Singer in sewing machines, Borden, Campbell, and Heinz in food processing, McCormick and International Harvester in agricultural equipment, American Tobacco in cigarettes, DuPont, Monsanto, and Dow in chemicals, and General Electric and Westinghouse in electrical equipment.

Interconnecting a Continent

In the postwar years, no industry was grander or more important than the railroads. Rapid, large-scale industrial growth would have been impossible without construction of an elaborate rail grid. Trains brought crops, livestock, and raw materials to processing and manufacturing centers and offered ready distribution for the finished products. They spurred and made workable thousands of new settlements in the West and connected established towns, cities, and entire regions with each other. The celebrated "golden spike" ceremony at Promontory Point, Utah, in 1869 marked the linkup of the Union Pacific line built westward from St. Louis and the Central Pacific's built eastward from California, symbolized the new transcontinental status of the United States, and gave hint of the economic colossus in the making.

As the chief commercial arteries for a truly national market, railroads became the nation's first "big business." In a golden age of railway building, track mileage rose from 35,000 at the end of the war to 93,000 by 1880 and to 163,000

The joining of the Union Pacific and Central Pacific railroads May 10, 1869, at Promontory Point, Utah, completed the country's first transcontinental railway and helped usher in the greatest economic expansion in the nation's history, lasting until the stock market crash of 1929. Celebrated by hundreds of dignitaries, laborers, and plain hangers-on in the Golden Spike ceremony, the linkup was a civil engineering tour-de-force, marked by enterprising private investment, federal underwriting, and a generous share of corruption.

by 1890, more than in all Europe. Use of this network increased even more rapidly. Freight tonnage miles, standing at 10 billion in 1865, grew to an astonishing 366 billion by the eve of World War I. Hauling cost per tonnage mile dropped steadily as local markets became regional and regional markets national.

The rail net could not have been built by entrepreneurs acting alone. To induce the mammoth construction projects, government, especially the federal government, gave the rail companies generous rights of way, ceding hundreds of thousands of choice acres on each side of the tracks. Financing construction called for enormous amounts of capital, much of which came from European investors betting on the American future as they had so successfully many times in the past. So large was this underwriting that it spurred the specialization of investment banking and eventually helped make Wall Street the financial capital of the world.

Railway pioneering in modern corporate finance and administration came at a price. Labor

problems over pay and safety abounded. Freight rates were a continual issue with farmers and manufacturers, many of whom felt exploited. The roads became the first industry to come under extensive government regulation, and conflicts over this control offered the Supreme Court some of its most important cases.

Organization of Big Capital

The railroads led the corporate way. Their success showed the importance of centralized organization and bold imagination. The pre-Civil War factory, often family-owned and making but one product, was typically one of several independent way stations between the raw material producer and end user. More and more of these businesses were now transformed into highly capitalized, vertically integrated, multifunctional enterprises in which central decisions controlled supply, production, marketing, and finance. These arrangements produced undreamed of economies of scale, dramatically reducing cost per unit.

Profits could be enormous, but competition was keen, often cutthroat. Innumerable mergers came about, many through such innovative schemes as the trust and holding company. In the first, stockholders in several related companies deposited their shares with trustees, thus ceding control to central directors. In the pyramidal holding company, the corporate entity at the top held enough shares of other companies to control their operations. Because the stock of these companies was typically scattered among many holders, central ownership of only a small fraction of shares could lead to control of an entire industry, even several industries. When New Jersey became the first state to permit such consolidation, the holding company was soon the combination of choice, though "trust" remained the standard term applied to large-scale business merging. Corporations became fewer and larger. In one 10-year period alone, 1895–1904, an average of 300 firms "disappeared" annually. In at least 50 industries, one company controlled 60 percent of production or more.

From the corporate point of view, the new consolidation was a sensible way of rationalizing economic life, reducing costs and competition. But its bent toward monopoly, coupled with the vast power that a few titans like Morgan, Carnegie, and Rockefeller wielded at the top, cast new doubt on whether the corporate interest, however economically compelling, could be reconciled with the public. Concentrated economic power became a salient political issue and one that called for deep constitutional soul searching.

Despite these concerns, there was no disputing the nation's economic advance. By 1910, the American domestic market was the world's largest. By the 1920s, the United States had less than 5 percent of the world's population but generated 40 percent of its industrial output. As volume went up, prices fell. Between 1880 and 1900, steelmaker Andrew Carnegie was able to reduce prices from $67 a ton to $17. The great, efficient industrial base was indispensable to American victories in World Wars I and II.

Astonishing growth did not come from technological and administrative innovation alone. The transcontinental nation was blessed with an abundance of natural resources, much of which was easily exploited. Its constant need for labor was met by waves of immigrants. Rates of entry,

Issuance of shares of corporate stock was the promissory of entrepreneurial capitalism. For the buyer-holder they were bets, sometimes risky, on future growth, capital gains, and dividends; for the issuer, they were the means of working with the capital of others, for ventures that could not otherwise be undertaken. The certificate, above, depicts the New York Stock Exchange (tall building), not yet the imposing "Wall Street" it would later become.

already high in the antebellum period, doubled, then tripled. Between 1905 and 1914, an average of 1 million persons a year came to the United States. Settling mainly in the larger cities of the seaboards, they took places in industry, manufacturing, and railroading—thousands of Chinese immigrants, for example, had built the Central Pacific's line to Promontory Point.

There were intangibles as well. For a socially and geographically mobile population of immigrants and descendants of immigrants, family status and social prestige counted less than material success. Accrued wealth was more likely to be plowed back into expanding business or acquiring more land or other material benefit than to pursue leisure, gracious living, or aristocratic standing. Production was a stronger engine than consumption. Personal decisions were more apt to be bounded by a material pragmatism than in more settled, traditional societies. If there was a uniquely American mindset, it was one in which moderate risk taking and optimism were fused with an almost mystical belief in the natural morality of work and competition.

Not least important, economic growth was underwritten by government and law. Industrial expansion called for public institutions and rules that were responsive to dynamic commercial interests. The more rigid structures of the Old World, reflecting as they often did the interests of clerical or hereditary aristocracies, a mandarin class, or a standing army, would not have served American needs nor been honored by American attitudes.

Response of Middling Government

It was natural to expect government and law to play the same importantly supportive role in industrialization that they had in antebellum growth. Even laissez-faire purists seldom objected to the bestowal of benefits. States liberalized incorporation laws and issued protective charters for the building of transport, utilities, and other projects of public importance. They used their borrowing power to subsidize railway construction, pledging future tax revenue to secure the bonds. Local governments devolved eminent domain power to companies where land or realty rights needed to be acquired, allowing these private entities to take private property for purely private purposes. The federal government raised or maintained tariffs to shelter home industries from foreign competition. It gave more than 131 million acres and the states an additional 49 million to railroads as part of their rights of way, in all an area larger than any state.

Later, many of these cedings and benefits would seem extremely generous, perhaps little more than giveaways. The private capitalist supplicating the elected official sometimes opened doors to bribery and corruption. Yet without friendly government and its largesse, the important transport and utility infrastructure would not have been built so quickly. Projects in unsettled or thinly settled areas of the West, many of which were still threatened by "hostiles"—unreconciled Indian tribes—would have been too risky to attract sufficient private capital. But with government support, the railway building was accelerated and created a national market much more quickly than would have otherwise been possible. In doing so, it also made the Harrimans, Hills, Vanderbilts, and many other enterprisers enormously wealthy.

Where new government was formed, as in the West, it was apt to be shaped by commercial needs—those of farmers, merchants, railways, and eventually large enterprise. Despite inefficiencies and occasional malfeasance, government generally won the confidence of investors and property owners that their holdings would be protected and opportunities left unfettered. Governmental stability and a business-friendly environment, American hallmarks, encouraged high rates of savings that, in turn, underwrote further investment. They served as well to attract large amounts of additional capital from Europe.

As corporations became larger, many evolving into trusts and monopolies, the disparity

A Creed for the Times

With no feudal or aristocratic traditions to bind it, social and economic mobility was probably greater in the United States in the last third of the nineteenth century than in any nation before. A beckoning frontier once geographic but now economic appeared to be perpetual. Opportunity was the byword and a better material life its command. Hard work, determination, individual responsibility, and freedom from interfering authority was the common prescription for success.

The combination often worked, on occasion spectacularly. It is not surprising that the writings of Horatio Alger should have loomed large in the popular culture of the day. Alger, a Unitarian minister, wrote more than 125 novels between 1865 and his death in 1899. Almost all were variations on a theme: A worthy boy or young man of humble origin overcomes various trials and hardships to achieve middle-class success, sometimes fame and fortune as well. These romantic tales touched a responsive moralistic chord. "Algerism," as it was later called, was a belief, almost religious in its power, that ambition, persistence, and good habits could overcome almost any obstacle and assure a steady and rewarding rise.

At a more philosophic notch, the values of freedom, individualism, enterprise, material striving, and success were given a "scientific," Darwinian rendition in the writings of the English sociologist Herbert Spencer and his American disciple William Graham Sumner. Social Darwinists, as adherents were called, drew biologic analogies for society. Spencer used such evolutionist terms as "natural selection" and "survival of the fittest" to explain historical change. Human society was evolving. Social and economic selection would produce higher forms just as biological selection did in nature.

Because action of the State would only interfere with this development, functions of government had to be held to the fewest possible. Spencer admitted "natural" selection might be cruel to some individuals, but interference could only harm society by perpetuating the socially and economically unfit. If left alone, society in the long run would be better and stronger. Casting this social theory as a set of "laws" that in the end were the expression of God's will, Spencer avoided the theological attack Darwin's biological theory of evolution suffered.

Social Darwinism had an extraordinary effect on the American mind. It was seized on by entrepreneurs to justify the new economic order and their own success within it, without notice or care that it did little to separate the captain of industry from the robber baron. Like the inspiring Alger stories, Spencer's ideas also touched many in the middle class whose material lives had visibly improved, as

between their size and power and that of government grew more dramatic. Concentration of enormous economic power in a few hands had no precedent, and excesses of the "robber barons" drew attention to the growing conflict between public purpose and private profit. Voices of protest also began to be heard from farmers, labor, and other interests, who felt victimized by big capital.

With the ideals of laissez-faire still dominant, government usually had neither the will nor heft to respond to these concerns nor be much of a countervailing force. The growth of public institutions had not matched that of business. In the 1870s, for example, the entire federal government employed only 50,000 civilians, three-quarters of whom were postal workers. The ratio of federal workers to general population was 1 to 2,900, compared to 1 to 100 a century later.

The balance shifted, but slowly. Some state legislatures began to be moved by demands from farmers, workers, and consumers for intervention when regulation by the market seemed to fail. At the federal level, Congress created the Interstate Commerce Commission in 1887, the first national regulatory agency, to investigate railway operations. In the 1890s, the Sherman Anti-Trust Act gave the federal government power to prosecute monopolies. Farmers and labor organized, the former entering electoral politics through

well as many immigrants and workers for whom such gain might still be a dream.

Spencer was lionized when he visited the United States in the 1880s. His best known and most readable work *Social Statics* eventually had American sales of nearly a half million copies. The "vogue of Spencer" was still strong enough at the turn of century that Justice Oliver Wendell Holmes, dissenting against application of the laissez-faire liberty of contract doctrine in *Lochner v. New York,* chided his majority colleagues that the Constitution "does not enact Mr. Herbert Spencer's *Social Statics.*"

Fittingly, Spencer's greatest American admirer was Andrew Carnegie, the diminutive Scotsman who had built a steel empire. Carnegie had come to the United States at 12, his family, like that of many immigrants, penniless. Bright, alert, personable, young Carnegie rose like an Alger hero; his later career assumed almost mythical proportions. Renown for applying the most advanced technology, cutting costs, and making full-capacity use of his mills, Carnegie pushed less efficient competitors to the wall. When workers at his large Homestead plant near Pittsburgh struck for higher wages, he crushed them. In what seemed like pages out of Spencer and Alger, the nation got much needed low-cost, high-quality steel and Carnegie, only in his forties, became the world's richest man.

In his popular, widely read essay "Wealth," he defended the "efficiency" of big industry, but tried to give his social Darwinist creed a humane face. The rich had a moral duty to plow their wealth back into good works with the same zeal they had shown in acquiring it. Carnegie set about doing just that. In the last half of his life, he turned almost exclusively to philanthropy and work for world peace. He built and stocked free libraries in thousands of American cities and towns, set up foundations and, without a high school education himself, endowed universities. He shocked his fellow magnates by urging high inheritance taxes so that millionaires would be encouraged to make bequests and their children acquire self-reliance. He worked hard but naively to head off the European conflict that led to World War I. Carnegie's way became a model for others who had become unimaginably rich, but it was more often exception than rule.

Though some of its elements continue to resonate in the American mind to the present day, Social Darwinism as a public philosophy could not overcome its lack of compassion and intellectual shortcomings. It mistakenly identified social evolution with progress and elevated economic efficiency and competitive success above all other values. Applied to social life, "survival of the fittest" was less a natural law or will of God than a justification for those on top being there. Social Darwinism was more a set of argumentative explanatory propositions than a proven science. Reaction to its severity helped spur theories of reform and calls for a kinder, gentler society.

the Populist Party. For several decades, pressures for reform vied with laissez-faire urgings of business. Reformers won partial victories through the Progressive wings of the two major parties but lost ground again after World War I. When the struggle was carried to the courts, unelected judges sympathetic to business often held against reform.

Laissez-Faire Constitutionalism

In the antebellum period, the Supreme Court's most important work dealt with the issues of federalism and Union. After the war, more and more it was asked to draw lines between what was public, thus regulatable, and what was private and free of government intervention. Neither the demands of business for government support nor of other interests for government regulation were consistent with well-settled laissez-faire preferences. As a result, legislative responses were mixed and often halting, as was the Court's review of them. It is not surprising that statute and decision often parted company.

Almost immediately after the war, the Court had to deal with an important fiscal problem left in its wake. To help pay for steeply rising military costs, Congress had passed the wartime Legal Tender Act, in which $450 million worth of United States notes were issued without backing by metal reserves. This "greenback" money was made legal tender at face value in all transactions. It soon depreciated, meeting with objections from creditors reluctant to accept it in payment of debt.

After avoiding appeals from the act during the war, the Court finally declared it unconstitutional in *Hepburn v. Griswold* in 1870, as it applied to contracts made before passage. The decision caused turmoil in commercial circles. After President Ulysses Grant, a strong supporter of paper money, appointed William Strong and Joseph Bradley, both sympathetic to the act, to the Court a year later, the issue was heard again. In *Knox v. Lee,* the Court reversed itself, sustaining broad Congressional power over currency.

The quick about-face led to cries of "court packing" and hurt the Court's reputation for consistency and independence. Citing the framers' fear of economic radicalism, critics charged the second decision violated the "spirit" of the Constitution. Though the framers had forbidden issuance of paper money by the states, they had said nothing about that power for the central government. *Knox* was a triumph for a constitutional reading not merely to meet exigencies unforeseen by the framers but to serve continuing needs they could not have anticipated either. Paper money was born of wartime necessity, but a modern economy could hardly have developed without it. The Court would not always be so astute.

That the Court's first ruling on the Fourteenth Amendment should affect not rights of former slaves but of white businessmen was a forewarning of the new constitutionalism to come. The decision dealt with a set of 1873 appeals from Louisiana known as the Slaughterhouse Cases (p. 255). Several butchers in New Orleans objected to a state law that confined livestock slaughter to one area of the city and created a monopoly by granting one company the exclusive right to engage in it or license others to do so. Close ties of the beneficiary to the state's Reconstruction government led to charges of corruption and bribery, which may well have been true. To many, the law aimed less at protecting public health then securing commercial

gains for a few persons at the expense of others. The excluded butchers argued that this deprived them of a right to work in an otherwise lawful trade, thus violating the new Amendment's provisions that no state may "abridge the privileges and immunities of citizens of the United States" nor "deprive any person of life, liberty, or property without due process of law."

Rejecting these claims, a majority of the Court made an important distinction between rights of national and state citizenship. The Amendment protected only the first, and those rights were limited to the citizen's relationship to the federal government. They did not include the right to work in a particular trade or business. Such a right was an aspect of state citizenship and so could be regulated by the state.

Though not seeming so at the time, the decision was to be of great consequence. First, despite Justice Samuel Miller's majority view that the Amendment was intended to protect civil rights of former slaves not the property of white businessmen, the decision greatly narrowed the Amendment's privileges and immunities clause. In doing so, it weakened the Amendment for civil rights protection.

Second, the theory of the dissenting justices would influence constitutional political economy until well into the twentieth century. Three of the four dissenters, including Stephen Field and Joseph Bradley, who became leading intellectual forces on the Court, argued that the Amendment's due process clause was not limited to procedural guarantees but protected substantive economic rights including entry into an otherwise lawful occupation. Insisting that the Amendment was not aimed at securing the rights of black persons alone, Field and Bradley argued for a much more potent instrument, one that would protect property rights against state interference. This formulation, later known as the doctrine of economic substantive due process, soon found fuller application in laissez-faire principles that protected a freedom to make contracts and limited state power to regulate business.

The Waite Court

Chief Justice Salmon Chase, who had been appointed Taney's successor during the Civil War, died in 1873. After a belabored search, President Grant chose Morrison R. Waite, an Ohio lawyer with limited public experience, as his successor. For the next 14 years, Waite led a Court dominated by several strong judicial personalities, including Miller, Field, Bradley and, later, John Marshall Harlan. By 1882, only three justices remained from the Chase period. Despite Field's persistent urging on behalf of substantive economic rights, a majority of the Waite Court resisted embracing a full-blown laissez-fair interpretation of the Constitution.

Many states and localities, especially in the West, had gone to great lengths to attract railroads and industry, even offering cash subsidies. This support was usually paid for by selling bonds, that is, by pledging future taxes against the debt. Caught in the financial crunch of a mid-1870s depression, many overextended communities simply repudiated their bonds. Disappointed holders eventually brought nearly 300 appeals from these actions to the Court. Generally, the justices drew a line between bonds issued to subsidize railroads and utilities, which were thought to be "public highways" even when built and operated by private companies, and bonds supporting other private enterprise. Only if future taxes were pledged for "public use" would the bonded debt be enforceable.*

Later, in *Stone v. Mississippi* (1880), the Court similarly held that a state could not grant away its future right to use police power to protect public health, safety, or morals. Mississippi had given a 25 year lottery charter to a private company, but a new constitution adopted a year later barred all lotteries. As it had in the bondholder cases, the Court prevented state and local governments, whether they were motivated by an excess of promotional zeal or simple venality, from bargaining

away future use of an inherent power. In this, the Court also moved away from the wide-ranging protection of public contracts the Marshall Court had fashioned, specifically narrowing the chief's holding in *New Jersey v. Wilson* 70 years before.

The Waite Court's most important work was in the Granger cases, several appeals from state regulation of business practices. By the 1870s, many farmers had grown resentful of the railroads and grain elevator companies on whom they depended for shipment of crops and storage until sale. These virtual monopolies were seen as using their dominant positions to gouge shippers with excessive or discriminatory rates. Grievances were especially keen in the Midwest, where farmers used the Grange and other agricultural organizations originally formed for educational purposes and cooperative marketing, to mobilize politically. The movement won control of several state legislatures, which then passed laws limiting the rates railroads and grain elevators could charge.

Several appeals from these enactments came before the Supreme Court in 1877. The best known was *Munn v. Illinois* (p. 260), in which a state law had fixed maximum storage rates for grain elevators in Chicago. The Court's 7-2 decision sustaining it was the salient ruling of the Waite period. Grain elevators, like railroads, were privately owned and operated, but their near-monopoly status and central place in the market cast them as businesses "affected with the public interest." As such, Chief Justice Waite wrote, they could be controlled "by the public for the public good," here through the state's police power. The principle was not new. Waite reached back to seventeenth-century English common law that admitted public regulation of wharves, and to American precedent of public control of bridges, ferries, and road vehicles. In adding grain elevators, he used the historic common law method of refitting old rules to new conditions, in this instance, to a modern market economy.

But Waite went further. Whether a business was clothed with the public interest was for the legislature, not the courts, to say. The owners of

* See, for example, *Loan Office Association v. Topeka,* 87 U.S. 655 (1874).

Retreat from a Cause

By the mid-1870s, slavery had been abolished, the Constitution amended, and the South at least partly reconstructed, or so it seemed. Northern political support for vigorous protection of the civil rights of the former slaves began to wane. For many, weary of war and division, the time for reconciliation seemed at hand so the nation might fully return to the improvement of material life, even the outright production of wealth.

On civil rights there were some grounds for optimism. In many parts of the South important progress had been made toward integration and equality before the law. The advances might have been first steps in the complex social revolution that would bring true equality for the Freedmen. But with the gradual return of white supremacists to control in almost all areas of the former Confederacy, these hopes were dashed. In the place of integration, however tentative, they built a caste system based on segregation of the races and a permeating discrimination, underwritten by the force of government through Jim Crow laws. This system remained largely intact for nearly 75 years at great cost to the region's economic recovery and at great deprivation to its black population.

The Supreme Court played an important doctrinal role in this development. Its narrow reading of the Fourteenth Amendment's privileges and immunities clause in the Slaughterhouse Cases was followed by others weakening the Civil War ammendments as a shield for protecting the rights of Southern blacks.

In *United States v. Cruikshank*, in 1876, the year Reconstruction was formally ended, the Court heard an appeal from the convictions of several Louisiana whites for the murder of more than 100 black men in the Colfax Massacre growing out of a dispute over the state's 1873 gubernatorial election. The government had brought the case under the Enforcement Act, a Reconstruction law designed to give effect to the Fourteenth and Fifteenth Amendments by making punishable conspiracies to forcibly deprive anyone of a constitutional right.

The Court unanimously overturned the convictions, again making a distinction between federal and state citizenship rights: The indictments had not alleged the denial of a federal right. Nor did the Fourteenth Amendment's due process or equal protection clauses apply because they were limits on state as opposed to private actions. And since the indictments failed to allege the murders were racially motivated, the Fifteenth Amendment's protection of the right to vote from discrimination because of race was not applicable either. Responsibility for punishing offenses like the Colfax murders, the Court said, lay with state authorities. But in the post-Reconstruction South, this usually meant little or no action would be taken at all. That result was hardly the Court's intention, yet there is little doubt that *Cruikshank* encouraged, at least did little to discourage, violence against black persons in Southern states.

such businesses were entitled to a reasonable return on their investment, but determining that return was also a matter of legislative discretion. For those objecting to such legislation, remedy lay at the polls, not in the courts. Waite also concluded that state rate setting did not conflict with federal regulation of interstate commerce; in any case, the effect on such commerce was indirect.

In a forceful dissent, Justice Field argued that the Fourteenth Amendment's due process clause prevented certain substantive property rights from being impaired by the states. This contention, a reprise of his dissent in the Slaughterhouse Cases, sharply contrasted with Waite's view that due process guaranteed only procedural rights. Field believed the Court's decision would put all property and business in a state at the "mercy of the legislature."

Despite Waite's triumph, the doctrine of business affected with the public interest would be largely neutralized in the years ahead. Finally persuaded by Field, the Court came to embrace a laissez-faire interpretation of the Fourteenth Amendment and the Constitution generally. The *Munn* doctrine did have

In the Civil Rights Cases (1883)—five appeals attacking the Civil Rights Act of 1875—the Court was yet more definite in limiting the scope of the Fourteenth Amendment. In the Act, the last and most ambitious of the Reconstruction laws, Congress had prohibited racial discrimination in inns, public transport, and in many other privately owned facilities accommodating the public. For authority, it used Section 5 of the Amendment, giving it "power to enforce, by appropriate legislation, the provisions of this article," meaning the Amendment.

The Court saw it otherwise. Justice Joseph Bradley held that the Amendment, overall, was a limit on state action and so did not reach the behavior of private parties, here the owners of the "public accommodations." Enforcement powers under Section 5 were limited to remedial measures where state action had restricted civil rights. Otherwise, Bradley said, the Amendment would be a license for the federal government to enact municipal codes. Responsibility for preventing discrimination by private persons or privately owned businesses was that of state law. Bradley admitted the Thirteenth Amendment, outlawing slavery, did reach private parties, but discrimination in public facilities, he argued, could not be interpreted as a renewal of slavery.

One dissenter, Justice John Marshall Harlan, a Kentucky Republican and former slaveholder, took a much broader view of the two amendments and argued that federal power could reach private discrimination under either. The Thirteenth, Harlan wrote, abolished not only slavery but the "badges of slavery" of which discrimination was one. Extrapolating from the doctrine of business affected with a public interest developed *Munn v. Illinois,* Harlan reasoned that if such businesses as inns and railways discriminated, they did so with tacit approval of the State and their acts were thus state action under the Fourteenth Amendment.

Harlan's view would eventually prevail but not until the 1960s. Bradley's more conservative interpretation of the amendments was closer to the understanding of the day. The Civil Rights Cases prevented Congress from legislating against private discrimination. Leaving the matter to the states only encouraged public and private discrimination now becoming the norm throughout the South.

In *Plessy v. Ferguson* (1896), the Court further limited the scope of the Fourteenth Amendment by severely qualifying its equal protection clause. It sustained a Louisiana law that required racial segregation on intrastate railroads. Here state action was present, but the Court held that it did not deny segregated black persons "equal protection of the laws" as long as such a law required the separate facilities be equal. That such facilities were seldom equal made a mockery of such laws and of the emergent "separate but equal" doctrine.

Again Harlan dissented alone, arguing that the Constitution was "color-blind" and eloquently restating his position in the Civil Rights Cases. His dissents in the two cases were well ahead of their time and are now better known than any majority or concurring opinions he wrote in 34 years on the Court. But the separate but equal doctrine remained prevailing law until *Plessy* was overruled in the School Desegregation cases, *Brown v. Board of Education,* in 1954.

the last word, but not until it was resurrected in the 1930s after the conflict over the New Deal. It then became what it had prematurely been in the 1870s: an important building block in restructuring the relationship between business and government in the modern industrial state.

The Fuller Court

In the 1880s, the Court began to adopt a more conservative posture on corporate property rights and the role of government in the marketplace. It grew less deferential to state regulations and more solicitous of entrepreneurial liberty. Time and again the Constitution was held to incorporate principles of laissez-faire, including strong preference for market control of economic life and a private ordering by contract over public control through political regulation. The Court used new possibilities afforded by the Fourteenth Amendment for judicial interdiction of state law and to read substantive economic rights into the Constitution through its due process protection.

The gradual shift to a more activist role came less from grand design than from the vicissitudes of personnel changes on the Court and the interest of several justices in individual liberties. Between 1880 and 1895, a dozen new justices arrived, seven in the six years 1888–1894 alone. Several, such as Rufus Peckham, George Shiras, and the new chief justice, Melville Fuller, had successful private law practices that included important railway work. Almost all, Democrats included, were economic conservatives.

Events also had their effect. Encouraged by *Munn* and responding to demands of farmers and consumer groups, many states had zealously enacted new regulations. The raft of laws from different jurisdictions often made it hard for railroads and other interstate businesses to operate effectively and at a profit. To some justices, these interventions were little more than class legislation to redistribute wealth. They tended to see corporations, the wealth producers, as servants of the general public good. Industrial violence, urban unrest, and farm protests were not so much calls for ameliorative policies to soften the harder edges of an industrial economy than harbingers of social revolution. The new justices were far more worried about threats to order and the security of property than their predecessors had been. Though their concern for the well-being of the country was genuine enough, their political science was problematic.

The rise of a laissez-faire jurisprudence was abetted by the works of two legal scholars, Thomas M. Cooley, who was also a state judge, and Christopher Tiedeman. Cooley's *Treatise on Constitutional Limitations,* which went through five editions after its first printing in 1868, was an influential work in American law until well into the twentieth century. He argued strongly for due process limits on state economic regulations where such laws seemed designed simply to transfer wealth from one segment of society to another. By linking due process to the older doctrine of vested rights, he broadened the reading of the Fourteenth Amendment, urging that it be a repository of protective substantive economic rights.

Tiedeman, more conservative than Cooley, would have reduced government's role to little more than administering the criminal law. In *A Treatise on the Limitations of Police Power in the United States* in 1886, he argued that property should be regulated only so it not be used to injure that of others. Courts had a primary task of protecting free market principles. His argument that freedom to make contracts was a protected substantive right influenced the Court's formulation of a Liberty of Contract doctrine in the 1890s.

Laissez-faire principles had been in constitutional law since the days of Marshall, but their full doctrinal ascendancy awaited tenure of the Fuller Court, 1888–1910. When Morrison Waite died in office, President Grover Cleveland turned to his friend and political ally, Melville Weston Fuller, a conservative property-conscious Democrat and corporate lawyer from Chicago, for his successor. Fuller proved a competent administrator and an amiable group leader, but not a great intellectual force on the Court. That role would be left to colleagues such as Field, Harlan, David Brewer, Horace Gray, and, not least, the new arrival in 1902, Oliver Wendell Holmes, who often disagreed with his more judicially activist brethren.

The Fuller Court took on a strong probusiness, antilabor cast, growing more activist as the elected branches of government, state and federal, became more responsive to demands for reform. In all, it struck down 90 state laws, 65 percent as many as the Court had in its entire first century. The vast majority dealt with economic regulations. Confronted by new federal interventions—administrative regulation of railroads, use of commerce power prosecutions to break up monopolies, and a peacetime tax on incomes—the Fuller Court weakened them or held them invalid. One important exception was a grudging acceptance of federal police power based on the commerce clause.

Substantive Due Process and Liberty of Contract

Substantive due process was the crown of laissez-faire jurisprudence and liberty of contract its most important jewel. Traditionally, due process referred to procedures government was obliged to follow before it could impose criminal punishment or other disability. These included rights to adequate notice, a hearing, confrontation of witnesses or accusers, and so on. Government might deprive a person of life, liberty, or property provided it adhered to such time-honored procedures. Broadly, due process protected against arbitrary government action. A substantive version was derived from the older doctrine of vested property rights: there were certain things government could not do to property no matter how it did them or what procedures it used. Individual justices such as Marshall and Story had sometimes spoken of vested rights as if they were protected by the Constitution, but the full Court had never gone that far.

The doctrine of substantive due process poured this old wine into a new bottle shaped by the Fourteenth Amendment. Except for police protection of public health, safety, or morals, it held that government could not interfere with or otherwise impair property. The view had been rejected in the Slaughterhouse Cases and in *Munn,* but two decisions in the mid-1880s opened the door to its eventual triumph.

In *Santa Clara County v. Southern Pacific* (1886), the Court found corporations to be "persons" within the meaning of the Fourteenth Amendment's provision that "no person shall be deprived of life, liberty, or property." This allowed corporate entities to avail themselves of whatever protection due process afforded. The following year in *Mugler v. Kansas,* it upheld a state prohibition law used to seize a brewery that had continued operations. But Justice Harlan stressed that the courts could look beyond regulatory means, that is, they could review "the substance of things" to see if restrictive provisions were suitably related to their ends. Though the state law was upheld, the decision was more important for this assertion of a far-reaching judicial review of state economic regulation. The Fieldian dissents in the Slaughterhouse Cases and *Munn* were gradually becoming the doctrine of the Court.

Formal enshrinement came in *Allgeyer v. Louisiana* (1897) in the form of liberty of contract. The state had enacted legislation regulating insurance companies. To enforce the policy against nonconforming out-of-state companies doing business in the state, it barred Louisianans from buying insurance, that is, from entering into contracts, with them. (Since the Court had earlier held insurance not to be interstate commerce in *Paul v. Virginia* (1869), the law could not be challenged as a burden on such commerce.) Allgeyer, a Louisiana resident, had bought insurance from a New York company that did not meet state standards. The Court held the restriction to violate his liberty to make otherwise valid contracts, a right protected by the due process clause of the Fourteenth Amendment.

The new doctrine did not mean states lost their police power to protect public health, safety, or morals. In *Holden v. Hardy,* for example, a year after *Allgeyer,* the Court took note of the unhealthy conditions in mines in upholding a Utah statute limiting miner's work to eight hours a day.

But how little the Court would defer to legislative judgment if it saw liberty of contract threatened became dramatically clear in *Lochner v. New York* (1905) (p. 276), a case that has come to symbolize the farthest reaches of laissez-faire constitutionalism. In its Bakeshop Act, New York had restricted work in bakeries to 10 hours a day and 60 hours a week. Legislative motives were mixed. Passed unanimously by its two houses, it was aimed partly at unsanitary conditions in the baking industry and dangers from exposure to flour dust, and partly at strengthening workers' bargaining position with employers. A majority of the Court saw the law as a labor measure, unconvinced that baking could be hazardous in the same way that mining was. If they could not be justified as a health measure, the work-hour restrictions infringed on workers' liberty to make employment contracts, that is, on the freedom to work as many hours as they pleased.

This statement of right was ironic to say the least, since the legislation had been enacted for

The Brahman Skeptic

Many constitutional scholars rank Oliver Wendell Holmes, Jr. the most able jurist to ever sit on the Supreme Court. In 30 years of service he wrote 873 opinions, more than any justice before or since. Many of these, for the Court and in dissent, are among the most memorable we have. His influence on constitutional interpretation, the reading of the common law, and the role of judges is prodigious.

Holmes was born into the Boston upper class. His father, for whom he was named, practiced medicine but was better known as an essayist and author of "The Autocrat at the Breakfast Table," a popular series in *The Atlantic Monthly,* which he cofounded. Young Holmes grew up in a secure, intellectually animated household in which Ralph Waldo Emerson and other New England cultural lights were frequent guests. He emerged independent of mind, self-confident, and possessed of a keen sense of duty, qualities that remained with him the rest of his life. He was 19 when the Civil War began and was one of the first to enlist in the 20th Massachusetts Volunteers. In the next four years, he fought in several of the war's great battles, including Antietam and Fredericksburg and was wounded three times, twice almost fatally. The harrowing experience reinforced in Holmes another trait: doubt about moral absolutes and an enduring skepticism of things not self-evident.

After the war, he returned to Harvard to study law. Though he entered practice, it was soon clear that legal scholarship was his true love. In spare hours he wrote articles and essays, mainly on the growth and development of the common law. In 1881, he put many of these together in a book *The Common Law,* perhaps the most important work in American jurisprudence. In it, Holmes moved away from the traditional formalism that dominated legal thinking and introduced a largely new perspective on the law and on the role of judges in shaping it.

Law was not a body of logically related, eternally fixed principles—"a brooding omnipresence in the sky," as he termed it—but rules that had evolved from more primitive origins. It was continuing to change according the "felt necessities of the time" through judging that was not yet fully conscious. Judges, Holmes said, decided

the benefit of bakery workers and with their wide support. Liberty of contract was not absolute, said Justice Peckham, who had also written the *Allgeyer* opinion, but it could be abridged only by genuine exercise of police power, that is, only to protect health, safety or morals. Who would decide the purpose of such laws? In the end, not the legislature elected by the people but the Supreme Court. Here Peckham and his four colleagues, surely knowing less about conditions in New York bakeries than the legislators who had passed the law, made a finding of fact from no evidence other than "common understanding"

that bakery work had never been thought to be an unhealthy trade requiring police legislation.

It was this usurping activism that made the decision controversial and called out dissents from four justices. Harlan, who supported liberty of contract and thought the doctrine should prevail unless health or safety needs could be shown, was persuaded that long working hours were harmful to bakers and, absent proof otherwise, the legislature's finding should hold. Holmes went further. In one of the most notable dissents in the Court's history, he attacked laissez-faire constitutionalism and its Social Darwinian un-cases first and then looked for logical reasons and precedents to justify their conclusions. That this left room for prejudice was unavoidable, but greater danger lay in judges not recognizing their "inarticulate premises," convincing themselves they were mere instruments for the discovery and application of objective, unchanging rules. Many lawyers and judges of Holmes's day considered these ideas heretical. But so powerfully were they stated that *The Common Law* sharply challenged more settled approaches and, eventually, became a basic work in two important new schools of legal thought, sociological jurisprudence and legal realism.

Soon after its publication, Holmes was appointed to the Supreme Judicial Court of Massachusetts, eventually becoming its chief justice. In 20 years on that court, he wrote more than 1,000 opinions, many them explications of the evolving common law. Their influence on tort and contract law was extensive.

Holmes was 61 when he was appointed by the Supreme Court by Theodore Roosevelt in 1902. He served until 1932, when failing health forced him to retire at 91, the oldest justice ever. He had continually asked chief justices under whom he served—Fuller, White, and Taft—to assign him more opinions. He worked quickly, and typically with brevity and eloquence; many of his opinions are marked by unusual beauty and power.

His view of the role of judges often caused him to part company with laissez-faire colleagues, whom he believed simply substituted their economic views for those of the legislature, cloaking them, wittingly

or not, with the mantle of constitutional requirement. His dissenting critique in *Lochner* is a classic statement of this analysis.

Holmes's perspective made him dubious about judicial activism, and he was willing to give great deference to legislative action, even experimentation, so long as it did not violate a specific constitutional limit. Ironically, he personally did not have much faith in most proposals for social and economic reform, believing they would do little good. Nor did he have a high opinion of most legislators. But as long as the political processes remained unclogged, the majority, as represented in the legislature, had a right to govern. Holmes, the conservative doubter, could accept even radical proposals with which he disagreed.

When his views were applied to free speech cases in the 1920s, the result was often liberal. Speech not posing a "clear and present danger" was protected, a standard Holmes formulated that would later become central to an expansive free speech doctrine. In the end, Holmes thought, "the best test of truth is the power of the thought to get itself accepted in the competition of the marketplace" [*Abrams v. United States,* 250 U. S. 616 at 630 (1919)]. Here, perhaps, the Darwinian pessimist who saw life as an unending clash of interests, revealed a basic faith after all.

Holmes and his wife, whom he outlived, had no children. He left his estate to the United States with a special provision, later known as the Holmes Devise, for the research and writing of a comprehensive history of the Supreme Court, a project after many delays now substantially finished.

derpinnings. The decision, he said, rested on "an economic theory which a large part of the country does not entertain." He argued for judicial self-restraint and recognition of "the right of the majority to embody their opinions into law." Yet despite the storm it created on and off the Court, *Lochner* and its expanded liberty of contract remained valid law until overruled in *West Coast Hotel v. Parrish* (1937), near the end of the New Deal crisis.

Was liberty of contract also part of the due process clause of the Fifth Amendment and thus a limit on federal power as well? The

Court's affirmative answer came three years after *Lochner* when it held the Erdman Act invalid in *Adair v. United States.* Using the commerce power, Congress had outlawed "yellow dog" contracts—employment agreements requiring that a worker not belong to a union and making later union membership cause for dismissal. The law had recognized that most workers in a modern industrial economy were employed by large companies and, that being so, their bargaining position in dealing with their employers was anything but equal. Yet in striking down the law, the Court ignored that liberty of contract made little sense as a protected right unless parties had something approaching bargaining parity. Again, a law to protect workers was invalidated in the name of their freedom. State attempts to outlaw yellow dog contracts were held to violate the Fourteenth Amendment in *Coppage v. Kansas* (1915).

Regulation by Commission? Not Entirely

In the great postwar railway boom, many states responded to cutthroat competition and complaints about rates by creating a new governmental device—the regulatory commission. The first bodies were empowered only to investigate rail operations and publish their findings, on the assumption that such exposure would be enough to counter rate excess and other abuses.

When buccaneer railroad men like Gould, Vanderbilt, and Huntington merely shrugged off adverse publicity, some legislatures tried to set maximum rates by law. But being diverse bodies elected to debate and formulate general policies, they were not expert or flexible enough for the continuous work of overseeing rates. Gradually, the task was turned over to the commissions, which then became hybrid bodies having a mix of legislative, executive, and judicial functions. As they grew in importance, the unelected commissioners, only indirectly accountable to the legislature or governor, became known as the fourth branch of government.

Rate setting by myriad state commissions had a balkanizing effect and as their number grew so did objections from railway companies. Though the Supreme Court had earlier upheld state rail regulation in one of the Granger cases heard with *Munn* in 1877, the railroads won a big victory in *Wabash, St. Louis, & Pacific Railway v. Illinois* (1886). The justices held that rate fixing for interstate shipments directly burdened interstate commerce, a matter only the federal government could sanction through its commerce power. Since there were no federal rate regulations at the time, the decision left a void in which much of the railway business—all that

was interstate—remained free of any rate supervision at all.

Because Congress had debated the possibility of railway regulation for several years, the justices and the railways probably anticipated what happened next. Within four months, Congress enacted and President Cleveland signed the Interstate Commerce Act creating the nation's first federal regulatory body, the Interstate Commerce Commission. It was headed by five commissioners appointed by the President to six-year terms arranged to expire unevenly. Though empowered to hear complaints, gather information from railways, subpoena witnesses, and issue cease and desist orders, it was not given rate-setting power per se. Cleveland appointed the eminent scholar-jurist Thomas Cooley the commission's first chairman.

Its early years were stormy. Not surprisingly, railways frequently challenged its findings, and the new agency depended on the courts to enforce its orders and to clarify vague provisions in the Interstate Commerce Act itself. It often ran into hostility, partly because of uneasiness about its blend of functions and partly because many, if not most, federal judges were committed to principles of laissez-faire. The Supreme Court, which had forced creation of the Commission, dealt it a blow in *Cincinnati, New Orleans & Texas Pacific Railway v. I.C.C.* (1896), holding that it lacked power to prescribe a rate schedule where it found one set by the carrier unreasonable. It took another decade before enough support was rallied in Congress in the Hepburn Act of 1906 to correct this narrow reading of the commission's powers.

The railway rate cases gave the Court chance to add another tenet to the doctrine of substantive due process. In *Chicago, Milwaukee & St. Paul Railway v. Minnesota* (1890), it held state rate setting to be judicially reviewable, striking down a law that had set up a regulatory commission but had not required notice and a hearing before rates were set or provided for an appeal to the courts. Not stopping with these procedural findings, the Court said the judiciary would also have power to decide the reasonableness of rates themselves.

It was not long before the Court did exactly that. In *Smyth v. Ames* (1897), it found an intrastate rate schedule set by the Nebraska legislature itself to be unreasonable. The rates, the Court said, did not offer "a fair return on fair value" of the assets of the railway and so deprived it of property without due process of law. The finding was made after protracted analysis of railway operations, including expenses, cost of construction and replacement, methods of asset valuation, and the like, all matters better suited for administrative deliberation. The standard was as circular as it was subjective. As critics pointed out, the value of a railway's assets was, in part, determined by the rates it could charge; the first could not be fully gauged until the second was set. Despite these difficulties, *Smyth v. Ames* remained constitutional authority for nearly 50 years until overruled in *Federal Power Commission v. Hope Natural Gas,* in 1944. The older case stood as a pillar of the Court's activist laissez-faire jurisprudence and a leading exercise of substantive due process.

Trust-busting? Sometimes

With ever-larger markets and the effects of sharp competition, it was logical for many businesses to look for greater security and profit through merger and other combination. Consolidation was thus a natural development in an expanding industrial economy, a sensible way to rationalize economic life, realize economies of scale, and produce greater overall wealth. Yet if unchecked, continued merging could eliminate all competition and overwhelm other economic interests, including those of labor, farmers, and consumers, to say nothing of losing some efficiencies that a competitive market might produce.

Agitation about the trusts grew steadily in the 1880s. Many states had acted to restrict them, but because the largest combinations were now economic giants marketing products through-out the country, these efforts usually had little effect. Pressure mounted for federal action, and after prolonged debate, Congress passed the Sherman Anti-Trust Act in July 1890, creating another interface of business and government. Under prevailing constitutional doctrine, it could not follow the innovative regulatory path it had in the Interstate Commerce Act three years earlier because most trusts, unlike railways, were not businesses "affected with the public interest." Instead, Congress looked to statutory restriction enforceable through civil and criminal penalties. Railroads and utilities almost had to be monopolies to be efficient, but other combinations could be broken up or headed off. If they were, so it was believed, the market could again be self-regulating.

The Sherman Act outlawed "every contract, combination in the form of trust or otherwise, or conspiracy in restraint of trade or commerce among the several states or with foreign nations." Those engaging in such practices were guilty of a misdemeanor, punishable by fine and imprisonment. Though emphatic, the legislation was not well drafted. Such terms as "trust," "combination," and "restraint of trade" were left undefined or ambiguous. Interpretation would need to be made by the courts as the government brought prosecutions.

The act was in the pattern of legislative reform of the time: growing political agitation by those hurt by new economic or social conditions, a responsive general enactment symbolically affirming a basic ideal—in this case, competitiveness of free markets—and later judicial clarification of its meaning in specific cases. The legislative-judicial division of labor was not new and remains a chief characteristic of American government. But here, the new act would be interpreted by a federal judiciary for the most part unfriendly to it. Here an intervention in the economy would be narrowed by judges and justices committed to laissez-faire, dubious about government regulation of property even if aimed at restoring free, competitive markets.

The Supreme Court first ruled on the Sherman Act in *United States v. E. C. Knight Co.* (1895) (p. 264), a prosecution of the American Sugar Refining Company, which had gained control of 98 percent of the nation's refining capacity. Speaking for a majority of eight, Chief Justice Fuller sustained a lower court's dismissal of the case, holding that Congress's power over interstate commerce—the constitutional basis for the act—did not extend to manufacturing or production, which were entirely local. Whatever effect their monopolization had on interstate trade, it was indirect and beyond Congress's reach.

The ruling was an important limit on the Sherman Act which, if kept from reaching manufacturing, would be left mainly to apply to railroads, clearly not Congress's intention. More important, the decision severely cut federal power over business and industry. By leaving regulation of manufacturing to the police power of the states, the Court refused to recognize that almost all giant combinations were interstate in operation and thus largely beyond the reach of any one state. It was clearly afraid that any other holding would give Congress sweeping power to regulate nearly all aspects of a manufacturing economy. Unsurprisingly, the decision encouraged a new wave of mergers. Even so, the Court kept the distinction between manufacturing and commerce until forced to retreat during the New Deal crisis.

When *E. C. Knight* was handed down, important industrial combinations in the country numbered about a dozen. A decade later, thanks to the legalizing of holding companies by New Jersey and Delaware, there were more than 300, created from the merging of more than 5,000 companies and plants. Consolidation became even more of a political issue. Public dismay and perhaps the justices' own concern about this rapid growth made the Court amenable to putting sharper teeth in the Sherman Act. When Theodore Roosevelt, who courted a reputation as a trust-buster, succeeded to the presidency after the assassination of William McKinley in September 1901, he ordered his Attorney General Philander Knox, to initiate a series of Sherman Act prosecutions. Two of these, against the Railway Trust and the Beef Trust, led to dramatic victories in the Supreme Court.

In the first, *Northern Securities Co. v. United States* (1904), the government sought to dissolve a holding company created by the banking and railway tycoons J. P. Morgan, James J. Hill, and E. H. Harriman. It had acquired majority stock in three railroads and then operated them on an integrated basis. The company contended that stock transfers or contracts were not part of interstate commerce and so were outside the Sherman Act. But the Court, retreating from *E. C. Knight,* held the act applicable to contracts made in restraint of trade. Four dissenters argued that Congress's

The influence of large, concentrated capital often dwarfed even the apparently hard-working federal government in the late Nineteenth century.

commerce power did not reach stock ownership and, in any event, the company's restraint on competition was reasonable since it was a natural ancillary to more efficient operations. The division cast doubt on whether the Sherman Act made all combinations illegal, as it seemed to say, or only those that were unreasonable.

In the government's case against the Beef Trust the following year, the Court took another step back from *E. C. Knight*. Here, the defendant contended that each of its activities was local and thus "manufacturing" under the Knight doctrine. But Justice Holmes, writing for a unanimous Court in *Swift & Co. v. United States*, held that the company's Chicago stockyards, though immediately local, were part of a "stream of commerce" among the states. Each of its operations in the shipment and sale of livestock was but a temporary interruption in an interstate current. This formulation narrowed the distinction between manufacturing and interstate commerce and, logically or not, allowed the Court to maintain exceptions to its general rule that manufacturing was not interstate commerce and not within Congress's reach.

Application of the Sherman Act took an unusual if perhaps not surprising turn in the Danbury Hatters Case, *Loewe v. Lawlor* that reached the Court in 1908. When a Connecticut hat company resisted unionization efforts, workers struck, and the national Hatters Union urged members of the American Federation of Labor to boycott company products. Loewe, the company owner, filed a civil suit under the Sherman Act, charging the union with conspiracy to restrain trade.

On appeal, the Court unanimously rejected the union's contention that it was not a combination under the act. Chief Justice Fuller held that Congress had not intended to exclude unions, though the law was unclear on the point as on many others. The decision left the Court in the anomalous position of having declared a national sugar monopoly to be local but a union's national boycott to be interstate commerce. The case reflected the Court's strong antiunion bias and readiness to sustain injunctions and other actions against organized labor. As a result of this judicial hostility, unions turned more and more

to the political arena. In the Clayton Anti-Trust Act of 1914, they succeeded in getting Congress to include some protection from antitrust penalties, by that "correcting" *Loewe v. Lawlor*. Additional relief came in the Norris-LaGuardia Act in the 1930s.

The scope of the Sherman Act was again the chief issue in *Standard Oil Co. v. United States* (1911), a well-publicized attempt by the Taft Administration to break up the Rockefeller oil trust. Though the Court unanimously upheld dissolution, it formulated the "rule of reason," which substantially narrowed antitrust powers. Chief Justice Edward White, who succeeded Fuller, held that the Act, though seeming to include all combinations in restraint of trade, was meant to reach only those that were unreasonable. In determining which were which, White said, the Court would look to traditional common law standards of reasonableness and thus not be left to its own discretion. Justice Harlan, who concurred in the result, was not so sure. He saw the rule of reason as an activist door to judicial legislating, much like the one the Court had opened in reviewing the reasonableness of railway rates in *Chicago, Milwaukee & St. Paul Railway* and in *Smyth v. Ames*. The rule of reason created new uncertainties for business, but gave the Court flexibility in deciding later anti-trust cases.

Income Tax? Not at All

The income tax provision of the Wilson-Gorman Act of 1894 was, along with the Interstate Commerce and Sherman Acts, one of Congress's three great attempts to deal with economic inequities of the late nineteenth century industrial age. Before the Civil War, the federal government was able to collect all the revenue it needed from tariffs, excises, and the sale of public lands. When these sources fell short of meeting the cost of the war, Congress enacted a law taxing incomes on a progressive scale. After the war it was reduced and shortly repealed. Its constitutional status was upheld by the Supreme Court in *Springer v. United States* (1880).

The peacetime income tax imposed by Wilson-Gorman, in part to meet government deficits caused by the depression of 1893, was simple and mild by modern standards: a flat 2 percent with an exemption of $4,000, which meant most working class persons were excluded. As taxes went, it was politically popular. Congress had recognized two salient facts of industrial capitalism: The chief forms of wealth had shifted markedly from realty and personal property to liquid capital assets and, in a steadily expanding economy, these assets had enormous earning power. Taxing only older forms of wealth seemed both inexpedient and unfair.

Nonetheless, the new measure was immediately challenged and, a year later, struck down by the Supreme Court in *Pollock v. Farmer's Loan & Trust Co.* (p. 267) Because of the importance of the issue and the Court's even division on one of its main questions (only eight justices participated), the case was reargued a few months later before all nine members of the Court. The result was virtually the same. For a majority of five, Chief Justice Fuller held the levy, which included income from land, to be a direct tax and thus unconstitutional in not being apportioned among the states according to population, as required of direct taxes by Article I-9.

Traditionally, direct taxes were those imposed on land or on "heads," that is, on persons alone rather than on their property or income. The apportionment requirement had been put into the Constitution to mollify Southern delegates who feared that a new central government might tax the South's large holdings in land and slaves, leaving northern commercial interests untouched. Apportioning such taxes among the states by population would make them politically unpalatable to the smaller, more densely populated states of the Northeast where manufacturing was a chief source of wealth and landholding per capita was small. Southerners believed that land or head levies would then be seen in the North as disproportionately burdensome. They were correct and such taxes were never levied by the federal government.

But did direct taxes go beyond those on land and heads? Precedent and original understanding seemed to say no. In *Hylton v. United States* (1796), the Court had found a federal levy on carriages not a direct tax but an excise. And in *Springer,* a general income tax as a wartime measure had been sustained. But Chief Justice Fuller brushed this history aside as "a century of error." Striking down Wilson-Gorman was one more notch on the Court's gunstock of laissez-faire. Though the tax was modest enough, the Court's majority worried about the possibility of greater and wider income levies in the future and, as Fuller said, of an "attack upon accumulated property by mere force of numbers." Such concern was evident in the heated rhetoric of Joseph Choate, the eminent counsel who represented the tax challengers. The tax, Choate told the Court, "is defended here upon principles as communistic, socialistic—what shall I call them—populistic as ever have been addressed to any political assembly in the world."*

Unlike *E. C. Knight, Lochner,* and *Adair,* which had to wait decades before being overruled, the Income Tax Case was soon "corrected." In 1909, a constitutional amendment was proposed giving Congress the power to tax income from any source, without apportionment. It was ratified as the Sixteenth Amendment in 1913, the first formal change in the Constitution since Reconstruction. Taxes on individual and corporate income eventually became the chief source of federal revenue. Rates have been dauntingly high at times, but without the mechanism or some huge equivalent source of government revenue, neither modern welfare capitalism nor twentieth century American military victories and superpower status would have been possible.

The Progressive Interlude

As protests against concentrated economic power grew, they became an important force in electoral politics. Farmers, who had not helped themselves by taking on excessive debt and

---

* Quoted in Melvin Urofsky, *The March of Liberty,* (New York: Alfred A. Knopf, 1988), 547.

chronically overproducing, were at the low end of the market chain and were among those hurt most by the dislocating forces of industrialism. Dissatisfied with the response of the two major parties, Southern and Midwestern farmers formed the People's Party. It became the chief vehicle for the Populist movement, which advocated freer currency, lower tariffs, higher commodity prices, and stricter regulation of railroads.

The party's first presidential candidate, James B. Weaver, polled more than a million votes, 8.5 percent of the total in 1892, the best third-party showing in 30 years. But the party and movement were unable to broaden their appeal to reach urban workers or overcome internal division between Southern and Midwestern constituents over race.

A severe depression in 1893 generated wider discontent that spread to the major parties. "Free silver" proponents captured control of the Democratic Party in 1896 and nominated the youthful William Jennings Bryan after his rousing "Cross of Gold" speech at the party's Chicago convention. Populists joined Democrats in support of Bryan against Republican William McKinley.

Many historians consider 1896 the most important election between the Civil War and the New Deal victory of Franklin Roosevelt in 1932. Running as the candidate of sound currency—a gold standard—and protectionism, McKinley successfully portrayed Bryan and his Populist supporters as radicals. Bryan won 22 states but not one in the Northeast and only a handful in the Midwest. Looking for class polarization, he found only a sectional one. Agrarian protest had failed again to make common cause with labor. When McKinley again defeated Bryan in 1900 and by a larger margin, Populism was dead as the chief vehicle for protest and reform.

The leading event of McKinley's first term was the war with Spain in the spring and early summer of 1898, in which the world's leading anticolonial power acquired colonies. The immediate cause was a Cuban revolt against Spanish rule and its brutal suppression which had taken nearly 100,000 Cuban lives. Sympathy for the Cuban revolutionaries, who had gotten much financial and material aid from American supporters, was whipped to a fevered pitch by a new journalistic phenomenon, the mass-circulation press.

When the American battleship *Maine*, sent to Cuba to "show the flag," blew up in Havana Harbor in what at first appeared to be sabotage, war was inevitable. (The explosion was later found to be caused by spontaneous combustion in one of the ship's magazines.) American victories against a weak, ineffectual Spanish army and navy were swift in the Caribbean and the Pacific. As a result, Cuba gained independence and the United States took over pieces of Spain's crumbling empire including Puerto Rico, the Philippines, and Guam.

The war had two other consequences, one immediate and political, the other longer-term and economic. It catapulted one of its highly visible heroes, Colonel Theodore Roosevelt to the governorship of New York later in 1898 and then to vice-presidential candidacy on McKinley's ticket in 1900. When McKinley was assassinated months later, the "damned cowboy," as detractors called him (he was actually the scion of a wealthy, aristocratic New York family), was president of the United States at 42, the youngest ever to serve. All this was just three years after he had led his "Rough Riders" in the charge to take San Juan Hill outside Santiago, Cuba. The energetic, activist Roosevelt, who championed reform and unnerved the Republican old guard, helped usher in the Progressive Era.

By propelling the United States into a position of a world power with colonial possessions, the war broadened American marketing horizons and diverted attention from unrest at home caused by extremes in the supply and demand fluctuations of industrial capitalism. By offering an outlet for the surpluses of an ever-expanding industrial base, successful penetration of overseas markets had stabilizing effects at home, strengthened proponents of free trade, and weakened protectionism. That such expansion was not the long-run answer to economic roller coaster rides or distributive inequities at home would become apparent in the Great Depression of the 1930s. Overseas economic expansion also made future clashes with other, like-minded rising powers, notably Germany and Japan, more probable.

The New Reform

The Progressive Era is more or less coextensive with the period 1901–1920, but Progressivism itself defies easy definition. It was more a persuasion or disposition than a well worked out, consistent ideology. It relied more on wide, coincident support for ameliorative policies than on a highly organized movement. Its political blanket, in fact, covered many interests. It inherited much of Populism's discontent, but its demographic center of gravity was more urban, Northeastern, and middle class. It was less nativist and xenophobic and, if concerned about the effect of millions of newcomers to the United States, it was not opposed to immigration. Activists came from a wide range of backgrounds, including the ranks of business, labor, universities, such older professions as law and such newer ones as journalism and social work, and of the churches, particularly the older Protestant denominations.

Progressivism had strength in wings of the two major parties and elected three successive presidents: Republicans Roosevelt in 1904, William Howard Taft in 1908, and Democrat Woodrow Wilson in 1912 and 1916. Its leading figures also included Jane Addams, the social work pioneer and founder of Chicago's Hull House, the academic economist Thorstein Veblen, the political journalist Herbert Croly, and Louis Brandeis, the Boston "people's attorney."

In pursuing political, economic, and social reforms, Progressives sought to curb concentrated private economic power, improve industrial work conditions, combat political corruption, and in general make government more efficient through "expert" management and more responsive to "the people." Action came at all levels. Locally, Progressives worked to restructure municipal government through home rule, the city manager system, and public regulation or ownership of transport and utilities. Much of the effort was aimed at reducing the influence of political bosses and machines.

In the states, they supported the secret ballot, open primary nominations, citizen initiative of legislation, the referendum (popular voting on laws directly), and the election and popular recall of judges. Nationally, they set up the Federal Reserve System to manage currency and gain greater monetary stability, and the Federal Trade Commission to prevent unfair methods of competition. They reinvigorated antitrust statutes and railroad regulation, expanded the civil service system, lowered tariffs, and enacted pure food and drug regulations, conservation measures, and antiprostitution laws.

Progressives were largely responsible for four Constitutional amendments between 1913 and 1920, the most concentrated amending since the addition of the Bill of Rights. Besides the Sixteenth that allowed Congress to levy an income tax without apportionment, the Seventeenth, in 1916 provided for direct popular election of Senators; the Eighteenth, in 1919 outlawed the sale, manufacture, and transport of intoxicating liquors; and the Nineteenth, in 1920 gave women the right to vote.

In all, Progressivism had mixed success. Many of its policies did remedy or reduce social and economic failings of laissez-faire industrial capitalism. Middle-class interest and participation in government were heightened, though many structural reforms such as initiative, referendum, and recall, proved to be largely symbolic. The use of vigorous positive government to control concentrated private power laid the groundwork for the modern administrative state that reached new breadth with the New Deal programs of the 1930s.

Yet Progressivism's faith in government by nonpartisan professionals applying rational or scientific principles to regulation, now seems at least partly misplaced. Such wide delegation of authority not only raised the issue of separation of power, it was not entirely compatible with the goal of widening citizen participation and public control over government. The new bureaucratic "fourth branch," operating in the name of the public, would often prove elusive of democratic accountability. Naively equating all their work with the public good, many Progressives did not see that reforms could sometimes serve selfish special interests every bit as much as the evils they were designed to remedy.

Progressive ideals were carried into World War I to transform that struggle into "the war to end wars" and thus to make the world safe for democracy. Some have said the movement died at the conference table at Versailles with Wilson's compromises or later in the Senate chamber with defeat of the League of Nations treaty. In fact, the thrust of Progressivism was spent by the war itself. The tremendous military effort overseas and mobilization at home diverted attention, imagination, and resources from reform and domestic concerns. These were never recaptured.

The White Court

Though the Constitution was amended four times, the constitutional success of Progressive reforms depended more on favorable interpretation of its laws and policies by the Supreme Court. The Court was accommodating in several important decisions, but it did not break decisively with laissez-faire. Instead, it allowed development of two parallel, sometimes conflicting lines of precedent, one consistent with activist limits on government's power, the other upholding several Progressive interventions in markets and the workplace.

This inconsistency was clearest during the period of Edward White's chief justiceship, 1910–1921, when the Court came under the influence of new Taft and Wilson appointees. Oliver Wendell Holmes, named by Roosevelt in 1902, had already become a critic of the majority's laissez-faire activism. Though Taft's one-term presidency, sandwiched between the longer and more dramatic tenures of Roosevelt and Wilson, was generally undistinguished, he made six appointments to the Court, the most since Washington. This was fitting perhaps for a president who took a special interest in the Court and later realized a life-long dream of becoming its chief justice.

One of the appointments was the elevation of White, who had been on the Court since 1894, to be chief after the death of Melville Fuller. It was the first time a chief justice had been chosen from the ranks of the associates. The most noteworthy of Taft's new appointees was Charles Evans Hughes, the Republican governor of New York. Hughes distinguished himself as an able jurist by the time he resigned in 1916 to accept the Republican nomination to run against President Wilson, to whom he narrowly lost. He was later reappointed as chief justice in 1930, and served through one of the Court's most difficult periods.

Wilson's appointments of James McReynolds, in 1914, and Louis Brandeis, in 1916, were two of the most contrasting in the history of the Court. Brandeis, the Boston corporate attorney famed for his pro bono work in Progressive causes, especially opposing concentrated economic power, was the Court's first justice of Jewish ancestry. The controversial nomination was a prelude to a distinguished career on the Court. McReynolds, Wilson's attorney general, seemed to leave his Progressivism behind when he joined the Court. He became a latter-day apostle of laissez-faire, and as a colleague showed himself to be an anti-Semite and an often disagreeable personality.

White, a courtly, approachable Southerner, proved skillful in furthering a spirit of cooperation among his disparate colleagues, though he was not markedly effective as an administrator. As an ex-Confederate soldier and son of a wealthy plantation owner, his nomination in 1894 symbolized the nation's continued sectional reconciliation. He was, after Roger Taney, the second Roman Catholic to sit on the Court.

Federal Police Power

Police power has resisted exact definition. In *Gibbons v. Ogden*, Marshall had referred to it as "that immense mass of legislation, which embraces everything within the territory of a State,

Attorney for the People

Louis Dembitz Brandeis was a controversial and, for many, an inspiring figure long before he reached the Supreme Court. He had had a long, unique career as a lawyer and, though never holding public office, had more influence on public affairs than most who did. Misgivings about the excesses of industrial capitalism allied him with the Progressive reform of his time.

Brandeis was born in Louisville, Kentucky, five years before the Civil War began. The families of both his parents had fled Bohemia after the failed 1848 democratic revolt in the Austro-Hungarian Empire. His father became a successful grain merchant and young Louis grew up in an upper middle class cultured household in which public affairs were the subject of continuous debate. He entered Harvard Law School at 18, later graduating with the highest grades in the school's history.

He and Samuel D. Warren, a Boston socialite, who was second in Brandeis's class, opened a local law practice. They soon prospered though neither was interested simply in making money. Together they wrote "The Right of Privacy" for the *Harvard Law Review,* arguing for recognition of a common law right. It became one of the most cited of all legal articles and helped establish a right to privacy in American law. When Warren left the partnership to run his family's business, Brandeis formed his own firm of Brandeis, Dunbar, and Nutter. He gained renown as a formidable courtroom advocate who had no peer in the mastery of facts, both of the case at hand and those of its larger social and economic context. Corporate clients often found that their lawyer knew more about their businesses than they did.

As Brandeis prospered—he became a millionaire in his early forties—he began to choose his clients. Where they could not afford his fees, he often represented them without pay, becoming a pioneer in such pro bono work. Increasingly, his practice became "public" as he entered cases against corrupt streetcar companies, monopolistic railroads, and gouging gas companies. He mediated labor disputes and drew up the first plans for savings bank life insurance and sliding scale utility rates. The press dubbed him "the people's attorney." In 1907, the State of Oregon hired him to defend its new maximum hours law for women workers before the Supreme Court. Working with his sister-in-law Florence Goldmark, a consumer activist, Brandeis put together his now famous fact-laden brief on the working conditions of women and the health and social benefits that could come from limiting the workday.

Had he never reached the Supreme Court, his influence on American law and legal practice would have been remarkable. His emphasis on wide factual support for legal argument became a model for advocacy. It placed Brandeis at the cen-

not surrendered to the general government," thus seeming to equate it with the reserved powers of the states themselves. In the License Cases (1847), Taney said it was "nothing more or less than the powers of government inherent in every sovereignty to the extent of its dominions." [46 U. S. 582 at 587]

After hundreds of cases in which it had been an issue before the Court, two things were clear: It was a basic regulatory power of state government and it could be used for the protection of public health, safety, and morals. In a few decisions, such as *Munn,* the Court went further, upholding purely economic regulation where a

ter of the new school of sociological jurisprudence, which stressed the social and economic effects of law in contrast to argument based solely on precedent and deductive principles. His moral view of legal practice is summed up in the striking observation that "a lawyer who has not studied economics and sociology is very apt to become a public enemy."*

Though a Republican most of his career, Brandeis joined Woodrow Wilson's presidential campaign in 1912. Wilson, who had not met Brandeis before, came to rely on him as a close advisor. Victorious, he planned to name Brandeis attorney general, but opposition within the Democratic Party forced him to change his mind. He continued to draw on Brandeis's private advice in formulating his administration's antitrust policy. When Justice Joseph Lamar died in 1916, Wilson nominated Brandeis for the Supreme Court. Heated Senate hearings on the nomination followed, often making front-page news. He was opposed by many business interests who feared a Progressive of his ability on the Court, and many of his old courtroom enemies came to Washington to testify against him. Some of the opposition was anti-Semitic. After four months he was confirmed, 47-22, becoming the first Jew to serve on the Court.

It was Brandeis's fate that most of his 23 years on the bench were those of the Taft and Hughes periods, when the Court was dominated by laissez-faire conservatives. Though more than 85 percent of his opinions were those for the Court, that is, for the majority, some of his most notable were in dissent or concurrence. In *Olmstead v. United States* (1928), he argued, prophetically, for a *constitutional* right of privacy. His eloquent concurring opinion defending freedom of speech in *Whitney v. California* (1927) urged application of the clear and present danger test to criminal syndicalism cases, a position the Court eventually accepted and extended years

later in *Brandenberg v. Ohio* (1969). Whether in the majority or dissent, he urged deference to legislative judgment in economic regulation partly so that states might have a wide range in which to experiment.

Though he generally supported the New Deal and had occasionally given informal advice to Franklin Roosevelt, Brandeis voted to strike down provisions of the National Industrial Recovery Act in *Panama Refining Co. v. Ryan* and *Schechter Poultry Corp. v. United States,* in 1935. That and his opposition to the Court-packing plan caused the president to distrust him, perhaps not fully appreciating Brandeis's skepticism about concentrated power whether it be corporate or governmental. Harsher critics had always seen Brandeis as a manipulating, devious figure, too sure of his own rightness. They may not have appreciated that his streak of independence was at least as wide as that of his public altruism.

Brandeis had a second career while on the Court, that of leader of the world Zionist movement. Though nonreligious, he had in middle age become interested in and then dedicated to the idea of establishing a Palestinian homeland for Jews. But he feuded with European Zionist leaders, notably Chaim Weizmann, and was eventually ousted from the leadership role, though he continued to be a force in the movement.

The Zionist activity and what were later revealed to be covert efforts to influence various public policies through his protégé Felix Frankfurter, would no doubt receive critical response today as not fully compatible with the role of a Supreme Court justice.

In failing health, Brandeis retired from the Court in 1939, a giant in American law and politics, ahead of his day in many ways, yet not at home with the dawning of big government.

* Quoted in Alpheus Thomas Mason, *Brandeis, A Free Man's Life* (New York: Viking Press, 1946), 246.

business was "affected with the public interest." But as Congress became more active in using the commerce power, the question of whether the federal government had police powers, that is, whether the commerce and other powers might be used for the protection of health, safety, and morals, came to the fore. Doubters argued that

the national government had only enumerated powers and those reasonably implied and that police power was mentioned nowhere in the Constitution.

The matter first came to the Court in *Champion v. Ames,* in 1901, dealing with a challenge to Congress's antilottery act of 1895, which forbade shipment of lottery tickets in interstate commerce. As mere pieces of paper, the tickets were not dangerous to commerce or transport as, say, explosives, chemicals, or diseased animals might be. The regulation was aimed at the presumed harm of lotteries, traditionally a matter for state police regulation. The justices recognized the import of the constitutional issue and were deeply divided over it. The case was first heard in February 1901, reargued in April but left undecided. It was heard again at the start of the Court's next term in October, but again left undecided. It was heard a fourth time in November 1902 and a fifth in December, before it was decided in February 1903, making it the most argued case in the Court's history.

Its 5-4 decision in what became known as the Lottery Case, upheld the act and the constitutionality of a federal police power. It recognized the antilottery law was a Congressional attempt to protect public morals not to regulate interstate business. The majority was concerned that if Congress could not bar the lottery tickets from interstate traffic, a no-man's land would exist subject to neither federal nor state control. The minority feared that upholding the act would empower Congress to regulate and possibly prohibit any item of interstate business. Speaking for the dissenters, Chief Justice Fuller took the familiar dual federalism position. Lotteries were historically a matter for state control; the federal government could bar the tickets only had it been given an enumerated power over gambling.

Harlan, for the majority, held the federal commerce power was plenary, with only "such limitations or restrictions as are prescribed by the Constitution." As such, it could be used to ban an item completely, even one whose harmful effects were not to the stream of commerce itself. The novelty of the decision was less in holding mere pieces of paper to be commerce or in the complete barring of them, than in permitting the commerce power to be used for noncommercial ends.

Progressives welcomed the decision and it encouraged a host of new federal reform measures.

Among the more innovative were the Pure Food and Drug Act in 1906, barring adulterated or misbranded foods from interstate commerce, the Meat Inspection Act, also in 1906, and the antiprostitution Mann Act in 1910, which barred the interstate transport of women for immoral purposes. These laws were eventually upheld by the White Court on authority of the Lottery Case.

The commerce power was not the only source of federal police regulation the Court was willing to uphold. In *McCray v. United States* (1904) (p. 274), it sustained a federal oleomargarine tax that imposed a rate on colored margarine 40 times higher than on uncolored. The law, a political victory for the dairy industry to hold down competition, was clearly prohibitory rather than revenue-raising in purpose and effect. Yet a majority of the Court refused to examine Congressional motives.

Since Congress's taxing power in Article I-8 is not limited to interstate commerce, the Court's unwillingness to go beyond the face of the margarine tax as an excise raised the possibility of federal regulation of almost any aspect of the economy until the Court partly retreated from the position in the 1920s. Heartened by the ruling, Progressive majorities in Congress used the tax power to prohibit, that is, tax out of existence, many items thought be to dangerous to their users and used it to gain compliance with various federal laws.

But the Court's willingness to sustain police aspects of the commerce power had its limits and these were soon reached. In 1916, Congress passed the Keating-Owen Child Labor Act, a jewel in the crown of Wilsonian Progressivism. Widespread employment of children in factories and mills had become a leading political issue. When state regulations proved ineffective, the matter reached the top of the national agenda. Keating-Owen barred interstate shipment of goods made wholly or in part by children under age 14 who had been permitted to work more than eight hours a day or six days a week. An attack on the law in *Hammer v. Dagenhart* (1918) found the justices again deeply divided. Rather than sustaining, as had been widely expected, a majority of five struck it down.

Justice William R. Day tried to distinguish goods made by children from lottery tickets, impure food, and other items the Court had said Congress might prohibit as harmful. Neither the products of child labor nor the purposes to which they were put were inherently harmful. He admitted the child worker might need protection, but whatever the harm, it lay in production, that is, in acts that took place before goods entered interstate commerce. Thus, Day fell back on the Court's earlier distinction between manufacturing and commerce in the Sugar Trust Case, one that it ignored when it chose to, to argue that manufacturing was local and subject only to state control.

In this classic reasoning of dual federalism, such nationally enumerated powers as that over interstate commerce were not plenary but limited by the Tenth Amendment, that is, by powers reserved to the states. It was the very analysis the Court had rejected in the Lottery Case. Day's argument was not helped by his misquote of the Tenth Amendment as "the powers not expressly delegated to the national government are reserved to the states." The word "expressly" had, of course, been expressly omitted from the amendment by Congress when it framed the Bill of Rights.

Though Day's opinion was subjected to close analysis in a notable dissent by Holmes, it survived as a limit on federal police use of the commerce clause until overruled in *United States v. Darby Lumber Co.* (1941). As *Hammer* made clear, several justices—here a majority—remained committed to the older federal-state balance in economic matters and to an underlying belief that basic changes in the relationship of government and the economy should be resisted at almost any cost. The case foreshadowed wider judicial resistance to government regulation in the 1920s.

State Regulation and the Brandeis Proof

As pressures for reform gained intensity, many states enacted laws limiting work hours. These were usually rationalized as health or safety measures. In upholding such a law for mine workers in *Holden v. Hardy,* but overturning one benefiting bakery workers in *Lochner v. New York,* the Court had revealed two doctrinal approaches that divided it until the late 1930s. Were reform enactments valid police health and safety measures or were they economic regulations restricting the liberty of contract?

When an Oregon law limiting the workday for women in factories and laundries to 10 hours was appealed in 1908, the Court had chance to resolve its differences. Louis Brandeis, still eight years away from being a justice himself, was retained by the state to defend before the Court. He chose an unusual strategy. Rather than arguing that *Lochner* should not apply or should be overruled, he responded to Justice Peckham's chief point that the link between the law and harmful work conditions had not been proven.

With the help of reform activists, Brandeis gathered an enormous amount of material from medical and governmental reports on the working conditions of women in the United States and Europe to show how long hours endangered women's health. He assembled the information into a remarkable legal brief unlike any the Supreme Court had seen before. Only two of its 112 pages dealt with legal precedents, the mainstay of most briefs. Almost 100 were given to excerpts from the different studies and reports.

In *Muller v. Oregon* (p, 280), the Court was unanimous in sustaining the law, its connection to a valid health concern having been shown. Though the Court's (and Brandeis's) premise that women were physically vulnerable and thus in need of special protection might be thought paternalistic today, the assumption was widely accepted at the time. For the Court, Justice David Brewer took the unusual step of acknowledging the "very copious collection" of information Brandeis had supplied.

The "Brandeis brief" was widely copied and became a vehicle for defending Progressive reform in the courts and for making judges and justices more aware of the underlying social and economic conditions that called forth regulatory legislation. The method had its drawbacks, however. Much "research" presented was thin and not carefully put together. Some data was technical and detailed and raised an issue of the competence of courts to fully evaluate it.

The Brandeis brief was an important practical application of "sociological jurisprudence," which held that judges should not limit themselves to legal precedent and authority in reviewing social legislation. The term had first been used by Roscoe Pound, a prolific legal scholar and law school dean, and came to denote a new school of legal thought for which Pound became chief theoretician. As an antidote to legal formalism and, not so incidentally, to laissez-faire activism, sociological jurisprudence contrasted sharply with the earlier ideas of Cooley and Tiedeman. Its principles are nowhere better stated than in Justice Holmes's memorable observation:

> "The life of law has not been logic; it has been experience. The felt necessities of the time, the prevalent moral and political theories, institutions of public policy, avowed or unconscious, even the prejudices which judges share with their fellow men, have a good deal more to do than the syllogism in determining the rule by which men should be governed."*

Implied in this view and in sociological jurisprudence generally is the idea that courts owe legislatures substantial deference in evaluating public policy. If a policy was unwise or mistaken, it could be corrected by the people through the elections.

Brandeis's success in *Muller* meant that the Court had accepted state regulation aimed at protecting the health of seemingly vulnerable groups even where such laws also had consequences affecting the liberty of contract. But what about measures that covered all or most working persons and were not limited to hours but included wage prescriptions? Such laws cut much closer to the heart of laissez-faire jurisprudence and its liberty of contract doctrine.

The matter came to the Court in *Bunting v. Oregon* (1917), in which a state's 10-hour day for all workers in manufacturing and time-and-a-half pay for overtime were challenged. A massive Brandeis brief was filed by Felix Frankfurter, then a young protégé of Brandeis, as counsel for the state. (Because he had been associated with the case at an earlier stage, Brandeis, now on the Court, recused himself on its appeal.)

The Court was split over the wage provision and the case was reargued twice before being decided, 6-3, for the state. The majority was persuaded that the overtime pay provision was not primarily a wage regulation but a penalty to discourage overtime and thus to protect workers' health. If a victory for reform, the division on the Court and the majority's reasoning showed that *Lochner,* though not mentioned in the opinion, had not been overruled *sub silentio,* as many had supposed after *Muller.* Decisions in the 1920s would confirm that wage legislation was not yet home free.

Revitalization of the I.C.C.

As the first experiment in federal regulation, the Interstate Commerce Act and its administrative creation the Interstate Commerce Commission, had been less than a complete success. Original shortcomings in the act had been compounded by narrow judicial interpretations of the Commission's powers. After long debate, Congress redrew the Commission's statutory charter in the Hepburn Act of 1906, finally giving it power to revise rates set by carriers and enforce them by its own orders. (Four years later Congress added the power to set rates originally.) The burden of taking an appeal to the courts was shifted from the Commission to the carriers. How much of the Commission's work was reviewable by the courts was left open and thus left to the courts to decide.

---

* Quoted in Morton Keller, *Affairs of State: Public Life in Late Nineteenth Century* America (Cambridge: Belknap Press of Harvard University, 1977), 346.

When that issue came to the Supreme Court, laissez-fairists who expected it to claim wide discretion to second-guess the Commission's decisions on rates were disappointed. In *I.C.C. v. Illinois Central Railroad* (1910), the Court said that it would review the Commission's orders only to see whether they had been properly authorized; it would not review substantive aspects of the Commission's rates. As for the agency's powers, the Court upheld the rate-setting delegation by Congress, both as to revision and original formulation.

By now, many railroads had come to prefer overall federal regulation to myriad state controls. In the Minnesota Rate Cases (1913), several carriers argued that federal regulations were now a bar to state rate setting. But the Court held that Congress had not empowered the I.C.C. to set uniform rates for all railroads; state intrastate regulation was valid so long as it did not conflict with interstate rates overseen by the Commission.

This last issue came up the following year in *Houston East and West Texas Railway v. United States,* otherwise known as the Shreveport Rate Case (p. 282), and led to a new extension of federal power. Several interstate railways had set intrastate per mile rates from Houston and Dallas to cities and towns in east Texas lower than those charged from Shreveport, Louisiana, to the same area. The disparity put shippers from Shreveport at a disadvantage in competing with Texas shippers for the east Texas market. The I.C.C. ruled that the lower intrastate rates burdened interstate commerce and ordered those from Houston and Dallas to be raised. By a 7-2 vote, the Court upheld the order, Justice Hughes observing that the federal commerce power, "complete and paramount," could not be impeded by local rivalries or by actions solely intrastate.

Mobilization for World War

After trying for nearly three years to influence yet stay out of the Great War, the largely stalemated European conflict that came to be called

World War I, the United States finally declared war on Germany in April 1917, allying with Britain and France. Its status as an active belligerent transformed American life. The war was run by Progressives—Wilson in the White House and large majorities drawn from the two major parties in Congress—and Progressive ideals tried to turn the struggle into a mission for democracy. Though war ended domestic reform, the emphasis the Progressives had put on the positive use of federal power proved vital to economic mobilization and final military victory.

Preparing the country and its industrial machine for modern, total war raised familiar constitutional questions: What was the proper balance between national and state authority within the federal system? Between Congress and the president? Between government and private property? Between government and individual liberties? For 50 years, the leading constitutional question had been how might a largely decentralized governmental system with a modest federal establishment deal with a rapidly expanding, rapidly centralizing industrial economy? This question now became one of how might that system harness the mighty economy and allocate vital resources for a great foreign military effort? The Progressives' answer, undoubtedly correct but not without cost, was to shift great power to the federal government and, within it, to the president, giving him and the Executive branch unaccustomed authority over private property and personal liberty.

In the summer of 1916, eight months before American entry, Congress authorized the president to take over the nation's railways in the event of war. When faced with a monstrous rail traffic jam on the East Coast that slowed down the movement of troops and resources during the war, Wilson used the power to take control of the rail net. Later, acting under supplemental Congressional legislation, the executive set rates for both inter- and intrastate shipping for the lines the government actually operated.

The centerpiece of Congressional wartime legislation was the Lever Act of August 1917, passed in the face of impending food and fuel shortages and rising prices. It gave the president power over both the production and distribution of fuel and foodstuffs, including, if needed, the setting of prices and fair trade practices. Debated for two months and strongly opposed by many Republicans and a sprinkling of anti-Wilson Democrats, the act was an unprecedented grant of authority to the executive and an extension of federal power to matters traditionally left to the states. Resting on the federal government's war rather than commerce power, it would have been unthinkable in peacetime.

It was accompanied by other emergency measures. Congress established a military draft with the Selective Service Act, censorship of the mails and radio and cable communications in the Trading with the Enemy Act, authorized takeover of telephone and telegraph lines, and in the War Prohibition Act (passed 10 days after the Armistice) barred manufacture and sale of alcoholic liquors. Made illegal were various activities deemed obstructive to the war effort in the Espionage Act and antiwar speech in the Sedition Act. In the Overman Act of May 1918, Congress authorized the president to coordinate and consolidate executive agencies for more efficient prosecution of the war, thus allowing him to all but rearrange the Executive branch.

Since the president alone could not personally exercise the myriad of powers Congress had delegated, a wide range of bureaus, commissions, boards, and other government entities was set up. This federal bureaucracy was largely temporary but it marked an acceptance of a larger federal role in economic life and prepared the country for even greater federal and executive responsibilities in later national emergencies.

Likening Wilson's great powers to those of Lincoln during the Civil War can be misleading. Lincoln faced an internal conflict for which there was no constitutional precedent. In the first months of the war he acted without Congressional authorization. Even later, in issuance of the Emancipation Proclamation, for example, he executed policies in many constitution-

ally gray areas, without supporting or empowering Congressional action. Wilson's "dictatorship" was authorized by Congress, which had also formally declared war. Powers delegated to Wilson far exceeded those Lincoln had. No president before had ever been ceded so much legislative authority. Dominated by Progressives, Wilson's Congress was sanguine about the use of federal and executive authority; Lincoln's, though firmly in the hands of his own party, was far less so.

The role of the Supreme Court was muted as it had been during the Civil War and as it would be in every other major war. The most important war measures never came before the Court or did so well after the war was over. One important exception was the military draft, which the Court upheld in The Selective Draft Law cases, in January 1918, on Congress's Article I-8 authority to "raise and support armies."

In *Northern Pacific Railway v. North Dakota* (1919) after the war, the Court sustained the power given the president to seize and operate railroads against a claim that it could not include rate setting for intrastate lines. Chief Justice White wrote that federal war powers could constitutionally preempt intrastate controls that would be binding in peacetime. In *Dakota Central Telephone v. South Dakota* (1919), it sustained government takeover of telephone and telegraph lines, citing the war powers.

The constitutionality of the Lever Act did not come before the Court until 1921. In *United States v. L. Cohen Grocery Co.*, a price-fixing section of it was held invalid, not because the government lacked such power during wartime, but because Congress had not established clear standards for determining which prices set by businesses were reasonable and which were not.

In all, the Court was approving. It did not stand in the way of the greatest shift of constitutional powers, albeit temporary, in the nation's history. The actions of Congress, the president, and the Court allowed a historically decentralized constitutional system and a private economy to mobilize for a great centralized public effort. It required no formal change in the constitutional structure. The war powers of the Constitution were asserted and, as temporary measures, sustained in their writ and found adequate to their task.

There were costs according to one's view. Laissez-fairists would never feel the economy was quite free again. Proponents of dual federalism would not see the federal system as in balance again. In the face of restrictions on speech and publication that the Court upheld in decisions immediately after the war, civil libertarians would see much of the wartime experience as repressive. For better or worse, the growth of central power within the federal system and of government intervention in the economy would be important continuing trends in American constitutional life. Concerns about wartime civil liberties would be renewed during World War II, but the earlier curtailment did not prove part of a lasting suppression. On the contrary, the Supreme Court soon began to develop principles for an expansive reading of the Bill of Rights.

Return to "Normalcy"

American disillusionment with the Treaty of Versailles that formally ended the war and defeat of its League covenant in the Senate marked the end of an era. Wilson, exhausted from campaigning for the treaty, suffered a stroke in October 1919 that left him partly paralyzed and largely ineffective the rest of his term. Much of the country now seemed weary from the two decades of crusading zeal at home and abroad that had commandeered its attention and resources. Politically, it was ready to change directions. With women voting for the first time in 1920, the handsome, genial, but limited Republican Warren G. Harding was elected president in a landslide. His campaign statement that what America needed was "not heroics but healing, not nostrums but normalcy," seemed to capture the mood of the time.

In many ways the 1920s were anything but normal. They brought a new sexual freedom and re-

action against established cultural authority. It was the golden age of sports and of the enormous popularity of movies and radio, which made mass entertainment a compelling cultural force. The mass-produced, inexpensive automobile offered a unique physical mobility and independence. The misplaced moralism of Prohibition became a boon for organized crime, which thoughtfully supplied Americans with the very commodity they had just outlawed. The "roaring" decade was populated with any number of exciting, gaudy figures.

The Twenties were a return to industrial expansion and the production of wealth at yet higher levels. The result was an unrivaled prosperity in which the United States achieved the highest standard of living the world had known. The popular Calvin Coolidge, who succeeded Harding as president, seemed to have it right in declaring that "The business of America is business!" Many believed that productivity, aided by the science of management and ever-new technology, could eventually end poverty itself.

There was certainly room for optimism. Employment was high and wages were rising after years of stagnation. Many companies shortened the work week to five days and several introduced annual paid vacations. Productivity gains were impressive. By middecade, the Ford assembly line in Detroit was turning out new cars at the rate of 360 an hour. Output no less extraordinary could be found in many other industries. The business leader was lionized as the voice of economic wisdom and the herald of a new age. As for government, much of the public expected that its role would be supportive and not interfering. In general, all three branches did their best to oblige.

The good times came to a crashing end with the stock market's precipitous fall in October 1929, leading to the deepest and most prolonged depression in history. The material gains of the decade had been real enough, but they masked grave weaknesses and deficiencies in the economic system. The uncritical probusiness optimism of the Twenties proved to be as myopic and naive as some of the reforming zeal of the Progressive period.

Taft and His Court

When Chief Justice White died in 1921, William Howard Taft was appointed his successor. The former president, who as an incumbent had suffered a crushing rejection in the 1912 election, running third behind Wilson and Roosevelt and carrying but two states, had lobbied hard for the job. It was, he confided to friends, the only one he ever really wanted. Never happy as president, Taft would find that now, at 64, his best days as a public servant were still ahead.

Though the Court he joined had on it two intellectually unconventional figures, Holmes and Brandeis, the other justices, including two Taft had appointed, shared his economic conservatism. The new chief later used his influence with Harding and Coolidge to advise on the selection of four new justices during the 1920s: George Sutherland, Pierce Butler, Edward Sanford, and Harlan Stone, virtually hand-picking Butler and Sutherland. He was disappointed only with Stone, a former law dean and a conservative, who soon began voting with Holmes and Brandeis.

Taft proved an effective leader. Naturally affable, most who knew him liked working with him. With Justice Willis Van Devanter, who wrote few

opinions, acting as a kind of foreman, the work of the Court moved along with unusual efficiency. Even Holmes and Brandeis, who often disagreed with Taft, acknowledged the chief's skill. How could someone who was so bad as president be so good as chief justice, Brandeis once asked his friend Felix Frankfurter.

Taft offered leadership off the Court as well. He lobbied successfully for more federal judges and for streamlining procedures in the federal courts. In 1925, he got Congress to pass the "Judges Bill," giving the Court full control of its docket. Until 1891, cases the Court heard depended largely by the initiative of litigants. Though the Court had then been given authority by Congress to review certain kinds of cases through the discretionary writ of certiorari, many from lower appellate courts continued to be reviewable by right of the parties. The Judges Bill meant that cases coming before the Court would be only those it chose to hear. This relieved congestion in the docket and allowed the Court to avoid many less important appeals. Taft also persuaded Congress to appropriate money for a new Supreme Court building, the "Marble Palace" it now occupies across from the Capitol, though construction was not finished until after his death.

The constitutional jurisprudence of the Taft Court was undeniably conservative despite the

This chamber in the U.S. capitol served as the courtroom of the Supreme Court from 1860 to 1935 after which the Court moved into its present imposing permanent home, the U.S. Supreme Court building across the street from the Capitol.

occasional moderating efforts of Holmes, Brandeis, and Stone. Though many reform measures were upheld, the Court's majority used the doctrinal tools of substantive due process, liberty of contract, and dual federalism to protect business and property from labor insurgency and government intervention.

No Again to Child Labor Reform

After the Child Labor Act was struck down in *Hammer v. Dagerhart,* Congress renewed its attack, using a different constitutional strategy. Eight months after the Court's decision, it passed the second Child Labor Act, imposing a 10 percent tax on the net profits of any company employing children. The measure, obviously meant to end child labor rather than raise revenue—had it done the latter, it would have been a policy failure—seemed on safe ground since the Court had upheld police use of the federal taxing power in the Oleomargarine Case, *McCray v. United States.*

But it met with near-unanimous opposition from the Court in *Bailey v. Drexel Furniture Co.* (1922) (p. 247), with even Holmes and Brandeis joining the majority. Taft rooted his opinion for the Court firmly in the principles of dual federalism: Where Congress taxed to penalize rather than raise revenue, it invaded powers reserved to the states under the Tenth Amendment. As for *McCray* and the federal police power cases, they had dealt with only "incidental" restraints, Taft said. The justices were clearly irked by the law's loose draftsmanship and transparent attempt to effect an ulterior social purpose. However worthy that end might be, responsibility for it was that of the states, Taft said. He ignored the fact that nowhere in the Constitution is it stated or implied that federal taxes are confined to raising revenue or are limited by the Tenth Amendment.

Despite this second defeat, the child labor issue remained critical. In 1924, Congress approved and sent to the states a Constitutional amendment that would give it power "to limit, regulate, and prohibit the labor of persons un-

der 18 years of age." Because of well-organized opposition from vested economic interests and from certain religious and states rights groups, the amendment moved slowly through the state legislatures. By the end of the decade, more states had rejected than ratified. Though states had police authority to regulate or end child labor, many had found the power politically difficult to use because such regulation could place local businesses at a disadvantage against competitors in states not regulating.

The amendment gained new support in the changed political and economic environment of the 1930s. By the end of that decade, 28 states had ratified, still eight short of the three-quarters needed. In 1941, the Court made the amendment unnecessary by overruling *Hammer v. Dagenhart* in *United States v. Darby Lumber Co.* For a quarter century between the two cases, a constitutional limbo bounded by state failure to regulate and the Court's federal disempowerment allowed child exploitation to continue despite large majorities in Congress that had tried three times to end it.

Liberty of Contract Renascent

A year after *Bailey,* the Court, taking up the issue of minimum wages, handed down one of its most striking laissez-faire decisions. At issue was a federal law setting minimum pay for women working in the District of Columbia. Its stated purpose was the protection of women's health and morals from poor living conditions caused by inadequate wages. Because the Court had earlier accepted a work-hour law that included an overtime pay provision in *Bunting v. Oregon,* it was widely thought it would go one step further and sustain the federal law. But in *Adkins v. Children's Hospital* (p. 289), Justice Sutherland, who was now becoming the intellectual leader of the most conservative justices, explained why the Court would not, in a classic statement of liberty of contract.

Wages, Sutherland said, were basic to the employment contract and must be determined by the marketplace not government fiat. Here the law forbade two competent parties "to freely contract with one another in respect to the price for which one shall render service to the other in a purely private employment where both are willing, perhaps anxious to agree." Freedom of contract was the general rule, restraint the exception, and the economic inequality of women did not create such an exception. In any case, Sutherland said, it would be unfair to place a remedial burden that belongs to "society as a whole" solely on the shoulders of employers. That higher minimum wage costs could in most cases be passed on to society as a whole, was ignored.

In revitalizing liberty of contract, *Adkins* dampened reform until well into the 1930s. It became one of the most cited of the Court's decisions until overruled in *West Coast Hotel v. Parrish,* in 1937, a case that signaled the beginning of the end of the Court's conflict with the New Deal. The effect of *Adkins* was particularly severe in the states. Many of the 115 state laws found unconstitutional by the Taft Court after Adkins were struck down as violating liberty of contract.

One of the more definitive of these rulings came in *Wolff Packing Co. v. Kansas Court of Industrial Relations* (1923) in which the Court reined in the "public interest" doctrine. Following a costly coal strike, Kansas had passed the Industrial Relations Act, requiring compulsory arbitration of all labor disputes in the food, clothing, fuel, and certain other industries declared to be affected with the public interest. The innovative enactment, unpopular with business and labor, set up a special court to hear the disputes and gave it power to restrict strikes and employer lockouts and, if needed, to set wages and work conditions.

The Court unanimously found the scheme to violate liberty of contract. Taft confined the public interest doctrine, which ran back to *Munn v. Illinois,* to common carriers, utilities and other publicly conferred monopolies, and to a handful of other businesses such as inns, historically thought to be affected with the public interest. The class could not be expanded by legislative declaration.

Though the decision appeared reasonable enough on the surface, the Court again paid little heed to the complex, integrated nature of the nation's modern economy. Applying standards better suited to an earlier day, it ignored a principle many observers thought commonplace after the war experience, that all basic economic activity affected the public interest. For them, the check on government regulation, absent a clearly stated constitutional limit, lay in politics rather than in a rigidly applied substantive doctrine read into the Constitution by the Court itself.

Protecting Against Labor Insurgency

The Court's probusiness activism had its reciprocal in a strong antilabor bias. With passage of the Clayton Act in 1913, labor leaders thought they had won protection from having the Sherman Act, intended to break up trusts, applied to unions. An important provision barred federal courts from issuing injunctions against picketing unless needed to prevent "an irreparable injury to property." They did not reckon on the Court giving this shield the narrowest possible reading. In *Duplex Printing Press v. Deering* (1921), in which New York unions had boycotted products of a Michigan company whose workers were on strike, the Court held the Clayton Act's anti-injunction provision protected only immediate parties to a suit not those in secondary boycotts. And in *American Steel Founderies v. Tri-City Trades Council,* decided the same year and one of Taft's first opinions, the Court held that even otherwise peaceful picketing could be intimidating and thus enjoinable.

In *Truax v. Corrigan* (1921), Taft held against an Arizona law that barred state courts from issuing injunctions to stop peaceful picketing. A union had picketed a restaurant, causing its business to drop by half. By removing the legal remedy of injunction, Taft said, the law deprived the business owner of a property right and thus violated due process. By singling out disputes between employer and employees, it also violated equal protection of the laws.

Later, applying a double standard, the Court turned a small, local strike—a few union stonecutters had refused to work on limestone cut by nonunion workers—into a secondary boycott burdening interstate commerce and justifying an injunction. The holding in *Bedford Cut Stone Co. v. Journeymen Stone Cutters Association* (1927) was out of keeping with the Court's prevailing theory dating to the Sugar Trust Case that all production was local and thus not part of interstate commerce. It was not until the Norris-LaGuardia Act of 1932, enacted during the Depression, that Congress removed from the courts power to enjoin peaceful strikes, picketing, and secondary boycotts.

*Property Versus Property:
Regulation of Land Use*

Growing urbanization and the congestion caused by rapid development in many areas created new constitutional issues in the public regulation of real property, sometimes setting one set of ownership rights against another. In Pennsylvania mining areas, coal companies often sold surface rights to land holdings, retaining the option to continue mining below. As streets and buildings came to be built on such holdings, surface owners, fearing collapse if mining continued, got the state to limit extraction under the improved areas. In *Pennsylvania Coal Co. v. Mahon* (1922), one of the Taft Court's landmark decisions, a company contended the regulation was a "taking" in violation of the Fifth Amendment's provision that private property could not "be taken for public use without just compensation." (Earlier, in *Chicago, Burlington & Quincy Railroad v. Chicago* (1897) the Court had held this part of the Amendment applicable to the states through the due process clause of the Fourteenth Amendment).

The Court agreed, Holmes holding that the shield of the takings clause was not limited to cases of physical intrusion or seizure by eminent domain. If regulation went "too far," the clause protected against loss of a right to use property or being put to higher costs for its use. Such loss of value called for just compensation from the government. The purpose of the takings clause, Holmes explained, was to keep the financial burdens imposed by a public policy from falling solely on an individual property owner and have them shared by the entire public.

The Court took a different view of zoning laws. Many cities and towns, finding historic nuisance law inadequate, enacted zoning regulations to control land use and development. In *Euclid v. Ambler Realty Co.* (1926), the Court upheld an ordinance that set out residential and commercial districts each with its own construction requirements. The regulation was a protection of the health, safety, and morals of the community, thus not a "taking." The majority apparently believed, as did many proponents of zoning, that such laws could increase land values by stabilizing use. If so, the decision was not as unfriendly to property rights as it might otherwise seem. In contrast to the takings decisions, it was a case of sustaining benefits to the many from burdens on a few.

For many Americans the Twenties were good times. The nation seemed carefree, entertained, and untroubled by foreign involvement. Prosperity was undeniable. Under these circumstances, the constitutional jurisprudence of the Taft Court, partly reviving the laissez-faire activism of the late nineteenth century, was never tested and found wanting as such review would be when bad times followed in the 1930s. A constitutional innocence could still reign with its stubborn belief at least in peacetime, that a decentralized, narrowly limited government of the past was sufficient public authority for the present and future. In rationalizing protection of large, powerful, impersonal economic interests, many justices spoke as though they were ruling on the property rights of beset individuals. They embraced a judicial activism that betrayed lack of trust in the wisdom of elected representatives and the efficacy of the ballot box and other political avenues to correct abuses and mistakes.

Like its postbellum predecessors, the Taft Court failed to fully appreciate qualitative changes that rapid, continued expansion and a giant industrial economy had wrought, that not all of these were positive, and that some of the social costs they imposed could be met only by remedial public action. The Taft Court was not reactionary, but neither was it perspicacious. Its constitutional policies did not cause the Depression that followed, but neither did they do much that would have helped avoid it. Instead, its jurisprudence made resistance to the reform efforts of the New Deal easier.

FURTHER READING

Laissez-Faire Constitutionalism and Industrial Capitalism

Berk, Gerald, Alternative Tracks: *The Constitution of American Industrial Order, 1865–1917* (1994)

Beth, Loren P., *The Development of the American Constitution, 1877–1917* (1971)

Cortner, Richard C., *The Iron Horse and the Constitution: The Railroads and the Transformation of the Fourteenth Amendment* (1993)

Ely, John Hart Jr, *The Chief Justiceship of Melville W. Fuller, 1888–1910* (1995)

Fiss, Owen M., *History of the Supreme Court of the United States, vol 8, Troubled Beginnings of the Modern State, 1888–1910* (1993)

Furer, Howard B., *The Fuller Court: 1888–1910* (1986)

Goodwyn, Lawrence, *Democratic Promise: The Populist Movement in America* (1976)

Kazin, Michael, *The Populist Persuasion: An American History* (1995)

Keller, Morton, *Affairs of State: Public Life in Late 19th Century America* (1977)

———, *Regulating a New Economy: Public Policy and Economic Change in America, 1900–1933*

Libecap, Gary D., *The Regulated Economy* (1994)

McCloskey, Robert G., *American Conservatism in the Age of Enterprise, 1865–1910* (1951)

Nelson, William E., *The Roots of American Bureaucracy, 1830–1900* (1982)

Ritter, Gretchen, *Goldbugs and Greenbacks: The Anti-Monopoly Tradition and the Politics of Politics of Finance in America, 1865–1896* (1997)

Robbins, William G., *Colony and Empire: The Capitalist Transformation of the American West* (1994)

Semonche, John E., *Charting the Future: The Supreme Court Responds to a Changing Society* (1978)

Skowronek, Stephen, *Building a New American State: The Expansion of National Administrative Capacity, 1877–1920* (1982)

Steeples, Douglas and David O. Whitten, *Democracy in Desparation: The Depression of 1893* (1998)

Stover, John F., *American Railroads,* 2nd ed. (1998)

Twiss, Benjamin R., *Lawyers and the Constitution: How Laissez Faire Come to the Supreme Court* (1942)

Wiebe, Robert H., *The Search for Order, 1877–1920* (1966)

Progressivism and Reform

Bickel, Alexander M. and Benno C. Schmidt, Jr., *History of the Supreme Court of the United States, vol 9, The Judiciary and Responsible Government, 1910–1921* (1984)

Eisenach, Eldon, *The Lost Promise of Progressivism* (1994)

Gillman, Howard, *The Constitution Besieged: The Rise and Demise of Lochner Era Police Powers Jurisprudence* (1993)

Hamm, Richard F., *Shaping the Eighteenth Amendment: Temperance Reform, Legal Culture and the Polity. 1880–1920* (1995)

Hoebeke, C. H., *The Road to Mass Democracy: Original Intent and the Seventeenth Amendment* (1995)

Hofstadter, Richard, *The Age of Reform: From Bryan to F.D.R.* (1955)

Kahn, Jonathan, *Budgeting Democracy: State Building and Citizenship in America, 1890–1928* (1997)

Keller, Morton, *Regulating a New Society: Public Policy and Social Change in America, 1900–1933* (1994)

Langum, David J., *Crossing over the Line: Legislating Morality and the Mann Act* (1994)

Milkis, Sidney M. and Jerome Mileur, eds., *Progressivism and the New Democracy* (1999)

Paulson, Ross Evans, *Liberty, Equality, and Justice: Civil Rights, Women's Rights, and the Regulation of Business, 1865–1932* (1997)

Pegram, Thomas R., *Battling Demon Rum: The Struggle for a Dry America, 1800–1933* (1988)

Purcell, Edward A., *Brandeis and the Progressive Constitution* (2000)

Rohr, John A., *To Run a Constitution: The Legitimacy of the Administrative State* (1986)

Ross, William G., *A Muted Fury: Populists, Progressives, and Labor Unions Confront the Courts, 1890–1937* (1993)

Sklar, Martin J., *The United States as a Developing Country: Studies in United States History in the Progressive Era and the 1920s* (1992)

Stid, Daniel, *The President as Statesman: Woodrow Wilson and the Constitution* (1998)

West, Robin, *Progressive Constitutionalism: Reconstructing the Fourteenth Amendment* (1994)

Wood, Stephen B., *Constitutional Politics in the Progressive Era: Child Labor and the Law* (1968)

The Taft Court and Return to 'Normalcy'

Burton, David H., *Taft, Holmes, and the 1920s Court* (1998)

Danelski, David J., *A Supreme Court Justice Is Appointed* (1964)

Kyvig, David E., *Repealing National Prohibition* (1979)

Shaffer, Buitler, *In Restraint of Trade: The Business Campaign Against Competition, 1918–1933* (1997)

Biographical

Fairman, Charles, *Mr. Justice Miller and the Supreme Court, 1862–1890* (1939)

Kens, Paul, *Justice Stephen Field: Shaping American Liberty from the Gold Rush to the Gilded Age* (1997)

King, Willard L., *Melville Weston Fuller: Chief Justice of the United States, 1888–1910* (1950)

Mason, Alpheus T., *William Howard Taft: Chief Justice* (1965)

McGrath, C. Peter, *Morrison R. Waite: The Triumph of Character* (1963)

Strum, Philippa, *Brandeis: Beyond Progressivism* (1993)

Swindler, William F., *Court and Constitution in the 20th Century: The Old Loyalty, 1889–1932* (1969)

Swisher, Carl B., *Stephen Field: Craftsman of the Law* (1930)

Stid, Daniel D., *The President as Statesman: Woodrow Wilson and the Constitution* (1998)

Urofsky, Melvin, *Louis D. Brandeis and the Progressive Tradition* (1981)

White, G. Edward, *Justice Oliver Wendell Holmes: Law and the Inner Self* (1993)

On Leading Cases

Kens, Paul, *Judicial Power and Reform Politics: The Anatomy of* Lochner v. New York (1990)

———, *Lochner v. New York: Economic Regulation on Trial* (1998)

Papke, David R., *The Pullman Case: The Clash of Labor and Capital in America* (1999)

CASES

The Slaughterhouse Cases

83 U.S. 36 (1873), 5-4
Opinion of the Court: Miller (Clifford, Davis, Hunt, Strong)
Dissenting: Bradley, Chase, Field, Swayne
Who has the stronger argument, Miller or the dissenters, with regard to the original purpose of the Fourteenth Amendment? The meaning it has come to have? Whose argument gives greater strength to the amendment? Whose is likely to have greater effect on economic development and why? What is the difference between privileges and immunities of national citizenship and those of state citizenship, according to Miller? To Field? Would Miller have interpreted the privileges and immunities clause of the Amendment differently had the case dealt with rights of a former slave? Would Bradley or Field? Would the dissenters make the Bill of Rights applicable to the states?

Miller, for the Court:

This statute is denounced not only as creating a monopoly and conferring odious and exclusive privileges upon a small number of persons at the expense of the great body of the community of New Orleans, but it is asserted that it deprives a large and meritorious class of citizens—the whole of the butchers of the city—of the right to exercise their trade, the business to which they have been trained and on which they depend for the support of themselves and their families, and that the unrestricted exercise of the business of butchering is necessary to the daily subsistence of the population of the city.

But a critical examination of the act hardly justifies these assertions.

It is true that it grants, for a period of twenty-five years, exclusive privileges. And whether those privileges are at the expense of the community in the sense of a curtailment of any of their fundamental rights, or even in the sense of doing them an injury, is a question open to considerations to be hereafter stated. But it is not true that it deprives the butchers of the right to exercise their trade, or imposes upon them any restriction incompatible with its successful pursuit . . .

The wisdom of the monopoly granted by the legislature may be open to question, but it is difficult to see a justification for the assertion that the butchers are deprived of the right to labor in their occupation, or the people of their daily service in preparing food . . .

It cannot be denied that the statute under consideration is aptly framed to remove from the more densely populated part of the city, the noxious slaughter-houses, and large and offensive collections of animals necessarily incident to the slaughtering business of a large city, and to locate them where the convenience, health, and comfort of the people require they shall be located. And it must be conceded that the means adopted by the act for this purpose are appropriate, are stringent, and effectual. But it is said that in creating a corporation for this purpose, and conferring upon it exclusive privileges—privileges which it is said constitute a monopoly—the legislature has exceeded its power . . .

The plaintiffs accepting this issue, allege that the statute is a violation of the Constitution of the United States in these several particulars: . . .

That it abridges the privileges and immunities of citizens of the United States;

That it denies to the plaintiffs the equal protection of the laws; and,

That it deprives them of their property without due process of law; contrary to the provisions of the first section of the fourteenth article of amendment.

This court is thus called upon for the first time to give construction to these articles . . .

The most cursory glance at these articles discloses a unity of purpose, when taken in connection with the history of the times, which cannot fail to have an important bearing on any question of doubt concerning their true meaning . . .

In [the Civil War] slavery, as a legalized social relation, perished. It perished as a necessity of the bitterness and force of the conflict. When the armies of freedom found themselves upon the soil of slavery they could do nothing less than free the poor victims whose enforced servitude was the foundation of the quarrel . . . . The proclamation of President Lincoln expressed an accomplished fact as to a large portion of the insurrectionary districts, when he declared slavery abolished in them all. But the war being over, those who had succeeded in re-establishing the authority of the Federal government were not content to permit this great act of emancipation to rest on the actual results of the contest or the proclamation of the

Executive . . . and they determined to place this main and most valuable result in the Constitution of the restored Union as one of its fundamental articles . . .

We do not say that no one else but the negro can share in this protection. Both the language and spirit of these articles are to have their fair and just weight in any question of construction. Undoubtedly while negro slavery alone was in the mind of the Congress which proposed the thirteenth article, it forbids any other kind of slavery, now or hereafter. If Mexican peonage or the Chinese coolie labor system shall develop slavery of the Mexican or Chinese race within our territory, this amendment may safely be trusted to make it void. And so if other rights are assailed by the States which properly and necessarily fall within the protection of these articles, that protection will apply, though the party interested may not be of African descent. But what we do say, and what we wish to be understood is, that in any fair and just construction of any section or phrase of these amendments, it is necessary to look to the purpose which we have said was the pervading spirit of them all, the evil which they were designed to remedy, and the process of continued addition to the Constitution, until that purpose was supposed to be accomplished, as far as constitutional law can accomplish it.

The first section of the fourteenth article, to which our attention is more specially invited, opens with a definition of citizenship—not only citizenship of the United States, but citizenship of the States. No such definition was previously found in the Constitution, nor had any attempt been made to define it by act of Congress . . . But it had been held by this court, in the celebrated Dred Scott case, only a few years before the outbreak of the civil war, that a man of African descent, whether a slave or not, was not and could not be a citizen of a State or of the United States. This decision, while it met the condemnation of some of the ablest statesmen and constitutional lawyers of the country, had never been overruled; and if it was to be accepted as a constitutional limitation of the right of citizenship, then all the negro race who had recently been made freemen, were still, not only not citizens, but were incapable of becoming so by anything short of an amendment to the Constitution.

To remove this difficulty primarily, and to establish a clear and comprehensive definition of citizenship which should declare what should constitute citizenship of the United States, and also citizenship of a State, the first clause of the first section was framed.

'All persons born or naturalized in the United States, and subject to the jurisdiction thereof, are citizens of the United States and of the State wherein they reside.'

The first observation we have to make on this clause is, that it puts at rest both the questions which we stated to have been the subject of differences of opinion. It declares that persons may be citizens of the United States without regard to their citizenship of a particular State, and it overturns the Dred Scott decision by making all persons born within the United States and subject to its jurisdiction citizens of the United States. That its main purpose was to establish the citizenship of the negro can admit of no doubt . . .

The next observation is more important in view of the arguments of counsel in the present case. It is, that the distinction between citizenship of the United States and citizenship of a State is clearly recognized and established. Not only may a man be a citizen of the United States without being a citizen of a State, but an important element is necessary to convert the former into the latter. He must reside within the State to make him a citizen of it, but it is only necessary that he should be born or naturalized in the United States to be a citizen of the Union.

It is quite clear, then, that there is a citizenship of the United States, and a citizenship of a State, which are distinct from each other, and which depend upon different characteristics or circumstances in the individual . . .

[T]he next paragraph of this same section . . . speaks only of privileges and immunities of citizens of the United States, and does not speak of those of citizens of the several States . . .

The language is, 'No State shall make or enforce any law which shall abridge the privileges or immunities of citizens of the United States.' It is a little remarkable, if this clause was intended as a protection to the citizen of a State against the legislative power of his own State, that the word citizen of the State should be left out when it is so carefully used, and used in contradistinction to citizens of the United States, in the very sentence which precedes it . . . [T]he change in phraseology was adopted understandingly and with a purpose.

Of the privileges and immunities of the citizen of the United States, and of the privileges and immunities of the citizen of the State, and what they respectively are, we will presently consider; but we wish to state here that it is only the former which are placed by this clause under the protection of the Federal Constitution, and that the latter, whatever they may be, are not intended to have any additional protection by this paragraph of the amendment.

If, then, there is a difference between the privileges and immunities belonging to a citizen of the United States as such, and those belonging to the citizen of the State as such the latter must rest for their security and protection where they have heretofore rested; for they are not embraced by this paragraph of the amendment . . .

[U]p to the adoption of the recent amendments, no claim or pretense was set up that . . . rights [of state citizenship] depended on the Federal government for their existence or protection, beyond the very few express limitations which the Federal Constitution imposed upon the States—such, for instance, as the prohibition against ex post facto laws, bills of attainder, and laws impairing the obligation of contracts. But with the exception of these and a few other restrictions, the entire domain of the privileges and immunities of citizens of the States . . . lay within the constitutional and legislative power of the States, and without that of the Federal government. Was it the purpose of the fourteenth amendment, by the simple declaration that no State should make or enforce any law which shall abridge the privileges and immunities of citizens of the United States, to transfer the security and protection of all the civil rights which we have mentioned, from the States to the Federal government? And where it is declared that Congress shall have the power to enforce that article, was it intended to bring within the power of Congress the entire domain of civil rights heretofore belonging exclusively to the States? . . .

We are convinced that no such results were intended by the Congress which proposed these amendments, nor by the legislatures of the States which ratified them.

Having shown that the privileges and immunities relied on in the argument are those which belong to citizens of the States as such, and that they are left to the State governments for security and protection, and not by this article placed under the special care of the Federal government, we may hold ourselves excused from defining the privileges and immunities of citizens of the United States which no State can abridge, until some case involving those privileges may make it necessary to do so.

But lest it should be said that no such privileges and immunities are to be found if those we have been considering are excluded, we venture to suggest some which own their existence to the Federal government, its National character, its Constitution, or its laws.

One of these is well described in the case of *Crandall v. Nevada*. It is said to be the right of the citizen of this great country, protected by implied guarantees of its constitution, 'to come to the seat of government to assert any claim he may have upon that government, to transact any business he may have with it, to seek its protection, to share its offices, to engage in administering its functions. He has the right of free access to its seaports, through which all operations of foreign commerce are conducted, to the sub-treasuries, land offices, and courts of justice in the several States.' . . .

Another privilege of a citizen of the United States is to demand the care and protection of the Federal government over his life, liberty, and property when on the high seas or within the jurisdiction of a foreign government. Of this there can be no doubt, nor that the right depends upon his character as a citizen of the United States. The right to peaceably assemble and petition for redress of grievances, the privilege of the writ of habeas corpus, are rights of the citizen guaranteed by the Federal Constitution. The right to use the navigable waters of the United States, however they may penetrate the territory of the several States, all rights secured to our citizens by treaties with foreign nations, are dependent upon citizenship of the United States, and not citizenship of a State. . . .

The argument has not been much pressed in these cases that the defendant's charter deprives the plaintiffs of their property without due process of law, or that it denies to them the equal protection of the law. The first of these [protections] has been in the Constitution since the adoption of the fifth amendment, as a restraint upon the Federal power. It is also to be found in some form of expression in the constitutions of nearly all the States, as a restraint upon the power of the States . . .

We are not without judicial interpretation . . . both State and National, of the meaning of this clause . . . [U]nder no construction of that provision . . . can the restraint imposed by the State of Louisiana upon the exercise of their trade by the butchers of New Orleans be held to be a deprivation of property within the meaning of that provision.

'Nor shall any State deny to any person within its jurisdiction the equal protection of the laws.'

In the light of the history of these amendments, and the pervading purpose of them, which we have already discussed, it is not difficult to give a meaning to this clause. The existence of laws in the States where the newly emancipated negroes resided, which discriminated with gross injustice and hardship against them as a class, was the evil to be remedied by this clause, and by it such laws are forbidden . . .

We doubt very much whether any action of a State not directed by way of discrimination against the negroes as a class, or on account of their race, will ever be held to come within the purview of this provision. It is so clearly a provision for that race and that emergency, that a strong case would be necessary for its application to any other . . .

[W]e do not see in [the Thirteenth, Fourteenth, and Fifteenth] Amendments any purpose to destroy the main features of the general system. Under the pressure of all the excited feeling growing out of the war, our statesmen have still believed that the existence of the State with powers for domestic and local government, including the regulation of civil rights— the rights of person and of property—was essential to the perfect working of our complex form of government, though they have thought proper to impose additional limitations on the States, and to confer additional power on that of the Nation . . .

The judgments of the Supreme Court of Louisiana in these cases are Affirmed.

Field (Bradley, Clark, Swayne), dissenting:

The question presented is, therefore, one of the gravest importance, not merely to the parties here, but to the whole country. It is nothing less than the question whether the recent amendments to the Federal Constitution protect the citizens of the United States against the deprivation of their common rights by State legislation . . . [T]he Fourteenth Amendment does afford such protection, and was so intended by the Congress which framed and the States which adopted it. . .

The first clause of this amendment determines who are citizens of the United States, and how their citizenship is created. Before its enactment there was much diversity of opinion among jurists and statesmen whether there was any such citizenship independent of that of the State, and, if any existed, as to the manner in which it originated. With a great number the opinion prevailed that there was no such citizenship independent of the citizenship of the State . . .

The first clause of the fourteenth amendment changes this whole subject, and removes it from the region of discussion and doubt. It recognizes in express terms, if it does not create, citizens of the United States, and it makes their citizenship dependent upon the place of their birth, or the fact of their adoption, and not upon the constitution or laws of any State or the condition of their ancestry. A citizen of a State is now only a citizen of the United States residing in that State. The fundamental rights, privileges, and immunities which belong to him as a free man and a free citizen, now belong to him as a citizen of the United States, and are not dependent upon his citizenship of any State. The exercise of these rights and privileges, and the degree of enjoyment received from such exercise, are always more or less affected by the condition and the local institutions of the State, or city, or town where he resides. They are thus affected in a State by the wisdom of its laws, the ability of its officers, the efficiency of its magistrates, the education and morals of its people, and by many other considerations. This is a result which follows from the constitution of society, and can never be avoided, but in no other way can they be affected by the action of the State, or by the residence of the citizen therein. They do not derive their existence from its legislation, and cannot be destroyed by its power.

The amendment does not attempt to confer any new privileges or immunities upon citizens, or to enumerate or define those already existing. It assumes that there are such privileges and immunities which belong of right to citizens as such, and ordains that they shall not be abridged by State legislation. If this inhibition has no reference to privileges and immunities of this character, but only refers . . . to such privileges and immunities as were before its adoption specially designated in the Constitution or necessarily implied as belonging to citizens of the United States, it was a vain and idle enactment, which accomplished nothing, and most unnecessarily excited Congress and the people on its passage. With privileges and immunities thus designated or implied no State could ever have interfered by its laws, and no new constitutional provision was required to inhibit such interference. The supremacy of the Constitution and the laws of the United States always controlled any State legislation of that character. But if the amendment refers to the natural and inalienable rights which belong to all citizens, the inhibition has a profound significance and consequence.

What, then, are the privileges and immunities which are secured against abridgment by State legislation?

In the first section of the Civil Rights Act Congress has given its interpretation to these terms, or at least has stated some of the rights which, in its judgment, these terms include; it has there declared that they include the right 'to make and enforce contracts, to sue, be parties and give evidence, to inherit, purchase, lease, sell, hold, and convey real and personal property, and to full and equal benefit of all laws and proceedings for the security of person and property.' That act, it is true, was passed before the Fourteenth Amendment, but the amendment was adopted . . . to obviate objections to the act, or . . . objections to legislation of a similar character, extending the protection of the National government over the common rights of all citizens of the United States. Accordingly, after its ratification, Congress re-enacted the act under the belief that whatever doubts may have previously existed of its validity, they were removed by the amendment.

The terms, privileges and immunities, are not new in the amendment; they were in the Constitution before the amendment was adopted. They are found in the second section of the fourth article, which declares that 'the citizens of each State shall be entitled to all privileges and immunities of citizens in the several States,' . . .

What the clause in question did for the protection of the citizens of one State against hostile and discriminating legislation of other States, the fourteenth amendment does for the protection of every citizen of the United States against hostile and discriminating legislation against him in favor of others, whether they reside in the same or in different States. If under the fourth article of the Constitution equality of privileges and immunities is secured between citizens of different States, under the Fourteenth Amendment the same equality is secured between citizens of the United States . . .

The Fourteenth Amendment places them under the guardianship of the National authority. All monopolies in any known trade or manufacture are an invasion of these privileges, for they encroach upon the liberty of citizens to acquire property and pursue happiness . . .

[E]quality of right, with exemption from all disparaging and partial enactments, in the lawful pursuits of life, throughout the whole country, is the distinguishing privilege of citizens of the United States. To them, everywhere, all pursuits, all professions, all avocations are open without other restrictions than such as are imposed equally upon all others of the same age, sex, and condition. The State may prescribe such regulations for every pursuit and calling of life as will promote the public health, secure the good order and advance the general prosperity of society, but when once prescribed, the pursuit or calling must be free to be followed by every citizen who is within the conditions designated, and will conform to the regulations. This is the fundamental idea upon which our institutions rest, and unless adhered to in the legislation of the country our government will be a republic only in name. The Fourteenth Amendment . . . makes it essential to the validity of the legislation of every State that this equality of right should be respected. How widely this equality has been departed from, how entirely rejected and trampled upon by the act of Louisiana, I have already shown. And it is to me a matter of profound regret that its validity is recognized by a majority of this court, for by it the right of free labor, one of the most sacred and imprescriptible rights of man, is violated . . . That only is a free government, in the American sense of the term, under which the inalienable right of every citizen to pursue his happiness is unrestrained, except by just, equal, and impartial laws.

Bradley, dissenting:

[A] law which prohibits a large class of citizens from adopting a lawful employment, or from following a lawful employment previously adopted, does deprive them of liberty as well as property, without due process of law. Their right of choice is a portion of their liberty; their occupation is their property. Such a law also deprives those citizens of the equal protection of the laws, contrary to the last clause of the section . . .

It is futile to argue that none but persons of the African race are intended to be benefited by this amendment. They may have been the primary cause of the amendment, but its language is general, embracing all citizens, and . . . was purposely so expressed.

The mischief to be remedied was not merely slavery and its incidents and consequences; but that spirit of insubordination and disloyalty to the National government which had troubled the country for so many years in some of the States, and that intolerance of free speech and free discussion which often rendered life and property insecure, and led to much unequal legislation. The amendment was an attempt to give voice to the strong National yearning for that time and that condition of things, in which American citizenship should be a sure guaranty of safety, and in

which every citizen of the United States might stand erect on every portion of its soil, in the full enjoyment of every right and privilege belonging to a freeman, without fear of violence or molestation.

But great fears are expressed that this construction of the amendment will lead to enactments by Congress interfering with the internal affairs of the States, and establishing therein civil and criminal codes of law for the government of the citizens, and thus abolishing the State governments in everything but name . . .

In my judgment no such practical inconveniences would arise. Very little, if any, legislation on the part of Congress would be required to carry the amendment into effect. Like the prohibition against passing a law impairing the obligation of a contract, it would execute itself. The point would be regularly raised, in a suit at law, and settled by final reference to the Federal court. As the privileges and immunities protected are only those fundamental ones which belong to every citizen, they would soon become so far defined as to cause but a slight accumulation of business in the Federal courts. Besides, the recognized existence of the law would prevent its frequent violation. But even if the business of the National courts should be increased, Congress could easily supply the remedy by increasing their number and efficiency. The great question is, What is the true construction of the amendment? When once we find that, we shall find the means of giving it effect. The argument from inconvenience ought not to have a very controlling influence in questions of this sort. The National will and National interest are of far greater importance.

Munn v. Illinois

94 U.S. 113 (1877), 7-2
Opinion of the Court: Waite, C.J. (Bradley, Clifford, Davis, Miller, Hunt, Swayne)
Dissenting: Field, Strong

Does the doctrine of business affected with a public interest developed by the Court offer a precise test of when a business can be regulated by the state, or does it, as Field argues, open the door to state regulation of any business? Who decides whether a business is affected with a public interest? For businesses so affected, who decides the validity regulations? The Court rejected the doctrine of substantive due process, as it had in The Slaughterhouse Cases (p. 000), but which decision leaves more room for its reassertion and why? Is the

Court's decision here likely to inhibit economic development, as Field suggests? Which opinion, Waite's or Field's, is the more judicially activist? Besides grain farmers and grain elevator operators, who is likely to benefit and who is likely to be hurt by this decision?

Waite, C.J., for the Court:

The question to be determined in this case is whether the general assembly of Illinois can, under the limitations upon the legislative power of the States imposed by the Constitution of the United States, fix by law the maximum of charges for the storage of grain in warehouses at Chicago and other places in the State having not less than one hundred thousand inhabitants . . .

It is claimed that such a law is repugnant . . . [t]o that part of Amendment 14 which ordains that no State shall 'deprive any person of life, liberty, or property, without due process of law, nor deny to any person within its jurisdiction the equal protection of the laws.' . . .

The Constitution contains no definition of the word 'deprive,' as used in the Fourteenth Amendment. To determine its signification, therefore, it is necessary to ascertain the effect which usage has given it . . .

While this provision of the amendment is new in the Constitution of the United States, as a limitation upon the powers of the States, it is old as a principle of civilized government. It is found in Magna Charta, and, in substance if not in form, in nearly or quite all the constitutions that have been from time to time adopted by the several States of the Union. By the Fifth Amendment, it was introduced into the Constitution of the United States as a limitation upon the powers of the national government, and by the Fourteenth, as a guaranty against any encroachment upon an acknowledged right of citizenship by the . . . States . . .

When one becomes a member of society, he necessarily parts with some rights or privileges which, as an individual not affected by his relations to others, he might retain . . . From this source come the police powers, . . . which, as was said by Mr. Chief Justice Taney in the License Cases, 'are nothing more or less than the powers of government inherent in every sovereignty, . . . that is to say, . . . the power to govern men and things.' Under these powers the government regulates the conduct of its citizens one towards another, and the manner in which each shall use his own property, when such regulation becomes necessary for the public good. In their exercise it has been customary in England from time immemorial, and in this country

from its first colonization, to regulate ferries, common carriers, hackmen, bakers, millers, wharfingers, innkeepers, &c., and in so doing to fix a maximum of charge to be made for services rendered, accommodations furnished, and articles sold. To this day, statutes are to be found in many of the States some or all these subjects; and we think it has never yet been successfully contended that such legislation came within any of the constitutional prohibitions against interference with private property . . .

This brings us to inquire as to the principles upon which this power of regulation rests, in order that we may determine what is within and what without its operative effect. Looking, then, to the common law, from whence came the right which the Constitution protects, we find that when private property is 'affected with a public interest, it ceases to be *juris privati* only.' This was said by Lord Chief Justice Hale more than two hundred years ago, in his treatise *De Portibus Maris*, and has been accepted without objection as an essential element in the law of property ever since. Property does become clothed with a public interest when used in a manner to make it of public consequence, and affect the community at large. When, therefore, one devotes his property to a use in which the public has an interest, he, in effect, grants to the public an interest in that use, and must submit to be controlled by the public for the common good . . .

[W]hen private property is devoted to a public use, it is subject to public regulation. It remains only to ascertain whether the warehouses of [Munn et al.] and the business which is carried on there, come within the operation of this principle . . .

[A]lthough in 1874 there were in Chicago fourteen warehouses adapted to this particular business, and owned by about thirty persons, nine business firms controlled them . . . Thus it is apparent that all the elevating facilities through which [the grain] 'of seven or eight great States of the West' must pass on the way 'to four or five of the States on the seashore' may be a 'virtual' monopoly.

Under such circumstances it is difficult to see why, if the common carrier, or the miller, or the ferryman, or the innkeeper, or the wharfinger, or the baker, or the cartman, or the hackney-coachman, pursues a public employment and exercises 'a sort of public office,' [Munn et al.] do not. They stand . . . in the very 'gateway of commerce,' and take toll from all who pass. Their business most certainly 'tends to a common charge, and is become a thing of public interest

The Waite Court, 1876, two years after the appointment of Morrison R. Waite as Chief Justice and a year before its historic decision in *Munn v. Illinois*. From left, Joseph Bradley, Stephen Field, Samuel Miller, Nathan Clifford, Waite, Noah Swayne, David Davis, William Strong, and Ward Hunt.

and use.' Every bushel of grain for its passage 'pays a toll, which is a common charge,' ... Certainly, if any business can be clothed 'with a public interest, and cease to be *juris privati* only,' this has been. It may not be made so by the operation of the Constitution of Illinois or this statute, but it is by the facts.

We also are not permitted to overlook the fact that, for some reason, the people of Illinois, when they revised their Constitution in 1870, saw fit to make it the duty of the general assembly to pass laws 'for the protection of producers, shippers, and receivers of grain and produce,' art. 13, sect. 7 ... This indicates very clearly that during the twenty years in which this peculiar business had been assuming its present 'immense proportions,' something had occurred which led the whole body of the people to suppose that remedies such as are usually employed to prevent abuses by virtual monopolies might not be inappropriate here. For our purposes we must assume that, if a state of facts could exist that would justify such legislation, it actually did exist when the statute now under consideration was passed ... Of the propriety of legislative interference within the scope of legislative power, the legislature is the exclusive judge ...

It matters not in this case that [Munn et al.]. had built their warehouses and established their business before the regulations complained of were adopted. What they did was from the beginning subject to the power of the body politic to require them to conform to such regulations as might be established by the proper authorities for the common good. They entered upon their business and provided themselves

with the means to carry it on subject to this condition. If they did not wish to submit themselves to such interference, they should not have clothed the public with an interest in their concerns. The same principle applies to them that does to the proprietor of a hackney-carriage, and as to him it has never been supposed that he was exempt from regulating statutes or ordinances because he had purchased his horses and carriage and established his business before the statute or the ordinance was adopted.

It is insisted, however, that the owner of property is entitled to a reasonable compensation for its use, even though it be clothed with a public interest, and that what is reasonable is a judicial and not a legislative question.

As has already been shown, the practice has been otherwise. In countries where the common law prevails, it has been customary from time immemorial for the legislature to declare what shall be a reasonable compensation under such circumstances, or, perhaps more properly speaking, to fix a maximum beyond which any charge made would be unreasonable. Undoubtedly, in mere private contracts, relating to matters in which the public has no interest, what is reasonable must be ascertained judicially. But this is because the legislature has no control over such a contract. So, too, in matters which do affect the public interest, and as to which legislative control may be exercised, if there are no statutory regulations upon the subject, the courts must determine what is reasonable. The controlling fact is the power to regulate at all. If that exists, the right to establish the maximum of charge, as one of the means of regulation, is implied. In fact, the common-law rule, which requires the charge to be reasonable, is itself a regulation as to price. Without it the owner could make his rates at will, and compel the public to yield to his terms, or forego the use.

But a mere common-law regulation of trade or business may be changed by statute. A person has no property, no vested interest, in any rule of the common law. That is only one of the forms of municipal law, and is no more sacred than any other. Rights of property which have been created by the common law cannot be taken away without due process; but the law itself, as a rule of conduct, may be changed at the will, or even at the whim, of the legislature, unless prevented by constitutional limitations. Indeed, the great office of statutes is to remedy defects in the common law as they are developed, and to adapt it to the changes of time and circumstances. To limit the rate of charge for services rendered in a public employment, or for the use of property in which the public has an interest, is only changing a regulation which existed before. It establishes no new principle in the law, but only gives a new effect to an old one.

We know that this is a power which may be abused; but that is no argument against its existence. For protection against abuses by legislatures the people must resort to the polls, not to the courts . . .

We conclude, therefore, that the statute in question is not repugnant to the Constitution of the United States.

Field, dissenting:

The principle upon which the opinion of the majority proceeds is . . . subversive of the rights of private property, heretofore believed to be protected by constitutional guaranties against legislative interference, and is in conflict with the authorities cited in its support . . .

The question presented, therefore, is one of the greatest importance—whether it is within the competency of a State to fix the compensation which an individual may receive for the use of his own property in his private business, and for his services in connection with it.

The declaration of the [Illinois] Constitution of 1870, that private buildings used for private purposes shall be deemed public institutions, does not make them so. The receipt and storage of grain in a build-

ing erected by private means for that purpose does not constitute the building a public warehouse. There is no magic in the language, though used by a constitutional convention, which can change a private business into a public one, or alter the character of the building in which the business is transacted . . . One might as well attempt to change the nature of colors, by giving them a new designation. [Munn et.al.] were no more public warehousemen . . . than the merchant who sells his merchandise to the public is a public merchant, or the blacksmith who shoes horses for the public is a public blacksmith; and it was a strange notion that by calling them so they would be brought under legislative control . . .

If this be sound law, if there be no protection, either in the principles upon which our republican government is founded, or in the prohibitions of the Constitution against such invasion of private rights, all property and all business in the State are held at the mercy of a majority of its legislature. The public has no greater interest in the use of buildings for the storage of grain than it has in the use of buildings for the residences of families, nor, indeed, any thing like so great an interest; and, according to the doctrine announced, the legislature may fix the rent of all tenements used for residences, without reference to the cost of their erection. If the owner does not like the rates prescribed, he may cease renting his houses. He has granted to the public, says the Court, an interest in the use of the buildings, and 'he may withdraw his grant by discontinuing the use; but, so long as he maintains the use, he must submit to the control.' . . .

[T]here is hardly an enterprise or business engaging the attention and labor of any considerable portion of the community, in which the public has not an interest in the sense in which that term is used by the Court in its opinion; and the doctrine which allows the legislature to interfere with and regulate the charges which the owners of property thus employed shall make for its use, that is, the rates at which all these different kinds of business shall be carried on, has never before been asserted . . . by any judicial tribunal in the United States.

No State 'shall deprive any person of life, liberty, or property without due process of law,' says the Fourteenth Amendment to the Constitution . . .

The same liberal construction which is required for the protection of life and liberty [in the Fourteenth Amendment], in all particulars in which life and liberty are of any value, should be applied to the protection of private property. If the legislature of a State, under pretense of providing for the public good, or for any other reason, can determine, against the consent of the owner, the uses to which private property shall be devoted, or the prices which the owner shall receive for its uses, it can deprive him of the property as completely as by a special act for its confiscation or destruction. If, for instance, the owner is prohibited from using his building for the purposes for which it was designed, it is of little consequence that he is permitted to retain the title and possession; or, if he is compelled to take as compensation for its use less than the expenses to which he is subjected by its ownership, he is, for all practical purposes, deprived of the property, as effectually as if the legislature had ordered his forcible dispossession . . .

There is nothing in the character of the business of the [Munn et al.] as warehousemen which called for the interference complained of in this case. Their buildings are not nuisances; their occupation of receiving and storing grain infringes upon no rights of others, disturbs no neighborhood, infects not the air, and in no respect prevents others from using and enjoying their property as to them may seem best. The legislation in question is nothing less than a bold assertion of absolute power by the State to control at its discretion the property and business of the citizen, and fix the compensation he shall receive . . . I deny the power of any legislature under our government to fix the price which one shall receive for his property of any kind. If the power can be exercised as to one article, it may as to all articles, and the prices of every thing, from a calico gown to a city mansion, may be the subject of legislative direction.

United States v. E. C. Knight Co.

156 U.S. 1 (1895), 8-1
Opinion of the Court: Fuller, C.J. (Brewer, Brown, Field, Gray, Jackson, Shiras, White)
Dissenting: Harlan

In passing the Sherman Anti-Trust Act in 1890, Congress made it unlawful to restrain trade in interstate or foreign commerce through contract, combination, or conspiracy. In 1892, the American Sugar Refining Company, already the major producer of sugar in the United States, purchased controlling stock in four other sugar companies, giving it control of 98 percent of American sugar production. The Justice Department prosecuted the company for

violation of the Sherman Act. The case, which bears the name of one of the purchased companies, was the first antitrust appeal heard by the Supreme Court. Though acknowledging the harm that monopolies may do, the Fuller's majority opinion casts the issues of the case largely in terms of national versus state power. How does Harlan's description of the problem differ? How does his conception of commerce and interstate commerce differ? In this regard, which is closer to Marshall's view in Gibbons v. Ogden (p. 206)? Can Fuller's opinion be described as one protecting property rights and Harlan's not? What is the likely effect of this decision on economic development? How does Harlan see the Court's decision as creating a vacuum of power? If the states have the power to reach production monopolies such as that created by the Sugar Trust, why did not more regulate them?

Fuller, C.J., for the Court:

By the purchase of the stock of the four Philadelphia refineries with shares of its own stock the American Sugar Refining Company acquired nearly complete control of the manufacture of refined sugar within the United States. The bill charged that the contracts under which these purchases were made constituted combinations in restraint of trade, and that in entering into them the defendants combined and conspired to restrain the trade and commerce in refined sugar among the several states and with foreign nations, contrary to the act of Congress of July 2, 1890 . . .

The fundamental question is whether, conceding that the existence of a monopoly in manufacture is established by the evidence, that monopoly can be directly suppressed under the act of Congress . . .

It cannot be denied that the power of a state to protect the lives, health, and property of its citizens, and to preserve good order and the public morals . . . is a power originally and always belonging to the states, not surrendered by them to the general government, nor directly restrained by the Constitution of the United States, and essentially exclusive. The relief of the citizens of each state from the burden of monopoly and the evils resulting from the restraint of trade among such citizens was left with the states to deal with, and this court has recognized their possession of that power even to the extent of holding that an employment or business carried on by private individuals, when it becomes a matter of such public interest and importance as to create a common charge or burden upon the citizen—in other words, when it becomes a practical monopoly . . . and by means of which a tribute can be exacted from the community—is subject to regulation by state legislative power. On the other hand, the power of Congress to regulate commerce among the several states is also exclusive. The Constitution does not provide that interstate commerce shall be free, but, by the grant of this exclusive power to regulate it, it was left free, except as Congress might impose restraints. Therefore . . . the failure of Congress to exercise this exclusive power in any case is an expression of its will that the subject shall be free from restrictions or impositions upon it by the several states, and if a law passed by a state in the exercise of its acknowledged powers comes into conflict with that will, the Congress and the state cannot occupy the position of equal opposing sovereignties, because the Constitution declares its supremacy, and that of the laws passed in pursuance thereof; and that which is not supreme must yield to that which is supreme . . . That which belongs to commerce is within the jurisdiction of the United States, but that which does not belong to commerce is within the jurisdiction of the police power of the state.

The argument is that the power to control the manufacture of refined sugar is a monopoly over a necessary of life, to the enjoyment of which by a large part of the population of the United States interstate commerce is indispensable, and that, therefore, the general government, in the exercise of the power to regulate commerce, may repress such monopoly directly, and set aside the instruments which have created it. But this argument cannot be confined to necessaries of life merely, and must include all articles of general consumption . . . Commerce succeeds to manufacture, and is not a part of it. The power to regulate commerce is the power to prescribe the rule by which commerce shall be governed, and is a power independent of the power to suppress monopoly. But it may operate in repression of monopoly whenever that comes within the rules by which commerce is governed, or whenever the transaction is itself a monopoly of commerce.

It is vital that the independence of the commercial power and of the police power, and the delimitation between them, however sometimes perplexing, should always be recognized and observed, for, while the one furnishes the strongest bond of union, the other is essential to the preservation of the autonomy of the states as required by our dual form of government . . .

It will be perceived how far-reaching the proposition is that the power of dealing with a monopoly directly may be exercised by the general government whenever interstate or international commerce may be ultimately affected. The regulation of commerce applies to the subjects of commerce, and not to matters of internal police. Contracts to buy, sell, or exchange goods to be transported among the several states, the transportation and its instrumentalities, and articles bought, sold, or exchanged for the purposes of such transit among the states, or put in the way of transit, may be regulated; but this is because they form part of interstate trade or commerce. The fact that an article is manufactured for export to another state does not of itself make it an article of interstate commerce, and the intent of the manufacturer does not determine the time when the article or product passes from the control of the state and belongs to commerce . . . There must be a point of time when they cease to be governed exclusively by the domestic law, and begin to be governed and protected by the national law of commercial regulation; and that moment seems to us to be a legitimate one for this purpose in which they commence their final movement from the state of their origin to that of their destination.' . . .

Contracts, combinations, or conspiracies to control domestic enterprise in manufacture, agriculture, mining, production in all its forms, or to raise or lower prices or wages, might unquestionably tend to restrain external as well as domestic trade, but the restraint would be an indirect result, however inevitable, and whatever its extent, and such result would not necessarily determine the object of the contract, combination, or conspiracy . . .

Slight reflection will show that, if the national power extends to all contracts and combinations in manufacture, agriculture, mining, and other productive industries, whose ultimate result may affect external commerce, comparatively little of business operations and affairs would be left for state control . . .

Congress did not attempt thereby to assert the power to deal with monopoly directly as such; or to limit and restrict the rights of corporations created by the states or the citizens of the states in the acquisition, control, or disposition of property; or to regulate or prescribe the price or prices at which such property or the products thereof should be sold; or to make criminal the acts of persons in the acquisition and control of property which the states of their residence or creation sanctioned or permitted . . . [W]hat the law struck at was combinations, contracts, and conspiracies to monopolize trade and commerce among the several states or with foreign nations; but the contracts and acts of the defendants related exclusively to the acquisition of the Philadelphia refineries and the business of sugar refining in Pennsylvania, and bore no direct relation to commerce between the states or with foreign nations. The object was manifestly private gain in the manufacture of the commodity, but not through the control of interstate or foreign commerce. It is true that the bill alleged that the products of these refineries were sold and distributed among the several states, and that all the companies were engaged in trade or commerce with the several states and with foreign nations; but this was no more than to say that trade and commerce served manufacture to fulfill its function. Sugar was refined for sale, and sales were probably made at Philadelphia for consumption, and undoubtedly for resale by the first purchasers throughout Pennsylvania and other states, and refined sugar was also forwarded by the companies to other states for sale. Nevertheless it does not follow that an attempt to monopolize, or the actual monopoly of, the manufacture was an attempt . . . to monopolize commerce, even though, in order to dispose of the product, the instrumentality of commerce was necessarily invoked . . .

Harlan, dissenting:

[T]his court assumes on the record before us that the result of the transactions disclosed . . . was the creation of a monopoly in the manufacture of a necessary of life. If this combination, so far as its operations necessarily or directly affect interstate commerce, cannot be restrained or suppressed under some power granted to Congress, it will be cause for regret that the patriotic statesmen who framed the Constitution did not foresee the necessity of investing the national government with power to deal with gigantic monopolies holding in their grasp, and injuriously controlling in their own interest, the entire trade among the states in food products that are essential to the comfort of every household in the land . . .

It would seem to be indisputable that no combination of corporations or individuals can . . . impose unlawful restraints upon interstate trade, whether upon transportation or upon such interstate intercourse and traffic as precede transportation, any more than it can . . . impose unreasonable restraints upon the completely internal traffic of a state . . . If it be true that a combination of corporations or individuals may, so far as the power of Congress is concerned, subject interstate trade, in any of its stages, to unlawful restraints, the conclusion is inevitable that the Constitution has failed to accomplish one primary object of the Union, which was to place commerce

among the states under the control of the common government of all the people, and thereby relieve or protect it against burdens or restrictions imposed, by whatever authority, for the benefit of particular localities or special interests . . .

The power of Congress covers and protects the absolute freedom of such intercourse and trade among the states as may or must succeed manufacture and precede transportation from the place of purchase. . . . Each part of such trade is then under the protection of Congress. And yet, by the opinion and judgment in this case . . . Congress is without power to protect the commercial intercourse that . . . purchasing necessarily involves against the restraints and burdens arising from the existence of combinations that meet purchasers, from whatever state they come, with the threat—for it is nothing more nor less than a threat—that they shall not purchase what they desire to purchase, except at the prices fixed by such combinations . . .

[C]itizens of the several states composing the Union are entitled of right to buy goods in the state where they are manufactured, or in any other state, without being confronted by an illegal combination whose business extends throughout the whole country . . . and which prevents such buying, except at prices arbitrarily fixed by it . . . [F]ree course of trade among the states cannot coexist with such combinations . . . Whatever improperly obstructs the free course of interstate intercourse and trade, as involved in the buying and selling of articles to be carried from one state to another, may be reached by Congress under its authority to regulate commerce among the states. The exercise of that authority so as to make trade among the states in all recognized articles of commerce absolutely free from unreasonable or illegal restrictions imposed by combinations is justified by an express grant of power to Congress, and would redound to the welfare of the whole country. I am unable to perceive that any such result would imperil the autonomy of the states, especially as that result cannot be attained through the action of any one state.

Undue restrictions or burdens upon the purchasing of goods in the market for sale, to be transported to other states, cannot be imposed, even by a state, without violating the freedom of commercial intercourse guaranteed by the Constitution. But if a state within whose limits the business of refining sugar is exclusively carried on may not constitutionally impose burdens upon purchases of sugar to be transported to other states, how comes it that combinations of corporations or individuals within the same state may not be prevented by the national government from putting unlawful restraints upon the purchasing of that article to be carried from the state in which such purchases are made? If the national power is competent to repress state action in restraint of interstate trade as it may be involved in purchases of refined sugar to be transported from one state to another state, surely it ought to be deemed sufficient to prevent unlawful restraints attempted to be imposed by combinations of corporations or individuals upon those identical purchases; otherwise illegal combinations of corporations or individuals may . . . do with impunity what no state can do . . .

To the general government has been committed the control of commercial intercourse among the states, to the end that it may be free at all times from any restraints except such as Congress may impose or permit for the benefit of the whole country. The common government of all the people is the only one that can adequately deal with a matter which directly and injuriously affects the entire commerce of the country, which concerns equally all the people of the Union, and which . . . cannot be adequately controlled by any one state. Its authority should not be so weakened by construction that it cannot reach and eradicate evils that, beyond all question, tend to defeat an object which that government is entitled, by the Constitution, to accomplish.

Pollock v. Farmers' Loan & Trust Co.

158 U.S. 601 (1895), 5-4

Opinion of the Court: Fuller, C.J. (Brewer, Field, Gray, Shiras)

Dissenting: Brown, Harlan, Jackson, White

Which opinion, Fuller's majority or Harlan's dissent, was more consistent with the precedent and understanding of the taxing power at the time? Is Harlan correct in stating that the framers were unclear about what they were doing when they put the requirement of direct tax into the Constitution? What ends might it have served? The Pollock decision was eventually undone by the Sixteenth Amendment. Without such a change, is it likely that Congress would ever have taxed incomes if the levy had to be apportioned among the states by population? Who gains or loses as a result of the decision in this case?

Fuller, C.J., for the Court:

[T]he Constitution divided federal taxation into two great classes—the class of direct taxes, and the class of duties, imposts, and excises—and prescribed two rules which qualified the grant of power as to each class.

The power to lay direct taxes, apportioned among the several states in proportion to their representation in the popular branch of Congress—representation based on population as ascertained by the census—was plenary and absolute, but to lay direct taxes without apportionment was forbidden. The power to lay duties, imposts, and excises was subject to the qualification that the imposition must be uniform throughout the United States.

Our previous decision was confined to the consideration of the validity of the tax on the income from real estate, and on the income from municipal bonds. The question thus limited was whether such taxation was direct, or not, in the meaning of the Constitution; and the Court went no further, as to the tax on the income from real estate, than to hold that it fell within the same class as the source whence the income was derived—that is, that a tax upon the realty and a tax upon the receipts therefrom were alike direct; while, as to the income from municipal bonds, that could not be taxed, because of want of power to tax the source, and no reference was made to the nature of the tax, as being direct or indirect.

We are now permitted to broaden the field of inquiry, and to determine to which of the two great classes a tax upon a person's entire income—whether derived from rents or products, or otherwise, of real estate, or from bonds, stocks, or other forms of personal property—belongs; and we are unable to conclude that the enforced subtraction from the yield of all the owner's real or personal property, in the manner prescribed, is so different from a tax upon the property itself that it is not a direct, but an indirect, tax, in the meaning of the Constitution . . .

We know of no reason for holding otherwise than that the words 'direct taxes,' on the one hand, and 'duties, imposts and excises,' on the other, were used in the Constitution in their natural and obvious sense. Nor, in arriving at what those terms embrace, do we perceive any ground for enlarging them beyond, or narrowing them within, their natural and obvious import at the time the Constitution was framed and ratified.

And, passing from the text, we regard the conclusion reached as inevitable, when the circumstances which surrounded the convention and controlled its action, and the views of those who framed and those who adopted the Constitution, are considered . . .

The founders anticipated that the expenditures of the states, their counties, cities, and towns, would chiefly be met by direct taxation on accumulated property, while they expected that those of the federal government would be for the most part met by indirect taxes. And in order that the power of direct taxation by the general government should not be exercised except on necessity and . . . should be so exercised as to leave the states at liberty to discharge their respective obligations, and should not be so exercised unfairly and discriminatingly . . . by a mere majority vote . . . the qualified grant was made . . .

It is said that a tax on the whole income of property is not a direct tax in the meaning of the Constitution, but a duty, and, as a duty, leviable without apportionment, whether direct or indirect. We do not think so. Direct taxation was not restricted in one breath, and the restriction blown to the winds in another . . .

The Constitution prohibits any direct tax, unless in proportion to numbers as ascertained by the census, and in the light of the circumstances to which we have referred, is it not an evasion of that prohibition to hold that a general unapportioned tax, imposed upon all property owners as a body for or in respect of their property, is not direct, in the meaning of the Constitution, because confined to the income therefrom?

Whatever the speculative views of political economists or revenue reformers may be, can it be properly held that the Constitution, taken in its plain and obvious sense, and with due regard to the circumstances attending the formation of the government, authorizes a general unapportioned tax on the products of the farm and the rents of real estate, although imposed merely because of ownership, and with no possible means of escape from payment, as belonging to a totally different class from that which includes the property from whence the income proceeds?

There can be but one answer, unless the constitutional restriction is to be treated as utterly illusory and futile, and the object of its framers defeated. We find it impossible to hold that a fundamental requisition deemed so important as to be enforced by two provisions, one affirmative and one negative, can be refined away by forced distinctions between that which gives value to property and the property itself.

Nor can we perceive any ground why the same reasoning does not apply to capital in personalty held for the purpose of income, or ordinarily yielding income,

and to the income therefrom. All the real estate of the country, and all its invested personal property, are open to the direct operation of the taxing power, if an apportionment be made according to the Constitution. The Constitution does not say that no direct tax shall be laid by apportionment on any other property than land; on the contrary, it forbids all unapportioned direct taxes; and we know of no warrant for excepting personal property from the exercise of the power . . .

The stress of the argument is thrown, however, on the assertion that an income tax is not a property tax at all; that it is not a real-estate tax, or a crop tax, or a bond tax; that it is an assessment upon the taxpayer on account of his money-spending power, as shown by his revenue for the year preceding the assessment; that rents received, crops harvested, interest collected, have lost all connection with their origin, and, although once not taxable, have become transmuted, in their new form, into taxable subject-matter—in other words, that income is taxable, irrespective of the source from whence it is derived . . .

We have unanimously held in this case that, so far as this law operates on the receipts from municipal bonds, it cannot be sustained, because it is a tax on the power of the states and on their instrumentalities to borrow money, and consequently repugnant to the Constitution. But if . . . the interest, when received, has become merely money in the recipient's pocket, and taxable as such, without reference to the source from which it came, the question is immaterial whether it could have been originally taxed at all or not . . . [I]t follows that if the revenue derived from municipal bonds cannot be taxed, because the source cannot be, the same rule applies to revenue from any other source not subject to the tax, and the lack of power to levy any but an apportional tax on real and personal property equally exists as to the revenue therefrom.

Admitting that this act taxes the income of property, irrespective of its source, still we cannot doubt that such a tax is necessarily a direct tax, in the meaning of the Constitution . . .

We have considered the act only in respect of the tax on income derived from real estate, and from invested personal property, and have not commented on so much of it as bears on gains or profits from business, privileges, or employments . . .

Being of opinion that so much of the sections of this law as lays a tax on income from real and personal property is invalid, we are brought to the question of the effect of that conclusion upon these sections as a whole . . .

According to the census, the true valuation of real and personal property in the United States in 1890 was $65,037,091,197, of which real estate with improvements thereon made up $39,544,544,333. Of course, from the latter must be deducted, in applying these sections, all unproductive property and all property whose net yield does not exceed $4,000; but, even with such deductions, it is evident that the income from realty formed a vital part of the scheme for taxation embodied therein. If that be stricken out, and also the income from all invested personal property, bonds, stocks, investments of all kinds, it is obvious that by far the largest part of the anticipated revenue would be eliminated, and this would leave the burden of the tax to be borne by professions, trades, employments, or vocations; and in that way what was intended as a tax on capital would remain, in substance, a tax on occupations and labor. We cannot believe that such was the intention of Congress. We do not mean to say that an act laying by apportionment a direct tax on all real estate and personal property, or the income thereof, might not also lay excise taxes on business, privileges, employments, and vocations. But this is not such an act, and the scheme must be considered as a whole. Being invalid as to the greater part, and falling, as the tax would, if any part were held valid, in a direction which could not have been contemplated, except in connection with the taxation considered as an entirety, we are constrained to conclude that sections 27 to 37, inclusive, of the act, which became a law, without the signature of the president, on August 28, 1894, are wholly inoperative and void.

Our conclusions may therefore be summed up as follows:

First. We adhere to the opinion already announced—that, taxes on real estate being indisputably direct taxes, taxes on the rents or income of real estate are equally direct taxes.

Second. We are of opinion that taxes on personal property, or on the income of personal property, are likewise direct taxes.

Third. The tax imposed by sections 27 to 37, inclusive, of the act of 1894, so far as it falls on the income of real estate, and of personal property, being a direct tax, within the meaning of the Constitution, and therefore unconstitutional and void, because not apportioned according to representation, all those sections, constitut-

ing one entire scheme of taxation, are necessarily invalid.

Harlan, (White) dissenting:

What are 'direct taxes,' within the meaning of the Constitution? In the convention of 1787, Rufus King asked what was the precise meaning of 'direct' taxation, and no one answered. The debates of that famous body do not show that any delegate attempted to give a clear, succinct definition of what, in his opinion, was a direct tax. Indeed, the report of those debates, upon the question now before us, is very meager and unsatisfactory . . .

A question so difficult to be answered by able statesmen and lawyers directly concerned in the organization of the present government can now, it seems, be easily answered, after a re-examination of documents, writings, and treatises on political economy, all of which . . . have been several times directly brought to the attention of this court. And whenever that has been done the result always, until now, has been that a duty on incomes, derived from taxable subjects, of whatever nature, was held not to be a direct tax within the meaning of the Constitution, to be apportioned among the states on the basis of population, but could be laid, according to the rule of uniformity, upon individual citizens, corporations, and associations, without reference to numbers in the particular states in which such citizens, corporations, or associations were domiciled . . .

From th[e] history of legislation and of judicial decisions, it is manifest:

That in the judgment of the members of this court, as constituted when the Hylton Case was decided (all of whom were statesmen and lawyers of distinction; two, Wilson and Paterson, being recognized as great leaders in the convention of 1787), the only taxes that could certainly be regarded as direct taxes, within the meaning of the Constitution, were capitation taxes and taxes on lands . . .

That from the foundation of the government, until 1861, Congress, following the declarations of the judges in the Hylton Case, restricted direct taxation to real estate and slaves, and in 1861 to real estate exclusively, and has never, by any statute, indicated its belief that personal property, however assessed or valued, was the subject of 'direct taxes' to be apportioned among the states . . .

That, in 1861 and subsequent years, Congress imposed, without apportionment among the states on the basis of numbers, but by the rule of uniformity, duties on income derived from every kind of property, real and personal, including income derived from rents, and from trades, professions, and employments, etc. And lastly—

That upon every occasion when it has considered the question whether a duty on incomes was a direct tax, within the meaning of the Constitution, this court has, without a dissenting voice, determined it in the negative, always proceeding on the ground that capitation taxes and taxes on land were the only direct taxes contemplated by the framers of the Constitution . . .

In its practical operation this decision withdraws from national taxation not only all incomes derived from real estate, but tangible personal property, 'invested personal property, bonds, stocks, investments of all kinds,' and the income that may be derived from such property . . . [A]ll such personal property and all incomes from real estate and personal property are placed beyond national taxation otherwise than by apportionment among the states on the basis simply of population. No such apportionment can possibly be made without doing gross injustice to the many for the benefit of the favored few in particular states. Any attempt upon the part of Congress to apportion among the states, upon the basis simply of their population, taxation of personal property or of incomes, would tend to arouse such indignation among the freemen of America that it would never be repeated. When, therefore, this court adjudges . . . that Congress cannot impose a duty or tax upon personal property, or upon income arising either from rents of real estate or from personal property, including invested personal property, bonds, stocks, and investments of all kinds, except by apportioning the sum to be so raised among the states according to population, it practically decides that, without an amendment of the Constitution . . . such property and incomes can never be made to contribute to the support of the national government . . .

I cannot assent to an interpretation of the Constitution that impairs and cripples the just powers of the national government in the essential matter of taxation, and at the same time discriminates against the greater part of the people of our country.

The practical effect of the decision today is to give to certain kinds of property a position of favoritism and advantage inconsistent with the fundamental principles of our social organization, and to invest them with power and influence that may be perilous to that portion of the American people upon whom

rests the larger part of the burdens of the government, and who ought not to be subjected to the dominion of aggregated wealth any more than the property of the country should be at the mercy of the lawless.

Champion v. Ames

188 U.S. 321 (1903), 5-4
Opinion of the Court: Harlan (Brown, Holmes, McKenna, White)
Dissenting: Brewer, Fuller, Peckham, Shiras
What were the various constitutional arguments raised against the Anti-Lottery Act? How did Harlan answer each of them? What power would Congress need to have to make the law constitutional for Fuller? What limits are there, in Harlan's view, to Congress's power to regulate by prohibiting interstate shipment?

Harlan, for the Court:
The general question arising upon this appeal involves the constitutionality of the . . . act of Congress . . . entitled 'An Act for the Suppression of Lottery Traffic through National and Interstate Commerce and the Postal Service . . .

[Champion] insists that the carrying of lottery tickets from one state to another state by an express company engaged in carrying freight and packages from state to state, although such tickets may be contained in a box or package, does not constitute . . . commerce among the states within the meaning of the clause of the Constitution . . . consequently, that Congress cannot make it an offense to cause such tickets to be carried from one state to another.

The government insists that express companies, when engaged, for hire, in the business of transportation from one state to another, are instrumentalities of commerce among the states; that the carrying of lottery tickets from one state to another is commerce which Congress may regulate; and that as a means of executing the power to regulate interstate commerce Congress may make it an offense against the United States to cause lottery tickets to be carried from one state to another . . .

What is the import of the word 'commerce' as used in the Constitution? It is not defined by that instrument. Undoubtedly, the carrying from one state to another by independent carriers of things or commodities that are ordinary subjects of traffic, and which have in themselves a recognized value in money, constitutes interstate commerce. But does not commerce among the several states include something more? Does not the carrying from one state to another, by independent carriers, of lottery tickets that entitle the holder to the payment of a certain amount of money therein specified, also constitute commerce among the states? . . .

The leading case under the commerce clause of the Constitution is *Gibbons v. Ogden*. Referring to that clause, Chief Justice Marshall said: 'The subject to be regulated is commerce; and our Constitution being, as was aptly said at the bar, one of enumeration, and not of definition, to ascertain the extent of the power it becomes necessary to settle the meaning of the word . . . Commerce, undoubtedly, is traffic, but it is something more; it is intercourse. It describes the commercial intercourse between nations and parts of nations, in all its branches, and is regulated by prescribing rules for carrying on that intercourse . . . It has been truly said that commerce, as the word is used in the Constitution, is a unit, every part of which is indicated by the term. If this be the admitted meaning of the word, in its application to foreign nations, it must carry the same meaning throughout the sentence, and remain a unit, unless there be some plain, intelligible cause which alters it. The subject to which the power is next applied is to commerce 'among the several states.' The word 'among' means intermingled with. A thing which is among others is intermingled with them. Commerce among the states cannot stop at the external boundary line of each state, but may be introduced into the interior. It is not intended to say that these words comprehend that commerce which is completely internal, which is carried on between man and man in a state, or between different parts of the same state, and which does not extend to or affect other states. Such a power would be inconvenient, and is certainly unnecessary. Comprehensive as the word 'among' is, it may very properly be restricted to that commerce which concerns more states than one . . . The genius and character of the whole government seem to be that its action is to be applied to all the external concerns of the nation, and to those internal concerns which affect the states generally; but not to those which are completely within a particular state, which do not affect other states, and with which it is not necessary to interfere, for the purpose of executing some of the general powers of the government.' . . .

[P]rior adjudications . . . sufficiently indicate the grounds upon which this court has proceeded when determining the meaning and scope of the commerce clause. They show that commerce among the states embraces navigation, intercourse, communication, traffic, the transit of persons, and the transmission of messages by telegraph. They also show that the power to regulate commerce among the several states is vested in Congress as absolutely as it would be in a single government, having in its constitution the same restrictions on the exercise of the power as are found in the Constitution of the United States; that such power is plenary, complete in itself, and may be exerted by Congress to its utmost extent, subject only to such limitations as the Constitution imposes upon the exercise of the powers granted by it; and that in determining the character of the regulations to be adopted Congress has a large discretion which is not to be controlled by the courts, simply because, in their opinion, such regulations may not be the best or most effective that could be employed.

We come, then, to inquire whether there is any solid foundation upon which to rest the contention that Congress may not regulate the carrying of lottery tickets from one state to another, at least by corporations or companies whose business it is, for hire, to carry tangible property from one state to another.

It was said in argument that lottery tickets are not of any real or substantial value in themselves, and therefore are not subjects of commerce. If that were conceded to be the only legal test as to what are to be deemed subjects of the commerce that may be regulated by Congress, we cannot accept as accurate the broad statement that such tickets are of no value . . .

We are of opinion that lottery tickets are subjects of traffic, and therefore are subjects of commerce, and the regulation of the carriage of such tickets from state to state, at least by independent carriers, is a regulation of commerce among the several states.

But it is said that the statute in question does not regulate the carrying of lottery tickets from state to state, but by punishing those who cause them to be so carried Congress in effect prohibits such carrying; that in respect of the carrying from one state to another of articles or things that are, in fact, or according to usage in business, the subjects of commerce, the authority given Congress was not to prohibit, but only to regulate. This view was earnestly pressed at the bar . . . and must be examined.

[T]he Constitution does not define what is to be deemed a legitimate regulation of interstate commerce . . . While our government must be acknowledged by all to be one of enumerated powers, the Constitution does not attempt to set forth all the means by which such powers may be carried into execution. It leaves to Congress a large discretion as to the means that may be employed in executing a given power ...

We have said that the carrying from state to state of lottery tickets constitutes interstate commerce, and that the regulation of such commerce is within the power of Congress under the Constitution. Are we prepared to say that a provision which is, in effect, a prohibition of the carriage of such articles from state to state is not a fit or appropriate mode for the regulation of that particular kind of commerce? If lottery traffic, carried on through interstate commerce, is a matter of which Congress may take cognizance and over which its power may be exerted, can it be possible that it must tolerate the traffic, and simply regulate the manner in which it may be carried on? Or may not Congress, for the protection of the people of all the states, and under the power to regulate interstate commerce, devise such means, within the scope of the Constitution, and not prohibited by it, as will drive that traffic out of commerce among the states?

In determining whether regulation may not under some circumstances properly take the from or have the effect of prohibition, the nature of the interstate traffic which it was sought by the act of May 2d, 1895, to suppress cannot be overlooked ...

[T]he power of Congress to regulate commerce among the states is plenary, is complete in itself, and is subject to no limitations except such as may be found in the Constitution. What provision in that instrument can be regarded as limiting the exercise of the power granted? What clause can be cited which, in any degree, countenances the suggestion that one may, of right, carry or cause to be carried from one state to another that which will harm the public morals? We cannot think of any clause of that instrument that could possibly be invoked by those who assert their right to send lottery tickets from state to state except the one providing that no person shall be deprived of his liberty without due process of law. We have said that the liberty protected by the Constitution embraces the right to be free in the enjoyment of one's faculties; 'to be free to use them in all lawful ways; to live and work where he will; to earn his livelihood by any lawful calling; to pursue any livelihood or avocation, and for that purpose to enter into all contracts which may be proper.' But surely it will not be said to be a part of anyone's liberty, as recognized by the supreme law of

the land, that he shall be allowed to introduce into commerce among the states an element that will be confessedly injurious to the public morals ...

Congress, by [the] act, does not assume to interfere with traffic or commerce in lottery tickets carried on exclusively within the limits of any state, but has in view only commerce of that kind among the several states. It has not assumed to interfere with the completely internal affairs of any state, and has only legislated in respect of a matter which concerns the people of the United States. As a state may, for the purpose of guarding the morals of its own people, forbid all sales of lottery tickets within its limits, so Congress, for the purpose of guarding the people of the United States against the 'widespread pestilence of lotteries' and to protect the commerce which concerns all the states, may prohibit the carrying of lottery tickets from one state to another. In legislating upon the subject of the traffic in lottery tickets, as carried on through interstate commerce, Congress only supplemented the action of those states—perhaps all of them—which, for the protection of the public morals, prohibit the drawing of lotteries, as well as the sale or circulation of lottery tickets, within their respective limits. It said, in effect, that it would not permit the declared policy of the states, which sought to protect their people against the mischiefs of the lottery business, to be overthrown or disregarded by the agency of interstate commerce. We should hesitate long before adjudging that an evil of such appalling character, carried on through interstate commerce, cannot be met and crushed by the only power competent to that end ...

It is said, however, that if, in order to suppress lotteries carried on through interstate commerce, Congress may exclude lottery tickets from such commerce, that principle leads necessarily to the conclusion that Congress may arbitrarily exclude from commerce among the states any article, commodity, or thing, of whatever kind or nature, or however useful or valuable, which it may choose, no matter with what motive, to declare shall not be carried from one state to another. It will be time enough to consider the constitutionality of such legislation when we must do so. The present case does not require the Court to declare the full extent of the power that Congress may exercise in the regulation of commerce among the states ... This power ... may not be exercised so as to infringe rights secured or protected by that instrument ... There is probably no governmental power that may not be exerted to the injury of the public. If what is done by Congress is manifestly in excess of the powers granted to it, then upon the courts will rest the duty of adjudging that its action is neither legal nor binding upon the people. But if what Congress does is within the limits of its power, and is simply unwise or injurious, the remedy is that suggested by Chief Justice Marshall in *Gibbons v. Ogden*, when he said: 'The wisdom and the discretion of Congress, their identity with the people, and the influence which their constituents possess at elections, are, in this, as in many other instances, as that, for example, of declaring war, the sole restraints on which they have relied, to secure them from its abuse. They are the restraints on which the people must often rely solely, in all representative governments.'

The whole subject is too important, and the questions suggested by its consideration are too difficult of solution, to justify any attempt to lay down a rule for determining in advance the validity of every statute that may be enacted under the commerce clause. We decide nothing more in the present case than that lottery tickets are subjects of traffic among those who choose to sell or buy them; that the carriage of such tickets by independent carriers from one state to another is therefore interstate commerce; that under its power to regulate commerce among the several states Congress—subject to the limitations imposed by the Constitution upon the exercise of the powers granted—has plenary authority over such commerce, and may prohibit the carriage of such tickets from state to state; and that legislation to that end . . . is not inconsistent with any limitation or restriction imposed upon the exercise of the powers granted to Congress.

Fuller, C.J. (Brewer, Peckham, Shiras) dissenting:
The naked question is whether the prohibition by Congress of the carriage of lottery tickets from one state to another by means other than the mails is within the powers vested in that body by the Constitution of the United States . . .

The power of the state to impose restraints and burdens on persons and property in conservation and promotion of the public health, good order, and prosperity is a power originally and always belonging to the states, not surrendered by them to the general government, nor directly restrained by the Constitution of the United States, and essentially exclusive, and the suppression of lotteries as a harmful business falls within this power, commonly called, of police.

It is urged, however, that because Congress is empowered to regulate commerce between the several

states, it, therefore, may suppress lotteries by prohibiting the carriage of lottery matter. Congress may, indeed, make all laws necessary and proper for carrying the powers granted to it into execution, and doubtless an act prohibiting the carriage of lottery matter would be necessary and proper to the execution of a power to suppress lotteries; but that power belongs to the states and not to Congress. To hold that Congress has general police power would be to hold that it may accomplish objects not entrusted to the general government, and to defeat the operation of the 10th Amendment . . .

When Chief Justice Marshall said that commerce embraced intercourse, he added, commercial intercourse, and this was necessarily so since, as Chief Justice Taney pointed out, if intercourse were a word of larger meaning than the word 'commerce,' it could not be substituted for the word of more limited meaning contained in the Constitution.

Is the carriage of lottery tickets from one state to another commercial intercourse?

The lottery ticket purports to create contractual relations, and to furnish the means of enforcing a contract right . . .

These contracts are not articles of commerce in any proper meaning of the word. They are not subjects of trade and barter offered in the market as something having an existence and value independent of the parties to them. They are not commodities to be shipped or forwarded from one state to another, and then put up for sale. They are like other personal contracts between parties which are completed by their signature and the transfer of the consideration. Such contracts are not interstate transactions, though the parties may be domiciled in different states. The policies do not take effect—are not executed contracts—until delivered by the agent in Virginia. They are, then, local transactions, and are governed by the local law. They do not constitute a part of the commerce between the states any more than a contract for the purchase and sale of goods in Virginia by a citizen of New York whilst in Virginia would constitute a portion of such commerce.' . . .

To say that the mere carrying of an article which is not an article of commerce in and of itself nevertheless becomes such the moment it is to be transported from one state to another, is to transform a non-commercial article into a commercial one simply because it is transported . . .

It would be to say that everything is an article of commerce the moment it is taken to be transported from place to place, and of interstate commerce if from state to state.

An invitation to dine, or to take a drive, or a note of introduction, all become articles of commerce under the ruling in this case, by being deposited with an express company for transportation. This in effect breaks down all the differences between that which is, and that which is not, an article of commerce, and the necessary consequence is to take from the states all jurisdiction over the subject so far as interstate communication is concerned. It is a long step in the direction of wiping out all traces of state lines, and the creation of a centralized government.

Does the grant to Congress of the power to regulate interstate commerce import the absolute power to prohibit it? . . .

It will not do to say—a suggestion which has heretofore been made in this case—that state laws have been found to be ineffective for the suppression of lotteries, and therefore Congress should interfere. The scope of the commerce clause of the Constitution cannot be enlarged because of present views of public interest . . .

The power to prohibit the transportation of diseased animals and infected goods over railroads or on steamboats is an entirely different thing, for they would be in themselves injurious to the transaction of interstate commerce, and, moreover, are essentially commercial in their nature. And the exclusion of diseased persons rests on different ground, for nobody would pretend that persons could be kept off the trains because they were going from one state to another to engage in the lottery business. However enticing that business may be, we do not understand these pieces of paper themselves can communicate bad principles by contact . . .

McCray v. United States

195 U. S. 27 (1904), 6-3
Opinion of the Court: White (Brewer, Day, Harlan, Holmes, McKenna)
Dissenting: Brown, Fuller, Peckham
At the urging of dairy farmers, Congress levied a tax of 10 cents a pound on oleomargarine colored to look like butter, but taxed uncolored oleomargarine at only one-quarter of a cent per pound. McCray, a margarine retailer, was fined $50 for purchasing colored margarine for resale on which only the lower tax had been paid.

Was the tax in this case intended to raise revenue? Who are the "real" antagonists? Was the Court justified in refus- *ing to look at the motives of Congress in levying the tax? Does the decision mean that Congress can tax an item—any item—so heavily that it will be destroyed commercially?*

White, C.J., for the Court:
Did Congress, in passing the acts which are assailed, exert a power not conferred by the Constitution?

That the acts in question on their face impose excise taxes which Congress had the power to levy is so completely established as to require only statement . . .

The summary which follows embodies the propositions contained in the assignments of error, and the substance of the elaborate argument by which those assignments are deemed to be sustained. Not denying the general power of Congress to impose excise taxes, and conceding that the acts in question, on their face, purport to levy taxes of that character, the propositions are these:

(a) That the power of internal taxation which the Constitution confers on Congress is given to that body for the purpose of raising revenue, and that the tax on artificially colored oleomargarine is void because it is of such an onerous character as to make it manifest that the purpose of Congress in levying it was not to raise revenue, but to suppress the manufacture of the taxed article.

(b) The power to regulate the manufacture and sale of oleomargarine being solely reserved to the several states, it follows that the acts in question, enacted by Congress for the purpose of suppressing the manufacture and sale of oleo-margarine, when artificially colored, are void, because usurping the reserved power of the states, and therefore exerting an authority not delegated to Congress by the Constitution.

(c) Whilst it is true so the argument proceeds that Congress, in exerting the taxing power conferred upon it, may use all means appropriate to the exercise of such power, a tax which is fixed at such a high rate as to suppress the production of the article taxed is not a legitimate means to the lawful end, and is therefore beyond the scope of the taxing power.

(d) As the tax levied by the acts which are assailed discriminates against oleomargarine artificially colored, and in favor of butter so colored, and creates an unwarranted and unreasonable distinction between the oleomargarine which is artificially colored and that which is not, and as the necessary operation and effect of the tax is to suppress the manufacture of artificially colored oleomargarine, and to aid the butter industry, therefore the acts are void. And with this proposition in mind it is insisted that wherever the judiciary is called upon to determine whether a power which Congress has exerted is within the authority conferred by the Constitution, the duty is to test the validity of the act, not merely by its face, or, to use the words of the argument, 'by the label placed upon it by Congress,' but by the necessary scope and effect of the assailed enactment . . .

It is, however, argued, if a lawful power may be exerted for an unlawful purpose, and thus, by abusing the power, it may be made to accomplish a result not intended by the Constitution, all limitations of power must disappear, and the grave function lodged in the judiciary, to confine all the departments within the authority conferred by the Constitution, will be of no avail. This, when reduced to its last analysis, comes to this: that, because a particular department of the government may exert its lawful powers with the object or motive of reaching an end not justified, therefore it becomes the duty of the judiciary to restrain the exercise of a lawful power wherever it seems to the judicial mind that such lawful power has been abused. But this reduces itself to this contention that, under our constitutional system, the abuse by one department of the government of its lawful powers is to be corrected by the abuse of its powers by another department.

The proposition, if sustained, would destroy all distinction between the powers of the respective departments of the government, would put an end to that confidence and respect for each other which it was the purpose of the Constitution to uphold, and would thus be full of danger to the permanence of our institutions . . .

It is, of course, true, as suggested, that if there be no authority in the judiciary to restrain a lawful exercise of power by another department of the government, where a wrong motive or purpose has impelled to the exertion of the power, that abuses of a power conferred may be temporarily effectual. The remedy for this, however, lies, not in the abuse by the judicial authority of its functions, but in the people, upon whom, after all, under our institutions, reliance must be placed for the correction of abuses committed in the exercise of a lawful power . . .

The decisions of this court from the beginning lend no support whatever to the assumption that the judiciary may restrain the exercise of lawful power on the assumption that a wrongful purpose or motive has caused the power to be exerted . . .

It being thus demonstrated that the motive or purpose of Congress in adopting the acts in question may not be inquired into, we are brought to consider the contentions relied upon to show that the acts assailed were beyond the power of Congress, putting entirely out of view all considerations based upon purpose or motive.

1. Undoubtedly, in determining whether a particular act is within a granted power, its scope and effect is to be considered. Applying this rule to the acts assailed, it is self-evident that on their face they levy an excise tax. That being their necessary scope and operation, it follows that the acts are within the grant of power. The argument to the contrary rests on the proposition that, although the tax be within the power, as enforcing it will destroy or restrict the manufacture of artificially colored oleomargarine, therefore the power to levy the tax did not obtain. This, however, is but to say that the question of power depends, not upon the authority conferred by the Constitution, but upon what may be the consequence arising from the exercise of the lawful authority.

Since . . . the taxing power conferred by the Constitution knows no limits except those expressly stated in that instrument, it must follow, if a tax be within the lawful power, the exertion of that power may not be judicially restrained because of the results to arise from its exercise . . .

2. The proposition that where a tax is imposed which is within the grant of powers, and which does not conflict with any express constitutional limitation, the courts may hold the tax to be void because it is deemed that the tax is too high, is absolutely disposed of by the opinions in the cases hitherto cited, and which expressly hold, to repeat again the language of one of the cases that 'The judicial department cannot prescribe to the legislative department limitations upon the exercise of its acknowledged powers. The power to tax may be exercised oppressively upon persons; but the responsibility of the legislature is not to the courts, but to the people by whom its members are elected.'

3. Whilst undoubtedly both the 5th and 10th Amendments qualify, in so far as they are applicable, all the provisions of the Constitution, nothing in those amendments operates to take away the grant of power to tax conferred by the Constitution upon Congress. The contention on this subject rests upon the theory that the purpose and motive of Congress in exercising its undoubted powers may be inquired into by the courts, and the proposition is therefore disposed of by what has been said on that subject.

The right of Congress to tax within its delegated power being unrestrained, except as limited by the Constitution, it was within the authority conferred on Congress to select the objects upon which an excise should be laid. It therefore follows that, in exerting its power, no want of due process of law could possibly result, because that body chose to impose an excise on artificially colored oleomargarine, and not upon natural butter artificially colored . . .

4. Lastly we come to consider the argument that, even though as a general rule a tax of the nature of the one in question would be within the power of Congress, in this case the tax should be held not to be within such power, because of its effect. This is based on the contention that, as the tax is so large as to destroy the business of manufacturing oleomargarine artificially colored to look like butter, it thus deprives the manufacturers of that article of their freedom to engage in a lawful pursuit, and hence, irrespective of the distribution of powers made by the Constitution, the taxing laws are void, because they violate those fundamental rights which it is the duty of every free government to safeguard, and which, therefore, should be held to be embraced by implied, though none the less potential, guaranties, or, in any event, to be within the protection of the due process clause of the 5th Amendment.

Let us concede, for the sake of argument only, the premise of fact upon which the proposition is based. Moreover, concede, for the sake of argument only, that even although a particular exertion of power by Congress was not restrained by any express limitation of the Constitution, if, by the perverted exercise of such power, so great an abuse was manifested as to destroy fundamental rights which no free government could consistently violate, that it would be the duty of the judiciary to hold such acts to be void upon the assumption that the Constitution, by necessary implication, forbade them.

Such concession, however, is not controlling in this case. This follows when the nature of oleomargarine, artificially colored to look like butter, is recalled. As we have said, it has been conclusively settled by this court that the tendency of that article to deceive the public into buying it for butter is such that the states may, in the exertion of their police powers, without violating the due process clause of the 14th Amendment, absolutely prohibit the manufacture of the article. It hence results, that even although it be true that the effect of the tax in question is to repress the manufacture of artificially colored oleomargarine, it cannot be said

that such repression destroys rights which no free government could destroy, and, therefore, no ground exists to sustain the proposition that the judiciary may invoke an implied prohibition, upon the theory that to do so is essential to save such rights from destruction. And the same considerations dispose of the contention based upon the due process clause of the 5th Amendment. That provision, as we have previously said, does not withdraw or expressly limit the grant of power to tax conferred upon Congress by the Constitution. From this it follows, as we have also previously declared, that the judiciary is without authority to avoid an act of Congress exerting the taxing power, even in a case where, to the judicial mind, it seems that Congress had, in putting such power in motion, abused its lawful authority by levying a tax which was unwise or oppressive, or the result of the enforcement of which might be to indirectly affect subjects not within the powers delegated to Congress.

Let us concede that if a case was presented where the abuse of the taxing power was so extreme as to be beyond the principles which we have previously stated, and where it was plain to the judicial mind that the power had been called into play, not for revenue, but solely for the purpose of destroying rights which could not be rightfully destroyed consistently with the principles of freedom and justice upon which the Constitution rests, that it would be the duty of the courts to say that such an arbitrary act was not merely an abuse of a delegated power, but was the exercise of an authority not conferred. This concession, however, like the one previously made, must be without influence upon the decision of this cause for the reasons previously stated; that is, that the manufacture of artificially colored oleomargarine may be prohibited by a free government without a violation of fundamental rights.

Lochner v. New York

198 U.S. 45 (1905), 5-4
Opinion of the Court: Peckham (Brewer, Brown, Fuller, McKenna)
Dissenting: Day, Harlan, Holmes, White
According to Peckham, what is the test of the validity of a state police power regulation? What does Peckham think the reasons for the regulation were? What evidence does he cite for challenging the legislature's factual finding? What does Peckham fear may happen if the law is sustained? How do the dissenters answer that fear? If facts as to the need for a regulation are un-

clear or uncertain, should there be no legislation? Should the matter be left entirely to the legislature's judgment or should the courts exercise review of that judgment? Is legislative motive relevant? How might motive be determined? Is the Court's decision here consistent with The Slaughterhouse Cases? With Munn v. Illinois?

Peckham, for the Court:

The indictment, it will be seen, charges that [Lochner] violated the 110th section of article 8, chapter 415, of the Laws of 1897, known as the labor law of the state of New York, in that he . . . unlawfully required and permitted an employee working for him to work more than sixty hours in one week . . .

The mandate of the statute, that 'no employee shall be required or permitted to work,' is the substantial equivalent of an enactment that 'no employee shall contract or agree to work,' more than ten hours per day; and, as there is no provision for special emergencies, the statute is mandatory in all cases. It is not an act merely fixing the number of hours which shall constitute a legal day's work, but an absolute prohibition upon the employer permitting, under any circumstances, more than ten hours' work to be done in his establishment. The employee may desire to earn the extra money which would arise from his working more than the prescribed time, but this statute forbids the employer from permitting the employee to earn it.

The statute necessarily interferes with the right of contract between the employer and employees, concerning the number of hours in which the latter may labor in the bakery of the employer. The general right to make a contract in relation to his business is part of the liberty of the individual protected by the 14th Amendment of the Federal Constitution. *Allgeyer v. Louisiana.* Under that provision no state can deprive any person of life, liberty, or property without due process of law. The right to purchase or to sell labor is part of the liberty protected by this amendment, unless there are circumstances which exclude the right. There are, however, certain powers, existing in the sovereignty of each state in the Union, somewhat vaguely termed police powers, the exact description and limitation of which have not been attempted by the courts. Those powers, broadly stated . . . relate to the safety, health, morals, and general welfare of the public . . .

The state, therefore, has power to prevent the individual from making certain kinds of contracts, and in regard to them the Federal Constitution offers no protection. If the contract be one which the state, in the le-

gitimate exercise of its police power, has the right to prohibit, it is not prevented from prohibiting it by the 14th Amendment. Contracts in violation of a statute, either of the Federal or state government, or a contract to let one's property for immoral purposes, or to do any other unlawful act, could obtain no protection from the Federal Constitution, as coming under the liberty of person or of free contract. Therefore, when the state, by its legislature, in the assumed exercise of its police powers, has passed an act which seriously limits the right to labor or the right of contract in regard to their means of livelihood between persons who are *sui juris* (both employer and employee), it becomes of great importance to determine which shall prevail—the right of the individual to labor for such time as he may choose, or the right of the state to prevent the individual from laboring, or from entering into any contract to labor, beyond a certain time prescribed by the state.

This court has recognized the existence and upheld the exercise of the police powers of the states in many cases which might fairly be considered as border ones . . . Among the later cases where the state law has been upheld by this court is that of *Holden v. Hardy.* A provision in the act of the legislature of Utah was there under consideration, the act limiting the employment of workmen in all underground mines or workings, to eight hours per day, 'except in cases of emergency, where life or property is in imminent danger.' It also limited the hours of labor in smelting and other institutions for the reduction or refining of ores or metals to eight hours per day, except in like cases of emergency. The act was held to be a valid exercise of the police powers of the state . . . It was held that the kind of employment, mining, smelting, etc., and the character of the employees in such kinds of labor, were such as to make it reasonable and proper for the state to interfere to prevent the employees from being constrained by the rules laid down by the proprietors in regard to labor . . .

[T]here is a limit to the valid exercise of the police power by the state . . . Otherwise the 14th Amendment would have no efficacy and the legislatures of the states would have unbounded power, and it would be enough to say that any piece of legislation was enacted to conserve the morals, the health, or the safety of the people; such legislation would be valid, no matter how absolutely without foundation the claim might be. The claim of the police power would be a mere pretext—become another and delusive name for the supreme sovereignty of the state to be exercised free from constitutional restraint. . . In every case that comes before this court, therefore, where legislation of this character is concerned, and where the protection of the Federal Constitution is sought, the question necessarily arises: Is this a fair, reasonable, and appropriate exercise of the police power of the state, or is it an unreasonable, unnecessary, and arbitrary interference with the right of the individual to his personal liberty, or to enter into those contracts in relation to labor which may seem to him appropriate or necessary for the support of himself and his family? Of course the liberty of contract relating to labor includes both parties to it. The one has as much right to purchase as the other to sell labor.

This is not a question of substituting the judgment of the Court for that of the legislature. If the act be within the power of the state it is valid, although the judgment of the Court might be totally opposed to the enactment of such a law. But the question would still remain: Is it within the police power of the state? and that question must be answered by the Court.

[W]hether this act is valid as a labor law . . . may be dismissed in a few words. There is no reasonable ground for interfering with the liberty of person or the right of free contract, by determining the hours of labor, in the occupation of a baker. There is no contention that bakers as a class are not equal in intelligence and capacity to men in other trades or manual occupations, or that they are not able to assert their rights and care for themselves without the protecting arm of the state, interfering with their independence of judgment and of action. They are in no sense wards of the state. Viewed in the light of a purely labor law, with no reference whatever to the question of health, we think that a law like the one before us involves neither the safety, the morals, nor the welfare, of the public, and that the interest of the public is not in the slightest degree affected by such an act. The law must be upheld, if at all, as a law pertaining to the health of the individual engaged in the occupation of a baker. It does not affect any other portion of the public than those who are engaged in that occupation. Clean and wholesome bread does not depend upon whether the baker works but ten hours per day or only sixty hours a week. The limitation of the hours of labor does not come within the police power on that ground.

It is a question of which of two powers or rights shall prevail—the power of the state to legislate or the right of the individual to liberty of person and freedom of contract. The mere assertion that the subject relates, though but in a remote degree, to the public health, does not necessarily render the enactment valid. The act must have a more direct relation, as a means to an end, and the end itself must be appropriate and legitimate, before an act can be held to be valid which interferes with the general right of an individual to be free in his person and in his power to contract in relation to his own labor . . .

[T]he limit of the police power has been reached and passed in this case. There is . . . no reasonable foundation for holding this to be necessary or appropriate as a health law to safeguard the public health, or the health of the individuals who are following the trade of a baker. If this statute be valid, and . . . a proper case is made out in which to deny the right of an individual . . . as employer or employee, to make contracts for the labor of the latter under the protection of the provisions of the Federal Constitution, there would seem to be no length to which legislation of this nature might not go. The case differs widely . . . from the expressions of this court in regard to laws of this nature, as stated in *Holden v. Hardy* . . .

[T]here can be no fair doubt that the trade of a baker, in and of itself, is not an unhealthy one to that degree which would authorize the legislature to interfere with the right to labor, and with the right of free contract on the part of the individual, either as employer or employee In looking through statistics regarding all trades and occupations, it may be true that the trade of a baker does not appear to be as healthy as some other trades, and is also vastly more healthy than still others. To the common understanding the trade of a baker has never been regarded as an unhealthy one. Very likely physicians would not recommend the exercise of that or of any other trade as a remedy for ill health. Some occupations are more healthy than others, but we think there are none which might not come under the power of the legislature to supervise and control the hours of working therein, if the mere fact that the occupation is not absolutely and perfectly healthy is to confer that right upon the legislative department of the government. It might be safely affirmed that almost all occupations more or less affect the health. There must be more than the mere fact of the possible existence of some small amount of unhealthiness to warrant legislative interference with liberty. It is unfortunately true that labor, even in any department, may possibly carry with it the seeds of unhealthiness. But are we all, on that account, at the mercy of legislative majorities? . . .

We do not believe in the soundness of the views which uphold this law. On the contrary, we think that such a law as this, although passed in the assumed exercise of the police power, and as relating to the public health, or the health of the employees named, is not within that power, and is invalid. The act is not, within any fair meaning of the term, a health law, but is an illegal interference with the rights of individuals, both employers and employees, to make contracts regarding labor upon such terms as they may think best, or which they may agree upon with the other parties to such contracts . . .

It was further urged on the argument that restricting the hours of labor in the case of bakers was valid because it tended to cleanliness on the part of the workers, as a man was more apt to be cleanly when not overworked, and if cleanly then his 'output' was also more likely to be so. What has already been said applies with equal force to this contention. We do not admit the reasoning to be sufficient to justify the claimed right of such interference. . . In our judgment it is not possible in fact to discover the connection between the number of hours a baker may work in the bakery and the healthful quality of the bread made by the workman. The connection, if any exist, is too shadowy and thin to build any argument for the interference of the legislature . . .

This interference on the part of the legislatures of the several states with the ordinary trades and occupations of the people seems to be on the increase . . .

It is impossible for us to shut our eyes to the fact that many of the laws of this character, while passed under what is claimed to be the police power for the purpose of protecting the public health or welfare, are, in reality, passed from other motives. We are justified in saying so when, from the character of the law and the subject upon which it legislates, it is apparent that the public health or welfare bears but the most remote relation to the law. The purpose of a statute must be determined from the natural and legal effect of the language employed; and whether it is or is not repugnant to the Constitution of the United States must be determined from the natural effect of such statutes when put into operation, and not from their proclaimed purpose.

It is manifest to us that the limitation of the hours of labor as provided for in this section of the statute under which the indictment was found, and [Lochner] convicted, has no such direct relation to, and no such substantial effect upon, the health of the employee, as to justify us in regarding the section as really a health law. It seems to us that the real object and purpose were simply to regulate the hours of labor between

the master and his employees (all being men, sui juris), in a private business, not dangerous in any degree to morals, or in any real and substantial degree to the health of the employees. Under such circumstances the freedom of master and employee to contract with each other in relation to their employment, and in defining the same, cannot be prohibited or interfered with, without violating the Federal Constitution.

Harlan (White, Day), dissenting:

Granting . . . that there is a liberty of contract which cannot be violated even under the sanction of direct legislative enactment, but assuming . . . that such liberty of contract is subject to such regulations as the state may reasonably prescribe for the common good and the well-being of society, what are the conditions under which the judiciary may declare such regulations to be in excess of legislative authority and void? . . . [T]he rule is universal that a legislative enactment, Federal or state, is never to be disregarded or held invalid unless it be, beyond question, plainly and palpably in excess of legislative power. In *Jacobson v. Massachusetts,* we said that the power of the courts to review legislative action in respect of a matter affecting the general welfare exists only 'when that which the legislature has done comes within the rule that, if a statute purporting to have been enacted to protect the public health, the public morals, or the public safety has no real or substantial relation to those objects, or is, beyond all question, a plain, palpable invasion of rights secured by the fundamental law.' If there be doubt as to the validity of the statute, that doubt must therefore be resolved in favor of its validity, and the courts must keep their hands off, leaving the legislature to meet the responsibility for unwise legislation . . .

I find it impossible, in view of common experience, to say that there is here no real or substantial relation between the means employed by the state and the end sought to be accomplished by its legislation . . .

We judicially know that the question of the number of hours during which a workman should continuously labor has been, for a long period, and is yet, a subject of serious consideration among civilized peoples, and by those having special knowledge of the laws of health. Suppose the statute prohibited labor in bakery and confectionery establishments in excess of eighteen hours each day. No one . . . could dispute the power of the state to enact such a statute. But the statute before us does not embrace extreme or exceptional cases. It may be said to occupy a middle ground in respect of the hours of labor. What is the true ground for the state to take between legitimate protection, by legislation, of the public health and liberty of contract is not a question easily solved, nor one in respect of which there is or can be absolute certainty . . .

It is enough for the determination of this case, and it is enough for this court to know, that the question is one about which there is room for debate and for an honest difference of opinion. There are many reasons of a weighty, substantial character, based upon the experience of mankind, in support of the theory that . . . more than ten hours' steady work each day, from week to week, in a bakery or confectionery establishment, may endanger the health and shorten the lives of the workmen, thereby diminishing their physical and mental capacity to serve the state and to provide for those dependent upon them.

If such reasons exist that ought to be the end of this case, for the state is not amenable to the judiciary, in respect of its legislative enactments, unless such enactments are plainly, palpably, beyond all question, inconsistent with the Constitution of the United States . . .

We are not to presume that the state of New York has acted in bad faith. Nor can we assume that its legislature acted without due deliberation, or that it did not determine this question upon the fullest attainable information and for the common good. We cannot say that the state has acted without reason, nor ought we to proceed upon the theory that its action is a mere sham. Our duty . . . is to sustain the statute as not being in conflict with the Federal Constitution, for the reason . . . it is not shown to be plainly and palpably inconsistent with that instrument. Let the state alone in the management of its purely domestic affairs, so long as it does not appear beyond all question that it has violated the Federal Constitution.

Holmes, dissenting:

This case is decided upon an economic theory which a large part of the country does not entertain. If it were a question whether I agreed with that theory, I should desire to study it further and long before making up my mind. But I do not conceive that to be my duty, because I strongly believe that my agreement or disagreement has nothing to do with the right of a majority to embody their opinions in law. It is settled by various decisions of this court that state constitutions and state laws may regulate life in many ways which we as legislators might think as injudicious . . . Sunday laws and usury laws are ancient examples. A more modern one is the

prohibition of lotteries. The liberty of the citizen to do as he likes so long as he does not interfere with the liberty of others to do the same, which has been a shibboleth for some well-known writers, is interfered with by school laws, by the Post Office, by every state or municipal institution which takes his money for purposes thought desirable, whether he likes it or not. The 14th Amendment does not enact Mr. Herbert Spencer's Social Statics. The other day we sustained the Massachusetts vaccination law. United States and state statutes and decisions cutting down the liberty to contract by way of combination are familiar to this court. Two years ago we upheld the prohibition of sales of stock on margins, or for future delivery, in the Constitution of California. The decision sustaining an eight-hour law for miners is still recent. *Holden v. Hardy.* Some of these laws embody convictions or prejudices which judges are likely to share. Some may not. But a Constitution is not intended to embody a particular economic theory, whether of paternalism and the organic relation of the citizen to the state or of laissez faire. It is made for people of fundamentally differing views, and the accident of our finding certain opinions natural and familiar, or novel, and even shocking, ought not to conclude our judgment upon the question whether statutes embodying them conflict with the Constitution of the United States . . .

[T]he word 'liberty,' in the 14th Amendment, is perverted when it is held to prevent the natural outcome of a dominant opinion, unless it can be said that a rational and fair man necessarily would admit that the statute proposed would infringe fundamental principles as they have been understood by the traditions of our people and our law. It does not need research to show that no such sweeping condemnation can be passed upon the statute before us. A reasonable man might think it a proper measure on the score of health. Men whom I certainly could not pronounce unreasonable would uphold it as a first installment of a general regulation of the hours of work. Whether in the latter aspect it would be open to the charge of inequality I think it unnecessary to discuss.

Muller v. Oregon

208 U.S. 412 (1908), 9-0
Opinion of the Court: Brewer (Day, Fuller, Harlan, Holmes, McKenna, Moody, Peckham, White)
Does the Court hold the state legislation not to interfere with liberty of contract or that liberty of contract must chival-

rously step aside to make room for paternalist protection? Can this case be distinguished from Lochner v. New York because the subjects of the law were women workers rather than workers in particular industry or because the evidence here is factually "richer" than in Lochner? Or are the two cases inconsistent?

Brewer, for the Court:

The single question is the constitutionality of the statute under which the [Muller] was convicted, so far as it affects the work of a female in a laundry . . .

We held in *Lochner v. New York,* that a law providing that no laborer shall be required or permitted to work in bakeries more than sixty hours in a week or ten hours in a day was not as to men a legitimate exercise of the police power of the state, but an unreasonable, unnecessary, and arbitrary interference with the right and liberty of the individual to contract in relation to his labor, and as such was in conflict with, and void under, the Federal Constitution. That decision is invoked by [Muller] as decisive of the question before us. But this assumes that the difference between the sexes does not justify a different rule respecting a restriction of the hours of labor.

In patent cases counsel are apt to open the argument with a discussion of the state of the art. It may not be amiss, in the present case, before examining the constitutional question, to notice the course of legislation, as well as expressions of opinion from other than judicial sources. In the brief filed by Mr. Louis D. Brandeis for [Oregon] is a very copious collection of all these matters . . .

The legislation and opinions . . . may not be, technically speaking, authorities, and in them is little or no discussion of the constitutional question presented to us for determination, yet they are significant of a widespread belief that woman's physical structure, and the functions she performs in consequence thereof, justify special legislation restricting or qualifying the conditions under which she should be permitted to toil. Constitutional questions . . . are not settled by even a consensus of present public opinion, for it is the peculiar value of a written constitution that it places in unchanging form limitations upon legislative action, and thus gives a permanence and stability to popular government which otherwise would be lacking. At the same time, when a question of fact is debated and debatable, and the extent to which a special constitutional limitation goes is affected by the truth in respect to that fact, a wide-

spread and long continued belief concerning it is worthy of consideration. We take judicial cognizance of all matters of general knowledge . . .

[T]he general right to contract in relation to one's business is part of the liberty of the individual, protected by the 14th Amendment to the Federal Constitution; yet it is equally well settled that this liberty is not absolute and extending to all contracts, and that a state may, without conflicting with the provisions of the 14th Amendment, restrict in many respects the individual's power of contract . . .

That woman's physical structure and the performance of maternal functions place her at a disadvantage in the struggle for subsistence is obvious. This is especially true when the burdens of motherhood are upon her. Even when they are not, by abundant testimony of the medical fraternity continuance for a long time on her feet at work, repeating this from day to day, tends to injurious effects upon the body, and, as healthy mothers are essential to vigorous offspring, the physical well-being of woman becomes an object of public interest and care in order to preserve the strength and vigor of the race.

Still again, history discloses the fact that woman has always been dependent upon man. He established his control at the outset by superior physical strength, may, without conflicting with the provisions and this control in various forms, with diminishing intensity, has continued to the present . . . [S]he has been looked upon in the courts as needing especial care that her rights may be preserved. Education was long denied her, and while now the doors of the schoolroom are opened and her opportunities for acquiring knowledge are great, yet even with that and the consequent increase of capacity for business affairs it is still true that in the struggle for subsistence she is not an equal competitor with her brother. Though limitations upon personal and contractual rights may be removed by legislation, there is that in her disposition and habits of life which will operate against a full assertion of those rights. She will still be where some legislation to protect her seems necessary to secure a real equality of right. Doubtless there are individual exceptions, and there are many respects in which she has an advantage over him; but looking at it from the viewpoint of the effort to maintain an independent position in life, she is not upon an equality. Differentiated by these matters from the other sex, she is properly placed in a class by herself, and legislation designed for her protection may be sustained, even when like legislation is not necessary for men, and could not be sustained. It is impossible to close one's eyes to the fact that she still looks to her brother and depends upon him. Even though all restrictions on political, personal, and contractual rights were taken away, and she stood, so far as statutes are concerned, upon an absolutely equal plane with him, it would still be true that she is so constituted that she will rest upon and look to him for protection; that her physical structure and a proper discharge of her maternal functions—having in view not merely her own health, but the well-being of the race—justify legislation to protect her from the greed as well as the passion of man. The limitations which this statute places upon her contractual powers, upon her right to agree with her employer as to the time she shall labor, are not imposed solely for her benefit, but also largely for the benefit of all. The two sexes differ in structure of body, in the functions to be performed by each, in the amount of physical strength, in the capacity for long continued labor, particularly when done standing, the influence of vigorous health upon the future well-being of the race, the self-reliance which enables one to assert full rights, and in the capacity to maintain the struggle for subsistence. This difference justifies a difference in legislation, and upholds that which is designed to compensate for some of the burdens which rest upon her . . .

For these reasons, and without questioning in any respect the decision in *Lochner v. New York,* we are of the opinion that it cannot be adjudged that the act in question is in conflict with the Federal Constitution, so far as it respects the work of a female in a laundry, and the judgment of the Supreme Court of Oregon is affirmed.

The Shreveport Rate Cases (Houston East and West Texas Railway Company v. United States)

234 U.S. 342 (1914), 7-2
Opinion for the Court: Hughes (White, McKenna, Holmes, Day, Van Devanter, J. Lamar)
Dissenting: Lurton, Pitney
Several railroads serving East Texas charged higher freight rates per mile for shipping from Shreveport, Louisiana, than from Dallas or Houston. The effect was to make transportation costs for in-state Texas shippers less than those for out-of-state shippers even though Dallas and Houston were farther from East Texas markets than was Shreveport. The Louisiana Rail-

way Commission filed a complaint with the Interstate Commerce Commission alleging discrimination against interstate commerce. In response and over the railroads objection, the ICC set maximum rates that could be charged on the Shreveport runs, thus making shipping costs from Shreveport comparable to those on intrastate runs on a per mile basis. The railroads appealed the ruling to the Federal Commerce Court and, losing there, to the Supreme Court.

What new reach of the federal commerce power is underwritten by this decision? What limits, if any, does Hughes put on it? Can the decision be reconciled with United States v. E. C. Knight Co., *or has that case been silently overruled? Who gains and loses as a result of this decision?*

Hughes, for the Court:

The Interstate Commerce Commission found that the interstate class rates out of Shreveport to named Texas points were unreasonable, and it established maximum class rates for this traffic. These rates, we understand, were substantially the same as the class rates fixed by the Railroad Commission of Texas, and charged by the carriers, for transportation for similar distances in that State. The Interstate Commerce Commission also found that the carriers maintained "higher rates from Shreveport to points in Texas" than were in force "from cities in Texas to such points under substantially similar conditions and circumstances," and that thereby "an unlawful and undue preference and advantage" was given to the Texas cities and a "discrimination" that was "undue and unlawful" was effected against Shreveport. In order to correct this discrimination, the carriers were directed to desist from charging higher rates for the transportation of any commodity from Shreveport to Dallas and Houston, respectively, and intermediate points, than were contemporaneously charged for the carriage of such commodity from Dallas and Houston toward Shreveport for equal distances, as the Commission found that relation of rates to be reasonable . . .

The point of the objection to the order is that, as the discrimination found by the Commission to be unjust arises out of the relation of intrastate rates, maintained under state authority, to interstate rates that have been upheld as reasonable, its correction was beyond the Commission's power. Manifestly, the order might be complied with, and the discrimination avoided, either by reducing the interstate rates from Shreveport to the level of the competing intrastate rates, or by raising these intrastate rates to the level of the interstate rates, or by such reduction in the one case and increase in the other as would result in equality. But it is urged that, so far as the interstate rates were sustained by the Commission as reasonable, the Commission was without authority to compel their reduction in order to equalize them with the lower intrastate rates. The holding of the Commerce Court was that the order relieved the appellants from further obligation to observe the intrastate rates, and that they were at liberty to comply with the Commission's requirements by increasing these rates sufficiently to remove the forbidden discrimination. The invalidity of the order in this aspect is challenged upon two grounds:

1. That Congress is impotent to control the intrastate charges of an interstate carrier even to the extent necessary to prevent injurious discrimination against interstate traffic; and

2. That, if it be assumed that Congress has this power, still it has not been exercised, and hence the action of the Commission exceeded the limits of the authority which has been conferred upon it.

. . . It is unnecessary to repeat what has frequently been said by this court with respect to the complete and paramount character of the power confided to Congress to regulate commerce among the several States. It is of the essence of this power that, where it exists, it dominates. Interstate trade was not left to be destroyed or impeded by the rivalries of local governments. The purpose was to make impossible the recurrence of the evils which had overwhelmed the Confederation and to provide the necessary basis of national unity by insuring "uniformity of regulation against conflicting and discriminating state legislation." By virtue of the comprehensive terms of the grant, the authority of Congress is at all times adequate to meet the varying exigencies that arise and to protect the national interest by securing the freedom of interstate commercial intercourse from local control.

Congress is empowered to regulate—that is, to provide the law for the government of interstate commerce . . . Its authority, extending to these interstate carriers as instruments of interstate commerce, necessarily embraces the right to control their operations in all matters having such a close and substantial relation to interstate traffic that the control is essential or appropriate to the security of that traffic, to the efficiency of the interstate service, and to the maintenance of conditions under which interstate commerce may be conducted upon fair terms and without molestation or hindrance. As it is competent for Congress to legislate to these ends, unquestionably it may seek their attainment by requiring that the agencies of interstate commerce shall not be used in such manner as to cripple, retard or destroy it. The fact that carriers are instruments of intrastate commerce, as well as of interstate commerce, does not derogate from the complete and paramount authority of Congress over the latter or preclude the Federal power from being exerted to prevent the intrastate operations of such carriers from being made a means of injury to that which has been confided to Federal care. Wherever the interstate and intrastate transactions of carriers are so related that the government of the one involves the control of the other, it is Congress, and not the State, that is entitled to prescribe the final and dominant rule, for otherwise Congress would be denied the exercise of its constitutional authority and the State, and not the Nation, would be supreme within the national field . . .

[Here the Court cited several decisions in which Congress's power to reach certain intrastate activity affecting interstate commerce was upheld.]

While these decisions sustaining the Federal power relate to measures adopted in the interest of the safety of persons and property, they illustrate the principle that Congress, in the exercise of its paramount power, may prevent the common instrumentalities of interstate and intrastate commercial intercourse from being used in their intrastate operations to the injury of interstate commerce. This is not to say that Congress possesses the authority to regulate the internal commerce of a State, as such, but that it does possess the power to foster and protect interstate commerce, and to take all measures necessary or appropriate to that end, although intrastate transactions of interstate carriers may thereby be controlled.

This principle is applicable here. We find no reason to doubt that Congress is entitled to keep the highways of interstate communication open to interstate traffic upon fair and equal terms. That an unjust discrimination in the rates of a common carrier, by which one person or locality is unduly favored as against another under substantially similar conditions of traffic, constitutes an evil is undeniable, and where this evil consists in the action of an interstate carrier in unreasonably discriminating against interstate traffic over its line, the authority of Congress to prevent it is equally clear. It is immaterial, so far as the protecting power of Congress is concerned, that the discrimination arises from intrastate rates, as compared with interstate rates. The use of the instrument of interstate commerce in a discriminatory manner so as to inflict injury upon that commerce, or some part thereof, furnishes abundant ground for Federal intervention. Nor can the attempted exercise of state authority alter the matter, where Congress has acted, for a State may not authorize the carrier to do that which Congress is entitled to forbid and has forbidden . . .

. . . It is for Congress to supply the needed correction where the relation between intrastate and interstate rates presents the evil to be corrected, and this it may do completely by reason of its control over the interstate carrier in all matters having such a close and substantial relation to interstate commerce that it is necessary or appropriate to exercise the control for the effective government of that commerce.

It is also clear that, in removing the injurious discriminations against interstate traffic arising from the relation of intrastate to interstate rates, Congress is not bound to reduce the latter below what it may deem to be a proper standard fair to the carrier and to the public. Otherwise, it could prevent the injury to interstate commerce only by the sacrifice of its judgment as to interstate rates. Congress is entitled to maintain its own standard as to these rates, and to forbid any discriminatory action by interstate carriers which will obstruct the freedom of movement of interstate traffic over their lines in accordance with the terms it establishes.

Having this power, Congress could provide for its execution through the aid of a subordinate body, and we conclude that the order of the Commission . . . cannot be held invalid upon the ground that it exceeded the authority which Congress could lawfully confer.

Hammer v. Dagenhart

247 U.S. 251 (1918), 5-4
Opinion of the Court: Day (McReynolds, Pitney, Van Devanter, White)
Dissenting: Brandeis, Holmes, Clark, McKenna
In the Federal Child Labor Act, Congress barred from shipment in interstate commerce goods made totally or in part by children under 14 or by children 14 to 16 who worked more than eight hours a day. With the support of a militant employer organization, Roland Dagenhart, whose two minor sons were affected by the act, sought to enjoin William C. Hammer, a U. S. attorney, from enforcing it.

How does Justice Day's conception of commerce differ from Marshall's in Gibbons v. Ogden? How does he distinguish Champion v. Ames and other federal police power cases? How does Holmes deal with these cases? Can the decision be distinguished from The Shreveport Rate Case? How does Day answer the charge that differing state laws on child labor gave a competitive advantage to industries in some states as opposed to others? Is Holmes's dissent based on opposition to child labor? What does Day believe would happen if the Child Labor law were to be upheld?

Day, for the Court:

The attack upon the act rests upon three propositions: First: It is not a regulation of interstate and foreign commerce; second: It contravenes the Tenth Amendment to the Constitution; third: It conflicts with the Fifth Amendment to the Constitution . . .

The power essential to the passage of this act, the government contends, is found in the commerce clause of the Constitution which authorizes Congress to regulate commerce with foreign nations and among the states . . .

[I]t is insisted that adjudged cases in this court establish the doctrine that the power to regulate given to Congress incidentally includes the authority to prohibit the movement of ordinary commodities and therefore that the subject is not open for discussion. The cases demonstrate the contrary. They rest upon the character of the particular subjects dealt with and the fact that the scope of governmental authority, state or national, possessed over them is such that the authority to prohibit is . . . but the exertion of the power to regulate.

The first of these cases is *Champion v. Ames*, the so-called Lottery Case, in which it was held that Congress might pass a law having the effect to keep the channels of commerce free from use in the transportation of tickets used in the promotion of lottery schemes. In *Hipolite Egg Co. v. United States*, this court sustained the power of Congress to pass the Pure Food and Drug Act, which prohibited the introduction into the states by means of interstate commerce of impure foods and drugs. In *Hoke v. United States*, this court sustained the constitutionality of the so-called 'White Slave Traffic Act', whereby the transportation of a woman in interstate commerce for the purpose of prostitution was forbidden . . .

In each of these instances the use of interstate transportation was necessary to the accomplishment of harmful results. In other words, although the power over interstate transportation was to regulate, that could only be accomplished by prohibiting the use of the facilities of interstate commerce to effect the evil intended.

This element is wanting in the present case. The thing intended to be accomplished by this statute is the denial of the facilities of interstate commerce to those manufacturers in the states who employ children within the prohibited ages. The act in its effect does not regulate transportation among the states, but aims to standardize the ages at which children may be employed in mining and manufacturing within the states. The goods shipped are of themselves harmless. The act permits them to be freely shipped after thirty days from the time of their removal from the factory. When offered for shipment, and before transportation begins, the labor of their production is over, and the mere fact that they were intended for interstate commerce transportation does not make their production subject to federal control under the commerce power.

Commerce 'consists of intercourse and traffic . . . and includes the transportation of persons and property, as well as the purchase, sale and exchange of commodities.' The making of goods and the mining of coal are not commerce, nor does the fact that these things are to be afterwards shipped, or used in interstate commerce, make their production a part thereof.

Over interstate transportation, or its incidents, the regulatory power of Congress is ample, but the production of articles, intended for interstate commerce, is a matter of local regulation. 'When the commerce begins is determined, not by the character of the commodity, nor by the intention of the owner to transfer it to another state for sale, nor by his preparation of it for transportation, but by its actual delivery to a common carrier for transportation, or the actual commencement of its transfer to another state.' This principle has been recognized often in this court. If it were otherwise, all manufacture intended for interstate shipment would be brought under federal control to the practical exclusion of the authority of the states, a result certainly not contemplated by the framers of the Constitution when they vested in Congress the authority to regulate commerce among the States.

It is further contended that the authority of Congress may be exerted to control interstate commerce in the shipment of child-made goods because of the effect of the circulation of such goods in other states where the evil of this class of labor has been recognized by local legislation, and the right to thus employ child labor has been more rigorously restrained than in the state of production. In other words, that the unfair competition, thus engendered, may be controlled by closing the channels of interstate commerce to manufacturers in those states where the local laws do not meet what Congress deems to be the more just standard of other states.

There is no power vested in Congress to require the states to exercise their police power so as to prevent possible unfair competition. Many causes may cooperate to give one state, by reason of local laws or

By striking down Congress's attempts to end child labor, in *Hammer v. Dagenhart* and *Bailey v. Drexel Furniture Co.* the Supreme Court allowed workplace scenes like this in a textile factory to continue.

conditions, an economic advantage over others. The commerce clause was not intended to give to Congress a general authority to equalize such conditions. In some of the states laws have been passed fixing minimum wages for women, in others the local law regulates the hours of labor of women in various employment. Business done in such states may be at an economic disadvantage when compared with states which have no such regulations; surely, this fact does not give Congress the power to deny transportation in interstate commerce to those who carry on business where the hours of labor and the rate of compensation for women have not been fixed by a standard in use in other states and approved by Congress.

The grant of power of Congress over the subject of interstate commerce was to enable it to regulate such commerce, and not to give it authority to control the states in their exercise of the police power over local trade and manufacture.

The grant of authority over a purely federal matter was not intended to destroy the local power always existing and carefully reserved to the states in the Tenth Amendment to the Constitution.

Police regulations relating to the internal trade and affairs of the states have been uniformly recognized as within such control . . .

That there should be limitations upon the right to employ children in mines and factories in the interest of their own and the public welfare, all will admit. That such employment is generally deemed to require regulation is shown by the fact that the brief of counsel states that every state in the Union has a law upon the subject, limiting the right to thus employ children. In North Carolina, the state wherein is located the factory in which the employment was had in the present case, no child under twelve years of age is permitted to work . . .

In interpreting the Constitution it must never be forgotten that the nation is made up of states to which are entrusted the powers of local government. And to them and to the people the powers not expressly delegated to the national government are reserved. The power of the states to regulate their purely internal affairs by such laws as seem wise to the local authority is inherent and has never been surrendered to the general government. To sustain this statute would not be in our judgment a recognition of the lawful exertion of Congressional authority over interstate commerce, but would sanction an invasion by the federal power of the control of a matter purely local in its character,

and over which no authority has been delegated to Congress in conferring the power to regulate commerce among the states . . .

In our view the necessary effect of this act is, by means of a prohibition against the movement in interstate commerce of ordinary commercial commodities to regulate the hours of labor of children in factories and mines within the states, a purely state authority. Thus the act in a two-fold sense is repugnant to the Constitution. It not only transcends the authority delegated to Congress over commerce but also exerts a power as to a purely local matter to which the federal authority does not extend. The far reaching result of upholding the act cannot be more plainly indicated than by pointing out that if Congress can thus regulate matters entrusted to local authority by prohibition of the movement of commodities in interstate commerce, all freedom of commerce will be at an end, and the power of the states over local matters may be eliminated, and thus our system of government be practically destroyed.

Holmes, (Brandeis, Clark, McKenna) dissenting:

The single question in this case is whether Congress has power to prohibit the shipment in interstate or foreign commerce of any product of a cotton mill situated in the United States, in which within thirty days before the removal of the product children under fourteen have been employed, or children between fourteen and sixteen have been employed more than eight hours in a day, or more than six days in any week, or between seven in the evening and six in the morning. The objection urged against the power is that the States have exclusive control over their methods of production and that Congress cannot meddle with them, and taking the proposition in the sense of direct intermeddling I agree to it and suppose that no one denies it. But if an act is within the powers specifically conferred upon Congress, it seems to me that it is not made any less constitutional because of the indirect effects that it may have . . . and that we are not at liberty upon such grounds to hold it void . . .

[T]he statute in question is within the power expressly given to Congress if considered only as to its immediate effects and that if invalid it is so only upon some collateral ground. The statute confines itself to prohibiting the carriage of certain goods in interstate or foreign commerce. Congress is given power to regulate such commerce in unqualified terms. It would not be argued today that the power to regulate does not include the power to prohibit. Regulation means the prohibition of something, and when interstate commerce is the matter to be regulated I cannot doubt that the regulation may prohibit any part of such commerce that Congress sees fit to forbid . . . [I]t is established by the Lottery Case and others that have followed it that a law is not beyond the regulative power of Congress merely because it prohibits certain transportation out and out . . .

The question then is narrowed to whether the exercise of its otherwise constitutional power by Congress can be pronounced unconstitutional because of its possible reaction upon the conduct of the States in a matter upon which . . . they are free from direct control . . . [T]he most conspicuous decisions of this court had made it clear that the power to regulate commerce and other constitutional powers could not be cut down or qualified by the fact that it might interfere with the carrying out of the domestic policy of any State.

The manufacture of oleomargarine is as much a matter of State regulation as the manufacture of cotton cloth. Congress levied a tax upon the compound when colored so as to resemble butter that was so great as obviously to prohibit the manufacture and sale. In a very elaborate discussion the present Chief Justice excluded any inquiry into the purpose of an act which apart from that purpose was within the power of Congress. Fifty years ago a tax on state banks, the obvious purpose and actual effect of which was to drive them . . . out of existence, was sustained, although the result was one that Congress had no constitutional power to require. The Court made short work of the argument as to the purpose of the Act. 'The Judicial cannot prescribe to the Legislative Departments of the Government limitations upon the exercise of its acknowledged powers.' So it well might have been argued that the corporation tax was intended under the guise of a revenue measure to secure a control not otherwise belonging to Congress, but the tax was sustained . . . And to come to cases upon interstate commerce notwithstanding *United States v. E. C. Knight Co.*, the Sherman Act has been made an instrument for the breaking up of combinations in restraint of trade and monopolies, using the power to regulate commerce as a foothold, but not proceeding because that commerce was the end actually in mind. The objection that the control of the States over production was interfered with was urged again and again but always in vain . . .

The Pure Food and Drug Act which was sustained in *Hipolite Egg Co. v. United States*, with the intimation that 'no trade can be carried on between the States to which it [the power of Congress to regulate commerce] does not extend,' applies not merely to articles that the changing opinions of the time condemn as intrinsically harmful but to others innocent in themselves, simply on the ground that the order for them was induced by a preliminary fraud. It does not matter whether the supposed evil precedes or follows the transportation. It is enough that in the opinion of Congress the transportation encourages the evil. I may add that in the cases on the so-called White Slave Act it was established that the means adopted by Congress as convenient to the exercise of its power might have the character of police regulations . . .

The notion that prohibition is any less prohibition when applied to things now thought evil I do not understand. But if there is any matter upon which civilized countries have agreed—far more unanimously than they have with regard to intoxicants and some other matters over which this country is now emotionally aroused—it is the evil of premature and excessive child labor . . .

[T]his court always had disavowed the right to intrude its judgment upon questions of policy or morals. It is not for this court to pronounce when prohibition is necessary to regulation if it ever may be necessary . . .

The Act does not meddle with anything belonging to the States. They may regulate their internal affairs and their domestic commerce as they like. But when they seek to send their products across the State line they are no longer within their rights. If there were no Constitution and no Congress their power to cross the line would depend upon their neighbors. Under the Constitution such commerce belongs not to the States but to Congress to regulate. It may carry out its views of public policy whatever indirect effect they may have upon the activities of the States. Instead of being encountered by a prohibitive tariff at her boundaries the State encounters the public policy of the United States which it is for Congress to express. The public policy of the United States is shaped with a view to the benefit of the nation as a whole. If . . . a State should take a different view of the propriety of sustaining a lottery from that which generally prevails, I cannot believe that the fact would require a different decision from that reached in *Champion v. Ames*. Yet in that case it would be said with quite as much force as in this that

Congress was attempting to intermeddle with the State's domestic affairs. The national welfare as understood by Congress may require a different attitude within its sphere from that of some self-seeking State.

Bailey v. Drexel Furniture Co.

259 U.S. 20 (1922), 8-1
Opinion of the Court: Taft, C.J. (Brandeis, Day, Holmes, McKenna, McReynolds, Pitney, Van Devanter)
Dissenting: Clarke
In the Child Labor Tax Law, Congress placed a 10 percent tax on the net profits of any mining company that employed children under age 16 or any factory that employed those under 14, or where children between 14 and 16 worked more than eight hours a day or six days a week. Drexel Furniture, which employed such children, paid the tax but sued J. W. Bailey, a regional collector for the Internal Revenue Service, for a refund.

Why did the Court hold that Congress cannot tax if the tax is intended to penalize? How does it conclude that Congress intended the tax to serve as a penalty rather than to raise revenue? What does Taft fear if the Court were to uphold the tax?

Taft, for the Court:
This case presents the question of the constitutional validity of the Child Labor Tax Law . . .

The law is attacked on the ground that it is a regulation of the employment of child labor in the states—an exclusively state function under the federal Constitution and within the reservations of the Tenth Amendment. It is defended on the ground that it is a mere excise tax levied by the Congress of the United States under its broad power of taxation conferred by section 8, article 1, of the federal Constitution. We must construe the law and interpret the intent and meaning of Congress from the language of the act. The words are to be given their ordinary meaning unless the context shows that they are differently used. Does this law impose a tax with only that incidental restraint and regulation which a tax must inevitably involve? Or does it regulate by the use of the so-called tax as a penalty? If a tax, it is clearly an excise. If it were an excise on a commodity or other thing of value, we might not be permitted under previous decisions of this court to infer solely from its heavy burden that the act intends a prohibition instead of a tax. But this act is more. It provides a heavy

exaction for a departure from a detailed and specified course of conduct in business. That course of business is that employers shall employ in mines and quarries, children of an age greater than 16 years; in mills and factories, children of an age greater than 14 years, and shall prevent children of less than 16 years in mills and factories from working more than 8 hours a day or 6 days in the week. If an employer departs from this prescribed course of business, he is to pay to the government one-tenth of his entire net income in the business for a full year. The amount is not to be proportioned in any degree to the extent or frequency of the departures, but is to be paid by the employer in full measure whether he employs 500 children for a year, or employs only one for a day. Moreover, if he does not know the child is within the named age limit, he is not to pay; that is to say, it is only where he knowingly departs from the prescribed course that payment is to be exacted. Scienters are associated with penalties, not with taxes. The employer's factory is to be subject to inspection at any time not only by the taxing officers of the Treasury, the Department normally charged with the collection of taxes, but also by the Secretary of Labor and his subordinates, whose normal function is the advancement and protection of the welfare of the workers. In the light of these features of the act, a court must be blind not to see that the so-called tax is imposed to stop the employment of children within the age limits prescribed. Its prohibitory and regulatory effect and purpose are palpable . . .

It is the high duty and function of this court in cases regularly brought to its bar to decline to recognize or enforce seeming laws of Congress, dealing with subjects not entrusted to Congress, but left or committed by the supreme law of the land to the control of the states. We cannot avoid the duty, even though it require us to refuse to give effect to legislation designed to promote the highest good. The good sought in unconstitutional legislation is an insidious feature, because it leads citizens and legislators of good purpose to promote it, without thought of the serious breach it will make in the ark of our covenant, or the harm which will come from breaking down recognized standards. In the maintenance of local self-government, on the one hand, and the national power, on the other, our country has been able to endure and prosper for near a century and a half.

Out of a proper respect for the acts of a coordinate branch of the government, this court has gone far to sustain taxing acts as such, even though there has been ground for suspecting, from the weight of the tax, it was intended to destroy its subject. But in the act before us the presumption of validity cannot prevail, because the proof of the contrary is found on the very face of its provisions. Grant the validity of this law, and all that Congress would need to do, hereafter, in seeking to take over to its control any one of the great number of subjects of public interest, jurisdiction of which the states have never parted with, and which are reserved to them by the Tenth Amendment, would be to enact a detailed measure of complete regulation of the subject and enforce it by a so-called tax upon departures from it. To give such magic to the word 'tax' would be to break down all constitutional limitation of the powers of Congress and completely wipe out the sovereignty of the states.

The difference between a tax and a penalty is sometimes difficult to define, and yet the consequences of the distinction in the required method of their collection often are important. Where the sovereign enacting the law has power to impose both tax and penalty, the difference between revenue production and mere regulation may be immaterial, but not so when one sovereign can impose a tax only, and the power of regulation rests in another. Taxes are occasionally imposed in the discretion of the Legislature on proper subjects with the primary motive of obtaining revenue from them and with the incidental motive of discouraging them by making their continuance onerous. They do not lose their character as taxes because of the incidental motive. But there comes a time in the extension of the penalizing features of the so-called tax when it loses its character as such and becomes a mere penalty, with the characteristics of regulation and punishment. Such is the case in the law before us. Although Congress does not invalidate the contract of employment or expressly declare that the employment within the mentioned ages is illegal, it does exhibit its intent practically to achieve the latter result by adopting the criteria of wrongdoing and imposing its principal consequence on those who transgress its standard.

The case before us cannot be distinguished from that of *Hammer v. Dagenhart*. Congress there enacted a law to prohibit transportation in interstate commerce of goods made at a factory in which there was employment of children within the same ages and for the same number of hours a day and days in a week as are penalized by the act in this case. This court held the law in that case to be void. It said: 'In our view the necessary effect of this act is, by means of a prohibition against the movement in interstate commerce of ordinary commercial commodities, to regulate the hours of labor of children in factories and mines within the states, a purely state authority.' . . .

The Congressional power over interstate commerce is, within its proper scope, just as complete and unlimited as the congressional power to tax, and the legislative motive in its exercise is just as free from judicial suspicion and inquiry. Yet when Congress threatened to stop interstate commerce in ordinary and necessary commodities, unobjectionable as subjects of transportation, and to deny the same to the people of a state in order to coerce them into compliance with Congress' regulation of state concerns, the Court said this was not in fact regulation of interstate commerce, but rather that of state concerns and was invalid. So here the so-called tax is a penalty to coerce people of a state to act as Congress wishes them to act in respect of a matter completely the business of the state government under the federal Constitution . . .

For the reasons given, we must hold the Child Labor Tax Law invalid.

Adkins v. Children's Hospital

261 U.S. 525 (1923), 5-3
Opinion of the Court: Sutherland (Butler, McKenna, McReynolds, Van Devanter)
Dissenting: Holmes, Sanford, Taft
Not participating: Brandeis

Liberty of contract receives its strongest and most defined statement in this case. Does Sutherland's opinion resolve the inconsistencies between Lochner v. New York and Muller v. Oregon? Continue them? Deepen them? Do any of the opinions in the case recognize that most employers and employees do not bargain over wages or, if they do, do so unequally? After striking a respectful tone for legislative judgment, Sutherland says that it must be ignored when "opposed to the Constitution." Does he make it clear how the Court in resolving such matters avoids making subjective judgments of its own? Now overruled, Adkins is widely regarded as an elegant statement of reactionary constitutional law. Might it also be seen as an early statement of feminism?

Sutherland, for the Court:

The question presented for determination by these appeals is the constitutionality of the Act of September 19, 1918, providing for the fixing of minimum wages for women and children in the District of Columbia . . .

The judicial duty of passing upon the constitutionality of an act of Congress is one of great gravity and delicacy. The statute here in question has successfully borne the scrutiny of the legislative branch of the government, which, by enacting it, has affirmed its validity, and that determination must be given great weight. This court, by an unbroken line of decisions from Chief Justice Marshall to the present day, has steadily adhered to the rule that every possible presumption is in favor of the validity of an act of Congress until overcome beyond rational doubt. But, if by clear and indubitable demonstration a statute be opposed to the Constitution, we have no choice but to say so. The Constitution, by its own terms, is the supreme law of the land, emanating from the people, the repository of ultimate sovereignty under our form of government. A congressional statute, on the other hand, is the act of an agency of this sovereign authority, and if it conflict with the Constitution must fall; for that which is not supreme must yield to that which is . . .

The statute now under consideration is attacked upon the ground that it authorizes an unconstitutional interference with the freedom of contract included within the guaranties of the due process clause of the Fifth Amendment. That the right to contract about one's affairs is a part of the liberty of the individual protected by this clause is settled by the decisions of this court and is no longer open to question . . . Within this liberty are contracts of employment of labor. In making such contracts, generally speaking, the parties have an equal right to obtain from each other the best terms they can as the result of private bargaining . . .

There is, of course, no such thing as absolute freedom of contract. It is subject to a great variety of restraints. But freedom of contract is, nevertheless, the general rule and restraint the exception, and the exercise of legislative authority to abridge it can be justified only by the existence of exceptional circumstances. Whether these circumstances exist in the present case constitutes the question to be answered . . .

In the Muller Case the validity of an Oregon statute, forbidding the employment of any female in certain industries more than 10 hours during any one day was upheld. The decision proceeded upon the theory that the difference between the sexes may justify a different rule respecting hours of labor in the case of women than in the case of men. It is pointed out that these consist in differences of physical structure, especially in respect of the maternal functions, and also in the fact that historically woman has always been dependent upon man, who has established his control by superior physical strength . . . But the ancient inequality of the sexes, otherwise than physical, as suggested in the Muller Case has continued 'with diminishing intensity.' In view of the great—not to say revolutionary—changes which have taken place since that utterance, in the contractual, political, and civil status of women, culminating in the Nineteenth Amendment, it is not unreasonable to say that these differences have now come almost, if not quite, to the vanishing point. In this aspect of the matter, while the physical differences must be recognized in appropriate cases, and legislation fixing hours or conditions of work may properly take them into account, we cannot accept the doctrine that women of mature age . . . require or may be subjected to restrictions upon their liberty of contract which could not lawfully be imposed in the case of men under similar circumstances. To do so would be to ignore all the implications to be drawn from the present day trend of legislation, as well as that of common thought and usage, by which woman is accorded emancipation from the old doctrine that she must be given special protection or be subjected to special restraint in her contractual and civil relationships. In passing, it may be noted that the instant statute applies in the case of a woman employer contracting with a woman employee as it does when the former is a man . . .

[T]he statute now under consideration . . . deal(s) with incidents of the employment having no necessary effect upon the heart of the contract; that is, the amount of wages to be paid and received. A law forbidding work to continue beyond a given number of hours leaves the parties free to contract about wages and thereby equalize whatever additional burdens may be imposed upon the employer as a result of the restrictions as to hours, by an adjustment in respect of the amount of wages. Enough has been said to show that the authority to fix hours of labor cannot be exercised except in respect of those occupations where work of long continued duration is detrimental to health. This court has been careful in every case where the question has been raised, to place its decision upon this limited authority of the Legislature to regulate hours of labor and to disclaim any purpose to uphold the legislation as fixing wages, thus recognizing an essential difference between the two . . .

[T]he statute in question . . . is not a law dealing with any business charged with a public interest or with public work, or to meet and tide over a temporary emergency. It has nothing to do with the character, methods or periods of wage payments. It does not prescribe hours of labor or conditions under which labor is to be done. It is not for the protection of persons under legal disability or for the prevention of fraud. It is simply and exclusively a price-fixing law, confined to adult women (for we are not now considering the provisions relating to minors), who are legally as capable of contracting for themselves as men. It forbids two parties having lawful capacity—under penalties as to the employer—to freely contract with one another in respect of the price for which one shall render service to the other in a purely private employment where both are willing, perhaps anxious, to agree, even though the consequence may be to oblige one to surrender a desirable engagement and the other to dispense with the services of a desirable employee . . .

The relation between earnings and morals is not capable of standardization. It cannot be shown that well-paid women safeguard their morals more carefully than those who are poorly paid. Morality rests upon other considerations than wages, and there is, certainly, no such prevalent connection between the two as to justify a broad attempt to adjust the latter with reference to the former . . .

The law takes account of the necessities of only one party to the contract. It ignores the necessities of the employer by compelling him to pay not less than a certain sum, not only whether the employee is capable of earning it, but irrespective of the ability of his business to sustain the burden, generously leaving him, of course, the privilege of abandoning his business as an alternative for going on at a loss . . . To the extent that the sum fixed exceeds the fair value of the services rendered, it amounts to a compulsory exaction from the employer for the support of a partially indigent person, for whose condition there rests upon him no peculiar responsibility, and therefore, in effect, arbitrarily shifts to his shoulders a burden which, if it belongs to anybody, belongs to society as a whole . . .

A statute requiring an employer to pay in money, to pay at prescribed and regular intervals, to pay the value of the services rendered, even to pay with fair relation to the extent of the benefit obtained from the service, would be understandable. But a statute which prescribes payment without regard to any of these things, and solely with relation to circumstances apart from the contract of employment, the business af-

fected by it, and the work done under it, is so clearly the product of a naked, arbitrary exercise of power that it cannot be allowed to stand under the Constitution of the United States . . .

Finally, it may be said that if, in the interest of the public welfare, the police power may be invoked to justify the fixing of a minimum wage, it may, when the public welfare is thought to require it, be invoked to justify a maximum wage. The power to fix high wages connotes, by like course of reasoning, the power to fix low wages. If, in the face of the guaranties of the Fifth Amendment, this form of legislation shall be legally justified, the field for the operation of the police power will have been widened to a great and dangerous degree . . . A wrong decision does not end with itself; it is a precedent, and, with the swing of sentiment, its bad influence may run from one extremity of the arc to the other . . .

It follows, from what has been said, that the act in question passes the limit prescribed by the Constitution, and accordingly the decrees of the court below are affirmed.

Taft, C.J., dissenting:

Legislatures in limiting freedom of contract between employee and employer by a minimum wage proceed on the assumption that employees, in the class receiving least pay, are not upon a full level of equality of choice with their employer and in their necessitous circumstances are prone to accept pretty much anything that is offered. They are peculiarly subject to the overreaching of the harsh and greedy employer. The evils of the sweating system and of the long hours and low wages which are characteristic of it are well known. . . . I agree that it is a disputable question in the field of political economy how far a statutory requirement of maximum hours or minimum wages may be a useful remedy for these evils, and whether it may not make the case of the oppressed employee worse than it was before. But it is not the function of this court to hold congressional acts invalid simply because they are passed to carry out economic views which the Court believes to be unwise or unsound . . .

The right of the Legislature under the Fifth and Fourteenth Amendments to limit the hours of employment on the score of the health of the employee . . . has been firmly established. As to that . . . the line had been pricked out so that it has become a well formulated rule. In *Holden v. Hardy*, it was applied to miners and rested on the unfavorable environment of employment in mining and smelting. In *Lochner v. New York,* it was held that restricting those employed in bakeries to 10 hours a day was an arbitrary and invalid interference with the liberty of contract secured by the Fourteenth Amendment. Then followed a number of cases beginning with *Muller v. Oregon,* sustaining the validity of a limit on maximum hours of labor for women . . . and following these cases came *Bunting v. Oregon.* In that case, this court sustained a law limiting the hours of labor of any person, whether man or woman, working in any mill, factory, or manufacturing establishment to 10 hours a day with a proviso as to further hours . . . The law covered the whole field of industrial employment and certainly covered the case of persons employed in bakeries. Yet the opinion in the Bunting Case does not mention the Lochner Case. No one can suggest any constitutional distinction between employment in a bakery and one in any other kind of a manufacturing establishment which should make a limit of hours in the one invalid, and the same limit in the other permissible. It is impossible for me to reconcile the Bunting Case and the Lochner Case, and I have always supposed that the Lochner Case was thus overruled *sub silentio.* Yet the opinion of the Court herein in support of its conclusion quotes from the opinion in the Lochner Case as one which has been sometimes distinguished but never overruled. Certainly there was no attempt to distinguish it in the Bunting Case.

However, the opinion herein does not overrule the Bunting Case in express terms, and therefore, I assume that the conclusion in this case rests on the distinction between a minimum of wages and a maximum of hours in the limiting of liberty to contract. I regret to be at variance with the Court as to the substance of this distinction. In absolute freedom of contract the one term is as important as the other, for both enter equally into the consideration given and received . . .

If I am right in thinking that the Legislature can find as much support in experience for the view that a sweating wage has as great and as direct a tendency to bring about an injury to the health and morals of workers, as for the view that long hours injure their health, then I respectfully submit that *Muller v. Oregon,* controls this case. The law which was there sustained forbade the employment of any female in any mechanical establishment or factory or laundry for more than 10 hours. This covered a pretty wide field

in women's work, and it would not seem that any sound distinction between that case, and this can be built up on the fact that the law before us applies to all occupations of women . . .

I am not sure from a reading of the opinion whether the Court thinks the authority of *Muller v. Oregon* is shaken by the adoption of the Nineteenth Amendment. The Nineteenth Amendment did not change the physical strength or limitations of women upon which the decision in *Muller v. Oregon* rests. The amendment did give women political power and makes more certain that legislative provisions for their protection will be in accord with their interests as they see them. But I do not think we are warranted in varying constitutional construction based on physical differences between men and women, because of the amendment.

Holmes, dissenting:

The question in this case is the broad one, Whether Congress can establish minimum rates of wages for women in the District of Columbia with due provision for special circumstances, or whether we must say that Congress had no power to meddle with the matter at all. To me . . . the power of Congress seems absolutely free from doubt. The end, to remove conditions leading to ill health, immorality and the deterioration of the race, no one would deny to be within the scope of constitutional legislation. The means are means that have the approval of Congress, of many States, and of those governments from which we have learned our greatest lessons . . . [I]n the present instance the only objection that can be urged is found within the vague contours of the Fifth Amendment, prohibiting the depriving any person of liberty or property without due process of law. To that I turn.

The earlier decisions upon the same words in the Fourteenth Amendment began within our memory and went no farther than an unpretentious assertion of the liberty to follow the ordinary callings. Later that innocuous generality was expanded into the dogma, Liberty of Contract. Contract is not specially mentioned in the text that we have to construe. It is merely an example of doing what you want to do, embodied in the word liberty. But pretty much all law consists in forbidding men to do some things that they want to do, and contract is no more exempt from law than other acts. Without enumerating all the restrictive laws that have been upheld I will mention a few that seem to me to have interfered with liberty of contract quite as seriously and directly as the one before us. Usury laws prohibit contracts by which a man receives more than so much interest for the money that he lends. Statutes of frauds restrict many contracts to certain forms. Some Sunday laws prohibit practically all contracts during one-seventh of our whole life. Insurance rates may be regulated . . . Employers of miners may be required to pay for coal by weight before screening . . . The responsibility of employers to their employees may be profoundly modified . . . Finally women's hours of labor may be fixed, *Muller v. Oregon* . . . and the principle was extended to men with the allowance of a limited overtime to be paid for 'at the rate of time and one-half of the regular wage,' in *Bunting v. Oregon.*

I confess that I do not understand the principle on which the power to fix a minimum for the wages of women can be denied by those who admit the power to fix a maximum for their hours of work . . . The bargain is equally affected whichever half you regulate. *Muller v. Oregon,* I take it, is as good law today as it was in 1908. It will need more than the Nineteenth Amendment to convince me that there are no differences between men and women, or that legislation cannot take those differences into account. I should not hesitate to take them into account if I thought it necessary to sustain this Act. But after *Bunting v. Oregon,* I had supposed that it was not necessary, and that *Lochner v. New York* would be allowed a deserved repose.

8

THE NEW DEAL: ECONOMIC AND CONSTITUTIONAL CRISIS

The day after Labor Day 1929, the American stock market had reached an all-time high. At 381.17, the Dow Jones Industrial Average had risen more than 80 points in a year, and quadrupled in four years. The market drifted downward later in the month but rallied back in early October. Few shareowners were worried. On October 16, the well-known Yale economist Irving Fisher declared that "stock prices have reached what looks like a permanently high plateau."* But on October 23, a huge drop came in the final hour of trading. The next day, "Black Thursday," prices plunged as nearly 13 million shares changed hands, small volume by modern standards but a record at the time. Selling continued the following week, reaching a fury on Tuesday, October 29, when the stock ticker ran two-and-a-half hours behind trades, which now reached 16.4 million shares, a level not seen again for 35 years. The Dow Industrials closed at 230.07; most other stocks were hit even harder. The party of the

1920s was over and, in time, so was a constitutional era.

The Great Decline

The Crash triggered the deepest, most sustained and thoroughgoing economic contraction in the nation's history and led to a worldwide depression. The slide in equities continued through the year and for the next four years, their shrinking indices describing the smashed economy itself. By November 1929, $30 billion in market wealth had disappeared, by mid-1932, losses grew to $75 billion, and the Dow Industrials were at 41.22, 11 percent of their high before the crash. Almost everything was scaled down. Businesses had lost much of their capital resources, individuals much of their life savings. Stronger companies cut back and laid off workers; less robust ones went bankrupt and closed. By 1932, manufacturing was only 54 percent of its 1929 level; in automobiles, the strongest industry of the 1920s, it was 25 percent. In all, production had receded to the level of 1913, a

---

* Quoted in John C. Galbraith, *The Great Crash,* 1929 (Boston: Houghton Mifflin, 1955), 75.

jarring setback for an economy bent on ever-accelerating growth.

Many banks had made unsound loans and failed, bringing ruin to depositors. Prices fell, those of commodities so precipitously that many heavily mortgaged farms went to foreclosure. In manufacturing the dried up demand was daunting. By the time many products reached market, their price had fallen below what it cost to make them. Among those hardest hit were industrial workers and their families. By the end of 1932, unemployment had reached 25 percent of the workforce, and many of those with jobs worked fewer hours. Deflation fed on itself: Lower production meant less work, which meant less income, which meant lower demand, which meant lower production. For an individual family or business, cutting back and doing with less made great economic sense. Collectively, however, it was tragic in its effect.

Economists generally agree there was no one cause of the Depression. The stock market crash set it off, but a dangerous slope had already been reached. Speculation had mushroomed by 1929, luring more and more persons into the market. Many used margin—money borrowed from their brokers—to buy more stocks until that debt reach $8.5 billion. Prices of companies were bid to astonishing heights, out of all proportion to their ability to pay dividends or maintain growth. The price of RCA, for example, one of the highest flyers of the Twenties, was well over $500 a share in today's dollars, without the company ever having paid a dividend.

A cyclical slowing down of many industries in the late 1920s was ignored by investors and speculators alike. Eventually, the froth in prices would have guaranteed a break in the market, but such a "correction" alone would not have caused the Depression. The economist John Kenneth Galbraith has pointed to several underlying weaknesses in the prosperous industrial economy of the 1920s. Income distribution had become increasingly skewed. Worker productivity during the decade rose far more than did average wages and salary. By 1929, those in the highest 5 per-

cent of income controlled about 25 percent of all earnings. Continued prosperity was too dependent on their sustained spending and investment, especially on such durable consumer goods as cars and housing, two of the booming industries of the 1920s. This was the income group most immediately affected by the crash in stocks. When it cut back—many in it were wiped out—an enormous slack in demand followed. Because of the pattern of income distribution, this loss was not easily made up by the general consumer.

The holding company structure, still dominant in many large industries including railroads and utilities, depended on an upward flow of dividends from operating companies to pay interest on the bonded debt of the upstream combinations. When this stream was interrupted, investment had to be cut back, often as the only choice besides bankruptcy. These central deflationary decisions in turn produced further retrenchment down the line. The banking structure served little better. Overextended with what had once been optimistic loans, many banks failed when business borrowers could not repay. "Runs" became epidemic. Depositors, many of whom were individuals, hearing of a failure elsewhere would rush to withdraw their money from an otherwise secure bank, causing it to fail or temporarily close.

Finally, there was international trade. Historically, the United States had been a debtor nation, borrowing capital overseas and meeting the interest and repaying the loans from a surplus of exports over imports. The European debt of World War I, however, had made the nation a creditor. To maintain international balance, the United States needed to import more than it exported so that borrowing nations could earn enough to repay their loans. High tariffs and the vitality of American exports now produced the opposite result. When worldwide deflation hit, European debtor countries either defaulted or drastically cut back imports from the United States. American foreign trade dropped from $10 billion in 1929 to $3 billion in 1932. The result was further losses, especially for foreign bond holders and farmers, many of whom depended on exporting agricultural surplus. Wheat, a big export crop, fell from $1.05 a bushel to just 39 cents.

One weakness led to another until a downward spiral was in full swing. Few leaders or experts could have predicted the debacle because few understood well enough the underlying economic flaws that later became all too apparent. Without such insight, they now found it difficult to suggest ways to reverse its course.

Failure of Policy and Imagination

Herbert Hoover was the Republican nominee in 1928, Calvin Coolidge having declined to run again. He won 58 percent of the popular vote and carried all but eight states against Democrat Alfred E. Smith of New York. He had first won public notice for his work in food and relief administration during and just after the World War, being hailed as the Great Humanitarian. Later he had ably served as secretary of commerce under both Harding and Coolidge. A hard-working, self-made man now of independent wealth, he had obvious executive ability and seemed far more suited for presidency than either of his Republican predecessors in the 1920s. In better times, he might well have led a resurgence of Republican Progressivism. But the Depression diverted nearly all the attention and energy of his administration. Ineffectiveness in dealing with the crisis dimmed whatever bright promise he had brought to the office.

Like many other leaders, Hoover was slow to grasp the enormity of the crisis—ironically, he had been one of the few in government in the 1920s to warn against excessive speculation. He was not helped by his arch-conservative Treasury Secretary Andrew Mellon, a holdover from the Harding and Coolidge days. While insisting publicly that an end to the decline was near, Mellon privately believed it should be allowed to go "right to the bottom," as a kind of social darwinian purge.

Hoover himself worked hard but with little success to moderate the crisis. Where the government had money, he increased public construction and urged state and local governments to do the same. He proposed a short moratorium on the payment of war reparations and other intergovernmental debt. In his preference for voluntary action, he gained pledges from business leaders not to cut wages of those still employed. The agreements held for a year or two before giving way to a mushrooming of sweatshops. He urged an increase in charity to give relief to the unemployed and near starving and set up committees of volunteers to solicit money. The results were far short of expectations.

More than talk and volunteer work were needed, yet Hoover resisted bolder initiatives. Along with many other leaders of the day, he was bound by fixed economic ideas, perhaps reinforced by his dramatic rise from early poverty. Though an able administrator, he lacked the political skill that in time of crisis might have allowed him to move others to new ends. As unemployment grew to nearly 15 million, state and local relief resources gave out. Hoover stubbornly resisted proposals for a federal relief program, believing a dole would unbalance the budget and create a class of public dependents. No unemployment insurance program of the sort many European countries had was in place to cushion the blow of job loss.

There is no clearer example of wrong-headed policy than Hoover's obsession with balancing the budget, a holy writ he shared with most other public leaders regardless of party or social philosophy. Even Hoover's 1932 opponent, Franklin Roosevelt, called for it during the presidential campaign. When government income dropped, deficits rose. If a family or company went into large debt, it made great sense to cut back costs and try to bring in more money to liquidate it. But what was rational for individual economic units might not be so for the unit of last resort, the federal government. If money, demand, and jobs had dried up through deflation,

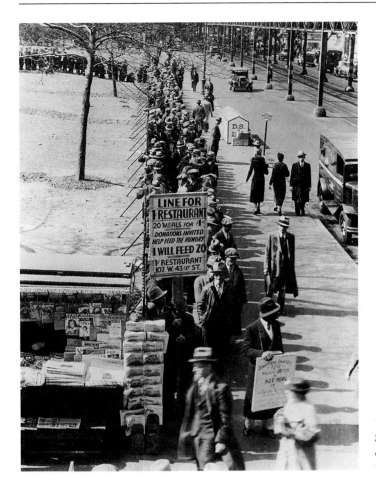

"Bread" lines, like this one near Times Square in New York in 1932, were a common daily scene in large cities as the Depression deepened.

it made sense to create them by going into even greater debt, say, by the deficit financing of massive work projects. Only government could do this, but the idea was yet too heretical for those who were running the country or wanted to. Instead, the well-intentioned president returned his own salary to the Treasury as a gesture of reducing the deficit.

One Hoover proposal that did dent deflation was that for the Reconstruction Finance Corporation (RFC), which Congress created early in 1932. The agency lent money to beleaguered banks, railways, and certain other businesses. The theory was orthodox: Get things moving by funneling stimulus in at the top and letting it trickle down. The RFC kept many banks from closing and shored up some railroads on the verge of bankruptcy, but as a main antideflationary thrust it was too little too late.

Hoover, Mellon, and many others believed too long that the decline would be self-correcting, as declines in the past had seemed to be. But this downward spiral was different; as it continued, it became worse. The expectation of more deflation produced more deflation. The crisis became as much a psychic as an economic depression. Despair and loss of confidence accompanied loss of work, long unemployment, and financial ruin. It was a vicious circle into which highest public leadership was unable to break.

Mandate for Change

The Democratic nomination in 1932 almost assured election against the now widely unpopular incumbent. Franklin D. Roosevelt, the governor of New York, emerged the winner from the crowded field. He had been assistant secretary of the Navy during the war and, in 1920, had been the vice presidential nominee on the defeated Democratic ticket headed by James Cox. His background was one of wealth and privilege, much like that of his distant cousin, Theodore Roosevelt. He was a person of ebullient, self-assured charm and persuasiveness, and considerable oratorical gifts, in marked contrast to Hoover's shy, dour personality. These skills and personal qualities allowed Roosevelt to deftly manipulate subordinates, the press, and Congressional opponents alike.

With the unending economic crisis the chief campaign issue, Roosevelt won 57 percent of the popular vote and carried all but six states, an almost mirror image of Hoover's victory four years before. The election marked an 18.5 percentage point swing away from Hoover's 1928 total and a 16.5 swing from Alfred E. Smith the Democratic nominee, to Roosevelt, the greatest four-year shift in presidential election history. Not before or since have voters so emphatically chosen a new deal.

Roosevelt had first used the term in accepting the Democratic nomination: "I pledge you, I pledge myself, to a New Deal for the American people." He returned to the theme often during the campaign and it became the collective name for his policies as president. Yet he outlined his program only in tantalizingly vague terms, promising benefits for farmers, workers, the jobless, and hard-pressed business. In all this his greatest asset was that he was not Hoover.

The electoral voice that called so loudly for change was moderate. Norman Thomas, the Socialist candidate, and William Z. Foster, the Communist, urged radical measures to partly or fully dismantle the capitalist system. Together, they polled fewer than a million votes, less than 2.5 percent of the total. Thomas's vote was less than his fellow Socialist Eugene Debs had gotten 12 years before. The faith of Americans in industrial capitalism as they knew it had been badly shaken, but they were not ready to abandon it or the constitutional system under which it had developed and flourished.

The One Hundred Days

Roosevelt took office on March 4, 1933, and immediately faced a banking crisis.* More than 5,000 institutions had failed in three years, resulting in deposit losses of $3.4 billion. Now, widespread withdrawals and cash hoarding had created a currency shortage that threatened to produce many more closures. In the week before inauguration, governors of 22 states had declared bank "holidays." Roosevelt's first action as president was to proclaim a national bank holiday that shut financial institutions including stock exchanges for a week. In the meantime, he drew up a remedial plan, resisting such radical solutions as government takeover of the banks, in favor of empowering the Federal Reserve to issue currency against bank assets and making gold hoarding illegal. He called Congress into immediate special session and gave it the plan the day it convened. It was enacted eight hours later.

Roosevelt seized the momentum of the banking action to get Congressional passage of more than a dozen important programs in the weeks that followed. When its special session ended on June 16, Congress had enacted, virtually under the president's direction, the most intensive, frenzied, and perhaps creative legislative program in history. The "One Hundred Days" has

---

* The Twentieth Amendment cut the lame duck period between election and office several weeks by moving presidential inaugurations up to January 20 and convening Congress fully 11 months earlier from December to January 3. It had been ratified a month earlier, but was not to take effect until the next election.

Repeal

Consumption of intoxicating drink has been a matter of social concern and legal policy since colonial times. Several states, beginning with Maine in 1851, have from time to time banned the manufacture or sale of alcoholic beverages. The temperance movement after the Civil War gained attention and adherents by focusing on the apparent link between drinking and various ills including crime, poverty, family abuse and neglect, promiscuity, liver damage, and absenteeism and incompetence in the workplace. Protestant evangelical churches, the Women's Christian Temperance Union, the Anti-Saloon League, and the Prohibition Party, which ran candidates in several presidential elections, were among the organizations and interests in the movement. It was strongest in the South and rural Midwest, weakest in urban areas of the Northeast and among Roman Catholics and immigrants, particularly those from Ireland and Germany. Temperance gained new strength when it became linked with women's suffrage and other reforms of the Progressive period that had wide middle class support.

By 1916, 21 states had banned saloons. With "drys" outnumbering "wets" two to one in the Congress elected that year, the drive for nationwide prohibition became irresistible. In December 1917, Congress adopted the Eighteenth Amendment, outlawing "the manufacture, sale, or transportation of intoxicating liquors" in the United States and also their import or export. Its ratification 13 months later was followed by an enforcement statute, the Volstead Act, defining "intoxicating liquors" to include any drink having an alcohol content greater than one-half of 1 percent, thus prohibiting beer and wine along with "hard" liquor. Criminal investigative powers were given to the Treasury Department. The act virtually ended the liquor business, which in its ramified manufacturing, distribution, and retail sales, was the nation's seventh largest.

As social policy, some early results of Prohibition were encouraging. Alcohol consumption dropped sharply as did arrests for drunkenness, cost of maintaining prisons, auto accidents attributable to drunk driving, and the treatment of diseases related to alcoholism. But by the mid-1920s, enforcement, never easy, grew increasingly problematic as violations of the Volstead Act multiplied. "Bootlegging," "speakeasies," and "bathtub gin" became common terms and a vast underground criminal enterprise directed by colorful but dangerous figures like Al Capone replaced the once legitimate liquor industry. The Roaring Twenties were dry on the surface but in many cities and towns distinctly damp underneath.

The Supreme Court decided several cases that lent support to enforcement. It upheld concurrent federal and state prosecution, broadened the

since been a model for every new president but never since approached for sheer sustained innovative law-making. In the haste, many details were overlooked, and some measures, frankly experimental, turned out to be impractical or unworkable. Yet these deficiencies mattered less than that action was taken and that new solutions were sought where old ones had failed.

Several measures gave direct temporary relief to beleaguered individuals and families. In creation of the Civilian Conservation Corps, 300,000 young men between 18 and 25 were hired to work in camps on road construction, reforestation, and other conservation projects. The Federal Emergency Relief Act gave $500 million to the states to directly aid families of the unemployed and create work projects for the employable. The Home Owners Refinancing Act offered loans to refinance small mortgages on nonfarm dwellings, and the emergency Farm Mortgage Act provided similar help to farmers. These acts prevented many foreclosures.

The Agricultural Adjustment Act (AAA) set out a daring national policy for dealing with long-standing problems of the depressed farm economy. It limited production and thus the price-deflating surplus farmers perennially produced in such basic commodities as corn, wheat, hogs, and dairy products. For voluntarily reducing acreage, a farmer received a subsidy

search and seizure of automobiles, and approved use of wiretap evidence against bootleggers. Yet enforcement was often haphazard, local officials were sometimes corrupt or uncooperative, and there were big breakdowns in urban areas.

Cynicism undermined respect for the law, and growing numbers of persons were coming to resent federal intrusion in their lives. For many, restrictions on drinking were at odds with new opportunities for personal freedom afforded by the auto- mobile and telephone and other modern consumer goods and portrayed so often in movies and radio. By 1928, sentiment for ending or modifying Prohibition entered the presidential election when Alfred E. Smith of New York ran as a wet. The Depression added another spur. Many business and labor leaders argued that repeal would restore an important industry, creating jobs and producing tax revenue; economically here was what there had been all too little of: demand chasing insufficient supply.

Opposition to Prohibition grew in both parties, and in February 1933, Congress did what it had never done before: It proposed an amendment to repeal an amendment. To reduce the chance that entrenched legislators in a handful of rural states might block ratification, it chose the option in Article V that requires assent by conventions called in each state. Except in ratification of the Constitution itself, the procedure had never been used. Approval was astonishingly swift. By early December, 36 states—the needed three-quarters—had ratified;

only one, South Carolina, rejected. Of 21 million voters who cast ballots, 73 percent voted for delegates favoring an end to Prohibition.

The Twenty-first Amendment merely repealed the Eighteenth; it did not make alcohol legal throughout the country. In fact, it barred the transport or import of "intoxicating liquors" into any state in violation of its laws, by that, allowing states wanting to remain dry to do so. Many did or gave that option to their incorporated cities and towns. Today, completely dry areas are difficult to find, but many states and communities have rigorously continued to regulate the time, place, and manner in which "intoxicating liquors" are advertised, bought, or consumed.

The once "noble experiment," Prohibition is now thought to have been a misguided folly or, worse, an attempt to impose rural prejudice and Victorian values on urban sophistication and individual liberty. Yet Prohibition did affect drinking. Alcohol consumption did not reach pre-Prohibition levels for nearly 30 years and never again approached levels of the nineteenth century. If partial success is a measure of effectiveness, as it must so often be in politics, then neither the temperance movement nor Prohibition can be judged complete failures. The error of Prohibition lay in its attempt to impose by law a standard of morality on a diverse population in which that standard was not universally shared, thus limiting the freedom of many who had no abusive habit.

---

paid for by a tax on processors of farm products. Farm income eventually rose, though many farmers never felt comfortable about holding land out of production or thinning herds. The Supreme Court later held tax provisions of the act unconstitutional.

In an ambitious scheme to revive business, the National Industrial Recovery Act (NIRA) authorized the president to set up committees in different industries, on which business and labor were represented. Their charge was to draw up industry "codes" of fair trade practices, maximum working hours, minimum wages, rules for collective bargaining, and the like. When approved by the president, a code had the force of

law. Another part of the act set up the Public Works Administration to put unemployed persons to work in a wide range of public projects from building schools and waterworks to painting post office murals. Eventually, $4.2 billion was spent on more than 30,000 projects. The Supreme Court later found code provisions of the act unconstitutional.

Several measures dealt with long-standing problems in the financial sector. In an executive decision later supported by a joint resolution of Congress, the president removed the nation from the gold standard. This meant, among other things, that holders of government bonds and bills of $20 or higher could no longer demand their gold equivalent. The action stimulated foreign trade, ended the drain of metal to Europe where creditors had been "cashing in" on the gold-backed paper, and caused stock and commodity prices to rise. The Truth in Securities Act required that new stock issues be publicly registered and certain information be disclosed to prospective buyers. The Glass-Steagall Banking Act created the Federal Bank Deposit Insurance Corporation (FDIC) to insure individual deposits up to $5,000 and restricted speculative activity by banks.

One of the most successful and far-reaching actions of the first One Hundred Days was the creation of the Tennessee Valley Authority (TVA). As an independent government corporation, it began the unified hydroelectric development in Tennessee and parts of six other states, in all, an area larger than most countries. Two earlier but scaled down versions of the project, the brainchild of Republican Senator George Norris of Nebraska, were approved by Congress but had been vetoed by Coolidge and Hoover who believed they would compete with private enterprise. Now Norris had Roosevelt's enthusiastic support and a far more ambitious plan was passed. In the next 20 years, more than 50 dams and power plants were built on the Tennessee and Cumberland Rivers and tributaries. They led to flood control, reclamation, reforestation, improved navigation, and the production of low-cost electricity, a boon for the entire region. The TVA harnessed the destructive power of an unruly river system and put it to productive use in what became a world model for the cooperation of government and private enterprise in regional development.

The "Second" New Deal

Many jump-start measures of the One Hundred Days were filled out or supplemented in the next three years in a continuous stream of reform legislation and executive directives. Federal spending grew enormously as did the size of the federal bureaucracy with its unending stream of new "alphabet" agencies.

Three important early initiatives were the creation of the Export-Import Bank (EXIM), the Securities and Exchange Commission (SEC), and the Federal Housing Administration (FHA). The first aimed at encouraging foreign trade by providing loans and credits to American exporters of agricultural and industrial products. The SEC was empowered to oversee stock market operations and prevent unfair trade practices. Concurrently, the Federal Reserve Board was given power to restrict the use of margin in stock purchases to curb speculation. The FHA ensured loans made by banks and other institutions for the repair and construction of private dwellings, to improve housing standards and create a sound system of home financing.

In his 1935 State of the Union message to Congress, Roosevelt outlined still other reform measures for aid to the elderly, the unemployed, small farmers, and labor. Creation of the Rural Electrification Administration (REA), for example, helped bring power to isolated areas. The Works Progress Administration (WPA), which replaced the Civil Works Administration, signaled Federal withdrawal from direct relief that was now left to states and communities, in favor of job creation through public projects. The Resettlement Administration (RA) helped destitute families in hard-hit rural and urban areas relocate in those more productive. The National Labor Relations Board (NLRB) was empowered to supervise collective bargaining elections and to define unfair labor practices by employers.

The most important measure of this period was the Social Security Act. It set up the social security system that guaranteed limited pensions for persons over 65, assisted the states in aiding the handicapped and dependent children, and set up a federal-state program of unemployment compensation. The massive project was paid for by payroll taxes on employers and employees, starting at 1 percent.

To say the New Deal was controversial is an understatement. It was strongly opposed by

Not all editorial cartoonists were enthusiastic about the New Deal.

many conservatives who saw it as trampling property rights and individual liberties and subverting an economic system that had served the country well. Administered by a dictatorial executive, it would lead to socialism or, worse, an American version of Communism. Critics on the left, disappointed in the New Deal's eclectic pragmatism, contended that it missed the chance to radically reconstruct capitalism and introduce rational, systematic economic planning to government.

Historians have disagreed about how much of a departure the New Deal was. For some, it was simply an extension of the Progressive tradition and its liberal values, providing a badly needed overhaul of capitalism but mainly preserving that economy. Others have argued that in embracing welfare and massive deficit spending, responding to class interests, and emphasizing federal bureaucratic power, it was a sharp break with the often moralistic, largely middle-class character of past reform. It is fair to say the New

Deal modified the capitalist economy and, in doing so, probably saved it. It redefined the purpose of government, expanding it, centralizing it, and by that creating for better and worse new interventions in business and in the lives of individuals. The New Deal may have appeared more radical than it was because it was preceded by a laissez-faire revival in the 1920s and the conservative, rigid leadership of the Hoover administration and most other government.

The New Deal was much less than a complete success. It stopped the economic decline, addressed desperate individual needs, and restored a measure of confidence about the future. But it did not end the Depression. In fact, a severe recession in 1937–1938 was a big setback. Full economic recovery and renewal of growth awaited the enormous economic stimulus of World War II.

What was the judgment of the American people? In the 1934 Congressional elections, Democrats gained nine seats in the House and nine in the Senate. It was only the second time in the two-party era that a majority party was able to increase its margin in both houses in a midterm election. The presidential election of 1936 was a virtual referendum on the New Deal. Roosevelt defeated the Republican Alfred Landon with 61 percent of the popular vote and won the electoral vote by an overwhelming 523-8, carrying every state but Maine and Vermont. In Congress, Democrats gained again and held historic edges of 76-16 in the Senate, 331-89 in the House. Voters spoke with a clarity seldom heard in national politics.

Judicial Resistance

The New Deal was completely experimental. Convinced that orthodoxy had failed, Roosevelt, without a great overall design, tried new things. Many innovative measures sailed in uncharted constitutional waters, at least for peacetime. Many shifted great powers away from the states to the federal government and intruded upon property rights. They challenged business supremacy and the hallowed idea of a self-regulating economy, and led to concerns about economic liberty. Almost all the programs shifted great power to the executive. Such changes had occurred before but they were during wartime for military need and were viewed as temporary. The New Deal measures did not rest on war powers and most were designed to be permanent.

The sway of laissez-faire did not completely die with the massive rejection of Hoover in 1932. Economic conservatives, including many federal judges, seemed bent on resisting the New Deal or at least slowing things down. They may have believed, as the Federalists had after Jefferson's election in the "Revolution of 1800," that the judiciary could serve as a bastion until the winds of change subsided. Interests defeated in one political arena were happy to continue the fight by carrying the conflict into another. Business and property

interests who were adversely affected by New Deal programs brought hundreds of suits to the federal courts, many of them raising constitutional issues. In all, federal judges issued nearly 1,500 injunctions against New Deal programs. Roosevelt's popularity was at new presidential heights yet his recovery program was anything but secure. Opponents, though in a minority, were often deeply alienated and uncompromising. "Roosevelt Hater" became of term of common usage, and many wore the badge proudly.

The Holdover Court

When Chief Justice Taft resigned early in 1930 because of failing health, Hoover named Charles Evans Hughes to succeed him. At 68, the former associate justice became the first person to twice serve on the Court and the oldest appointed chief. He was confirmed over strong objections from liberals who said, perhaps unjustifiably, that he had become too closely associated with business. Later in 1930, Hoover chose Owen J. Roberts to replace Edward Sanford, who had died unexpectedly, as it happened the same day as Taft resigned. It was a pivotal appointment in the constitutional battle to come. Roberts, a conservative Republican, had experience in private practice and as a law professor. He had made his name as a special U.S. attorney in the probe of the Teapot Dome Scandal in the 1920s, and was believed by some to harbor presidential ambitions. When Holmes retired in 1932, Hoover replaced a giant with a giant. His choice, Benjamin Cardozo, chief judge of New York's highest court and an accomplished legal scholar, was generally thought to be the leading state court judge of his day. Hoover's Supreme Court appointments were one of the few bright spots of his presidency.

The new appointees along with Willis Van Devanter, James McReynolds, Pierce Butler, George Sutherland, Louis Brandeis, and Harlan Stone were the sitting Court when Roosevelt was inaugurated in March 1933. Their average age was 67, their average length of service, 10 years. Three—Brandeis, Stone, and Cardozo—could be expected to support reform measures and forego using judicial power to protect economic liberty, though for Brandeis this was tempered by opposition to bigness in almost any form.

Four—Van Devanter, McReynolds, Butler, and Sutherland—later to be called the Four Horsemen after the Apocalypse vision in the New Testament Book of Revelations, were unreconstructed laissez-faire conservatives. Hughes and Roberts were more difficult to classify. Despite liberal objections to his nomination, Hughes recognized the need for new initiatives in the crisis and, by that measure at least, was sympathetic to the New Deal. Roberts, who had no clear judicial philosophy, was often the deciding vote on the closely divided Court.

The Court's success in scuttling parts of the New Deal would not have been possible but for an accident of circumstance. Roosevelt had no chances to appoint new justices during his entire first term, the first president so denied since James Monroe. The Court he faced at his second inauguration in January 1936 was the same one that had been in place four years before. Now, all nine justices were over 60, six over 70. With an average age of 71, it was the oldest Court in history. Where the executive and legislature had undergone a dramatic change of leadership as a result of national crisis, the third branch remained intact. For opponents of the New Deal, this was providential; supporters saw it as a flaw in the constitutional system.

First Response

In two decisions early in 1934 it appeared that a majority of the Court, including the Hoover appointees, might be receptive to New Deal initiatives and experimentation. Though federal legislation was not at issue, the Court upheld state programs that incorporated New Deal goals of debtor relief and price stabilization.

In *Home Building & Loan Association v. Blaisdell* (p. 319), it sustained the Minnesota Mortgage Moratorium Act, which permitted beleaguered home owners and farmers who could not make their mortgage payments, to delay foreclosure for

The Supreme Court in 1934 before it began to hold New Deal programs unconstitutional. Front from left: Louis Brandeis, Willis Van Devanter, Charles Evans Hughes, C.J., James McReynolds, and George Sutherland. Back: Owen Roberts, Pierce Butler, Harlan Stone, and Benjamin Cardozo.

Public Servant Extraordinair

Though he was a corporate attorney by trade and a highly successful one, few figures of the twentieth century contributed more to public service or with a keener sense of duty than Charles Evans Hughes. He looked like a patrician and radiated authority in a way that often gave him a Washington-like bearing of commanding aloofness. Few would have thought of calling him "Charlie." He sprang from a modest but unusual background. His parents, an immigrant Welsh minister and the daughter of a minister, doted on his education, which was mostly at home. The values of humility, hard work, and moral concern they instilled in their only child remained with Hughes his entire life. He was precocious, learning to read at three, reciting classics at six, and mastering several languages before his teens. He graduated from high school at 13, was later first in his law school class at Columbia, and got the highest score ever recorded on the difficult New York State bar exam.

He joined a leading New York City law firm and later married the daughter of one of the senior partners. A hard-driving intensity took a toll on him physically, as it would several times in his life, and he left law practice for the less pressured work of teaching law, at Cornell. Though attracted by the intellectual stimulation of the academic world, he gave in to his father-in-law's

entreaties and returned to law practice two years later, soon becoming a leading figure before New York courts.

His first public role was that of special counsel to a state legislative committee investigating corruption among utility companies and in the insurance business. Success in these efforts led state Republicans to draft him to run for governor in 1906. He won and was reelected in 1908 after turning down an invitation from William Howard Taft to be his vice-presidential running mate. As governor the former corporate attorney initiated many progressive reforms, including the

---

a year or more. The program assumed that general economic conditions or at least those of the mortgagors might improve in that time so that payments could be resumed and loss of home or farm avoided. The law did not cancel debt, but in granting a delay in repayment it changed or could change the terms of almost every mortgage contract in the state. Chief Justice Hughes's opinion for the Court sustaining the impairment of these contracts is striking in its recognition of economic exigency. "While emergency does not create power," Hughes argued, "emergency may furnish the occasion for the exercise of power."

He came close to saying that even a peacetime government might do things in a crisis that would otherwise be forbidden to it. Roosevelt could not have put it better.

Weeks later, the Court upheld a New York statute that aimed to halt the downward spiral of prices in the state's dairy industry by setting minimum and maximum prices for retail sale of milk. The Court had routinely struck down this kind of law in the past when it was applied to businesses outside the narrow range of those "affected with the public interest." But in *Nebbia v. New York*, Justice Roberts, brushing aside liberty

nation's first compulsory workman's compensation program.

He was appointed to the Supreme Court by Taft in 1910 and soon established himself as a moderate on matters of reform and economic regulation, frequently rejecting liberty of contract arguments. In 1916, the Republicans nominated him to run for president against the incumbent Woodrow Wilson. Hughes had not actively tried for the nomination and resigned from the Court when he got it. On election night, he appeared to be the winner, but late returns gave California to Wilson by fewer than 4,000 votes, enabling the president to gain an electoral vote majority of 277-254.

Hughes returned to private law practice in New York. When Harding was elected in 1920, he accepted appointment as secretary of state, a post in which he served with distinction until 1925. He chaired the Washington Disarmament Conference in 1921–1922, taking the lead in negotiating one of the first modern arms control treaties, limiting world naval forces. Again he suffered the effects of overwork and resigned to return to law practice. In the late 1920s, he served briefly as a judge on the International Court of Justice in the Hague. In 1930, he was Hoover's choice to succeed Taft as chief justice, becoming the only person to serve twice on the Court.

The assignment would be the most difficult of Hughes's life, as the nation sank into the Depression and the Court entered one of its most troubled periods. His intellectual brilliance, administrative ability, and diplomacy made Hughes a masterful leader. Felix Frankfurter, who later served under him, once said that "to see [Hughes] preside was like witnessing Toscanini lead an orchestra."* But all of Hughes's skill could not reconcile the deep philosophical division among the justices or prevent the Court from clashing with the New Deal. In this, Hughes failed as chief justice. His instinct for compromise and moderation led him to preside rather than forcefully take the Court to new ground early in the New Deal. But in contributing to the defeat of Roosevelt's Court-Packing Plan and in steering the Court's dramatic change of direction in 1937, he helped it retain identity and independence. He remained chief justice until 1941, retiring at 79.

He had had a remarkable, if not entirely happy, public career. Warm and relaxed with family and close friends, he was enormously self-contained in his public work. He had no political cronies, no circle of advisors, and built no political machine. Yet he was a person to whom others naturally looked for leadership. An unusual sense of duty led him to accept responsibility even when he did not seek it. For Hughes this meant working hard to do good things well. The moral probity he learned as a child, he carried into public life. He saw himself as others often did, a straight arrow in a political world where many quivers were bent.

* Quoted in Alpheus Thomas Mason, *Harlan Fiske Stone: Pillar of the Law,* (New York: Viking Press, 1956), 789.

---

of contract doctrine, held that "a state is free to adopt whatever economic policy may be deemed to promote public welfare." [291 U.S. 502 at 537 (1934)] The ruling greatly enlarged the public interest category and was a big step away from economic due process.

Though New Dealers took heart from these decisions, the Court remained closely divided, with the laissez-faire justices dissenting as a bloc in each. In *Blaisdell,* Sutherland argued forcefully that the decision ignored the clear words of the contracts clause in Article I-10 and the framers' intent that states not have power to compromise creditor rights even during times of economic distress. In *Nebbia,* McReynolds saw the New York law as benefiting one group—dairy farmers—at the expense of another—consumers—and thus interfering with entrepreneurial liberty and violating substantive due process. That these dissents were not the dying gasps of laissez-faire jurisprudence was soon evident.

New Deal legislation came before the Court for the first time in *Panama Refining Co. v. Ryan,* decided early in 1935. In its oil marketing provisions, the NIRA had authorized the president to bar "hot" oil—production that exceeded quotas set by different oil-producing states—from interstate commerce. Like many other parts of the act, they aimed to put a floor under prices by limiting production; thus bringing it into line with the slowdown in demand. The Court was tried by the vagueness of the legislation, partly the result of haste in its drafting, and by sloppiness of its administration. The decision against the government struck a hard blow because it went beyond these obvious defects to the issue of delegation. Chief Justice Hughes held that Congress had not set out clear guidelines for the president for using the great power it had given him. For the first time the Court had struck down a Congressional delegation of power to the executive. In a lone dissent, Justice Cardozo argued to sustain on grounds of national emergency.

The Court's objections were largely unanticipated by government counsel who had given only a few pages to the delegation question in their brief. The decision left the rest of the NIRA intact, but it was now clear that it and other programs depending on extensive delegation would have difficulty with the Court. The decision also meant that the oil industry returned to unregulated destructive competition.

Two months later, the government won a victory in three appeals collectively known as the Gold Clause Cases. In these the Court upheld a Congressional act that nullified clauses in private debt contracts that required payments be made in gold rather than paper. Aimed at conserving gold reserves, the act was held to be within Congress's monetary power, despite its breach in the obligation of contracts. Since the contractual provisions for payment in gold were held not to be commodity contracts but only those for payment of money, the more formidable question of federal control of production was avoided.

"Black Monday" and Beyond

Early in May 1935 the Court, in *Railroad Retirement Board v. Alton,* struck down a federal law that required railroad companies to contribute to a pension program for retired railway workers. Though

the plan was not an integral part of the New Deal program, the case was important for two reasons. First, the decision did not rest only on deficiencies of draftsmanship or procedural defects, but went to a constitutional issue. In the Court's view, because the pension plan was unrelated to matters of health, safety, or efficiency, it went beyond Congress's commerce power. Second, the 5-4 decision was written by Justice Roberts, whose support had been vital to the victories in *Blaisdell, Nebbia,* and the Gold Clause cases. With the sweeping decision in *Alton,* Roberts had announced his alliance with the conservative four to form an anti-New Deal majority. It confirmed Roosevelt's worst fears about Roberts and about the fate of more central New Deal programs about to come before the Court.

On May 27, known as "Black Monday," the Court announced three decisions that rocked the New Deal. In *Schechter v. United States* (p. 323), it unanimously held the NIRA unconstitutional. The owners of a poultry slaughterhouse in New York City were charged with violating the wages and hours and fair trade provisions of the act's poultry code. Chief Justice Hughes found the delegation of power to the president to draw up industry codes, which Roosevelt later redelegated to industry groups, to be without clear guidelines. This defect was theoretically curable through redrafting. It was Hughes's second objection that buried the NIRA: The Schechter business—and by implication, thousands of others covered by NIRA codes—was mainly local. The company's importation of poultry from other states had only "indirect" consequence for interstate commerce, Hughes said, thus breathing new life into the old distinction between "direct" and "indirect" effects. As such, its business was not in interstate commerce and thus not subject to the NIRA. In what seemed to be an about-face from his position in *Blaisdell,* Hughes added that extraordinary conditions did not create or enlarge constitutional power.

In the second case, the Court unanimously struck down the Frazier-Lemke Emergency Farm Mortgage Act. It had been designed to reduce foreclosures by allowing farmers to repurchase their properties at reappraised, lower values and to do so by borrowing at 1 percent interest. In *Louisville Bank v. Radford,* Brandeis spoke for the Court, holding that though the federal government in contrast to the states might lawfully impair the obligation of contracts, it could not take private property—here the mortgage holder's rights—without just compensation as required by the Fifth Amendment. In the third decision, *Humphrey's Executor v. United States,* the Court, unanimous again, thwarted the president's power to bring independent regulatory commissions into line with New Deal policies, by holding that he did not have unlimited power to remove their commissioners.

The Black Monday decisions, like others against the New Deal, reflected genuine concern about delegation, draftsmanship, and crude administration. Complaints against the overbureaucratization and petty interference of the National Recovery Administration, the agency created by the NIRA, had been mounting for some time. But the decisions, especially *Schechter,* went further and struck at the basic federal and executive power Roosevelt claimed he had. After Black Monday, the president began to complain more loudly to associates about the "nine old men" and, fearing worse to come, became convinced the Court would now be a formidable obstacle to economic recovery.

Worse did come in the Court's next term. In *United States v. Butler* (p. 330) decided in January 1936, the Court took a restrictive view of Congress's power to tax and spend. The casualty this time was the Agricultural Adjustment Act passed during the One Hundred Days as the centerpiece of the New Deal farm program. So that subsidies could be paid to farmers for voluntarily reducing acreage, the act placed a tax on mills and other commodity processors. Unlike the NIRA, the AAA scheme seemed to be working. Farm income had risen substantially and debt declined. Despite this, Justice Roberts, writing for a majority of six that included the chief justice, held that the tax, like the one in *Bailey v. Drexel Furniture Co.,* the second

child labor case, was not really a tax at all. Since its proceeds went not to general revenue but were used to "buy" compliance with the program, the tax was actually a means for regulating agricultural production a matter reserved to the states. Roberts admitted that Congress could spend for the general welfare, but held that that power was limited by the Tenth Amendment. Otherwise it would be free to use its tax and spending powers to regulate any aspect of economic life. In a sharp dissent, Justice Stone, joined by Brandeis and Cardozo, took issue with this tortured reasoning. Arguing that the program was constitutional under Congress's power to spend for the general welfare, he urged greater deference be given to legislative judgment. Courts, he said in pointedly Holmesian terms, "are not the only agencies of government that must be assumed to have the capacity to govern."

A month later, the New Deal won its only victory in the Court in the two years 1935 and 1936. It came in *Ashwander v. Tennessee Valley Authority* where insurgent shareholders of a utility company challenged the government's sale of electricity generated as a by-product of its dam construction. With only Justice McReynolds dissenting, Chief Justice Hughes upheld such sale on ground of Congress's power to build dams for national defense and, under Article IV-3, power to dispose of property acquired. Perhaps waiting for another day, the Court did not deal with the innovative and more controversial planning aspects of the TVA. For a brief time the decision quieted the mounting criticism of the Court for its anti-New Deal decisions.

In March, the Court by a vote of 5-4, struck down the Bituminous Coal Conservation Act, passed a year earlier to deal with low wages, labor unrest, and ruinous competition in the coal industry. Based on Congress's commerce power, the act set minimum prices at the minehead and called for collective bargaining to fix wages and hours. But in *Carter v. Carter Coal Co.* (p. 326), Justice Sutherland, invoking the doctrine of dual federalism, held the labor provisions void, citing the Sugar Trust Case and its distinction between

Longevity in the Robe

When the exasperated Franklin Roosevelt called the Supreme Court "the nine old men," he was facing the most superannuated Court in history. But his comment called attention to a striking phenomenon: The Court has always been "old." For reasons not fully understood, most justices have led unusually long lives. (Professors and other moralists may try to convince students that it is because of the encounter with hard, demanding work. But if there is such effect, it may lie as much in the enormous deference given the robe and to the great power wielded by those who wear it.) The average life span of 95 former justices now deceased (all males) is 73.7 years. In comparison, that for 36 deceased presidents is only 69.6. The justices' average life span is shorter than that which males of 54, (the average age of justices at appointment) might expect today, but since most of the justices lived during periods in which life expectancy for both men and women was lower than that of today by many years, their average of nearly 74 years is unusual.

For those appointed for life or good behavior, longevity translates into lengthy tenures in office.

Of 100 justices who have completed their terms, the average length of service is 16.1 years, much longer than that of elected members in the federal government. It is more than three times longer than the average of 5.2 years for 41 presidents. Twelve Justices served 30 years or more, 23 others served between 20 and 30 years.

Is longevity in office a problem or a blessing? The question has both physical and political measure. Some of the greatest justices did some of their best work in their 70s or 80s, Holmes, Brandeis, and John Marshall, among them. Both Holmes and Cardozo were nearly 62 before they were appointed. Earl Warren was 62 when he became chief justice, Taft nearly 64, and Hughes nearly 68. Other justices—Black, Brennan, the first Harlan, and Miller, among them—were powerful forces on the Court even in their late years.

But a closer look also reveals another picture. Nearly half the 100 former justices—48—died in office. Thirty-five others retired for reasons of health or simply the weight of advanced years. Only 17 of the 100 left the Court in good health. For nine it was to pursue other careers, one to avoid a conflict of interest, and one under charges of unethical behavior. Only six justices have left the

---

production and commerce. The relationship between employer and employee was a local one. Labor disputes dealt with an aspect of production and thus had only indirect effect on interstate commerce. That being the case, they could be regulated only by state authority. Here Sutherland ignored *amici* briefs filed by several states urging federal action as the only way to stabilize the industry.

The conservative majority was not finished. In June, in *Morehead v. New York ex. rel. Tipaldo*, they struck down a model New York minimum wage law for women and children, on authority of *Adkins v. Childrens Hospital.* Justice Butler reasserted the doctrine of liberty of contract, arguing that it prevented any state interference with work contracts. Public reaction to the decision was overwhelmingly negative; hundreds of newspaper editorials attacked it while few came to its defense. Even the Republican presidential nominee Landon dissociated himself from it.

Battle Lost, War Won

Roosevelt was now convinced the laissez-faire justices on the Court would systematically dismantle the New Deal. Never in so short a time— 13 months—had the Court overturned so many acts of Congress. He now believed the National Labor Relations and Social Security Acts were in mortal danger. Yet he was muted in his public criticism of the Court during the 1936 election campaign, clearly biding his time until voters had spoken on the New Deal.

Roosevelt's Plan

The president saw the emphatic result at the polls as a green light to move against the Court. He first thought about proposing a constitutional amendment that would require a two-

Court simply to enjoy retirement before being overtaken by a marked decline in abilities.

Several justices became mentally infirm while on the bench and some of these refused or were reluctant to step down. Blair, Grier, Swayne, Field, and McKenna, for example, were probably in the early stages of Alzheimer's disease or other dementia in their last months or years on the Court. No opinions could be assigned to them and their constructive contribution to the Court's work all but vanished. Most of this was hidden from the public. Even vigorous giants like Holmes and Brandeis slowed markedly when they became old, old men, Holmes frequently falling asleep during oral argument and in conference. Other justices have suffered the effects of various physical ailments including stroke, heart disease, Parkinson's disease, pernicious anemia, crippling arthritis, deafness, and failing vision. There is no way of knowing with exactness how and in what manner these physical failings affected the quality of the Court's work, but it is hard to imagine it was for the better.

The New Deal revealed how very long tenure could put the Court at odds with the elected branches. With justices having average tenure of 16.1 years, a new president and Congress is likely to share power with a Court on which the average member has already served eight years. In ordinary times, the disparity might be unimportant or even salutary, since the constitutional system is not one of absolute majority rule and has room for a continuing counterweight to the majority of the moment. But when the country has markedly changed political course as it did in the 1930s, judicial "lag" can be substantial and precipitate a constitutional crisis.

Incumbent justices may, of course, "read the election returns." But they are not required to do so and can deliberately ignore a message that is loud and clear. In the long run the Court catches up; if nothing else mortality tables take their toll. Though some presidents—Monroe, Franklin Roosevelt, and Carter—have gone through entire four-year terms without an appointment, new vacancies have occurred on an average of one every 1.9 years. This has allowed great new national governing coalitions, such as those forming with the elections of Jefferson, Jackson, Lincoln, and Franklin Roosevelt, eventually to restock the Court in their own image. In the not-so-long run, however, "politically old" justices often have their way.

thirds vote of the Court before an act of Congress could be held unconstitutional or one that would abolish the Court's power to review federal legislation altogether. This strategy was rejected as too slow and too risky since opponents would need to succeed in only 13 state legislatures to defeat it. It would also tacitly concede the strength of the Court's laissez-faire interpretations.

Instead, he and Attorney General Homer Cummings decided to ask Congress to use its Article III powers to restructure the federal judiciary, enlarging its size to give the president a chance to appoint new judges and justices sympathetic to the New Deal. Whenever a federal judge or justice with 10 years of service or more did not retire within six months of reaching age 70, the president could appoint an additional judge to that court. New appointments would be limited to 6 on the Supreme Court and 44 for all other federal courts together. Since only three members of the Supreme Court were under 70, this would allow Roosevelt to enlarge the Court to as many as 15 Justices.

Submitted to Congress in February 1937 as the Judiciary Reorganization Plan, it hit like a bombshell and became known immediately and forever after as the Court-Packing Plan. It proved sharply divisive even among New Dealers and brought to the foreground the new, complicating issue of judicial independence. The constitutional crisis that arrayed two branches of government against a third was now escalated and brought to a head.

Changing the size of the Court—"packing" or "unpacking" it—was hardly a new idea and was fully within Congress's Article III power. Congress had reduced the Court from six to five justices in 1801, restored it to six in 1802, increased it to nine in 1837, to ten in 1863, reduced it to seven in 1865, and restored it again to nine in 1869. But here, Roosevelt, famed for his political sagacity, badly miscalculated. Misgivings about the threat to judicial independence were fed by the president's tactics. Though the purpose of the plan was transparent, Roosevelt contended the present justices needed help because age was preventing them from getting their work done. In a letter to the Senate Judiciary Committee, Chief Justice Hughes supplied docket statistics to show this was not the case and that with more justices the Court might well become less efficient. "There would be more judges to hear, more judges to confer, more judges to discuss, more judges to be convinced and to decide," Hughes said.* The plan was also publicly opposed by Brandeis who, at a vigorous 80, was the Court's oldest member. Roosevelt was seen as devious both in keeping the plan secret until giving it to Congress and in not directly dealing with the Court's interpretation of the Constitution. For many, he had transformed the issue of the Court's obstructionism into one of its independence.

The Switch in Time

Despite criticism of the president and reservations many in Congress had about tampering with the basic structure of the Court, the plan had many supporters who had not forgotten the reason it had been introduced. The possibility that it might be enacted apparently affected constitutional views of at least one justice.

On March 29, the Court announced a stunning 5-4 decision to uphold a Washington State minimum wage law for women similar to the one in New York it had struck down the year before. In went further still and overruled *Adkins v. Childrens Hospital,* the 1922 case that had served

---

* U.S. Senate Committee on the Judiciary, 75th Cong., 1st Sess. *Reorganization of the Federal Judiciary,* Hearings, S.1392 (Washington: Government Printing Office, 1937), Part 3, 491, quoted in William E. Leuchtenberg, *The Supreme Court Reborn: The Constitutional Revolution in the Age of Roosevelt* (New York: Oxford University Press, 1995), 140–141.

to revive liberty of contract. Writing for the majority in *West Coast Hotel Co. v. Parrish,* (p. 334) Chief Justice Hughes made clear the decision was an emphatic move away from substantive due process. State police power could go beyond the traditional protection of health, safety, and morals to include "welfare of the people" and "interests of the community" without violating liberty of contract. Here regulation of wages was no different from regulation of hours. Hughes also observed that greater deference was owed to legislative judgments.

Justice Owen Roberts, with the majority in the New York case the year before, was the fifth vote in *Parrish.* The crossing of the aisle did not go unnoticed and was widely attributed to the threat of the Court-Packing Plan. It was later called by one wit, "The switch in time that save nine." Yet, it is often overlooked that *Parrish* was decided in conference in December, two months before the Court-Packing Plan was made public. Roberts, who had a wavering judicial philosophy, had announced there that he would vote to uphold the Washington State statute.

It was soon apparent that the *Parrish* decision was not intended to be an isolated "correction." Two weeks later in *NLRB v. Jones & Laughlin Co.* (p. 337), Chief Justice Hughes used the "stream of commerce" theory to revive a broad conception of federal power over commerce and to sustain one of the New Deal's most controversial laws, the National Labor Relations Act that, among other things, removed obstacles to union organizing and required employers to engage in collective bargaining. Noting that labor strife at plants of companies operating on a national scale could threaten interstate commerce, Hughes narrowed the distinction between production and commerce, totally abandoning the direct-indirect effects test. Again the decision was 5-4 and again Roberts was the majority's fifth vote.

The following month in the companion cases of *Steward Machine Co. v. Davis* (p. 341) and *Helvering v. Davis,* the Court upheld important provisions of the Social Security Act, Justice Cardozo writing the opinions in both. At issue in the first was the unemployment compensation feature and Congress's payroll tax on employers to pay for benefits. In ruling for a majority of five, Cardozo held the plan, which required state unemployment compensation programs conform to certain standards before they could share federal benefits, to be within Congress's power to tax and spend. He refused to recognize Tenth Amendment limits on these powers and, by that, silently repudiated Roberts' narrow view of such authority in *United States v. Butler* the year before.

In *Helvering*, Cardozo sustained the old age benefits provision of the act on the same expansive nationalist theory of the tax power. Observing that the law was passed to deal with calamitous conditions "the laws of the separate states cannot deal with effectively," [301 U.S. 619 at 645 (1937)] he upheld federal power to tax for the general welfare. The Court had now moved decisively away from the doctrine of dual federalism.

Just before these decisions, Justice Van Devanter announced his retirement at the end of the Court's term. This and the Court's change of course doomed the Court-Packing Plan, which was still before Congress. To the relief of many Democrats, enlarging the Court now seemed unnecessary. In July, with the president stubbornly refusing to withdraw it, the plan died in Senate committee. Though the New Deal had triumphed over the Court, the Court-packing fight handed Roosevelt the worse setback of his presidency and revealed fissures in his New Deal constituency that were never fully repaired.

What accounted for the Court's reversal of course? First, seven of the nine justices did not, in the main, change their views. The four laissez-faire conservatives were as adamantly opposed to legitimating the New Deal in 1937 as they had been before. The two who shifted were Hughes and Roberts, more importantly Roberts, since the chief justice had often been uncomfortable in voting with the laissez-fairists. The old saying that "the justices read the election returns" may have been true here. If so, it is a hopeful sign for democratic government that the nonelected branch can bow to an uncommonly strong electoral voice

when that voice speaks, as it did in November 1936. Mounting public criticism of the Court from the press and legal profession may also have been important. The threat of enlarging the Court cannot be ruled out. Had the Court continued to undercut the New Deal recovery program in 1937 as it had in 1935 and 1936, the Court-Packing Plan might well have been enacted. Had he remained an unreconstructed New Deal opponent, Roberts, the youngest of the justices—he was to serve nine more years—would no doubt have found life on the Court with a host of Roosevelt appointees uncomfortable.

Aftermath

Whatever Roosevelt's setback on the Court-Packing Plan, the New Deal was now safe from judicial scuttling. If its programs failed it would not be for want of constitutional power to enact them. The Supreme Court's dramatic retreat ended the constitutional crisis and made structural reform a moot point. It also portended a momentous change in the constitutional system every bit as great as changes that were transforming the nation's political economy.

The Roosevelt Court

The president wasted no time in filling the vacant seat created by Van Devanter's retirement. He chose a loyal New Deal senator from Alabama, Hugo Black, then 51. The appointment was controversial. Black had meager law training, no prior judicial experience except for brief service as a police court judge, and no legal scholarship to his credit. His qualifications were altogether political. Shortly after his confirmation, disclosure that he had briefly been a member of the Ku Klux Klan as a young man created a furor that was quelled only when Black, in a radio address to the country, disowned the Klan and his one-time membership. It was not an auspicious start to one of the longest, most important, and most liberal of all Court tenures.

Justice of the Judicial Process

Benjamin Cardozo was on the Supreme Court only six years, from 1932 until his death from a stroke in 1938 at 68. Much of that time he suffered from coronary disease, despite his robust appearance. Not a laissez-faire conservative, he was often cast as a dissenter in the Court's most important cases, a part he was not accustomed to playing. His great majority opinions in the two Social Security Act cases and in *Palko v. Connecticut* (1937), formulating the "ordered liberty" standard for selectively incorporating rights in the Bill of Rights into the due process clause of the Fourteenth Amendment thereby setting new boundaries for state and federal power, were among his last on the Court.

Many believed Cardozo should have come to the Court much sooner. As chief judge of the New York Court of Appeals, the highest in the state, he was widely acknowledged to be the most able state appellate judge in the country. In the 1920s, Taft, who as president had once offered Cardozo a federal judgeship, used his influence with Harding and Coolidge to discourage his appointment, apparently believing Cardozo would vote with the "liberals," Holmes and Brandeis. When Holmes retired in 1932, there was as close to being a public demand for Cardozo's appointment as perhaps ever for a prospective justice. But Cardozo was a Democrat, there were already two New Yorkers on the Court, and Brandeis filled the "Jewish seat." Justice Harlan Stone, a New Yorker, offered to resign to make room for Cardozo. William Borah, an Idaho Republican and a power in the Senate, told Hoover that Cardozo "belonged as much to Idaho as to New York." The president was persuaded.

Cardozo was descended from a long line of Sephardic Jews who fled persecution in Spain and Portugal to come to the Dutch colony of New Amsterdam in the late 1600s. Over the years, many intermarried and became leaders in the New York social and cultural worlds and in law and politics. Cardozo's father had been a state judge but was forced to resign

Other vacancies now came quickly. Justice Sutherland resigned in June 1938, Cardozo died later in the year, Brandeis retired early in 1939, Butler died later that year, and McReynolds, last of the Four Horsemen, resigned early in 1941. Months later, Hughes himself retired. By then, only Justices Stone and Roberts remained from the Court that had struck at the New Deal. Denied in his proposal for restructuring, Roosevelt could now "pack" the Court through traditional appointments.

His second was that of Stanley Reed, 54, his solicitor general. To replace Cardozo, he chose the peppery Harvard law professor Felix Frankfurter, 57, who though a political activist and long-time New Deal advisor, brought a background of legal scholarship to the Court in the tradition of Story and Holmes. Brandeis was succeeded by William O. Douglas, 41, chairman of the Securities and Exchange Commission and a former law professor, the youngest appointee of the twentieth century. Frank Murphy, 50, the attorney general and former governor of Michigan, was named to replace Butler. Robert H. Jackson, 49, Murphy's successor as attorney general, succeeded McReynolds. When the chief justice retired, Roosevelt elevated Justice Stone to that office and appointed James F. Byrnes, 62, a South Carolina senator as the new associate

under a cloud of corruption charges stemming from his association with Boss Tweed's notorious Tammany Hall political machine. Though young Ben was only two, the scandal hung over the family for years and the future Supreme Court justice later seemed bent on atoning for his father's fall. Cardozo's mother died a few years later when he was nine, and he was raised by an older sister, Ellen. They remained very close, living in the family home the rest of their lives, neither ever marrying. Like Charles Evans Hughes, young Cardozo was tutored at home. One of his instructors was the author Horatio Alger, who inspired in the young boy a love of literature and language, so often evident later in elegantly crafted legal opinions.

Cardozo became a practicing lawyer without finishing his studies at Columbia Law School. His legal acumen quickly won respect from fellow lawyers, and in 1913 he was appointed the New York Court of Appeals, becoming its chief in 1926. He excelled as a common law judge. In several important decisions in torts and contracts, he ingeniously applied old law to new circumstances, making the changes seem like natural, logical, almost compelling extensions of established principles. In *MacPherson v. Buick* (1916), one of his earliest and best known opinions, he held the car manufacturer liable to a driver injured when a defective wheel collapsed, even though it was not shown to have been careless and had no contractual relationship with the driver. The decision laid the foundation for modern product liability law for "inherently dangerous" instruments, expanding older common law principles of negligence to fit conditions of the new industrial age.

In *The Nature of the Judicial Process,* in 1921, Cardozo set out to explain how common law judges—at least Judge Cardozo—reached their decisions. Its four short chapters, which have become a classic statement on the judge as maker of law, had been presented as the Storrs lectures at Yale a year earlier. At the conclusion of the first, given to an overflow audience, Cardozo received a spontaneous standing ovation, not a usual response to a jurisprudential talk.

He outlined four methods: philosophy, emphasizing the logic and symmetry of the law; history; tradition, referring to customs and practices of a trade or business; and sociology, by which he meant the social policies and values implicit in legal rules. He tried to reconcile the need for stability and continuity in the law with that for change and progress. It is easy to understand the great appeal this juristic philosophy had for a nation and society in perpetual change yet having an almost ever-present yearning for permanence. For many, it broke a path between rigid oracular formalism on the one side, and the almost nihilistic relativism of legal realism on the other.

These views were an important contribution to sociological jurisprudence but they were largely wasted on Cardozo's laissez-faire colleagues on the Supreme Court who either failed to appreciate the subtle juxtaposing of judicial fallibility and judicial opportunity, or were determined to ignore it.

justice. Byrnes resigned a year later, in 1942, at Roosevelt's request to serve as the president's chief assistant for wartime economic mobilization. Roosevelt then made his last appointment, that of Wiley Rutledge, 49, an Iowa Democrat and federal appellate judge.

In all, Roosevelt, who had no vacancies to fill during his first term, made nine appointments, filling eight seats, as many as had George Washington himself. His appointees, with widely differing backgrounds and personalities, had two things in common: They were New Deal Democrats loyal to the president and were all relatively young, having an average age at appointment of 51.6 years. When Rutledge took his seat in October 1943, the average age of the justices was 57.1 years, 14 years younger than the Court of 1936–1937.

The new Court, though pro-New Deal, would soon have its own divisions. But before these became apparent, it made emphatic its expansive view of federal power over the economy through the commerce clause. In *Mulford v. Smith* (1939), it upheld marketing quotas in the Agricultural Adjustment Act of 1938 (passed after the Court had held the AAA of 1933 invalid in *United States v. Butler*), aimed at reducing surplus production, against a challenge that it was an unconstitutional interference with powers of the states under the Tenth Amendment. Justice Roberts, writing for the Court, admitted his majority opinion in *Butler* was mistaken.

In *United States v. Darby Lumber Co.* (1941) (p. 344), the Court unanimously sustained one of the last New Deal enactments, the Fair Labor Standards Act of 1938, which set minimum wages and maximum hours for all employees "engaged in commerce or in the production of goods for commerce." A few years earlier, such a scope to federal power would have made the act unconstitutional on its face. To enforce its provisions, goods made in violation of the act would be kept from interstate commerce. In sustaining the act, Justice Stone reaffirmed Congress's power to reach production and to use complete prohibition as a regulating device. Doing so, he announced that *Hammer v. Dagenhart,* the Child Labor Case, was overruled.

How far the new Court was willing to go became evident the following year in *Wickard v. Filburn* (p. 347), in which a wheat farmer challenged a penalty imposed for growing wheat in excess of his allotted quota. In this instance, the extra wheat—about 12 acres—was used entirely to feed livestock on the farm on which it was grown and so never entered commerce at all. Nonetheless, the Court, speaking through Justice Jackson, unanimously upheld the penalty. Though the amount of wheat was trivial and privately consumed, Jackson argued that it removed demand from the market, thus undermining the purpose of the supply quota program. The decision obliterated any remaining distinctions between direct versus indirect effects on interstate commerce or between production for commercial use and that for private.

The New Constitutional Order

The New Deal failed in its chief task, that of ending the Great Depression. The recession in 1937 sent unemployment back to 10 million in 1938. By most measures, the economy was still operating well below its pre-Depression capacity. But New Deal programs were eminently successful in keeping the Depression from getting worse, that is, in halting the deflationary spiral and in starting economic recovery. Not least, they provided immedi-

The "Roosevelt Court", 1941, after the appointment of Justice Stone as Chief Justice. Front from left: Stanley Reed, Owen Roberts, Stone, Hugo Black, and Felix Frankfurter. Back: James Byrnes, William O. Douglas, Frank Murphy, and Robert Jackson. All but Stone and Roberts were appointed by Franklin Roosevelt.

ate and long-term relief to millions of jobless workers, destitute farmers, and others victimized by the crisis. These achievements may have kept the country from politically lurching to the extreme left or right, a distinct possibility had the Depression worsened. All of which prompted the historian Samuel Eliot Morrison with deliberate irony, to hail Roosevelt as "the most effective American conservative since Alexander Hamilton."*

The New Deal transformed the constitutional order, giving it the shape familiar to contemporary Americans. It greatly accelerated the long-term shift of power in the federal system to the center. "Administrative state" and "welfare state" came to be terms used to describe new federal intervention in economic life through regulatory use of the tax, spending, and commerce powers and the government's acceptance of substantial responsibility for individual economic security. These changes would be realized only through a federal bureaucracy grown so vast and independent that it would at times defy control by either Congress or the president.

Federal expansion did not come at the expense of state police powers, which themselves were permanently enlarged. But the states were dwarfed by the national government in the coordinated welfare and regulatory programs of "cooperative federalism," losing much of their policy-making autonomy in these ventures.

The new balance in the federal system was complemented by a new balance within the central government between Congress and the president. Unlike great power shifts to the executive during war, those of the New Deal were not designed to be temporary. Many of the great powers given the president were traditionally legislative. He and his administration became a kind of chief legislator submitting policy initiatives, in many cases, systematic legislative programs, to Congress for debate and deliberation. It is a pattern that has continued to the present.

These changes required changes in the Constitution. However, they came about not through amendments, of which there were none during the New Deal, but interpretation by the Supreme Court, that is, through basic changes in constitutional doctrine. The laissez-faire jurisprudence that dominated constitutional understanding for 75 years was completely abandoned. Economic due process and liberty of contract, so often the means for blocking state and federal governments from the regulation of business, markets, and work conditions, ceased to be constitutional "requirements." Dual federalism would no longer frustrate federal power because of unnamed reserved powers in the states. In the new "national supremacy federalism," as Justice Stone put it, the Tenth Amendment was but "a truism," describing where unmentioned powers that were not federal lay, rather than being a grant of independent powers to the states limiting the federal government. The Civil War had laid to rest the idea of a dual sovereignty in which states and central government were equals. The New Deal conflict did the same for dual federalism in which federal power was partly defined by state power.

The transformation called for a change in the role of the Court itself. Abandonment of laissez-faire would require the Court to defer to legislative judgment on the wisdom of economic regulations rather than substitute its own preferences as though they were constitutional commands. This would mean less judicial protection for property rights, a departure from the Court's historic mission dating to Marshall and from the conception many, if not most, framers had of the third branch.

The new Court was to make this point in several early cases, but perhaps none more important than *United States v. Carolene Products* (1938). In upholding the federal Filled Milk Act, which barred a type of evaporated skimmed milk from interstate commerce, it simply accepted Congress's declaration that such milk was injurious to health, despite the legislation's transparent aid to certain dairy interests. From now on, Justice

---

* Samuel Eliot Morrison, *History of the American People*, (New York: Oxford University Press, 1965), 987.

Stone said, economic regulatory legislation would violate due process only if it was not based "on some rational basis within the knowledge and experience of the legislators." [304 U.S. 144 at 152] This standard, presuming economic regulation to be reasonable until proved otherwise and placing the burden of that proof on those who would challenge, gave Congress and state legislatures a wide berth in making economic policy.

But Stone made an important distinction in footnote 4 of his opinion, little noticed at the time, but now the most cited aside in the Court's history. He said there would be a narrower presumption of constitutionality, that is, a wider judicial scrutiny, when a law dealt with personal liberties or rights as opposed to those of property. The reason, Stone said, was that those affected by such laws—individuals and "insular minorities"—could not as easily defend their interests through the ordinary ways of politics as could property. Critics have pointed out that

Stone's distinction is not supported by the text of the Constitution and is quite at odds with the intent of the framers. Today his rationale seems simplistic. Some civil liberties interests—the media, for example—are far more powerful than many small property interests, and civil rights interests often have a lobbying power rivaling that of business. But Stone's reasoning represented a remarkable change in judicial sensitivity and echoed the New Deal's concern with basic fairness in the work of democratic government.

The distinction between personal and property rights foretold a momentous change in the Court's work. Starting in the 1940s and continuing to the present, half or more of the cases coming before the Court have dealt with civil liberties or rights. As the Court partly withdrew from one area of review, it moved ever more into another. In doing so, it built an expansive constitutional law of rights and liberties. This was one of the most important legacies of the Court's losing battle with the New Deal.

FURTHER READING

Economic Crisis and Political Innovation

Badger, Anthony, *The New Deal* (1988)

Bellush, Barnard, *The Failure of the N.R.A.* (1978)

Dawson, Nelson, *Louis D. Brandeis, Felix Frankfurter, and the New Deal* (1980)

Friedel, Frank, *Franklin D. Roosevelt: A Rendezvous with Destiny* (1990)

Galbraith, John Kenneth, *The Great Crash* (1954)

Gordon, Colin, *New Deals: Business, Labor, and Politics in America, 1920–1935* (1994)

Irons, Peter, *New Deal Lawyers* (1982)

Leuchtenberg, William E., *Franklin D. Roosevelt and the New Deal: 1932–1940* (1963)

Reagan, Patrick D., *Designing a New America: The Origins of the New Deal* (2000)

Schlesinger, Arthur M., *The Age of Roosevelt*, 3 vols (1957–1960)

Schwartz, Jordan A., *The Interregnum of Despair: Hoover, Congress, and the Depression* (1970)

Sitkoff, Harvey ed., *Fifty Years Later: The New Deal Reevaluated* (1985)

Temin, Peter, *Lessons from the Great Depression* (1989)

The New Deal and the Supreme Court

Baker, Leonard, *Back to Back: The Duel Between FDR and the Supreme Court* (1967)

Jackson, Robert H., *The Struggle for Judicial Supremacy* (1941)

Leonard, Charles A., *A Search for Judicial Philosophy: Mr. Justice Roberts and the Constitutional Revolution of 1937* (1971)

Leuchtenberg, William E., *The Supreme Court Reborn: The Constitutional Revolution in the Age of Roosevelt* (1995)

Maidment, Richard A., *The Judicial Response to the New Deal: The U.S. Supreme Court and Economic Regulation, 1934–1936* (1992)

White, G. Edward, *The Constitution and the New Deal* (2000)

The New Constitutional Era

Cushman, Barry, *Rethinking the New Deal: The Structure of Constitutional Revolution* (1998)

Eden, Robert, ed., *The New Deal and Its Legacy: Critique and Reappraisal* (1989)

Pritchett, C. Herman, *The Roosevelt Court: A Study in Judicial Politics and Values* (1948)

Biographical

Arkes, Hadley, *The Return of George Sutherland: Restoring a Jurisprudence of Natural Rights* (1994)

Burns, James MacGregor, *Roosevelt: The Lion and the Fox* (1956)

Freidel, Frank, *Franklin D. Roosevelt: A Rendezvous with Destiny* (1990)

Mason, Alpheus Thomas, *Harlan Fiske Stone: Pillar of the Law* (1956)

Pusey, Merlo J., *Charles Evans Hughes*, 2 vols (1951)

On Leading Cases

Cortner, Richard C., *The Jones & Laughlin Case* (1970)

_____, *The Wagner Act Cases* (1964)

Purcell, Edward A. Jr., *Brandeis and the Progression Constitution* (2000) (*Erie Railroad v. Tompkins*)

CASES

Home Building & Loan Association v. Blaisdell

290 U.S. 398 (1934), 5-4

Opinion of the Court: Hughes, C.J. (Brandeis, Cardozo, Roberts, Stone)

Dissenting: Butler, McReynolds, Sutherland, Van Devanter

What aspects of the Minnesota law redeem it for the Court? When does an emergency exist? Can Hughes's quote from McCulloch v. Maryland *that "a constitution is intended to endure for ages to come and, consequently, to be adopted to the various crises of human affairs," be reconciled with Sutherland's statement that a provision of the Constitution "does not mean one thing at one time and an entirely different thing at another time"? What are the implications of Hughes's view for constitutional interpretation in general? Is there anything left of the contracts clause after this decision? See* United States Trust v. New Jersey.

Hughes, C.J., for the Court:

[The Home Building and Loan Association] contests the validity of chapter 339 of . . . the Minnesota Mortgage Moratorium Law, as being repugnant to the contract clause (Article 1, s 10) and the due process and equal protection clauses of the Fourteenth Amendment of the Federal Constitution. The statute was sustained by the Supreme Court of Minnesota and the case comes here on appeal.

The act provides that, during the emergency declared to exist, relief may be had through authorized judicial proceedings with respect to foreclosures of mortgages, and execution sales, of real estate; that

sales may be postponed and periods of redemption may be extended . . . The act is to remain in effect 'only during the continuance of the emergency and in no event beyond May 1, 1935.' No extension of the period for redemption and no postponement of sale is to be allowed which would have the effect of extending the period of redemption beyond that date . . .

The statute does not impair the integrity of the mortgage indebtedness. The obligation for interest remains. The statute does not affect the validity of the sale or the right of a mortgagee-purchaser to title in fee, or his right to obtain a deficiency judgment, if the mortgagor fails to redeem within the prescribed period. Aside from the extension of time, the other conditions of redemption are unaltered . . .

In determining whether the provision for this temporary and conditional relief exceeds the power of the state by reason of the clause in the Federal Constitution prohibiting impairment of the obligations of contracts, we must consider the relation of emergency to constitutional power, the historical setting of the contract clause, the development of the jurisprudence of this Court in the construction of that clause, and the principles of construction which we may consider to be established.

Emergency does not create power. Emergency does not increase granted power or remove or diminish the restrictions imposed upon power granted or reserved. The Constitution was adopted in a period of grave emergency. Its grants of power to the federal government and its limitations of the power of the States were determined in the light of emergency, and they are not altered by emergency. What power was thus granted and what limitations were thus imposed are questions which have always been, and always will be, the subject of close examination under our constitutional system.

While emergency does not create power, emergency may furnish the occasion for the exercise of power . . . Thus, the war power of the federal government is not created by the emergency of war, but it is a power given to meet that emergency. It is a power to wage war successfully, and thus it permits the harnessing of the entire energies of the people in a supreme cooperative effort to preserve the nation. But even the war power does not remove constitutional limitations safeguarding essential liberties. When the provisions of the Constitution, in grant or restriction, are specific, so particularized as not to admit of construction, no question is presented. Thus, emergency would not permit a state to have more than two Senators in the Congress, or permit the election of President by a general popular vote without regard to the number of electors to which the States are respectively entitled, or permit the States to 'coin money' or to 'make anything but gold and silver coin a tender in payment of debts.' But, where constitutional grants and limitations of power are set forth in general clauses, which afford a broad outline, the process of construction is essential to fill in the details. That is true of the contract clause . . .

In the construction of the contract clause. the debates in the Constitutional Convention are of little aid. But the reasons which led to the adoption of that clause, and of the other prohibitions of section 10 of article 1, are not left in doubt, and have frequently been described with eloquent emphasis. The widespread distress following the revolutionary period and the plight of debtors had called forth in the States an ignoble array of legislative schemes for the defeat of creditors and the invasion of contractual obligations. Legislative interferences had been so numerous and extreme that the confidence essential to prosperous trade had been undermined and the utter destruction of credit was threatened . . .

To ascertain the scope of the constitutional prohibition, we examine the course of judicial decisions in its application. These put it beyond question that the prohibition is not an absolute and is not to be read with literal exactness like a mathematical formula . . .

The inescapable problems of construction have been: What is a contract? What are the obligations of contracts? What constitutes impairment of these obligations? What residuum of power is there still in the States, in relation to the operation of contracts, to protect the vital interests of the community? . . .

The obligations of a contract are impaired by a law which renders them invalid, or releases or extinguishes them and impairment, as above noted, has been predicated of laws which without destroying contracts derogate from substantial contractual rights . . . Undoubtedly, whatever is reserved of state power must be consistent with the fair intent of the constitutional limitation of that power. The reserved power cannot be construed so as to destroy the limitation, nor is the

Farm foreclosures grew increasingly common during the Depression as plunging commodity prices forced defaults on mortgage payments. Minnesota's experiment with a one-year moratorium survived a challenge in the Supreme Court in *Home Building & Loan Association v. Blaisdell.* Foreclosure sales like the one here in Iowa in 1932 were sometimes greeted by an angry crowd of other farmers.

limitation to be construed to destroy the reserved power in its essential aspects. They must be construed in harmony with each other. This principle precludes a construction which would permit the state to adopt as its policy the repudiation of debts or the destruction of contracts or the denial of means to enforce them. But it does not follow that conditions may not arise in which a temporary restraint of enforcement may be consistent with the spirit and purpose of the constitutional provision and thus be found to be within the range of the reserved power of the state to protect the vital interests of the community. It cannot be maintained that the constitutional prohibition should be so construed as to prevent limited and temporary interpositions with respect to the enforcement of contracts if made necessary by a great public calamity such as fire, flood, or earthquake. The reservation of state power appropriate to such extraordinary conditions may be deemed to be as much a part of all contracts as is the reservation of state power to protect the public interest in the other situations to which we have referred. And, if state power exists to give temporary relief from the enforcement of contracts in the presence of disasters due to physical causes such as fire, flood, or earthquake, that power cannot be said to be nonexistent when the urgent public need demanding such relief is produced by other and economic causes . . .

[T]he question is no longer merely that of one party to a contract as against another, but of the use of reasonable means to safeguard the economic structure upon which the good of all depends.

It is no answer to say that this public need was not apprehended a century ago, or to insist that what the provision of the Constitution meant to the vision of that day it must mean to the vision of our time. If by the statement that what the Constitution meant at the time of its adoption it means today, it is intended to say that the great clauses of the Constitution must be confined to the interpretation which the framers, with the conditions and outlook of their time, would have placed upon them, the statement carries its own refutation. It was to guard against such a narrow conception that Chief Justice Marshall uttered the memorable warning: 'We must never forget, that it is a constitution we are expounding,' 'a constitution intended to endure for ages to come, and, consequently, to be adapted to the various crises of human affairs.' When we are dealing with the words of the Constitution, said this Court in *Missouri v. Holland,*

'we must realize that they have called into life a being the development of which could not have been foreseen completely by the most gifted of its begetters . . . The case before us must be considered in the light of our whole experience and not merely in that of what was said a hundred years ago.' . . .

The vast body of law which has been developed was unknown to the fathers, but it is believed to have preserved the essential content and the spirit of the Constitution. With a growing recognition of public needs and the relation of individual right to public security, the Court has sought to prevent the perversion of the clause through its use as an instrument to throttle the capacity of the states to protect their fundamental interests . . . And the germs of the later decisions are found in the early cases of the Charles River Bridge and the West River Bridge, which upheld the public right against strong insistence upon the contract clause. The principle of this development is, as we have seen, that the reservation of the reasonable exercise of the protective power of the state is read into all contracts . . .

Applying the criteria established by our decisions, we conclude:

1. An emergency existed in Minnesota which furnished a proper occasion for the exercise of the reserved power of the state to protect the vital interests of the community. The declarations of the existence of this emergency by the Legislature and by the Supreme Court of Minnesota cannot be regarded as a subterfuge or as lacking in adequate basis. The finding of the Legislature and state court has support in the facts of which we take judicial notice . . .

2. The legislation was addressed to a legitimate end; that is, the legislation was not for the mere advantage of particular individuals but for the protection of a basic interest of society.

3. In view of the nature of the contracts in question— mortgages of unquestionable validity—the relief afforded and justified by the emergency, in order not to contravene the constitutional provision, could only be of a character appropriate to that emergency, and could be granted only upon reasonable conditions.

4. The conditions upon which the period of redemption is extended do not appear to be unreasonable . . .

5. The legislation is temporary in operation. It is limited to the exigency which called it forth . . .

We are of the opinion that the Minnesota statute as here applied does not violate the contract clause of the Federal Constitution. Whether the legislation is wise or unwise as a matter of policy is a question with which we are not concerned . . .

Sutherland, dissenting:
The effect of the Minnesota legislation, though serious enough in itself, is of trivial significance compared with the far more serious and dangerous inroads upon the limitations of the Constitution which are almost certain to ensue as a consequence naturally following any step beyond the boundaries fixed by that instrument . . .

A provision of the Constitution, it is hardly necessary to say, does not admit of two distinctly opposite interpretations. It does not mean one thing at one time and an entirely different thing at another time . . .

The whole aim of construction, as applied to a provision of the Constitution, is to discover the meaning, to ascertain and give effect to the intent of its framers and the people who adopted it. The necessities which gave rise to the provision, the controversies which preceded, as well as the conflicts of opinion which were settled by its adoption, are matters to be considered to enable us to arrive at a correct result. The history of the times, the state of things existing when the provision was framed and adopted should be looked to in order to ascertain the mischief and the remedy . . . [W]e should place ourselves in the condition of those who framed and adopted it. And, if the meaning be at all doubtful, the doubt should be resolved . . . in a way to forward the evident purpose with which the provision was adopted.

An application of these principles to the question under review removes any doubt . . . that the contract impairment clause denies to the several states the power to mitigate hard consequences resulting to debtors from financial or economic exigencies by an impairment of the obligation of contracts of indebtedness . . .

The present exigency is nothing new. From the beginning of our existence as a nation, periods of depression, of industrial failure, of financial distress, of unpaid and unpayable indebtedness, have alternated with years of plenty. The vital lesson that expenditure beyond income begets poverty, that public or private extravagance, financed by promises to pay, either must end in complete or partial repudiation or the promises be fulfilled by self-denial and painful effort, though constantly taught by bitter experience, seems never to be learned; and the attempt by legislative devices to shift the misfortune of the debtor to the shoulders of the creditor without coming into conflict with the contract impairment clause has been persistent and oft-repeated . . .

It is quite true that an emergency may supply the occasion for the exercise of power, dependent upon the nature of the power and the intent of the Constitution with respect thereto. The emergency of war furnishes an occasion for the exercise of certain of the war powers. This the Constitution contemplates, since they cannot be exercised upon any other occasion. The existence of another kind of emergency authorizes the United States to protect each of the states of the Union against domestic violence. But we are here dealing, not with a power granted by the Federal Constitution, but with the state police power, which exists in its own right. Hence the question is, not whether an emergency furnishes the occasion for the exercise of that state power, but whether an emergency furnishes an occasion for the relaxation of the restrictions upon the power imposed by the contract impairment clause; and the difficulty is that the contract impairment clause forbids state action under any circumstances, if it have the effect of impairing the obligation of contracts. That clause restricts every state power in the particular specified, no matter what may be the occasion. It does not contemplate that an emergency shall furnish an occasion for softening the restriction or making it any the less a restriction upon state action in that contingency than it is under strictly normal conditions.

The Minnesota statute either impairs the obligation of contracts or it does not . . . A statute which materially delays enforcement of the mortgagee's contractual right of ownership and possession does not modify the remedy merely; it destroys, for the period of delay, all remedy so far as the enforcement of that right is concerned. The phrase 'obligation of a contract' in the constitutional sense imports a legal duty to perform the specified obligation of that contract, not to substitute and perform, against the will of one of the parties, a different, albeit equally valuable, obligation. And a state, under the contract impairment clause, has no more power to accomplish such a substitution than has one of the parties to the contract against the will of the other. It cannot do so either by acting directly upon the contract or by bringing about the result under the guise of a statute in form acting only upon the remedy . . .

I quite agree with the opinion of the Court that whether the legislation under review is wise or unwise is a matter with which we have nothing to do.

Whether it is likely to work well or work ill presents a question entirely irrelevant to the issue. The only legitimate inquiry we can make is whether it is constitutional. If it is not, its virtues, if it have any, cannot save it; if it is, its faults cannot be invoked to accomplish its destruction. If the provisions of the Constitution be not upheld when they pinch as well as when they comfort, they may as well be abandoned.

Schechter Poultry Corp. v. United States

295 U.S. 495 (1935), 9-0
Opinion of the Court: Hughes, C.J. (Brandeis, Butler, McReynolds, Roberts, Stone, Sutherland, Van Devanter)
Concurring: Cardozo

Owners of the corporation were convicted for conspiring to violate the Code of Fair Competition for the Live Poultry Industry drawn up for the New York metropolitian area, under the N.I.R.A.

Why does the Schechter business not come under "the stream of commerce" concept presented by the Court in Swift Packing Co. v. United States *and* Stafford v. Wallace? *In the long run, which is the more telling objection to the National Industrial Recovery Act, its excessive delegation and poor draftsmanship or application of one of its propounded codes to this corporation? Has Hughes revived the distinctions of* E. C. Knight Co. v. United States *without saying so? What does Cardozo's opinion add to this decision?*

Hughes, C.J., for the Court:

The Question of the Delegation of Legislative Power . . . The Constitution provides that 'All legislative powers herein granted shall be vested in a Congress of the United States, which shall consist of a Senate and House of Representatives.' Article 1, s 1. And the Congress is authorized 'To make all Laws which shall be necessary and proper for carrying into Execution' its general powers. Article 1, s 8, par. 18. The Congress is not permitted to abdicate or to transfer to others the essential legislative functions with which it is thus vested.

. . . Section 3 of the Recovery Act is without precedent. It supplies no standards for any trade, industry, or activity. It does not undertake to prescribe rules of conduct to be applied to particular states of fact determined by appropriate administrative procedure. Instead of prescribing rules of conduct, it authorizes the making of codes to prescribe them. For that legislative undertaking, section 3 sets up no standards,

aside from the statement of the general aims of rehabilitation, correction, and expansion described in section 1. In view of the scope of that broad declaration and of the nature of the few restrictions that are imposed, the discretion of the President in approving or prescribing codes, and thus enacting laws for the government of trade and industry throughout the country, is virtually unfettered . . . [C]ode-making authority thus conferred is an unconstitutional delegation of legislative power . . .

The Question of the Application of the Provisions of the Live Poultry Code to Intrastate Transactions. Although the validity of the codes (apart from the question of delegation) rests upon the commerce clause of the Constitution, section 3(a) of the act is not . . . limited to interstate and foreign commerce . . . [I]t would appear that section 3(a) was designed to authorize codes without that limitation. But under section 3(f) of the act penalties are confined to violations of a code provision 'in any transaction in or affecting interstate or foreign commerce.' This aspect of the case presents the question whether the particular provisions of the Live Poultry Code, which the defendants were convicted for violating and for having conspired to violate, were within the regulating power of Congress.

These provisions relate to the hours and wages of those employed by defendants in their slaughterhouses in Brooklyn and to the sales there made to retail dealers and butchers.

Were these transactions 'in' interstate commerce? Much is made of the fact that almost all the poultry coming to New York is sent there from other states. But the code provisions, as here applied, do not concern the transportation of the poultry from other states to New York, or the transactions of the commission men or others to whom it is consigned, or the sales made by such consignees to defendants. When defendants had made their purchases, whether at the West Washington Market in New York City or at the railroad terminals serving the city, or elsewhere, the poultry was trucked to their slaughterhouses in Brooklyn for local disposition. The interstate transactions in relation to that poultry then ended. Defendants held the poultry at their slaughterhouse markets for slaughter and local sale to retail dealers and butchers who in turn sold directly to consumers. Neither the slaughtering nor the sales by defendants were transactions in interstate commerce.

The undisputed facts thus afford no warrant for the argument that the poultry handled by defendants at their slaughterhouse markets was in a 'current' or

Cartoonist Harry Outhwaite's stark comment on the Supreme Court's decision in *Schechter Poultry Corp. v. United States.*

'flow' of interstate commerce, and was thus subject to congressional regulation. The mere fact that there may be a constant flow of commodities into a state does not mean that the flow continues after the property has arrived and has become commingled with the mass of property within the state and is there held solely for local disposition and use. So far as the poultry here in question is concerned, the flow in interstate commerce had ceased. The poultry had come to a permanent rest within the state. It was not held, used, or sold by defendants in relation to any further transactions in interstate commerce and was not destined for transportation to other states. Hence decisions which deal with a stream of interstate commerce—where goods come to rest within a state temporarily and are later to go forward in interstate commerce—and with the regulations of transactions involved in that practical continuity of movement, are not applicable here.

Did the defendants' transactions directly 'affect' interstate commerce so as to be subject to federal regulation? The power of Congress extends, not only to the regulation of transactions which are part of interstate commerce, but to the protection of that commerce from injury. It matters not that the injury may be due to the conduct of those engaged in intrastate operations. Thus, Congress may protect the safety of those employed in interstate transportation, 'no matter what may be the source of the dangers which threaten it.' . . .

The instant case is not of that sort . . . Defendants have been convicted, not upon direct charges of injury to interstate commerce or of interference with persons engaged in that commerce, but of violations of certain provisions of the Live Poultry Code and of conspiracy to commit these violations. Interstate commerce is brought in only upon the charge that violations of these provisions—as to hours and wages of employees and local sales—'affected' interstate commerce.

In determining how far the federal government may go in controlling intrastate transactions upon the ground that they 'affect' interstate commerce, there is a necessary and well-established distinction between direct and indirect effects. The precise line can be drawn only as individual cases arise, but the distinction is clear in principle. Direct effects are illustrated by the railroad cases we have cited, as, e.g., the effect of failure to use prescribed safety appliances on railroads which are the highways of both interstate and intrastate commerce, injury to an employee engaged in interstate transportation by the negligence of an employee engaged in an intrastate movement, the fixing of rates for intrastate transportation which unjustly discriminate against interstate commerce. But where the effect of intrastate transactions upon interstate commerce is merely indirect, such transactions remain within the domain of state power. If the commerce clause were construed to reach all enterprises and transactions which could be said to have an indirect effect upon interstate commerce, the federal authority would embrace practically all the activities of the people, and the authority of the state over its domestic concerns would exist only by sufferance of the federal government . . .

The question of chief importance relates to the provisions of the code as to the hours and wages of those employed in defendants' slaughterhouse markets. It is plain that these requirements are imposed in order to govern the details of defendants' management of their local business. The persons employed in slaughtering and selling in local trade are not employed in interstate commerce. Their hours and wages have no direct relation to interstate commerce. The question of how many hours these employees should work and what they should be paid differs in no essential respect from similar questions in other local businesses which handle commodities brought into a state and there dealt in as a part of its internal commerce . . . If the federal government may determine the wages and hours of employees in the internal commerce of a state, because of their relation to cost and prices and their indirect effect upon interstate commerce, it would seem that a similar control might be exerted over other elements of cost, also affecting prices, such as the number of employees, rents, advertising, methods of doing business, etc. All the processes of production and distribution that enter into cost could likewise be controlled . . .

The government also makes the point that efforts to enact state legislation establishing high labor standards have been impeded by the belief that, unless similar action is taken generally, commerce will be diverted from the states adopting such standards, and that this fear of diversion has led to demands for federal legislation on the subject of wages and hours. The apparent implication is that the federal authority under the commerce clause should be deemed to extend to the establishment of rules to govern wages and hours in intrastate trade and industry generally throughout the country, thus overriding the authority of the states to deal with domestic problems arising from labor conditions in their internal commerce.

It is not the province of the Court to consider the economic advantages or disadvantages of such a centralized system. It is sufficient to say that the Federal Constitution does not provide for it . . . [T]he authority of the federal government may not be pushed to such an extreme as to destroy the distinction, which the commerce clause itself establishes, between commerce 'among the several States' and the internal concerns of a state . . .

Cardozo, concurring:

Here, in the case before us, is an attempted delegation not confined to any single act nor to any class or group of acts identified or described by reference to a standard. Here in effect is a roving commission to inquire into evils and upon discovery correct them . . .

[T]here is no standard, definite or even approximate, to which legislation must conform . . . If codes of fair competition are codes eliminating 'unfair' methods of competition ascertained upon inquiry to prevail in one industry or another, there is no unlawful delegation of legislative functions when the President is directed to inquire into such practices and denounce them when discovered. For many years a like power has been committed to the Federal Trade Commission with the approval of this court in a long series of decisions. Delegation in such circumstances is born of the necessities of the occasion. The industries of the country are too many and diverse to make it possible for Congress . . . to legislate directly with adequate appreciation of varying conditions. Nor is the substance of the power changed because the President may act at the instance of trade or industrial associations having special knowledge of the facts. Their function is strictly advisory; it is the imprimatur of the President that begets the quality of law . . .

But there is another conception of codes of fair competition, their significance and function, which leads to very different consequences, though it is one that is struggling now for recognition and acceptance. By this other conception a code is not to be restricted to the elimination of business practices that would be characterized by general acceptation as oppressive or unfair. It is to include whatever ordinances may be desirable or helpful for the well-being or prosperity of the industry affected. In that view, the function of its adoption is not merely negative, but positive; the planning of improvements as well as the extirpation of abuses. What is fair, as thus conceived, is not something to be contrasted with what is unfair or fraudulent or tricky. The extension becomes as wide as the field of industrial regulation. If that conception shall prevail, anything that Congress may do within the limits of the commerce clause for the betterment of business may be done by the President upon the recommendation of a trade association by calling it a code. This is delegation running riot. No such plenitude of power is susceptible of transfer. The statute, however, aims at nothing less, as one can learn both from its terms and from the administrative practice under it . . .

The code does not confine itself to the suppression of methods of competition that would be classified as unfair according to accepted business standards or accepted norms of ethics. It sets up a comprehensive body of rules to promote the welfare of the industry, if not the welfare of the nation, without reference to standards, ethical or commercial, that could be known or predicted in advance of its adoption. One of the new rules . . . is aimed at an established practice, not unethical or oppressive, the practice of selective buying. Many others could be instanced as open to the same objection if the sections of the code were to be examined one by one . . . Even if the statute itself had fixed the meaning of fair competition by way of contrast with practices that are oppressive or unfair, the code outruns the bounds of the authority conferred. What is excessive is not sporadic or superficial. It is deep-seated and pervasive. The licit and illicit sections are so combined and welded as to be incapable of severance without destructive mutilation.

But there is another objection, far-reaching and incurable, aside from any defect of unlawful delegation.

If this code had been adopted by Congress itself, and not by the President on the advice of an industrial association, it would even then be void, unless authority to adopt it is included in the grant of power 'to regulate commerce with foreign nations, and among the several States.'

I find no authority in that grant for the regulation of wages and hours of labor in the intrastate transac-

tions that make up the defendants' business . . . There is a view of causation that would obliterate the distinction between what is national and what is local in the activities of commerce . . . Activities local in their immediacy do not become interstate and national because of distant repercussions. What is near and what is distant may at times be uncertain. There is no penumbra of uncertainty obscuring judgment here. To find immediacy or directness here is to find it almost everywhere . . .

Carter v. Carter Coal Co.

298 U.S. 238 (1936), 5-4
Opinion of the Court: Sutherland (Butler, McReynolds, Van Devanter, Roberts
Dissenting: Brandeis, Cardozo, Hughes, Stone
In the Bituminous Coal Act of 1935, Congress put a 15 percent tax on coal production to underwrite various proposals of a coal industry commission with regard to wages, hours, working conditions, and fair competition. The commission's recommendations were voluntary, but a 90 percent rebate of the tax was given to companies that complied. Carter and other shareholders in the Carter Coal Co. sued the company to keep it from joining the program on grounds that the Coal Act was unconstitutional.

How do Sutherland and Cardozo differ in their interpretation of "direct" and "indirect" effects on interstate commerce? Have the terms taken on a life of their own for the Court or do they make distinctions that are important and substantial? If upholding the Bituminous Coal Conservation Act would, as Sutherland fears, bring any economic activity within the reach of Congress, what would the checks be, if any, on such power? In this case, a brief for the Government cited Swift & Co. v. United States, Stafford v. Wallace, *and the* Shreveport Rate Case *in defense of the act. Do these precedents provide a sufficient constitutional base for upholding the act or would a new conception of Congress's commerce power be necessary?*

Sutherland for the Court:

Certain recitals contained in the act plainly suggest that its makers were of opinion that its constitutionality could be sustained under some general federal power, thought to exist, apart from the specific grants of the Constitution . . . [They] are to the effect that the distribution of bituminous coal is of national interest, affecting the health and comfort of the people and the general welfare of the Nation; that this circumstance, together with the necessity of maintaining just and rational relations between the public, owners, producers, and employees, and the right of the public to constant and adequate supplies at reasonable prices, require regulation of the industry as the act provides . . .

The proposition . . . that the power of the federal government inherently extends to purposes affecting the Nation as a whole with which the states severally cannot deal or cannot adequately deal, and the related notion that Congress, entirely apart from those powers delegated by the Constitution, may enact laws to promote the general welfare, have never been accepted . . . by this court. . .

[T]he general purposes which the act recites . . . are beyond the power of Congress except so far, and only so far, as they may be realized by an exercise of some specific power granted by the Constitution. Proceeding by a process of elimination . . . we shall find no grant of power which authorizes Congress to legislate in respect of these general purposes unless it be found in the commerce clause—and this we now consider.

. . . Since the validity of the act depends upon whether it is a regulation of interstate commerce, the nature and extent of the power conferred upon Congress by the commerce clause becomes the determinative question in this branch of the case. The commerce clause vests in Congress the power 'To regulate Commerce with foreign Nations, and among the several States, and with the Indian Tribes.' The function to be exercised is that of regulation. The thing to be regulated is the commerce described. In exercising the authority conferred by this clause of the Constitution, Congress is powerless to regulate anything which is not commerce, as it is powerless to do anything about commerce which is not regulation. We first inquire, then—What is commerce? . . . No all-embracing definition has ever been formulated. The question is to be approached both affirmatively and negatively—that is to say, from the points of view as to what it includes and what it excludes. . .

As used in the Constitution, the word 'commerce' is the equivalent of the phrase 'intercourse for the purposes of trade,' and includes transportation, purchase, sale, and exchange of commodities between the citizens of the different states. And the power to regulate commerce embraces the instruments by which commerce is carried on—'traffic, intercourse, trade, navigation, communication, the transit of per-

sons, and the transmission of messages by telegraph—indeed, every species on commercial intercourse among the several states.' . . .

That commodities produced or manufactured within a state are intended to be sold or transported outside the state does not render their production or manufacture subject to federal regulation under the commerce clause. As this court said in *Coe v. Errol,* 'Though intended for exportation, they may never be exported—the owner has a perfect right to change his mind—and until actually put in motion, for some place out of the state, or committed to the custody of a carrier for transportation to such place, why may they not be regarded as still remaining a part of the general mass of property in the state?' It is true that this was said in respect of a challenged power of the state to impose a tax; but the query is equally pertinent where the question, as here, is with regard to the power of regulation . . .

One who produces or manufactures a commodity, subsequently sold and shipped by him in interstate commerce, whether such sale and shipment were originally intended or not, has engaged in two distinct and separate activities. So far as he produces or manufactures a commodity, his business is purely local. So far as he sells and ships, or contracts to sell and ship, the commodity to customers in another state, he engages in interstate commerce. In respect of the former, he is subject only to regulation by the state; in respect of the latter, to regulation only by the federal government . . .

Extraction of coal from the mine is the aim and the completed result of local activities. Commerce in the coal mined is not brought into being by force of these activities, but by negotiations, agreements and circumstances entirely apart from production. Mining brings the subject-matter of commerce into existence. Commerce disposes of it . . .

[T]he effect of the labor provisions of the act, including those in respect of minimum wages, wage agreements, collective bargaining, and the Labor Board and its powers, primarily falls upon production and not upon commerce; and confirms the further resulting conclusion that production is a purely local activity. It follows that none of these essential antecedents of production constitutes a transaction in or forms any part of interstate commerce. Everything which moves in interstate commerce has had a local origin. Without local production somewhere, interstate commerce, as now carried on, would practically disappear. Nevertheless, the local character of mining, of manufacturing, and of crop growing is a fact, and remains a fact, whatever may be done with the products . . .

Another group of cases, of which *Swift & Company v. United States,* is an example, rest upon the circumstance that the acts in question constituted direct interferences with the 'flow' of commerce among the states. In the Swift Case, live stock was consigned and delivered to stockyards—not as a place of final destination, but, as the Court said in *Stafford v. Wallace,* 'a throat through which the current flows.' The sales which ensued merely changed the private interest in the subject of the current without interfering with its continuity. It was nowhere suggested in these cases that the interstate commerce power extended to the growth or production of the things which, after production, entered the flow. If the Court had held that the raising of the cattle, which were involved in the Swift Case, including the wages paid to and working conditions of the herders and others employed in the business, could be regulated by Congress, that decision and decisions holding similarly would be in point; for it is that situation, and not the one with which the Court actually dealt, which here concerns us . . .

The restricted field covered by the Swift and kindred cases is illustrated by the Schechter Case. There the commodity in question, although shipped from another state, had come to rest in the state of its destination, and, as the Court pointed out, was no longer in a current or flow of interstate commerce. The Swift doctrine was rejected as inapposite. In the Schechter Case the flow had ceased. Here it had not begun. The difference is not one of substance. The applicable principle is the same . . .

[W]e are brought to the final and decisive inquiry, whether here that effect is direct . . . or indirect . . .

Whether the effect of a given activity or condition is direct or indirect is not always easy to determine. The word 'direct' implies that the activity or condition invoked or blamed shall operate proximately—not mediately, remotely, or collaterally—to produce the effect. It connotes the absence of an efficient intervening agency or condition. And the extent of the effect bears no logical relation to its character. The distinction between a direct and an indirect effect turns, not upon the magnitude of either the cause or the effect, but entirely upon the manner in which the effect has been brought about. If the production by one man of a sin-

gle ton of coal intended for interstate sale and shipment, and actually so sold and shipped, affects interstate commerce indirectly, the effect does not become direct by multiplying the tonnage, or increasing the number of men employed, or adding to the expense or complexities of the business, or by all combined . . .

Much stress is put upon the evils which come from the struggle between employers and employees over the matter of wages, working conditions, the right of collective bargaining, etc., and the resulting strikes, curtailment, and irregularity of production and effect on prices; and it is insisted that interstate commerce is greatly affected thereby. But, in addition to what has just been said, the conclusive answer is that the evils are all local evils over which the federal government has no legislative control. The relation of employer and employee is a local relation . . .

The only perceptible difference between [the Schechter] case and this is that in the Schechter Case the federal power was asserted with respect to commodities which had come to rest after their interstate transportation; while here, the case deals with commodities at rest before interstate commerce has begun. That difference is without significance. The federal regulatory power ceases when interstate commercial intercourse ends; and, correlatively, the power does not attach until interstate commercial intercourse begins . . .

The conclusion is unavoidable that the price-fixing provisions of the code are so related to and dependent upon the labor provisions as conditions, considerations, or compensations, as to make it clearly probable that the latter being held bad, the former would not have been passed. The fall of the latter, therefore, carries down with it the former . . .

Hughes, C.J., dissenting in part:

I agree that the stockholders were entitled to bring their suits; that, in view of the question whether any part of the act could be sustained, the suits were not premature; that the so-called tax is not a real tax, but a penalty; that the constitutional power of the federal government to impose this penalty must rest upon the commerce clause, as the government concedes; that production—in this case mining—which precedes commerce is not itself commerce; and that the power to regulate commerce among the several states is not a power to regulate industry within the state.

The power to regulate interstate commerce embraces the power to protect that commerce from injury, whatever may be the source of the dangers which threaten it, and to adopt any appropriate means to that end. Second Employers' Liability Cases. Congress thus has adequate authority to maintain the orderly conduct of interstate commerce and to provide for the peaceful settlement of disputes which threaten it. But Congress may not use this protective authority as a pretext for the exertion of power to regulate activities and relations within the states which affect interstate commerce only indirectly. Otherwise, in view of the multitude of indirect effect, Congress in its discretion could assume control of virtually all the activities of the people to the subversion of the fundamental principle of the Constitution. If the people desire to give Congress the power to regulate industries within the state, and the relations of employers and employees in those industries, they are at liberty to declare their will in the appropriate manner, but it is not for the Court to amend the Constitution by judicial decision . . .

But that is not the whole case. The act also provides for the regulation of the prices of bituminous coal sold in interstate commerce and prohibits unfair methods of competition in interstate commerce. Undoubtedly transactions in carrying on interstate commerce are subject to the federal power to regulate that commerce and the control of charges and the protection of fair competition in that commerce are familiar illustrations of the exercise of the power, as the Interstate Commerce Act, the Packers and Stockyards Act and the Anti-Trust Acts abundantly show . . .

The marketing provisions in relation to interstate commerce can be carried out as provided in part 2 without regard to the labor provisions contained in part 3. That fact, in the light of the congressional declaration of separability, should be considered of controlling importance.

In this view, the act, and the code for which it provides, may be sustained in relation to the provisions for marketing in interstate commerce, and the decisions of the courts below, so far as they accomplish that result, should be affirmed.

Cardozo, dissenting in part:
[S]o far as the act is directed to interstate transactions . . . sales made in such conditions constitute interstate commerce, and do not merely 'affect' it. To regulate the price for such transactions is to regulate commerce itself, and not alone its antecedent conditions or its ultimate consequences . . . Prices in interstate transactions may not be regulated by the states.

They must therefore be subject to the power of the Nation unless they are to be withdrawn altogether from governmental supervision. If such a vacuum were permitted, many a public evil incidental to interstate transactions would be left without a remedy. This does not mean, of course, that prices may be fixed for arbitrary reasons or in an arbitrary way. The commerce power of the Nation is subject to the requirement of due process like the police power of the states. Heed must be given to similar considerations of social benefit or detriment in marking the division between reason and oppression. The evidence is overwhelming that Congress did not ignore those considerations in the adoption of this act . . .

Regulation of prices being an exercise of the commerce power in respect of interstate transactions, the question remains whether it comes within that power as applied to intrastate sales where interstate prices are directly or intimately affected. Mining and agriculture and manufacture are not interstate commerce considered by themselves, yet their relation to that commerce may be such that for the protection of the one there is need to regulate the other. Sometimes it is said that the relation must be 'direct' to bring that power into play. In many circumstances such a description will be sufficiently precise to meet the needs of the occasion. But a great principle of constitutional law is not susceptible of comprehensive statement in an adjective. The underlying thought is merely this, that 'the law is not indifferent to considerations of degree.' . . . Perhaps, if one group of adjectives is to be chosen in preference to another, 'intimate' and 'remote' will be found to be as good as any. At all events, 'direct' and 'indirect,' even if accepted as sufficient, must not be read too narrowly. A survey of the cases shows that the words have been interpreted with suppleness of adaptation and flexibility of meaning. The power is as broad as the need that evokes it . . .

[T]he prices for intrastate sales of coal have so inescapable a relation to those for interstate sales that a system of regulation for transactions of the one class is necessary to give adequate protection to the system of regulation adopted for the other . . .

The commerce clause being accepted as a sufficient source of power, the next inquiry must be whether the power has been exercised consistently with the Fifth Amendment. In the pursuit of that inquiry, *Nebbia v. New York,* lays down the applicable principle. There a statute of New York prescribing a minimum price for milk was upheld against the objection that price-fixing was forbidden by the Fourteenth Amendment. We found it a sufficient reason to uphold the challenged system that 'the conditions or practices in an industry make unrestricted competition an inadequate safeguard of the consumer's interests, produce waste harmful to the public, threaten ultimately to cut off the supply of a commodity needed by the public, or portend the destruction of the industry itself.' . . .

All this may be said, and with equal, if not greater force, of the conditions and practices in the bituminous coal industry, not only at the enactment of this statute in August, 1935, but for many years before. Overproduction was at a point where free competition had been degraded into anarchy. Prices had been cut so low that profit had become impossible for all except a lucky handful. Wages came down along with prices and with profits. There were strikes, at times nation-wide in extent, at other times spreading over broad areas and many mines, with the accompaniment of violence and bloodshed and misery and bitter feeling . . . During the twenty-three years between 1913 and 1935, there were nineteen investigations or hearings by Congress or by specially created commissions with reference to conditions in the coal mines. The hope of betterment was faint unless the industry could be subjected to the compulsion of a code. In the weeks immediately preceding the passage of this act the country was threatened once more with a strike of ominous proportions. The plight of the industry was not merely a menace to owners and to mine workers, it was and had long been a menace to the public, deeply concerned in a steady and uniform supply of a fuel so vital to the national economy.

Congress was not condemned to inaction in the face of price wars and wage wars so pregnant with disaster. Commerce had been choked and burdened; its normal flow had been diverted from one state to another; there had been bankruptcy and waste and ruin alike for capital and for labor. The liberty protected by the Fifth Amendment does not include the right to persist in this anarchic riot.

United States v. Butler

297 U.S. 1 (1936), 6-3

Opinion of the Court: Roberts (Butler, Hughes, McReynolds, Sutherland, Van Devanter)

Dissenting: Brandeis, Cardozo, Stone

Butler, appointed a receiver for the bankrupt Hoosac Mills, a Massachusetts cotton processor, refused to pay a federal

processing tax under the Agricultural Adjustment Act of 1933. Money raised by the tax was used to subsidize farmers for cutting production and thus to stabilize farm prices.

Does the "general welfare" qualification in Article I-9 of the Constitution mean that federal spending must be confined to the powers enumerated in Article I-8 and those implied from them or does it give Congress additional power going beyond Article I-8? Are Roberts's objections to the Agricultural Adjustment Act based on a view of the federal system? Of the enumeration of powers to Congress? Of the economic system? Of individual liberty? Are the fears expressed in the last paragraphs of his opinion justified? How does he describe judicial review? How close does this come to the way in which the Court actually makes decisions? How do Roberts and Stone differ on the power of Congress to tax and spend? To regulate local activities? To coerce individuals?

Roberts for the Court:

First . . . the [processing] tax can only be sustained by ignoring the avowed purpose and operation of the act, and holding it a measure merely laying an excise upon processors to raise revenue for the support of government. Beyond cavil the sole object of the legislation is to restore the purchasing power of agricultural products to a parity with that prevailing in an earlier day; to take money from the processor and bestow it upon farmers who will reduce their acreage for the accomplishment of the proposed end, and, meanwhile, to aid these farmers during the period required to bring the prices of their crops to the desired level . . .

It is inaccurate and misleading to speak of the exaction from processors prescribed by the challenged act as a tax, or to say that as a tax it is subject to no infirmity. A tax, in the general understanding of the term, and as used in the Constitution, signifies an exaction for the support of the government. The word has never been thought to connote the expropriation of money from one group for the benefit of another. We may concede that the latter sort of imposition is constitutional when imposed to effectuate regulation of a matter in which both groups are interested and in respect of which there is a power of legislative regulation. But manifestly no justification for it can be found unless as an integral part of such regulation . . .

Second . . . the government asserts that even if [Butler, et.al.] may question the propriety of the appropriation embodied in the statute, their attack must fail because article 1, s 8 of the Constitution, authorizes the contemplated expenditure of the funds raised by the tax. This contention presents the great and the controlling question in the case. We approach its decision with a sense of our grave responsibility to render judgment in accordance with the principles established for the governance of all three branches of the government . . .

There should be no misunderstanding as to the function of this court in such a case. It is sometimes said that the Court assumes a power to overrule or control the action of the people's representatives. This is a misconception. The Constitution is the supreme law of the land ordained and established by the people. All legislation must conform to the principles it lays down. When an act of Congress is appropriately challenged in the courts as not conforming to the constitutional mandate, the judicial branch of the government has only one duty; to lay the article of the Constitution which is invoked beside the statute which is challenged and to decide whether the latter squares with the former. All the Court does, or can do, is to announce its considered judgment upon the question. The only power it has, if such it may be called, is the power of judgment. This Court neither approves nor condemns any legislative policy. Its delicate and difficult office is to ascertain and declare whether the legislation is in accordance with, or in contravention of, the provisions of the Constitution; and, having done that, its duty ends . . .

[T]he act under review does not purport to regulate transactions in interstate or foreign commerce. Its stated purpose is the control of agricultural production, a purely local activity, in an effort to raise the prices paid the farmer. Indeed, the government does not attempt to uphold the validity of the act on the basis of the commerce clause, which, for the purpose of the present case, may be put aside as irrelevant.

The clause thought to authorize the legislation . . . confers upon the Congress power 'to lay and collect Taxes, Duties, Imposts and Excises, to pay the Debts and provide for the common Defence and general Welfare of the United States . . .' It is not contended that this provision grants power to regulate agricultural production upon the theory that such legislation would promote the general welfare. The government concedes that the phrase 'to provide for the general welfare' qualifies the power 'to lay and collect taxes.' The view that the clause grants power to provide for the general welfare, independently of the taxing power, has never been authoritatively accepted . . . The true construction undoubtedly is that the only

thing granted is the power to tax for the purpose of providing funds for payment of the nation's debts and making provision for the general welfare.

Nevertheless, the government asserts that warrant is found in this clause for the adoption of the Agricultural Adjustment Act. The argument is that Congress may appropriate and authorize the spending of moneys for the 'general welfare'; that the phrase should be liberally construed to cover anything conducive to national welfare; that decision as to what will promote such welfare rests with Congress alone, and the courts may not review its determination; and, finally, that the appropriation under attack was in fact for the general welfare of the United States.

The Congress is expressly empowered to lay taxes to provide for the general welfare. Funds in the Treasury as a result of taxation may be expended only through appropriation. Article 1, s 9, cl. 7. They can never accomplish the objects for which they were collected, unless the power to appropriate is as broad as the power to tax. The necessary implication from the terms of the grant is that the public funds may be appropriated 'to provide for the general welfare of the United States.' These words cannot be meaningless, else they would not have been used. The conclusion must be that they were intended to limit and define the granted power to raise and to expend money . . .

[T]he power to tax is not unlimited, its confines are set in the clause which confers it, and not in those of section 8 which bestow and define the legislative powers of the Congress. It results that the power of Congress to authorize expenditure of public moneys for public purposes is not limited by the direct grants of legislative power found in the Constitution.

But the adoption of the broader construction leaves the power to spend subject to limitations . . .

We are not now required to ascertain the scope of the phrase 'general welfare of the United States' or to determine whether an appropriation in aid of agriculture falls within it. Wholly apart from that question, another principle embedded in our Constitution prohibits the enforcement of the Agricultural adjustment Act. The act invades the reserved rights of the states. It is a statutory plan to regulate and control agricultural production, a matter beyond the powers delegated to the federal government. The tax, the appropriation of the funds raised, and the direction for their disbursement, are but parts of the plan. They are but means to an unconstitutional end.

From the accepted doctrine that the United States is a government of delegated powers, it follows that those not expressly granted, or reasonably to be implied from such as are conferred, are reserved to the states or to the people. To forestall any suggestion to the contrary, the Tenth Amendment was adopted. The same proposition, otherwise stated, is that powers not granted are prohibited. None to regulate agricultural production is given, and therefore legislation by Congress for that purpose is forbidden . . .

The power of taxation, which is expressly granted, may, of course, be adopted as a means to carry into operation another power also expressly granted. But resort to the taxing power to effectuate an end which is not legitimate, not within the scope of the Constitution, is obviously inadmissible.

Third. If the taxing power may not be used as the instrument to enforce a regulation of matters of state concern with respect to which the Congress has no authority to interfere, may it . . . be employed to raise the money necessary to purchase a compliance which the Congress is powerless to command? The government asserts that whatever might be said against the validity of the plan, if compulsory, it is constitutionally sound because the end is accomplished by voluntary cooperation. There are two sufficient answers to the contention. The regulation is not in fact voluntary. The farmer, of course, may refuse to comply, but the price of such refusal is the loss of benefits. The amount offered is intended to be sufficient to exert pressure on him to agree to the proposed regulation. The power to confer or withhold unlimited benefits is the power to coerce or destroy . . .

But if the plan were one for purely voluntary cooperation it would stand no better so far as federal power is concerned. At best, it is a scheme for purchasing with federal funds submission to federal regulation of a subject reserved to the states.

It is said that Congress has the undoubted right to appropriate money to executive officers for expenditure under contracts between the government and individuals; that much of the total expenditures is so made. But appropriations and expenditures under contracts for proper governmental purposes cannot justify contracts which are not within federal power. And contracts for the reduction of acreage and the control of production are outside the range of that power. An appropriation to be expended by the United States under contracts calling for violation of a state law clearly would offend the Constitution. Is a

statute less objectionable which authorizes expenditure of federal moneys to induce action in a field in which the United States has no power to intermeddle? The Congress cannot invade state jurisdiction to compel individual action; no more can it purchase such action . . .

Congress has no power to enforce its commands on the farmer to the ends sought by the Agricultural Adjustment Act. It must follow that it may not indirectly accomplish those ends by taxing and spending to purchase compliance. The Constitution and the entire plan of our government negative any such use of the power to tax and to spend as the act undertakes to authorize. It does not help to declare that local conditions throughout the nation have created a situation of national concern; for this is but to say that whenever there is a widespread similarity of local conditions, Congress may ignore constitutional limitations upon its own powers and usurp those reserved to the states. If, in lieu of compulsory regulation of subjects within the states' reserved jurisdiction, which is prohibited, the Congress could invoke the taxing and spending power as a means to accomplish the same end, clause 1 of section 8 of article 1 would become the instrument for total subversion of the governmental powers reserved to the individual states.

If the act before us is a proper exercise of the federal taxing power, evidently the regulation of all industry throughout the United States may be accomplished by similar exercises of the same power. It would be possible to exact money from one branch of an industry and pay it to another branch in every field of activity which lies within the province of the states. The mere threat of such a procedure might well induce the surrender of rights and the compliance with federal regulation as the price of continuance in business. A few instances will illustrate the thought . . .

A possible result of sustaining the claimed federal power would be that every business group which thought itself underprivileged might demand that a tax be laid on its vendors or vendees, the proceeds to be appropriated to the redress of its deficiency of income . . .

Until recently no suggestion of the existence of any such power in the federal government has been advanced. The expressions of the framers of the Constitution, the decisions of this court interpreting that instrument and the writings of great commentators will be searched in vain for any suggestion that there exists in the clause under discussion or elsewhere in the Constitution, the authority whereby every provision and every fair, implication from that instrument may be subverted, the independence of the individual states obliterated, and the United States converted into a central government exercising uncontrolled police power in every state of the Union, superseding all local control or regulation of the affairs or concerns of the states.

Stone, dissenting:

[C]ertain propositions . . . should have controlling influence in determining the validity of the act. They are:

1. The power of courts to declare a statute unconstitutional is subject to two guiding principles of decision which ought never to be absent from judicial consciousness. One is that courts are concerned only with the power to enact statutes, not with their wisdom. The other is that while unconstitutional exercise of power by the executive and legislative branches of the government is subject to judicial restraint, the only check upon our own exercise of power is our own sense of self-restraint. For the removal of unwise laws from the statute books appeal lies, not to the courts, but to the ballot and to the processes of democratic government.

2. The constitutional power of Congress to levy an excise tax upon the processing of agricultural products is not questioned. The present levy is held invalid, not for any want of power in Congress to lay such a tax to defray public expenditures, including those for the general welfare, but because the use to which its proceeds are put is disapproved.

3. As the present depressed state of agriculture is nation wide in its extent and effects, there is no basis for saying that the expenditure of public money in aid of farmers is not within the specifically granted power of Congress to levy taxes to 'provide for the . . . general welfare.' . . .

It is with these preliminary and hardly controverted matters in mind that we should direct our attention to the pivot on which the decision of the Court is made to turn. It is that a levy unquestionably within the taxing power of Congress may be treated as invalid because it is a step in a plan to regulate agricultural production and is thus a forbidden infringement of state power. The levy is not any the less an exercise of taxing power because it is intended to defray an expenditure for the general welfare rather than for some other support of government. Nor is the levy and collection of the tax pointed to as effecting the regulation. While all federal taxes inevitably have some influence on the internal economy of the states, it is not contended that the levy of a processing tax upon manufacturers using agricultural products as raw material has any perceptible regulatory effect upon either their production or manufacture . . . Here regulation, if any there be, is accomplished not by the tax, but by the method by which its proceeds are expended, and would equally be accomplished by any like use of public funds, regardless of their source . . .

Of the assertion that the payments to farmers are coercive, it is enough to say that no such contention is pressed by the taxpayer, and no such consequences were to be anticipated or appear to have resulted from the administration of the act. The suggestion of coercion finds no support in the record or in any data showing the actual operation of the act. Threat of loss, not hope of gain, is the essence of economic coercion . . .

It is upon the contention that state power is infringed by purchased regulation of agricultural production that chief reliance is placed. It is insisted that, while the Constitution gives to Congress, in specific and unambiguous terms, the power to tax and spend, the power is subject to limitations which do not find their origin in any express provision of the Constitution and to which other expressly delegated powers are not subject . . .

The power of Congress to spend is inseparable from persuasion to action over which Congress has no legislative control . . . It makes no difference that there is a promise to do an act which the condition is calculated to induce. Condition and promise are alike valid since both are in furtherance of the national purpose for which the money is appropriated . . .

The spending power of Congress is in addition to the legislative power and not subordinate to it. This independent grant of the power of the purse, and its very nature, involving in its exercise the duty to insure expenditure within the granted power, presuppose freedom of selection among divers ends and aims, and the capacity to impose such conditions as will render the choice effective. It is a contradiction in terms to say that there is power to spend for the national welfare, while rejecting any power to impose conditions reasonably adapted to the attainment of the end which alone would justify the expenditure . . .

The limitation now sanctioned must lead to absurd consequences. The government may give seeds to farmers, but may not condition the gift upon their being planted in places where they are most needed or even planted at all. The government may give money to the unemployed, but may not ask that those who get it shall give labor in return, or even use it to support their families. It may give money to sufferers from earthquake, fire, tornado, pestilence, or flood, but may not impose conditions, health precautions, designed to prevent the spread of disease, or induce the movement of population to safer or more sanitary areas. All that, because it is purchased regulation infringing state powers, must be left for the states, who are unable or unwilling to supply the necessary relief . . . Do all its activities collapse because, in order to effect the permissible purpose in myriad ways the money is paid out upon terms and conditions which influence action of the recipients within the states, which Congress cannot command? . . . If the expenditure is for a national public purpose, that purpose will not be thwarted because payment is on condition which will advance that purpose. The action which Congress induces by payments of money to promote the general welfare, but which it does not command or coerce, is but an incident to a specifically granted power, but a permissible means to a legitimate end. If appropriation in aid of a program of curtailment of agricultural production is constitutional, and it is not denied that it is, payment to farmers on condition that they reduce their crop acreage is constitutional. It is not any the less so because the farmer at his own option promises to fulfill the condition . . .

The power to tax and spend is not without constitutional restraints. One restriction is that the purpose must be truly national. Another is that it may not be used to coerce action left to state control. Another is the conscience and patriotism of Congress and the Executive . . .

A tortured construction of the Constitution is not to be justified by recourse to extreme examples of reckless congressional spending which might occur if courts could not prevent—expenditures which . . . would be possible only by action of a legislature lost to all sense of public responsibility. Such suppositions are addressed to the mind accustomed to believe that it is the business of courts to sit in judgment on the wisdom of legislative action. Courts are not the only agency of government that must be assumed to have capacity to govern . . .

[T]he power to tax and spend includes the power to relieve a nationwide economic maladjustment by conditional gifts of money.

West Coast Hotel Co. v. Parrish

300 U.S. 379 (1937), 5-4
Opinion of the Court: Hughes, C.J. (Brandeis, Cardozo, Roberts, Stone)
Dissenting: Butler, McReynolds, Sutherland, Van Devanter

Parrish, a chambermaid working for the West Coast Hotel was not paid the minimum wage mandated for women and minors by Washington state law. She sued her employer to recover wages due.

Is there any way the Court's decision can be reconciled with Sutherland's conception of judicial review? Do Hughes and Sutherland differ mainly about the flexibility of the Constitution as written or about who will decide what it means? After citing reasons the legislature had for enactment of the law, Hughes supplies additional ones based on "common knowlege." Is this consistent with the legislature being "entitled to its judgment"? Does Sutherland's view of judicial review take into account that the Constitution is often unclear and, still more often, silent? Is this case mainly about the reach of regulatory power or about the role of judges?

Hughes, C.J., for the Court:

This case presents the question of the constitutional validity of the minimum wage law of the state of Washington . . .

The Supreme Court of Washington has upheld the minimum wage statute of that state. It has decided that the statute is a reasonable exercise of the police power of the state. In reaching that conclusion, the state court has invoked principles long established by this Court in the application of the Fourteenth Amendment. The state court has refused to regard the decision in the Adkins Case as determinative and has pointed to our decisions both before and since that case as justifying its position. We are of the opinion that this ruling of the state court demands on our part a re-examination of the Adkins Case. The importance of the question, in which many states having similar laws are concerned, the close division by which the decision in the Adkins Case was reached, and the economic conditions which have supervened, and in the light of which the reasonableness of the exercise of the protective power of the state must be considered, make it not only appropriate, but we think imperative, that in deciding the present case the subject should receive fresh consideration . . .

The principle which must control our decision is not in doubt. The constitutional provision invoked is the due process clause of the Fourteenth Amendment governing the states, as the due process clause invoked in the Adkins Case governed Congress. In each case the violation alleged by those attacking minimum wage regulation for women is deprivation of freedom of contract. What is this freedom? The Constitution does not speak of freedom of contract. It speaks of liberty and prohibits the deprivation of liberty without due process of law. In prohibiting that deprivation, the Constitution does not recognize an absolute and uncontrollable liberty. Liberty in each of its phases has its history and connotation. But the liberty safeguarded is liberty in a social organization which requires the protection of law against the evils which menace the health, safety, morals, and welfare of the people. Liberty under the Constitution is thus necessarily subject to the restraints of due process, and regulation which is reasonable in relation to its subject and is adopted in the interests of the community is due process.

This essential limitation of liberty in general governs freedom of contract in particular . . .

This power under the Constitution to restrict freedom of contract has had many illustrations. That it may be exercised in the public interest with respect to contracts between employer and employee is undeniable. Thus statutes have been sustained limiting employment in underground mines and smelters to eight hours a day; in requiring redemption in cash of store orders or other evidences of indebtedness issued in the payment of wages; in forbidding the payment of seamen's wages in advance; in making it unlawful to contract to pay miners employed at quantity rates upon the basis of screened coal instead of the weight of the coal as originally produced in the mine; in prohibiting contracts limiting liability for injuries to employees; in limiting hours of work of employees in manufacturing establishments; and in maintaining workmen's compensation laws. In dealing with the relation of employer and employed, the Legislature has necessarily a wide field of discretion in order that there may be suitable protection of health and safety, and that peace and good order may be promoted through regulations designed to insure wholesome conditions of work and freedom from oppression.

The point that has been strongly stressed that adult employees should be deemed competent to make their own contracts was decisively met nearly forty years ago in Holden v. Hardy, where we pointed out the inequality in the footing of the parties. We said:

'The legislature has also recognized the fact, which the experience of legislators in many states has corroborated, that the proprietors of these establishments and their operatives do not stand upon an equality, and that their interests are, to a certain extent, conflicting. The former naturally desire to obtain as much labor as possible from their employees, while the latter are often induced by the fear of discharge to conform to regulations which their judgment, fairly exercised, would pronounce to be detrimental to their health or strength. In other words, the proprietors lay down the rules, and the laborers are practically constrained to obey them. In such cases self-interest is often an unsafe guide, and the legislature may properly interpose its authority.'

And we added that the fact 'that both parties are of full age, and competent to contract, does not necessarily deprive the state of the power to interfere, where the parties do not stand upon an equality, or where the public heath demands that one party to the contract shall be protected against himself.' 'The state still retains an interest in his welfare, however reckless he may be . . .

It is manifest that this established principle is peculiarly applicable in relation to the employment of women in whose protection the state has a special interest. That phase of the subject received elaborate consideration in *Muller v. Oregon* (1908), where the constitutional authority of the state to limit the working hours of women was sustained . . .

[T]he decision in the Adkins Case was a departure from the true application of the principles governing the regulation by the state of the relation of employer and employed. Those principles have been reenforced by our subsequent decisions. Thus in *Radice v. New York*, we sustained the New York statute which restricted the employment of women in restaurants at night. In *O'Gorman & Young v. Hartford Fire Insurance Company*, which upheld an act regulating the commissions of insurance agents, we pointed to the presumption of the constitutionality of a statute dealing with a subject within the scope of the police power and to the absence of any factual foundation of record for deciding that the limits of power had been transcended. In *Nebbia v. New York*, dealing with the New

York statute providing for minimum prices for milk, the general subject of the regulation of the use of private property and of the making of private contracts received an exhaustive examination, and we again declared that if such laws 'have a reasonable relation to a proper legislative purpose, and are neither arbitrary nor discriminatory, the requirements of due process are satisfied'; that 'with the wisdom of the policy adopted, with the adequacy or practicability of the law enacted to forward it, the courts are both incompetent and unauthorized to deal'; that 'times without number we have said that the Legislature is primarily the judge of the necessity of such an enactment, that every possible presumption is in favor of its validity, and that though the Court may hold views inconsistent with the wisdom of the law, it may not be annulled unless palpably in excess of legislative power.'

With full recognition of the earnestness and vigor which characterize the prevailing opinion in the Adkins Case, we find it impossible to reconcile that ruling with these well-considered declarations. What can be closer to the public interest than the health of women and their protection from unscrupulous and overreaching employers? And if the protection of women is a legitimate end of the exercise of state power, how can it be said that the requirement of the payment of a minimum wage fairly fixed in order to meet the very necessities of existence is not an admissible means to that end? The Legislature of the state was clearly entitled to consider the situation of women in employment, the fact that they are in the class receiving the least pay, that their bargaining power is relatively weak, and that they are the ready victims of those who would take advantage of their necessitous circumstances. The Legislature was entitled to adopt measures to reduce the evils of the 'sweating system,' the exploiting of workers at wages so low as to be insufficient to meet the bare cost of living, thus making their very helplessness the occasion of a most injurious competition. The Legislature had the right to consider that its minimum wage requirements would be an important aid in carrying out its policy of protection. The adoption of similar requirements by many states evidences a deep-seated conviction both as to the presence of the evil and as to the means adapted to check it. Legislative response to that conviction cannot be regarded as arbitrary or capricious and that is all we have to decide. Even if the wisdom of the policy be regarded as debatable and its effects uncertain, still the Legislature is entitled to its judgment.

There is an additional and compelling consideration which recent economic experience has brought into a strong light. The exploitation of a class of workers who are in an unequal position with respect to bargaining power and are thus relatively defenseless against the denial of a living wage is not only detrimental to their health and well being, but casts a direct burden for their support upon the community. What these workers lose in wages the taxpayers are called upon to pay. The bare cost of living must be met. We may take judicial notice of the unparalleled demands for relief which arose during the recent period of depression and still continue to an alarming extent despite the degree of economic recovery which has been achieved. It is unnecessary to cite official statistics to establish what is of common knowledge through the length and breadth of the land. While in the instant case no factual brief has been presented, there is no reason to doubt that the state of Washington has encountered the same social problem that is present elsewhere. The community is not bound to provide what is in effect a subsidy for unconscionable employers. The community may direct its law-making power to correct the abuse which springs from their selfish disregard of the public interest. The argument that the legislation in question constitutes an arbitrary discrimination, because it does not extend to men, is unavailing. This Court has frequently held that the legislative authority, acting within its proper field, is not bound to extend its regulation to all cases which it might possibly reach. The Legislature 'is free to recognize degrees of harm and it may confine its restrictions to those classes of cases where the need is deemed to be clearest.' If 'the law presumably hits the evil where it is most felt, it is not to be overthrown because there are other instances to which it might have been applied.' There is no 'doctrinaire requirement' that the legislation should be couched in all embracing terms. This familiar principle has repeatedly been applied to legislation which singles out women, and particular classes of women, in the exercise of the state's protective power. Their relative need in the presence of the evil, no less than the existence of the evil itself, is a matter for the legislative judgment.

Our conclusion is that the case of *Adkins v. Children's Hospital*, should be, and it is, overruled. The judgment of the Supreme Court of the state of Washington is affirmed.

Sutherland, dissenting:

Under our form of government, where the written Constitution, by its own terms, is the supreme law, some agency, of necessity, must have the power to say the final word as to the validity of a statute assailed as unconstitutional. The Constitution makes it clear that the power has been entrusted to this court when the question arises in a controversy within its jurisdiction; and so long as the power remains there, its exercise cannot be avoided without betrayal of the trust.

It has been pointed out many times, as in the Adkins Case, that this judicial duty is one of gravity and delicacy; and that rational doubts must be resolved in favor of the constitutionality of the statute. But whose doubts, and by whom resolved? Undoubtedly it is the duty of a member of the Court, in the process of reaching a right conclusion, to give due weight to the opposing views of his associates; but in the end, the question which he must answer is not whether such views seem sound to those who entertain them, but whether they convince him that the statute is constitutional or engender in his mind a rational doubt upon that issue ... And in passing upon the validity of a statute, he discharges a duty imposed upon him, which cannot be consummated justly by an automatic acceptance of the views of others which have neither convinced, nor created a reasonable doubt in, his mind. If upon a question so important he thus surrender his deliberate judgment, he stands forsworn. He cannot subordinate his convictions to that extent and keep faith with his oath or retain his judicial and moral independence.

The suggestion that the only check upon the exercise of the judicial power, when properly invoked, to declare a constitutional right superior to an unconstitutional statute is the judge's own faculty of self-restraint, is both ill considered and mischievous. Self-restraint belongs in the domain of will and not of judgment. The check upon the judge is that imposed by his oath of office, by the Constitution, and by his own conscientious and informed convictions; and since he has the duty to make up his own mind and adjudge accordingly, it is hard to see how there could be any other restraint ...

It is urged that the question involved should now receive fresh consideration, among other reasons, because of 'the economic conditions which have supervened'; but the meaning of the Constitution does not change with the ebb and flow of economic events. We frequently are told in more general words that the Constitution must be construed in the light of the present. If by that it is meant that the Constitution is made up of living words that apply to every new condition which they include, the statement is quite true. But to say, if that be intended, that the words of the Constitution mean today what they did not mean when written—that is, that they do not apply to a situation now to which they would have applied then—is to rob that instrument of the essential element which continues it in force as the people have made it until they, and not their official agents, have made it otherwise ...

The judicial function is that of interpretation; it does not include the power of amendment under the guise of interpretation. To miss the point of difference between the two is to miss all that the phrase 'supreme law of the land' stands for and to convert what was intended as inescapable and enduring mandates into mere moral reflections.

If the Constitution, intelligently and reasonably construed in the light of these principles, stands in the way of desirable legislation, the blame must rest upon that instrument, and not upon the Court for enforcing it according to its terms. The remedy in that situation—and the only true remedy—is to amend the Constitution ...

Coming, then, to a consideration of the Washington statute, it first is to be observed that it is in every substantial respect identical with the statute involved in the Adkins Case. Such vices as existed in the latter are present in the former. And if the Adkins Case was properly decided, as we who join in this opinion think it was, it necessarily follows that the Washington statute is invalid ...

National Labor Relations Board v. Jones & Laughlin Steel Corp.

301 U.S. 1 (1937), 5-4

Opinion of the Court: Hughes, C.J. (Brandeis, Cardozo, Roberts, Stone)

Dissenting: Butler, McReynolds, Sutherland, Van Devanter

Under the National Labor Relations Act of 1935, the N.L.R.B. had ordered the company to end discriminatory practices against union members in hiring and tenure. When the company failed to comply, the Board petitioned to have the order enforced.

Since its holding on the reach of federal commerce power in this case does not rely on such older concepts as direct versus indirect effect or stream of commerce, on what is it based? Are any clear limits articulated? Have Hughes's views of the commerce power changed from those he gave in Schechter Poultry Corp. v. United States*? Has the Court overruled* Schechter *without saying so?*

Hughes, C.J., for the Court:

First. The Scope of the Act. The act is challenged in its entirety as an attempt to regulate all industry, thus invading the reserved powers of the States over their local concerns . . .

We think it clear that the National Labor Relations Act may be construed so as to operate within the sphere of constitutional authority. The jurisdiction conferred upon the Board, and invoked in this instance, is found in section 10(a), which provides:

'Sec. 10(a). The Board is empowered, as hereinafter provided, to prevent any person from engaging in any unfair labor practice affecting commerce.'

The critical words of this provision, prescribing the limits of the Board's authority in dealing with the labor practices, are 'affecting commerce.' The act specifically defines the 'commerce' to which it refers section 2(6):

'The term 'commerce' means trade, traffic, commerce, transportation, or communication among the several States, or between the District of Columbia or any Territory of the United States and any State or other Territory, or between any foreign country and any State, Territory, or the District of Columbia, or within the District of Columbia or any Territory, or between points in the same State but through any other State or any Territory or the District of Columbia or any foreign country.'

There can be no question that the commerce thus contemplated by the act (aside from that within a Territory or the District of Columbia) is interstate and foreign commerce in the constitutional sense. The act also defines the term 'affecting commerce' section 2(7):

'The term 'affecting commerce' means in commerce, or burdening or obstructing commerce or the free flow of commerce, or having led or tending to lead to a labor dispute burdening or obstructing commerce or the free flow of commerce.'

This definition is one of exclusion as well as inclusion. The grant of authority to the Board does not purport to extend to the relationship between all industrial employees and employers. Its terms do not impose collective bargaining upon all industry regardless of effects upon interstate or foreign commerce. It purports to reach only what may be deemed to burden or obstruct that commerce and, thus qualified, it must be construed as contemplating the exercise of control within constitutional bounds. It is a familiar principle that acts which directly burden or obstruct interstate or foreign commerce, or its free flow, are within the reach of the congressional power. Acts having that effect are not rendered immune because they grow out of labor disputes. It is the effect upon commerce, not the source of the injury, which is the criterion . . .

Second. The Unfair Labor Practices in Question . . . Thus, in its present application, the statute goes no further than to safeguard the right of employees to self-organization and to select representatives of their own choosing for collective bargaining or other mutual protection without restraint or coercion by their employer.

That is a fundamental right. Employees have as clear a right to organize and select their representatives for lawful purposes as [Jones & Laughlin] has to organize its business and select its own officers and agents. Discrimination and coercion to prevent the free exercise of the right of employees to self-organization and representation is a proper subject for condemnation by competent legislative authority. Long ago we stated the reason for labor organizations. We said that they were organized out of the necessities of the situation; that a single employee was helpless in dealing with an employer; that he was dependent ordinarily on his daily wage for the maintenance of himself and family; that, if the employer refused to pay him the wages that he thought fair, he was nevertheless unable to leave the employ and resist arbitrary and unfair treatment; that union was essential to give laborers opportunity to deal on an equality with their employer. We reiterated these views when we had under consideration the Railway Labor Act of 1926. Fully recognizing the legality of collective action on the part of employees in order to safeguard their proper interests, we said that Congress was not required to ignore this right but could safeguard it . . .

Third. The application of the Act to Employees Engaged in Production . . . [Jones & Laughlin] says that, whatever may be said of employees engaged in interstate commerce, the industrial relations and activities in the manufacturing department of [it's] enterprise are not subject to federal regulation. The argument rests upon the proposition that manufacturing in itself is not commerce . . .

We do not find it necessary to determine whether these features of [corporation's] business dispose of the asserted analogy to the 'stream of commerce' cases. The instances in which that metaphor has been used are but particular, and not exclusive, illustrations of the protective power which the government invokes in support of the present act. The congressional authority to protect interstate commerce from burdens and obstructions is not limited to transactions which can be deemed to be an essential part of a 'flow' of interstate or foreign commerce. Burdens and obstructions may be due to injurious action springing from other sources. The fundamental principle is that the power to regulate commerce is the power to enact 'all appropriate legislation' for its 'protection or advancement'; to adopt measures 'to promote its growth and insure its safety'; 'to foster, protect, control, and restrain.' That power is plenary and may be exerted to protect interstate commerce 'no matter what the source of the dangers which threaten it.' Although activities may be intrastate in character when separately considered, if they have such a close and substantial relation to interstate commerce that their control is essential or appropriate to protect that commerce from burdens and obstructions, Congress cannot be denied the power to exercise that control. Undoubtedly the scope of this power must be considered in the light of our dual system of government and may not be extended so as to embrace effects upon interstate commerce so indirect and remote that to embrace them, in view of our complex society, would effectually obliterate the distinction between what is national and what is local and create a completely centralized government. The question is necessarily one of degree . . .

That intrastate activities, by reason of close and intimate relation to interstate commerce, may fall within federal control is demonstrated in the case of carriers who are engaged in both interstate and intrastate transportation. There federal control has been found essential to secure the freedom of interstate traffic from interference or unjust discrimination and to promote the efficiency of the interstate service. It is manifest that intrastate rates deal primarily with a local activity. But in rate making they bear such a close relation to interstate rates that effective control of the one must embrace some control over the other . . .

The close and intimate effect which brings the subject within the reach of federal power may be due to activities in relation to productive industry although the industry when separately viewed is local . . .

It is thus apparent that the fact that the employees here concerned were engaged in production is not determinative. The question remains as to the effect upon interstate commerce of the labor practice involved. In the Schechter Case we found that the effect there was so remote as to be beyond the federal power. To find 'immediacy or directness' there was to find it 'almost everywhere,' a result inconsistent with the maintenance of our federal system. In the Carter Case, the Court was of the opinion that the provisions of the statute relating to production were invalid upon several grounds—that there was improper delegation of legislative power, and that the requirements not only went beyond any sustainable measure of protection of interstate commerce but were also inconsistent with due process. These cases are not controlling here.

Fourth. Effects of the Unfair Labor Practice in [Jones & Laughlin's] Enterprise. Giving full weight to [the corporation's] contention with respect to a break in the complete continuity of the 'stream of commerce' by reason of [its] manufacturing operations, the fact remains that the stoppage of those operations by industrial strife would have a most serious effect upon interstate commerce. In view of [its] far-flung activities, it is idle to say that the effect would be indirect or remote. It is obvious that it would be immediate and might be catastrophic. We are asked to shut our eyes to the plainest facts of our national life and to deal with the question of direct and indirect effects in an intellectual vacuum. Because there may be but indirect and remote effects upon interstate commerce in connection with a host of local enterprises throughout the country, it does not follow that other industrial activities do not have such a close and intimate relation to interstate commerce as to make the presence of industrial strife a matter of the most urgent national concern. When industries organize themselves on a national scale, making their relation to interstate commerce the dominant factor in their activities, how can it be maintained that their industrial labor relations constitute a forbidden field into which Congress may not enter when it is necessary to protect interstate commerce from the paralyzing consequences of industrial war? We have often said that interstate commerce itself is a practical conception. It is equally true that interferences with that commerce must be appraised by a judgment that does not ignore actual experience.

Experience has abundantly demonstrated that the recognition of the right of employees to self-organization and to have representatives of their own choosing for the purpose of collective bargaining is often an essential condition of industrial peace. Refusal to confer and negotiate has been one of the most prolific causes of strife . . .

The steel industry is one of the great basic industries of the United States, with ramifying activities affecting interstate commerce at every point . . . Instead of being beyond the pale, we think that it presents in a most striking way the close and intimate relation which a manufacturing industry may have to interstate commerce and we have no doubt that Congress had constitutional authority to safeguard the right of [Jones & Laughlin's] employees to self-organization and freedom in the choice of representatives for collective bargaining . . .

Our conclusion is that the order of the Board was within its competency and that the act is valid as here applied.

McReynolds, (Butler, Sutherland, Van Devanter) dissenting:

The Court . . . departs from well-established principles followed in *Schechter Poultry Corporation v. United States*, and *Carter v. Carter Coal Co* . . .

By its terms the Labor Act extends to employers—large and small—unless excluded by definition, and declares that, if one of these interferes with, restrains, or coerces any employee regarding his labor affiliations, etc., this shall be regarded as unfair labor practice. And a 'labor organization' means any organization of any kind or any agency or employee representation committee or plan which exists for the purpose in whole or in part of dealing with employers concerning grievances, labor disputes, wages, rates of pay, hours of employment or conditions of work . . .

The argument in support of the Board affirms: 'Thus the validity of any specific application of the preventive measures of this Act depends upon whether industrial strife resulting from the practices in the particular enterprise under consideration would be of the character which Federal power could control if it occurred. If strife in that enterprise could be controlled, certainly it could be prevented.' . . .

Any effect on interstate commerce by the discharge of employees shown here would be indirect and remote in the highest degree, as consideration of the facts will show. In No. 419 ten men out of ten thousand were discharged; in the other cases only a few. The immediate effect in the factor may be to create discontent among all those employed and a strike may follow, which, in turn, may result in reducing production, which ultimately may reduce the volume of goods moving in interstate commerce. By this chain of indirect and progressively remote events we finally reach the evil with which it is said the legislation under consideration undertakes to deal. A more remote and indirect interference with interstate commerce or a more definite invasion of the powers reserved to the states is difficult, if not impossible, to imagine . . .

We are told that Congress may protect the 'stream of commerce' and that one who buys raw material without the state, manufactures it therein, and ships the output to another state is in that stream. Therefore it is said he may be prevented from doing anything which may interfere with its flow.

This, too, goes beyond the constitutional limitations heretofore enforced. If a man raises cattle and regularly delivers them to a carrier for interstate shipment, may Congress prescribe the conditions under which he may employ or discharge helpers on the ranch? The products of a mine pass daily into interstate commerce; many things are brought to it from other states. Are the owners and the miners within the power of Congress in respect of the latter's tenure and discharge? May a mill owner be prohibited from closing his factory or discontinuing his business because so to do would stop the flow of products to and from his plant in interstate commerce? May employees in a factory be restrained from quitting work in a body because this will close the factory and thereby stop the flow of commerce? May arson of a factory be made a federal offense whenever this would interfere with such flow? If the business cannot continue with the existing wage scale, may Congress command a reduction? If the ruling of the Court just announced is adhered to, these questions suggest some of the problems certain to arise . . .

There is no ground on which reasonably to hold that refusal by a manufacturer, whose raw materials come from states other than that of his factory and whose products are regularly carried to other states, to bargain collectively with employees in his manufacturing plant, directly affects interstate commerce. In such business, there is not one but two distinct movements or streams in interstate transportation. The first brings in raw material and there ends. Then follows manufacture, a separate and local activity. Upon completion of this and not before, the second distinct movement or stream in interstate commerce begins and the products go to other states. Such is the common course for small as well as large industries. It is unreasonable and unprecedented to say the commerce clause confers upon Congress power to govern relations between employers and employees in these local activities. In Schechter's Case we condemned as unauthorized by the commerce clause assertion of federal power in respect of commodities which had come to rest after interstate transportation. And, in Carter's Case, we held Congress lacked power to regulate labor relations in respect of commodities before interstate commerce has begun.

It is gravely stated that experience teaches that if an employer discourages membership in 'any organization of any kind' 'in which employees participate, and which exists for the purpose in whole or in part of dealing with employers concerning grievances, labor disputes, wages, rates of pay, hours of employment or conditions of work,' discontent may follow and this in turn may lead to a strike, and as the outcome of the strike there may be a block in the stream of interstate commerce. Therefore Congress may inhibit the discharge! Whatever effect any cause of discontent may ultimately have upon commerce is far too indirect to justify congressional regulation. Almost anything—marriage, birth, death—may in some fashion affect commerce.

That Congress has power by appropriate means, not prohibited by the Constitution, to prevent direct and material interference with the conduct of interstate commerce is settled doctrine. But the interference struck at must be direct and material, not some mere possibility contingent on wholly uncertain events...

The things inhibited by the Labor Act relate to the management of a manufacturing plant—something distinct from commerce and subject to the authority of the state. And this may not be abridged because of some vague possibility of distant interference with commerce...

The right to contract is fundamental and includes the privilege of selecting those with whom one is willing to assume contractual relations. This right is un-duly abridged by the act now upheld. A private owner is deprived of power to manage his own property by freely selecting those to whom his manufacturing operations are to be entrusted.

Steward Machine Co. v. Davis

301 U.S. 548 (1937), 5-4
Opinion of the Court: Cardozo (Brandeis, Hughes, Roberts, Stone)
Dissenting: Butler, McReynolds, Sutherland, Van Devanter

The company, which was subject to a federal payroll tax in accordance with unemployment compensation provisions of the Social Security Act, sued to recover tax paid.

Is the decision here consistent with Butler v. United States? *Is it based on factors not considered in* Butler? *In the statutory scheme, a state would gain by accepting a federal reward, but it could also just say no. Can that choice be said to be free of coercion?*

Cardozo for the Court:

The validity of the tax imposed by the Social Security Act on employers of eight or more is here to be determined...

The assault on the statute proceeds on an extended front. Its assailants take the ground that the tax is not an excise; that it is not uniform throughout the United States as excises are required to be; that its exceptions are so many and arbitrary as to violate the Fifth Amendment; that its purpose was not revenue, but an unlawful invasion of the reserved powers of the states; and that the states in submitting to it have yielded to coercion and have abandoned governmental functions which they are not permitted to surrender...

The tax, which is described in the statute as an excise, is laid with uniformity throughout the United States as a duty, an impost, or an excise upon the relation of employment...

The subject matter of taxation open to the power of the Congress is as comprehensive as that open to the power of the states, though the method of apportionment may at times be different. 'The Congress shall have Power to lay and collect Taxes, Duties, Imposts and Excises.' Article 1, s 8. If the tax is a direct one, it shall be apportioned according to the census or enumeration. If it is a duty, impost, or excise, it shall be uniform throughout the United States. Together, these classes include every form of tax appropriate to sovereignty. Whether the tax is to be classified as an 'excise' is in truth not of critical importance. If not that, it is an 'impost' or a 'duty' A capitation or other 'direct' tax it certainly is not . . . .

The tax being an excise, its imposition must conform to the canon of uniformity. There has been no departure from this requirement. According to the settled doctrine, the uniformity exacted is geographical, not intrinsic . . . .

The excise is not void as involving the coercion of the states in contravention of the Tenth Amendment or of restrictions implicit in our federal form of government.

The proceeds of the excise when collected are paid into the Treasury at Washington, and thereafter are subject to appropriation like public moneys generally. No presumption can be indulged that they will be misapplied or wasted. Even if they were collected in the hope or expectation that some other and collateral good would be furthered as an incident, that without more would not make the act invalid . . . The case for [Steward Machine] is built on the contention that here an ulterior aim is wrought into the very structure of the act, and what is even more important that the aim is not only ulterior, but essentially unlawful. In particular, the 90 per cent credit is relied upon as supporting that conclusion. But before the statute succumbs to an assault upon these lines, two propositions must be made out by the assailant. There must be a showing in the first place that separated from the credit the revenue provisions are incapable of standing by themselves. There must be a showing in the second place that the tax and the credit in combination are weapons of coercion, destroying or impairing the autonomy of the states. The truth of each proposition being essential to the success of the assault, we pass for convenience to a consideration of the second, without pausing to inquire whether there has been a demonstration of the first.

To draw the line intelligently between duress and inducement, there is need to remind ourselves of facts as to the problem of unemployment that are now matters of common knowledge. The relevant statistics are gathered in the brief of counsel for the government. Of the many available figures a few only will be mentioned. During the years 1929 to 1936, when the country was passing through a cyclical depression, the number of the unemployed mounted to unprecedented heights. Often the average was more than 10 million; at times a peak was attained of 16 million or more. Disaster to the breadwinner meant disaster to dependents. Accordingly the roll of the unemployed, itself formidable enough, was only a partial roll of the destitute or needy. The fact developed quickly that the states were unable to give the requisite relief. The problem had become national in area and dimensions. There was need of help from the nation if the people were not to starve. It is too late today for the argument . . . that in a crisis so extreme the use of the moneys of the nation to relieve the unemployed and their dependents is a use for any purpose narrower than the promotion of the general welfare. The nation responded to the call of the distressed. Between January 1, 1933, and July 1, 1936, the states (according to statistics submitted by the government) incurred obligations of $689,291,802 for emergency relief; local subdivisions an additional $775,675,366. In the same period the obligations for emergency relief incurred by the national government were $2,929,307,125, or twice the obligations of states and local agencies combined. According to the President's budget message for the fiscal year 1938, the national government expended for public works and unemployment relief for the three fiscal years 1934, 1935, and 1936, the stupendous total of $8,681,000,000 . . .

In the presence of this urgent need for some remedial expedient, the question is . . . whether the expedient adopted has overlept the bounds of power. The assailants of the statute say that its dominant end and aim is to drive the state Legislatures under the whip of economic pressure into the enactment of unemployment compensation laws at the bidding of the central government. Supporters of the statute say that its operation is not constraint, but the creation of a larger freedom, the states and the nation joining in a cooperative endeavor to avert a common evil. Before Congress acted, unemployment compensation insurance was still, for the most part, a project and no more. Wisconsin was the pioneer. Her statute was adopted in 1931. At times bills for such insurance were introduced elsewhere, but they did not reach the stage of law. In 1935, four states (California, Massachusetts, New Hampshire, and New York) passed unemployment laws on the eve of the adoption of the Social Security Act, and two others did likewise after the federal act and later in the year. The statutes differed to some extent in type, but were directed to a common end. In 1936, twenty-eight other states fell in line, and eight more the present year. But if states had been holding back before the passage of the federal law, inaction was not owing, for the most part, to the lack of sympathetic interest. Many held back through alarm lest in laying such a toll upon their industries, they would place themselves in a position of economic disadvantage as compared with neighbors or competitors. Two consequences ensued. One was that the freedom of a state to contribute its fair share to the solution of a national problem was paralyzed by fear. The other was that in so far as there was failure by the states to contribute relief according to the measure of their capacity, a disproportionate burden, and a mountainous one, was laid upon the resources of the government of the nation.

The Social Security Act is an attempt to find a method by which all these public agencies may work together to a common end. Every dollar of the new taxes will continue in all likelihood to be used and needed by the nation as long as states are unwilling, whether through timidity or for other motives, to do what can be done at home. At least the inference is permissible that Congress so believed, though retaining undiminished freedom to spend the money as it pleased . . .

Who then is coerced through the operation of this statute? Not the taxpayer. He pays in fulfillment of the mandate of the local legislature. Not the state. Even now she does not offer a suggestion that in passing the unemployment law she was affected by duress. For all that appears, she is satisfied with her choice, and would be sorely disappointed if it were now to be annulled. The difficulty with the [company's] contention is that it confuses motive with coercion. 'Every tax is in some measure regulatory. To some extent it interposes an economic impediment to the activity taxed as compared with others not taxed.' In like manner every rebate from a tax when conditioned upon conduct is in some measure a temptation. But to hold that motive or temptation is equivalent to coercion is to plunge the law in endless difficulties. The outcome of such a doctrine is the acceptance of a philosophical determinism by which choice becomes impossible . . .

United States v. Butler is cited by [the company] as a decision to the contrary. There a tax was imposed on processors of farm products, the proceeds to be paid to farmers who would reduce their acreage and crops under agreements with the Secretary of Agriculture, the plan of the act being to increase the prices of cer-

tain farm products by decreasing the quantities produced. The Court held (1) that the so-called tax was not a true one the proceeds being earmarked for the benefit of farmers complying with the prescribed conditions, (2) that there was an attempt to regulate production without the consent of the state in which production was affected, and (3) that the payments to farmers were coupled with coercive contracts, unlawful in their aim and oppressive in their consequences. The decision was by a divided court, a minority taking the view that the objections were untenable. None of them is applicable to the situation here developed.

(a) The proceeds of the tax in controversy are not earmarked for a special group.

(b) The unemployment compensation law which is a condition of the credit has had the approval of the state and could not be a law without it.

(c) The condition is not linked to an irrevocable agreement, for the state at its pleasure may repeal its unemployment law, terminate the credit, and place itself where it was before the credit was accepted.

(d) The condition is not directed to the attainment of an unlawful end, but to an end, the relief of unemployment, for which nation and state may lawfully cooperate.

The statute does not call for a surrender by the states of powers essential to their quasi sovereign existence . . .

A wide range of judgment is given to the several states as to the particular type of statute to be spread upon their books . . . What they may not do, if they would earn the credit, is to depart from those standards which in the judgment of Congress are to be ranked as fundamental . . .

There is argument . . . that the moneys when withdrawn are to be devoted to specific uses, the relief of unemployment, and that by agreement for such payment the quasi-sovereign position of the state has been impaired, if not abandoned. But again there is confusion between promise and condition. Alabama is still free, without breach of an agreement to change her system over night. No officer or agency of the national government can force a compensation law upon her or keep it in existence. No officer or agency of that government, either by suit or other means, can supervise or control the application of the payments.

Finally and chiefly, abdication is supposed to follow from section 904 of the statute and the parts of section 903 that are complementary thereto. By these the Secretary of the Treasury is authorized and directed to receive and hold in the Unemployment Trust Fund all moneys deposited therein by a state agency for a state unemployment fund and to invest in obligations of the United States such portion of the fund as is not in his judgment required to meet current withdrawals. We are told that Alabama in consenting to that deposit has renounced the plenitude of power inherent in her statehood.

The same pervasive misconception is in evidence again. All that the state has done is to say in effect through the enactment of a statute that her agents shall be authorized to deposit the unemployment tax receipts in the Treasury at Washington. The statute may be repealed. The consent may be revoked. The deposits may be withdrawn. The moment the state commission gives notice to the depository that it would like the moneys back, the Treasurer will return them. To find state destruction there is to find it almost anywhere. With nearly as much reason one might say that a state abdicates its functions when it places the state moneys on deposit in a national bank . . .

The inference of abdication thus dissolves in thinnest air when the deposit is conceived of as dependent upon a statutory consent, and not upon a contract effective to create a duty. By this we do not intimate that the conclusion would be different if a contract were discovered. Even sovereigns may contract without derogating from their sovereignty. The states are at liberty, upon obtaining the consent of Congress, to make agreements with one another. We find no room for doubt that they may do the like with Congress if the essence of their statehood is maintained without impairment. Alabama is seeking and obtaining a credit of many millions in favor of her citizens out of the Treasury of the nation. Nowhere in our scheme of government—in the limitations express or implied of our Federal Constitution—do we find that she is prohibited from assenting to conditions that will assure a fair and just requital for benefits received . . .

United States v. Darby Lumber Co.

312 U.S. 100 (1941), 8-0

Opinion of the Court: Stone (Black, Douglas, Frankfurter, Hughes, Murphy, Reed, Roberts)

How does Congress's direct regulation of wages and hours eliminate "unfair competition"? What is "unfair competition"? Has the Court returned to Marshall's concept of the commerce power? Does the ban on interstate shipment upheld here differ from that in Champion v. Ames? How should the Tenth Amendment be understood, according to Stone? Is this different from its meaning in the past? Does this case present a conflict between the State of Georgia and the United States? Does the decision confirm the fears of laissez-faire justices in E. C. Knight v. United States, Hammer v. Dagenhart, Champion v. Ames, and other cases that abandonment of such distinctions as commerce/production, direct/indirect effect, regulation/prohibition would leave Congress free to regulate any economic activity?*

Stone, C.J., for the Court:

The two principal questions . . . are, first, whether Congress has constitutional power to prohibit the shipment in interstate commerce of lumber manufactured by employees whose wages are less than a prescribed minimum or whose weekly hours of labor at that wage are greater than a prescribed maximum, and, second, whether it has power to prohibit the employment of workmen in the production of goods 'for interstate commerce' at other than prescribed wages and hours. A subsidiary question is whether in connection with such prohibitions Congress can require the employer subject to them to keep records showing the hours worked each day and week by each of his employees including those engaged 'in the production and manufacture of goods to wit, lumber, for 'interstate commerce.'" . . .

The Fair Labor Standards Act set up a comprehensive legislative scheme for preventing the shipment in interstate commerce of certain products and commodities produced in the United States under labor conditions as respects wages and hours which fail to conform to standards set up by the Act. Its purpose.. is to exclude from interstate commerce goods produced for the commerce and to prevent their production for interstate commerce, under conditions detrimental to the maintenance of the minimum standards of living necessary for health and general well-being; and to prevent the use of interstate commerce as the means of competition in the distribution of goods so produced, and as the means of spreading and perpetuating such substandard labor conditions among the workers of the several states . . .

The indictment charges that [Darby] is engaged, in the state of Georgia, in the business of acquiring raw materials, which he manufactures into finished lumber with the intent, when manufactured, to ship it in interstate commerce to customers outside the state, and that he does in fact so ship a large part of the lumber so produced. There are numerous counts charging [Darby] with the shipment in interstate commerce from Georgia to points outside the state of lumber in the production of which, for interstate commerce, [Darby] has employed workmen at less than the prescribed minimum wage or more than the prescribed maximum hours without payment to them of any wage for overtime. Other counts charge the employment by [Darby] of workmen in the production of lumber for interstate commerce at wages of less than 25 cents an hour or for more than the maximum hours per week without payment to them of the prescribed overtime wage. Still another count charges . . . failure to keep records showing the hours worked each day a week by each of his employees as required by s 11(c) and the regulation of the administrator, and also that [Darby] unlawfully failed to keep such records of employees engaged 'in the production and manufacture of goods, to-wit lumber, for interstate commerce.' . . .

The prohibition of shipment of the proscribed goods in interstate commerce. Section 15(a)(1) prohibits . . . the shipment in interstate commerce, of goods produced for interstate commerce by employees whose wages and hours of employment do not conform to the requirements of the Act. Since this section is not violated unless the commodity shipped has been produced under labor conditions prohibited by s 6 and s 7, the only question arising under the commerce clause with respect to such shipments is whether Congress has the constitutional power to prohibit them.

While manufacture is not of itself interstate commerce the shipment of manufactured goods interstate is such commerce and the prohibition of such shipment by Congress is indubitably a regulation of the commerce. The power to regulate commerce . . . extends not only to those regulations which aid, foster and protect the commerce, but embraces those which prohibit it. It is conceded that the power of Congress to prohibit transportation in interstate commerce includes noxious articles,; stolen articles, kidnapped persons, and articles such as intoxicating liquor or convict made goods, traffic in which is forbidden or restricted by the laws of the state of destination.

But it is said that the present prohibition falls within the scope of none of these categories; that while the prohibition is nominally a regulation of the commerce its motive or purpose is regulation of wages and hours of persons engaged in manufacture, the control of which has been reserved to the states and upon which Georgia and some of the states of destination have placed no restriction; that the effect of the present statute is not to exclude the prescribed articles from interstate commerce in aid of state regulation, but instead, under the guise of a regulation of interstate commerce, it undertakes to regulate wages and hours within the state contrary to the policy of the state which has elected to leave them unregulated.

The power of Congress over interstate commerce . . . acknowledges no limitations, other than are prescribed by the constitution. [It] can neither be enlarged nor diminished by the exercise or non-exercise of state power. Congress, following its own conception of public policy concerning the restrictions which may appropriately be imposed on interstate commerce, is free to exclude from the commerce articles whose use in the states for which they are destined it may conceive to be injurious to the public health, morals or welfare, even though the state has not sought to regulate their use . . .

The motive and purpose of the present regulation are plainly to make effective the Congressional conception of public policy that interstate commerce should not be made the instrument of competition in the distribution of goods produced under substandard labor conditions, which competition is injurious to the commerce and to the states from and to which the commerce flows. The motive and purpose of a regulation of interstate commerce are matters for the legislative judgment upon the exercise of which the Constitution places no restriction and over which the courts are given no control. 'The judicial cannot prescribe to the legislative departments of the government limitations upon the exercise of its acknowledged power'. Whatever their motive and purpose, regulations of commerce which do not infringe some constitutional prohibition are within the plenary power conferred on Congress by the Commerce Clause. Subject only to that limitation . . . that the prohibition of the shipment interstate of goods produced under the forbidden substandard labor conditions is within the constitutional authority of Congress.

In the more than a century which has elapsed since the decision of *Gibbons v. Ogden*, these principles of constitutional interpretation have been so long and repeatedly recognized by this Court as applicable to the Commerce Clause, that there would be little occasion for repeating them now were it not for the decision of this Court twenty-two years ago in *Hammer v. Dagenhart*. In that case it was held by a bare majority of the Court over the powerful and now classic dissent of Mr. Justice Holmes setting forth the fundamental issues involved, that Congress was without power to exclude the products of child labor from interstate commerce. The reasoning and conclusion of the Court's opinion there cannot be reconciled with the conclusion which we have reached, that the power of Congress under the Commerce Clause is plenary to exclude any article from interstate commerce subject only to the specific prohibitions of the Constitution.

Hammer v. Dagenhart has not been followed. The distinction on which the decision was rested that Congressional power to prohibit interstate commerce is limited to articles which in themselves have some harmful or deleterious property—a distinction which was novel when made and unsupported by any provision of the Constitution—has long since been abandoned . . .

The conclusion is inescapable that *Hammer v. Dagenhart*, was a departure from the principles which have prevailed in the interpretation of the commerce clause both before and since the decision and that such vitality, as a precedent . . . has long since been exhausted. It should be and now is overruled.

Validity of the wage and hour requirements. Section 15(a)(2) and ss 6 and 7 require employers to conform to the wage and hour provisions with respect to all employees engaged in the production of goods for interstate commerce. As [Darby's] employees are not alleged to be 'engaged in interstate commerce' the validity of the prohibition turns on . . . whether the employment, under other than the prescribed labor standards, of employees engaged in the production of goods for interstate commerce is so related to the commerce and so affects it as to be within the reach of the power of Congress to regulate it . . .

Congress was not unaware that most manufacturing businesses shipping their product in interstate commerce make it in their shops without reference to its ultimate destination and then after manufacture select some of it for shipment interstate and some intrastate according to the daily demands of their business, and that it would be practically impossible, without disrupting manufacturing businesses, to restrict the prohibited kind of production to the particular pieces of lumber, cloth, furniture or the like which later move in interstate rather than intrastate commerce . . .

Congress, having by the present Act adopted the policy of excluding from interstate commerce all goods produced for the commerce which do not conform to the specified labor standards, it may choose the means reasonably adapted to the attainment of the permitted end, even though they involve control of intrastate activities. Such legislation has often been sustained with respect to powers, other than the commerce power granted to the national government, when the means chosen, although not themselves within the granted power, were nevertheless deemed appropriate aids to the accomplishment of some purpose within an admitted power of the national government. A familiar like exercise of power is the regulation of intrastate transactions which are so commingled with or related to interstate commerce that all must be regulated if the interstate commerce is to be effectively controlled. Similarly Congress may require inspection and preventive treatment of all cattle in a disease infected area in order to prevent shipment in interstate commerce of some of the cattle without the treatment. It may prohibit the removal, at destination, of labels required by the Pure Food & Drugs Act, to be affixed to articles transported in interstate commerce. And we have recently held that Congress in the exercise of its power to require inspection and grading of tobacco shipped in interstate commerce may compel such inspection and grading of all tobacco sold at local auction rooms from which a substantial part but not all of the tobacco sold is shipped in interstate commerce . . .

Congress, to attain its objective in the suppression of nationwide competition in interstate commerce by goods produced under substandard labor conditions, has made no distinction as to the volume or amount of shipments in the commerce or of production for commerce by any particular shipper or producer. It recognized that in present day industry, competition by a small part may affect the whole and that the total effect of the competition of many small producers may be great. The legislation aimed at a whole embraces all its parts.

So far as *Carter v. Carter Coal Co.* is inconsistent with this conclusion, its doctrine is limited in principle by the decisions under the Sherman Act and the National Labor Relations Act, which we have cited and which we follow.

Our conclusion is unaffected by the Tenth Amendment . . . The amendment states but a truism that all is retained which has not been surrendered. There is nothing in the history of its adoption to suggest that it was more than declaratory of the relationship between the national and state governments as it had been established by the Constitution before the amendment or that its purpose was other than to allay fears that the new national government might seek to exercise powers not granted, and that the states might not be able to exercise fully their reserved powers.

From the beginning and for many years the amendment has been construed as not depriving the national government of authority to resort to all means for the exercise of a granted power which are appropriate and plainly adapted to the permitted end. Whatever doubts may have arisen of the soundness of that conclusion they have been put at rest by the decisions under the Sherman Act and the National Labor Relations Act which we have cited . . .

Validity of the wage and hour provisions under the Fifth Amendment. Both provisions are minimum wage requirements compelling the payment of a minimum standard wage with a prescribed increased wage for overtime of 'not less than one and one-half times the regular rate' at which the worker is employed. Since our decision in *West Coast Hotel Co. v. Parrish*, it is no longer open to question that the fixing of a minimum wage is within the legislative power and that the bare fact of its exercise is not a denial of due process under the Fifth more than under the Fourteenth Amendment. Nor is it any longer open to question that it is within the legislative power to fix maximum hours. Similarly the statute is not objectionable because applied alike to both men and women.

Wickard v. Filburn

317 U.S. 111 (1942), 9-0
Opinion of the Court: Jackson (Black, Byrnes, Douglas, Frankfurter, Murphy, Reed, Roberts, Stone)
Filburn sought to enjoin the secretary of agriculture from enforcing a penalty against him for growing wheat in excess of the marketing quota for his farm, as imposed by a 1941 amendment to the Agricultural Adjustment Act of 1938.

How does this decision go beyond that in Darby v. United States? *Who gains and loses as a result of it? Did Congress intend the marketing regulations to reach such actions as Filburn's? Can the decision be distinguished from*

Schechter Poultry Corp. v. United States? *Is there now any economic activity that can be said to be beyond Congress's reach? See* Garcia v. San Antonio Metropolitan Transit Authority. *Any noncommercial activity? See* United States v. Lopez.

Jackson for the Court:
The general scheme of the Agricultural Adjustment Act of 1938 as related to wheat is to control the volume moving in interstate and foreign commerce in order to avoid surpluses and shortages and the consequent abnormally low or high wheat prices and obstructions to commerce. Within prescribed limits and by prescribed standards the Secretary of Agriculture is directed to ascertain and proclaim each year a national acreage allotment for the next crop of wheat, which is then apportioned to the states and their counties, and is eventually broken up into allotments for individual farms . . .

It is urged that under the Commerce Clause . . . Congress does not possess the power it has in this instance sought to exercise. The question would merit little consideration since our decision in *United States v. Darby*, sustaining the federal power to regulate production of goods for commerce except for the fact that this Act extends federal regulation to production not intended in any part for commerce but wholly for consumption on the farm. The Act includes a definition of 'market' and its derivatives so that as related to wheat in addition to its conventional meaning it also means to dispose of 'by feeding to poultry or livestock which, or the products of which, are sold, bartered, or exchanged, or to be so disposed of.' Hence, marketing quotas not only embrace all that may be sold without penalty but also what may be consumed on the premises. Wheat produced on excess acreage is designated as 'available for marketing' as so defined and the penalty is imposed thereon. Penalties do not depend upon whether any part of the wheat either within or without the quota is sold or intended to be sold. The sum of this is that the Federal Government fixes a quota including all that the farmer may harvest for sale or for his own farm needs, and declares that wheat produced on excess acreage may neither be disposed of nor used except upon payment of the penalty or except it is stored as required by the Act or delivered to the Secretary of Agriculture.

[Filburn] says that this is a regulation of production and consumption of wheat. Such activities are, he urges, beyond the reach of Congressional power under the Commerce Clause, since they are local in character, and their effects upon interstate commerce are at most 'indirect.' In answer the Government argues that the statute regulates neither production nor consumption, but only marketing; and, in the alternative, that if the Act does go beyond the regulation of marketing it is sustainable as a 'necessary and proper' implementation of the power of Congress over interstate commerce.

The Government's concern lest the Act be held to be a regulation of production or consumption rather than of marketing is attributable to a few dicta and decisions of this Court which might be understood to lay it down that activities such as 'production,' 'manufacturing,' and 'mining' are strictly 'local' and, except in special circumstances which are not present here, cannot be regulated under the commerce power because their effects upon interstate commerce are, as matter of law, only 'indirect.' Even today, when this power has been held to have great latitude, there is no decision of this Court that such activities may be regulated where no part of the product is intended for interstate commerce or intermingled with the subjects thereof. We believe that a review of the course of decision under the Commerce Clause will make plain, however, that questions of the power of Congress are not to be decided by reference to any formula which would give controlling force to nomenclature such as 'production' and 'indirect' and foreclose consideration of the actual effects of the activity in question upon interstate commerce.

At the beginning Chief Justice Marshall described the Federal commerce power with a breadth never yet exceeded. He made emphatic the embracing and penetrating nature of this power by warning that effective restraints on its exercise must proceed from political rather than from judicial processes.

For nearly a century, however, decisions of this Court under the Commerce Clause dealt rarely with questions of what Congress might do in the exercise of its granted power under the Clause and almost entirely with the permissibility of state activity which it was claimed discriminated against or burdened interstate commerce. During this period there was perhaps little occasion for the affirmative exercise of the commerce power, and the influence of the Clause on American life and law was a negative one, resulting almost wholly from its operation as a restraint upon the powers of the states. In discussion and decision the point of reference instead of being what was 'necessary and proper' to the exercise by Congress of its granted power, was often some concept of sovereignty thought to be implicit in the status of statehood. Certain activities such as 'production,' 'manufacturing,' and 'mining' were occasionally said to be within the province of state governments and beyond the power of Congress under the Commerce Clause.

It was not until 1887 with the enactment of the Interstate Commerce Act that the interstate commerce power began to exert positive influence in American law and life. This first important federal resort to the commerce power was followed in 1890 by the Sherman Anti-Trust Act and, thereafter, mainly after 1903, by many others. These statutes ushered in new phases of adjudication, which required the Court to approach the interpretation of the Commerce Clause in the light of an actual exercise by Congress of its power thereunder . . .

The Court's recognition of the relevance of the economic effects in the application of the Commerce Clause exemplified by this statement has made the mechanical application of legal formulas no longer feasible. Once an economic measure of the reach of the power granted to Congress in the Commerce Clause is accepted, questions of federal power cannot be decided simply by finding the activity in question to be 'production' nor can consideration of its economic effects be foreclosed by calling them 'indirect.' . . .

Whether the subject of the regulation in question was 'production,' 'consumption,' or 'marketing' is, therefore, not material for purposes of deciding the question of federal power before us. That an activity is of local character may help in a doubtful case to determine whether Congress intended to reach it. The same consideration might help in determining whether in the absence of Congressional action it would be permissible for the state to exert its power on the subject matter, even though in so doing it to some degree affected interstate commerce. But even if [Filburn's] activity be local and though it may not be regarded as commerce, it may still, whatever its nature, be reached by Congress if it exerts a substantial economic effect on interstate commerce and this irrespective of whether such effect is what might at some earlier time have been defined as 'direct' or 'indirect.' . . .

The maintenance by government regulation of a price for wheat undoubtedly can be accomplished as effectively by sustaining or increasing the demand as by limiting the supply. The effect of the statute before us is to restrict the amount which may be produced for market and the extent as well to which one may forestall resort to the market by producing to meet his own needs. That [Filburn's] own contribution to the demand for wheat may be trivial by itself is not enough to remove him from the scope of federal regulation where, as here, his contribution, taken together with that of many others similarly situated, is far from trivial.

It is well established by decisions of this Court that the power to regulate commerce includes the power to regulate the prices at which commodities in that commerce are dealt in and practices affecting such prices. One of the primary purposes of the Act in question was to increase the market price of wheat and to that end to limit the volume thereof that could affect the market. It can hardly be denied that a factor of such volume and variability as home-consumed wheat would have a substantial influence on price and market conditions. This may arise because being in marketable condition such wheat overhangs the market and if induced by rising prices tends to flow into the market and check price increases. But if we assume that it is never marketed, it supplies a need of the man who grew it which would otherwise be reflected by purchases in the open market. Home-grown wheat in this sense competes with wheat in commerce. The stimulation of commerce is a use of the regulatory function quite as definitely as prohibitions or restrictions thereon. This record leaves us in no doubt that Congress may properly have considered that wheat consumed on the farm where grown if wholly outside the scheme of regulation would have a substantial effect in defeating and obstructing its purpose to stimulate trade therein at increased prices.

It is said, however, that this Act, forcing some farmers into the market to buy what they could provide for themselves, is an unfair promotion of the markets and prices of specializing wheat growers. It is of the essence of regulation that it lays a restraining hand on the self-interest of the regulated and that advantages from the regulation commonly fall to others. The conflicts of economic interest between the regulated and those who advantage by it are wisely left under our system to resolution by the Congress under its more flexible and responsible legislative process. Such conflicts rarely lend themselves to judicial determination. And with the wisdom, workability, or fairness, of the plan of regulation we have nothing to do.

IV

THE MODERN
CONSTITUTION

9

PRESIDENTIAL POWER
AND DIVIDED GOVERNMENT

The New Deal's activist, innovative response to the Great Depression ushered in the modern constitutional era of vastly augmented national and executive authority and responsibility. Victory in World War II elevated the nation to superpower status and made the presidency the world's most powerful office. The postwar world saw emergence of the "welfare state," greater public regulation of markets, and management of economic growth. Internationally, peace was quickly followed by the Cold War with the Soviet Union and its Communist allies that lasted to the 1990s. These foreign and domestic changes redrew the institutional balance of power within the national government, which is our concern here, and transformed the American federal system, the topic of the next chapter.

The framers of the Constitution could not have imagined any of this. Yet, Ironically, their chief task had been to propose a national government far stronger than the one existing at the time. Well aware of the defects of one-branch legislative government under the Continental Congress and the Articles of Confederation, they wanted to diversify functions within the central government,

but agonized about executive power and how to balance and coordinate it with legislative. Creating a more powerful central government, they divided power within it among legislative, executive, and judicial tasks.

The framers also realized that too much separation and independence in this functional specification could create stalemate and prevent coherent policy from being formulated so that the government could act when needed. Their solution of giving separated branches several overlapping powers and responsibilities was for Madison the consummate arrangement. In the twentieth century, Justice Robert Jackson put the matter concisely: "While the Constitution diffuses power the better to secure liberty, it also contemplates that the practice will integrate the dispersed powers into a workable government. It enjoins upon its branches separateness but interdependence, autonomy but reciprocity."*

Yet this statement of the ideal masks several problems. Because the branches have different

---

* *Youngstown Sheet and Tube Co. v. Sawyer,* 343 U.S. 579 at 635 (1952).

structure and different functions, each has proved responsive to different interests. This has often made it easier for a determined minority to block a policy or a change of direction than for other interests, perhaps amounting to a majority, to bring government to act. This bias toward the negative is not necessarily bad—it clearly limits power—but the separated power places an extra burden on the task of marshaling diverse interests that is usually necessary before government can move decisively on critical issues or even reflect majority will. Political accountability is apt to be less certain than in more unified constitutional systems.

By coordinating diverse interests, political parties have served as an important extragovernmental antidote to separate power in both war and peacetime. Lincoln benefited from a strong Republican Party in working with Congress and state governors during the Civil War. In the New Deal, a strong party, endorsed by the electorate, organized and harmonized executive and legislative efforts to formulate innovative policies. Later it helped overcome opposition from a judiciary that relied on separated power to undermine those policies. In periods in which parties have been less robust, such as the late nineteenth century and the present, the national government has found it harder to speak with one voice.

For better or worse, functionally separated power is central to the constitutional system and deeply rooted in the American political mind. Electorally, it is repeatedly endorsed, whether by design or inadvertence, in the time-honored practice of ticket splitting. Having the chance to choose a president and Congress of the same party and thus reduce the friction of separated power, modern voters have refused it more often than not. The majority of one or both houses of Congress has been of a different party than the president in 32 of the 56 years since 1946.

Weighed against the problem of coordinating power is the one of checking it. In the modern constitutional era, this has raised important new questions of presidential authority to involve the United States in war, to make agreements with other nations, deal with domestic issues arising from the exigencies of foreign policy, and about the role Congress in these matters. Growth of federal responsibility in domestic affairs has produced a proliferation of administrative offices and agencies. This formidable bureaucracy, the "fourth branch" of government, has challenged democracy's need to hold nonelected government accountable to the elected. In addition, many responsibilities assumed by the federal government do not fall neatly into the familiar "executive, legislative, and judicial" analysis.

Experimentation with hybrid offices and procedures has generated constitutional issues of boundary and function for each of the three co-equal branches and between each and the public. Are there limits, for example, to Congress's power to "expose" witnesses and others through use of its investigative authority in the age of mass media? To what extent are policies of the national government and actions of its officers, including the president, shielded from legal challenges by ordinary citizens or aggrieved individuals in the age of ready litigation?

Answers to the modern questions of separated power have not come through formal changes in the Constitution. None of the last six amendments, beginning with the twenty-second in 1951 has conferred new powers on government. And, except for the twenty-fourth protecting the right to vote from the burden of poll taxes and the twenty-sixth lowering the voting age to 18, none has removed or narrowed powers of government. Important constitutional change has come through new practices and through reinterpretation of existing powers. In this, the Supreme Court has been called upon repeatedly to review boundary and functional issues, including those affecting its own branch.

It is fair to say that most of the modern changes in national power were neither foreseen nor intended by those who drafted the Constitution. Alien though many of these would have been in 1787, it is much less certain that the astute founders of the nation would see them as such today were they alive and framing new government.

War and National Security

Starting with World War II, the United States has faced almost continuous international crises. This has included four major wars, a long "cold" one under the threat of mutual mass destruction, and a score of lesser military engagements around the world. These conflicts placed unprecedented demands on the ability of American government to protect the nation's security and pursue its interests abroad while maintaining constitutional government at home.

The framers anticipated future war and foreign crises and conferred an array of diplomatic and military powers on the central government but characteristically divided them between the legislative and executive branches. In Article I, Congress was given the power to declare war, raise, support, and regulate an army and navy, and to mobilize the militia to deal with insurrection or invasion. Besides its general law-making authority, its power over the purse allows it to underwrite or not the cost of war and foreign policy. The president is vested with diplomatic authority in Article II and generally charged with executing the laws. But his chief source of war power is his cryptic designation as commander in chief of the armed forces. In practice, these assignments have meant that Congress may declare and support war, but only the president can wage it. In the international world of the late twentieth century, it is the president, rather than Congress, who would probably initiate it.

In only five of nine American wars—the War of 1812, the Mexican War, the Spanish-American War, and World Wars I and II—has Congress declared war. Only in 1812 did the matter of hostilities get anything close to full debate. In the Civil War, Korea, Vietnam, and the Persian Gulf, Congress approved and later supported major presidential initiatives. Though presidents have often consulted with Congressional leaders, most other military commitments abroad have been made by the president acting alone. These have numbered more than 100 since 1789.

The premium that modern warfare's complex technology places on speed and secrecy has made the open, deliberative Congress the junior member of the constitutional partnership. The shift of power to the president, though prudent and unavoidable, nonetheless raises important constitutional issues. What are its domestic limits over the rights of persons and property and in the face of opposition in Congress or public opinion? Since the Constitution says so little about the president's war power, what is the constitutional justification for its modern development?

The Supreme Court dealt definitively with the last question in *United States v. Curtiss-Wright Export Corp.* (1936) (p. 404). Congress had authorized President Roosevelt, at his discretion, to place an embargo on American arms sales to Peru and Bolivia, who were at war over disputed territory in the Chaco region. Charged with violating the embargo, the company contended the authorization was an unconstitutional delegation of legislative power. Not only did the Court hold otherwise, it went further in justifying the president's action. Justice Sutherland argued that the national government's sovereignty in foreign affairs was a condition of its existence as a nation among other nations; it did not depend on an express grant in the Constitution. Since the president was the "sole organ of the federal government in the field of international relations" his power to deal with other nations did not depend on an express grant in the Constitution or on Congressional authorization. It was inherent in national sovereignty.

Roosevelt's Wartime "Dictatorship"

Fighting and winning World War II called for a vastly greater effort than did World War I, in which American military action was on a much smaller scale and largely confined to one country.

The second war was truly global and included European, Asian, and African theaters of operation, required greater mobilization at home, and carried with it less certainty that defeat could be avoided. American participation lasted three-and-a-half years compared to 18 months in World War I.

Constitutional limits were stretched even further than in 1861 and 1917 as the federal government and the president assumed many new powers. Some were authorized by Congress, but many were not. Few came before the Supreme Court, and without judicial review their outer limits remained vague. They may have been whatever it took to wage war successfully. Yet no one pretended these powers were permanent or could be used for ends unrelated to the war. In Franklin D. Roosevelt's hands they had overwhelming public support. Where not authorized by statute, Congress gave them recognition and support whenever it appropriated money for implementation. Though the war was still raging in Europe and Asia in 1944, there was never a doubt that Roosevelt, like Lincoln in 1864, would submit his war stewardship to the public in a free, open, scheduled election. He easily won an unprecedented fourth term. In all, prosecuting the war raised fewer constitutional issues than did the Civil War or World War I, partly because of the precedents established in those two conflicts. World War II removed any remaining doubt that the Constitution could be adapted to waging large-scale war and mobilizing the nation to that end.

Even before American entry, Congress had passed the Selective Service Act of 1940, setting up military conscription, and the Lend-Lease Act early in 1941, allowing war supplies to be given to Great Britain. They gave the president wide discretionary powers. Immediately after Pearl Harbor, Congress passed the first War Powers Act, a reprise of the Overman Act of World War I, giving the president nearly unlimited authority to organize the executive branch and redelegate his own wartime authority. The second War Powers Act a few months later gave Roosevelt control over the national economy

that went far beyond Wilson's World War I authority. Included were powers to regulate production and ration critical goods and services including food and fuel.

Roosevelt created a vast array of wartime agencies and offices simply by executive decree, which left their precise constitutional status uncertain. More than a hundred had been set up by the end of 1942. Few of their policies or programs were challenged in the courts; of those that were, few cases were heard by the Supreme Court. In almost all those, such as *Yakus v. United States* (1944) and *Steuart & Co. v. Bowles* (1944), in which price and rent controls were at issue, the Court sustained the government.

The most dramatic of Roosevelt's actions affecting property were his seizures of war plants to end strikes that interfered with production. In these he simply issued proclamations, citing his powers as commander in chief. In what was now becoming a familiar pattern, Congress then enacted legislation giving the president seizure power. The constitutionality of these takeovers, which numbered more than 30 before the war was over, never came before the Supreme Court.

The most extreme and constitutionally dubious presidential domestic act during the war was the removal of 112,000 persons of Japanese descent from their homes on the West Coast in 1942 and relocating them in detention camps in interior states for the rest of the war. Seventy thousand were American citizens, many of whom were native-born. Though none had been charged with a crime and there was no evidence of spying or sabotage, internment was believed necessary for national security. In the early months of the war, a Japanese attack on the West Coast could not be ruled out, and alarmists believed the loyalty of many Japanese-Americans was suspect. The Pearl Harbor "sneak" attack and reports of Japanese atrocities also fanned long-standing anti-Japanese sentiment in Western states into popular hysteria. The detention centers were in no sense the concentration camps the world was learning of in Nazi-occupied Europe, but they were forced confinement and a gross violation of the civil liberties of persons not guilty of wrongdoing.

The Relocation Program, as internment was called, was first set up by presidential order, which Roosevelt based on his authority as commander in chief. Later, Congress enacted supporting legislation. Several legal challenges to it were eventually heard by the Supreme Court, but a majority of the justices sustained various aspects of the program and avoided ruling on the constitutionality of the detention itself. The most important of these cases was *Korematsu v. United States* (1944) (p. 407) in which the defendant had refused to report to an assembly center, the first step in internment, instead remaining behind in what was now for him a restricted area. Justice Black upheld Korematsu's conviction for six members of the Court, but limited his opinion to the government's power to exclude Korematsu from a designated military area and require him to report to an assembly center. As Black saw it, the grounds were not race or ancestry but military urgency and need. This, he admitted, worked a hardship on the Japanese-Americans, but "hardships are a part of war and war is an aggregation of hardships."

Justices Roberts, Murphy, and Jackson each dissented. They were unwilling to separate the detention question from other aspects of the Relocation Program. Absent evidence of disloyalty, they would not allow claims of military necessity to justify classifying and punishing persons because of ancestry alone. Murphy argued that questions of disloyalty should be dealt with individual by individual as would be the case with other charges of wrongdoing.

The unfairness of the Relocation Program weighed heavily on the American conscience. In 1948, Congress offered compensation if property loss could be shown, but proof was often difficult and only a fraction of the claims were paid. In the 1980s, a commission set up by Congress to review the circumstances that led to the program concluded, with benefit of hindsight, that its creation was not justified by military need of the time. In 1988, Congress passed and President Reagan signed legislation that offered a formal apology and reparations to nearly 70,000 surviving former internees.

As in the Civil War and World War I, the Constitution was stretched but not broken. Little doubt remained that it was adaptable to waging of large-scale war and that its peacetime form and substance could be retained or completely restored at war's end. The extraordinary discretionary powers given to or asserted by the president and acquiesced by Congress and the Supreme Court, and the new intrusions on personal lives and property were tolerable only so far as they were assumed to be temporary and necessary for final victory. Had the war gone beyond its nearly four years or had victory been in doubt or not been complete, strains might have developed that would have permanently changed the constitutional system.

Korea and the Cold War

The unconditional surrender of Germany and Japan brought total victory, but what followed was not exactly peace and, domestically, clearly not a return to "normalcy." The uneasy wartime alliance with the Soviet Union was transformed into a bipolar rivalry that kept the international world in a state of perpetual tension. Soviet aims appeared to include the subversion of democratic and capitalist states and the consummation of global Communism. American policy became geared to resisting and containing this expansionism at all cost. The ideological rivalry between Communism and democratic government came to have an almost religious force that made compromise between the two sides difficult. Hanging over everything was the threat of mutual mass destruction through nuclear weapons, many of which each side permanently aimed at the other. The United States entered this Cold War almost before the guns of World War II fell silent. It was not clear then nor would it be for many years after whether the Cold War was prelude to a massively destructive World War III or a substitute for it.

Cold War demands raised constitutional issues about the president's unilateral power to put the United States into a major fighting war and the claim of prerogative power in the domestic economy. Concerns about espionage and subversion caused internal security measures to clash with established civil liberties. New use of the treaty power, dealt with in the next section, affected the balance in the federal system.

When Communist North Korea invaded the Republic of South Korea allied with the United States in June 1950, President Harry Truman immediately sent American troops stationed in Japan to the peninsula without asking or waiting for Congressional approval. His quick discretionary action almost certainly saved South Korea from being overrun and clearly showed American resolve, just one year after Chinese Communist forces had completed takeover of mainland China, to resist Communist expansion by force if necessary. But, as it turned out, Truman's action committed the United States not to a quick expulsion of North Korea from South, but to a major regional war in which Chinese forces eventually entered on a large scale and which resulted in 33,000 American deaths and 100,000 wounded in more than three years of fighting.

The day after North Korea's invasion, the United Nations Security Council met to condemn the aggression and to ask member states to aid South Korea. (The Soviet Union, which had been boycotting the Council, was not present to veto this resolution.) Truman relied on the Council's act as legal justification for his military orders, calling the conflict a "police action," though the United States had not signed the U.N.'s Article 43 agreement for using troops in peacekeeping operations. Congress never declared war but, as it had many times before, underwrote presidential action with legislation expanding the armed forces and building up the supply of weapons and war material. The ambiguous constitutional status of the fighting produced several legal challenges, but the Supreme Court refused to hear them.

An important objection to the president's domestic wartime authority did arise and find its way to the top. In April 1952 after the Wage Stabilization Board was unable to effect a new labor-management agreement in the steel industry, the United Steelworkers called a nationwide strike that would halt nearly all steel production. The day before the strike was to start, Truman ordered Secretary of Commerce, Charles Sawyer to take possession of the steel mills and keep them operating. He cited the emergency conditions of the Korean fighting and the need for uninterrupted production of steel. Since no federal laws permitted the United States to seize private property under these circumstances, he could not rely on statutory authority. He based his order, instead, on general executive powers as president and commander in chief.

A suit filed by steel companies to stop this action reached the Supreme Court in a matter of days. In *Youngstown Sheet & Tube Co. v. Sawyer,* the Steel Seizure Case (p. 411), a Court now made up entirely of Roosevelt and Truman appointees held against the president, 6-3. Seven justices, including each of the six in the majority, wrote individual opinions. Black's, for the Court, rejected the claim of executive prerogative based on implied powers as commander in chief or on inherent presidential powers in foreign affairs. He sidestepped the question of emergency. In domestic matters, the president could not do that for which he had no specific grant from the Constitution or authorization from Congress.

Several concurring justices were not willing to go so far in limiting presidential authority. Frankfurter argued that the president had statutory means at his disposal for delaying harmful strikes, namely power to invoke an 80-day "cooling off" period provided by the Taft-Hartley Act of 1947. (The act, an anathema to organized labor, had been passed over Truman's veto, five years before.) Jackson was unwilling to hold the president totally without inherent powers in domestic matters. But those powers were weakest where Congress, rather than being silent, had addressed the issue at hand and, as in Taft-Hartley, refrained from giving the president the power he now asserted. Chief Justice Vinson dissented, arguing that the president had discretionary powers in times of national crisis or emergency. He cited the extraordinary actions taken by Lincoln in the first weeks after the firing on Fort Sumter and Roosevelt's defense plant seizures during World War II.

Though seven of the nine justices held that the president might have inherent powers in domestic affairs, at least in emergency situations, the vote against Truman in the Steel Seizure Case has served as a basis for resisting later claims of inherent domestic authority. The decision in the case also set off a 53-day strike but one that did not substantially impair the war effort.

The early Cold War trials of Julius and Ethel Rosenberg, Alger Hiss, and Klaus Fuchs focused attention on possible widespread Communist espionage and government infiltration and raised sharp concerns about internal security. Under pressure from conservatives and moderates, Truman set up a loyalty review program that included an F.B.I. check of federal employees, covering nearly 5 million persons between 1947 and 1953. These investigations produced 26,000 "cases" that went before a loyalty review board. About 60 percent of these persons got final clearance. Seven thousand resigned and about 500 others were dismissed on loyalty charges. The investigations and firings raised several civil liberties questions.

The status of the American Communist Party was another Cold War constitutional issue. Was the organization, which had about 50,000 members, simply an unpopular political party taking its ideological cues from Moscow and so could otherwise be safely ignored? Or was it a conspiratorial group bent on overthrowing the government with covert help from the country's chief international adversary? Here again, conservative and moderate voices won out over liberal in the Executive branch and in Congress. The Truman administration arrested and prosecuted the 11 leaders of the party under the 1940 Alien Registration Act otherwise known as the Smith Act, which made it a crime to advocate violent overthrow of the government or to organize or be a member of a group advocating overthrow.

Convictions in these cases were upheld by the Supreme Court in *Dennis v. United States* (1951), one of its most important postwar freedom of speech cases. But in *Yates v. United States* six years later, the Court refused to uphold convictions of second-rank party leaders because the trial court had not distinguished between advocating violent overthrow as a step toward action from advocating it in the abstract. Congress also made wide use—some would say, misuse—of its investigatory powers on the issue of internal security, though its most aggressive hearings produced little legislation.

In 1950 over the president's veto, Congress passed the Internal Security Act, also known as the McCarran Act. It required the Communist Party to register with the Justice Department as a subversive organization and thus disclose its membership, sources of income, and details of other activities. But the party refused to register and a long legal battle followed. In *Communist Party v. Subversive Activities Control Board* (1961), the government's right to register subversive organizations and get information from them was sustained, but the Supreme Court overturned convictions of individual party members who had refused to register because the requirement violated the Fifth Amendment is privilege against self-incrimination. (By imposing various disabilities on party members in the Communist Control Act of 1954, Congress had all but outlawed the organization, thus a possibility that merely registering as a member would be incriminating.) The McCarran Act proved all but unenforceable, but by the 1960s it no longer mattered. The Communist Party was shown to be ineffectual, public opinion ceased to be rattled by it, and attempts to get it to register seemed more like opera-bouffe than protection of internal security.

It is hard to assess the degree to which internal security was in jeopardy in the early years of the Cold War. Instances of espionage were proved, but the possibility of overthrowing the government appears to have been next to zero. The perception of danger in those quasi-war conditions led to substantial legislative and executive intrusion into the lives and careers of many persons.

Vietnam and Beyond

The Korean War and the threat of Communist subversion in government were main issues in the 1952 election won by World War II hero Dwight Eisenhower and the Republicans, who captured control of both houses of Congress for the first time in 24 years. The Korean conflict, now stalemated, ended in a truce in 1953, but the Cold War continued for nearly 40 years. Despite such flash points as the Hungarian Revolt, the Berlin standoff, and the Cuban missile crisis, American forces did not fight in a shooting war again until committed to Indochina in the 1960s.

Fearing that Vietcong rebels and their North Vietnamese allies would undermine and overthrow the non-Communist government of South Vietnam and thus destabilize Southeast Asia, President John Kennedy, elected in 1960, increased the number of American military advisors with the South Vietnamese army from a handful to more than 16,000 by 1963, a number far greater than needed for merely training and advising. When the war did not go well, Kennedy's successor, Lyndon Johnson, gradually increased American participation. In August 1964, after a reported attack by North Vietnamese gunboats on an American destroyer in the Gulf of Tonkin, Johnson asked Congress to pass a resolution he had drafted, authorizing him as commander in chief, to "take all necessary measures to repel any armed attack against the forces of the United States and to prevent further aggression." This Congress did, unanimously in the House and with only two dissenting votes in the Senate.

Johnson interpreted the resolution as carte blanche for expanding the war. Braced by a landslide election victory over Senator Barry Goldwater later in 1964, he committed large numbers of American troops, most of them conscripts. By 1965, 300,000 were in Vietnam, by 1968 more than a half million. They were supported by a massive bombing of North Vietnam, in tonnage greater than all the bombs dropped on Germany and Japan in World War II. The war, which would eventually be lost, took more than 50,000 American lives and $140 billion in resources; it all but halted Johnson's liberal Great Society social programs. It also produced wide public protest, resistance to the draft, and distrust of government, and eventually drove Johnson from office. He declined to run in 1968, his popularity had plummeted in five years.

As Johnson's successor, Richard Nixon scaled back use of American ground troops and eventually opened direct peace talks with the North Vietnamese in Paris. At the same time, he increased the bombing and mined harbors in the North and, without informing Congress, conducted months of secret, massive bombing of Vietcong sanctuaries in neighboring Cambodia, formally a neutral country. Later American ground forces were sent into Cambodia and Laos to pursue the enemy and cut supply routes. For this expansion of the war, Nixon relied not on the Gulf of Tonkin resolution, which Congress had earlier revoked, but on the claim of powers as commander in chief to expand the war zone to neutral countries if he thought it necessary. In June 1973, after four years of the war under the Nixon administration, the United States and North Vietnam signed the Paris Peace Agreement providing for withdrawal of all remaining American forces. Two years later, North Vietnamese and Vietcong forces completed the conquest of South Vietnam.

The Supreme Court repeatedly refused to review constitutional issues raised by the war, concluding decisions were best left to the two popular branches. Several cases in lower federal courts, such as *Mora v. McNamara* (1967), in which three servicemen challenged the president's authority to commit troops to fight an undeclared war, were held to raise political questions, thus not resolvable by judicial decision. The Court declined to hear appeals from these rulings.

Though Congress consistently supported Americanization of the war and continued to appropriate billions of dollars to supply troops and material, members had become increasingly critical of Nixon's war actions and the growth of what many now called the "imperial presidency." In 1973, Congress passed the War Powers Resolution in an attempt to reassert its role in warmaking and in committing American forces.

Though the act affirms the president's right to send American forces into combat without Congress's approval if the United States or one of its territories is attacked, other provisions try to restrict executive discretion to put the nation in war. Where the president has committed troops and Congress has not assented by a declaration of war or other supportive acts, he must withdraw them within 60 to 90 days. Military action beyond that period would need Congressional approval. Even if Congress approved the president's action, it could call for immediate withdrawal of forces by a concurrent resolution of both houses not subject to presidential veto. The act was vetoed by Nixon but became law when Congress overrode.

Nixon and all later presidents have questioned the constitutionality of the act and refused to admit being bound by it. Though they have consulted with and reported to Congress, they have done so citing their authority as commander in chief rather than the statutory requirements of the act. The War Powers Resolution has not stopped presidents from taking military action outside U. S. territory without getting Congressional approval. Instances include President Jimmy Carter's attempt to rescue American hostages held by Iran in 1980; President Ronald Reagan's deployment of military advisors to El Salvador in 1981, marines to Lebanon in 1983, invasion of Grenada in 1983, and bombing of Libya in 1986; President

George Bush's invasion of Panama in 1989, and deployment of troops to Somalia in 1992; President Bill Clinton's intervention in Haiti in 1994, stationing troops in Bosnia in 1996, commitment of American air power to play the major role in the NATO bombing of Kosovo in 1999 and of ground troops to a later peacekeeping role in that Yugoslav province.

The nation's only large-scale conflict since Vietnam—the Persian Gulf War in 1991—did not raise an issue under the War Powers Resolution. In response to Iraq's invasion of Kuwait and its threat to Saudi Arabia and world oil supplies, President Bush coordinated a massive buildup of the land, sea, and air forces of 23 nations with United Nations support but without express Congressional authorization. This included stationing more than 500,000 American troops. Before launching the attack against Iraq in January 1991, Bush asked for and got Congressional approval for use of American military force to free Kuwait. The fighting was limited to an intensive five-week air bombardment of Iraq and a swift four-day land offensive that smashed the Iraqi army and liberated Kuwait but left Saddam Hussein in power in Baghdad.

The War Powers Resolution is unlikely to be yielded to by presidents, unlikely to be repealed by Congress, and unlikely to be reviewed by the Supreme Court. Its effect is more symbolic than practical.

Constitutional questions about the roles of the president and Congress in starting and waging war remain, and exact boundaries between the two branches are still vague. More than ever, modern warfare and threats to national security call for swift, sometimes covert action often based on secret intelligence and, politically, for speaking clearly in one voice. The force of these circumstances favors a continued shift of responsibility to the president and away from Congress. Tension between the two branches over military action is likely to be greatest and public support most problematic when American interests are not well defined or where operations prove less than successful. Between failure in Vietnam and success in the Persian Gulf and Kosovo lies a vast range of fortune. The effectiveness of Congress in checking the president will depend largely on its representation of public opinion, which in the age of modern communications the president has unusual power to mold.

Diplomacy and Foreign Affairs

War and military action are not the only matters of foreign policy the Constitution commits the president and Congress to sharing, nor about which powers have gradually shifted to the president. In diplomacy, as in war, the framers made the president the nation's chief but not only voice. To augment this, the first Congress created the Department of State in the Executive branch responsible to the president. Article II gives the president power to make treaties and to appoint and receive ambassadors. In these matters he must act with the "advice and consent" of the Senate and, for treaties, must have the approval of two-thirds of the Senate. The ambassadorial power has produced few constitutional questions, but treaties, which under Article VI become "the supreme law of the land," have at times been the source of great controversy and conflict between the branches.

Partly for this reason and partly because treaties are unwieldy for many matters that must be negotiated, sometimes secretly, with foreign nations over continuing issues, presidents have often resorted to executive agreements that bypass the Senate. Neither provided for nor forbidden by the Constitution, these instruments have produced constitutional uncertainties of their own.

Article I-10 bars the states from making treaties or alliances and leaves no doubt that the president and Congress alone speak for the nation in foreign affairs. Underscoring this primacy, the Logan Act of 1799 makes any unauthorized private negotiation with foreign governments to influence American foreign policy a criminal act, though no one has ever been convicted under it.

The Supreme Court has been nearly as reticent about ruling on treaties and executive agreements as it has about making war.

Treaties and Treaty-Making

A treaty is typically negotiated with a foreign nation by a team of persons chosen and directed by the president, often through the State Department. If the treaty is important, the delegation may include one or more members of Congress. Presidents learned a lesson from the disastrous Senate fate of the League of Nations treaty for which President Wilson failed to include any members of Congress in the American representation at the Versailles negotiations. Once agreement has been reached and drafted, the president submits it to the Senate for ratification. Approved, it becomes a binding international agreement and, if applicable, governing domestic law.

Some treaties, such as those that define certain individual rights, are self-executing, that is, they need no implementing legislation. Most, however, call for statutory support, in many cases for appropriations, to give their terms effect. This gives the House, where all spending bills must originate, a role to play despite the precedent Washington set by refusing its demand for information on the Jay Treaty negotiations. In practice, presidents often work closely with leaders of House and Senate foreign affairs committees to win support for treaties.

The scope and constitutional effect of treaties have been more controversial than the process of making them. Can the national government, for example, achieve an end through treaty that it could not through its constitutionally enumerated and implied powers? Is it important that the supremacy clause of Article VI refers to acts of Congress made in "pursuance of the Constitution" but refers to treaties made "under authority of the United States"? These questions came before the Supreme Court in *Missouri v. Holland* (1920) (p. 400), in which a state tried to enjoin enforcement of the Migratory Bird Treaty Act of 1918, passed by Congress to augment a treaty signed with Great Britain and Canada to protect migratory birds. Before the treaty a statutory attempt to regulate the killing of migratory birds had been struck down by a lower court as beyond Congress's granted powers and an invasion of those reserved to states under the Tenth Amendment. Missouri now made the same argument against a statute designed to give effect to a treaty.

Speaking for the Court, Justice Holmes held that the fate of migratory birds was a matter of national interest and since the birds did not respect national boundaries, their protection was an appropriate subject for a treaty. Congress had "necessary and proper" authority to carry out such a treaty. In this ruling, Holmes acknowledged the possibility that Congress and the federal government might acquire powers through treaties made under "authority of the United States" that they did not have under Article I to make laws "pursuant to the Constitution."

This unsettled matter came to the fore after World War II and the United States signing the United Nations Charter and its Covenant on Human Rights. Concern stemmed from the possibility that those international agreements could commit and possibly subordinate American military forces to U. N. direction and that rights could be created that would be enforceable in American courts without regard to American laws. These anxieties, which touched old chords of prewar isolationism, also reflected pent-up conservative reaction to years of aggressive foreign policy leadership by Presidents Roosevelt and Truman.

In 1952, at the urging of several states and an array of interests including the American Bar Association, the Ohio Republican Senator John W. Bricker introduced a constitutional amendment to limit the effect given to treaties and to close the door seemingly opened by *Missouri v. Holland*. A treaty or agreement would become effective only through "legislation which would be valid in the absence of a treaty." The "Bricker Amendment" was debated for nearly two years. It was opposed by the newly elected Eisenhower who, with other

critics, argued that it would tie the nation's hands in foreign affairs. When a toned down version came to a vote in February 1954, it fell one vote short of the two-thirds needed to sent it to the states for ratification. When Democrats regained control of Congress later that year, interest in the amendment faded rapidly.

In the early Cold War years, the United States entered into several collective security treaties, including those of NATO, SEATO, and CENTO, as essential blocks of containment policy. Though they called for substantial international commitment by the United States, few of their provisions had much effect on domestic affairs.

If a state law cannot stand in the way of a treaty, may a federal statute do so? Here again, the Constitution is silent. The Supreme Court has assumed that treaty and Congressional act have equal constitutional status and in *Whitney v. Robertson* (1888) it developed a practical rule of thumb where the two may be in conflict: "the last in date will control the other." [124 U.S. 190 at 194]

The Constitution offers no guidelines about how a treaty may be abrogated. The question arose when President Carter formally recognized mainland Communist China—the People's Republic of China—and withdrew recognition from the Nationalist Government of Taiwan as the government of China. In doing so, Carter announced termination of a defense treaty with the Taiwan government. Several senators challenged this action in *Goldwater v. Carter* (1979), arguing that the president must first get consent of the Senate as he is required to do in making a treaty. Though the justices were divided in their reasoning, a majority of six ordered the suit dismissed, four on the ground that it was a political question committed by the Constitution to the other branches.

Executive Agreements

Existing executive agreements outnumber treaties by nearly 20 to 1. Hundreds are made with other nations every year and most deal with such routine matters as postal regulations, patent rights, and the status of nationals, which would be cumbersome to make the subject of a treaty. Many have been previously authorized by Congress. Texas and Hawaii became United States possessions through executive agreements authorized by Congress. The Lend-Lease Act early in 1941 before American entry into World War II gave the president discretion to "sell, transfer, lease, or lend" war materials to countries he believed were vital to American defense. Executive agreements that followed resulted in a vast American underwriting of Great Britain's resistance to Nazi Germany.

Other agreements, however, including some of great importance have been based on the president's authority as commander in chief or his prerogative in foreign affairs, alone. In the Hull-Lothian destroyers-for-bases agreement with Great Britain in 1940, Roosevelt transferred 50 over-aged warships in exchange for 99-year leases on several British naval bases in the Caribbean and North Atlantic. Though the arrangement strengthened American defenses, it also raised constitutional and statutory questions about the disposal of United States property. Presidents Roosevelt and Truman made extensive use of executive agreements during the war. These included the secret accords with allies at the Cairo, Yalta, and Potsdam conferences that decided much of the postwar political shape of Europe and Asia. Since then, every president has used the executive agreement as an important instrument of foreign policy, entering into accords, secret and otherwise, with other nations. As with the war powers, the need to act quickly and sometimes covertly has been an important consideration. Critics have worried about presidential accountability in these deals and their effect on the constitutional partnership of the president and Congress in foreign affairs.

Some constitutional questions raised by executive agreements have been addressed by the Supreme Court. President Roosevelt's formal recognition of the Soviet Union in 1933 was followed by an executive agreement known as the Litvinov Assignment. Among other things, it gave the federal government possession of certain once-private Russian assets in the United States that had been appropriated by the Soviet government after the Russian Revolution. In *United States v. Belmont* (1937), creditors of the former holders of these assets who appeared to have rights under New York state law sued the United States for their possession. The Court denied the claim, holding that the executive agreement was a valid international compact and, like a treaty, became the "law of the land," state rules notwithstanding.

The Court reaffirmed this position four years later in *United States v. Pink* also growing out of the Litvinov Assignment. Justice Douglas held that the president, exercising his undisputed power to recognize foreign governments, had an implied power to remove obstacles to that recognition—here conflicting claims to appropriated assets—through agreements. An executive agreement overrode state law with which it was in conflict. These decisions narrowed the distinction between treaties and executive agreements in their domestic effect. Whether executive agreements can override a conflicting federal statute is doubtful but remains unsettled.

The effect of executive agreements on property rights was again before the Court in *Dames & Moore Co. v. Regan* (p. 439) (1981), a case growing out of settlement of the Iran hostage crisis. In November 1979, 66 Americans had been seized by a mob at the U. S. embassy in Tehran and later held by the Iranian government. To get their release after more than 15 months of captivity and a failed military effort to free them, President Carter made several concessions in an executive agreement. Included among them was the protection of previously frozen Iranian assets in the United States from American creditors. To carry out this provision, Carter issued executive orders nullifying prejudgment attachments of these assets and ending all pending legal actions against Iran by American nationals. These were to be heard later by a special arbitration panel agreed to by the two countries.

Dames & Moore, which had already filed a suit against the Iranian government for money allegedly owed on a contract, argued that the president had no authority to interfere with judicial redress of property wrongs. Though the Court was unanimous in rejecting the claim, it did not base its decision on an inherent foreign policy authority of the president to displace judicial claims. Instead, it interpreted previous acts of Congress as approving claim settlement by executive agreement where American nationals had sued foreign states.

The Court has been emphatic that agreements may not extinguish private rights guaranteed by the Constitution. In *Reid v. Covert* (1957), it held that a status-of-forces agreement governing the stationing of American soldiers in Germany could not make civilian dependents charged with crimes subject to military courts-martial that would deprive them of jury trials guaranteed by the Fifth Amendment. Specific prohibitions of the Constitution were limits on treaties and executive agreements. As Justice Black observed, "It would be completely anomalous to say that a treaty need not comply with the Constitution when such an agreement can be overridden by a statute that must conform to that instrument." [354 U.S. 1 at 17]

Holding Office

Except for the president, vice president, and members of Congress, all other officers and employees of the federal government are appointed and hold their positions for fixed terms or "good behavior." Article II-2 provides for appointment of "ambassadors, other public ministers and consuls, judges of the Supreme Court, and other officers of the United States." Except for impeachment, which is assigned to Congress and limited to "treason, bribery, or other high crimes and misdemeanors," the Constitution says nothing about removal. Critical issues have arisen partly because of the Constitution's reticence and partly because of the obvious importance of determining who is to be entrusted or not with executive or judicial power. In recent

years attempts to limit the number of terms or years elected members of Congress may serve have raised additional constitutional questions.

Appointment

In dividing yet linking power, the framers characteristically "balanced" the executive and legislative branches in making appointments. For Supreme Court justices and the executive officers mentioned in Article II, the president appoints with "advice and consent of the Senate." But for offices that Congress may later create—in effect, all lower federal courts and nearly the entire Executive branch—Congress may vest appointment of "such inferior officers" in the president, the courts, or in the heads of departments. It may also set such qualifications as age, citizenship, or residence for holders of these offices. It may not, however, retain the power of appointment itself. In *Buckley v. Valeo* (1976), for example, the Supreme Court held the Federal Election Campaign Act of 1973 violated the separation of powers principle of Article II-2 in its requirement that a majority of Federal Election Commissioners be appointed by the presiding officer of the Senate and the Speaker of the House.

The framers' insistence on separating power is also evident in the Article I-6 requirement barring members of Congress from holding executive or judicial office during their service in the legislature. Senators and Representatives who have been appointed to the Cabinet or the Supreme Court have resigned their seats.

"Employees" are a third class of appointees, accounting for 98 percent or more of the federal civilian workforce. Unlike primary and inferior officers, their appointments are not limited by constitutional restraints. The civil service system set up by Congress in 1889 and expanded several times since, now governs most of these hires.

Though the Constitution imposes no obligation on the Senate to approve nominations, rejections are infrequent. Customarily Supreme Court nominees get the closest scrutiny. Of more than 130 candidacies for the Court, only

12 have failed to win Senate confirmation; those of six others were withdrawn by the president, chiefly because confirmation seemed doubtful. In recent years, televised nomination hearings of the Senate Judiciary Committee have become commonplace and led to nationwide debate of the candidacies of Robert Bork in 1987 and Clarence Thomas in 1991. Typically Senate rejections have been based on concerns about professional competence or on partisan objections to a nominee's views on substantive legal issues.

The Senate has usually been more deferring on nominations of Cabinet officers, in the belief that the president should have wide berth in the choice of his highest subordinates. Yet because department and agency heads also make policy and administer programs Congress has passed, strong partisan reservations about a nominee's political views have sometimes resulted in rejections, as have embarrassing ethical disclosures. Nominations have less difficulty if the president and a majority of the Senate are of the same party.

The infrequency of formal rejection understates the Senate's power to advise and consent. For example, there is no way of knowing how often nominations have not been made because advance consultation with Senate leaders revealed strong opposition. Where the federal office to be filled is in a state rather than in Washington, it is customary for the president to defer to the views of the Senator or Senators of the state if they are members of his party. A breach of this "Senatorial courtesy" may lead to a rejection of the president's nominee if the objecting Senator tells the chamber that he or she finds the nominee "personally offensive."

If a vacancy occurs while the Senate is not in session, Article II-2 allows the president to make a "recess" appointment by which a nominee may serve until the end of the Senate's next session. Theoretically at least, this gives a president chance to appoint temporarily someone the Senate might not otherwise confirm and thus compromise the Senate's part in appointments.

In creating offices Congress has usually vested the appointment power in the president

or in department heads, but on a few occasions it has given it to "courts of law," the third party mentioned in Article II-2. In sustaining court appointment of election supervisors in *Ex parte Siebold* (1879), the Supreme Court, mindful of the separation of powers, held that such assignment must not be incongruous with the judicial function. A modern controversy grew out of the independent counsel provisions of the Ethics in Government Act of 1978, passed after the Watergate scandal. In part, the act is designed to deal with suspected wrongdoing by high-ranking executive officers for which the prosecuting vigor of the Justice Department might be suspect. In a specific case, the attorney general may ask a designated panel of three federal judges, called the "Special Division," to appoint an independent counsel and define his or her prosecuting jurisdiction.

This arrangement was challenged in *Morrison v. Olson* (1988) (p. 452), in which a Justice Department officer was alleged to have made false and misleading statements to a Congressional committee. Olson refused to cooperate with an independent counsel, contending that she was a primary not an "inferior" officer and so should have been appointed directly by the president. The Supreme Court held otherwise, noting that the independent counsel had limited jurisdiction, did not make policy, and could be removed for just cause by the attorney general. The appointments clause in Article II-2, it said, gave Congress discretion to vest appointment of such inferior Executive branch officers in the judiciary if Congress thought it proper.

Removal

Though the power to appoint is more important politically than that to remove, because many more persons are appointed, removal has produced greater constitutional controversy. The chief reason is that the Constitution is silent, except about impeachment. Can, for example, the president remove without the approval of Congress? Can Congress in creating an office put restrictions on the removal of officers appointed? To what extent are cases of removal reviewable by the courts? Answers have been supplied by legislation, executive practice, and judicial interpretation.

By the Executive. The first question came up almost immediately when the State Department was created by the first Congress. After much debate about how the secretary might be removed, a majority concluded that the power lay with the president alone. This action, known as the "Decision of 1789," appeared to settle matters at least for Cabinet officers. Controversies have arisen when removal is tied to a leading political issue of the day. When President Jackson, seeking to shift funds from the United States Bank to state banks, removed his secretary of the Treasury without consulting Congress, an angry legislature did no more than pass a resolution of censure. Removal took a more poisonous turn in the conflict between President Andrew Johnson and the Radical Republican Congress during Reconstruction. In the Tenure of Office Act in 1867, Congress made it unlawful for the president to remove any officer appointed with the advice and consent of the Senate, without approval of the Senate. Johnson disregarded the law, which had been passed over his veto and which he believed to be unconstitutional, when he unilaterally removed Secretary of War Edwin Stanton. The action was an important event leading to his impeachment. Congress repealed the Tenure of Office Act in 1887.

The Supreme Court did not make a full-dress review of the removal question until *Myers v. United States* (1926). In 1920, President Wilson summarily dismissed a postmaster in Portland, Oregon, before his four-year term had expired. Myers sued for back salary contending the president had violated a Congressional statute, dating to 1876, which called for the Senate's approval in removal of all first-, second-, and third-class postmasters. Chief Justice Taft's opinion rejecting the claim is one of the longest in the Court's history and one of the most expansive of presidential power. The president's removal power could be derived directly from the Constitution's grant of the executive power and its charge that the laws be faithfully executed. Taft's central reasoning was practical: The president cannot administer the laws unaided and so must be able to control those who assist him and for whom he is responsible. But the former president's opinion was cast so broadly that it appeared to say the president had unlimited power to remove any executive officials, not just ones directly responsible to him.

The Court confronted an application of this sweeping theory nine years later in *Humphrey's Executor v. United States* (1935) (p. 402). Humphrey had been one of seven commissioners of the Federal Trade Commission, appointed first by President Coolidge and reappointed by President Hoover. In 1933, President Roosevelt, believing Humphrey's views on economic policy were incompatible with aims of the New Deal, removed him. After Humphrey's death a short time later, his estate sued for back salary from the time of removal till death. It was argued that Roosevelt had violated the Federal Trade Commission Act, which limited removal to reasons of "inefficiency, neglect of duty, or malfeasance in office," none of which the president had cited.

In the Court's decision, one of three hostile to the New Deal handed down on "Black Monday" May 1, 1935, Justice Sutherland distinguished the case from *Myers*. Humphrey was not an executive department officer responsible directly to the president nor one, like Myers, exercising largely nondiscretionary administrative duties. As the member of an independent regulatory agency, Humphrey performed "quasi-legislative, quasi-judicial" functions besides being an administrator. As such, Congress intended that he be independent of executive control and could therefore place restrictions on removal. Though not overruling *Myers*, which dealt with a purely administrative executive officer, the Court disregarded Taft's broad dictum.

The principle of *Humphrey's Executor* was extended in *Wiener v. United States* (1958) in which President Eisenhower had removed a member of the War Claims Commission appointed by

President Truman, simply to replace him with a Republican. In setting up the temporary commission after World War II, Congress apparently assumed the commissioners would serve until the agency's work was finished and made no provisions for removal. Justice Frankfurter held for a unanimous Court that the commission was a quasi-judicial agency and its members were protected against removal except for just cause, whether Congress provided so or not.

Removal of "mere" employees of the Executive branch is governed by federal civil service laws. In the Hatch Act of 1939, Congress provided for the removal of civil servants who engaged in political activities, and in *United Public Workers v. Mitchell* (1947), the Supreme Court held it not to interfere with employees' freedom of speech. The loyalty review program set up by President Truman in 1947 provided for removal of workers found to be security risks by a loyalty review board. Lower federal courts held that due process in removal was not necessary because public employment was not a constitutional right. When the Supreme Court was divided 4-4 on this issue in *Bailey v. Richardson* (1951), the inferior rulings were allowed to stand.

While the independent counsel law was in effect, the appointed attorneys, who were formally placed in the Justice Department and considered to be "inferior officers" in the Constitution's terms, could be removed only by the Attorney General and only for just cause. This arrangement was held not to be an unconstitutional limit on executive authority in *Morrison v. Olson* in 1988.

By Impeachment. Article II-4 gives Congress the power to impeach civil officers of the federal government, meaning members of the executive and judicial branches. The House initiates proceedings by majority vote and acts as the prosecuting party (Article I-2). Trial is before the Senate acting as jury (Article I-3). Conviction is by two-thirds vote and carries with it removal from office and possible disqualification from future appointment. Since it is not a criminal proceeding, it does not prevent later indictment in a court of law.

Article II-4 provides that impeachment may be for "treason, bribery, or other high crimes and misdemeanors." Despite this limit, the first impeachment, which resulted in the conviction and removal of Judge John Pickering in 1803, was for intemperate judicial conduct and mental illness rather than criminal activity. The impeachment of Justice Samuel Chase, an outspoken Federalist, by a Jeffersonian Congress a year later was for his political partisanship rather than criminality. His acquittal by the Senate was a rebuke to those who wanted to turn impeachment into an instrument for removing political opponents.

Because it is cumbersome and halts the work of Congress, impeachment has been resorted to infrequently. Charges have been brought against only three members of the Executive branch, Presidents Andrew Johnson in 1868 and Bill Clinton in 1999, and Secretary of War William Belknap in 1876. Johnson and Clinton were acquitted and Belknap resigned before trial. Besides Pickering and Chase, 10 other federal judges have been impeached. Six were convicted, including three in the 1980s, three acquitted, and one resigned.

Preparation of impeachment charges by the House in the Watergate scandal led to the resignation of President Richard Nixon in 1974. The strong possibility of impeachment was a fact in the resignation of Justice Abe Fortas in 1969 after disclosure that he had accepted a retainer fee from a foundation.

Persistent calls from conservative groups for the impeachment of Chief Justice Earl Warren in the 1960s and introduction of a House resolution to impeach Justice William O. Douglas in 1970 were based on partisan objections to their court opinions and constitutional philosophy rather than accusations of wrongdoing. Tradition, the unwieldy nature of impeachment, and the enormous power of modern communications media to report and to focus public attention, make it improbable that impeachment can now be used successfully for strictly partisan purposes. The Constitution's clear and complete commitment of the matter to Congress makes it improbable that the Supreme Court will review impeachment questions. When it was asked to do so by the impeached federal judge Walter Nixon, Jr., in *Nixon v. United States* in 1993, because his Senate trial had been before a designated committee rather than the full Senate, the Court held the matter a political question for the Senate alone to decide.

From Congress. Impeachment does not apply to members of the legislative branch, who are not "civil officers of the United States" under Article II-4. However, Article I-5 gives each house of Congress power to expel a member by two-thirds vote or to punish for "disorderly behavior". Except in the cases of 14 Senators and three Representatives expelled in 1861 for supporting the rebellion, each house has used the procedure only once. Though expulsion need not require criminality, Congress has preferred to discipline members through milder forms of punishment such as censure or loss of seniority.

Each house also has power under Article I-5 to judge the qualifications of members. This has been used from time to time to exclude, that is, not to seat, a Senator or Representative-elect and can be exercised by simple majority vote. Qualifications mentioned in the Constitution include age (at least 25 years to serve in the House, 30 in the Senate), citizenship (at least seven years for the House, nine for the Senate), residence in the state represented, the holding of no other federal office, and since ratification of the Fourteenth Amendment, loyalty to the United States. Of 13 members-elect excluded (three by the Senate, ten by the House), only three failed to meet the constitutional qualifications—in their cases, citizenship and residence. Five were excluded for disloyalty during the Civil War. The remaining five were not seated for several extra-constitutional reasons including polygamy, sedition, malfeasance, and misconduct.

The question of whether Congress may validly add to the qualifications mentioned in the Con-

stitution, as it had in the last cases, came before Supreme Court in *Powell v. McCormack* (1969) (p. 432). In January 1967 at the opening of the 90th Congress, the House voted to exclude New York Representative Adam Clayton Powell for various improprieties including misuse of government funds. Powell, who had been elected the preceding fall to his thirteenth consecutive term, challenged the constitutionality of the action in court and asked for back salary. In 1968, with the case pending, he was reelected, permitted to take his seat, fined, and stripped of his seniority. When in the following year he appealed an adverse lower court decision in his suit, the Supreme Court held that Congress could refuse to seat an elected member only for failure to meet those qualifications stated in the Constitution. This did not mean that Congress might not expel a member for its own reasons, but since Powell had not been seated at all in the 90th Congress, his was a case of exclusion. Whether the Court would review a matter of expulsion, which is not qualified by other constitutional provisions except the two-thirds vote, or consider it a political question, is uncertain.

Term Limits

From colonial times to the present, concern that long and entrenched holding of power by elected officials would render republican government less responsive and less accountable has led to support for frequent elections, short terms, and limited reeligibility. Washington's disinterest in a third presidential term, which he very likely would have won, established a popular informal "two-term" tradition that lasted for more than 150 years. When it was broken by Franklin Roosevelt seeking and winning a third term in 1940 and a fourth in 1944, a postwar reaction produced the Twenty-second Amendment, limiting presidential eligibility to two elected terms or to one if an incumbent has succeeded to the office as vice president and served more than two years of the predecessor's term.

The President and the Prosecutor

On February 12, 1999, President William Jefferson Clinton was acquitted in an impeachment trial in the U. S. Senate in two roll call votes, 55-45 and 50-50, cast largely along party lines, that fell far short of the two-thirds majority needed for conviction and removal from office. The charges brought against him by the Republican-controlled House, based on a report of an independent counsel, accused him of lying under oath and obstructing justice in the sexual harassment case of *Jones v. Clinton.*

Constitutional issues in the matter were partly overshadowed by partisan rancor over the president's behavior and over tactics of the independent counsel, Kenneth Starr. A former judge but with no previous experience as a prosecutor, Starr had been appointed in 1994 to investigate Clinton's financial dealings during the time he was governor of Arkansas. Though that inquiry produced little to implicate Clinton in wrongdoing, in 1998 Starr received taped telephone conversations of Monica Lewinsky, a former White House intern, that indicated she and the president may have had sexual encounters in the White House. If true, the information indicated Clinton had perjured himself in depositions given in the Jones suit. Starr's investigation then turned to Clinton's sexual conduct and his veracity under oath, eventually producing the report to the House of Representatives concluding that the president had committed impeachable offenses.

Amid strident charges that Clinton was morally unfit to continue as president and equally strident ones that Starr had conducted a political vendetta based on little more than sexual indiscretions, public opinion remained unusually discriminating. Polls consistently showed that a large majority condemned Clinton's behavior yet gave him high approval for job performance and opposed removing him from office. There is little doubt that this support for Clinton as president kept many Democratic and a few Republican senators from voting to convict in the impeachment trial.

The Clinton saga did little to clarify the uncertain "high crimes and misdemeanors" the Constitution specifies in Article II-4 as impeachable offenses in addition to those of treason and bribery. Lying under oath and obstructing justice seemed to qualify, but those missteps in Clinton's case were not connected with use of presidential power or with any matter of public policy or other conduct of government. They were related only to personal behavior however reckless that behavior may have been.

In important ways, Clinton's impeachment was a mirror image of Andrew Johnson's. The main charge against Johnson—that he violated the Tenure of Office Act by firing Secretary of War Edwin M. Stanton—spoke to deep policy differences between the president and Congress on the chief political issue of the day—how to reconstruct the Southern states for full reentry into the Union. Johnson's defense, unlike Clinton's, was that the law he had violated not only was not criminal, but was itself unconstitutional, a view the Supreme Court confirmed 60 years later in *Myers v. United States.* The case against Clinton came closer to "high crimes and misdemeanors" but Clinton's acts, unlike Johnson's, had no fundamental political weight in the conduct of the presidency, a matter public opinion seemed to recognize.

In contrast, the most successful presidential impeachment was the one that never took place. By removing himself from office in July 1974, Richard Nixon headed off Watergate impeachment charges that were being prepared by the House of Representatives. The main count, obstruction of justice in investigation of the break-in, dealt with criminal use of executive power, which is probably closer to what the framers generally understood to be among impeachable high crimes and misdemeanors. Whether impeachment can be based on minor crimes, civil wrongs such as malfeasance or nonfeasance of a duty, obstruction of constitutionally enacted legislation, or simply deep policy differences, is still not firmly established. In the end, an impeachable offense will probably be what the Congress of the moment, informed by public opinion, says it is.

The major institutional casualty of the Clinton impeachment was not the presidency, which the public saw as separated from its holder, but the office of independent counsel. Created by the Ethics in Government Act of 1978 and renewed every five years except in 1992 when it was allowed to expire, only to be renewed again in 1994, it was allowed to lapse a second and perhaps final time in June 1999.

Concerns that Starr had abused his powers were added to long-standing misgivings about the office in the scheme of separated powers, to sink any chance of renewal. In the 19 years of the law's life, 20 independent counsels, operating with their own staff and unlimited budgets—in all, nearly $200 million was spent—were appointed to investigate more than a score of high-ranking officials in Republican and Democratic administrations. Unlike Starr, most completed their work with dispatch and in slightly more cases than not, cleared the figures investigated.

Debate over the office reveals the fundamental political tension between the need for objective investigation and the need for accountability. Suspicion that the Justice Department may at times be politically influenced when faced with investigating executive officers, especially the president, and may not command public confidence in doing so must be balanced against creation of an agency that may be nearly a law unto itself. Prosecution is an executive function, yet the independent counsel law had counsels appointed by the judiciary and, though locating them in the Executive branch, left them almost totally independent of the attorney general. The Supreme Court upheld the constitutionality of this arrangement in *Morrison v. Olson* in 1988, yet Justice Scalia's dissenting opinion, a decade before the Starr investigation, was prophetic:

> The mini-Executive that is the independent counsel . . . operating in an area where so little is law and so much is discretion, is intentionally cut off from the unifying influence of the Justice Department and from the perspective that multiple responsibilities provide. What would normally be regarded as a technical violation . . . may in his or her small world assume the proportions of an indictable offense. What would normally be regarded as an investigation that has reached the level of pursuing such picayune matters that it should be concluded, may to him or her be an investigation that ought to go on for another year. How frightening it must be to have your own independent counsel and staff appointed, with nothing else to do but to investigate you until investigation is no longer worthwhile . . . And to have that counsel and staff decide, with no basis for comparison, whether what you have done is bad enough, willful enough, provable enough, to warrant an indictment.

Without the independent counsel law, the attorney general retains power to appoint a special counsel to investigate executive officers, as he or she did before the Ethics in Government Act was passed. Situations may arise again where the attorney general and the Justice Department do not seem sufficiently disinterested or able to command public confidence for an objective investigation of high-ranking members of its own administration. In such cases, a more distanced prosecutor might be enviable.

The balance between independence and accountability is one of the oldest problems in democratic political organization. Where it is best struck is not likely to have permanent answer in political or constitutional debate, despite the consensus that allowed the troublesome independent counsel law die.

The electoral advantages legislative incumbency have often led to reelection rates of more than 90 percent. Concern about such "permanence" and about the responsiveness of government generally spurred a grass-roots movement in the 1980s and early 1990s to limit legislative terms. In a number of states these efforts also produced laws imposing limits on the reeligibility of persons elected to Congress. In 1995, Arkansas's establishment of such limits through an amendment to its constitution was struck down by the Supreme Court in *United States Term Limits v. Thornton* (p. 458).Though Article I allows states to establish voter qualifications and prescribe "times, places and manner" of holding Congressional elections, the Court said it did not empower them to alter or add to qualifications for membership already set out in the Article, namely those of age, citizenship, and residence. The decision had no effect on a state's power to set term limits for state offices; term limits for Congress, however, would require a constitutional amendment.

In response to the Thornton decision, voters in Missouri adopted a "scarlet letter" amendment to the state's constitution that required the inscription "Disregarded voters' instruction on term limits" be printed on ballots next to the names of incumbent Missouri Congressional candidates who did not support a federal constitutional amendment that would authorize term limits and the inscription "Declined to pledge to support term limits" by the names of nonincumbent candidates who did not make such a pledge. Challenged by a nonincumbent who refused to make the pledge, The Supreme Court struck down the state amendment in *Cook v. Gralike,* 2001. It held unanimously that a state constitutional amendment affecting candidates for federal office was not a power reserved to the state under the Tenth Amendment because reserved powers were those that preceded creation of the Constitution. Nor could the state amendment be sustained as a delegated power under Article 1-4 authorizing the states to regulate the manner of holding Congressional elections because it was not a procedural regulation but an attempt to "dictate electoral outcomes" by favoring a class of candidates.

The Bounds of Office

In setting out three branches of government, the framers paid most attention to Congress, which they assumed would be the dominant branch. In the presidency, they gave the world a new political office, but left its powers general and, for the most part, its boundaries undefined. Though aware that cooperation between executive and legislature would be needed, they were also concerned with limiting government. Friction and conflict, reinforced by coequality and independence, would be part of power checking power. Beyond the mutual checks in law-making, treaty-making, and appointments, the framers said little about how the branches were to deal with each other. This left many uncertainties but also room for the practical experience of later generations to better define the boundaries of separated power.

Executive Privilege and Information

In Article II-3, the president must "from time to time give Congress information on the state of the union." For modern presidents this requirement has become an annual occasion to outline the administration's general political direction and call for legislative and public support. But in day-to-day law-making Congress needs a great deal of information, often highly specific, from the executive. At the same time, the president has need to protect state "secrets," which often have to do with national security, and for confidentiality in communicating with subordinates. Usually these interbranch matters are handled routinely in a spirit of cooperation. Mutual accommodation sometimes fails because the intelligence sought is central to important political conflict between the president or other members of the executive branch and majority powers in Congress. Complicating things is the possibility that executive reluctance to provide information may hide constitutionally questionable or even illegal acts or that Congress may want information less for a legislative purpose than to weaken the executive politically.

Decisions by the first president established certain lines for executive privilege (the term itself was not used until the 1950s) that have served as precedents. Washington substantially complied with Congress's first investigation—a House inquiry in 1792 into the defeat of General Arthur St. Clair's expedition against Indians in the Northwest Territory. But he concluded the president could and should withhold papers the disclosure of which might "injure the public." In 1796, Washington refused the House's request for documents having to do with negotiations of the Jay Treaty with Great Britain, saying the House played no part in treaty-making.

The courts have generally avoided these struggles, leaving them to be resolved through political means. But the possibility of conflict between the executive and the judiciary became apparent in the treason trial of Aaron Burr. Chief Justice Marshall issued a subpoena *duces tecum*—an order to appear in court with certain documents—to President Jefferson to get a letter believed useful to the defense. Jefferson refused to appear but sent the letter, albeit stating he was doing so voluntarily, and a showdown was avoided. Until the Watergate crisis, most executive-judicial conflicts over information affected relatively minor matters that, if reviewed by the Supreme Court, usually resulted in the executive claim being upheld. For example, in *United States v. Reynolds* (1953), decided during the Korean War, the spouses of three civilians killed in a military plane crash sued for damages asking for certain documents from the U. S. Air Force. The Court recognized an executive right to withhold information that might compromise national security even if it was needed in adjudication.

During the Eisenhower, Kennedy, and Johnson administrations, claims of an absolute privilege, usually citing national security, were heard more often. The Nixon presidency eventually brought the matter to the constitutional foreground.

The Arrogation of Power

After his victory in 1968, Nixon faced a strong Democratic Congress and what he saw as an entrenched, nearly uncontrolled bureaucracy. He resolved to use executive power against liberal forces in government.

To curb many spending programs enacted during the Johnson years, Nixon used the device of budgetary impoundment—the freezing of funds already appropriated by Congress for an agency or program but not yet spent. Impounding was not new—other presidents, starting with Jefferson, had used it on occasion—but never before had it been an instrument of concerted executive policy. Nixon's impoundments, which affected more than 100 programs and $15 billion, were greater than those of all other presidents combined.

Though Congress had occasionally authorized the freezing of funds, Nixon had no express constitutional or general statutory authority to do so himself. He lamely defended his actions as needed to curb inflation. Critics charged that impounding had the effect of crippling programs duly created and funded by Congress as part of national policy. Not using this money also ran counter to the president's constitutional obligation to "faithfully execute the laws." The administration's reply curiously resembled Lincoln's to Taney when he ignored the chief justice's habeas corpus order in *Ex parte Merryman:* The president must look beyond individual laws and weigh his actions by their effect on all the laws. But in Nixon's case, the extraordinary executive claim was made in peacetime in the face of no national crisis.

In 1974, dealing with a president weakened by the Watergate scandal, Congress passed the Budget and Impoundment Act, which placed limits on presidential impounding and required Congressional approval in certain circumstances. Nixon's practice was the subject of more than 50 suits in the federal courts, only one of which, *Train v. City of New York* (1975), involving the Clean Water Act, reached the Supreme Court. He was out of office by then, and the Court held only that the act did not permit presidential withholding of funds appropriated for its enforcement. It did not rule on the constitutionality of impoundment.

Nixon's reelection in 1972 by the largest popular vote margin in history seemed to confirm the correctness of his aggressive presidency and embattled course with Congress and parts of the bureaucracy. Clearly he did not lack popular support. Some observers began to refer to the "plebiscitory presidency," a political arrangement in which the executive leader, as the only nationally elected figure except for the vice-president, acts with broad discretion, checked not so much by a Congress dominated by "special interests" and too fragmented to govern, as by the people directly through elections. These in turn become national plebiscites on his policies. The model was congenial to a president who had antagonized or largely cut himself off from the administrative elite in various executive agencies and from the committees of Congress that, with the president and the courts, have traditionally made up American governmental pluralism.

There is more than enough irony here to go around. The strong, activist presidency, glorified by liberals and by liberal presidents from Wilson to Franklin Roosevelt to John Kennedy and Lyndon Johnson, found its embodiment in a conservative bent on undoing liberal programs. The president who billed himself as a constitutional "strict constructionist" carried presidential authority to the edge of the constitutional envelope and perhaps beyond. Had the Watergate scandal not intervened, the plebiscitory presidency would no doubt have been greatly strengthened by the end of Nixon's second term.

The Watergate Crisis

Nixon's antagonistic presidency left him especially vulnerable to political mishaps. His view of himself as perpetually beset by enemies on every side—a curious character bend given his success and popularity—almost guaranteed mishaps would occur. On June 17, 1972, Washington, D.C.

police apprehended several persons who had broken into the offices of the Democratic National Committee to install bugging equipment. They worked for the Committee to Re-elect the President (CREEP), which Nixon had set up to bypass the Republican National Committee. There was no immediate evidence that the president had ordered the break-in or had even known that it was to take place, and the incident had little effect on the election campaign that fall. Months afterward, thanks in part to investigative work by two *Washington Post* reporters, suspicion of a direct White House connection to the burglary grew. So did the belief that Nixon, whether personally involved or not, was protecting those who were.

In February 1973, the Senate set up a Select Committee, chaired by Senator Sam Ervin, of North Carolina, to investigate criminal activity during the 1972 campaign. New evidence linked CREEP to other break-ins, illegal wiretapping, and money laundering. Things heated up further when a White House aide told the committee that conversations in the presidential Oval Office were routinely and secretly taped. This record would presumably show what Nixon knew of the break-in and when he knew it. It became a new focus of the investigation and eventually of a claim of executive privilege that would turn Watergate into a constitutional crisis.

The committee asked for several of the tapes, but Nixon refused to deliver them citing an executive privilege from the separation of powers. The committee then asked a federal court to issue a subpoena *duces tecum* on the president to turn them over, but the court refused, sustaining the president's right to withhold information or materials from the Legislative branch. Nixon did agree to the appointment of a special prosecutor in the Justice Department to investigate the possibility of executive involvement in the Watergate matter.

His new attorney general Eliot Richardson chose Archibald Cox of the Harvard Law School, once solicitor general in the Kennedy administration. Cox soon asked for the tapes and when

Nixon again refused, got a subpoena *duces tecum* from a grand jury investigating the Watergate crime. When Nixon still refused, Cox applied to a federal district court which ordered Nixon to release them. The president appealed this decision to the federal Court of Appeals in Washington, which held against him in *Nixon v. Sirica*. He then offered Cox a summary of the tapes, which Cox refused insisting the president obey the court order. At this point, Nixon ordered the attorney general, who as the hiring agent had power to dismiss Cox, to fire him and so presumably end the investigation. Richardson refused and resigned. His replacement, solicitor general Robert Bork carried out the president's order.

Though the firing was not illegal, a public uproar followed. It was now clear that Nixon was desperately trying to suppress evidence, and public support began to fall away rapidly. It was also clear that unless the Watergate matter could be resolved quickly, the nation faced a constitutional crisis. The separation of powers threatened a governmental stalemate that would leave the nation's chief executive ineffective in both domestic and foreign affairs.

Under pressure, the attorney general appointed a new Special Prosecutor Leon Jaworski, who soon requested the tapes but was refused. In March 1974, Jaworski got a federal grand jury indictment of the former Nixon assistants H. R. Haldeman and John Erlichman and former attorney general John Mitchell on charges of obstructing justice in connection with the break-in. It named the president as an unindicted coconspirator. Now Jaworski issued a new subpoena *duces tecum* because the tapes were needed in the criminal trials of the three subordinates. Nixon released edited transcripts of the tapes and went to federal court to quash the subpoena, citing executive privilege. Judge John Sirica denied the motion, and Jaworski asked the Supreme Court to hear Nixon's appeal directly and immediately, which it did.

The Court's unanimous decision in *United States v. Nixon* (p. 434) eight weeks later marked the end of the Nixon presidency. Chief Justice Burger

admitted that the president's need for privacy and confidentiality in communicating with his subordinates gave him a presumptive conditional executive privilege derived from the separation of powers, but he rejected Nixon's claim to an unqualified executive privilege against demands of the judicial process. The need for information having to do with the guilt or innocence of other parties in a pending criminal case limited the privilege. Confidential materials, Burger wrote, could be looked at by the trial judge *in camera* to determine which portions were needed for trial. Nixon was ordered to produce the tapes, which showed complicity in the Watergate cover-up, that is, in the crime of conspiring to obstruct justice. Less than three weeks later, with the House of Representatives preparing articles of impeachment, Nixon became the first and only president to resign the office.

Executive privilege was further limited three years later in *Nixon v. Administrator of General Services*. Though the privilege might survive a president's tenure, the Court held it was not violated by a Congressional act that gave custody of Nixon's papers and tapes to the head of the General Services Administration and allowed them to be screened by archivists.

Since *United States v. Nixon* (p. 432), lower courts have approved subpoenas on each president since Nixon, in pending criminal or civil cases. Because each has complied, usually by testifying on videotape, the courts have not had to clarify further the limits of executive privilege. The balance struck in *United States v. Nixon* might be different were the president's claim to be based on national security or secrets of state rather than the need for confidentiality in speaking with subordinates. The full implication of the Court basing the presumptive privilege in the president's constitutional powers remains unclear as well.

Politically, the immediate effect of the Watergate crisis was to weaken the presidency. In the 1970s, Congress reasserted itself in the War Powers Resolution, the Budget and Impoundment

Control Act, and the National Emergency Act, which provided procedures for declaring and ending "national emergencies." It also created the Congressional Budget Office and the increased use of legislative vetoes.

Nixon's elected vice president, Spiro Agnew, resigned in 1973 after entering a plea bargain on a charge of income tax evasion. Republican Representative Gerald Ford was then named vice president under the twenty-fifth Amendment, which, whenever the vice presidency is vacant, authorizes the president to "nominate a Vice-President who shall take office upon confirmation by a majority vote of both houses of Congress." When Nixon resigned, Ford became the nation's first nonelected president. Neither Ford nor the Democrat Jimmy Carter, who narrowly defeated him in 1976, were very successful as chief executives in the 1970s, but the post-Watergate environment hostile to presidential power did not last. Long-run shifts of authority and responsibilities to the president, the pragmatic price of modern government, resumed with the election of Ronald Reagan in 1980.

Immunities

The president and Congress each need discretion to perform their functions, the president to administer programs and otherwise execute the laws, Congress to freely debate what the laws should be and enact them. Groups and individuals hurt or disadvantaged by these actions may try to block them or recover damages through lawsuit. The framers foresaw the danger for Congress and wrote certain protections into Article I-6, but were silent about a shield for the executive. Personal civil or criminal liability of the president and chief executive officers for acts in office or before taking office has raised several important constitutional issues.

Executive. Politically, executive immunity has many features of executive privilege, but rests on different legal considerations. It sets the president's need to be free to act without challenge or enjoinder by lawsuits against the rule of law that every person is civilly and criminally accountable for their acts.

Judicial blocking of presidential enforcement of a law or policy was largely disposed of in *Mississippi v. Johnson* (1869) in which the state had tried to enjoin President Andrew Johnson's enforcement of a Reconstruction statute. The Supreme Court held that a litigant had no power to stop or impede execution of a law when the president's act was discretionary or depended on political judgment. Only after the fact could the president be challenged in court. Whether this rule also applied to the few nondiscretionary, ministerial duties of the office was not decided.

Immunity is less well-settled when a plaintiff claiming injury from the president's official acts tries to hold him personally liable. In *Nixon v. Fitzgerald* (1982), the Supreme Court held 5-4 that the president had absolute immunity from civil damages arising from his official acts. A civilian analyst employed by the air force alleged he was fired at Nixon's orders for "whistle-blowing" testimony given to Congress on defense contract cost overruns. Justice Lewis Powell held that the "singular importance" of the president's duties require his energies and attention be free from the distractions of private lawsuits. He concluded that the protections against presidential misconduct were impeachment, Congressional oversight, and scrutiny by the press. Presidential civil damage immunity continues even after leaving office for acts while in office. Four dissenters argued that the bestowal of blanket immunity removed the president from the rule of law. In the companion case of *Harlow v. Fitzgerald,* however, high-ranking executive officials were held to have only qualified civil immunity, not extending to acts that violated rights of which a reasonable person would be aware.

The president does not have immunity from criminal charges. Very probably impeachment would take place before the filing of such charges, as would have been the case in the Watergate crisis had not Nixon resigned. Conviction in impeachment does not prevent such charges from being filed. In Nixon's case, the closest the nation has come to criminal indictment of a president or former president, President Ford used his pardoning power in Article II-2 to grant Nixon "a full, free, and absolute pardon ... for all offenses against the United States" during his time as president.

Can a president be sued for civil damages for alleged wrongs committed before becoming president? This was the question the Court faced in *Clinton v. Jones* (1997) (p.464), in which an Arkansas state employee sued President Bill Clinton for alleged sexual harassment while he was governor of the state. Since official presidential acts were not at issue, the president's attorneys argued the lawsuit would be distracting from the presidential responsibilities. The Court disagreed, holding unanimously that the plaintiff did not need to wait until Clinton's term had ended before pursuing her claim and that the case could be tried in a way that would accommodate the president's schedule. Though the suit, remanded, was later dismissed for lack of merit, the decision in *Clinton v. Jones* allowed pretrial investigation to continue while Clinton was in office. This, in turn, led indirectly to revelations of the Lewinsky scandal, the president's sexual dalliance with a White House intern.

In another development growing out of Jones's suit, Clinton became the first sitting president to be cited for civil contempt. The trial judge found that he had given in a deposition "intentionally false, misleading, and evasive answers that were designed to obstruct the judicial process."* He was ordered to pay expenses incurred by the judge and by Jones's attorneys in traveling to Washington, D.C. to take the deposition and in any work resulting from the objectionable testimony—nearly $90,000 in all. Since Clinton did not appeal the citation its constitutionality remains less than certain. (In a later formal agreement with a special prosecutor, he admitted he had not been truthful.)

Legislative. To keep law-making free of executive or judicial impediment, the framers wrote versions of two hard-won English parliamentary rights into Article I-6 of the Constitution. The first gives immunity from arrest when attending or going to and from a Congressional session. The protection does not apply to criminal matters and is now of little relevance since civil arrests for breaches of contract or nonpayment of debt, common in the eighteenth century, are generally disallowed today.

Of greater consequence is the second shield, that "for any speech or debate in either House, they shall not be questioned in any other place." Originally intended to protect members from suits for libel or slander, the clause was treated expansively by the Supreme Court in *Kilbourne v. Thompson* (1881). The Speaker of the House was sued for false arrest in ordering that a recalcitrant witness in an investigatory hearing be jailed for contempt of Congress. The Court held that the clause protected not just speech and debate on the floor, but all things normally done in a legislative session, including the conduct of hearings and investigations.

The Court elaborated on and limited this view in *Gravel v. United States* (1972), in which Senator Mike Gravel made public portions of what came to be called the Pentagon Papers, classified documents on American military policy in Vietnam, which he obtained clandestinely. Gravel convened a special session of the Public Works Subcommittee on Public Buildings, which he chaired. With the press in attendance, he read selections from the documents into the subcommittee's record. Later he arranged for their publication with a private book publisher. On his reading of portions to the subcommittee, the Court held Gravel was not subject to jurisdiction of a federal grand jury that investigated release of the Papers. It also extended protection of the Speech and Debate Clause to Gravel's aide because of the importance of aides in legislative work. But the Court held the speech and debate shield did not extend to such nonlegislative acts arranging for private publication. About

---

* *The New York Times,* April 13, 1999, 1.

these, Gravel and his aide could be required to testify.

The speech and debate protection does not give a member of Congress immunity from libel action for defamatory statements made in press releases or in newsletters to constituents, even if those statements were made first on the Senate floor. In *Hutcheson v. Proxmire* (1979), the Court held that publication of such statements was "not part of the legislative function." [443 U.S. 111 at 133]

Earlier, in *United States v. Brewster* (1972), the Speech and Debate Clause was held not to bar indictment of a Senator for receiving a bribe. Though the shield was protection against inquiry into the motives for legislative action, the Court noted the charge against Brewster was taking a bribe, not the legislative end the bribe was intended to obtain.

Legislative Power Delegated and Retained

The separating of power has needed constant adjustment to enable the national government to deal with complex modern domestic and foreign problems. Nowhere has the shift to greater executive power been more dramatic than in Congress's empowerment of the executive and its creation of federal agencies that make and enforce rules. Except during the New Deal, this development has produced fewer constitutional questions than one might expect. Those that have arisen have tended to exercise the formalism of the legal mind more than the pragmatism of the political.

Creation of the Administrative State

An old axiom in Anglo-American law holds that a power once delegated cannot be redelegated. Though the Supreme Court still occasionally refers to it, the doctrine is rarely invoked. If it were, Congress, which is granted great powers by the Constitution, could delegate nothing.

Here again, the Constitution itself is of little help; it neither provides for delegation nor prohibits it. Congress and the courts have each recognized that some shift of discretionary rule-making to other branches is essential to effective government. The legislative process is ponderous and deliberate. Its aggregation of interests and collective mechanics is well suited to discover final ends and formulate general policies to reach them. But legislatures lacking time and expertness are less well suited for dealing with the details of those policies or with problems that may arise in carrying them out. Nor is it possible for a legislature to anticipate all future events that may call for discretionary adjustments to realize general ends. In this sense, legislators are in much the same position as constitution-makers. Limitations were all the more telling as the national government has become a regulator of the domestic economy and a superpower in the international world.

Congress may make some delegations contingent on executive determination that certain conditions exist. More commonly Congress simply sets a goal and prescribes broad standards to guide the president or administrators in what Marshall called "filling up the details." Sometimes these standards have been no more specific than "reasonable rates" (for the Interstate Commerce Commission), "uniform methods of competition" (the Federal Trade Commission), "public convenience, interest, and necessity" (Federal Communications Commission), or "fair and equitable" (the World War II Office of Price Administration).

Today the president, executive agencies, and independent regulatory commissions operate under several thousand laws that delegate discretionary rule-making authority, the results of which fill dozens of volumes of the Federal Code of Regulations. From time to time, Congress has also delegated quasi-legislative power to the judicial branch. Under its Article III power to create lower federal courts, for example, Congress has authorized the Supreme Court to prescribe procedural rules for them.

The Supreme Court has held Congressional delegating unconstitutional only three times, all during the New Deal. In *Panama Refining Co. v. Ryan* (1935) and *Schechter v. United States* (1936), the Court invalidated broad, loosely drafted delegations in the National Industrial Recovery Act. The statute gave the president law-making authority without a clear declaration of policy, adequate guidelines, or the requirement of initial fact-finding. When it struck down the Guffey Coal Act in *Carter v. Carter Coal Co.* a year later, it was partly for the same reasons and partly because responsibility for drafting a code of industry regulations was given to private parties, in this case, representatives of the coal industry. Though Congress has since been more careful in drafting delegatory legislation, these decisions are best appreciated as historical anomalies, artifacts of the laissez-faire Court's battle with the New Deal. The inclusion of private parties in delegation schemes was later upheld in *Currin v. Wallace* (1939) when the Court sustained a veto Congress had given farmers with regard to marketing proposals made by the secretary of agriculture.

Today, the judicial check on delegation is likely to rest on interpretation of the statutory intent of Congress rather than on supposed constitutional requirements. Where the Court holds against executive acts on a delegation issue, it concludes that Congress did not intend such delegation rather than that it lacked the power to make it. This allows Congress to reinstate the delegation by revising the statute. As with most negative rulings resting on statutory interpretation, the Court's check lies in forcing the legislature, if it wants to retain the policy, to reconsider and clarify its position.

The Legislative Veto

In delegating power, it is not surprising that Congress should try to retain some corrective control, short of passing new legislation or repealing an existing law. It has sometimes resorted to the legislative veto, so called because it requires one or both houses to approve or at least not disapprove a particular executive decision before that decision can have final legal effect. The veto arrays pragmatic considerations of obtaining executive accountability against a doctrinaire through intuitively appealing adherence of the principle of separating power.

The legislative veto was first used in 1932 when Congress gave President Hoover vast discretionary authority to reorganize the Executive branch with a proviso that his plans would not become law if either house disapproved. Later that year and after his defeat by Roosevelt, he issued executive orders consolidating nearly 60 government agencies and programs. The House of Representatives rejected all of them in a single vote. From then until the early 1980s, the legislative veto was included in more than 200 delegatory laws, including the War Powers Resolution in 1973, the Budget Impoundment Act of 1974, and the Nuclear Non-Proliferation Act of 1978.

Critics of the veto argue that it is inconsistent with law-making provisions of the Presentment Clause of Article I-7, which requires that all bills passed by Congress be given to the president for signature or veto. The legislative veto is said to reverse the process by making Executive proposals subject to Congressional approval. In *Immigration and Naturalization Service v. Chadha* (1983) (p. 441), the Supreme Court agreed with the critics and struck down an amendment to the Naturalization Act of 1952 giving either house a veto in decisions to suspend deportations of illegal aliens. Chadha, a foreign graduate student whose visa had expired, persuaded the I.N.S. to let him remain in the United States. This determination, along with that for several other aliens, was vetoed by the House.

Chief Justice Burger held the veto to violate the Presentment Clause and, as a one-house veto, also the bicameral requirements of Article I-1 and Article I-7. More broadly, he found it inconsistent with the separation of powers; Congress had power to pass laws but not to participate in their execution. In a long dissenting opinion, Justice Byron White argued that the decision, invalidating 50 years of practice, made accountability of executive and independent regulatory agencies much less certain.

After *Chadha,* Congress began using its control over appropriations to give Senate and House committees opportunities to intervene informally in various programs. Executive agencies have generally accepted these "underground" vetoes as the price for Congress's continued willingness to broadly delegate discretionary authority.

Hybrid Offices and Mixed Functions

The Constitution goes far toward separating legislative, executive, and judicial power at the same time that it provides specific checks and balances of one branch against another. Yet it says nothing at all about a mixing or combining functions that the practical considerations of governing in a complex modern world would seem to demand. One of Congress's earliest innovative attempts to fill this constitutional blank was the creation of the Interstate Commerce Commission in 1887. Congress set up in the Executive branch an agency that had more than simply administrative tasks and was not totally controlled by the president. Other so-called independent regulatory agencies followed, including the Federal Trade Commission, the Federal Communications Commission, and the National Labor Relations Board.

Typically these agencies have executive power to carry out legislative policies, but they also make rules having the force of law, and may adjudicate disputes of parties who are in their regulatory domain. In *Humphrey's Executor* the Supreme Court justified the "independence" of these commissions in the Executive branch by referring to them as performing "quasi-legislative, quasi-judicial" functions. With this view, the Court moved away from the notion of three discrete governmental functions as though they were essences that could never be combined in the same body.

But in recent years, Congress has created several offices that the Supreme Court has thought

to raise constitutional issues of the separated power. In the early 1980's a combination of new tax cuts proposed by President Reagan and a sharp recession sent an already high federal debt to a new record of nearly $2 trillion. Because a popular president refused to support either tax increases or cuts in defense spending, Congress, which found it politically painful to cut "nonessential" domestic programs, cast about for a way to reduce the deficit without taking direct responsibility for specific cuts.

The scheme adopted in 1985 was the Gramm-Rudman-Hollings Act, formally titled the Balanced Budget Emergency Control Act. The deficit was to be reduced annually until a balance was reached. If Congress did not raise taxes, which it probably would not do without the president's support, or make enough spending cuts, which in the past at least, it had shown little will to do, the comptroller general as head of the General Accounting Office, an auditing arm of Congress, was empowered to make across-the-board cuts in all programs so the annual reduction schedule could be met. Several members of Congress who had voted against the act, including Representative Mike Synar, immediately filed suit against Comptroller General Charles A. Bowsher, arguing that it unconstitutionally violated the separation of powers.

In *Bowsher v. Synar* (1986), (p. 447) the Supreme Court agreed, 7-2. Chief Justice Burger held for the majority that the responsibilities given the comptroller general under the act, that is, carrying out the Congressional mandate to reduce the budget deficit, were executive. But the comptroller general, though appointed by the president, can be removed only by Congress and was thus a legislative officer. Through this formalistic analysis, Burger concluded that the Gramm-Rudman Act was unconstitutional because it retained executive functions in the Legislative branch. Soon after the decision, Congress amended the act, substituting the director of the Office of Management and Budget (O.M.B.), an executive branch official, for the comptroller general.

Mixed functions was also the issue in a challenge to the Ethics in Government Act in *Morrison v. Olson* in 1988 (p. 452),noted earlier. Passed in 1978 in response to the Watergate Scandal, it provided for appointment of an independent prosecutor to investigate charges of misconduct against high executive officials. On application by the attorney general, a panel of three federal judges could appoint an independent counsel and specify his or her jurisdiction. To avoid the possibility of a summary firing as had occurred with Archibald Cox, the first Watergate independent counsel, the law allowed dismissal by the attorney general but only for just cause, not at will. The Supreme Court, held this arrangement not to violate the separation of powers. Mindful of the conflict of interest that could arise if the Executive branch were faced with investigating one of its own high-ranking officers, Chief Justice Rehnquist argued that Congress had power under Article II-2 to assign appointment of an "inferior" officer to the Judicial branch. Nor did the limit on the attorney general's removal power unconstitutionally interfere with executive authority. The decision, in contrast to *Bowsher,* embraces a more flexible view of the separation of powers.

This was again evident in the Court's sustaining constitutionality of the United States Sentencing Commission, an unusual agency Congress had set up in the Judicial branch in the Sentencing Reform Act of 1984. Concerned about the need for uniformity in federal sentencing, it empowered the commission to set out binding sentencing guidelines for various federal crimes. Its seven members, at least three of whom had to be federal judges, were appointed by the president and were removable by him. In *Mistretta v. United States* (1989), Justice Harry Blackmun held that judicial independence was not compromised by placing the commission in the Judicial branch or by requiring judges serve on it and share their power with nonjudges or by giving the President powers to appoint and remove them from the commission. Nor did Congress excessively delegate legislative power

to the commission whose part in setting out sentencing guidelines and rules was "particularly appropriate."

After several years of debating the issue, Congress passed the Line Item Veto Act in 1996, authorizing the president to strike out specific spending provisions or tax benefits in appropriations bills, a power similar to that possessed by several governors over state legislation. Instead of being forced to sign or veto an entire bill, which often might contain pet "pork barrel" projects of individual members of Congress, the president could sign and veto single items. Where he did so, the struck items would not become law unless within 30 days Congress passed a bill restoring them (which could itself be subject to presidential veto). In the law's first 18 months, President Clinton used his new power more than 80 times. Challenges to two of these actions were brought by aggrieved parties, New York City hospitals that would have benefited from vetoed funds and a group of Idaho potato farmers who would have received a particular tax benefit. In the cases, consolidated as *Clinton v. City of New York* (1998) (p. 468), the Supreme Court held the line item veto unconstitutional as a violation of the law-making procedures of Article I-7. There was no provision in the Constitution, Justice Stevens declared, "that authorizes the President to enact, to amend, or repeal statutes."

Congressional Investigation

The power of Congress to inform itself, though not mentioned in the Constitution, is clearly implied from its law-making authority. Through standing or ad hoc committees, each chamber has conducted formal investigations dating to the House's 1792 inquiry into the disastrous St. Clair expedition. Now dozens of hearings take place each year. The vast majority raise no constitutional issues of separation of power or of individual rights. They have produced valuable information Congress has used to enact legislation

The Man Who Followed Warren

His appointment was something of a surprise. On May 21, 1969, President Nixon nominated Warren Earl Burger to become chief justice of the Supreme Court; he was confirmed two weeks later. Burger had been an able though not distinguished judge on the District of Columbia Federal Court of Appeals and was almost totally unknown to the general public. He was a critic of judicial activism, a conservative on many legal issues including matters of criminal justice, and ethically had an unblemished record. These characteristics appealed to the president, who in his fifth month of office faced not only appointing a successor to Earl Warren but an opportunity to begin to remake the liberal Court Warren had led.

That the chief justiceship was vacant at all was the result of political happenstance. A year earlier, Warren had informed then-President Johnson that he intended to retire and would leave as soon as Johnson chose a successor. The president quickly nominated his old friend and political confidant, Associate Justice Abe Fortas. Before Fortas could be confirmed, it was revealed that the former Washington lawyer had accepted a retainer fee from a private foundation after he had joined the Court. In October 1968, he asked that his name be withdrawn. With only a month to go before the presidential election, Republicans anticipating victory were determined to deny the lameduck Johnson an opportunity to fill the chief justiceship. Johnson did not make another nomination, and Warren stayed on until the new president, in this case his old California political foe, could make the appointment.

Burger had grown up in humble circumstances in St. Paul, Minnesota. He turned down a scholarship to Princeton because it would not have permitted him to help with family finances. Instead, he worked his way through two years at the University of Minnesota and attended law school—St. Paul College of Law, now William Mitchell College of Law—at night. He later joined a St. Paul law firm and taught law at his alma mater as an adjunct Professor. He soon became active in civil reform in St. Paul and in Republican state politics. He was floor manager of former-governor Harold Stassen's presidential candidacies at the 1948 and 1952 Republican conventions. When Stassen withdrew in 1952, Burger helped swing delegates from Minnesota and several other states to Eisenhower. The following

or to review the performance of executive officials and the operation of laws already passed. Many also have important effect on public opinion.

Questioning high administration officials, if sometimes unwelcome by the executive, is commonplace and is usually effected in a spirit of cooperation. Executive privilege, which the president may claim, is not available to subordinates, though on rare occasions presidents have or-

dered them to withhold certain information. Most constitutional issues arising from Congressional investigations have come from encounters with nongovernmental witnesses. These have raised questions of the scope and relevance of the investigation, the power of Congress to compel cooperation, and the legal rights of uncooperative witnesses. The Supreme Court has walked a fine line between not interfering with a legitimate basic power of a coequal branch and the protec-

year he was appointed assistant attorney general for the civil division of the Justice Department. In 1956, Eisenhower appointed him to the federal appellate bench.

Burger served 17 years as chief justice, longer than all but three other chiefs. He was not notably effective as jurisprudential leader, being more of an advocate than conciliator or consensus-builder. Even here, the intellectual poles of the Burger Court were represented by William Rehnquist on the right and William Brennan on the left. Burger was not the most enthusiastic justice in consolidating Warren advances in civil liberties. He took the lead in narrowing several Warren Court criminal justice decisions and on limiting the access of litigants to the federal courts. He advocated greater constitutional accommodation of public aid to parochial schools and, as shown in several cases in this chapter, a more formal view of separated powers, one that underscored independence of the three branches. Burger's best known and probably most important opinion was that for a unanimous Court in *United States v. Nixon,* which in an ironic twist, ended the presidency of the person who had appointed him.

Burger's greatest contribution as chief justice may have been his off-the-bench work on behalf of court administrative reform. In this arena, his efforts rival those of Taft. He was a leading force in creation of the Institution for Court Management for training professional court administrators, and the National Center for State Courts, for pooling state judicial resources. He advocated six-person juries, now used in many federal jurisdictions, and worked toward improving the quality of trial lawyers in the federal courts.

His initiatives were felt in the Supreme Court as well. Oral arguments were shortened from two hours to one. On opinion day, justices read summaries rather than the full text of their opinions from the bench. Administrative support for the Justices was increased. Burger's efforts helped relieve the overload of cases at all levels of the federal judiciary. On his retirement in 1986, the Conference of State Chief Justices and State Court Administrators paid him high tribute, resolving that he had done "more than any person in history to improve the operation of our nation's courts."*

A large man with strong, even features, a deep well-modulated voice, and a shock of flowing white hair, the chief justice seemed almost cast for the role by Hollywood. Though he was often criticized as being austere and aloof from his fellow justices, those who worked for him in the Justice Department and on the Court usually felt differently. He maintained especially close relationships with his clerks. A regular feature of their Saturday workday was lunch prepared by the chief justice, an accomplished cook, in a small kitchen he had installed in his chambers.

Burger was one of the few justices to enjoy productive years of retirement. He enthusiastically and energetically chaired the five-year Bicentennial Commission for celebrating the two hundredth anniversary of the Constitution. He died on June 22, 1995, only months after publishing the book *It Is So Ordered: A Constitution Unfolds.*

* Quoted in Clare Cushman, ed., *The Supreme Court Justices* (Washington: Congressional Quarterly Press, 1995), 483–484.

---

tion of individual rights against abuse of that power.

Early on, Congress assumed it had inherent power to cite for contempt and punish private citizens who endangered its work. This power was upheld but limited in a noninvestigatory case in which a man who had offered a bribe to a Congressman was brought before the Speaker of the House and declared guilty of contempt. In *Anderson v. Dunn* (1821), the Court sus-

tained the contempt power as necessary for self-preservation, but imprisonment had to end with the next adjournment of Congress. Congress passed remedial legislation in 1857 partly because of this limit and partly to turn contempt cases over to the courts so that it would not be burdened with proceedings that often proved lengthy. A subpoenaed witness who refused to appear or to "answer any question pertinent to the question under inquiry" would be guilty of a misdemeanor punishable by a fine and imprisonment up to a year.

In *McGrain v. Dougherty* (1927), a case growing out of Congress's investigation of former Attorney General Harry Dougherty's failure to prosecute apparent wrongdoers in the well-publicized Teapot Dome oil-lease scandal, the Court clarified the scope of Congress's enforceable investigatory authority. Dougherty's brother, Mally, subpoenaed to appear refused to do so, claiming that the purpose of the inquiry was not to gather information for legislation but to put his brother on trial. The Supreme Court, though observing that the Senate did not have a general right to pry into private affairs, held that an inquiry into whether the Justice Department had properly discharged its duties would be presumed to serve a legislative purpose unless shown otherwise. That being so, a witness could refuse to cooperate only if the questions asked were "not pertinent to the matter under inquiry."

McCarthyism

Early Cold War concerns about Communist infiltration of government and other institutions led to dramatic new use of the investigatory power and, in the hands of demagogic figures, to abuses of individual liberties. In February 1950, an obscure first-term Republican Senator from Wisconsin, Joseph McCarthy, charged that 205 card-carrying Communists were still working in the State Department and shaping its policies. Though unable to prove these charges, which were later found baseless by the Senate Foreign Relations Committee, McCarthy became a force in American politics overnight.

With the election of Dwight Eisenhower in 1952, the Republicans captured control of the Senate and McCarthy became chair of its Permanent Subcommittee on Investigations. From there he launched more than 150 inquiries into Communist activity in high levels of government, universities, business and professional organizations, and labor unions. Thousands of

witnesses were called, many innocent of Communist association, to have their past or present loyalty questioned—often by unnamed accusers on undisclosed evidence. Those who dared to invoke their Fifth Amendment privilege against self-incrimination were labeled "Fifth Amendment Communists." Accusations got daily headlines as McCarthy proved himself a shrewd manipulator of media coverage. Those who might have sued for defamation could not because McCarthy refused to be specific outside the confines of Congress, where what he said was protected by the Speech and Debate Clause of Article I-6.

The counterpart of McCarthy's committee in the House was the Un-American Activities Committee (HUAC), created in 1938. It made a name for itself after the war by investigating the alleged espionage of Alger Hiss in the State Department and supposed Communist influence in the film industry. Neither McCarthy's committee nor HUAC uncovered even one Communist in a high place and their inquiries were not central to later legislation. As their chairmen cheerfully admitted, the chief purpose was to publicize and expose, and thus make the public aware of threats to internal security.

This "educating" use of the investigatory power, though not new or sinister in itself, was carried to a witch-hunting extreme. These inquiries cost many persons their jobs, careers, and friends, leaving them blacklisted with no adequate way to clear their names. Beyond this extreme, the probes were generally based on political opinion and association. As the net of publicity was cast more widely, it snared those merely "soft" on Communism, which included many liberals who simply had reservations about Cold War policies.

When the Supreme Court came to rein in the investigatory power in *Watkins v. United States* (1957) (p. 418), McCarthy had already fallen. Early in 1954, he charged that Communists had infiltrated the Army Signal Corps at Fort Monmouth, New Jersey. The Army, in turn, accused McCarthy of seeking preferential treatment for a former aid who was then in uniform. Lengthy, sensational televised hearings followed that exposed McCarthy to the nation as an irresponsible, bullying character assassin. With the urging of the president, who had denounced McCarthy's tactics, the Senate voted to censure him. He was never a power again.

The work and influence of HUAC, however, continued. Watkins, a labor union officer called to testify, answered questions about his past Communist association but refused to answer those about past activities of persons he knew to be former Communists, claiming the questions were not relevant to the committee's inquiry. In an opinion written by Chief Justice Earl Warren, the Supreme Court overturned his conviction for contempt. In setting up HUAC the House had not described its purpose with "sufficient pertinency" so that a witness could judge whether the questions put to him had to do with the committee's legislative purpose. (In the 1857 contempt law under which Watkins was convicted, only failure to answer a "pertinent" question was a crime.) More broadly Warren said that inquiry could not be an end in itself, since compelling a testimony about unorthodox or unpopular beliefs could interfere with freedom of speech.

The Watkins decision brought a storm of criticism upon the Court. In Congress, several proposals were introduced to curb its authority, including one to remove contempt prosecutions from its appellate review. These efforts were unsuccessful, partly because the Court soon retreated from its position. In *Barenblatt v. United States* (1959), it sustained the contempt conviction of a HUAC witness who had refused to answer questions about his beliefs and membership in a Communist club at the University of Michigan. Justice John M. Harlan, II held that the pertinence of the questions had been shown, even though the committee had not been much more forthcoming than it had been with Watkins. The government's interest in self-preservation outweighed Barenblatt's free speech rights.

In a series of contempt cases in the early 1960s, the Court again tightened the procedural reins on HUAC by closely examining the "pertinence" requirement for specific questions and the general authorizing elements of the committee's investigatory power. Yet it deferred to the separation of powers by not reviewing Congress's motives or the general scope of its authority. Nor did the Court assert the primacy of free speech rights over Congress's power to inquire. A partial thawing of the Cold War in the 1960s and ebbing public concern about subversion caused HUAC power to decline. In 1975, the committee was abolished by the House.

Later Issues

The free speech question arose again in 1975, this time as a ground for blocking a subpoena for documents. The Senate Judiciary Subcommittee on Internal Security had issued a subpoena on a bank to get financial records of a group that had protested the Vietnam War and run coffeehouses near military bases. Since the records included a list of contributors, the group argued they were protected by the First Amendment's freedoms of speech and association. In *Eastland v. U.S. Servicemen's Fund,* Chief Justice Burger denied the claim, saying the subpoenas were issued to further an inquiry Congress had the power to make.

Witnesses in judicial proceedings and legislative hearings may invoke the Fifth Amendment's privilege against self-incrimination to avoid testimony they believe could be used against them in a criminal case. The right may be overcome by a grant of immunity from any prosecution based on testimony given. When the recipient is a legislative witness already under indictment, the grant can pose a conflict between legislature and judiciary. This happened in the Watergate affair when several witnesses before Senator Ervin's Senate committee were granted immunity to compel their testimony, over the objection of the special prosecutor. Though the Supreme Court held in *Kastigar v. United States*

(1972) that an immunized witness may be prosecuted for criminal acts they may be required to discuss, none of the prosecuting evidence may come from the testimony.

The issue arose again when the Senate granted immunity to Colonel Oliver North in its investigation of the Iran-Contra affair in 1986. North was later prosecuted and convicted on several criminal counts having to do with the affair. In *United States v. North* (1991), the Supreme Court reversed on the ground that the trial judge did not find out whether North's televised testimony before the Senate's committee may have influenced witnesses at his trial. In circumstances like these, the Congressional committee must weigh the political and legislative value of the testimony against the chance that a later conviction for wrongdoing will not be sustained.

The Modern Court

When Franklin Roosevelt won reelection for a third term in 1940, the Supreme Court was a different body and institution than it had been in the battle over the New Deal four years before. Roosevelt appointees, now a majority of the Court, had begun to transform its constitutional jurisprudence. Foreshadowed by Justice Stone's Footnote Four in the 1937 Carolene Products case, review of government economic regulation became more circumspect and, substantively, laissez-faire economic principles were no longer constitutional requirements.

But the new deference to legislative judgment would not be general. Stone had suggested that laws affecting the "political processes," such as the right to vote and communicate, and those directed at "insular minorities" might get greater scrutiny. His footnote was essentially a new job description for the Court as it retreated from one vicinity to build in another. Cases presenting issues of individual rights and freedoms came to occupy half or more of its docket. The shift began almost immediately after the "Roosevelt Court" was in place and reached its zenith

in the Warren Court a generation later. There was only a modest retreat in the later Burger and Rehnquist Courts.

Role in the Separation of Powers

The power and influence of the Court has ebbed and flowed throughout its history. Without sword or purse and without the republican authority that comes with being elected, it has often seemed a junior partner in the national triumvirate, "the least dangerous branch" that Hamilton had described in *The Federalist Papers*. Yet the Constitution is a legal document, and issues arising under it are inevitably cast in legal terms. When Marshall declared in *Marbury v. Madison* that "it is emphatically the province and duty of the judicial department to say what the law is," he capitalized on this simple fact. When a law is alleged to violate the Constitution, saying what the law is is to interpret the Constitution. At times this power of review can make the Judicial branch first among equals. It can also cast the Court as the arbiter of separated power at the same time it may be a party of interest.

Recognizing that conflict may reside in these roles, the Court has been cautious in ruling on the basic powers of the elected branches. Its reticence has contributed importantly to the growth of modern presidential authority. In the realm of war power, as we have seen, the Court's review is close to nonexistent. The theoretical basis for not interfering with work assigned to another branch is the doctrine of "political questions." First used by Chief Justice Taney in *Luther v. Borden* (1849), the term is misleading, since most important decisions deal with political matters. But Taney used it to refer to issues that the Constitution has seemed to commit to the president or to Congress, such as the guarantee to each state of a republican form of government and the protection of each state from domestic violence in Article IV-4. These were also matters for which readily applicable judicial standards were lacking and for which courts would have difficulty enforcing decisions.

The Court has consistently held arguments appealing to the Guarantee Clause of Article IV-4 present nonjusticiable political questions. When Oregon voters used the initiative process in the state constitution, to directly enact a 2 percent tax on utility companies, the companies refused to pay it. They argued that the law, not having been enacted by a legislature, violated the guarantee of a republican form of government in which laws are made by representatives, not voters directly. In *Pacific States Telephone and Telegraph v. Oregon* (1912), the Court refused jurisdiction, holding the matter a political not judicial question. Remedy lay with Congress, which has responsibility for the guarantee and could enforce it by refusing to admit representatives from the state if it concluded the government was not republican in form.

In *Coleman v. Miller* (1939), an aggrieved party challenged whether Kansas could ratify the Child Labor Amendment after once rejecting it and 13 years after Congress had sent it to the states. The Court held the issues were political questions in keeping with Congress's power to propose amendments in Article V and therefore must be decided by Congress.

Seven years later, the Court held the matter of reapportioning Congressional legislative districts, challenged under the Guarantee Clause, was also a political question the Courts were ill-suited to decide. In *Colegrove v. Green* (1946), Justice Frankfurter wrote that ordering a state legislature to reapportion itself would take the Court into a "political thicket" interfering with "the very being of Congress." [329 U.S. 549 at 554, 556] In this instance, there were wide population disparities among Illinois Congressional districts because they had not been redrawn since 1901. Population inequality in static legislative districts was widespread and reduced the representation of urban and suburban areas that had seen large population gains while allowing representation of rural areas that had suffered declines. Again, the Court said the remedy lay with Congress.

But in 1962 in *Baker v. Carr* (p. 424), it took a very different stand, holding that the federal courts could hear reapportionment challenges that were based on the equal protection clause of the Fourteenth Amendment under which, it said, there were settled, judicially applicable standards of fairness. *Baker* did not decide that the districts—in this case those in Tennessee—were malapportioned, only that federal courts might hear cases raising the issue. It opened the door to an array of apportionment cases, leading eventually to development of the "one person, one vote" requirement that districts be almost equal in population.

Of doctrinal importance in *Baker* was Justice William Brennan's formula for identifying political questions. They were issues in which there was or would be one or more of the following: a textual Constitutional commitment to another branch, a lack of judicially discoverable standards, nonjudicial discretion called for through an initial policy decision, a lack of respect shown by the courts for another branch, a need for adherence to a political decision already made, or embarrassment from "multifarious pronouncements from various departments."

In the tenor of *Baker,* the Court narrowed the political questions doctrine in several later decisions. In *Powell v. McCormick,* for example, it rejected the argument that Congress's decision to exclude a member was wholly a "political" one. And in *Davis v. Bandemer* (1986), it held that gerrymandering—the exotic shaping of election districts to under- or overrepresent partisan interests—was not a political question that should be left entirely to the legislature. In this case, Indiana Democrats had challenged the Republican-controlled legislature's redrawing of districts as unconstitutionally discriminatory. On the merits, the Court did not find the districts unfair, but the decision opened the door to judicial review of gerrymander issues.

The later Rehnquist Court has been sensitive about guarding its role as preeminent interpreter of the Constitution against usurpation by Congress. In the Religious Freedom Restoration Act of 1993, Congress tried to establish a standard for interpreting the Free Exercise Clause of the First

Amendment that recognized a right broader than that contained in the Court's own interpretation. In *City of Boerne v. Flores* (1997), the Court reacted by holding that Congress could neither limit a constitutional right that had been declared by the Court nor, as in this case, add to one. Borrowing from *Marbury v. Madison,* it observed, "When the Court has interpreted the Constitution, it has acted within the province of the Judicial Branch, which embraces the duty to say what the law is."

Deciding to Decide

The political question doctrine, which helps to define boundaries of the branches, is also an exercise in judicial self-restraint and is complemented by other principles and practices the Court has developed if not always followed. These follow from a sense of judicial modesty and prudence that tempers the Court's review of the acts of co-equal branches that have, as the Court does not, republican authority to govern. They also show awareness that the Court may be most powerful when it appears to be least political. "Overstepping," on the other hand, can bring retaliation from a president who may find ways to circumvent a decision or from a Congress that may change the Court's structure or appellate jurisdiction or "correct" it by proposing a Constitutional amendment.

Boundaries the Court has set out between federal judicial power and state government that have helped to shape the modern federal system are discussed in the next chapter.

Interpreting Law. In *Ashwander v. Tennessee Valley Authority* (1936), in which the Court rejected a constitutional challenge to the New Deal's great regional development project, Justice Brandeis argued in a concurring opinion that the court need not have reached the issue of constitutionality. As he saw it, the dispute was simply one between a utility company and a group of shareholders. The concurrence was particularly notable because Brandeis formulated a set of guidelines, not entirely original with him, for ruling on statutes that came under constitu-

tional challenge. The Ashwander rules, as they have become called, can also be read as statements of judicial deference to the legislature.

The main points were that the Court (1) should not anticipate a question of constitutional law or make a constitutional ruling unless absolutely necessary, (2) should not cast a constitutional ruling more broadly than that needed to decide a case, (3) if possible, should base a decision on statutory rather than constitutional grounds, and (4) if several readings of a statute are possible, should prefer that which avoids finding the law unconstitutional. Appearing in a concurring opinion, these guidelines were not and have never been officially adopted by the Court, but they have become generally followed.

Jurisdiction and Justiciability. Jurisdiction, the authority to hear a case, is the door to judicial power. For the federal courts, it is set out generally in Article III-2, which specifies nine kinds of cases or controversies. These are defined by party (the United States, two or more states, citizens of different states, ambassadors, and public ministers) and by subject (questions arising under the Constitution, federal laws and treaties, or admiralty and maritime law). The Supreme Court's original jurisdiction—its authority to hear a suit from its start—is confined to a small range of cases completely described in Article III-3. In all other cases, the Court has appellate jurisdiction as regulated by Congress. In its power to create lower courts, Congress can within the Article III confines of "cases" or "controversies," set out both original and appellate jurisdiction of those courts.

Within the jurisdictional prescriptions, the Supreme Court has great discretion in the cases that it and lower federal courts hear and decide. It has developed standards of justiciability for determining whether a case is fit for judicial decision. Each of these standards, like the doctrine of political questions itself, contains an element of self-restraint that narrows or confines judicial power. For example, the Court has interpreted "cases" and "controversies" describing federal jurisdiction in Article III to mean that it will hear only true adversary proceedings—disputes between parties whose rights or interests are in actual conflict—not those that are collusive or merely friendly.

Similarly, the Court will not rule on hypothetical questions or give merely advisory opinions. It had decided against the latter when it politely refused President Washington's request for advice on provisions in a 1793 treaty with France. Referring to the separation of powers, it told the president it could give opinions only on issues in litigation before it, a stand that kept the Court from evolving, at least in part, as a legal advisor to the president.

Other self-imposed limits include ripeness, mootness, and standing. The first two are matters of timing. A lack of ripeness, as the metaphor suggests, refers to a dispute not yet ready in its factual development for adjudication, that is, for a court to determine legal rights, wrongs, injuries, and remedies. The Court considers cases moot and not given to further proceeding when factual developments have ended the conflict between parties, at least about legal rights. In *DeFunis v. Odegaard* (1974), for example, the Court held that a suit challenging a law school's admissions policy giving preferential treatment to some black applicants, by a white applicant first denied admission, was moot. The applicant, who had been admitted pending the litigation, would graduate before the Court could reach a decision on the merits of the case. An important exception to the mootness doctrine applies to women challenging restrictions on abortion, since pregnancy in most instances would probably have ended before rights could be resolved in court.

Standing to sue is another aspect of justiciability and refers to who may maintain a lawsuit in the federal courts and who may not. The chief requirement in satisfying standing is that the plaintiff have a sufficient personal interest in suit, which usually means allegation of personal injury or deprivation of a right. Problems arise when plaintiffs challenge government action but can claim only that someone else has been injured or that they have been injured only in common with all other citizens or taxpayers.

When a taxpayer challenged a federal grant-in-aid program providing money to states for maternal and child health care as being an intrusion on state power reserved under the Tenth Amendment and thus an unconstitutional use of her tax money, in *Frothingham v.* Mellon (1923), the Supreme "Court held that she lacked standing to sue. Speaking for a unanimous court, Justice Sutherland held for a unanimous Court that a taxpayer's interest in the use of federal funds was "comparatively minute and indeterminable." In holding that there was no generalized "citizen standing" to challenge government acts, the Court was clearly concerned that federal taxpayer suits could produce litigious challenges to nearly every national expenditure and thus transform the federal courts into general reviewers of almost all acts of Congress.

It is a measure of the liberal judicial activism of the Warren years that the Court should partly retreat from this position and make the federal courts more receptive to general citizen challenges to governmental acts. In *Flast v. Cohen* (1968) (p. 427), it sustained standing for a taxpayer who claimed the use of federal education funds to aid students in parochial schools violated the First Amendment's establishment clause requiring separation of church and state. Chief Justice Warren held that Flast had met the two requirements of federal taxpayer standing. Her challenge was to spending under the taxing and spending clause of Article I-8 rather than to expenditures incidental to Congress's other enumerated powers, and she had alleged the spending violated a specific Constitutional prohibition rather than a generalized limit such as the Tenth Amendment, argued in *Frothingham*. As expected, the decision opened the federal courts to a barrage of taxpayer suits challenging the constitutionality of various federal policies without a showing of personal injury or harm.

In the 1970s, the more conservative Burger Court began to narrow the application of *Flast*. In *United States v. Richardson* (1974), taxpayer standing was denied in a suit asserting that Congress's failure to disclose the budget of the Central Intelligence Agency was a violation of Article I-9 that requires publication of public expenditures. The Court said the suit did not directly

When the Court Chose a President

The decision in *Bush v. Gore* (p. 470) effectively ended the 2000 presidential contest, 35 days after voters went to the polls. In its ruling, the Rehnquist Court, which often sees itself, correctly or not, as pledged to the principle of self-restraint, wrote a bold new chapter in judicial activism.

The election of 2000, won by Governor George W. Bush with 271 electoral votes to 267 for Vice President Albert Gore, was the closest since 1876; the popular vote, which Gore won by four-tenths of 1 percent, was the closest since 1960. For five weeks, the outcome hinged on Florida's 25 electoral votes. The state's returns the day after the election showed Bush the winner by 1,784 votes, a hairline three-one hundredths of 1 percent of nearly six million cast. The next a statewide machine recount (mandated by Florida law wherever a margin of victory is less than one-half of 1 percent), again showed Bush the winner but by only 327, later increased to 930 when several thousand absentee ballots were counted.

Exercising a right under Florida law, Gore asked for a hand recount of ballots in 4 of the state's 67 counties, all heavily Democratic. When Florida Secretary of State, Katherine Harris, charged with certifying the state's election results, refused to waive the statutory deadline so that manual recounting then underway could be completed, the Florida Supreme Court, at Gore's petition, voted unanimously to extend the deadline 12 days until November 26 and ordered the results of the hand recounting to be included in the eventual certification.

This led to a tedious but well-televised spectacle of teams closely examining each ballot card to determine whether it had been punched through for Bush, for Gore, both or neither. Disputes arose about whether a valid vote had been cast where the small punched out part of the card—a "chad"—was still attached to the card and, if it was, how many corners had to be loosened. Most controversial were ballots that were merely "dimpled," that is, indented but not punched through at all. The counties applied different standards in making these decisions and, in one county, different standards at different stages of the recount.

At the expiration of the new deadline of November 26 and with hand recounting not completed in one county and discontinued in another, the secretary of state certified the results at that point as official, with Bush still leading by 537 votes. The following day Gore sued to contest the official certification. Under Florida law this required the challenger to show that enough legal votes were rejected "to change or place in doubt the result of the election." After a hurried one-and-a-half day trial in which Gore's lawyers were held not to have proved the case, an appeal was taken to the Florida Supreme Court. Four days later, December 8, this time sharply divided 4-3, the Court overruled the trial court and ordered an immediate manual recount of all "undervotes" in the state, that is, of those ballots which machines had not recorded a vote for president, about 45,000 in all. It also ordered that all hand recounted tallies already completed, including those after the extended deadline, be included in the statewide total. The court, offering only the spare guidance that a legal vote was one "in which there is a clear indication of the intent of the voter," remanded the case to a trail judge for execution. After a hearing, the judge decided to allow each of the 67 county canvassing boards to set its own standards for detecting voter intent. Looming over the entire matter and contributing to haste was the apparent deadline of December 12, the last day federal law allows the state legislature to appoint a slate of presidential electors if it believes a valid slate has not been chosen.

At this point, Bush filed an emergency petition with the United States Supreme Court to halt the manual recounting. The Court issued a temporary injunction late Saturday, December 9, heard oral argument, Monday, December 11, and issued its decision at 10 p.m. Tuesday, December 12. By a vote of 7-2, in an unsigned per curiam opinion (very likely written by Justice O'Connor or Justice Kennedy), it held the recount order of the Florida Supreme Court, at least as it stood, to violate the equal protection clause of the Fourteenth Amendment by failing to provide a uniform standard for hand counting. (The Court also noted the state court's failure to include an additional 110,000 "overvotes"—ballots read by machines having more than one vote for president—in its recount order.)

The state court had not met the minimum requirement for non-arbitrary treatment of voters necessary to secure the fundamental right. Florida's basic command for the count of legally cast votes is to consider the "intent of the voter." This is unobjectionable as an abstract proposition and a starting principle. The problem inheres in the absence of specific standards to ensure its equal application. The formulation of uniform rules to determine intent based on these recruiting circumstances is practicable and, we conclude, necessary.

The Court was also concerned about procedures, noting that the Florida court did not specify who would recount the ballots. The county canvassing boards were forced to pull together ad hoc teams comprised of judges from various circuits who had no previous training in handling and interpreting ballots. Furthermore, while others were permitted to observe, they were prohibited from objecting the recount. The recount process . . . is inconsistent with the minimum procedures necessary to protect the fundamental right of each voter in the special instance of a statewide recount under authority of a single judicial officer.

What to do about these defects, however, divided the justices more sharply. Five of the seven in the majority—O'Connor, Kennedy, Rehnquist, Scalia, and Thomas—concluded that because "the recount cannot be conducted in compliance with the requirements of equal protection and due process without substantial additional work." there was no chance that that could be done by the apparent deadline of December 12 (which was also the day of the Court's decision). Thus they voted to reverse the Florida Supreme Court's recount order.

On this point, two justices of the majority—Souter and Breyer—dissented and argued for remanding the case to the Florida Supreme Court with instructions to establish uniform standards for manual recounting and allowing it the remaining five days until December 18, the day the electors actually meet, to do so. Souter, admitting that the hand counting of even the 60,000 undervotes in five days was "a tall order," thought the state courts should have opportunity to try.

Justices Stevens and Ginsberg, who joined the dissenting views of Souter and Breyer on the re-

mand question, also dissented on the constitutional issues, finding no violation of equal protection or due process in the lack of uniform standards, the procedures for recounting, or the Florida Supreme Court's order that the partial recounts completed earlier be accepted, as made.

Three justices of the majority—Rehnquist, Scalia and Thomas—argued in a concurring opinion that by ordering a hand recount and by changing deadlines for certification, the Florida Supreme Court has also violated Article II-1 of the Constitution, which specifies that it is the state legislature, not the judiciary, that decides "the manner" of choosing electors. On this point, four justices dissented, arguing that the state supreme court rather than usurping the legislature's role had merely interpreted implementing statutes the legislature had passed.

The decision of five members of the majority thus ended the presidential election contest. The decision of seven members finding fault with the Florida Supreme Court may have done so anyway because there was small chance that a constitutionally acceptable recount process could have been mounted and actual counting completed in five days.

Reaction to the decision was as predictably divided as the contest of the Florida vote and the election itself had been. Some analysts praised the Court for ending the drawn out, chaotic, and constitutionally uncertain process and for heading off an even greater constitutional crisis. Others criticized the decision and its activism as usurping process underway in the state courts that might had led to greater clarity of the state's vote and possibly revealing a different winner.

What might have happened had the Court not intervened and refused to hear the case? The matter is speculative, of course, but if the recount had given Gore the greater number of votes and he was certified the winner, the lack of uniform standards would almost certainly have clouded its legitimacy. Also, the Florida legislature, controlled by the Republicans, and arguing that the recounting was flawed, very likely would have exercised its legal right to appoint a slate of electors, this one pledged to Bush. With competing slates in the field, the matter would have been thrust into the hands of the new Congress convening in January, only days away from the

(Continued)

presidential inauguration. Which, if either, slate would have been accepted? If neither, would Gore be the winner because he had the majority of remaining electoral votes or would the election be given to the House of Representatives because he did not have a majority of all 538 electoral votes? Who would decide these questions? With Republicans holding a slim margin in the House and the Senate evenly divided with Gore himself in his last days as vice president holding the tie-breaking vote, a protracted and rancorous debate could have been expected, followed by yet another close decision, the legitimacy of which would be far from clear. If not a constitutional crisis, it would have been a constitutional spectacle beyond parallel.

A second question may also be asked: Did the Court do serious damage to its own authority by a ruling that effectively chose the president? The Court has had many reputational ups and downs in its history, but for the most part it has steered clear of the fray of electoral politics. Public opinion, measured in polls immediately after the decision, was considerably more supportive of the Court than critical. History's reading, however, may well ponder what Justice Robert Jackson once said of the Court: "If there were a super Supreme Court, a substantial proportion of our reversals . . . would also be reversed. We are not final because we are infallible, but we are infallible only because we are final." [concurring in *Brown v. Allen*, 344 U S 443, 540 (1953)]

challenge an appropriation and, reiterating *Frothingham*, held the plaintiff had not suffered a personal injury from the failure of disclosure. In *Valley Forge Christian College v. Americans United for the Separation of Church and State* (1982), plaintiffs tried to block conveyance of several vacated army hospital buildings to a church-supported college arguing that it would violate the Establishment Clause. They were held not to have standing under the *Flast* rule. The Court said the property transfer was not under Congress's taxing and spending authority in Article I-8 but under Article IV-3 provisions allowing it to dispose of property belonging to the United States. In *Allen v. Wright* (1984), a group of black taxpayers was held to lack standing to challenge methods used by the Internal Revenue Service to determine whether certain tax-exempt private schools discriminated by race and thus violated the terms of federal law granting tax exempt status to educational institutions. The plaintiffs, the Court said, had not shown that IRS administrative practices made desegregation of their school district more difficult.

Like the doctrine of political questions, the rules of standing, ripeness, and mootness, and against advisory opinions self-imposed restraint. Though the Court may widen or narrow them from time to time, all have the effect of limiting the scope of judicial power. Doctrines of self-restraint are useful, perhaps even vital, to legitimating the authority of a nonelected body that rules on the meaning of the Constitution and places limits on its elected coequal branches. At the same time, the discretionary character of the doctrines has allowed the Court to influence policy through them without directly appearing to do so.

Composition and Change

The work of the Supreme Court—the kinds of cases its hears, its activism or self-restraint, its deferring to or checking of Congress and the president—also depends on the political views, jurisprudential skills, and personalities of the justices who sit on it.

When Justice Stone succeeded Chief Justice Hughes in 1941, he presided over a past-New Deal Court on which Most had served for four years or less. Under Stone, the "Roosevelt Court" completed the ratification of Congress's new regulatory power under the commerce clause. Its deference to legislative judgment on economic matters was generally carried to state authority as well. But as the Court turned more and more to matters of individual rights, signs of a new activism and new internal discord began to appear.

An able jurist, Stone proved ineffective as leader of the new Court, the members of which he once called "a team of wild horses." Though all the Roosevelt appointees were New Dealers, most had come from successful political careers and none had had important judicial experience. By temperament, most were highly individualist. Inevitably, there were clashes of personality and judicial philosophy. By the time of Stone's death in 1946, two poles were evident. One, centering around Justices Black and Douglas, represented a more activist judicial review, less attention to precedent, and a tendency to move toward absolutism in claims of rights and liberties. The other, centering around Justices Frankfurter and Jackson, stood for a more traditional self-restraint, more concern for continuity in the law, and a greater willingness to balance public and governmental interests against those of individual rights. Dissenting and concurring opinions greatly increased.

President Harry Truman chose his close friend Fred Vinson as Stone's successor, believing the affable former Treasury secretary might be able to unify the Court. The hope proved vine as Vinson, without much experience in the law, was found to be intellectually inferior to most of his colleagues. Dealing with the tensions produced by internal security cases and those demanding a reinterpretation of equal protection and other rights, the Court grew more divided than ever. Cases decided unanimously dropped to an all-time low. If the Vinson Court had an identity, it was supplied by a middle group of justices that included Vinson and other Truman appointees: the Republican Senator Harold Burton, the Democrats Tom Clark, who had been Truman's attorney general, Sherman Minton, a federal judge, and the Roosevelt holdover Stanley Reed. They often voted to sustain government action. None possessed the style or originality of the more polarized justices.

Vinson died less than a year after the election of Dwight Eisenhower, and the moderate Republican president chose Earl Warren, the moderate Republican California governor who had been first his rival then supporter for the 1952 nomination, as the new chief justice. The judicially inexperienced but politically skillful Warren was successful where Stone and Vinson had failed, in unifying the Court and giving it direction.

Under Warren's leadership, the Court embraced a liberal activism unparalleled in its history, its decisions having substantial effect on American political, social, and cultural life. Starting with the school desegregation case in Warren's first year, the Court read an extensive protection of civil rights into the constitutional requirement of equal protection. It gave an expansive interpretation the various freedoms of speech, press, association, and exercise of religion in the First Amendment and substantially broadened due process and trial rights for those suspected or accused of crimes. Its civil rights decisions ended de jure racial segregation and radically changed race relations. In this, the Court acted where other branches had been unwilling or unable, much as its reapportionment decisions broke a similar long-standing deadlock in fair representation. These matters are explored in Volume II.

Though nominally the Warren Court began with the chief's appointment in October 1953, its period of greatest activism came later with the appointment of several liberal justices. They included William Brennan, a state court judge named by Eisenhower in 1957; Arthur Goldberg, a former labor lawyer and secretary of labor appointed by President Kennedy in 1962; Abe Fortas, a leading Washington lawyer appointed by President Johnson to replace Goldberg in 1965; and Thurgood Marshall, a leading civil rights attorney and later solicitor general appointed by Johnson in 1967, the first African-American to serve on the Court. Joining Warren and the pre-Warren activists Black and Douglas, the newcomers formed a strong majority for constitutional innovation. Potter Stewart, a fed-

Reading (into) the Constitution

The Supreme Court's power to review the constitutionality of governmental actions is now well-settled, but how active or restrained the Court should be in this important role continues to be a matter of sharp debate that has swirled about the modern Court. The sustained activism of the Warren period and later retreat under Chief Justices Burger and Rehnquist have honed the dispute and focused new attention on how the Constitution should be interpreted.

Critics of judicial activism emphasize the need for continuity and stability in determining constitutional meaning. They argue that the words and provisions of the Constitution should receive literal or "plain meaning" interpretation where possible and, in any case, be given strict reading rather than broad construction. If the constitutional text is not clear, then every effort should be made to determine and remain faithful to the original intent of the framers in drafting the text. Formidable weight should be given to historical context, tradition, and legal precedent. Wherever possible, important constitutional change should come through the amendment process. This jurisprudential approach today is often called "interpretivism."

Critics of it, who are sometimes unwieldingly called "noninterpretivists," are apt to see the Constitution as a "living document," the meaning of which, to borrow from Justice Oliver Wendell Holmes, should meet the "felt necessities" of the time. Thoughtful noninterpretivists do not dispute the importance of constitutional text and the intent of the framers, but they see those sources as only the beginning, not end, of constitutional interpretation. In emphasizing the need for flexibility and

adaptability, noninterpretivists point out that the constitutional text often does not yield "plain meaning" and that the original intent of the framers may not always be easily discoverable. They see the Constitution as a statement of broad principles and purposes that allow flexible application to modern circumstances and conditions. Many noninterpretivists go further and argue that the fundamental issue is not what the Constitution says or was intended to say, but what it *should* mean. They would allow various extraconstitutional principles, such as those drawn from natural law, political or moral philosophy, social science, or simply contemporary societal values, to be used to clarify, establish, or even create constitutional meaning. All noninterpretivists hold that the formal amendment process is too cumbersome to maintain adequate flexibility and would soon become strained were it to be the chief vehicle for constitutional change.

Though noninterpretivism is a modern term, the approach is consistent with the emphatic position struck by Chief Justice Hughes in the 1934 Blaisdell case to explain why the Court would uphold a state moratorium on mortgage payments even though the law appeared to be a clear violation of the contracts clause of Article I-10. Writing at a time in which the country faced a great economic emergency, Hughes argued that particular provisions of the Constitution need not be confined "to the interpretation which the framers, with the conditions and outlook of their time, would have placed upon them." Non-interpretivist activism reached its zenith during the Warren period and remains a vital element in determining constitutional meaning, particularly in the realm of civil liberties and civil rights. In the words of Justice William Brennan:

eral judge appointed by Eisenhower in 1958 and Byron White, a Kennedy appointee who had been in the Justice Department, were more moderate members of the Court. John Marshall Harlan, grandson of the first Justice Harlan, appointed by Eisenhower in 1955, and joined Justice Frankfurter as an oft-dissenting advocate of judicial self-restraint.

The Warren Court was partly an accident. The Warren and Brennan appointments were "mistakes" in the sense that Eisenhower believed he had chosen moderates, Republican in the one case, Democrat in the other. Their backgrounds, especially Warren's, gave little hint that each would become a leading proponent of an activist liberal constitutional jurisprudence.

The Constitution is not a static document whose meaning on every detail is fixed for all time by the life experience of the Framers. We have recognized in a wide variety of constitutional contexts that the practices that were in place at the time any particular guarantee was enacted into the Constitution do not necessarily fix forever the meaning of the guarantee. To be truly faithful to the Framers, "our use of the history of their time must limit itself to broad purposes, not specific practices." [Marsh v. Chambers, 463 U.S. 783 (1983), dissenting opinion]

Interpretivists respond by arguing that this approach makes the nine nonelected, life-term justices not only law-makers but constitution-amenders. When given license to go beyond the "four corners" of the document, justices can read their own values and preferences into it, becoming at best philosopher kings, at worst merely partisan advocates. Interpretivists prefer that new constitutional values be first espoused by elected branches of government. In their view, the judicial reading of extraconstitutional moral or philosophical principles into the Constitution:

> . . . teaches disrespect for the actual institutions of the American polity. These institutions are designed to achieve compromise, to slow change, to dilute absolutisms. They embody wholesome inconsistencies. They are designed, in short, to do things that abstract generalizations about the just society tend to bring into contempt . . . In a constitutional democracy the moral content of the law must be given by the morality of the framer or the legislator, never the judge. The sole task of the latter—and it is a task quite large enough for anyone's wisdom, skill, and virtue—is to translate the framer's or legislator's morality into a rule to govern unforeseen circumstances. That abstinence from giving his own desires free play, that continuing and self-conscious renunciation of power, that is the morality of the jurist."*

Thoughtful interpretivists do not claim to have a complete theory for discovering or establishing constitutional meaning, but merely that the interpretavist approach is in Justice Antonin Scalia terms "the lesser evil."†

The modern debate between interpretivists and noninterpretivists is part of a long-standing dialogue about various elements of the constitutional system, including the role of the Court among coequal branches of government, the competence of judges and the institutional capacity of courts to exercise wide political discretion and, not least, the balance to be drawn between majority rule and individual rights. The argument has never had definitive resolution and is not likely get it in the future. Nor has the Supreme Court ever adopted a single, unified theory of constitutional interpretation. Forced to deal with the many pragmatic considerations of resolving conflict in cases coming before them, most justices have avoided taking polar positions in the debate and have tolerated inconsistencies in their own interpretative positions.

This jurisprudence has helped guide an eighteenth-century document into the twenty-first century with its text and provisions largely intact. That the Constitution has been amended only 27 times (18 if the first 10, the Bill of Rights, is considered a single amending event) is a remarkable testimony to the interpretative role of the Supreme Court.

* Judge Robert Bork, "Tradition and Morality in Constitutional Law," in Mark W. Cannon and David M. O'Brien, eds., *Views from the Bench: The Judiciary and Constitutional Politics*, (Chatham, N.J.: Chatham House Publishers, 1985) 169, 171–172.
† Antonin Scalia, "Originalism: The Lesser Evil," 57 *Cincinnati Law Review* 849 (1989).

For this reason, there never was an "Eisenhower Court," though the president made three other appointments. Five new justices in a two-term presidency would ordinarily be enough to reshape the Court or at least bend it to reflect national political shifts, in this case toward the post-New Deal moderate, consolidating Republicanism that Eisenhower's two clear-cut election victories represented. In contrast, the new justices of the 1960s more closely reflected the liberal Democratic politics of their nominating presidents, Kennedy and Johnson.

Criticism of the Warren Court was similar to that heard of other activist courts: the reading of new rules into the Constitution, light regard for precedent, indifference to doctrinal reasoning, and judicial "legislating" that substituted the values of the justices for those of elected representatives. But where other aggressive Courts defended interests of an entrenched elite, the Warren Court's activist decisions, as the legal historian G. Edward White put it, "benefited blacks, disadvantaged suburban voters, atheists, criminals, pornographers, and the poor."*

A reaction to the extensive and rapid-fire constitutional changes was to be expected. It was made certain by the foundering of Johnson's liberal presidency and the election of Richard Nixon in 1968 and landslide reelection in 1972. Warren retired in 1969, allowing Nixon to appoint Warren Burger, a federal appellate judge, as chief justice. Nixon appointed three other justices in the next three years: Harry Blackmun, also a federal appellate judge, in 1970 to replace Fortas who had resigned; Lewis Powell, a lawyer in private practice, who succeeded Black on his death in 1972, and William Rehnquist, assistant attorney general, to replace Harlan who retired in 1972. By then the Warren Court was no longer.

The "Nixon Court" became the Burger Court with the appointments of John Paul Stevens, a federal appellate judge, by President Gerald Ford in 1975, and Sandra Day O'Connor, an Arizona state court judge and the first woman to sit on the Court, by President Ronald Reagan in 1981. The one Democratic president between 1969 and 1992, Jimmy Carter, had no appointments during his one term, 1977–1981.

It cannot be said that the more conservative Burger Court turned back the clock set in the Warren years. Faced with problems of giving effect to new rights, it was generally consolidating. Gains in civil rights were largely maintained, if not extended, as the Court came to deal with such complex "later" issues of discrimination as de facto segregation in the North and affirmative action. It embraced a less rigorous separation of church and state than its predecessor and was more willing to balance the needs of

state and community against "absolute" First Amendment freedoms and the due process rights of criminal defendants. More often than not, these shifts took the form of narrowing Warren Court decisions than overruling them. Landmark cases of the Warren period remained almost intact. Indeed, wholesale overruling or disregard of earlier work would have offended a conservative's respect for precedent and continuity. In a few areas—gender equality, abortion, and capital punishment—the Burger Court extended rights beyond the Warren scope. These matters are also discussed in Volume II.

As several cases in this chapter have shown, the Burger Court took a more formal view of the separation of powers between the president and Congress. With some exceptions, such as *United States v. Nixon,* it was more apt to defer to the elected branches when judicial power was at issue. As several cases in the next chapter will show, it also proved to be more sensitive to federalism and the rights of states than any Court of recent years. Despite these concerns, the Burger Court lacked the unifying themes of its predecessor. Much less often were decisions based on broad principles, ringing moral imperatives, or a manifest optimism about new uses of judicial power. More often they reflected pragmatic, sometimes gray technical concerns, fine distinctions, and a skepticism about the competence of judges to solve society's problems. In a larger sense, the Burger Court probably reflected the nation's wider doubt and uncertainty about government itself.

When Burger retired in 1986, President Reagan chose Justice William Rehnquist, who though 17 years younger had been on the Court almost as long as Burger, to succeed him. The vacant seat was filled by Antonin Scalia, a federal appellate judge of outspoken conservative persuasion. With the retirement of Powell in 1988, Reagan appointed Anthony Kennedy, also from the federal appellate bench. Following the retirements of William Brennan in 1990 after 34 years and Thurgood Marshall in 1991, President George Bush the elder appointed David Souter and Clarence Thomas, both federal appeals

---

* *The American Judicial Tradition: Profiles of Leading American Judges* (New York: Oxford University Press, 1988), 341.

The Supreme Court, 2002. From left: Clarence Thomas, Antonin Scalia, Sandra Day O'Connor, Anthony Kennedy, David Souter, Stephen Breyer, John Paul Stevens, William Rehnquist, C. J., and Ruth Bader Ginsberg.

judges. The retirements of White in 1993 and Blackmun in 1994 gave President Clinton opportunity to appoint Ruth Bader Ginsberg and Stephen Breyer, also federal appeals judges.

The Rehnquist Court has distinguished itself by effecting a so far minor, but nonetheless controversial, shift in the federal system toward states rights, discussed in the next chapter, mainly by limiting the outer reaches of Congress's power to regulate interstate commerce as it touches state government. Viewed from the long perspective of constitutional development, the work and philosophy of the Rehnquist Court has not been greatly different from that of the Burger. Both were products of a conserv-

ative political shift in the country reflected in presidential Republicanism between 1969 and 1993 and in the plurality victories of Clinton, a moderate Democrat, in 1992 and 1996. In the political environment at the turn of the century, neither Warren-like liberal activism nor sustained leaps from the Court in any constitutional direction seem probable. The growing tendency to appoint professional judges to the Court has contributed to this development and reinforced it. The last eight appointees and 12 of the last 14 have come from the appellate bench, in all but one case, the federal bench. The chief justice is the only member of the present Court without earlier judicial experience.

FURTHER READING

The Conduct of War and Diplomacy

Adler, David Gray and Larry N. George, eds., *The Constitution and the Conduct of American Foreign Policy* (1996)

Burgess, Susan A., *Contest for Constitutional Authority* (1992)

Ely, John Hart, *War and Responsibility: Constitutional Lessons of Vietnam and Its Aftermath* (1993)

Fisher, Louis, *Presidential War Power* (1995)

Franck, Thomas M., *Political Questions/Judicial Answers: Does the Rule of Law Apply to Foreign Affairs?* (1992)

Fried, Albert, *Communism in America: A History in Documents* (1997)

Glennon, Michael J., *Constitutional Diplomacy* (1990)

Henkin, Louis, *Constitutionalism, Democracy, and Foreign Affairs* (1989)

———, *Foreign Affairs and the Constitution* (1972)

Hogan, Michael J., *A Cross of Iron: Harry S Truman and the Origins of the National Security State, 1945–1954* (1998)

Koh, Harold Hongju, *The National Security Constitution: Sharing Power after the Iran-Contra Affair* (1990)

Licht, Robert A. and Robert A Goldwin, eds., *Foreign Policy and the Constitution* (1990)

Lofgren, Charles A., *"Government from Reflection and Choice": Constitutional Essays on War Foreign Relations, and Federalism* (1986)

May, Christopher, *In the Name of War: Judicial Review and the War Powers Since 1918* (1989)

McCormick, Thomas J., *America's Half Century: United States Foreign Policy in the Cold War* (1989)

Reveley, W. Taylor, III, *War Powers of the President and Congress* (1981)

Rossiter, Clinton, *The Supreme Court and the Commander in Chief* (1976)

Silverstein, Gordon, *Imbalance of Powers: Constitutional Interpretation and the Making of American Foreign Policy* (1996)

Stern, Gary M. and Morton H. Halperin, eds., *The United States Constitution and the Power to Go to War* (1993)

Vile, M. J. C., *The Constitution and the Sword* (1967)

Westerfield, Donald L., *War Powers: The President, Congress, and the Question of War* (1996)

Wormuth, Francis D. and Firmage, Edward B., *To Chain the Dogs of War: The War Power of Congress in History and Law* (1989)

Executive Ascendency

Baker, Nancy V., *Conflicting Loyalties: Law and Politics in the Attorney General's Office, 1789–1990* (1992)

Barber, Sotirios, *The Constitution and the Delegation of Congressional Power* (1975)

Berger, Roaul, *Executive Privilege: A Constitutional Myth* (1974)

Bessette, Joseph, and Tulis, Jeffrey, *The President and the Constitutional Order* (1981)

Caplan, Theodore, *The Tenth Justice: The Solicitor General and the Rule of Law* (1987)

Corwin, Edward S., *The President: Office and Powers*, 5th ed. (1984)

Cox, Gary W. and Samuel Kernell, *The Politics of Divided Government* (1991)

Crovitz, L. Gordon and Jeremy A. Rabkin eds, *The Fettered Presidency: Legal Constraints on the Executive Branch* (1989)

Dickinson, Matthew J., *Bitter Harvest: FDR, Presidential Power and the Growth of the Executive Branch* (1996)

Eastland, Terry, *Ethics, Politics, and the Independent Counsel: Executive Power, Executive Vice, 1789–1989* (1989)

Fausold, Martin L. and Alan Shank, eds., *The Constitution and the American Presidency* (1991)

Fiorina, Morris, *Divided Government* (1992)

Fisher, Louis, *Constitutional Structures* (1990)

———, *Presidential Spending Power* (1975)

———, *Constitutional Conflicts between Congress and the President* (1997)

Franklin, Daniel P., *Extraordinary Measures: The Exercise of Prerogative Powers in the United States* (1989)

Galderisi, Peter F., ed., *Divided Government: Change, Uncertainty, and the Constitutional Order* (1996)

Galambos, Louis, ed., *The New American State: Bureaucracies and Policies since World War II* (1987)

Gerhardt, Michael, *The Federal Appointments Process: A Constitutional and Historical Analysis* (2000)

Gilbert, Robert E., *Managing Crisis: Presidential Disability and the Twenty-Fifth Amendment* (2000)

Harriger, Katy J., *Independent Justice: the Federal Special Prosecutor in American Politics* (1992)

Hoffman, Daniel, *Governmental Secrecy and the Founding Fathers: A Study in Constitutional Controls* (1981)

Jones, Charles O., *The Presidency in a Separated System* (1994)

Kurland, Philip B., *Watergate and the Constitution* (1978)

Kutler, Stanley I., *The Wars of Watergate: The Last Crisis of Richard Nixon* (1990)

Robinson, Donald L., *"To the best of my ability": The Presidency and the Constitution* (1987)

Rose, Gary L., *The American Presidency Under Siege* (1997)

Salokar, Rebecca Mae, *The Solicitor General: The Politics of Law* (1992)

Thurber, James A., *Rivals for Power: Presidential-Congressional Relations* (1996)

Congressional Power

Campbell, Colton C. and John F. Stack, eds., *Congress Confronts the Court: The Struggle for Legitimacy and Authority in Lawmaking* (2001)

Craig, Barbara, *The Legislature Veto: Congressional Control of Regulation* (1983)

Gerhardt, Michael J., *The Federal Impeachment Process: A Constitutional and Historical Analysis* (1996)

Goodman, Walter, *The Committee: The Extraordinary Career of the House Un-American Activities Committee* (1968)

Jones, Gordon S. and Marini, John A., eds., *The Imperial Congress: Crisis in the Separation of Powers* (1988)

Katzman, Robert A., *Courts and Congress* (1997)

Korn, Jessica, *The Power of Separating: American Constitutionalism and the Myth of the Legislative Veto* (1996)

Mayhew, David R., *Divided We Govern: Party Control, Lawmaking, and Investigations, 1946–1990* (1991)

Murphy, Walter F., *Congress and the Court: A Case Study in the American Political Process* (1962)

Posner, Richard A., *An Affair of State: The Investigation, Impeachment, and Trial of President Clinton* (1999)

Pritchett, C. Herman, *Congress versus the Supreme Court, 1957–1960* (1961)

Schmidhauser, John R. and Larry L. Berg, *The Supreme Court and Congress: Conflict and Interaction, 1945–1968* (1972)

Schrecker, Ellen, *The Age of McCarthyism: A Brief History with Documents* (1994)

————, *Many Are the Crimes: McCarthyism in America* (1998)

Sundquist, James L., *The Decline and Resurgence of Congress* (1981)

Volcansek, Mary L., *Judicial Impeachment: Noen Called It Justice* (1993)

The Modern Court

Bickel, Alexander M., *The Supreme Court and the Idea of Progress* (1978)

Blasi, Vincent, *The Burger Court: The Counterrevolution That Wasn't* (1983)

Brenner, Saul and Harold J. Spaeth, *Stare Indecisis: The Alteration of Precedent on the Supreme Court, 1946–1992* (1995)

Brigham, John, *Cult of the Court* (1987)

Brisbin, Jr., Richard A., *Justice Antonin Scalia and the Conservative Revival* (1997)

Davis, Sue, *Justice Rehnquist and the Constitution* (1989)

Freyer, Tony, ed., *Justice Hugo Black and Modern America* (1990)

Friedelbaum, Stanley H., *The Rehnquist Court: In Pursuit of Judicial Conservatism* (1993)

Funston, Richard Y., *Constitutional Counterrevolution? The Warren Court and the Burger Court: Judicial Policy Making in Modern America* (1977)

Horwitz, Morton J., *The Warren Court and the Pursuit of Justice* (1998)

Hockett, Jeffrey D., *New Deal Justice: the Constitutional Jurisprudence of Hugo L. Black, Felix Frankfurter, and Robert H. Jackson* (1996)

Kahn, Ronald, *The Supreme Court and Constitutional Theory, 1953–1993* (1994)

Lamb, Charles M. and Stephen C. Halpern, eds., *The Burger Court: Political and Judicial Profiles* (1991)

Lasser, William, *The Limits of Judicial Power: The Supreme Court in American Politics* (1988)

Lewis, Frederick P., *The Context of Judicial Activism: The Endurance of the Warren Court Legacy in a Collective Age* (1999)

Maveety, Nancy, *Justice Sandra Day O'Connor: Strategist on the Supreme Court* (1996)

Nagel, Robert F., *Constitutional Cultures: The Mentality and Consequences of Judicial Review* (1989)

Pacelle, Jr., Richard L., *The Transformation of the Supreme Court's Agenda: From the New Deal to the Reagan Administration* (1991)

Parrish, Michael E., *Felix Frankfurter and His Times* (1982)

Pritchett, C. Herman, *The Roosevelt Court: A Study in Judicial Politics and Values* (1948)

Schwartz, Herman, ed., *The Burger Years: Rights and Wrongs in the Supreme Court, 1969–1986* (1987)

Sickels, Robert J., *John Paul Stevens and the Constitution* (1988)

Smith, Christopher E., *Justice Antonin Scalia and the Supreme Court's Conservative Moment* (1993)

Sunstein, Cass, *One Case at a Time: Judicial Minimalism on the Supreme Court* (1999)

Urofsky, Melvin I., *Division and Discord: The Supreme Court under Stone and Vinson, 1941–1953* (1997)

Witt, Elder, *A Different Justice: Reagan and the Supreme Court* (1986)

Wolfe, Christopher, The Rise of Modern Judicial Review: From Constitutional Interpretation to Judge-Made Law (1986)

Yackle, Larry, *Reclaiming the Federal Courts* (1994)

Yalof, David A., *Pursuit of Justices, Presidential Politics and The Pursuit of Supreme Court Nominees* (1999)

Yarbrough, Tinsley E., *The Rehnquist Court and the Constitution* (2000)

On Leading Cases

Cortner, Richard C., *Civil Rights and Public Accommo-dations: The Heart of Atlanta Motel and McClung Cases* (2001)

Craig, Barbara H., *Chadha: The Story of an Epic Consti-tutional Struggle* (1988)

Dionne, Jr., E. J. and William Kristol, *Bush v. Gore: The Court Cases and the Commentary*, (2001)

Irons, Peter, *Justice at War: The Story of the Japanese-American Internment Cases* (1983)

Marcus, Maeva, *Truman and the Steel Seizure Case: The Limits of Presidential Power* (1987)

Weeks, Kent M., *Adam Clayton Powell and the Supreme Court* (1971) (*Powell v. McCormick*)

Westin, Alan F., *Anatomy of a Constitutional Law Case* (1958)

CASES

Missouri v. Holland

252 U.S. 416 (1920), 7-2

Opinion of the Court: Holmes (Brandeis, Clark, Day, McKenna, McReynolds, White)

Dissenting: Pitney, Van Devanter

Concern of farmers and conservation groups about the killing of insect-eating migratory birds led Congress in 1913 to pass the Migratory Bird Act that forbade the killing of certain species. The law was shortly held unconstitutional in lower federal courts as beyond Congress's legislative authority. In 1916, the United States entered into a treaty with Great Britain, acting on behalf of Canada, to deal with the migratory bird problem. Two years later, Congress, pursuing terms of the treaty, enacted the Migratory Bird Treaty Act, which, like the 1913 law, prohibited the killing of certain species that migrated between the United States and Canada. Responding to hunting and states rights interests, Missouri brought suit against Holland, a federal game warden, to enjoin him from enforcing provisions of the act against two Missouri hunters who had violated it. The state ar-gued that the federal law encroached upon powers reserved to the states under the Tenth Amendment. Did the Court, in effect, give Congress a free hand to reach any subject it chose, as long as it was through the treaty power? Two years before this deci-sion, in Hammer v. Dagenhart, *the Court held that Congress could not reach child labor through its commerce power. Could Congress, following the decision here, outlaw child labor by ne-gotiating a treaty to that effect with another nation? What would have been the constitutional effect had the Court upheld Missouri's challenge? What did Holmes mean by his statement, "We must consider what this country has become in deciding what that (the Tenth) amendment has reserved"? Holmes al-lows that there may be qualifications on the treaty-making power, but they "must be ascertained in a different way." Does he say what that way is?*

Holmes, for the Court:

This is a bill in equity brought by the State of Missouri to prevent a game warden of the United States from attempting to enforce the Migratory Bird Treaty Act of July 3, 1918, and the regulations made by the Sec-retary of Agriculture in pursuance of the same. The ground of the bill is that the statute is an unconstitu-tional interference with the rights reserved to the States by the Tenth Amendment, and that the acts of [Holland] done and threatened under that authority invade the sovereign right of the State and contra-vene its will manifested in statutes. The State also al-leges a pecuniary interest, as owner of the wild birds within its borders and otherwise. . . .

[T]he question raised is the general one whether the treaty and statute are void as an interference with the rights reserved to the States.

To answer this question it is not enough to refer to the Tenth Amendment, reserving the powers not del-egated to the United States, because by Article 2, Sec-tion 2, the power to make treaties is delegated expressly, and by Article 6 treaties made under the au-thority of the United States, along with the Constitu-tion and laws of the United States made in pursuance thereof, are declared the supreme law of the land. If the treaty is valid there can be no dispute about the validity of the statute under Article 1, Section 8, as a necessary and proper means to execute the powers of the Government. . . .

It is said that a treaty cannot be valid if it infringes the Constitution, that there are limits, therefore, to the treaty-making power, and that one such limit is that what an act of Congress could not do unaided, in derogation of the powers reserved to the States, a treaty cannot do. An earlier act of Congress that attempted by itself and not in pursuance of a treaty to regulate the killing of migratory birds within the States had been held bad in the District Court. *United States v. Shauver, United States v. McCullagh,* Those decisions were supported by arguments that migratory birds were owned by the States in their sovereign capacity for the benefit of their people, and that under cases like *Geer v. Connecticut,* this control was one that Congress had no power to displace. The same argument is supposed to apply now with equal force.

Whether the two cases cited were decided rightly or not they cannot be accepted as a test of the treaty power. Acts of Congress are the supreme law of the land only when made in pursuance of the Constitution, while treaties are declared to be so when made under the authority of the United States. It is open to question whether the authority of the United States means more than the formal acts prescribed to make the convention. We do not mean to imply that there are no qualifications to the treaty-making power; but they must be ascertained in a different way. It is obvious that there may be matters of the sharpest exigency for the national well being that an act of Congress could not deal with but that a treaty followed by such an act could, and it is not lightly to be assumed that, in matters requiring national action, 'a power which must belong to and somewhere reside in every civilized government' is not to be found. What was said in that case with regard to the powers of the States applies with equal force to the powers of the nation in cases where the States individually are incompetent to act. We are not yet discussing the particular case before us but only are considering the validity of the test proposed. With regard to that we may add that when we are dealing with words that also are a constituent act, like the Constitution of the United States, we must realize that they have called into life a being the development of which could not have been foreseen completely by the most gifted of its begetters. It was enough for them to realize or to hope that they had created an organism; it has taken a century and has cost their successors much sweat and blood to prove that they created a nation. The case before us must be considered in the light of out whole experience and not merely in that of what was said a hundred years ago. The treaty in question does not contravene any prohibitory words to be found in the Constitution. The only question is whether it is

forbidden by some invisible radiation from the general terms of the Tenth Amendment. We must consider what this country has become in deciding what that amendment has reserved.

The State as we have intimated founds its claim of exclusive authority upon an assertion of title to migratory birds, an assertion that is embodied in statute. No doubt it is true that as between a State and its inhabitants the State may regulate the killing and sale of such birds, but it does not follow that its authority is exclusive of paramount powers. To put the claim of the State upon title is to lean upon a slender reed. Wild birds are not in the possession of anyone; and possession is the beginning of ownership. The whole foundation of the State's rights is the presence within their jurisdiction of birds that yesterday had not arrived, tomorrow may be in another State and in a week a thousand miles away. If we are to be accurate we cannot put the case of the State upon higher ground than that the treaty deals with creatures that for the moment are within the state borders, that it must be carried out by officers of the United States within the same territory, and that but for the treaty the State would be free to regulate this subject itself.

As most of the laws of the United States are carried out within the States and as many of them deal with matters which in the silence of such laws the State might regulate, such general grounds are not enough to support Missouri's claim. Valid treaties of course 'are as binding within the territorial limits of the States as they are elsewhere throughout the dominion of the United States.' No doubt the great body of private relations usually fall within the control of the State, but a treaty may override its power . . . [I]t only remains to consider the application of established rules to the present case.

Here a national interest of very nearly the first magnitude is involved. It can be protected only by national action in concert with that of another power. The subject matter is only transitorily within the State and has no permanent habitat therein. But for the treaty and the statute there soon might be no birds for any powers to deal with. We see nothing in the Constitution that compels the Government to sit by while a food supply is cut off and the protectors of our forests and our crops are destroyed. It is not sufficient to rely upon the States. The reliance is vain, and were it otherwise, the question is whether the United States is forbidden to act. We are of opinion that the treaty and statute must be upheld.

Humphrey's Executor v. United States

295 U.S. 602 (1935), 9-0

Opinion of the Court: Sutherland (Brandeis, Butler, Cardozo, Hughes, McReynolds, Roberts, Stone, Van Devanter)

Samuel Rathbun, executor of the estate of William E. Humphrey sued the United States to recover salary allegedly owed the deceased as a member of the Federal Trade Commission from October 8, 1933, when he was removed from office by the President, to the time of his death, February 14, 1934.

Why are so-called independent regulatory commissions qualitatively different from other agencies of the Executive branch, according to the Court? How does the Court distinguish Myers v. United States? *Does it make sense that the president should have the power to hire but not fire? What political difference would it make if the president had power to remove commissioners like Humphrey at will? To whom are regulatory commissions now responsible?*

Sutherland, for the Court:

. . . [T]he following questions are certified:

'1. Do the provisions of section 1 of the Federal Trade Commission Act, stating that 'any commissioner may be removed by the President for inefficiency, neglect of duty, or malfeasance in office', restrict or limit the power of the President to remove a commissioner except upon one or more of the causes named?

'If the foregoing question is answered in the affirmative, then—

'2. If the power of the President to remove a commissioner is restricted or limited . . . is such a restriction or limitation valid under the Constitution of the United States?'

The Federal Trade Commission Act creates a commission of five members to be appointed by the President by and with the advice and consent of the Senate, and section 1 provides: 'Not more than three of the commissioners shall be members of the same political party. The first commissioners appointed shall continue in office for terms of three, four, five, six, and seven years, respectively, from the date of the taking effect of this Act, the term of each to be designated by the President, but their successors shall be appointed for terms of seven years, except that any person chosen to fill a vacancy shall be appointed only for the unexpired term of the commissioner whom he shall succeed. The commission shall choose a chairman from its own membership

. . . Any commissioner may be removed by the President for inefficiency. neglect of duty, or malfeasance in office.' . . .

First. The question first to be considered is whether, by the provisions of section 1 of the Federal Trade Commission Act already quoted, the President's power is limited to removal for the specific causes enumerated therein . . .

The commission is to be nonpartisan; and it must, from the very nature of its duties, act with entire impartiality. It is charged with the enforcement of no policy except the policy of the law. Its duties are neither political nor executive, but predominantly quasi-judicial and quasi-legislative. Like the Interstate Commerce Commission, its members are called upon to exercise the trained judgment of a body of experts 'appointed by law and informed by experience.'

The legislative reports in both houses of Congress clearly reflect the view that a fixed term was necessary to the effective and fair administration of the law. In the report to the Senate, the Senate Committee on Interstate Commerce, in support of the bill which afterwards became the act in question, after referring to the provision fixing the term of office at seven years, so arranged that the membership would not be subject to complete change at any one time . . .

The debates in both houses demonstrate that the prevailing view was that the Commission was not to be 'subject to anybody in the government but . . . only to the people of the United States'; free from 'political domination or control' or the 'probability or possibility of such a thing'; to be 'separate and apart from any existing department of the government—not subject to the orders of the President.' . . .

Thus, the language of the act, the legislative reports, and the general purposes of the legislation as reflected by the debates, all combine to demonstrate the congressional intent to create a body of experts who shall gain experience by length of service; a body which shall be independent of executive authority, except in its selection, and free to exercise its judgment without the leave or hindrance of any other official or any department of the government. To the accomplishment of these purposes . . . Congress was of opinion that length and certainty of tenure would vitally contribute. And to hold that, nevertheless, the members of the commission continue in office at the mere will of the President, might be to thwart . . . the very ends which Congress sought to realize by definitely fixing the term of office.

We conclude that the intent of the act is to limit the executive power of removal to the causes enumerated, the existence of none of which is claimed here; and we pass to the second question.

Second. To support its contention that the removal provision of section 1, as we have just construed it, is an unconstitutional interference with the executive power of the President, the government's chief reliance is *Myers v. United States* . . . Nevertheless, the narrow point actually decided was only that the President had power to remove a postmaster of the first class, without the advice and consent of the Senate as required by act of Congress. In the course of the opinion of the Court, expressions occur which tend to sustain the government's contention, but these are beyond the point involved and, therefore, do not come within the rule of stare decisis. In so far as they are out of harmony with the views here set forth, these expressions are disapproved. . . .

The office of a postmaster is so essentially unlike the office now involved that the decision in the Myers Case cannot be accepted as controlling our decision here. A postmaster is an executive officer restricted to the performance of executive functions. He is charged with no duty at all related to either the legislative or judicial power. The actual decision in the Myers Case finds support in the theory that such an officer is merely one of the units in the executive department and, hence, inherently subject to the exclusive and illimitable power of removal by the Chief Executive, whose subordinate and aid he is. Putting aside dicta, which may be followed if sufficiently persuasive but which are not controlling, the necessary reach of the decision goes far enough to include all purely executive officers. It goes no farther; much less does it include an officer who occupies no place in the executive department and who exercises no part of the executive power vested by the Constitution in the President.

The Federal Trade Commission is an administrative body created by Congress to carry into effect legislative policies embodied in the statute in accordance with the legislative standard therein prescribed, and to perform other specified duties as a legislative or as a judicial aid. Such a body cannot in any proper sense be characterized as an arm or an eye of the executive. Its duties are performed without executive leave and, in the contemplation of the statute, must be free from executive control. In administering the provisions of the statute in respect of 'unfair methods of competi-

tion,' that is to say, in filling in and administering the details embodied by that general standard, the commission acts in part quasi-legislatively and in part quasi-judicially. In making investigations and reports thereon for the information of Congress under section 6, in aid of the legislative power, it acts as a legislative agency. Under section 7, which authorizes the commission to act as a master in chancery under rules prescribed by the Court, it acts as an agency of the judiciary. To the extent that it exercises any executive function, as distinguished from executive power in the constitutional sense, it does so in the discharge and e ffectuation of its quasi-legislative or quasi-judicial powers, or as an agency of the legislative or judicial departments of the government.

If Congress is without authority to prescribe causes for removal of members of the trade commission and limit executive power of removal accordingly, that power at once becomes practically all-inclusive in respect of civil officers with the exception of the judiciary provided for by the Constitution. The Solicitor General, at the bar, apparently recognizing this to be true, with commendable candor, agreed that his view in respect of the removability of members of the Federal Trade Commission necessitated a like view in respect of the Interstate Commerce Commission and the Court of Claims. We are thus confronted with the serious question whether not only the members of these quasi-legislative and quasi-judicial bodies, but the judges of the legislative Court of Claims, exercising judicial power, continue in office only at the pleasure of the President.

We think it plain under the Constitution that illimitable power of removal is not possessed by the President in respect of officers of the character of those just named. The authority of Congress, in creating quasi-legislative or quasi-judicial agencies, to require them to act in discharge of their duties independently of executive control cannot well be doubted; and that authority includes, as an appropriate incident, power to fix the period during which they shall continue, and to forbid their removal except for cause in the meantime. For it is quite evident that one who holds his office only during the pleasure of another cannot be depended upon to maintain an attitude of independence against the latter's will.

The fundamental necessity of maintaining each of the three general departments of government entirely free from the control or coercive influence, direct or indirect, of either of the others, has often been stressed and is hardly open to serious question. So much is implied in the very fact of the separation of the powers of these departments by the Constitution; and in the rule which recognizes their essential co-equality. The sound application of a principle that makes one master in his own house precludes him from imposing his control in the house of another who is master there. . . .

The power of removal here claimed for the President falls within this principle, since its coercive influence threatens the independence of a commission, which is not only wholly disconnected from the executive department, but which, as already fully appears, was created by Congress as a means of carrying into operation legislative and judicial powers, and as an agency of the legislative and judicial departments. . . .

The result of what we now have said is this: Whether the power of the President to remove an officer shall prevail over the authority of Congress to condition the power by fixing a definite term and precluding a removal except for cause will depend upon the character of the office; the Myers decision, affirming the power of the President alone to make the removal, is confined to purely executive officers; and as to officers of the kind here under consideration, we hold that no removal can be made during the prescribed term for which the officer is appointed, except for one or more of the causes named in the applicable statute.

United States v. Curtiss-Wright Export Corp.

299 U.S. 304 (1936), 7-1
Opinion of the Court: Sutherland (Brandeis, Butler,
   Cardozo, Hughes, Roberts, Van Devanter)
Dissenting: McReynolds
Not participating: Stone
What reasons does the Court give for holding that the national government has exclusive power in foreign affairs? On what grounds does Sutherland argue that the president has power in foreign affairs that "would not be admissible were domestic affairs alone involved"? Can a power that does not depend on a constitutional grant be limited by the Constitution? What are the limits of such a power? Is the notion of inherent power compatible with limited or constitutional government? What would be the political effect of the Court holding the other way in this case?

Sutherland, for the Court:

On January 27, 1936, an indictment was returned in the court below, the first count of which charges that [Curtiss-Wright], beginning with the 29th day of May, 1934, conspired to sell in the United States certain arms of war, namely, fifteen machine guns, to Bolivia, a country then engaged in armed conflict in the Chaco, in violation of the Joint Resolution of Congress approved May 28, 1934, and the provisions of a proclamation issued on the same day by the President of the United States pursuant to authority conferred by section 1 of the resolution . . .

First. It is contended that by the Joint Resolution the going into effect and continued operation of the resolution was conditioned (a) upon the President's judgment as to its beneficial effect upon the re-establishment of peace between the countries engaged in armed conflict in the Chaco; (b) upon the making of a proclamation, which was left to his unfettered discretion, thus constituting an attempted substitution of the President's will for that of Congress; (c) upon the making of a proclamation putting an end to the operation of the resolution, which again was left to the President's unfettered discretion; and (d) further, that the extent of its operation in particular cases was subject to limitation and exception by the President, controlled by no standard. In each of these particulars, [Curtiss-Wright urges] that Congress abdicated its essential functions and delegated them to the Executive.

Whether, if the Joint Resolution had related solely to internal affairs, it would be open to the challenge that it constituted an unlawful delegation of legislative power to the Executive, we find it unnecessary to determine. The whole aim of the resolution is to affect a situation entirely external to the United States, and falling within the category of foreign affairs. The determination which we are called to make, therefore, is whether the Joint Resolution, as applied to that situation, is vulnerable to attack under the rule that forbids a delegation of the lawmaking power. In other words, assuming (but not deciding) that the challenged delegation, if it were confined to internal affairs, would be invalid, may it nevertheless be sustained on the ground that its exclusive aim is to afford a remedy for a hurtful condition within foreign territory?

It will contribute to the elucidation of the question if we first consider the differences between the powers of the federal government in respect of foreign or external affairs and those in respect of domestic or internal affairs. That there are differences between them, and that these differences are fundamental, may not be doubted.

The two classes of powers are different, both in respect of their origin and their nature. The broad statement that the federal government can exercise no powers except those specifically enumerated in the Constitution, and such implied powers as are necessary and proper to carry into effect the enumerated powers, is categorically true only in respect of our internal affairs. In that field, the primary purpose of the Constitution was to carve from the general mass of legislative powers then possessed by the states such portions as it was thought desirable to vest in the federal government, leaving those not included in the enumeration still in the states. That this doctrine applies only to powers which the states had is self-evident. And since the states severally never possessed international powers, such powers could not have been carved from the mass of state powers but obviously were transmitted to the United States from some other source. During the Colonial period, those powers were possessed exclusively by and were entirely under the control of the Crown. By the Declaration of Independence, 'the Representatives of the United States of America' declared the United (not the several) Colonies to be free and independent states, and as such to have 'full Power to levy War, conclude Peace, contract Alliances, establish Commerce and to do all other Acts and Things which Independent States may of right do.'

As a result of the separation from Great Britain by the colonies, acting as a unit, the powers of external sovereignty passed from the Crown not to the colonies severally, but to the colonies in their collective and corporate capacity as the United States of America. Even before the Declaration, the colonies were a unit in foreign affairs, acting through a common agency—namely, the Continental Congress, composed of delegates from the thirteen colonies. That agency exercised the powers of war and peace, raised an army, created a navy, and finally adopted the Declaration of Independence. Rulers come and go; governments end and forms of government change; but sovereignty survives. A political society cannot endure without a supreme will somewhere. Sovereignty is never held in suspense. When, therefore, the external sovereignty of Great Britain in respect of the colonies ceased, it immediately passed to the Union. . . .

The Union existed before the Constitution, which was ordained and established among other things to form 'a more perfect Union.' Prior to that event, it is clear that the Union, declared by the Articles of Confederation to be 'perpetual,' was the sole possessor of external sovereignty, and in the Union it remained without change save in so far as the Constitution in express terms qualified its exercise. . . .

It results that the investment of the federal government with the powers of external sovereignty did not depend upon the affirmative grants of the Constitution. The powers to declare and wage war, to conclude peace, to make treaties, to maintain diplomatic relations with other sovereignties, if they had never been mentioned in the Constitution, would have vested in the federal government as necessary concomitants of nationality. Neither the Constitution nor the laws passed in pursuance of it have any force in foreign territory unless in respect of our own citizens and operations of the nation in such territory must be governed by treaties, international understandings and compacts, and the principles of international law. As a member of the family of nations, the right and power of the United States in that field are equal to the right and power of the other members of the international family. Otherwise, the United States is not completely sovereign. The power to acquire territory by discovery and occupation, the power to expel undesirable aliens, the power to make such international agreements as do not constitute treaties in the constitutional sense, none of which is expressly affirmed by the Constitution, nevertheless exist as inherently inseparable from the conception of nationality. This the Court recognized, and in each of the cases cited found the warrant for its conclusions not in the provisions of the Constitution, but in the law of nations. . . .

Not only, as we have shown, is the federal power over external affairs in origin and essential character different from that over internal affairs, but participation in the exercise of the power is significantly limited. In this vast external realm, with its important, complicated, delicate and manifold problems, the President alone has the power to speak or listen as a representative of the nation. He makes treaties with the advice and consent of the Senate; but he alone negotiates. Into the field of negotiation the Senate cannot intrude; and Congress itself is powerless to invade it. . . .

It is important to bear in mind that we are here dealing not alone with an authority vested in the President by an exertion of legislative power, but with such an authority plus the very delicate, plenary and exclusive power of the President as the sole organ of the federal government in the field of international relations—a power which does not require as a basis for its exercise an act of Congress, but which, of course, like every other governmental power, must be exercised in subordination to the applicable provisions of the Constitution. It is quite apparent that if, in the maintenance of our international relations, embarrassment . . . is to be avoided and success for our aims achieved, congressional legislation which is to be made effective through negotiation and inquiry within the international field must often accord to the President a degree of discretion and freedom from statutory restriction which would not be admissible were domestic affairs alone involved. Moreover, he, not Congress, has the better opportunity of knowing the conditions which prevail in foreign countries, and especially is this true in time of war. He has his confidential sources of information. He has his agents in the form of diplomatic, consular and other officials. Secrecy in respect of information gathered by them may be highly necessary, and the premature disclosure of it productive of harmful results. Indeed, so clearly is this true that the first President refused to accede to a request to lay before the House of Representatives the instructions, correspondence and documents relating to the negotiation of the Jay Treaty—a refusal the wisdom of which was recognized by the House itself and has never since been doubted. . . .

The marked difference between foreign affairs and domestic affairs in this respect is recognized by both houses of Congress in the very form of their requisitions for information from the executive departments. In the case of every department except the Department of State, the resolution directs the official to furnish the information. In the case of the State Department, dealing with foreign affairs, the President is requested to furnish the information 'if not incompatible with the public interest.' A statement that to furnish the information is not compatible with the public interest rarely, if ever, is questioned.

When the President is to be authorized by legislation to act in respect of a matter intended to affect a situation in foreign territory, the legislator properly bears in mind the important consideration that the form of the President's action—or, indeed, whether he shall act at all—may well depend, among other things, upon the nature of the confidential information which he has or may thereafter receive, or upon the effect which his action may have upon our foreign relations. This consideration, in connection with what we have already said on the subject discloses the unwisdom of requiring Congress in this field of governmental power to lay down narrowly definite standards by which the President is to be governed. . . .

In the light of the foregoing observations, it is evident that this court should not be in haste to apply a general rule which will have the effect of condemning legislation like that under review as constituting an unlawful delegation of legislative power. The principles which justify such legislation find overwhelming support in the unbroken legislative practice which has prevailed almost from the inception of the national government to the present day. . . .

Practically every volume of the United States Statutes contains one or more acts or joint resolutions of Congress authorizing action by the President in respect of subjects affecting foreign relations, which either leave the exercise of the power to his unrestricted judgment, or provide a standard far more general than that . . . with regard to domestic affairs. . . .

The result of holding that the joint resolution here under attack is void and unenforceable as constituting an unlawful delegation of legislative power would be to stamp this multitude of comparable acts and resolutions as likewise invalid. And while this court may not, and should not, hesitate to declare acts of Congress, however many times repeated, to be unconstitutional if beyond all rational doubt it finds them to be so, an impressive array of legislation . . . enacted by nearly every Congress from the beginning of our national existence to the present day, must be given unusual weight in the process of reaching a correct determination of the problem. A legislative practice such as we have here . . . but marked by the movement of a steady stream for a century and a half of time, goes a long way in the direction of proving the presence of unassailable ground for the constitutionality of the practice. . . .

[B]oth upon principle and in accordance with precedent, we conclude there is sufficient warrant for the broad discretion vested in the President to determine whether the enforcement of the statute will have a beneficial effect upon the re-establishment of peace in the affected countries; whether he shall make proclamation to bring the resolution into operation; whether and when the resolution shall cease to operate and to make proclamation accordingly; and to prescribe limitations and exceptions to which the enforcement of the resolution shall be subject.

Korematsu v. United States

323 U.S. 214 (1944), 6-3
Opinion of the Court: Black (Douglas, Reed, Rutledge, Stone)
Concurring: Frankfurter
Dissenting: Jackson, Murphy, Roberts

A year earlier in Hirabayashi v. United States, *the Court upheld an 8 p.m. to 6 a.m. World War II curfew on all persons of Japanese ancestry living in West Coast military districts as reasonable and necessary to prevent espionage and sabotage. The following case arose from a challenge to a second military program—the evacuation of Japanese-Americans from their West Coast homes.*

Is this a case of national security or of individual rights? The views of Black and Murphy are very far apart. Is there any way to reconcile them? Is Murphy's solution to the security problem practical? Should the Court have taken into account that fear of a Japanese invasion was later shown to have been largely unfounded? Does Jackson support or oppose the evacuation order? Support or oppose the Court's hearing of this case? Can the Court's decision be distinguished from Ex parte Milligan?

Black, for the Court:

[Korematsu], an American citizen of Japanese descent, was convicted in a federal district court for remaining in San Leandro, California, a "Military Area," contrary to Civilian Exclusion Order No. 34 of the Commanding General of the Western Command, U.S. Army, which directed that, after May 9, 1942, all persons of Japanese ancestry should be excluded from that area. No question was raised as [his] loyalty to the United States . . .

. . . [A]ll legal restrictions which curtail the civil rights of a single racial group are immediately suspect. That is not to say that all such restrictions are unconstitutional. It is to say that courts must subject them to the most rigid scrutiny. Pressing public necessity may sometimes justify the existence of such restrictions; racial antagonism never can.

. . . [P]rosecution of [Korematsu] was begun by information charging violation of an Act of Congress, of March 21, 1942, which provides that

> . . . whoever shall enter, remain in, leave, or commit any act in any military area or military zone prescribed, under the authority of an Executive order of the President, by the Secretary of War, or by any military commander designated by the Secretary of War, contrary to the restrictions applicable to any such area or zone or contrary to the order of the Secretary of War or any such military commander, shall, if it appears that he knew or should have known of the existence and extent of the restrictions or order and that his act was in violation thereof, be guilty of a misdemeanor and upon conviction shall be liable to a fine of not to exceed $5,000 or to imprisonment for not more than one year, or both, for each offense.

Exclusion Order No. 34, which [Korematsu] knowingly and admittedly violated, was one of a number of military orders and proclamations, all of which were substantially based upon Executive Order No. 9066. That order, issued after we were at war with Japan, declared that

> the successful prosecution of the war requires every possible protection against espionage and against sabotage to national defense material, national defense premises, and national defense utilities . . .

In the light of the principles we announced in the Hirabayashi case, we are unable to conclude that it was beyond the war power of Congress and the Executive to exclude those of Japanese ancestry from the West Coast war area at the time they did. True, exclusion from the area in which one's home is located is a far greater deprivation than constant confinement to the home from 8 p.m. to 6 a.m. Nothing short of apprehension by the proper military authorities of the gravest imminent danger to the public safety can constitutionally justify either. But exclusion from a threatened area, no less than curfew, has a definite and close relationship to the prevention of espionage and sabotage. The military authorities, charged with the primary responsibility of defending our shores, concluded that curfew provided inadequate protection and ordered exclusion. They did so, as pointed out in our Hirabayashi opinion, in accordance with Congressional authority to the military to say who should, and who should not, remain in the threatened areas . . .

Here, as in the Hirabayashi case, we cannot reject as unfounded the judgment of the military authorities and of Congress that there were disloyal members of that population, whose number and strength could not be precisely and quickly ascertained. We cannot say that the war-making branches of the Government did not have ground for believing that, in a critical hour, such persons could not readily be isolated and separately dealt with, and constituted a menace to the national defense and safety which demanded that prompt and adequate measures be taken to guard against it.

Like curfew, exclusion of those of Japanese origin was deemed necessary because of the presence of an unascertained number of disloyal members of the group, most of whom we have no doubt were loyal to this country. It was because we could not reject the finding of the military authorities that it was impossible to bring about an immediate segregation of the disloyal from the loyal that we sustained the validity of the curfew order as applying to the whole group. In the instant case, temporary exclusion of the entire group was rested by the military on the same ground. The judgment that exclusion of the whole group was, for the same reason, a military imperative answers the contention that the exclusion was in the nature of group punishment based on antagonism to those of Japanese origin. That there were members of the group who retained loyalties to Japan has been con-firmed by investigations made subsequent to the exclusion. Approximately five thousand American citizens of Japanese ancestry refused to swear unqualified allegiance to the United States and to renounce allegiance to the Japanese Emperor, and several thousand evacuees requested repatriation to Japan.

We uphold the exclusion order as of the time it was made and when the petitioner violated it. In doing so, we are not unmindful of the hardships imposed by it upon a large group of American citizens. But hardships are part of war, and war is an aggregation of hardships. All citizens alike, both in and out of uniform, feel the impact of war in greater or lesser measure. Citizenship has its responsibilities, as well as its privileges, and, in time of war, the burden is always heavier. Compulsory exclusion of large groups of citizens from their homes, except under circumstances of direst emergency and peril, is inconsistent with our basic governmental institutions. But when, under conditions of modern warfare, our shores are threatened by hostile forces, the power to protect must be commensurate with the threatened danger . . .

It is said that we are dealing here with the case of imprisonment of a citizen in a concentration camp solely because of his ancestry, without evidence or inquiry concerning his loyalty and good disposition towards the United States. Our task would be simple, our duty clear, were this a case involving the imprisonment of a loyal citizen in a concentration camp because of racial prejudice. Regardless of the true nature of the assembly and relocation centers—and we deem it unjustifiable to call them concentra-

Japanese Americans with personal belongings waiting at the Santa Anita reception center in Los Angeles for evacuation to internment camps under an army war emergency order, April 1942.

tion camps, with all the ugly connotations that term implies—we are dealing specifically with nothing but an exclusion order. To cast this case into outlines of racial prejudice, without reference to the real military dangers which were presented, merely confuses the issue. Korematsu was not excluded from the Military Area because of hostility to him or his race. He was excluded because we are at war with the Japanese Empire, because the properly constituted military authorities feared an invasion of our West Coast and felt constrained to take proper security measures, because they decided that the military urgency of the situation demanded that all citizens of Japanese ancestry be segregated from the West Coast temporarily, and, finally, because Congress, reposing its confidence in this time of war in our military leaders—as inevitably it must—determined that they should have the power to do just this. There was evidence of disloyalty on the part of some, the military authorities considered that the need for action was great, and time was short. We cannot—by availing ourselves of the calm perspective of hindsight—now say that, at that time, these actions were unjustified.

Murphy, dissenting:
This exclusion of "all persons of Japanese ancestry, both alien and non-alien," from the Pacific Coast area on a plea of military necessity in the absence of martial law ought not to be approved. Such exclusion goes over "the very brink of constitutional power," and falls into the ugly abyss of racism.

In dealing with matters relating to the prosecution and progress of a war, we must accord great respect and consideration to the judgments of the military authorities who are on the scene and who have full knowledge of the military facts. The scope of their discretion must, as a matter of necessity and common sense, be wide. And their judgments ought not to be overruled lightly by those whose training and duties ill-equip them to deal intelligently with matters so vital to the physical security of the nation.

At the same time, however, it is essential that there be definite limits to military discretion, especially where martial law has not been declared. Individuals must not be left impoverished of their constitutional rights on a plea of military necessity that has neither substance nor support. Thus, like other claims conflicting with the asserted constitutional rights of the individual, the military claim must subject itself to the judicial process of having its reasonableness determined and its conflicts with other interests reconciled . . .

The judicial test of whether the Government, on a plea of military necessity, can validly deprive an individual of any of his constitutional rights is whether the deprivation is reasonably related to a public danger that is so "immediate, imminent, and impending" as not to admit of delay and not to permit the intervention of ordinary constitutional processes to alleviate the danger. Civilian Exclusion Order No. 34, banishing from a prescribed area of the Pacific Coast "all persons of Japanese ancestry, both alien and non-alien," clearly does not meet that test. Being an obvious racial discrimination, the order deprives all those within its scope of the equal protection of the laws as guaranteed by the Fifth Amendment. It further deprives these individuals of their constitutional rights to live and work where they will, to establish a home where they choose and to move about freely. In excommunicating them without benefit of hearings, this order also deprives them of all their constitutional rights to procedural due process. Yet no reasonable relation to an "immediate, imminent, and impending" public danger is evident to support this racial restriction, which is one of the most sweeping and complete deprivations of constitutional rights in the history of this nation in the absence of martial law.

It must be conceded that the military and naval situation in the spring of 1942 was such as to generate a very real fear of invasion of the Pacific Coast, accompanied by fears of sabotage and espionage in that area. The military command was therefore justified in adopting all reasonable means necessary to combat these dangers. In adjudging the military action taken in light of the then apparent dangers, we must not erect too high or too meticulous standards; it is necessary only that the action have some reasonable relation to the removal of the dangers of invasion, sabotage and espionage. But the exclusion, either temporarily or permanently, of all persons with Japanese blood in their veins has no such reasonable relation. And that relation is lacking because the exclusion order necessarily must rely for its reasonableness upon the assumption that all persons of Japanese ancestry may have a dangerous tendency to commit sabotage and espionage and to aid our Japanese enemy in other ways . . .

The main reasons relied upon by those responsible for the forced evacuation . . . do not prove a reasonable relation between the group characteristics of Japanese Americans and the dangers of invasion, sabotage and espionage. The reasons appear, instead, to be largely an accumulation of much of the misinformation, half-truths and insinuations that for years have been directed against Japanese Americans by people with racial and economic prejudices—the same people who have been among the foremost advocates of the evacuation. A military judgment based upon such racial and sociological considerations is not entitled to the great weight ordinarily given the judgments based upon strictly military considerations . . .

The military necessity which is essential to the validity of the evacuation order . . . resolves itself into a few intimations that certain individuals actively aided the enemy, from which it is inferred that the entire group of Japanese Americans could not be trusted to be or remain loyal to the United States. No one denies, of course, that there were some disloyal persons of Japanese descent on the Pacific Coast who did all in their power to aid their ancestral land. Similar disloyal activities have been engaged in by many persons of German, Italian and even more pioneer stock in our country. But to infer that examples of individual disloyalty prove group disloyalty and justify discriminatory action against the entire group is to deny that, under our system of law, individual guilt is the sole basis for deprivation of rights. Moreover, this inference, which is at the very heart of the evacuation orders, has been used in support of the abhorrent and despicable treatment of minority groups by the dictatorial tyrannies which this nation is now pledged to destroy. To give constitutional sanction to that inference in this case, however well intentioned may have been the military command on the Pacific Coast, is to adopt one of the cruelest of the rationales used by our enemies to destroy the dignity of the individual and to encourage and open the door to discriminatory actions against other minority groups in the passions of tomorrow.

No adequate reason is given for the failure to treat these Japanese Americans on an individual basis by holding investigations and hearings to separate the loyal from the disloyal, as was done in the case of persons of German and Italian ancestry. It is asserted merely that the loyalties of this group "were unknown and time was of the essence." Yet nearly four months elapsed after Pearl Harbor before the first exclusion order was issued; nearly eight months went by until the last order was issued, and the last of these "subversive" persons was not actually removed until almost eleven months had elapsed. Leisure and deliberation seem to have been more of the essence than speed. And the fact that conditions were not such as to warrant a declaration of martial law adds strength to the belief that the factors of time and

military necessity were not as urgent as they have been represented to be . . .

It seems incredible that, under these circumstances, it would have been impossible to hold loyalty hearings for the mere 112,000 persons involved—or at least for the 70,000 American citizens—especially when a large part of this number represented children and elderly men and women. Any inconvenience that may have accompanied an attempt to conform to procedural due process cannot be said to justify violations of constitutional rights of individuals.

I dissent, therefore, from this legalization of racism. Racial discrimination in any form and in any degree has no justifiable part whatever in our democratic way of life. It is unattractive in any setting, but it is utterly revolting among a free people who have embraced the principles set forth in the Constitution of the United States. All residents of this nation are kin in some way by blood or culture to a foreign land. Yet they are primarily and necessarily a part of the new and distinct civilization of the United States. They must, accordingly, be treated at all times as the heirs of the American experiment, and as entitled to all the rights and freedoms guaranteed by the Constitution.

Jackson, dissenting:

Much is said of the danger to liberty from the Army program for deporting and detaining these citizens of Japanese extraction. But a judicial construction of the due process clause that will sustain this order is a far more subtle blow to liberty than the promulgation of the order itself. A military order, however unconstitutional, is not apt to last longer than the military emergency. Even during that period, a succeeding commander may revoke it all. But once a judicial opinion rationalizes such an order to show that it conforms to the Constitution, or rather rationalizes the Constitution to show that the Constitution sanctions such an order, the Court for all time has validated the principle of racial discrimination in criminal procedure and of transplanting American citizens. The principle then lies about like a loaded weapon, ready for the hand of any authority that can bring forward a plausible claim of an urgent need. Every repetition imbeds that principle more deeply in our law and thinking and expands it to new purposes . . . A military commander may overstep the bounds of constitutionality, and it is an incident. But if we review and approve, that passing incident becomes the doctrine of the Constitution. There it has a generative power of its own, and all that it creates will be in its own image. Nothing better illustrates this danger than does the Court's opinion in this case . . .

I should hold that a civil court cannot be made to enforce an order which violates constitutional limitations even if it is a reasonable exercise of military authority. The courts can exercise only the judicial power, can apply only law, and must abide by the Constitution, or they cease to be civil courts and become instruments of military policy.

Of course, the existence of a military power resting on force, so vagrant, so centralized, so necessarily heedless of the individual, is an inherent threat to liberty. But I would not lead people to rely on this Court for a review that seems to me wholly delusive. The military reasonableness of these orders can only be determined by military superiors. If the people ever let command of the war power fall into irresponsible and unscrupulous hands, the courts wield no power equal to its restraint. The chief restraint upon those who command the physical forces of the country, in the future as in the past, must be their responsibility to the political judgments of their contemporaries and to the moral judgments of history.

My duties as a justice, as I see them, do not require me to make a military judgment as to whether General DeWitt's evacuation and detention program was a reasonable military necessity. I do not suggest that the courts should have attempted to interfere with the Army in carrying out its task. But I do not think they may be asked to execute a military expedient that has no place in law under the Constitution. I would reverse the judgment and discharge the prisoner.

Youngstown Sheet & Tube Co. v. Sawyer

343 U.S. 579 (1952), 6-3
Opinion of the Court: Black
Concurring: Burton, Clark, Douglas, Frankfurter, Jackson
Dissenting: Vinson, Minton, Reed
What do the majority justices hold with regard to inherent presidential power? Implied presidential power? What role does Congressional action play in the decision? How do Black and Jackson differ in their analysis of this case? Is Jackson's three-part guide helpful in reaching decisions about presidential power? Do examples of presidential action cited in Vinson's dissent comprehend the action taken by President Truman? Why did Truman not invoke the Taft-Hartley Act? Are there any checks, other than the constitutional ones applied by the Court, on a president's claim of

inherent power to deal with emergency situations? Is the decision in this case consistent with Curtiss-Wright Corp. v. United States? With Korematsu v. United States? *In which, Korematsu or Youngstown was the president's decision more problematic? In which was national security more at risk?*

Black, for the Court:
We are asked to decide whether the President was acting within his constitutional power when he issued an order directing the Secretary of Commerce to take possession of and operate most of the Nation's steel mills. The mill owners argue that the President's order amounts to lawmaking, a legislative function which the Constitution has expressly confided to the Congress and not to the President. The Government's position is that the order was made on findings of the President that his action was necessary to avert a national catastrophe which would inevitably result from a stoppage of steel production, and that in meeting this grave emergency the President was acting within the aggregate of his constitutional powers as the Nation's Chief Executive and the Commander in Chief of the Armed Forces of the United States . . .

The President's power, if any, to issue the order must stem either from an act of Congress or from the Constitution itself. There is no statute that expressly authorizes the President to take possession of property as he did here. Nor is there any act of Congress to which our attention has been directed from which such a power can fairly be implied. Indeed, we do not understand the Government to rely on statutory authorization for this seizure. . . .

Moreover, the use of the seizure technique to solve labor disputes in order to prevent work stoppages was not only unauthorized by any congressional enactment; prior to this controversy, Congress had refused to adopt that method of settling labor disputes. When the Taft-Hartley Act was under consideration in 1947, Congress rejected an amendment which would have authorized such governmental seizures in cases of emergency. Apparently it was thought that the technique of seizure, like that of compulsory arbitration, would interfere with the process of collective bargaining. Consequently, the plan Congress adopted in that Act did not provide for seizure under any circumstances. Instead, the plan sought to bring about settlements by use of the customary devices of mediation, conciliation, investigation by boards of inquiry, and public reports. In some instances temporary injunctions were authorized to provide cooling-off periods. All this failing, unions were left free to strike after a secret vote by employees as to whether they wished to accept their employers' final settlement offer.

It is clear that if the President had authority to issue the order he did, it must be found in some provisions of the Constitution. And it is not claimed that express constitutional language grants this power to the President. The contention is that presidential power should be implied from the aggregate of his powers under the Constitution. Particular reliance is placed on provisions in Article II which say that 'the executive Power shall be vested in a President...'; that 'he shall take Care that the Laws be faithfully executed'; and that he 'shall be Commander in Chief of the Army and Navy of the United States.'

The order cannot properly be sustained as an exercise of the President's military power as Commander in Chief of the Armed Forces. The Government attempts to do so by citing a number of cases upholding broad powers in military commanders engaged in day-to-day fighting in a theater of war. Such cases need not concern us here. Even though 'theater of war' be an expanding concept, we cannot with faithfulness to our constitutional system hold that the Commander in Chief of the Armed Forces has the ultimate power as such to take possession of private property in order to keep labor disputes from stopping production. This is a job for the Nation's lawmakers, not for its military authorities.

Nor can the seizure order be sustained because of the several constitutional provisions that grant executive power to the President. In the framework of our Constitution, the President's power to see that the laws are faithfully executed refutes the idea that he is to be a lawmaker. The Constitution limits his functions in the lawmaking process to the recommending of laws he thinks wise and the vetoing of laws he thinks bad. And the Constitution is neither silent nor equivocal about who shall make laws which the President is to execute. The first section of the first article says that 'All legislative Powers herein granted shall be vested in a Congress of the United

Charles Sawyer, President Truman's Secretary of Commerce was not smiling when he reluctantly followed his boss's order to seize privately-owned steel mills to head off a strike in June 1952 during the Korean War. Nor could he have been happy when the Supreme Court, days later, ruled that he and the president had acted unconstitutionally.

States . . .' After granting many powers to the Congress, Article I goes on to provide that Congress may 'make all Laws which shall be necessary and proper for carrying into Execution the foregoing Powers and all other Powers vested by this Constitution in the Government of the United States, or in any Department or Officer thereof.'

The President's order does not direct that a congressional policy be executed in a manner prescribed by Congress—it directs that a presidential policy be executed in a manner prescribed by the President. The preamble of the order itself . . . proclaims these policies as rules of conduct to be followed, and again, like a statute, authorizes a government official to promulgate additional rules and regulations consistent with the policy proclaimed and needed to carry that policy into execution. The power of Congress to adopt such public policies as those proclaimed by the order is beyond question. It can authorize the taking of private property for public use. It can makes laws regulating the relationships between employers and employees, prescribing rules designed to settle labor disputes, and fixing wages and working conditions in certain fields of our economy. The Constitution did not subject this lawmaking power of Congress to presidential or military supervision or control. . . .

The Founders of this Nation entrusted the law making power to the Congress alone in both good and bad times.

Jackson, concurring:

A judge, like an executive adviser, may be surprised at the poverty of really useful and unambiguous authority applicable to concrete problems of executive power as they actually present themselves. Just what our forefathers did envision, or would have envisioned had they foreseen modern conditions, must be divined from materials almost as enigmatic as the dreams Joseph was called upon to interpret for Pharaoh. A century and a half of partisan debate and scholarly speculation yields no net result but only supplies more or less apt quotations from respected sources on each side of any question. They largely cancel each other . . .

We may well begin by a somewhat over-simplified grouping of practical situations in which a President may doubt, or others may challenge, his powers, and by distinguishing roughly the legal consequences of this factor of relativity.

1. When the President acts pursuant to an express or implied authorization of Congress, his authority is at its maximum, for it includes all that he possesses in his own right plus all that Congress can delegate. In these circumstances, and in these only, may he be said . . . to personify the federal sovereignty. If his act is held unconstitutional under these circumstances, it usually means that the Federal Government as an undivided whole lacks power. A seizure executed by the President pursuant to an Act of Congress would be supported by the strongest of presumptions and the widest latitude of judicial interpretation, and the burden of persuasion would rest heavily upon any who might attack it.

2. When the President acts in absence of either a congressional grant or denial of authority, he can only rely upon his own independent powers, but there is a zone of twilight in which he and Congress may have concurrent authority, or in which its distribution is uncertain. Therefore, congressional inertia, indifference or quiescence may sometimes, at least as a practical matter, enable, if not invite, measures on independent presidential responsibility. In this area, any actual test of power is likely to depend on the imperatives of events and contemporary imponderables rather than on abstract theories of law.

3. When the President takes measures incompatible with the expressed or implied will of Congress, his power is at its lowest ebb, for then he can rely only upon his own constitutional powers minus any constitutional powers of Congress over the matter. Courts can sustain exclusive Presidential control in such a case only be disabling the Congress from acting upon the subject. Presidential claim to a power at once so conclusive and preclusive must be scrutinized with caution, for what is at stake is the equilibrium established by our constitutional system.

Into which of these classifications does this executive seizure of the steel industry fit? It is eliminated from the first by admission, for it is conceded that no congressional authorization exists for this seizure . . .

Can it then be defended under flexible tests available to the second category? It seems clearly eliminated from that class because Congress has not left seizure of private property an open field but has covered it by three statutory policies inconsistent with this seizure. In cases where the purpose is to supply needs of the Government itself, two courses are provided: one, seizure of a plant which fails to comply with obligatory orders placed by the Government, another, condemnation of facilities, including temporary use under the power of eminent domain. The third is applicable where it is the general economy of the country that is to be protected rather than exclusive governmental interests. None of these were invoked. In choosing a different and inconsistent way of his own, the President cannot claim that it is necessitated or invited by failure of Congress to legislate upon the occasions, grounds and methods for seizure of industrial properties.

This leaves the current seizure to be justified only by the severe tests under the third grouping, where it can be supported only by any remainder of executive power after subtraction of such powers as Congress may have over the subject. In short, we can sustain the President only by holding that seizure of such strikebound industries is within his domain and beyond control by Congress. . . .

I am not persuaded . . . that the executive branch, like the Federal Government as a whole, possesses only delegated powers. The purpose of the Constitution was not only to grant power, but to keep it from getting out of hand. However, because the President does not enjoy unmentioned powers does not mean that the mentioned ones should be narrowed by a niggardly construction. Some clauses could be made almost unworkable, as well as immutable, by refusal to indulge some latitude of interpretation for changing times. I . . . give to the enumerated powers the scope and elasticity afforded by what seem to be reasonable practical implications instead of the rigidity dictated by a doctrinaire textualism.

The Solicitor General seeks the power of seizure in three clauses of the Executive Article, the first reading, 'The executive Power shall be vested in a President of the United States of America.' Lest I be thought to exaggerate, I quote the interpretation which his brief puts upon it: 'In our view, this clause constitutes a grant of all the executive powers of which the Government is capable.' If that be true, it is difficult to see why the forefathers bothered to add several specific items, including some trifling ones. . . .

I cannot accept the view that this clause is a grant in bulk of all conceivable executive power but regard it as an allocation to the presidential office of the generic powers thereafter stated.

The clause on which the Government next relies is that 'The President shall be Commander in Chief of the Army and Navy of the United States . . .' These cryptic words have given rise to some of the most persistent controversies in our constitutional history. Of course, they imply something more than an empty title . . . It undoubtedly puts the Nation's armed forces under Presidential command. Hence, this loose appellation is sometimes advanced as support for any Presidential action, internal or external, involving use of force, the idea being that it vests power to do anything, anywhere, that can be done with an army or navy. . . .

[N]o doctrine that the Court could promulgate would seem to me more sinister and alarming than that a President whose conduct of foreign affairs is so largely uncontrolled, and often even is unknown, can vastly enlarge his mastery over the internal affairs of the country by his own commitment of the Nation's armed forces to some foreign venture. I do not, however, find it necessary or appropriate to consider the legal status of the Korean enterprise to discountenance argument based on it.

Assuming that we are in a war de facto, whether it is or is not a war de jure, does that empower the Commander-in-Chief to seize industries he thinks necessary to supply our army? The Constitution expressly places in Congress power 'to raise and support Armies' and 'to provide and maintain a Navy.' This certainly lays upon Congress primary responsibility for supplying the armed forces. Congress alone controls the raising of revenues and their appropriation and may determine in what manner and by what means they shall be spent for military and naval procurement . . . Congress can take over war supply as a Government enterprise. On the other hand, if Congress sees fit to rely on free private enterprise collectively bargaining with free labor for support and maintenance of our armed forces can the Executive because of lawful disagreements incidental to that process, seize the facility for operation upon Government-imposed terms?

There are indications that the Constitution did not contemplate that the title Commander-in-Chief of the Army and Navy will constitute him also Commander-in-Chief of the country, its industries and its inhabitants. He has no monopoly of 'war powers,' whatever they are. While Congress cannot deprive the President of the command of the army and navy, only Congress can provide him an army or navy to command. It is also empowered to make rules for the 'Government and Regulation of land and naval forces,' by which it may to some unknown extent impinge upon even command functions. . . .

We should not use this occasion to circumscribe, much less to contract, the lawful role of the President as Commander-in-Chief. I should indulge the widest latitude of interpretation to sustain his exclusive function to command the instruments of national force, at least when turned against the outside world for the security of our society. But, when it is turned inward, not because of rebellion but because of a lawful economic struggle between industry and labor, it should have no such indulgence. His command power is not such an absolute as might be implied from that office in a militaristic system but is subject to limitations consistent with a constitutional Republic whose law and policy-making branch is a representative Congress. The purpose of lodging dual titles in one man was to insure that the civilian would control the military, not to enable the military to subordinate the presidential office . . . What the power of command may include I do not try to envision, but I think it is not a military prerogative, without support of law, to seize persons or property because they are important or even essential for the military and naval establishment.

The third clause in which the Solicitor General finds seizure powers is that 'he shall take Care that the Laws be faithfully executed . . .' That authority must be matched against words of the Fifth Amendment that 'No person shall be . . . deprived of life, liberty, or property, without due process of law . . .' One gives a governmental authority that reaches so far as there is law, the other gives a private right that authority shall go no farther. These signify about all there is of the principle that ours is a government of laws, not of men, and that we submit ourselves to rulers only if under rules.

The Solicitor General lastly grounds support of the seizure upon nebulous, inherent powers never expressly granted but said to have accrued to the office from the customs and claims of preceding administrations. The plea is for a resulting power to deal with a crisis or an emergency according to the necessities of the case, the unarticulated assumption being that necessity knows no law. . . .

The claim of inherent and unrestricted presidential powers has long been a persuasive dialectical weapon in political controversy . . .

The Solicitor General, acknowledging that Congress has never authorized the seizure here, says practice of prior Presidents has authorized it. He seeks color of legality from claimed executive precedents, chief of which is President Roosevelt's seizure of June 9, 1941, of the California plant of the North American Aviation Company. Its superficial similarities with the present case, upon analysis, yield to dis-

tinctions so decisive that it cannot be regarded as even a precedent, much less an authority for the present seizure.

The appeal, however, that we declare the existence of inherent powers ex necessitate to meet an emergency asks us to do what many think would be wise, although it is something the forefathers omitted. They knew what emergencies were, knew the pressures they engender for authoritative action, knew, too, how they afford a ready pretext for usurpation. We may also suspect that they suspected that emergency powers would tend to kindle emergencies. Aside from suspension of the privilege of the writ of habeas corpus in time of rebellion or invasion, when the public safety may require it, they made no express provision for exercise of extraordinary authority because of a crisis. . . .

In view of the ease, expedition and safety with which Congress can grant and has granted large emergency powers, certainly ample to embrace this crisis, I am quite unimpressed with the argument that we should affirm possession of them without statute. Such power either has no beginning or it has no end. If it exists, it need submit to no legal restraint. I am not alarmed that it would plunge us straightway into dictatorship, but it is at least a step in that wrong direction. . . .

The executive action we have here originates in the individual will of the President and represents an exercise of authority without law. No one, perhaps not even the President, knows the limits of the power he may seek to exert in this instance and the parties affected cannot learn the limit of their rights. We do not know today what powers over labor or property would be claimed to flow from Government possession if we should legalize it, what rights to compensation would be claimed or recognized, or on what contingency it would end.

Vinson, C.J., (Minton, Reed) dissenting:

Those who suggest that this is a case involving extraordinary powers should be mindful that these are extraordinary times. . . .

In 1950, when the United Nations called upon member nations 'to render every assistance' to repel aggression in Korea, the United States furnished its vigorous support. For almost two full years, our armed forces have been fighting in Korea, suffering casualties of over 108,000 men. Hostilities have not abated. The 'determination of the United Nations to continue its action in Korea to meet the aggression' has been reaffirmed. Congressional support of the action in Korea has been manifested by provisions for increased military manpower and equipment and for economic stabilization . . .

Congress recognized the impact of these defense programs upon the economy. Following the attack in Korea, the President asked for authority to requisition property and to allocate and fix priorities for scarce goods. In the Defense Production Act of 1950, Congress granted the powers requested and, in addition, granted power to stabilize prices and wages and to provide for settlement of labor disputes arising in the defense program. The Defense Production Act was extended in 1951, a Senate Committee noting that in the dislocation caused by the programs for purchase of military equipment 'lies the seed of an economic disaster that might well destroy the military might we are straining to build.' Significantly, the Committee examined the problem 'in terms of just one commodity, steel,' and found 'a graphic picture of the over-all inflationary danger growing out of reduced civilian supplies and rising incomes.' Even before Korea, steel production at levels above theoretical 100% capacity was not capable of supplying civilian needs alone. Since Korea, the tremendous military demand for steel has far exceeded the increases in productive capacity. This Committee emphasized that the shortage of steel, even with the mills operating at full capacity, coupled with increased civilian purchasing power, presented grave danger of disastrous inflation . . .

One is not here called upon even to consider the possibility of executive seizure of a farm, a corner grocery store or even a single industrial plant. Such considerations arise only when one ignores the central fact of this case—that the Nation's entire basic steel production would have shut down completely if there had been no Government seizure. Even ignoring for the moment whatever confidential information the President may possess as 'the Nation's organ for foreign affairs,' the uncontroverted affidavits in this record amply support the finding that 'a work stoppage would immediately jeopardize and imperil our national defense.' . . . Accordingly, if the President has any power under the Constitution to meet a critical situation in the absence of express statutory authorization, there is no basis whatever for criticizing the exercise of such power in this case . . .

The steel mills were seized for a public use. The power of eminent domain, invoked in that case, is an essential attribute of sovereignty and has long been recognized as a power of the Federal Government. [The companies] cannot complain that any provision in the Constitution prohibits the exercise of the power of eminent domain in this case. The Fifth Amendment provides: 'nor shall private property be taken for public use, without just compensation.' It is no bar to this seizure for . . . [they] are assured of receiving the required just compensation.

Admitting that the Government could seize the mills, [the companies] claim that the implied power of eminent domain can be exercised only under an Act of Congress; under no circumstances, they say, can that power be exercised by the President unless he can point to an express provision in enabling legislation. . . .

Under this view, the President is left powerless at the very moment when the need for action may be most pressing and when no one, other than he, is immediately capable of action. Under this view, he is left powerless because a power not expressly given to Congress is nevertheless found to rest exclusively with Congress. . . .

A review of executive action demonstrates that our Presidents have on many occasions exhibited the leadership contemplated by the Framers when they made the President Commander in Chief, and imposed upon him the trust to 'take Care that the Laws be faithfully executed.' With or without explicit statutory authorization, Presidents have at such times dealt with national emergencies by acting promptly and resolutely to enforce legislative programs, at least to save those programs until Congress could act. Congress and the courts have responded to such executive initiative with consistent approval.

Our first President displayed at once the leadership contemplated by the Framers. When the national revenue laws were openly flouted in some sections of Pennsylvania, President Washington, without waiting for a call from the state government, summoned the militia and took decisive steps to secure the faithful execution of the laws. When international disputes engendered by the French revolution threatened to involve this country in war, and while congressional policy remained uncertain, Washington issued his Proclamation of Neutrality. Hamilton, whose defense of the Proclamation has endured the test of time, invoked the argument that the Executive has the duty to do that which will preserve peace until Congress acts and, in addition, pointed to the need for keeping the Nation informed of the requirements of existing laws and treaties as part of the faithful execution of the laws . . .

Jefferson's initiative in the Louisiana Purchase, the Monroe Doctrine, and Jackson's removal of Government deposits from the Bank of the United States further serve to demonstrate by deed what the Framers described by word when they vested the whole of the executive power in the President.

Without declaration of war, President Lincoln took energetic action with the outbreak of the War Between the States. He summoned troops and paid them out of the Treasury without appropriation therefor. He proclaimed a naval blockade of the Confederacy and seized ships violating that blockade. Congress, far from denying the validity of these acts, gave them express approval. The most striking action of President Lincoln was the Emancipation Proclamation, issued in aid of the successful prosecution of the War Between the States, but wholly without statutory authority.

In an action furnishing a most apt precedent for this case, President Lincoln without statutory authority directed the seizure of rail and telegraph lines leading to Washington. Many months later, Congress recognized and confirmed the power of the President to seize railroads and telegraph lines and provided criminal penalties for interference with Government operation. This Act did not confer on the President any additional powers of seizure. Congress plainly rejected the view that the President's acts had been without legal sanction until ratified by the legislature. Sponsors of the bill declared that its purpose was only to confirm the power which the President already possessed. Opponents insisted a statute authorizing seizure was unnecessary and might even be construed as limiting existing Presidential powers....

In *In re Neagle,* this Court held that a federal officer had acted in line of duty when he was guarding a Justice of this Court riding circuit. It was conceded that there was no specific statute authorizing the President to assign such a guard. In holding that such a statute was not necessary, the Court broadly stated the question as follows: '(The President) is enabled to fulfill the duty of his great department, expressed in the phrase that 'he shall take care that the laws be faithfully executed.' 'Is this duty limited to the enforcement of acts of Congress or of treaties of the United States according to their express terms, or does it include the rights, duties and obligations growing out of the Constitution itself, our international relations, and all the protection implied by the nature of the government under the Constitution?'...

President Hayes authorized the widespread use of federal troops during the Railroad Strike of 1877. President Cleveland also used the troops in the Pullman Strike of 1895 and his action is of special significance. No statute authorized this action. No call for help had issued from the Governor of Illinois; indeed Governor Altgeld disclaimed the need for supplemental forces. But the President's concern was that federal laws relating to the free flow of interstate commerce and the mails be continuously and faithfully executed without interruption. To further this aim his agents sought and obtained the injunction upheld by this Court in *In re Debs,* The Court scrutinized each of the steps taken by the President to insure execution of the 'mass of legislation' dealing with commerce and the mails and gave his conduct full approval. Congress likewise took note of this use of Presidential power to forestall apparent obstacles to the faithful execution of the laws. By separate resolutions, both the Senate and the House commended the Executive's action....

During World War I, President Wilson established a War Labor Board without awaiting specific direction by Congress... [T]he Board had as its purpose the prevention of strikes and lockouts interfering with the production of goods needed to meet the emergency. Effectiveness of War Labor Board decision was accomplished by Presidential action, including seizure of industrial plants. Seizure of the Nation's railroads was also ordered by President Wilson.

Beginning with the Bank Holiday Proclamation and continuing through World War II, executive leadership and initiative were characteristic of President Franklin D. Roosevelt's administration. In 1939, upon the outbreak of war in Europe, the President proclaimed a limited national emergency for the purpose of strengthening our national defense. By May of 1941, the danger from the Axis belligerents having become clear, the President proclaimed 'an unlimited national emergency' calling for mobilization of the Nation's defenses to repel aggression. The President took the initiative in strengthening our defenses by acquiring rights from the British Government to establish air bases in exchange for overage destroyers...

Some six months before Pearl Harbor, a dispute at a single aviation plant at Inglewood, California, interrupted a segment of the production of military aircraft. In spite of the comparative insignificance of this work stoppage to total defense production as contrasted with the complete paralysis now threatened by a shutdown of the entire basic steel industry, and even though our armed forces were not then engaged in combat, President Roosevelt ordered the seizure of the plant 'pursuant to the powers vested in (him) by the Constitution and laws of the United States, as President of the United States of America and Commander in Chief of the Army and Navy of the United States.' The Attorney General (Jackson) vigorously proclaimed that the President had the moral duty to keep this Nation's defense effort a 'going concern.' His ringing moral justification was coupled with a legal justification equally well stated:

'The Presidential proclamation rests upon the aggregate of the Presidential powers derived from the Constitution itself and from statutes enacted by the Congress.' . . .

This is but a cursory summary of executive leadership. But it amply demonstrates that Presidents have taken prompt action to enforce the laws and protect the country whether or not Congress happened to provide in advance for the particular method of execution. At the minimum, the executive actions reviewed herein sustain the action of the President in this case. And many of the cited examples of Presidential practice go far beyond the extent of power necessary to sustain the President's order to seize the steel mills. The fact that temporary executive seizures of industrial plants to meet an emergency have not been directly tested in this Court furnishes not the slightest suggestion that such actions have been illegal. Rather, the fact that Congress and the courts have consistently recognized and given their support to such executive action indicates that such a power of seizure has been accepted throughout our history. . . .

The President reported to Congress the morning after the seizure that he acted because a work stoppage in steel production would immediately imperil the safety of the Nation by preventing execution of the legislative programs for procurement of military equipment. And, while a shutdown could be averted by granting the price concessions requested by [the companies], granting such concessions would disrupt the price stabilization program also enacted by Congress. Rather than fail to execute either legislative program, the President acted to execute both.

Much of the argument in this case has been directed at straw men. We do not now have before us the case of a President acting solely on the basis of his own notions of the public welfare. Nor is there any question of unlimited executive power in this case.

The President himself closed the door to any such claim when he sent his Message to Congress stating his purpose to abide by any action of Congress, whether approving or disapproving his seizure action. Here, the President immediately made sure that Congress was fully informed of the temporary action he had taken only to preserve the legislative programs from destruction until Congress could act.

The absence of a specific statute authorizing seizure of the steel mills as a mode of executing the laws . . . has not until today been thought to prevent the President from executing the laws. Unlike an administrative commission confined to the enforcement of the statute under which it was created, or the head to a department when administering a particular statute, the President is a constitutional officer charged with taking care that a 'mass of legislation' be executed. Flexibility as to mode of execution to meet critical situations is a matter of practical necessity. . . .

In this case, there is no statute prohibiting the action taken by the President in a matter not merely important but threatening the very safety of the Nation. Executive inaction in such a situation, courting national disaster, is foreign to the concept of energy and initiative in the Executive as created by the Founding Fathers . . .

Watkins v. United States

354 U.S. 178 (1957), 6-1
Opinion of the Court: Warren (Black, Brennan, Douglas, Harlan)
Concurring: Frankfurter
Dissenting: Clark
Not participating: Burton, Whittaker
Watkins was convicted of violating 2 U.S.C. § 192, making it a misdemeanor for a witness before a Congressional committee to refuse to answer questions "pertinent to the question under inquiry." Called to testify before the House Subcommittee on Un-American Activities (HUAC), he spoke freely about his own activities and associations but refused to say whether he knew certain other persons to have been members of the Communist Party. He argued that the questions were outside of the scope of the Committee's activities and not relevant to its work.

Why must a Congressional witness be apprised of the pertinency of questions put to him or her? Has the Court held that Watkins had a free speech right not to answer? Do you believe Watkins did not understand the purpose of the inquiry or how the questions he refused to answer were perti-

nent to it? Is Congress's investigatory power enumerated? Implied? Inherent? How much does this decision limit that power? According to Warren, "There is no Congressional power to expose for the sake of exposure." Should Congress have power to investigate for the purpose of informing or alerting public opinion?

Warren, C.J., for the Court:

We start with several basic premises on which there is general agreement. The power of the Congress to conduct investigations is inherent in the legislative process. That power is broad. It encompasses inquiries concerning the administration of existing laws, as well as proposed or possibly needed statutes. It includes surveys of defects in our social, economic or political system for the purpose of enabling the Congress to remedy them. It comprehends probes into departments of the Federal Government to expose corruption, inefficiency or waste. But, broad as is this power of inquiry, it is not unlimited. There is no general authority to expose the private affairs of individuals without justification in terms of the functions of the Congress. This was freely conceded by the Solicitor General in his argument of this case. Nor is the Congress a law enforcement or trial agency. These are functions of the executive and judicial departments of government. No inquiry is an end in itself; it must be related to, and in furtherance of, a legitimate task of the Congress. Investigations conducted solely for the personal aggrandizement of the investigators or to "punish" those investigated are indefensible.

It is unquestionably the duty of all citizens to cooperate with the Congress in its efforts to obtain the facts needed for intelligent legislative action. It is their unremitting obligation to respond to subpoenas, to respect the dignity of the Congress and its committees, and to testify fully with respect to matters within the province of proper investigation. This, of course, assumes that the constitutional rights of witnesses will be respected by the Congress as they are in a court of justice. The Bill of Rights is applicable to investigations as to all forms of governmental action. Witnesses cannot be compelled to give evidence against themselves. They cannot be subjected to unreasonable search and seizure. Nor can the First Amendment freedoms of speech, press, religion, or political belief and association be abridged . . .

In the decade following World War II, there appeared a new kind of congressional inquiry unknown in prior periods of American history. Principally this was the result of the various investigations into the threat of subversion of the United States Government, but other subjects of congressional interest also contributed to the changed scene. This new phase of legislative inquiry involved a broad-scale intrusion into the lives and affairs of private citizens. It brought before the courts novel questions of the appropriate limits of congressional inquiry. Prior cases, like *Kilbourn, McGrain* and *Sinclair* had defined the scope of investigative power in terms of the inherent limitations of the sources of that power. In the more recent cases, the emphasis shifted to problems of accommodating the interest of the Government with the rights and privileges of individuals. The central theme was the application of the Bill of Rights as a restraint upon the assertion of governmental power in this form . . .

Abuses of the investigative process may imperceptibly lead to abridgment of protected freedoms. The mere summoning of a witness and compelling him to testify, against his will, about his beliefs, expressions or associations is a measure of governmental interference. And when those forced revelations concern matters that are unorthodox, unpopular, or even hateful to the general public, the reaction in the life of the witness may be disastrous. This effect is even more harsh when it is past beliefs, expressions or associations that are disclosed and judged by current standards, rather than those contemporary with the matters exposed. Nor does the witness alone suffer the consequences. Those who are identified by witnesses, and thereby placed in the same glare of publicity, are equally subject to public stigma, scorn and obloquy. Beyond that, there is the more subtle and immeasurable effect upon those who tend to adhere to the most orthodox and uncontroversial views and associations in order to avoid a similar fate at some future time. That this impact is partly the result of nongovernmental activity by private persons cannot relieve the investigators of their responsibility for initiating the reaction . . .

Accommodation of the congressional need for particular information with the individual and personal interest in privacy is an arduous and delicate task for any court. We do not underestimate the difficulties that would attend such an undertaking. It is manifest that, despite the adverse effects which follow upon compelled disclosure of private matters, not all such inquiries are barred. *Kilbourn v. Thompson* teaches that such an investigation into individual affairs is invalid if unrelated to any legislative purpose. That is beyond the powers conferred upon the Congress in the Constitution. *United States v. Rumely* makes it plain that the

In the 1950's, the House UnAmerican Activities drew upon Congressional investigating power to hold public hearin̦s on suspected Communist infiltration of American institutions, including labor unions, universities, churches, and the film industry. Here in the house Caucus Room, G. Bromley Oxman, facing camera, a left-of-center Methodist bishop and outspoken critic of the committee, is sworn to testify about his past political affiliations, June 1953. Eight months later in similar hearings in Chicago, the committee called John T. Watkins, a vice president of the Farm Equipment Workers Union and former Communist. His refusal to answer questions gave rise to the constitutional and statutory issues of *Watkins v. United States.*

mere semblance of legislative purpose would not justify an inquiry in the face of the Bill of Rights. The critical element is the existence of, and the weight to be ascribed to, the interest of the Congress in demanding disclosures from an unwilling witness. We cannot simply assume, however, that every congressional investigation is justified by a public need that overbalances any private rights affected. To do so would be to abdicate the responsibility placed by the Constitution upon the judiciary to insure that the Congress does not unjustifiably encroach upon an individual's [354 U.S. 199] right to privacy nor abridge his liberty of speech, press, religion or assembly.

[Watkins] has earnestly suggested that the difficult questions of protecting these rights from infringement by legislative inquiries can be surmounted in this case because there was no public purpose served in his interrogation. His conclusion is based upon the thesis that the Subcommittee was engaged in a program of exposure for the sake of exposure. The sole purpose of the inquiry, he contends, was to bring down upon himself and others the violence of public reaction because of their past beliefs, expressions and associations. In support of this argument, petitioner has marshalled an impressive array of evidence that some Congressmen have believed that such was their duty, or part of it.

We have no doubt that there is no congressional power to expose for the sake of exposure. The public is, of course, entitled to be informed concerning the workings of its government. That cannot be inflated into a general power to expose where the predominant result can only be an invasion of the private rights of individuals. But a solution to our problem is not to be found in testing the motives of committee members for this purpose. Such is not our function. Their motives alone would not vitiate an investigation which had been instituted by a House of Congress if that assembly's legislative purpose is being served.

. . . The theory of a committee inquiry is that the committee members are serving as the representatives of the parent assembly in collecting information for a legislative purpose. Their function is to act as the eyes and ears of the Congress in obtaining facts upon which the full legislature can act . . .

An essential premise in this situation is that the House or Senate shall have instructed the committee members on what they are to do with the power delegated to them. It is the responsibility of the Congress, in the first instance, to insure that compulsory process is used only in furtherance of a legislative purpose. That requires that the instructions to an investigating committee spell out that group's jurisdiction and purpose with sufficient particularity. Those instructions are embodied in the authorizing resolution. That document is the committee's charter. Broadly drafted and loosely worded, however, such resolutions can leave tremendous latitude to the discretion of the investigators. The more vague the committee's charter is, the greater becomes the possibility that the committee's specific actions are not in conformity with the will of the parent House of Congress.

The authorizing resolution of the Un-American Activities Committee was adopted in 1938, when a select committee, under the chairmanship of Representative Dies, was created. Several years later, the Committee was made a standing organ of the House with the same mandate. It defines the Committee's authority as follows:

> The Committee on Un-American Activities, as a whole or by subcommittee, is authorized to make from time to time investigations of (1) the extent, character, and objects of un-American propaganda activities in the United States, (2) the diffusion within the United States of subversive and un-American propaganda that is instigated from foreign countries or of a domestic origin and attacks the principle of the form of government as guaranteed by our Constitution, and (3) all other questions in relation thereto that would aid Congress in any necessary remedial legislation.

It would be difficult to imagine a less explicit authorizing resolution. Who can define the meaning of "un-American"? What is that single, solitary "principle of the form of government as guaranteed by our Constitution"? There is no need to dwell upon the language, however. At one time, perhaps, the resolution might have been read narrowly to confine the Committee to the subject of propaganda. The events that have transpired in the fifteen years before the interrogation of petitioner make such a construction impossible at this date.

The members of the Committee have clearly demonstrated that they did not feel themselves restricted in any way to propaganda in the narrow sense of the word. Unquestionably, the Committee conceived of its task in the grand view of its name. Un-American activities were its target, no matter how or where manifested. Notwithstanding the broad purview of the Committee's experience, the House of Representatives repeatedly approved its continuation. Five times it extended the life of the special committee. Then it made the group a standing committee of the House. A year later, the Committee's charter was embodied in the Legislative Reorganization Act. On five occasions, at the beginning of sessions of Congress, it has made the authorizing resolution part of the rules of the House. On innumerable occasions, it has passed appropriation bills to allow the Committee to continue its efforts.

Combining the language of the resolution with the construction it has been given, it is evident that the preliminary control of the Committee exercised by the House of Representatives is slight or nonexistent. No one could reasonably deduce from the charter the kind of investigation that the Committee was directed to make. As a result, we are asked to engage in a process of retroactive rationalization. Looking backward from the events that transpired, we are asked to uphold the Committee's actions unless it appears that they were clearly not authorized by the charter. As a corollary to this inverse approach, the Government urges that we must view the matter hospitably to the power of the Congress—that, if there is any legislative purpose which might have been furthered by the kind of disclosure sought, the witness must be punished for withholding it. No doubt every reasonable indulgence of legality must be accorded to the actions of a coordinate branch of our Government. But such deference cannot yield to an unnecessary and unreasonable dissipation of precious constitutional freedoms.

The Government contends that the public interest at the core of the investigations of the Un-American Activities Committee is the need by the Congress to be informed of efforts to overthrow the Government by force and violence, so that adequate legislative safeguards can be erected. From this core, however, the Committee can radiate outward infinitely to any topic thought to be related in some way to armed insurrection. The outer reaches of this domain are known only by the content of "un-American activities." Remoteness of subject can be aggravated by a probe for a depth of detail even farther removed from any basis of legislative action. A third dimension is added when the investigators turn their attention to the past to collect minutiae on remote topics, on the hypothesis that the past may reflect upon the present . . .

. . . An excessively broad charter like that of the House Un-American Activities Committee places the courts in an untenable position if they are to strike a balance between the public need for a particular interrogation and the right of citizens to carry on their affairs free from unnecessary governmental interference. It is impossible in such a situation to ascertain whether any legislative purpose justifies the disclosures sought, and, if so, the importance of that information to the Congress in furtherance of its legislative function. The reason no court can make this critical judgment is that the House of Representatives itself has never made it. Only the legislative assembly initiating an investigation can assay the relative necessity of specific disclosures.

Absence of the qualitative consideration of petitioner's questioning by the House of Representatives aggravates a serious problem, revealed in this case, in the relationship of congressional investigating committees and the witnesses who appear before them. Plainly, these committees are restricted to the missions delegated to them, i.e., to acquire certain data to be used by the House or the Senate in coping with a problem that falls within its legislative sphere. No witness can be compelled to make disclosures on matters outside that area. This is a jurisdictional concept of pertinency drawn from the nature of a congressional committee's source of authority. It is not wholly different from nor unrelated to the element of pertinency embodied in the criminal statute under which petitioner was prosecuted. When the definition of jurisdictional pertinency is as uncertain and wavering as in the case of the Un-American Activities Committee, it becomes extremely difficult for the Committee to limit its inquiries to statutory pertinency . . .

The appropriate statute is found in 2 U.S.C. § 192. It provides:

> Every person who having been summoned as a witness by the authority of either House of Congress to give testimony . . . refuses to answer any question pertinent to the question under in-

quiry, shall be deemed guilty of a misdemeanor, punishable by a fine of not more than $1,000 nor less than $100 and imprisonment in a common jail for not less than one month nor more than twelve months.

In fulfillment of their obligation under this statute, the courts must accord to the defendants every right which is guaranteed to defendants in all other criminal cases. Among these is the right to have available, through a sufficiently precise statute, information revealing the standard of criminality before the commission of the alleged offense. Applied to persons prosecuted under § 192, this raises a special problem in that the statute defines the crime as refusal to answer "any question pertinent to the question under inquiry." Part of the standard of criminality, therefore, is the pertinency of the questions propounded to the witness.

The problem attains proportion when viewed from the standpoint of the witness who appears before a congressional committee. He must decide at the time the questions are propounded whether or not to answer . . . An erroneous determination on his part, even if made in the utmost good faith, does not exculpate him if the court should later rule that the questions were pertinent to the question under inquiry.

It is obvious that a person compelled to make this choice is entitled to have knowledge of the subject to which the interrogation is deemed pertinent. That knowledge must be available with the same degree of explicitness and clarity that the Due Process Clause requires in the expression of any element of a criminal offense. The "vice of vagueness" must be avoided here, as in all other crimes. There are several sources that can outline the "question under inquiry" in such a way that the rules against vagueness are satisfied. The authorizing resolution, the remarks of the chairman or members of the committee, or even the nature of the proceedings themselves, might sometimes make the topic clear. This case demonstrates, however, that these sources often leave the matter in grave doubt.

The first possibility is that the authorizing resolution itself will so clearly declare the "question under inquiry" that a witness can understand the pertinency of questions asked him. The Government does not contend that the authorizing resolution of the Un-American Activities Committee could serve such a purpose. Its confusing breadth is amply illustrated by the innumerable and diverse questions into which the Committee has inquired under this charter since 1938. If the "question under inquiry" were stated with such sweeping and uncertain scope, we doubt that it would withstand an attack on the ground of vagueness . . .

No aid is given as to the "question under inquiry" in the action of the full Committee that authorized the creation of the Subcommittee before which petitioner appeared. The Committee adopted a formal resolution giving the Chairman the power to appoint subcommittees ". . . for the purpose of performing any and all acts which the Committee as a whole is authorized to do." In effect, this was a device to enable the investigations to proceed with a quorum of one or two members and sheds no light on the relevancy of the questions asked of petitioner . . .

The final source of evidence as to the "question under inquiry" is the Chairman's response when petitioner objected to the questions on the grounds of lack of pertinency. The Chairman then announced that the Subcommittee was investigating "subversion and subversive propaganda." This is a subject at least as broad and indefinite as the authorizing resolution of the Committee, if not more so.

Having exhausted the several possible indicia of the "question under inquiry," we remain unenlightened as to the subject to which the questions asked petitioner were pertinent. Certainly, if the point is that obscure after trial and appeal, it was not adequately revealed to petitioner when he had to decide at his peril whether or not to answer. Fundamental fairness demands that no witness be compelled to make such a determination with so little guidance. Unless the subject matter has been made to appear with undisputable clarity, it is the duty of the investigative body, upon objection of the witness on grounds of pertinency, to state for the record the subject under inquiry at that time and the manner in which the propounded questions are pertinent thereto. To be meaningful, the explanation must describe what the topic under inquiry is and the connective reasoning whereby the precise questions asked relate to it.

The statement of the Committee Chairman in this case, in response to petitioner's protest, was woefully inadequate to convey sufficient information as to the pertinency of the questions to the subject under inquiry. Petitioner was thus not accorded a fair opportunity to determine whether he was within his rights in refusing to answer, and his conviction is necessarily invalid under the Due Process Clause of the Fifth Amendment.

Clark, dissenting:

I think the Committee here was acting entirely within its scope, and that the purpose of its inquiry was set out with "undisputable clarity." In the first place, the authorizing language . . . must be read as a whole, not dissected. It authorized investigation into subversive activity, its extent, character, objects, and diffusion. While the language might have been more explicit than using such words as "un-American," or phrases like "principle of the form of government," still, these are fairly well understood terms . . . Our cases indicate that, rather than finding fault with the use of words or phrases, we are bound to presume that the action of the legislative body in granting authority to the Committee was with a legitimate object "if [the action] is capable of being so construed." Before we can deny the authority, "it must be obvious that" the Committee has "exceeded the bounds of legislative power." The fact that the Committee has often been attacked has caused close scrutiny of its acts by the House as a whole, and the House has repeatedly given the Committee its approval. "Power" and "responsibility" have not been separated. But the record in this case does not stop here. It shows that, at the hearings involving Watkins, the Chairman made statements explaining the functions of the Committee. And, furthermore, Watkins' action at the hearing clearly reveals that he was well acquainted with the purpose of the hearing. It was to investigate Communist infiltration into his union. This certainly falls within the grant of authority from the Reorganization Act, and the House has had ample opportunity to limit the investigative scope of the Committee if it feels that the Committee has exceeded its legitimate bounds.

The Court makes much of petitioner's claim of "exposure for exposure's sake," and strikes at the purposes of the Committee through this catch phrase. But we are bound to accept as the purpose of the Committee that stated in [its charter], together with the statements of the Chairman at the hearings involved here. Nothing was said of exposure. The statements of a single Congressman cannot transform the real purpose of the Committee into something not authorized by the parent resolution. The Court indicates that the questions propounded were asked for exposure's sake, and had no pertinency to the inquiry. It appears to me that they were entirely pertinent to the announced purpose of the Committee's inquiry. Undoubtedly Congress has the power to inquire into the subjects of communism and the Communist Party. As a corollary of the congressional power to inquire into such subject matter, the Congress, through its committees, can legitimately seek to identify individual members of the Party.

The pertinency of the questions is highlighted by the need for the Congress to know the extent of infiltration of communism in labor unions. This technique of infiltration was that used in bringing the downfall of countries formerly free but now still remaining behind the Iron Curtain . . . If the parties about whom Watkins was interrogated were Communists and collaborated with him, as a prior witness indicated, an entirely new area of investigation might have been opened up. Watkins' silence prevented the Committee from learning this information which could have been vital to its future investigation. The Committee was likewise entitled to elicit testimony showing the truth or falsity of the prior testimony of the witnesses who had involved Watkins and the union with collaboration with the Party. If the testimony was untrue, a false picture of the relationship between the union and the Party leaders would have resulted. For these reasons, there were ample indications of the pertinency of the questions.

Baker v. Carr

369 U.S. 186 (1952), 6-2
Opinion of the Court: Brennan (Black, Douglas, Warren)
Concurring: Clark, Douglas, Stewart
Dissenting: Frankfurter, Harlan
Not participating: Whittaker
The case was an appeal by several Tennessee voters from a ruling by a three-judge federal district court that their suit challenging the malapportionment of state legislature districts presented a nonjusticiable question and should be dismissed.

Did the Court hold the Tennessee legislative districts were malapportioned? The three opinions here represent highly contrasting positions. How do they differ from each other on the role of the courts in the separation of power? On the competence of courts in questions of legislative malapportion-

ment? On their interpretation of text of the Constitution? On the meaning of democracy? What does Frankfurter mean when he says that Brennan's approach requires the Court to choose "among competing theories of political philosophy"? Does his own? Does Frankfurter say the matter is a political question the courts cannot decide or that there has been no constitutional violation or both? Who gained and lost as a result of the Court's decision?

Brennan, for the Court:
[T]he District Court to have read the cited cases as compelling the conclusion that since [Baker et al.] sought to have a legislative apportionment held unconstitutional, their suit presented a 'political question' and was therefore nonjusticiable. We hold that this challenge to an apportionment presents no nonjusticiable 'political question.' . . .

[T]he mere fact that the suit seeks protection of a political right does not mean it presents a political question . . . [I]t is argued that apportionment cases, whatever the actual wording of the complaint, can involve no federal constitutional right except one resting on the guaranty of a republican form of government, and that complaints based on that clause have been held to present political questions which are nonjusticiable.

We hold that the claim pleaded here neither rests upon nor implicates the Guaranty Clause and that its justiciability is therefore not foreclosed by our decisions of cases involving that clause . . . [Baker et al.] claim that they are being denied equal protection is justiciable, and if 'discrimination is sufficiently shown, the right to relief under the equal protection clause is not diminished by the fact that the discrimination relates to political rights. 'To show why we reject the argument based on the Guaranty Clause, we must examine the authorities under it. But because there appears to be some uncertainty as to why those cases did present political questions, and specifically as to whether this apportionment case is like those cases, we deem it necessary first to consider the contours of the 'political question' doctrine. . . .

[I]n the Guaranty Clause cases and in the other 'political question' cases, it is the relationship between the judiciary and the coordinate branches of the Federal Government, and not the federal judiciary's relationship to the States, which gives rise to the 'political question.'

We have said that 'In determining whether a question falls within (the political question) category, the appropriateness under our system of government of attributing finality to the action of the political departments and also the lack of satisfactory criteria for a judicial determination are dominant considerations.' The nonjusticiability of a political question is primarily a function of the separation of powers ... Deciding whether a matter has in any measure been committed by the Constitution to another branch of government, or whether the action of that branch exceeds whatever authority has been committed, is itself a delicate exercise in constitutional interpretation, and is a responsibility of this Court as ultimate interpreter of the Constitution. To demonstrate this requires no less than to analyze representative cases and to infer from them the analytical threads that make up the political question doctrine. We shall then show that none of those threads catches this case.

Foreign relations: There are sweeping statements to the effect that all questions touching foreign relations are political questions. Not only does resolution of such issues frequently turn on standards that defy judicial application, or involve the exercise of a discretion demonstrably committed to the executive or legislature; but many such questions uniquely demand single-voiced statement of the Government's views. Yet it is error to suppose that every case or controversy which touches foreign relations lies beyond judicial cognizance. Our cases in this field seem invariably to show a discriminating analysis of the particular question posed, in terms of the history of its management by the political branches, of its susceptibility to judicial handling in the light of its nature and posture in the specific case, and of the possible consequences of judicial action. For example, though a court will not ordinarily inquire whether a treaty has been terminated, since on that question 'governmental action ... must be regarded as of controlling importance,' if there has been no conclusive 'governmental action' then a court can construe a treaty and may find it provides the answer. Though a court will not undertake to construe a treaty in a manner inconsistent with a subsequent federal statute, no similar hesitancy obtains if the asserted clash is with state law. ...

Dates of duration of hostilities: Though it has been stated broadly that 'the power which declared the necessity is the power to declare its cessation, and what the cessation requires,' here too analysis reveals isolatable reasons for the presence of political questions, underlying this Court's refusal to review the political

departments' determination of when or whether a war has ended. Dominant is the need for finality in the political determination, for emergency's nature demands 'A prompt and unhesitating obedience,' Moreover, 'the cessation of hostilities does not necessarily end the war power. It was stated in *Hamilton v. Kentucky Distilleries & W. Co.* that the war power includes the power 'to remedy the evils which have arisen from its rise and progress' and continues during that emergency. But deference rests on reason, not habit. The question in a particular case may not seriously implicate considerations of finality—e.g., a public program of importance (rent control) yet not central to the emergency effort. Further, clearly definable criteria for decision may be available. In such case the political question barrier falls away ...

It is apparent that several formulations which vary slightly according to the settings in which the questions arise may describe a political question, although each has one or more elements which identify it as essentially a function of the separation of powers. Prominent on the surface of any case held to involve a political question is found a textually demonstrable constitutional commitment of the issue to a coordinate political department; or a lack of judicially discoverable and manageable standards for resolving it; or the impossibility of deciding without an initial policy determination of a kind clearly for non-judicial discretion; or the impossibility of a court's undertaking independent resolution without expressing lack of the respect due coordinate branches of government; or an unusual need for unquestioning adherence to a political decision already made; or the potentiality of embarrassment from multifarious pronouncements by various departments on one question.

Unless one of these formulations is inextricable from the case at bar, there should be no dismissal for non-justiciability on the ground of a political question's presence. The doctrine of which we treat is one of 'political questions,' not one of 'political cases.' ...

But it is argued that this case shares the characteristics of decisions that constitute a category not yet considered, cases concerning the Constitution's guaranty, in Art. IV, s 4, of a republican form of government. A conclusion as to whether the case at bar does present a political question cannot be confidently reached until we have considered those cases with special care. We shall discover that Guaranty Clause claims involve those elements which define a 'political question,' and for that reason and no other, they are non-justiciable. In particular, we shall discover that the non-justiciability of such claims has nothing to do with their touching upon matters of state governmental organization.

Republican form of government: . . . Clearly, several factors were thought by the Court in *Luther [v. Borden]* to make the question there 'political': the commitment to the other branches of the decision as to which is the lawful state government; the unambiguous action by the President, in recognizing the charter government as the lawful authority; the need for finality in the executive's decision; and the lack of criteria by which a court could determine which form of government was republican.

But the only significance that *Luther* could have for our immediate purposes is in its holding that the Guaranty Clause is not a repository of judicially manageable standards which a court could utilize independently in order to identify a State's lawful government. The Court has since refused to resort to the Guaranty Clause . . . as the source of a constitutional standard for invalidating state action. . . .

Just as the Court has consistently held that a challenge to state action based on the Guaranty Clause presents no justiciable question so has it held . . . that challenges to congressional action on the ground of inconsistency with that clause present no justiciable question. In *Georgia v. Stanton*, the State sought by an original bill to enjoin execution of the Reconstruction Acts, claiming that it already possessed 'A republican State, in every political, legal, constitutional, and juridical sense,' and that enforcement of the new Acts 'Instead of keeping the guaranty against a forcible overthrow of its government by foreign invaders or domestic insurgents, . . . is destroying that very government by force.' Congress had clearly refused to recognize the republican character of the government of the suing State. It seemed to the Court that the only constitutional claim that could be presented was under the Guaranty Clause, and Congress having determined that the effects of the recent hostilities required extraordinary measures to restore governments of a republican form, this Court refused to interfere with Congress' action at the behest of a claimant relying on that very guaranty. . . .

We come, finally, to the ultimate inquiry whether our precedents as to what constitutes a non-justiciable 'political question' bring the case before us under the umbrella of that doctrine. A natural beginning is to note whether any of the common characteristics which we have been able to identify and label descrip-

tively are present. We find none: The question here is the consistency of state action with the Federal Constitution. We have no question decided, or to be decided, by a political branch of government coequal with this Court. Nor do we risk embarrassment of our government abroad, or grave disturbance at home if we take issue with Tennessee as to the constitutionality of her action here challenged. Nor need [Baker et al.] . . . ask the Court to enter upon policy determinations for which judicially manageable standards are lacking. Judicial standards under the Equal Protection Clause are well developed and familiar, and it has been open to courts since the enactment of the Fourteenth Amendment to determine . . . that a discrimination reflects no policy, but simply arbitrary and capricious action.

This case does . . . involve the allocation of political power within a State, and [Baker et al.] might conceivably have added a claim under the Guaranty Clause. Of course, as we have seen, any reliance on that clause would be futile. But because any reliance on the Guaranty Clause could not have succeeded it does not follow that [they] may not be heard on the equal protection claim which in fact they tender. . . .

We conclude then that the non-justiciability of claims resting on the Guaranty Clause which arises from their embodiment of questions that were thought 'political,' can have no bearing upon the justiciability of the equal protection claim presented in this case. . . .

Clark, Concurring:

The Court holds that [Baker et al.] have alleged a cause of action. However, it refuses to award relief here—although the facts are undisputed—and fails to give the District Court any guidance whatever . . . I believe it can be shown that this case is distinguishable from earlier cases dealing with the distribution of political power by a State, that a patent violation of the Equal Protection Clause of the United States Constitution has been shown, and that an appropriate remedy may be formulated. . . .

The controlling facts cannot be disputed. . . . The frequency and magnitude of the inequalities in the present districting admit of no policy whatever. An examination of Table I accompanying this opinion, conclusively reveals that the apportionment picture in Tennessee is a topsy-turvical of gigantic proportions. This is not to say that some of the disparity cannot be explained, but when the entire table is examined—comparing the voting strength of counties of like population as well as contrasting that of the smaller with the larger counties—it leaves but one conclusion, namely that Tennessee's apportionment is a crazy quilt without rational basis. . . .

The truth is that—although this case has been here for two years and has had over six hours' argument (three times the ordinary case) and has been most carefully considered over and over again by us in Conference and individually—no one, not even the State nor the dissenters, has come up with any rational basis for Tennessee's apportionment statute. . . .

Although I find the Tennessee apportionment statute offends the Equal Protection Clause, I would not consider intervention by this Court into so delicate a field if there were any other relief available to the people of Tennessee. But the majority of the people of Tennessee have no 'Practical opportunities for exerting their political weight at the polls' to correct the existing 'invidious discrimination.' Tennessee has no initiative and referendum. I have searched diligently for other 'practical opportunities' present under the law. I find none other than through the federal courts. The majority of the voters have been caught up in a legislative strait jacket. Tennessee has an 'informed, civically militant electorate' and 'an aroused popular conscience,' but it does not sear 'the conscience of the people's representatives.' This is because the legislative policy has riveted the present seats in the Assembly to their respective constituencies, and by the votes of their incumbents a reapportionment of any kind is prevented. The people have been rebuffed at the hands of the Assembly; they have tried the constitutional convention route, but since the call must originate in the Assembly it, too, has been fruitless. They have tried Tennessee courts with the same result, and Governors have fought the tide only to flounder. It is said that there is recourse in Congress and perhaps that may be, but from a practical standpoint this is without substance. To date Congress has never undertaken such a task in any State. We therefore must conclude that the people of Tennessee are stymied and without judicial intervention will be saddled with the present discrimination in the affairs of their state government . . .

Frankfurter (Harlan), dissenting:

The Court today reverses a uniform course of decision established by a dozen cases, including one by which the very claim now sustained was unanimously rejected only five years ago. The impressive body of rulings thus cast aside reflected the equally uniform

course of our political history regarding the relationship between population and legislative representation—a wholly different matter from denial of the franchise to individuals because of race, color, religion or sex. Such a massive repudiation of the experience of our whole past in asserting destructively novel judicial power demands a detailed analysis of the role of this Court in our constitutional scheme. Disregard of inherent limits in the effective exercise of the Court's 'judicial Power' not only presages the futility of judicial intervention in the essentially political conflict of forces by which the relation between population and representation has time out of mind been and now is determined. It may well impair the Court's position as the ultimate organ of 'the supreme Law of the Land' in that vast range of legal problems, often strongly entangled in popular feeling, on which this Court must pronounce. The Court's authority—possessed of neither the purse nor the sword—ultimately rests on sustained public confidence in its moral sanction. Such feeling must be nourished by the Court's complete detachment, in fact and in appearance, from political entanglements and by abstention from injecting itself into the clash of political forces in political settlements.

A hypothetical claim resting on abstract assumptions is now for the first time made the basis for affording illusory relief for a particular evil . . . The claim is hypothetical and the assumptions are abstract because the Court does not vouchsafe the lower courts—state and federal—guidelines for formulating specific, definite, wholly unprecedented remedies for the inevitable litigations that today's umbrageous disposition is bound to stimulate in connection with politically motivated reapportionments in so many States. In such a setting, to promulgate jurisdiction . . . is as devoid of reality as 'a brooding omnipresence in the sky,' for it conveys no intimation what relief, if any, a District Court is capable of affording that would not invite legislatures to play ducks and drakes with the judiciary. For this Court to direct the District Court to enforce a claim to which the Court has over the years consistently found itself required to deny legal enforcement and at the same time to find it necessary to withhold any guidance to the lower court how to enforce this turnabout, new legal claim, manifests an odd—indeed an esoteric—conception of judicial propriety . . .

[T]oday's decision empowers the courts of the country to devise what should constitute the proper composition of the legislatures of the fifty States. If state courts should for one reason or another find themselves unable to discharge this task, the duty of doing so is put on the federal courts or on this Court, if State views do not satisfy this Court's notion of what is proper districting. . . .

[T]here is not under our Constitution a judicial remedy for every political mischief, for every undesirable exercise of legislative power. The Framers carefully and with deliberate forethought refused so to enthrone the judiciary. In this situation . . . appeal for relief does not belong here. Appeal must be to an informed, civically militant electorate. In a democratic society like ours, relief must come through an aroused popular conscience that sears the conscience of the people's representatives . . .

The present case involves all of the elements that have made the Guarantee Clause cases non-justiciable. It is, in effect, a Guarantee Clause claim masquerading under a different label. But it cannot make the case more fit for judicial action that [Baker et al.] invoke the Fourteenth Amendment rather than Art. IV, s 4, where, in fact, the gist of their complaint is the same—unless it can be found that the Fourteenth Amendment speaks with greater particularity to their situation . . . But where judicial competence is wanting, it cannot be created by invoking one clause of the Constitution rather than another . . .

In invoking the Equal Protection Clause, [Baker et al.] assert that the distortion of representative government complained of is produced by systematic discrimination against them, by way of 'a debasement of their votes . . .' Does this characterization, with due regard for the facts from which it is derived, add anything to [Baker et al.'s] case?

At first blush, this charge of discrimination based on legislative under-representation is given the appearance of a more private, less impersonal claim, than the assertion that the frame of government is askew. [They] appear as representatives of a class that is prejudiced as a class, in contradistinction to the polity in its entirety. However, the discrimination relied on is the deprivation of what [Baker et al.] conceive to be their proportionate share of political influence. This, of course, is the practical effect of any allocation of power within the institutions of government. Hardly any distribution of political authority that could be assailed as rendering government non-republican would fail similarly to operate to the prejudice of some groups, and to the advantage of others, within the body politic. It would be ingenuous not to see, or consciously blind to deny, that the real battle over the initiative and referendum, or over a delegation of power to local rather than state-wide authority, is the battle between forces whose influence is disparate among the various organs of government to whom power may be given. No shift of power but works a corresponding shift in political influence among the groups composing a society.

What, then, is this question of legislative apportionment? [Baker et al.] invoke the right to vote and to have their votes counted. But they are permitted to vote and their votes are counted. They go to the polls, they cast their ballots, they send their representatives to the state councils. Their complaint is simply that the representatives are not sufficiently numerous or powerful—in short, that Tennessee has adopted a basis of representation with which they are dissatisfied. Talk of 'debasement' or 'dilution' is circular talk. One cannot speak of 'debasement' or 'dilution' of the value of a vote until there is first defined a standard of reference as to what a vote should be worth. What is actually asked of the Court in this case is to choose among competing bases of representation—ultimately, really, among competing theories of political philosophy—in order to establish an appropriate frame of government for the State of Tennessee and thereby for all the States of the Union.

In such a matter, abstract analogies which ignore the facts of history deal in unrealities; they betray reason. This is not a case in which a State has, through a device however oblique and sophisticated, denied Negroes or Jews or redheaded persons a vote, or given them only a third or a sixth of a vote. What Tennessee illustrates is an old and still widespread method of representation—representation by local geographical division, only in part respective of population—in preference to others, others . . . more appealing. [Baker et al.] contest this choice and seek to make this Court the arbiter of the disagreement. They would make the Equal Protection Clause the charter of adjudication, asserting that the equality which it guarantees comports, if not the assurance of equal weight to every voter's vote, at least the basic conception that representation ought to be proportionate to population, a standard by reference to which the reasonableness of apportionment plans may be judged.

To find such a political conception legally enforceable in the broad and unspecific guarantee of equal protection is to rewrite the Constitution. Certainly, 'equal protection' is no more secure a foundation for judicial judgment of the permissibility of varying forms of representative government than is 'Republican Form.' Indeed since 'equal protection of the laws' can only mean an equality of persons standing in the same relation to whatever governmental action is challenged, the determination whether treatment is equal presupposes a determination concerning the nature of the relationship. This, with respect to apportionment, means an inquiry into the theoretic base of representation in an acceptably republican state. For a court could not determine the equal-protection issue without in fact first determining the Republican-Form issue, simply because what is reasonable for equal-protection purposes will depend upon what frame of government, basically, is allowed. To divorce 'equal protection' from 'Republican Form' is to talk about half a question . . .

Manifestly, the Equal Protection Clause supplies no clearer guide for judicial examination of apportionment methods than would the Guarantee Clause itself. Apportionment, by its character, is a subject of extraordinary complexity, involving—even after the fundamental theoretical issues concerning what is to be represented in a representative legislature have been fought out or compromised—considerations of geography, demography, electoral convenience, economic and social cohesions or divergencies among particular local groups, communications, the practical effects of political institutions like the lobby and the city machine, ancient traditions and ties of settled usage, respect for proven incumbents of long experience and senior status, mathematical mechanics, censuses compiling relevant data, and a host of others. Legislative responses throughout the country to the reapportionment demands of the 1960 Census have glaringly confirmed that these are not factors that lend themselves to evaluations of a nature that are the staple of judicial determinations or for which judges are equipped to adjudicate by legal training or experience or native wit. And this is the more so true because in every strand of this complicated, intricate web of values meet the contending forces of partisan politics. The practical significance of apportionment is that the next election results may differ because of it. Apportionment battles are overwhelmingly party or intra-party contests. It will add a virulent source of friction and tension in federal-state relations to embroil the federal judiciary in them.

Flast v. Cohen

392 U.S. 93 (1968), 8-1
Opinion of the Court: Warren, C.J. (Black, Brennan, Marshall, White)
Concurring: Douglas, Fortas, Stewart
Dissenting: Harlan

When may a federal taxpayer have standing to challenge federal spending? Is Warren's reasoning clear on this point? What would the consequences be of allowing general taxpayers to sue? How might it change the balance in the political system? Would it make the system more democratic or less?

Warren, C.J., for the Court:

In *Frothingham v. Mellon* this Court ruled that a federal taxpayer is without standing to challenge the constitutionality of a federal statute. That ruling has stood for 45 years as an impenetrable barrier to suits against Acts of Congress brought by individuals who can assert only the interest of federal taxpayers. In this case, we must decide whether the Frothingham barrier should be lowered when a taxpayer attacks a federal statute on the ground that it violates the Establishment and Free Exercise Clauses of the First Amendment.

[Flast and six other taxpayers] filed suit . . . enjoin the allegedly unconstitutional expenditure of federal funds under Titles I and II of the Elementary and Secondary Education Act of 1965 . . . [I]t is clear from the complaint that they were resting their standing to maintain the action solely on their status as federal taxpayers. [Cohen, et al.], who are charged by Congress with administering the Elementary and Secondary Education Act of 1965, were sued in their official capacities . . .

Although the barrier *Frothingham* erected against federal taxpayer suits has never been breached, the decision has been the source of some confusion, and the object of considerable criticism. The confusion has developed as commentators have tried to determine whether *Frothingham* establishes a constitutional bar to taxpayer suits or whether the Court was simply imposing a rule of self-restraint which was not constitutionally compelled . . .

Whatever the merits of the current debate over *Frothingham*, its very existence suggests that we should undertake a fresh examination of the limitations upon standing to sue in a federal court and the application of those limitations to taxpayer suits . . .

Standing is an aspect of justiciability, and, as such, the problem of standing is surrounded by the same complexities and vagaries that inhere in justiciability.

Standing has been called one of "the most amorphous [concepts] in the entire domain of public law." Some of the complexities peculiar to standing problems result because standing "serves, on occasion, as a shorthand expression for all the various elements of justiciability." In addition, there are at work in the standing doctrine the many subtle pressures which tend to cause policy considerations to blend into constitutional limitations.

Despite the complexities and uncertainties, some meaningful form can be given to the jurisdictional limitations placed on federal court power by the concept of standing. The fundamental aspect of standing is that it focuses on the party seeking to get his complaint before a federal court, and not on the issues he wishes to have adjudicated. The "gist of the question of standing" is whether the party seeking relief has alleged such a personal stake in the outcome of the controversy as to assure that concrete adverseness which sharpens the presentation of issues upon which the court so largely depends for illumination of difficult constitutional questions.

In other words, when standing is placed in issue in a case, the question is whether the person whose standing is challenged is a proper party to request an adjudication of a particular issue, and not whether the issue itself is justiciable . . .

When the emphasis in the standing problem is placed on whether the person invoking a federal court's jurisdiction is a proper party to maintain the action, the weakness of the Government's argument in this case becomes apparent. The question whether a particular person is a proper party to maintain the action does not, by its own force, raise separation of powers problems related to improper judicial interference in areas committed to other branches of the Federal Government. Such problems arise, if at all, only from the substantive issues the individual seeks to have adjudicated. Thus, in terms of Article III limitations on federal court jurisdiction, the question of standing is related only to whether the dispute sought to be adjudicated will be presented in an adversary context and in a form historically viewed as capable of judicial resolution. It is for that reason that the emphasis in standing problems is on whether the party invoking federal court jurisdiction has "a personal stake in the outcome of the controversy," *Baker v. Carr,* and whether the dispute touches upon "the legal relations of parties having adverse legal interests." *Aetna Life Insurance Co. v. Haworth.* A taxpayer may or may not have the requisite personal stake in the outcome, depending upon the circumstances of the particular case. Therefore, we find no absolute bar in Article III to suits by federal taxpayers challenging allegedly unconstitutional federal taxing and spending programs. There remains, however, the problem of determining the circumstances under which a federal taxpayer will be deemed to have the personal stake and interest that impart the necessary concrete adverseness to such litigation so that standing can be conferred on the taxpayer qua taxpayer consistent with the constitutional limitations of Article III . . .

The nexus demanded of federal taxpayers has two aspects to it. First, the taxpayer must establish a logical link between that status and the type of legislative enactment attacked. Thus, a taxpayer will be a proper party to allege the unconstitutionality only of exercises of congressional power under the taxing and spending clause of Art. I, § 8, of the Constitution. It will not be sufficient to allege an incidental expenditure of tax funds in the administration of an essentially regulatory statute . . . Secondly, the taxpayer must establish a nexus between that status and the precise nature of the constitutional infringement alleged. Under this requirement, the taxpayer must show that the challenged enactment exceeds specific constitutional limitations imposed upon the exercise of the congressional taxing and spending power, and not simply that the enactment is generally beyond the powers delegated to Congress by Art. I, § 8. When both nexuses are established, the litigant will have shown a taxpayer's stake in the outcome of the controversy, and will be a proper and appropriate party to invoke a federal court's jurisdiction.

[Flast et al.] . . . have satisfied both nexuses to support their claim of standing under the test we announce today. Their constitutional challenge is made to an exercise by Congress of its power under Art. I, § 8, to spend for the general welfare, and the challenged program involves a substantial expenditure of federal tax funds. In addition, [they] have alleged that the challenged expenditures violate the Establishment and Free Exercise Clauses of the First Amendment. Our history vividly illustrates that one of the specific evils feared by those who drafted the Establishment Clause and fought for its adoption was that the taxing and spending power would be used to favor one religion over another or to support religion in general . . .

The allegations of the taxpayer in *Frothingham v. Mellon* were quite different from those made in this case, and the result in *Frothingham* is consistent with the test of taxpayer standing announced today. The taxpayer in *Frothingham* attacked a federal spending program, and she, therefore, established the first nexus required. However, she lacked standing because her constitutional attack was not based on an allegation that Congress, in enacting the Maternity Act of 1921, had breached a specific limitation upon its taxing and spending power . . .

We have noted that the Establishment Clause of the First Amendment does specifically limit the taxing and spending power conferred by Art. I, § 8. Whether the Constitution contains other specific limitations can be determined only in the context of future cases. However, whenever such specific limitations are found, we believe a taxpayer will have a clear stake as a taxpayer in assuring that they are not breached by Congress. Consequently, we hold that a taxpayer will have standing consistent with Article III to invoke federal judicial power when he alleges that congressional action under the taxing and spending clause is in derogation of those constitutional provisions which operate to restrict the exercise of the taxing and spending power. The taxpayer's allegation in such cases would be that his tax money is being extracted and spent in violation of specific constitutional protections against such abuses of legislative power. Such an injury is appropriate for judicial redress, and the taxpayer has established the necessary nexus between his status and the nature of the allegedly unconstitutional action to support his claim of standing to secure judicial review . . .

While we express no view at all on the merits of [the taxpayers'] claims in this case, their complaint contains sufficient allegations under the criteria we have outlined to give them standing to invoke a federal court's jurisdiction for an adjudication on the merits.

Harlan, dissenting:

The problems presented by this case are narrow and relatively abstract, but the principles by which they must be resolved involve nothing less than the proper functioning of the federal courts, and so run to the roots of our constitutional system. The nub of my view is that the end result of *Frothingham v. Mellon* was correct . . .

Apparently the Court has repudiated the emphasis in *Frothingham* upon the amount of the plaintiff's tax bill, only to substitute an equally irrelevant emphasis upon the form of the challenged expenditure.

The Court's second criterion is similarly unrelated to its standard for the determination of standing. The intensity of a plaintiff's interest in a suit is not measured, even obliquely, by the fact that the constitutional provision under which he claims is, or is not, a "specific limitation" upon Congress' spending powers . . . I am quite unable to understand how, if a taxpayer believes that a given public expenditure is unconstitutional, and if he seeks to vindicate that belief in a federal court, his interest in the suit can be said necessarily to vary according to the constitutional provision under which he states his claim . . .

The Court's position is . . . that, because of the Establishment Clause's historical purposes, taxpayers retain rights under it quite different from those held by them under other constitutional provisions.

The difficulties with this position are several . . . [G]iven the ultimate obscurity of the Establishment Clause's historical purposes, it is inappropriate for this Court to draw fundamental distinctions among the several constitutional commands upon the supposed authority of isolated dicta extracted from the clause's complex history. In particular, I have not found, and the opinion of the Court has not adduced, historical evidence that properly permits the Court to distinguish, as it has here, among the Establishment Clause, the Tenth Amendment, and the Due Process Clause of the Fifth Amendment as limitations upon Congress' taxing and spending powers.

It seems to me clear that public actions, whatever the constitutional provisions on which they are premised, may involve important hazards for the continued effectiveness of the federal judiciary. Although I believe such actions to be within the jurisdiction conferred upon the federal courts by Article III of the Constitution, there surely can be little doubt that they strain the judicial function and press to the limit judicial authority. There is every reason to fear that unrestricted public actions might well alter the allocation of authority among the three branches of the Federal Government. It is not, I submit, enough to say that the present members of the Court would not seize these opportunities for abuse, for such actions would, even without conscious abuse, go far toward the final transformation of this Court into the Council of Revision which, despite Madison's support, was rejected by the Constitutional Convention . . .

[T]here is available a resolution of this problem that entirely satisfies the demands of the principle of separation of powers. This Court has previously held that individual litigants have standing to represent the public interest, despite their lack of economic or other personal interests, if Congress has appropriately authorized such suits . . . I would adhere to that principle.

Powell v. McCormick

395 U.S. 486 (1969), 7-1
Opinion of the Court: Warren, C.J. (Black, Brennan,
    Harlan, Marshall, White)
Concurring: Douglas
Dissenting: Stewart

How does this decision change the "political question" doctrine? How does the Court distinguish between Congress's power to exclude and its power to expel? Is the Court's narrow reading of the Qualifications Clause reasonable? How might Article I-5 stating that "each House shall be the judge . . . of the qualifications of its members," need to be written to convince Warren that the House might constitutionally exclude Powell? Does the decision in this case mean that the House might not exclude a convicted criminal, avowed racist, or advocate of violent overthrow of the government, so long as he or she was duly elected and met the age, citizenship, and residency requirements of Article I-2? Does the decision in this case lay groundwork for judicial review of impeachment?

Warren, C.J., for the Court:

In November, 1966 . . . Adam Clayton Powell, Jr., was duly elected from the 18th Congressional District of New York to serve in the . . . House of Representatives for the 90th Congress. However, pursuant to a House resolution [following charges that he had misappropriated funds], he was not permitted to take his seat. Powell (and some of the voters of his district) then filed suit [against the Speaker and certain officers of the House] . . . claiming that the House could exclude him only if it found he failed to meet the standing requirements of age, citizenship, and residence contained in Art. I, § 2, of the Constitution—requirements the House specifically found Powell met and thus had excluded him unconstitutionally . . .

[McCormick, et al.] maintain that, even if this case is otherwise justiciable, it presents only a political question . . .

[Their] . . . contention is that . . . under Art. I, 5, there has been a "textually demonstrable constitutional commitment" to the House of the "adjudicatory power" to determine Powell's qualifications. Thus, it is argued that the House, and the House alone, has power to determine who is qualified to be a member.

In order to determine whether there has been a textual commitment to a coordinate department of the Government, we must interpret the Constitution. In other words, we must first determine what power the Constitution confers upon the House through Art. I, § 5, before we can determine to what extent, if any, the exercise of that power is subject to judicial review. [McCormick, et al.] maintain that the House has broad power under § 5, and, they argue, the House may determine which are the qualifications necessary for membership. On the other hand, [Powell, et al.] allege that the Constitution provides that an elected representative may be denied his seat only if the House finds he does not meet one of the standing qualifications expressly prescribed by the Constitution.

If examination of § 5 disclosed that the Constitution gives the House judicially unreviewable power to set qualifications for membership and to judge whether prospective members meet those qualifications, further review of the House determination might well be barred by the political question doctrine. On the other hand, if the Constitution gives the House power to judge only whether elected members possess the three standing qualifications set forth in the Constitution, further consideration would be necessary to determine whether any of the other formulations of the political question doctrine are "inextricable from the case at bar."

In other words, whether there is a "textually demonstrable constitutional commitment of the issue to a coordinate political department" of government and what is the scope of such commitment are questions we must resolve for the first time in this case. For, as we pointed out in *Baker v. Carr*, "[d]eciding whether a matter has in any measure been committed by the Constitution to another branch of government, or whether the action of that branch exceeds whatever authority has been committed, is itself a delicate exercise in constitutional interpretation, and is a responsibility of this Court as ultimate interpreter of the Constitution."

In order to determine the scope of any "textual commitment" under Art. I, § 5, we necessarily must determine the meaning of the phrase to "be the Judge of the Qualifications of its own Members."

[Powell, et al.] argue that the records of the debates during the Constitutional Convention; available commentary from the post-Convention, pre-ratification period, and early congressional applications of Art. I, § 5, support their construction of the section. [McCormick, et al.] insist, however, that a careful examination of the pre-Convention practices of the English Parliament and American colonial assemblies demonstrates that, by 1787, a legislature's power to judge the qualifications of its members was generally understood to encompass exclusion or expulsion on the ground that an individual's character or past conduct rendered him unfit to serve. When the Constitution and the debates over its adoption are thus viewed in historical perspective, [they] argue, it becomes clear that the "qualifications" expressly set forth in the Constitution were not meant to limit the long-recognized legislative power to exclude or expel at will, but merely to establish "standing incapacities," which could be altered only by a constitutional amendment. Our examination of the relevant historical materials leads us to the conclusion that [Powell, et al.] are correct, and that the Constitution leaves the House without authority to exclude any person, duly elected by his constituents, who meets all the requirements for membership expressly prescribed in the Constitution . . .

Relying heavily on Charles Warren's analysis of the Convention debates, [Powell, et al.] argue that the proceedings manifest the Framers' unequivocal intention to deny either branch of Congress the authority to add to or otherwise vary the membership qualifications expressly set forth in the Constitution. We do not completely agree, for the debates are subject to other interpretations. However, we have concluded that the records of the debates, viewed in the context of the bitter struggle for the right to freely choose representatives which had recently concluded in England and in light of the distinction the Framers made between the power to expel and the power to exclude, indicate that [their] ultimate conclusion is correct . . .

. . . [T]he Convention's decision to increase the vote required to expel, because that power was "too important to be exercised by a bare majority," while at the same time not similarly restricting the power to judge qualifications, is compelling evidence that they considered the latter already limited by the standing qualifications previously adopted . . .

The debates at the state conventions also demonstrate the Framers' understanding that the qualifications for members of Congress had been fixed in the Constitution . . .

As clear as these statements appear, [McCormick, et al.] dismiss them as "general statements . . . directed to other issues." They suggest that far more relevant is Congress' own understanding of its power to judge qualifications as manifested in post-ratification exclusion cases. Unquestionably, both the House and the Senate have excluded members-elect for reasons other than their failure to meet the Constitution's standing qualifications. For almost the first 100 years of its existence, however, Congress strictly limited its power to judge the qualifications of its members to those enumerated in the Constitution . . .

Had the intent of the Framers emerged from these materials with less clarity, we would nevertheless have been compelled to resolve any ambiguity in favor of a narrow construction of the scope of Congress' power to exclude members-elect. A fundamental principle of our representative democracy is, in Hamilton's words, "that the people should choose whom they please to govern them." As Madison pointed out at the Convention, this principle is undermined as much by limiting whom the people can select as by limiting the franchise itself. In apparent agreement with this basic philosophy, the Convention adopted his suggestion limiting the power to expel. To allow essentially that same power to be exercised under the guise of judging qualifications would be to ignore Madison's warning, borne out in the Wilkes case and some of Congress' own post-Civil War exclusion cases, against "vesting an improper & dangerous power in the Legislature." Moreover, it would effectively nullify the Convention's decision to require a two-thirds vote for expulsion. Unquestionably, Congress has an interest in preserving its institutional integrity, but, in most cases, that interest can be sufficiently safeguarded by the exercise of its power to punish its members for disorderly behavior and, in extreme cases, to expel a member with the concurrence of two-thirds. In short, both the intention of the Framers, to the extent it can be determined, and an examination of the basic principles of our democratic system persuade us that the Constitution does not vest in the Congress a discretionary power to deny membership by a majority vote.

For these reasons, we have concluded that Art. I, § 5, is, at most, a "textually demonstrable commitment" to Congress to judge only the qualifications expressly set forth in the Constitution. Therefore, the "textual commitment" formulation of the political question doctrine does not bar federal courts from adjudicating [Powell's] claims.

Stewart, dissenting:

I believe that events which have taken place since certiorari was granted in this case on November 18, 1968, have rendered it moot, and that the Court should therefore refrain from deciding the novel, difficult, and delicate constitutional questions which the case presented at its inception.

The essential purpose of this lawsuit by Congressman Powell and members of his constituency was to regain the seat from which he was barred by the 90th Congress. That purpose, however, became impossible of attainment on January 3, 1969, when the 90th Congress passed into history and the 91st Congress came into being. On that date, [their] prayer for a judicial decree restraining enforcement of House Resolution No. 278 and commanding the [McCormick, et al.] to admit Congressman Powell to membership in the 90th Congress became incontestably moot.

[They] assert that actions of the House of Representatives of the 91st Congress have prolonged the controversy raised by Powell's exclusion and preserved the need for a judicial declaration in this case . . . [T]o the contrary, that the conduct of the present House of Representatives confirms the mootness of the . . . suit against the 90th Congress. Had Powell been excluded from the 91st Congress, he might argue that there was a "continuing controversy" concerning the exclusion attacked in this case. And such an argument might be sound even though the present House of Representatives is a distinct legislative body, rather than a continuation of its predecessor, and though any grievance caused by conduct of the 91st Congress is not redressable in this action. But on January 3, 1969, the House of Representatives of the 91st Congress admitted Congressman Powell to membership, and he now sits as the Representative of the 18th Congressional District of New York. With the 90th Congress terminated and Powell now a member of the 91st, it cannot seriously be contended that there remains a judicial controversy between these parties over the power of the House of Representatives to exclude Powell and the power of a court to order him reseated. Understandably, neither the Court nor [Powell, et al.] advance the wholly untenable proposition

that the continuation of this case can be founded on the infinitely remote possibility that Congressman Powell, or any other Representative, may someday be excluded for the same reasons or in the same manner. And because no foreseeable possibility of such future conduct exists, [McCormick, et al.] have met their heavy burden of showing that "subsequent events made it absolutely clear that the allegedly wrongful behavior could not reasonably be expected to recur."

United States v. Nixon

418 U.S. 683 (1974), 8-0
Opinion of the Court: Burger, C.J. (Black, Brennan, Douglas, Marshall, Powell, Stewart, White)
Not participating: Rehnquist
What was the Court's reason for holding that the president did not have an absolute executive privilege? What factors did it weigh against what other factors? Was the text of the Constitution important in this decision? When might a president validly claim executive privilege? Is executive privilege stronger or weaker as a result of this decision? From the standpoint of the interests and needs of the three branches, is this decision self-serving in placing those of one over the arguably constitutional claims of another?

Burger, C.J., for the Court:

. . . [A] grand jury of the United States District Court for the District of Columbia returned an indictment charging seven named individuals with various offenses, including conspiracy to defraud the United States and to obstruct justice. Although he was not designated as such in the indictment, the grand jury named the President, among others, as an unindicted coconspirator . . . [U]pon motion of the Special Prosecutor, a subpoena *duces tecum* was issued . . . to the President by the United States District Court . . . This subpoena required the production . . . of certain tapes, memoranda, papers, transcripts or other writings relating to certain precisely identified meetings between the President and others . . . [T]he President's counsel filed . . . a motion to quash the subpoena . . . This motion was accompanied by a formal claim of privilege. . . .

[T]he District Court denied the motion to quash and the motions to expunge and for protective orders. It further ordered 'the President or any subordinate officer, official, or employee with custody or control of the documents or objects subpoenaed,' to deliver to the District Court . . .

In the District Court, the President's counsel argued that the court lacked jurisdiction to issue the subpoena because the matter was an intra-branch dispute between a subordinate and superior officer of the Executive Branch and hence not subject to judicial resolution . . .

Under the authority of Art. II, s 2, Congress has vested in the Attorney General the power to conduct the criminal litigation of the United States Government. It has also vested in him the power to appoint subordinate officers to assist him in the discharge of his duties. Acting pursuant to those statutes, the Attorney General has delegated the authority to represent the United States in these particular matters to a Special Prosecutor with unique authority and tenure. The regulation gives the Special Prosecutor explicit power to contest the invocation of executive privilege in the process of seeking evidence deemed relevant to the performance of these specially delegated duties . . .

Here . . . it is theoretically possible for the Attorney General to amend or revoke the regulation defining the Special Prosecutor's authority. But he has not done so. So long as this regulation remains in force the Executive Branch is bound by it, and indeed the United States as the sovereign composed of the three branches is bound to respect and to enforce it. Moreover, the delegation of authority to the Special Prosecutor in this case is not an ordinary delegation by the Attorney General to a subordinate officer: with the authorization of the President, the Acting Attorney General provided in the regulation that the Special Prosecutor was not to be removed without the 'consensus' of eight designated leaders of Congress.

In light of the uniqueness of the setting in which the conflict arises, the fact that both parties are officers of the Executive Branch cannot be viewed as a barrier to justiciability. It would be inconsistent with the applicable law and regulation, and the unique facts of this case to conclude other than that the Special Prosecutor has standing to bring this action and that a justiciable controversy is presented for decision . . .

In a case such as this, however, where a subpoena is directed to a President of the United States, appellate review, in deference to a coordinate branch of Government, should be particularly meticulous to ensure that the standards of Rule 17(c) have been correctly applied. From our examination of the materials submitted by the Special Prosecutor to the District Court in support of his motion for the subpoena, we are persuaded that the District Court's denial of the President's motion to quash the subpoena was consistent with Rule 17(c). We also conclude that the Special Prosecutor has made a sufficient showing to justify a subpoena for production before trial. The subpoenaed materials are not available from any other source, and their examination and processing should not await trial in the circumstances shown . . .

Having determined that the requirements of Rule 17(c) were satisfied, we turn to the claim that the subpoena should be quashed because it demands 'confidential conversations between a President and his close advisors that it would be inconsistent with the public interest to produce.' The first contention is a broad claim that the separation of powers doctrine precludes judicial review of a President's claim of privilege. The second contention is that if he does not prevail on the claim of absolute privilege, the Court should hold as a matter of constitutional law that the privilege prevails over the subpoena *duces tecum*.

In the performance of assigned constitutional duties each branch of the Government must initially interpret the Constitution, and the interpretation of its powers by any branch is due great respect from the others. The President's counsel, as we have noted, reads the Constitution as providing an absolute privilege of confidentiality for all Presidential communications. Many decisions of this Court, however, have unequivocally reaffirmed the holding of *Marbury v. Madison,* that '(i)t is emphatically the province and duty of the judicial department to say what the law is.'

No holding of the Court has defined the scope of judicial power specifically relating to the enforcement of a subpoena for confidential Presidential communications for use in a criminal prosecution, but other exercises of power by the Executive Branch and the Legislative Branch have been found invalid as in conflict with the Constitution. In a series of cases, the Court interpreted the explicit immunity conferred by express provisions of the Constitution on Members of the House and Senate by the Speech or Debate Clause. Since this Court has consistently exercised the power to construe and delineate claims arising under express powers, it must follow that the Court has authority to interpret claims with respect to powers alleged to derive from enumerated powers.

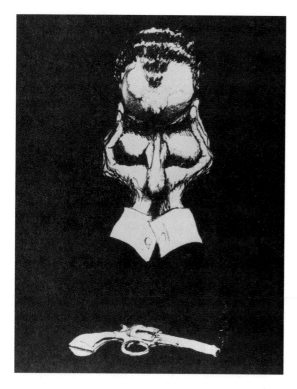

In this Oliphant cartoon "The Smoking Gun" in 1974, President Richard Nixon contemplates metaphorical reference to the discovery of incriminating White House tapes he eventually was ordered to surrender. They confirmed suspicion that he had obstructed investigation of the Watergate breakin by ordering aides to take part in a cover up of the crime.

. . . In support of his claim of absolute privilege, the President's counsel urges two grounds, one of which is common to all governments and one of which is peculiar to our system of separation of powers. The first ground is the valid need for protection of communications between high Government officials and those who advise and assist them in the performance of their manifold duties; the importance of this confidentiality is too plain to require further discussion. Human experience teaches that those who expect public dissemination of their remarks may well temper candor with a concern for appearances and for their own interests to the detriment of the decision-making process. Whatever the nature of the privilege of confidentiality of Presidential communications in the exercise of Art. II powers, the privilege can be said to derive from the supremacy of each branch within its own assigned area of constitutional duties. Certain powers and privileges flow from the nature of enumerated powers; the protection of the confidentiality of Presidential communications has similar constitutional underpinnings . . .

The second ground asserted by the President's counsel in support of the claim of absolute privilege rests on the doctrine of separation of powers. Here it is argued that the independence of the Executive Branch within its own sphere insulates a President from a judicial subpoena in an ongoing criminal prosecution, and thereby protects confidential Presidential communications.

However, neither the doctrine of separation of powers, nor the need for confidentiality of high-level communications, without more, can sustain an absolute, unqualified Presidential privilege of immunity from judicial process under all circumstances. The President's need for complete candor and objectivity from advisers calls for great deference from the courts. However, when the privilege depends solely on the broad, undifferentiated claim of public interest in the confidentiality of such conversations, a confrontation with other values arises. Absent a claim of need to protect military, diplomatic, or sensitive national security secrets, we find it difficult to accept the argument that even the very important interest in confidentiality of Presidential communications is significantly diminished by production of such material for in camera inspection with all the protection that a district court will be obliged to provide.

The impediment that an absolute, unqualified privilege would place in the way of the primary constitutional duty of the Judicial Branch to do justice in criminal prosecutions would plainly conflict with the function of the courts under Art. III. In designing the structure of our Government and dividing and allocating the sovereign power among three co-equal branches, the Framers of the Constitution sought to provide a comprehensive system, but the separate powers were not intended to operate with absolute independence. 'While the Constitution diffuses power the better to secure liberty, it also contemplates that practice will integrate the dispersed powers into a workable government. It enjoins upon its branches separateness but interdependence, autonomy but reciprocity.' To read the Art. II powers of the President as providing an absolute privilege as against a subpoena essential to enforcement of criminal statutes on no more than a generalized claim of the public interest in confidentiality of nonmilitary and nondiplomatic discussions would upset the constitutional balance of 'a workable government' and gravely impair the role of the courts under Art. III.

Since we conclude that the legitimate needs of the judicial process may outweigh Presidential privilege, it is necessary to resolve those competing interests in a manner that preserves the essential functions of each branch. The right and indeed the duty to resolve that question does not free the Judiciary from according high respect to the representations made on behalf of the President.

The expectation of a President to the confidentiality of his conversations and correspondence, like the claim of confidentiality of judicial deliberations, for example, has all the values to which we accord deference for the privacy of all citizens and, added to those values, is the necessity for protection of the public interest in candid, objective, and even blunt or harsh opinions in Presidential decision-making. A President and those who assist him must be free to explore alternatives in the process of shaping policies and making decisions and to do so in a way many would be unwilling to express except privately. These are the considerations justifying a presumptive privilege for Presidential communications. The privilege is fundamental to the operation of Government and inextricably rooted in the separation of powers under the Constitution. In *Nixon v. Sirica,* the Court of Appeals

held that such Presidential communications are 'presumptively privileged,' and this position is accepted by both parties in the present litigation. We agree with Mr. Chief Justice Marshall's observation, therefore, that '(i)n no case of this kind would a court be required to proceed against the president as against an ordinary individual.'

But this presumptive privilege must be considered in light of our historic commitment to the rule of law. This is nowhere more profoundly manifest than in our view that 'the twofold aim (of criminal justice) is that guilt shall not escape or innocence suffer.' We have elected to employ an adversary system of criminal justice in which the parties contest all issues before a court of law. The need to develop all relevant facts in the adversary system is both fundamental and comprehensive. The ends of criminal justice would be defeated if judgments were to be founded on a partial or speculative presentation of the facts. The very integrity of the judicial system and public confidence in the system depend on full disclosure of all the facts, within the framework of the rules of evidence. To ensure that justice is done, it is imperative to the function of courts that compulsory process be available for the production of evidence needed either by the prosecution or by the defense . . .

In this case the President challenges a subpoena served on him as a third party requiring the production of materials for use in a criminal prosecution; he does so on the claim that he has a privilege against disclosure of confidential communications. He does not place his claim of privilege on the ground they are military or diplomatic secrets. As to these areas of Art. II duties the courts have traditionally shown the utmost deference to Presidential responsibilities . . . No case of the Court, however, has extended this high degree of deference to a President's generalized interest in confidentiality. Nowhere in the Constitution, as we have noted earlier, is there any explicit reference to a privilege of confidentiality, yet to the extent this interest relates to the effective discharge of a President's powers, it is constitutionally based.

The right to the production of all evidence at a criminal trial similarly has constitutional dimensions. The Sixth Amendment explicitly confers upon every defendant in a criminal trial the right 'to be confronted with the witnesses against him' and 'to have compulsory process for obtaining witnesses in his favor.' Moreover, the Fifth Amendment also guarantees that no person shall be deprived of liberty without due process of law. It is the manifest duty of the courts to vindicate those guarantees, and to accomplish that it is essential that all relevant and admissible evidence be produced.

In this case we must weigh the importance of the general privilege of confidentiality of Presidential communications in performance of the President's responsibilities against the inroads of such a privilege on the fair administration of criminal justice. The interest in preserving confidentiality is weighty indeed and entitled to great respect. However, we cannot conclude that advisers will be moved to temper the candor of their remarks by the infrequent occasions of disclosure because of the possibility that such conversations will be called for in the context of a criminal prosecution.

On the other hand, the allowance of the privilege to withhold evidence that is demonstrably relevant in a criminal trial would cut deeply into the guarantee of due process of law and gravely impair the basic function of the courts. A President's acknowledged need for confidentiality in the communications of his office is general in nature, whereas the constitutional need for production of relevant evidence in a criminal proceeding is specific and central to the fair adjudication of a particular criminal case in the administration of justice. Without access to specific facts a criminal prosecution may be totally frustrated. The President's broad interest in confidentiality of communications will not be vitiated by disclosure of a limited number of conversations preliminarily shown to have some bearing on the pending criminal cases.

We conclude that when the ground for asserting privilege as to subpoenaed materials sought for use in a criminal trial is based only on the generalized interest in confidentiality, it cannot prevail over the fundamental demands of due process of law in the fair administration of criminal justice. The generalized assertion of privilege must yield to the demonstrated, specific need for evidence in a pending criminal trial . . .

Here the District Court treated the material as presumptively privileged, proceeded to find that the Special Prosecutor had made a sufficient showing to rebut the presumption, and ordered an *in camera* examination of the subpoenaed material. On the basis of our examination of the record we are unable to conclude that the District Court erred in ordering the inspection. Accordingly we affirm the order of the District Court that subpoenaed materials be transmitted to that court. We now turn to the important question of the District Court's responsibilities in conducting the *in camera* examination of Presidential materials or communications delivered under the compulsion of the subpoena *duces tecum* . . .

It is elementary that *in camera* inspection of evidence is always a procedure calling for scrupulous protection against any release or publication of material not found by the court, at that stage, probably admissible in evidence and relevant to the issues of the trial for which it is sought. That being true of an ordinary situation, it is obvious that the District Court has a very heavy responsibility to see to it that Presidential conversations, which are either not relevant or not admissible, are accorded that high degree of respect due the President of the United States. Mr. Chief Justice Marshall, sitting as a trial judge in the Burr case was extraordinarily careful to point out that '(i)n no case of this kind would a court be required to proceed against the president as against an ordinary individual.' Marshall's statement cannot be read to mean in any sense that a President is above the law, but relates to the singularly unique role under Art. II of a President's communications and activities, related to the performance of duties under that Article. Moreover, a President's communications and activities encompass a vastly wider range of sensitive material than would be true of any 'ordinary individual.' It is therefore necessary in the public interest to afford Presidential confidentiality the greatest protection consistent with the fair administration of justice. The need for confidentiality even as to idle conversations with associates in which casual reference might be made concerning political leaders within the country or foreign statesmen is too obvious to call for further treatment. We have no doubt that the District Judge will at all times accord to Presidential records that high degree of deference suggested in *United States v. Burr* and will discharge his responsibility to see to it that until released to the Special Prosecutor no *in camera* material is revealed to anyone. This burden applies with even greater force to excised material; once the decision is made to excise, the material is restored to its privileged status and should be returned under seal to its lawful custodian.

Since this matter came before the Court during the pendency of a criminal prosecution, and on representations that time is of the essence, the mandate shall issue forthwith.

Dames & Moore v. Regan

453 U.S. 654 (1981), 9-0

Opinion of the Court: Rehnquist (Blackmun, Brennan, Burger, Marshall, Powell, Stevens, Stewart, White)

Does the Court hold that the president acted under powers delegated to him by Congress, those implied in Article II, or those inherent in the executive? In what way can it be argued that Congress assented to the hostage agreement? Congress was "silent" in this case as it was in Youngstown Sheet & Tube Corp. v. Sawyer. *Why are the results different? President Carter had failed diplomatically and militarily to free the American hostages. Does the decision here make* Dames & Moore, *and possibly other companies with valid contractual claims totally unrelated to the crisis, pay for the failure?*

Rehnquist, for the Court:

[W]e are obviously deciding only one more episode in the never-ending tension between the President exercising the executive authority in a world that presents each day some new challenge with which he must deal and the Constitution under which we all live and which no one disputes embodies some sort of system of checks and balances.

On November 4, 1979, the American Embassy in Tehran was seized and our diplomatic personnel were captured and held hostage. In response to that crisis, President Carter, acting pursuant to the International Emergency Economic Powers Act [IEEPA], declared a national emergency . . . and blocked the removal or transfer of "all property and interests in property of the Government of Iran. . . .

On December 19, 1979, Dames & Moore filed suit . . . against the Government of Iran, the Atomic Energy Organization of Iran, and a number of Iranian banks . . . [alleging it] was a party to a written contract with the Atomic Energy Organization . . . Under the contract, [it] was to conduct site studies for a proposed nuclear power plant in Iran . . . [T]he Atomic Energy Organization terminated the agreement for its own convenience on June 30, 1979. [Dames & Moore] contended, however, that it was owed $3,436,694.30 plus interest for services performed under the contract prior to the date of termination. The District Court issued orders of attachment directed against property of the defendants, and the property of certain Iranian banks was then attached to secure any judgment that might be entered against them.

On January 20, 1981, the Americans held hostage were released by Iran pursuant to an Agreement entered into the day before [which] . . . stated that "[I]t is the purpose of [the United States and Iran] . . . to terminate all litigation as between the Government of each party and the nationals of the other, and to bring about the settlement and termination of all such claims through binding arbitration." In furtherance of this goal, the Agreement called for the establishment of an Iran-United States Claims Tribunal which would arbitrate any claims not settled within six months. Awards of the Claims Tribunal are to be "final and binding" and "enforceable . . . in the courts of any nation in accordance with its laws." Under the Agreement, the United States is obligated "to terminate all legal proceedings in United States courts involving claims of United States persons and institutions against Iran and its state enterprises, to nullify all attachments and judgments obtained therein, to prohibit all further litigation based on such claims, and to bring about the termination of such claims through binding arbitration." . . .

The parties and the lower courts, confronted with the instant questions, have all agreed that much relevant analysis is contained in *Youngstown Sheet & Tube Corp. v. Sawyer.* Justice Black's opinion for the Court in that case, involving the validity of President Truman's effort to seize the country's steel mills in the wake of a nationwide strike, recognized that "[t]he President's power, if any, to issue the order must stem either from an act of Congress or from the Constitution itself." Justice Jackson's concurring opinion elaborated in a general way the consequences of different types of interaction between the two democratic branches in assessing Presidential authority to act in any given case. When the President acts pursuant to an express or implied authorization from Congress, he exercises not only his powers but also those delegated by Congress. In such a case the executive action "would be supported by the strongest of presumptions and the widest latitude of judicial interpretation, and the burden of persuasion would rest heavily upon any who might attack it." When the President acts in the absence of congressional authorization he may enter "a zone of twilight in which he and Congress may have concurrent authority, or in which its distribution is uncertain." In such a case the analysis becomes more complicated, and the validity of the President's action, at least so far as separation-of-pow-

ers principles are concerned, hinges on a consideration of all the circumstances which might shed light
on the views of the Legislative Branch toward such action, including "congressional inertia, indifference or
quiescence." Finally, when the President acts in contravention of the will of Congress, "his power is at its
lowest ebb," and the Court can sustain his actions
"only by disabling the Congress from acting upon the
subject."

Although we have in the past found and do today
find Justice Jackson's classification of executive actions into three general categories analytically useful,
we should be mindful of Justice Holmes' admonition,
quoted by Justice Frankfurter in *Youngstown* (concurring opinion) that "[t]he great ordinances of the
Constitution do not establish and divide fields of
black and white." Justice Jackson himself recognized
that his three categories represented "a somewhat
over-simplified grouping," and it is doubtless the case
that executive action in any particular instance falls,
not neatly in one of three pigeonholes, but rather at
some point along a spectrum running from explicit
congressional authorization to explicit congressional
prohibition. This is particularly true as respects cases
such as the one before us, involving responses to
international crises the nature of which Congress
can hardly have been expected to anticipate in any
detail . . .

This Court has previously recognized that the congressional purpose in authorizing blocking orders is
"to put control of foreign assets in the hands of the
President . . . ." *Propper v. Clark* (1949). Such orders
permit the President to maintain the foreign assets at
his disposal for use in negotiating the resolution of a
declared national emergency. The frozen assets serve
as a "bargaining chip" to be used by the President
when dealing with a hostile country. Accordingly, it is
difficult to accept [Dames & Moore's] argument because the practical effect of it is to allow individual
claimants throughout the country to minimize or
wholly eliminate this "bargaining chip" through attachments, garnishments, or similar encumbrances
on property. Neither the purpose the statute was enacted to serve nor its plain language supports such a
result.

Because the President's action in nullifying the attachments and ordering the transfer of the assets was
taken pursuant to specific congressional authorization, it is "supported by the strongest of presumptions
and the widest latitude of judicial interpretation, and

the burden of persuasion would rest heavily upon any
who might attack it." *Youngstown* (Jackson, J., concurring). Under the circumstances of this case, we cannot say that [Dames & Moore] has sustained that
heavy burden. A contrary ruling would mean that the
Federal Government as a whole lacked the power exercised by the President, and that we are not prepared to say.

Although we have declined to conclude that the
IEEPA or the Hostage Act directly authorizes the
President's suspension of claims for the reasons
noted, we cannot ignore the general tenor of Congress' legislation in this area in trying to determine
whether the President is acting alone or at least with
the acceptance of Congress . . . Congress cannot anticipate and legislate with regard to every possible action
the President may find it necessary to take or every
possible situation in which he might act. Such failure
of Congress specifically to delegate authority does not,
"especially . . . in the areas of foreign policy and national security," imply "congressional disapproval" of
action taken by the Executive. *Haig v. Agee* (1981). On
the contrary, the enactment of legislation closely related to the question of the President's authority in a
particular case which evinces legislative intent to accord the President broad discretion may be considered
to "invite" "measures on independent presidential responsibility," *Youngstown* (Jackson, J., concurring). At
least this is so where there is no contrary indication of
legislative intent and when, as here, there is a history
of congressional acquiescence in conduct of the sort
engaged in by the President. It is to that history which
we now turn.

Not infrequently in affairs between nations, outstanding claims by nationals of one country against
the government of another country are "sources of
friction" between the two sovereigns. To resolve these
difficulties, nations have often entered into agreements
settling the claims of their respective nationals . . .
Consistent with that principle, the United States
has repeatedly exercised its sovereign authority to settle the claims of its nationals against foreign countries.
Though those settlements have sometimes been made
by treaty, there has also been a long-standing practice
of settling such claims by executive agreement without
the advice and consent of the Senate. Under such
agreements, the President has agreed to renounce or
extinguish claims of United States nationals against
foreign governments in return for lump-sum payments or the establishment of arbitration procedures.

To be sure, many of these settlements were encouraged by the United States claimants themselves, since a claimant's only hope of obtaining any payment at all might lie in having his Government negotiate a diplomatic settlement on his behalf . . . It is clear that the practice of settling claims continues today. Since 1952, the President has entered into at least 10 binding settlements with foreign nations . . .

Crucial to our decision today is the conclusion that Congress has implicitly approved the practice of claim settlement by executive agreement. This is best demonstrated by Congress' enactment of the International Claims Settlement Act of 1949 . . . [in which it] created the International Claims Commission, now the Foreign Claims Settlement Commission, and gave it jurisdiction to make final and binding decisions with respect to claims by United States nationals against settlement funds. By creating a procedure to implement future settlement agreements, Congress placed its stamp of approval on such agreements. . . .

In addition to congressional acquiescence in the President's power to settle claims, prior cases of this Court have also recognized that the President does have some measure of power to enter into executive agreements without obtaining the advice and consent of the Senate. In *United States v. Pink,* for example, the Court upheld the validity of the Litvinov Assignment, which was part of an Executive Agreement whereby the Soviet Union assigned to the United States amounts owed to it by American nationals so that outstanding claims of other American nationals could be paid . . .

In light of all of the foregoing—the inferences to be drawn from the character of the legislation Congress has enacted in the area, such as the IEEPA and the Hostage Act, and from the history of acquiescence in executive claims settlement—we conclude that the President was authorized to suspend pending claims . . . As Justice Frankfurter pointed out in *Youngstown,* "a systematic, unbroken, executive practice, long pursued to the knowledge of the Congress and never before questioned . . . may be treated as a gloss on 'Executive Power' vested in the President by s 1 of Art. II." Past practice does not, by itself, create power, but "long-continued practice, known to and acquiesced in by Congress, would raise a presumption that the [action] had been [taken] in pursuance of its consent . . . ." Such practice is present here and such a presumption is also appropriate. In light of the fact that Congress may be considered to have consented to the President's action in suspending claims, we cannot say that action exceeded the President's powers.

Our conclusion is buttressed by the fact that the means chosen by the President to settle the claims of American nationals provided an alternative forum, the Claims Tribunal, which is capable of providing meaningful relief . . . The President's power to [nullify attachments] does not depend on his provision of a forum whereby claimants can recover on those claims. The fact that the President has provided such a forum here means that the claimants are receiving something in return for the suspension of their claims, namely, access to an international tribunal before which they may well recover something on their claims. . . .

Just as importantly, Congress has not disapproved of the action taken here. Though Congress has held hearings on the Iranian Agreement itself, Congress has not enacted legislation, or even passed a resolution, indicating its displeasure with the Agreement. Quite the contrary, the relevant Senate Committee has stated that the establishment of the Tribunal is "of vital importance to the United States." We are thus clearly not confronted with a situation in which Congress has in some way resisted the exercise of Presidential authority.

Finally, we re-emphasize the narrowness of our decision. We do not decide that the President possesses plenary power to settle claims, even as against foreign governmental entities . . . But where, as here, the settlement of claims has been determined to be a necessary incident to the resolution of a major foreign policy dispute between our country and another, and where, as here, we can conclude that Congress acquiesced in the President's action, we are not prepared to say that the President lacks the power to settle such claims.

Immigration and Naturalization Service v. Chadha

462 U.S. 919 (1983), 7-2

Opinion of the Court: Burger (Blackmun, Brennan, Marshall, O'Connor, Stevens)

Concurring: Powell

Dissenting: Rehnquist, White

Has the majority of the Court given an excessively formal reading to the constitutional requirements of the separation of powers, or has it restored a fundamental distinction important to the constitutional system? Burger gives a primacy to the text of the Constitution. What other considerations may be relevant in arriving at constitutional meaning in this case? White, in dissent, emphasizes the apparent practical effects of the decision. Are they a good or sufficient reason for denying the constitutional challenge? On what grounds would Powell decide this case? Should a practice, like the legislative veto, become constitutional if it is not specifically prohibited by the Constitution and is employed without complaint for a long period of time? Have changes that have taken place in the balance of power between the president and Congress had a bearing on the opinions in this case? If so, which ones? Does the decision in this case affect the War Powers Act? Aside from Chadha and other aliens affected, is it possible to say what interests gain and lose by this decision?

Burger, C.J., for the Court:

[The appeal] . . . presents a challenge to the constitutionality of the provision in s 244(c)(2) of the Immigration and Nationality Act, 8, authorizing one House of Congress, by resolution, to invalidate the decision of the Executive Branch, pursuant to authority delegated by Congress to the Attorney General of the United States, to allow a particular deportable alien to remain in the United States.

Chadha is an East Indian who was born in Kenya and holds a British passport. He was lawfully admitted to the United States in 1966 on a nonimmigrant student visa. His visa expired on June 30, 1972. On October 11, 1973, the District Director of the Immigration and Naturalization Service ordered Chadha to show cause why he should not be deported for having "remained in the United States for a longer time than permitted." . . . [A] deportation hearing was held before an immigration judge on January 11, 1974. Chadha conceded that he was deportable for overstaying his visa and the hearing was adjourned to enable him to file an application for suspension of deportation . . . Section 244(a)(1) [of the Immigration and Nationality Act, which provides in part that] the Attorney General may, in his discretion, suspend deportation . . . in the case of an alien . . . whose deportation would . . . result in extreme hardship to the alien or to his spouse, parent, or child, who is a citizen of the United States" . . .

Explicit and unambiguous provisions of the Constitution prescribe and define the respective functions of the Congress and of the Executive in the legislative process. Since the precise terms of those familiar provisions are critical to the resolution of this case, we set

them out verbatim. Art. I provides: "All legislative Powers herein granted shall be vested in a Congress of the United States, which shall consist of a Senate and a House of Representatives." Art. I, s 1. "Every Bill which shall have passed the House of Representatives and the Senate, shall, before it becomes a Law, be presented to the President of the United States; . . ." "Every Order, Resolution, or Vote to which the Concurrence of the Senate and House of Representatives may be necessary (except on a question of Adjournment) shall be presented to the President of the United States; and before the Same shall take Effect, shall be approved by him, or being disapproved by him, shall be repassed by two thirds of the Senate and House of Representatives, according to the Rules and Limitations prescribed in the Case of a Bill."

The records of the Constitutional Convention reveal that the requirement that all legislation be presented to the President before becoming law was uniformly accepted by the Framers. Presentment to the President and the Presidential veto were considered so imperative that the draftsmen took special pains to assure that these requirements could not be circumvented. During the final debate on Art. I, s 7, cl. 2, James Madison expressed concern that it might easily be evaded by the simple expedient of calling a proposed law a "resolution" or "vote" rather than a "bill." As a consequence, Art. I, s 7, cl. 3, was added.

The decision to provide the President with a limited and qualified power to nullify proposed legislation by veto was based on the profound conviction of the Framers that the powers conferred on Congress were the powers to be most carefully circumscribed. It is beyond doubt that lawmaking was a power to be shared by both Houses and the President . . .

The President's role in the lawmaking process also reflects the Framers' careful efforts to check whatever propensity a particular Congress might have to enact oppressive, improvident, or ill-considered measures . . . The Court also has observed that the Presentment Clauses serve the important purpose of assuring that a "national" perspective is grafted on the legislative process: "The President is a representative of the people just as the members of the Senate and of the House are, and it may be, at some times, on some subjects, that the President elected by all the people is rather more representative of them all than are the members of either body of the Legislature whose constituencies are local and not countrywide . . . ." *Myers v. United States.*

The bicameral requirement of Art. I, ss 1, 7 was of scarcely less concern to the Framers than was the

Presidential veto and indeed the two concepts are interdependent. By providing that no law could take effect without the concurrence of the prescribed majority of the Members of both Houses, the Framers reemphasized their belief, already remarked upon in connection with the Presentment Clauses, that legislation should not be enacted unless it has been carefully and fully considered by the Nation's elected officials. In the Constitutional Convention debates on the need for a bicameral legislature, James Wilson, later to become a Justice of this Court, commented: "Despotism comes on mankind in different shapes. Sometimes in an Executive, sometimes in a military, one. Is there danger of a Legislative despotism? Theory and practice both proclaim it. If the Legislative authority be not restrained, there can be neither liberty nor stability; and it can only be restrained by dividing it within itself, into distinct and independent branches. In a single house there is no check, but the inadequate one, of the virtue and good sense of those who compose it." Hamilton argued that a Congress comprised of a single House was antithetical to the very purposes of the Constitution. Were the Nation to adopt a Constitution providing for only one legislative organ, he warned: "we shall finally accumulate, in a single body, all the most important prerogatives of sovereignty, and thus entail upon our posterity one of the most execrable forms of government that human infatuation ever contrived. Thus we should create in reality that very tyranny which the adversaries of the new Constitution either are, or affect to be, solicitous to avert." *The Federalist* No. 22.

This view was rooted in a general skepticism regarding the fallibility of human nature . . .

We see therefore that the Framers were acutely conscious that the bicameral requirement and the Presentment Clauses would serve essential constitutional functions. The President's participation in the legislative process was to protect the Executive Branch from Congress and to protect the whole people from improvident laws. The division of the Congress into two distinctive bodies assures that the legislative power would be exercised only after opportunity for full study and debate in separate settings. The President's unilateral veto power, in turn, was limited by the power of two thirds of both Houses of Congress to overrule a veto thereby precluding final arbitrary action of one person. It emerges clearly that the prescription for legislative action in Art. I, ss 1, 7 represents the Framers' decision that the legislative power of the Federal government be exercised in accord with a single, finely wrought and exhaustively considered, procedure. . . .

Examination of the action taken here by one House pursuant to s 244(c)(2) reveals that it was essentially legislative in purpose and effect. In purporting to exercise power defined in Art. I, s 8, cl. 4 to "establish an uniform Rule of Naturalization," the House took action that had the purpose and effect of altering the legal rights, duties and relations of persons, including the Attorney General, Executive Branch officials and Chadha, all outside the legislative branch. Section 244(c)(2) purports to authorize one House of Congress to require the Attorney General to deport an individual alien whose deportation otherwise would be cancelled under s 244. The one-House veto operated in this case to overrule the Attorney General and mandate Chadha's deportation; absent the House action, Chadha would remain in the United States. Congress has acted and its action has altered Chadha's status.

The legislative character of the one-House veto in this case is confirmed by the character of the Congressional action it supplants. Neither the House of Representatives nor the Senate contends that, absent the veto provision in s 244(c)(2), either of them, or both of them acting together, could effectively require the Attorney General to deport an alien once the Attorney General, in the exercise of legislatively delegated authority, had determined the alien should remain in the United States. Without the challenged provision in s 244(c)(2), this could have been achieved, if at all, only by legislation requiring deportation. Similarly, a veto by one House of Congress under s 244(c)(2) cannot be justified as an attempt at amending the standards set out in s 244(a)(1), or as a repeal of s 244 as applied to Chadha. Amendment and repeal of statutes, no less than enactment, must conform with Art. I. . . .

The nature of the decision implemented by the one-House veto in this case further manifests its legislative character. After long experience with the clumsy, time consuming private bill procedure, Congress made a deliberate choice to delegate to the Executive Branch, and specifically to the Attorney General, the authority to allow deportable aliens to remain in this country in certain specified circumstances. It is not disputed that this choice to delegate authority is precisely the kind of decision that can be implemented only in accordance with the procedures set out in Art. I. Disagreement with the Attorney General's decision on Chadha's deportation—that is,

Congress' decision to deport Chadha—no less than Congress' original choice to delegate to the Attorney General the authority to make that decision, involves determinations of policy that Congress can implement in only one way; bicameral passage followed by presentment to the President. Congress must abide by its delegation of authority until that delegation is legislatively altered or revoked. . . .

Finally, we see that when the Framers intended to authorize either House of Congress to act alone and outside of its prescribed bicameral legislative role, they narrowly and precisely defined the procedure for such action. There are but four provisions in the Constitution, explicit and unambiguous, by which one House may act alone with the unreviewable force of law, not subject to the President's veto:

(a) The House of Representatives alone was given the power to initiate impeachments. Art. I, s 2, cl. 6;

(b) The Senate alone was given the power to conduct trials following impeachment on charges initiated by the House and to convict following trial. Art. I, s 3, cl. 5;

(c) The Senate alone was given final unreviewable power to approve or to disapprove presidential appointments. Art. II, s 2, cl. 2;

(d) The Senate alone was given unreviewable power to ratify treaties negotiated by the President. Art. II, s 2, cl. 2.

Clearly, when the Draftsmen sought to confer special powers on one House, independent of the other House, or of the President, they did so in explicit, unambiguous terms. These carefully defined exceptions from presentment and bicameralism underscore the difference between the legislative functions of Congress and other unilateral but important and binding one-House acts provided for in the Constitution. These exceptions are narrow, explicit, and separately justified; none of them authorize the action challenged here. On the contrary, they provide further support for the conclusion that Congressional authority is not to be implied and for the conclusion that the veto provided for in s 244(c)(2) is not authorized by the constitutional design of the powers of the Legislative Branch.

Since it is clear that the action by the House under s 244(c)(2) was not within any of the express constitutional exceptions authorizing one House to act alone, and equally clear that it was an exercise of legislative power, that action was subject to the standards prescribed in Article I. The bicameral requirement, the Presentment Clauses, the President's veto, and Congress' power to override a veto were intended to erect enduring checks on each Branch and to protect the people from the improvident exercise of power by mandating certain prescribed steps. To preserve those checks, and maintain the separation of powers, the carefully defined limits on the power of each Branch must not be eroded. To accomplish what has been attempted by one House of Congress in this case requires action in conformity with the express procedures of the Constitution's prescription for legislative action: passage by a majority of both Houses and presentment to the President.

The veto authorized by s 244(c)(2) doubtless has been in many respects a convenient shortcut; the "sharing" with the Executive by Congress of its authority over aliens in this manner is, on its face, an appealing compromise. In purely practical terms, it is obviously easier for action to be taken by one House without submission to the President; but it is crystal clear from the records of the Convention, contemporaneous writings and debates, that the Framers ranked other values higher than efficiency. The records of the Convention and debates in the States preceding ratification underscore the common desire to define and limit the exercise of the newly created federal powers affecting the states and the people. There is unmistakable expression of a determination that legislation by the national Congress be a step-by-step, deliberate and deliberative process.

The choices we discern as having been made in the Constitutional Convention impose burdens on governmental processes that often seem clumsy, inefficient, even unworkable, but those hard choices were consciously made by men who had lived under a form of government that permitted arbitrary governmental acts to go unchecked. There is no support in the Constitution or decisions of this Court for the proposition that the cumbersomeness and delays often encountered in complying with explicit Constitutional standards may be avoided, either by the Congress or by the President. With all the obvious flaws of delay, untidiness, and potential for abuse, we have not yet found a better way to preserve freedom than by making the exercise of power subject to the carefully crafted restraints spelled out in the Constitution.

We hold that the Congressional veto provision in s 244(c)(2) is . . . unconstitutional.

Powell, concurring:

... [T]he House's action appears clearly adjudicatory. The House did not enact a general rule; rather it made its own determination that six specific persons did not comply with certain statutory criteria. It thus undertook the type of decision that traditionally has been left to other branches ...

The impropriety of the House's assumption of this function is confirmed by the fact that its action raise the very danger the Framers sought to avoid—the exercise of unchecked power. in decided whether Chadha deserves to be deported, Congress is not subject to any internal constraints that prevent it from arbitrarily depriving him of the right to remain in this country. Unlike the judiciary or an administrative agency, Congress is not bound by established substantive rules. Nor is it subject to procedural safeguards, such as the right to counsel and a hearing before an impartial tribunal, that are present when a court or an agency adjudicates individual rights. The only effective constraint on Congress' power is political, but Congress is most accountable politically when it prescribes rules of general applicability. When it decides rights of specific persons, those rights are subject to "the tyranny of a shifting majority." ...

The Court's decision, based on the Presentment Clauses, Art. I, s 7, cls. 2 and 3, apparently will invalidate every use of the legislative veto. The breadth of this holding gives one pause. Congress has included the veto in literally hundreds of statutes, dating back to the 1930s. Congress clearly views this procedure as essential to controlling the delegation of power to administrative agencies. One reasonably may disagree with Congress' assessment of the veto's utility, but the respect due its judgment as a coordinate branch of Government cautions that our holding should be no more extensive than necessary to decide this case. In my view, the case may be decided on a narrower ground. When Congress finds that a particular person does not satisfy the statutory criteria for permanent residence in this country it has assumed a judicial function in violation of the principle of separation of powers. Accordingly, I concur only in the judgment ...

White, dissenting:

Today the Court not only invalidates s 244(c)(2) of the Immigration and Nationality Act, but also sounds the death knell for nearly 200 other statutory provisions in which Congress has reserved a "legislative veto." For this reason, the Court's decision is of surpassing importance. And it is for this reason that the Court would have been well-advised to decide the case, if possible, on the narrower grounds of separation of powers, leaving for full consideration the constitutionality of other congressional review statutes operating on such varied matters as war powers and agency rule-making, some of which concern the independent regulatory agencies.

The prominence of the legislative veto mechanism in our contemporary political system and its importance to Congress can hardly be overstated. It has become a central means by which Congress secures the accountability of executive and independent agencies. Without the legislative veto, Congress is faced with a Hobson's choice: either to refrain from delegating the necessary authority, leaving itself with a hopeless task of writing laws with the requisite specificity to cover endless special circumstances across the entire policy landscape, or in the alternative, to abdicate its law-making function to the executive branch and independent agencies. To choose the former leaves major national problems unresolved; to opt for the latter risks unaccountable policymaking by those not elected to fill that role. Accordingly, over the past five decades, the legislative veto has been placed in nearly 200 statutes. The device is known in every field of governmental concern: reorganization, budgets, foreign affairs, war powers, and regulation of trade, safety, energy, the environment and the economy....

The history of the legislative veto also makes clear that it has not been a sword with which Congress has struck out to aggrandize itself at the expense of the other branches—the concerns of Madison and Hamilton. Rather, the veto has been a means of defense, a reservation of ultimate authority necessary if Congress is to fulfill its designated role under Article I as the nation's lawmaker. While the President has often objected to particular legislative vetoes, generally those left in the hands of congressional committees, the Executive has more often agreed to legislative review as the price for a broad delegation of authority. To be sure, the President may have preferred unrestricted power, but that could be precisely why Congress thought it essential to retain a check on the exercise of delegated authority

For all these reasons, the apparent sweep of the Court's decision today is regrettable. The Court's Article I analysis appears to invalidate all legislative vetoes irrespective of form or subject. Because the legislative veto is commonly found as a check upon rule-making by administrative agencies and upon broad-based policy decisions of the Executive Branch, it is particularly unfortunate that the Court reaches its decision in a case involving the exercise of a veto over deportation decisions regarding particular individuals. Courts should always be wary of striking statutes as unconstitutional; to strike an entire class of statutes based on consideration of a somewhat atypical and more-readily indictable exemplar of the class is irresponsible . . .

If the legislative veto were as plainly unconstitutional as the Court strives to suggest, its broad ruling today would be more comprehensible. But, the constitutionality of the legislative veto is anything but clear cut. The issue divides scholars, courts, attorneys general, and the two other branches of the National Government. If the veto devices so flagrantly disregarded the requirements of Article I as the Court today suggests, I find it incomprehensible that Congress, whose members are bound by oath to uphold the Constitution, would have placed these mechanisms in nearly 200 separate laws over a period of 50 years.

The reality of the situation is that the constitutional question posed today is one of immense difficulty over which the executive and legislative branches—as well as scholars and judges—have understandably disagreed. That disagreement stems from the silence of the Constitution on the precise question: The Constitution does not directly authorize or prohibit the legislative veto. Thus, our task should be to determine whether the legislative veto is consistent with the purposes of Art. I and the principles of Separation of Powers which are reflected in that Article and throughout the Constitution. We should not find the lack of a specific constitutional authorization for the legislative veto surprising, and I would not infer disapproval of the mechanism from its absence. From the summer of 1787 to the present the government of the United States has become an endeavor far beyond the contemplation of the Framers. Only within the last half century has the complexity and size of the Federal Government's responsibilities grown so greatly that the Congress must rely on the legislative veto as the most effective if not the only means to insure their role as the nation's lawmakers. But the wisdom of the Framers was to anticipate that the nation would grow and new problems of governance would require different solutions. Accordingly, our Federal Government was intentionally chartered with the flexibility to respond to contemporary needs without losing sight of

fundamental democratic principles. This was the spirit in which Justice Jackson penned his influential concurrence in the Steel Seizure Case . . .

The power to exercise a legislative veto is not the power to write new law without bicameral approval or presidential consideration. The veto must be authorized by statute and may only negative what an Executive department or independent agency has proposed. On its face, the legislative veto no more allows one House of Congress to make law than does the presidential veto confer such power upon the President. Accordingly, the Court properly recognizes that it "must establish that the challenged action under s 244(c)(2) is of the kind to which the procedural requirements of Art. I, s 7 apply" and admits that "not every action taken by either House is subject to the bicameralism and presentation requirements of Art. I." . . .

[T]he Court believes that the legislative veto we consider today is best characterized as an exercise of legislative or quasi-legislative authority. Under this characterization, the practice does not, even on the surface, constitute an infringement of executive or judicial prerogative. The Attorney General's suspension of deportation is equivalent to a proposal for legislation. The nature of the Attorney General's role as recommendatory is not altered because s 244 provides for congressional action through disapproval rather than by ratification. In comparison to private bills, which must be initiated in the Congress and which allow a Presidential veto to be overriden by a two-thirds majority in both Houses of Congress, s 244 augments rather than reduces the executive branch's authority. So understood, congressional review does not undermine . . . the "weight and dignity" that attends the decisions of the Executive Branch.

Nor does s 244 infringe on the judicial power, as Justice Powell would hold. Section 244 makes clear that Congress has reserved its own judgment as part of the statutory process. Congressional action does not substitute for judicial review of the Attorney General's decisions. The Act provides for judicial review of the refusal of the Attorney General to suspend a deportation and to transmit a recommendation to Congress. But the courts have not been given the authority to review whether an alien should be given permanent status; review is limited to whether the Attorney General has properly applied the statutory standards for essentially denying the alien a recommendation that his deportable status be changed by the Congress. Moreover, there is no constitutional obligation to provide any judicial review whatever for a failure to suspend deportation . . .

I do not suggest that all legislative vetoes are necessarily consistent with separation of powers principles. A legislative check on an inherently executive function, for example that of initiating prosecutions, poses an entirely different question. But the legislative veto device here—and in many other settings—is far from an instance of legislative tyranny over the Executive. It is a necessary check on the unavoidably expanding power of the agencies, both executive and independent, as they engage in exercising authority delegated by Congress. . . .

I regret the destructive scope of the Court's holding. It reflects a profoundly different conception of the Constitution than that held by the Courts which sanctioned the modern administrative state. Today's decision strikes down in one fell swoop provisions in more laws enacted by Congress than the Court has cumulatively invalidated in its history . . .

Bowsher v. Synar

478 U.S. 714 (1986), 7-2
Opinion of the Court: Burger, C.J. (Brennan, Marshall, O'Connor, Powell, White)
Concurring: Stevens
Dissenting: Blackmun, White
Representative Mike Synar and 11 other members of Congress sued to have the act, which gave ultimate budget-cutting responsibilities to the Comptroller General Charles Bowsher, declared unconstitutional.

The Emergency Deficit Control Act was one of the most ambitious enactments of the 1980s. Did the Court's decision correct a fundamental flaw in constitutional understanding, as Burger says, or was its objection to the law trivial, as White says? According to the Court, what are the differences between legislative and executive functions, according to the Court? On what grounds does Burger argue that the act gave executive power to the comptroller general? That the comptroller general is controlled by the Congress? How does Stevens's analysis of the infirmity of the act differ from Burger's? Aside from the parties to the case, what private or governmental interests are likely to gain and lose as a result of this decision?

Burger, C.J., for the Court:

The question presented by these appeals is whether the assignment by Congress to the Comptroller Gen-

eral of the United States of certain functions under the Balanced Budget and Emergency Deficit Control Act of 1985 violates the doctrine of separation of powers.

On December 12, 1985, the President signed into law the Balanced Budget and Emergency Deficit Control Act of 1985, popularly known as the "Gramm-Rudman-Hollings Act." The purpose of the Act is to eliminate the federal budget deficit. To that end, the Act sets a "maximum deficit amount" for federal spending for each of fiscal years 1986 through 1991. The size of that maximum deficit amount progressively reduces to zero in fiscal year 1991. If in any fiscal year the federal budget deficit exceeds the maximum deficit amount by more than a specified sum, the Act requires across-the-board cuts in federal spending to reach the targeted deficit level, with half of the cuts made to defense programs and the other half made to non-defense programs. The Act exempts certain priority programs from these cuts.

These "automatic" reductions are accomplished through a rather complicated procedure, spelled out in s 251, the so-called "reporting provisions" of the Act. Each year, the Directors of the Office of Management and Budget (OMB) and the Congressional Budget Office (CBO) independently estimate the amount of the federal budget deficit for the upcoming fiscal year. If that deficit exceeds the maximum targeted deficit amount for that fiscal year by more than a specified amount, the Directors of OMB and CBO independently calculate, on a program-by-program basis, the budget reductions necessary to ensure that the deficit does not exceed the maximum deficit amount. The Act then requires the Directors to report jointly their deficit estimates and budget reduction calculations to the Comptroller General.

The Comptroller General, after reviewing the Directors' reports, then reports his conclusions to the President. The President in turn must issue a "sequestration" order mandating the spending reductions specified by the Comptroller General. There follows a period during which Congress may by legislation reduce spending to obviate, in whole or in part, the need for the sequestration order. If such reductions are not enacted, the sequestration order becomes effective and the spending reductions included in that order are made . . .

The Constitution does not contemplate an active role for Congress in the supervision of officers charged with the execution of the laws it enacts. The President appoints "Officers of the United States" with the "Advice and Consent of the Senate . . . ."

Art. II, s 2. Once the appointment has been made and confirmed, however, the Constitution explicitly provides for removal of Officers of the United States by Congress only upon impeachment by the House of Representatives and conviction by the Senate. An impeachment by the House and trial by the Senate can rest only on "Treason, Bribery or other high Crimes and Misdemeanors." Article II, s 4. A direct congressional role in the removal of officers charged with the execution of the laws beyond this limited one is inconsistent with separation of powers . . .

In light of these precedents [*Myers v. United States, Humphrey's Executor v. United States, and Wiener v. United States*], we conclude that Congress cannot reserve for itself the power of removal of an officer charged with the execution of the laws except by impeachment. To permit the execution of the laws to be vested in an officer answerable only to Congress would, in practical terms, reserve in Congress control over the execution of the laws. As the District Court observed: "Once an officer is appointed, it is only the authority that can remove him, and not the authority that appointed him, that he must fear and, in the performance of his functions, obey." The structure of the Constitution does not permit Congress to execute the laws; it follows that Congress cannot grant to an officer under its control what it does not possess.

Our decision in *INS v. Chadha* (1983), supports this conclusion. In *Chadha*, we struck down a one-House "legislative veto" provision by which each House of Congress retained the power to reverse a decision Congress had expressly authorized the Attorney General to make . . . To permit an officer

controlled by Congress to execute the laws would be, in essence, to permit a congressional veto. Congress could simply remove, or threaten to remove, an officer for executing the laws in any fashion found to be unsatisfactory to Congress. This kind of congressional control over the execution of the laws, *Chadha* makes clear, is constitutionally impermissible.

The dangers of congressional usurpation of Executive Branch functions have long been recognized. "[T]he debates of the Constitutional Convention, and the Federalist Papers, are replete with expressions of fear that the Legislative Branch of the National Government will aggrandize itself at the expense of the other two branches." *Buckley v. Valeo* (1976). Indeed, we also have observed only recently that "[t]he hydraulic pressure inherent within each of the separate Branches to exceed the outer limits of its power, even to accomplish desirable objectives, must be resisted." *Chadha* With these principles in mind, we turn to consideration of whether the Comptroller General is controlled by Congress.

[Bowsher et al.] urge that the Comptroller General performs his duties independently and is not subservient to Congress. . . .

The critical factor lies in the provisions of the statute defining the Comptroller General's office relating to removability. Although the Comptroller General is nominated by the President from a list of three individuals recommended by the Speaker of the House of Representatives and the President pro tempore of the Senate, and confirmed by the Senate, he is removable only at the initiative of Congress. He may be removed not only by impeachment but also by

As the lead plaintiff, Congressman Mike Synar had reason to smile after the Supreme Court's decision in *Bowsher v. Synar*. A key provision of the Balanced Budget and Emergency Deficit Control Act of 1985, which Synar had opposed, was held unconstitutional.

joint resolution of Congress "at any time" resting on any one of the following bases: (i) permanent disability; (ii) inefficiency; (iii) neglect of duty; (iv) malfeasance; or (v) a felony or conduct involving moral turpitude. . . .

It is clear that Congress has consistently viewed the Comptroller General as an officer of the Legislative Branch. The Reorganization Acts of 1945 and 1949, for example, both stated that the Comptroller General and the GAO are "a part of the legislative branch of the Government." Similarly, in the Accounting and Auditing Act of 1950, Congress required the Comptroller General to conduct audits "as an agent of the Congress."

Over the years, the Comptrollers General have also viewed themselves as part of the Legislative Branch. In one of the early Annual Reports of Comptroller General, the official seal of his office was described as reflecting "the independence of judgment to be exercised by the General Accounting Office, subject to the control of the legislative branch. . . . The combination represents an agency of the Congress independent of other authority auditing and checking the expenditures of the Government as required by law and subjecting any questions arising in that connection to quasi-judicial determination." Later, Comptroller General Warren, who had been a Member of Congress for 15 years before being appointed Comptroller General, testified: "During most of my public life . . . I have been a member of the legislative branch. Even now, although heading a great agency, it is an agency of the Congress, and I am an agent of the Congress." And, in one conflict during Comptroller General McCarl's tenure, he asserted his independence of the Executive Branch, stating: "Congress . . . is . . . the only authority to which there lies an appeal from the decision of this office . . . I may not accept the opinion of any official, inclusive of the Attorney General, as controlling my duty under the law."

Against this background, we see no escape from the conclusion that, because Congress has retained removal authority over the Comptroller General, he may not be entrusted with executive powers. The remaining question is whether the Comptroller General has been assigned such powers in the Balanced Budget and Emergency Deficit Control Act of 1985.

The primary responsibility of the Comptroller General under the instant Act is the preparation of a "report." This report must contain detailed estimates of projected federal revenues and expenditures. The report must also specify the reductions, if any, necessary to reduce the deficit to the target for the appropriate fiscal year. The reductions must be set forth on a program-by-program basis.

In preparing the report, the Comptroller General is to have "due regard" for the estimates and reductions set forth in a joint report submitted to him by the Director of CBO and the Director of OMB, the President's fiscal and budgetary adviser. However, the Act plainly contemplates that the Comptroller General will exercise his independent judgment and evaluation with respect to those estimates. The Act also provides that the Comptroller General's report "shall explain fully any differences between the contents of such report and the report of the Directors."

[Bowsher et al.] suggest that the duties assigned to the Comptroller General in the Act are essentially ministerial and mechanical so that their performance does not constitute "execution of the law" in a meaningful sense. On the contrary, we view these functions as plainly entailing execution of the law in constitutional terms. Interpreting a law enacted by Congress to implement the legislative mandate is the very essence of "execution" of the law. Under s 251, the Comptroller General must exercise judgment concerning facts that affect the application of the Act. He must also interpret the provisions of the Act to determine precisely what budgetary calculations are required. Decisions of that kind are typically made by officers charged with executing a statute.

The executive nature of the Comptroller General's functions under the Act is revealed in s 252(a)(3) which gives the Comptroller General the ultimate authority to determine the budget cuts to be made. Indeed, the Comptroller General commands the President himself to carry out . . . the directive of the Comptroller General as to the budget reductions. . . .

Congress of course initially determined the content of the Balanced Budget and Emergency Deficit Control Act; and undoubtedly the content of the Act determines the nature of the executive duty. However, as *Chadha* makes clear, once Congress makes its choice in enacting legislation, its participation ends. Congress can thereafter control the execution of its enactment only indirectly—by passing new legislation. By placing the responsibility for execution of the Balanced Budget and Emergency Deficit Control Act in the hands of an officer who is subject to removal only by itself, Congress in effect has retained control over the execution of the Act and has intruded into the executive function. The Constitution does not permit such intrusion. . . .

No one can doubt that Congress and the President are confronted with fiscal and economic problems of unprecedented magnitude, but "the fact that a given law or procedure is efficient, convenient, and useful in facilitating functions of government, standing alone, will not save it if it is contrary to the Constitution. Convenience and efficiency are not the primary objectives—or the hallmarks—of democratic government . . . ." *Chadha.*

We conclude that the District Court correctly held that the powers vested in the Comptroller General under s 251 violate the command of the Constitution that the Congress play no direct role in the execution of the laws. Accordingly, the judgment and order of the District Court are affirmed.

Stevens (Marshall), concurring:

When this Court is asked to invalidate a statutory provision that has been approved by both Houses of the Congress and signed by the President, particularly an Act of Congress that confronts a deeply vexing national problem, it should only do so for the most compelling constitutional reasons. I agree with the Court that the "Gramm-Rudman-Hollings" Act contains a constitutional infirmity so severe that the flawed provision may not stand. I disagree with the Court, however, on the reasons why the Constitution prohibits the Comptroller General from exercising the powers assigned to him by s 251(b) and s 251(c)(2) of the Act. It is not the dormant, carefully circumscribed congressional removal power that represents the primary constitutional evil. Nor do I agree with the conclusion of both the majority and the dissent that the analysis depends on a labeling of the functions assigned to the Comptroller General as "executive powers." Rather, I am convinced that the Comptroller General must be characterized as an agent of Congress because of his long-standing statutory responsibilities; that the powers assigned to him under the Gramm-Rudman-Hollings Act require him to make policy that will bind the Nation; and that, when Congress, or a component or an agent of Congress, seeks to make policy that will bind the Nation, it must follow the procedures mandated by Article I of the Constitution—through passage by both Houses and presentment to the President. In short, Congress may not exercise its fundamental power to formulate national policy by delegating that power to one of its two Houses, to a legislative committee, or to an individual agent of the Congress such as the Speaker of the House of Representatives, the Sergeant at Arms of the Senate, or the Director of the Congressional Budget Office. That principle, I believe, is applicable to the Comptroller General.

White, dissenting:

The Court, acting in the name of separation of powers, takes upon itself to strike down the Gramm-Rudman-Hollings Act, one of the most novel and far-reaching legislative responses to a national crisis since the New Deal. The basis of the Court's action is a solitary provision of another statute that was passed over 60 years ago and has lain dormant since that time . . . I will not purport to speak to the wisdom of the policies incorporated in the legislation the Court invalidates; that is a matter for the Congress and the Executive, both of which expressed their assent to the statute barely half a year ago. I will, however, address the wisdom of the Court's willingness to interpose its distressingly formalistic view of separation of powers as a bar to the attainment of governmental objectives through the means chosen by the Congress and the President in the legislative process established by the Constitution. Twice in the past four years I have expressed my view that the Court's recent efforts to police the separation of powers have rested on untenable constitutional propositions leading to regrettable results. Today's result is even more misguided. . . . [T]he Court's decision rests on a feature of the legislative scheme that is of minimal practical significance and that presents no substantial threat to the basic scheme of separation of powers. . . .

Before examining the merits of the Court's argument, I wish to emphasize what . . . the Court quite pointedly and correctly does not hold: namely, that "executive" powers of the sort granted the Comptroller by the Act may only be exercised by officers removable at will by the President. The Court's apparent unwillingness to accept this argument, which has been tendered in this Court by the Solicitor General, is fully consistent with the Court's long-standing recognition that it is within the power of Congress under the "Necessary and Proper" Clause, Art. I, s 8, to vest authority that falls within the Court's definition of executive power in officers who are not subject to removal at will by the President and are therefore not under the President's direct control. In an earlier day, in which simpler notions of the role of government in society prevailed, it was perhaps plausible to insist that all "executive" officers be subject to an unqualified Presidential removal power, but with the advent and triumph of the administrative state and the accompanying multiplication of the tasks undertaken by the Federal Government, the Court has been virtually compelled to recognize that Congress may reasonably deem it "necessary and proper" to vest some among the broad new array of governmental functions in officers who are free from the partisanship that may be expected of agents wholly dependent upon the President . . .

[T]he powers exercised by the Comptroller General under the Gramm-Rudman-Hollings Act are not such that vesting them in an officer not subject to removal at will by the President would in itself improperly interfere with Presidential powers. Determining the level of spending by the Federal Government is not by nature a function central either to the exercise of the President's enumerated powers or to his general duty to ensure execution of the laws; rather, appropriating funds is a peculiarly legislative function, and one expressly committed to Congress by Art. I, s 9, which provides that "No Money shall be drawn from the Treasury, but in Consequence of Appropriations made by Law." In enacting Gramm-Rudman-Hollings, Congress has chosen to exercise this legislative power to establish the level of federal spending by providing a detailed set of criteria for reducing expenditures below the level of appropriations in the event that certain conditions are met. Delegating the execution of this legislation—that is, the power to apply the Act's criteria and make the required calculations—to an officer independent of the President's will does not deprive the President of any power that he would otherwise have or that is essential to the performance of the duties of his office. Rather, the result of such a delegation, from the standpoint of the President, is no different from the result of more traditional forms of appropriation: under either system, the level of funds available to the Executive Branch to carry out its duties is not within the President's discretionary control. To be sure, if the budget-cutting mechanism required the responsible officer to exercise a great deal of policy-making discretion, one might argue that having created such broad discretion Congress had some obligation based upon Art. II to vest it in the Chief Executive or his agents. In Gramm-Rudman-Hollings, however, Congress has done no such thing; instead, it has created a precise and articulated set of criteria designed to minimize the degree of policy choice exercised by the officer executing the statute and to ensure that the relative spending priorities es-

tablished by Congress in the appropriations it passes into law remain unaltered. Given that the exercise of policy choice by the officer executing the statute would be inimical to Congress' goal in enacting "automatic" budget-cutting measures, it is eminently reasonable and proper for Congress to vest the budget-cutting authority in an officer who is to the greatest degree possible nonpartisan and independent of the President and his political agenda and who therefore may be relied upon not to allow his calculations to be colored by political considerations. Such a delegation deprives the President of no authority that is rightfully his.

If . . . the assignment of "executive" powers under Gramm-Rudman-Hollings to an officer not removable at will by the President would not in itself represent a violation of the constitutional scheme of separated powers, the question remains whether, as the Court concludes, the fact that the officer to whom Congress has delegated the authority to implement the Act is removable by a joint resolution of Congress should require invalidation of the Act. The Court's decision . . . is based on a syllogism: the Act vests the Comptroller with "executive power"; such power may not be exercised by Congress or its agents; the Comptroller is an agent of Congress because he is removable by Congress; therefore the Act is invalid. I have no quarrel with the proposition that the powers exercised by the Comptroller under the Act may be characterized as "executive" in that they involve the interpretation and carrying out of the Act's mandate. I can also accept the general proposition that although Congress has considerable authority in designating the officers who are to execute legislation, the constitutional scheme of separated powers does prevent Congress from reserving an executive role for itself or for its "agents." I cannot accept, however, that the exercise of authority by an officer removable for cause by a joint resolution of Congress is analogous to the impermissible execution of the law by Congress itself, nor would I hold that the congressional role in the removal process renders the Comptroller an "agent" of the Congress, incapable of receiving "executive" power. . . .

[T]he Court baldly mischaracterizes the removal provision when it suggests that it allows Congress to remove the Comptroller for "executing the laws in any fashion found to be unsatisfactory"; in fact, Congress may remove the Comptroller only for one or more of five specified reasons, which "although not so narrow as to deny Congress any leeway, circumscribe Congress' power to some extent by providing a basis for judicial review of congressional removal." . . . [M]ore to the point, the Court overlooks or deliberately ignores the decisive difference between the congressional removal provision and the legislative veto struck down in *Chadha:* under the Budget and Accounting Act, Congress may remove the Comptroller only through a joint resolution, which by definition must be passed by both Houses and signed by the President. In other words, a removal of the Comptroller under the statute satisfies the requirements of bicameralism and presentment laid down in *Chadha.* . . .

Realistic consideration of the nature of the Comptroller General's relation to Congress thus reveals that the threat to separation of powers conjured up by the majority is wholly chimerical. The power over removal retained by the Congress is not a power that is exercised outside the legislative process as established by the Constitution, nor does it appear likely that it is a power that adds significantly to the influence Congress may exert over executive officers through other, undoubtedly constitutional exercises of legislative power and through the constitutionally guaranteed impeachment power. Indeed, the removal power is so constrained by its own substantive limits and by the requirement of Presidential approval "that, as a practical matter, Congress has not exercised, and probably will never exercise, such control over the Comptroller General that his non-legislative powers will threaten the goal of dispersion of power, and hence the goal of individual liberty, that separation of powers serves."

The majority's contrary conclusion rests on the rigid dogma that, outside of the impeachment process, any "direct congressional role in the removal of officers charged with the execution of the laws . . . is inconsistent with separation of powers." Reliance on such an unyielding principle to strike down a statute posing no real danger of aggrandizement of congressional power is extremely misguided and insensitive to our constitutional role. The wisdom of vesting "executive" powers in an officer removable by joint resolution may indeed be debatable—as may be the wisdom of the entire scheme of permitting an unelected official to revise the budget enacted by Congress—but such matters are for the most part to be worked out between the Congress and the President through the legislative process, which affords each branch ample opportunity to defend its interests. The Act vesting budget-cutting

authority in the Comptroller General represents Congress' judgment that the delegation of such authority to counteract ever-mounting deficits is "necessary and proper" to the exercise of the powers granted the Federal Government by the Constitution; and the President's approval of the statute signifies his unwillingness to reject the choice made by Congress. Under such circumstances, the role of this Court should be limited to determining whether the Act so alters the balance of authority among the branches of government as to pose a genuine threat to the basic division between the lawmaking power and the power to execute the law. Because I see no such threat, I cannot join the Court in striking down the Act.

Morrison v. Olson

487 U.S. 654 (1988), 7-1
Opinion of the Court: Rehnquist, C.J. (Blackmun, Brennan, Marshall, O'Connor, Stevens, White)
Dissenting: Scalia
Not participating: Kennedy

A report of the House Judiciary Committee, following its investigation of the Justice Department's role in a controversy between the House and the Environmental Protection Agency (EPA), suggested that Theodore Olson, an official in the Justice Department, had given false testimony in the investigation and that two officials of the EPA had obstructed the investigation by wrongfully withholding certain documents. The report asked the attorney general, under the Ethics in Government Act of 1978, to seek appointment of an independent counsel to investigate the allegations. Alexia Morrison was eventually appointed by the Special Division, itself created by the act. When Olson and the EPA officials were served with grand jury subpoenas at Morrison's urging, they moved to quash them, arguing that the Ethics in Government Act provisions for appointment of an independent counsel were unconstitutional.

How many separation of powers questions did the Court need to decide? What was its rationale in each? What is the significance of the distinction between "principal" and "inferior" officers? Does Rehnquist make clear what the essential executive powers are that cannot be compromised by actions of other branches? Is Rehnquist's concept of separation of powers consistent with the Court's in Immigration and Naturalization Service v. Chadha and Bowsher v. Synar? What are the advantages and disadvantages of having a special independent counsel investigate and possibly prosecute high-ranking members of the Executive branch?

Rehnquist, C.J., for the Court:

This case presents us with a challenge to the independent counsel provisions of the Ethics in Government Act of 1978. We hold today that these provisions of the Act do not violate the Appointments Clause of the Constitution, Art. II, § 2, cl. 2, or the limitations of Article III, nor do they impermissibly interfere with the President's authority under Article II in violation of the constitutional principle of separation of powers . . .

The parties do not dispute that "[t]he Constitution for purposes of appointment . . . divides all its officers into two classes." As we stated in *Buckley v. Valeo:* "Principal officers are selected by the President with the advice and consent of the Senate. Inferior officers Congress may allow to be appointed by the President alone, by the heads of departments, or by the Judiciary." The initial question is, accordingly, whether [Morrison] is an "inferior" or a "principal" officer. If she is the latter, as the Court of Appeals concluded, then the Act is in violation of the Appointments Clause.

The line between "inferior" and "principal" officers is one that is far from clear, and the Framers provided little guidance into where it should be drawn . . . We need not attempt here to decide exactly where the line falls between the two types of officers, because, in our view, [Morrison] clearly falls on the "inferior officer" side of that line. Several factors lead to this conclusion.

First, [Morrison] is subject to removal by a higher Executive Branch official. Although [Morrison] may not be "subordinate" to the Attorney General (and the President) insofar as she possesses a degree of independent discretion to exercise the powers delegated to her under the Act, the fact that she can be removed by the Attorney General indicates that she is, to some degree, "inferior" in rank and authority.

Second, [Morrison] is empowered by the Act to perform only certain, limited duties. An independent counsel's role is restricted primarily to investigation and, if appropriate, prosecution for certain federal crimes. Admittedly, the Act delegates to [Morrison] "full power and independent authority to exercise all investigative and prosecutorial functions and powers of the Department of Justice," but this grant of authority does not include any authority to formulate policy for the Government or the Executive Branch, nor does it give [Morrison] any administrative duties outside of those necessary to operate her office. The

Act specifically provides that, in policy matters, [Morrison] is to comply to the extent possible with the policies of the Department . . .

Third, [Morrison's] office is limited in jurisdiction. Not only is the Act itself restricted in applicability to certain federal officials suspected of certain serious federal crimes, but an independent counsel can only act within the scope of the jurisdiction that has been granted by the Special Division pursuant to a request by the Attorney General. Finally, [Morrison's] office is limited in tenure. There is concededly no time limit on the appointment of a particular counsel. Nonetheless, the office of independent counsel is "temporary" in the sense that an independent counsel is appointed essentially to accomplish a single task, and when that task is over, the office is terminated, either by the counsel herself or by action of the Special Division. Unlike other prosecutors, [Morrison] has no ongoing responsibilities that extend beyond the accomplishment of the mission that she was appointed for and authorized by the Special Division to undertake. In our view, these factors relating to the "ideas of tenure, duration . . . and duties" of the independent counsel, are sufficient to establish that [Morrison] is an "inferior" officer in the constitutional sense . . .

This does not, however, end our inquiry under the Appointments Clause. [Olson, et al.] argue that, even if [Morrison] is an "inferior" officer, the Clause does not empower Congress to place the power to appoint such an officer outside the Executive Branch. They contend that the Clause does not contemplate congressional authorization of "interbranch appointments," in which an officer of one branch is appointed by officers of another branch. The relevant language of the Appointments Clause is worth repeating. It reads: ". . . but the Congress may by Law vest the Appointment of such inferior Officers, as they think proper, in the President alone, in the courts of Law, or in the Heads of Departments." On its face, the language of this "excepting clause" admits of no limitation on interbranch appointments. Indeed, the inclusion of "as they think proper" seems clearly to give Congress significant discretion to determine whether it is "proper" to vest the appointment of, for example, executive officials in the "courts of Law." . . .

We do not mean to say that Congress' power to provide for interbranch appointments of "inferior officers" is unlimited. In addition to separation of powers concerns, which would arise if such provisions for appointment had the potential to impair the constitutional functions assigned to one of the branches . . . In this case, however, we do not think it impermissible for Congress to vest the power to appoint independent counsel in a specially created federal court. We thus disagree with the Court of Appeals' conclusion that there is an inherent incongruity about a court having the power to appoint prosecutorial officers. We have recognized that courts may appoint private attorneys to act as prosecutor for judicial contempt judgments . . . Congress of course was concerned when it created the office of independent counsel with the conflicts of interest that could arise in situations when the Executive Branch is called upon to investigate its own high-ranking officers. If it were to remove the appointing authority from the Executive Branch, the most logical place to put it was in the Judicial Branch. In the light of the Act's provision making the judges of the Special Division ineligible to participate in any matters relating to an independent counsel they have appointed, we do not think that appointment of the independent counsel by the court runs afoul of the constitutional limitation on "incongruous" interbranch appointments.

[Olson, et al.] next contend that the powers vested in the Special Division by the Act conflict with Article III of the Constitution. We have long recognized that by the express provisions of Article III, the judicial power of the United States is limited to "Cases" and "Controversies." As a general rule, we have broadly stated that "executive or administrative duties of a non-judicial nature may not be imposed on judges holding office under Art. III of the Constitution." The purpose of this limitation is to help ensure the independence of the Judicial Branch and to prevent the judiciary from encroaching into areas reserved for the other branches . . .

Most importantly, the Act vests in the Special Division the power to choose who will serve as independent counsel and the power to define his or her jurisdiction. Clearly, once it is accepted that the Appointments Clause gives Congress the power to vest the appointment of officials such as the independent counsel in the "courts of Law," there can be no Article III objection to the Special Division's exercise of that power, as the power itself derives from the Appointments Clause, a source of authority for judicial action that is independent of Article III.

[Olson, et al.] contend, however, that the Division's Appointments Clause powers do not encompass the power to define the independent counsel's jurisdiction. We disagree. In our view, Congress' power under the Clause to vest the "Appointment" of inferior officers in the courts may, in certain circumstances, allow Congress to give the courts some discretion in defining the nature and scope of the appointed official's authority. Particularly when, as here, Congress creates a temporary "office" the nature and duties of which will by necessity vary with the factual circumstances giving rise to the need for an appointment in the first place, it may vest the power to define the scope of the office in the court as an incident to the appointment of the officer pursuant to the Appointments Clause. This said, we do not think that Congress may give the Division unlimited discretion to determine the independent counsel's jurisdiction. In order for the Division's definition of the counsel's jurisdiction to be truly "incidental" to its power to appoint, the jurisdiction that the court decides upon must be demonstrably related to the factual circumstances that gave rise to the Attorney General's investigation and request for the appointment of the independent counsel in the particular case.

The Act also vests in the Special Division various powers and duties in relation to the independent counsel that, because they do not involve appointing the counsel or defining his or her jurisdiction, cannot be said to derive from the Division's Appointments Clause authority . . .

Leaving aside for the moment the Division's power o terminate an independent counsel, we do not think that Article III absolutely prevents Congress from vesting these other miscellaneous powers in the Special Division pursuant to the Act. As we observed above, one purpose of the broad prohibition upon the courts' exercise of "executive or administrative duties of a non-judicial nature," is to maintain the separation between the judiciary and the other branches of the Federal Government by ensuring that judges do not encroach upon executive or legislative authority or undertake tasks that are more properly accomplished by those branches . . . The Act simply does not give the Division the power to "supervise" the independent counsel in the exercise of his or her investigative or prosecutorial authority. And the functions that the Special Division is empowered to perform are not inherently "Executive"; indeed, they are directly analogous to functions that federal judges perform in other contexts, such as deciding whether to allow disclosure of matters occurring before a grand jury or awarding attorney's fees.

We are more doubtful about the Special Division's power to terminate the office of the independent counsel pursuant to § 596(b)(2) . . . [T]he power to terminate, especially when exercised by the Division on its own motion, is "administrative" to the extent that it requires the Special Division to monitor the progress of the proceedings of the independent counsel and come to a decision as to whether the counsel's job is "completed." It also is not a power that could be considered typically "judicial," as it has few analogues among the court's more traditional powers. Nonetheless, we do not, as did the Court of Appeals, view this provision as a significant judicial encroachment upon executive power or upon the prosecutorial discretion of the independent counsel . . .

Nor do we believe . . . that the Special Division's exercise of the various powers specifically granted to it under the Act poses any threat to the "impartial and independent federal adjudication of claims within the judicial power of the United States." We reach this conclusion for two reasons. First, the Act as it currently stands gives the Special Division itself no power to review any of the actions of the independent counsel or any of the actions of the Attorney General with regard to the counsel. Accordingly, there is no risk of partisan or biased adjudication of claims regarding the independent counsel by that court. Second, the Act prevents members of the Special Division from participating in any judicial proceeding concerning a matter which involves such independent counsel while such independent counsel is serving in that office or which involves the exercise of such independent counsel's official duties, regardless of whether such independent counsel is still serving in that office . . . We think both the special court and its judges are sufficiently isolated by these statutory provisions from the review of the activities of the independent counsel so as to avoid any taint of the independence of the judiciary such as would render the Act invalid under Article III . . .

We now turn to consider whether the Act is invalid under the constitutional principle of separation of powers. Two related issues must be addressed: the first is whether the provision of the Act restricting the Attorney General's power to remove the independent counsel to only those instances in which he can show "good cause," taken by itself, impermissibly interferes with the President's exercise of his constitutionally appointed functions. The second is whether, taken as a whole, the Act violates the separation of powers by reducing the President's ability to control the prosecutorial powers wielded by the independent counsel . . .

Unlike both *Bowsher* and *Myers*, this case does not involve an attempt by Congress itself to gain a role in the removal of executive officials other than its established powers of impeachment and conviction. The Act instead puts the removal power squarely in the hands of the Executive Branch; an independent counsel may be removed from office, "only by the personal action of the Attorney General, and only for good cause." There is no requirement of congressional approval of the Attorney General's removal decision, though the decision is subject to judicial review. In our view, the removal provisions of the Act make this case more analogous to *Humphrey's Executor v. United States* and *Wiener v. United States,* than to *Myers* or *Bowsher* . . .

Considering for the moment the "good cause" removal provision . . . [t]here is no real dispute that the functions performed by the independent counsel are "executive" in the sense that they are law enforcement functions that typically have been undertaken by officials within the Executive Branch. . . . [T]he independent counsel is an inferior officer under the Appointments Clause, with limited jurisdiction and tenure and lacking policymaking or significant administrative authority. Although the counsel exercises no small amount of discretion and judgment in deciding how to carry out his or her duties under the Act, we simply do not see how the President's need to control the exercise of that discretion is so central to the functioning of the Executive Branch as to require as a matter of constitutional law that the counsel be terminable at will by the President.

Nor do we think that the "good cause" removal provision . . . impermissibly burdens the President's power to control or supervise the independent counsel, as an executive official, in the execution of his or her duties under the Act. This is not a case in which the power to remove an executive official has been completely stripped from the President, thus providing no means for the President to ensure the "faithful execution" of the laws. Rather, because the independent counsel may be terminated for "good cause," the Executive, through the Attorney General, retains ample authority to assure that the counsel is competently performing his or her statutory responsibilities in a manner that comports with the provisions of the Act. Although we need not decide in this case exactly what is encompassed within the term "good cause" under the Act, the legislative history of the removal provision also makes clear that the Attorney General may remove an independent counsel for "misconduct." . . . We do not think that this limitation as it presently stands sufficiently deprives the President of control over the independent counsel to interfere impermissibly with his constitutional obligation to ensure the faithful execution of the laws.

The final question to be addressed is whether the Act, taken as a whole, violates the principle of separation of powers by unduly interfering with the role of the Executive Branch. Time and again we have reaffirmed the importance in our constitutional scheme of the separation of governmental powers into the three coordinate branches . . .

We observe first that this case does not involve an attempt by Congress to increase its own powers at the expense of the Executive Branch. Unlike some of our previous cases, most recently *Bowsher v. Synar,* this case simply does not pose a "dange[r] of congressional usurpation of Executive Branch functions." Indeed, with the exception of the power of impeachment—which applies to all officers of the United States—Congress retained for itself no powers of control or supervision over an independent counsel. The Act does empower certain Members of Congress to request the Attorney General to apply for the appointment of an independent counsel, but the Attorney General has no duty to comply with the request, although he must respond within a certain time limit. Other than that, Congress' role under the Act is limited to receiving reports or other information and oversight of the independent counsel's activities, functions that we have recognized generally as being incidental to the legislative function of Congress.

Similarly, we do not think that the Act works any judicial usurpation of properly executive functions. As should be apparent from our discussion of the Appointments Clause above, the power to appoint inferior officers such as independent counsel is not, in itself, an "executive" function in the constitutional sense, at least when Congress has exercised its power to vest the appointment of an inferior office in the "courts of Law." We note nonetheless that, under the Act, the Special Division has no power to appoint an independent counsel *sua sponte;* it may only do so upon the specific request of the Attorney General, and the courts are specifically prevented from reviewing the At-

torney General's decision not to seek appointment. In addition, once the court has appointed a counsel and defined his or her jurisdiction, it has no power to supervise or control the activities of the counsel . . . [T]he various powers delegated by the statute to the Division are not supervisory or administrative, nor are they functions that the Constitution requires be performed by officials within the Executive Branch. The Act does give a federal court the power to review the Attorney General's decision to remove an independent counsel, but in our view this is a function that is well within the traditional power of the judiciary.

Finally, we do not think that the Act "impermissibly undermine[s]" the powers of the Executive Branch, or disrupts the proper balance between the coordinate branches [by] prevent[ing] the Executive Branch from accomplishing its constitutionally assigned functions, It is undeniable that the Act reduces the amount of control or supervision that the Attorney General and, through him, the President exercises over the investigation and prosecution of a certain class of alleged criminal activity. The Attorney General is not allowed to appoint the individual of his choice; he does not determine the counsel's jurisdiction; and his power to remove a counsel is limited.

Nonetheless, the Act does give the Attorney General several means of supervising or controlling the prosecutorial powers that may be wielded by an independent counsel. Most importantly, the Attorney General retains the power to remove the counsel for "good cause," a power that we have already concluded provides the Executive with substantial ability to ensure that the laws are "faithfully executed" by an independent counsel. No independent counsel may be appointed without a specific request by the Attorney General, and the Attorney General's decision not to request appointment if he finds "no reasonable grounds to believe that further investigation is warranted" is committed to his unreviewable discretion. The Act thus gives the Executive a degree of control over the power to initiate an investigation by the independent counsel. In addition, the jurisdiction of the independent counsel is defined with reference to the facts submitted by the Attorney General, and once a counsel is appointed, the Act requires that the counsel abide by Justice Department policy unless it is not "possible" to do so. Notwithstanding the fact that the counsel is to some degree "independent" and free from Executive supervision to a greater extent than other federal prosecutors, in our view, these features of the Act give the

Executive Branch sufficient control over the independent counsel to ensure that the President is able to perform his constitutionally assigned duties.

In sum, we conclude today that it does not violate the Appointments Clause for Congress to vest the appointment of independent counsel in the Special Division; that the powers exercised by the Special Division under the Act do not violate Article III; and that the Act does not violate the separation of powers principle by impermissibly interfering with the functions of the Executive Branch.

Scalia, dissenting:

The Court concedes that "[t]here is no real dispute that the functions performed by the independent counsel are 'executive'," though it qualifies that concession by adding "in the sense that they are 'law enforcement' functions that typically have been undertaken by officials within the Executive Branch." . . . There is no possible doubt that the independent counsel's functions fit this description. She is vested with the full power and independent authority to exercise all investigative and prosecutorial functions and powers of the Department of Justice [and] the Attorney General. Governmental investigation and prosecution of crimes is a quintessentially executive function.

As for the second question, whether the statute before us deprives the President of exclusive control over that quintessentially executive activity: the Court . . . points out that the President, through his Attorney General, has at least some control. That concession is alone enough to invalidate the statute, but I cannot refrain from pointing out that the Court greatly exaggerates the extent of that "some" Presidential control. "Most importan[t]" among these controls, the Court asserts, is the Attorney General's "power to remove the counsel for 'good cause.'" . . . As we recognized in *Humphrey's Executor v. United States* . . . limiting removal power to 'good cause'" is an impediment to, not an effective grant of, Presidential control. We said that limitation was necessary with respect to members of the Federal Trade Commission, which we found to be "an agency of the legislative and judicial departments," and "wholly disconnected from the executive department," because it is quite evident that one who holds his office only during the pleasure of another cannot be depended upon to maintain an attitude of independence against the latter's will . . .

We should say here that the President's constitutionally assigned duties include complete control over investigation and prosecution of violations of the law, and that the inexorable command of Article II is clear and definite: the executive power must be vested in the President of the United States.

Is it unthinkable that the President should have such exclusive power, even when alleged crimes by him or his close associates are at issue? No more so than that Congress should have the exclusive power of legislation, even when what is at issue is its own exemption from the burdens of certain laws . . . No more so than that this Court should have the exclusive power to pronounce the final decision on justiciable cases and controversies, even those pertaining to the constitutionality of a statute reducing the salaries of the Justices. A system of separate and coordinate powers necessarily involves an acceptance of exclusive power that can theoretically be abused . . . While the separation of powers may prevent us from righting every wrong, it does so in order to ensure that we do not lose liberty. The checks against any branch's abuse of its exclusive powers are twofold: first, retaliation by one of the other branch's use of its exclusive powers: Congress, for example, can impeach the executive who willfully fails to enforce the laws; the executive can decline to prosecute under unconstitutional statutes; and the courts can dismiss malicious prosecutions. Second, and ultimately, there is the political check that the people will replace those in the political branches (the branches more "dangerous to the political rights of the Constitution," who are guilty of abuse. Political pressures produced special prosecutors—for Teapot Dome and for Watergate, for example—long before this statute created the independent counsel.

Under our system of government, the primary check against prosecutorial abuse is a political one. The prosecutors who exercise this awesome discretion are selected, and can be removed, by a President whom the people have trusted enough to elect. Moreover, when crimes are not investigated and prosecuted fairly, non-selectively, with a reasonable sense of proportion, the President pays the cost in political damage to his administration. If federal prosecutors "pick people that [they] thin[k] [they] should get, rather than cases that need to be prosecuted," if they amass many more resources against a particular prominent individual, or against a particular class of political protesters, or against members of a particular political party, than the gravity of the alleged offenses or the record of successful prosecutions seems to warrant, the unfairness will come home to roost in the Oval Office . . . That result, of course, was precisely what the Founders had in mind when they provided that all executive powers would be exercised by a single Chief Executive . . .

It is, in other words, an additional advantage of the unitary Executive that it can achieve a more uniform application of the law. Perhaps that is not always achieved, but the mechanism to achieve it is there. The mini-Executive that is the independent counsel, however, operating in an area where so little is law and so much is discretion, is intentionally cut off from the unifying influence of the Justice Department, and from the perspective that multiple responsibilities provide. What would normally be regarded as a technical violation (there are no rules defining such things), may in his or her small world assume the proportions of an indictable offense. What would normally be regarded as an investigation that has reached the level of pursuing such picayune matters that it should be concluded, may to him or her be an investigation that ought to go on for another year. How frightening it must be to have your own independent counsel and staff appointed, with nothing else to do but to investigate you until investigation is no longer worthwhile—with whether it is worthwhile not depending upon what such judgments usually hinge on, competing responsibilities. And to have that counsel and staff decide, with no basis for comparison, whether what you have done is bad enough, willful enough, and provable enough, to warrant an indictment. How admirable the constitutional system that provides the means to avoid such a distortion.

U. S. Term Limits v. Thornton

514 U.S. 1218 (1995), 5-4
Opinion of the Court: Stevens (Souter, Ginsberg, Breyer)
Concurring: Kennedy
Dissenting: Thomas (Rehnquist, O'Connor, Scalia)
Why, in the majority's view, does the Constitution not permit states to impose term limits on members of Congress? How is Powell v. McCormick relevant to this case? How do Stevens and Thomas differ in their interpretation of constitutional text? The intent of the framers? Historical practice? What does Thomas mean when he says that the national and state governments "face different default rules"? Is this a new the- *ory of federalism? What might the rules be? What differences would term limits make politically?*

Stevens, for the Court:
The Constitution sets forth qualifications for membership in the Congress of the United States. Article I, 2, cl. 2, which applies to the House of Representatives, provides: "No Person shall be a Representative who shall not have attained to the Age of twenty five Years, and been seven Years a Citizen of the United States, and who shall not, when elected, be an Inhabitant of that State in which he shall be chosen."

Article I, 3, cl. 3, which applies to the Senate, similarly provides: "No Person shall be a Senator who shall not have attained to the Age of thirty Years, and been nine Years a Citizen of the United States, and who shall not, when elected, be an Inhabitant of that State for which he shall be chosen."

Today's cases present a challenge to an amendment to the Arkansas State Constitution that prohibits the name of an otherwise-eligible candidate for Congress from appearing on the general election ballot if that candidate has already served three terms in the House of Representatives or two terms in the Senate. The Arkansas Supreme Court held that the amendment violates the Federal Constitution. We agree with that holding. Such a state-imposed restriction is contrary to the "fundamental principle of our representative democracy," embodied in the Constitution, that "the people should choose whom they please to govern them." Allowing individual States to adopt their own qualifications for congressional service would be inconsistent with the Framers' vision of a uniform National Legislature representing the people of the United States. If the qualifications set forth in the text of the Constitution are to be changed, that text must be amended. . . .

. . . [T]he constitutionality of Amendment 73 depends critically on the resolution of two distinct issues. The first is whether the Constitution forbids States from adding to or altering the qualifications specifically enumerated in the Constitution. The second is, if the Constitution does so forbid, whether the fact that Amendment 73 is formulated as a ballot access restriction rather than as an outright disqualification is of constitutional significance. Our resolution of these issues draws upon our prior resolution of a related but distinct issue: whether Congress has the power to add to or alter the qualifications of its Members.

Twenty-six years ago, in *Powell v. McCormack,* we reviewed the history and text of the Qualifications Clauses in a case involving an attempted exclusion of a duly elected Member of Congress. The principal issue was whether the power granted to each House in Art. I, 5, to judge the "Qualifications of its own Members" includes the power to impose qualifications other than those set forth in the text of the Constitution. In an opinion by Chief Justice Warren for eight Members of the Court, we held that it does not. Because of the obvious importance of the issue, the Court's review of the history and meaning of the relevant constitutional text was especially thorough. We therefore begin our analysis today with a full statement of what we decided in that case. . . .

We ultimately accepted that contention, concluding that the House of Representatives has no "authority to exclude any person, duly elected by his constituents, who meets all the requirements for membership expressly prescribed in the Constitution." In reaching that conclusion, we undertook a detailed historical review to determine the intent of the Framers. Though recognizing that the Constitutional Convention debates themselves were inconclusive, we determined that the "relevant historical materials" reveal that Congress has no power to alter the qualifications in the text of the Constitution. . . .

Powell thus establishes two important propositions: first, that the "relevant historical materials" compel the conclusion that, at least with respect to qualifications imposed by Congress, the Framers intended the qualifications listed in the Constitution to be exclusive; and second, that that conclusion is equally compelled by an understanding of the "fundamental principle of our representative democracy . . . that the people should choose whom they please to govern them." . . .

. . . [A]fter examining *Powell's* historical analysis and its articulation of the "basic principles of our democratic system," we reaffirm that the qualifications for service in Congress set forth in the text of the Constitution are "fixed," at least in the sense that they may not be supplemented by Congress.

Our reaffirmation . . . does not necessarily resolve the specific questions presented in these cases. For petitioners argue that whatever the constitutionality of additional qualifications for membership imposed by Congress, the historical and textual materials discussed in *Powell* do not support the conclusion that the Constitution prohibits additional qualifications imposed by States. In the absence of such a constitutional prohibition, petitioners argue, the Tenth Amendment and the principle of reserved powers require that States be allowed to add such qualifications. . . .

Petitioners argue that the Constitution contains no express prohibition against state-added qualifications, and that Amendment 73 is therefore an appropriate exercise of a State's reserved power to place additional restrictions on the choices that its own voters may make. We disagree for two independent reasons. First, we conclude that the power to add qualifications is not within the "original powers" of the States, and thus is not reserved to the States by the Tenth Amendment. Second, even if States possessed some original power in this area, we conclude that the Framers intended the Constitution to be the exclusive source of qualifications for members of Congress, and that the Framers thereby "divested" States of any power to add qualifications . . .

Contrary to petitioners' assertions, the power to add qualifications is not part of the original powers of sovereignty that the Tenth Amendment reserved to the States. Petitioners' Tenth Amendment argument misconceives the nature of the right at issue because that Amendment could only "reserve" that which existed before . . .

With respect to setting qualifications for service in Congress, no such right existed before the Constitution was ratified. The contrary argument overlooks the revolutionary character of the government that the Framers conceived. Prior to the adoption of the Constitution, the States had joined together under the Articles of Confederation . . . After the Constitutional Convention convened, the Framers were presented with, and eventually adopted a variation of, "a plan not merely to amend the Articles of Confederation but to create an entirely new National Government with a National Executive, National Judiciary, and a National Legislature." In adopting that plan, the Framers envisioned a uniform national system, rejecting the notion that the Nation was a collection of States, and instead creating a direct link between the National Government and the people of the United States. In that National Government, representatives owe primary allegiance not to the people of a State, but to the people of the Nation . . .

This conclusion is consistent with our previous recognition that, in certain limited contexts, the power to regulate the incidents of the federal system is not a reserved power of the States, but rather is delegated by the Constitution. Thus, we have noted that "[w]hile, in a loose sense, the right to vote for representatives in Congress is sometimes spoken of as a right derived from the states, . . . this statement is true only in the sense that the states are authorized by the Constitution, to legislate on the subject as provided by 2 of Art. I." . . .

In short, as the Framers recognized, electing representatives to the National Legislature was a new right, arising from the Constitution itself. The Tenth Amendment thus provides no basis for concluding that the States possess reserved power to add qualifications to those that are fixed in the Constitution. Instead, any state power to set the qualifications for membership in Congress must derive not from the reserved powers of state sovereignty, but rather from the delegated powers of national sovereignty. In the absence of any constitutional delegation to the States of power to add qualifications to those enumerated in the Constitution, such a power does not exist.

Even if we believed that States possessed as part of their original powers some control over congressional qualifications, the text and structure of the Constitution, the relevant historical materials, and, most importantly, the "basic principles of our democratic system" all demonstrate that the Qualifications Clauses were intended to preclude the States from exercising any such power and to fix as exclusive the qualifications in the Constitution . . .

The available affirmative evidence indicates the Framers' intent that States have no role in the setting of qualifications . . .

We also find compelling the complete absence in the ratification debates of any assertion that States had the power to add qualifications. In those debates, the question whether to require term limits, or "rotation," was a major source of controversy . . .

The Federalists' responses to those criticisms and proposals addressed the merits of the issue, arguing that rotation was incompatible with the people's right to choose. . . . Hamilton argued that the representatives' need for reelection rather than mandatory rotation was the more effective way to keep representatives responsive to the people, because "[w]hen a man knows he must quit his station, let his merit be what it may, he will turn his attention chiefly to his own emolument."

Regardless of which side has the better of the debate over rotation, it is most striking that nowhere in the extensive ratification debates have we found any statement by either a proponent or an opponent of rotation that the draft constitution would permit States to require rotation for the representatives of their own citizens. If the participants in the debate had believed that the States retained the authority to impose term limits, it is inconceivable that the Federalists would not have made this obvious response to the arguments of the pro-rotation forces. The absence in an otherwise freewheeling debate of any suggestion that States had the power to impose additional qualifications unquestionably reflects the Framers' common understanding that States lacked that power.

In short, if it had been assumed that States could add additional qualifications, that assumption would have provided the basis for a powerful rebuttal to the arguments being advanced. The failure of intelligent and experienced advocates to utilize this argument must reflect a general agreement that its premise was unsound, and that the power to add qualifications was one that the Constitution denied the States . . .

Our conclusion that States lack the power to impose qualifications vindicates the same "fundamental principle of our representative democracy" that we recognized in *Powell,* namely that "the people should choose whom they please to govern them."

. . . [T]he *Powell* Court recognized that an egalitarian ideal—that election to the National Legislature should be open to all people of merit—provided a critical foundation for the Constitutional structure . . .

Similarly, we believe that state-imposed qualifications, as much as congressionally imposed qualifications, would undermine the second critical idea recognized in *Powell:* that an aspect of sovereignty is the right of the people to vote for whom they wish. Again, the source of the qualification is of little moment in assessing the qualification's restrictive impact.

Finally, state-imposed restrictions, unlike the congressionally imposed restrictions at issue in *Powell,* violate a third idea central to this basic principle: that the right to choose representatives belongs not to the States, but to the people . . . [T]he Framers, in perhaps their most important contribution, conceived of a Federal Government directly responsible to the people, possessed of direct power over the people, and chosen directly, not by States, but by the people. The Framers implemented this ideal most clearly in the provision, extant from the beginning of the Republic, that calls for the Members of the House of Representatives to be "chosen every second Year by the People of the several States." Art. I, 2, cl. 1. Following the adoption of the 17th Amendment in 1913, this ideal was extended to elections for the Senate. The Congress of the United States, therefore, is not a confederation of nations in which separate sovereigns are represented by appointed delegates, but is instead a body composed of representatives of the people . . .

Permitting individual States to formulate diverse qualifications for their representatives would result in a patchwork of state qualifications, undermining the uniformity and the national character that the Framers envisioned and sought to ensure . . . Such a patchwork would also sever the direct link that the Framers found so critical between the National Government and the people of the United States . . .

In sum, the available historical and textual evidence, read in light of the basic principles of democracy underlying the Constitution and recognized by this Court in *Powell*, reveal the Framers' intent that neither Congress nor the States should possess the power to supplement the exclusive qualifications set forth in the text of the Constitution.

Petitioners argue that, even if States may not add qualifications, Amendment 73 is constitutional because it is not such a qualification, and because Amendment 73 is a permissible exercise of state power to regulate the "Times, Places and Manner of Holding Elections." We reject these contentions.

Unlike [sections] 1 and 2 of Amendment 73, which create absolute bars to service for long-term incumbents running for state office, 3 merely provides that certain Senators and Representatives shall not be certified as candidates and shall not have their names appear on the ballot. They may run as write-in candidates and, if elected, they may serve . . .

In our view, Amendment 73 is an indirect attempt to accomplish what the Constitution prohibits Arkansas from accomplishing directly. As the plurality opinion of the Arkansas Supreme Court recognized, Amendment 73 is an "effort to dress eligibility to stand for Congress in ballot access clothing," because the "intent and the effect of Amendment 73 are to disqualify congressional incumbents from further service." We must, of course, accept the State Court's view of the purpose of its own law: we are thus authoritatively informed that the sole purpose of [section] 3 of Amendment 73 was to attempt to achieve a result that is forbidden by the Federal Constitution. Indeed, it cannot be seriously contended that the intent behind Amendment 73 is other than to prevent the election of incumbents. The preamble of Amendment 73

states explicitly: "[T]he people of Arkansas . . . herein limit the terms of elected officials." Sections 1 and 2 create absolute limits on the number of terms that may be served. There is no hint that [section] 3 was intended to have any other purpose.

Petitioners do, however, contest the Arkansas Supreme Court's conclusion that the Amendment has the same practical effect as an absolute bar. They argue that the possibility of a write-in campaign creates a real possibility for victory, especially for an entrenched incumbent. One may reasonably question the merits of that contention. Indeed, we are advised by the state court that there is nothing more than a faint glimmer of possibility that the excluded candidate will win. Our prior cases, too, have suggested that write-in candidates have only a slight chance of victory. Petitioners are correct that incumbents may occasionally win reelection as write-in candidates, there is no denying that the ballot restrictions will make it significantly more difficult for the barred candidate to win the election. In our view, an amendment with the avowed purpose and obvious effect of evading the requirements of the Qualifications Clauses by handicapping a class of candidates cannot stand . . .

Petitioners make the related argument that Amendment 73 merely regulates the "Manner" of elections, and that the Amendment is therefore a permissible exercise of state power under Article I, 4, cl. 1 (the Elections Clause) to regulate the "Times, Places and Manner" of elections. We cannot agree.

A necessary consequence of petitioners' argument is that Congress itself would have the power to "make or alter" a measure such as Amendment 73. Art. I, 4, cl. 1. That the Framers would have approved of such a result is unfathomable. As our decision in *Powell* and our discussion above make clear, the Framers were particularly concerned that a grant to Congress of the authority to set its own qualifications would lead inevitably to congressional self-aggrandizement and the upsetting of the delicate constitutional balance. Petitioners would have us believe, however, that even as the Framers carefully circumscribed congressional power to set qualifications, they intended to allow Congress to achieve the same result by simply formulating the regulation as a ballot access restriction under the Elections Clause. We refuse to adopt an interpretation of the Elections Clause that would so cavalierly disregard what the Framers intended to be a fundamental constitutional safeguard.

Moreover, petitioners' broad construction of the Elections Clause is fundamentally inconsistent with the Framers' view of that Clause. The Framers intended the Elections Clause to grant States authority to create procedural regulations, not to provide States with license to exclude classes of candidates from federal office . . .

The merits of term limits, or "rotation," have been the subject of debate since the formation of our Constitution, when the Framers unanimously rejected a proposal to add such limits to the Constitution. The cogent arguments on both sides of the question that were articulated during the process of ratification largely retain their force today. Over half the States have adopted measures that impose such limits on some offices either directly or indirectly, and the Nation as a whole, notably by constitutional amendment, has imposed a limit on the number of terms that the President may serve. Term limits, like any other qualification for office, unquestionably restrict the ability of voters to vote for whom they wish. On the other hand, such limits may provide for the infusion of fresh ideas and new perspectives, and may decrease the likelihood that representatives will lose touch with their constituents. It is not our province to resolve this longstanding debate.

We are, however, firmly convinced that allowing the several States to adopt term limits for congressional service would effect a fundamental change in the constitutional framework. Any such change must come not by legislation adopted either by Congress or by an individual State, but rather—as have other important changes in the electoral process—through the Amendment procedures set forth in Article V. The Framers decided that the qualifications for service in the Congress of the United States be fixed in the Constitution and be uniform throughout the Nation. That decision reflects the Framers' understanding that Members of Congress are chosen by separate constituencies, but that they become, when elected, servants of the people of the United States . . .

Thomas, dissenting:
It is ironic that the Court bases today's decision on the right of the people to "choose whom they please to govern them." Under our Constitution, there is only one State whose people have the right to "choose whom they please" to represent Arkansas in Congress. The Court holds, however, that neither the elected legislature of that State nor the people themselves

(acting by ballot initiative) may prescribe any qualifications for those representatives. The majority therefore defends the right of the people of Arkansas to "choose whom they please to govern them" by invalidating a provision that won nearly 60% of the votes cast in a direct election and that carried every congressional district in the State.

. . . Nothing in the Constitution deprives the people of each State of the power to prescribe eligibility requirements for the candidates who seek to represent them in Congress. The Constitution is simply silent on this question. And where the Constitution is silent, it raises no bar to action by the States or the people.

Because the majority fundamentally misunderstands the notion of "reserved" powers, I start with some first principles. Contrary to the majority's suggestion, the people of the States need not point to any affirmative grant of power in the Constitution in order to prescribe qualifications for their representatives in Congress, or to authorize their elected state legislators to do so.

Our system of government rests on one overriding principle: all power stems from the consent of the people. To phrase the principle in this way, however, is to be imprecise about something important to the notion of "reserved" powers. The ultimate source of the Constitution's authority is the consent of the people of each individual State, not the consent of the undifferentiated people of the Nation as a whole . . .

When they adopted the Federal Constitution, of course, the people of each State surrendered some of their authority to the United States (and hence to entities accountable to the people of other States as well as to themselves). They affirmatively deprived their States of certain powers, see, e.g., Art. I, 10, and they affirmatively conferred certain powers upon the Federal Government, see, e.g., Art. I, 8. Because the people of the several States are the only true source of power, however, the Federal Government enjoys no authority beyond what the Constitution confers: the Federal Government's powers are limited and enumerated . . .

In each State, the remainder of the people's powers—"[t]he powers not delegated to the United States by the Constitution, nor prohibited by it to the States," are either delegated to the state government or retained by the people. The Federal Constitution does not specify which of these two possibilities obtains; it is up to the various state constitutions to declare which powers the people of each State have delegated to their state government. As far as the Federal Constitution is concerned, then, the States can exercise all powers that the Constitution does not withhold from them. The Federal Government and the States thus face different default rules: where the Constitution is silent about the exercise of a particular power—that is, where the Constitution does not speak either expressly or by necessary implication—the Federal Government lacks that power and the States enjoy it.

These basic principles are enshrined in the Tenth Amendment, which declares that all powers neither delegated to the Federal Government nor prohibited to the States "are reserved to the States respectively, or to the people." With this careful last phrase, the Amendment avoids taking any position on the division of power between the state governments and the people of the States: it is up to the people of each State to determine which "reserved" powers their state government may exercise. But the Amendment does make clear that powers reside at the state level except where the Constitution removes them from that level. All powers that the Constitution neither delegates to the Federal Government nor prohibits to the States are controlled by the people of each State.

To be sure, when the Tenth Amendment uses the phrase "the people," it does not specify whether it is referring to the people of each State or the people of the Nation as a whole. But the latter interpretation would make the Amendment pointless: there would have been no reason to provide that where the Constitution is silent about whether a particular power resides at the state level, it might or might not do so. In addition, it would make no sense to speak of powers as being reserved to the undifferentiated people of the Nation as a whole, because the Constitution does not contemplate that those people will either exercise power or delegate it. The Constitution simply does not recognize any mechanism for action by the undifferentiated people of the Nation. Thus, the amendment provision of Article V calls for amendments to be ratified not by a convention of the national people, but by conventions of the people in each State or by the state legislatures elected by those people. Likewise, the Constitution calls for Members of Congress to be chosen State by State, rather than in nationwide elections. Even the selection of the President surely the most national of national figures—is accomplished by an electoral college made up of delegates

chosen by the various States, and candidates can lose a Presidential election despite winning a majority of the votes cast in the Nation as a whole.

In short, the notion of popular sovereignty that undergirds the Constitution does not erase state boundaries, but rather tracks them. The people of each State obviously did trust their fate to the people of the several States when they consented to the Constitution; not only did they empower the governmental institutions of the United States, but they also agreed to be bound by constitutional amendments that they themselves refused to ratify. See Art. V (providing that proposed amendments shall take effect upon ratification by three-quarters of the States). At the same time, however, the people of each State retained their separate political identities . . .

The majority begins by announcing an enormous and untenable limitation on the principle expressed by the Tenth Amendment. According to the majority, the States possess only those powers that the Constitution affirmatively grants to them or that they enjoyed before the Constitution was adopted; the Tenth Amendment "could only 'reserve' that which existed before." From the fact that the States had not previously enjoyed any powers over the particular institutions of the Federal Government established by the Constitution, the majority derives a rule precisely opposite to the one that the Amendment actually prescribes . . .

The majority's essential logic is that the state governments could not "reserve" any powers that they did not control at the time the Constitution was drafted. But it was not the state governments that were doing the reserving. The Constitution derives its authority instead from the consent of the people of the States. Given the fundamental principle that all governmental powers stem from the people of the States, it would simply be incoherent to assert that the people of the States could not reserve any powers that they had not previously controlled.

The Tenth Amendment's use of the word "reserved" does not help the majority's position. If someone says that the power to use a particular facility is reserved to some group, he is not saying anything about whether that group has previously used the facility. He is merely saying that the people who control the facility have designated that group as the entity with authority to use it. The Tenth Amendment is similar: the people of the States, from whom all governmental powers stem, have specified that all powers not prohibited to the States by the Federal Constitution are reserved "to the States respectively, or to the people."

The majority is therefore quite wrong to conclude that the people of the States cannot authorize their state governments to exercise any powers that were unknown to the States when the Federal Constitution was drafted. Indeed, the majority's position frustrates the apparent purpose of the Amendment's final phrase. The Amendment does not pre-empt any limitations on state power found in the state constitutions, as it might have done if it simply had said that the powers not delegated to the Federal Government are reserved to the States. But the Amendment also does not prevent the people of the States from amending their state constitutions to remove limitations that were in effect when the Federal Constitution and the Bill of Rights were ratified . . .

. . . [T]he people of Arkansas do enjoy "reserved" powers over the selection of their representatives in Congress. Purporting to exercise those reserved powers, they have agreed among themselves that the candidates covered by [section] 3 of Amendment 73—those whom they have already elected to three or more terms in the House of Representatives or to two or more terms in the Senate—should not be eligible to appear on the ballot for reelection, but should nonetheless be returned to Congress if enough voters are sufficiently enthusiastic about their candidacy to write in their names. Whatever one might think of the wisdom of this arrangement, we may not override the decision of the people of Arkansas unless something in the Federal Constitution deprives them of the power to enact such measures.

The majority settles on "the Qualifications Clauses" as the constitutional provisions that Amendment 73 violates. Because I do not read those provisions to impose any unstated prohibitions on the States, it is unnecessary for me to decide whether the majority is correct to identify Arkansas' ballot-access restriction with laws fixing true term limits or otherwise prescribing "qualifications" for congressional office . . . [T]he Qualifications Clauses are merely straightforward recitations of the minimum eligibility requirements that the Framers thought it essential for every Member of Congress to meet. They restrict state power only in that they prevent the States from abolishing all eligibility requirements for membership in Congress . . .

It is radical enough for the majority to hold that the Constitution implicitly precludes the people of the States from prescribing any eligibility requirements for the congressional candidates who seek their votes. This holding, after all, does not stop with negating the term limits that many States have seen fit to impose on their Senators and Representatives. Today's decision also means that no State may disqualify congressional candidates whom a court has found to be mentally incompetent, who are currently in prison, or who have past vote-fraud convictions . . .

In order to invalidate [section] 3 of Amendment 73, however, the majority must go farther. The bulk of the majority's analysis—like Part II of my dissent addresses the issues that would be raised if Arkansas had prescribed "genuine, unadulterated, undiluted term limits." But as the parties have agreed, Amendment 73 does not actually create this kind of disqualification. It does not say that covered candidates may not serve any more terms in Congress if reelected, and it does not indirectly achieve the same result by barring those candidates from seeking reelection. It says only that if they are to win reelection, they must do so by write-in votes . . .

. . . [T]oday's decision reads the Qualifications Clauses to impose substantial implicit prohibitions on the States and the people of the States. I would not draw such an expansive negative inference from the fact that the Constitution requires Members of Congress to be a certain age, to be inhabitants of the States that they represent, and to have been United States citizens for a specified period. Rather, I would read the Qualifications Clauses to do no more than what they say.

Clinton v. Jones

520 U.S. 681 (1997), 9-0
Opinion of the Court: Stevens (Rehnquist, Ginsberg, Kennedy, O'Connor, Scalia, Souter, Thomas)
Concurring: Breyer

Is this a civil liberties case or one of presidential power? Do you think the Court would have made the same decision or been unanimous in it, had the justices anticipated that letting the lawsuit against Clinton go forward would uncover a scandal and lead to the president's impeachment? Does the decision rest simply on the degree of anticipated interference with the president's conduct of his office? What are the significant differences between this decision and that of Mississippi v. Johnson?

Stevens, for the Court:

This case raises a constitutional and a prudential question concerning the Office of the President of the United States. [Paula Jones], a private citizen, seeks to recover damages from the current occupant of that office based on actions allegedly taken before his term began. The President submits that in all but the most exceptional cases the Constitution requires federal courts to defer such litigation until his term ends and that, in any event, respect for the office warrants such a stay. Despite the force of the arguments supporting the President's submissions, we conclude that they must be rejected . . .

[Jones's] allegations principally describe events that are said to have occurred . . . during an official conference held at the Excelsior Hotel in Little Rock, Arkansas. The Governor [now the President] delivered a speech at the conference; [Jones]—working as a state employee—staffed the registration desk. She alleges that [a state police officer] persuaded her to leave her desk and to visit the Governor in a business suite at the hotel, where he made "abhorrent" sexual advances that she vehemently rejected. She further claims that her superiors at work subsequently dealt with her in a hostile and rude manner, and changed her duties to punish her for rejecting those advances. Finally, she alleges that after [Governor Clinton] was elected President . . . various persons authorized to speak for the [him] publicly branded her a liar by denying that the incident had occurred . . .

Only three sitting Presidents have been defendants in civil litigation involving their actions prior to taking office. Complaints against Theodore Roosevelt and Harry Truman had been dismissed before they took office; the dismissals were affirmed after their respective inaugurations. Two companion cases arising out of an automobile accident were filed against John F. Kennedy in 1960 during the Presidential campaign. After taking office, he unsuccessfully argued that his status as Commander in Chief gave him a right to a stay under the Soldiers' and Sailors' Civil Relief Act of 1940. The motion for a stay was denied by the District Court, and the matter was settled out of court. Thus, none of those cases sheds any light on the constitutional issue before us.

The principal rationale for affording certain public servants immunity from suits for money damages arising out of their official acts is inapplicable to unofficial conduct. In cases involving prosecutors, legislators, and judges we have repeatedly explained that the immunity serves the public interest in enabling such officials to perform their designated functions effectively without fear that a particular decision may give rise to personal liability . . .

That rationale provided the principal basis for our holding that a former President of the United States was "entitled to absolute immunity from damages liability predicated on his official acts." Our central concern [in *Nixon v. Fitzgerald*] was to avoid rendering the President "unduly cautious in the discharge of his official duties."

This reasoning provides no support for an immunity for unofficial conduct. As we explained in *Fitzgerald*, "the sphere of protected action must be related closely to the immunity's justifying purposes." Because of the President's broad responsibilities, we recognized in that case an immunity from damages claims arising out of official acts extending to the "outer perimeter of his authority." But we have never suggested that the President, or any other official, has an immunity that extends beyond the scope of any action taken in an official capacity.

Moreover, when defining the scope of an immunity for acts clearly taken within an official capacity, we have applied a functional approach. "Frequently our decisions have held that an official's absolute immunity should extend only to acts in performance of particular functions of his office." Hence, for example, a judge's absolute immunity does not extend to actions performed in a purely administrative capacity. As our opinions have made clear, immunities are grounded in "the nature of the function performed, not the identity of the actor who performed it."

[The president's] effort to construct an immunity from suit for unofficial acts grounded purely in the identity of his office is unsupported by precedent . . .

[His] strongest argument supporting his immunity claim is based on the text and structure of the Constitution. He does not contend that the occupant of the Office of the President is "above the law," in the sense that his conduct is entirely immune from judicial scrutiny. The President argues merely for a postponement of the judicial proceedings that will determine whether he violated any law. His argument is grounded in the character of the office that was created by Article II of the Constitution, and relies on separation of powers principles that have structured our constitutional arrangement since the founding.

As a starting premise, [he] contends that he occupies a unique office with powers and responsibilities so vast and important that the public interest demands that he devote his undivided time and attention to his public duties. He submits that—given the nature of the office—the doctrine of separation of powers places limits on the authority of the Federal Judiciary to interfere with the Executive Branch that would be transgressed by allowing this action to proceed . . .

It does not follow, however, that separation of powers principles would be violated by allowing this action to proceed. The doctrine of separation of powers is concerned with the allocation of official power among the three co-equal branches of our Government . . .

Of course the lines between the powers of the three branches are not always neatly defined. But in this case there is no suggestion that the Federal Judiciary is being asked to perform any function that might in some way be described as "executive." [Jones] is merely asking the courts to exercise their core Article III jurisdiction to decide cases and controversies. Whatever the outcome of this case, there is no possibility that the decision will curtail the scope of the official powers of the Executive Branch. The litigation of questions that relate entirely to the unofficial conduct of the individual who happens to be the President poses no perceptible risk of misallocation of either judicial power or executive power.

Rather than arguing that the decision of the case will produce either an aggrandizement of judicial power or a narrowing of executive power, [the president] contends that—as a by product of an otherwise traditional exercise of judicial power—burdens will be placed on the President that will hamper the performance of his official duties . . . As a factual matter, [he] contends that this particular case . . . may impose an unacceptable burden on the President's time and energy, and thereby impair the effective performance of his office.

[His] predictive judgment finds little support in either history or the relatively narrow compass of the issues raised in this particular case. As we have already noted, in the more than 200 year history of the Republic, only three sitting Presidents have been subjected to suits for their private actions. If the past is any indicator, it seems unlikely that a deluge of such litigation will ever engulf the Presidency. As for the case at hand, if properly managed by the District Court, it appears to us highly unlikely to occupy any substantial amount of [the president's] time.

Of greater significance, [the president] errs by presuming that interactions between the Judicial Branch and the Executive, even quite burdensome interactions, necessarily rise to the level of constitutionally forbidden impairment of the Executive's ability to perform its constitutionally mandated functions . . .

The fact that a federal court's exercise of its traditional Article III jurisdiction may significantly burden the time and attention of the Chief Executive is not sufficient to establish a violation of the Constitution. Two long settled propositions, first announced by Chief Justice Marshall, support that conclusion.

First, we have long held that when the President takes official action, the Court has the authority to determine whether he has acted within the law . . .

Second, it is also settled that the President is subject to judicial process in appropriate circumstances. Although Thomas Jefferson apparently thought otherwise, Chief Justice Marshall, when presiding in the treason trial of Aaron Burr, ruled that a subpoena *duces tecum* could be directed to the President. We unequivocally and emphatically endorsed Marshall's position when we held that President Nixon was obligated to comply with a subpoena commanding him to produce certain tape recordings of his conversations with his aides. *United States v. Nixon.* As we explained, "neither the doctrine of separation of powers, nor the need for confidentiality of high level communications, without more, can sustain an absolute, unqualified Presidential privilege of immunity from judicial process under all circumstances."

Sitting Presidents have responded to court orders to provide testimony and other information with sufficient frequency that such interactions between the Judicial and Executive Branches can scarcely be thought a novelty. President Monroe responded to written interrogatories, President Nixon . . . produced tapes in response to a subpoena duces tecum, President Ford complied with an order to give a deposition in a criminal trial, and President Clinton has twice given videotaped testimony in criminal proceedings. Moreover, sitting Presidents have also voluntarily complied with judicial requests for testimony. President Grant gave a lengthy deposition in a criminal case under such circumstances, and President Carter similarly gave videotaped testimony for use at a criminal trial.

. . . If the Judiciary may severely burden the Executive Branch by reviewing the legality of the President's official conduct, and if it may direct appropriate process to the President himself, it must follow that the federal courts have power to determine the legality of his unofficial conduct. The burden on the President's time and energy that is a mere by product of such review surely cannot be considered as onerous as the direct burden imposed by judicial review and the occasional invalidation of his official actions. We therefore hold that the doctrine of separation of powers does not require federal courts to stay all private actions against the President until he leaves office . . .

[W]e are persuaded that it was an abuse of discretion for the District Court to defer the trial until after the President leaves office. Such a lengthy and categorical stay takes no account whatever of the [Jones's] interest in bringing the case to trial. The complaint was filed within the statutory limitations period—albeit near the end of that period—and delaying trial would increase the danger of prejudice resulting from the loss of evidence, including the inability of witnesses to recall specific facts, or the possible death of a party.

. . . We think the District Court may have given undue weight to the concern that a trial might generate unrelated civil actions that could conceivably hamper the President in conducting the duties of his office. If and when that should occur, the court's discretion would permit it to manage those actions in such fashion (including deferral of trial) that interference with the President's duties would not occur. But no such impingement upon the President's conduct of his office was shown here.

We add a final comment on two matters that are discussed at length in the briefs: the risk that our decision will generate a large volume of politically motivated harassing and frivolous litigation, and the danger that national security concerns might prevent the President from explaining a legitimate need for a continuance.

We are not persuaded that either of these risks is serious. Most frivolous and vexatious litigation is terminated at the pleading stage or on summary judgment, with little if any personal involvement by the defendant. Moreover, the availability of sanctions provides a significant deterrent to litigation directed at the President in his unofficial capacity for purposes of political gain or harassment. History indicates that the likelihood that a significant number of such cases will be filed is remote. Although scheduling problems may arise, there is no reason to assume that the District Courts will be either unable to accommodate the President's needs or unfaithful to the tradition— especially in matters involving national security— of giving "the utmost deference to Presidential responsibilities." . . .

If Congress deems it appropriate to afford the President stronger protection, it may respond with appropriate legislation . . .

The Federal District Court has jurisdiction to decide this case. Like every other citizen who properly invokes that jurisdiction, [Jones] has a right to an orderly disposition of her claims.

Breyer, concurring:

I agree with the majority that the Constitution does not automatically grant the President an immunity from civil lawsuits based upon his private conduct . . .

In my view, however, once the President sets forth and explains a conflict between judicial proceeding and public duties, the matter changes. At that point, the Constitution permits a judge to schedule a trial in an ordinary civil damages action . . . only within the constraints of a constitutional principle—a principle that forbids a federal judge in such a case to interfere with the President's discharge of his public duties. I have no doubt that the Constitution contains such a principle applicable to civil suits, based upon Article II's vesting of the entire "executive Power" in a single individual, implemented through the Constitution's structural separation of powers, and revealed both by history and case precedent.

I recognize that this case does not require us now to apply the principle specifically, thereby delineating its contours; nor need we now decide whether lower courts are to apply it directly or categorically through the use of presumptions or rules of administration. Yet I fear that to disregard it now may appear to deny it . . . Further, if the majority is wrong in predicting the future infrequency of private civil litigation against sitting Presidents, acknowledgement and future delineation of the constitutional principle will prove a practically necessary institutional safeguard. For these reasons, I think it important to explain how the Constitution's text, history, and precedent support this principle of judicial noninterference with Presidential functions in ordinary civil damages actions . . .

The majority points to the fact that private plaintiffs have brought civil damage lawsuits against a sitting President only three times in our Nation's history; and it relies upon the threat of sanctions to discourage, and "the court's discretion" to manage, such actions so that "interference with the President's duties would not occur." I am less sanguine. Since 1960, when the last such suit was filed, the number of civil lawsuits filed annually in Federal District Courts has increased from under 60,000 to about 240,000; the number of federal district judges has increased from 233; the time and expense associated with both discovery and trial have increased; an increasingly complex economy has led to increasingly complex sets of statutes, rules and regulations, that often create potential liability, with or without fault. And this Court has now made clear that such lawsuits may proceed against a sitting President. The consequence, as the Court warned in *Fitzgerald,* is that a sitting President, given "the visibility of his office," could well become "an easily identifiable target for suits for civil damages." The threat of sanctions could well discourage much unneeded litigation, but some lawsuits (including highly intricate and complicated ones) could resist ready evaluation and disposition; and individual district court procedural rulings could pose a significant threat to the President's official functions . . .

. . . I agree with the majority's determination that a constitutional defense must await a more specific showing of need; I do not agree with what I believe to be an understatement of the "danger." And I believe that ordinary case management principles are unlikely to prove sufficient to deal with private civil lawsuits for damages unless supplemented with a constitutionally based requirement that district courts schedule proceedings so as to avoid significant interference with the President's ongoing discharge of his official responsibilities.

. . . It may well be that the trial of this case cannot take place without significantly interfering with the President's ability to carry out his official duties. Yet, I agree with the majority that there is no automatic temporary immunity and that the President should have to provide the District Court with a reasoned explanation of why the immunity is needed; and I also agree that, in the absence of that explanation, the court's postponement of the trial date was premature. For those reasons, I concur in the result.

Clinton v. City of New York

524 U.S. 417 (1998), 6-3

Opinion of the Court: Stevens (Rehnquist, Ginsberg, Souter, Stevens, Thomas)

Concurring: Kennedy

Dissenting in part: Breyer, O'Conner, Scalia

In the Line Item Veto Act of 1996, Congress gave the president power to cancel certain types of provisions in larger bills he signed into law. Two such "vetoes" by President Clinton were at issue in this case: cancellation of Section 4722(c) of the Balanced Budget Act of 1997 and Section 968 of the Taxpayer Relief Act of 1997. The first struck out waiver of the federal government's right to recoup $2.6 billion in taxes New York had levied against medicare providers. The second

struck out an option given to certain food refiners and processors to defer recognition of capital gains if they sold their stock to eligible farmers cooperatives. Parties showing injury by these cancellations—the City of New York, several hospitals, and two health care workers' unions in the first; the Snake River (Idaho) farmers cooperative and one of its members in the second—challenged the constitutionality of the Line Item Veto Act.

What does the Constitution say about unilateral presidential action of the sort provided for in the Line Item Veto Act? On what grounds does Stevens conclude that such action is constitutionally forbidden? Is the decision consistent with the Court's theory of law-making in Immigration and Naturalization Service v. Chadha? *Why would Congress enhance the role of the role of the president in law-making at its own expense? Is it possible to say who the future gainers and losers will be as a result of this decision?*

Stevens, for the Court:

The Line Item Veto Act gives the President the power to "cancel in whole" three types of provisions that have been signed into law: "(1) any dollar amount of discretionary budget authority; (2) any item of new direct spending; or (3) any limited tax benefit." It is undisputed that the New York case involves an "item of new direct spending" and that the Snake River case involves a "limited tax benefit" as those terms are defined in the Act. It is also undisputed that each of those provisions had been signed into law pursuant to Article I, §, of the Constitution before it was canceled.

The Act requires the President to adhere to precise procedures whenever he exercises his cancellation authority. In identifying items for cancellation he must consider the legislative history, the purposes, and other relevant information about the items. He must determine, with respect to each cancellation, that it will "(i) reduce the Federal budget deficit; (ii) not impair any essential Government functions; and (iii) not harm the national interest." Moreover, he must transmit a special message to Congress notifying it of each cancellation within five calendar days (excluding Sundays) after the enactment of the canceled provision. It is undisputed that the President meticulously followed these procedures in these cases.

A cancellation takes effect upon receipt by Congress of the special message from the President. If, however, a "disapproval bill" pertaining to a special message is enacted into law, the cancellations set forth in that message become "null and void." The Act sets forth a detailed expedited procedure for the

Flanked by several members of Congress, President Bill Clinton signs the line-item veto bill, April 9, 1996. Clinton used the new power, which allowed presidential veto of individual items in appropriation bills, more than 80 times before it was held unconstitutional.

consideration of a "disapproval bill," but no such bill was passed for either of the cancellations involved in these cases. A majority vote of both Houses is sufficient to enact a disapproval bill. The Act does not grant the President the authority to cancel a disapproval bill, but he does, of course, retain his constitutional authority to veto such a bill.

. . . [U]nder the plain text of the statute, the two actions of the President that are challenged in these cases prevented one section of the Balanced Budget Act of 1997 and one section of the Taxpayer Relief Act of 1997 "from having legal force or effect." The remaining provisions of those statutes, with the exception of the second canceled item in the latter, continue to have the same force and effect as they had when signed into law.

In both legal and practical effect, the President has amended two Acts of Congress by repealing a portion of each. "[R]epeal of statutes, no less than enactment, must conform with Art. I." There is no provision in the Constitution that authorizes the President to enact, to amend, or to repeal statutes. Both Article I and Article II assign responsibilities to the President that directly relate to the lawmaking process, but neither addresses the issue presented by these cases. The President "shall from time to time give to the Congress Information on the State of the Union, and recommend to their Consideration such Measures as he shall judge necessary and expedient. . . ." Art. II, §3. Thus, he may initiate and influence legislative proposals. Moreover, after a bill has passed both Houses of

Congress, but "before it become[s] a Law," it must be presented to the President. If he approves it, "he shall sign it, but if not he shall return it, with his Objections to that House in which it shall have originated, who shall enter the Objections at large on their Journal, and proceed to reconsider it." Art. I, §7, cl. 2. His "return" of a bill, which is usually described as a "veto," is subject to being overridden by a two-thirds vote in each House.

There are important differences between the President's "return" of a bill pursuant to Article I, §7, and the exercise of the President's cancellation authority pursuant to the Line Item Veto Act. The constitutional return takes place before the bill becomes law; the statutory cancellation occurs after the bill becomes law. The constitutional return is of the entire bill; the statutory cancellation is of only a part. Although the Constitution expressly authorizes the President to play a role in the process of enacting statutes, it is silent on the subject of unilateral Presidential action that either repeals or amends parts of duly enacted statutes.

There are powerful reasons for construing constitutional silence on this profoundly important issue as equivalent to an express prohibition. The procedures governing the enactment of statutes set forth in the text of Article I were the product of the great debates and compromises that produced the Constitution itself. Familiar historical materials provide abundant support for the conclusion that the power to enact statutes may only "be exercised in accord with a single, finely wrought and exhaustively considered, procedure." Our first President understood the text of the Presentment Clause as requiring that he either "approve all the parts of a Bill, or reject it in toto." What has emerged in these cases from the President's exercise of his statutory cancellation powers, however, are truncated versions of two bills that passed both Houses of Congress. They are not the product of the "finely wrought" procedure that the Framers designed . . .

The Government advances two related arguments to support its position that despite the unambiguous provisions of the Act, cancellations do not amend or repeal properly enacted statutes in violation of the Presentment Clause. First, relying primarily on *Field v. Clark*, the Government contends that the cancellations were merely exercises of discretionary authority granted to the President by the Balanced Budget Act and the Taxpayer Relief Act read in light of the previously enacted Line Item Veto Act. Second, the Government submits that the substance of the authority to cancel tax and spending items "is, in practical effect, no more and no less than the power to 'decline to spend' specified sums of money, or to 'decline to implement' specified tax measures." Neither argument is persuasive.

In *Field v. Clark*, the Court upheld the constitutionality of the Tariff Act of 1890. That statute contained a "free list" of almost 300 specific articles that were exempted from import duties "unless otherwise specially provided for in this act." Section 3 was a special provision that directed the President to suspend that exemption for sugar, molasses, coffee, tea, and hides "whenever, and so often" as he should be satisfied that any country producing and exporting those products imposed duties on the agricultural products of the United States that he deemed to be "reciprocally unequal and unreasonable . . ." The section then specified the duties to be imposed on those products during any such suspension . . .

. . . [*Field*] identifies three critical differences between the power to suspend the exemption from import duties and the power to cancel portions of a duly enacted statute. First, the exercise of the suspension power was contingent upon a condition that did not exist when the Tariff Act was passed: the imposition of "reciprocally unequal and unreasonable" import duties by other countries. In contrast, the exercise of the cancellation power within five days after the enactment of the Balanced Bud-

get and Tax Reform Acts necessarily was based on the same conditions that Congress evaluated when it passed those statutes. Second, under the Tariff Act, when the President determined that the contingency had arisen, he had a duty to suspend; in contrast, while it is true that the President was required by the Act to make three determinations before he canceled a provision, those determinations did not qualify his discretion to cancel or not to cancel. Finally, whenever the President suspended an exemption under the Tariff Act, he was executing the policy that Congress had embodied in the statute. In contrast, whenever the President cancels an item of new direct spending or a limited tax benefit he is rejecting the policy judgment made by Congress and relying on his own policy judgment. Thus, the conclusion in *Field v. Clark* that the suspensions mandated by the Tariff Act were not exercises of legislative power does not undermine our opinion that cancellations pursuant to the Line Item Veto Act are the functional equivalent of partial repeals of Acts of Congress that fail to satisfy Article I, §7 . . .

. . . [T]his Court has recognized that in the foreign affairs arena, the President has "a degree of discretion and freedom from statutory restriction which would not be admissible were domestic affairs alone involved." *United States v. Curtiss-Wright Export Corp.* "Moreover, he, not Congress, has the better opportunity of knowing the conditions which prevail in foreign countries." More important, when enacting the statutes discussed in *Field*, Congress itself made the decision to suspend or repeal the particular provisions at issue upon the occurrence of particular events subsequent to enactment, and it left only the determination of whether such events occurred up to the President. The Line Item Veto Act authorizes the President himself to effect the repeal of laws, for his own policy reasons, without observing the procedures set out in Article I, §7. The fact that Congress intended such a result is of no moment. Although Congress presumably anticipated that the President might cancel some of the items in the Balanced Budget Act and in the Taxpayer Relief Act, Congress cannot alter the procedures set out in Article I, §7, without amending the Constitution.

Neither are we persuaded by the Government's contention that the President's authority to cancel new direct spending and tax benefit items is no greater than his traditional authority to decline to spend appropriated funds. The Government has reviewed in some detail the series of statutes in which Congress has given the Executive broad discretion over the expenditure of appropriated funds. For example, the First Congress appropriated "sum[s] not exceeding" specified amounts to be spent on various Government operations. In those statutes, as in later years, the President was given wide discretion with respect to both the amounts to be spent and how the money would be allocated among different functions. It is argued that the Line Item Veto Act merely confers comparable discretionary authority over the expenditure of appropriated funds. The critical difference between this statute and all of its predecessors, however, is that unlike any of them, this Act gives the President the unilateral power to change the text of duly enacted statutes. None of the Act's predecessors could even arguably have been construed to authorize such a change.

The Balanced Budget Act of 1997 is a 500-page document that became "Public Law 105-33" after three procedural steps were taken: (1) a bill containing its exact text was approved by a majority of the Members of the House of Representatives; (2) the Senate approved precisely the same text; and (3) that text was signed into law by the President. The Constitution explicitly requires that each of those three steps be taken before a bill may "become a law." Art. I, §7. If one paragraph of that text had been omitted at any one of those three stages, Public Law 105-33 would not have been validly enacted. If the Line Item Veto Act were valid, it would authorize the President to create a different law—one whose text was not voted on by either House of Congress or presented to the President for signature. Something that might be known as "Public Law 105-33 as modified by the President" may or may not be desirable, but it is surely not a document that may "become a law" pursuant to the procedures designed by the Framers of Article I, §7, of the Constitution.

If there is to be a new procedure in which the President will play a different role in determining the final text of what may "become a law," such change must come not by legislation but through the amendment procedures set forth in Article V of the Constitution.

Kennedy, concurring:

A nation cannot plunder its own treasury without putting its Constitution and its survival in peril. The statute before us, then, is of first importance, for it seems undeniable the Act will tend to restrain persis-

tent excessive spending. Nevertheless, for the reasons given by Justice Stevens in the opinion for the Court, the statute must be found invalid. Failure of political will does not justify unconstitutional remedies.

I write to respond to my colleague Justice Breyer, who observes that the statute does not threaten the liberties of individual citizens, a point on which I disagree . . .

The principal object of the statute, it is true, was not to enhance the President's power to reward one group and punish another, to help one set of taxpayers and hurt another, to favor one State and ignore another. Yet these are its undeniable effects. The law establishes a new mechanism which gives the President the sole ability to hurt a group that is a visible target, in order to disfavor the group or to extract further concessions from Congress. The law is the functional equivalent of a line item veto and enhances the President's powers beyond what the Framers would have endorsed.

It is no answer, of course, to say that Congress surrendered its authority by its own hand; nor does it suffice to point out that a new statute, signed by the President or enacted over his veto, could restore to Congress the power it now seeks to relinquish. That a congressional cession of power is voluntary does not make it innocuous . . .

The Constitution is not bereft of controls over improvident spending. Federalism is one safeguard, for political accountability is easier to enforce within the States than nationwide. The other principal mechanism, of course, is control of the political branches by an informed and responsible electorate. Whether or not federalism and control by the electorate are adequate for the problem at hand, they are two of the structures the Framers designed for the problem the statute strives to confront. The Framers of the Constitution could not command statesmanship. They could simply provide structures from which it might emerge. The fact that these mechanisms, plus the proper functioning of the separation of powers itself, are not employed, or that they prove insufficient, cannot validate an otherwise unconstitutional device. With these observations, I join the opinion of the Court.

Breyer, dissenting:

. . . In my view the Line Item Veto Act does not violate any specific textual constitutional command, nor does it violate any implicit Separation of Powers principle. Consequently, I believe that the Act is con-stitutional . . .

[T]he power the Act conveys is the right kind of power. It is "executive." As explained above, an exer-cise of that power "executes" the Act. Conceptually speaking, it closely resembles the kind of delegated authority-to spend or not to spend appropriations, to change or not to change tariff rates-that Congress has frequently granted the President, any differences be-ing differences in degree, not kind . . .

. . . [O]ne cannot say that the Act "encroaches" upon Congress' power, when Congress retained the power to insert, by simple majority, into any future appropriations bill, into any section of any such bill, or into any phrase of any section, a provision that says the Act will not apply . . . Congress also retained the power to "disapprov[e]," and thereby reinstate, any of the President's cancellations. And it is Con-gress that drafts and enacts the appropriations statutes that are subject to the Act in the first place-and thereby defines the outer limits of the Presi-dent's cancellation authority. Thus this Act is not the sort of delegation "without . . . sufficient check" that concerns Justice Kennedy. Indeed, the President acts only in response to, and on the terms set by, the Congress.

Nor can one say that the Act's basic substantive ob-jective is constitutionally improper, for the earliest Congresses could have, see Part II, supra, and often did, confer on the President this sort of discretionary authority over spending . . .

Nor can one say the Act's grant of power "aggran-dizes" the Presidential office. The grant is limited to the context of the budget. It is limited to the power to spend, or not to spend, particular appropriated items, and the power to permit, or not to permit, specific limited exemptions from generally applica-ble tax law from taking effect. These powers, as I will explain in detail, resemble those the President has exercised in the past on other occasions. The delega-tion of those powers to the President may strengthen the Presidency, but any such change in Executive Branch authority seems minute when compared with the changes worked by delegations of other kinds of authority that the Court in the past has upheld . . .

In sum, I recognize that the Act before us is novel. In a sense, it skirts a constitutional edge. But that edge has to do with means, not ends. The means cho-sen do not amount literally to the enactment, repeal, or amendment of a law. Nor, for that matter, do they

amount literally to the "line item veto" that the Act's title announces. Those means do not violate any basic Separation of Powers principle. They do not improp-erly shift the constitutionally foreseen balance of power from Congress to the President. Nor, since they comply with Separation of Powers principles, do they threaten the liberties of individual citizens. They represent an experiment that may, or may not, help representative government work better. The Constitu-tion, in my view, authorizes Congress and the Presi-dent to try novel methods in this way. Consequently, with respect, I dissent.

Bush v. Gore

___ U.S. ___ (2000), 7-2.
Per Curiam: (Rehnquist, C.J., O'Connor, Souter, Scalia, Kennedy, Thomas, Breyer)
Concurring: Rehnquist, C.J. (Scalia, Thomas)
Dissenting in part: Souter, Breyer
Dissenting: Stevens (Ginsberg)
For background on this case, see When the Supreme Court Chose a President. p. 390-392

Should the Court have heard this case? Would it have been criticized had it not? Once it did decide to decide was there any ruling that would have been fair to all sides? What is "fair"? Does the Per Curiam opinion show respect or disrespect for the rights of states? If there was very little time left in which recounting might be completed, as Jus-tice Souter admits, what would have been the situation had it been allowed to continue but time ran out before completion? Is the disagreement between the majority and the dissenters one about the interpretation of statutes and constitutional provisions? The weight each should be given? The role of courts and the Court? Who should be president? What would have been the outcome of the elec-tion had Congress eventually decided outstanding mat-ters? Would that process and results have been better or worse than this decision?

Per Curiam:

The petition presents the following questions: whether the Florida Supreme Court established new standards for resolving Presidential election contests, thereby vi-olating Art II, §1, cl. 2, of the United States Constitu-tion and failing to comply with 3 U.S.C. Section 5, and whether the use of standardless manual re-counts violates the Equal Protection and Due Process Clauses. With respect to the equal protection question, we find a violation of the Equal Protection Clause. . . .

The right to vote is protected in more than the initial allocation of the franchise. Equal protection applies as well as to the manner of its exercise. Having once granted the right to vote on equal terms, the State may not, by later arbitrary and disparate treatment, value one person's vote over that of another. . . .

. . . The question before us . . . is whether the recount procedures the Florida Supreme Court has adopted are consistent with its obligation to avoid arbitrary and disparate treatment of the members of its electorate.

Much of the controversy seems to revolve around ballot cards designed to be perforated by a stylus but which, either through error or deliberate omission, have not been perforated with sufficient precision for a machine to count them. In some cases a piece of the card—a chad—is hanging, say by two corners. In other cases there is no separation at all, just an indentation.

The Florida Supreme Court has ordered that the intent of the voter be discerned from such ballots. For purposes of resolving the equal protection challenge, it is not necessary to decide whether Florida Supreme Court has the authority under the legislative scheme for resolving election disputes to define what a legal vote is and to mandate a manual recount implementing that definition. The recount mechanisms implemented in response to the decisions of the Florida Supreme Court do not satisfy the minimum requirement for non-arbitrary treatment of voters necessary to secure the fundamental right. Florida's basic command for the count of legally cast votes is to consider the "intent of the voter." This is unobjectionable as an abstract proposition and a starting principle. The problem inheres in the absence of specific standards to ensure its equal protection. The formulation of uniform rules to determine intent based on these recurring circumstances is practicable and, we conclude, necessary.

The law does now refrain from searching for the intent of the actor in a multitude of circumstances; and in some cases the general command to ascertain intent is not susceptible to much further refinement. In this instance, however, the question is not whether to believe a witness but how to interpret the marks or holes or scratches on an inanimate object, a piece of cardboard or paper which, it is said, might not have registered as a vote during the machine count. The factfinder confronts a thing, not a person. The search for intent can be confined by specific rules designed to ensure uniform treatment.

The want of those rules here has led to unequal evaluation of ballots in various respects. See *Gore v. Harris,* (Wells, J., dissenting) ("Should a county canvassing board count or not count a 'dimpled chad' where the voter is able to successfully dislodge the chad in every other contest on the ballot? Here, the county canvassing boards disagree.") As seems to have been acknowledged at oral argument, the standards for accepting or rejecting contested ballots might vary not only from county to county but indeed within a single county from one recount team to another. . . .

Gov. George W. Bush's narrow election night victory over Vice-President Albert Gore in Florida resulted in Democratic challenges to the machine count in three of the state's 67 counties. Here in a manual recount in Palm Beach Country, Judge Charles Burton, chairman of the county canvassing board, examines a punch card ballot to determine the intent of its voter. The recount revealed little change from the original machine count. Statewide manual recounting, ordered later by the Florida Supreme Court, was stopped by the U.S. Supreme Court in *Bush v. Gore.*

. . . At oral argument, respondents estimated there are as many as 110,000 overvotes statewide. As a result, the citizen whose ballot was not read by a machine because he failed to vote for a candidate in a way readable by a machine may still have his vote counted in a manual recount; on the other hand, the citizen who marks two candidates in a way discernible by the machine will not have the same opportunity to have his vote count, even if a manual examination of the ballot would reveal the requisite indicia of intent. Furthermore, the citizen who marks two candidates, only one of which is discernible by the machine, will still have his vote counted even though it should have been read as an invalid ballot. The State Supreme Court's inclusion of vote counts based on these variant standards exemplifies concerns with the remedial processes that were under way.

That brings the analysis to yet a further equal protection problem. The votes certified by the court included a partial total from one county, Miami-Dade. The Florida Supreme Court's decision thus gives no assurance that the recounts included a final certification must be complete. Indeed, it is respondent's submission that it would be consistent with the rules of the recount procedures to include whatever partial counts are done by the time of final certification, and we interpret the Florida Supreme Court's decision to permit this. This accommodation no doubt results from the truncated contest period established by the Florida Supreme Court in Bush I, at respondents' own urging. The press of time does not diminish the constitutional concern. A desire for speed is not a general excuse for ignoring equal protection guarantees.

In addition to these difficulties the actual process by which the votes were to be counted under the Florida Supreme Court's decision raises further concerns. That order did not specify who would recount the ballots. The county canvassing boards were forced to pull together ad hoc teams comprised of judges from various Circuits who had no previous training in handling and interpreting ballots. Furthermore, while others were permitted to observe, they were prohibited from objecting during the recount.

The recount process, in its features here described, is inconsistent with the minimum procedures necessary to protect the fundamental right of each voter in the special instance of a statewide recount under the authority of a single state judicial officer. . . .

The question before the Court is not whether local entities, in the exercise of their expertise, may develop different systems for implementing elections. Instead, we are presented with a situation where a state court with the power to assure uniformity has ordered a statewide recount with minimal procedural safeguards. When a court orders a statewide remedy, there must be at least some assurance that the rudimentary requirements of equal treatment and fundamental fairness are satisfied.

Given the Court's assessment that the recount process underway was probably being conducted in an unconstitutional manner, the Court stayed the order directing the recount so it could hear this case and render an expedited decision. The contest provision, as it was mandated by the State Supreme Court, is not well calculated to sustain the confidence that all citizens must have in the outcome of elections. The State has not shown that its procedures include the necessary safeguards. The problem, for instance, of the estimated 110,000 overvotes has not been addressed, although [state] Chief Justice Wells called attention to the concern in his dissenting opinion.

Upon due consideration of the difficulties identified to this point, it is obvious that the recount cannot be conducted in compliance with the requirements of equal protection and due process without substantial additional work. It would require not only the adoption (after opportunity for argument) of adequate statewide standards for determining what is a legal vote, and practicable procedures to implement them, but also orderly judicial review of any disputed matters that might arise. In addition, the Secretary of State has advised that the recount of only a portion of the ballots requires that the vote tabulation equipment be used to screen out undervotes, a function for which the machines were not designed. If a recount of overvotes were also required, perhaps even a second screening would be necessary. Use of the equipment for this purpose, and any new software developed for it, would have to be evaluated for accuracy by the Secretary of State, as required by Fla. Stat. §101.015.

The Supreme Court of Florida has said that the legislature intended the State's electors to "participat[e] fully in the federal electoral process," as provided in 3 U.S.C. s. 5. That statute, in turn, requires that any controversy or contest that is designed to lead to a conclusive selection of electors be completed by December 12. That date is upon us, and there is no recount procedure in place under the State Supreme Court's order that comports with minimal constitutional standards. Because it is evident that any recount seeking to meet the December 12 date will be unconstitutional for the reasons we have discussed, we reverse the judgment of the Supreme Court of Florida ordering a recount to proceed.

Seven Justices of the Court agreed that there are constitutional problems with the recount ordered by the Florida Supreme Court that demand a remedy. The only disagreement is as to the remedy. Because the Florida Supreme Court has said that the Florida Legislature intended to obtain the safe-harbor benefits of 3 U.S.C. s.5, Justice Breyer's proposed remedy—remanding to the Florida Supreme Court for its ordering of a constitutionally proper contest until December 18—contemplates action in violation of the Florida election code, and hence could not be a part of an "appropriate" order authorized by Fla. Stat. §102.168(8).

None are more conscious of the vital limits of judicial authority than are the members of this Court, and none stand more in admiration of the Constitution's design to leave the selection of the President to the people, through their legislatures, and to the political sphere. When contending parties invoke the process of the courts, however, it becomes an unsought responsibility to resolve the federal and constitutional issues the judicial system has been forced to confront.

The judgment of the Supreme Court of Florida is reversed, and the case is remanded for further proceedings not inconsistent with this opinion.

Rehnquist, concurring:

We join the per curiam opinion. We write separately because we believe there are additional grounds that require us to reverse the Florida Supreme Court's decision.

... Article II, §1, cl. 2, provides that "[e]ach State shall appoint, in such Manner as the Legislature thereof may direct," electors for President and Vice President. (emphasis added.) ...

In *McPherson v. Blacker* (1892), we explained that Art. II, §1, cl. 2, "convey[s] the broadest power of determination" and "leaves it to the legislature exclusively to define the method" of appointment. ld., at 27. A significant departure from the legislative scheme for appointing Presidential electors presents a federal constitutional question.

3 U.S.C., s.5 informs our application of Art II, §1, cl. 2, to the Florida statutory scheme, which, as the Florida Supreme Court acknowledged, took that statute into account. Section 5 provides that the State's selection of electors "shall be conclusive, and shall govern in the counting of the electoral votes" if the electors are chosen under laws enacted prior to election day, and if the selection process is completed six days prior to the meeting of the electoral college. As we noted in Bush v. Palm Beach County Canvassing Board.

"Since §5 contains a principle of federal law that would assure finality of the State's determination if made pursuant to a state law in effect before the election, a legislative wish to take advantage of the 'safe harbor' would counsel against any construction of the Election Code that Congress might deem to be a change in the law."

If we are to respect the legislature's Article II powers, therefore, we must ensure that post-election state court actions do not frustrate the legislative desire to attain the "safe harbor" provided by §5.

In Florida, the legislature has chosen to hold statewide elections to appoint the State's 25 electors. Importantly, the legislature has delegated the authority to run the elections and to oversee election disputes to the Secretary of State and to state circuit courts. ...

Acting pursuant to its constitutional grant of authority, the Florida Legislature has created a detailed, if not perfectly crafted, statutory scheme that provides for appointment of Presidential electors by direct election ...

... [I]n a Presidential election the clearly expressed intent of the legislature must prevail. ...

The scope and nature of the remedy ordered by the Florida Supreme Court jeopardizes the "legislative wish" to take advantage of the safe harbor provided by 3 U.S.C. s.5., December 12, 2000, is the last date for a final determination of the Florida electors that will satisfy §5. Yet in the late afternoon of December 8th—four days before this deadline—the Supreme Court of Florida ordered recounts of tens of thousands of so-called "undervotes" spread through 64 of the State's 67 counties. This was done in a search for elusive—perhaps delusive—certainty as to the exact count of 6 million votes. But no one claims that these ballots have not previously been tabulated; they were initially read by voting machines at the time of the election, and thereafter reread by virtue of Florida's automatic recount provision. No one claims there was any fraud in the election. The Supreme Court of Florida ordered this additional recount under the provision of the election code giving the circuit judge the authority to provide relief that is "appropriate under such circumstances."

Given all these factors, and in light of the legislative intent identified by the Florida Supreme Court to bring Florida within the "safe harbor" provision of 3 U.S.C. s.5, the remedy prescribed by the Supreme Court of Florida cannot be deemed an "appropriate" one as of December 8. It significantly departed from the statutory framework in place on November 7, and authorized open-ended further proceedings which could not be completed by December 12, thereby preventing a final determination by that date.

For these reasons, in addition to those given in the per curiam, we would reverse.

Stevens, dissenting:

The federal questions that ultimately emerged in this case are not substantial. Article II provides that "[e]ach State shall appoint, in such Manner as the Legislature thereof may direct, a Number of Electors." It does not create state legislatures out of whole cloth, but rather takes them as they come—as creatures born of, and constrained of, their state constitutions. Lest there be any doubt, we stated over 100 years ago in *McPherson v. Blacker*, (1982), that "[w]hat is forbidden or required to be done by a State" in the Article II context "is forbidden or required of the legislative power under state constitutions as they exist." In the same vein, we also observed that "[t]he [State's] legislative power is the supreme authority except as limited by the constitution of the State." The legislative power in Florida is subject to judicial review pursuant to Article V of the Florida Constitution, and nothing in Article II of the Federal Constitution frees the state legislature from the constraints in the state constitution that created it. . . .

It hardly needs stating that Congress, pursuant to 3 U.S.C. s.5 did not impose any affirmative duties upon the States that their governmental branches could "violate." . . . Neither §5 nor Article II grants federal judges any special authority to substitute their views for those of the state judiciary on matters of state law.

Nor are petitioners correct in asserting that the failure of the Florida Supreme Court to specify in detail the precise manner in which the "intent of the voter," is to be determined rises to the level of a constitutional violation. We found such a violation when individual votes within the same State were weighted unequally, but we have never before called into question the substantive standard by which a State determines that a vote has been legally cast.

Admittedly, the use of differing standards for determining voter intent in different counties employing similar voting systems may raise serious concerns. Those concerns are alleviated—if not eliminated—by the fact that a single impartial magistrate will ultimately adjudicate all objections arising from the recount process. . . .

In the interest of finality, however, the majority effectively order the disenfranchisement of an unknown number of voters whose ballots reveal their intent—and are therefore legal votes under state law—but were for some reason rejected by ballot-counting machines. It does so on the basis of the deadlines set forth in Title 3 of the United States Code. But, as I have already noted, those provisions merely provide rules of decision for Congress to follow when selecting among conflicting states of electors. They do not prohibit a State from counting what the majority concedes to be legal votes until a bona fide winner is determined. . . .

What must underlie petitioner's entire federal assault on the Florida election procedures is an unstated lack of confidence in the impartiality and capacity of the state judges who would make the critical decisions if the vote count were to proceed. Otherwise, their position is wholly without merit. The endorsement of that position by the majority of this Court can only lend credence to the most cynical appraisal of the work of judges throughout the land. It is confidence in the men and women who administer the judicial system that is the true backbone of the rule of law. Time will one day heal the wound to that confidence that will be inflicted by today's decision. One thing, however, is certain. Although we may never know with complete certainty the identity of the winner of this year's Presidential election, the identity of the loser is perfectly clear. It is the Nation's confidence in the judge as an impartial guardian of the rule of the law.

Souter, dissenting in part:

As will be clear, I am in substantial agreement with the dissenting opinions of Justice Stevens, Justice Ginsberg, and Justice Breyer. I write separately only to say how straightforward the issues before us really are.

There are three issues: whether the State Supreme Court's interpretation of the statute providing for a contest of the state election results somehow violates 3 U.S.C. s.5 whether that court's construction of the state statutory provisions governing contests impermissibly changes a state law from what the State's legislature has provided, in violation of Article II, §1, cl.2, of the national Constitution; and whether the manner of interpreting markings on disputed ballots failing to cause machines to register votes for President (the undervote ballots) violates the equal protection or due process guaranteed by the Fourteenth Amendment. None of these issues is difficult to describe or to resolve.

The 3 U.S.C. s.5 issue is not serious. That provision sets certain conditions for treating a State's certification of Presidential electors as conclusive in the event that a dispute over recognizing those electors must be resolved in the Congress under 3 U.S.C. s.15. Conclusiveness requires selection under a legal scheme in place before the election, with results determined at least six days before the date set for casting electoral votes. But no State is required to conform to §5 if it cannot do that (for whatever reason); the sanction for failing to satisfy the conditions under §5 is simply loss of what has been called its "safe harbor."

And even that determination is to be made, if made anywhere, in the Congress.

The second matter here goes to the State Supreme Court's interpretation of certain terms in the state statute governing election "contests." . . . The issue is whether the judgment of the state supreme court has displaced the state legislature's provisions for election contests: is the law as declared by the court different from the provisions made by the legislature, to which the national Constitution commits responsibility for determining how each State's Presidential electors are chosen? . . .

. . . None of the state court's interpretations is unreasonable to the point of displacing the legislative enactment quoted. As I will note below, other interpretations were of course possible, and some might have been better than those adopted by the Florida court's majority; the two dissects from the majority opinion of that court and various briefs submitted to us set out alternatives. But the majority view is in each instance within the bounds of reasonable interpretation, and the law as declared is consistent with Article II.

. . . Whatever people of good will and good sense may argue about the merits of the Florida court's reading, there is not warrant for saying that it transcends the limits of reasonable statutory interpretation to the point of supplanting the statute enacted by the "legislature" within the meaning of Article II

In sum, the interpretations by the Florida court raise no substantial question under Article II. . . .

It is only on the third issue before us that there is a meritorious argument for relief, as this Court's Per Curiam opinion recognizes. It is an issue that might well have been dealt with adequately by the Florida courts if the state proceedings had not been interrupted, and if not disposed of at the state level it could have been considered by the Congress in any electoral vote dispute. But because the course of state proceedings has been interrupted, time is short, and the issue is before us, I think it sensible for the Court to address it.

Petitioners have raised an equal protection claim (or, alternatively, a due process claim, in the charge that unjustifiably disparate standards are applied in different electoral jurisdictions to otherwise identical facts. It is true that the Equal Protection Clause does not forbid the use of a variety of voting mechanisms within a jurisdiction, even though different mechanisms will have different levels of effectiveness in recording voters' intentions; local variety can be justified by concerns about cost, the potential value of innovation, and so on. But evidence in the record here suggests that a different order of disparity obtains under rules for determining a voter's intent that have been applied (and could continue to be applied) to identical types of ballots used in identical brands of machines and exhibiting identical physical characteristics (such as "hanging" or "dimpled" chads). I can conceive of not legitimate state interest served by these differing treatments of the expressions of voters' fundamental rights. The differences appear wholly arbitrary.

In deciding what to do about this, we should take account of the fact that the electoral votes are due to be cast in six days. I would therefore remand the case to the courts of Florida with instructions to establish uniform standards for evaluating the several types of ballots that have prompted differing treatments, to be applied within and among counties when passing on such identical ballots in any further recounting (or successive recounting) that the courts might order.

Unlike the majority, I see no warrant for this Court to assume that Florida could not possibly comply with this requirement before the date set for the meeting of electors, December 18. Although one of the dissenting justices of the State Supreme Court estimated that disparate standards potentially affected 170,000 votes, the number at issue is significantly smaller. The 170,000 figure apparently represents all uncounted votes, both undervotes (those for which no Presidential choice was recorded by a machine) and overvotes (those rejected because of votes for more than one candidate). But as Justice Breyer has pointed out, no showing has been made of legal overvotes uncounted, and counsel for Gore made an uncontradicted representation to the Court that the statewide total of undervotes is about 60,000. To recount these manually would be a tall order, but before this Court stayed the effort to do that the courts of Florida were ready to do their best to get that job done. There is no justification for denying the State the opportunity to try to count all disputed ballots now.

10

THE NEW FEDERAL SYSTEM

Federalism or a federal system divides power between a central or national government and governments of regions, provinces, or states. In contrast to a unitary arrangement, in which an all-powerful central government may delegate to subdivisions, powers of central and provincial governments in a federal system derive from a constitution, independently of each other.

The American Constitution creates a federal system but does not define federalism or even use the term. For the framers, federalism was the answer, perhaps the only one, to the chief problem they faced: how to meld 13 largely independent sovereignties into a stronger union. Since this union could only be forged by persuasion and not by force, it came to rest on an imaginative construction filled with compromises and riddled with ambiguities. Without a federal system, there would have been no union, at least not one differing much from the Articles of Confederation. In the late eighteenth century, the federal system was probably the strongest American union constitution-making could devise.

Federal systems offer many supposed advantages: accommodation of diversity, opportunity for experimentation, and the republican efficiency of having many governmental decisions made locally. Supposed disadvantages include the absence of uniformity, difficulty in mobilizing power on a large scale, and multiple points of governmental conflict. For the framers, these positives and negatives were less important than finding a common ground on which the states could stand to form a stronger union.

The Constitution recognizes the states as the constituent units at some points and "the people" at others. Article VI makes the central government supreme, but the central government is one of delegated not residual powers. Powers not given to it by the Constitution and not among those denied to the states are, in the Tenth Amendment, reserved to "the states respectively, or to the People."

This ingenious arrangement left much unsettled. Despite later nationalizing developments and such important decisions as *McCulloch v. Maryland, Martin v. Hunter's Lessee,* and *Cohens v. Virginia,* the matter of retained state sovereignty remained unresolved until the Civil War. The defeat of secession created a new federal system and established national supremacy beyond doubt. Constitutional amendments coming out of the war placed new restrictions on the states. Left unresolved was the matter of whether powers reserved to the states by the Tenth Amendment were also independent limits on authority of the national government. As we have seen, this question had ups and downs for more than 60 years until settled by the New Deal crisis. In the oft-quoted term of Justice Stone in *United States v. Darby* (1941), the Tenth Amendment stated but a "truism"—it was merely a description of where unaccounted-for powers resided, not an independent constitutional grant to the states that could stand against the central government.

The outcome of the New Deal conflict and the redirection of the Supreme Court created a second new federal system, marked by two great developments. The first was the central government's nearly total control over the national economy through Congress's commerce and taxing powers, now given great new reach. The second saw new restrictions placed on state power in the name of individual liberties. Protections in the Bill of Rights, once applicable only to the central government, were gradually extended to the states, and restrictions first imposed on the states by the Civil War amendments were revitalized. These changes were not effected by constitution amendment; they were products of judicial reinterpretation of powers already vested and limits already set.

The changes have not meant a withering away of state government. Instead, governments in the 50 states and in most of the more than 80,000 local units including counties, municipalities, school districts, and the like, has grown enormously in the second half of the twentieth century. Like the national government, they assumed new responsibilities and have intervened more widely in everyday life. The second new federal system, as the first, has seen a shift in the division of power between the center and periphery. But where the first resulted from a war defeating secession, the second was the product of the same modern developments that affected the balance of power within the central government:

an interdependent economy and ever-larger national marketplace, assumption of new social responsibilities by government, and an increasingly prominent role of the United States in world affairs.

This chapter deals with the relationship of state and national powers in the modern federal system: the new reach of federal power and the possible conflict of state power with national law. The state powers include taxation and spending, regulation of intrastate commerce, and the police power—the authority to promote the public health, safety, and welfare of state citizens. Issues of state power and property rights are the subject of Chapter 11.

Debate between nationalists and state power proponents over the balance in the federal system is as old as the Constitution itself and will no doubt continue as long as federalism is a chief feature of American government. At different times, different political interests have attached themselves to one side or the other. Nationalists have included conservative defenders of property rights during the antebellum period, Radical Republicans during Reconstruction, industrial capitalists in the late nineteenth century, Progressives, and later, New Dealers in the early twentieth century, and in more recent times, civil rights advocates. Defenders of states have included antebellum slaveholders and small entrepreneurs, late nineteenth century economic reformers, early twentieth century economic conservatives, and later, racial segregationists and advocates of deregulation. Some interests, such as the railroads, have freely taken the nationalist or the state-power position depending on which was better serving, unembarrassed by constitutional inconstancy.

The Reach of Federal Legislation

The "Constitutional revolution" that followed the New Deal crisis in the late 1930s was only the formal recognition of the vast changes that had taken place in government and in the federal system. In assuming new regulatory functions and creating new social programs, the national government used its commerce, tax, and spending powers in new ways to reach ends often different from those of the past. Many of these policies took federal power into places once reserved for the states. The constitutional revolution was the Roosevelt Court's recognition of the great changes wrought by the Depression and the New Deal's response to it. That revolution transformed the commerce power into an almost unlimited federal grant, not merely over interstate business, but over almost anything having to do with the economy. The constitutional issues raised were not ones of federal supremacy, now well settled, but of what limits, if any, the requirements of a federal system placed on national power.

Police Regulation of Private Acts

In the 1960s, after several Southern states did not move expeditiously to end racial discrimination in hotels, restaurants, and other private businesses serving the public after the Supreme Court had declared "separate but equal" treatment to be unconstitutional, Congress used the commerce power to outlaw such practices. The Civil Rights Act of 1964 was challenged the same year it was passed, in the companion cases of *Heart of Atlanta Motel v. United States* (p. 506) and *Katzenbach v. McClung*. The argument made was that the facilities, a motel and a restaurant, were local and thus removed from interstate commerce. In unanimously rejecting it, the Supreme Court sustained a broad new reach for the commerce clause as a source of national police power.

The motel, in downtown Atlanta, served a transient clientele, many of whom were interstate travelers. Speaking for a unanimous Court, Justice Clark held that Congress had power to reach and regulate even local businesses if their operations had to do with interstate commerce. The case of the restaurant, Ollie's Barbecue, was more difficult since all its customers were local and all its food was bought locally. Clark observed that some food sold to the restaurant by local suppliers had originated out of state. He then held that Congress had a "rational basis" for

concluding that such a local business when aggregated with other similar local businesses could affect interstate commerce by reducing through discrimination the amount of food purchased and served. Such local practices might also deter industries from other states from relocating. In accepting this attenuated link, the Court appeared to underwrite an almost unlimited reach of the commerce power to economic matters. Congress also used the power in the 1964 act to legislate against discrimination in employment and again in the Civil Rights Act of 1968 to bar discrimination in the sale or rental of most housing.

Elsewhere, Congress has used the expanded commerce power to enact federal criminal law, such as in the Organized Crime Control and Consumer Credit Protection Acts of 1970. Title IX of the former, dealing with Racketeer Influenced and Corrupt Organizations (RICO), aims at preventing organized crime from infiltrating businesses in interstate commerce. When the ban on "loan-sharking"—extortionate credit practices—in the Consumer Credit Protection Act was challenged in *Perez v. United States* (1971), the Court reaffirmed the new breadth of the commerce power to deal with crime. It sustained federal prosecution for an act entirely local and having no apparent link to organized crime, on the ground that Congress could decide that loan-sharking was a national problem.

Concluding that its commerce power was unlimited by the federal system, however, was premature. In *United States v. Lopez* (1995) (p. 531), the Supreme Court, 5-4, invalidated the Gun-Free School Zones Act of 1990 that made it a federal crime to possess a gun within 1,000 feet of a school. In overturning the conviction of a high school student who had brought a gun to school, Chief Justice Rehnquist held that the law neither regulated commercial activity nor required there be a link to interstate commerce. When a federal law is not directed at the channels of interstate commerce or the protection of persons or things in interstate commerce, the activity regulated must bear a "substantial relation" to that commerce. Otherwise, Rehnquist wrote, the Court would "pile inference upon inference" to convert the commerce authority to "a general police power of the sort retained by the States." Similarly, in *Jones v. United States,* (2000), the Court curbed the reach of Congress's commerce power by holding that a federal anti-arson law making it a crime to damage or destroy property used in interstate commerce did not apply to an owner-occupied private residence not used for commercial purposes.

The decision was the first since the New Deal period to hold a Congressional act directed at private behavior was beyond the commerce power. The full significance of *Lopez* is not yet clear, but Rehnquist's statement that a constitution enumerating powers "presupposes something not enumerated," suggests the Court may hold the commerce power to be something less than plenary and limited, in its far reaches at least, by the federal system. This was the position of the same narrow majority in *United States v. Morrison,* (2000) (p. 556), in which a civil provision of the Violence Against Women Act of 1994, permitting victims of gender motivated crimes to sue their alleged attackers in federal courts, was struck down. Observing that such crimes were not "in any sense of the phrase, economic activity," the Court, through Chief Justice Rehnquist, held the provision to be beyond Congress's power to regulate interstate commerce.

Federal Regulation of State Government

Direct federal regulation of the states as governmental or political entities would be inimical to a federal system, against the intent and vision of the framers, and no doubt politically unacceptable. Such an arrangement would turn the nation into a unitary system, reducing the states to mere administrative arms of the central government. Yet the increasing reach of federal power, particularly in dealing with an integrated economy, has touched the governmental operations of the states. When is such intrusion simply a valid extension of national power and when is it limited by the fact of a federal system?

Congress used the commerce power in 1938 to pass the Fair Labor Standards Act (FLSA) to establish a minimum wage and maximum working hours. The act, upheld in *United States v. Darby* (1941) as applied to a business that was mainly local, now covers almost all workers in the private sector. When Congress amended the act's wage and hour provisions to cover employees of state and local government in 1974 the extension was challenged as a violation of the Tenth Amendment. In *National League of Cities v. Usery* (1976), to the surprise of many, the Court held the new coverage unconstitutional, the first limiting of Congress's commerce power since the days of the anti-New Deal Court in the 1930s. A five-member majority led by then-Associate Justice Rehnquist held that a state's power to set the wages and working hours of its employees "to carry out integral governmental functions" was an attribute of state sovereignty. The FLSA extension thus tried to regulate the "states as states."

In several cases immediately following, the Court tried to draw distinctions, some of which were fine, between governmental functions that were "integral" and those not, especially where the functions included the sorts of activities also performed by private enterprise. Finally, in *Garcia v. San Antonio Metropolitan Transit Authority* (1985) (p. 515) where the FLSA provisions had been applied to employees of a city-owned bus company, it gave up the effort and reversed the National League decision. Instead of finding the transit operations were integral or not integral, the Court held the distinction to be "illusory" and unworkable. Justice Blackmun, who left the *National League* majority to join its four dissenters, spoke for an equally narrow majority. The protection of state interests was to be found not in a limiting content of the Tenth Amendment, but in the workings of the national government, particularly in representation of the states in the Senate. The dissenters argued that Senators were members of the national government, not simply representatives of their states. In their view the Court still had an important role to play in protecting state sovereignty needed to maintain a federal system.

Since the New Deal, Congress has used its spending power to induce states to regulate in areas where it seemed not to have power itself or preferred not to use it. Such conditional grants, sometimes referred to as "cooperative federalism," had been upheld in *Steward Machine Co. v. Davis* (1937) as inducement to states to set up unemployment insurance programs. But a latter-day challenge to conditional grants developed in *South Dakota v. Dole* (1987) (p. 523), in which state officials sued the secretary of transportation to prevent her from withdrawing federal highway funds. Concerned about minors killed while driving intoxicated, Congress amended the Surface Transportation Act in 1984 to authorize withholding highway funds from states that had not raised their legal drinking age to 21. The Court held these kinds of conditional grants were valid so long as spending was for the general welfare as required by Article I-8, and the conditions were clearly related to the spending and did not induce states to undertake unconstitutional acts. The Court also held the conditions in this case did not violate the Twenty-first Amendment, which gave the states authority to regulate the use of intoxicating liquors.

In the Low-Level Radioactive Waste Policy Act of 1980, Congress addressed problems created by the disposal of nuclear waste, relying on its commerce and spending powers. Amended in 1985, the act was designed to take pressure off the three national waste sites in South Carolina, Nevada, and Washington State by inducing every state to make in-state arrangements for disposal or enter into regional compacts with other states to do so. As "incentives," it set increasingly high surcharges on disposal at the national sites, with the proceeds going to states that were complying with the act. States not arranging for disposal, in-state or regionally, would also be required to "take title" to waste generated in the state. As its legal owner, the state would then be liable for damage or harm the waste might cause.

New York challenged these requirements as violating state rights guaranteed by the Tenth Amendment in *New York v. United States* (1992) (p. 525). The Supreme Court upheld the act,

including the surcharges, as valid measures to motivate states to act, but held in New York's favor on the "take title" provision. On this point, Justice O'Connor writing for the Court's majority, said that in forcing ownership on the state as an alternative to regulation, Congress had "crossed the line distinguishing encouragement from coercion." Congress could reward states for actions or could preempt state regulations that were inconsistent with national policy, but it could not order states to take particular action or to administer a federal program.

Federal command of a different sort was at issue in *Printz v. United States* (1997) (p. 537). The so-called Brady Act, a gun control law passed in 1993, required local law enforcement officials to make background checks on handgun purchasers to find out whether they met federal restrictions. In *Printz,* the Court, 5-4, agreed with the contention of two county sheriffs that Congress could not "conscript" state or local officials to administer part of a federal regulatory program. Dissenting justices argued that Congress pursuing its delegated powers could place affirmative obligations on state officials as it could on ordinary citizens. In their view, the Tenth Amendment meant only that federal powers were limited to those affirmatively granted by the Constitution; it did not impose independent restrictions on those powers.

The same majority in *Printz* and *Lopez* has held states to have sovereign immunity from being sued by plaintiffs making claims under federal regulatory laws. These decisions further redraw the boundary separating federal authority from state prerogatives, enhancing and enlarging the latter. In *Seminole Tribe v. Florida,* 1996, a section of the Indian Gaming Regulatory Act that allowed tribes to sue in federal court where states refused to negotiate about establishing gambling casinos on reservations, was held to violate the Eleventh Amendment despite Congress having nearly complete authority (and the states none) to enact laws related to Indian affairs.

Three 5-4 decisions in 1999 carried the doctrine of sovereign immunity to suits brought in state courts. In *Alden v. Maine* (p. 542), 65 state probation officers sued for premium

Chief Justice Conservative

William Hubbs Rehnquist was born in Milwaukee, Wisconsin, in 1924 and grew up in one of its suburbs, the son of a successful paper salesman. He served in the air force in World War II, went to college at Stanford under the G.I. Bill, earned graduate political science degrees at Stanford and Harvard, and later returned to Stanford to study law. After graduating first in his class (Sandra Day, later O'Connor and still later a fellow associate justice of the Supreme Court, was third in the same class), he served as Justice Robert Jackson's law clerk.

He was an outspoken political conservative from his early youth. After he moved to Phoenix, Arizona, to practice law, he entered Republican politics and soon became a force in the conservative wing of the state party. After Richard Nixon's election in 1968, Rehnquist was named associate attorney general to head the Office of the Legal Counsel, a post in which he represented the new administration's views to Congress. His performance and his "law and order" views on criminal justice issues and advocacy of judicial self-restraint impressed the president, who chose him to succeed the retiring conservative justice John M. Harlan, II, in 1971.

With three other Nixon appointees, Warren Burger, Harry Blackmun, and Lewis Powell, Rehnquist was part of the nucleus of what eventually became the "Burger Court," a moderately conservative successor to the Warren Court. He emerged as one of the Court's intellectual leaders and most conservative members, less interested in looking for majority consensus than in being true to his own values. He did not hesitate to dissent, as in *Roe v. Wade* (1973), the abortion rights case. Points made in several of his dissents have later been taken up in majority opinions. He was influential in leading the Burger Court to narrow many of the Warren Court's more controversial criminal justice decisions.

overtime pay under the federal Fair Labor Standards Act (FLSA), which provided that such suits could be filed in state courts. In *College Savings Bank v. Florida* and *Florida v. College Savings Bank,* a private company marketing special certificates of deposit tailored for parents saving for college tuition, sued the state under the Trademark Remedy Classification Act (the first case) and the Patent Remedy Clarification Act (the second) for patent infringement and trademark violation after the state began to market similar instruments. In each case, the Court expanded the immunity shield for states by holding that federal legislation forcing them to be defendants in their own courts against private plaintiffs violated the Tenth Amendment.

A year later in *Kimel v. Florida Board of Regents* (p. 548), in which several college professors sued in federal court under the federal Age Discrimination in Employment Act (ADEA) seeking to prove discriminatory acts by state's university system, the Court held the suits to be barred by the Eleventh Amendment. It conceded that Congress's power to enforce the equal protection provisions of the Fourteenth Amendment, on which the ADEA was based, might overcome the Eleventh Amendment and state sovereign immunity. But it held the substantive age discrimination standards the ADEA imposed in this case were "disproportion-

On Burger's retirement in 1986, President Reagan nominated Rehnquist to be the nation's sixteenth Chief Justice. His constitutional jurisprudence and conservative record on civil rights fired liberal opposition to the appointment. He was eventually confirmed by the Senate, 65-33.

As chief justice, Rehnquist has placed greater value on building consensus and has moved closer to the center of his Court. It may be equally true that the center of the conservative Court has moved closer to Rehnquist's views. He has become an effective manager of the Court's work, winning praise from fellow justices for fairness and efficient leadership in the Court's weekly conference. His informal, sometimes playful style is anything but conservative and is credited with improving cordiality among the justices. In sharp contrast to the sometimes stiff formality his predecessor, the current chief justice has been known to play practical jokes and, at informal gatherings, lead fellow justices and clerks in singing Broadway show tunes.

Rehnquist is widely read outside of the law particularly in history, literature, and biography. Since becoming chief justice, he has published two popular books on the Court and constitutional law: *The Supreme Court: How It Was, How It Is,* in 1988, and *Grand Inquest: The Historic Impeachments of Justice Samuel Chase and President Andrew Johnson,* in 1992.

One observer has described him as "the most powerful figure in American law since Earl Warren." This is a high estimate, yet there is little doubt that in more than a quarter century on the Court, Rehnquist's largely unwavering political and judicial philosophy has had a substantial influence on the Court's constitutional law. He has repeatedly opposed extension of individual liberties at the expense of majority rule and electoral accountability. This "democratic" model leads to a more restrained role for judges and justices who, he has said, do not have "a roving commission to second-guess Congress, state legislatures, and state and federal administrative officials concerning what is best for the country."

Rehnquist has placed the highest value on federalism, advocating that its balance be shifted away from the center by preserving and expanding the powers and responsibilities of state and local government. Where this has called for judicial activism, as in *United States v. Lopez* (1995), for example, the chief justice has been willing to put aside values of self-restraint to advance toward a more state-centered federalism. His constitutional values have been well-defined, consistent, and heard for many years. Only their impact is yet in doubt.

---

ate to any unconstitutional conduct that conceivably could be targeted by the Act."

The Court reached a similar conclusion about the Americans with Disabilities Act of 1990 insofar as the law gave a right to disabled state employees to sue for damages in federal courts if they believed their state employer had not provided reasonable at-work accommodations for their disabilities. With the same 5-4 split, the Court in *Board of Trustees of the University of Alabama v. Garrett,* (2001), held that the states had Eleventh Amendment immunity from being sued in federal courts and that such immunity was not overcome by Congress's Fourteenth Amendment equal protection power because it was "entirely

rational and therefore constitutional for a state employer to conserve scarce financial resources by hiring employees who are able to use existing facilities."

The Court declined, however, to extend sovereign immunity in *Reno v. Condon,* (2000) (p. 553), where it unanimously upheld the federal Driver's Privacy Protection Act regulating disclosure of information contained in state motor vehicle department records. It distinguished *New York v. United States* and *Printz,* holding that the Act, though placing restrictions on states where they chose to disclose information, had not required them "in their sovereign capacity to regulate their own citizens."

How far the emerging sovereign immunity doctrine will carry is yet unclear. States may become more vigorous in asserting the defense in suits brought against them by private parties under federal laws. But the immunity shield may be less about denying Congress power to make uniform regulations than about how these regulations are to be enforced. In the case of the FLSA, for example, persons claiming to be injured by state violations can still have their claims asserted in lawsuits brought by the federal government to enforce its own laws. The sovereign immunity cases are one more indication that federalism continues to be the chief fault line in the Rehnquist Court.

Federal Supremacy: Preemption

Where concurrent national and state powers conflict, national supremacy in Article VI-2 requires the state power to give way. The Supreme Court affirmed this preemption in case of the treaty-making power in *Missouri v. Holland* (1920). But conflict between federal and state action is more likely with Congressional domestic legislation, and its incidence has grown as the activities of federal and state government have increased. Congress has sometimes anticipated clashes and has expressly stated to what extent, if any, an enactment should preempt related state laws, sometimes including "savings" clauses. But more often than not, Congressional intent on preemption is unclear. This has left its discovery and the task of sifting through the inconsistencies between the federal and state laws to the courts. Though a great many cases have arisen from federal laws regulating commerce, the Supreme Court's most definitive statement on preemption came in the Cold War sedition case, *Pennsylvania v. Nelson* (1956) (p. 504).

Nelson, a member of the Communist Party, was convicted under a Pennsylvania law making it a crime to advocate violent overthrow of the federal government. He appealed arguing that the state law was completely preempted by the Smith Act of 1940, in which Congress similarly made advocacy of violent overthrow a crime.

Chief Justice Warren, speaking for the Court, held the Smith Act preemptive as a pervasive federal regulatory scheme. In it Congress had addressed a dominant federal interest and had intended to occupy the field because of a need for national uniformity. Response to the decision was strongly negative both in and outside of Congress. Three years later, the Court gave it narrower effect in *Uphaus v. Wyman,* holding that Congress had not intended to preempt state laws aimed at protecting state government from subversion.

Though the criteria for determining preemption in *Nelson* were reasonable, they often proved difficult to apply in specific circumstances. Because of this, the Court has been cautious in inferring preemptive intent where the federal statute is ambiguous. Generally it has tried to discover whether a concurrent state law is an obstacle to Congressional purposes. The Court has usually been more willing to hold that state laws are not preempted where they deal with public health or safety rather than commerce.

A few examples illustrate how the preemption doctrine may turn on factual particulars. In *City of Burbank v. Lockheed Air Terminal* (1972), a local noise abatement ordinance barring jet aircraft takeoffs between 11 p.m. and 7 a.m. at a privately owned airport was held preempted by federal aviation regulations. The Court said the need for efficient control of air traffic made the federal rules pervasively national. In *Geier v. American Honda Motor Co.,* 2000, a state's tort law allowing an accident victim to sue an auto manufacturer for injuries sustained because its car had not been equipped with air bags, was held to be preempted by provisions of the federal National Traffic and Motor Vehicle Safety Act that required that some but not all cars be equipped with passive restraints.

But in *Pacific Gas & Electric Co. v. State Energy Resource and Development Commission* in 1983, the Court held the federal Atomic Energy Act, though occupying the "entire field of safety concerns," did not preempt a California moratorium on construction of new nuclear power plants for reasons other than safety. A year later, in *Silkwood v. Kerr-McGee,* the Act was held not to preempt state tort law that awarded punitive damages to a radiation victim injured at a nuclear plant that was federally licensed and met federal safety regulations. Similarly, in *Cipollone v. Liggett Group* (1992), a federal requirement that the dangers of smoking be placed on cigarette packs was held to preempt state tort law that permitted damage suits based on the manufacturer's failure to warn of the dangers of smoking. Not preempted, however, were the state's tort laws permitting recovery for breach of warranty, intentional fraud, or conspiracy to conceal or misrepresent material facts.

The lack of clarity in many federal laws on the preemption question and the difficulty the courts have in discovering Congressional intent, often puts them in a position of policy-making. But since the decisions here are based on statutory rather than constitutional construction, Congress can override a judicial finding if it concludes legislative intent was wrongly interpreted, by simply amending its law.

Mutual Tax Immunities

The doctrine of intergovernmental tax immunity holds that federal and state governments and their instrumentalities are each exempt from taxation by the other. Though once a highly developed feature of the federal system, it is now a mere shadow of its former self. Since the Constitution is silent about whether one government may tax another, the doctrine is entirely of judicial construction and has had favor with different courts. It is traceable to Marshall's opinion in *McCulloch v. Maryland,* holding that the state could not impose a tax on the Baltimore branch of the United States Bank. His reasoning was based on the apparent inconsistency of the federal government being supreme and, at the same time, being taxable, possibly destructively, by a state power.

It was not until after the Civil War that the doctrine was given two-way effect. In *Collector v. Day* (1871), the Court, which had earlier held

that a state could not tax the income of federal officeholders, ruled that a state judge's salary was not subject to the Civil War federal income tax. The constitutional basis for the immunity, Justice Nelson explained, was the Tenth Amendment. In place of the national supremacy that underwrote federal immunity, was the need to protect states as states in the federal system.

From there, correlative immunities multiplied. One notable advance came in *Pollock v. Farmers Loan and Trust* (1895), in which the Court held interest from state or municipal bonds was not taxable by the federal government. Philosophically congenial with laissez-faire economics, intergovernmental immunity by the early 1930s had come to apply to wide range of federal and state taxes. Included were state levies applied to such items as income from federally leased land, gasoline sold to the federal government, and royalties on federally registered patents. Federal taxes included those on the sale of a motorcycle to local police, and on private income derived from leasing state-owned lands. On the other hand, federal income tax was upheld on fees of professional consultants paid by state government, federal customs duties were held to apply to scientific equipment imported by a state university, and a federal admissions tax was sustained on tickets to games played by teams of a state university. Earlier the Court had upheld federal liquor taxes where applied to state-run retail liquor sales. In these cases, many decided 5-4, the Court purportedly distinguished between whether the taxes were on "essential" or "nonessential" government activity and whether or not they imposed an "excessive burden." This unenviable task also offered a chance for extensive judicial policymaking.

After the financial needs of federal and state governments grew desperate in the Great Depression, tax immunity was less and less functional. Starting with *Helvering v. Mountain Producers Corp.* (1938), in which a federal tax on private oil revenues from state-leased lands was upheld, the Roosevelt Court began to rein in the tax immunity doctrine. In *Graves v. New York ex. rel. O'Keefe* (1939), it overruled *Collector v. Day* and made the income of state employees subject to the federal income tax and that of federal employees subject to state tax. It abandoned that part of the doctrine that treated a tax on income as a tax on the source of the income. This principle was extended two years later in *Alabama v. King & Boozer*, to a state sales tax applied to material used by a federal contractor even though the burden of the tax could be passed on to the federal government.

Two later cases illustrate the limits and remaining vitality of intergovernmental tax immunity. To reduce evasion of federal estate taxes by holders of unregistered state and local bonds (those issued simply to the bearers), Congress removed the federal income tax exemption from interest on such bonds. South Carolina challenged this action, arguing that it violated the Tenth Amendment and would force the state and local governments to pay higher interest and thus raise the cost of financing government capital operations. In *South Carolina v. Baker* (1988), the Court rejected the claim, holding there was no constitutional reason why interest income should be treated differently from income received from other kinds of contracts with state government. Further, Justice Brennan held, states have no constitutional entitlement to issue bonds that pay the lowest possible interest rates. The decision overruled that part of the Pollock case that had held income from state bonds to be free from taxation.

The following year, in *Davis v. Michigan Department of the Treasury,* the Court ruled that a state may not discriminate between state and federal employees in its levy of an income tax. Here, Michigan had given a tax exemption to retirement benefits derived from state employment but not those from federal work. The Court held the Michigan provisions violated the doctrine of intergovernmental immunity by favoring retired state and local public workers over federal.

Judicial Federalism

The relationship of federal and state courts has been an important and special aspect of the development of the federal system. Though usually informed by the principles of comity—deference given by one jurisdiction to the decisions of another—the relationship has been marked by uncertainty and sometimes acrimony. It has been at the center of debates between nationalists and proponents of states rights and in many liberal-conservative struggles over property rights and more recently over civil rights and civil liberties.

Article III-2 describes federal jurisdiction but says nothing about the role of state courts or about appeals from state courts to the United States Supreme Court. In the Judiciary Act of 1789, the first Congress set up the lower federal courts and the first rules of judicial federalism. It calmed states rights fears by allowing state courts to hear federal questions—those raising issues under the Constitution, treaties, or federal laws. But it also provided that where such questions were ruled on by the highest court of a state, they could be appealed to the United States Supreme Court. The constitutionality of this provision had been upheld in *Martin v. Hunter's Lessee* (1816) against a Virginia claim that a ruling on rights under the Jay Treaty by its highest court was final. And in *Cohens v. Virginia* (1821), the Supreme Court held that its appellate jurisdiction extended to state criminal cases in which a federal question had arisen even where the appellant was not a citizen of the state.

In all, the 1789 Act gave the Supreme Court appellate jurisdiction over decisions of state supreme courts where they had (1) upheld a state law against a claim that it violated Constitution, a federal law, or a treaty, (2) held a federal law or treaty unconstitutional, or (3) denied a claim under the Constitution or federal law. It was not until the Removal Act of 1875 that Congress began to give lower federal courts original and removal jurisdiction that was coextensive with the Supreme Court's appellate jurisdiction on federal questions. Before then, lower federal courts heard mainly admiralty and maritime cases and those of diversity of citizenship—cases between residents of different states. In placing new constitutional restrictions on the states, the fourteenth Amendment greatly increased the federal questions that could and did arise, thus further increasing opportunity for federal judicial review of state court decisions. Gradual application of the Bill of Rights to the states through the due process clause of the Fourteenth Amendment had an even greater effect on the Supreme Court's overseeing role and profoundly changed the relationship of federal and state courts.

Despite this important shift in judicial federalism, a state supreme court's interpretation of the state constitution or state law remains final and, absent a federal question, not reviewable by the U.S. Supreme Court. State courts handle more than 90 percent of all cases filed—nearly 30,000,000 a year. These include tort claims, contractual disputes, property transfers, criminal matters, divorces, and other domestic conflict. Only a small fraction of these cases ever present a federal question. Most litigation begins and ends in the state courts.

The Matter of Federal Common Law

Common law is called judge-made because its rules and principles derive not from the "positive" law of statutes and constitutions, but from long-standing judicial recognition of certain practices or customs and the shaping of them into "law." Such rules may be superseded by legislative enactment, but absent that, they importantly fill the interstices of positive law. At the nation's founding, all common law was state law,

and on a given issue there could be, theoretically at least, as many rules as there were states.

Creation of the federal courts added a new complexity. In the Judiciary Act of 1789, Congress required those courts to follow "the laws of the several states," meaning the law of the state in which the federal court was located. Because of an expanding national marketplace and more manufacturers and other entrepreneurs coming to do business in two or more states, commercial markets tended to develop uniform practices, predictable behavior on which merchants rely. But often these efficiencies were at odds with a diversity of governing legal rules that were the product of common law developing in one state largely independent of its development in another.

The situation was an anathema to Justice Story, a leading legal scholar of his day and long an advocate of a uniform commercial law. In *Swift v. Tyson* (1842), a federal diversity of citizenship case brought in New York over a contract, Story was able to persuade all his Taney Court colleagues to free the federal courts from the apparent strictures of the Judiciary Act and, in doing so, open the door to a federal commercial common law. Story interpreted the "laws" to which the act required adherence, to refer to state and local statutory law not to law formed by previous state court decisions, that is, not to state common law.

New York common law, Story said, was not law pronounced by the sovereign state but by its courts in attempting to devise legal rules from customs and practices of multistate commercial transactions. If a federal court believed such law to be mistaken, it was free to ignore and formulate a different rule, that is, to create federal common law that would serve as precedent in federal courts. *Swift v. Tyson* did not change state common law but it offered the means for creating a different body of law, which Story correctly anticipated would supply much greater and needed uniformity to commercial activity, at least in those cases brought to federal courts.

Swift was an important step in the legal nationalization of commercial markets and it protected multistate businesses against the idiosyncrasies that might have developed in the common law of different states. It also increased the power of the federal courts, which in the late nineteenth and early twentieth centuries were generally more conservative and sympathetic to business interests than were many state courts. One of the long-run effects of *Swift v. Tyson* was to allow business to get around state common law where it was more restrictive than federal. It is not surprising that the *Swift* rule became a target of Progressives and other reform-minded groups.

Normally there is only one court in which a lawsuit may be filed. But the diversity of citizenship jurisdiction of the federal courts allows a plaintiff living in a different state than the defendant to sue in either federal or state court in the defendant's home state. *Swift v. Tyson* meant that in commercial litigation the substantive law applied might be different in federal court than in the state. So a plaintiff could do "forum shopping"—choose the jurisdiction, federal or state, in which the law was more favorable. This sometimes led to blatant abuses in which a plaintiff in the same state as the defendant, manufactured diversity by setting up minimum formal residence in another state in order to file the case in the federal courts.

"Old Swifty," as the doctrine came to be called, was ended in a stroke in *Erie Railroad v. Tompkins* in 1938. Tompkins had been struck by a freight train while walking along the railroad tracks. Though the accident occurred in Pennsylvania and the defendant did much of its business in Pennsylvania, Tompkins sued in a federal court in New York where the railroad was chartered. He did this because Pennsylvania law would probably have held Tompkins to be a trespasser on the tracks and thus owed no liability by the railroad. Federal common law, on the other hand, would probably allow recovery. Justice Brandeis, long a critic of the *Swift* rule, wrote for a majority of seven and pointed out

different problems *Swift* had created. Declaring "there is no federal common law," he overruled the case.

Coming from the early Roosevelt Court, *Erie v. Tompkins* may seem paradoxical in its antinationalist effect. But by the 1930s, *Swift v. Tyson* had grown less important as a mechanism for gaining uniformity in commercial law. By then, most states had adopted uniform commercial codes drawn up by the National Conference of Commissioners on Uniform State Laws, and the variations from state to state were fewer than they had once been. Further, state and interregional animosities, once so characteristic of American federalism, had moderated, making the need for a diversity jurisdiction less important.

On substantive questions of law, *Erie* required federal courts to apply the common law of the state in which they were located. Soon after the case, Congress enacted the Federal Rules of Civil Procedure reforming procedures in the federal courts. All federal courts are governed by these rules regardless of what state procedural rules may be. This division of applicable law is not always tidy, since the line between a procedural and a substantive question may not always be clear.

Despite Brandeis's emphatic statement, *Erie* did not completely end federal common law. In many areas, neither state statutes nor court decisions are applicable enough to decide a question. In such cases, federal judges make common law, though their decisions no longer form a separate body of it as they once did.

Federal Supervisory Authority

Despite the principle of comity, the lower federal courts can be asked to check alleged unconstitutional state acts in cases already under state jurisdiction. Such petitioning, which often seeks to enjoin state officials or gain the release of state-held prisoners on writs of habeas corpus, has been a source of tension within the dual court system created by federalism.

Enjoining State Officials. The Eleventh Amendment bars federal courts from hearing suits against a state by an out-of-state citizen, but in *Osborn v. Bank of United States* (1824) and in *Ex parte Young* (1908), the Supreme Court held that it did not bar suits brought in federal courts against state officials. In *Young,* shareholders of a railroad subject to new state rate regulations won a temporary injunction against the state attorney general. It kept him from enforcing the rates until it could be determined whether they were confiscatory and thus a violation of the due process clause of the Fourteenth Amendment. *Young* was not a popular decision, and two years later Congress required that injunctions of state laws by federal courts be issued only by three-judge panels with a direct appeal to the Supreme Court. Ironically, federal injunctive power, sustained by a conservative court to protect corporate shareholders, has often been used, especially during the Warren years, on behalf criminal defendants against allegedly unconstitutional acts.

The power was greatly expanded in *Dombrowski v. Pfister* (1967), in which a three-judge federal district court had denied Dombrowski's request that Louisiana officials be enjoined from prosecuting or threatening to prosecute an organization he headed, under state subversion statutes. He had argued that the statutes violated the First Amendment and were used to harass him in order to get the organization's records. The Supreme Court reversed, upholding federal injunctive relief because the state statutes were clearly unconstitutional and continual threats of prosecution had a chilling effect on freedom of speech.

The decision opened the door to scores of suits by criminal defendants seeking federal injunctions against state prosecutors. This prompted reconsideration of the matter by the Burger Court in *Younger v. Harris* (1971). Indicted under a California criminal syndicalism statute similar to an Ohio statute the Court had held unconstitutional two years before, Harris got a federal injunction against his California prosecutor. But the Supreme Court, dis-

tinguishing *Dombrowski,* held it should not have been issued. It found no showing of harassment or bad-faith prosecution. Justice Black's opinion for the Court, a paean to federalism, underlined the importance of comity and the narrow circumstances that would allow federal courts to intervene in pending state cases.

Removal of State Cases. Technically, habeas corpus—"you have the body," in literal translation—is a judicial writ that may be petitioned for by a person jailed or otherwise held. If issued, it orders the detaining authority to bring the person before the court and explain the reasons for detention. In most cases, the practical effect of the writ is to allow a convicted person to assert that errors made at trial denied a constitutional right. All courts, state and federal, have the power to issue writs on officers in their own jurisdiction. But in the Habeas Corpus Act of 1867, the Reconstruction Congress gave lower federal courts authority to issue the writ on state officials. By that, it empowered them to review state criminal convictions, including those that may have been upheld by the highest court of the state. Though first aimed at protecting federal officers in the South from harassment by local officials and at gaining the release of former slaves held unlawfully, the act has become a means for federal intervention in state criminal justice proceedings.

Federal judges issued the writ generously during the Warren years. The state cases "reviewed" were a way by which new criminal justice rights of the Warren Court could be applied to the states and meant that petitioners did not have to appeal to the Supreme Court. In *Fay v. Noia* (1963), for example, the Court ruled that the writ could be issued even if state prisoners had not raised their federal constitutional claims in state court, so long as they had not deliberately bypassed state procedures. As a result, federal habeas corpus petitions from state prisoners rose ninefold to more than 9,000 annually between 1961 and 1971. Also increasing dramatically was the resentment of state judges, who complained that convictions upheld in the highest state courts could be overturned by a single federal district court judge.

It is not surprising that the more conservative and state-minded Burger and Rehnquist Courts should cut back on the supervisory role of the lower federal courts. In *Stone v. Powell* (1976), the Court held that if state courts had given chance for a full and fair hearing of federal constitutional claims, those issues could not be raised again through federal habeas corpus action. In *Coleman v. Thompson* (1991), in which the attorney for a death row prisoner had missed a deadline for filing an appeal, the Court departed from *Fay v. Noia* to hold that inadvertent failure of a defendant's lawyer to raise a constitutional right or to meet a state court deadline was not ground for granting the habeas corpus writ. Finally, in *Brecht v. Abrahamson* (1993), the Court held that petitioning state prisoners must show that an alleged state trial error had "a substantial and injurious effect" on the jury's verdict rather than the state needing to prove such error "harmless beyond reasonable doubt."

Adequate and Independent State Grounds. The Judiciary Act of 1789 gave the Supreme Court appellate jurisdiction over state cases raising federal questions but not over those presenting only questions of state law. Rulings by the highest state courts on purely state law matters were final. The Supreme Court reaffirmed the independence of state courts on purely state law in *Murdoch v. Memphis* (1873), setting out principles that became known as the doctrine of adequate and independent state grounds. Freely translated, this means that if a state decision appealed to the Supreme Court rests on both federal and state law and the state ground alone is enough to support the decision, the decision will stand even if the Court finds the state court's reliance on federal law to have been in error.

In the 1970s, this long-standing doctrine began to get new attention and force. It was congenial with the Burger Court's version of cooperative federalism and its determination to show greater deference to the state judiciaries. Also, as that Court's slowness to expand Warren Court criminal justice decisions became clear, many liberal proponents of individual rights looked to state courts to go beyond federal protections in what has sometimes been called the "new judicial federalism." All state constitutions contain Bills of Rights, many provisions of which are similar if not identical to those in the federal Bill of Rights. Moreover, many state constitutions contain rights on such matters as privacy, environmental protection, and collective bargaining not expressly found in the federal Constitution.

One of the difficulties in applying the adequate and independent state grounds principle is that many state cases that contain both federal and state bases for decision are unclear on which there has been reliance. The problem was addressed by the Supreme Court in *Michigan v. Long* (1983) (p. 512), in which the Michigan Supreme Court had reversed a criminal conviction because a search on which it was based violated the Fourth Amendment of the federal Constitution and Article I-2 of the Michigan Constitution. The U. S. Supreme Court reversed, holding that in its settled interpretation of the Fourth Amendment the search was constitutional. But might it still have been unconstitutional under the Michigan Constitution? For the Court, Justice O'Connor held that where it was not clear which of two grounds were the basis of decision, the Supreme Court would presume the state court had relied on federal law. For the adequate and independent state grounds principle to apply, the state court would need to make its reliance on state law or constitution clear in a "plain statement."

Many civil liberties-minded state courts took the requirement in *Long* seriously. There are now several hundred cases in which state supreme courts have given individual rights identical in federal and state constitutions broader interpretation than called for by the federal. Though this has heartened proponents of the new judicial federalism, optimism may be precariously placed. Historically, state supreme courts have not been in the forefront of the protection of individual rights. State constitutions are usually easier to amend than the federal, and state judges, many of whom are elected, are more subject to political and popular pressures than are their federal counterparts.

State Regulation of Interstate Commerce

One of the chief economic aims of the framers was to prevent states from erecting trade barriers against one another to favor local interests against those out of state. Believing such balkanizing, would inhibit economic growth and be a barrier to unity perhaps even leading to hostilities, they nationalized power over interstate commerce and at the same time placed limits on state powers. Among the latter were restrictions on coining of money, issuance of bills of credit, entering into trade pacts, and the taxing of imports or exports except to execute inspection laws.

In Article I-8 they committed the regulation of interstate and foreign commerce to Congress, but remained silent on whether states might regulate interstate commerce directly, incidentally, or at all. The matter is further complicated by states having unquestioned power to regulate commerce within their borders, to tax, and to exercise police powers for the protection of public health, safety, and welfare. When Congress does deal with interstate or foreign commerce, its regulations are supreme and any state laws in conflict must give way. But through much of the nation's early history, Congress did little regulating of interstate commerce.

In its 1852 *Cooley v. Board of Wardens* decision, the Supreme Court had rejected two theories of the commerce power in favor of a third. Unlike the taxing power, the power over commerce was not the fully concurrent one that would leave the states free to act in the absence of opposing federal laws. Nor did the

Court accept the so-called dormant power theory, that vestment of commerce power in Congress meant that states could not regulate at all, whether Congress had exercised its power or not. Instead, the "Cooley Rule," sometimes called the theory of selective exclusion, held that where Congress had been silent, states might regulate provided the matter at hand did not call for a uniform rule; if uniformity was necessary, states could not regulate.

Cooley was a bridge to modern commerce clause interpretation, but it raised as many questions as it answered. Commerce, unlike law and politics, usually did not observe state lines, and the distinction between inter- and intrastate commerce became increasingly artificial. Economic growth, as the framers had foreseen, called for a national marketplace uninhibited by state barriers. Many businesses, including the fastest growing, were multistate in operation and products routinely crossed state lines. At the same time, states had valid revenue needs and valid police responsibilities to protect state and local citizens. How could these be realized without discriminating against out-of-state businesses or favoring in-state? This has become the central question of the modern commerce power. We examine it here looking at how states have regulated transport, the access of out-of-state sellers to in-state markets, and the access of out-of-state buyers to in-state resources.

Transport

Two cases of the Roosevelt Court with contrasting results illustrate the Court's general method. A South Carolina law had barred trucks more than 90 feet wide or more than 10 tons gross weight from roads in the state, but all other states permitted the standard width of 96 inches and all but four permitted weights greater than 10 tons. In upholding the state's regulations in *South Carolina State Highway Dept. v. Barnwell Bros.* (1938), the Court stressed the state law's safety features and, in *Cooley* fashion, the local nature of highway regulations. Noting that the regulations applied equally to intra- and interstate traffic, it concluded the burdens on the second were not unreasonable. If *Barnwell* might be decided differently today, it would probably be because of the changed nature of highways and highway traffic rather than application of a different analysis.

In *Southern Pacific v. Arizona* (1945) (p. 500), the Court dealt with a the state's Train Limit Law that barred passenger trains of more than 14 cars and freight trains of more than 70. Here the Court was less persuaded of safety gains and more impressed that the car limits were a burden falling more heavily on interstate runs than on those entirely within the state. The two decisions show that states may regulate interstate transport for police ends, but the burdens imposed must not be substantial or fall more heavily on interstate commerce. The Court has recognized that out-of-state interests, unlike in-state, have less influence in the state legislature and thus less chance of politically checking burdensome regulations. The South Carolina weight and width limits, for example, which fell mainly on in-state interests, were modified by the legislature three months after *Barnwell*.

Later transport cases have not freed the Court from close scrutiny of safety regulations. In *Bibb v. Navaho Freight Lines* (1959), it invalidated an Illinois law that required all trucks to have contoured, as opposed to flat, mudguards. Flat mudguards were legal in 45 other states and were actually required in one. The Court held that the contoured guards, having no safety advantages, unacceptably burdened interstate commerce. An Iowa law at issue in *Kassel v. Consolidated Freightways* (1981), barred 65-foot double-trailers, which meant that interstate trucking companies using them had to route their vehicles around the state or reload to smaller ones at the state line. The Court found that any reduction in accidents from the use or smaller trucks was offset by a probable increase that would result from greater truck mileage.

Incoming Commerce

Though the Court has not found the task of separating permissible state regulations and taxes from impermissible an easy task, two basic principles are clear. First, states have a valid interest in the health of the local economy, the safety and well-being of the citizenry, the conservation of local resources, and the fair financing of government programs and operations. Second, the national interest requires that out-of-state commercial interests not be discriminated against inadvertently or by design, to the advantage of local business. As a few examples will show, these principles are often in conflict.

Where a Wisconsin city made it illegal to sell milk not processed at pasteurization plants within five miles from the city, the Court found public health concerns were outweighed by the discrimination against out-of-state milk producers. In *Dean Milk Co. v. City of Madison* (1951), it held that valid health concerns could be met by "reasonable nondiscriminatory alternatives," such as having city inspectors go to more distant plants and charging the cost of such inspection to the producers.

In *Hunt v. Washington State Applegrowers Advertising Commission* (1977), the Court struck down a North Carolina apple labeling regulation that disallowed any state's grading information to be shown, ostensibly to guard against consumer fraud. Having a substantial apple industry of its own, North Carolina had discriminated against competing Washington State growers by not allowing labels that showed that Washington's strict grading, which could denote high-quality apples.

Where the Court has been persuaded by health or safety claims, it has sustained regulations even if their burden fell more heavily on out-of-state than in-state business. As an environmental conservation measure, Minnesota had banned the sale of milk in plastic, unrefillable containers but permitted sale in paperboard milk cartons. The Court upheld the measure in

Minnesota v. Cloverleaf Creamery (1981) despite its obvious boon for the large in-state paper products industry.

The Court went yet further in accepting a discriminatory effect in *Maine v. Taylor* (1986) (p. 520), in which the state had banned the importation of live baitfish to protect local fish from lethal parasites often carried by imports. The total ban was permissible because there was no reasonable, less discriminatory alternative for combating the parasites and protecting the state's fragile aquatic balance.

Outright economic protectionism untempered by health or safety gain is almost certain to be struck down as it was in *Wyoming v. Oklahoma* (1992), in which Oklahoma had required power companies in the state buy at least 10 percent of their coal from Oklahoma mines.

In raising revenue, states may tax those who benefit from state services. But levies on property, income, or sales may raise commerce clause questions if they fall on out-of-state businesses. In *Complete Auto Transit v. Brady* (1977), the Court developed a four-part test for analyzing the validity of such taxes when they affect interstate commerce. Mississippi had placed a 5 percent levy on the gross income from Mississippi operations of intra- and interstate companies. A Michigan corporation that unloaded new cars shipped into Mississippi by train and then trucked them to local dealers, challenged the tax as one imposed on "the privilege of doing business" in interstate commerce. The Court overruled earlier decisions and held such taxes were valid if they (1) were on activity having a substantial connection with the state, (2) were fairly apportioned, (3) did not discriminate against interstate business, and (4) were fairly related to state services such as police and fire protection.

The new test was stretched in *Commonwealth Edison v. Montana* (1981) to uphold a 30 percent tax on coal mined in the state. Despite a showing that 90 percent of the coal was shipped to other states, the Court held the tax did not discriminate against interstate commerce because it fell at an equal rate on all buyers. That the scheme allowed Montana to export much of the burden of its state budget to consumers who had no political representation in the state, did not persuade the Court otherwise.

Growth in mail order catalog sales in recent years has hurt local retail merchants and offered an inviting target for state revenue taxation. In *Quill v. North Dakota* (1992), a state *use* tax (the equivalent of sales tax for goods bought out of state) that required collection by the out-of-state seller, was challenged by an office supplies company that had annual sales of $1,000,000 in North Dakota but no employees, offices, or property in the state. All sales were by direct mail or telephone. The Court held the tax, though not violating due process, burdened interstate commerce because the company lacking a physical presence in the state, did not have the needed "substantial connection" with the state. The Court noted the absence of national legislation and stressed that Congress could authorize the states to collect use taxes on catalog sales.

Tax schemes that work to effect local protection, even though indirectly, are readily struck down. In *West Lynn Creamery v. Healy* (1994), an out-of-state milk dealer challenged a Massachusetts policy that required contributions to a state "Dairy Equalization Fund" based on milk sold in the state, regardless of where it was produced. The Court held the scheme to be an unconstitutional burden on interstate commerce because the fund was used to subsidize the troubled Massachusetts dairy industry, in part to allow it to compete with lower-cost out-of-state producers.

State taxation may also raise a constitutional issue when it applies to goods imported from other countries. The commerce clause gives Congress the power to regulate foreign and interstate commerce, while the exports-imports clause of Article I-10 bars the states from taxing imports or exports for raising revenue. The framers feared that states with large ports might heavily tax foreign goods and so discriminate against other states in which some of the goods would eventually be sold. In *Brown v. Maryland* (1827), the Marshall Court had drawn a line with the "original package" doctrine, excluding imports from state levies as long as they remained in their shipping containers. But in *Michelin Tire Corp. v. Wages* (1976), the Court retreated from this rule by upholding a value-based property tax applied to imported tires and accessories stored in their original containers in a warehouse awaiting distribution to retail outlets. It held that neither *Brown* nor the export-import clause barred states from including imports in nondiscriminatory uniform taxes on inventory warehoused in the state.

Outgoing Commerce and State Resources

Many of the issues created by the regulation or taxation of out-of-state sellers also arise where states have tried to limit out-of-state use of resources or local production. The Supreme Court has long held that discrimination against out-of-state consumers would violate commerce clause principles. In *Hood v. DuMond* (1949), for example, it ruled that New York could not ensure the supply of milk for local markets by barring in-state companies from processing milk to serve Massachusetts markets.

Similarly, in *Philadelphia v. New Jersey* (1978) (p. 509), it held that the state could not try to extend the life of its dwindling landfill sites for disposing of liquid and solid waste by closing them to waste from other states. The Court recognized the state's environmental goal, but viewed the state's restriction as a form of protectionism to fence out a national problem. The following year in *Hughes v. Oklahoma,* it departed from a previously held legal fiction that all wild animals within a state were "owned" by the state and were thus not in interstate commerce. Though admitting the state's valid conservation interest, it overturned an Oklahoma statute that barred the export of minnows taken in Oklahoma waters.

Nor may a state prevent a private power company from selling locally generated power to out-of-state users. In *New England Power Co. v. New Hampshire* (1982), the Court held that state-imposed priorities requiring that the needs of in-state consumers be served first, was unconstitutional. Finally, the Court has disallowed discriminatory taxation that had a subsidization effect in the use of landfills. In *Oregon Waste Systems v. Department of Environmental Quality* (1994), it held that a tax on out-of-state waste three times higher than that on in-state, even though fair as to disposal cost, was invalid as a form of protectionism. That it was an attempt to protect resources rather than economic interests did not matter.

The Court has taken a different view where the state is a "market participant," that is, a producer or seller itself rather than a regulator or taxing authority. For example, in *Hughes v. Alexandria Scrap Corp.* (1976), the Court upheld a Maryland policy in which the state, to rid itself of abandoned cars, paid in-state scrap dealers a premium for crushed hulks but refused to buy any from out-of-state dealers. In *Reeves v. Stake* (1980), the Court did not limit a state's permissible market participatory actions to environmental matters. In contrast to its decision in *New England Power* in which the state acted as a regulator, it upheld a South Dakota policy of giving in-state cement buyers preference at state-owned cement plants during periods of shortage. In these cases, in which the state owns the resources and discriminates in favor of its citizens, the Court has treated the policy as a form of in-state welfare rather than a protectionist burden on interstate commerce.

The distinction, however, may be a fine one. In *White v. Massachusetts Council of Construction Employees* (1983), for example, the Court upheld an order by the mayor of Boston that at least half the workers in construction projects paid for by the city be Boston residents. Because such preferential policies are typically economically inefficient for the state's general taxpayers, the Court has, in effect, relied on the political forces within the state to act as a check on discriminatory excess.

Interstate Relations

Issues of federalism also arise from relations between and among the states. The framers, all too aware of conflicts that had arisen among 13 near-independent states, addressed this element of federalism at several important points. In Article I-10 they barred states from making compacts with each other without the consent of Congress. In Article IV-1 each state is required to give "full faith and credit" to official proceedings of other states. In Article IV-2, citizens of each state are entitled to the "privileges and immunities of citizens of the several states." Also in Article IV-2, states are required to return fugitives from justice to the state having jurisdiction over the crime.

Full Faith and Credit

In the interest of national unity and to discourage one state from nullifying the effect of valid acts in another, the framers required that each recognize the official proceedings of all others. Article IV-1 transforms comity, long a principle of international law, from courtesy to legal duty. The first Congress quickly passed legislation requiring the judicial proceedings and public records of a state be honored in the courts of all other states. This holds even where a decision would not have been permitted under a second state's laws or public policy. That state may ask only whether the issuing court had jurisdiction on which to base its decision; it may not take up substantive issues in the case.

Divorce actions have created a problem where a state, Nevada for example, has granted divorces liberally by requiring that only one spouse need to have lived in the state and only for a few days or weeks. Concern that these divorces were, in effect, ex parte decrees that might foreclose all marital issues in the home state, led the Court to hold in *Estin v. Estin* (1948) that a divorce decree might be "divisible." The decree granted by the short-term residence of one party would be binding on the matter of marital status, but not conclusive of such other questions as child custody, alimony, and disposition of property.

Privileges and Immunities

The privileges and immunities obligation imposed by Article IV-2 requiring each state to treat citizens of another state as it would its own, is distinct from the privileges and immunities clause of the fourteenth Amendment that bars a state from abridging rights associated with the national citizenship. Though the Article IV-2 requirement does not say what privileges and immunities are, the framers hoped to prevent discrimination against citizens of other states and, by that, to foster national unity.

Yet the Supreme Court has held the clause not to prevent all distinctions between state and out-of-state citizens. For example, states may charge out-of-state students at state-run colleges and universities higher tuition, charge out-of-state residents higher fees for hunting licenses, and require out-of-state lawyers and other professionals to show higher levels of competence to practice in the state. The Court has found that such distinctions serve "substantial state interests" and that local residents have had to pay more taxes to support educational institutions or upkeep of the public domain.

Less well-justified distinctions, however, are likely to be struck down. For example, in *Toomer v. Witsell* (1948), the Court invalidated a South Carolina license fee of $2,500 for out-of-state citizens compared to a $25 fee charged state residents for the privilege of shrimp trawling in the state's coastal waters. In *Supreme Court of New Hampshire v. Piper* (1985), the Court held that though a state might impose absolute residency requirements for voting and holding elective office, it could not bar an out-of-state lawyer from practicing solely because she was a nonresident.

The Court has closely scrutinized durational residency requirements that out-of-state citizens must satisfy before becoming eligible for state benefits or privileges. Using the equal protection clause of the Fourteenth Amendment and the right to travel, it ruled invalid any residency requirement for welfare benefits or medical care in *Shapiro v. Thompson* (1969), and a one-year requirement for voting in *Dunn v. Blaustein* (1972). On the other hand, it upheld a one-year requirement for getting a divorce in *Sosna v. Iowa* (1975), and for an out-of-state student to be eligible for in-state tuition rates at a state university in *Vlandis v. Kline* (1973).

The privileges and immunities clause of Article IV-2 has not developed more fully because the Court in dealing with alleged state discrimination has often found it easier to use equal protection principles of the Fourteenth Amendment or, if economic claims are at issue, those of the commerce clause. In *Saenz v. Roe*, 1999, it drew on the largely dormant privileges and immunities clause of the Fourteenth Amendment to invalidate state welfare provisions that limited new residents at first to the level of benefits they would have received in their home states.

Rendition

The full faith and credit obligation does not include enforcement of another state's criminal laws. But the so-called rendition clause of Article IV-2 requires a state to return or "extradite" a fugitive from criminal justice. This obligation was upheld in *Kentucky v. Dennison* (1861), in which Kentucky asked the governor of Ohio return a person charged with helping a slave to escape. But Chief Justice Taney, possibly recognizing that the Ohio governor would not return the fugitive even if ordered by the Court, held the Court lacked authority to force him to do so. The ruling, on the eve the Civil War, though a setback for the slaveholding interest, was also a late bow to state sovereignty. It nonetheless remained a precedent for more than a century. During that time, the vast majority of apprehended criminal fugitives were

returned to their jurisdictional states on request and without incident. In the rare case in which rendition was refused it was usually because of belief that the fugitive was probably innocent and a victim of prejudice or had not had a fair trial, as in the case of one of the rape defendants in the notorious 1930s Scottsboro Case who had fled Alabama to Michigan.

Dennison was finally overruled in *Puerto Rico v. Branstad* (1987). The Court held it had been based on "a now discredited view of federal-state relations" and that the federal courts had full power to order a governor to observe the requirement of the rendition clause. If a state requests the return of a fugitive, courts of the asylum state may ask only whether the person has been charged with a crime in the demanding state and whether he or she is in fact a fugitive. That the crime charged may not be one in the asylum state is irrelevant.

Interstate Disputes

If a disagreement between two or more states has not been resolved by political negotiation and is brought to litigation, Article III-2 refers it directly to the Supreme Court under its original jurisdiction. The framers realized that courts within states would be unsuitable forums for interstate disputes. Though suits between states are not common, they are apt to be factually complex. Because of this and to prevent its time from being taken up with drawn out trials, the Court has usually appointed a "Special Master"—a member of the Supreme Court bar skilled in the subject matter in dispute—to act as a fact finder, hearing witnesses and receiving other evidence. The master's findings are submitted to the Court, which may then hear argument on them. The Court is free to accept the master's report as final, make changes, or reject it.

The law applied to interstate disputes may be state, federal, or even international, as circumstances require. Decisions in interstate disputes have led to a small body of what may be called interstate common law.

Interstate Compacts

Article I-10, the Constitution's great negative on state powers, forbids states to enter into treaties, alliances, or confederations, thus giving the national government a monopoly in foreign affairs. The section also bars them from entering into agreements or compacts with each other without the consent of Congress. Here, the framers' chief concerns were that regional trade barriers not be formed and that state power not be made greater at the expense of national. Despite or perhaps because of these limits on state authority, interstate compacts have proved highly constructive instruments and have raised few constitutional issues.

Through the first quarter of the twentieth century, there were fewer than 40 interstate compacts and many dealt with unimportant boundary or land cession issues. Since then, states have made scores of formal agreements on a wide range of matters, allowing them to be addressed on a wider, regional basis. These have included transport, conservation, pollution control, utility regulation, crime control, and contingent planning for emergencies and disasters. Though the compact has been only a footnote to the much larger text of government centralization, it has served to invigorate state initiative and responsibility.

Congress has sometimes authorized compacts in advance; more often it has approved them after the fact. Despite clear wording in Article I-10, the Supreme Court has ruled that Congress need not give express approval. In *Virginia v. Tennessee* (1893), Virginia disputed a 90-year-old boundary agreement because it had never been approved by Congress. But Justice Field held that so long as a compact did not increase the powers of the states at the national government's expense or diminish the sovereignty of other states, it need not have express approval. This practical rule is still followed and relieves Congress of the burden of looking at every agreement between two or more states. It was reaffirmed in *United States Steel v. Multi-State Tax Commission* (1978), holding Congressional approval was not needed for an 21-state compact to set up an apparatus for auditing multistate taxpayers.

A compact once made, however, joins federal statutes and treaties as supreme law, and a signer state may not withdraw from it unilaterally. In *West Virginia ex. rel. Dyer v. Sims* (1951), the Court overturned a ruling of the West Virginia Supreme Court that provisions of an eight-state compact entered into in 1940 to control pollution of the Ohio River system, violated the state's constitution. Normally, the Court accepts a state supreme court's interpretation of its constitution as final, but here, it felt free to uphold the compact because it affected rights of other states. As with other disputes between states, those of interstate compacts are subject to the Court's original jurisdiction, and all questions raised may be decided by the Court with finality.

FURTHER READING

Modern Federalism

Anton, Thomas, *American Federalism and Public Policy* (1989)

Beer, Samuel H., *To Make a Nation: A Rediscovery of American Federalism* (1993)

Conlin, Timothy, *The New Federalism: Intergovernmental Reform from Nixon to Reagan* (1988)

_____, From New Federalism to Devolution: Twenty-Five Years of Intergovernmental Reform (1998)

Davis, S. Rufus, The Federal Principle: A Journey Through Time in Quest of Meaning (1978)

Donohue, John D., *Disunited States* (1997)

Dye, Thomas R., *American Federalism: Competition Among Governments* (1990)

Elazar, Daniel, *American Federalism: The View from the States* (1984)

Friedelbaum, Stanley H., *The Rehnquist Court: In Pursuit of Judicial Conservatism* (1993)

Gittel, Marilyn, *State Politics and the New Federalism* (1986)

Goldwin, Robert A. and William A. Schambra, eds., *How Federal Is the Constitution?* (1987)

Goodwin, Frank, *The Supreme Court's Federalism, Real or Imagined?* (2001)

Hall, Kermit L., ed., *Federalism: A Nation of States* (1987)

Kettl, Donald F., *The Regulation of American Federalism* (1983)

Lofgren, Charles A., *"Government from Reflection and Choice": Constitutional Essays on War Foreign Relations, and Federalism* (1986)

Ostrom, Vincent, *The Meaning of American Federalism: Constituting a Self-Governing Society* (1991)

Peterson, Paul E., *The Price of Federalism* (1995)

————, Barry G. Rabe, and Kenneth K. Wong, *When Federalism Works* (1986)

Posner, Paul L., *The Politics of Unfunded Mandates: Whither Federalism* (1998)

Reagan, Michael D., *The New Federalism* (1972)

Redish, Martin, *The Constitution as Political Structure* (1995)

Riker, William, *Federalism: Origin, Operation, Significance* (1964)

Scheiber, Harry N. and Malcolm M. Feeley, eds., *Power Divided: Essays on the Theory and Practice of Federalism* (1988)

Schmidhauser, John, *The Supreme Court as Final Arbitrator of Federal-State Relations* (1958)

Shapiro, David L., *Federalism: A Dialogue* (1995)

Walker, David B., *The Rebirth of Federalism: Slouching toward Washington* (1995)

————, *Toward a Functioning Federalism* (1981)

Wright, Deil S., *Understanding Intergovernmental Relations* (1979)

Zimmerman, Joseph F., *Federal Preemption: The Silent Revolution* (1991)

The Judiciary in a Nation of States

Fino, Susan P., *The Role of the State Supreme Courts in the New Judicial Federalism* (1987)

Fish, Peter Graham, *The Politics of Federal Judicial Administration* (1973)

Frieson, Jennifer, *State Constitutional Law* (1995)

Latzer, Barry, *State Constitutions and Criminal Justice* (1991)

Stumpf, Harry and Culver, John, *The Problems of State Courts* (1992)

Tarr, G. Alan, ed., *Constitutional Politics in the States: Contemporary Controversies and Historical Patterns* (1996)

Tarr, G. Alan, *Understanding State Constitutions* (1998)

Tarr, G. Alan and Porter, Mary C., *State Supreme Courts in State and Nation* (1988)

CASES

Southern Pacific Co. v. Arizona

325 U.S. 761 (1945), 7-2

Opinion of the Court: Stone, C.J. (Frankfurter, Jackson, Murphy, Reed, Roberts, Rutledge)

Dissenting: Black, Douglas

Arizona sued to recover penalties against the company for violating its Train Limit Law, limiting trains operated in the state to 14 passenger cars or 70 freight cars.

What is the Court's test for determining whether a state regulation of commerce affecting interstate commerce may be upheld? How is the Court's formulation more defined than that in Cooley v. Board of Wardens? *Since Congress did not establish a national minimum length for trains, why does this not imply, under the Cooley rule, that the matter does not require uniform regulation and should thus be left to the states? What is the role of the Court where Congress has been silent? Is Black's dissent based mainly on the rights*

of states and thus on considerations of federalism, or on the need to prevent a regulatory void? What interests gain and lose as a result of this decision?

Stone, C.J., for the Court:

Congress, although asked to do so, has declined to pass legislation specifically limiting trains to seventy cars. We are therefore brought to [Southern Pacific's] principal contention, that the state statute contravenes the commerce clause of the Federal Constitution.

Although the commerce clause conferred on the national government power to regulate commerce, its possession of the power does not exclude all state power of regulation. Ever since *Willson v. Black-Bird Creek Marsh* and *Cooley v. Board of Wardens* it has been recognized that, in the absence of conflicting legislation by Congress, there is a residuum of power in the state to make laws governing matters of local concern which nevertheless in some measure affect interstate commerce or even, to some extent, regulate it. Thus the states may regulate matters which, because of their number and diversity, may never be adequately dealt with by Congress. When the regulation of matters of local concern is local in character and effect, and its impact on the national commerce does not seriously interfere with its operation, and the consequent incentive to deal with them nationally is slight, such regulation has been generally held to be within state authority.

But ever since *Gibbons v. Ogden* the states have not been deemed to have authority to impede substantially the free flow of commerce from state to state, or to regulate those phases of the national commerce which, because of the need of national uniformity, demand that their regulation, if any, be prescribed by a single authority. Whether or not this long recognized distribution of power between the national and the state governments is predicated upon the implications of the commerce clause itself, or upon the presumed intention of Congress, where Congress has not spoken, the result is the same.

In the application of these principles some enactments may be found to be plainly within and others plainly without state power. But between these extremes lies the infinite variety of cases in which regulation of local matters may also operate as a regulation of commerce, in which reconciliation of the conflicting claims of state and national power is to be attained only by some appraisal and accommodation of the competing demands of the state and national interests involved.

For a hundred years it has been accepted constitutional doctrine that the commerce clause, without the aid of Congressional legislation, thus affords some protection from state legislation inimical to the national commerce, and that in such cases, where Congress has not acted, this Court, and not the state legislature, is under the commerce clause the final arbiter of the competing demands of state and national interests.

Congress has undoubted power to redefine the distribution of power over interstate commerce. It may either permit the states to regulate the commerce in a manner which would otherwise not be permissible, or exclude state regulation even of matters of peculiarly local concern which nevertheless affect interstate commerce.

But in general Congress has left it to the courts to formulate the rules thus interpreting the commerce clause in its application, doubtless because it has appreciated the destructive consequences to the commerce of the nation if their protection were withdrawn, and has been aware that in their application state laws will not be invalidated without the support of relevant factual material which will 'afford a sure basis' for an informed judgment. Meanwhile, Congress has accommodated its legislation, as have the states, to these rules as an established feature of our constitutional system. There has thus been left to the states wide scope for the regulation of matters of local state concern, even though it in some measure affects the commerce, provided it does not materially restrict the free flow of commerce across state lines, or interfere with it in matters with respect to which uniformity of regulation is of predominant national concern.

Hence the matters for ultimate determination here are the nature and extent of the burden which the state regulation of interstate trains, adopted as a safety measure, imposes on interstate commerce, and whether the relative weights of the state and national interests involved are such as to make inapplicable the rule, generally observed, that the free flow of interstate commerce and its freedom from local restraints in matters requiring uniformity of regulation are interests safeguarded by the commerce clause from state interference. . . .

The findings show that the operation of long trains, that is trains of more than fourteen passenger and more than seventy freight cars, is standard practice over the main lines of the railroads of the United States, and that, if the length of trains is to be regulated at all, national uniformity in the regulation adopted, such as only Congress can prescribe, is practically indispensable to the operation of an efficient and economical national railway system. On many railroads passenger trains of more than fourteen cars and freight trains of more than seventy cars are operated, and on some systems freight trains are run ranging from one hundred and twenty-five to one hundred and sixty cars in length. Outside of Arizona, where the length of trains is not restricted, [Southern Pacific] runs a substantial proportion of long trains. In 1939 on its comparable route for through traffic through Utah and Nevada from 66 to 85% of its freight trains were over 70 cars in length and over 43% of its passenger trains included more than fourteen passenger cars.

In Arizona, approximately 93% of the freight traffic and 95% of the passenger traffic is interstate. Because of the Train Limit Law [Southern Pacific] is required to haul over 30% more trains in Arizona than would otherwise have been necessary. The record shows a definite relationship between operating costs and the length of trains, the increase in length resulting in a reduction of operating costs per car. The additional cost of operation of trains complying with the Train Limit Law in Arizona amounts for the two railroads traversing that state to about $1,000,000 a year. The reduction in train lengths also impedes efficient operation. More locomotives and more manpower are required; the necessary conversion and reconversion of train lengths at terminals and the delay caused by breaking up and remaking long trains upon entering and leaving the state in order to comply with the law, delays the traffic and diminishes its volume moved in a given time, especially when traffic is heavy. . . .

The unchallenged findings leave no doubt that the Arizona Train Limit Law imposes a serious burden on the interstate commerce conducted by [Southern Pacific]. It materially impedes the movement of [its] interstate trains through that state and interposes a substantial obstruction to the national policy proclaimed by Congress, to promote adequate, economical and efficient railway transportation service. Enforcement of the law in Arizona, while train lengths remain unregulated or are regulated by varying standards in other states, must inevitably result in an impairment of uniformity of efficient railroad operation because the railroads are subjected to regulation which is not uniform in its application. Compliance with a state statute limiting train lengths requires interstate trains of a length lawful in other states to be broken up and reconstituted as they enter each state according as it may impose varying limitations upon train lengths. The alternative is for the carrier to conform to the lowest train limit restriction of any of the states through which its trains pass, whose laws thus control the carriers' operations both within and without the regulating state.

Although the seventy car maximum for freight trains is the limitation which has been most commonly proposed, various bills introduced in the state legislatures provided for maximum freight train lengths of from fifty to one hundred and twenty-five cars, and maximum passenger train lengths of from ten to eighteen cars. With such laws in force in states which are interspersed with those having no limit on train lengths, the confusion and difficulty with which interstate operations would be burdened under the varied system of state regulation and the unsatisfied need for uniformity in such regulation, if any, are evident. . . .

If one state may regulate train lengths, so may all the others, and they need not prescribe the same maximum limitation. The practical effect of such regulation is to control train operations beyond the boundaries of the state exacting it because of the necessity of breaking up and reassembling long trains at the nearest terminal points before entering and after leaving the regulating state. The serious impediment to the free flow of commerce by the local regulation of train lengths and the practical necessity that such regulation, if any, must be prescribed by a single body having a nation-wide authority are apparent.

The trial court found that the Arizona law had no reasonable relation to safety, and made train operation more dangerous. Examination of the evidence and the detailed findings makes it clear that this conclusion was rested on facts found which indicate that such increased danger of accident and personal injury as may result from the greater length of trains is more than offset by the increase in the number of accidents resulting from the larger number of trains when train lengths are reduced. In considering the effect of the statute as a safety measure, therefore, the factor of controlling significance for present purposes is not whether there is basis for the conclusion of the Arizona Supreme Court that the increase in length of trains beyond the statutory maximum has an adverse effect upon safety of operation. The decisive question is whether in the circumstances the total effect of the law as a safety measure in reducing accidents and casualties is so slight or problematical as not to outweigh the national interest in keeping interstate commerce free from interferences which seriously impede it and subject it to local regulation which does not have a uniform effect on the interstate train journey which it interrupts . . .

We think . . . that the Arizona Train Limit Law, viewed as a safety measure, affords at most slight and dubious advantage, if any, over unregulated train lengths, because it results in an increase in the number of trains and train operations and the consequent increase in train accidents of a character generally more severe than those due to slack action. Its undoubted effect on the commerce is the regulation, without securing uniformity, of the length of trains operated in interstate commerce, which lack is itself a primary cause of preventing the free flow of commerce by delaying it and by substantially increasing its cost and impairing its efficiency. In these respects the case differs from those where a state, by regulatory measures affecting the commerce, has removed or reduced safety hazards without substantial interference with the interstate movement of trains. Such are measures abolishing the car stove, requiring locomotives to be supplied with electric headlights, providing for full train crews, and for the equipment of freight trains with cabooses. . . .

Here we conclude that the state does go too far. Its regulation of train lengths, admittedly obstructive to interstate train operation, and having a seriously adverse effect on transportation efficiency and economy, passes beyond what is plainly essential for safety since it does not appear that it will lessen rather than increase the danger of accident. Its attempted regulation of the operation of interstate trains cannot establish nation-wide control such as is essential to the maintenance of an efficient transportation system, which Congress alone can prescribe. The state interest cannot be preserved at the expense of the national interest by an enactment which regulates interstate train lengths without securing such control, which is a matter of national concern. . . .

[The state] especially rel[ies] on the full train crew cases and also on *South Carolina Highway Dept. v. Barnwell Bros.*, as supporting the state's authority to regulate the length of interstate trains. While the full train crew laws undoubtedly placed an added financial burden on the railroads in order to serve a local interest, they did not obstruct interstate transportation or seriously impede it. They had no effects outside the state beyond those of packing up and setting down the extra employees at the state boundaries; they involved no wasted use of facilities or serious impairment of transportation efficiency, which are among the factors of controlling weight here. . . .

South Carolina State Highway Dept. v. Barnwell Bros. was concerned with the power of the state to regulate the weight and width of motor cars passing interstate over its highways, a legislative field over which the state has a far more extensive control than over interstate railroads. In that case, and in *Maurer v. Hamilton*, we were at pains to point out that there are few subjects of state regulation affecting interstate commerce which are so peculiarly of local concern as is the use of the state's highways.

Unlike the railroads local highways are built, owned and maintained by the state or its municipal subdivisions. The state is responsible for their safe and economical administration. Regulations affecting the safety of their use must be applied alike to intrastate and interstate traffic. The fact that they affect alike shippers in interstate and intrastate commerce in great numbers, within as well as without the state, is a safeguard against regulatory abuses. Their regulation is akin to quarantine measures, game laws, and like local regulations of rivers, harbors, piers, and docks, with respect to which the state has exceptional scope for the exercise of its regulatory power, and which, Congress not acting, have been sustained even though they materially interfere with interstate commerce.

The contrast between the present regulation and the full train crew laws in point of their effects on the commerce, and the like contrast with the highway safety regulations, in point of the nature of the subject of regulation and the state's interest in it, illustrate and emphasize the considerations which enter into a determination of the relative weights of state and national interests where state regulation affecting interstate commerce is attempted. Here examination of all the relevant factors makes it plain that the state interest is outweighed by the interest of the nation in an adequate, economical and efficient railway transportation service, which must prevail.

Black, dissenting:

[W]hether it is in the interest of society for the length of trains to be governmentally regulated is a matter of public policy. Someone must fix that policy—either the Congress, or the state, or the courts. A century and a half of constitutional history and government admonishes this Court to leave that choice to the elected legislative representatives of the people themselves, where it properly belongs both on democratic principles and the requirements of efficient government.

I think that legislatures, to the exclusion of courts, have the constitutional power to enact laws limiting train lengths, for the purpose of reducing injuries brought about by 'slack movements.' Their power is not less because a requirement of short trains might increase grade crossing accidents. This latter fact raises an entirely different element of danger which is itself subject to legislative regulation. For legislatures may, if necessary, require railroads to take appropriate steps to reduce the likelihood of injuries at grade crossings. And the fact that grade crossing improvements may be expensive is no sufficient reason to say that an unconstitutional 'burden' is put upon a railroad even though it be an interstate road. . . .

There have been many sharp divisions of this Court concerning its authority, in the absence of congressional enactment, to invalidate state laws as violating the Commerce Clause . . . [E]ven the broadest exponents of judicial power in this field have not heretofore expressed doubt as to a state's power, absent a paramount congressional declaration, to regulate interstate trains in the interest of safety. For as early as 1913, this Court, speaking through Mr. Justice Hughes, later Chief Justice, referred to 'the settled principle that, in the absence of legislation by Congress, the states are not denied the exercise of that power to secure safety in the physical operation of railroad trains within their territory, even though such trains are used in interstate commerce. That has been the law since the beginning of railroad transportation.' Until today, the oft-repeated principles of that case have never been repudiated in whole or in part. . . .

[M]any employees have been seriously injured and killed in the past, and that many more are likely to be so in the future, because of 'slack movement' in trains. Everyday knowledge as well as direct evidence presented at the various hearings, substantiates the report of the Senate Committee that the danger from slack movement is greater in long trains than in short trains. It may be that offsetting dangers are possible in the operation of short trains. The balancing of these probabilities, however, is not in my judgment a matter for judicial determination, but one which calls for legislative consideration. Representatives elected by the people to make their laws, rather than judges appointed to interpret those laws, can best determine the policies which govern the people. That at least is the basic principle on which our democratic society rests.

Pennsylvania v. Nelson

350 U.S. 497 (1956), 6-3
Opinion of the Court: Warren, C.J. (Clark, Douglas, Frankfurter, Harlan)
Dissenting: Burton, Minton, Reed
What are the criteria for preemption or supercession of state law by federal? What reasons does Warren give for why supercession is reasonable or desirable in this case? Are analogies to preemptive federal regulation of interstate commerce valid or not? Has the Court here substituted its judgment for that of Congress, as Reed suggests, or has it interpreted Congress's intent correctly? If Congress has not been clear about supercession or has not thought about it, is it the Court's responsibility to decide the matter? Since Congress has extensively and repeatedly made seditious acts against the federal government criminal, why would more than 40 states do the same?

Warren, C.J., for the Court:

Steve Nelson, an acknowledged member of the Communist Party, was convicted in the Court of Quarter Sessions of Allegheny County, Pennsylvania, of a violation of the Pennsylvania Sedition Act and sentenced to imprisonment for twenty years and to a fine of $10,000 and to costs of prosecution in the sum of $13,000 . . . The Supreme Court of Pennsylvania, recognizing but not reaching many alleged serious trial errors and conduct of the trial court infringing upon [Nelson's] right to due process of law, decided the case on the narrow issue of supersession of the state law by the Federal Smith Act. . . .

The precise holding of the [Pennsylvania] court, and all that is before us for review, is that the Smith Act of 1940, as amended in 1948, which prohibits the knowing advocacy of the overthrow of the Government of the United States by force and violence, supersedes the enforceability of the Pennsylvania Sedition Act which proscribes the same conduct. . . .

It should be said at the outset that [our] decision . . . does not affect the right of States to enforce their sedition laws at times when the Federal Government has not occupied the field and is not protecting the entire country from seditious conduct. The distinction between the two situations was clearly recognized by the court below. . . .

In this case, we think that each of several tests of supersession is met.

First, '(t)he scheme of federal regulation (is) so pervasive as to make reasonable the inference that Congress left no room for the States to supplement it.' The Congress determined in 1940 that it was necessary for it to re-enter the field of anti-subversive legislation, which had been abandoned by it in 1921. In that year, it enacted the Smith Act which proscribes advocacy of the overthrow of any government—federal, state or local—by force and violence and organization of and knowing membership in a group which so advocates. Conspiracy to commit any of these acts is punishable under the general criminal conspiracy provisions. [Here, the Court considers the antisedition provisions of the Internal Security Act of 1950 and the Communist Control Act of 1954]. . . .

We examine these Acts only to determine the congressional plan. Looking to all of them in the aggregate, the conclusion is inescapable that Congress has intended to occupy the field of sedition. Taken as a whole, they evince a congressional plan which makes it reasonable to determine that no room has been left for the States to supplement it. Therefore, a state sedition statute is superseded regardless of whether it purports to supplement the federal law. As was said by Mr. Justice Holmes in *Charleston & Western Carolina R. Co. v. Varnville Furniture Co.*: 'When Congress has taken the particular subject-matter in hand, coincidence is as ineffective as opposition, and a state law is not to be declared a help because it attempts to go farther than Congress has seen fit to go.'

Second, the federal statutes 'touch a field in which the federal interest is so dominant that the federal system (must) be assumed to preclude enforcement of state laws on the same subject.' Congress has . . . accordingly proscribed sedition against all government in the nation—national, state and local. Congress declared that these steps were taken 'to provide for the common defense, to preserve the sovereignty of the United States as an independent nation, and to guarantee to each State a republican form of government . . .' Congress having thus treated seditious conduct as a matter of vital national concern, it is in no sense a local enforcement problem. . . .

Third, enforcement of state sedition acts presents a serious danger of conflict with the administration of the federal program. Since 1939, in order to avoid a hampering of uniform enforcement of its program by sporadic local prosecutions, the Federal Government has urged local authorities not to intervene in such matters, but to turn over to the federal authorities immediately and unevaluated all information concerning subversive activities. . . .

In his brief, the Solicitor General states that forty-two States plus Alaska and Hawaii have statutes which in some form prohibit advocacy of the violent overthrow of established government. These statutes are entitled anti-sedition statutes, criminal anarchy laws, criminal syndicalist laws, etc. Although all of them are primarily directed against the overthrow of the United States Government, they are in no sense uniform. And our attention has not been called to any case where the prosecution has been successfully directed against an attempt to destroy state or local government. . . .

Should the States be permitted to exercise a concurrent jurisdiction in this area, federal enforcement would encounter . . . conflict engendered by different criteria of substantive offenses.

Since we find that Congress has occupied the field to the exclusion of parallel state legislation, that the dominant interest of the Federal Government precludes state intervention, and that administration of state Acts would conflict with the operation of the federal plan. . . .

Reed (Burton, Minton), dissenting:
Congress has not, in any of its statutes relating to sedition, specifically barred the exercise of state power to punish the same Acts under state law. . . .

First, the Court relies upon the pervasiveness of the antisubversive legislation embodied in the Smith Act of 1940, the Internal Security Act of 1950, and the Communist Control Act of 1954. It asserts that these Acts in the aggregate mean that Congress has occupied the 'field of sedition' to the exclusion of the States. The 'occupation of the field' argument has been developed by this Court for the Commerce Clause and legislation thereunder to prevent partitioning of this country by locally erected trade barriers. . . .

But the federal sedition laws are distinct criminal statutes that punish willful advocacy of the use of force against 'the government of the United States or the government of any State.' These criminal laws proscribe certain local activity without creating any statutory or administrative regulation. There is, consequently, no question as to whether some general congressional regulatory scheme might be upset by a coinciding state plan. In these circumstances the conflict should be clear and direct before this Court reads a congressional intent to void state legislation into the federal sedition acts. . . .

[I]t is quite apparent that since 1940 Congress has been keenly aware of the magnitude of existing state legislation proscribing sedition. It may be validly assumed that in these circumstances this Court should not void state legislation without a clear mandate from Congress.

We cannot agree that the federal criminal sanctions against sedition directed at the United States are of such a pervasive character as to indicate an intention to void state action.

Secondly, the Court states that the federal sedition statutes touch a field 'in which the federal interest is so dominant' they must preclude state laws on the same subject... The Court in *[Hines v.] Davidowitz* ruled that federal statutes compelling alien registration preclude enforcement of state statutes requiring alien registration. We read Davidowitz to teach nothing more than that when the Congress provided a single nation-wide integrated system of regulation so complete as that for aliens' registration (with fingerprinting, a scheduling of activities, and continuous information as to their residence), the Act bore so directly on our foreign relations as to make it evident that Congress intended only one uniform national alien registration system.

We look upon the Smith Act as a provision for controlling incitements to overthrow by force and violence the Nation, or any State, or any political subdivision of either. Such an exercise of federal police power carries... no such dominancy over similar state powers as might be attributed to continuing federal regulations concerning foreign affairs or coinage, for example. In the responsibility of national and local governments to protect themselves against sedition, there is no 'dominant interest.'...

Thirdly, the Court finds ground for abrogating Pennsylvania's anti-sedition statute because, in the Court's view, the State's administration of the Act may hamper the enforcement of the federal law... The Court's attitude as to interference seems to us quite contrary to that of the Legislative and Executive Departments. Congress was advised of the existing state sedition legislation when the Smith Act was enacted and has been kept current with its spread. No declaration of exclusiveness followed....

Mere fear by courts of possible difficulties does not seem to us in these circumstances a valid reason for ousting a State from exercise of its police power. Those are matters for legislative determination.

Finally, and this one point seems in and of itself decisive, there is an independent reason for reversing the Pennsylvania Supreme Court. The Smith Act appears in Title 18 of the United States Code, which Title codifies the federal criminal laws. Section 3231 of that Title provides: 'Nothing in this title shall be held to take away or impair the jurisdiction of the courts of the several States under the laws thereof.' That declaration springs from the federal character of our Nation. It recognizes the fact that maintenance of order and fairness rests primarily with the States. The section was first enacted in 1825 and has appeared successively in the federal criminal laws since that time. This Court has interpreted the section to mean that

States may provide concurrent legislation in the absence of explicit congressional intent to the contrary. The majority's position in this case cannot be reconciled with that clear authorization of Congress.

Heart of Atlanta Motel v. United States

379 U.S. 241 (1964), 9-0
Opinion of the Court: Clark (Brennan, Harlan, Stewart, Warren, White)
Concurring: Black, Douglas, Goldberg
What connection did Congress and the Court make between race discrimination and interstate commerce? Following Clark's reasoning, are there any theoretical or practical limits to the use of the federal commerce power to end discrimination by privately owned businesses serving the public? What is Douglas's theory for upholding the use of federal power to end private discrimination? Does it raise constitutional questions?

Clark, for the Court:
This is a declaratory judgment action attacking the constitutionality of Title II of the Civil Rights Act of 1964. In addition to declaratory relief, the complaint sought an injunction restraining the enforcement of the Act and damages against [the government] based on allegedly resulting injury in the event compliance was required...

... [T]he Heart of Atlanta Motel... has 216 rooms available to transient guests... It is readily accessible to interstate highways 75 and 85 and state highways 23 and 41. [It] solicits patronage from outside the State of Georgia through various national advertising media, including magazines of national circulation; it maintains over 50 billboards and highway signs within the State, soliciting patronage for the motel; it accepts convention trade from outside Georgia and approximately 75% of its registered guests are from out of State. Prior to passage of the Act, the motel had followed a practice of refusing to rent rooms to Negroes, and it alleged that it intended to continue to do so. In an effort to perpetuate that policy, this suit was filed.

The [motel] contends that Congress, in passing this Act, exceeded its power to regulate commerce under Art. I, of the Constitution; that the Act violates the Fifth Amendment because [the motel] is deprived of the right to choose its customers and operate its business as it wishes, resulting in a taking of its liberty and property without due process of law and a taking

President Lyndon Johnson signing the Civil Rights Act of 1964, Title II of which outlawed racial discrimination in privately-owned public accommodations in interstate commerce. To Johnson's left (right in photo) are Sen. Walter Mondale (Minn.), later Vice President, and Solicitor General Thurgood Marshall, whom Johnson would soon appoint to the Supreme Court. Congress's use of commerce power to fashion Title II was upheld by the Supreme Court in *Heart of Atlanta Motel v. United States.*

of its property without just compensation; and, finally, that, by requiring [it] to rent available rooms to Negroes against its will, Congress is subjecting it to involuntary servitude in contravention of the Thirteenth Amendment . . .

The [Civil Rights Act of 1964] as finally adopted was most comprehensive, undertaking to prevent, through peaceful and voluntary settlement, discrimination in voting as well as in places of accommodation and public facilities, federally secured programs, and in employment. Since Title II is the only portion under attack here, we confine our consideration to those public accommodation provisions . . .

The Senate Commerce Committee made it quite clear that the fundamental object of Title II was to vindicate "the deprivation of personal dignity that surely accompanies denials of equal access to public establishments." At the same time, however, it noted that such an objective has been and could be readily achieved "by congressional action based on the commerce power of the Constitution." Our study of the legislative record, made in the light of prior cases, has brought us to the conclusion that Congress possessed ample power in this regard, and we have therefore not considered the other grounds relied upon. This is not to say that the remaining authority upon which it acted was not adequate, a question upon which we do not pass, but merely that, since the commerce power is sufficient for our decision here, we have considered it alone . . .

While the Act, as adopted, carried no congressional findings, the record of its passage through each house is replete with evidence of the burdens that discrimination by race or color places upon interstate commerce . . . This testimony included the

fact that our people have become increasingly mobile, with millions of people of all races traveling from State to State; that Negroes in particular have been the subject of discrimination in transient accommodations, having to travel great distances to secure the same; that often they have been unable to obtain accommodations, and have had to call upon friends to put them up overnight, and that these conditions had become so acute as to require the listing of available lodging for Negroes in a special guidebook which was itself "dramatic testimony to the difficulties" Negroes encounter in travel. These exclusionary practices were found to be nationwide, the Under Secretary of Commerce testifying that there is "no question that this discrimination in the North still exists to a large degree" and in the West and Midwest as well. This testimony indicated a qualitative, as well as quantitative, effect on interstate travel by Negroes. The former was the obvious impairment of the Negro traveler's pleasure and convenience that resulted when he continually was uncertain of finding lodging. As for the latter, there was evidence that this uncertainty stemming from racial discrimination had the effect of discouraging travel on the part of a substantial portion of the Negro community. This was the conclusion not only of the Under Secretary of Commerce, but also of the Administrator of the Federal Aviation Agency, who wrote the Chairman of the Senate Commerce Committee that it was his belief that air commerce is adversely affected by the denial to a substantial segment of the traveling public of adequate and desegregated public accommodations. We shall not burden this opinion with further details, since the voluminous testimony presents overwhelming evidence that discrimination by hotels and motels impedes interstate travel.

The power of Congress to deal with these obstructions depends on the meaning of the Commerce Clause. Its meaning was first enunciated 140 years ago by the great Chief Justice John Marshall in *Gibbons v. Ogden* . . .

In short, the determinative test of the exercise of power by the Congress under the Commerce Clause is simply whether the activity sought to be regulated is "commerce which concerns more States than one" and has a real and substantial relation to the national interest. Let us now turn to this facet of the problem.

That the "intercourse" of which the Chief Justice spoke included the movement of persons through more States than one was settled as early as 1849, in the Passenger Cases, where Mr. Justice McLean stated: "That the transportation of passengers is a part of commerce is not now an open question." Again in 1913, Mr. Justice McKenna, speaking for the Court, said: "Commerce among the States, we have said, consists of intercourse and traffic between their citizens, and includes the transportation of persons and property." . . . Nor does it make any difference whether the transportation is commercial in character . . .

The same interest in protecting interstate commerce which led Congress to deal with segregation in interstate carriers and the white slave traffic has prompted it to extend the exercise of its power to gambling, to criminal enterprises, to deceptive practices in the sale of products, to fraudulent security transactions, to misbranding of drugs, to wages and hours, to members of labor unions, to crop control, to discrimination against shippers, to the protection of small business from injurious price-cutting, to resale price maintenance, to professional football, and to racial discrimination by owners and managers of terminal restaurants.

That Congress was legislating against moral wrongs in many of these areas rendered its enactments no less valid. In framing Title II of this Act, Congress was also dealing with what it considered a moral problem. But that fact does not detract from the overwhelming evidence of the disruptive effect that racial discrimination has had on commercial intercourse. It was this burden which empowered Congress to enact appropriate legislation, and, given this basis for the exercise of its power, Congress was not restricted by the fact that the particular obstruction to interstate commerce with which it was dealing was also deemed a moral and social wrong.

It is said that the operation of the motel here is of a purely local character. But, assuming this to be true, "[i]f it is interstate commerce that feels the pinch, it does not matter how local the operation which applies the squeeze." . . .

Thus, the power of Congress to promote interstate commerce also includes the power to regulate the local incidents thereof, including local activities in both the States of origin and destination, which might have a substantial and harmful effect upon that commerce. One need only examine the evidence which we have discussed above to see that Congress may—as it has—prohibit racial discrimination by motels serving travelers, however "local" their operations may appear.

Nor does the Act deprive [owners of the motel] of liberty or property under the Fifth Amendment. The commerce power invoked here by the Congress is a specific and plenary one authorized by the Constitution itself. The only questions are: (1) whether Congress had a rational basis for finding that racial discrimination by motels affected commerce, and (2) if it had such a basis, whether the means it selected to eliminate that evil are reasonable and appropriate. If they are, [the motel] has no "right" to select its guests as it sees fit, free from governmental regulation.

There is nothing novel about such legislation. Thirty-two States now have it on their books either by statute or executive order, and many cities provide such regulation. Some of these Acts go back four-score years. It has been repeatedly held by this Court that such laws do not violate the Due Process Clause of the Fourteenth Amendment . . .

We find no merit in the remainder of [the motel's] contentions, including that of "involuntary servitude." . . .

We therefore conclude that the action of the Congress in the adoption of the Act as applied here to a motel which concededly serves interstate travelers is within the power granted it by the Commerce Clause of the Constitution, as interpreted by this Court for 140 years. It may be argued that Congress could have pursued other methods to eliminate the obstructions it found in interstate commerce caused by racial discrimination. But this is a matter of policy that rests entirely with the Congress, not with the courts. How obstructions in commerce may be removed—what means are to be employed—is within the sound and exclusive discretion of the Congress. It is subject only to one caveat—that the means chosen by it must be reasonably adapted to the end permitted by the Constitution. We cannot say that its choice here was not so adapted. The Constitution requires no more.

Douglas, concurring:

Though I join the Court's opinions, I am somewhat reluctant . . . to rest solely on the Commerce Clause. My reluctance is not due to any conviction that Congress lacks power to regulate commerce in the interests of human rights. It is, rather, my belief that the right of people to be free of state action that discriminates against them because of race, like the "right of persons to move freely from State to State occupies a more protected position in our constitutional system than does the movement of cattle, fruit, steel and coal across state lines." (*Edwards v. California*) Moreover, when we come to the problem of abatement . . . the result reached by the Court is, for me, much more obvious as a protective measure under the Fourteenth Amendment than under the Commerce Clause. For the former deals with the constitutional status of the individual, not with the impact on commerce of local activities or vice versa . . .

A decision based on the Fourteenth Amendment would have a more settling effect, making unnecessary litigation over whether a particular restaurant or inn is within the commerce definitions of the Act or whether a particular customer is an interstate traveler. Under my construction, the Act would apply to all customers in all the enumerated places of public accommodation. And that construction would put an end to all obstructionist strategies, and finally close one door on a bitter chapter in American history.

Philadelphia v. New Jersey

437 U.S. 617 (1978), 7-2
Opinion of the Court: Stewart (Blackmun, Brennan, Marshall, Powell, Stevens, White)
Dissenting: Burger, Rehnquist
Under what circumstances, if any, would the Court have upheld the New Jersey restrictions on out-of-state use of landfills? Do Stewart and Rehnquist disagree on how to characterize solid waste? The desirability of conserving landfill resources? Or a principle of federalism? Does the decision, in effect, allow a larger and less pressed state to "dump" on a smaller one with a more acute waste disposal problem? If so, is this discrimination involving interstate commerce?

Stewart, for the Court:

A New Jersey law prohibits the importation of most "solid or liquid waste which originated or was collected outside the territorial limits of the State . . ." In this case we are required to decide whether this statutory prohibition violates the Commerce Clause of the United States Constitution.

The statutory provision . . . took effect in early 1974. In pertinent part it provides: "No person shall bring into this State any solid or liquid waste which originated or was collected outside the territorial limits of the State, except garbage to be fed to swine in the State of New Jersey, until the commissioner [of the State Department of Environmental Protection] shall determine that such action can be permitted without endangering the public health, safety and welfare and has promulgated regulations permitting and regulating the treatment and disposal of such waste in this State." . . .

Immediately affected by these developments were the operators of private landfills in New Jersey, and several cities in other States that had agreements with these operators for waste disposal. They brought suit against New Jersey and its Department of Environmental Protection in state court, attacking the statute and regulations on a number of state and federal grounds. . . .

Although the Constitution gives Congress the power to regulate commerce among the States, many subjects of potential federal regulation under that power inevitably escape congressional attention "because of their local character and their number and diversity." In the absence of federal legislation, these subjects are open to control by the States so long as they act within the restraints imposed by the Commerce Clause itself. The bounds of these restraints appear nowhere in the words of the Commerce Clause, but have emerged gradually in the decisions of this Court giving effect to its basic purpose. . . .

The opinions of the Court through the years have reflected an alertness to the evils of "economic isolation" and protectionism, while at the same time recognizing that incidental burdens on interstate commerce may be unavoidable when a State legislates to safeguard the health and safety of its people. Thus, where simple economic protectionism is effected by state legislation, a virtually per se rule of invalidity has been erected. The clearest example of such legislation is a law that overtly blocks the flow of interstate commerce at a State's borders. But where other legislative objectives are credibly advanced and there is no patent

New Jersey's attempt to conserve its land-fill resources by barring privately-owned sites like the one here from receiving garbage from sources outside the state was at issue in *Philadelphia v. New Jersey*, 1978. The state later phased out most sites in favor of other means of disposal, including shipping to Pennsylvania.

discrimination against interstate trade, the Court has adopted a much more flexible approach. . . .

The crucial inquiry, therefore, must be directed to determining whether ch. 363 is basically a protectionist measure, or whether it can fairly be viewed as a law directed to legitimate local concerns, with effects upon interstate commerce that are only incidental.

The purpose of ch. 363 is set out in the statute itself as follows: "The Legislature finds and determines that . . . the volume of solid and liquid waste continues to rapidly increase, that the treatment and disposal of these wastes continues to pose an even greater threat to the quality of the environment of New Jersey, that the available and appropriate land fill sites within the State are being diminished, that the environment continues to be threatened by the treatment and disposal of waste which originated or was collected outside the State, and that the public health, safety and welfare require that the treatment and disposal within this State of all wastes generated outside of the State be prohibited." . . .

[Philadelphia and the landfill operators] strenuously contend that ch. 363, "while outwardly cloaked 'in the currently fashionable garb of environmental protection' . . . is actually no more than a legislative effort to suppress competition and stabilize the cost of solid waste disposal for New Jersey residents . . ." They cite passages of legislative history suggesting that the problem addressed by ch. 363 is primarily financial: Stemming the flow of out-of-state waste into certain landfill sites will extend their lives, thus delaying the day when New Jersey cities must transport their waste to more distant and expensive sites.

[New Jersey] on the other hand, den[ies] that ch. 363 was motivated by financial concerns or economic protectionism. In the words of their brief, "[n]o New Jersey commercial interests stand to gain advantage over competitors from outside the state as a result of the ban on dumping out-of-state waste." Noting that New Jersey landfill operators are among the plaintiffs, the [New Jersey] brief argues that "[t]he complaint is not that New Jersey has forged an economic preference for its own commercial interests, but rather that it has denied a small group of its entrepreneurs an economic opportunity to traffic in waste in order to protect the health, safety and welfare of the citizenry at large."

This dispute about ultimate legislative purpose need not be resolved, because its resolution would not be relevant to the constitutional issue to be decided in this case. Contrary to the evident assumption of the state court and the parties, the evil of protectionism can reside in legislative means as well as legislative ends. Thus, it does not matter whether the ultimate aim of ch. 363 is to reduce the waste disposal costs of New Jersey residents or to save remaining open lands from pollution, for we assume New Jersey has every right to protect its residents' pocketbooks as well as their environment. And it may be assumed as well that New Jersey may pursue those ends by slowing the flow of all waste into the State's remaining landfills, even though interstate commerce may incidentally be affected. But whatever New Jersey's ultimate purpose, it may not be accomplished by discriminating against articles of commerce coming from outside the State unless there is some reason, apart from their origin, to treat them differently. Both on its face and in its plain effect, ch. 363 violates this principle of nondiscrimination.

The Court has consistently found parochial legislation of this kind to be constitutionally invalid, whether the ultimate aim of the legislation was to assure a steady supply of milk by erecting barriers to allegedly ruinous outside competition, or to create jobs by keeping industry within the State, or to preserve the State's financial resources from depletion by fencing out indigent immigrants. In each of these cases, a presumably legitimate goal was sought to be achieved by the illegitimate means of isolating the State from the national economy.

Also relevant here are the Court's decisions holding that a State may not accord its own inhabitants a preferred right of access over consumers in other States to natural resources located within its borders. These cases stand for the basic principle that a "State is without power to prevent privately owned articles of trade from being shipped and sold in interstate commerce on the ground that they are required to satisfy local demands or because they are needed by the people of the State."

The New Jersey law at issue in this case falls squarely within the area that the Commerce Clause puts off limits to state regulation. On its face, it imposes on out-of-state commercial interests the full burden of conserving the State's remaining landfill space. It is true that in our previous cases the scarce natural resource was itself the article of commerce, whereas here the scarce resource and the article of commerce are distinct. But that difference is without consequence. In both instances, the State has overtly moved to slow or freeze the flow of commerce for protectionist reasons. It does not matter that the State has shut the article of commerce inside the State in one case and outside the State in the other. What is crucial is the attempt by one State to isolate itself from a problem common to many by erecting a barrier against the movement of interstate trade.

[New Jersey] argue[s] that not all laws which facially discriminate against out-of-state commerce are forbidden protectionist regulations. In particular, they point to quarantine laws, which this Court has repeatedly upheld even though they appear to single out interstate commerce for special treatment. In [New Jersey's] view, ch. 363 is analogous to such health-protective measures, since it reduces the exposure of New Jersey residents to the allegedly harmful effects of landfill sites.

It is true that certain quarantine laws have not been considered forbidden protectionist measures, even though they were directed against out-of-state commerce. But those quarantine laws banned the importation of articles such as diseased livestock that required destruction as soon as possible because their very movement risked contagion and other evils. Those laws thus did not discriminate against interstate commerce as such, but simply prevented traffic in noxious articles, whatever their origin.

The New Jersey statute is not such a quarantine law. There has been no claim here that the very movement of waste into or through New Jersey endangers health, or that waste must be disposed of as soon and as close to its point of generation as possible. The harms caused by waste are said to arise after its disposal in landfill sites, and at that point, as New Jersey concedes, there is no basis to distinguish out-of-state waste from domestic waste. If one is inherently harmful, so is the other. Yet New Jersey has banned the former while leaving its landfill sites open to the latter. The New Jersey law blocks the importation of waste in an obvious effort to saddle those outside the State with the entire burden of slowing the flow of refuse into New Jersey's remaining landfill sites. . . .

Today, cities in Pennsylvania and New York find it expedient or necessary to send their waste into New Jersey for disposal, and New Jersey claims the right to close its borders to such traffic. Tomorrow, cities in New Jersey may find it expedient or necessary to send their waste into Pennsylvania or New York for disposal, and those States might then claim the right to close their borders. The Commerce Clause will protect New Jersey in the future, just as it protects her neighbors now, from efforts by one State to isolate itself in the stream of interstate commerce from a problem shared by all. The judgment is reversed.

Rehnquist (Burger), dissenting:

A growing problem in our Nation is the sanitary treatment and disposal of solid waste. For many years, solid waste was incinerated. Because of the significant environmental problems attendant on incineration, however, this method of solid waste disposal has declined in use in many localities, including New Jersey. "Sanitary" landfills have replaced incineration as the principal method of disposing of solid waste. In ch. 363 . . . the State of New Jersey legislatively recognized the unfortunate fact that landfills also present extremely serious health and safety problems. First, in New Jersey, "virtually all sanitary landfills can be expected to produce leachate, a noxious and highly polluted liquid which is seldom visible and frequently pollutes . . . ground and surface waters." The natural decomposition process which occurs in landfills also produces large quantities of methane and thereby presents a significant explosion hazard. Landfills can also generate "health hazards caused by rodents, fires and scavenger birds" and, "needless to say, do not help New Jersey's aesthetic appearance nor New Jersey's noise or water or air pollution problems."

The health and safety hazards associated with landfills present [New Jersey] with a currently unsolvable dilemma. Other, hopefully safer, methods of disposing of solid wastes are still in the development stage and cannot presently be used. But [it] obviously cannot completely stop the tide of solid waste that its citizens will produce in the interim. For the moment, therefore, [it] must continue to use sanitary landfills to dispose of New Jersey's own solid waste despite the critical environmental problems thereby created.

The question presented in this case is whether New Jersey must also continue to receive and dispose of solid waste from neighboring States, even though these will inexorably increase the health problems discussed above. The Court answers this question in the affirmative. New Jersey must either prohibit all landfill operations, leaving itself to cast about for a presently nonexistent solution to the serious problem of disposing of the waste generated within its own borders, or it must accept waste from every portion of the United States, thereby multiplying the health and safety problems which would result if it dealt only with such wastes generated within the State. [P]ast precedents establish that the Commerce Clause does not present [New Jersey] with such a Hobson's choice. . . .

The Court recognizes that States can prohibit the importation of items "'which, on account of their existing condition, would bring in and spread disease, pestilence, and death, such as rags or other substances infected with the germs of yellow fever or the virus of small-pox, or cattle or meat or other provisions that are diseased or decayed or otherwise, from their condition and quality, unfit for human use or consumption.'" As the Court points out, such "quarantine laws have not been considered forbidden protectionist measures, even though they were directed against out-of-state commerce."

. . . [T]hese cases are dispositive of the present one. Under them, New Jersey may require germ-infected rags or diseased meat to be disposed of as best as possible within the State, but at the same time prohibit the importation of such items for disposal at the facilities that are set up within New Jersey for disposal of such material generated within the State. The physical fact of life that New Jersey must somehow dispose of its own noxious items does not mean that it must serve as a depository for those of every other State. Similarly, New Jersey should be free under our past precedents to prohibit the importation of solid waste because of the health and safety problems that such waste poses to its citizens. The fact that New Jersey continues to, and indeed must continue to, dispose of its own solid waste does not mean that New Jersey may not prohibit the importation of even more solid waste into the State. I simply see no way to distinguish solid waste, on the record of this case, from germ-infected rags, diseased meat, and other noxious items.

Michigan v. Long

463 U.S. 1032 (1983), 6-3
Opinion of the Court: O'Connor (Berger, Powell, Rehnquist, White)
Concurring: Blackmun
Dissenting: Brennan, Stevens

What is the Court's theory for not reviewing state court judgments that rest on "adequate and independent state grounds"? Why should the Court review state court decisions at all? Why this one? How great a burden does the rule announced by the Court place on state supreme courts? Which opinion, O'Connor's or Stevens's, shows greater respect for state courts? What is the significance of Stevens's observation that "fifteen years ago, we did not review any such cases"? Is this a case if judicial activism or judicial self-restraint?

O'Connor, for the Court:

In *Terry v. Ohio*, we upheld the validity of a protective search for weapons in the absence of probable cause to arrest because it is unreasonable to deny a police officer the right "to neutralize the threat of physical harm," when he possesses an articulable suspicion that an individual is armed and dangerous. We did not, however, expressly address whether such a protective search for weapons could extend to an area beyond the person in the absence of probable cause to arrest. In the present case, David Long was convicted for possession of marijuana found by police in the passenger compartment and trunk of the automobile that he was driving. The police searched the passenger compartment because they had reason to believe that the vehicle contained weapons potentially dangerous to the officers. We hold that the protective search of the passenger compartment was reasonable under the principles articulated in *Terry* and other decisions of this Court. We also examine Long's argument that the decision below rests upon an adequate and independent state ground. . . .

Before reaching the merits, we must consider Long's argument that we are without jurisdiction to decide this case because the decision below rests on an adequate and independent state ground. The court below referred twice to the state constitution in its opinion, but otherwise relied exclusively on federal law. Long argues that the Michigan courts have provided greater protection from searches and seizures under the state constitution than is afforded under the Fourth Amendment, and the references to the state constitution therefore establish an adequate and independent ground for the decision below. . . .

Although we have announced a number of principles in order to help us determine whether various forms of references to state law constitute adequate and independent state grounds, we openly admit that we have thus far not developed a satisfying and consistent approach for resolving this vexing issue. . . .

[The] ad hoc method of dealing with cases that involve possible adequate and independent state grounds is antithetical to the doctrinal consistency that is required when sensitive issues of federal-state relations are involved. Moreover, none of the various methods of disposition that we have employed thus far recommends itself as the preferred method that we should apply to the exclusion of others, and we therefore determine that it is appropriate to reexamine our treatment of this jurisdictional issue in order to achieve the consistency that is necessary. . . .

Respect for the independence of state courts, as well as avoidance of rendering advisory opinions, have been the cornerstones of this Court's refusal to decide cases where there is an adequate and independent state ground. It is precisely because of this . . . that we do not wish to continue to decide issues of state law that go beyond the opinion that we review,

or to require state courts to reconsider cases to clarify the grounds of their decisions. Accordingly, when, as in this case, a state court decision fairly appears to rest primarily on federal law, or to be interwoven with the federal law, and when the adequacy and independence of any possible state law ground is not clear from the face of the opinion, we will accept as the most reasonable explanation that the state court decided the case the way it did because it believed that federal law required it to do so. If a state court chooses merely to rely on federal precedents as it would on the precedents of all other jurisdictions, then it need only make clear by a plain statement in its judgment or opinion that the federal cases are being used only for the purpose of guidance, and do not themselves compel the result that the court has reached. In this way, both justice and judicial administration will be greatly improved. If the state court decision indicates clearly and expressly that it is alternatively based on bona fide separate, adequate, and independent grounds, we, of course, will not undertake to review the decision.

This approach obviates in most instances the need to examine state law in order to decide the nature of the state court decision, and will at the same time avoid the danger of our rendering advisory opinions. It also avoids the unsatisfactory and intrusive practice of requiring state courts to clarify their decisions to the satisfaction of this Court. We believe that such an approach will provide state judges with a clearer opportunity to develop state jurisprudence unimpeded by federal interference, and yet will preserve the integrity of federal law. . . .

The principle that we will not review judgments of state courts that rest on adequate and independent state grounds is based, in part, on "the limitations of our own jurisdiction." The jurisdictional concern is that we not render an advisory opinion . . . [I]n determining . . . whether we have jurisdiction to review a case that is alleged to rest on adequate and independent state grounds, we merely assume that there are no such grounds when it is not clear from the opinion itself that the state court relied upon an adequate and independent state ground and when it fairly appears that the state court rested its decision primarily on federal law.

Our review of the decision below under this framework leaves us unconvinced that it rests upon an independent state ground. Apart from its two citations to the state constitution, the court below relied exclusively on its understanding of *Terry* and other federal cases. Not a single state case was cited to support the state court's holding that the search of the passenger compartment was unconstitutional . . . The references to the state constitution in no way indicate that the decision below rested on grounds in any way independent from the state court's interpretation of federal law. Even if we accept that the Michigan constitution has been interpreted to provide independent protection for certain rights also secured under the Fourth Amendment, it fairly appears in this case that the Michigan Supreme Court rested its decision primarily on federal law.

Rather than dismissing the case, or requiring that the state court reconsider its decision on our behalf solely because of a mere possibility that an adequate and independent ground supports the judgment, we find that we have jurisdiction in the absence of a plain statement that the decision below rested on an adequate and independent state ground. . . .

The court below held . . . that Deputy Howell's entry into the vehicle cannot be justified under the principles set forth in *Terry* because "*Terry* authorized only a limited pat-down search of a person suspected of criminal activity" rather than a search of an area. Although Terry did involve the protective frisk of a person, we believe that the police action in this case is justified by the principles that we have already established in Terry and other cases. . . .

The decision of the Michigan Supreme Court is reversed, and the case is remanded for further proceedings not inconsistent with this opinion.

Stevens, dissenting:
The jurisprudential questions presented in this case are far more important than the question whether the Michigan police officer's search of [Long's] car violated the Fourth Amendment. The case raises profoundly significant questions concerning the relationship between two sovereigns—the State of Michigan and the United States of America.

The Supreme Court of the State of Michigan expressly held "that the deputies' search of the vehicle was proscribed by the Fourth Amendment of the United States Constitution and art. 1, s 11 of the Michigan Constitution." The state law ground is clearly adequate to support the judgment, but the question whether it is independent of the Michigan Supreme Court's understanding of federal law is more difficult. Four possible

ways of resolving that question present themselves: (1) asking the Michigan Supreme Court directly, (2) attempting to infer from all possible sources of state law what the Michigan Supreme Court meant, (3) presuming that adequate state grounds are independent unless it clearly appears otherwise, or (4) presuming that adequate state grounds are not independent unless it clearly appears otherwise. This Court has, on different occasions, employed each of the first three approaches; never until today has it even hinted at the fourth. In order to "achieve the consistency that is necessary," the Court today undertakes a reexamination of all the possibilities. It rejects the first approach as inefficient and unduly burdensome for state courts, and rejects the second approach as an inappropriate expenditure of our resources. Although I find both of those decisions defensible in themselves, I cannot accept the Court's decision to choose the fourth approach over the third—to presume that adequate state grounds are intended to be dependent on federal law unless the record plainly shows otherwise. . . .

It appears to be common ground that any rule we adopt should show "respect for state courts, and [a] desire to avoid advisory opinions." And I am confident that all members of this Court agree that there is a vital interest in the sound management of scarce federal judicial resources. All of those policies counsel against the exercise of federal jurisdiction. They are fortified by my belief that a policy of judicial restraint—one that allows other decisional bodies to have the last word in legal interpretation until it is truly necessary for this Court to intervene—enables this Court to make its most effective contribution to our federal system of government. . . .

Until recently we had virtually no interest in cases of this type. Thirty years ago, this Court reviewed only one. Indeed, that appears to have been the only case during the entire 1952 Term in which a state even sought review of a decision by its own judiciary. Fifteen years ago, we did not review any such cases, although the total number of requests had mounted to three. Some time during the past decade, perhaps about the time of the 5-to-4 decision in *Zacchini v. Scripps-Howard Broadcasting Co.* (1977), our priorities shifted. The result is a docket swollen with requests by states to reverse judgments that their courts have rendered in favor of their citizens. I am confident that a future Court will recognize the error of this allocation of resources. When that day comes, I think it likely that the Court will also reconsider the propriety of to-day's expansion of our jurisdiction.

Garcia v. San Antonio Metropolitan Transit Authority

469 U.S. 528 (1985), 5-4
Opinion of the Court: Blackmun (Brennan, Marshall, Stevens, White)
Dissenting: Burger, O'Connor, Powell, Rehnquist
In the early 1980s, the Department of Labor ruled that the minimum wage and overtime pay provisions of federal Fair Labor Standards Act (FLSA), which Congress originally en-acted to regulate private employment, be applied to the San Antonio Metropolitan Transit System (SAMTA), a munici-pally owned regional mass transit authority. Garcia and sev-eral other SAMTA employees brought suit against the authority for overtime pay under the FLSA. Has the Court de-clared the nonexistence of state sovereignty in regard to the reach of federal commerce power, in favor of state representa-tion in the national government? Does O'Connor, dissenting, illuminate the line of state sovereignty that Blackmun says is now almost impossible to draw? Is she concerned about the de-cline of state sovereignty or with the growth of federal power? What does she mean by "spirit of the Constitution"? Is the ex-tension of the Fair Labor Standards Act a major impediment for state power and independence or is it more a nominal, though symbolic, interference? If state interests are represented in Congress, how might those of only a minority of states be protected? Are states represented in the executive?

Blackmun, for the Court:
We revisit in these cases an issue raised in *National League of Cities v. Usery* (1976). In that litigation, this Court, by a sharply divided vote, ruled that the Com-merce Clause does not empower Congress to enforce the minimum-wage and overtime provisions of the Fair Labor Standards Act (FLSA) against the States "in areas of traditional governmental functions." Although *Na-tional League of Cities* supplied some examples of "tradi-tional governmental functions," it did not offer a general explanation of how a "traditional" function is to be distinguished from a "nontraditional" one. Since then, federal and state courts have struggled with the task . . . of identifying a traditional function for purposes of state immunity under the Commerce Clause. . . .

Our examination of this "function" standard ap-plied in these and other cases over the last eight years now persuades us that the attempt to draw the bound-aries of state regulatory immunity in terms of "tradi-tional governmental function" is not only unworkable but is also inconsistent with established principles of federalism and, indeed, with those very federalism principles on which *National League of Cities* purported to rest. That case, accordingly, is overruled. . . .

Were SAMTA a privately owned and operated en-terprise, it could not credibly argue that Congress ex-ceeded the bounds of its Commerce Clause powers in prescribing minimum wages and overtime rates for SAMTA's employees. Any constitutional exemption from the requirements of the FLSA therefore must rest on SAMTA's status as a governmental entity rather than on the "local" nature of its operations. . . .

[C]ourts have held that regulating ambulance ser-vices, licensing automobile drivers, operating a munici-pal airport, performing solid waste disposal, and operating a highway authority are functions protected under *National League of Cities*. At the same time, courts have held that issuance of industrial development bonds, regulation of intrastate natural gas sales, regula-tion of traffic on public roads, regulation of air trans-portation, operation of a telephone system, leasing and sale of natural gas, operation of a mental health facility, and provision of in-house domestic services for the aged and handicapped are not entitled to immunity. We find it difficult, if not impossible, to identify an organizing principle that places each of the cases in the first group on one side of a line and each of the cases in the second group on the other side. The constitutional distinction between licensing drivers and regulating traffic, for ex-ample, or between operating a highway authority and operating a mental health facility, is elusive at best.

Thus far, this Court itself has made little headway in defining the scope of the governmental functions deemed protected under *National League of Cities*. In that case the Court set forth examples of protected and unprotected functions, but provided no explana-tion of how those examples were identified. . . .

We rejected the possibility of making immunity turn on a purely historical standard of "tradition" . . . The most obvious defect of a historical approach to state immunity is that it prevents a court from accom-modating changes in the historical functions of States, changes that have resulted in a number of once-pri-vate functions like education being assumed by the States and their subdivisions. At the same time, the only apparent virtue of a rigorous historical standard, namely, its promise of a reasonably objective measure for state immunity, is illusory. Reliance on history as an organizing principle results in line-drawing of the most arbitrary sort; the genesis of state governmental functions stretches over a historical continuum from before the Revolution to the present, and courts would have to decide by fiat precisely how long-standing a pattern of state involvement had to be for federal regulatory authority to be defeated. . . .

A non-historical standard for selecting immune governmental functions is likely to be just as unworkable as is a historical standard. The goal of identifying "uniquely" governmental functions, for example, has been rejected by the Court in the field of governmental tort liability in part because the notion of a "uniquely" governmental function is unmanageable. Another possibility would be to confine immunity to "necessary" governmental services, that is, services that would be provided inadequately or not at all unless the government provided them. The set of services that fits into this category, however, may well be negligible. The fact that an unregulated market produces less of some service than a State deems desirable does not mean that the State itself must provide the service; in most if not all cases, the State can "contract out" by hiring private firms to provide the service or simply by providing subsidies to existing suppliers. It also is open to question how well equipped courts are to make this kind of determination about the workings of economic markets.

We believe, however, that there is a more fundamental problem at work here, a problem that explains why the Court was never able to provide a basis for the governmental/proprietary distinction in the intergovernmental tax-immunity cases and why an attempt to draw similar distinctions with respect to federal regulatory authority under *National League of Cities* is unlikely to succeed regardless of how the distinctions are phrased. The problem is that neither the governmental/proprietary distinction nor any other that purports to separate out important governmental functions can be faithful to the role of federalism in a democratic society. The essence of our federal system is that within the realm of authority left open to them under the Constitution, the States must be equally free to engage in any activity that their citizens choose for the common weal, no matter how unorthodox or unnecessary anyone else—including the judiciary—deems state involvement to be. Any rule of state immunity that looks to

the "traditional," "integral," or "necessary" nature of governmental functions inevitably invites an unelected federal judiciary to make decisions about which state policies it favors and which ones it dislikes . . . [T]he States cannot serve as laboratories for social and economic experiment if they must pay an added price when they meet the changing needs of their citizenry by taking up functions that an earlier day and a different society left in private hands. In the words of Justice Black: "There is not, and there cannot be, any unchanging line of demarcation between essential and non-essential governmental functions. Many governmental functions of today have at some time in the past been non-governmental. The genius of our government provides that, within the sphere of constitutional action, the people—acting not through the courts but through their elected legislative representatives—have the power to determine as conditions demand, what services and functions the public welfare requires." *Helvering v. Gerhardt,* (concurring opinion).

We therefore now reject, as unsound in principle and unworkable in practice, a rule of state immunity from federal regulation that turns on a judicial appraisal of whether a particular governmental function is "integral" or "traditional." Any such rule leads to inconsistent results at the same time that it disserves principles of democratic self-governance, and it breeds inconsistency precisely because it is divorced from those principles. If there are to be limits on the Federal Government's power to interfere with state functions—as undoubtedly there are—we must look elsewhere to find them. . . .

The central theme of *National League of Cities* was that the States occupy a special position in our constitutional system and that the scope of Congress' authority under the Commerce Clause must reflect that position. . . .

What has proved problematic is not the perception that the Constitution's federal structure imposes limitations on the Commerce Clause, but rather the nature and content of those limitations. One approach to defining the limits on Congress' authority to regulate the States under the Commerce Clause is to identify certain underlying elements of political sovereignty that are deemed essential to the States' "separate and independent existence." This approach obviously underlay the Court's use of the "traditional governmental function" concept in *National League of Cities.* It also has led to the separate requirement that the challenged federal statute "address matters that are indisputably 'attribute[s] of state sovereignty,'" quoting *National League of Cities.* In *National League of Cities* itself, for example, the Court concluded that decisions by a State concerning the wages and hours of its employees are an "undoubted attribute of state sovereignty." The opinion did not explain what aspects of such decisions made them such an "undoubted attribute." . . . The point of the inquiry, however, has remained to single out particular features of a State's internal governance that are deemed to be intrinsic parts of state sovereignty.

We doubt that courts ultimately can identify principled constitutional limitations on the scope of Congress' Commerce Clause powers over the States merely by relying on a priori definitions of state sovereignty. In part, this is because of the elusiveness of objective criteria for "fundamental" elements of state sovereignty, a problem we have witnessed in the search for "traditional governmental functions." There is, however, a more fundamental reason: the sovereignty of the States is limited by the Constitution itself. A variety of sovereign powers, for example, are withdrawn from the States by Article I, s 10. Section 8 of the same Article works an equally sharp contraction of state sovereignty by authorizing Congress to exercise a wide range of legislative powers and (in conjunction with the Supremacy Clause of Article VI) to displace contrary state legislation. By providing for final review of questions of federal law in this Court, Article III curtails the sovereign power of the States' judiciaries to make authoritative determinations of law. Finally, the developed application, through the Fourteenth Amendment, of the greater part of the Bill of Rights to the States limits the sovereign authority that States otherwise would possess to legislate with respect to their citizens and to conduct their own affairs.

The States unquestionably do "retai[n] a significant measure of sovereign authority." *EEOC v. Wyoming,* (Powell, dissenting). They do so, however, only to the extent that the Constitution has not divested them of their original powers and transferred those powers to the Federal Government. . . .

[T]o say that the Constitution assumes the continued role of the States is to say little about the nature of that role . . . The power of the Federal Government is a "power to be respected" as well, and the fact that the States remain sovereign as to all powers not vested in Congress or denied them by the Constitution offers no guidance about where the frontier between state and federal power lies. In short, we have no license to employ freestanding conceptions of state sovereignty

when measuring congressional authority under the Commerce Clause. . . .

Apart from the limitation on federal authority inherent in the delegated nature of Congress' Article I powers, the principal means chosen by the Framers to ensure the role of the States in the federal system lies in the structure of the Federal Government itself. It is no novelty to observe that the composition of the Federal Government was designed in large part to protect the States from overreaching by Congress. The Framers thus gave the States a role in the selection both of the Executive and the Legislative Branches of the Federal Government. The States were vested with indirect influence over the House of Representatives and the Presidency by their control of electoral qualifications and their role in Presidential elections. U.S. Const., Art. I, s 2, and Art. II, s 1. They were given more direct influence in the Senate, where each State received equal representation and each Senator was to be selected by the legislature of his State. Art. I, s 3. The significance attached to the States' equal representation in the Senate is underscored by the prohibition of any constitutional amendment divesting a State of equal representation without the State's consent. Art. V.

The extent to which the structure of the Federal Government itself was relied on to insulate the interests of the States is evident in the views of the Framers . . . [They] chose to rely on a federal system in which special restraints on federal power over the States inhered principally in the workings of the National Government itself, rather than in discrete limitations on the objects of federal authority. State sovereign interests, then, are more properly protected by procedural safeguards inherent in the structure of the federal system than by judicially created limitations on federal power.

The effectiveness of the federal political process in preserving the States' interests is apparent even today in the course of federal legislation. On the one hand, the States have been able to direct a substantial proportion of federal revenues into their own treasuries in the form of general and program- specific grants in aid . . . Moreover, at the same time that the States have exercised their influence to obtain federal support, they have been able to exempt themselves from a wide variety of obligations imposed by Congress under the Commerce Clause . . . The fact that some federal statutes such as the FLSA extend general obligations to the States cannot obscure the extent to which the political position of the States in the federal system has served to minimize the burdens that the States bear under the Commerce Clause.

[T]he fundamental limitation that the constitutional scheme imposes on the Commerce Clause to protect the "States as States" is one of process rather than one of result. . . .

Insofar as the present cases are concerned, then, we need go no further than to state that we perceive nothing in the overtime and minimum-wage requirements of the FLSA, as applied to SAMTA, that is destructive of state sovereignty or violative of any constitutional provision. SAMTA faces nothing more than the same minimum-wage and overtime obligations that hundreds of thousands of other employers, public as well as private, have to meet.

In these cases, the status of public mass transit simply underscores the extent to which the structural protections of the Constitution insulate the States from federally imposed burdens. When Congress first subjected state mass-transit systems to FLSA obligations in 1966, and when it expanded those obligations in 1974, it simultaneously provided extensive funding for state and local mass transit through UMTA. In the two decades since its enactment, UMTA has provided over $22 billion in mass-transit aid to States and localities. In 1983 alone, UMTA funding amounted to $3.7 billion. As noted above, SAMTA and its immediate predecessor have received a substantial amount of UMTA funding, including over $12 million during SAMTA's first two fiscal years alone. In short, Congress has not simply placed a financial burden on the shoulders of States and localities that operate mass-transit systems, but has provided substantial countervailing financial assistance as well, assistance that may leave individual mass-transit systems better off than they would have been had Congress never intervened at all in the area. Congress' treatment of public mass transit reinforces our conviction that the national political process systematically protects States from the risk of having their functions in that area handicapped by Commerce Clause regulation.

This analysis makes clear that Congress' action in affording SAMTA employees the protections of the wage and hour provisions of the FLSA contravened no affirmative limit on Congress' power under the Commerce Clause. The judgment of the District Court therefore must be reversed.

Of course, we continue to recognize that the States occupy a special and specific position in our constitutional system and that the scope of Congress' authority under the Commerce Clause must reflect that

position. But the principal and basic limit on the federal commerce power is that inherent in all congressional action—the built-in restraints that our system provides through state participation in federal governmental action. The political process ensures that laws that unduly burden the States will not be promulgated. In the factual setting of these cases the internal safeguards of the political process have performed as intended. . . .

[T]he Court in [*National League of Cities*] attempted to articulate affirmative limits on the Commerce Clause power in terms of core governmental functions and fundamental attributes of state sovereignty. But the model of democratic decision-making the Court there identified underestimated, in our view, the solicitude of the national political process for the continued vitality of the States. Attempts by other courts since then to draw guidance from this model have proved it both impracticable and doctrinally barren. In sum, in *National League of Cities* the Court tried to repair what did not need repair.

We do not lightly overrule recent precedent. We have not hesitated, however, when it has become apparent that a prior decision has departed from a proper understanding of congressional power under the Commerce Clause. Due respect for the reach of congressional power within the federal system mandates that we do so now.

Powell (Burger, O'Connor, Rehnquist), dissenting:

Whatever effect the Court's decision may have in weakening the application of stare decisis, it is likely to be less important than what the Court has done to the Constitution itself. A unique feature of the United States is the federal system of government guaranteed by the Constitution and implicit in the very name of our country. Despite some genuflecting in the Court's opinion to the concept of federalism, today's decision effectively reduces the Tenth Amendment to meaningless rhetoric when Congress acts pursuant to the Commerce Clause. The Court holds that the Fair Labor Standards Act (FLSA) "contravened no affirmative limit on Congress' power under the Commerce Clause" to determine the wage rates and hours of employment of all state and local employees. In rejecting the traditional view of our federal system, the Court states: "Apart from the limitation on federal authority inherent in the delegated nature of Congress' Article I powers, the principal means chosen by the Framers to ensure the role of the States in the federal system lies in the structure of the Federal Government itself." . . .

In our federal system, the States have a major role that cannot be pre-empted by the National Government. As contemporaneous writings and the debates at the ratifying conventions make clear, the States' ratification of the Constitution was predicated on this understanding of federalism. Indeed, the Tenth Amendment was adopted specifically to ensure that the important role promised the States by the proponents of the Constitution was realized. . . .

[T]he harm to the States that results from federal overreaching under the Commerce Clause is not simply a matter of dollars and cents. Nor is it a matter of the wisdom or folly of certain policy choices. Rather, by usurping functions traditionally performed by the States, federal overreaching under the Commerce Clause undermines the constitutionally mandated balance of power between the States and the Federal Government, a balance designed to protect our fundamental liberties . . .

Although the Court's opinion purports to recognize that the States retain some sovereign power, it does not identify even a single aspect of state authority that would remain when the Commerce Clause is invoked to justify federal regulation. . . .

As I view the Court's decision today as rejecting the basic precepts of our federal system and limiting the constitutional role of judicial review, I dissent.

O'Connor (Powell, Rehnquist), dissenting:

The Court overrules *National League of Cities v. Usery* on the grounds that it is not "faithful to the role of federalism in a democratic society. The essence of our federal system," the Court concludes, "is that within the realm of authority left open to them under the Constitution, the States must be equally free to engage in any activity that their citizens choose for the common weal . . . ." *National League of Cities* is held to be inconsistent with this narrow view of federalism because it attempts to protect only those fundamental aspects of state sovereignty that are essential to the States' separate and independent existence, rather than protecting all state activities "equally."

In my view, federalism cannot be reduced to the weak "essence" distilled by the majority today. There is more to federalism than the nature of the constraints that can be imposed on the States in "the realm of authority left open to them by the Constitution." The central issue of federalism, of course, is

whether any realm is left open to the States by the Constitution—whether any area remains in which a State may act free of federal interference . . . The true "essence" of federalism is that the States as States have legitimate interests which the National Government is bound to respect even though its laws are supreme. If federalism so conceived and so carefully cultivated by the Framers of our Constitution is to remain meaningful, this Court cannot abdicate its constitutional responsibility to oversee the Federal Government's compliance with its duty to respect the legitimate interests of the States. . . .

It is not enough that the "end be legitimate"; the means to that end chosen by Congress must not contravene the spirit of the Constitution. Thus many of this Court's decisions acknowledge that the means by which national power is exercised must take into account concerns for state autonomy . . . The operative language of these cases varies, but the underlying principle is consistent: state autonomy is a relevant factor in assessing the means by which Congress exercises its powers.

This principle requires the Court to enforce affirmative limits on federal regulation of the States to complement the judicially crafted expansion of the interstate commerce power. *National League of Cities v. Usery* represented an attempt to define such limits. The Court today rejects *National League of Cities* and washes its hands of all efforts to protect the States. . . .

The last two decades have seen an unprecedented growth of federal regulatory activity, as the majority itself acknowledges . . . Today, as federal legislation and coercive grant programs have expanded to embrace innumerable activities that were once viewed as local, the burden of persuasion has surely shifted, and the extraordinary has become ordinary. For example, recently the Federal Government has, with this Court's blessing, undertaken to tell the States the age at which they can retire their law enforcement officers, and the regulatory standards, procedures, and even the agenda which their utilities commissions must consider and follow. The political process has not protected against these encroachments on state activities, even though they directly impinge on a State's ability to make and enforce its laws. With the abandonment of *National League of Cities,* all that stands between the remaining essentials of state sovereignty and Congress is the latter's underdeveloped capacity for self-restraint.

The problems of federalism in an integrated national economy are capable of more responsible resolution than holding that the States as States retain no status apart from that which Congress chooses to let them retain. The proper resolution . . . lies in weighing state autonomy as a factor in the balance when interpreting the means by which Congress can exercise its authority on the States as States. It is insufficient, in assessing the validity of congressional regulation of a State pursuant to the commerce power, to ask only whether the same regulation would be valid if enforced against a private party. That reasoning, embodied in the majority opinion, is inconsistent with the spirit of our Constitution. It remains relevant that a State is being regulated, as *National League of Cities* and every recent case have recognized . . .

It has been difficult for this Court to craft bright lines defining the scope of the state autonomy protected by *National League of Cities*. Such difficulty is to be expected whenever constitutional concerns as important as federalism and the effectiveness of the commerce power come into conflict. Regardless of the difficulty, it is and will remain the duty of this Court to reconcile these concerns in the final instance. That the Court shuns the task today by appealing to the "essence of federalism" can provide scant comfort to those who believe our federal system requires something more than a unitary, centralized government. I would not shirk the duty acknowledged by *National League of Cities* . . . and I share Justice Rehnquist's belief that this Court will in time again assume its constitutional responsibility.

Maine v. Taylor

477 U.S. 131 (1986), 8-1
Opinion of the Court: Blackmun (Brennan, Burger, Marshall, O'Connor, Powell, Rehnquist, White)
Dissenting: Stevens

Taylor, owner of a baitfish business in Maine, imported live baitfish despite a state law barring such importation. He was indicted under a federal statute making it a federal crime to transport fish in interstate commerce in violation of state law. He moved to dismiss the indictment on the ground that the Maine statute unconstitutionally burdened interstate commerce. Maine intervened to defend the validity of the statute.

Does the decision in this case rest mainly on the idiosyncratic facts of the case or does it derive from principles developed for determining when and where a state's police power may constitutionally burden interstate commerce? What might such principles be? How can this decision be reconciled with Philadelphia v. New Jersey?

Blackmun, for the Court:
The Commerce Clause of the Constitution grants Congress the power "[t]o regulate Commerce with foreign Nations, and among the several States, and with the Indian Tribes." Art. I, 8, cl. 3. "Although the Clause thus speaks in terms of powers bestowed upon Congress, the Court long has recognized that it also limits the power of the States to erect barriers against interstate trade." Maine's statute restricts interstate trade in the most direct manner possible, blocking all inward shipments of live baitfish at the State's border. Still . . . this fact alone does not render the law unconstitutional. The limitation imposed by the Commerce Clause on state regulatory power "is by no means absolute," and "the States retain authority under their general police powers to regulate matters of 'legitimate local concern,' even though interstate commerce may be affected."

In determining whether a State has overstepped its role in regulating interstate commerce, this Court has distinguished between state statutes that burden interstate transactions only incidentally, and those that affirmatively discriminate against such transactions. While statutes in the first group violate the Commerce Clause only if the burdens they impose on interstate trade are "clearly excessive in relation to the putative local benefits," statutes in the second group are subject to more demanding scrutiny. The Court explained in *Hughes v. Oklahoma*, that once a state law is shown to discriminate against interstate commerce "either on its face or in practical effect," the burden falls on the State to demonstrate both that the statute "serves a legitimate local purpose," and that this purpose could not be served as well by available nondiscriminatory means . . .

The evidentiary hearing on which the District Court based its conclusions was one before a Magistrate. Three scientific experts testified for the prosecution and one for the defense. The prosecution experts testified that live baitfish imported into the State posed two significant threats to Maine's unique and fragile fisheries. First, Maine's population of wild fish—including its own indigenous golden shiners—would be placed at risk by three types of parasites prevalent in out-of-state baitfish, but not common to wild fish in Maine. Second, nonnative species inadvertently included in shipments of live baitfish could disturb Maine's aquatic ecology to an unpredictable extent by competing with native fish for food or habitat, by preying on native species, or by disrupting the environment in more subtle ways.

The(y) . . . further testified that there was no satisfactory way to inspect shipments of live baitfish for parasites or commingled species. According to their testimony, the small size of baitfish and the large quantities in which they are shipped made inspection for commingled species "a physical impossibility." Parasite inspection posed a separate set of difficulties because the examination procedure required destruction of the fish. Although statistical sampling and inspection techniques had been developed for salmonids (i. e., salmon and trout), so that a shipment could be certified parasite-free based on a standardized examination of only some of the fish, no scientifically accepted procedures of this sort were available for baitfish.

[Taylor's] expert [witness] denied that any scientific justification supported Maine's total ban on the importation of baitfish. He testified that none of the three parasites discussed by the prosecution witnesses posed any significant threat to fish in the wild and that sampling techniques had not been developed for baitfish precisely because there was no need for them. He further testified that professional baitfish farmers raise their fish in ponds that have been freshly drained to ensure that no other species is inadvertently collected.

Weighing all the testimony, the Magistrate concluded that both prongs of the *Hughes* test were satisfied, and accordingly that [Taylor's] motion to dismiss the indictment should be denied. [Taylor] filed objections, but the District Court, after an independent review of the evidence, reached the same conclusions . . .

No matter how one describes the abstract issue whether "alternative means could promote this local purpose as well without discriminating against interstate commerce," the more specific question whether scientifically accepted techniques exist for the sampling and inspection of live baitfish is one of fact, and the District Court's finding that such techniques have not been devised cannot be characterized as clearly erroneous. Indeed, the record probably could not support a contrary finding. Two prosecution witnesses testified to the lack of such procedures, and [Taylor's] expert conceded the point, although he disagreed about the need for such tests. That Maine has

allowed the importation of other freshwater fish after inspection hardly demonstrates that the District Court clearly erred in crediting the corroborated and uncontradicted expert testimony that standardized inspection techniques had not yet been developed for baitfish. This is particularly so because the text of the permit statute suggests that it was designed specifically to regulate importation of salmonids, for which, the experts testified, testing procedures had been developed.

. . . [Taylor] does not argue that sampling and inspection procedures already exist for baitfish; he contends only that such procedures "could be easily developed." Perhaps this is also what the Court of Appeals meant to suggest. Unlike the proposition that the techniques already exist, the contention that they could readily be devised enjoys some support in the record. [Taylor's] expert testified that developing the techniques "would just require that those experts in the field . . . get together and do it." He gave no estimate of the time and expense that would be involved, however, and one of the prosecution experts testified that development of the testing procedures for salmonids had required years of heavily financed research. In light of this testimony, we cannot say that the District Court clearly erred in concluding that the development of sampling and inspection techniques for baitfish could be expected to take a significant amount of time.

. . . A State must make reasonable efforts to avoid restraining the free flow of commerce across its borders, but it is not required to develop new and unproven means of protection at an uncertain cost. [Taylor], of course, is free to work on his own or in conjunction with other bait dealers to develop scientifically acceptable sampling and inspection procedures for golden shiners; if and when such procedures are developed, Maine no longer may be able to justify its import ban. The State need not join in those efforts, however, and it need not pretend they already have succeeded.

. . . [W]e cannot say that the District Court clearly erred in finding that substantial scientific uncertainty surrounds the effect that baitfish parasites and nonnative species could have on Maine's fisheries. Moreover, we agree with the District Court that Maine has a legitimate interest in guarding against imperfectly understood environmental risks, despite the possibility that they may ultimately prove to be negligible. "[T]he constitutional principles underlying the commerce clause cannot be read as requiring the State of Maine to sit idly by and wait until potentially irreversible environmental damage has occurred or until the scientific community agrees on what disease organisms are or are not dangerous before it acts to avoid such consequences."

Nor do we think that much doubt is cast on the legitimacy of Maine's purposes by what the Court of Appeals took to be signs of protectionist intent. Shielding in-state industries from out-of-state competition is almost never a legitimate local purpose, and state laws that amount to "simple economic protectionism" consequently have been subject to a "virtually per se rule of invalidity." [But] there is little reason in this case to believe that the legitimate justifications the State has put forward for its statute are merely a sham or a "post hoc rationalization." . . .

The other evidence of protectionism . . . is no more persuasive. The fact that Maine allows importation of salmonids, for which standardized sampling and inspection procedures are available, hardly demonstrates that Maine has no legitimate interest in prohibiting the importation of baitfish, for which such procedures have not yet been devised. Nor is this demonstrated by the fact that other States may not have enacted similar bans, especially given the testimony that Maine's fisheries are unique and unusually fragile. Finally, it is of little relevance that fish can swim directly into Maine from New Hampshire. As the Magistrate explained: "The impediments to complete success . . . cannot be a ground for preventing a state from using its best efforts to limit [an environmental] risk."

The Commerce Clause significantly limits the ability of States and localities to regulate or otherwise burden the flow of interstate commerce, but it does not elevate free trade above all other values. As long as a State does not needlessly obstruct interstate trade or attempt to "place itself in a position of economic isolation," it retains broad regulatory authority to protect the health and safety of its citizens and the integrity of its natural resources. The evidence in this case amply supports the District Court's findings that Maine's ban on the importation of live baitfish serves legitimate local purposes that could not adequately be served by available nondiscriminatory alternatives. This is not a case of arbitrary discrimination against interstate commerce; the record suggests that Maine has legitimate reasons, "apart from their origin, to treat [out-of-state baitfish] differently."

Stevens, dissenting:

There is something fishy about this case. Maine is the only State in the Union that blatantly discriminates against out-of-state baitfish by flatly prohibiting their importation. Although golden shiners are already present and thriving in Maine (and, perhaps not coincidentally, the subject of a flourishing domestic industry), Maine excludes golden shiners grown and harvested (and, perhaps not coincidentally, sold) in other States. This kind of stark discrimination against out-of-state articles of commerce requires rigorous justification by the discriminating State. "When discrimination against commerce of the type we have found is demonstrated, the burden falls on the State to justify it both in terms of the local benefits flowing from the statute and the unavailability of nondiscriminatory alternatives adequate to preserve the local interests at stake."

Like the District Court, the Court concludes that uncertainty about possible ecological effects from the possible presence of parasites and nonnative species in shipments of out-of-state shiners suffices to carry the State's burden of proving a legitimate public purpose. The Court similarly concludes that the State has no obligation to develop feasible inspection procedures that would make a total ban unnecessary. It seems clear, however, that the presumption should run the other way. Since the State engages in obvious discrimination against out-of-state commerce, it should be put to its proof. Ambiguity about dangers and alternatives should actually defeat, rather than sustain, the discriminatory measure.

This is not to derogate the State's interest in ecological purity. But the invocation of environmental protection or public health has never been thought to confer some kind of special dispensation from the general principle of nondiscrimination in interstate commerce. "A different view, that the ordinance is valid simply because it professes to be a health measure, would mean that the Commerce Clause of itself imposes no restraints on state action other than those laid down by the Due Process Clause, save for the rare instance where a state artlessly discloses an avowed purpose to discriminate against interstate goods." If Maine wishes to rely on its interest in ecological preservation, it must show that interest, and the infeasibility of other alternatives, with far greater specificity. Otherwise, it must further that asserted interest in a manner far less offensive to the notions of comity and cooperation that underlie the Commerce Clause.

...Maine's unquestionable natural splendor notwithstanding, the State has not carried its substantial burden of proving why it cannot meet its environmental concerns in the same manner as other States with the same interest in the health of their fish and ecology.

South Dakota v. Dole

483 U.S. 203 (1987), 7-2
Opinion of the Court: Rehnquist, C.J. (Blackmun, Marshall, Powell, Scalia, Stevens, White)
Dissenting: Brennan, O'Connor
South Dakota challenged the constitutionality of a federal highway statute that conditioned the state's receipt of federal highway funds on its adoption of a minimum drinking age of 21.

Why does Rehnquist say that the Twenty-first Amendment is not a bar to federal spending in this case? What constitutional limits are there on Congress's spending power? To what extent have states been "coerced" by the federal policy at issue?

Rehnquist, C.J., for the Court:
The Constitution empowers Congress to "lay and collect Taxes, Duties, Imposts, and Excises, to pay the Debts and provide for the common Defence and general Welfare of the United States." Art. I, s 8, cl. 1. Incident to this power, Congress may attach conditions on the receipt of federal funds, and has repeatedly employed the power "to further broad policy objectives by conditioning receipt of federal moneys upon compliance by the recipient with federal statutory and administrative directives." *Fullilove v. Klutznick* (1980). The breadth of this power was made clear in *United States v. Butler* (1936), where the Court, resolving a long-standing debate over the scope of the Spending Clause, determined that "the power of Congress to authorize expenditure of public moneys for public purposes is not limited by the direct grants of legislative power found in the Constitution." Thus, objectives not thought to be within Article I's "enumerated legislative fields," may nevertheless be attained through the use of the spending power and the conditional grant of federal funds.

The spending power is of course not unlimited, but is . . . subject to several general restrictions articulated in our cases. The first of these limitations is derived from the language of the Constitution itself: the exercise of the spending power must be in pursuit of "the

general welfare." In considering whether a particular expenditure is intended to serve general public purposes, courts should defer substantially to the judgment of Congress. Second, we have required that if Congress desires to condition the States' receipt of federal funds, it "must do so unambiguously . . . , enabl[ing] the States to exercise their choice knowingly, cognizant of the consequences of their participation." *Pennhurst State School and Hospital v. Halderman.* Third, our cases have suggested . . . that conditions on federal grants might be illegitimate if they are unrelated "to the federal interest in particular national projects or programs." *Massachusetts v. United States* (1978). Finally, we have noted that other constitutional provisions may provide an independent bar to the conditional grant of federal funds.

South Dakota does not seriously claim that [the federal act] is inconsistent with any of the first three restrictions mentioned above . . . Congress found that the differing drinking ages in the States created particular incentives for young persons to combine their desire to drink with their ability to drive, and that this interstate problem required a national solution. The means it chose to address this dangerous situation were reasonably calculated to advance the general welfare. The conditions upon which States receive the funds, moreover, could not be more clearly stated by Congress. And the State itself, rather than challenging the germaneness of the condition to federal purposes, admits that it "has never contended that the congressional action was . . . unrelated to a national concern in the absence of the Twenty-first Amendment." Indeed, the condition imposed by Congress is directly related to one of the main purposes for which highway funds are expended—safe interstate travel. This goal of the interstate highway system had been frustrated by varying drinking ages among the States. A Presidential commission appointed to study alcohol-related accidents and fatalities on the Nation's highways concluded that the lack of uniformity in the States' drinking ages created "an incentive to drink and drive" because "young persons commut[e] to border States where the drinking age is lower." Presidential Commission on Drunk Driving, Final Report (1983) . . . Congress conditioned the receipt of federal funds in a way reasonably calculated to address this particular impediment to a purpose for which the funds are expended.

The remaining question about the validity of [the act] and the basic point of disagreement between the parties—is whether the Twenty-first Amendment constitutes an "independent constitutional bar" to the conditional grant of federal funds. [South Dakota], relying on its view that the Twenty-first Amendment prohibits direct regulation of drinking ages by Congress, asserts that "Congress may not use the spending power to regulate that which it is prohibited from regulating directly under the Twenty-first Amendment." Brief for [South Dakota]. But our cases show that this "independent constitutional bar" limitation on the spending power is not of the kind [South Dakota] suggests. . . .

We have also held that a perceived Tenth Amendment limitation on congressional regulation of state affairs did not concomitantly limit the range of conditions legitimately placed on federal grants . . .

[T]he "independent constitutional bar" limitation on the spending power is not, as [South Dakota] suggests, a prohibition on the indirect achievement of objectives which Congress is not empowered to achieve directly. Instead, we think that the language in our earlier opinions stands for the unexceptionable proposition that the power may not be used to induce the States to engage in activities that would themselves be unconstitutional. Thus, for example, a grant of federal funds conditioned on invidiously discriminatory state action or the infliction of cruel and unusual punishment would be an illegitimate exercise of the Congress' broad spending power. But no such claim can be or is made here. Were South Dakota to succumb to the blandishments offered by Congress and raise its drinking age to 21, the State's action in so doing would not violate the constitutional rights of anyone.

Our decisions have recognized that in some circumstances the financial inducement offered by Congress might be so coercive as to pass the point at which "pressure turns into compulsion." *Steward Machine Co. v. Davis*. Here, however, Congress has directed only that a State desiring to establish a minimum drinking age lower than 21 lose a relatively small percentage of certain federal highway funds. [South Dakota] contends that the coercive nature of this program is evident from the degree of success it has achieved. We cannot conclude, however, that a conditional grant of federal money of this sort is unconstitutional simply by reason of its success in achieving the congressional objective.

When we consider . . . that all South Dakota would lose if she adheres to her chosen course as to a suitable minimum drinking age is 5% of the funds otherwise obtainable under specified highway grant programs, the argument as to coercion is shown to be more rhetoric than fact . . .

Here Congress has offered relatively mild encouragement to the States to enact higher minimum drinking ages than they would otherwise choose. But the enactment of such laws remains the prerogative of the States not merely in theory but in fact. Even if Congress might lack the power to impose a national minimum drinking age directly, we conclude that encouragement to state action found in [the act] is a valid use of the spending power.

Brennan, dissenting:

I agree with Justice O'Connor that regulation of the minimum age of purchasers of liquor falls squarely within the ambit of those powers reserved to the States by the Twenty-first Amendment. Since States possess this constitutional power, Congress cannot condition a federal grant in a manner that abridges this right. The Amendment, itself, strikes the proper balance between federal and state authority. I therefore dissent.

O'Connor, dissenting:

The Court today upholds the National Minimum Drinking Age Amendment, as a valid exercise of the spending power conferred by Article I, s 8. But s 158 is not a condition on spending reasonably related to the expenditure of federal funds and cannot be justified on that ground. Rather, it is an attempt to regulate the sale of liquor, an attempt that lies outside Congress' power to regulate commerce because it falls within the ambit of s 2 of the Twenty-first Amendment . . .

When Congress appropriates money to build a highway, it is entitled to insist that the highway be a safe one. But it is not entitled to insist as a condition of the use of highway funds that the State impose or change regulations in other areas of the State's social and economic life because of an attenuated or tangential relationship to highway use or safety. Indeed, if the rule were otherwise, the Congress could effectively regulate almost any area of a State's social, political, or economic life on the theory that use of the interstate transportation system is somehow enhanced. If, for example, the United States were to condition highway moneys upon moving the state capital, I suppose it might argue that interstate transportation is facilitated by locating local governments in places easily accessible to interstate highways—or, conversely, that highways might become overburdened if they had to carry traffic to and from the state capital. In my mind, such a relationship is hardly more attenuated than the one which the Court finds supports [the act] . . .

There is a clear place at which the Court can draw the line between permissible and impermissible conditions on federal grants. It is the line identified in the Brief for the National Conference of State Legislatures et al. as Amici Curiae: "Congress has the power to spend for the general welfare, it has the power to legislate only for delegated purposes . . . The appropriate inquiry, then, is whether the spending requirement or prohibition is a condition on a grant or whether it is regulation. The difference turns on whether the requirement specifies in some way how the money should be spent, so that Congress' intent in making the grant will be effectuated. Congress has no power under the Spending Clause to impose requirements on a grant that go beyond specifying how the money should be spent. A requirement that is not such a specification is not a condition, but a regulation, which is valid only if it falls within one of Congress' delegated regulatory powers."

This approach harks back to *United States v. Butler* (1936), the last case in which this Court struck down an Act of Congress as beyond the authority granted by the Spending Clause . . .

While *Butler's* authority is questionable insofar as it assumes that Congress has no regulatory power over farm production, its discussion of the spending power and its description of both the power's breadth and its limitations remain sound. The Court's decision in *Butler* also properly recognizes the gravity of the task of appropriately limiting the spending power. If the spending power is to be limited only by Congress' notion of the general welfare, the reality, given the vast financial resources of the Federal Government, is that the Spending Clause gives "power to the Congress to tear down the barriers, to invade the states' jurisdiction, and to become a parliament of the whole people, subject to no restrictions save such as are self-imposed." *United States v. Butler*. This . . . was not the framers' plan and it is not the meaning of the Spending Clause.

Our later cases are consistent with the notion that, under the spending power, the Congress may only condition grants in ways that can fairly be said to be related to the expenditure of federal funds. For example, in *Oklahoma v. CSC* (1947), the Court upheld ap-plication of the Hatch Act to a member of the Oklahoma State Highway Commission who was employed in connection with an activity financed in part by loans and grants from a federal agency. This condition is appropriately viewed as a condition relating to how federal moneys were to be expended. Other conditions that have been upheld by the Court may be viewed as independently justified under some regulatory power of the Congress. Thus, in *Fullilove v. Klutznick* (1980), the Court upheld a condition on federal grants that 10% of the money be "set aside" for contracts with minority business enterprises. But the Court found that the condition could be justified as a valid regulation under the commerce power and s 5 of the Fourteenth Amendment. . . .

As discussed above, a condition that a State will raise its drinking age to 21 cannot fairly be said to be reasonably related to the expenditure of funds for highway construction. The only possible connection, highway safety, has nothing to do with how the funds Congress has appropriated are expended. Rather than a condition determining how federal highway money shall be expended, it is a regulation determining who shall be able to drink liquor. As such it is not justified by the spending power.

Of the other possible sources of congressional authority for regulating the sale of liquor only the commerce power comes to mind . . . [T]he regulation of the age of the purchasers of liquor, just as the regulation of the price at which liquor may be sold, falls squarely within the scope of those powers reserved to the States by the Twenty-first Amendment . . . Accordingly, Congress simply lacks power under the Commerce Clause to displace state regulation of this kind.

New York v. United States

505 U.S. 144 (1992), 6-3
Opinion of the Court: O'Connor (Kennedy, Rehnquist, Souter, Scalia, Thomas)
Dissenting: Stevens, White
To deal with a shortage of disposal sites for low-level radioactive waste, Congress enacted the Low-Level Radioactive Waste Policy Amendments Act of 1985 requiring states, either alone or in regional compacts with other states, to make provisions for disposing of waste generated within their borders. States that did not comply by a particular date were required, on the request of the waste's owner, to take title to and possession of the waste and become liable for damages

that might be produced by it. New York State and two of its counties sued to have the act declared unconstitutional

Why is a federal requirement that states "take title" unconstitutional? Does the Court object to the means chosen by Congress or to the reach of its power? Does the provision strike at the heart of federalism as a practical matter? As a matter of principle? How, in O'Connor's view, does it undermine democratic accountability? Are the United States and New York state the real antagonists in this case? How, if at all, can this case be distinguished from South Dakota v. Dole? *From* Garcia v. San Antonio Metropolitan Transit Authority?

O'Connor, for the Court:

This case implicates one of our Nation's newest problems of public policy and perhaps our oldest question of constitutional law. The public policy issue involves the disposal of radioactive waste: In this case, we address the constitutionality of three provisions of the Low-Level Radioactive Waste Policy Amendments Act of 1985 The constitutional question . . . consists of discerning the proper division of authority between the Federal Government and the States. We conclude that while Congress has substantial power under the Constitution to encourage the States to provide for the disposal of the radioactive waste generated within their borders, the Constitution does not confer upon Congress the ability simply to compel the States to do so. We therefore find that only two of the Act's three provisions at issue are consistent with the Constitution's allocation of power to the Federal Government . . .

Congress exercises its conferred powers subject to the limitations contained in the Constitution. Thus, for example, under the Commerce Clause Congress may regulate publishers engaged in interstate commerce, but Congress is constrained in the exercise of that power by the First Amendment. The Tenth Amendment likewise restrains the power of Congress, but this limit is not derived from the text of the Tenth Amendment itself, which . . . is essentially a tautology. Instead, the Tenth Amendment confirms that the power of the Federal Government is subject to limits that may, in a given instance, reserve power to the States. The Tenth Amendment thus directs us to determine, as in this case, whether an incident of state sovereignty is protected by a limitation on an Article I power . . .

This framework has been sufficiently flexible over the past two centuries to allow for enormous changes in the nature of government. The Federal Govern-

ment undertakes activities today that would have been unimaginable to the Framers in two senses; first, because the Framers would not have conceived that any government would conduct such activities; and second, because the Framers would not have believed that the Federal Government, rather than the States, would assume such responsibilities. Yet the powers conferred upon the Federal Government by the Constitution were phrased in language broad enough to allow for the expansion of the Federal Government's role. Among the provisions of the Constitution that have been particularly important in this regard, three concern us here.

First, the Constitution allocates to Congress the power "[t]o regulate Commerce . . . among the several States." Interstate commerce was an established feature of life in the late 18th century . . . The volume of interstate commerce and the range of commonly accepted objects of government regulation have, however, expanded considerably in the last 200 years, and the regulatory authority of Congress has expanded along with them. As interstate commerce has become ubiquitous, activities once considered purely local have come to have effects on the national economy, and have accordingly come within the scope of Congress' commerce power . . .

The Court's broad construction of Congress' power under the Commerce and Spending Clauses has of course been guided, as it has with respect to Congress' power generally, by the Constitution's Necessary and Proper Clause, which authorizes Congress "[t]o make all Laws which shall be necessary and proper for carrying into Execution the foregoing Powers."

Finally, the Constitution provides that "the Laws of the United States . . . shall be the supreme Law of the Land . . . any Thing in the Constitution or Laws of any State to the Contrary notwithstanding." As the Federal Government's willingness to exercise power within the confines of the Constitution has grown, the authority of the States has correspondingly diminished to the extent that federal and state policies have conflicted. We have observed that the Supremacy Clause gives the Federal Government "a decided advantage in th[e] delicate balance" the Constitution strikes between state and federal power.

The actual scope of the Federal Government's authority with respect to the States has changed over the years, therefore, but the constitutional structure underlying and limiting that authority has not. In the end, just as a cup may be half empty or half full, it makes no difference whether one views the question at issue in this case as one of ascertaining the limits of the power delegated to the Federal Government under the affirmative provisions of the Constitution or one of discerning the core of sovereignty retained by the States under the Tenth Amendment. Either way, we must determine whether any of the three challenged provisions of the Low-Level Radioactive Waste Policy Amendments Act of 1985 oversteps the boundary between federal and state authority.

[New York does] not contend that Congress lacks the power to regulate the disposal of low level radioactive waste. Space in radioactive waste disposal sites is frequently sold by residents of one State to residents of another. Regulation of the resulting interstate market in waste disposal is therefore well within Congress' authority under the Commerce Clause. [New York] likewise do[es] not dispute that under the Supremacy Clause Congress could, if it wished, pre-empt state radioactive waste regulation. [New York] contend[s] only that the Tenth Amendment limits the power of Congress to regulate in the way it has chosen. Rather than addressing the problem of waste disposal by directly regulating the generators and disposers of waste, [it] argue[s], Congress has impermissibly directed the States to regulate in this field . . .

[T]his is not a case in which Congress has subjected a State to the same legislation applicable to private parties.

. . . [I]nstead [it] concerns the circumstances under which Congress may use the States as implements of regulation; that is, whether Congress may direct or otherwise motivate the States to regulate in a particular field or a particular way. Our cases have established a few principles that guide our resolution of the issue.

As an initial matter, Congress may not simply "commandee[r] the legislative processes of the States by directly compelling them to enact and enforce a federal regulatory program." *Hodel v. Virginia Surface Mining & Reclamation Assn., Inc.* (1981). . . .

While Congress has substantial powers to govern the Nation directly, including in areas of intimate concern to the States, the Constitution has never been understood to confer upon Congress the ability to require the States to govern according to Congress' instructions . . . In Chief Justice Chase's much-quoted words, "the preservation of the States, and the maintenance of their governments, are as much within the design and care of the Constitution as the preservation of

the Union and the maintenance of the National government. The Constitution, in all its provisions, looks to an indestructible Union, composed of indestructible States." *Texas v. White* (1869) . . .

This is not to say that Congress lacks the ability to encourage a State to regulate in a particular way, or that Congress may not hold out incentives to the States as a method of influencing a State's policy choices. Our cases have identified a variety of methods, short of outright coercion, by which Congress may urge a State to adopt a legislative program consistent with federal interests. Two of these methods are of particular relevance here.

First, under Congress' spending power, "Congress may attach conditions on the receipt of federal funds." *South Dakota v. Dole.* Such conditions must (among other requirements) bear some relationship to the purpose of the federal spending, otherwise, of course, the spending power could render academic the Constitution's other grants and limits of federal authority. Where the recipient of federal funds is a State, as is not unusual today, the conditions attached to the funds by Congress may influence a State's legislative choices. *Dole* was one such case: The Court found no constitutional flaw in a federal statute directing the Secretary of Transportation to withhold federal highway funds from States failing to adopt Congress' choice of a minimum drinking age. Similar examples abound.

Second, where Congress has the authority to regulate private activity under the Commerce Clause, we have recognized Congress' power to offer States the choice of regulating that activity according to federal standards or having state law pre-empted by federal regulation. . . .

By either of these two methods, as by any other permissible method of encouraging a State to conform to federal policy choices, the residents of the State retain the ultimate decision as to whether or not the State will comply. If a State's citizens view federal policy as sufficiently contrary to local interests, they may elect to decline a federal grant. If state residents would prefer their government to devote its attention and resources to problems other than those deemed important by Congress, they may choose to have the Federal Government rather than the State bear the expense of a federally mandated regulatory program, and they may continue to supplement that program to the extent state law is not preempted. Where Congress encourages state regulation rather than compelling it, state governments remain responsive to the local electorate's preferences; state officials remain accountable to the people.

By contrast, where the Federal Government compels States to regulate, the accountability of both state and federal officials is diminished. If the citizens of New York, for example, do not consider that making provision for the disposal of radioactive waste is in their best interest, they may elect state officials who share their view. That view can always be preempted under the Supremacy Clause if it is contrary to the national view, but in such a case it is the Federal Government that makes the decision in full view of the public, and it will be federal officials that suffer the consequences if the decision turns out to be detrimental or unpopular. But where the Federal Government directs the States to regulate, it may be state officials who will bear the brunt of public disapproval, while the federal officials who devised the regulatory program may remain insulated from the electoral ramifications of their decision. Accountability is thus diminished when, due to federal coercion, elected state officials cannot regulate in accordance with the views of the local electorate in matters not preempted by federal regulation.

With these principles in mind, we turn to the three challenged provisions of the Low-Level Radioactive Waste Policy Amendments Act of 1985 . . .

The first set of incentives works in three steps. First, Congress has authorized States with disposal sites to impose a surcharge on radioactive waste received from other States. Second, the Secretary of Energy collects a portion of this surcharge and places the money in an escrow account. Third, States achieving a series of milestones receive portions of this fund.

The first of these steps is an unexceptionable exercise of Congress' power to authorize the States to burden interstate commerce. . . .

The second step, the Secretary's collection of a percentage of the surcharge, is no more than a federal tax on interstate commerce, which [New York] do[es] not claim to be an invalid exercise of either Congress' commerce or taxing power.

The third step is a conditional exercise of Congress' authority under the Spending Clause: Congress has placed conditions—the achievement of the milestones—on the receipt of federal funds. . . .

The Act's first set of incentives, in which Congress has conditioned grants to the States upon the States' attainment of a series of milestones, is thus well within the authority of Congress under the Commerce and Spending Clauses. Because the first set of incentives is supported by affirmative constitutional grants of power to Congress, it is not inconsistent with the Tenth Amendment.

In the second set of incentives, Congress has authorized States and regional compacts with disposal sites gradually to increase the cost of access to the sites, and then to deny access altogether, to radioactive waste generated in States that do not meet federal deadlines. As a simple regulation, this provision would be within the power of Congress to authorize the States to discriminate against interstate commerce. Where federal regulation of private activity is within the scope of the Commerce Clause, we have recognized the ability of Congress to offer States the choice of regulating that activity according to federal standards or having state law pre-empted by federal regulation.

This is the choice presented to non-sited States by the Act's second set of incentives: States may either regulate the disposal of radioactive waste according to federal standards by attaining local or regional self-sufficiency, or their residents who produce radioactive waste will be subject to federal regulation authorizing sited States and regions to deny access to their disposal sites. The affected States are not compelled by Congress to regulate, because any burden caused by a State's refusal to regulate will fall on those who generate waste and find no outlet for its disposal, rather than on the State as a sovereign. A State whose citizens do not wish it to attain the Act's milestones may devote its attention and its resources to issues its citizens deem more worthy; the choice remains at all times with the residents of the State, not with Congress. The State need not expend any funds, or participate in any federal program, if local residents do not view such expenditures or participation as worthwhile. Nor must the State abandon the field if it does not accede to federal direction; the State may continue to regulate the generation and disposal of radioactive waste in any manner its citizens see fit.

The Act's second set of incentives thus represents a conditional exercise of Congress' commerce power, along the lines of those we have held to be within Congress' authority. As a result, the second set of incentives does not intrude on the sovereignty reserved to the States by the Tenth Amendment.

The take title provision is of a different character. This third so-called "incentive" offers States, as an alternative to regulating pursuant to Congress' direction, the option of taking title to and possession of the low level radioactive waste generated within their borders and becoming liable for all damages waste generators suffer as a result of the States' failure to do so promptly. In this provision, Congress has crossed the line distinguishing encouragement from coercion . . .

The take title provision offers state governments a "choice" of either accepting ownership of waste or regulating according to the instructions of Congress. Respondents do not claim that the Constitution would authorize Congress to impose either option as a free-standing requirement. On one hand, the Constitution would not permit Congress simply to transfer radioactive waste from generators to state governments. Such a forced transfer, standing alone, would in principle be no different than a congressionally compelled subsidy from state governments to radioactive waste producers. The same is true of the provision requiring the States to become liable for the generators' damages. Standing alone, this provision would be indistinguishable from an Act of Congress directing the States to assume the liabilities of certain state residents. Either type of federal action would "commandeer" state governments into the service of federal regulatory purposes, and would for this reason be inconsistent with the Constitution's division of authority between federal and state governments. On the other hand, the second alternative held out to state governments—regulating pursuant to Congress' direction—would, standing alone, present a simple command to state governments to implement legislation enacted by Congress . . . [T]he Constitution does not empower Congress to subject state governments to this type of instruction . . .

The take title provision appears to be unique. No other federal statute has been cited which offers a state government no option other than that of implementing legislation enacted by Congress. Whether one views the take title provision as lying outside Congress' enumerated powers, or as infringing upon the core of state sovereignty reserved by the Tenth Amendment, the provision is inconsistent with the federal structure of our Government established by the Constitution.

Respondents raise a number of objections to this understanding of the limits of Congress' power.

The United States proposes three alternative views of the constitutional line separating state and federal authority. While each view concedes that Congress generally may not compel state governments to regulate pursuant to federal direction, each purports to

find a limited domain in which such coercion is permitted by the Constitution.

First, the United States argues that the Constitution's prohibition of congressional directives to state governments can be overcome where the federal interest is sufficiently important to justify state submission. This argument contains a kernel of truth: In determining whether the Tenth Amendment limits the ability of Congress to subject state governments to generally applicable laws, the Court has in some cases stated that it will evaluate the strength of federal interests in light of the degree to which such laws would prevent the State from functioning as a sovereign; that is, the extent to which such generally applicable laws would impede a state government's responsibility to represent and be accountable to the citizens of the State. The Court has more recently departed from this approach. But whether or not a particularly strong federal interest enables Congress to bring state governments within the orbit of generally applicable federal regulation, no Member of the Court has ever suggested that such a federal interest would enable Congress to command a state government to enact state regulation. No matter how powerful the federal interest involved, the Constitution simply does not give Congress the authority to require the States to regulate. The Constitution instead gives Congress the authority to regulate matters directly and to pre-empt contrary state regulation. Where a federal interest is sufficiently strong to cause Congress to legislate, it must do so directly; it may not conscript state governments as its agents.

Second, the United States argues that the Constitution does, in some circumstances, permit federal directives to state governments. Various cases are cited for this proposition, but none support it. Some of these cases discuss the well established power of Congress to pass laws enforceable in state courts . . .

Third, the United States, supported by the three sited regional compacts as amici, argues that the Constitution envisions a role for Congress as an arbiter of interstate disputes. The United States observes that federal courts, and this Court in particular, have frequently resolved conflicts among States. Many of these disputes have involved the allocation of shared resources among the States, a category perhaps broad enough to encompass the allocation of scarce disposal space for radioactive waste. The United States suggests that if the Court may resolve such interstate disputes, Congress can surely do the same under the

Commerce Clause. The regional compacts support this argument with a series of quotations from *The Federalist* and other contemporaneous documents, which the compacts contend demonstrate that the Framers established a strong National Legislature for the purpose of resolving trade disputes among the States. Brief for Rocky Mountain Low-Level Radioactive Waste Compact et al. as Amici Curiae 17, and . 16.

While the Framers no doubt endowed Congress with the power to regulate interstate commerce in order to avoid further instances of the interstate trade disputes that were common under the Articles of Confederation, the Framers did not intend that Congress should exercise that power through the mechanism of mandating state regulation. The Constitution established Congress as "a superintending authority over the reciprocal trade" among the States, *The Federalist* No. 42, by empowering Congress to regulate that trade directly, not by authorizing Congress to issue trade-related orders to state governments. . . .

The sited state respondents focus their attention on the process by which the Act was formulated. They correctly observe that public officials representing the State of New York lent their support to the Act's enactment. A Deputy Commissioner of the State's Energy Office testified in favor of the Act . . . [They] note that the Act embodies a bargain among the sited and unsited States, a compromise to which New York was a willing participant and from which New York has reaped much benefit. [It] then pose[s] what appears at first to be a troubling question: How can a federal statute be found an unconstitutional infringement of state sovereignty when state officials consented to the statute's enactment?

The answer follows from an understanding of the fundamental purpose served by our Government's federal structure. The Constitution does not protect the sovereignty of States for the benefit of the States or state governments as abstract political entities, or even for the benefit of the public officials governing the States. To the contrary, the Constitution divides authority between federal and state governments for the protection of individuals. State sovereignty is not just an end in itself: "Rather, federalism secures to citizens the liberties that derive from the diffusion of sovereign power." *Coleman v. Thompson* (1991) (Blackmun, J., dissenting). . . .

Where Congress exceeds its authority relative to the States, therefore, the departure from the constitutional plan cannot be ratified by the "consent" of state officials . . .

Some truths are so basic that, like the air around us, they are easily overlooked. Much of the Constitution is concerned with setting forth the form of our government, and the courts have traditionally invalidated measures deviating from that form. The result may appear "formalistic" in a given case to partisans of the measure at issue, because such measures are typically the product of the era's perceived necessity. But the Constitution protects us from our own best intentions: It divides power among sovereigns and among branches of government precisely so that we may resist the temptation to concentrate power in one location as an expedient solution to the crisis of the day. The shortage of disposal sites for radioactive waste is a pressing national problem, but a judiciary that licensed extra-constitutional government with each issue of comparable gravity would, in the long run, be far worse.

States are not mere political subdivisions of the United States. State governments are neither regional offices nor administrative agencies of the Federal Government. The positions occupied by state officials appear nowhere on the Federal Government's most detailed organizational chart . . .

The Federal Government may not compel the States to enact or administer a federal regulatory program. The Constitution permits both the Federal Government and the States to enact legislation regarding the disposal of low level radioactive waste. The Constitution enables the Federal Government to pre-empt state regulation contrary to federal interests, and it permits the Federal Government to hold out incentives to the States as a means of encouraging them to adopt suggested regulatory schemes. It does not, however, authorize Congress simply to direct the States to provide for the disposal of the radioactive waste generated within their borders.

White (Stevens, Blackmun), concurring in part and dissenting in part:

My disagreement with the Court's analysis begins at the basic descriptive level of how the legislation at issue in this case came to be enacted. The Court goes some way toward setting out the bare facts, but its omissions cast the statutory context of the take title provision in the wrong light. To read the Court's version of events, see *ante*, at 2-3, one would think that Congress was the sole proponent of a solution to the Nation's low-level radioactive waste problem. Not so. The Low-Level Radioactive Waste Policy Act of 1980 and its amendatory 1985 Act, resulted from the efforts of state leaders to achieve a state-based set of remedies to the waste problem. They sought not federal pre-emption or intervention, but rather congressional sanction of interstate compromises they had reached . . .

New York's actions subsequent to enactment of the 1980 and 1985 Acts fairly indicate its approval of the interstate agreement process embodied in those laws within the meaning of Art. I, s 10, cl. 3, of the Constitution, which provides that "[n]o State shall, without the Consent of Congress, . . . enter into any Agreement or Compact with another State." First, the States—including New York—worked through their Governors to petition Congress for the 1980 and 1985 Acts . . . [T]hese statutes are best understood as the products of collective state action, rather than as impositions placed on States by the Federal Government. Second, New York acted in compliance with the requisites of both statutes in key respects, thus signifying its assent to the agreement achieved among the States as codified in these laws. After enactment of the 1980 Act and pursuant to its provision in s 4(a)(2), New York entered into compact negotiations with several other northeastern States before withdrawing from them to "go it alone." . . .

The Court's distinction between a federal statute's regulation of States and private parties for general purposes, as opposed to a regulation solely on the activities of States, is unsupported by our recent Tenth Amendment cases. In no case has the Court rested its holding on such a distinction. Moreover, the Court makes no effort to explain why this purported distinction should affect the analysis of Congress' power under general principles of federalism and the Tenth Amendment . . . An incursion on state sovereignty hardly seems more constitutionally acceptable if the federal statute that "commands" specific action also applies to private parties. The alleged diminution in state authority over its own affairs is not any less because the federal mandate restricts the activities of private parties . . .

Though I disagree with the Court's conclusion that the take title provision is unconstitutional, I do not read its opinion to preclude Congress from adopting a similar measure through its powers under the Spending or Commerce Clauses. The Court makes clear that its objection is to the alleged "commandeer[ing]" quality of the take title provision. As its discussion of the surcharge and rebate incentives reveals, the spending power offers a means of enacting a take title provision under the Court's standards.

Congress could, in other words, condition the payment of funds on the State's willingness to take title if it has not already provided a waste disposal facility . . .

Similarly, should a State fail to establish a waste disposal facility by the appointed deadline (under the statute as presently drafted, January 1, 1996, s 2021e(d)(2)(C)), Congress has the power pursuant to the Commerce Clause to regulate directly the producers of the waste . . .

Finally, our precedents leave open the possibility that Congress may create federal rights of action in the generators of low-level radioactive waste against persons acting under color of state law for their failure to meet certain functions designated in federal-state programs . . .

The ultimate irony of the decision today is that in its formalistically rigid obeisance to "federalism," the Court gives Congress fewer incentives to defer to the wishes of state officials in achieving local solutions to local problems. This legislation was a classic example of Congress acting as arbiter among the States in their attempts to accept responsibility for managing a problem of grave import. The States urged the National Legislature not to impose from Washington a solution to the country's low-level radioactive waste management problems. Instead, they sought a reasonable level of local and regional autonomy consistent with Art. I, s 10, cl. 3, of the Constitution. By invalidating the measure designed to ensure compliance for recalcitrant States, such as New York, the Court upsets the delicate compromise achieved among the States and forces Congress to erect several additional formalistic hurdles to clear before achieving exactly the same objective.

United States v. Lopez

115 S.Ct. 1624 (1995), 5-4
Opinion of the Court: Rehnquist, C.J. (O'Connor, Scalia)
Concurring: Kennedy, Thomas
Dissenting: Breyer, Souter, Stevens

Does enumeration of power mean there must be something not enumerated and thus withheld? Is it the Court's view that carrying a handgun to school is not commerce or that it does not have a substantial effect on interstate commerce? What is the difference between "effect" and "substantial effect"? Does such a distinction resurrect the direct versus indirect effects analysis of years past or does it simply refer to matter of degree? Are the supposed negative links between quality of education and violence in the schools and between education and national economic well-being as described in Breyer's dissent Congress's reasons for passage of the act, or is it Breyer's speculation? If Breyer's interpretation of the scope of the commerce clause is correct, is there any activity that would not, in the aggregate, be related to commerce and thus to interstate commerce? Is it relevant to the constitutional issues in the case that Lopez had been indicted under Texas law and, presumably, would have been prosecuted under it had the federal action not been taken?

Rehnquist, C.J., for the Court:

In the Gun-Free School Zones Act of 1990, Congress made it a federal offense "for any individual knowingly to possess a firearm at a place that . . . is a school zone." The Act neither regulates a commercial activity nor contains a requirement that the possession be connected in any way to interstate commerce. We hold that the Act exceeds the authority of Congress "[t]o regulate Commerce . . . among the several States . . . ."

On March 10, 1992, [Lopez], who was then a 12th-grade student, arrived at Edison High School in San Antonio, Texas, carrying a concealed .38 caliber handgun and five bullets. Acting upon an anonymous tip, school authorities confronted [Lopez], who admitted that he was carrying the weapon. He was arrested and charged under Texas law with firearm possession on school premises. The next day, the state charges were dismissed after federal agents charged [him] . . . with violating the Gun-Free School Zones Act of 1990 . . .

We start with first principles. The Constitution creates a Federal Government of enumerated powers. As James Madison wrote, "[t]he powers delegated by the proposed Constitution to the federal government are few and defined. Those which are to remain in the State governments are numerous and indefinite." *The Federalist* No. 45. This constitutionally mandated division of authority "was adopted by the Framers to ensure protection of our fundamental liberties." *Gregory v. Ashcroft* (1991) "Just as the separation and independence of the coordinate branches of the Federal Government serves to prevent the accumulation of excessive power in any one branch, a healthy balance of power between the States and the Federal Government will reduce the risk of tyranny and abuse from either front." . . .

The Court, through Chief Justice Marshall, first defined the nature of Congress' commerce power in *Gibbons v. Ogden* (1824): "Commerce, undoubtedly, is traffic, but it is something more: it is intercourse. It describes the commercial intercourse between nations, and parts of nations, in all its branches, and is regulated by prescribing rules for carrying on that intercourse." The commerce power "is the power to regulate; that is, to prescribe the rule by which commerce is to be governed. This power, like all others vested in Congress, is complete in itself, may be exercised to its utmost extent, and acknowledges no limitations, other than are prescribed in the constitution." The *Gibbons* Court, however, acknowledged that limitations on the commerce power are inherent in the very language of the Commerce Clause. "It is not intended to say that these words comprehend that commerce, which is completely internal, which is carried on between man and man in a State, or between different parts of the same State, and which does not extend to or affect other States. Such a power would be inconvenient, and is certainly unnecessary. . . .

Jones & Laughlin Steel, Darby, and *Wickard* ushered in an era of Commerce Clause jurisprudence that greatly expanded the previously defined authority of Congress under that Clause. In part, this was a recognition of the great changes that had occurred in the way business was carried on in this country. Enterprises that had once been local or at most regional in nature had become national in scope. But the doctrinal change also reflected a view that earlier Commerce Clause cases artificially had constrained the authority of Congress to regulate interstate commerce.

But even these modern-era precedents which have expanded congressional power under the Commerce Clause confirm that this power is subject to outer limits. In *Jones & Laughlin Steel,* the Court warned that the scope of the interstate commerce power "must be considered in the light of our dual system of government and may not be extended so as to embrace effects upon interstate commerce so indirect and remote that to embrace them, in view of our complex society, would effectually obliterate the distinction between what is national and what is local and create a completely centralized government." . . . Since that time, the Court has heeded that warning and undertaken to decide whether a rational basis existed for concluding that a regulated activity sufficiently affected interstate commerce . . .

Consistent with this structure, we have identified three broad categories of activity that Congress may regulate under its commerce power. First, Congress may regulate the use of the channels of interstate commerce . . . Second, Congress is empowered to regulate and protect the instrumentalities of interstate commerce, or persons or things in interstate commerce, even though the threat may come only from intrastate activities . . . Finally, Congress' commerce authority includes the power to regulate those activities having a substantial relation to interstate commerce, i.e., those activities that substantially affect interstate commerce.

Within this final category, admittedly, our case law has not been clear whether an activity must "affect" or "substantially affect" interstate commerce in order to be within Congress' power to regulate it under the Commerce Clause . . . We conclude, consistent with the great weight of our case law, that the proper test requires an analysis of whether the regulated activity "substantially affects" interstate commerce.

We now turn to consider the power of Congress, in the light of this framework, to enact s 922(q). The first two categories of authority may be quickly disposed of: s 922(q) is not a regulation of the use of the channels of interstate commerce, nor is it an attempt to prohibit the interstate transportation of a commodity through the channels of commerce; nor can s 922(q) be justified as a regulation by which Congress has sought to protect an instrumentality of interstate commerce or a thing in interstate commerce. Thus, if s 922(q) is to be sustained, it must be under the third category as a regulation of an activity that substantially affects interstate commerce.

. . . [W]e have upheld a wide variety of congressional Acts regulating intrastate economic activity where we have concluded that the activity substantially affected interstate commerce. Examples include the regulation of intrastate coal mining, intrastate extortionate credit transactions, restaurants utilizing substantial interstate supplies, inns and hotels catering to interstate guests, and production and consumption of home-grown wheat. These examples are by no means exhaustive, but the pattern is clear. Where economic activity substantially affects interstate commerce, legislation regulating that activity will be sustained . . .

Section 922(q) is a criminal statute that by its terms has nothing to do with "commerce" or any sort of economic enterprise, however broadly one might define those terms. Section 922(q) is not an essential part of a larger regulation of economic activity, in which the regulatory scheme could be undercut unless the intrastate activity were regulated. It cannot, therefore, be sustained under our cases upholding regulations of activities that arise out of or are connected with a commercial transaction, which viewed in the aggregate, substantially affects interstate commerce.

Second, s 922(q) contains no jurisdictional element which would ensure, through case-by-case inquiry, that the firearm possession in question affects interstate commerce. For example, in *United States v. Bass* (1971), the Court interpreted former 18 U.S.C. s 1202(a), which made it a crime for a felon to "receiv[e], posses[s], or transpor[t] in commerce or affecting commerce . . . any firearm." The Court interpreted the possession component of s 1202(a) to require an additional nexus to interstate commerce both because the statute was ambiguous and because "unless Congress conveys its purpose clearly, it will not be deemed to have significantly changed the federal-state balance." The *Bass* Court set aside the conviction because although the Government had demonstrated that Bass had possessed a firearm, it had failed "to show the requisite nexus with interstate commerce." The Court thus interpreted the statute to reserve the constitutional question whether Congress could regulate, without more, the "mere possession" of firearms . . . Unlike the statute in *Bass*, s 922(q) has no express jurisdictional element which might limit its reach to a discrete set of firearm possessions that additionally have an explicit connection with or effect on interstate commerce.

Although as part of our independent evaluation of constitutionality under the Commerce Clause we of course consider legislative findings, and indeed even congressional committee findings, regarding effect on interstate commerce, the Government concedes that "[n]either the statute nor its legislative history contain[s] express congressional findings regarding the effects upon interstate commerce of gun possession in a school zone." We agree with the Government that Congress normally is not required to make formal findings as to the substantial burdens that an activity has on interstate commerce. But to the extent that congressional findings would enable us to evaluate the legislative judgment that the activity in question substantially affected interstate commerce, even though no such substantial effect was visible to the naked eye, they are lacking here . . .

The Government's essential contention . . . is that we may determine here that s 922(q) is valid because possession of a firearm in a local school zone does indeed substantially affect interstate commerce. Brief for United States 17. The Government argues that possession of a firearm in a school zone may result in violent crime and that violent crime can be expected to affect the functioning of the national economy in two ways. First, the costs of violent crime are substantial, and, through the mechanism of insurance, those costs are spread throughout the population. Second, violent crime reduces the willingness of individuals to travel to areas within the country that are perceived to be unsafe. The Government also argues that the presence of guns in schools poses a substantial threat to the educational process by threatening the learning environment. A handicapped educational process, in turn, will result in a less productive citizenry. That, in turn, would have an adverse effect on the Nation's economic well-being. As a result, the Government argues that Congress could rationally have concluded that s 922(q) substantially affects interstate commerce. . . .

The Government admits, under its "costs of crime" reasoning, that Congress could regulate not only all violent crime, but all activities that might lead to violent crime, regardless of how tenuously they relate to interstate commerce. Similarly, under the Government's "national productivity" reasoning, Congress could regulate any activity that it found was related to the economic productivity of individual citizens: family law (including marriage, divorce, and child custody), for example. Under the theories that the Government presents in support of s 922(q), it is difficult to perceive any limitation on federal power, even in areas such as criminal law enforcement or education where States historically have been sovereign. Thus, if we were to accept the Government's arguments, we are hard-pressed to posit any activity by an individual that Congress is without power to regulate . . .

Admittedly, a determination whether an intrastate activity is commercial or noncommercial may in some cases result in legal uncertainty. But, so long as Congress' authority is limited to those powers enumerated in the Constitution, and so long as those enumerated powers are interpreted as having judicially enforceable outer limits, congressional legislation under the Commerce Clause always will engender "legal uncertainty." As Chief Justice Marshall stated in *McCulloch v. Maryland* (1819): "The [federal] government is acknowledged by all to be one of enumerated powers. The principle, that it can exercise only the powers granted to it . . . is now universally admitted. But the question respecting the extent of the powers actually granted, is perpetually arising, and will probably continue to arise, as long as our system shall exist." The Constitution mandates this uncertainty by withholding from Congress a plenary police power that would authorize enactment of every type of legislation. Congress has operated within this framework of legal uncertainty ever since this Court determined that it was the judiciary's duty "to say what the law is." *Marbury v. Madison* (1803). Any possible benefit from eliminating this "legal uncertainty" would be at the expense of the Constitution's system of enumerated powers . . .

These are not precise formulations, and in the nature of things they cannot be. But we think they point the way to a correct decision of this case. The possession of a gun in a local school zone is in no sense an economic activity that might, through repetition elsewhere, substantially affect any sort of interstate commerce. [Lopez] was a local student at a local school; there is no indication that he had recently moved in interstate commerce, and there is no requirement that his possession of the firearm have any concrete tie to interstate commerce.

To uphold the Government's contentions here, we would have to pile inference upon inference in a manner that would bid fair to convert congressional authority under the Commerce Clause to a general police power of the sort retained by the States. Admittedly, some of our prior cases have taken long steps down that road, giving great deference to congressional action. The broad language in these opinions has suggested the possibility of additional expansion, but we decline here to proceed any further. To do so would require us to conclude that the Constitution's enumeration of powers does not presuppose something not enumerated, and that there never will be a distinction between what is truly national and what is truly local. This we are unwilling to do.

Breyer (Ginsberg, Souter, Stevens), dissenting:
The issue in this case is whether the Commerce Clause authorizes Congress to enact a statute that makes it a crime to possess a gun in, or near, a school . . . [T]he statute falls well within the scope of the

commerce power as this Court has understood that power over the last half-century. . . .

First, the power to "regulate Commerce . . . among the several States," encompasses the power to regulate local activities insofar as they significantly affect interstate commerce. As the majority points out, the Court, in describing how much of an effect the Clause requires, sometimes has used the word "substantial" and sometimes has not. . . . And, as the majority also recognizes in quoting Justice Cardozo, the question of degree (how much effect) requires an estimate of the "size" of the effect that no verbal formulation can capture with precision. . . .

Second, in determining whether a local activity will likely have a significant effect upon interstate commerce, a court must consider, not the effect of an individual act (a single instance of gun possession), but rather the cumulative effect of all similar instances (i.e., the effect of all guns possessed in or near schools). . . .

Third, the Constitution requires us to judge the connection between a regulated activity and interstate commerce, not directly, but at one remove. Courts must give Congress a degree of leeway in determining the existence of a significant factual connection between the regulated activity and interstate commerce—both because the Constitution delegates the commerce power directly to Congress and because the determination requires an empirical judgment of a kind that a legislature is more likely than a court to make with accuracy. The traditional words "rational basis" capture this leeway. Thus, the specific question before us, as the Court recognizes, is not whether the "regulated activity sufficiently affected interstate commerce," but, rather, whether Congress could have had "a rational basis" for so concluding. . . .

Applying these principles to the case at hand, we must ask whether Congress could have had a rational basis for finding a significant (or substantial) connection between gun-related school violence and interstate commerce . . . Numerous reports and studies—generated both inside and outside government—make clear that Congress could reasonably have found the empirical connection that its law, implicitly or explicitly, asserts . . .

For one thing, reports, hearings, and other readily available literature make clear that the problem of guns in and around schools is widespread and extremely serious. These materials report, for example, that four percent of American high school students

(and six percent of inner-city high school students) carry a gun to school at least occasionally, that 12 percent of urban high school students have had guns fired at them, that 20 percent of those students have been threatened with guns, and that, in any 6-month period, several hundred thousand schoolchildren are victims of violent crimes in or near their schools. And, they report that this widespread violence in schools throughout the Nation significantly interferes with the quality of education in those schools . . . Based on reports such as these, Congress obviously could have thought that guns and learning are mutually exclusive. And, Congress could therefore have found a substantial educational problem—teachers unable to teach, students unable to learn—and concluded that guns near schools contribute substantially to the size and scope of that problem.

Having found that guns in schools significantly undermine the quality of education in our Nation's classrooms, Congress could also have found, given the effect of education upon interstate and foreign commerce, that gun-related violence in and around schools is a commercial, as well as a human, problem. Education, although far more than a matter of economics, has long been inextricably intertwined with the Nation's economy. When this Nation began, most workers received their education in the workplace . . . As public school enrollment grew in the early 20th century, the need for industry to teach basic educational skills diminished. But, the direct economic link between basic education and industrial productivity remained. Scholars estimate that nearly a quarter of America's economic growth in the early years of this century is traceable directly to increased schooling, that investment in "human capital" (through spending on education) exceeded investment in "physical capital" by a ratio of almost two to one,); and that the economic returns to this investment in education exceeded the returns to conventional capital investment. . . .

Finally, there is evidence that, today more than ever, many firms base their location decisions upon the presence, or absence, of a work force with a basic education . . . In light of this increased importance of education to individual firms, it is no surprise that half of the Nation's manufacturers have become involved with setting standards and shaping curricula for local schools, that 88 percent think this kind of involvement is important, that more than 20 States have recently passed educational reforms to attract new business, and that business magazines have begun to rank cities according to the quality of their schools. . . .

[G]uns in the hands of six percent of inner-city high school students and gun-related violence throughout a city's schools must threaten the trade and commerce that those schools support. The only question, then, is whether the latter threat is (to use the majority's terminology) "substantial." And, the evidence of (1) the extent of the gun-related violence problem, (2) the extent of the resulting negative effect on classroom learning, and (3) the extent of the consequent negative commercial effects, when taken together, indicate a threat to trade and commerce that is "substantial." At the very least, Congress could rationally have concluded that the links are "substantial."

Specifically, Congress could have found that gun-related violence near the classroom poses a serious economic threat (1) to consequently inadequately educated workers who must endure low paying jobs, and (2) to communities and businesses that might (in today's "information society") otherwise gain, from a well-educated work force, an important commercial advantage, of a kind that location near a railhead or harbor provided in the past. Congress might also have found these threats to be no different in kind from other threats that this Court has found within the commerce power, such as the threat that loan sharking poses to the "funds" of "numerous localities," and that unfair labor practices pose to instrumentalities of commerce . . . Congress has written that "the occurrence of violent crime in school zones" has brought about a "decline in the quality of education" that "has an adverse impact on interstate commerce and the foreign commerce of the United States." The violence-related facts, the educational facts, and the economic facts, taken together, make this conclusion rational. And, because under our case law, the sufficiency of the constitutionally necessary Commerce Clause link between a crime of violence and interstate commerce turns simply upon size or degree, those same facts make the statute constitutional . . .

The majority's holding—that s 922 falls outside the scope of the Commerce Clause—creates three serious legal problems. First, the majority's holding runs contrary to modern Supreme Court cases that have upheld congressional actions despite connections to interstate or foreign commerce that are less significant than the effect of school violence. In *Perez*

v. United States, the Court held that the Commerce Clause authorized a federal statute that makes it a crime to engage in loan sharking ("[e]xtortionate credit transactions") at a local level. The Court said that Congress may judge that such transactions, "though purely intrastate, . . . affect interstate commerce." Presumably, Congress reasoned that threatening or using force, say with a gun on a street corner, to collect a debt occurs sufficiently often so that the activity (by helping organized crime) affects commerce among the States. But, why then cannot Congress also reason that the threat or use of force—the frequent consequence of possessing a gun—in or near a school occurs sufficiently often so that such activity (by inhibiting basic education) affects commerce among the States? The negative impact upon the national economy of an inability to teach basic skills seems no smaller (nor less significant) than that of organized crime . . .

The second legal problem the Court creates comes from its apparent belief that it can reconcile its holding with earlier cases by making a critical distinction between "commercial" and noncommercial "transaction[s]." That is to say, the Court believes the Constitution would distinguish between two local activities, each of which has an identical effect upon interstate commerce, if one, but not the other, is "commercial" in nature . . . Although the majority today attempts to categorize *Perez, McClung,* and *Wickard* as involving intrastate "economic activity," ante, at 1630, the Courts that decided each of those cases did not focus upon the economic nature of the activity regulated. Rather, they focused upon whether that activity affected interstate or foreign commerce. . . .

The third legal problem created by the Court's holding is that it threatens legal uncertainty in an area of law that, until this case, seemed reasonably well settled. Congress has enacted many statutes (more than 100 sections of the United States Code), including criminal statutes (at least 25 sections), that use the words "affecting commerce" to define their scope. . . .

In sum, to find this legislation within the scope of the Commerce Clause would permit "Congress . . . to act in terms of economic . . . realities." . . . Upholding this legislation would do no more than simply recognize that Congress had a "rational basis" for finding a significant connection between guns in or near schools and (through their effect on education) the interstate and foreign commerce they threaten.

Printz v. United States

521 U.S. 898 (1997), 5-4
Opinion of the Court: Scalia (Kennedy, Rehnquist,)
Concurring: (O'Connor, Thomas)
Dissenting: (Breyer, Ginsberg, Souter, Stevens)
Where do Scalia and Stevens disagree on what the Constitution permits or requires? How does this decision affect the balance between state and federal power? Is the effect significant? Is the decision consistent with New York v. United States? *With* Garcia v. San Antonio Metropolitan Transit Authority? *Apart from the parties to the case and those affected by the Brady Act, who are likely to gain and lose the most from the concept of federalism articulated by Scalia?*

Scalia, for the Court:

The question presented in these cases is whether certain interim provisions of the Brady Handgun Violence Prevention Act, commanding state and local law enforcement officers to conduct background checks on prospective handgun purchasers and to perform certain related tasks, violate the Constitution . . .

In 1993, Congress amended the GCA [the Gun Control Act of 1968] by enacting the Brady Act. The Act requires the Attorney General to establish a national instant background check system by November 30, 1998 . . . [A] firearms dealer who proposes to transfer a handgun must first receive from the transferee a statement (the Brady Form) containing the name, address and date of birth of the proposed transferee along with a sworn statement that the transferee is not among any of the classes of prohibited purchasers, verify the identity of the transferee by examining an identification document, provide the "chief law enforcement officer" (CLEO) of the transferee's residence with notice of the contents (and a copy) of the Brady Form. With some exceptions, the dealer must then wait five business days before consummating the sale, unless the CLEO earlier notifies the dealer that he has no reason to believe the transfer would be illegal . . .

. . . When a CLEO receives the required notice of a proposed transfer from the firearms dealer, the CLEO must "make a reasonable effort to ascertain within 5 business days whether receipt or possession would be in violation of the law, including research in whatever State and local record keeping systems are available and in a national system designated by the Attorney General." . . .

. . . Jay Printz and Richard Mack, the CLEOs for Ravalli County, Montana, and Graham County, Arizona, respectively, filed separate actions challenging the constitutionality of the Brady Act's interim provisions . . .

. . . [I]t is apparent that the Brady Act purports to direct state law enforcement officers to participate, albeit only temporarily, in the administration of a federally enacted regulatory scheme. Regulated firearms dealers are required to forward Brady Forms not to a federal officer or employee, but to the CLEOs, whose obligation to accept those forms is implicit in the duty imposed upon them to make "reasonable efforts" within five days to determine whether the sales reflected in the forms are lawful. While the CLEOs are subjected to no federal requirement that they prevent the sales determined to be unlawful (it is perhaps assumed that their state law duties will require prevention or apprehension), they are empowered to grant, in effect, waivers of the federally prescribed 5-day waiting period for handgun purchases by notifying the gun dealers that they have no reason to believe the transactions would be illegal.

[Printz and Mack] here object to being pressed into federal service, and contend that congressional action compelling state officers to execute federal laws is unconstitutional. Because there is no constitutional text speaking to this precise question, the answer to the CLEOs' challenge must be sought in historical understanding and practice, in the structure of the Constitution, and in the jurisprudence of this Court . . .

[They] contend that compelled enlistment of state executive officers for the administration of federal programs is, until very recent years at least, unprecedented. The Government contends, to the contrary, that "the earliest Congresses enacted statutes that required the participation of state officials in the implementation of federal laws." . . . Conversely if, as [Printz and Mack] contend, earlier Congresses avoided use of this highly attractive power, we would have reason to believe that the power was thought not to exist.

The Government observes that statutes enacted by the first Congresses required state courts to record applications for citizenship, to transmit abstracts of citizenship applications and other naturalization records to the Secretary of State, and to register aliens seeking naturalization and issue certificates of registry. It may well be, however, that these requirements applied only in States that authorized their courts to conduct naturalization proceedings . . .

These early laws establish, at most, that the Constitution was originally understood to permit imposition of an obligation on state judges to enforce federal prescriptions, insofar as those prescriptions related to matters appropriate for the judicial power . . . It is understandable why courts should have been viewed distinctively in this regard; unlike legislatures and executives, they applied the law of other sovereigns all the time. The principle underlying so called "transitory" causes of action was that laws which operated elsewhere created obligations in justice that courts of the forum state would enforce. The Constitution itself, in the Full Faith and Credit Clause, Art. IV, § 1, generally required such enforcement with respect to obligations arising in other States.

For these reasons, we do not think the early statutes imposing obligations on state courts imply a power of Congress to impress the state executive into its service . . .

Not only do the enactments of the early Congresses, as far as we are aware, contain no evidence of an assumption that the Federal Government may command the States' executive power in the absence of a particularized constitutional authorization, they contain some indication of precisely the opposite assumption . . .

To complete the historical record, we must note that there is not only an absence of executive commandeering statutes in the early Congresses, but there is an absence of them in our later history as well, at least until very recent years. The Government points to the Act of August 3, 1882, which enlisted state officials "to take charge of the local affairs of immigration in the ports within such State, and to provide for the support and relief of such immigrants therein landing as may fall into distress or need of public aid"; to inspect arriving immigrants

Vice President Albert Gore, and Attorney General Janet Reno with James and Sara Brady after President Clinton signed the Brady Gun Control Bill in 1993. The former press secretary for President Ronald Reagan was shot in the head by John Hinckley in an attempt to assassinate Reagan in 1981. Left permanently disabled, Brady, with his wife, led the lobbying of Congress to pass gun control legislation.

and exclude any person found to be a "convict, lunatic, idiot," or indigent; and to send convicts back to their country of origin "without compensation." The statute did not, however, mandate those duties, but merely empowered the Secretary of the Treasury "to enter into contracts with such State . . . officers as may be designated for that purpose by the governor of any State." . . .

The Government points to a number of federal statutes enacted within the past few decades that require the participation of state or local officials in implementing federal regulatory schemes. Some of these are connected to federal funding measures, and can perhaps be more accurately described as conditions upon the grant of federal funding than as mandates to the States; others, which require only the provision of information to the Federal Government, do not involve the precise issue before us here, which is the forced participation of the States' executive in the actual administration of a federal program . . .

The constitutional practice we have examined above tends to negate the existence of the congressional power asserted here, but is not conclusive. We turn next to consideration of the structure of the Constitution, to see if we can discern among its "essential postulates." . . . a principle that controls the present cases.

It is incontestible that the Constitution established a system of "dual sovereignty." Although the States surrendered many of their powers to the new Federal Government, they retained "a residuary and inviolable sovereignty," . . .

The Framers' experience under the Articles of Confederation had persuaded them that using the States as the instruments of federal governance was both ineffectual and provocative of federal state conflict. Preservation of the States as independent political entities being the price of union, and "[t]he practicality of making laws, with coercive sanctions, for the States as political bodies" having been, in Madison's words, "exploded on all hands," the Framers rejected the concept of a central government that would act upon and through the States, and instead designed a system in which the state and federal governments would exercise concurrent authority over the people . . . The Constitution . . . contemplates that a State's government will represent and remain accountable to its own citizens. As Madison expressed it: "[T]he local or municipal authorities form distinct and independent portions of the supremacy, no more subject, within their respective spheres, to the general authority than the general authority is subject to them, within its own sphere." The Federalist No. 39.

This separation of the two spheres is one of the Constitution's structural protections of liberty . . . To quote Madison once again: "In the compound republic of America, the power surrendered by the people is first divided between two distinct governments, and then the portion allotted to each subdivided among distinct and separate departments. Hence a double security arises to the rights of the people. The different governments will control each other, at the same time that each will be controlled by itself." The Federalist No. 51 . . .

Finally, and most conclusively in the present litigation, we turn to the prior jurisprudence of this Court. Federal commandeering of state governments is such a novel phenomenon that this Court's first experience with it did not occur until the 1970's, when the Environmental Protection Agency promulgated regulations requiring States to prescribe auto emissions testing, monitoring and retrofit programs, and to designate preferential bus and carpool lanes. The Courts of Appeals for the Fourth and Ninth Circuits invalidated the regulations on statutory grounds in order to avoid what they perceived to be grave constitutional issues; and the District of Columbia Circuit invalidated the regulations on both constitutional and statutory grounds. After we granted certiorari to review the statutory and constitutional validity of the regulations, the Government declined even to defend them, and instead rescinded some and conceded the invalidity of those that remained . . .

. . . [L]ater opinions of ours have made clear that the Federal Government may not compel the States to implement, by legislation or executive action, federal regulatory programs. In *Hodel v. Virginia Surface Mining & Reclamation Assn., Inc.* and *FERC v. Mississippi*, we sustained statutes against constitutional challenge only after assuring ourselves that they did not require the States to enforce federal law . . . We warned that "this Court never has sanctioned explicitly a federal command to the States to promulgate and enforce laws and regulations,"

When we were at last confronted squarely with a federal statute that unambiguously required the States to enact or administer a federal regulatory program, our decision should have come as no surprise. At issue in *New York v. United States*, were the so called "take title" provisions of the Low Level Radioactive Waste Policy Amendments Act of 1985, which required States either to enact legislation providing for the disposal of radioactive waste generated within their borders, or to take title to, and possession of the waste—effectively requiring the States either to legislate pursuant to Congress's directions, or to implement an administrative solution. We concluded that Congress could constitutionally require the States to do neither. "The Federal Government," we held, "may not compel the States to enact or administer a federal regulatory program."

The Government contends that is distinguishable on the following ground: unlike the "take title" provisions invalidated there, the background check provision of the Brady Act does not require state legislative or executive officials to make policy, but instead issues a final directive to state CLEOs. It is permissible, the Government asserts, for Congress to command state or local officials to assist in the implementation of federal law so long as "Congress itself devises a clear legislative solution that regulates private conduct" and requires state or local officers to provide only "limited, non policymaking help in enforcing that law." "[T]he constitutional line is crossed only when Congress compels the States to make law in their sovereign capacities." . . .

Even assuming, moreover, that the Brady Act leaves no "policymaking" discretion with the States, we fail to see how that improves rather than worsens the intrusion upon state sovereignty . . .

The Government also maintains that requiring state officers to perform discrete, ministerial tasks specified by Congress does not violate the principle of New York because it does not diminish the accountability of state or federal officials. This argument fails even on its own terms. By forcing state governments to absorb the financial burden of implementing a federal regulatory program, Members of Congress can take credit for "solving" problems without having to ask their constituents to pay for the solutions with higher federal taxes. And even when the States are not forced to absorb the costs of implementing a federal program, they are still put in the position of taking the blame for its burdensomeness and for its defects . . .

Finally, the Government puts forward a cluster of arguments that can be grouped under the heading: "The Brady Act serves very important purposes, is most efficiently administered by CLEOs during the in-

terim period, and places a minimal and only temporary burden upon state officers." . . . Assuming all the mentioned factors were true, they might be relevant if we were evaluating whether the incidental application to the States of a federal law of general applicability excessively interfered with the functioning of state governments. But where, as here, it is the whole object of the law to direct the functioning of the state executive, and hence to compromise the structural framework of dual sovereignty, such a "balancing" analysis is inappropriate. It is the very principle of separate state sovereignty that such a law offends, and no comparative assessment of the various interests can overcome that fundamental defect . . .

We held in *New York* that Congress cannot compel the States to enact or enforce a federal regulatory program. Today we hold that Congress cannot circumvent that prohibition by conscripting the State's officers directly. The Federal Government may neither issue directives requiring the States to address particular problems, nor command the States' officers, or those of their political subdivisions, to administer or enforce a federal regulatory program. It matters not whether policymaking is involved . . . ; such commands are fundamentally incompatible with our constitutional system of dual sovereignty.

Stevens, (Souter, Ginsberg, Breyer) dissenting:

When Congress exercises the powers delegated to it by the Constitution, it may impose affirmative obligations on executive and judicial officers of state and local governments as well as ordinary citizens. This conclusion is firmly supported by the text of the Constitution, the early history of the Nation, decisions of this Court, and a correct understanding of the basic structure of the Federal Government.

These cases do not implicate the more difficult questions associated with congressional coercion of state legislatures addressed in *New York v. United States*. Nor need we consider the wisdom of relying on local officials rather than federal agents to carry out aspects of a federal program, or even the question whether such officials may be required to perform a federal function on a permanent basis. The question is whether Congress, acting on behalf of the people of the entire Nation, may require local law enforcement officers to perform certain duties during the interim needed for the development of a federal gun control program. It is remarkably similar to the question, heavily debated by the Framers of the Constitution, whether the Congress could require state agents to collect federal taxes. Or the question whether Congress could impress state judges into federal service to entertain and decide cases that they would prefer to ignore.

Indeed, since the ultimate issue is one of power, we must consider its implications in times of national emergency. Matters such as the enlistment of air raid wardens, the administration of a military draft, the mass inoculation of children to forestall an epidemic, or perhaps the threat of an international terrorist, may require a national response before federal personnel can be made available to respond. If the Constitution empowers Congress and the President to make an appropriate response, is there anything in the Tenth Amendment, "in historical understanding and practice, in the structure of the Constitution, [or] in the jurisprudence of this Court," that forbids the enlistment of state officers to make that response effective? More narrowly, what basis is there in any of those sources for concluding that it is the Members of this Court, rather than the elected representatives of the people, who should determine whether the Constitution contains the unwritten rule that the Court announces today?

Perhaps today's majority would suggest that no such emergency is presented by the facts of these cases. But such a suggestion is itself an expression of a policy judgment. And Congress' view of the matter is quite different from that implied by the Court today . . .

Unlike the First Amendment, which prohibits the enactment of a category of laws that would otherwise be authorized by Article I, the Tenth Amendment imposes no restriction on the exercise of delegated powers. Using language that plainly refers only to powers that are "not" delegated to Congress, it provides: "The powers not delegated to the United States by the Constitution, nor prohibited by it to the States, are reserved to the States respectively, or to the people."

The Amendment confirms the principle that the powers of the Federal Government are limited to those affirmatively granted by the Constitution, but it does not purport to limit the scope or the effectiveness of the exercise of powers that are delegated to Congress . . .

There is not a clause, sentence, or paragraph in the entire text of the Constitution of the United States that supports the proposition that a local police officer can ignore a command contained in a statute enacted by Congress pursuant to an express delegation of power enumerated in Article I . . .

Indeed, the historical materials strongly suggest that the Founders intended to enhance the capacity of the federal government by empowering it—as a part of the new authority to make demands directly on individual citizens—to act through local officials. Hamilton made clear that the new Constitution, "by extending the authority of the federal head to the individual citizens of the several States, will enable the government to employ the ordinary magistracy of each, in the execution of its laws." The Federalist No. 27. Hamilton's meaning was unambiguous; the federal government was to have the power to demand that local officials implement national policy programs. As he went on to explain: "It is easy to perceive that this will tend to destroy, in the common apprehension, all distinction between the sources from which [the state and federal governments] might proceed; and will give the federal government the same advantage for securing a due obedience to its authority which is enjoyed by the government of each State." . . .

Bereft of support in the history of the founding, the Court rests its conclusion on the claim that there is little evidence the National Government actually exercised such a power in the early years of the Republic . . . [W]e have never suggested that the failure of the early Congresses to address the scope of federal power in a particular area or to exercise a particular authority was an argument against its existence. That position, if correct, would undermine most of our post-New Deal Commerce Clause jurisprudence . . .

. . . Absent even a modicum of textual foundation for its judicially crafted constitutional rule, there should be a presumption that if the Framers had actually intended such a rule, at least one of them would have mentioned it.

The Court's "structural" arguments are not sufficient to rebut that presumption. The fact that the Framers intended to preserve the sovereignty of the several States simply does not speak to the question whether individual state employees may be required to perform federal obligations, such as registering young adults for the draft, creating state emergency response commissions designed to manage the release of hazardous substances, collecting and reporting data on underground storage tanks that may pose an environmental hazard, and reporting traffic fatalities, and missing children, to a federal agency . . .

Perversely, the majority's rule seems more likely to damage than to preserve the safeguards against tyranny provided by the existence of vital state governments. By limiting the ability of the Federal Government to enlist state officials in the implementation of its programs, the Court creates incentives for the National Government to aggrandize itself. In the name of State's rights, the majority would have the Federal Government create vast national bureaucracies to implement its policies. This is exactly the sort of thing that the early Federalists promised would not occur, in part as a result of the National Government's ability to rely on the magistracy of the states . . .

Alden v. Maine

527 U.S. 706 (1999), 5-4
Opinion of the Court: Kennedy (Rehnquist, O'Connor, Scalia, Thomas)
Dissenting: Souter (Breyer, Ginsberg, Stevens)
On what constitutional principles does Kennedy base a nonconsenting state's immunity from lawsuit? Why is neither Congress's exercise of a delegated power nor the command of the federal supremacy clause enough to overcome state sovereign immunity? What limits to state sovereignty, if any, does Kennedy see? Where do Kennedy and Stevens disagree on history? On the requirements of constitutional structure? How much of a disadvantage would it be to a state not to have immunity from lawsuit? Which opinion, Kennedy's or Stevens's, reflects judicial self-restraint as opposed to activism?

Kennedy, for the Court:
In 1992, a group of probation officers filed suit against their employer, the State of Maine, in the United States District Court for the District of Maine. The officers alleged the State had violated the overtime provisions of the Fair Labor Standards Act of 1938 (FLSA), as amended . . . While the suit was pending, this Court decided *Seminole Tribe of Fla. v. Florida* (1996), which made it clear that Congress lacks power under Article I to abrogate the States' sovereign immunity from suits commenced or prosecuted in the federal courts. Upon consideration of *Seminole Tribe*, the District Court dismissed petitioners' action, and the Court of Appeals affirmed. Petitioners then filed the same action in state court. The state trial court dismissed the suit on the basis of sovereign immunity, and the Maine Supreme Judicial Court affirmed.

The Maine Supreme Judicial Court's decision conflicts with the decision of the Supreme Court of Arkansas, *Jacoby v. Arkansas Dept. of Ed.*, and calls into question the constitutionality of the provisions of the FLSA purporting to authorize private actions against States in their own courts without regard for consent. In light of the importance of the question presented and the conflict between the courts, we granted certiorari . . .

. . . [A]s the Constitution's structure, and its history, and the authoritative interpretations by this Court make clear, the States' immunity from suit is a fundamental aspect of the sovereignty which the States enjoyed before the ratification of the Constitution, and which they retain today (either literally or by virtue of their admission into the Union upon an equal footing with the other States) except as altered by the plan of the Convention or certain constitutional Amendments . . .

The States thus retain "a residuary and inviolable sovereignty." They are not relegated to the role of mere provinces or political corporations, but retain the dignity, though not the full authority, of sovereignty.

The generation that designed and adopted our federal system considered immunity from private suits central to sovereign dignity . . .

Despite the persuasive assurances of the Constitution's leading advocates and the expressed understanding of the only state conventions to address the issue in explicit terms, this Court held, just five years after the Constitution was adopted, that Article III authorized a private citizen of another State to sue the State of Georgia without its consent. *Chisholm v. Georgia* . . .

An initial proposal to amend the Constitution was introduced in the House of Representatives the day after *Chisholm* was announced; the proposal adopted as the Eleventh Amendment was introduced in the Senate promptly following an intervening recess. Congress turned to the latter proposal with great dispatch; little more than two months after its introduction it had been endorsed by both Houses and forwarded to the States . . .

. . . [T]he swiftness and near unanimity with which the Eleventh Amendment was adopted suggest "either that the Court had not captured the original understanding, or that the country had changed its collective mind most rapidly." The more reasonable interpretation, of course, is that regardless of the views of four Justices in *Chisholm,* the country as a whole—which had adopted the Constitution just five years earlier—had not understood the document to strip the States' of their immunity from private suits . . .

Not only do the ratification debates and the events leading to the adoption of the Eleventh Amendment reveal the original understanding of the States' constitutional immunity from suit, they also underscore the importance of sovereign immunity to the founding generation. Simply put, "The Constitution never would have been ratified if the States and their courts were to be stripped of their sovereign authority except as expressly provided by the Constitution itself." *Atascadero State Hospital v. Scanlon* . . .

The Court has been consistent in interpreting the adoption of the Eleventh Amendment as conclusive evidence "that the decision in *Chisholm* was contrary to the well-understood meaning of the Constitution," and that the views expressed by Hamilton, Madison, and Marshall during the ratification debates, and by Justice Iredell in his dissenting opinion in *Chisholm,* reflect the original understanding of the Constitution . . .

. . . The Eleventh Amendment confirmed rather than established sovereign immunity as a constitutional principle; it follows that the scope of the States' immunity from suit is demarcated not by the text of the Amendment alone but by fundamental postulates implicit in the constitutional design . . .

In this case we must determine whether Congress has the power, under Article I, to subject non-consenting States to private suits in their own courts . . . [T]he fact that the Eleventh Amendment by its terms limits only "[t]he Judicial power of the United States" does not resolve the question . . .

While the constitutional principle of sovereign immunity does pose a bar to federal jurisdiction over suits against non-consenting States, this is not the only structural basis of sovereign immunity implicit in the constitutional design. Rather, "[t]here is also the postulate that States of the Union, still possessing attributes of sovereignty, shall be immune from suits, without their consent, save where there has been 'a surrender of this immunity in the plan of the convention.'" This separate and distinct structural principle is not directly related to the scope of the judicial power established by Article III, but inheres in the system of federalism established by the Constitution. In exercising its Article I powers Congress may subject the States to private suits in their own courts only if there is "compelling evidence" that the States were required to surrender this power to Congress pursuant to the constitutional design.

[Alden, etal.] contend the text of the Constitution and our recent sovereign immunity decisions establish that the States were required to relinquish this portion of their sovereignty. We turn first to these sources.

Article I, §8 grants Congress broad power to enact legislation in several enumerated areas of national concern. The Supremacy Clause, furthermore, provides: "This Constitution, and the Laws of the United States which shall be made in Pursuance thereof . . . , shall be the supreme Law of the Land; and the Judges in every State shall be bound thereby, any Thing in the Constitution or Laws of any state to the Contrary notwithstanding."

It is contended that, by virtue of these provisions, where Congress enacts legislation subjecting the States to suit, the legislation by necessity overrides the sovereign immunity of the States.

As is evident from its text, however, the Supremacy Clause enshrines as "the supreme Law of the Land" only those federal Acts that accord with the constitutional design. Appeal to the Supremacy Clause alone merely raises the question whether a law is a valid exercise of the national power . . .

The Constitution, by delegating to Congress the power to establish the supreme law of the land when acting within its enumerated powers, does not foreclose a State from asserting immunity to claims arising under federal law merely because that law derives not from the State itself but from the national power . . . We reject any contention that substantive federal law by its own force necessarily overrides the sovereign immunity of the States. When a State asserts its immunity to suit, the question is not the primacy of federal law but the implementation of the law in a manner consistent with the constitutional sovereignty of the States.

Nor can we conclude that the specific Article I powers delegated to Congress necessarily include, by virtue of the Necessary and Proper Clause or otherwise, the incidental authority to subject the States to private suits as a means of achieving objectives otherwise within the scope of the enumerated powers . . .

There are isolated statements in some of our cases suggesting that the Eleventh Amendment is inapplicable in state courts. This, of course, is a truism as to the literal terms of the Eleventh Amendment. As we have explained, however, the bare text of the Amendment is not an exhaustive description of the States' constitutional immunity from suit. The cases, furthermore, do not decide the question presented here—whether the States retain immunity from private suits in their own courts notwithstanding an attempted abrogation by the Congress . . .

Whether Congress has authority under Article I to abrogate a State's immunity from suit in its own courts is, then, a question of first impression. In determining whether there is "compelling evidence" that this derogation of the States' sovereignty is "inherent in the constitutional compact," we continue our discussion of history, practice, precedent, and the structure of the Constitution.

We look first to evidence of the original understanding of the Constitution. Petitioners contend that because the ratification debates and the events surrounding the adoption of the Eleventh Amendment focused on the States' immunity from suit in federal courts, the historical record gives no instruction as to the founding generation's intent to preserve the States' immunity from suit in their own courts.

We believe, however, that the founders' silence is best explained by the simple fact that no one, not even the Constitution's most ardent opponents, suggested the document might strip the States of the immunity. In light of the overriding concern regarding the States' war-time debts, together with the well known creativity, foresight, and vivid imagination of the Constitution's opponents, the silence is most instructive. It suggests the sovereign's right to assert immunity from suit in its own courts was a principle so well established that no one conceived it would be altered by the new Constitution . . .

Similarly, while the Eleventh Amendment by its terms addresses only "the Judicial power of the United States," nothing in *Chisholm,* the catalyst for the Amendment, suggested the States were not immune from suits in their own courts . . .

The language of the Eleventh Amendment, furthermore, was directed toward the only provisions of the constitutional text believed to call the States' immunity from private suits into question. Although Article III expressly contemplated jurisdiction over suits between States and individuals, nothing in the Article or in any other part of the Constitution suggested the States could not assert immunity from private suit in

their own courts or that Congress had the power to abrogate sovereign immunity there.

Finally, the Congress which endorsed the Eleventh Amendment rejected language limiting the Amendment's scope to cases where the States had made available a remedy in their own courts. Implicit in the proposal, it is evident, was the premise that the States retained their immunity and the concomitant authority to decide whether to allow private suits against the sovereign in their own courts.

In light of the language of the Constitution and the historical context, it is quite apparent why neither the ratification debates nor the language of the Eleventh Amendment addressed the States' immunity from suit in their own courts. The concerns voiced at the ratifying conventions, the furor raised by *Chisholm,* and the speed and unanimity with which the Amendment was adopted, moreover, underscore the jealous care with which the founding generation sought to preserve the sovereign immunity of the States. To read this history as permitting the inference that the Constitution stripped the States of immunity in their own courts and allowed Congress to subject them to suit there would turn on its head the concern of the founding generation—that Article III might be used to circumvent state-court immunity. In light of the historical record it is difficult to conceive that the Constitution would have been adopted if it had been understood to strip the States of immunity from suit in their own courts and cede to the Federal Government a power to subject non-consenting States to private suits in these fora.

Our historical analysis is supported by early congressional practice, which provides "contemporaneous and weighty evidence of the Constitution's meaning." Although early Congresses enacted various statutes authorizing federal suits in state court, we have discovered no instance in which they purported to authorize suits against non-consenting States in these fora. The "numerousness of these statutes [authorizing suit in state court], contrasted with the utter lack of statutes" subjecting States to suit, "suggests an assumed absence of such power." It thus appears early Congresses did not believe they had the power to authorize private suits against the States in their own courts . . .

Even the recent statutes, moreover, do not provide evidence of an understanding that Congress has a greater power to subject States to suit in their own courts than in federal courts . . .

The theory and reasoning of our earlier cases suggest the States do retain a constitutional immunity from suit in their own courts. We have often described the States' immunity in sweeping terms, without reference to whether the suit was prosecuted in state or federal court...

As it is settled doctrine that neither substantive federal law nor attempted congressional abrogation under Article I bars a State from raising a constitutional defense of sovereign immunity in federal court, see Part II-A-1, supra, our decisions suggesting that the States retain an analogous constitutional immunity from private suits in their own courts support the conclusion that Congress lacks the Article I power to subject the States to private suits in those fora.

Our final consideration is whether a congressional power to subject non-consenting States to private suits in their own courts is consistent with the structure of the Constitution. We look both to the essential principles of federalism and to the special role of the state courts in the constitutional design.

... [F]ederalism requires that Congress treat the States in a manner consistent with their status as residuary sovereigns and joint participants in the governance of the Nation...

[Alden etal.] contend that immunity from suit in federal court suffices to preserve the dignity of the States. Private suits against non-consenting States, however, present "the indignity of subjecting a State to the coercive process of judicial tribunals at the instance of private parties," regardless of the forum. Not only must a State defend or default but also it must face the prospect of being thrust, by federal fiat and against its will, into the disfavored status of a debtor, subject to the power of private citizens to levy on its treasury or perhaps even government buildings or property which the State administers on the public's behalf...

... A power to press a State's own courts into federal service to coerce the other branches of the State, furthermore, is the power first to turn the State against itself and ultimately to commandeer the entire political machinery of the State against its will and at the behest of individuals...

It is unquestioned that the Federal Government retains its own immunity from suit not only in state tribunals but also in its own courts. In light of our constitutional system recognizing the essential sovereignty of the States, we are reluctant to conclude that the States are not entitled to a reciprocal privilege.

Underlying constitutional form are considerations of great substance. Private suits against non-consenting States—especially suits for money damages—may threaten the financial integrity of the States. It is indisputable that, at the time of the founding, many of the States could have been forced into insolvency but for their immunity from private suits for money damages. Even today, an unlimited congressional power to authorize suits in state court to levy upon the treasuries of the States for compensatory damages, attorney's fees, and even punitive damages could create staggering burdens, giving Congress a power and a leverage over the States that is not contemplated by our constitutional design....

A general federal power to authorize private suits for money damages would place unwarranted strain on the States' ability to govern in accordance with the will of their citizens. Today, as at the time of the founding, the allocation of scarce resources among competing needs and interests lies at the heart of the political process. While the judgment creditor of the State may have a legitimate claim for compensation, other important needs and worthwhile ends compete for access to the public fisc. Since all cannot be satisfied in full, it is inevitable that difficult decisions involving the most sensitive and political of judgments must be made. If the principle of representative government is to be preserved to the States, the balance between competing interests must be reached after deliberation by the political process established by the citizens of the State, not by judicial decree mandated by the Federal Government and invoked by the private citizen...

Congress cannot abrogate the States' sovereign immunity in federal court; were the rule to be different here, the National Government would wield greater power in the state courts than in its own judicial instrumentalities.

The resulting anomaly cannot be explained by reference to the special role of the state courts in the constitutional design... It would be an unprecedented step, however, to infer from the fact that Congress may declare federal law binding and enforceable in state courts the further principle that Congress' authority to pursue federal objectives through the state judiciaries exceeds not only its power to press other branches of the State into its service but even its control over the federal courts themselves. The conclusion would imply that Congress may in some cases act only through instrumentalities of the States...

In light of history, practice, precedent, and the structure of the Constitution, we hold that the States retain immunity from private suit in their own courts, an immunity beyond the congressional power to abrogate by Article I legislation.

The constitutional privilege of a State to assert its sovereign immunity in its own courts does not confer upon the State a concomitant right to disregard the Constitution or valid federal law. The States and their officers are bound by obligations imposed by the Constitution and by federal statutes that comport with the constitutional design . . .

Sovereign immunity, moreover, does not bar all judicial review of state compliance with the Constitution and valid federal law. Rather, certain limits are implicit in the constitutional principle of state sovereign immunity.

The first of these limits is that sovereign immunity bars suits only in the absence of consent. Many States, on their own initiative, have enacted statutes consenting to a wide variety of suits. The rigors of sovereign immunity are thus "mitigated by a sense of justice which has continually expanded by consent the suability of the sovereign."

The States have consented, moreover, to some suits pursuant to the plan of the Convention or to subsequent constitutional amendments. In ratifying the Constitution, the States consented to suits brought by other States or by the Federal Government.

We have held also that in adopting the Fourteenth Amendment, the people required the States to surrender a portion of the sovereignty that had been preserved to them by the original Constitution, so that Congress may authorize private suits against non-consenting States pursuant to its §5 enforcement power . . .

The second important limit to the principle of sovereign immunity is that it bars suits against States but not lesser entities. The immunity does not extend to suits prosecuted against a municipal corporation or other governmental entity which is not an arm of the State. Nor does sovereign immunity bar all suits against state officers. Some suits against state officers are barred by the rule that sovereign immunity is not limited to suits which name the State as a party if the suits are, in fact, against the State. The rule, however, does not bar certain actions against state officers for injunctive or declaratory relief. Even a suit for money damages may be prosecuted against a state officer in his individual capacity for unconstitutional or wrongful conduct fairly attributable to the officer himself, so long as the relief is sought not from the state treasury but from the officer personally.

The principle of sovereign immunity as reflected in our jurisprudence strikes the proper balance between the supremacy of federal law and the separate sovereignty of the States. Established rules provide ample means to correct ongoing violations of law and to vindicate the interests which animate the Supremacy Clause. That we have, during the first 210 years of our constitutional history, found it unnecessary to decide the question presented here suggests a federal power to subject non-consenting States to private suits in their own courts is unnecessary to uphold the Constitution and valid federal statutes as the supreme law.

Souter (with Breyer, Ginsburg, and Stevens), dissenting:

In *Seminole Tribe of Fla. v. Florida*, a majority of this Court invoked the Eleventh Amendment to declare that the federal judicial power under Article III of the Constitution does not reach a private action against a State, even on a federal question. In the Court's conception, however, the Eleventh Amendment was understood as having been enhanced by a "background principle" of state sovereign immunity (understood as immunity to suit) that operated beyond its limited codification in the Amendment, dealing solely with federal citizen-state diversity jurisdiction. To the *Seminole Tribe* dissenters, of whom I was one, the Court's enhancement of the Amendment was at odds with constitutional history and at war with the conception of divided sovereignty that is the essence of American federalism.

Today's issue arises naturally in the aftermath of the decision in *Seminole Tribe*. The Court holds that the Constitution bars an individual suit against a State to enforce a federal statutory right under the Fair Labor Standards Act of 1938 (FLSA) when brought in the State's courts over its objection. In thus complementing its earlier decision, the Court of course confronts the fact that the state forum renders the Eleventh Amendment beside the point, and it has responded by discerning a simpler and more straightforward theory of state sovereign immunity than it found in *Seminole Tribe*: a State's sovereign immunity from all individual suits is a "fundamental aspect" of state sovereignty "confirm[ed]" by the Tenth Amendment. As a consequence, *Seminole Tribe's* contorted reliance on the Eleventh Amendment and its background was presumably unnecessary; the Tenth would have done the work with an economy that the majority in *Seminole Tribe* would have welcomed. Indeed, if the Court's current reasoning is correct, the Eleventh Amendment itself was unnecessary . . .

. . . There is no evidence that the Tenth Amendment constitutionalized a concept of sovereign immunity as inherent in the notion of statehood, and no evidence that any concept of inherent sovereign immunity was understood historically to apply when the sovereign sued was not the font of the law. Nor does the Court fare any better with its subsidiary lines of reasoning, that the state-court action is barred by the scheme of American federalism, a result supposedly confirmed by a history largely devoid of precursors to the action considered here. The Court's federalism ignores the accepted authority of Congress to bind States under the FLSA and to provide for enforcement of federal rights in state court. The Court's history simply disparages the capacity of the Constitution to order relationships in a Republic that has changed since the founding . . .

. . . There is almost no evidence that the generation of the Framers thought sovereign immunity was fundamental in the sense of being unalterable. Whether one looks at the period before the framing, to the ratification controversies, or to the early republican era, the evidence is the same. Some Framers thought sovereign immunity was an obsolete royal prerogative inapplicable in a republic; some thought sovereign immunity was a common-law power defeasible, like other common-law rights, by statute; and perhaps a few thought, in keeping with a natural law view distinct from the common-law conception, that immunity was inherent in a sovereign because the body that made a law could not logically be bound by it. Natural law thinking on the part of a doubtful few will not, however, support the Court's position . . .

. . . To the extent that States were thought to possess immunity, it was perceived as a prerogative of the sovereign under common law. And where sovereign immunity was recognized as barring suit, provisions for recovery from the State were in order, just as they had been at common law in England . . .

. . . At all events, the state ratifying conventions' felt need for clarification on the question of state suability demonstrates that uncertainty surrounded the matter even at the moment of ratification. This uncer-

tainty set the stage for the divergent views expressed in *Chisholm* . . .

The Court's rationale for today's holding based on a conception of sovereign immunity as somehow fundamental to sovereignty or inherent in statehood fails for the lack of any substantial support for such a conception in the thinking of the founding era. The Court cannot be counted out yet, however, for it has a second line of argument looking not to a clause-based reception of the natural law conception or even to its recognition as a "background principle," but to a structural basis in the Constitution's creation of a federal system. Immunity, the Court says, "inheres in the system of federalism established by the Constitution," its "contours [being] determined by the founders' understanding, not by the principles or limitations derived from natural law," Again, "[w]e look both to the essential principles of federalism and to the special role of the state courts in the constitutional design." That is, the Court believes that the federal constitutional structure itself necessitates recognition of some degree of state autonomy broad enough to include sovereign immunity from suit in a State's own courts, regardless of the federal source of the claim asserted against the State. If one were to read the Court's federal structure rationale in isolation from the preceding portions of the opinion, it would appear that the Court's position on state sovereign immunity might have been rested entirely on federalism alone. If it had been, however, I would still be in dissent, for the Court's argument that state court sovereign immunity on federal questions is inherent in the very concept of federal structure is demonstrably mistaken . . .

. . . [T]he general scheme of delegated sovereignty as between the two component governments of the federal system was clear, and was succinctly stated by Chief Justice Marshall: "In America, the powers of sovereignty are divided between the government of the Union, and those of the States. They are each sovereign, with respect to the objects committed to it, and neither sovereign with respect to the objects committed to the other." *McCulloch v. Maryland* . . .

Hence the flaw in the Court's appeal to federalism. The State of Maine is not sovereign with respect to the national objective of the FLSA. It is not the authority that promulgated the FLSA, on which the right of action in this case depends . . .

. . . Maine has advanced no "'valid excuse,' for its courts' refusal to hear federal-law claims in which Maine is a defendant, and sovereign immunity cannot be that excuse, simply because the State is not sovereign with respect to the subject of the claim against it . . ."

Yet today the Court has no qualms about saying frankly that the federal right to damages afforded by Congress under the FLSA cannot create a concomitant private remedy. The right was "made for the benefit of" petitioners . . . but despite what has long been understood as the necessary consequence of law," they have no action. It will not do for the Court to respond that a remedy was never available where the right in question was against the sovereign. A State is not the sovereign when a federal claim is pressed against it, and even the English sovereign opened itself to recovery and, unlike Maine, provided the remedy to complement the right. To the Americans of the founding generation it would have been clear (as it was to Chief Justice Marshall) that if the King would do right, the democratically chosen Government of the United States could do no less . . .

The Court has swung back and forth with regrettable disruption on the enforceability of the FLSA against the States, but if the present majority had a defensible position one could at least accept its decision with an expectation of stability ahead. As it is, any such expectation would be naïve. The resemblance of today's state sovereign immunity to the *Lochner* era's industrial due process is striking. The Court began this century by imputing immutable constitutional status to a conception of economic self-reliance that was never true to industrial life and grew insistently fictional with the years, and the Court has chosen to close the century by conferring like status on a conception of state sovereign immunity that is true neither to history nor to the structure of the Constitution. I expect the Court's late essay into immunity doctrine will prove the equal of its earlier experiment in laissez-faire, the one being as unrealistic as the other, as indefensible, and probably as fleeting.

Kimel v. Florida Board of Regents

528 U S 62 (2000), 5-4

Opinion of the Court: O'Connor (Rehnquist, Scalia;
     Parts I, II, IV, Kennedy, Thomas; Part III,
Stevens, Souter, Ginsberg, Breyer)
Concurring in part, dissenting in part: Stevens,
     Kennedy, Souter, Thomas, Ginsberg, Breyer)
*What is the Court's theory of "state sovereign immunity"?
What is the constitutional and historical reasoning that*
leads Stevens to disagree? Under what circumstances, if any, might Congress be able to address possible age discrimination by an employer state? Can this decision be reconciled with Garcia v. San Antonio Metropolitan Transit Authority?

O'Connor, for the Court:

The Age Discrimination in Employment Act of 1967 (ADEA) makes it unlawful for an employer, including a State, "to fail or refuse to hire or to discharge any individual or otherwise discriminate against any individual . . . because of such individual's age." . . . [T]hree sets of plaintiffs filed suit under the Act, seeking money damages for their state employers' alleged discrimination on the basis of age . . . [W]e are asked to consider whether the ADEA contains a clear statement of Congress' intent to abrogate the States' Eleventh Amendment immunity and, if so, whether the ADEA is a proper exercise of Congress' constitutional authority. We conclude that the ADEA does contain a clear statement of Congress' intent to abrogate the States' immunity, but that the abrogation exceeded Congress' authority under Sec. 5 of the Fourteenth Amendment.

The ADEA makes it unlawful for an employer to fail or refuse to hire or to discharge any individual or otherwise discriminate against any individual with respect to his compensation, terms, conditions, or privileges of employment, because of such individual's age. The Act also provides several exceptions to this broad prohibition. For example, an employer may rely on age where it "is a bona fide occupational qualification reasonably necessary to the normal operation of the particular business." The Act also permits an employer to engage in conduct otherwise prohibited by . . . if the employer's action "is based on reasonable factors other than age," or if the employer "discharge[s] or otherwise discipline[s] an individual for good cause." . . .

. . . When first passed in 1967, the ADEA applied only to private employers . . . In 1974 . . . Congress extended application of the ADEA's substantive requirements to the States . . .

. . . [The act] now permits an individual to bring a civil action "against any employer (including a public agency) in any Federal or State court of competent jurisdiction." [It] defines "[p]ublic agency" to include "the Government of a State or political subdivision thereof," and "any agency of . . . a State, or a political subdivision of a State." . . .

In April, 1995, a group of current and former faculty and librarians of Florida State University, including J. Daniel Kimel, Jr., the named petitioner in one of today's cases, filed suit against the Florida Board of Regents in the United States District Court for the Northern District of Florida. The complaint was subsequently amended to add as plaintiffs current and former faculty and librarians of Florida International University. The plaintiffs, all over age 40, alleged that the Florida Board of Regents refused to require the two state universities to allocate funds to provide previously agreed upon market adjustments to the salaries of eligible university employees. The plaintiffs contended that the failure to allocate the funds violated both the ADEA and the Florida Civil Rights Act of 1992, because it had a disparate impact on the base pay of employees with a longer record of service, most of whom were older employees. The plaintiffs sought backpay, liquidated damages, and permanent salary adjustments as relief. The Florida Board of Regents moved to dismiss the suit on the grounds of Eleventh Amendment immunity . . .

The Eleventh Amendment states:

> The Judicial power of the United States shall not be construed to extend to any suit in law or equity, commenced or prosecuted against one of the United States by Citizens of another State, or by Citizens or Subjects of any Foreign State.

Although today's cases concern suits brought by citizens against their own States, this Court has long "understood the Eleventh Amendment to stand not so much for what it says, but for the presupposition . . . which it confirms." Accordingly, for over a century now, we have made clear that the Constitution does not provide for federal jurisdiction over suits against non-consenting States. Petitioners nevertheless contend that the States of Alabama and Florida must defend the present suits on the merits because Congress abrogated their Eleventh Amendment immunity in the ADEA. To determine whether petitioners are correct, we must resolve two predicate questions: first, whether Congress unequivocally expressed its intent to abrogate that immunity, and second, if it did, whether Congress acted pursuant to a valid grant of constitutional authority.

To determine whether a federal statute properly subjects States to suits by individuals, we apply a simple but stringent test: "Congress may abrogate the States' constitutionally secured immunity from suit in federal court only by making its intention unmistakably clear in the language of the statute." We agree with petitioners that the ADEA satisfies that test . . . Read as a whole, the plain language of these provisions clearly demonstrates Congress' intent to subject the States to suit for money damages at the hands of individual employees.

This is not the first time we have considered the constitutional validity of the 1974 extension of the ADEA to state and local governments. In *EEOC v. Wyoming*, we held that the ADEA constitutes a valid exercise of Congress' power "[t]o regulate Commerce . . . among the several States," and that the Act did not transgress any external restraints imposed on the commerce power by the Tenth Amendment. Because we found the ADEA valid under Congress' Commerce Clause power, we concluded that it was unnecessary to determine whether the Act also could be supported by Congress' power under Sec. 5 of the Fourteenth Amendment. Resolution of today's cases requires us to decide that question.

In *Seminole Tribe of Florida v. Florida*, we held that Congress lacks power under Article I to abrogate the States' sovereign immunity. "Even when the Constitution vests in Congress complete lawmaking authority over a particular area, the Eleventh Amendment prevents congressional authorization of suits by private parties against unconsenting States."

. . . Section 5 of the Fourteenth Amendment, however, does grant Congress the authority to abrogate the States' sovereign immunity. In *Fitzpatrick v. Bitzer*, we recognized that "the Eleventh Amendment, and the principle of state sovereignty which it embodies, are necessarily limited by the enforcement provisions of Sec. 5 of the Fourteenth Amendment." Since our decision in *Fitzpatrick*, we have reaffirmed the validity of that congressional power on numerous occasions. Accordingly, the private petitioners in these cases may maintain their ADEA suits against the States of Alabama and Florida if, and only if, the ADEA is appropriate legislation under Sec. 5.

The Fourteenth Amendment provides, in relevant part:

> Section 1. . . . No State shall make or enforce any law which shall abridge the privileges or immunities of citizens of the United States; nor shall any State deprive any person of life, liberty, or property, without due process of law; nor deny to any person within its jurisdiction the equal protection of the laws . . .

Section 5. The Congress shall have power to enforce, by appropriate legislation, the provisions of this article.

As we recognized most recently in *City of Boerne v. Flores,* Sec. 5 is an affirmative grant of power to Congress: "It is for Congress in the first instance to "determin[e] whether and what legislation is needed to secure the guarantees of the Fourteenth Amendment," and its conclusions are entitled to much deference." Congress' Sec. 5 power is not confined to the enactment of legislation that merely parrots the precise wording of the Fourteenth Amendment. Rather, Congress' power "to enforce" the Amendment includes the authority both to remedy and to deter violation of rights guaranteed thereunder by prohibiting a somewhat broader swath of conduct, including that which is not itself forbidden by the Amendment's text.

Nevertheless, we have also recognized that the same language that serves as the basis for the affirmative grant of congressional power also serves to limit that power. For example, Congress cannot "decree the substance of the Fourteenth Amendment's restrictions on the States ... It has been given the power "to enforce," not the power to determine what constitutes a constitutional violation." The ultimate interpretation and determination of the Fourteenth Amendment's substantive meaning remains the province of the Judicial Branch. In *City of Boerne,* we noted that ... "[t]here must be a congruence and proportionality between the injury to be prevented or remedied and the means adopted to that end."

In *City of Boerne,* we applied that "congruence and proportionality" test and held that the Religious Freedom Restoration Act of 1993 (RFRA) was not appropriate legislation under Sec. 5. We first noted that the legislative record contained very little evidence of the unconstitutional conduct purportedly targeted by RFRA's substantive provisions. Rather, Congress had uncovered only "anecdotal evidence" that, standing alone, did not reveal a "widespread pattern of religious discrimination in this country." Second, we found that RFRA is "so out of proportion to a supposed remedial or preventive object that it cannot be understood as responsive to, or designed to prevent, unconstitutional behavior."

Last Term, we ... held that the [Patent Remedy Act], which subjected States to patent infringement suits, was not appropriate legislation under Sec. 5 of the Fourteenth Amendment. [It] failed to meet our congruence and proportionality test first because "Congress identified no pattern of patent infringement by the States, let alone a pattern of constitutional violations." Moreover, because it was unlikely that many of the acts of patent infringement affected by the statute had any likelihood of being unconstitutional, we concluded that the scope of the Act was out of proportion to its supposed remedial or preventive objectives. Instead, "[t]he statute's apparent and more basic aims were to provide a uniform remedy for patent infringement and to place States on the same footing as private parties under that regime." While we acknowledged that such aims may be proper congressional concerns under Article I, we found them insufficient to support an abrogation of the States' Eleventh Amendment immunity after *Seminole Tribe.*

Applying the same "congruence and proportionality" test in these cases, we conclude that the ADEA is not "appropriate legislation" under Sec. 5 of the Fourteenth Amendment. Initially, the substantive requirements the ADEA imposes on state and local governments are disproportionate to any unconstitutional conduct that conceivably could be targeted by the Act. We have considered claims of unconstitutional age discrimination under the Equal Protection Clause three times. In all three cases, we held that the age classifications at issue did not violate the Equal Protection Clause. Age classifications, unlike governmental conduct based on race or gender, cannot be characterized as "so seldom relevant to the achievement of any legitimate state interest that laws grounded in such considerations are deemed to reflect prejudice and antipathy." Older persons, again, unlike those who suffer discrimination on the basis of race or gender, have not been subjected to a "'history of purposeful unequal treatment.'" Old age also does not define a discrete and insular minority because all persons, if they live out their normal life spans, will experience it ... [A]ge is not a suspect classification under the Equal Protection Clause.

States may discriminate on the basis of age without offending the Fourteenth Amendment if the age classification in question is rationally related to a legitimate state interest. The rationality commanded by the Equal Protection Clause does not require States to match age distinctions and the legitimate interests they serve with razor-like precision. As we have explained, when conducting rational basis review,

[With]we will not overturn such [government action] unless the varying treatment of different groups or persons is so unrelated to the achievement of any combination of legitimate purposes that we can only conclude that the [government's] actions were irrational.

In contrast, when a State discriminates on the basis of race or gender, we require a tighter fit between the discriminatory means and the legitimate ends they serve ... Under the Fourteenth Amendment, a State may rely on age as a proxy for other qualities, abilities, or characteristics that are relevant to the State's legitimate interests. The Constitution does not preclude reliance on such generalizations. That age proves to be an inaccurate proxy in any individual case is irrelevant ...

... Our Constitution permits States to draw lines on the basis of age when they have a rational basis for doing so at a class-based level, even if it "is probably not true" that those reasons are valid in the majority of cases.

Judged against the backdrop of our equal protection jurisprudence, it is clear that the ADEA is "so out of proportion to a supposed remedial or preventive object that it cannot be understood as responsive to, or designed to prevent, unconstitutional behavior." The Act, through its broad restriction on the use of age as a discriminating factor, prohibits substantially more state employment decisions and practices than would likely be held unconstitutional under the applicable equal protection, rational basis standard. The ADEA makes unlawful, in the employment context, all "discriminat[ion] against any individual ... because of such individual's age." ...

That the ADEA prohibits very little conduct likely to be held unconstitutional, while significant, does not alone provide the answer to our [Fourteenth Amendment] Sec. 5 inquiry. Difficult and intractable problems often require powerful remedies, and we have never held that Sec. 5 precludes Congress from enacting reasonably prophylactic legislation. Our task is to determine whether the ADEA is in fact just such an appropriate remedy or instead merely an attempt to substantively redefine the States' legal obligations with respect to age discrimination. One means by which we have made such a determination in the past is by examining the legislative record containing the reasons for Congress' action. "The appropriateness of remedial measures must be considered in light of the evil presented. Strong measures appropriate to address one harm may be an unwarranted response to another lesser one."

Our examination of the ADEA's legislative record confirms that Congress' 1974 extension of the Act to the States was an unwarranted response to a perhaps inconsequential problem. Congress never identified any pattern of age discrimination by the States, much less any discrimination whatsoever that rose to the level of constitutional violation. The evidence compiled by petitioners to demonstrate such attention by Congress to age discrimination by the States falls well short of the mark. That evidence consists almost entirely of isolated sentences clipped from floor debates and legislative reports ...

Petitioners place additional reliance on Congress' consideration of a 1966 report prepared by the State of California on age discrimination in its public agencies ... Like the assorted sentences petitioners cobble together from a decade's worth of congressional reports and floor debates, the California study does not indicate that the State had engaged in any unconstitutional age discrimination. In fact, the report stated that the majority of the age limits uncovered in the state survey applied in the law enforcement and firefighting occupations. Those age limits were not only permitted under California law at the time, but are also currently permitted under the ADEA. Even if the California report had uncovered a pattern of unconstitutional age discrimination in the State's public agencies at the time, it nevertheless would have been insufficient to support Congress' 1974 extension of the ADEA to every State of the Union. The report simply does not constitute "evidence that [unconstitutional age discrimination] had become a problem of national import."

Finally, the United States' argument that Congress found substantial age discrimination in the private sector, is beside the point. Congress made no such findings with respect to the States. Although we also have doubts whether the findings Congress did make with respect to the private sector could be extrapolated to support a finding of unconstitutional age discrimination in the public sector, it is sufficient for these cases to note that Congress failed to identify a widespread pattern of age discrimination by the States.

A review of the ADEA's legislative record as a whole, then, reveals that Congress had virtually no reason to believe that state and local governments were unconstitutionally discriminating against their employees on the basis of age. Although that lack of support is not determinative of the Sec. 5 inquiry, Congress' failure to uncover any significant pattern of unconstitutional discrimination here confirms that Congress had no reason to believe that broad prophylactic legislation was necessary in this field. In light of the indiscriminate scope of the Act's substantive requirements, and the lack of evidence of widespread and unconstitutional age discrimination by the States, we hold that the ADEA is not a valid exercise of Congress' power under Sec. 5 of the Fourteenth Amendment. The ADEA's purported abrogation of the States' sovereign immunity is accordingly invalid.

Our decision today does not signal the end of the line for employees who find themselves subject to age discrimination at the hands of their state employers. We hold only that, in the ADEA, Congress did not validly abrogate the States' sovereign immunity to suits by private individuals. State employees are protected by state age discrimination statutes, and may recover money damages from their state employers, in almost every State of the Union. Those avenues of relief remain available today, just as they were before this decision.

Because the ADEA does not validly abrogate the States' sovereign immunity, however, the present suits must be dismissed. Accordingly, the judgment of the Court of Appeals is affirmed.

Stevens, dissenting in part:
Congress' power to regulate the American economy includes the power to regulate both the public and the private sectors of the labor market. Federal rules outlawing discrimination in the workplace, like the regulation of wages and hours or health and safety standards, may be enforced against public as well as private employers. In my opinion, Congress' power to authorize federal remedies against state agencies that violate federal statutory obligations is coextensive with its power to impose those obligations on the States in the first place. Neither the Eleventh Amendment nor the doctrine of sovereign immunity places any limit on that power.

The application of the ancient judge-made doctrine of sovereign immunity in cases like these is supposedly justified as a free-standing limit on congressional authority, a limit necessary to protect States' "dignity and respect" from impairment by the National Government. The Framers did not, however, select the Judicial Branch as the constitutional guardian of those state in-

terests. Rather, the Framers designed important structural safeguards to ensure that when the National Government enacted substantive law (and provided for its enforcement), the normal operation of the legislative process itself would adequately defend state interests from undue infringement.

It is the Framers' compromise giving each State equal representation in the Senate that provides the principal structural protection for the sovereignty of the several States. The composition of the Senate was originally determined by the legislatures of the States, which would guarantee that their interests could not be ignored by Congress. The Framers also directed that the House be composed of Representatives selected by voters in the several States . . .

Whenever Congress passes a statute, it does so against the background of state law already in place; the propriety of taking national action is thus measured by the metric of the existing state norms that Congress seeks to supplement or supplant. The persuasiveness of any justification for overcoming legislative inertia and taking national action, either creating new federal obligations or providing for their enforcement, must necessarily be judged in reference to state interests, as expressed in existing state laws. The precise scope of federal laws, of course, can be shaped with nuanced attention to state interests. The Congress also has the authority to grant or withhold jurisdiction in lower federal courts. The burden of being haled into a federal forum for the enforcement of federal law thus can be expanded or contracted as Congress deems proper, which decision, like all other legislative acts, necessarily contemplates state interests. Thus, Congress can use its broad range of flexible legislative tools to approach the delicate issue of how to balance local and national interests in the most responsive and careful manner. It is quite evident, therefore, that the Framers did not view this Court as the ultimate guardian of the States' interest in protecting their own sovereignty from impairment by "burdensome" federal laws.

Federalism concerns do make it appropriate for Congress to speak clearly when it regulates state action. But, when it does so, as it has in these cases, we can safely presume that the burdens the statute imposes on the sovereignty of the several States were taken into account during the deliberative process leading to the enactment of the measure. Those burdens necessarily include the cost of defending against enforcement proceedings and paying whatever penalties might be incurred for violating the statute. In my judgment, the question whether those enforcement proceedings should be conducted exclusively by federal agencies, or may be brought by private parties as well, is a matter of policy for Congress to decide. In either event, once Congress has made its policy choice, the sovereignty concerns of the several States are satisfied, and the federal interest in evenhanded enforcement of federal law, explicitly endorsed in Article VI of the Constitution does not countenance further limitations. There is not a word in the text of the Constitution supporting the Court's conclusion that the judge-made doctrine of sovereign immunity limits Congress' power to authorize private parties, as well as federal agencies, to enforce federal law against the States. The importance of respecting the Framers' decision to assign the business of lawmaking to the Congress dictates firm resistance to the present majority's repeated substitution of its own views of federalism for those expressed in statutes enacted by the Congress and signed by the President.

The Eleventh Amendment simply does not support the Court's view. As has been stated before, the Amendment only places a textual limitation on the diversity jurisdiction of the federal courts . . . Here . . . private petitioners did not invoke the federal courts' diversity jurisdiction; they are citizens of the same State as the defendants, and they are asserting claims that arise under federal law. Thus, today's decision . . . rests entirely on a novel judicial interpretation of the doctrine of sovereign immunity, which the Court treats as though it were a constitutional precept. It is nevertheless clear to me that, if Congress has the power to create the federal rights that these petitioners are asserting, it must also have the power to give the federal courts jurisdiction to remedy violations of those rights, even if it is necessary to "abrogate" the Court's "Eleventh Amendment" version of the common law defense of sovereign immunity to do so.

Reno v. Condon

528 U S 141 (2000), 9-0

Opinion of the Court: Rehnquist (Stevens, O'Conner, Scalia, Kennedy, Souter, Thomas, Ginsberg, Breyer)

On what constitutional power has Congress based the Driver's Privacy Protection Act? What "principles of federalism contained in the Tenth Amendment" might make such exer- *cise of power unconstitutional? Why did they not in this case? Can the decision here be distinguished from that of* Printz v. United States *or has the Court partially retreated from its states rights position in that case?*

Rehnquist, C.J., for the Court:

The Driver's Privacy Protection Act of 1994 (DPPA or Act) regulates the disclosure of personal information contained in the records of state motor vehicle departments (DMVs). We hold that, in enacting this statute, Congress did not run afoul of the federalism principles enunciated in *New York v. United States* and *Printz v. United States.*

The DPPA regulates the disclosure and resale of personal information contained in the records of state DMVs. State DMVs require drivers and automobile owners to provide personal information, which may include a person's name, address, telephone number, vehicle description, Social Security number, medical information, and photograph, as a condition of obtaining a driver's license or registering an automobile. Congress found that many States, in turn, sell this personal information to individuals and businesses. These sales generate significant revenues for the States . . .

The DPPA establishes a regulatory scheme that restricts the States' ability to disclose a driver's personal information without the driver's consent. The DPPA generally prohibits any state DMV, or officer, employee, or contractor thereof, from "knowingly disclos[ing] or otherwise mak[ing] available to any person or entity personal information about any individual obtained by the department in connection with a motor vehicle record." The DPPA defines "personal information" as any information "that identifies an individual, including an individual's photograph, social security number, driver identification number, name, address (but not the 5-digit zip code), telephone number, and medical or disability information, but not including information on vehicular accidents, driving violations, and driver's status." . . .

The DPPA's ban on disclosure of personal information does not apply if drivers have consented to the release of their data . . . States may not imply consent from a driver's failure to take advantage of a state-afforded opportunity to block disclosure, but must rather obtain a driver's affirmative consent to disclose the driver's personal information for use in surveys, marketing, solicitations, and other restricted purposes.

The DPPA's prohibition of nonconsensual disclosures is also subject to a number of statutory exceptions. For example, the DPPA requires disclosure of personal information:

> for use in connection with matters of motor vehicle or driver safety and theft, motor vehicle emissions, motor vehicle product alterations, recalls, or advisories, performance monitoring of motor vehicles and dealers by motor vehicle manufacturers, and removal of non-owner records from the original owner records of motor vehicle manufacturers to carry out the purposes of Titles I and IV of the Anti-Car Theft Act of 1992, the Automobile Information Disclosure Act, the Clean Air Act, and Chapters 301, 305, and 321-331 of Title 49.

. . . The DPPA's provisions do not apply solely to States. The Act also regulates the resale and redisclosure of drivers' personal information by private persons who have obtained that information from a state DMV. In general, the Act allows private persons who have obtained drivers' personal information for one of the aforementioned permissible purposes to further disclose that information for any one of those purposes. If a State has obtained drivers' consent to disclose their personal information to private persons generally and a private person has obtained that information, the private person may redisclose the information for any purpose. Additionally, a private actor who has obtained drivers' information from DMV records specifically for direct marketing purposes may resell that information for other direct marketing uses, but not otherwise. Any person who rediscloses or resells personal information from DMV records must, for five years, maintain records identifying to whom the records were disclosed and the permitted purpose for the resale or redisclosure.

The DPPA establishes several penalties to be imposed on States and private actors that fail to comply with its requirements. The Act makes it unlawful for any "person" knowingly to obtain or disclose any record for a use that is not permitted under its provisions, or to make a false representation in order to obtain personal information from a motor vehicle record. Any person who knowingly violates the DPPA may be subject to a criminal fine. Additionally, any person who knowingly obtains, discloses, or uses information from a state motor vehicle record for a use

other than those specifically permitted by the DPPA may be subject to liability in a civil action brought by the driver to whom the information pertains . . . [A] state agency that maintains a "policy or practice of substantial noncompliance" with the Act may be subject to a civil penalty imposed by the United States Attorney General of not more than $5,000 per day of substantial noncompliance.

South Carolina law conflicts with the DPPA's provisions. Under that law, the information contained in the State's DMV records is available to any person or entity that fills out a form listing the requester's name and address and stating that the information will not be used for telephone solicitation . . .

Following the DPPA's enactment, South Carolina and its Attorney General, respondent Condon, filed suit in the United States District Court for the District of South Carolina, alleging that the DPPA violates the Tenth and Eleventh Amendments to the United States Constitution . . .

The United States asserts that the DPPA is a proper exercise of Congress' authority to regulate interstate commerce under the Commerce Clause. The United States bases its Commerce Clause argument on the fact that the personal identifying information that the DPPA regulates is a "thin[g] in interstate commerce," and that the sale or release of that information in interstate commerce is therefore a proper subject of congressional regulation. We agree with the United States' contention. The motor vehicle information which the States have historically sold is used by insurers, manufacturers, direct marketers, and others engaged in interstate commerce to contact drivers with customized solicitations. The information is also used in the stream of interstate commerce by various public and private entities for matters related to interstate motoring. Because drivers' information is, in this context, an article of commerce, its sale or release into the interstate stream of business is sufficient to support congressional regulation. We therefore need not address the Government's alternative argument that the States' individual, intrastate activities in gathering, maintaining, and distributing drivers' personal information has a sufficiently substantial impact on interstate commerce to create a constitutional base for federal legislation.

But the fact that drivers' personal information is, in the context of this case, an article in interstate commerce does not conclusively resolve the constitutionality of the DPPA. In *New York* and *Printz*, we held federal statutes invalid not because Congress lacked legislative authority over the subject matter, but because those statutes violated the principles of federalism contained in the Tenth Amendment. In *New York*, Congress commandeered the state legislative process by requiring a state legislature to enact a particular kind of law. We said:

> While Congress has substantial powers to govern the Nation directly, including in areas of intimate concern to the States, the Constitution has never been understood to confer upon Congress the ability to the require the States to govern according to Congress' instructions.

In *Printz*, we invalidated a provision of the Brady Act which commanded "state and local enforcement officers to conduct background check on prospective handgun purchasers. We said:

> We held in *New York* that Congress cannot compel the States to enact or enforce a federal regulatory program. Today we hold that Congress cannot circumvent that prohibition by conscripting the States' officers directly. The Federal Government may neither issue directives requiring the States to address particular problems nor command the States' officers, or those of their political subdivisions to administer or enforce a federal regulatory program.

South Carolina contends that the DPPA violates the Tenth Amendment because it "thrusts upon the States all of the day-to-day responsibility for administering its complex provisions," and thereby makes "state officials the unwilling implementors of federal policy," South Carolina emphasizes that the DPPA requires the State's employees to learn and apply the Act's substantive restrictions, which are summarized above, and notes that these activities will consume the employees' time and thus the State's resources. South Carolina further notes that the DPPA's penalty provisions hang over the States as a potential punishment should they fail to comply with the Act.

We agree with South Carolina's assertion that the DPPA's provisions will require time and effort on the part of state employees, but reject the State's argument that the DPPA violates the principles laid down in either *New York* or *Printz*. We think, instead,

that this case is governed by our decision in South *Carolina v. Baker*. In *Baker*, we upheld a statute that prohibited States from issuing unregistered bonds because the law "regulate[d] state activities," rather than "seek[ing] to control or influence the manner in which States regulate private parties." We further noted:

> The NGA [National Governor's Association] nonetheless contends that Sec. 310 has commandeered the state legislative and administrative process because many state legislatures had to amend a substantial number of statutes in order to issue bonds in registered form and because state officials had to devote substantial effort to determine how best to implement a registered bond system. Such "commandeering" is, however, an inevitable consequence of regulating a state activity. Any federal regulation demands compliance. That a State wishing to engage in certain activity must take administrative and sometimes legislative action to comply with federal standards regulating that activity is a commonplace that presents no constitutional defect.

Like the statute at issue in *Baker*, the DPPA does not require the States in their sovereign capacity to regulate their own citizens. The DPPA regulates the States as the owners of databases. It does not require the South Carolina Legislature to enact any laws or regulations, and it does not require state officials to assist in the enforcement of federal statutes regulating private individuals. We accordingly conclude that the DPPA is consistent with the constitutional principles enunciated in *New York* and *Printz*.

As a final matter, we turn to South Carolina's argument that the DPPA is unconstitutional because it regulates the States exclusively. The essence of South Carolina's argument is that Congress may only regulate the States by means of "generally applicable" laws, or laws that apply to individuals as well as States. But we need not address the question whether general applicability is a constitutional requirement for federal regulation of the States, because the DPPA is generally applicable. The DPPA regulates the universe of entities that participate as suppliers to the market for motor vehicle information—the States as initial suppliers of the information in interstate commerce and private resellers or redisclosers of that information in commerce.

United States v. Morrison

529 U.S. 598 (2000), 5-4
Opinion of the Court: Rehnquist, C.J. (O'Connor, Scalia, Kennedy, Thomas)
Dissenting: Breyer (Stevens, Souter, Ginsberg)
This civil suit in which the United States intervened was brought under the Violence Against Women Act of 1994 (42 United States Code, s. 42).

Does this case differ significantly from United States v. Lopez? *Could Congress have done anything in the Violence against Women Act that would have met the Court's objection to it? What is the immediate point of dispute between the majority and the dissenters? Do they have a longer-term disagreement about constitutional interpretation as Justice Souter suggests? If so, what is it? Is it possible to distinguish between what is economic and noneconomic? Should the Court try?*

Rehnquist, C.J., for the Court:

Petitioner Christy Brzonkala enrolled at Virginia Polytechnic Institute (Virginia Tech) in the fall of 1994. In September of that year, Brzonkala met respondents Antonio Morrison and James Crawford, who were both students at Virginia Tech and members of its varsity football team. Brzonkala alleges that, within 30 minutes of meeting Morrison and Crawford, they assaulted and repeatedly raped her.... Brzonkala alleges that this attack caused her to become severely emotionally disturbed and depressed. She sought assistance from a university psychiatrist, who prescribed antidepressant medication. Shortly after the rape Brzonkala stopped attending classes and withdrew from the university ...

Brzonkala sued Morrison, Crawford, and Virginia Tech. Her complaint alleged that Morrison's and Crawford's attack violated s. 13981 ... Morrison and Crawford moved to dismiss this complaint on the grounds that ... s. 13981's civil remedy is unconstitutional. The United States intervened to defend s. 13981's constitutionality....

... In *Lopez* we held that the Gun-Free School Zones Act of 1990, which made it a federal crime to knowingly possess a firearm in a school zone, exceeded Congress' authority under the Commerce Clause. Several significant considerations ...

First, we observed that [The Gun Free School Zones Act] was "a criminal statute that by its terms has nothing to do with 'commerce' or any sort of economic enterprise, however broadly one might define those terms." ...

... *Lopez*'s review of Commerce Clause case law demonstrates that in those cases where we have sustained federal regulation of intrastate activity based upon the activity's substantial effects on interstate commerce, the activity in question has been some sort of economic endeavor.

The second consideration that we found important ... was that the statute contained "no express jurisdictional element which might limit its reach to a discrete set of firearm possessions that additionally have an explicit connection with or effect on interstate commerce." ...

Third, we noted that neither [the Gun Free School Zones Act] "'nor its legislative history contain[s] express congressional findings regarding the effects upon interstate commerce of gun possession in a school zone.'" While "Congress normally is not required to make formal findings as to the substantial burdens that an activity has on interstate commerce," the existence of such findings may "enable us to evaluate the legislative judgment that the activity in question substantially affect[s] interstate commerce, even though no such substantial effect [is] visible to the naked eye."

Finally, our decision in *Lopez* rested in part on the fact that the link between gun possession and a substantial effect on interstate commerce was attenuated. The United States argued that the possession of guns may lead to violent crime, and that violent crime "can be expected to affect the functioning of the national economy in two ways. First, the costs of violent crime are substantial, and, through the mechanism of insurance, those costs are spread throughout the population. Second, violent crime reduces the willingness of individuals to travel to areas within the country that are perceived to be unsafe." The Government also argued that the presence of guns at schools poses a threat to the educational process, which in turn threatens to produce a less efficient and productive workforce, which will negatively affect national productivity and thus interstate commerce.

We rejected these "costs of crime" and "national productivity" arguments because they would permit Congress to "regulate not only all violent crime, but all activities that might lead to violent crime, regardless of how tenuously they relate to interstate commerce." ... We noted that, under this but-for reasoning ... Congress could regulate any activity that is found was related to the economic productivity of individual citizens: family law (including marriage, divorce, and child custody), for example. Under the[se] theories; it is difficult to perceive any limitation on federal power, even in areas such as criminal law enforcement or education where States historically have been sovereign. Thus, if we were to accept the Government's arguments, we are hard pressed to posit any activity by an individual that Congress is without power to regulate.

With these principles underlying our Commerce Clause jurisprudence as reference points, the proper resolution of the present cases is clear. Gender-motivated crimes of violence are not, in any sense of the phrase, economic activity. While we need not adopt a categorical rule against aggregating the effects of any noneconomic activity in order to decide these cases, thus far in our Nation's history our cases have upheld Commerce Clause regulation of intrastate activity only where that activity is economic in nature.

Like the Gun-Free School Zones act at issue in *Lopez,* 13981 contains no jurisdictional element establishing that the federal cause of action is in pursuance of Congress' power to regulate interstate commerce. . . .

In contrast with the lack of congressional findings that we faced in *Lopez,* s. 13981 is supported by numerous findings regarding the serious impact that gender-motivated violence h as on victims and their families. But the existence of congressional findings is not sufficient, by itself, to sustain the constitutionality of Commerce Clause legislation. As we stated in *Lopez,* "'[S]imply because Congress may conclude that a particular activity substantially affects interstate commerce does not necessarily make it so.'" Rather, "'[w]hether particular operations affect interstate commerce sufficiently to come under the constitutional power of Congress to regulate them is ultimately a judicial rather than a legislative question, and can be settled finally only by this Court.'"

. . . Congress' findings are substantially weakened by the fact that they rely so heavily on a method of reasoning that we have already rejected as unworkable if we are to maintain the Constitution's enumeration of powers. Congress found that gender-motivated violence affects interstate commerce

> by deterring potential victims from traveling interstate, from engaging in employment in interstate business, and from transacting with business, and in places involved in interstate commerce; by diminishing national productivity, increasing medical and other costs, and decreasing the supply of and the demand for interstate products.

Given these findings and petitioner's arguments, the concern that we expresses in *Lopez* that Congress might use the Commerce Clause to completely obliterate the Constitution's distinction between national and local authority seems well founded. The reasoning that petitioners advance seeks to follow the but-for causal chain from the initial occurrence of violent crime)the suppression of which has always been the prime object of the States' police power) to every attenuated effect upon interstate commerce. If accepted, petitioners' reasoning would allow Congress to regulate any crime as long as the nationwide, aggregated impact of that crime has substantial effects on employment, production, transit, or consumption. Indeed, if Congress may regulate gender-motivated violence, it would be able to regulate murder or any other type of violence since gender-motivated violence, as a subset of all violent crime, is certain to have lesser economic impacts than the larger class of which it is a part.

Petitioners' reasoning, moreover, will not limit Congress to regulating violence but may, as we suggested in *Lopez,* be applied equally as well to family law and other areas of traditional state regulation since the aggregate effect of marriage, divorce, and childrearing on the national economy is undoubtedly significant. Congress may have recognized this specter when it expressly precluded s. 13981 from being used in the family law context. Under our written Constitution, however, the limitation of congressional authority is not solely a matter of legislative grace.

We accordingly reject the argument that Congress may regulate noneconomic, violent criminal conduct based solely on that conduct's aggregate effect on interstate commerce. The Constitution requires a distinction between what is truly national and what is truly local. In recognizing this fact we preserve one of the few principles that has been consistent since the Clause was adopted. The regulation and punishment of intrastate violence that is not directed at the instrumentalities, channels, or goods involved in interstate commerce has always been the province of the States. Indeed, we can think of no better example of the police power, which the Founders denied the National Government and reposed in the States, than the suppression of violent crime and vindication of its victims. . . .

Petitioner Brzonkala's complaint alleges that she was the victim of a brutal assault. . . . If the allegations here are true, no civilized system of justice could fail to provide her a remedy for the conduct of respondent Morrison. But under our federal system that remedy must be provided by the Commonwealth of Virginia, and not by the United States.

Souter, dissenting:

... Congress has the power to legislate with regard to activity that, in the aggregate, has a substantial effect on interstate commerce. The fact of such a substantial effect is not an issue for the courts in the first instance, *ibid.*, but for the Congress, whose institutional capacity for gathering evidence and taking testimony far exceeds ours. By passing legislation, Congress indicates its conclusion, whether explicitly or not, that facts support its exercise of the commerce power. The business of the courts is to review the congressional assessment, not for soundness but simply for the rationality of concluding that a jurisdictional basis exists in fact. See *ibid.* Any explicit findings that Congress chooses to make, though not dispositive of the question of rationality, may advance judicial review by identifying factual authority on which Congress relied. ...

One obvious difference from *United States v. Lopez,* is the mountain of data assembled by Congress, here showing the effects of violence against women on interstate commerce. Passage of the Act in 1994 was preceded by four years of hearings, which included testimony from physicians and law professors; from survivors of rape and domestic violence; and from representatives of state law enforcement and private business. The record includes reports on gender bias from task forces in 21 States, and we have the benefit of specific factual findings in the eight separate Reports issued by Congress and its committees over the long course leading to enactment. ...

Congress thereby explicitly states the predicate for the exercise of its Commerce Clause power. Is its conclusion irrational in view of the data amassed? True, the methodology of particular studies may be challenged, and some of the figures arrived at may be disputed. But the sufficiency of the evidence before Congress to provide a rational basis for the finding cannot seriously be questioned. ...

The Act would have passed muster at any time between *Wickard* [*v. Filburn*] in 1942 and *Lopez* in 1995, a period in which the law enjoyed a stable understanding that congressional power under the Commerce Clause, complemented by the authority of the Necessary and Proper Clause extended to all activity that, when aggregated, has a substantial effect on interstate commerce. ...

The fact that the Act does not pass muster before the Court today is therefore proof, to a degree that *Lopez* was not, that the Court's nominal adherence to the substantial effects test is merely that. Although a new jurisprudence has not emerged with any distinctness, it is clear that some congressional conclusions about obviously substantial, cumulative effects on commerce are being assigned lesser values than the once-stable doctrine would assign them. These devaluations are accomplished not by any express repudiation of the substantial effects test or its application through the aggregation of individual conduct, but by supplanting rational basis scrutiny with a new criterion of review. ...

All of this convinces me that today's ebb of the commerce power rests on error, and at the same time leads me to doubt that the majority's view will prove to be enduring law. There is yet one more reason for doubt. Although we sense the presence of [*Carter v.*] *Carter Coal, Schechter* [*Poultry Corp. v. United States*], and [*National League of Cities v.*] *Usery* once again, the majority embraces them only at arm's-length. Where such decisions once stood for rules, today's opinion points to considerations by which substantial effects are discounted. Cases standing for the sufficiency of substantial effects are not overruled; cases overruled since 1937 are not quite revived. The Court's thinking betokens less clearly a return to the conceptual straitjackets of *Schechter* and *Carter Coal* and *Usery* than to something like the unsteady state of obscenity law between *Redrup v. New York,* (1967) and *Miller v. California,* (1973), a period in which the failure to provide a workable definition left this Court to review each case ad hoc. As our predecessors learned then, the practice of such ad hoc review cannot preserve the distinction between the judicial and the legislative, and this Court, in any event, lacks the institutional capacity to maintain such a regime for very long. This one will end when the majority realizes that the conception of the commerce power for which it entertains hopes would inevitably fail the test expressed in Justice Holmes's statement that "[t]he first call of a theory of law is that it should fit the facts." The facts that cannot be ignored today are the facts of integrated national commerce and a political relationship between States and Nation much affected by their respective treasuries and constitutional modifications adopted by the people. The federalism of some earlier time is no more adequate to account for those facts today than the theory of laissez-faire was able to govern the national economy 70 years ago.

11

PROPERTY RIGHTS
IN THE AGE OF REGULATION

The economic and social crisis of the Great Depression exposed grave weaknesses in industrial capitalism. The response of the New Deal, built on earlier reform efforts, was to modify the capitalist political economy by creation of an "administrative state" in which government assumed new responsibilities through regulatory intervention in markets and the sponsorship of social welfare programs. The system of regulated welfare capitalism that emerged paid more attention to harmful economic, social, and environmental effects that could accompany economic development. It also recognized that in an ever-more integrated and centralized economy, collisions of interests could often have a wide, even national effect and that the public interest might not always be served by market operations alone.

These developments witnessed an enormous growth in the size and importance of government. In 1930, federal, state, and local public spending together was only 10 percent of the gross national product. By 1970, it had grown to more than 30 percent and by 1985 to an all-time high of more than 35. Federal spending, only 2.5 percent of the gross national product in

1930, had risen ninefold to more than 22 percent by 1985. Corresponding increases took place in taxation and in government borrowing. Civilians employed in government doubled between 1930 and 1960 and doubled again by 1985. If everything that government does is regulation, as some have said, then the regulatory state had arrived.

The "constitutional revolution" that followed the New Deal has ratified the administrative state and supported this growth. Through its tax, spending, and commerce powers, the national government has assumed now an almost unlimited regulatory power over the economy. Though the balance in the federal system markedly tilts toward the center, the states have also assumed new regulatory functions through their police powers. In much of its review of social and economic policy of either level of government, the Supreme Court has deferred to legislative judgment to an extent unimagined in earlier times.

Misgivings about the growth of the administrative state, however, have been part of a larger conservative trend and a new polarization in American politics starting in the late 1960s. Growing dissatisfaction with the Vietnam War, political assassinations, and scandal in high office contributed to a disenchantment with governmental authority generally. Economic developments had an effect as well. The oil-driven energy crisis of the 1970s on top of war expenditures led to a decade of high inflation, high interest rates, an ever-larger national debt, and a slowdown of economic growth and productivity.

Politically, the nation entered an era of divided government. The election of Richard Nixon in 1968 began a period of presidential Republicanism in which the White House was held by conservative Republicans 20 of the next 24 years. During most of that time, power was shared with a Congress controlled by moderate Democrats. Though this alignment was entirely reversed during the Clinton presidency, the national government remained divided, with conservatives controlling one branch and moderates the other. One important result was a slowing down of the advance of the regulatory state and new attention given to economic development and, correspondingly, to rights of property.

The change is best represented by the Reagan presidency. Arguing that government—too much of it—was the main cause of the nation's economic ills, Reagan won decisive victories in 1980 and 1984. His program was one of economic stimulus through tax cuts, deregulation, and new spending limits on social welfare programs. It included a clear ideological preference for dealing with problems, wherever possible, through markets and voluntary associations rather than government, and within government, for state and local rather than federal policy-making. Military spending was the only important budget area not coming under constrictive pressure. The Reagan years were marked by much lower inflation, lower interest rates, and renewed economic growth that led to a boom worldwide. But partly because of the tax cuts and increased military spending, neither the annual federal deficits nor accumulated debt was reduced. Deficits ended, at least temporarily, with a resurgence of growth and productivity in the late 1990s under a Democratic president and a Republican Congress, creating an even more favorable economic environment.

For all the moderate-conservative politics of the last quarter century, the regulatory administrative state has not been dismantled. Its growth has been slowed and, in some instances, halted, but government regulation and intervention continue to be a part of modern capitalism. Business, perhaps surprisingly, has generally taken an accommodating stance, being satisfied that policy-makers remain sensitive to the economic cost and inefficiency that regulatory controls and federal intervention in markets often impose. Its criticism of the liberal orthodoxy of the post-New Deal welfare state notwithstanding, business has tended to prefer predictability, stability, and moderation to wholesale deregulation.

In the 1970s, the Supreme Court began to question the long-standing distinction between personal and property rights and the wisdom of leaving the latter largely to the discretion legislatures who all too often, it was charged, come under the influence of "special interests." Though no such distinction can be found in the text of the Constitution or in the intent of the framers, advocates of greater recognition of property rights argued that it would serve not just economic well-being, but individual liberty as well. The Burger and Rehnquist Courts have been friendlier to economic rights than any Court since that of the early New Deal, yet only modest constitutional change had occurred by century's end. One reason perhaps is that new judicial protection called for new judicial activism, a matter troubling to many conservative justices.

Economic Due Process Interred

Renewed interest in property rights has not come through a revival of economic substantive due process doctrine. The New Deal victory over the Supreme Court marked the end of that doctrine in American constitutional law. The Court withdrew from deciding whether legislatures had authority to enact particular economic regulations. No longer were such laws be struck down because they were, in the view of the justices, unreasonable.

How far the Court had moved away from the overseeing of state regulation of business became dramatically evident in *Williamson v. Lee Optical Co.* (1955) (p. 557). Before the Court was an Oklahoma law that required a medical prescription whenever an optician duplicated eyeglass lenses or fit old lenses into new frames. The law appeared to be without rational police basis and simply to favor one economic interest over another. In upholding it, the Court hypothesized rational purposes it might serve, however far-fetched. On economic regulation, then, if the legislature did not offer rational reasons for enactment, the Court might think up some that it might have used. In this deference to the legislature, Justice Douglas said that anyone claiming to be hurt by the law should look for remedy in the political branches rather than the courts.

In *Ferguson v. Skrupa* (1963) (p. 567), it became clear that the Court would sustain legislative regulatory judgment if it could be supported by almost any fact known or reasonably inferable. In upholding a Kansas law that limited the practice of debt adjustment to licensed attorneys and simply favored one occupational interest over another, Justice Black wrote, "We refuse to sit as a super-legislature to weigh the wisdom of [economic] legislation." The due process clause thus imposed almost no limit on state regulation of economic matters.

Greater power of states in regulating business was partly offset by another feature of post-New Deal constitutional change: the Court's willingness to sustain nearly unlimited federal power to regulate commerce. This has enhanced the so-called dormant commerce power—the residual power said to exist in the commerce clause when Congress has been "silent," that is, when it has not acted to regulate interstate commerce. Such silence leaves the Court the arbiter of state regulations bearing on interstate commerce and allows it to use the dormant commerce power to strike them down. As we have seen in the preceding chapter, the Court is most apt to do this if it finds that state restrictions disfavor out-of-state interests without advancing a strong police power end. The dormant commerce power may thus be used to protect property rights but only to prevent discrimination against out-of-state interests and so maintain an open marketplace among the states. In such cases, the Court may weigh the reasonableness of economic legislation.

The Contracts Clause Revived

Once the most litigated clause in the Constitution, Article I-10's bar of states from "impairing the obligations of contracts" had declined in importance after the Civil War when the Supreme Court began to use the broader doctrine of substantive due process to defend property against regulation. The clause appeared to reach its nadir in the Depression era case of *Home Building & Loan Association v. Blaisdell* (1934), which upheld a state-imposed moratorium on mortgage payments. Though the law was intended to meet a grave economic emergency and did not extinguish debt, its validation moved the Court further from the contracts clause restriction than it had ever gone. The decision also fitted nicely with the Court's later deference to legislative judgment on economic regulation and its abandonment of substantive due process.

El Paso v. Simmons (1965) was typical of the new approach. A Texas law permitted persons who had bought land from the state with a small down payment but failed to make interest payments to reclaim their tract later by paying the back interest, provided no third-party rights had been asserted in the meantime. When Texas amended the law to place a five-year limit on reinstatement of a claim, it was challenged as a violation of the original land contract. The Court acknowledged the impairment but nonetheless upheld the law as a way of curbing land speculation and reducing uncertainty over titles. Against the contracts clause, the Court gave a wide berth to the power of state legislatures to protect the general welfare.

But with the coming of the Burger Court, it became clear that the contracts clause was not yet to be read out of the Constitution. In *United States Trust v. New Jersey* (1977) (p. 568) the Court struck down a state law that removed a contractual protection for bondholders. In a 1920s interstate compact, New York and New Jersey had created the Port Authority of New York and New Jersey (PATH) to develop and manage transportation in the New York harbor area. In 1962, the states authorized PATH to take over a bankrupt railway with the proviso that operating revenue pledged to secure the bonds that financed the project would not be used to absorb other railway expenses. But in 1974, responding to a national energy crisis, the two states withdrew the pledge so that operating revenues earmarked to secure the bonds could be used to pay for other mass transit projects. By a 4-3 vote, the Court held the action an unconstitutional impairment of contractual obligation rather than simply the exercise of a police power, Justice Blackmun noting that there were other ways of promoting mass transit. The Court also suggested that it did not think the energy shortage was comparable to the economic emergency faced at the time of *Blaisdell.*

In *Allied Structural Steel v. Spannaus* the following year, the Court found a state law affecting private contractual obligation to be an unconstitutional impairment. Minnesota had required that a company closing business operations in the state must grant employees with 10 or more years of service pension benefits whether such benefits were in the company's pension contract or not. The effect was to increase the obligations of one party to a private contract. In striking it down, the Court offered a set of measured standards: The impairment must be substantial, not temporary to deal with emergency conditions, and not be a police action needed to remedy an "important and general social problem."

United States Trust, Allied Structural Steel, and later decisions make it clear that the Court is neither willing to bury the contracts clause, as many thought it had, nor restore it to former heights. For example, it later sustained a state law that limited the price increases a natural gas supplier could charge a public utility even though the regulation conflicted with contracts already in force. In *Energy Reserves Group v. Kansas Power & Light* (1983), it held the law to be an important consumer protection from price fluctuations created by federal deregulation. Similarly, in *Keystone Bituminous Coal Ass'n. v. DeBenedictus* (1987), it upheld a Pennsylvania law that limited the amount of coal a mining company could remove under an area with surface buildings. The company had contracts with the owners of the buildings in which they had waived damage claims that might result from further mining. Stating that the constitutional bar to impairing the obligations of contracts "is not to be read literally," Justice Stevens held the police power interest in preventing environmental damage from mining operations justified the restriction.

Modern contract clause decisions suggest that successful claims against state regulations are possible, but what is required of the claimant's proof means that the courts will have the discretionary task of judging whether legislation reasonably promotes the public welfare.

Eminent Domain and the Takings Clause

Eminent domain is the government's authority to take or seize private property for public use. It is an incident of sovereignty distinct from the general police power or the power to tax. The so-called takings clause of the Fifth Amendment— "nor shall private property be taken for public use without just compensation"—implicitly recognizes eminent domain as a sovereign power at the same time that it places an important restriction on it. Generally, the eminent domain power is exercised against real as opposed to personal, financial, or intangible property, as when private land is taken to build a highway, clear a slum, or protect the environment. Just compensation for property taken ensures that the cost of public improvement will be borne by all rather than by one or a few owners.

In *Barron v. Baltimore* (1833), the protection of the takings clause was held to limit only the national government. With ratification of the Fourteenth Amendment and its due process limit on state power after the Civil War, the Supreme Court eventually amended this rule. In *Chicago, Burlington & Quincy Railroad v. Chicago* (1897) it held that "just compensation" for seized property, in this case for street widening, was part of due process of law and thus an applicable limit on state power. As land development accelerated and uses grew more complex, courts were increasingly called on to decide what the takings clause required or permitted. The Supreme Court has now heard scores of cases in which state or local regulation of land use or other property rights has been constitutionally challenged under the takings clause. The Rehnquist Court in particular has given increasing attention to the issue. Here we look at three aspects of the eminent domain power: what is "public use," what constitutes a "taking," and what satisfies "just compensation." The Court's decisions, like those holding on state power to regulate interstate commerce, often show an admirable ad hoc balancing of interests but fall short of providing clear theoretical guidelines.

Public Use

Public purpose or use is the basic rationale for eminent domain. Without it, there can be no taking of private property even with just compensation. In giving the term broad interpretation, the Supreme Court now defers largely to legislative judgment. This means that the constitutionally required public purpose for the taking of property may be coextensive with a legislature's conception of its police power to protect health, safety, morals, or general welfare. Public use may benefit only some of the public, as in the construction of a housing project, for example, or may be indirect and diffused, as when the eminent domain power is devolved so that land can be acquired to build a privately owned railway or utility.

The leading modern case is *Berman v. Parker* (1954), in which the Supreme Court unanimously upheld a taking of several acres of privately owned property for an urban renewal project in Washington, D.C. A department store owner had objected to the plan as applied to him because his property was not slum housing and would simply be transferred to other private owners for development. In rejecting this claim, the Court held that even property that was not substandard could be taken as part of a comprehensive redevelopment plan for an area.

In a more recent decision, *Hawaii Housing Authority v. Midkiff* (1984) (p. 575), the Court went further in giving broad meaning to public use. The Hawaii legislature, aiming to break up the tight ownership of land by a few persons, gave tenants with long-term leases the right to acquire title to the property they occupied through eminent domain. The dispossessed landlords would then be paid "just compensation." The Court held that the redistributive effect of the law was not disproof that it was "rationally related to a conceivable public purpose"—here the social and economic problems created by long-standing land oligopoly. Using the same broad reasoning, lower courts have consistently upheld use of eminent domain to take land for industrial development by private corporations.

What Is a Taking?

Determining whether a government act has "taken" property has proved more difficult than whether a public use has been served. It has led to hard thinking about what may be held to be a property right for which compensation is due.

From its first review of a comprehensive zoning ordinance in *Euclid v. Ambler Realty* (1926), the Court has upheld local land use plans against property owners alleging loss of value. As long as the zoning regulations advance an arguable police power end, do not destroy the primary value of the property, and do not shift the economic cost of regulation to one or to a small group of owners, the diminished land value is not a taking that calls for compensation. The Court's modern balancing approach in which it weighs social, economic, or environmental gains against the diminution of property value, was evident in *Keystone Bituminous Coal Ass'n. v. DeBenedictus,* already noted. The requirement that a mining company leave a portion of its coal in the ground for surface support, was held not a taking.

"Landmark" zoning, in which the chief regulatory aim is the preservation of aesthetic values, came before the Court in *Penn Central v. City of New York* (1978) (p. 571). An ordinance required that proposed changes to buildings designated as historic landmarks needed approval by the city's Landmarks Preservation Commission. When the commission rejected the railroad's plan to build a 55-story office building above Grand Central Terminal, its historic Beaux Arts structure that had landmark status, the railroad challenged the denial as an unconstitutional taking. The Court disagreed, Justice Brennan holding that the restriction was in keeping with a comprehensive plan to preserve historic buildings and did not affect the primary use of the structure as a rail terminal. He also noted that a mitigating feature of the city's ordinance allowing a regulated landowner to transfer "air rights" to other, nonlandmark property was evidence of the law's reasonableness.

The Rehnquist Court has shown less willingness to simply defer to legislative judgment on local land use regulations. In *Nollan v. California Coastal Commission* (1987), for example, it held that conditioning a permit for rebuilding a beach house on the owners to allow public access to the beach amounted to a taking of property. A similar result was reached in *Lucas v. South Carolina Coastal Council* (1992) (p. 577). Lucas had bought an ocean-front tract intending to build a house similar to others on nearby property, only to have

the commission in the interest of environmental protection issue a ruling forbidding new construction. Though the regulation was within the state's police powers, the Court concluded that it had left Lucas's land nearly worthless and held it a taking requiring compensation.

The Court went further still in *Palazzolo v. Rhode Island* (2001), in which a waterfront property owner challenged the state's building restrictions on an area it had designated as protected "coastal wetlands," even though he knew the restrictions were in effect before he bought the land. Upholding the right to challenge (though not deciding whether they amounted to a "taking"), the Court said that a state could not put an "expiration date" on the takings clause nor absolve itself from having to defend its land designation simply because the property had changed hands. In an echo of Chief Justice Roger Taney's time-tested developmental reasoning in the Charles River Bridge case, it added, "Future generations, too, have a right to challenge unreasonable limitations on the use and value of land."

Physical occupation of private property by government or by another private owner with the government's authorization may be subject to just compensation. Thus in *Loretto v. Teleprompter Manhattan CATV Corp.* (1982), the Court struck down a New York City ordinance that for the payment of one dollar allowed cable television lines to be installed in an apartment building. It held that installation was a permanent taking of part of the building. But government occupation in emergencies produced by war or natural disaster has not usually been held a taking. In *Miller v. Schoene* (1928), Virginia's attempt to protect apple crops by authorizing destruction of infected cedar trees within two miles of any apple orchard was held not an entry and taking that called for compensation.

The Court dealt with impairment of property by incidental, nonregulatory government action in *United States v. Causby* (1946). A chicken farm next to a military air base had been ruined by continuous overflights at a height of 80 feet. The Court held that the owner's air space had been invaded and that the economic damage amounted to a taking of property.

The takings clause usually does not apply to property interests not having to do with land. Taxes, for example, are not takings however high they may be. The Rehnquist Court, however, has been willing to consider takings clause challenges brought by private utility companies to governmentally set rates. In *Duquesne Light Co. v. Barasch* (1989), the Court's first constitutional review of utility rates since the New Deal period, it rejected the company's claim that the rates constituted a taking because of an allegedly unfair method of calculation. Observing that the Constitution required no one formula, it held that a rate would not be a taking unless it was "confiscatory," that is, so low that it would "destroy the property for all purposes for which it was acquired." Though the rate was upheld, the decision leaves open the door for courts to decide when a rate level may violate the takings clause.

Just Compensation

The Constitution does not prevent government from taking property but only that such impairment or loss be for public use and be justly compensated. Normally just compensation is whatever the property is worth in a free and open market. This ignores worth that is of interest to the owner alone, such as sentimental attachment. If worth is in dispute, the Supreme Court has usually left the matter to lower courts, not exercising review.

Though most just compensation cases are routine, some have presented issues of assessment. For example, in *United States v. Sioux Nation of Indians* (1980), the Supreme Court finding the United States had violated a treaty in taking over Indian lands in 1877, held that the tribe was due $17 million the land had been worth at the time and 5 percent annual compounded interest since, in all nearly $100 million.

If government action has affected property and no payment has been made, the property owner may bring an "inverse condemnation" proceeding for compensation. Normally, if the action is found to be a taking, the government can either stop or continue and pay fair market value for a permanent taking. In keeping with its new interest in eminent domain cases, however, the Rehnquist Court has modified this rule. In *First English Evangelical Lutheran Church v. Los Angeles County* (1987), it held that even if the government stopped, it must pay just compensation for a temporary taking.

FURTHER READING

Ackerman, Alan T., *Current Condemnation Law: Takings, Compensation, and Benefits* (1994)

Ackerman, Bruce, *Private Property and the Constitution* (1977)

Coyle, Dennis J., *Property Rights and the Constitution: Shaping Society Through Land Use Regulation* (1993)

Dorne, James A. and Maine, Henry G., eds., *Economic Liberties and the Judiciary* (1987)

Ely, James W., *The Guardian of Every Other Right: The Constitutional History of Property Rights* (1992)

Epstein, Richard, *Takings: Private Property and the Power of Eminent Domain* (1985)

Fischel, William, *Regulatory Takings: Law, Economics, and Policy* (1995)

Hopperton, Robert J., *Standards of Judicial Review in the Supreme Court Land Use Opinions* (1998)

Levy, Leonard, *A License to Steal: Forfeiture of Property* (1996)

Macedo, Stephen, *The New Right v. the Constitution* (1986)

Mercuro, Nicholas, *Taking Property and Just Compensation* (1992)

Munzer, *A Theory of Property* (1990)

Paul, Ellen Frankel, *Property Rights and Eminent Domain* (1987)

Schultz, David A., *Property, Power, and American Democracy* (1992)

Sunstein, Cass R., *After the Rights Revolution: Reconceiving the Regulatory State* (1990)

CASES

Williamson v. Lee Optical Co.

348 U.S. 483 (1955), 8-0
Opinion of the Court: Douglas (Black, Burton, Clark, Frankfurter, Minton, Reed, Warren)
Not participating: Harlan

Who gains and who loses as a result of this decision? Does the Court require any showing of a rational basis for economic regulation? Are economic interests now entirely without protection against regulatory legislation? What role, if any, does Douglas leave for the Court to play in reviewing economic regulations?

Douglas, for the Court:

This suit was instituted in the District Court to have an Oklahoma law declared unconstitutional and to enjoin state officials from enforcing it, for the reason that it allegedly violated various provisions of the Federal Constitution. . . .

The effect of [the law] is to forbid the optician from fitting or duplicating lenses without a prescription from an ophthalmologist or optometrist. In practical effect, it means that no optician can fit old glasses into new frames or supply a lens, whether it be a new lens or one to duplicate a lost or broken lens, without a prescription. The District Court conceded that it was in the competence of the police power of a State to regulate the examination of the eyes. But it rebelled at the notion that a State could require a prescription from an optometrist or ophthalmologist 'to take old lenses and place them in new frames and then fit the completed spectacles to the face of the eyeglass wearer.' It held that such a requirement was not 'reasonably and rationally related to the health and welfare of the people.' The court found that through mechanical devices and ordinary skills the optician could take a broken lens or a fragment thereof, measure its power, and reduce it to prescriptive terms. The court held that 'Although on this precise issue of duplication, the legislature in the instant regulation was dealing with a matter of public interest, the particular means chosen are neither reasonably necessary nor reasonably related to the end sought to be achieved.' It was, accordingly, the opinion of the court that this provision of the law violated the Due Process Clause by arbitrarily interfering with the optician's right to do business . . .

The Oklahoma law may exact a needless, wasteful requirement in many cases. But it is for the legislature, not the courts, to balance the advantages and disadvantages of the new requirement. It appears that in many cases the optician can easily supply the new frames or new lenses without reference to the old written prescription. It also appears that many written prescriptions contain no directive data in regard to fitting spectacles to the face. But in some cases the directions contained in the prescription are essential, if the glasses are to be fitted so as to correct the particular defects of vision or alleviate the eye condition. The legislature might have concluded that the frequency of occasions when a prescription is necessary was sufficient to justify this regulation of the fitting of eyeglasses. Likewise, when it is necessary to duplicate a lens, a written prescription may or may not be necessary. But the legislature might have concluded that one was needed often enough to require one in every case. Or the legislature may have concluded that eye examinations were so critical, not only for correction of vision but also for detection of latent ailments or diseases, that every change in frames and every duplication of a lens should be accompanied by a prescription from a medical expert. To be sure, the present law does not require a new examination of the eyes every time the frames are changed or the lenses duplicated. For if the old prescription is on file with the optician, he can go ahead and make the new fitting or duplicate the lenses. But the law need not be in every respect logically consistent with its aims to be constitutional. It is enough that there is an evil at hand for correction, and that it might be thought that the particular legislative measure was a rational way to correct it.

The day is gone when this Court uses the Due Process Clause of the Fourteenth Amendment to strike down state laws, regulatory of business and industrial conditions, because they may be unwise, improvident, or out of harmony with a particular school of thought. We emphasize again what Chief Justice Waite said in *Munn v. State of Illinois* 'For protection against abuses by legislatures the people must resort to the polls, not to the courts.' . . .

An eyeglass frame, considered in isolation, is only a piece of merchandise. But an eyeglass frame is not used in isolation, . . . it is used with lenses; and lenses, pertaining as they do to the human eye, enter the field of health. Therefore, the legislature might conclude that to regulate one effectively it would have to regulate the other. Or it might conclude that both the sellers of frames and the sellers of lenses were in a business where advertising should be limited or even abolished in the public interest. The advertiser of frames may be using his ads to bring in customers who will buy lenses. If the advertisement of lenses is to be abolished or controlled, the advertising of frames must come under the same restraints; or so the legislature might think. We see no constitutional reason why a State may not treat all who deal with the human eye as members of a profession was should use no merchandising methods for obtaining customers . . .

Ferguson v. Skrupa

372 U.S. 726 (1963), 9-0
Opinion of the Court: Black (Brennan, Clark, Douglas, Goldberg, Stewart, White, Warren)
Concurring: Harlan

Why do economic regulations have a presumptive constitutionality? What, if anything, would be required for the Court to strike down a law like the one in this case? Does Black's position leave weak economic interests to the mercy of strong in the legislature? Has the Court gone too far in refusing to review the substantive aspects of economic regulation?

Black, for the Court:

[W]e are asked to review the judgment of a three-judge District Court enjoining, as being in violation of the Due Process Clause of the Fourteenth Amendment, a Kansas statute making it a misdemeanor for any person to engage 'in the business of debt adjusting' except as an incident to 'the lawful practice of law in this state.' The statute defines 'debt adjusting' as 'the making of a contract, express, or implied with a particular debtor whereby the debtor agrees to pay a certain amount of money periodically to the person engaged in the debt adjusting business who shall for a consideration distribute the same among certain specified creditors in accordance with a plan agreed upon.'

The complaint, filed by Skrupa doing business as 'Credit Advisors,' alleged that Skrupa was engaged in the business of 'debt adjusting' as defined by the statute, that his business was a 'useful and desirable' one, that his business activities were not 'inherently immoral or dangerous' or in any way contrary to the public welfare, and that therefore the business could not be 'absolutely prohibited' by Kansas. The three-

judge court heard evidence by Skrupa tending to show the usefulness and desirability of his business and evidence by the state officials tending to show that 'debt adjusting' lends itself to grave abuses against distressed debtors, particularly in the lower income brackets, and that these abuses are of such gravity that a number of States have strictly regulated 'debt adjusting' or prohibited it altogether. . . .

The only case discussed by the court below as support for its invalidation of the statute was *Commonwealth v. Stone* (1959), in which the Superior Court of Pennsylvania struck down a statute almost identical to the Kansas act involved here. In *Stone* the Pennsylvania court held that the State could regulate, but could not prohibit, a 'legitimate' business. Finding debt adjusting, called 'budget planning' in the Pennsylvania statute, not to be 'against the public interest' and concluding that it could 'see no justification for such interference' with this business, the Pennsylvania court ruled that State's statute to be unconstitutional. In doing so, the Pennsylvania court relied heavily on *Adams v. Tanner* (1917), which held that the Due Process Clause forbids a State to prohibit a business which is 'useful' and not 'inherently immoral or dangerous to public welfare.'

Both the District Court in the present case and the Pennsylvania court in *Stone* adopted the philosophy of *Adams v. Tanner,* and cases like it, that it is the province of courts to draw on their own views as to the morality, legitimacy, and usefulness of a particular business in order to decide whether a statute bears too heavily upon that business and by so doing violates due process. Under the system of government created by our Constitution, it is up to legislatures, not courts, to decide on the wisdom and utility of legislation. There was a time when the Due Process Clause was used by this Court to strike down laws which were thought unreasonable, that is, unwise or incompatible with some particular economic or social philosophy. In this manner the Due Process Clause was used, for example, to nullify laws prescribing maximum hours for work in bakeries, outlawing 'yellow dog' contracts, setting minimum wages for women, and fixing the weight of loaves of bread. This intrusion by the judiciary into the realm of legislative value judgments was strongly objected to at the time, particularly by Mr. Justice Holmes and Mr. Justice Brandeis. Dissenting from the Court's invalidating a state statute which regulated the resale price of theatre and other tickets, Mr. Justice Holmes said, 'I think the proper course is to recognize that a state Legislature can do whatever it sees fit to do unless it is restrained by some express prohibition in the Constitution of the United States or of the State, and that Courts should be careful not to extend such prohibitions beyond their obvious meaning by reading into them conceptions of public policy that the particular Court may happen to entertain.' . . .

The doctrine that prevailed in, *Lochner, Coppage, Adkins, Burns*, and like cases—that due process authorizes courts to hold laws unconstitutional when they believe the legislature has acted unwisely—has long since been discarded. We have returned to the original constitutional proposition that courts do not substitute their social and economic beliefs for the judgment of legislative bodies, who are elected to pass laws . . . Legislative bodies have broad scope to experiment with economic problems, and this Court does not sit to 'subject the state to an intolerable supervision hostile to the basic principles of our government and wholly beyond the protection which the general clause of the Fourteenth Amendment was intended to secure.' It is now settled that States 'have power to legislate against what are found to be injurious practices in their internal commercial and business affairs, so long as their laws do not run afoul of some specific federal constitutional prohibition, or of some valid federal law.' . . .

[R]eliance on *Adams v. Tanner* is as mistaken as would be adherence to *Adkins v. Children's Hospital*, overruled by *West Coast Hotel Co. v. Parrish* (1937) . . . [T]he Kansas Legislature was free to decide for itself that legislation was needed to deal with the business of debt adjusting. Unquestionably, there are arguments showing that the business of debt adjusting has social utility, but such arguments are properly addressed to the legislature, not to us. We refuse to sit as a 'super-legislature to weigh the wisdom of legislation,' and we emphatically refuse to go back to the time when courts used the Due Process Clause 'to strike down state laws, regulatory of business and industrial conditions, because they may be unwise, improvident, or out of harmony with a particular school of thought.' Nor are we able or willing to draw lines by calling a law 'prohibitory' or 'regulatory.' Whether the legislature takes for its textbook Adam Smith, Herbert Spencer, Lord Keynes, or some other is no concern of ours. The Kansas debt adjusting statute may be wise or unwise. But relief, if any be needed, lies not with us but with the body constituted to pass laws for the State of Kansas.

Nor is the statute's exception of lawyers a denial of equal protection of the laws to non-lawyers. Statutes create many classifications which do not deny equal protection; it is only 'invidious discrimination' which offends the Constitution. The business of debt adjusting gives rise to a relationship of trust in which the debt adjuster will, in a situation of insolvency, be marshaling assets in the manner of a proceeding in bankruptcy. The debt adjuster's client may need advice as to the legality of the various claims against him remedies existing under state laws governing debtor-creditor relationships, or provisions of the Bankruptcy Act—advice which a non-lawyer cannot lawfully give him. If the State of Kansas wants to limit debt adjusting to lawyers, the Equal Protection Clause does not forbid it.

United States Trust v. New Jersey

431 U.S. 1 (1977), 4-3
Opinion of the Court: Blackmun (Rehnquist, Stevens)
Concurring: Burger
Dissenting: Brennan, Marshall, White
Not participating: Powell, Stewart

An agreement between New Jersey and New York in 1962 barred the Port Authority of New York and New Jersey, a bi-state agency created by the two states in 1921, from subsidizing passenger rail service with any revenues or reserves pledged as security for bonds issued by the Authority. However, in 1974, in order to use such pledged assets to expand mass transit, the states passed concurrent laws retroactively repealing the 1962 agreement. United States Trust of New York, a trustee for and holder of Port Authority bonds, sued for declaratory relief, arguing that the repeal impaired the obligation of the states' contract with the bondholders, in violation of the Contract Clause of the Constitution.

What was the contract impaired in this case? Is the difference between this case and Home Building and Loan Association v. Blaisdell *one of degree, that is, on how dire the emergency was, or are the differences more profound? Are the differences between Blaisdell and Brennan mainly over the importance of expanding mass transit in the New York Harbor area? Is Blackmun substituting his evaluation of the "important purposes" of the state for the states'? Are the states freer to alter the obligation of private contracts than those they have made themselves? Who are the opposing interests in this case? What interests in the future are likely to be affected?*

Blackmun, for the Court:

At the time the Constitution was adopted, and for nearly a century thereafter, the Contract Clause was one of the few express limitations on state power. The many decisions of this Court involving the Contract Clause are evidence of its important place in our constitutional jurisprudence. Over the last century, however, the Fourteenth Amendment has assumed a far larger place in constitutional adjudication concerning the States. We feel that the present role of the Contract Clause is largely illuminated by two of this Court's decisions. In each, legislation was sustained despite a claim that it had impaired the obligations of contracts.

Home Building & Loan Assn. v. Blaisdell is regarded as the leading case in the modern era of Contract Clause interpretation. At issue was the Minnesota Mortgage Moratorium Law, enacted in 1933, during the depth of the Depression and when that State was under severe economic stress, and appeared to have no effective alternative . . . A closely divided Court, in an opinion by Mr. Chief Justice Hughes, observed that "emergency may furnish the occasion for the exercise of power," and that the constitutional question presented in the light of an emergency is whether the power possessed embraces the particular exercise of it in response to particular conditions . . .

This Court's most recent Contract Clause decision is *El Paso v. Simmons.* That case concerned a 1941 Texas statute that limited to a 5-year period the reinstatement rights of an interest-defaulting purchaser of land from the State . . . This Court held that "it is not every modification of a contractual promise that impairs the obligation of contract under federal law." It observed that the State "has the 'sovereign right . . . to protect the . . . general welfare of the people'" and "'we must respect the "wide discretion on the part of the legislature in determining what is and what is not necessary,"' . . .

Both of these cases eschewed a rigid application of the Contract Clause to invalidate state legislation. Yet neither indicated that the Contract Clause was without meaning in modern constitutional jurisprudence, or that its limitation on state power was illusory. Whether or not the protection of contract rights comports with current views of wise public policy, the Contract Clause remains a part of our written Constitution. We therefore must attempt to apply that constitutional provision to the instant case with due respect for its purpose and the prior decisions of this Court . . .

Although the Contract Clause appears literally to proscribe "any" impairment, this Court observed in *Blaisdell* that "the prohibition is not an absolute one and is not to be read with literal exactness like a mathematical formula." Thus, a finding that there has been a technical impairment is merely a preliminary step in resolving the more difficult question whether that impairment is permitted under the Constitution. In the instant case, as in *Blaisdell,* we must attempt to reconcile the strictures of the Contract Clause with the "essential attributes of sovereign power," necessarily reserved by the States to safeguard the welfare of their citizens.

The trial court concluded that repeal of the 1962 covenant was a valid exercise of New Jersey's police power because repeal served important public interests in mass transportation, energy conservation, and environmental protection. Yet the Contract Clause limits otherwise legitimate exercises of state legislative authority, and the existence of an important public interest is not always sufficient to overcome that limitation . . . Moreover, the scope of the State's reserved power depends on the nature of the contractual relationship with which the challenged law conflicts.

The States must possess broad power to adopt general regulatory measures without being concerned that private contracts will be impaired, or even destroyed, as a result. Otherwise, one would be able to obtain immunity from state regulation by making private contractual arrangements . . .

Yet private contracts are not subject to unlimited modification under the police power. The Court in *Blaisdell* recognized that laws intended to regulate existing contractual relationships must serve a legitimate public purpose. A State could not "adopt as its policy the repudiation of debts or the destruction of contracts or the denial of means to enforce them." Legislation adjusting the rights and responsibilities of contracting parties must be upon reasonable conditions and of a character appropriate to the public purpose justifying its adoption. As is customary in reviewing economic and social regulation, however, courts properly defer to legislative judgment as to the necessity and reasonableness of a particular measure.

When a State impairs the obligation of its own contract, the reserved powers doctrine has a different basis. The initial inquiry concerns the ability of the State to enter into an agreement that limits its power to act in the future. As early as *Fletcher v. Peck,* the Court considered the argument that "one legislature cannot abridge the powers of a succeeding legislature." It is often stated that "the legislature cannot bargain away the police power of a State." Stone v. Mississippi. This doctrine requires a determination of the State's power to create irrevocable contract rights in the first place, rather than an inquiry into the purpose or reasonableness of the subsequent impairment. In short, the Contract Clause does not require a State to adhere to a contract that surrenders an essential attribute of its sovereignty . . .

. . . In applying this standard, however, complete deference to a legislative assessment of reasonableness and necessity is not appropriate because the State's self-interest is at stake. A governmental entity can always find a use for extra money, especially when taxes do not have to be raised. If a State could reduce its financial obligations whenever it wanted to spend the money for what it regarded as an important public purpose, the Contract Clause would provide no protection at all . . .

Mass transportation, energy conservation, and environmental protection are goals that are important, and of legitimate public concern. [New Jersey] contends that these goals are so important that any harm to bondholders from repeal of the 1962 covenant is greatly outweighed by the public benefit. We do not accept this invitation to engage in a utilitarian comparison of public benefit and private loss . . . [A] State cannot refuse to meet its legitimate financial obligations simply because it would prefer to spend the money to promote the public good, rather than the private welfare of its creditors. We can only sustain the repeal of the 1962 covenant if that impairment was both reasonable and necessary to serve the admittedly important purposes claimed by the State.

The more specific justification offered for the repeal of the 1962 covenant was the States' plan for encouraging users of private automobiles to shift to public transportation. The States intended to discourage private automobile use by raising bridge and tunnel tolls and to use the extra revenue from those tolls to subsidize improved commuter railroad service. [New Jersey] contends that repeal of the 1962 covenant was necessary to implement this plan because the new mass transit facilities could not possibly be self-supporting and the covenant's "permitted deficits" level had already been exceeded. We reject this justification because the repeal was neither necessary to achievement of the plan nor reasonable in light of the circumstances.

The determination of necessity can be considered on two levels. First, it cannot be said that total repeal of the covenant was essential; a less drastic modification would have permitted the contemplated plan without

entirely removing the covenant's limitations on the use of Port Authority revenues and reserves to subsidize commuter railroads. Second, without modifying the covenant at all, the States could have adopted alternative means of achieving their twin goals of discouraging automobile use and improving mass transit. [New Jersey] contends however, that choosing among these alternatives is a matter for legislative discretion. But a State is not completely free to consider impairing the obligations of its own contracts on a par with other policy alternatives. Similarly, a State is not free to impose a drastic impairment when an evident and more moderate course would serve its purposes equally well . . .

. . . [T]he need for mass transportation in the New York metropolitan area was not a new development, and the likelihood that publicly owned commuter railroads would produce substantial deficits was well known. As early as 1922, over a half century ago, there were pressures to involve the Port Authority in mass transit. It was with full knowledge of these concerns that the 1962 covenant was adopted. Indeed, the covenant was specifically intended to protect the pledged revenues and reserves against the possibility that such concerns would lead the Port Authority into greater involvement in deficit mass transit.

During the 12-year period between adoption of the covenant and its repeal, public perception of the importance of mass transit undoubtedly grew because of increased general concern with environmental protection and energy conservation. But these concerns were not unknown in 1962, and the subsequent changes were of degree, and not of kind. We cannot say that these changes caused the covenant to have a substantially different impact in 1974 than when it was adopted in 1962. And we cannot conclude that the repeal was reasonable in the light of changed circumstances.

We therefore hold that the Contract Clause of the United States Constitution prohibits the retroactive repeal of the 1962 covenant.

Brennan, (White, Marshall) dissenting:

Decisions of this Court for at least a century have construed the Contract Clause largely to be powerless in binding a State to contracts limiting the authority of successor legislatures to enact laws in furtherance of the health, safety, and similar collective interests of the polity. In short, those decisions established the principle that lawful exercises of a State's police powers stand paramount to private rights held under contract. Today's decision, in invalidating the New Jersey Legislature's 1974 repeal of its predecessor's 1962 covenant, rejects this previous understanding and remolds the Contract Clause into a potent instrument for overseeing important policy determinations of the state legislature. At the same time, by creating a constitutional safe haven for property rights embodied in a contract, the decision substantially distorts modern constitutional jurisprudence governing regulation of private economic interests. I might understand, though I could not accept, this revival of the Contract Clause were it in accordance with some coherent and constructive view of public policy. But elevation of the Clause to the status of regulator of the municipal bond market at the heavy price of frustration of sound legislative policymaking is as demonstrably unwise as it is unnecessary . . .

One of the fundamental premises of our popular democracy is that each generation of representatives can and will remain responsive to the needs and desires of those whom they represent. Crucial to this end is the assurance that new legislators will not automatically be bound by the policies and undertakings of earlier days. In accordance with this philosophy, the Framers of our Constitution conceived of the Contract Clause primarily as protection for economic transactions entered into by purely private parties, rather than obligations involving the State itself. The Framers fully recognized that nothing would so jeopardize the legitimacy of a system of government that relies upon the ebbs and flows of politics to "clean out the rascals" than the possibility that those same rascals might perpetuate their policies simply by locking them into binding contracts . . .

I would not want to be read as suggesting that the States should blithely proceed down the path of repudiating their obligations, financial or otherwise. Their credibility in the credit market obviously is highly dependent on exercising their vast lawmaking powers with self-restraint and discipline . . . [I]n the final analysis, there is no reason to doubt that [United States Trust's] financial welfare is being adequately policed by the political processes and the bond marketplace itself.

Penn Central Transportation Co. v. City of New York

438 U.S. 104 (1978), 6-3
Opinion of the Court: Brennan (Blackmun, Marshall, Powell, Stewart, White)
Dissenting: Burger, Rehnquist, Stevens
Did the cost of achieving a public benefit fall entirely on Penn Central? Mainly? Unfairly? Why does the Court say that landmark designation did not interfere with Penn Central's "pri-

mary expectation" concerning use of the property in question? According to Brennan, whose judgment should determine whether compensation is required? According to Rehnquist?

Brennan, for the Court:
The question presented is whether a city may, as part of a comprehensive program to preserve historic landmarks and historic districts, place restrictions on the development of individual historic landmarks—in addition to those imposed by applicable zoning ordinances—without effecting a "taking" requiring the payment of "just compensation." Specifically, we must decide whether the application of New York City's Landmarks Preservation Law to the parcel of land occupied by Grand Central Terminal has "taken" its owners' property in violation of the Fifth and Fourteenth Amendments.

Over the past 50 years, all 50 States and over 500 municipalities have enacted laws to encourage or require the preservation of buildings and areas with historic or aesthetic importance. These nationwide legislative efforts have been precipitated by two concerns. The first is recognition that, in recent years, large numbers of historic structures, landmarks, and areas have been destroyed without adequate consideration of either the values represented therein or the possibility of preserving the destroyed properties for use in economically productive ways. The second is a widely shared belief that structures with special historic, cultural, or architectural significance enhance the quality of life for all. Not only do these buildings and their workmanship represent the lessons of the past and embody precious features of our heritage, they serve as examples of quality for today . . .

New York City, responding to similar concerns and acting pursuant to a New York State enabling Act, adopted its Landmarks Preservation Law in 1965. The city acted from the conviction that "the standing of [New York City] as a world-wide tourist center and world capital of business, culture and government" would be threatened if legislation were not enacted to protect historic landmarks and neighborhoods from precipitate decisions to destroy or fundamentally alter their character. The city believed that comprehensive measures to safeguard desirable features of the existing urban fabric would benefit its citizens in a variety of ways: e.g., fostering "civic pride in the beauty and noble accomplishments of the past"; protecting and enhancing "the city's attractions to tourists and visitors"; "support[ing] and stimul[ating] business and industry"; "strengthen[ing] the economy of the city"; and promoting "the use of historic districts, landmarks, interior landmarks and scenic landmarks for the education, pleasure and welfare of the people of the city."

The New York City law is typical of many urban landmark laws in that its primary method of achieving its goals is not by acquisitions of historic properties, but rather by involving public entities in land-use decisions affecting these properties and providing services, standards, controls, and incentives that will encourage preservation by private owners and users. While the law does place special restrictions on landmark properties as a necessary feature to the attainment of its larger objectives, the major theme of the law is to ensure the owners of any such properties both a "reasonable return" on their investments and maximum latitude to use their parcels for purposes not inconsistent with the preservation goals.

The operation of the law can be briefly summarized. The primary responsibility for administering the law is vested in the Landmarks Preservation Commission (Commission), a broad based, 11-member agency assisted by a technical staff. The Commission first performs the function, critical to any landmark preservation effort, of identifying properties and areas that have "a special character or special historical or aesthetic interest or value as part of the development, heritage or cultural characteristics of the city, state or nation." If the Commission determines, after giving all interested parties an opportunity to be heard, that a building or area satisfies the ordinance's criteria, it will designate a building to be a "landmark," situated on a particular "landmark site," or will designate an area to be a "historic district," After the Commission makes a designation, New York City's Board of Estimate, after considering the relationship of the designated property "to the master plan, the zoning resolution, projected public improvements and any plans for the renewal of the area involved," may modify or disapprove the designation, and the owner may seek judicial review of the final designation decision. Thus far, 31 historic districts and over 400 individual landmarks have been finally designated, and the process is a continuing one . . .

This case involves the application of New York City's Landmarks Preservation Law to Grand Central Terminal (Terminal). The Terminal, which is owned by the Penn Central Transportation Co. and its affiliates (Penn Central), is one of New York City's most famous buildings. Opened in 1913, it is regarded not only as

providing an ingenious engineering solution to the problems presented by urban railroad stations, but also as a magnificent example of the French beaux-arts style.

The Terminal is located in midtown Manhattan . . . The Terminal itself is an eight-story structure which Penn Central uses as a railroad station and in which it rents space not needed for railroad purposes to a variety of commercial interests. The Terminal is one of a number of properties owned by Penn Central in this area of midtown Manhattan. The others include the Barclay, Biltmore, Commodore, Roosevelt, and Waldorf-Astoria Hotels, the Pan-American Building and other office buildings along Park Avenue, and the Yale Club. At least eight of these are eligible to be recipients of development rights afforded the Terminal by virtue of landmark designation . . .

Before considering [Penn Central's] specific contentions, it will be useful to review the factors that have shaped the jurisprudence of the Fifth Amendment injunction "nor shall private property be taken for public use, without just compensation." The question of what constitutes a "taking" for purposes of the Fifth Amendment has proved to be a problem of considerable difficulty. While this Court has recognized that the "Fifth Amendment's guarantee . . . [is] designed to bar Government from forcing some people alone to bear public burdens which, in all fairness and justice, should be borne by the public as a whole," *Armstrong v. United States* (1960), this Court, quite simply, has been unable to develop any "set formula" for determining when "justice and fairness" require that economic injuries caused by public action be compensated by the government, rather than remain disproportionately concentrated on a few persons . . .

In engaging in these essentially ad hoc, factual inquiries, the Court's decisions have identified several factors that have particular significance. The economic impact of the regulation on the claimant and, particularly, the extent to which the regulation has interfered with distinct investment-backed expectations are, of course, relevant considerations. So, too, is the character of the governmental action. A "taking" may more readily be found when the interference with property can be characterized as a physical invasion by government than when interference arises from some public program adjusting the benefits and burdens of economic life to promote the common good.

"Government hardly could go on if to some extent values incident to property could not be diminished without paying for every such change in the general law," *Pennsylvania Coal Co. v. Mahon* (1922), and this Court has accordingly recognized, in a wide variety of contexts, that government may execute laws or programs that adversely affect recognized economic values. Exercises of the taxing power are one obvious example. A second are the decisions in which this Court has dismissed "taking" challenges on the ground that, while the challenged government action caused economic harm, it did not interfere with interests that were sufficiently bound up with the reasonable expectations of the claimant to constitute "property" for Fifth Amendment purposes . . .

More importantly for the present case, in instances in which a state tribunal reasonably concluded that "the health, safety, morals, or general welfare" would be promoted by prohibiting particular contemplated uses of land, this Court has upheld land-use regulations that destroyed or adversely affected recognized real property interests. Zoning laws are, of course, the classic example . . .

Zoning laws generally do not affect existing uses of real property, but "taking" challenges have also been held to be without merit in a wide variety of situations when the challenged governmental actions prohibited a beneficial use to which individual parcels had previously been devoted and thus caused substantial individualized harm. . . .

In contending that the New York City law has "taken" their property in violation of the Fifth and Fourteenth Amendments, [Penn Central] make[s] a series of arguments, which . . . essentially urge that any substantial restriction imposed pursuant to a landmark law must be accompanied by just compensation if it is to be constitutional. . . .

[It] first observe[s] that the airspace above the Terminal is a valuable property interest. They urge that the Landmarks Law has deprived them of any gainful use of their "air rights" above the Terminal and that, irrespective of the value of the remainder of their parcel, the city has "taken" their right to this super-adjacent airspace, thus entitling them to "just compensation" measured by the fair market value of these air rights.

Apart from our own disagreement with [its] characterization of the effect of the New York City law, the submission that [it] may establish a "taking" simply by showing that they have been denied the ability to exploit a property interest that they heretofore had believed was available for development is quite simply untenable. Were this the rule, this Court would have erred not only in upholding laws restricting the development of air rights, but also in approving those prohibiting both the subjacent, development of particular parcels. "Taking" jurisprudence does not divide a single parcel into discrete segments and attempt to determine whether rights in a particular segment have been entirely abrogated. In deciding whether a particular governmental action has effected a taking, this Court focuses rather both on the character of the action and on the nature and extent of the interference with rights in the parcel as a whole—here, the city tax block designated as the "landmark site."

Secondly, [Penn Central] focusing on the character and impact of the New York City law, argue[s] that it effects a "taking" because its operation has significantly diminished the value of the Terminal site . . . [It] argue[s] that New York City's regulation of individual landmarks is fundamentally different from zoning or from historic-district legislation because the controls imposed by New York City's law apply only to individuals who own selected properties.

Stated baldly, [Penn Central's] position appears to be that the only means of ensuring that selected owners are not singled out to endure financial hardship for no reason is to hold that any restriction imposed on individual landmarks pursuant to the New York City scheme is a "taking" requiring the payment of "just compensation." Agreement with this argument would, of course, invalidate not just New York City's law, but all comparable landmark legislation in the Nation. We find no merit in it . . .

Equally without merit is the related argument that the decision to designate a structure as a landmark "is inevitably arbitrary or at least subjective, because it is basically a matter of taste," thus unavoidably singling out individual landowners for disparate and unfair treatment. The argument has a particularly hollow ring in this case. For [Penn Central] not only did not seek judicial review of either the designation or of the denials of the certificates of appropriateness and of no exterior effect, but do not even now suggest that the Commission's decisions concerning the Terminal were in any sense arbitrary or unprincipled. But, in any event, a landmark owner has a right to judicial review of any Commission decision, and . . . there is no basis whatsoever for a conclusion that courts will have any greater difficulty identifying arbitrary or discriminatory action in the context of landmark regulation than in the context of classic zoning or indeed in any other context . . .

In any event, [Penn Central's] repeated suggestions that they are solely burdened and unbenefited is factually inaccurate. This contention overlooks the fact that the New York City law applies to vast numbers of structures in the city in addition to the Terminal— all the structures contained in the 31 historic districts and over 400 individual landmarks, many of which are close to the Terminal. Unless we are to reject the judgment of the New York City Council that the preservation of landmarks benefits all New York citizens and all structures, both economically and by improving the quality of life in the city as a whole—which we are unwilling to do—we cannot conclude that the owners of the Terminal have in no sense been benefited by the Landmarks Law. Doubtless [Penn Central believes it is] more burdened than benefited by the law . . . [T]he New York City law does not interfere in any way with the present uses of the Terminal. Its designation as a landmark not only permits but contemplates that [Penn Central] may continue to use the property precisely as it has been used for the past 65 years: as a railroad terminal containing office space and concessions. So the law does not interfere with what must be regarded as Penn Central's primary expectation concerning the use of the parcel. More importantly, on this record, we must regard the New York City law as permitting Penn Central not only to profit from the Terminal but also to obtain a "reasonable return" on its investment . . .

On this record, we conclude that the application of New York City's Landmarks Law has not effected a "taking" of [Penn Central's] property. The restrictions imposed are substantially related to the promotion of the general welfare and not only permit reasonable beneficial use of the landmark site but also afford [it] opportunities further to enhance not only the Terminal site proper but also other properties.

Rehnquist (Burger, Stevens), dissenting:

Of the over one million buildings and structures in the city of New York, [the City has] singled out 400 for designation as official landmarks. The owner of a building might initially be pleased that his property has been chosen by a distinguished committee of architects, historians, and city planners for such a singular distinction. But he may well discover, as Penn Central Transportation Co. did here, that the landmark designation imposes upon him a substantial

cost, with little or no offsetting benefit except for the honor of the designation. The question in this case is whether the cost associated with the city of New York's desire to preserve a limited number of "landmarks" within its borders must be borne by all of its taxpayers or whether it can instead be imposed entirely on the owners of the individual properties . . .

The Fifth Amendment provides in part: "nor shall private property be taken for public use, without just compensation." In a very literal sense, the actions of [the City] violated this constitutional prohibition. Before the city of New York declared Grand Central Terminal to be a landmark, Penn Central could have used its "air rights" over the Terminal to build a multistory office building, at an apparent value of several million dollars per year. Today, the Terminal cannot be modified in any form, including the erection of additional stories, without the permission of the Landmark Preservation Commission, a permission which [Penn Central], despite good-faith attempts, [has] so far been unable to obtain. Because the Taking Clause of the Fifth Amendment has not always been read literally, however, the constitutionality of [the City's] actions requires a closer scrutiny of this Court's interpretation of the three key words in the Taking Clause—"property," "taken," and "just compensation." . . .

As Mr. Justice Holmes pointed out in *Pennsylvania Coal Co. v. Mahon*, "the question at bottom" in an eminent domain case "is upon whom the loss of the changes desired should fall." The benefits that [the City] believe[s] will flow from preservation of the Grand Central Terminal will accrue to all the citizens of New York City. There is no reason to believe that [Penn Central] will enjoy a substantially greater share of these benefits. If the cost of preserving Grand Central Terminal were spread evenly across the entire population of the city of New York, the burden per person would be in cents per year—a minor cost [the City] would surely concede for the benefit accrued. Instead, however, [the City] would impose the entire cost of several million dollars per year on Penn Central. But it is precisely this sort of discrimination that the Fifth Amendment prohibits . . .

Of all the terms used in the Taking Clause, "just compensation" has the strictest meaning. The Fifth Amendment does not allow simply an approximate compensation but requires "a full and perfect equivalent for the property taken . . . The legislature may determine what private property is needed for public purposes—that is a question of a political and legislative character; but when the taking has been ordered, then the question of compensation is judicial. It does not rest with the public, taking the property, through Congress or the legislature, its representative, to say what compensation shall be paid, or even what shall be the rule of compensation. The Constitution has declared that just compensation shall be paid, and the ascertainment of that is a judicial inquiry." *Monongahela Navigation Co. v. United States . . .*

Over 50 years ago, Mr. Justice Holmes, speaking for the Court, warned that the courts were "in danger of forgetting that a strong public desire to improve the public condition is not enough to warrant achieving the desire by a shorter cut than the constitutional way of paying for the change." *Pennsylvania Coal Co. v. Mahon.* The Court's opinion in this case demonstrates that the danger thus foreseen has not abated.

Hawaii Housing Authority v. Midkiff

467 U.S. 229 (1984), 8-0
Opinion of the Court: O'Connor (Blackmun, Brennan, Burger, Powell, Rehnquist, Stevens, White)
Not participating: Marshall
What weight does the Court give to the ends of the Land Reform Act? To the means? According to the Court, are there any limits on the use of eminent domain as long as just compensation is paid? What keeps Hawaii's action from being merely that of taking from A to give to B? Does government have more freedom to take from A to give to B in its taxing or regulatory powers than in the use of eminent domain?

O'Connor, for the Court:

The Fifth Amendment of the United States Constitution provides . . . that "private property [shall not] be taken for public use, without just compensation." These cases present the question whether the Public Use Clause of that Amendment, made applicable to the States through the Fourteenth Amendment, prohibits the State of Hawaii from taking, with just compensation, title in real property from lessors and transferring it to lessees in order to reduce the concentration of ownership . . . in the State. We conclude that it does not.

The Hawaiian Islands were originally settled by Polynesian immigrants from the western Pacific. These settlers developed an economy around a feudal land tenure system in which one island high chief, the ali'i nui, controlled the land and assigned it for develop-

ment to certain subchiefs. The subchiefs would then reassign the land to other lower ranking chiefs, who would administer the land and govern the farmers and other tenants working it. All land was held at the will of the ali'i nui and eventually had to be returned to his trust. There was no private ownership of land.

Beginning in the early 1800's, Hawaiian leaders and American settlers repeatedly attempted to divide the lands of the kingdom among the crown, the chiefs, and the common people. These efforts proved largely unsuccessful, however, and the land remained in the hands of a few. In the mid-1960's, after extensive hearings, the Hawaii Legislature discovered that, while the State and Federal Governments owned almost 49% of the State's land, another 47% was in the hands of only 72 private landowners. The legislature further found that 18 landholders, with tracts of 21,000 acres or more, owned more than 40% of this land and that on Oahu, the most urbanized of the islands, 22 landowners owned 72.5% of the . . . titles. The legislature concluded that concentrated land ownership was responsible for skewing the State's residential . . . market, inflating land prices, and injuring the public tranquillity and welfare.

To redress these problems, the legislature decided to compel the large landowners to break up their estates. The legislature considered requiring large landowners to sell lands which they were leasing to homeowners. However, the landowners strongly resisted this scheme, pointing out the significant federal tax liabilities they would incur. Indeed, the landowners claimed that the federal tax laws were the primary reason they previously had chosen to lease, and not sell, their lands. Therefore, to accommodate the needs of both lessors and lessees, the Hawaii Legislature enacted the Land Reform Act of 1967 (Act), which created a mechanism for condemning residential tracts and for transfer-ring ownership of the condemned fees simple to existing lessees. By condemning the land in question, the Hawaii Legislature intended to make the land sales involuntary, thereby making the federal tax consequences less severe while still facilitating the redistribution. . . .

Under the Act's condemnation scheme, tenants living on single-family residential lots within developmental tracts at least five acres in size are entitled to ask the Hawaii Housing Authority (HHA) to condemn the property on which they live. When 25 eligible tenants, or tenants on half the lots in the tract, whichever is less, file appropriate applications, the

Act authorizes HHA . . . to designate some or all of the lots in the tract for acquisition. It then acquires, at prices set either by condemnation trial or by negotiation between lessors and lessees, the former fee owners' full "right, title, and interest" in the land.

After compensation has been set, HHA may sell the land titles to tenants who have applied for fee simple ownership . . . In practice, funds to satisfy the condemnation awards have been supplied entirely by lessees. While the Act authorizes HHA to issue bonds and appropriate funds for acquisition, no bonds have issued and HHA has not supplied any funds for condemned lots. . . .

[Midkiff et al.] filed suit . . . asking that the Act be declared unconstitutional and that its enforcement be enjoined. . . .

The starting point for our analysis of the Act's constitutionality is the Court's decision in *Berman v. Parker* (1954). In *Berman,* the Court held constitutional the District of Columbia Redevelopment Act of 1945. That Act provided both for the comprehensive use of the eminent domain power to redevelop slum areas and for the possible sale or lease of the condemned lands to private interests. In discussing whether the takings authorized by that Act were for a "public use," the Court stated:

"We deal, in other words, with what traditionally has been known as the police power. An attempt to define its reach or trace its outer limits is fruitless, for each case must turn on its own facts. The definition is essentially the product of legislative determinations addressed to the purposes of government, purposes neither abstractly nor historically capable of complete definition. Subject to specific constitutional limitations, when the legislature has spoken, the public interest has been declared in terms well-nigh conclusive. In such cases the legislature, not the judiciary, is the main guardian of the public needs to be served by social legislation, whether it be Congress legislating concerning the District of Columbia . . . or the States legislating concerning local affairs. . . . This principle admits of no exception merely because the power of eminent domain is involved. . . ."

The Court explicitly recognized the breadth of the principle it was announcing, noting:

"Once the object is within the authority of Congress, the right to realize it through the exercise of eminent domain is clear. For the power of eminent domain is merely the means to the end. . . . Once the object is within the authority of Congress, the means by which it will be attained is also for Congress to determine. Here one of the means chosen is the use of private enterprise for redevelopment of the area. [Midkiff et al.] argue that this makes the project a taking from one businessman for the benefit of another businessman. But the means of executing the project are for Congress and Congress alone to determine, once the public purpose has been established."

The "public use" requirement is thus coterminous with the scope of a sovereign's police powers.

There is, of course, a role for courts to play in reviewing a legislature's judgment of what constitutes a public use, even when the eminent domain power is equated with the police power. But the Court in *Berman* made clear that it is "an extremely narrow" one . . . [T]he Court has made clear that it will not substitute its judgment for a legislature's judgment as to what constitutes a public use "unless the use be palpably without reasonable foundation." *United States v. Gettysburg Electric R. Co.* (1896). . . .

On this basis, we have no trouble concluding that the Hawaii Act is constitutional. The people of Hawaii have attempted, much as the settlers of the original 13 Colonies did, to reduce the perceived social and economic evils of a land oligopoly traceable to their monarchs. The land oligopoly has, according to the Hawaii Legislature, created artificial deterrents to the normal functioning of the State's residential land market and forced thousands of individual homeowners to lease, rather than buy, the land underneath their homes. Regulating oligopoly and the evils associated with it is a classic exercise of a State's police powers . . .

Nor can we condemn as irrational the Act's approach to correcting the land oligopoly problem. The Act presumes that when a sufficiently large number of persons declare that they are willing but unable to buy lots at fair prices the land market is malfunctioning. When such a malfunction is signaled, the Act authorizes HHA to condemn lots in the relevant tract. The Act limits the number of lots any one tenant can purchase and authorizes HHA to use public funds to ensure that the market dilution goals will be achieved. This is a comprehensive and rational approach to identifying and correcting market failure. . . .

When the legislature's purpose is legitimate and its means are not irrational, our cases make clear that empirical debates over the wisdom of takings—no less than debates over the wisdom of other kinds of socioeconomic legislation—are not to be carried out in the federal courts. Redistribution . . . correct deficiencies in the market determined by the state legislature to be attributable to land oligopoly is a rational exercise of the eminent domain power. . . .

The mere fact that property taken outright by eminent domain is transferred in the first instance to private beneficiaries does not condemn that taking as having only a private purpose. The Court long ago rejected any literal requirement that condemned property be put into use for the general public . . . As the unique way titles were held in Hawaii skewed the land market, exercise of the power of eminent domain was justified. The Act advances its purposes without the State's taking actual possession of the land. In such cases, government does not itself have to use property to legitimate the taking; it is only the taking's purpose, and not its mechanics, that must pass scrutiny under the Public Use Clause. . . .

The State of Hawaii has never denied that the Constitution forbids even a compensated taking of property when executed for no reason other than to confer a private benefit on a particular private party. A purely private taking could not withstand the scrutiny of the public use requirement; it would serve no legitimate purpose of government and would thus be void. But no purely private taking is involved in these cases. The Hawaii Legislature enacted its Land Reform Act not to benefit a particular class of identifiable individuals but to attack certain perceived evils of concentrated property ownership in Hawaii—a legitimate public purpose. Use of the condemnation power to achieve this purpose is not irrational. Since we assume for purposes of these appeals that the weighty demand of just compensation has been met, the requirements of the Fifth and Fourteenth Amendments have been satisfied.

Lucas v. South Carolina Coastal Council

505 U.S. 1003 (1992), 6-3
Opinion of the Court: Scalia (O'Connor, Rehnquist, Thomas, White)
Concurring: Kennedy
Dissenting: Blackmun, Stevens
Separate statement: Souter
When does a land regulation become a taking? What would a landowner need to prove in order to win compensation for an imposed regulation? In what circumstances, if any, might land be regulated without compensation? Does Scalia say there may be inherent rights attaching to some parcels of land? Can this decision be reconciled with the Penn Central case? With Hawaii Housing Authority v. Midkiff?

Scalia, for the Court:

In 1986, David H. Lucas paid $975,000 for two residential lots on the Isle of Palms in Charleston County, South Carolina, on which he intended to build single-family homes. In 1988, however, the South Carolina Legislature enacted the Beachfront Management Act, which had the direct effect of barring [him] from erecting any permanent habitable structures on his two parcels. A state trial court found that this prohibition rendered Lucas's parcels "valueless." This case requires us to decide whether the Act's dramatic effect on the economic value of Lucas's lots accomplished a taking of private property under the Fifth and Fourteenth Amendments requiring the payment of "just compensation." . . .

Prior to Justice Holmes's exposition in *Pennsylvania Coal Co. v. Mahon* (1922), it was generally thought that the Takings Clause reached only a "direct appropriation" of property, or the functional equivalent of a "practical ouster of [the owner's] possession," *Transportation Co. v. Chicago* (1879). Justice Holmes recognized in *Mahon,* however, that if the protection against physical appropriations of private property was to be meaningfully enforced, the government's power to redefine the range of interests included in the ownership of property was necessarily constrained by constitutional limits. If, instead, the uses of private property were subject to unbridled, uncompensated qualification under the police power, "the natural tendency of human nature [would be] to extend the qualification more and more until at last private property disappear[ed]." These considerations gave birth in that case to the oft-cited maxim that, "while property may be regulated to a certain extent, if regulation goes too far it will be recognized as a taking."

Nevertheless, our decision in *Mahon* offered little insight into when, and under what circumstances, a given regulation would be seen as going "too far" for purposes of the Fifth Amendment. In 70-odd years of succeeding "regulatory takings" jurisprudence, we have generally eschewed any 'set formula' for determining how far is too far . . . We have, however, described at least two discrete categories of regulatory action as compensable without case-specific inquiry into the public interest advanced in support of the restraint. The first encompasses regulations that compel the property owner to suffer a physical "invasion" of his property. In general (at least with regard to permanent invasions), no matter how minute the intrusion, and no matter how weighty the public purpose behind it, we have required compensation. For example, in *Loretto v. Teleprompter Manhattan CATV Corp.* (1982), we determined that New York's law requiring landlords to allow television cable companies to emplace cable facilities in their apartment buildings constituted a taking, even though the facilities occupied at most only 1 1/2 cubic feet of the landlords' property . . .

The second situation in which we have found categorical treatment appropriate is where regulation denies all economically beneficial or productive use of land. As we have said on numerous occasions, the Fifth Amendment is violated when land-use regulation "does not substantially advance legitimate state interests or denies an owner economically viable use of his land."

We have never set forth the justification for this rule. Perhaps it is simply, as Justice Brennan suggested [in *Penn Central Transportation Co. v. City of New York*], that total deprivation of beneficial use is, from the landowner's point of view, the equivalent of a physical appropriation. Surely, at least, in the extraordinary circumstance when no productive or economically beneficial use of land is permitted, it is less realistic to indulge our usual assumption that the legislature is simply "adjusting the benefits and burdens of economic life," in a manner that secures an "average reciprocity of advantage" to everyone concerned. And the functional basis for permitting the government, by regulation, to affect property values without compensation—that "Government hardly could go on if to some extent values incident to property could not be diminished without paying for every such change in the general law,"—does not apply to the relatively rare situations where the government has deprived a landowner of all economically beneficial uses.

On the other side of the balance, affirmatively supporting a compensation requirement, is the fact that regulations that leave the owner of land without economically beneficial or productive options for its use—typically, as here, by requiring land to be left substantially in its natural state—carry with them a heightened risk that private property is being pressed into some form of public service under the guise of mitigating serious public harm. . . . The many statutes on the books, both state and federal, that provide for the use of eminent domain to impose servitudes on private scenic lands preventing developmental uses, or to acquire such lands altogether, suggest the practical equivalence in this setting of negative regulation and appropriation . . .

We think . . . that there are good reasons for our frequently expressed belief that when the owner of real property has been called upon to sacrifice all economically beneficial uses in the name of the common good, that is, to leave his property economically idle, he has suffered a taking. . . .

[M]any of our prior opinions have suggested that "harmful or noxious uses" of property may be proscribed by government regulation without the requirement of compensation . . . The "harmful or noxious uses" principle was the Court's early attempt to describe in theoretical terms why government may, consistent with the Takings Clause, affect property values by regulation without incurring an obligation to compensate— a reality we nowadays acknowledge explicitly with respect to the full scope of the State's police power. . . .

When it is understood that "prevention of harmful use" was merely our early formulation of the police power justification necessary to sustain (without compensation) any regulatory diminution in value . . . it becomes self-evident that noxious-use logic cannot serve as a touchstone to distinguish regulatory "takings"—which require compensation—from regulatory deprivations that do not require compensation . . . [T]he legislature's recitation of a noxious-use justification cannot be the basis for departing from our categorical rule that total regulatory takings must be compensated. If it were, departure would virtually always be allowed. The South Carolina Supreme Court's approach would essentially nullify *Mahon's* affirmation of limits to the non-compensable exercise of the police power. Our cases provide no support for this: None of them that employed the logic of "harmful use" prevention to sustain a regulation involved an allegation that the regulation wholly eliminated the value of the claimant's land.

Where the State seeks to sustain regulation that deprives land of all economically beneficial use, we think it may resist compensation only if the logically antecedent inquiry into the nature of the owner's estate shows that the proscribed use interests were not part of his title to begin with. This accords . . . with our "takings" jurisprudence, which has traditionally been guided by the understandings of our citizens regarding the content of, and the State's power over, the "bundle of rights" that they acquire when they obtain title to property. It seems to us that the property owner necessarily expects the uses of his property to be restricted, from time to time, by various measures newly enacted by the State in legitimate exercise of its police powers; "[a]s long recognized, some values are enjoyed under an implied limitation and must yield to the police power." *Pennsylvania Coal Co. v. Mahon* . . . In the case of land, however, we think the notion pressed by the Council that title is somehow held subject to the "implied limitation" that the State may subsequently eliminate all economically valuable use is inconsistent with the historical compact recorded in the Takings Clause that has become part of our constitutional culture.

Where "permanent physical occupation" of land is concerned, we have refused to allow the government to decree it anew (without compensation), no matter how weighty the asserted "public interests" involved . . . We believe similar treatment must be accorded confiscatory regulations, i.e., regulations that prohibit all economically beneficial use of land: Any limitation so severe cannot be newly legislated or decreed (without compensation), but must inhere in the title itself, in the restrictions that background principles of the State's law of property and nuisance already place upon land ownership. . . .

On this analysis, the owner of a lake-bed, for example, would not be entitled to compensation when he is denied the requisite permit to engage in a landfilling operation that would have the effect of flooding others' land. Nor the corporate owner of a nuclear generating plant, when it is directed to remove all improvements from its land upon discovery that the plant sits astride an earthquake fault. Such regulatory action may well have the effect of eliminating the land's only economically productive use, but it does not proscribe a productive use that was previously permissible under relevant property and nuisance principles. The use of these properties for what are now expressly prohibited purposes was always unlawful, and (subject to other constitutional limitations) it was open to the State at any point to make the implication of those background principles of nuisance and property law explicit . . . [T]his recognition that the Takings Clause does not require compensation when an owner is barred from putting land to a use that is proscribed by those "existing rules or understandings" is surely unexceptional. When, however, a regulation that declares "off-limits" all economically productive or beneficial uses of land goes beyond what the relevant background principles would dictate, compensation must be paid to sustain it.

The "total taking" inquiry we require today will ordinarily entail (as the application of state nuisance law ordinarily entails) analysis of, among other things, the degree of harm to public lands and resources, or adjacent private property, posed by the claimant's proposed activities, the social value of the claimant's activities and their suitability to the locality in question and the relative ease with which the alleged harm can be avoided through measures taken by the claimant and the government (or adjacent private landowners) alike. The fact that a particular use has long been engaged in by similarly situated owners ordinarily imports a lack of any common-law prohibition (though changed circumstances or new knowledge may make what was previously permissible no longer so). So also does the fact that other landowners, similarly situated, are permitted to continue the use denied to the claimant.

It seems unlikely that common-law principles would have prevented the erection of any habitable or productive improvements on [Lucas's] . . . The question, however, is one of state law to be dealt with on remand. We emphasize that to win its case South Carolina must do more than proffer the legislature's declaration that the uses Lucas desires are inconsistent with the public interest . . . Instead, as it would be required to do if it sought to restrain Lucas in a common-law action for public nuisance, South Carolina must identify background principles of nuisance and property law that prohibit the uses he now intends in the circumstances in which the property is presently found. Only on this showing can the State fairly claim that, in proscribing all such beneficial uses, the Beachfront Management Act is taking nothing.

Blackmun, dissenting:

The State of South Carolina prohibited Lucas from building a permanent structure on his property from 1988 to 1990. Relying on an unreviewed (and implausible) state trial court finding that this restriction left Lucas' property valueless, this Court granted review to determine whether compensation must be paid in cases where the State prohibits all economic use of real estate. According to the Court, such an occasion never has arisen in any of our prior cases, and the Court imagines that it will arise "relatively rarely" or only in "extraordinary circumstances." Almost certainly it did not happen in this case.

Nonetheless, the Court presses on . . . and creates simultaneously a new categorical rule and an exception (neither of which is rooted in our prior case law, common law, or common sense) . . . I question the Court's wisdom in issuing sweeping new rules to decide such a narrow case. . . .

This Court repeatedly has recognized the ability of government, in certain circumstances, to regulate property without compensation no matter how adverse the financial effect on the owner may be. More than a century ago, the Court explicitly upheld the right of States to prohibit uses of property injurious to public health, safety, or welfare without paying compensation: "A prohibition simply upon the use of property for purposes that are declared, by valid legislation, to be injurious to the health, morals, or safety of the community, cannot, in any just sense, be deemed a taking or an appropriation of property." *Mugler v. Kansas.* On this basis, the Court upheld an ordinance effectively prohibiting operation of a previously lawful brewery, although the "establishments will become of no value as property."

Mugler was only the beginning in a long line of cases . . .

In none . . . did the Court suggest that the right of a State to prohibit certain activities without paying compensation turned on the availability of some residual valuable use. Instead, the cases depended on whether the government interest was sufficient to prohibit the activity, given the significant private cost . . .

The Court makes sweeping and, in my view, misguided and unsupported changes in our takings doctrine. While it limits these changes to the most narrow subset of government regulation—those that eliminate all economic value from land—these changes go far beyond what is necessary to secure Lucas' private benefit.

APPENDICES

A. Reading a Supreme Court Decision

When the Supreme Court decides a case it applies political power in the form of judicial authority to resolve or settle a dispute. The Opinion of the Court, unanimous or representing a majority of the justices (in rare instances, a mere plurality), attempts to explain and justify what has been decided. Because opinions are technical legal documents and often deal with complex issues, they require careful yet aggressive reading and rereading. Understanding and mastery of opinions is likely to demand greater time and greater effort than would most text of similar length that students encounter in college study.

For these reasons, most students of law—undergraduate or professional—find it useful to outline a decision and its accompanying opinion(s) in a page or two. This summary is sometimes called a "brief" of a case. It is valuable for two reasons. First, the very process of doing it—of discerning relevant facts, identifying key issues, and grasping the rationale used to decide them—is likely to yield an intellectual mastery of the case that mere conventional reading would not. Second, one's outlines or briefs provide an excellent source of review for research papers and examinations.

In the beginning, briefing may seem difficult and time consuming, but with experience most students become adept and efficient. There is no single correct or universal form for a brief, and many students develop their own idiosyncratic style. A good outline, however, should contain the following features:

I. Title and Other Heading Material
    This includes the "name" of the case, the year it was decided, the vote of the justices, and the name of the justice writing the Opinion of the Court. For example:
    Humphrey's Executor v. United States (1935), 9-0, Sutherland

II. Circumstances of the Case
    Who is suing whom about what? Important here are the essential facts that triggered the dispute

between the parties and of any larger context—political, economic, or social—in which it arose. Brevity is desirable. Students first starting to make briefs tend to include too much detail. The more concise the statement of relevant facts, the better the Court's opinion has been read. Most constitutional law cases deal with an act of government—a statute, regulation, policy, or other undertaking—that is challenged as not conforming to the Constitution. It is important to identify the specific constitutional provision that is at issue. For example:

> *Humphrey, appointed to the Federal Trade Commission by President Hoover in 1931, was removed by President Franklin Roosevelt in 1933. Roosevelt believed Humphrey, an economic conservative, to be unsympathetic with the New Deal and said he did not have "full confidence" in his policies and actions on the Commission. The Federal Trade Commission Act, which created the FTC, provides that its seven commissioners, each appointed to a seven-year term, may be removed by the president "for inefficiency, neglect of duty, or malfeasance in office." Since Roosevelt had not alleged any such behavior, Humphrey believed he had been wrongly dismissed and sued to recover back salary. On behalf of the president, the government argued that the dismissal was within the statutory provisions and that, in any case, the president had unlimited constitutional power to removed executive officers. Humphrey died while the case was in the lower courts; the executor of his estate carried the appeal to the Supreme Court.*

III. The Issue(s) of the Case and the Court's Decision
    The issue or issues are the heart of the case. As the Court defined the facts, what question or questions did it resolve? If the issues are stated in question form, the Court's decision can be stated as a simple "yes" or "no." For example:

1. Did the president have power to remove Humphrey under the FTC Act for the reasons he stated? No.

2. If not, are the provisions of the Act a valid constitutional limitation on the president's power to remove officers of the Executive branch? Yes.

IV. The Court's Reasoning

What rationale or explanation did the Court offer to support its decision? Why did the Court uphold or invalidate the challenged government action? What interpretation or meaning did it give to the relevant constitutional provision or doctrine in the case? The Court's rendition of the Constitution may be more important than its immediate decision in the case, particularly if the dispute between the parties was relatively inconsequential. For example:

> On the first issue, Congress in creating the FTC as an independent regulatory commission intended it to be nonpartisan because its functions are largely quasi-legislative and quasi-judicial. The fixed terms of office and limited removal provisions, which are clearly and unambiguously stated, indicate the Commission was to be relatively free from political control. On the second, the statute's removal provisions do not violate the president's constitutional removal powers. Those powers are not unlimited and, in any case, do not extend to offices of a quasi-legislative, quasi-judicial character if Congress decided otherwise in creating them.

V. Developmental Consequences

Why has the case been included in this book? Two lines of inquiry should be pursued. First, how has the meaning of the Constitution been clarified or changed as a result of the Court's decision? For example, what existing doctrine, if any, has been broadened or narrowed? What important cases, if any, are affirmed, overruled, or simple ignored? (Some of these questions may be answered under Part IV.) Second, besides the parties to the case, who are the likely gainers and losers as a result of the decision? What was (or in the future may be) the likely effect of the decision on outstanding political, economic, or social questions or conflict? Since there often may be little or no discussion of nonlegal consequences in the Court's opinion, this part of the brief calls for a contextual analy-sis and, where consequences may not yet be fully clear, for speculation. For example:

> In narrowing presidential removal power, the decision was a departure from an important precedent established only nine years before in Myers v. United States, *in which the Court upheld presidential removal of postmasters despite Congress's attempt to place limits on such actions. Myers* was *distinguished but not overruled. A statement in it that the president's removal power extended even to members of regulatory commissions was held to be merely a dictum and thus not binding on the Court in* Humphrey *because removal of quasi-legislative, quasi-judicial officers was not at issue in* Myers. Humphrey *strengthened the independence of regulatory commissions by protecting commissioners from partisan removal if their policies differed from those of the president. However, it also made it more difficult for a president to coordinate economic policy in the Executive branch. Politically, the decision was setback for the New Deal and stiffened Roosevelt's determination to curb the Supreme Court.*

VI. Other Voices

In many cases, the justices are not unanimous; they may disagree about the outcome of the dispute before them or, even agreeing, may differ on the reasons supporting the decision. Occasionally, justices who differ may express their views through concurring or dissenting opinions. A concurrence supports the Court's decision but on different grounds. A dissent, which has no force of law, states the reasons why the writer voted against the decision. Though these differing opinions may help illuminate the discussion the justices had in conference before deciding the case, most are of slight long-term consequence. Occasionally, however, points made in a concurrence or dissent help more fully to frame the issues of the case and thus add to our understanding and help us evaluate the majority's reasoning. In unusual circumstances, concurring or dissenting opinions may eventually be transformed from the proverbial "voice in the wilderness" to tomorrow's prevailing theory or doctrine. Many of the latter kinds of concurring and dissenting opinions have been included in the cases in this book. A brief should include a concise statement of how the views expressed significantly differ from those in the majority opinion.

B. Law in the Library and on the Internet

Legal research usually requires access to primary and leading secondary legal sources. Normally these are not fully available in most public or college libraries but may be found in law school libraries, bar association libraries, and those of some agencies of state and local government. They may also be found, almost completely, on the internet.

Primary sources are laws themselves and the opinions of courts that apply laws in specific cases and thus interpret and clarify their meaning. Laws include constitutions, treaties, and statutes passed by Congress and state legislatures, ordinances enacted by local government, and regulations issued by federal and state administrative agencies. Legal decisions are those made by federal, state, and local courts at both trial and appellate levels. Most appellate and some trial decisions are accompanied by opinions of the judge or judges in the case, explaining why they decided as they did.

Secondary sources include a variety of books, articles, and reports that supply helpful clarifications of law and commentary on recent trends and developments. These statements do not have the binding effect of judicial opinions, but they are often widely read and influential. They include legal treatises and annotations, legal encyclopedias, scholarly books and articles on the law, jurisprudence, and legal history. Particularly important are law review articles written by scholars and law students in journals published by law schools.

In the Library

All new laws passed by Congress and state legislatures are collected and published. *Statutes at Large,* for example, contains all acts of Congress including resolutions and joint resolutions. Treaties and diplomatic agreements of the United States are collected and published by the State Department in *United States Treaties and Other International Agreements.* As federal laws are amended, repealed, or supplemented, they are consolidated every six years in the *United States Code,* systematically arranged under 50 subjects called Titles. Since 1936, the administrative regulations of federal agencies as well as executive proclamations and orders appear in the *Federal Register,* published daily. These actions are periodically consolidated in the *Code of Federal Regulations,* organized under 50 Titles closely paralleling

those of the *United States Code.* Each of the 50 states publishes the laws enacted by its legislature and rules issued by its regulatory agencies. Only well-stocked law libraries are likely to have a complete collection of these state volumes. Laws and regulations produced by local government are published but are usually not available beyond the official libraries and records of local government.

Decisions of the U.S. Supreme Court are published officially by the federal government in *United States Reports.* They are also collected and published by West Publishing Company as *The Supreme Court Reporter* and by the Lawyers Cooperative as *The Lawyer's Edition.* Both include extensive annotations and *The Lawyer's Edition,* excerpts of briefs filed by opposing counsel. All three sources contain all official actions of the Supreme Court and the full text of all opinions written by the justices. Any published opinion in a case may be found through the case's citation, for example, *Baker v. Carr,* 369 U.S.186 (1962) refers to volume 369 of the *United States Reports,* p. 186, the first page of the decision.

Recent decisions of the Supreme Court are given quick but temporary paperbound publication as "advance sheets" or "slip" opinions until they are included in permanent bound volumes. *United States Law Week* contains the full text of decisions announced the previous week as well as a report of recent docket actions taken by the Court. A few newspapers, such as *the New York Times,* publish excerpts of important Supreme Court opinions the day after announcement.

Decisions and opinions of the 12 federal Courts of Appeal are published by West Publishing as *The Federal Reporter,* now in its fourth series. Decisions and opinions of the federal District Courts (the trial level of the federal judiciary), are found in West's *Federal Supplement.* Most states publish the complete rulings of their appellate courts and many of their trial courts. West also publishes regional collections of the decisions and opinions of state supreme courts.

Law review articles are indexed in the *Index to Legal Periodicals* which covers more than 400 publications. Other articles may be located in various periodical indexes, such as the Social Sciences Index, Public Affairs Information Service, Political Abstracts, and the Reader's Guide. Relevant books may be located through card catalogs and conventional library research. Many leading reference works on constitutional development, constitutional interpretation, and the Supreme Court accompany chapters or are listed in the General Supplementary Bibliography of this book.

On the Internet

Law libraries are expensive to build and maintain and access to them may be limited to law students and legal professionals. Because there are relatively few of these libraries, lack of proximity may also make using them difficult. For this reason the internet has been a boon not only for lawyers, but for anyone doing legal research, including undergraduate students and members of the general public. The disadvantage to using the internet lies in the level of accuracy and reliability of information. Electronic errors may occur, and the information presented may not have the editorial quality control usually applied to print publications.

All primary and most secondary legal sources can be found on the internet though not (at least yet) at a single site. Many of the best sites are oriented toward lawyers in practice, but almost all contain some of the primary and basic secondary sources described earlier. A few of the more useful sites are described next. The list is not exhaustive, and the searcher will easily find links to other sites.

Findlaw Resources, **http://www.findlaw.com/** An all-purpose, partly fee-based commercial site. Laws and legal decisions are organized by subject and by court. Includes free access to a database of all U.S. Supreme Court cases since 1893, the individual cases of which may be downloaded. Contains information on the Supreme Court's calendar, rules, and briefs filed by counsel, and general coverage of legal news.

Legal Information Institute (LII), **http://supct. law.cornell.edu/supct/** A noncommercial site sponsored by Cornell University Law School and oriented mainly toward the Supreme Court. Provides access to nearly all the Court's opinions since 1990 and to more than 600 of its leading decisions since 1793. Tracks current cases as they move through stages of review and makes available synopses of current decisions on the day of announcement. Many links to other sites are included.

FLITE (Federal Legal Information Through Electronics), **http://www.fedworld.gov/supct/** A noncommercial site sponsored by the Technical Ad-

ministration of the U.S. Department of Commerce. Contains complete text of all 7,407 Supreme Court decisions from 1937 to 1975, any one of which may be downloaded as an ASCII text file. The same data base may be accessed through the Villanova Center for Law and Policy at Villanova University, **http://www.law.vill.edu/.**

InfoSynthesis, **http://www.usscplus.com/** A partly fee-based site commercial site that contains all Supreme Court decisions from 1907 and leading cases going back to 1793. Makes available the text of the 1,000 cases that have been the most cited by the Court itself, as well as decisions of the Court's current term.

The Oyez Project, **http://www.court.it-services. nwu.edu/** A noncommercial site sponsored by Northwestern University, offering access to current and many historic Supreme Court decisions. A unique feature is the availability of more than 900 hours of recorded, unedited oral arguments made before the Court. These are delivered by streaming audio or CD.

Jurist, The Legal Education Network, **http://www. jurist.law.pitt.edu/** A noncommercial site sponsored by the University of Pittsburgh School of Law and affiliated law schools in several countries. Oriented toward the teaching and study of law, it allows searching of federal case law and legislation. Contains book reviews of recent legal monographs, news of law schools, conferences, as well as guides to many legal subjects and current legal issues.

The U.S. Supreme Court, **http://www. supremecourtus.gov/** The Court's own web site, containing comprehensive information on the Court's docket and procedures. Also makes available for recent cases the text of slip opinions (those of cases yet to be published in bound volumes.

Medill School of Journalism, **http://www.medill. nwu.edu/docket/** Sponsored by Northwestern University and oriented toward journalists, the site offers coverage of Court's docket and brief journalistic descriptions of cases decided during the last two terms of the Court.

The West Group, Online Legal Services, **http:// www.westgroup.com/** A fully fee-based site of West Publishing that has full coverage of all the Supreme Court's decisions and of others that are reported in the company's print publications mentioned earlier. Access is free to students and faculty at law schools contractually subscribing to the service.

Lexis-Nexus, **http://www.lexis.com/** Like the West Group, a fully fee-based service with comprehensive coverage of the Supreme Court's decisions. Available to law schools and law firms.

Law and Politics Book Review, **http://www. polsci.wvu.edu/lpbr/** Sponsored by the Law and Politics section of the American Political Science Association, it offers reviews of a wide range of books dealing with the law and legal issues.

Administrative Office of the U.S. Courts, **http:// www.uscourt.gov/** Offers general information on the

federal courts as well as statistical and other data on caseloads, judicial appointments, and other aspects of the federal judiciary.

National Center for State Courts, **http://www. ncsc.dni.us/** Offers similar information on state courts and links to sites of hundreds of state and local courts in the United States.

C.   Getting to the Court: The Supreme Court and the American Judiciary

Litigation—a legal case—is a formalized way of settling a dispute between two or more parties that may be individuals, groups, organizations, or agencies of government. Resolution by judicial authority has the effect of distributing benefits and costs that, in the immediate, take the form of rights granted or denied and obligations imposed or avoided. If a party claiming a right wins, the right is affirmed and a reciprocal obligation is imposed on the losing side. If the claimant loses, the right is denied and the winning side avoids an obligation. Rights and obligations or their respective denial and avoidance are easily translated into the resources or valuable things that underlay the dispute. In most cases, this is money or economic gain, but it may also include power, opportunity, status, freedom, security, information, or well-being.

Cases begin in a trial court or other tribunal said to have original jurisdiction. Such courts apply legal principles to specific findings of fact in the disputes before them. The finder of fact may be a jury or simply the presiding judge. If the side losing at trial believes an error in the application of law has been made, it may appeal to a higher court. In appellate review no witnesses are called, no new evidence is introduced, and normally no new questions may be raised. Because of the double jeopardy provision of the Fifth Amendment to the Constitution, acquittals of defendants in criminal cases may not be appealed by the government.

The American judicial system is a complex arrangement of courts—federal and state, trial and appellate, general and specialized—in which justices, judges, and magistrates hear a great range of legal disputes. At the summit is the U.S. Supreme Court. With few exceptions, cases coming before it have passed through two or more lower courts. See Figure C.1

At the base of the federal judiciary are 94 District Courts, at least one in each state, the District of Columbia, and four American territories. These are trial courts of general jurisdiction empowered to hear both civil and criminal cases. With few exceptions cases are heard by a single judge, but the number of judges assigned to a district court depends on its workload. The court for the Southern District of New York, for example, the largest of the district courts, has 28. Jurisdiction is limited to cases raising a "federal question"—an issue arising under federal laws, treaties, or the Constitution—or in which there is diversity of citizenship (opposing parties residing in different states) and the monetary claim is above a fixed amount. The district courts dispose of about 270,000 cases a year. Attached to each district court are one or more full- or part-time magistrates and bankruptcy judges. Magistrates are appointed by the district courts and have a range of judicial duties depending on the court. These usually include the conduct of many pretrial proceedings and the trying of minor civil and criminal cases. Bankruptcy judges, appointed by the regional Courts of Appeal, handle the hundreds of thousands of federal bankruptcy cases filed each year.

Decisions may be appealed to 12 Federal Courts of Appeal. Eleven are organized regionally into circuits of three or more states. The twelfth is in Washington, D.C. Their size varies, ranging from six judges in the First Circuit (Maine, New Hampshire, Massachusetts,

FEDERAL   STATE
                                                                 (typical)

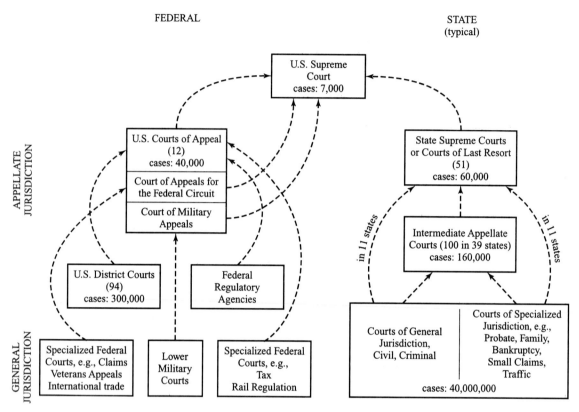

APPELLATE JURISDICTION

GENERAL JURISDICTION

Figure C.1 The American Judicial System, Lines of Appeal, Annual Number of Cases

Rhode Island, and Puerto Rico) to 28 in the Ninth Circuit (Washington State, Oregon, California, Montana, Idaho, Nevada, Arizona, Alaska, and Hawaii). Normally appeals are heard by rotating panels of three judges, though exceptional cases may come before the court's entire roster of judges sitting *en banc*. The Courts of Appeal dispose of about 55,000 cases a year, including appeals of rulings from federal regulatory agencies. Losing parties may petition the U.S. Supreme Court for review.

The federal judiciary also has a number of specialized trial and appellate tribunals. These include bankruptcy courts, which operate within the district court system; the United States Tax Court, hearing appeals from rulings of the Internal Revenue Service; the U.S.

Court of Federal Claims, hearing monetary claims against the U.S. government; the U.S. Court of Military Appeals, hearing appeals from military courts martial; the U.S. Court of Veterans Appeals, hearing cases from the Board of Veterans Appeals in the Veterans Administration; the U.S. Court of International Trade, hearing cases arising under trade and import laws; and the Court of Appeals for the Federal Circuit, having jurisdiction over patent, trademark, and copyright disputes and hearing appeals from several of the specialized courts. Losing parties may petition the United States Supreme Court for review.

State court systems vary considerably with no two exactly alike. All, however, have trial courts of general jurisdiction, though in some states criminal cases are heard in separate courts. All states also have a variety of specialized trial courts, typically dealing with probate, family, tax, small claims, and traffic matters. It is in these lower state courts, general and specialized, that most of the judicial work of the country is done. The exact number of cases disposed of annually is not known, but an educated estimate would be about 40,000,000, heard by more than 30,000 judges.

In most states, cases disposed of by lower courts can be appealed to an intermediate level appellate court, as in the federal system. All states have an appellate court of last resort, usually called the Supreme Court, though in New York and Maryland it is the Court of Appeals. Texas and Oklahoma also maintain a Court of Criminal Appeals as the court of last resort for criminal cases. Eleven of the less populated states—Maine, Mississippi, Montana, Nebraska, Nevada, New Hampshire, Rhode Island, South Dakota, Vermont, West Virginia, and Wyoming—do not have intermediate appellate courts. In these states, trial decisions may be appealed directly to the state supreme court. Intermediate state appellate courts dispose of approximately 160,000 cases a year, those of last resort, about 60,000. The jurisdiction of state courts is determined by state law, but generally, unless limited as to subject matter, may include any question of law—statutory, common, administrative, or constitutional—that the federal Constitution or Congress has not reserved exclusively for federal courts.

The U.S. Supreme Court is the ultimate American court of last resort. Though more than 99 percent of its work is appellate, it does have limited original jurisdiction in which it is the court of first and final resort. This jurisdiction, set out in Article III-2 of the Constitution, includes cases involving ambassadors and those in which a state is a party, usually against another state over a disputed boundary or water rights. An exercise of original jurisdiction does not mean a trial is actually held in the Court—the justices would hardly have time for that. Instead, the case is assigned to a Special Master, often a retired judge appointed by the Court, who hears it and files a report with the Court, which it usually accepts but is free to reject or modify. Cases under the Court's original jurisdiction cases seldom number more than four or five a year. The Court has had fewer than 200 in its history.

Though all other cases before the Court are informally called "appeals," there are actually three routes to Supreme Court appellate review: appeal, certification, and certiorari. Cases in the first category, "on appeal," are those in which a lower court has declared a law to violate the federal Constitution or in which a state court has upheld a state law challenged as violating the federal Constitution. Though Congress, having power to change the Supreme Court's appellate jurisdiction, once made review of such cases mandatory, the justices often sidestepped the requirement by summarily affirming the lower court's decision without opinion or, in state cases, dismissing appeals "for want of a substantial federal question." In 1988, at the Court's urging, Congress officially made the "on appeal" what it had nearly already become, discretionary. The only exceptions are cases arising under a few statutes, such as the Voting Rights Act, where Congress has provided that disputes initially heard by special three-judge district courts have mandatory appeal directly to the Supreme Court.

In certification the request for review comes not from one of the parties but the federal court of appeals itself, in a pending case. The presiding judges interrupt the case to seek clarification of a question of federal law by "certifying" it to the Supreme Court. It is a seldom exercised appellate route, and the Court is not obliged to accept such requests.

Most of the nearly 8,000 cases the Court is asked to hear each year arrive by the third route, the petition for a writ of certiorari, in which the losing party in the court below asks the Court for review. For the Court the matter is entirely discretionary. It takes a case up by granting the writ, literally from the Latin, "to be informed."

The Court today has nearly total control of its appellate docket. This is important since it gives the Court opportunity to pick and choose from a wide range of cases petitioned, allowing the justices to set their own agenda of issues and questions to be addressed.

In a typical year, the Supreme Court accepts fewer than 150 of the cases for review, about one in six of those from the federal Courts of Appeal, one in fifty from state courts of last resort. The chance of the Supreme Court eventually being asked to hear a case filed in an American court is about one in 6,000 and about one in 350,000 that it would be one the Court would give full review. Though this is but a small window on the body of judicial work of the country, the cases the Court does hear include many raising important current political, legal, and constitutional issues.

Exactly what kinds of cases is the Court likely to accept for review? Here it has supplied a partial answer in its own formal guidelines contained in Rule 10 governing certiorari petitions:

> A petition . . . will be granted only for compelling reasons. The following, although neither controlling nor fully measuring the Court's discretion, indicate the character of the reasons the Court considers:
>
> (a) a United States court of appeals has entered a decision in conflict with the decision of another United States court of appeals on the same important matter; has decided an important federal question in a way that conflicts with a decision by a state court of last resort; or has so far departed from the accepted and usual course of judicial proceedings, or sanctioned such a departure by a lower court, as to call for an exercise of this Court's supervisory power;
>
> (b) a state court of last resort has decided an important federal question in a way that conflicts with the decision of another state court of last resort or of a United States court of appeals;
>
> (c) a state court or a United States court of appeals has decided an important question of federal law that has not been, but should be, settled by this Court, or has decided an important federal question in a way that conflicts with relevant decisions of this Court.

Other considerations also come into play. For example, the Court accepts nearly three-quarters of appeals brought on behalf of the federal government by the solicitor general, the Justice Department's chief litigating officer. This high percentage reflects the public importance of many of the cases to which the United States has been a party. Cases in which a large number of "outside" but interested parties have filed *amicus curiae*—"friend of the court"—briefs are more likely to be accepted by the Court than other cases. As with the solicitor general's appeals, these briefs, representing interests beyond those of the immediate parties to the case, often reflect the public importance of issues presented in the cases.* Finally, there is little doubt that the political ideology and personal preferences of individual justices play a role in the Court's selection of cases.

If the Court refuses to hear a case, the decision of the court below, whether federal or state, is final. However, there can be no legal inference from the Court's refusal of review that it has affirmed or looked with favor on the lower court's decision. State supreme court cases that do not raise a question of federal law or right are not reviewable by the Supreme Court. In those, decisions of the state court on matters of state law and the state constitution is final.

---

* See Gregory A. Caldeira and John R. Wright, "Organized Interests and Agenda Setting in the U.S. Supreme Court," *American Political Science Review* 82 (1988), 1109–1127.

D.   Reaching a Decision: The Supreme Court at Work

Of the 8,000 or so cases the Supreme Court is asked to hear in a given year, only 110 to 130 are accepted for full argument and review. These have been winnowed and sifted by the justices and their law clerks. Should four or more justices vote to hear a case, it is put on the Court's review schedule. A handful of other cases, usually involving relatively inconsequential issues and little more than simple error correction, may be dealt with summarily, that is, without full dress review. These decisions are *per curiam*—"by the Court"—with unsigned opinions offering little elaboration. Though fully binding on the parties, they usually have little value as precedent.

Where a case is scheduled for full review, the appealing party (appellant or petitioner) has 45 days in which to submit a legal brief of the case and the opposing party (appellee or respondent) thereafter 30 days to file a reply brief. These documents, along with the opinion of the lower court from which the case is appealed, are the Court's main review materials. They must be submitted in 40 copies and not exceed 50 pages. The Court requires that they include, among other things, a description of the issues presented for review, citation of statutes, ordinances, treaties, or constitutional provisions relevant to the case, a factual statement of the case, a detailed argument based on points of fact and law, and a conclusion stating the relief sought. Briefs may also contain important supportive factual material.

At this stage, *amicus curiae*—"friend of the court"— briefs may be received from various interest groups and other organizations who, as outside third parties, are concerned less with the fate of the adversaries than with the legal and constitutional issues of the case and how the Court's decision might affect their members.

Once the justices have had time to review the briefs, the case is scheduled for oral argument before the full Court in the Court's courtroom. This part of the case is open to the public, and counsel for each side is given one-half hour, though in exceptional cases more time may be allowed. What begins as a presentation (simply reading a written statement aloud is strongly discouraged) is often quickly transformed into a colloquy, with the justices interrupting, sometimes peppering, counsel with questions and comments.

Later the same week, the case and others recently argued are discussed in a conference of all nine justices. A nonbinding vote is taken to reach a preliminary disposition. The case is then assigned one of the justices who, if the Court has not been unanimous, has voted with the majority, for writing the Opinion of the Court stating and explaining the decision reached.

When the justice has written a draft of the opinion, it is circulated among the other justices, who may make suggestions or even raise objections. The original draft may then be modified and recirculated. This stage may take several weeks, even months, and include negotiations over points of law or explanation. Occasionally, a justice may change his or her vote; on rare occasions in a close case, this may change the majority to a minority and vice-versa. Only after the final draft has been circulated and it has the signatures of a majority of the justices does it become the Opinion of the Court in a decided case.

A justice who has voted with the majority on disposition but who cannot fully agree with the majority's reasoning may write a concurring opinion. A justice who disagrees with the majority's decision may write a dissenting opinion. Though there is a majority for deciding the case, the Court may occasionally be so fragmented that there is no majority supporting one line of reasoning for the decision. In these instances, the

Opinion of the Court is based on a simple plurality. Such opinions have considerably less force as precedents; fortunately, they are few in number. Should the Court be divided 4-4 because a justice has been absent or there is a temporary vacancy, the case remains undecided and the decision of the lower court stands. The Court will not decide a case with fewer than seven justices participating.

The final step is public announcement of the decision on one of the Court's "opinion days," scheduled weekly or biweekly during the latter half of its term. These are held in the Court's courtroom with the parties, the press, and interested members of the public who usually include a number of Washington tourists, in attendance. The justice who has written the Opinion of the Court usually gives a brief summary of it, perhaps including an excerpt, rather than reading it in its entirety. Justices writing concurring or dissenting opinions may do likewise with their positions.

A decision by the Court affirms or reverses the decision of the court below. In some cases, the Court "remands," that is, sends the case back to the lower Court with specific instructions on proceeding with it further.

The traditional October Term of the Court, beginning the first Monday of October, now runs the full year, with a summer recess starting in late June or early July. During the working part of the term, the justices alternate between two weeks of hearing oral arguments and conference discussion and two weeks of reading briefs, research of cases, and opinion writing. Oral arguments are heard Mondays through Wednesdays, the Court usually getting through 12 cases in a week.

Conferences are held Wednesday afternoons and all day Friday. They are presided over by the chief justice, who first briefly summarizes each case argued that week and states his views on how it should be decided. In turn, each associate justice in order of seniority is given time to comment as each case is discussed. If the chief justice is in the majority after vote has been taken, he has responsibility for assigning the opinion to an associate justice or retaining it himself. Should he be in the minority, the most senior associate in the majority assigns the opinion. The conferences are strictly closed, no one other than the nine justices is even allowed in the room. There is no public record of their deliberations.

The work of the law clerks is vital to the Court's operations. Several clerk positions are assigned to each justice, who hires the clerks to fill them, usually for one term of the Court. Most clerks are recent graduates with distinguished academic records at leading law schools. These talented persons become the justice's "right arms" in the research and analysis of cases. They do most of the initial reading of the several thousand petitions for writs of certiorari, summarizing them and making recommendations. Of cases scheduled for review, the clerks often do research on the questions of law. Some justices entrust their clerks to prepare drafts of opinions, confining their own role to supervision and final editing. Even justices writing opinions themselves usually rely heavily on their clerks for research and editorial assistance.

The Court is a collegial body; its decisions are collective efforts and the procedures that lead to them call for the participation of all nine members. Yet, for the most part the justices work with a great deal of independence and in isolation from each other. Each has his or her own suite of offices and own staff in the form of the law clerks. By the time the justices reach conference discussion, for example, it is likely that most have already made up their minds about the cases on the table and it is not likely that a great deal of persuasion will take place. As Justice Lewis Powell once observed, "For the most part, perhaps as much as 90 percent of our total time, we function as nine small, independent law firms."*

---

* Lewis F. Powell, Jr., "What the Justices Are Saying . . . ," *American Bar Association Journal* 62 (1976), 1454

E.   Justices of the Supreme Court

Justice	Year Appt.	Appointing President	Party	State	Previous Position	Age at Appt.	Yrs on Court	Departure
1 John Jay	1789	Washington	Fed	N.Y.	Diplomat	52	6	1795, res.
2 John Rutledge	1789	Washington	Fed	S.C.	State Judge	43	2	1791, res.
3 William Cushing	1789	Washington	Fed	Mass.	State Judge	50	22	1810, d.
4 James Wilson	1789	Washington	Fed	Pa.	Lawyer	47	9	1798, d.
5 John Blair, Jr.	1789	Washington	Fed	Va.	State Judge	57	6	1796, ret.
6 James Iredell	1790	Washington	Fed	N.C.	Lawyer	38	10	1799, d.
7 Thomas Johnson	1791	Washington	Fed	Md.	State Judge	58	1	1793, ret.
8 William Patterson	1793	Washington	Fed	N.J.	Gov., N.J.	47	13	1806, d.
9 Samuel Chase	1796	Washington	Fed	Md.	State Judge	54	15	1811, d.
10 Oliver Ellsworth	1796	Washington	Fed	Conn.	Senator	50	4	1800, ill.
11 Bushrod Washington	1798	J. Adams	Fed	Va.	Lawyer	36	31	1829, d.
12 Alfred Moore	1799	J. Adams	Fed	N.C.	State Judge	44	4	1804, ret.
13 John Marshall	1801	J. Adams	Fed	Va.	Sec. State	45	34	1835, d.
14 William Johnson	1804	Jefferson	D-Rep	S.C.	State Judge	52	30	1834, d.
15 Henry Livingston	1806	Jefferson	D-Rep	N.Y.	State Judge	49	16	1823, d.
16 Thomas Todd	1807	Jefferson	D-Rep	Ky.	State Judge	42	19	1826, d.
17 Gabriel Duvall	1811	Madison	D-Rep	Md.	Fed. Admin.	58	23	1835, ret.
18 Joseph Story	1811	Madison	D-Rep	Mass.	State Legis.	32	34	1845, d.
19 Smith Thompson	1823	Monroe	D-Rep	N.Y.	Navy Sec.	55	20	1843, d.

20	Robert Trimble	1826	J. Q. Adams	D-Rep	Ky.	Fed Judge	49	2	1828, d.
21	John McLean	1829	Jackson	Dem	Ohio	Post. Gen.	43	32	1861, d.
22	Henry Baldwin	1830	Jackson	Dem	Pa.	Lawyer	49	14	1844, d.
23	James Wayne	1835	Jackson	Dem	Ga.	Cong. Rep.	45	32	1867, d.
24	Roger Taney	1836	Jackson	Dem	Md.	Lawyer	58	28	1864, d.
25	Philip Barbour	1836	Jackson	Dem	Va.	Fed Judge	52	5	1841, d.
26	John Catron	1837	Jackson	Dem	Tenn.	Lawyer	51	28	1865, d.
27	John McKinley	1837	Van Buren	Dem	Ala.	Senator	57	15	1852, d.
28	Peter Daniel	1841	Van Buren	Dem	Va.	Fed Judge	56	19	1860, d.
29	Samuel Nelson	1845	Tyler	Dem	N.Y.	State Judge	52	28	1872, ret.
30	Levi Woodbury	1846	Polk	Dem	N.H.	Senator	56	6	1851, d.
31	Robert Grier	1846	Polk	Dem	Pa.	State Judge	52	23	1870, ill.
32	Benjamin Curtis	1851	Fillmore	Whig	Mass.	Lawyer	42	6	1857, res.
33	John Campbell	1853	Pierce	Dem	Ala.	Lawyer	41	8	1861, res.
34	Nathan Clifford	1858	Buchanan	Dem	Maine	Lawyer	54	23	1881, d.
35	Noah Swayne	1862	Lincoln	Rep	Ohio	Lawyer	57	19	1881, ret.
36	Samuel Miller	1862	Lincoln	Rep	Iowa	Lawyer	46	28	1890, d.
37	David Davis	1862	Lincoln	Rep	Ill.	State Judge	47	14	1877, res.
38	Stephen Field	1863	Lincoln	Dem	Calif	State Judge	46	35	1897, ill.
39	Salmon Chase	1864	Lincoln	Rep	Ohio	Lawyer	56	8	1873, d.
40	William Strong	1870	Grant	Rep	Pa.	Lawyer	61	11	1880, ret.
41	Joseph Bradley	1870	Grant	Rep	N.J.	Lawyer	56	22	1892, d.
42	Ward Hunt	1872	Grant	Rep	N.Y.	State Judge	62	9	1882, ill.
43	Morrison Waite	1874	Grant	Rep	Ohio	State Govt.	57	14	1888, d.
44	John M. Harlan	1877	Hayes	Rep	Ky.	Lawyer	44	34	1911, d.
45	William Woods	1880	Hayes	Rep	Ga.	Fed Judge	56	6	1887, d.
46	Stanley Matthews	1881	Garfield	Rep	Ohio	Lawyer	56	8	1889, d.
47	Horace Gray	1881	Arthur	Rep	Mass.	State Judge	53	21	1902, d,
48	Samuel Blatchford	1882	Arthur	Rep	N.Y.	Fed Judge	62	11	1893, d.
49	Lucius Lamar	1888	Cleveland	Dem	Miss.	Interior Sec.	62	5	1893, d.
50	Melville Fuller	1888	Cleveland	Dem	Ill.	Lawyer	55	22	1910, d.
51	David Brewer	1889	Harrison	Rep	Kans.	Fed Judge	52	20	1910, d.
52	Henry Brown	1890	Harrison	Rep	Mich.	Fed Judge	54	15	1906, ill.
53	George Shiras, Jr.	1892	Harrison	Rep	Pa.	Lawyer	60	10	1903, ret.
54	Howell Jackson	1893	Harrison	Dem	Tenn.	Fed Judge	60	2	1895, d.
55	Edward White	1894	Cleveland	Dem	La.	Senator	48	27	1921, d.
56	Rufus Peckham	1895	Cleveland	Dem	N.Y.	State Judge	57	14	1909, d.
57	Joseph McKenna	1898	McKinley	Rep	Calif.	Atty. Gen.	54	27	1925, ill.
58	Oliver W. Holmes, Jr.	1902	T. Roosevelt	Rep	Mass.	State Judge	61	29	1932, ret.
59	William Day	1903	T. Roosevelt	Rep	Ohio	Fed Judge	63	20	1922, ret.
60	William Moody	1906	T. Roosevelt	Rep	Mass.	Atty. Gen.	52	4	1910, ill.
61	Horace Lurton	1909	Taft	Dem	Tenn.	Fed Judge	65	5	1914, d.

62	Chas. Evans Hughes	1910	Taft	Rep	N.Y.	Gov., N.Y.	48	6	1916, res.
63	Willis Van Devanter	1910	Taft	Rep	Wyo.	Fed Judge	51	26	1937, ret.
64	Joseph Lamar	1910	Taft	Dem	Ga.	State Judge	53	5	1916, d.
65	Mahlon Pitney	1912	Taft	Rep	N.J.	State Judge	54	11	1922, ill.
66	James McReynolds	1914	Wilson	Dem	Tenn.	Atty. Gen.	52	26	1941, ret.
67	Louis Brandeis	1916	Wilson	Rep	Mass.	Lawyer	59	23	1939, ret.
68	John Clarke	1916	Wilson	Dem	Ohio	Fed Judge	59	6	1922, res.
69	Wm. Howard Taft	1921	Harding	Rep	Ohio	Law Prof.	63	9	1930, ret.
70	George Sutherland	1922	Harding	Rep	Utah	Senator	60	15	1938, ret.
71	Pierce Butler	1922	Harding	Dem	Minn.	Lawyer	56	17	1939, d.
72	Edward Sanford	1923	Harding	Rep	Tenn.	Fed Judge	57	7	1930, d.
73	Harlan Stone	1925	Coolidge	Rep	N.Y.	Atty. Gen.	52	21	1946, d.
74	Chas. Evans Hughes	1930	Hoover	Rep	N.Y.	Lawyer	68	11	1941, ret.
75	Owen Roberts	1930	Hoover	Rep	Pa.	Law Prof.	55	15	1945, res.
76	Benjamin Cardozo	1932	Hoover	Dem	N.Y.	State Judge	61	6	1938, d.
77	Hugo Black	1937	F. Roosevelt	Dem	Ala.	Senator	51	34	1971, ill.
78	Stanley Reed	1938	F. Roosevelt	Dem	Ky.	Sol. Gen.	53	19	1957, ret.
79	Felix Frankfurter	1939	F. Roosevelt	indp.	Mass.	Law Prof.	56	24	1962, ill.
80	William O. Douglas	1939	F. Roosevelt	Dem	Conn.	SEC Chr.	40	37	1975, ill.
81	Frank Murphy	1940	F. Roosevelt	Dem	Mich.	Atty. Gen.	49	9	1949, d.
82	James Byrnes	1941	F. Roosevelt	Dem	S.C.	Senator	62	1	1942, res.
83	Robert Jackson	1941	F. Roosevelt	Dem	N.Y.	Atty. Gen.	49	13	1954, d.
84	Wiley Rutledge	1943	F. Roosevelt	Dem	Iowa	Fed Judge	48	7	1949, d.
85	Harold Burton	1945	Truman	Rep	Ohio	Senator	57	13	1958, ill.
86	Fred Vinson	1946	Truman	Dem	Ky.	Treas. Sec.	56	7	1953, d.
87	Tom Clark	1949	Truman	Dem	Tex.	Atty. Gen.	49	18	1967, ret.
88	Sherman Minton	1949	Truman	Dem	Ind.	Fed Judge	58	7	1956, ill.
89	Earl Warren	1953	Eisenhower	Rep	Calif.	Gov., Calif.	62	16	1969, ret.
90	John M. Harlan II	1955	Eisenhower	Rep	N.Y.	Fed Judge	55	16	1971, ill.
91	William Brennan	1956	Eisenhower	Dem	N.J.	State Judge	50	34	1990, ret.
92	Charles Whittaker	1957	Eisenhower	Rep	Mo.	Fed Judge	56	5	1962, ret.
93	Potter Stewart	1958	Eisenhower	Rep	Ohio	Fed Judge	43	23	1981, ret.
94	Byron White	1962	Kennedy	Dem	Colo.	Dep. A-G	44	31	1993, ret.
95	Arthur Goldberg	1962	Kennedy	Dem	Ill.	Labor Sec.	54	3	1965, res.
96	Abe Fortas	1965	Johnson	Dem	Tenn.	Fed Admin.	55	4	1969, res.
97	Thurgood Marshall	1967	Johnson	Dem	N.Y.	Fed Judge	58	24	1991, ret.
98	Warren Burger	1969	Nixon	Rep	Minn.	Fed Judge	61	17	1986, ret.
99	Harry Blackmun	1970	Nixon	Rep	Minn.	Fed Judge	61	24	1994, ret.
100	Lewis Powell, Jr.	1971	Nixon	Dem	Va.	Lawyer	64	15	1987, ret.
101	William Rehnquist	1971	Nixon	Rep	Ariz.	Asst. A-G	47		
102	John Paul Stevens	1975	Ford	Rep	Ill.	Fed Judge	55		
103	Sandra D. O'Connor	1981	Reagan	Rep	Ariz.	State Judge	51		

104	Antonin Scalia	1986	Reagan	Rep	Va.	Fed Judge	50
105	Arthur Kennedy	1988	Reagan	Rep	Calif.	Fed Judge	51
106	David Souter	1990	Bush	Rep	N.H.	Fed Judge	51
107	Clarence Thomas	1991	Bush	Rep	Ga.	Fed Judge	43
108	Ruth Ginsberg	1993	Clinton	Dem	N.Y.	Fed Judge	60
109	Stephen Breyer	1994	Clinton	Dem	Mass.	Fed Judge	56

Note: Previous positions are in the federal government unless otherwise stated.

Years on court are rounded to nearest full year.

Departure: d., died in office; ill., resignation because of infirmities; ret., retired; res., resigned. In some instances retirement was associated with general disability or that of advanced age.

F.   The Historic Supreme Courts

John Jay, C. J., 1789–1795

1789	Rutledge	Cushing	Wilson	Blair		
1790	Rutledge	Cushing	Wilson	Blair	Iredell	
1791	**Johnson**	Cushing	Wilson	Blair	Iredell	
1793	**Paterson**	Cushing	Wilson	Blair	Iredell	

John Rutledge, C. J., 1795

| 1795 | Paterson | Cushing | Wilson | Blair | Iredell |

Oliver Ellsworth, C. J., 1796–1800

1796	Paterson	Cushing	Wilson	**Chase**	Iredell
1798	Paterson	Cushing	**Washington**	Chase	Iredell
1799	Paterson	Cushing	Washington	Chase	**Moore**

John Marshall, C. J., 1801–1835

1801	Paterson	Cushing	Washington	Chase	Moore	
1804	Paterson	Cushing	Washington	Chase	**Johnson**	
1806	**Livingston**	Cushing	Washington	Chase	Johnson	
1807	Livingston	Cushing	Washington	Chase	Johnson	**Todd**
1811	Livingston	**Story**	Washington	**Duvall**	Johnson	Todd
1823	**Thompson**	Story	Washington	Duvall	Johnson	Todd
1826	Thompson	Story	Washington	Duvall	Johnson	**Trimble**
1829	Thompson	Story	Washington	Duvall	Johnson	**McLean**
1830	Thompson	Story	**Baldwin**	Duvall	Johnson	McLean
1835	Thompson	Story	Baldwin	Duvall	**Wayne**	McLean

Roger Taney, C. J., 1836–1864

| 1836 | Thompson | Story | Baldwin | **Barbour** | Wayne | McLean | | |
| 1837 | Thompson | Story | Baldwin | Barbour | Wayne | McLean | **Catron** | **McKinley** |

1841	Thompson	Story	Baldwin	**Daniel**	Wayne	McLean	Catron	McKinley	
1845	**Nelson**	**Woodbury**	Baldwin	Daniel	Wayne	McLean	Catron	McKinley	
1846	Nelson	Woodbury	**Grier**	Daniel	Wayne	McLean	Catron	McKinley	
1851	Nelson	**Curtis**	Grier	Daniel	Wayne	McLean	Catron	McKinley	
1863	Nelson	Curtis	Grier	Daniel	Wayne	McLean	Catron	**Campbell**	
1858	Nelson	**Clifford**	Grier	Daniel	Wayne	McLean	Catron	Campbell	
1862	Nelson	Clifford	Grier	**Miller**	Wayne	**Swayne**	Catron	**Davis**	
1863	Nelson	Clifford	Grier	Miller	Wayne	Swayne	Catron	Davis	**Field**

Salmon Chase, C. J., 1864–1873

1864	Nelson	Clifford	Grier	Miller	Wayne	Swayne	Catron	Davis	Field
1865	Nelson	Clifford	Grier	Miller	(vacant)	Swayne	Catron	Davis	Field
1867	Nelson	Clifford	Grier	Miller	(vacant)	Swayne	(vacant)	Davis	Field
1870	Nelson	Clifford	**Strong**	Miller	**Bradley**	Swayne	Davis	Field	
1872	**Hunt**	Clifford	Strong	Miller	Bradley	Swayne	Davis	Field	

Morrison Waite, C. J., 1874–1888

1874	Hunt	Clifford	Strong	Miller	Bradley	Swayne	Davis	Field	
1877	Hunt	Clifford	Strong	Miller	Bradley	Swayne	**Harlan**	Field	
1880	Hunt	Clifford	**Woods**	Miller	Bradley	Swayne	Harlan	Field	
1881	Hunt	**Gray**	Woods	Miller	Bradley	**Matthews**	Harlan	Field	
1882	**Blatchford**	Gray	Woods	Miller	Bradley	Matthews	Harlan	Field	

Melville Fuller, C. J., 1888–1910

1888	Blatchford	Gray	**L. Lamar**	Miller	Bradley	Matthews	Harlan	Field	
1889	Blatchford	Gray	L. Lamar	Miller	Bradley	**Brewer**	Harlan	Field	
1890	Blatchford	Gray	L. Lamar	**Brown**	Bradley	Brewer	Harlan	Field	
1892	Blatchford	Gray	L. Lamar	Brown	**Shiras**	Brewer	Harlan	Field	
1893	Blatchford	Gray	**Jackson**	Brown	Shiras	Brewer	Harlan	Field	
1894	**White**	Gray	Jackson	Brown	Shiras	Brewer	Harlan	Field	
1895	White	Gray	**Peckham**	Brown	Shiras	Brewer	Harlan	Field	
1898	White	Gray	Peckham	Brown	Shiras	Brewer	Harlan	**McKenna**	
1902	White	**Holmes**	Peckham	Brown	Shiras	Brewer	Harlan	McKenna	
1903	White	Holmes	Peckham	Brown	**Day**	Brewer	Harlan	McKenna	
1906	White	Holmes	Peckham	**Moody**	Day	Brewer	Harlan	McKenna	
1909	White*	Holmes	**Lurton**	Moody	Day	Brewer	Harlan	McKenna	

Edward White, C. J., 1910–1921

1910	**VanD'vanter**	Holmes	Lurton	**J. Lamar**	Day	**Hughes**	Harlan	McKenna	
1912	VanD'vanter	Holmes	Lurton	J. Lamar	Day	Hughes	**Pitney**	McKenna	
1914	VanD'vanter	Holmes	**McReynolds**	J. Lamar	Day	Hughes	Pitney	McKenna	
1916	VanD'vanter	Holmes	McReynolds	**Brandeis**	Day	**Clarke**	Pitney	McKenna	

William Howard Taft, C. J., 1921–1930

1921	VanD'vanter	Holmes	McReynolds	Brandeis	Day	Clarke	Pitney	McKenna	
1922	VanD'vanter	Holmes	McReynolds	Brandeis	**Butler**	**Sutherland**	Pitney	McKenna	

1923	VanD'vanter	Holmes	McReynolds	Brandeis	Butler	Sutherland	**Sanford**	McKenna
1925	VanD'vanter	Holmes	McReynolds	Brandeis	Butler	Sutherland	Sanford	**Stone**

Charles Evans Hughes, C. J., 1930–1941

1930	VanD'vanter	Holmes	McReynolds	Brandeis	Butler	Sutherland	**Roberts**	Stone
1932	VanD'vanter	**Cardozo**	McReynolds	Brandeis	Butler	Sutherland	Roberts	Stone
1937	**Black**	Cardozo	McReynolds	Brandeis	Butler	Sutherland	Roberts	Stone
1938	Black	Cardozo	McReynolds	Brandeis	Butler	**Reed**	Roberts	Stone
1939	Black	**Frankfurter**	McReynolds	**Douglas**	Butler	Reed	Roberts	Stone
1940	Black	Frankfurter	McReynolds	Douglas	**Murphy**	Reed	Roberts	Stone*

Harlan Fiske Stone, C. J., 1941–1946

1941	Black	Frankfurter	**Byrnes**	Douglas	Murphy	Reed	Roberts	**Jackson**
1943	Black	Frankfurter	**Rutledge**	Douglas	Murphy	Reed	Roberts	Jackson
1945	Black	Frankfurter	Rutledge	Douglas	Murphy	Reed	**Burton**	Jackson

Fred Vinson, C. J., 1946–1953

1946	Black	Frankfurter	Rutledge	Douglas	Murphy	Reed	Burton	Jackson
1949	Black	Frankfurter	**Minton**	Douglas	**Clark**	Reed	Burton	Jackson

Earl Warren, C. J., 1953–1969

1953	Black	Frankfurter	Minton	Douglas	Clark	Reed	Burton	Jackson
1955	Black	Frankfurter	Minton	Douglas	Clark	Reed	Burton	**Harlan**
1956	Black	Frankfurter	**Brennan**	Douglas	Clark	Reed	Burton	Harlan
1957	Black	Frankfurter	Brennan	Douglas	Clark	**Whittaker**	Burton	Harlan
1958	Black	Frankfurter	Brennan	Douglas	Clark	Whittaker	**Stewart**	Harlan
1962	Black	**Goldberg**	Brennan	Douglas	Clark	**White**	Stewart	Harlan
1965	Black	**Fortas**	Brennan	Douglas	Clark	White	Stewart	Harlan
1967	Black	Fortas	Brennan	Douglas	**Marshall**	White	Stewart	Harlan

Warren Burger, C. J., 1969–1986

1969	Black	Fortas	Brennan	Douglas	Marshall	White	Stewart	Harlan
1970	Black	**Blackmun**	Brennan	Douglas	Marshall	White	Stewart	**Rehnquist**
1972	**Powell**	Blackmun	Brennan	Douglas	Marshall	White	Stewart	Rehnquist
1975	Powell	Blackmun	Brennan	**Stevens**	Marshall	White	Stewart	Rehnquist
1981	Powell	Blackmun	Brennan	Stevens	Marshall	White	**O'Connor**	Rehnquist*

William Rehnquist, C. J., 1986–

1986	Powell	Blackmun	Brennan	Stevens	Marshall	White	O'Connor	**Scalia**
1988	**Kennedy**	Blackmun	Brennan	Stevens	Marshall	White	O'Connor	Scalia
1990	Kennedy	Blackmun	**Souter**	Stevens	Marshall	White	O'Connor	Scalia
1991	Kennedy	Blackmun	Souter	Stevens	**Thomas**	White	O'Connor	Scalia
1993	Kennedy	Blackmun	Souter	Stevens	Thomas	**Ginsberg**	O'Connor	Scalia
1994	Kennedy	**Breyer**	Souter	Stevens	Thomas	Ginsberg	O'Connor	Scalia

* Elevated to chief justice

G. American National Elections, 1788–2000

	Presidential Vote					Congressional Seats					
		Percent of				Senate			House		
Year	Candidate (Winner in Capitals)	Popular Vote	Electoral Vote	States Carried		Majority Party		Minority Party	Majority Party		Minority Party
1788	WASHINGTON (Fed)	*	69	11	1788	Ad	17	Op	9	Ad	38	Op	26
					1790	F	16	DR	13	F	37	DR	33
1792	WASHINGTON (Fed)	*	132	16	1792	F	17	DR	13	DR	57	F	48
					1794	F	19	DR	13	F	54	DR	52
1796	J. ADAMS (Fed)	*	71	10	1796	F	20	DR	12	F	58	DR	48
	Jefferson (Dem-Rep)	*	69	7	1798	F	12	DR	13	F	64	DR	52
1800	JEFFERSON (Dem-Rep)	*	73	8	1800	DR	18	F	14	DR	69	F	36
	J. Adams	*	69	7	1802	DR	25	F	9	DR	102	F	39
1804	JEFFERSON (Dem-Rep)	*	162	15	1804	DR	27	F	7	DR	116	F	25
	Pinckney (Fed)	*	14	2	1806	DR	28	F	6	DR	118	F	24
1808	MADISON (Dem-Rep)	*	122	12	1808	DR	28	F	6	DR	94	F	48
	Pinckney (Fed)	*	47	5	1810	DR	30	F	6	DR	108	F	46
1812	MADISON (Dem-Rep)	*	128	11	1812	DR	27	F	9	DR	112	F	68
	Clinton (Fed)	*	89	7	1814	DR	25	F	11	DR	117	F	65
1816	MONROE (Dem-Rep)	*	183	16	1816	DR	34	F	10	DR	141	F	42
	King (Fed)	*	34	3	1818	DR	35	F	7	DR	156	F	27
1820	MONROE (Dem-Rep)	*	231	24	1820	DR	44	F	4	DR	158	F	25
	(unopposed)				1822	DR	44	F	4	DR	187	F	26
1824	J. Q. ADAMS (Dem-Rep)	31	84	7	1824	Ad	26	J	20	Ad	105	J	97
	Jackson (Dem-Rep)	41	99	11	1826	J	28	Ad	20	J	119	Ad	94
	Crawford (Dem-Rep)	11	41	2								
	Clay (Dem-Rep)	13	37	3								
1828	JACKSON (Dem)	56	178	15	1828	D	26	NR	22	D	139	NR	74
	J. Q. Adams (Nat Rep)	44	83	9	1830	D	25	NR	21	D	141	NR	58
1832	JACKSON (Dem)	54	219	16	1832	D	20	NR	20	D	147	AM	53
	Clay (Nat Rep)	37	49	5	1834	D	27	W	25	D	145	W	98
1836	VAN BUREN (Dem)	51	170	15	1836	D	30	W	18	D	108	W	107
	Harrison (Whig)	37	73	7	1838	D	28	W	22	D	124	W	118
1840	HARRISON (Whig)	53	234	19	1840	W	28	D	22	W	133	D	102
	Van Buren (Dem) (TYLER, 1841)**	47	60	7	1842	W	28	D	25	D	143	W	79
1844	POLK (Dem)	50	170	15	1844	D	31	W	25	D	143	W	77
	Clay (Whig)	48	105	10	1846	D	36	W	21	W	115	D	108
1848	TAYLOR (Whig)	47	163	15	1848	D	35	W	25	D	112	W	109
	Cass (Dem) (FILLMORE, 1851)**	42	127	15	1850	D	35	W	24	D	140	W	88
1852	PIERCE (Dem)	51	254	27	1852	D	38	W	22	D	159	W	71
	Scott (Whig)	44	42	4	1854	D	40	R	15	R	108	D	83
1856	BUCHANAN (Dem)	45	174	19	1856	D	36	R	20	D	118	R	93
	Fremont (Rep)	33	114	11	1858	D	36	R	26	R	114	D	92
	Fillmore (Whig-Am)	22	8	1								
1860	LINCOLN (Rep)	40	180	18	1860	R	31	D	10	R	105	D	43
	Breckinridge (So Dem)	18	72	11	1862	R	36	D	9	R	102	D	75

Year	Candidate				Year								
	Bell (Con Union)	13	39	3									
	Douglas (Dem)	29	12	1									
1864	LINCOLN (Rep)	55	212	22	1864	U	42	D	10	U	149	D	42
	McClellan (Dem)	45	21	3	1866	R	42	D	11	R	143	D	49
	(JOHNSON, 1865)**												
1868	GRANT (Rep)	53	214	26	1868	R	56	D	11	R	149	D	63
	Seymour (Dem)	47	80	7	1870	R	52	D	17	D	134	R	104
1872	GRANT (Rep)	56	286	29	1872	R	49	D	19	R	194	D	92
	Greeley (Dem)	44	42	5	1874	R	45	D	29	D	169	R	109
1876	HAYES (Rep)	48	185	21	1876	R	39	D	36	D	153	R	140
	Tilden (Dem)	51	184	17	1878	D	42	R	33	D	149	R	130
1880	GARFIELD (Rep)	48	214	19	1880	R	37	D	37	R	147	D	135
	Hancock (Dem)	48	155	19	1882	R	38	D	36	D	197	R	118
	(ARTHUR, 1882)**												
1884	CLEVELAND (Dem)	49	219	20	1884	R	43	D	34	D	183	R	140
	Blaine (Rep)	48	182	18	1886	R	39	D	37	D	169	R	152
1888	HARRISON (Rep)	48	233	20	1888	R	39	D	37	R	166	D	159
	Cleveland (Dem)	49	168	18	1890	R	47	D	39	D	235	R	88
1892	CLEVELAND (Dem)	46	277	25	1892	D	44	R	38	D	218	R	127
	Harrison (Rep)	43	145	15	1894	R	43	D	39	R	234	D	105
	Weaver (Pop)	9	22	4									
1896	MCKINLEY (Rep)	51	271	23	1896	R	47	D	34	R	204	D	113
	Bryan (Dem, Pop)	47	176	22	1898	R	53	D	26	R	185	D	163
1900	MCKINLEY (Rep)	52	292	28	1900	R	55	D	31	R	197	D	151
	Bryan (Dem)	46	155	17	1902	R	57	D	33	R	208	D	178
	(T. ROOSEVELT, 1901)**												
1904	T. ROOSEVELT (Rep)	56	336	32	1904	R	57	D	33	R	250	D	136
	Parker (Dem)	38	140	13	1906	R	61	D	31	R	222	D	164
1908	TAFT (Rep)	52	321	29	1908	R	61	D	32	R	219	D	172
	Bryan (Dem)	43	162	17	1910	R	51	D	41	D	238	R	161
1912	WILSON (Dem)	42	435	40	1912	D	51	R	44	D	291	R	127
	T. Roosevelt (Prog)	27	88	6	1914	D	56	R	40	D	230	R	196
	Taft (Rep)	23	8	2									
1916	WILSON (Dem)	49	277	30	1916	D	53	R	42	D	216	R	210
	Hughes (Rep)	46	254	18	1918	R	49	D	47	R	240	D	190
1920	HARDING (Rep)	60	404	37	1920	R	59	D	37	R	303	D	131
	Cox (Dem)	34	127	11	1922	R	51	D	43	R	225	D	205
	(COOLIDGE, 1922)**												
1924	COOLIDGE (Rep)	54	382	35	1924	R	56	D	39	R	247	D	183
	Davis (Dem)	29	136	12	1926	R	49	D	46	R	237	D	195
	LaFollette (Prog)	17	13	1									
1928	HOOVER (Rep)	58	444	40	1928	R	56	D	39	R	267	D	167
	Smith (Dem)	41	87	8	1930	R	48	D	47	D	220	R	214
1932	F. ROOSEVELT (Dem)	57	472	42	1932	D	60	R	35	D	310	R	117
	Hoover (Rep)	40	59	6	1934	D	69	R	25	D	319	R	103
1936	F. ROOSEVELT (Dem)	61	523	46	1936	D	76	R	16	D	331	R	89
	Landon (Rep)	37	8	2	1938	D	69	R	23	D	261	R	164
1940	F. ROOSEVELT (Dem)	55	449	38	1940	D	66	R	28	D	268	R	162
	Wilkie (Rep)	45	82	10	1942	D	58	R	37	D	218	R	208
1944	F. ROOSEVELT (Dem)	54	432	36	1944	D	56	R	38	D	242	R	190

Year	Candidate (Party)				Year								
	Dewey (Rep)	46	99	12	1946	R	51	D	45	R	246	D	188
	(TRUMAN, 1945)**												
1948	TRUMAN (Dem)	50	303	30	1948	D	54	R	42	D	263	R	171
	Dewey (Rep)	45	189	15	1950	D	49	R	47	D	235	R	199
	Thurmond (SR Dem)	2	39	3									
1952	EISENHOWER (Rep)	56	442	39	1952	R	48	D	47	R	221	D	212
	Stevenson (Dem)	44	89	9	1954	D	48	R	47	D	232	R	203
1956	EISENHOWER (Rep)	57	457	41	1956	D	49	R	47	D	232	R	199
	Stevenson (Dem)	42	73	7	1958	D	62	R	34	D	280	R	152
1960	KENNEDY (Dem)	49	303	22	1960	D	65	R	35	D	261	R	176
	Nixon (Rep)	49	219	26	1962	D	67	R	33	D	258	R	174
	Byrd (Dem)	2	15	2									
	(JOHNSON, 1963)**												
1964	JOHNSON (Dem)	61	486	45	1964	D	68	R	32	D	295	R	140
	Goldwater (Rep)	38	52	6	1966	D	64	R	36	D	248	R	187
1968	NIXON (Rep)	43	301	31	1968	D	57	R	43	D	244	R	191
	Humphrey (Dem)	43	191	15	1970	D	54	R	44	D	255	R	180
	Wallace (Am Indp)	14	46	5									
1972	NIXON (Rep)	61	520	49	1972	D	56	R	42	D	242	R	192
	McGovern (Dem)	38	17	2	1974	D	61	R	37	D	291	R	144
	(FORD, 1974)***												
1976	CARTER (Dem)	50	297	24	1976	D	61	R	38	D	290	R	145
	Ford (Rep)	48	240	27	1978	D	58	R	41	D	276	R	159
1980	REAGAN (Rep)	51	489	44	1980	R	53	D	46	D	244	R	191
	Carter (Dem)	47	49	7	1982	R	54	D	46	D	269	R	166
	Anderson (Indp)	7	0	0									
1984	REAGAN (Rep)	59	525	49	1984	R	53	D	47	D	253	R	182
	Mondale (Dem)	41	13	2	1986	D	54	R	46	D	258	R	177
1988	BUSH (Rep)	53	426	41	1988	D	55	R	45	D	260	R	175
	Dukakis (Dem)	46	111	10	1990	D	56	R	45	D	267	R	167
1992	CLINTON (Dem)	43	370	33	1992	D	57	R	43	D	258	R	176
	Bush (Rep)	38	168	18	1994	R	52	D	48	R	230	D	204
	Perot (Ref)	19	0	0									
1996	CLINTON (Dem)	49	379	32	1996	R	55	D	45	R	226	D	207
	Dole (Rep)	41	159	19	1998	R	54	D	45	R	222	D	212
	Perot (Ref)	8	0	0									
2000	Bush (Rep)	48	271	30	2000	R	50	D	49	R	221	D	211
	Gore (Dem)	48	267	20									
	Nader (Green)	3	0	0									

* Popular vote not nationally tabulated until election of 1820.

** Vice president succeeded to office on death of incumbent.

*** Vice president succeeded to office on resignation of incumbent.

Presidential party abbreviations: Fed, Federalist; Dem-Rep, Democratic-Republican; Dem Democratic; Nat Rep, National Republican; Rep, Republican; Whig Am, Whig American; So Dem, Southern Democratic; Con Un, Constitutional Union; Pop, Populist; Prog, Progressive; SR Dem, States Rights Democratic: Am Indp, American Independent; Indp, Independent; Ref, Reform.

Congressional party abbreviations: Ad, Administration supporters; Op, opposition; F, Federalist; DR, Democratic-Republican; J, Jacksonian; NR, Nationalist Republican; AM, Anti-Masonic; W, Whig; U, Unionist; D, Democratic; R, Republican

GLOSSARY OF LEGAL AND CONSTITUTIONAL TERMS

abstention A doctrine under which federal courts refrain from deciding federal issues in state cases if the case can be decided on state law.

adjudication The hearing and resolution of issues in a legal case.

administrative law The law dealing with the powers, structure, procedures, and policies of regulatory agencies.

admiralty law The law governing maritime matters including shipping, navigation, and acts on the high seas.

adversary proceeding A legal action in which contending parties with opposing interests frame the issues to be decided.

advisory opinion A judicial opinion on legal issues not arising in an adversarial proceeding. It is usually requested by a legislature or an executive agency.

affidavit A sworn written statement of facts.

affirm To uphold or confirm an earlier judgment, usually that of a lower court.

a fortiori With greater or stronger reason.

allegation A charge or contention of fact that is to be legally proven.

amicus curiae Literally, friend of the court. A person or organization permitted to submit a brief in a lawsuit to which they are not one of the adversarial parties, usually because they have interests to protect that are at issue in the case.

appeal A request that a ruling or decision of a lower court be reviewed by a higher court.

appellant A losing party in a lower court that asks for review of that court's judgment by a higher court.

appellate jurisdiction The power of a higher court to review and correct errors made by a lower.

appellee The party against whom an appeal is taken to a higher court.

arbitrary Unreasonable, usually referring a governmental act.

bill of attainder An act by a legislature directly imposing punishment or legal disability on a person without benefit of trial. It is barred to the federal government and the states under Article I-9 and I-10 of the Constitution.

brief A written statement of legal arguments submitted by counsel in a lawsuit; the summary of a given case.

case law The law based on judicial decisions, in contrast to that contained in statutes or administrative rules.

case or controversy A legal action based on a claim of actual injury to personal interests in contrast to the raising of merely hypothetical or abstract questions of law; a requirement of Article III-2 for the exercise of the jurisdiction of the federal courts.

cause of action A statement of facts entitling a person to seek judicial relief; a case or complaint.

certification A procedure by which a lower court in a pending case asks a higher court to rule on a specific issue of law that it needs to have clarified or resolved or in order to continue the case.

certiorari, writ of An order of a higher court to a lower to have the record of a case sent up for review; the chief method by which the U. S. Supreme Court exercises appellate review.

civil action A lawsuit in which one party sues another to enforce a right or redress or prevent a wrong, in contrast to a criminal action brought by government to enforce criminal law.

civil law Law dealing with civil rather than criminal matters, for example, contracts, torts, property.

civil liberties, rights Freedoms of individuals protected by constitutions and certain statutes. Examples include the exercise of religion, the right to speak and publish, to have due process, and the equal protection of law.

class action A lawsuit brought by one or more persons not only for themselves but on behalf of a group or class of others in similar circumstances.

collateral attack An attempt to defeat a judgment by bringing an action, other than an appeal, in another court.

comity The respect or discretionary courtesy one sovereign gives to the legal actions of another, for example the federal government to the states, the states to each other, or one nation to another.

common law A body of law based on the judgments of courts in which earlier decisions serve as binding precedents for later cases, in contrast to statutes enacted by legislatures. Historically, a system of judge-made law originating in medieval England and based, initially at least, on usage and custom.

complaint A formal statement in which the party bringing a lawsuit states the reasons for the action.

concurring opinion An opinion by an appellate judge or justice agreeing with the decision in the case, but disagreeing with its rationale or offering different or additional reasons for it.

concurrent powers Those exercised by both state and federal governments, such as the power to tax.

consent decree A court-enforced agreement based on the consent of the parties in a civil case or administrative proceeding.

contempt A punishable act that disobeys a court order or that hinders, embarrasses, or lessens the dignity of a judicial or legislative proceeding.

constitutional courts Federal courts established under Article III-1 of the Constitution, for example the Supreme Court, the 12 Courts of Appeal, and the district courts.

criminal case A judicial action brought by a government prosecutor to enforce a criminal law.

criminal law Law dealing with noncivil matters, for example, robbery, homicide, or the sale or possession of illegal materials.

damages A monetary award in a civil case to compensate for a proven injury or loss; in the case of punitive damages, also to penalize egregious conduct

declaratory judgment A judicial ruling stating the rights, duties, or status of the parties, but not accompanied by an award of damages.

de facto Actual, in fact. In contrast to *de jure.*

defendant The party who is sued in a civil action or indicted in a criminal.

de jure Legal, duly authorized. In contrast to *de facto.*

demurrer A motion of the defendant in a civil case asserting that even if the facts alleged in the complaint are true, they are legally insufficient to maintain the suit.

de mininus Minimal, trifling; not sufficiently important for adjudication.

de novo Anew; for a second consideration by a court.

dictum (pl: dicta) A statement or observation in a court's opinion that is incidental to and not necessary for the decision in the case at hand and thus not binding on future cases. In contrast to holding. Also *obiter dictum.*

discovery The pretrial stage of factual investigation including the taking of testimony in written depositions.

dismissal Termination of a case by court order.

dissenting opinion An opinion by an appellate judge or justice disagreeing with the decision in a case.

distinguish Reasoning by a court that finds an earlier similar case sufficiently different from the case at hand that it does not serve as a controlling precedent.

diversity jurisdiction The authority of federal courts to hear civil cases between citizens of different states.

docket The record of cases to be heard by a court during a given term.

due process of law The fundamentally fair procedures that government must follow before it may deprive any person of life, liberty, or property.

eminent domain The power of government or authorized private parties to take private property for public use. The Fifth Amendment to the Constitution requires that such taking be met with "just compensation."

en banc The sitting of an appellate court with all judges or justices present, rather than hearing by a panel.

enjoin Judicially to order that a party do or refrain from doing a specific act; to issue an injunction.

equity A branch of the common law that provides for remedies, such as injunction and specific performance to prevent legal injuries, in contrast to law awarding damages for injuries that have occurred. Historically, equity evolved from flexible rules devised to mitigate the sometimes harsh and rigid requirements of common law, thereby emphasizing the court's basic sense of fairness.

error, writ of An order by an appellate court to a lower court to furnish the records of a case for review; before 1925, the chief method by which cases reached the U. S. Supreme Court and one over which the Court had little discretion.

ex parte On behalf of one party; a judicial proceeding without the presence an adversary party, for example, a habeas corpus hearing.

ex post facto **law** A retroactive criminal law making an act a crime that was not a crime when it was done or making punishment for a crime greater than it was when the crime was committed. Federal and state governments are barred from passing such laws under Article I-9 and I-10 of the Constitution.

ex rel. Literally, on the relation of. Refers to the name of a party on whose behalf an agency of government sues another party.

federal question A legal issue arising under the Constitution, a treaty, federal statute, regulation, or executive order.

felony The most serious category of crimes, including homicide, rape, and robbery, punishable by more than a year in prison.

fiduciary A person in a position of trust; one who handles the property of others, for example a banker or trustee.

grand jury A group of enpaneled citizens authorized to examine prosecutorial or independently gathered evidence against specific persons and to decide whether it is sufficient to support a criminal indictment.

habeas corpus, **writ of** A judicial order to a government officer holding someone in custody to bring the prisoner before the court so the legality of detention may be determined.

harmless error A trial error held by an appellate court not to be important enough to have affected the outcome of the trial or support reversing the trial judgment.

holding The specific legal ruling in a case; that part of the court's opinion that is considered binding as precedent for future decisions, in contrast to a dictum.

implied powers Authority of the national government that may be reasonably inferred from powers expressly delegated to it in the Constitution; specifically, power derived from the "necessary and proper" clause of Article I-8-18.

immunity Exemption from criminal prosecution or civil suit.

in camera In private; referring to matters taken up in the judge's private chambers or from which the public is excluded.

incorporation In constitutional law, the process by which rights in the Bill of Rights were held to be part of due process of law and thus included in the due process clause of the Fourteenth Amendment as limits on the powers of the states.

indictment A formal criminal charge brought by a grand jury after examination of prosecutorial evidence.

in forma pauperis Literally, in the manner of a pauper; a special status given to indigent persons, particularly in taking appeals, in which they are exempt from certain fees or procedural requirements.

information A criminal charge against a named person brought in a prosecutor's affidavit to a judge. It is used in state jurisdictions that do not indict by grand jury.

inherent powers Authority of the national government not based on delegated or implied powers but inferred from the existence of the United States as a sovereign nation in the international world.

injunction A court order that a party do or refrain from doing a specified act.

in personam A lawsuit brought against a person rather than against property (*in rem*).

in re In the matter of, concerning; refers to a named party about whom a judicial matter has been taken up.

in rem A lawsuit brought against property rather than a person (*in personam*).

inter alia Literally, among other things.

interlocutory decree A temporary judgment before a matter has been conclusively determined.

ipse dixit Asserted but not proved

judicial notice Recognition by a court of certain facts, usually matters of common knowledge, without requiring one side or the other to submit formal proof.

judicial review Appellate examination of lower court proceedings for errors of law; in constitutional law, the power of a court to affirm or strike down governmental acts on constitutional grounds.

jurisdiction The authority of a court to hear a case; the geographical area included in such authority.

jurisprudence Legal philosophy; a body of legal decisions.

justiciable The quality of being suitable for judicial consideration and decision.

legislative courts Federal courts, such as the U.S. Court of Claims, established by Congress under Article I-8, as distinguished from constitutional courts created under Article III-1.

litigant A party to a lawsuit or legal action.

magistrate A judge of a lower court; in the federal courts, a judicial officer in a district court authorized to handle certain pretrial matters and minor civil and criminal proceedings.

majority opinion The opinion of an appellate court supported by more than half but not all judges or justices, explaining the decision of the court.

mandamus, writ of A court order to a governmental officer to perform a nondiscretionary, ministerial duty.

mandate An order of a court that its decision or ruling in a case be executed.

martial law A declared condition under which the military assumes the powers of government in domestic territory during an emergency or crisis; the law prevailing under such circumstances.

merits The substantive issues of a lawsuit in contrast to those having to do with procedure or jurisdiction. A decision "on the merits" is one in which the substantive issues have been heard and decided on the evidence in the case.

ministerial duty A specified duty of a public officer not calling for the discretion or judgment of policy.

misdemeanor A category of crimes less serious than felonies, punishable by fines or imprisonment of not more than a year.

mistrial A trial terminated before completion, usually because procedural error or misconduct prevented a fair trial from continuing, or because a jury has been unable to reach a decision.

mootness Status of a legal issue or question that has resolved itself or, because of changed conditions, is no longer an active controversy between the parties to a case.

motion An formal request by a party to a lawsuit to the court for a specified ruling on an issue in the case or on the case itself.

natural law Principles of human conduct believed to derive from God or nature, applicable to all persons and preceding human law; the law that conforms to a basic desire to act rationally and morally.

Opinion of the Court A statement announcing the judgment of a court explaining its reasoning and supported by at least a majority of the judges or justices participating in the case. In contrast to concurring or dissenting opinions, the Opinion of the Court is a basis of precedent.

original jurisdiction Authority of a court to try a case originally, in contrast to hearing appeals of cases already tried.

overrule To nullify or deny, as when a higher court reverses the ruling of a lower court or when it supersedes an earlier decision of its own.

per curiam Literally, by the court. Term given to an unsigned, usually short opinion written collectively by an appellate court. Such opinions may issued when the legal questions need little explanation or when the court is deeply divided.

per se By itself, inherently

petitioner The party bringing a lawsuit; plaintiff in contrast to respondent. In the Supreme Court, the term may refer to the party seeking review.

petit jury Trial jury, as distinguished from grand jury.

plaintiff The party bringing a civil complaint or lawsuit, in contrast to the defendant.

pleading A written statement of facts and argument filed by a party in a lawsuit, for example the plaintiff's complaint or defendant's response.

plenary A reference to power that is full, complete, or exclusive, for example the federal government's power in foreign affairs.

plurality opinion An opinion that states the judgment of an appellate court but in its particular reasoning is supported by less than a majority of the judges or justices participating and, for that reason, is not considered binding in future cases.

police power The broad regulatory power of government to protect public health, safety, morals, and welfare.

political question A legal question that a court believes is more appropriately decided by the executive or legislative branches than the judicial, for example, the legality of military hostilities or whether a state has a republican form of government.

precedent An earlier court decision thought to be analogous or so similar to the present case that it cannot be distinguished from it and therefore must guide or control the decision in the present case.

preemption The condition in which an area of policy or authority once open to the states or shared by the states and the federal government has been superseded or occupied exclusively by the federal authority.

preliminary injunction A temporary restraining order issued at the beginning of a lawsuit forbidding one of the parties from carrying out an act that is at issue in the case.

prima facie Literally, at first sight, on its face. Refers to evidence or an entire complaint that is strong enough to be presumptively valid unless convincingly refuted.

procedural due process Fundamental fairness in the way and manner in which government deals with the liberty and property of individuals, usually referring to procedural protections, such as the right to notice, to confront witnesses, etc., as distinguished from substantive rights, such as freedom of speech.

prohibition, writ of An order from a higher to a lower court that it cease to hear a particular case, usually on the ground that it belongs in another court.

public law Law dealing with the powers and responsibilities of government, including constitutions and certain statutes, administrative rules, and judicial decisions.

quash To void, vacate, or suppress, as when a court throws out an indictment

ratio decidendi Literally, the reason for deciding. The holding of a case setting out the court's reasons for what it did, in contrast to statements of dicta.

recuse To disqualify oneself, as where a judge withdraws from hearing a case because of bias or conflict of interest.

remand To send back; the return of a case from a higher court to a lower usually with specific instructions on how to proceed further.

remedy The legal means for preventing or correcting a wrong or enforcing a right.

res judicata Literally, the matter adjudicated. A principle that forecloses further litigation of an issue between the parties to a case, except for an appeal, after the issue has been competently decided.

reserved powers Powers of a government not constitutionally delegated elsewhere or implied from those that are. Under the Tenth Amendment, for example, authority not delegated to the national government nor denied to the states is reserved to the states.

respondent The party against whom a suit is filed or an appeal taken.

reverse To overturn, as when an appellate court rules that the trial court should have rendered a decision for the other side in a case.

ripeness Readiness for legal decision or review, which usually means the issues in a case are not hypothetical and the parties have exhausted all other means of remedy or resolution. This prevents the premature hearing of cases.

sedition The crime of inciting rebellion or advocating violent overthrow of the government.

selective incorporation The case-by-case method the Supreme Court has used to hold that certain rights in the Bill of Rights are part of due process of law and thus serve as limits on state power through the due process clause of the Fourteenth Amendment

show cause A court order requiring a party to appear and show reason why the court should not take certain action, often the issuance of an injunction.

sovereign immunity Exemption of the government from being sued without its consent.

sovereignty Supremacy of authority or rule; self-governing; the ultimate power of government to make binding decisions and resolve conflicts.

special master An officer appointed by a court to receive evidence and then present findings and conclusions to the court, which rules on them. Almost always

used by the Supreme Court in hearing cases under its original jurisdiction.

specific performance A court order that a party perform certain obligations incurred under contract, as distinguished from an award of damages for breach of contract.

standing The requirement that a party bringing a lawsuit allege a direct and sufficiently substantial injury for which there is a legal remedy

stare decisis Literally, let the decision stand. Reliance on precedent; the principle that rules of law established in earlier cases are binding in later cases that are similar to or cannot be distinguished from the earlier.

state action Conduct or developments for which a state or local government is responsible directly or indirectly rather than being purely a private matter. In constitutional law, the conduct or action that is subject to limits imposed by the Fourteenth or Fifteenth Amendments or by Article I-10 of the Constitution.

states rights Powers reserved to the states under the Tenth Amendment. In constitutional doctrine, opposition to increasing the power of the national government at the expense of the states; emphasis on state power and responsibility within the federal system.

statute of limitations A law setting a time limit for bringing specified types of lawsuits or criminal prosecutions. Most statutes defining crimes have a statute of limitations provision.

statutory law Laws enacted by legislatures, in contrast to case law established in binding judicial decisions.

stay A court order halting the execution of a judgment, usually temporary until further legal consideration can be given to an issue in the matter.

strict construction A narrow interpretation of the text of a law or legal document. In constitutional doctrine, the view that the Constitution, particularly in its grant of powers to the national government, should be interpreted in terms of its exact language rather than broadly or liberally.

sua sponte Literally, of its own will. Voluntary, without prompting or suggestion.

subpoena Literally, under penalty. A legal order directing a person to appear in court or other official proceeding to give testimony.

subpoena duces tecum Literally, under penalty bring with you. An order that a person under subpoena bring with him or her certain records, documents, or other material, or to turn these over to a court.

sub silentio Literally, under silence. A court action without express acknowledgment, as when a precedent is abandoned without the case or cases on which it stood being overruled.

substantive due process The inclusion of certain concrete, nonprocedural rights, such as freedom of speech or, at one time, freedom to make contracts, in the requirements of due process of law, thus generally putting them beyond the power of government to abridge.

summary judgment A court decision resolving a case or legal dispute where it becomes clear that opposing parties do not disagree about the facts; a decision based on a ruling of law rather than a finding of fact.

three-judge court A special federal panel of district and appellate court judges invoked to expedite the hearing of certain cases or issues. Normally appeals from the rulings of such courts may be taken directly to the Supreme Court.

tort A civil rather than criminal wrong committed by one person against another, for example injury to person or property through negligence, the remedy for which is an award of damages.

ultra vires Literally, beyond powers. Action of a government officer or agency that exceeds vested legal authority.

vacate To set aside or annul, as when a higher court rescinds the judgment of a lower.

vagueness Lack of clarity; a defect in a law that violates the due process requirement that clear notice be given of what is lawful and unlawful.

venue The geographical area of a court's jurisdiction; the location of a trial.

vested rights Rights believed to be so basic that they may not be interfered with by government. Historically, certain rights to property.

warrant A court order allowing a competent authority to carry out a specified act, for example a search or an arrest.

writ A court order requiring that something be done or not done.

GENERAL AND SUPPLEMENTAL BIBLIOGRAPHY FOR VOLUME I

(Works specific to individual chapters are found at the end of each chapter)

General and Major Reference Works

Biskupic, Joan and Elder Witt, *Guide to the United States Supreme Court*, 3rd ed., 2 vols (1997)

Chase, Harold W. and Craig R. Ducat, *The Constitution and What It Means Today* (1978)

Corwin, Edward S., *The Constitution of the United States: Analysis and Interpretation* (1973)

Cushman, Clare, *The Supreme Court Justices: Illustrated Biographies* (1993)

Epstein, Lee, Jeffrey A. Segal, Harold J. Spaeth, and Thomas G. Walker, *The Supreme Court Compendium: Data, Decisions, and Development* (1994)

Friedman, Leon and Fred I. Israel, *Justices of the United States Supreme Court, 1789–1991*, 5 vols (1992)

Hall, Kermit L., ed., *The Oxford Companion to the Supreme Court of the United States* (1992)

——, *United States Constitutional and Legal History: Major Historical Essays*, 20 vols (1987)

——, (compiler), *A Comprehensive Bibliography of American Constitutional and Legal History*, 5 vols (1984)

——, *Oxford Guide to United States Supreme Court Opinions* (1999)

Johnson, John W., ed., *Historic United States Court Cases, 1690–1990: An Encyclopedia* (1992)

Levy, Leonard, Kenneth W. Karst, and Dennis J. Mahoney, eds., *The Encyclopedia of the American Constitution*, 4 vols (1986)

Nelson, William E. and John P. Reid, *The Literature of American Legal History* (1985)

Nowak, John E. and Ronald D. Rotunda, *Constitutional Law*, 4th ed. (1991)

Peltason, J. W., *Understanding the Constitution* (1994)

Pritchett, C. Herman, *The American Constitution*, 3rd, ed. (1977)

Tribe, Laurence H., *American Constitutional Law*, 2nd. ed. (1988)

Urofsy, Melvin I. and Paul Finkleman, eds., *Documents of American Constitutional and Legal History*, 2 vols (2001)

Vile, John R., *Encyclopedia of Constitutional Amendments, Proposed Amendments, and Amending Issues, 1789–1995* (1996)

American Political and Constitutional Development

Ackerman, Bruce, *Private Property and the Constitution* (1977)

Adler, David G., ed., *The Constitution and the Conduct of American Foreign Policy* (1996)

Aldrich, John, *Why Parties? The Origin and Transformation of Political Parties in America* (1995)

Beard, Charles A., *An Economic Interpretation of the Constitution* (1935)

Belz, Herman, *A Living Constitution or Fundamental Law? American Constitutionalism in Historical Perspective* (1998)

Bensel, Richard Franklin, *Sectionalism and American Political Development, 1880–1980* (1984)

Benson, Paul R., Jr., *The Supreme Court and the Commerce Clause, 1937–1970* (1970)

Best, Judith A., *A Choice of the People? Debating the Electoral College* (1996)

Bickel, Alexander M. and Benno C. Schmidt, Jr., *History of the Supreme Court of the United States*, vol 9, *The Judiciary and Responsible Government, 1910–1921* (1984)

Bland, Randall W., *The Black Robe and the Bald Eagle: The Supreme Court and Foreign Police of the United States, 1789–1961* (1999)

Bloomfield, Maxwell, *Peaceful Revolution: Constitutional Change and American Culture from Progressivism to the New Deal* (2000)

Brandwein, Pamela, *Reconstructing Reconstruction: The Supreme Court and the Production of Historical Truth* (1999)

Bruchey, Stuart, *The Wealth of a Nation: The Economic History of the United States* (1989)

Campbell, Ballard C., *The Growth of American Government: Governance from the Cleveland Era to the Present* (1995)

Chambers, William and Walter Dean Burnham, eds., *The American Party System* (1975)

Chandler, Jr., Alfred D., *The Railroads: The Nation's First Big Business* (1965)

Chandler, Ralph Clark, ed., *The Centennial History of the American Administrative State* (1987)

Conkin, Paul K., *FDR and the Origins of the Welfare State* (1967)

Crosskey, W. W. and William Jeffrey, Jr., *Politics and the Constitution in the History of the United States* (1980)

Currie, David P. *The Constitution and the Supreme Court, 1789–1986*, 2 vols. (1990)

Davis, David Brion, *The Boisterous Sea of Liberty: A Documentary History of America from Discovery Through the Civil War* (1998)

———, *The Problem of Slavery in the Age of Revolution, 1770–1823* (1975)

Degler, Carl N., *Out of Our Past: Forces That Shaped Modern America* (1984)

De Rosa, Marshall L., *The Politics of Dissolution: The Quest for National Identity and the American Civil War* (1998)

De Tocqueville, Alexis, *Democracy in America*, 2 vols (Vintage ed., 1954)

Dulles, Foster and Melvyn Dubofsky, *Labor in America, a History*, 4th ed. (1984)

Dunne, Gerald T., *Monetary Decisions of the Supreme Court* (1960)

Eisner, Marc Allen, *Regulatory Politics in Transition* (1993)

Ericson, David F., *The Shaping of American Liberalism: The Debates over Ratification, Nullification, and Slavery* (1993)

Ericson, David F. and Louisa Bertch Green, eds., *The Liberal Tradition American Politics: Reassessing the Legacy of American Liberalism* (1999)

Fairman, Charles, *History of the Supreme Court of the United States*, vols 6–7, *Reconstruction and Reunion* (1971, 1987)

Farber, Daniel A. and Suzanna Sherry, *A History of the American Constitution* (1990)

Finkelman, Paul and Stephen E. Gottlieb, eds., *Toward a Usable Past: Liberty under State Constitutions* (1991)

Firmage, Edward B., *To Chain the Dogs of War: The War Power of Congress in History and Law* (1989)

Fiss, Owen M., *History of the Supreme Court of the United States*, vol 8, *Troubled Beginnings of the Modern State, 1888–1910* (1993)

Frankfurter, Felix, *The Commerce Clause Under Marshall, Taney and Waite* (1937)

Freehling, William W., *The Road to Disunion: Secessionists at Bay, 1776–1854* (1990)

Friedman, Lawrence M., *A History of American Law* (1973)

Friedman, Lawrence M. and Harry N. Scheiber, *American Law and the Constitutional Order: Historical Perspectives* (1992)

Gates, John B., *The Supreme Court and Partisan Realignment: A Macro- and Microlevel Perspective* (1992)

Gerhardt, Michael J., *The Federal Impeachment Process: A Constitutional and Historical Analysis* (1996)

Goebel, Julius Jr., *History of the Supreme Court of the United States*, vol 1, *Antecedents and Beginnings to 1801* (1971)

Gordon, John Steele, *Hamilton's Blessing: The Extraordinary Life and Times of Our National Debt* (1997)

Greenstone, J. David, *The Lincoln Persuasion: Remaking American Liberalism* (1993)

Haines, Charles Grove, *The American Doctrine of Judicial Supremacy* (1932)

Hall, Kermit L., *The Magic Mirror: Law in American History* (1989)

Hammond, Bray, *Banks and Politics in America from the Revolution to the Civil War* (1957)

Hardaway, Robert M., *The Electoral College and the Constitution: The Case for Preserving Federalism* (1994)

Haskins, George L. and Herbert A. Johnson, *History of the Supreme Court of the United States*, vol 2, *Foundations of Power: John Marshall, 1801–1815* (1981)

Hickok, Eugene W., Jr. and Gary L. McDowell, *Our Peculiar Security: The Written Constitution and Limited Government* (1993)

Horwitz, Morton J., *The Transformation of American Law, 1780–1860* (1977)

Hovencamp, Herbert, *Enterprise and American Law, 1836–1937* (1991)

Howe, Daniel Walker, *The Political Culture of the American Whigs* (1979)

Huntington, Samuel P., *American Politics: The Promise of Disharmony* (1981)

Hurst, J. Willard, *A Legal History of Money in the United States* (1973)

———, *Law and the Conditions of Freedom in Nineteenth Century United States* (1956)

Hyman, Harold and Wiecek, William, *Equal Justice Under Law: Constitutional Development, 1835–1875* (1982)

Jacoby, Sanford, *Modern Manors: Welfare Capitalism since the New Deal* (1997)

Kammen, Michael, *A Machine That Would Go by Itself: The Constitution in American Culture* (1987)

Karl, Barry D., *The Uneasy State: The United States from 1915 to 1945* (1983)

Keller, Morton, *Regulating a New Society: Public Policy and Social Change in America, 1900–1933* (1994)

———, *Regulating a New Economy: Public Policy and Economic Change in America, 1900–1933* (1996)

Kelly, Alfred H., Winfred A. Harbison, and Herman Belz, *The American Constitution, Its Origins and Development*, 2 vols, 7th ed. (1991)

Knupfer, Peter B., *The Union As It Is: Constitutional Unionism and Sectional Compromise, 1787–1861* (1991)

Koistinen, Paul A. C., *Mobilizing for Modern War: The Political Economy of American Warfare, 1865–1919* (1997)

Kurland, Philip B., *Politics, the Constitution, and the Warren Court* (1970)

Kyvig, David E., *Explicit and Authentic Acts: Amending the United States Constitution, 1776–1995* (1996)

Levin, Daniel Lessard, *Representing Popular Sovereignty: The Constitution in American Political Culture* (1999)

Levinson, Sanford, ed., *Responding to Imperfection: The Theory and Practice of Constitutional Amendment* (1995)

Lipset, Seymour Martin, *The First New Nation* (1963)

———, *American Exceptionalism: A Double-Edged Sword* (1996)

Lively, Donald E., *Foreshadows of the Law: Supreme Court Dissents and Constitutional Development* (1992)

Longley, Lawrence D. and Neil R. Pierce, *The Electoral College Primer* (1996)

Lowi, Theodore J., *The End of Liberalism: Ideology, Power, and the Crisis of Public Authority* (1968, rev. ed., 1979)

Lynd, Staughton, *Class Conflict, Slavery, and the U. S. Constitution* (1967)

Mason, Alpheus T., *The Supreme Court from Taft to Burger* (1979)

Mayer, George H., *The Republican Party, 1854–1964* (1964)

McClosky, Robert G., *The Modern Supreme Court* (1972)

McCraw, Thomas K., *Prophets of Regulation* (1984)

McDonald, Forrest, *A Constitutional History of the United States* (1982)

———, *States Rights and the Union: Imperium in Imperio, 1776–1876* (2000)

Miller, Arthur Selwyn, *The Supreme Court and American Capitalism* (1968)

Moore, Wayne D., *Constitutional Rights and Powers of the People* (1998)

Morgan, Iwan W., *Beyond the Liberal Consensus: A Political History of the United States Since 1965* (1995)

Murphy, Paul L., *The Constitution in Crisis Times, 1918–1969* (1972)

Nardulli, Peter F., ed., *The Constitution and American Political Development: An Institutional Perspective* (1992)

Nedelsky, Jennifer, *Private Property and the Limits of American Constitutionalism* (1991)

Nelson, William E., *The Roots of American Bureaucracy, 1830–1900* (1982)

Nieman, Donald G., ed., *The Constitution, Law, and American Life: Critical Aspects of the Nineteenth Century Experience* (1992)

———, *Promises to Keep: African Americans and the Constitutional Order, 1776 to the Present*

Noble, Charles, *Welfare As We Know It: A Political History of the American Welfare State* (1997)

Orren, Karen, *Belated Feudalism: Labor, the Law, and Liberal Development in the United States* (1991)

Patterson, James T., *Grand Expectations: The United States, 1945–1974* (1996)

Powell, H. Jefferson, *The Constitution and the Attorneys General* (1998)

Richards, Michael P., *The Ferocious Engine of Democracy: A History of the American Presidency*, 2 vols (1995)

Robertson, David Brian, *Capital, Labor, and the State: The Battle for American Labor Markets from the Civil War to the New Deal* (2000)

Rohr, John A., *To Run a Constitution: The Legitimacy of the Administrative State* (1986)

Rosenbloom, David, *Federal Service and the Constitution: The Development of the Public Employment Relationship* (1971)

Ross, William G., *A Muted Fury: Populists, Progressives, and Labor Unions Confront the Courts, 1890–1937* (1993)

Rutland, Robert, *The Democrats from Jefferson to Carter* (1979)

Scalia, Laura, *America's Jeffersonian Experiment: Remaking State Constitutions, 1820–1850* (1999)

Schram, Peter W. and Bradford Wilson, eds., American Political Parties and Constitutional Politics (1993)

Schudson, Michael, *The Good Citizen: A History of American Civic Life* (1998)

Schwartz, Bernard, *A History of the Supreme Court* (1993)

———, *The Warren Court: A Retrospective* (1996)

Sellers, M. N. S., *American Republicanism: Roman Ideology in the United States Constitution* (1994)

Semonche, John E., *Keeping the Faith: A Cultural History of the U. S. Supreme Court* (1998)

Shafer, Byron E., ed., *The End of Realignment? Interpreting American Electoral Eras* (1991)

Sherry, Michael S., *In the Shadow of War: The United States since the 1930s* (1995)

Shipan, Charles R., *Designing Judicial Review: Interest Groups, Congress, and Communications Policy* (1997)

Skowronek, Stephen, *The Politics Presidents Make: Leadership from John Adams to George Bush* (1993)

Smith, Rogers M., *Civic Ideals: Conflicting Visions of Citizenship in U.S. History* (1997)

Stephenson, Jr., Donald Grier, *Campaigns and the Court: The U.S. Supreme Court in Presidential Elections* (1999)

Stoner, Jr., James R., *Common Law and Liberal Theory: Coke, Hobbes, and the Origins of American Constitutionalism* (1992)

Swift, Elaine K., *The Making of an American Senate: Reconstitutive Change in Congress, 1787–1841* (1996)

Swindler, William F., *Court and Constitution in the Twentieth Century*, 2 vols (1969, 1970)

Swisher, Carl B., *American Constitutional Development* (1954)

———, *History of the Supreme Court of the United States*, vol 5, *The Taney Period, 1836–1864* (1974)

Tulis, Jeffrey K., *The Rhetorical Presidency* (1987)

Tushnet, Mark V., *The Warren Court in Historical Perspective* (1993)

Urofsky, Melvin, *A March of Liberty* (1988)

Vile, John R., *Rewriting the United States Constitution: An Examination of Proposals from Reconstruction to the Present* (1991)

Vose, Clement E., *Constitutional Change: Amendment Politics and Supreme Court Litigation Since 1900* (1972)

Waldstreicher, David, *In the Midst of Perpetual Fetes: The Making of American Nationalism, 1776–1820* (1997)

Warren, Charles, *The Supreme Court in United States History* (1922)

Weiss, Thomas and Donald Schaefer, eds., *American Economic Development in Historical Perspective* (1994)

Whaples, Robert and Dianne C. Betts., eds., *Historical Perspectives on the American Economy: Selected Readings* (1995)

White, G. Edward, *The American Judicial Tradition: Profiles of Leading American Judges* 2nd ed. (1988)

———, *History of the Supreme Court of the United States*, vols 3–4: *The Marshall Court and Cultural Change, 1815–1835* (1988)

———, *Intervention and Detachment: Essays in Legal History and Jurisprudence* (1994)

Wiebe, Robert H., *Self-Rule: A Cultural History of American Democracy* (1995)

Wiecek, William M., *The Lost World of Classical Legal Thought: Law and Ideology in America, 1886–1997* (1998)

———, *Constitutional Development in a Modernizing Society: The United States, 1803–1917* (1985)

———, *The Sources of Anti-Slavery Constitutionalism in America, 1760–1848* (1977)

Wills, Garry, *A Necessary Evil: A History of American Distrust of Government* (1999)

Wilson, Bradford and Ken Matsugi, eds., *The Supreme Court and American Constitutionalism*, (1998)

Witte, John F., *The Politics and Development of the Federal Income Tax* (1985)

Wright, Benjamin F., *The Contract Clause of the Constitution* (1938)

Wright, Gavin, *The Political Economy of the Cotton South: Households, Markets, and Wealth in the Nineteenth Century* (1978)

Zieger, Robert, *American Workers, American Unions, 1920–1985* (1986)

Constitutional Theory and Interpretation

Ackerman, Bruce, *We the People: Foundations* (1991)

———, *We the People: Transformations* (1998)

Agresto, John, *The Supreme Court and Constitutional Democracy* (1984)

Anastaplo, George, *The Amendments to the Constitution: An Interpretation* (1995)

Arkes, Hadley, *The Return of George Sutherland: Restoring a Jurisprudence of Natural Rights* (1994)

———, *Beyond the Constitution* (1990)

Baker, Thomas E., *The Most Wonderful Work . . . : Our Constitution Interpreted* (1996)

Barber, Sotirios A., *On What the Constitution Means* (1984)

———, *The Constitution of Judicial Power* (1993)

Berger, Raoul, *Government by Judiciary* (1977)

Berns, Walter, *Taking the Constitution Seriously* (1987)

Bickel, Alexander M., *The Least Dangerous Branch* (1962)

———, *The Morality of Consent* (1975)

Black, Hugo, *A Constitutional Faith* (1968)

Bobbit, Philip, *Constitutional Fate* (1984)

Bork, Robert, *The Tempting of America* (1989)

Brandon, Mark E., *Free in the World: American Slavery and Constitutional Failure* (1998)

Brisbin, Jr., Richard A., *Justice Antonin Scalia and the Conservative Revival* (1997)

Burgess, Susan A., *Contest for Constitutional Authority* (1992)

Carter, Leif, *Contemporary Constitutional Lawmaking: The Supreme Court and the Art of Politics* (1985)

Choper, Jesse H., *The Supreme Court and the Political Branches: Judicial Review in the National Political Process: A Functional Reconsideration of the Role of the Supreme Court* (1980)

Clayton, Cornell and Howard Gillman, eds., *The Supreme Court in American Politics: New Institutionalist Interpretations* (1999)

Conant, Michael, *The Constitution and the Economy: Objective Theory and Critical Commentary* (1991)

Couter, Robert D., *The Strategic Constitution* (2000)

Dworkin, Ronald, *Taking Rights Seriously* (1977)

Edelman, Martin, *Democratic Theories and the Constitution* (1984)

Ely, John Hart, *Democracy and Distrust: A Theory of Judicial Review* (1980)

_____, *On Constitutional Ground* (1996)

Franck, Matthew J., *Against the Imperial Judiciary: The Supreme Court v. the Sovereignty of the People* (1996)

Gerber, Scott Douglas, *To Secure These Rights: the Declaration of Independence and Constitutional Interpretation* (1995)

Gerhardt, Michael, et at., *Constitutional Theory: Arguments and Perspectives* (2000)

Goldstein, Leslie Friedman, *In Defense the Text* (1991)

Goldwin, Robert A. and Licht, Robert A., eds., *The Spirit of the Constitution: Five Conversations* (1990)

Gordon, David, ed., *Secession, State, and Liberty* (1998)

Grasso, Kenneth L. and Cicelia Rodriguez Castillo, eds., *Liberty Under Law: American Constitutionalism, Yesterday, Today, and Tomorrow* (1997)

Griffin, Stephen M., *American Constitutionalism: From Theory to Politics* (1996)

Hardin, Russell, *Liberalism, Constitutionalism and Democracy,* (1999)

Harris II, William F., *The Interpretable Constitution* (1993)

Harwood, Sterling, *Judicial Activism, A Restrained Defense,* rev. ed. (1996)

Hoffman, Daniel N., *Our Elusive Constitution: Silences, Paradoxes, Priorities* (1997)

Jacobson, Gary, *Pragmatism, Statesmanship, and the Supreme Court* (1977)

_____, *The Supreme Court and the Decline of Constitutional Aspiration* (1984)

Jaffa, Harry, *Original Intent and the Framers of the Constitution* (1994)

Kahn, Paul W., *The Reign of Law:* Marbury v. Madison *and the Construction of America* (1997)

_____, *Legitimacy and History: Self-Government in American Constitutional Theory* (1993),

Kahn, Ronald, *The Supreme Court and Constitutional Theory, 1953–1993* (1994)

Kalman, Laura, *The Strange Case of Legal Liberalism* (1996)

Ketcham, Ralph, *Framed for Posterity: The Enduring Philosophy of the Constitution* (1993)

Keynes, Edward, *Liberty, Property, and Privacy: Toward a Jurisprudence of Substantive Due Process* (1996)

Kreml, William P., *The Constitutional Divide: The Public and Private Sectors in American Law* (1997)

Lamb, Charles, *Supreme Court Activism and Restraint* (1982)

Levinson, Sanford, *Constitutional Faith* (1988)

Levy, Leonard, *Original Intent and the Framers' Constitution* (1988)

Lewis, Frederick, *The Context of Judicial Activism: Endurance of the Warren Court Legacy in a Conservative Age* (1999)

Lipkin, Robert J., *Constitutional Revolutions: Pragmatism and the Role of Judicial Review in American Constitutionalism* (2000)

Maltz, Earl M., *Rethinking Constitutional Law: Originalism, Interventionism, and the Politics of Judicial Review* (1994)

Mansfield, Jr., Harvey C., *America's Constitutional Soul* (1991)

McCann, Michael W. and Gerald L. Houseman, eds., *Judging the Constitution: Critical Essays on Judicial Lawmaking* (1989)

McClellan, James, *Joseph Story and the American Constitution: A Study in Political and Legal Thought* (1971)

Moore, Wayne D., *Constitutional Rights and the Powers of the People* (1996)

Nagel, Robert F., *Constitutional Cultures: The Mentality and Consequences of Judicial Review* (1989)

_____, *Judicial Power and the American Character: Censoring Ourselves in an Anxious Age* (1994)

Peretti, Terri Jennings, *In Defense of a Political Court* (1999)

Perry, Michael, *The Constitution and the Courts: Law or Politics* (1994)

Powe, Jr., Lucas A., *The Warren Court and American Politics* (2000)

Redish, Martin H., *The Constitution as Political Structure* (1995)

Richards, David A. J., *Conscience and the Constitution: History, Theory, and Law of the Reconstruction Amendments* (1993)

Scalia, Antonin, *A Matter of Interpretation: Federal Courts and the Law* (1997)

Schambra, William A., ed., *As Far As Republican Principles Will Admit: Essays by Martin Diamond* (1992)

Schultz, David A. and Christopher E. Smith, *The Jurisprudential Vision of Justice Antonin Scalia* (1996)

Smith, Christopher, *Justice Antonin Scalia and the Supreme Court: The Conservative Moment* (1993)

Smith, Rogers, *Liberalism and American Constitutional Law* (1985)

Smith, Steven D., *The Constitution and the Pride of Reason* (1998)

Snowiss, Sylvia, *Judicial Review and the Law of the Constitution* (1990)

Sosin, J. M., *The Aristocracy of the Long Robe: The Origins of Judicial Review in America* (1989)

Strum, Phillipa, *The Supreme Court and Political Questions,* (1974)

Sunderland, Lane V., *Popular Government and the Supreme Court: Securing the Public and Private Rights* (1996)

Sunstein, Cass R., *The Partial Constitution* (1993)

_____, *One Case at a Time: Judicial Minimalism on the Supreme Court* (1999)

Tribe, Laurence, *Constitutional Choices* (1985)

Tribe, Laurence H. and Michael C. Dorf, *On Reading the Constitution* (1991)

Tushnet, Mark, *Red, White, and Blue: A Critical Analysis of Constitutional Law* (1988)

_____, *Taking the Constitution away from the Courts* (1999)

Van Sickel, Robert W., *Not a Particularly Different Voice: The Jurisprudence of Sandra Day O'Connor* (1998)

Vile, M. J. C., *Constitutionalism and the Separation of Powers* (1967)

Wellington, Harry H., Interpreting the Constitution: *The Supreme Court and the Process of Adjudication* (1990)

Whittington, Keith E., *Constitutional Interpretation: Textual Meaning, Original Intent and Judicial Review*

_____, *Constitutional Construction: Divided Powers and Constitutional Meaning* (1999)

Wolfe, Christopher, *The Rise of Judicial Review: From Constitutional Interpretation to Judge-Made Law* (1986)

_____, *Judicial Activism* (1991)

The Supreme Court: The Institution and Its Work

Abraham, Henry, *Justices and Presidents: A Political History of Appointments to the Supreme Court,* 3rd ed. (1992)

Atkinson, David N., *Leaving the Bench: Supreme Court Justices at the End* (1999)

Barnum, David G., *The Supreme Court and American Democracy* (1993)

Baum, Lawrence, *The Supreme Court* (1998)

Casper, Gerhard and Richard A. Posner, *The Workload of the Supreme Court* (1976)

Clayton, Cornell W. and Howard Gillman, eds., *Supreme Court Decision Making: New Institutional Approaches* (1999)

Cooper, Philip J., *Battles on the Bench: Conflicts Inside the Supreme Court* (1995)

Cooper, Phillip J. and Howard Ball, *The United States Supreme Court: From the Inside Out* (1996)

Danelski, David J., *A Supreme Court Justice Is Appointed* (1964)

Davis, Richard, *Decisions and Images: The Supreme Court and the Press* (1994)

Dickson, Del, ed., *The Supreme Court in Conference* (2001)

Epstein, Lee, *Conservatives in Court* (1985)

Epstein, Lee and Jack Knight, *The Choices Justices Make* (1998)

Flax, Jane, *The American Dream in Black and White: The Clarence Thomas Hearings* (1998)

Franck, Matthew and Richard Stevens, eds., *Sober as a Judge: The Supreme Court and Republican Liberty* (1999)

Greenberg, Ellen, *The Supreme Court Explained* (1997)

Halpern, Stephen C. and Charles M. Lamb, eds., *Supreme Court Activism and Restraint* (1982)

Maltese, John Anthony, *The Selling of Supreme Court Nominees* (1995)

Marshall, Thomas, *Public Opinion and the Supreme Court* (1989)

Massaro, John, *Supremely Political: The Role of Ideology and Presidential Management in Unsuccessful Supreme Court Nominations* (1990)

McGuire, Kevin T., *The Supreme Court Bar: Legal Elites in the Washington Community* (1993)

Murphy, Walter L., *Elements of Judicial Strategy* (1964)

O'Brien, David M., *Storm Center: The Supreme Court in American Politics* (1986)

Pacelle, Richard L., *The Transformation of the Supreme Court's Agenda: From the New Deal to the Reagan Administration* (1991)

Perry, Barbara A., *A "Representative" Court? The Impact of Race, Religion and Gender on Appointments* (1991)

_____, *The Priestly Tribe: The Supreme Court's Image in the American Mind* (1999)

Perry, Jr., H. W., *Deciding to Decide: Agenda Setting in the United States Supreme Court* (1991)

Rehnquist, William H., *The Supreme Court: How It Was, How It Is* (1987)

Schwartz, Bernard, *How the Supreme Court Decides Cases* (1996)

Segal, Jeffrey A. and Spaeth, Harold J., *The Supreme Court and the Attitudinal Model* (1993)

Silverstein, Mark, *Judicious Choices: The New Politics of Supreme Court Confirmations* (1994)

Smolla, Rodney and Neal Devins, eds., *A Year in the Life of the Supreme Court* (1995)

Spaeth, Harold J. and Saul Brenner, eds., *Studies in United States Supreme Court Behavior* (1990)

Spaeth, Harold J. and Jeffrey A. Segal, *Majority Rule or Minority Will: Adherence to Precedent on the U. S. Supreme Court* (1999)

Steamer, Robert J., *Chief Justice: Leadership and the Supreme Court* (1986)

Stearns, Maxwell L., *Constitutional Process: A Social Choice Analysis of Supreme Court Decision Making* (2000)

Sunstein, Cass R., *One Case at a Time: Judicial Minimalism on the Supreme Court* (1999)

Tribe, Laurence, *God Save This Honorable Court: How the Choice of Supreme Court Justices Shapes Our History* (1988)

Wasby, Stephen J., *The Supreme Court in the Federal Judicial System* (1993)

Judicial Biography

Hugo L. Black:

Ball, Howard, *Hugo L. Black: Cold Steel Warrior* (1996)

Magee, James, *Mr. Justice Black, Absolutist on the Court* (1980)

Newman, Roger K, *Hugo Black, A Biography* (1994)

Louis D. Brandeis:

Baker, Leonard, *Brandeis and Frankfurter: A Dual Biography* (1986)

Mason, Alpheus T., *Brandeis—A Free Man's Life* (1946)

Paper, Lewis J., *Brandeis* (1983)

Strum, Philippa, *Louis D. Brandeis: Justice for the People* (1984)

Benjamin Cardozo:

Kaufman, Andrew L., *Cardozo* (1998)

Polenberg, Eric, *The World of Benjamin Cardozo* (1997)

Posner, Richard A., *Cardozo: A Study in Reputation* (1990)

Salmon P. Chase:

Blue, Frederick J., *Salmon P. Chase: A Life in Politics* (1987)

Hyman, Harold M., *The Reconstruction Justice of Salmon P. Chase* (1997)

Niven, John, *Salmon P. Chase, A Biography* (1995)

David Davis:

King, William L., *Lincoln's Manager: David Davis* (1960)

Douglas, William O.:

Simon, James F., *Independent Journey: The Life of William O. Douglas* (1990)

Stephen J. Field:

Kens, Paul, *Justice Stephen Field: Shaping American Liberty from the Gold Rush to the Gilded Age* (1997)

Swisher, Carl B., *Stephen J. Field: Craftsman of the Law* (1969)

Abe Fortas:

Kalman, Laura, *Abe Fortas: A Biography* (1990)

Murphy, Bruce Allen, *Fortas: The Rise and Ruin of a Supreme Court Justice* (1988)

Felix Frankfurter:

Baker, Leonard, *Brandeis and Frankfurter: A Dual Biography* (1986)

Baker, Liva, *Felix Frankfurter* (1969)

Urofsky, Melvin I., *Felix Frankfurter: Judicial Restraint and Individual Liberties* (1991)

Melville W. Fuller:

King, Willard. L., *Melville Weston Fuller: Chief Justice of the United States, 1888–1910* (1967)

Arthur Goldberg:

Stebenne, David, *Arthur J. Goldberg: New Deal Liberal* (1996)

John Marshall Harlan, I:

Beth, Loren P., *John Marshall Harlan: The Last Whig Justice* (1992)

Lathan, F. B., *The Great Dissenter—John Marshall Harlan* (1970)

Yarbrough, Tinsley E., *Judicial Enigma: The First Justice Harlan* (1995)

John Marshall Harlan, II:

Yarbrough, Tinsley E., *John Marshall Harlan: Great Dissenter of the Warren Court* (1992)

Oliver Wendell Holmes, Jr.:

Alschular, Albert, *Law Without Values: The Life, Work, and Legacy of Justice Holmes* (2000)

Baker, Liva, *The Justice from Beacon Hill: The Life and Times of Oliver Wendell Holmes* (1991)

Bowen, Catherine Drinker, *A Yankee from Olympus: Justice Holmes and His Family* (1944)

Howe, Mark De Wolfe, *Justice Oliver Wendell Holmes: The Proving Years, 1870–1882* (1963)

_____, *Justice Oliver Wendell Holmes: The Shaping Years, 1841–1870* (1957)

Novick, Sheldon, *Honorable Justice: The Life of Oliver Wendell Holmes* (1989)

White, G. Edward, *Justice Oliver Wendell Holmes: Law and the Inner Self* (1993)

Charles Evans Hughes:

Pusey, Merlo J., *Charles Evans Hughes* (1951)

John Jay:

Johnson, Herbert A., *John Jay, 1745–1829* (1970)

William Johnson:

Morgan, Donald G., *Justice William Johnson, the First Dissenter: The Career and Constitutional Philosophy of a Jeffersonian Judge* (1954)

John Marshall:

Baker, Leonard, *John Marshall: A Life in Law* (1974)

Beveridge, Albert. J., *The Life of John Marshall* (1916)

Johnson, Herbert A., *The Chief Justiceship of John Marshall, 1801–1835* (1997)

Smith, Jean Edward, *John Marshall: Definer of a Nation* (1996)

Stites, Francis N., *John Marshall, Defender of the Constitution* (1981)

Thurgood Marshall:

Rowan, Carl T., *Dream Makers, Dream Breakers: The World of Justice Thurgood Marshall* (1993)

Tushnet, Mark V., *Making Constitutional Law: Thurgood Marshall and the Supreme Court, 1961–1991* (1997)

Williams, Juan, *Thurgood Marshall: American Revolutionary* (1998)

Samuel F. Miller:

Fairman, Charles, *Mr. Justice Miller and the Supreme Court, 1862–1890* (1939)

Frank Murphy:

Fine, Sidney, *Frank Murphy*, 3 vols (1974–1985)

Howard, J. Woodford, *Mr. Justice Murphy: A Political Biography* (1968)

Sandra Day O'Connor:

Maveety, Nancy, *Justice Sandra Day O'Connor: Strategist on the Supreme Court* (1996)

Lewis F. Powell:

Jeffries, John C., *Justice Lewis F. Powell, Jr.* (1994)

Harlan F. Stone

Konefsky, S. J., *Chief Justice Stone and the Supreme Court* (1946)

Mason, Alpheus T., *Harlan Fiske Stone: Pillar of the Law* (1956)

Joseph Story:

Dunne, Gerald T., *Justice Joseph Story and the Rise of the Supreme Court* (1970)

Newmyer, R. Kent, *Supreme Court Justice Joseph Story: Statesman of the Old Republic* (1985)

George Sutherland:

Paschal, Joel Francis, *Mr. Justice Sutherland, A Man Against the State* (1951)

William Howard Taft:

Anderson, Judith Icke, *William Howard Taft: An Intimate History* (1981)

Mason, Alpheus T., *William Howard Taft: Chief Justice* (1965)

Pringle, H., *The Life and Times of William Howard Taft* (1939)

Roger B. Taney:

Lewis, Walker, *Without Fear of Favor: A Biography of Chief Justice Roger Brooke Taney* (1965)

Swisher, Carl B., *Roger B. Taney* (1935)

Morrison R. Waite:

Magrath, C. Peter, *Morrison R. Waite: The Triumph of Character* (1963)

Earl Warren:

Cray, Ed, *Chief Justice: A Biography of Earl Warren* (1997)

Katcher, L., *Earl Warren: A Political Biography* (1967)

Pollack, J. H., Earl Warren: *The Judge Who Changed America* (1979)

White, G. Edward, *Earl Warren: A Public Life* (1982)

Byron R. White:

Hutchinson, Dennis J., *The Man Who Was Whizzer White* (1998)

Edward D. White:

Highsaw, Robert Baker, *Edward Douglass White: Defender of the Conservative Faith* (1981)

INDEX OF CASES

Cases excerpted are in **boldface.**

Ableman v. Booth, 62 U.S. 506 (1859), 139, **170–172**

Abrams v. United States, 250 U.S. 616 (1919), 233

Adair v. United States, 208 U.S. 161 (1908), 233, 238

Adkins v. Children's Hospital, 261 U.S. 525 (1923), 251–252, **289–293,** 310, 312

Alabama v. King & Boozer, 314 U.S. 1 (1941), **488**

Alden v. Maine, 527 U.S. 706 (1999), 483–484, **542–548**

Allgeyer v. Louisiana, 165 U.S. 578 (1897), 231, 232

Allied Structural Steel Co. v. Spannaus, 438 U.S. 234 (1978), 562

American Insurance Co. v. Cantor, 1 Pet. 511 (1828), 75, 130

American Steel Foundaries v. Tri-City Central Trades Council, 257 U.S. 184 (1921), 252

Amistad, The (see United States v. The Amistad)

Anderson v. Dunn, 6 Wheat. 24 (1821), 383

Antelope, The, 10 Wheat. 66 (1825), 127

Ashwander v. Tennessee Valley Authority, 297 U.S. 288 (1936), 309, 388

Bailey v. Drexel Furniture Co., 259 U.S. 20 (1922), 251, **288–289,** 309

Bailey v. Richardson, 341 U.S. 918 (1951), 368

Baker v. Carr, 369 U.S. 186 (1962), 93, 387, **424–429**

Barenblatt v. United States, 360 U.S. 109 (1959), 385

Barron v. Baltimore, 32 U.S. 243 (1833), 84, 88, 90, **116–117,** 191, 563

Belmont (see United States v. Belmont)

Berman v. Parker, 348 U.S. 26 (1954), 563

Bibb v. Navaho Frieght Lines, 386 U.S. 976 (1959), 492

Board of Trustees of University of Alabama v. Garrett, 121 S.Ct. 955 (2001), 485

Bowsher v. Synar, 478 U.S. 714 (1986), 380, **447–452**

Brewster (see United States v. Brewster)

Brecht v. Abraham, 507 U.S. 619 (1993), 492

Brown v. Allen, 344 U.S. 443 (1953), 392

Brown v. Board of Education, 347 U.S. 483 (1954), 229

Brown v. Maryland, (1827), 12 Wheat 419 (1827), 496

Buckley v. Valeo (1976), 424 U.S. 1 (1976), 365

Bunting v. Oregon, 243 U.S. 426 (1917), 246, 251

Burbank, City of v. Lockheed Air Terminal, 411 U.S. 624 (1973), 486

Bush v. Gore, ___ U.S. ___ (2000), 390–392, **472–478**

Butler (see United States v. Butler)

Carolene Products Co. (see United States v. Carolene Products Co.)

Carter v. Carter Coal Co., 298 U.S. 238 (1936), 309–310, **326–330,** 379

Causby (see United States v. Causby)

Champion v. Ames, 188 U.S. 321 (1903), 243–244, 245, **270–274**

Charles River Bridge v. Warren Bridge, 36 U.S. 420 (1837), 139, 194, 199, 200–201, **212–216,** 564

Chicago, Burlington & Quincy Railroad v. Chicago, 166 U.S. 226, (1897), 253, 563

Chicago, Milwaukee & St. Paul Railway v. Minnesota, 134 U.S. 418 (1890), 234, 237

Child Labor Case, The (see Hammer v. Dagenhart)

Chisholm v. Georgia, 2 U.S. 419, (1793), 72, 73, **97–99**

Cincinnati, New Orleans & Texas Pacific Railway v. Interstate Commerce Commission, 162 U.S. 184 (1896), 234

Cipollone v. Liggett Group, 505 U.S. 346 (1992), 487

City of Boerne v. Flores, 521 U.S. 507 (1997), 388

Civil Rights Cases, The, 109 U.S. 3 (1883), 229

Clinton v. City of New York, 524 U.S. 417 (1998), 381, **468–472**

Clinton v. Jones, 520 U.S. 681 (1997), 370, 377, **464–468**

Cohens v. Virginia, 19 U.S. 264 (1821), 86, 87, **108–110,** 194, 479, 488

Colegrove v. Green, 328 U.S. 459 (1946), 387

Coleman v. Miller, 307 U.S. 433 (1939), 387

Coleman v. Thompson, 501 U.S. 722, (1991), 492

Collector v. Day, 78 U.S. 113, (1871), 487, 488

College Savings Bank v. Florida, 527 U.S. 666 (1999), 484

Commonwealth Edison v. Montana, 453 U.S. 609 (1981), 495

Communist Party v. Subversive Activities Control Board, 367 U.S. 1 (1961), 359

Complete Auto Transit v. Brady, 430 U.S. 274 (1977), 495

Cook v. Gralike, ___ U.S. ___, (2001), 372

Cooley v. Board of Wardens, 53 U.S. 299 (1852), 90, 139, 200, **216–218,** 493

Coppage v. Kansas, 236 U.S. 1, (1915), 234

Cruikshank (see United States v. Cruikshank)

Cummings v. Missouri, 71 U.S. 277 (1867), 158

Curtiss-Wright Corp. (see United States v. Curtiss-Wright Corp.)

Dakota Central Telephone Co. v. South Dakota, 250 U.S. 163 (1919), 248

Dames & Moore v. Regan, 453 U.S. 654 (1981), 364–365, **439–441**

Darby Lumber Co. (see United States v. Darby Lumber Co.)

Dartmouth College v. Woodward, 17 U.S. 517 (1819), 193, 194, 199, **203–206**

Davis v. Bandemer, 478 U.S. 109 (1986), 387

Davis v. Michigan Department of Treasury, 489 U.S. 803 (1989), 488

Dean Milk Co. v. City of Madison, 340 U.S. 349 (1951), 494

DeFunis v. Odegaard, 415 U.S. 312, (1974), 389

Dennis v. United States, 341 U.S. 494 (1951), 359

Dombrowski v. Pfister, 380 U.S. 479 (1967), 491

Dred Scott v. Sandford, 60 U.S. 393 (1857), 81, 135 (map), 136–138, 139, 141, 145, 147, 149, 157, 158, **166–170**

Dunn v. Blaustein, 405 U.S. 330 (1972), 498

Duplex Printing Press v. Deering, 254 U.S. 433, (1921), 251

Duquesne Light Co, v. Barasch, 488 U.S. 299 (1989), 565

Eakin v. Raub, 12 S. & R. 330 (Pa., 1825), **103–104**

Eastland v. United States Servicemen's Fund, 421 U.S. 491 (1975), 385

E. C. Knight Co. (see United States v. E. C. Knight Co.)

E.E.O.C. v. Wyoming, 460 U.S. 226 (1983),

El Paso v. Simmons, 379 U.S. 497 (1965), 561

Energy Reserves Group v. Kansas Power & Light Co., 459 U.S. 400 (1983), 562

Erie Railroad v. Tompkins, 304 U.S. 64 (1938), 199, 490

Estin v. Estin, 334 U.S. 531 (1948), 497

Euclid v. Ambler Realty Co., 272 U.S. 365 (1926), 253, 563

Ex parte (see name of party)

Fairfax's Devisee v. Hunter's Lessee, 7 Cranch 603 (1813), 86

Fay v. Noia, 372 U.S. 391 (1963), 491, 492

Federal Power Commission v. Hope Natural Gas Co., 320 U.S. 551 (1944), 235

Ferguson v. Skrupa, 372 U.S. 726 (1963), 561, **567–568**

First English Evangelical Lutheran Church v. Los Angeles County, 482 U.S. 304 (1987), 565

Flast v. Cohen, 392 U.S. 83 (1968), 389, **429–432**

Fletcher v. Peck, 10 U.S. 87 (1810), 85, 192–193, **202–203**

Florida v. College Savings Bank, 527 U.S. 627 (1999), 484

Frothingham v. Mellon, 262 U.S. 447 (1923), 389

Garcia v. San Antonio Metropolitan Transit Authority, 469 U.S. 528 (1985), 482, **515–520**

Garland, Ex parte, 4 Wall. 333 (1867), 158, 160

Geier v. American Honda Motor Co., 529 U.S. 861 (2000), 486

Georgia v. Stanton, 6 Wall. 50 (1867), 159

Gibbons v. Ogden, 22 U.S. 1 (1824), 87–90, 194, 196–197, **206–211,** 241

Gold Clause Cases, 294 U.S. 240, 317, 330 (1935), 308

Goldwater v. Carter, 444 U.S. 996 (1979), 363

Gravel v. United States, 408 U.S. 606 (1972), 377–378

Graves v. New York ex. rel. O'Keefe, 306 U.S. 466 (1939), 488

Groves v. Slaughter, 15 Pet. 449 (1841), 128, 197

Hammer v. Dagenhart, 247 U.S. 251 (1918), 244, 245, 251, **284–288,** 316

Harlow v. Fitzgerald, 457 U.S. 800 (1982) 376

Hawaii Housing Authority v. Midkiff, 467 U.S. 229 (1984), 563, **575–577**

Hayburn's Case, 2 Dall. 409 (1792) 72

Heart of Atlanta Motel, Inc. v. United States, 379 U.S. 241 (1964), 481, **506–509**

Helvering v. Davis, 301 U.S. 619 (1937), 312

Helvering v. Mountain Producers Corp., 303 U.S. 376 (1938), 487–488

Hepburn v. Griswold, 75 U.S. 603 (1870), 226

Holden v. Hardy, 169 U.S. 366 (1898), 231, 245

Home Building & Loan Association v. Blaisdell, 290 U.S. 398 (1934), 305–306, 307, 308, **319–323,** 561, 562

Hood v. DuMond, 336 U.S. 525 (1949), 496

Houston East and West Texas Railway Co. v. United States (see Shreveport Rate Case)

Hughes v. Oklahoma, 441 U.S. 322 (1979), 496

Humphrey's Executor v. United States, 295 U.S. 602 (1935), 309, 367–368, 380, **402–404**

Hunt v. Washington State Apple Advertising Commission, 432 U.S. 333 (1977), 494

Hutchinson v. Proxmire, 443 U.S. 111 (1979), 378

Hylton v. United States, 3 Dall. 171 (1796), 73, 80, 238

I.C.C. v. Illinois Central Railroad, 215 U.S. 452 (1910), 247

Immigration and Naturalization Service v. Chadha, 462 U.S. 919 (1983), 379–380, **441–447**

In re (see name of party)

Jones v. United States, 526 U. S. 227 (2000), 482

Jones v. Van Zandt, 5 How. 215 (1847), 128–129

Kassel v. Consolidated Freightways, 450 U.S. 662 (1981), 492

Kastigar v. United States, 406 U.S. 441 (1972), 385–386

Katzenbach v. McClung, 379 U.S. 294 (1964), 481

Kentucky v. Dennison, 24 How. 66 (1861), 498

Keystone Bituminous Coal Association v. DeBenedictis, 480 U.S. 470 (1987), 562, 564

Kilbourne v. Thompson, 103 U.S. 168 (1881), 377

Kimel v. Florida Board of Regents, 528 U.S. 62 (2000), 484, **548–553**

Knox v. Lee, 12 Wall. 457 (1871), 226

Korematsu v. United States, 323 U.S. 214 (1944), 357, **407–411**

L. Cohen Grocery Co. (see United States v. L. Cohen Grocery Co.)

License Cases, The, 46 U.S. 504 (1847), 197, 242

Lochner v. New York, 198 U.S. 45 (1905), 225, 231–233, 238, 245, **276–280**

Loewe v. Lawlor, 208 U.S. 275 (1908), 237

Lopez (see United States v. Lopez)

Loretto v. Teleprompter Manhattan CATV Corp., 458 U.S. 419 (1972), 564

Lottery Case, The, (see Champion v. Ames)

Louisville Bank v. Radford, 295 U.S. 555 (1935), 309

Lucas v. South Carolina Coastal Council, 505 U.S. 1003 (1992), 564, **577–580**

Luther v. Borden, 7 How. 1 (1849), 92–93, **117–120,** 159, 194, 386

MacPherson v. Buick, 272 N.Y. 382 (1916) 315

Maine v. Taylor, 477 U.S. 131 (1986), 495, **520–523**

Marbury v. Madison, 5 U.S. 137 (1803), 50, 73, 80–82, 88, **99–103,** 386, 388

Marsh v. Chambers, 463 U.S. 783 (1983), 395

Martin v. Hunter's Lessee, 1 Wheat. 304 (1816), 86, **104–108,** 197, 479, 488

Martin v. Mott, 12 Wheat. 19 (1827), 77

McCardle, Ex parte, 7 U.S. 506 (1869), 159, **179–180**

McCray v. United States, 195 U.S. 27 (1904), 244, 251, **274–276**

McCulloch v. Maryland, 17 U.S. 315 (1819), 81, 86–87, 88, 90, 93, **110–116,** 194, 479, 487

McGrain v. Dougherty, 273 U.S. 135 (1927), 384

Merryman, Ex parte, 17 Fed. Case 9487 (1861), 139, 148–149, 373

Michelin Tire Corp. v. Wages, 423 U.S. 276 (1976), 496

Michigan v. Long, 462 U.S. 1032 (1983), 492, **512–514**

Miller v. Schoene, 276 U.S. 272 (1928), 564

Milligan, Ex parte, 71 U.S. 2 (1866), 149, 158, **174–178**

Minnesota v. Clover Leaf Creamery Co., 449 U.S. 456 (1981), 494–495

Minnesota Rate Cases, 230 U.S. 252 (1913), 247

Mississippi v. Johnson, 4 Wall. 475 (1867), 159, **178–179,** 376

Missouri v. Holland, 252 U.S. 416 (1920), 362–363, **400–401,** 486

Mistretta v. United States, 488 U.S. 361 (1989), 381

Mora v. McNamara, 389 U.S. 934 (1967), 360

Morehead v. New York ex. rel. Tipaldo, 298 U.S. 587 (1935), 310

Morrison (see United States v. Morrison)

Morrison v. Olson, 487 U.S. 654 (1988), 366, 368, 371, 381, **452–458**

Mugler v. Kansas, 123 U.S. 623 (1887), 231

Mulford v. Smith, 307 U.S. 38 (1939), 315

Muller v. Oregon, 208 U.S. 412 (1908), 245, 246, **280–282**

Munn v. Illinois, 94 U.S. 113 (1877), 227–229, 230, 231, 234, 242, 252, **260–264**

Murdoch v. Memphis, 20 Wall. 590 (1873), 492

Myers v. United States, 272 U.S. 52 (1926), 65, 157, 367, 371

National Labor Relations Board v. Jones & Laughlin Steel Corp., 301 U.S. 1 (1937), 312, **337–341**

National League of Cities v. Usery, 426 U.S. 833 (1976), 482

Nebbia v. New York, 291 U.S. 502 (1934), 306–307, 308

New England Power Co. v. New Hampshire, 455 U.S. 331 (1982), 496

New Jersey v. Wilson, 11 U.S. 164 (1812), 193, 227

New York v. Miln, 6 U.S. 102 (1837), 197, **211–212**

New York v. United States, 505 U.S. 144 (1992), 483, 485, **525–531**

Nixon (see U.S. v. Nixon)

Nixon v. Administrator of General Services, 433 U.S. 425 (1977), 375

Nixon v. Fitzgerald, 457 U.S. 731 (1982), 376

Nixon v. Sirica, 487 F.2d. 700 (D.C. Cir., 1973), 375

Nixon v. United States, 506 U.S. 224 (1993), 369

Nollan v. California Coastal Commission, 483 U.S. 825 (1987), 564

Northern Pacific Railway v. North Dakota ex. rel. Langer, 250 U.S. 135 (1919), 248

Northern Securities Co. v. United States, 193 U.S. 197 (1904), 236

Ogden v. Saunders, 25 U.S. 212 (1827), 194–195, 196

Olmstead v. United States, 277 U.S. 438 (1928), 243

Oregon Waste Systems v. Department of Environmental Quality (1994), 496

Osborn v. Bank of United States, 9 Wheat. 738 (1824), 87, 491

Pacific Gas & Electric Co. v. State Energy Resource and Development Commission, 461 U.S. 190 (1983), 486

Pacific States Telephone and Telegraph Co. v. Oregon, 223 U.S. 118 (1912), 387

Palazzolo v. Rhode Island, ___ U.S. ___ (2001), 564

Palko v. United States, 302 U.S. 319 (1937), 314

Panama Refining Co. v. Ryan, 293 U.S. 338 (1935), 243, 307–308, 379

Passenger Cases, The, 48 U.S. 282 (1849), 198

Paul v. Virginia, 8 Wall. 168 (1869), 231

Penn Central Transportation Co. v. New York City, 438 U.S. 104 (1978), 564, **571–575**

Pennsylvania v. Nelson, 350 U.S. 497 (1956), 486, **504–506**

Pennsylvania v. Wheeling and Belmont Bridge Co., 12 How. 518 (1852), 200

Pennsylvania Coal Co. v. Mahon, 260 U.S. 393 (1922), 253

Perez v. United States, 402 U.S. 146 (1971), 481

Permioli v. New Orleans, 44 U.S. 589 (1845), 131

Peters (see United States v. Peters)

Philadelphia v. New Jersey, 437 U.S. 617 (1978), 496, **509–512**

Pink (see United States v. Pink)

Plessy v. Ferguson, 163 U.S. 537 (1896), 229

Pollock v. Farmer's Loan & Trust Co., 158 U.S. 601 (1895), 238, **267–270,** 487

Powell v. McCormick, 395 U.S. 486 (1969), 369, 387, **432–434**

Prigg v. Pennsylvania, 16 Pet. 539 (1842), 128, **164–166**

Printz v. United States, 521 U.S. 898 (1997), 481, 485, **537–542**

Prize Cases, The, 67 U.S. 635 (1863), 147, **172–174**

Puerto Rico v. Branstad, 483 U.S. 219 (1987), 498

Quill Corp. v. North Dakota, 504 U.S. 298 (1992), 495

Railroad Retirement Board v. Alton Railway, 295 U.S. 330 (1935), 308

Reeves v. Stake, 447 U.S. 429 (1980), 496

Reid v. Covert, 354 U.S. 1 (1957), 365

Reno v. Condon, 528 U.S. 141 (2000), 485, **553–555**

Richardson (see United States v. Richardson)

Roe v. Wade, 410 U.S. 113 (1973), 484

Saenz v. Roe, 526 U.S. 489 (1999), 498

Santa Clara v. Southern Pacific, 118 U.S. 394 (1886), 231

Schechter Poultry Corp. v. United States, 295 U.S. 495 (1935), 243, 308, 309, **323–326,** 379

Selective Draft Law Cases, The, 245 U.S. 366 (1918), 77, 248

Seminole Tribe of Florida v. Florida, 517 U.S. 1125 (1996), 483

Shapiro v. Thompson, 394 U.S. 618 (1969), 498

Shreveport Rate Case, The, 234 U.S. 342 (1914), 247, **282–284**

Siebold, Ex parte, 100 U.S. 371 (1879), 366

Silkwood v. Kerr-McGee Corp., 464 U.S. 238 (1984), 487

Sioux Nation of Indians (see United States v. Sioux Nation of Indians)

Slaughterhouse Cases, The, 16 Wall. 36 (1873), 226, 228, 231, **255–260**

Smyth v. Ames, 169 U.S. 466 (1898), 235, 237

Sosna v. Iowa, 419 U.S. 393 (1975), 498

South Carolina v. Baker, 485 U.S. 505 (1988), 488

South Carolina State Highway Dept. v. Barnwell Bros., 303 U.S. 177 (1938), 493–494

South Dakota v. Dole, 483 U.S. 203 (1987), 483, **523–525**

Southern Pacific Co. v. Arizona, 325 U.S. 761 (1945), **500–504**

Springer v. United States, 102 U.S. 586 (1880), 237, 238

Standard Oil v. United States, 221 U.S. 1 (1911), 237

Steel Seizure Case, The (see Youngstown Sheet and Tube Co. v. Sawyer)

Steuart & Bros. v. Bowles, 322 U.S. 398 (1944), 356

Steward Machine Co. v. Davis, 301 U.S. 548 (1937), 312, **341–344,** 483

Stone v. Mississippi, 101 U.S. 814 (1880), 227

Stone v. Powell, 428 U.S. 465 (1976), 492

Strader v. Graham, 10 How. 82 (1851), 129, 137

Sturges v. Crowninshield, 17 U.S. 120 (1819), 193–194

Supreme Court of New Hampshire v. Piper, 470 U.S. 274 (1985), 497

Swift v. Tyson, 16 Pet. 1 (1842), 194, 197, 198, 488–489

Swift & Co. v. United States, 196 U.S. 375 (1905), 237

Texas v. White, 78 U.S. 700 (1869), 159, 161, **181–182**

Toomer v. Witsell, 334 U.S. 385 (1948), 497

Train v. City of New York, 420 U.S. 35 (1975), 373

Truax v. Corrigan, 257 U.S. 312 (1921), 252

Tyler v. Wilkinson, 24 F. Cas. 472 (No. 14,312) (1827), 198

United States v. The Amistad, 40 U.S. 518 (1841), 128

United States v. Belmont, 301 U.S. 324 (1937), **364**

United States v. Brewster, 408 U.S. 501 (1972), 378

United States v. Butler, 297 U.S. 1 (1936), 309, 313, 315, **330–334**

United States v. Carolene Products Co., 304 U.S. 144 (1938), 317, 386

United States v. Causby, 328 U.S. 256 (1946), 564

United States v. Cruikshank, 92 U.S. 542 (1876), 228

United States v. Curtiss-Wright Export Corp., 299 U.S. 304 (1936), 355, **404–407**

United States v. Darby Lumber Co., 312 U.S. 100 (1941), 245, 251, 316, **344–347,** 482

United States v. E. C. Knight Co., 156 U.S. 1 (1895), 236, 237, 238, 245, 253, **264–267,** 309

United States v. L. Cohen Grocery Co., 255 U.S. 81 (1921), 248

United States v. Lopez, 514 U.S. 549 (1995), 481–482, 483, **531–536**

United States v. Morrison, 529 U.S. 598 (2000), 482, **556–558**

United States v. Nixon, 418 U.S. 683 (1974), 375, 383, **434–438**

United States v. Peters, 9 U.S. 115 (1809), 85

United States v. Pink, 315 U.S. 203 (1942), 364

United States v. Richardson, 418 U.S. 166 (1974), 389

United States v. Sioux Nation of Indians, 448 U.S. 371 (1980), 565

United States Steel Corp. v. Multi-State Tax Commission, 434 U.S. 452 (1978), 499

United States Trust Co. v. New Jersey, 431 U.S. 1 (1977), 562, **568–571**

U.S. Term Limits, Inc. v. Thornton, 514 U.S. 779 (1995), 372, **458–464**

Uphaus v. Wyman, 360 U.S. 72 (1959), 486

Vallandigham, Ex parte, 68 U.S. 243 (1864), 149

Virginia v. Tennessee, 148 U.S. 503 (1893), 499

Vlandis v. Kline, 412 U.S. 441 (1973), 498

Wabash, St. Louis & Pacific Railway v. Illinois, 118 U.S. 557 (1886), 234

Ware v. Hylton, 3 U.S. 198 (1796), 72, 85

Watkins v. United States, 354 U.S. 178 (1957), 384–385, **418–424**

West Coast Hotel Co. v. Parrish, 300 U.S. 379 (1937), 233, 252, 312, **334–337**

White v. Massachusetts Council of Construction Employees (1983), 496

Whitney v. Robertson, 124 U.S. 190 (1888), 363

Weiner v. United States, 357 U.S. 349 (1958), 367

West Lynn Creamery v. Healy, 512 U.S. 186 (1994), 495

West River Bridge Co. v. Dix, 6 How. 507 (1848), 194

West Virginia ex rel. Dyer v. Sims, 341 U.S. 22 (1951), 499

Whitney v. California, 274 U.S. 357 (1927), 243

Wickard v. Filburn, 317 U.S. 111 (1942), 316, **347–349**

Williamson v. Lee Optical Co., 348 U.S. 483 (1955), 561, **566–567**

Willson v. Blackbird Creek Marsh Co., 27 U.S. 244 (1829), 197

Wolff Packing Co. v. Kansas Court of Industrial Relations, 262 U.S. 522 (1923), 252

Worcester v. Georgia, 6 Pet. 515 (1832), 90–91

Wyoming v. Oklahoma, 502 U.S. 437 (1992), 495

Yakus v. United States, 321 U.S. 414 (1944), 356

Yates v. United States, 354 U.S. 298 (1957), 359

Young, Ex parte, 209 U.S. 123 (1908), 491

Younger v. Harris, 401 U.S. 37 (1971), 491

Youngstown Sheet & Tube Co. v. Sawyer, 343 U.S. 579 (1952), 358, 359, **411–418**

INDEX OF SUBJECTS

Abolitionist movement, 123–126
Abolitionists, 123–126, 132
Adams, John, 25, 33, 37, 74, 82
 revolutionary figure, 17, 19, 20 (quoted)
 as President, 69–71, 79, 80, 84, 86
Adams, John Quincy, 75, 78, 91, 126, 128, 130
Adams, Samuel, 15, 38
Addams, Jane, 240
Administrative state, 378–379, 559–560
Advisory opinions, 66
Africans, 8
Age Discrimination in Employment Act (ADEA), 484
Agnew, Spiro, 376
Agricultural Adjustment Act of 1933, 300, 309, 315
Agricultural Adjustment Act of 1938, 315
Alabama, 92, 143, 156
Albany Plan, 16
Alger, Horatio, 224, 315
Alien and Sedition Acts, 50, 70, 79
Alien Registration Act of 1940 (see Smith Act)
American Antislavery Society, 124
American Federation of Labor, 237
American Party (see Know Nothing Party)
American Revenue Act (The Sugar Act), 14
American Revolution
 disputes leading to, 14–18
 debate leading to, 18–22
 earlier non-fighting, 19–20
 as a conservative rebellion, 20
 British defeat, 26–27
 government during, 25–26
 republican state constitutions, 29–31
 reception statutes and common law, 31–32
American Sugar Refining Co., 236
Americans with Disabilities Act of 1990, 485
Amicus curiae brief, 588, 589
Amistad The (the vessel), 127–128
Annapolis Convention, 33
Anti-Federalism, 47–54
Anti-Federalists, 47–54, 63, 67, 68, 71, 73, 77
Anti-New Deal Court, 304–310
Anti-Saloon League, 301
Anti-trust policy, 235–237
Appointment power, 365–366

Arizona, 131
Arkansas, 123, 145, 154, 156
Army Signal Corps, 384
Article I, 355, 363, 372
Article I-1, 379
Article I-2, 41, 82, 121, 112, 368
Article I-3, 82, 368
Article I-4, 372
Article I-5, 369
Article I-6, 376, 377, 384
Article I-7, 379
Article I-8, 65, 73, 76, 77, 78, 88, 126, 244, 389, 493
Article I-9, 121, 146, 159, 238, 389
Article I-10, 85, 90, 159, 188, 192–196, 362, 394, 495, 497, 561
Article II, 362
Article II-1, 88, 146, 392
Article II-2, 75, 130, 146, 365, 366, 377, 381
Article II-3, 372
Article II-4, 82, 369, 370
Article III, 311, 378
Article III-1, 79
Article III-2, 80, 159, 388, 488, 498, 587
Article III-3, 83, 143, 388
Article IV-1, 497
Article IV-2, 121, 122, 126, 128, 129, 497
Article IV-3, 75, 130, 309, 390
Article IV-4, 92–93, 126, 160, 386–387
Article V, 301
Article VI, 72, 188, 362, 479, 486
Article VII, 42, 47
Articles of Confederation, 3, 13, 25, 27–29, 32–34, 42, 44, 47, 49, 54, 55, 479
 summarized, 28
Atomic Energy Act of 1954, 486
Ashwander Rules, 388
Austin, Stephen, 130

Balanced Budget and Emergency Deficit Control Act of 1985 (see Gramm-Rudman-Hollings Act)
Baldwin, Henry, 90, 128, 197, 199
Baltimore, 90
Baltimore, Lord, 10
Barbour, Philip, 197

Battle of New Orleans, 76, 77
Battle of San Jacinto, 130
Beecher, Lyman, 124
Belknap, William, 368
Bell, John, 141
Benet, Stephen Vincent, 195
Berlin crisis, 360
Bicentennial Commission, 383
Bill of Rights, 3, 46, 48, 50, 54–55, 90, 155, 249, 314, 395, 480, 489, 492
Bituminous Coal Conservation Act of 1934, 309
Black Codes, 154
Black, Hugo, 310, 313, 357, 358, 365, 393, 561
"Black Monday", 308–309, 367
Blackmun, Harry, 381, 396, 482, 484
Blackstone, William, 31
Blair, John, 71, 72, 311
Board of Trade, 12
Board of Veterans Appeals, Veterans Administration, 586
Bolivia, 355
Borah, William, 314
Bork, Robert, 366, 375
Boss Tweed, 315
Boston, 15, 16
Boston Tea Party, 15
Bosnia, 361
Boucher, Jonathan, 18
Bowsher, Charles, 380
Bradley, Joseph, 226, 227
Brady Gun Control Act of 1993, 483
Brandeis brief, 245–246
Brandeis, Louis, 138, 388, 490
    Progressive figure, 240, 241, 245
    profile, 242–243
    on Taft Court, 250, 251
    during New Deal, 304, 305, 309, 310, 311, 312, 314
Breckenridge, John C., 141, 142
Brennan, William J., 310, 383, 387, 393, 394, 396, 488, 564
    on constitutional interpretation, 45, 394–395
Brewer, David, 230, 245
Breyer, Stephen, 391, 397
Bricker Amendment, 363
Bricker, John W., 363
Brooks, Preston, 135–136
Brown, John, 135
Bryan, William Jennings, 239
Buchanan, James, 135, 136, 147
Budget and Impoundment Act, 373, 375, 379
Bureaucracy, 354
Burger Court, 394, 396, 484, 491, 492, 560
Burger, Warren, 375, 379, 380, 385, 396, 397, 484
    profile, 382–383
Burgoyne, Gen. John, 26
Burke, Edmund, 14
Burr, Aaron, 69, 82, 83, 373

Burr treason trial, 82–83
Burton, Harold, 393
Bush, George H. W., 361, 397
Bush, George W., 75, 390–392
Butler, Pierce, 37
Butler, Pierce, 250, 304, 305, 310, 314
Byrnes, James F., 314

Cabinet, The, 66, 366
Cadwalader, George, 148
Cairo Conference, 364
Calhoun, John C., 70, 76, 78, 130, 132, 143
    ideas of, 94–95, 124–125, 136, 197
    profile, 124–125
California, 131, 132, 158
Cambodia, 360
Canada, 76, 363
Capitalism, 220
Capone, Al, 301
Cardozo, Benjamin, 304, 305, 308, 309, 310, 313
    profile, 314–315
Cardozo, Ellen, 315
Carnegie, Andrew, 222, 225
Carter, Jimmy, 311, 361, 363, 376, 396
Catron, John, 136, 147, 197
CENTO (Central Treaty Organization), 363
Central Intelligence Agency, 389
Central Pacific Railroad, 220, 221, 223
Certification, 587
Certiorari, writ of, 587
    Supreme Court's Rule 10 guidelines for granting, 588 (quoted)
Chase, Salmon P., 126, 132, 136
    as Chief Justice, 149, 157, 158, 159, 160, 161, 227
Chase, Samuel, 82, 368
Child Labor Act of 1919, 251
Child Labor Amendment, 387
Chinese Communists, 358
Choate, Joseph, 238
Church of England, 10
Church of Rome, 10
Cinque, Joseph, 128
Civil liberties (see also Bill of Rights, First, Fifth, and Fourteenth Amendments)
    Constitutional provisions before Bill of Rights, 46
    during Civil War, 146–147, 148–150
    during Reconstruction, 162
    World War II internments, 356–357
    Cold War anti-communism, 359–360
    Congressional investigations, 381–386
Civil rights, 155, 226, 228–229, xxx479
Civil War, 2–3, 46, 70, 145–153, 232, 355, 356, 357
    conflicts of 1850's as prelude to, 132–140
    election of 1860, 140–143
    Southern secession, 142–143, 145

Confederate Constitution, 144
  strengths and weaknesses of two sides, 145–146
  internal security and civil liberty, 146–147, 148–150
  legal status of the war, 147–148
  Lincoln at Gettysburg, 150–151
  status of slavery, 150–152
  growth of federal power, 152–153
Civil Rights Act of 1866, 155
Civil Rights Act of 1875, 229
Civil Rigths Act of 1964, 481
Civil Works Administration, 302
Civilian Conservation Corps, 300
Clark, Tom, 393, 481
Clay, Henry, 51, 76, 78, 91, 93, 123, 130, 132, 197
Clayton Anti-trust Act of 1914, 237, 252
Cleveland, Grover, 75, 230, 234
Clifford, Nathaniel, 147
Clinton, George, 54, 67
Clinton, William, 82, 158, 361, 368, 370–371, 377, 381, 397
Coercive Acts, 15
Cohen brothers, Philip and Mendes, 86
Cold War, The, 353, 357, 358, 359, 360, 384–385
Colfax Massacre, 228
Colonial assemblies, 11–12, 38
Colonial charters and compacts, 11, 13–14, 29
Colonial period:
  society, 7–9
  economy, 9–10
  religious tolerance, 10–11
  government, 11–13
  law, 13–14
Colonial suffrage, 12
Colorado, 131
Columbia University, 306, 315
Commentaries on American Law (Kent), 199
Commentaries on the Constitution (Story), 84, 199
Commentaries on the Laws of England (Blackstone), 31
Commerce, regulation of
  British-colonial, 9–10, 14–15
  Marshall's nationalism, 87–90
  common law aspects, 188–190
  obligation of contracts, 192–196
  growth of national marketplace, 196–200
  laissez faire constitutionalism, 225–238
  liberty of contract, 230–234, 251–252
  Interstate Commerce Commision, 234–235, 246–247
  anti-trust action, 235–237
  federal police power in Progressive period, 241–245
  state police power in Progressive period, 245–246
  New Deal programs, 299–304
  modern federal power, 481–482
  modern state power, 493–496
  modern property rights and, 560–565
Committee of Style, 42
Committee to Reelect the President (CREEP), 374

Common law
  English and colonial, 13, 31, 70
  reception statutes governing, 31
  American, 188–192, 199
  federal, 489–490
Common Law, The, (Holmes), 189, 232–233
"Common Sense" (Paine), 19
Communism, 357, 358
Communist Control Act of 1954, 359
Communist Party, 359, 486
Communists, 359, 360, 384–385
Compromise of 1850, The, 132, 133, 134 (map)
Concord, Mass., 16
Confederacy, The, 143, 144–152 passim
Confederate Constitution, 144
Confederation debt, 64, 66
Conference of State Chief Justices and State Court
  Administrators, 383
Congress
  framed in Constitution, 41
  creation of lower federal judiciary, 71–72
  Reconstruction plans, 158–160
  delegation of power, 378–379
  legislative veto, 379–380
  investigatory power, 381–386
Congressional investigation
  early precedents, 381–384
  McCarthyism, 384–385
  later issues, 385–386
Connecticut, 11, 14, 29, 52, 92
Conscription Act of 1863, 153
Constitution, The
  veneration of, 3
  framing of, 38–47
  opposition to, 47–48
  defense of, 48–51
  ratification of, 51–54
  addition of the Bill of Rights, 54–55
  the union formed by, 55–56
Constitutional amendments (see specific amendment)
Constitutional articles (see specific article)
Constitutional Convention, 4, 33, 37–47
  accord on ends, 38–39
  delegates to, 37–38
  plans introduced, 39–44
  scheme of the Constitution, 43
  unfinished work, 45–47
Constitutional interpretation, 44–45, 84–85, 394–395
Constitutional precedents, 65–66
Constitutional Union Party, 141, 142
Constitutionalism, 1–4, 13–14, 27
Continental Army, 26
Continental Congress, 15–18, 25, 27, 40, 50
  under Articles of Confederation, 28, 29, 32, 33, 38, 40, 51,
    64, 129, 141

Consumer Credit Protection Act of 1970, 481
Contracts clause, 42, 188, 192–196, 199, 561–562
Cooley, Thomas, 230, 234, 246
Coolidge, Calvin, 249, 250, 297, 302, 314, 367
Cooper, James Fenimore, 131
Cornell University, 306
Cornwallis, Gen. Lord, 27
Corporations, 190–192, 221–225, 235–237, 296
Cotton "gin", 123
Cotton, John, 10
Court of Appeals for the Federal Circuit, 586
Court packing,
    by Federalists, 79
    by Radical Republicans, 226
    Roosevelt's plan, 307, 311–313
Covenent on Human Rights, 363
Crevecoeuer, Hector St. John de, 8
Crittenden, John J., 143
Crittenden Compromise, 143
Croly, Herbert, 240
Cox, Archibald, 374–375, 381
Cox, James, 299
Critical Period, The, 32–34 (see also Articles of Confederation)
Cuba, 239
Cuban missile crisis, 360
Cummings, Homer, 311
Curtis, Benjamin, 137, 157, 200

Dartmouth College, 193
Davis, David, 147, 149, 158
Davis, Jefferson, 141, 143, 144
Day, William R., 245
Declaration of Independence, 17–18, 19–20, 25, 26, 30, 31, 38, 47, 54, 55, 82, 150–151
    document, 21–23
Declaratory Act of 1766, 18
Debs, Eugene, 299
"Decision of 1789", 367
Delaware, 52, 145
Democracy in America (de Tocqueville), 91
Democratic element in Constitution, 46–47
Democratic Party, 91, 92, 136, 137, 139, 155, 239, 243, 299
Democrats, 140–141, 304
Department of Finance, 25
"Devil and Daniel Webster, The" (Benet), 195
Dickinson, John, 18, 19, 25, 33
Diplomacy and foreign affairs (see also war and national security)
    treaties and treaty-making, 362–363
    executive agreements, 363–365
Direct tax, 42, 73, 122, 238
Discourse on the Constitution of the United States, A (Calhoun), 124
Disquisition on Government, A (Calhoun), 124
District of Columbia (see Washington, D.C.)
Dominion theory, 19

Dorr, Thomas, 92
Dougherty, Harry, 384
Dougherty, Mally, 384
Douglas, Stephen A., 133–134, 136, 137, 139–140, 141, 142
Douglas, William O., 314, 364, 368, 393, 561
Douglass, Frederick, 124
Driver's Privacy Protection Act of 1994, 485
Duane, William J., 94
Dulany, Daniel, 18
Duvall, Gabriel, 84, 138, 195

East India Tea Company, 15
Economic development
    in antebellum period, 185–187
    Constitution as enabler, 187–188
    common law aspects, 188–190
    incorporation, 190–192
    obligation of contracts, 192–196
    development of a national marketplace, 196–200
    new property versus old, 200–201
    post Civil War economic order, 220
    railway building, 220–221
    organization of corporate capital, 221–223
    response of government, 223–225
    laissez faire constitutionalism, 225–238
    liberty of contract, 230–234, 251–252
    regulation of interstate commerce, 234–235, 246–247
    anti-trust action, 235–237
    income tax, 237–238
    federal police power, 241–245
    state police power, 245–246
    World War I mobilization, 247–249
    post-war prosperity, 249–250
    labor insurgency, 252–253
    land use regulation, 253–254
    stock market crash, 295
    Great Depression, 295–304
    New Deal reform, 299–304
Economic radicalism in states, 33, 39, 42
Eighth Amendment, 55
Eighteenth Amendment, 240, 301
Eisenhower, Dwight, 360, 363, 367, 382–383, 384, 393, 394–395
El Salvador, 361
Elections, national (1788–2000), 596–598
Electoral College, 41, 74–75
Eleventh Amendment, 72, 86, 87, 144, 483–485, 491
Ellsworth, Oliver, 71, 72, 73, 79
Emancipation Proclamation, 152, 248
Embargo Act of 1807, 76
Embargo, Jefferson's, 75–76
Emergency Relief Act of 1933, 300
Emerson, John, 137
Emerson, Ralph Waldo, 195, 232
Eminent domain, 191–192, 562–565

public use, 563

takings clause, 563–565

just compensation, 565

England (see Great Britain)

English Bill of Rights, 13

English legal legacy, 13–14

Erlichman, John, 375

Ervin Committee (Senate Select Committee), 374, 385

Ervin, Sam, 374

Espionage Act, 248

Established churches, 10–11

Ethics in Government Act of 1978, 366, 371

Everett, Edward, 141, 150

Executive Agreements, 363–365

Export-Import Bank, 302

Fair Labor Standards Act of 1938 (FLSA), 316, 482, 484, 486

Fairfax, Thomas, 86

Farm Mortgage Act of 1933, 300

Federal Courts of Appeal, 585–587

Federal Code of Regulations, 378

Federal Communications Commission, 378, 380

Federal Court of Appeals, District of Columbia, 382

Federal Courts, structure and jurisdiction, 71–72

Federal Deposit Insurance Corporation (FDIC), 302

Federal District Courts, 585–586

Federal Election Campaign Act of 1973, 365

Federal Election Commissioners, 365

Federal Housing Administration (FHA), 302

Federal judiciary

created by Congress, 71

curbed by Eleventh Amendment, 72

Federalist-Republican conflict over, 79–83

judicial federalism, 488–493

modern structure of 585–587

lines of appeal, 585–586

Federal preemption, 486–487

Federal Reserve Board, 299, 302

Federal Rules of Civil Procedure, 490

Federal Trade Commission, 367, 378, 380

Federal Trade Commission Act of 1914, 367

Federalism, 33, 47, 49–50, 83, 90

modern federal system, 479–499 passim

Federalist government, 63–71

Federalist Papers, The, 49–51, 68, 71, 88, 386

No. 10, 49, 57–61 (document), 67

No. 39, 49

No. 84, 46

No. 85, 49

Federalist Party, 69

Federalists, 48–54, 67, 70–79 passim, 188, 304

Federal-state relations

federal regulation of state government, 482–486

federal preemption, 486–487

mutual tax immunities, 487–488

judicial federalism, 488–493

federal common law, 489–490

federal supervisory authority, 490–493

Field, Stephen, 158, 226, 227, 311, 499

Fifth Amendment, 55

just compensation, 90, 191, 253, 309, 562

due process, 126, 141

grand jury indictment, 149

self incrimination, 359, 384

double jeopardy, 585

Fifteenth Amendment, 156, 219, 228

Fillmore, Millard, 136

Filled Milk Act, 317

First Amendment, 3, 55, 70, 90, 387, 390, 393, 491

First Reconstruction Act of 1867, 156

First Report on Public Credit, 64

Fisher, Irving, 295

Fletcher, Robert, 192

Florida, 52, 75, 123, 129, 143, 156, 160, 390–392

Florida Supreme Court, 390–392

Four Horsemen, The, 305–310

Fourth Amendment, 55, 490

Fourteenth Amendment, 55, 219

due process, 90, 155, 226, 228–29, 230, 231, 234, 314, 489, 491

privileges and immunities, 226, 228

equal protection, 228, 387, 391, 484, 498

loyalty to the United States, 369

Force Bill of 1833, 94

Ford, Gerald, 376, 377, 396

Fort Sumter, 145

Fortas, Abe, 368, 382, 393

Foster, William Z., 299

France, 13, 14, 17, 64, 65, 69, 76, 123, 150, 247

Frankfurter, Felix, 197, 243, 246, 250, 307, 314, 358, 368, 387, 393, 394

Franklin, Benjamin, 52

Revolutionary figure, 12, 17, 18, 25

profile, 16–17

at Constitutional convention, 37, 38, 42

Frazier-Lemke Emergency Farm Mortgage Act of 1934, 308–309

Free Soil Party, 126, 132, 133, 136

Freedmen, 154–156, 160, 161, 228–229

Freedmen's Bureau, 155

Freeport Doctrine, 140

Fremont, John C., 136

French and Indian War, 14

French Republic, 69

French Revolution, 64, 67, 73

Fuchs, Klaus, 359

Fugitive Slave Act of 1793, 127, 128

Fugitive slaves, 122, 126–129, 132

Fuller Court, 229–238

Fuller, Melville, 230, 233, 236, 237, 238, 241, 244

Fulton, Robert, 87, 196

Gadsden Purchase, 129, 133, 185
Galbraith, John Kenneth, 298
Gallatin, Albert, 75
Garrison, William Lloyd, 124, 125, 126
General Accounting Office, 380
Germany, 219, 240, 247, 357, 360, 364
Gerry, Elbridge, 37, 42
Gettysburg Address, 150–151
Gettysburg, Battle of, 150
George III, 16
Georgia, 41, 52, 72, 90–91, 125, 143, 156, 192
Georgia-Cherokee crisis. 90–91
Gibbons, Thomas, 87–89, 196
Ginsberg, Ruth Bader, 391, 397
Gladstone, William, 2
Glass-Steagall Banking Act of 1933, 302
Glorious Revolution, The, 12, 13, 19
Goldberg, Arthur, 393
Goldmark, Florence, 242
Goldwater, Barry, 360
Gore, Albert, 75, 390–392
Gould, Jay, 234
Gramm-Rudman-Hollings Act of 1985 (Balanced Budget
    and Emergency Deficit Control Act), 380
Granada, 361
*Grand Inquest: The Historic Impeachments of Justice Samuel Chase
    and President Andrew Johnson* (Rehnquist), 485
Grange, The, 227
Grant, Ulysses S., 146, 156, 159, 160, 226, 227
Gravel, Mike, 377–378
Gray, Horace, 230
Great Britain, 11–20 passim, 26–27, 29, 32, 66, 76, 78, 129,
    131, 150, 152, 185, 219, 247, 363, 364
Great Compromise, The, 40
Great Debate, The, 14–15
Great Depression, The, 29, 30, 186, 240, 295–304 passim,
    481, 487
Greeley, Horace, 150, 160
Grier, Robert, 136, 147, 311
Guffey Coal Act, 379
Gulf of Tonkin Resolution, 360
Gun Free School Zones Act of 1990, 481

Habeas Corpus Act of 1863, 149
Habeas Corpus Act of 1867, 491
Haiti, 361
Haldeman, H. R., 375
Hamilton, Alexander, 18, 19, 33, 51, 69, 70, 75, 83, 87, 317
    at Constitutional convention, 37, 39, 42, 44
    in *The Federalist*, 46, 49, 72, 386
    profile, 68–69
    as Treasury Secretary, 64–65, 66, 188
Hancock, John, 38, 52

Harding, Warren G., 249, 250, 307, 314
Hat Act of 1732, 10
Hatch Act of 1939, 368
Harlan, John Marshall, 227, 230, 232, 237, 244, 310, 314
Harlan, John Marshall, III, 385, 396
Harriman, E. H. 223, 236
Harris, Katherine, 390
Harrison, Benjamin, 75
Hartford Convention, 77
Harvard University, 141, 199, 232, 242, 374, 484
Hawaii, 364
Hayes, Rutherford B., 75, 160, 161
Hayne, Robert Y., 195
Health of justices, 310–311
Henry, Patrick, 18, 38, 48, 51
Hepburn Act of 1906, 234, 246
Hill, James J., 223, 236
Hiss, Alger, 359, 384
Hofstadter, Richard, 125, 195
Holmes, Oliver Wendell, 85, 138, 237, 250, 251, 253, 304,
    310, 311, 363
    legal scholar, 189, 198, 246, 314, 394
    critic of laissez faire activism, 225, 230, 241
    profile, 232–233
Holmes Devise, The, 233
Homeowners Refinancing Act of 1933, 300
Hoover Adminstration, 297–298, 304
Hoover, Herbert, 297, 298, 299, 302, 304, 305, 307, 314,
    367, 379
Hopkinson, David, 87
Horwitz, Morton J., 189
House UnAmerican Activities Committee (HUAC),
    384–385
Houston, Sam, 130, 143
Hughes, Charles Evans, 304
    early service as associate justice, 137, 241
    Chief Justice during New Deal, 305, 308, 309, 310, 312,
        313, 314, 315, 392, 394
    profile, 306–307
Hull-Lothian Agreement, 364
Hungarian Revolt, 360
Hunter, David, 86
Hurst, J. Willard, 187, 192
Hutchinson, Thomas, 17
Hybrid offices, 354
Hylton, Daniel, 72

Idaho, 133
Inherent power, 355, 358–359
Illinois, 29, 92, 387
Immigration, 223
Immigration and Naturalization Service (INS), 379
Immunities, 376–378
    executive, 376–377
    legislative, 377–378

Impeachment, 368–371
  of Samuel Chase, 82
  of Andrew Johnson, 156–158, 368, 370–371
  of William Clinton, 158, 368, 370–371
Implied powers, 65, 68–69, 86–87, 88
Incorporation of businesses, 190–191, 221–223
Independent counsel, 370–371, 374–375, 381
Indian Gaming Regulatory Act, 483
Indiana, 29, 92
Indians (Native Americans), 8, 26, 145, 483, 565
  Creeks, 52, 65
  Cherokees, 90–91
Industrial capitalism, 3, 220–238
  post Civil War new economic order, 220
  organization of big capital, 221–225
  laissez faire constitutionalism, 225–238
Intergovernmental tax immunities, 487–488
Internal improvements, 77–78, 93
Internal Revenue Service (IRS), 390–391, 586
Internal Security Act of 1950, see McCarran Act
International Court of Justice, 307
Interpretivism, 394–395
Interstate Commerce Act of 1887, 234, 237, 246
Interstate Commerce Commission (ICC), 224, 234–235,
  246–247, 380
Interstate relations
  full faith and credit, 497
  privileges and immunities, 497–498
  rendition, 498
  interstate disputes, 499
  interstate compacts, 499
Investigatory power (see Congressional investigations)
Iran-Contra Affair, 386
Iran Hostage Crisis, 364
Iraq, 361
Iredell, James, 71
Iron Act of 1750, 10
It Is So Ordered: A Constitution Unfolds (Burger), 383

Jackson, Andrew, 75, 76, 78, 85, 87, 91–95, 130, 139, 153,
  157, 197, 199, 311, 367
Jackson, Robert, 314, 316, 353, 357, 358, 393, 484
Jacksonian democracy
  new party system, 91–92
  demise of property qualifications for voting, 92
  strong presidency, 93–94
  nullification crisis, 94–95
  economic growth, 185–187
James II, 12
Japan, 240, 356, 357, 360
Japanese-Americans, internment of, 150, 356–357
Jaworski, Leon, 375
Jay, John, 25, 49, 66, 68, 69, 71, 72, 73
Jay's Treaty, 66, 72, 86, 362, 373, 488
Jefferson, Thomas, 17, 18, 19, 30, 37, 50, 51, 63, 70, 95, 150, 197

as Secretary of State, 65, 66, 87
opposition to Hamilton, 66–68
as party figure, 67–68, 69, 74–75
as President, 73–76, 79–80, 82, 84, 85, 86, 311, 373
Johnson, Andrew, 82, 154–158, 159, 161, 367, 368,
  370–371, 376
Johnson, Lyndon, 360, 373, 374, 382, 393, 395, 396
Johnson, William, 83, 89, 90, 199
Johnson, William Samuel, 37, 42
Joint Committee of Fifteen, 154
Joint Committee on the Conduct of the War, 146–147
Judges Bill of 1925, 250
Judicial federalism
  federal common law, 587–588
  federal supervisory authority, 588–591
Judicial review, doctrine of, 31, 80–82
Judiciary Act of 1789, 71–72, 80, 82, 86, 488, 489, 492
Judiciary Act of 1801, 79
Judiciary Reorganization Plan, 311
Jurisdiction, 388–391, 587–588
Justice Department, 359, 366, 374, 384, 394
Justiciability, 388–391, 587–588

Kansas, 131, 134, 136, 140, 387
Kansas Territory, 133
Kansas-Nebraska Act of 1854, 133–134, 135 (map), 136
Keating-Owen Child Labor Act of 1916, 244
Kendall, Amos, 125
Kennedy, Anthony, 391, 396
Kennedy, John, 360, 373, 374, 393, 394, 395
Kent, James, 31, 199
Kentucky, 145
King, Rufus, 37, 42
King's College, 68
Know Nothing Party, 136
Knights of the White Camellia, 160
Knox, Henry 63
Knox, Philander, 236
Korean War, 147, 355, 357–359, 360, 373
Kosovo, 361, 362
Ku Klux Klan, 160, 313
Kurland, Philip B., 81
Kuwait, 361

Labor, organized, 252–253
Laissez faire capitalism, 220–225, 225–254 passim
Laissez faire constitutionalism, 225–238, 250–254, 304–312,
  317
Lamar, Joseph, 243
Landon, Alfred, 304, 310
Laos, 360
Law (see also common law)
  reception statutes, 31
  property, 188–189
  antebellum transformation of, 188–192

contracts, 189–190
torts, 190
of incorporation, 190–191
eminent domain, 191–192
bankruptcy, 193–194
Law clerks, Supreme Court, 588, 589, 590
League of Nations Treaty, 241, 249, 362
Lebanon, 361
Lee, Arthur, 18
Lee, Richard Henry, 17, 38, 48
Lee, Robert E., 150, 154
Legal Tender Act, 225
"Letters from a Pennsylvania Farmer" (Dickinson), 19
Lend-Lease Act of 1941, 364
Leonard, Daniel, 18
Lever Act of 1917, 247–248
Lewinsky, Monica, 370
Lewinsky scandal, 370, 377
Lexington, Mass., 16, 18
Liberty of contract, 230–234, 251–252
Libya, 361
Lincoln, Abraham, 95, 127, 153, 154, 155, 158, 160, 161, 162,
        195, 248, 311, 354, 359, 373
    debates with Douglas, 139–140
    1860 election, 140–142
    Southern secession, 142–143, 145
    curtailment of civil liberties, 146–147, 148–149
    legal status of the war, 147–148
    at Gettysburg, 150–151
    status of slavery 150–152
    Emancipation Proclamation, 152
Lincoln-Douglas debates, 139–140
Line Item Veto Act of 1996, 381
Litvinov Assignment, 364
Livingston, Robert, 17, 196
Livingston, William Brockholst, 83
Locke, John, 19, 187
Logan Act of 1799, 362
Louisiana, 123, 131, 154, 156, 160
Louisiana Purchase, 74–75, 123, 130, 133, 137, 185
Low-Level Radioactive Waste Policy Act of 1980, 483
Loyalists, 17, 26, 27, 32, 86

MacDonald, Forrest, 46
Madison, James, 33, 64, 69, 70, 80, 95
    at Constitutional convention, 37, 38, 39, 42, 44, 143
    role in Ratification, 48
    political theorist 49–50, 124–125, 353
    profile, 50–51
    in Federal Congress, 54
    opposition to Hamilton, 66–68
    party organizer, 67–68
    as President, 76–78, 79, 85, 93, 198
Magna Carta, 13
Maine, 92, 123

Maine, The, 239
Mann Act of 1910, 244
Marbury, William, 80
Martin, Denny, 86
Martin, Luther, 48, 87
Martineau, Harriet, 124
Marshall Court, 3, 187, 188, 192–197
Marshall, John, 51, 127, 130, 138, 139, 192–199 passim, 201,
        231, 241, 310, 317, 373, 378, 394
    early Marshall Court, 79–83
    nationalism, 83–91
    profile, 84–85
Marshall, Thurgood, 393, 396
Marx, Karl, 125
Maryland, 86–87, 92, 145
Mason, George, 30, 37, 39, 42, 48
Massachusetts, 15–16, 29, 40, 52, 92, 123
Mayflower Compact, 14
Maysville Road bill, 93
McCardle, William H., 159
McCarran Act (Internal Security Act of 1950), 359
McCarthy, Joseph, 384–385
McCarthyism, 384–385
McCulloch, James, 86
McKenna, Joseph, 311
McKinley, John, 197
McKinley, William, 236, 239
McLean, John, 90, 128, 137, 197
McReynolds, James, 241, 304, 305, 307, 309, 314
Meat Inspection Act of 1906, 244
Mellon, Andrew, 297, 298
Mercantilism, 9–10
Merryman, John, 148
Mexican Cession, 129, 131, 132
Mexican War, 131–132, 152, 355
Mexico, 83, 129, 130–131, 185
Mexico City, 131
Michigan, 29, 123
Michigan Constitution, 492
Michigan Supreme Court, 492
Migratory Bird Treaty Act of 1918, 362–363
Miller, Samuel Freeman, 147, 158, 226, 227, 310
Milligan, Lambdin, 149
Minnesota Territory, 137
Minton, Sherman, 393
Mississippi, 128, 156
Missouri, 123, 133, 145, 158
Missouri Compromise, 123, 131, 133, 134 (map), 136, 137,
        141, 143
Missouri crisis, 123
Mitchell, John, 375
Molasses Act of 1733, 10
Monroe Doctrine, 78, 85
Monroe, James, 78, 305, 310
Montgomery Convention, 143, 145

Morgan, J. P., 222, 236
Morris, Gouverneur, 37, 42, 44, 188
Morris, Richard, 69
Morris, Robert, 25, 37, 38, 64
Morrison, Samuel Eliot, 317
Murphy, Frank, 314, 357

Napoleon, 75, 76
Napoleonic Wars, 75–76
National Bank of United States
    First, 61, 77, 87
    Second, 77, 86, 93–94, 138, 153, 199
National Banking Act of 1863, 153
National Conference of Commissioners on Uniform State Laws, 490
National Emergency Act, 376
National Industrial Recovery Act of 1933 (NIRA), 301, 307, 308, 309, 379
National Labor Relations Act of 1936, 310, 312
National Labor Relations Board (NLRB), 302, 380
National Recovery Administration, 309
National Traffic and Motor Vehicle Safety Act, 486
National security (see War and national security)
Nationalist Chinese, 363
Nationalists, 480
NATO (North Atlantic Treaty Organization), 361, 363
Nature of the Judicial Process, The (Cardozo), 315
Nebraska Territory, 133
Necessary and Proper Clause 41, 48, 65 (see also implied powers)
Nelson, Samuel, 137, 147, 487
Netherlands, The, 64
Nevada, 131, 481
New Deal, 3, 4, 81, 187, 254, 339, 367, 480, 481, 559, 560
    failure of Hoover administration, 297–298
    Roosevelt's election, 299
    One Hundred Days, The, 299–302, 309
    "second" New Deal, 302–304
    judicial resistence, 304–310
    court packing plan, 310–312
    "switch in time", the, 312–313
    "Roosevelt Court", the, 313–316
    new constitutional order, 316–318
New Jersey, 52, 92, 222
New Hampshire, 52
New Mexico, 131
New Mexico Territory, 132
New Orleans, 226
New York Court of Appeals, 315
New York Provincial Congress, 18
New York, 26, 27, 52, 68, 87, 92, 483
New York City, 64
New York City Landmarks Commission, 564
Ninth Amendment, 55
Nineteenth Amendment, 240

Nixon, Richard, 360, 361, 368, 371, 373–377 passim, 382, 396, 484, 560
Nixon, Walter F., 369
Non-Importation Act of 1806, 76
Noninterpretivism, 394–395
Norris, George, 302
Norris-LaGuardia Act of 1932, 237, 253
North, Lord Frederick, 15
North, Oliver, 386
North Carolina, 52, 145, 156
North Korea, 358
North Vietnam, 360
Northern Democrats, 130, 140–141, 150
Northwest Ordinance of 1787, 29, 129, 131
Northwest Territory, 373
Nuclear Non-proliferation Act of 1978, 379
Nullification, 94–95
Nullification crisis, 94–95, 123

O'Connor, Sandra Day, 391, 396, 484, 492
Office of Legal Council, Justice Department, 484
Office of Management and Budget, 380
Office of Price Administration, 378
Office-holding
    appointment, 365–366
    removal, 65, 366–369
    term limits, 369, 372
Ogden, Aaron, 87–89, 196
Ohio, 29
Oklahoma, 131
Oklahoma Territory, 145
Old Bailey, 8
Olive Branch Petition, 16
One Hundred Days, The, 299–302, 309
Oregon, 133, 160
Oregon Territory, 129, 133
Organized Crime Control Act of 1970, 481
Original intent, 44–45, 88
Original jurisdiction, 76, 498, 587
Original package doctrine, 90, 496
Osborn, Ralph, 87
Otis, James, 18
Overman Act, 248, 356

Paine, Thomas, 18, 19
Panama, 361
Paris Peace Accords, 360
Parliament, 10, 12–13, 14–19
Parrington, Vernon, 69
Patent Remedy Clarification Act, 484
Paterson, William, 37, 40
Peace of Ghent, 76, 77
Pearl Harbor, 356
Peckham, Rufus, 230, 232, 245
Penn, William, 10, 11

Pennsylvania, 40, 52, 128
Pentagon Papers, 377
People's Party, 239
People's Republic of China, 1, 363
Persian Gulf War, 147, 355, 361, 362
Peru, 355
Philadelphia, 26, 37–38, 64, 67
Phillips, Wendell, 124, 126
Pickering, John, 82, 157, 368
Pickering, Timothy, 70
Pinckney, Charles, 37
Pinckney, William, 87
Pittsburgh, 67
Political parties, 67–68, 144
Poor Richard's Almanack (Franklin), 16
Police power,
   federal, 241–245, 480–482
   state, 493–497
Political economy
   of Framers, 45
   of Hamilton, 64–65, 69
   of slavery, 122–123
   antebellum, 185–201
   of industrial capitalism, 220–238
   stock market crash and depression, 295–298
   of New Deal, 299–304
Political questions doctrine, 93, 369, 386–387
Polk, James K., 130, 131
Popular sovereignty, 132, 133–135, 137, 140
Populism, 240
Populist Party, 225
Populists, 239
Port Authority of New York and New Jersey (PATH), 562
Potsdam Conference, 364
Potter, David, 133
Pound, Roscoe, 246
Powell, Adam Clayton, 369
Powell, Lewis, 376, 396, 484, 590
Precedent, 88–89
Primogeniture, 13
Privy Council, 12, 17
Progressives, 240–248
Progressivism, 240–241
Prohibition, 249, 300–301
Prohibition Party, 300
Promontory Point, 220–221, 223
Property, 30, 34
Public Works Administration, 301
Public Works Subcommittee on Public Buildings, 377
Pure Food and Drug Act of 1906, 244
Puritans, 10–11

Quakers, 10
Quitrent, 13

Racketeer Influenced and Corrupt Organizations Act (RICO), 481
Radical Republicans, 154–161 passim, 367
Railway building, 220–221, 223
Railway regulation, 234–235, 246–247
Randolph, Edmund, 37, 39, 42, 63
Randolph, John, 76
Ratification, 51–54
Reagan, Ronald, 357, 361, 376, 380, 396, 485, 560
Reapportionment, 387
Reception statutes, 31
Reconstruction
   Johnson's plan, 157–158
   Congressional plans, 158–160
   impeachment of Johnson, 160–162
   problematic Supreme Court, 162–164
   end of Reconstruction, 164–166
Reconstruction Finance Corporation (RFC), 298
Reed, Stanley, 314, 393
Rehnquist, William, 381, 383, 391, 392, 396, 481–482, profile, 482–483
Rehnquist Court, 387–388, 394, 397, 486, 492, 560, 564, 565
Religious Freedom Restoration Act of 1993, 387
Relocation program, 356–357
Removal Act of 1875, 489
Removal power, 65, 366–369
Repeal, 300–301
Report on the Subject of Manufactures, 65
Republican Constitutionalism, 73–79
   Louisiana Purchase, 74–75
   Jefferson's embargo, 75–76
   War of 1812, 76–77
   Internal improvements, 77–78
   end of era of, 78–79
Republican National Committee, 374
Republican Party (Jeffersonian), 51, 67–68, 70, 73–76, 91
Republican Party (modern), 126, 136, 306, 354
Republican state constitutions during and after Revolution, 29–31
Republicans (Jeffersonian), 67–68, 70, 73–87, 193
Republicans (modern), 136, 140–141, 152
Reserved powers (see Tenth Amendment)
Resettlement Adminstration (RA), 302
Revolution, The (see American Revolution)
"Revolution of 1800", 73, 82, 83, 304
Rhode Island, 11, 14, 37, 52, 92
Richardson, Eliot, 374
"Right of Privacy, The" (Warren and Brandeis), 242
Roane, Spencer, 86
Roberts, Owen J., 304, 305, 306, 309, 312, 313, 314, 316, 357
Rockefeller, John D., 222
Roosevelt Court, 313–316
Roosevelt, Franklin
   1932 campaign and election, 297, 299

New Deal leadership, 243, 299–313 passim, 367
    appointment of Roosevelt Court, 314–315, 358, 386, 393
    World War II leadership, 150, 355–357, 364
    break of two-term tradition, 369
Roosevelt, Theodore, 233, 236, 239, 240, 493
Rosenberg, Julius and Ethel, 359
Rural Electrification Administration (REA), 302
Russian Revolution, 364
Rutledge, John, 37, 71, 72
Rutledge, Wiley, 315

Saddam Hussein, 361
Sanford, Edward, 250, 304
Sanford, John, 137
Santa Ana, 130
Saudi Arabia, 361
Sawyer, Charles, 358
Scalia, Antonin, 371, 391, 392, 395, 396
Scott, Dred, 137
Scott, Winfield, 94, 131
SEATO (Southeast Asia Treaty Organization), 363
Secession, 142–143, 145
Second Amendment, 55
Securities and Exchange Commission (SEC), 302
Sedition Act of 1918, 248
Selective Service Act of 1917, 248
Selective Service Act of 1940, 356
Senate Foreign Relations Committee, 384
Senate Judiciary Committee, 312, 366
Senate Judiciary Subcommittee on Internal Security, 385
Senate Permanent Subcommittee on Investigations, 384
Senatorial courtesy, 366
Sentencing Reform Act of 1984, 381
Separation of powers, 30, 31, 45, 353–397 passim
    war and national security, 355–362
    diplomacy and foreign affairs, 362–365
    appointments and removals, 365–369
    independent counsel, 370–371, 374–375, 381
    executive privilege and information, 372–373
    Nixon arrogation of power, 373–374
    Watergate crisis, 374–376
    immunities, executive and legislative, 376–378
    creation of administrative state, 378–379, 559–560
    legislative veto, 379–380
    other hybrid offices and mixed functions, 380–381
Seven Years War, The, 14
Seventh Amendment, 55
Seventeenth Amendment, 240
Seward, William, 136, 140
Seymour, Horatio, 160
Shaw, George Bernard, 2
Shays, Daniel, 31
Shays's Rebellion, 31–32
Sherman Anti-Trust Act of 1890, 224, 235–237, 252

Sherman, Roger, 17, 37
Sherman, William T., 146
Shiras, George, 230
Sirica, John, 375
Sixth Amendment, 55
Sixteenth Amendment, 238, 240
Slavery, 3, 4, 41, 55
    and the Constitution, 37–38, 121–122
    political economy of, 122–123
    in the territories, 122–136 passim
    Missouri Compromise, 123
    in the Supreme Court, 127–129, 136–139
    fugitive slave problem, 126–127
    Compromise of 1850, 132–134
    Kansas conflict, 133–136
    founding of modern Republican Party, 136
    Lincoln-Douglas debates, 139–140
    in Confederate Constitution, 144
    legal status of during Civil War, 150–152
Slave trade, 41, 121, 126, 132, 143, 152
Smith, Alfred E., 297, 299, 301
Smith Act (Alien Registration Act of 1940), 359, 486
Social Darwinism, 224–225
Social Security Act of 1935, 302, 310, 312
Social Statics (Spencer), 225
Sociological jurisprudence, 243, 246
Solicitor General, 588
Somalia, 361
Sons of Liberty, 14
Souter, David, 391, 397
South Carolina, 41, 52, 94–95, 142–143, 145, 156, 160, 301, 483
"South Carolina Exposition" (Calhoun), 94–95
South Korea, 358
South Vietnam, 360
Southern Democrats, 140–141
Southern Whigs, 130, 136
Southwest expansion
    Texas question, 130–131
    war with Mexico, 131
    backlash, 131–132
Soviet Union, 353, 357, 358, 364
Spain, 13, 17, 64, 75, 129, 130
Spanish-American War, 239, 355
Speaker of the House of Representatives, 365, 377, 383
Special Division, 366
Special Master, 498, 587
Speech and Debate Clause (see Article I-6)
Spencer, Herbert, 224–225
Stamp Act Congress, 14, 18
Stamp Act, The, 14–15
Standing to sue, 389
Stanton, Edwin M., 156, 367
Stare decisis, 31, 88

Starr, Kenneth, 370–371
Stassen, Harold, 382
State bills of rights, 30, 31
State constitutions, 29–31
State court systems, 587
State Department, 362, 384
States rights, 94–95
    Eleventh Amendment, 72
    internal improvements, 77–78
    jurisdictional challenge of, 85–86
    supremacy of national power, 86–91
    nullification, 94–95
    secession, 142–143, 145
    state regulation of interstate commerce, 196–200, 493–497
    federal regulation of states, 482–489
    federal supervisory authority over state courts, 490–493
Stephens, Alexander, 132, 143, 154
Stevens, John Paul, 381, 391, 396, 562
Stevens, Thaddeus, 154
Stewart, Potter, 394
Stock market crash, 249, 295–297
Stone, Harlan, 250, 251, 304, 305, 309, 314, 316, 317, 318, 386, 392, 480
Stowe, Harriet Beecher, 127
Story, Joseph, 31, 51, 84, 85, 86, 89, 128, 138, 193, 195, 197, 201, 231, 314, 489
    profile, 198–199
Strong, William, 226
St. Clair, Arthur, 373
St. Clair Expedition, 373, 381
Substantive due process, 230–234, 251–252, 560–561
Sugar Act (American Revenue Act), 14, 18
Sumner, Charles, 135–136, 138, 154
Sumner, William Graham, 225
Supreme Court
    pre-Marshall Court, 71–73
    early Marshall Court, 79–83
    Marshall profile, 80–81
    Marshall's nationalism, 83–91
    Taney Court, 3, 187, 188, 197–201, 489
    Taney profile, 138–139
    Civil War decisions, 147–150
    Reconstruction decisions, 162–164
    antebellum contracts clause, 192–196
    antebellum commerce clause, 196–200
    Story profile, 198–199
    new property, 200–201
    laissez faire constitutionalism, 225–238
    Waite Court, 227–229
    Fuller Court, 229–230
    substantive due process, liberty of contract, 230–234
    Holmes profile, 232–233
    Interstate Commerce Commission, 234–235, 246–247
    anti-trust action, 235–237
    income tax, 237–238

White Court, 241–245
    Brandeis profile, 242–243
    federal, state police power, 241–246
    Taft Court, 249–254
    anti-New Deal Court, 304–310
    longevity, health of justices, 310–311
    Hughes profile, 306–307
    court packing plan, 310–312
    Cardozo profile, 314–315
    Roosevelt Court, 313–318
    in World War II, 356–356
    and Cold War, 357–360
    Warren Court, 3, 196, 383, 386, 393, 394, 395–396, 484, 491, 492
    Burger profile, 382–383
    Burger Court, 394, 396, 484, 491, 492, 560
    role in separation of powers, 386–388
    activism and self-restraint, 388–392,
    choosing a president, 390–392
    canons of intepretation, 44–45, 84–85, 394–395
    composition and change, 392–397
    modern reach of federal legislation, 480–488
    Rehnquist profile, 484–485
    Rehnquist Court, 387–388, 394, 397, 486, 492, 560, 564, 565
    judicial federalism, 488, 493
    modern state regulation of interstate commerce, 493–497
    interstate relations, 497–499
    modern property rights, 559–565
    modern paths to, 585–588
    at work, 588–590
    internal procedures, 588–590
    law clerks, 588, 589, 590
    Justices of the Court (biographical listing), 590–593
    the historic Courts from Jay to Rehnquist, 593–595
Supreme Court: How It Was, How It Is, The (Rehnquist), 485
Surface Transportation Act of 1984, 483
Sutherland, George, 250, 251–252, 304, 305, 309–310, 355
Swayne, Noah, 147, 158, 311
Synar, Mike, 380

Taft, William Howard
    as president, 240, 241, 307
    as chief justice, 233, 250, 251, 252, 304, 367, 383
Taft-Hartley Act of 1947, 358–359
Taiwan, 363
Tammany Hall, 315
Taney, Roger, 94, 158, 241
    political questions doctrine, 93
    slavery decisions, 128, 129, 137, 498
    Civil War decisions, 147, 149, 373
    economic development decisions, 197, 199, 201, 242, 564
    profile, 138–139
Taney Court, 3, 187, 188, 197–201, 489
Tariff of Abominations of 1828, 94–95

Tariffs, 64, 94–95, 296
Taxation of the colonies, 14–19
  debate over, 18–19
Taxes (see also Tariffs)
  excise, 73
  direct, 42, 122, 238
  income, 237–238
  regulatory, 244, 251, 309, 313
  intergovernmental immunity from, 487–488
Taylor, Zachery, 132
Tea Act of 1773, 15
Teapot Dome Scandal, 304, 384
Tennessee, 143, 145, 154, 155, 387
Tennessee Valley Authority, 302
Tenth Amendment, 55, 77, 389, 479–480
  as basis for state regulatory power, 187
  as independent limit on federal power, 245, 251, 309, 313, 363, 485
  abandonment as limit on federal power, 316, 317
  new emphasis on by Rehnquist Court, 482, 483, 488
Tenure of Office Act of 1867, 65, 156, 157, 367, 370
Term limits, 369, 372
Texas, 123, 131, 143, 154, 156, 364
Texas annexation, 129
Third Amendment, 55
Thirteenth Amendment, 152, 219, 229
Thomas, Clarence, 366, 391, 392, 397
Thomas, Norman, 299
Three-Fifths Clause, 41, 122
Tiedeman, Christopher, 230, 246
Tilden, Samuel J., 160
Todd, Thomas, 83
Toqueville, Alexis de, 1, 91
Townshend Acts of 1767, 15
Trademark Remedy Classification Act, 484
Trading with the Enemy Act, 248
Treason, 83, 143–144
Treatise on Constitutional Limitations (Cooley), 230
Treatise on the Limitations of Police Power in the United States (Tiedeman), 230
Treaty-making, 65, 362–365
Treaty of Guadalupe Hidalgo, 131
Treaty of Paris, 27, 72, 86
Truman, Harry, 358, 359, 363, 364, 368
Truth in Securities Act of 1933, 302
Twelfth Amendment, 75
Twenty-first Amendment, 301, 483
Twenty-second Amendment, 369
Tyler, John, 92, 130

Uncle Tom's Cabin (Stowe), 127
Underground Railroad, 126, 127, 129
Union Pacific Railroad, 220
United Nations, 361
United Nations Charter, 363

United Nations Security Council, 358
United States Court of Claims, 586
United States Court of Military Appeals, 586
United States Court of International Trade, 586
United States Court of Veterans Appeals, 586
United States Tax Court, 586
University of Michigan, 385
Utah, 131
Utah Territory, 132

Vallandigham, Clement, 149
Van Buren, Martin, 84, 92, 130, 197
Van Devanter, Willis, 250, 304, 313
Vanderbilt, Cornelius, 223, 234
Veblen, Thorstein, 240
Vera Cruz, 131
Vietnam War, 93, 147, 355, 360–361, 362, 560
Vinson Court, 393
Vinson, Fred, 359, 393
Violence Against Women Act of 1994, 482
Virginia, 40, 52, 64, 72, 86, 143, 145, 156
Virginia and Kentucky Resolutions, 50, 70, 77, 95
Virginia Constitution, 50
Virginia Court of Appeals, 86
Virginia Declaration of Rights, 30
Virginia Plan, 39, 40–41, 42, 50
Volstead Act, 301

Wade, Ben, 158
Wade-Davis Bill of 1864, 154
Wage Stabilization Board, 358
Waite Court, 227–229
Waite, Morrison, 227–229, 230
Wall Street, 221, 295–296
War and national security
  tensions with Britain and France, 69–70
  War of 1812, 51, 76–77, 152, 355
  Mexican War, 131
  Civil War, 145–150, 148
  Spanish-American War, 239–240
  World War I, 247–249, 362, 364
  World War II, 355–357
  Cold War, 357–360, 363–365
  Korean War, 357–359
  Vietnam War, 360–361
  Persian Gulf War, 361–362
War of 1812, 51, 76–77, 152, 355
War Powers Act of 1941, 356
War Powers Resolution of 1973, 361, 375, 379
War Prohibition Act of 1918, 248
Warren, Charles, 196
Warren, Earl, 310, 368, 382–383, 385, 393, 394, 485, 486
Warren, Samuel D., 242
Warren Court, 3, 196, 383, 386, 393, 394, 395–396, 484, 491, 492

Washington, Bushrod, 194
Washington, George
   as war leader, 16, 17, 25, 26, 27, 33, 51, 52, 68
   at the Constitutional convention, 37, 38
   as President, 54, 63, 65–66, 68, 70, 71, 72, 82, 84, 315,
      362, 369, 373, 389
Washington, D.C., 76, 79, 126, 132, 143
Washington Disarmament Conference, 307
Washington State, 133, 483
Watergate scandal, 366, 368, 371, 373, 374–376, 381, 385
Wayne, James, 147, 197
"Wealth" (Carnegie), 225
Weaver, James B., 239
Webster, Daniel, 51, 87, 88, 95, 130, 193, 199
   profile, 194–195
Weizmann, Chaim, 243
West Virginia, 145
Whig Party, 91, 92, 194, 195
Whigs, 93, 95
Whiskey Rebellion, 67
White, Byron, 379–380, 394
White, Edward, 233, 237, 241, 250
White, G. Edward, 396
White Court, 241
Whitman, Walt, 131
Whitney, Eli, 122
William and Mary College, 84

William Mitchell College of Law (St. Paul College of Law), 382
Williams, Roger, 11
Wills, Garry, 150
Wilmot, David, 131
Wilmot Proviso, 132, 195
Wilson, James, 18, 37, 39, 52, 71, 72
Wilson, Woodrow, 240, 241, 243, 247, 248, 250, 307, 362, 367
Wilson-Gorman Act of 1894, 237–238
Winthrop, John, 10
Wirt, William, 87
Wisconsin, 29
Women's Christian Temperance Union, 300
Woodbury, Levi, 129
Woolens Act of 1699, 10
Works Progress Adminstration (WPA), 302
World War I, 152, 153, 225, 241, 247–249, 355, 356, 357
World War II, 150, 152, 249, 303, 355–357, 360, 363, 364
Wright, Benjamin, 56
Wyoming, 131

Yale University, 315
Yalta conference, 364
Yates, Robert, 48
Yorktown, Battle of, 27

Zionism, 243
Zoning, 253